DATE DUE

		PRINTED IN U.S.A.	

Literature Criticism from 1400 to 1800

Guide to Gale Literary Criticism Series

For criticism on	Consult these Gale series
Authors now living or who died after December 31, 1959	*CONTEMPORARY LITERARY CRITICISM (CLC)*
Authors who died between 1900 and 1959	*TWENTIETH-CENTURY LITERARY CRITICISM (TCLC)*
Authors who died between 1800 and 1899	*NINETEENTH-CENTURY LITERATURE CRITICISM (NCLC)*
Authors who died between 1400 and 1799	*LITERATURE CRITICISM FROM 1400 TO 1800 (LC)* *SHAKESPEAREAN CRITICISM (SC)*
Authors who died before 1400	*CLASSICAL AND MEDIEVAL LITERATURE CRITICISM (CMLC)*
Black writers of the past two hundred years	*BLACK LITERATURE CRITICISM (BLC)*
Authors of books for children and young adults	*CHILDREN'S LITERATURE REVIEW (CLR)*
Dramatists	*DRAMA CRITICISM (DC)*
Hispanic writers of the late nineteenth and twentieth centuries	*HISPANIC LITERATURE CRITICISM (HLC)*
Native North American writers and orators of the eighteenth, nineteenth, and twentieth centuries	*NATIVE NORTH AMERICAN LITERATURE (NNAL)*
Poets	*POETRY CRITICISM (PC)*
Short story writers	*SHORT STORY CRITICISM (SSC)*
Major authors from the Renaissance to the present	*WORLD LITERATURE CRITICISM, 1500 TO THE PRESENT (WLC)*

ISSN 0740-2880

Volume 32

Literature Criticism from 1400 to 1800

Critical Discussion of the Works
of Fifteenth-, Sixteenth-, Seventeenth-, and
Eighteenth-Century Novelists, Poets, Playwrights,
Philosophers, and Other Creative Writers.

Jennifer Allison Brostrom, Editor

Mary L. Onorato
Associate Editor

Gerald R. Barterian
Assistant Editor

GALE

DETROIT · NEW YORK · TORONTO · LONDON

STAFF

Jennifer Allison Brostrom, *Editor*

Mary L. Onorato, *Associate Editor*

Gerald R. Barterian, Ondine Le Blanc, *Assistant Editors*

Susan M. Trosky, *Managing Editor*

Marlene S. Hurst, *Permissions Manager*
Margaret A. Chamberlain, Maria Franklin, *Permissions Specialists*
Susan Salas, Diane Cooper, Michele Lonoconus, Maureen Puhl, Shalice Shah,
Kimberly F. Smilay, Barbara A. Wallace, *Permissions Associates*
Sarah Chesney, Edna M. Hedblad, Margaret McAvoy-Amato, Tyra Y. Phillips,
Permissions Assistants

Victoria B. Cariappa, *Research Manager*
Alicia Noel Biggers, Julia C. Daniel, Tammy Nott, Michele Pica, Tracie A. Richardson, *Research Associates*

Mary Beth Trimper, *Production Director*
Deborah Milliken, *Production Assistant*

Sherrell Hobbs, *Macintosh Artist*
Pamela A. Hayes, *Photography Coordinator*
Robert Duncan, *Scanner Operator*
Randy Bassett, *Image Database Supervisor*

∞™ This book is printed on acid-free paper that meets the minimum requirements of American National Standard for Information Sciences—Permanence Paper for Printed Library Materials, ANSI Z39.48-1984.

Library of Congress Catalog Card Number 94-29718
ISBN 0-8103-9277-1
ISSN 0740-2880
Printed in the United States of America

10 9 8 7 6 5 4 3 2 1

Contents

Preface   vii

Acknowledgments   xi

Preface

L *iterature Criticism from 1400 to 1800 (LC)* presents criticism of world authors of the fifteenth through eighteenth centuries. The literature of this period reflects a turbulent time of radical change that saw the rise of modern European drama, the birth of the novel and personal essay forms, the emergence of newspapers and periodicals, and major achievements in poetry and philosophy. Many of these historical forces continue to influence modern art and society. *LC,* therefore, provides valuable insight into the art, life, thought, and cultural transformations that took place during these centuries.

Scope of the Series

LC provides an introduction to the great poets, dramatists, novelists, essayists, and philosophers of the fifteenth through eighteenth centuries; and to the most significant interpretations of these authors' works. Because criticism of this literature spans nearly six hundred years, an overwhelming amount of scholarship confronts the student. *LC* therefore organizes this material into volumes addressing specific historical and cultural topics, for example, "Literature of the Spanish Golden Age," or "Literature and the New World." Every attempt is made to reprint the most noteworthy, relevant, and educationally valuable essays available.

Readers should note that there is a separate Gale reference series devoted exclusively to Shakespearean studies. Although belonging properly to the period covered in *LC,* William Shakespeare has inspired such a tremendous and ever-growing corpus of secondary material that the editors have deemed it best to give his works extensive coverage in a separate series, *Shakespearean Criticism.*

Each author entry in *LC* presents a survey of critical response to an author's oeuvre. Early criticism is offered to indicate initial responses, later selections document any rise or decline in literary reputations, and retrospective analyses provide students with modern views. The size of each author entry is a relative reflection of the scope of criticism available in English. Every attempt has been made to identify and include the seminal essays on each author's work and to include recent commentary providing modern perspectives.

The need for *LC* among students and teachers of literature and history was suggested by the proven usefulness of Gale's *Contemporary Literary Criticism (CLC), Twentieth-Century Literary Criticism (TCLC),* and *Nineteenth-Century Literature Criticism (NCLC),* which excerpt criticism of works by nineteenth- and twentieth-century authors. There is no duplication of critical material in any of these literary criticism series. Major authors may appear more than once in one or more of the series because of the great quantity of critical material available, and his or her relevance to a variety of thematic topics.

Thematic Approach

Beginning with Volume 12, all the authors in each volume of *LC* are organized around such themes as specific literary or philosophical movements, writings surrounding important political and historical events, the philosophy and art associated with eras of cultural transformation, and the literature of specific social or ethnic groups. Each volume contains a topic entry providing a historical and literary overview, and several author entries, which examine major representatives of the featured period.

Organization of the Book

Each entry consists of the following elements: author or thematic heading, introduction, list of principal works, annotated works of criticism (each preceded by a bibliographical citation), and a bibliography of further reading. Also, most author entries contain author portraits and other illustrations.

- The **Author Heading** consists of the author's full name, followed by birth and death dates. (If an author wrote consistently under a pseudonym, the pseudonym is used in the author heading, with the real name given in parentheses on the first line of the biographical and critical introduction.) Also located here are any name variations under which an author wrote, including transliterated forms for authors whose native languages use nonroman alphabets. Uncertain birth or death dates are indicated by question marks. Topic entries are preceded by a **Thematic Heading,** which simply states the subject of the entry.

- The **Introduction** to each entry provides social and historical background important to understanding the criticism, and an overview of the biography and career of the featured author.

- Most *LC* author entries include **Portraits** of the author. Many entries also contain illustrations of materials pertinent to an author's career, including author holographs, title pages, letters, or representations of important people, places, and events in an author's life.

- The **List of Principal Works** is ordered chronologically, by date of first book publication, identifying the genre of each work. In the case of foreign authors whose works have been translated into English, the title and date of the first English-language edition are given in brackets beneath the foreign-language listing. Unless otherwise indicated, dramas are dated by first performance, not first publication.

- **Criticism** is arranged chronologically in each author entry to provide a useful perspective on changes in critical evaluation over time. For the purpose of easy identification, the critic's name and the date of first composition or publication of the critical work are given at the beginning of each piece of criticism. Unsigned criticism is preceded by the title of the source in which it appeared. All titles by the author featured in the critical entry are printed in boldface type. Publication information (such as publisher names and book prices) and some parenthetical numerical references (such as footnotes or page and line references to specific editions of works) have been occasionally deleted to provide smoother reading of the text.

- Critical essays are prefaced by **Annotations** as an additional aid to students using *LC*. These explanatory notes may provide several types of useful information, including: the reputation of a critic, the importance of a work of criticism, the commentator's individual approach to literary criticism, the intent of the criticism, and the growth of critical controversy or changes in critical trends regarding an author's work. In some cases, these notes cross-reference the work of critics within the entry who agree or disagree with each other.

- A complete **Bibliographical Citation** of the original essay or book follows each piece of criticism.

- An annotated bibliography of **Further Reading** appears at the end of each entry and suggests resources for additional study. In some cases, significant essays for which the editors could not obtain reprint rights are included here.

Cumulative Indexes

Each volume of *LC* includes a cumulative **Author Index** listing all the authors that have appeared in the following sources published by Gale: *Contemporary Literary Criticism, Twentieth-Century Literary Criticism, Nineteenth-Century Literature Criticism, Literature Criticism from 1400 to 1800, and Classical and Medieval Literature Criticism,* along with cross-references to the Gale series *Short Story Criticism, Poetry Criticism, Children's Literature Review, Authors in the News, Contemporary Authors, Contemporary Authors Autobiography Series, Contemporary Authors Bibliographical Series, Dictionary of Literary Biography, Concise Dictionary of Literary Biography, Something about the Author, Something about the Author Autobiography Series, and Yesterday's Authors of Books for Children.* Readers will welcome this cumulative author index as a useful tool for locating an author within the various series. The index, which includes authors' birth and death dates, is particularly valuable for those authors who are identified with a certain period but whose death dates cause them to be placed in another, or for those authors whose careers span two periods. For example, F. Scott Fitzgerald is found in *TCLC,* yet a writer often associated with him, Ernest Hemingway, is found in *CLC.*

Beginning with Volume 12, *LC* includes a cumulative **Topic Index** that lists all literary themes and topics treated in *LC, NCLC, TCLC,* and the *CLC* Yearbook. Each volume of *LC* also includes a cumulative **Nationality Index** in which authors' names are arranged alphabetically under their respective nationalities and followed by the numbers of the volumes in which they appear.

Each volume of *LC* also includes a cumulative **Title Index,** an alphabetical listing of all literary works discussed in the series. Each title listing includes the corresponding volume and page numbers where criticism may be located. Foreign-language titles that have been translated followed by the tiles of the translation—for example, *El ingenioso hidalgo Don Quixote de la Mancha (Don Quixote).* Page numbers following these translated titles refers to all pages on which any form of the titles, either foreign-language or translated, appear. Title of novels, dramas, nonfiction books, and poetry, short story, or essays collections are printed in italics, while individual poems, short stories, and essays are printed in roman type within quotation marks.

A Note to the Reader

When writing papers, students who quote directly from any volume in the Literary Criticism Series may use the following general forms to footnote reprinted criticism. The first example pertains to material drawn from periodicals, the second to material reprinted from books.

T. S. Eliot, "John Donne," *The Nation and the Athenaeum,* 33 (9 June 1923), 321-32; excerpted and reprinted in *Literature Criticism from 1400 to 1800,* Vol. 10, ed. James E. Person, Jr. (Detroit: Gale Research, 1989), pp. 28-9.

Clara G. Stillman, *Samuel Butler: A Mid-Victorian Modern* (Viking Press, 1932); excerpted and reprinted in *Twentieth-Century Literary Criticism,* Vol. 33, ed. Paula Kepos (Detroit: Gale Research, 1989), pp. 43-5.

Suggestions Are Welcome

Since the series began, features have been added to *LC* in response to various suggestions, including a nationality index, a Literary Criticism Series topic index, and thematic organization of entries.

Readers who wish to suggest new features, themes or authors to appear in future volumes, or who have other suggestions, are cordially invited to write to the editor.

ACKNOWLEDGMENTS

The editors wish to thank the copyright holders of the excerpted criticism included in this volume and the permissions managers of many book and magazine publishing companies for assisting us in securing reprint rights. We are also grateful to the staffs of the Detroit Public Library, the Library of Congress, the University of Detroit Mercy Library, Wayne State University Purdy/Kresge Library Complex, and the University of Michigan Libraries for making their resources available to us. Following is a list of the copyright holders who have granted us permission to reprint material in the volume of *LC*. Every effort has been made to trace copyright, but if omissions have been made, please let us know.

COPYRIGHT EXCERPTS IN *LC*, VOLUME 32, WERE REPRINTED FROM THE FOLLOWING PERIODICALS:

The American Political Science Review, v. LXX, September, 1976. Copyright, 1976, by The American Political Science Association. Reprinted by permission of the publisher.—*The Centennial Review*, v. XXIX, Summer, 1985 for "Rhetorical Strategy and the Fiction of Audience in More's 'Utopia' " by Ann W. Astell. © 1985 by The Centennial Review. Reprinted by permission of the publisher and the author.—*Church History*, v. 56, March, 1987. © 1987, The American Society of Church History. Reprinted by permission of the publisher.—*ELH*, v. 57, Fall, 1990 for "The 'New Atlantis' and the Uses of Utopia" by Denise Albanese. Copyright © 1990 by The Johns Hopkins University Press. All rights reserved. Reprinted by permission of the publisher and the author.—*English Literary Renaissance*, v. 6, 1976. Copyright © 1976 by English Literary Renaissance. Reprinted by permission of the publisher.—*German Life and Letters*, v. 41, July, 1988. Reprinted by permission of the publisher.—*International Review of Social History*, v. VII, 1962. Reprinted by permission of the publisher.—*Journal of Medieval and Renaissance Studies*, v. 20, Fall, 1990. Copyright © 1990 by Duke University Press. Reprinted with permission.—*Journal of the History of Ideas*, v. X, June, 1954 for "The Social Responsibilities of Science in 'Utopia' 'New Atlantis' and After" by Robert P. Adams; v. XV, June, 1949 for "Bacon's Man of Science" by Moody E. Prior; v. XXXXVIIII, July-September, 1988. Copyright 1954, renewed 1982; copyright 1949, renewed 1977; copyright 1988 Journal of the History of Ideas, Inc. All reprinted by permission of the Johns Hopkins University Press and the authors.—*Moreana*, November, 1971, v. 9-10, September, 1973. Reprinted by permission of the publisher.—*Renaissance Quarterly*, v. XLIII, Autumn, 1990. Copyright © 1990 by the Renaissance Society of America, Inc. Reprinted by permission of the publisher.—*Romance Languages Annual*, v. 4, 1992. Reprinted by permission of the publisher.—*Sixteenth Century Journal*, v. XXII, Summer, 1991. Copyright © 1991 by The Sixteenth Century Journal Publishers, Inc., Kirksville, Missouri. All rights reserved. Reprinted by permission of the publisher.—*Stanford Italian Review*, v. V, Fall, 1985. Reprinted by permission of the publisher and the author.—*Texas Studies in Literature and Language*, v. XXXIV, Summer, 1992 for "More's Place in 'No Place': The Self-Fashioning Transaction in 'Utopia' " by John Freeman. Copyright © 1992 by the University of Texas Press. Reprinted by permission of the publisher and the author.—*Utopian Studies*, v. 1, 1987. Reprinted by permission of the publisher. *Yale French Studies*, n. 49, 1973. Copyright © Yale French Studies, 1973. Reprinted by permission of the publisher.

COPYRIGHT EXCERPTS IN *LC*, VOLUME 32, WERE REPRINTED FROM THE FOLLOWING BOOKS:

Archer, John Michael. From *Sovereignty and Intelligence: Spying and Court Culture in the English Renaissance*. Stanford University Press, 1993. Copyright © 1993 by the Board of Trustees of Leland Stanford Junior University. Reprinted with the permission of the publishers, Stanford University Press.—Berneri, Marie Louise. From *Journey Through Utopia*. Routledge, 1950. Copyright 1950 by Routledge & Kegan Paul Ltd., London. Reprinted by permission of the publisher.—Bloch, Ernst. From *The Principle of Hope*. Neville Plaice, Stephen Plaice and Paul Knight, trans. Basil Blackwell, 1986. English translation © Basil Blackwell 1986. Reprinted by permission of the publisher.—Bonansea, Bernardino M. From *Tommaso Campanella Renaissance Pioneer of Modern Thought*. The Catholic University of America Press, 1969. © Copyright 1969 by The Catholic University of America Press, Inc. All

Utopian Literature of the Renaissance

INTRODUCTION

The concept of utopia as a literary form originated with Sir Thomas More's depiction of a fictional commonwealth in *Utopia* (1516), which inspired many imaginary societies of the sixteenth and seventeenth centuries and influenced efforts at social reform extending into the twentieth century. Such ideals as equality between the sexes, religious toleration, and preventative medicine have their roots in utopian literature; as do several important tenets of modern communism and socialism. Renaissance utopian works are characterized by several common factors: a belief in the possibility of social reconstruction through an assertion of human willpower, a sense of pessimism concerning present social conditions balanced by a feeling of optimism about the future, a communal approach to the distribution of property, a pervasive concern with society as a whole rather than with the experience of individuals, and a belief in the utility of social institutions—among the most consistently emphasized of which is education.

While the principal structural elements of More's *Utopia* served as a stock formula for other utopian works (for example, the location of the utopian society at a distance from the familiar world, often with an ocean voyage leading to a shipwreck or chance landing on the shores of an ideal commonwealth); thematic sources for utopian literature are found in prominent western cultural traditions, including the classical myth of a Golden Age, the ideal city-state of Plato's *Republic*, and the Christian conception of paradise. Frank E. Manuel and Fritzie P. Manuel comment: "The two ancient beliefs that molded and nurtured utopia—the Judeo-Christian faith in a paradise created with the world and destined to endure beyond it, and the Hellenic myth of an ideal, beautiful city built by men for men without the assistance and often in defiance of the gods—were deeply embedded in the consciousness of Europeans." Some critics have also suggested an inspiration for utopian literature in the transition between the Medieval and Renaissance worlds, viewing the utopian aspiration for a cohesive community as a reaction against the increasingly divisive and individualistic aspects of society during the sixteenth and seventeenth centuries—a nostalgic longing for the unified city community and Christian worldview of the Middle Ages. The changing conception of reality associated with New World exploration and scientific discovery during the Renaissance has also been cited as a possibe influence in the development of utopian literature. While works of Renaissance utopian literature share common structural and thematic origins, there is great variation in the specific solutions to societal problems proposed by different authors. Marie Louise Berneri commented: "Thomas More abolishes property but retains family institutions and slavery; Campanella, though a staunch Catholic, wants to abolish marriage and the family; Andreae borrows many of his ideas from More and Campanella but puts his faith in a new religious reformation which would go deeper than that inspired by Luther; Bacon wants to preserve private property and a monarchial government but believes that the happiness of mankind can be achieved through scientific progress."

In 1595, Sir Philip Sidney praised the new genre of utopian literature in his *Defense of Poesie,* ranking utopia, along with poetry, above philosophy and history as more persuasive than philosophical argument. In general, however, there was little critical discussion about utopian literature during the Renaissance, and the form did not receive detailed academic consideration until the nineteenth century, when utopian writings were becoming increasingly concerned with advocating realistic social reform and less focused on fictional conventions of the genre. The twentieth century has witnessed a surge of critical interest in utopian thought, with scholars of diverse fields examining works of the Renaissance for their political, historical, scientific, and literary value. Many have observed the decline of utopian fiction during the current century, noting the far more prevalent modern penchant for dystopia, or anti-utopia. Questioning the authenticity of a utopian author's intent is a common characteristic of contemporary scholarship on Renaissance utopian thought, with many critics emphasizing the satirical, as well as idealistic, implications of utopian works. Finally, a common twentieth-century criticism of the viability of utopian thought is that it tends to ignore the unpredictable, passionate, or irrational aspects of human nature, demonstrating a naive expectation that people will respond unselfishly to reason.

---

*REPRESENTATIVE WORKS

Alberti, Leone Battista
  De re aedificatoria 1485
Andreae, Johann Valentin
  Christianopolis 1619

Averlino, Antonio (also known as Filarete)
> Sforzinda 1461-1464

Bacon, Francis
> The New Atlantis 1627

Bruno, Giordano
> Lo spaccio de la bestia trionfante [The Expul
> sion of the Triumphant Beast] 1584

Campanella, Tommaso
> La Città del Sole [City of the Sun] 1602

Comenius, Johann Amos
> De Rerum Humanarum Emendatione Consul
> tatio Catholica [General Consultation on an
> Improvement of All Things Human] 1666

Contarini, Cardinal Gasparo
> De Magistratibus et Republica Venetorum Libri
> Quinque 1543

Doni, Antonio Francesco
> I Mondi celesti, terrestri, et infernali 1552

de Guevara, Antonio
> Libro llamado Relox de los principes 1529

Hartlib, Samuel
> Macaria 1641

Landi, Ortensio
> Commentario delle piu notabili, et mostruose
> cose d'Italia 1548

Martini, Francesco di Giorgio
> Trattato di architettura 1481

More, Sir Thomas
> Utopia 1516

Müntzer, Thomas
> Protestation 1524

*Includes works completed or published between the years 1400
and 1700.

OVERVIEWS

Marie Louise Berneri (essay date 1950)

SOURCE: "Utopias of the Renaissance," in *Journey
Through Utopia*, 1950. Reprint by The Beacon Press,
1951, pp. 52-58.

[*In the following excerpt from her critical study of
utopian literature, Berneri argues that "though the
utopias of Thomas More, Campanella and Andreae
embody to a great extent the spirit of the Renaissance,
they are also a reaction against it."*]

From the Greek ideal commonwealths we now pass to
those of the Renaissance. This does not mean that
during this gap of fifteen centuries the mind of man
had ceased to be interested in building imaginary societies, and a complete survey of utopian thought should
describe its manifestations during the Roman Empire

and even more during the following period which is
generally, and unjustly, called the Dark Ages. In many
legends of that time one finds that the utopian dream
assumes a primitive form as in the early Greek myths.

With the theological thought of the Middle Ages the
ideal commonwealths are projected in the next world
either, in the mystic and philosophic manner of St
Augustine's *De Civitate Dei*, or in the poetical and
naive fashion of the narrative of the great Irish traveller St Brendan. This intrepid monk tells how, during
one of his travels, his ship was driven towards the
north, and how after fifteen days he and his companions reached a country where they saw cathedrals of
crystal and where day followed day without night and
they landed on an island which was the abode of the
blessed. Though in this 6th century legend, Utopia is
identified with Paradise, the combination of actual travels with the vision of an ideal island is a feature which
will be found in many later utopias.

If the utopian writers of the Renaissance owe a great
deal to Greek philosophy they are also indebted to the
Christian Fathers and to later theologians. St Thomas
Aquinas's *De Regimine Principum*, written during the
13th century, contains some passages which are worth
quoting because they express ideas common to almost
all the utopias of the Renaissance. Firstly that human
happiness is dependent on ethical principles as well as
material comfort:

> For an individual to lead a good life two things are
> required. The first and most important is to act in a
> virtuous manner, for virtue is that by which one
> lives well; the second, which is secondary and as it
> were instrumental, is a sufficiency of those bodily
> goods whose use is necessary to an act of virtue.

The self-sufficiency of the city and surrounding country is the ideal to be achieved:

> Now there are two ways in which an abundance of
> food-stuffs can be supplied to a city. The first is
> where the soil is so fertile that it nobly provides for
> all the necessities of human life. The second is by
> trade, through which the necessities of life are
> brought to the town from different places. But it is
> quite clear that the first means is better. For the
> higher a thing is the more self-sufficient it is; since
> whatever needs another's help is by that very fact
> proven inferior. But that city is more fully self-
> sufficient which the surrounding country supplies
> with all its vital needs, than is another which must
> obtain these supplies by trade. A city which has an
> abundance of food from its own territory is more
> dignified than one which is provisioned by
> merchants. It is safer, too, for the importing of
> supplies can be prevented whether owing to the
> uncertain outcome of wars or to the many dangers
> of the road, and thus the city may be overcome
> through lack of food.

St Thomas Aquinas perceived the disruptive effect of commerce upon the community:

> Again, if the citizens themselves devote their lives to matters of trade the way will be opened to many vices. For since the object of trading leads especially to the making of money, greed is awakened in the hearts of citizens through the pursuit of trade. The result is that everything in the city will be offered for sale; confidence will be destroyed and the way opened to all kinds of trickery; each one will work only for his own profit, despising the public good: the cultivation of virtue will fail, since honour, virtue's reward, will be bestowed upon everyone. Thus in such a city civic life will be corrupted.

It would have been impossible for the Renaissance writers to model their ideal commonwealth entirely upon those of the Greek thinkers, for the structure of the society they had before their eyes was fundamentally different from that of ancient Greece. The Athenian or Spartan city, with its watertight division between citizen and slaves, its primitive economy based almost exclusively on agriculture, could not be transplanted into the society of the sixteenth century without undergoing some radical changes.

The most important change was in regard to manual labour. For Plato manual work was merely a necessity of life and should be left to the slaves and artisans, while a special caste busied itself with the affairs of State. The experience of the mediaeval city had shown, on the contrary, that the whole community was capable of governing itself through its guilds and city councils, and this community was entirely composed of producers. Thus work had acquired an important and respected position which it did not altogether lose with the breaking up of communal institutions.

All the utopists of the Renaissance insist that work is a duty for all citizens and some of them, like Campanella and Andreae, maintain that all work, even the most menial, is honourable. Nor was this a mere statement of principle; it was reflected in the institutions which gave equal rights to the labourer as to the craftsman, to the peasant as to the school-master. These utopian institution deprived work of its mercenary character by abolishing wages and trade, and they further endeavoured to make work pleasant by reducing the number of working hours. These institutions, which strike us as modern, had in fact existed in the mediaeval city where hired labour was practically non-existent and where manual labour was no token of inferiority, while the idea that work must be pleasant was a current one and was well expressed in this mediaeval Kuttenberg Ordinance which says: "Every one must be pleased with his work, and no one shall, while doing nothing, appropriate for himself what others have produced by applicationand work, because laws must be a shield for application and work." The utopian idea of

a short working day which to us, accustomed to think of the past in terms of the nineteenth century, seems a very radical one, does not appear such an innovation, if it is compared with an ordinance of Ferdinand the First relative to the Imperial coal mines, which settled the miner's day at eight hours. And according to Thorold Rogers, in fifteenth century England men worked forty-eight hours a week.

During the fourteenth and fifteenth centuries the cities gradually lost their independence, their prosperity began to decline and soon the most abject poverty prevailed generally among working people. But the experience of the free cities was not lost and was consciously or unconsciously assimilated in the constitution of ideal states.

The utopias of the Renaissance introduced, however, some important innovations. The mediaeval city had not succeeded in allying itself with the peasantry and this had been one of the chief causes of its decay. The peasant had remained in a condition of slavery and, though in England serfdom had been abolished, in most European countries the peasants were enduring conditions not dissimilar from those of the Helots in Sparta. The utopian writers of the sixteenth and seventeenth century realised, as St Thomas Aquinas had done, that a stable society must integrate the town and the countryside, craftsmen and peasants, and that agricultural work should be given an honoured position equal to that of the other crafts.

The importance given in utopian writings to the scientific cultivation of the land was probably inspired by the work done by the monasteries in this field. Other features of monastic life, such as the rigid time-tables, the meals taken in common, the uniformity and austerity of clothes, the considerable amount of time devoted to study and prayer were also included in the constitutions of ideal cities.

Of more importance than the experiences of the past, however, is the direct influence that the movements of the Renaissance and the Reformation have had on utopian thought. This influence is a complex one for, though the utopias of Thomas More, Campanella and Andreae embody to a great extent the spirit of the Renaissance, they are also a reaction against it.

The splendid artistic and scientific movement of the Renaissance was accompanied by a disintegration of society. The assertion ofman's individuality, the development of his critical faculties, and the widening of knowledge, had consolidated the destruction of the collective spirit of the Middle Ages and undermined the unity of the Christian world. The Renaissance furthermore had led to the formation of a class of "intellectuals" by creating a division between the worker and the technician, the craftsman and the artist, the mason and the architect. A new aristocracy was born; not, at first, based on wealth and power, but on intelligence and knowledge. Burckhardt, the brilliant apologist of the Renaissance, admits that this movement "was anti-popular, that through it Europe became for the first time sharply divided into the cultivated and the uncultivated classes."

This division quickened the disintegration of society. The rising power of the nobles and the kings was no longer held in check by the Communes, and led to continuous and exhausting warfare. The old associations had been broken up and nothing had come to take their place. The condition of the people grew increasingly worse until it reached that abject poverty so powerfully described in More's *Utopia*.

The utopias of the Renaissance represented a reaction against its extreme individualism and were an effort to create a new unity among nations. For this purpose they sacrificed the most cherished conquests of the Renaissance; Thomas More the scholar and humanist, the patron of painters and friend of Erasmus, produced an utopia where the lack of individuality is evident— from the uniformity of the houses and clothes to the adherence to a strict routine of work; where artistic manifestations are completely absent; where the "unique" man of the Renaissance is replaced by a "standard" man. Except for Rabelais, who is in a category of his own, all the other utopian writers are as parsimonious as More, in their allowance of personal freedom.

If these utopias represented a reaction against the movement of the Renaissance they also anticipate its logical outcome. The development of the individuality had taken place in a minority at the expense of the majority. A cathedral built according to the plan conceived by one artist, more clearly expresses his individuality than one built by the common efforts of an association, but the workmen who execute the plan have less chance to develop their personalities.

In the political sphere the initiative also passed from the people to a few individuals. The condottieri, the princes, kings and bishops, dispensed justice, waged wars, contracted alliances, regulated commerce and production: all tasks which had been previously undertaken by the communes, guilds or city councils. The Renaissance which had allowed the development of the individual also created the state which became the negation of the individual.

The utopias of the Renaissance try to offer a solution to the problems facing a society in the process of evolving a new form of organisation.

As has often been pointed out, the discovery of the New World gave a new impetus to utopian thought, but it played only a secondary role, and one can safely assume that had More never read Vespucci's travels he would have imagined an ideal commonwealth in a different setting, like Campanella or Andreae who did not bother to consult travel books before they described their ideal cities. The main impetus came from the need to replace the associations, and the philosophical and religious systems of the Middle Ages, with new ones.

Next to the utopias we find, as we did in Greece under similar circumstances, the elaboration of ideal constitutions which sought a solution in political reforms rather than in the establishment of a completely new system of society. Among the creators of ideal constitutions of that period, Jean Bodin probably exerted the greatest influence. This French philosopher strongly resisted the temptation of wishing to build "a Republic in the imagination and without effect such as those which Plato and Thomas More, the chancellor of England, have imagined." He believed, like Aristotle, that private property and family institutions should remain untouched, but that a strong state should be created which would be able to maintain the unity of the nation. At the time when Bodin wrote his *Republic* (1557), France was torn by religious wars, and there began to grow up a movement in favour of a monarchical state which would be strong enough to prevent religious struggles but which would at the same time allow political and religious freedom. Bodin's theories on the state answered these preoccupations and his works were read with interest all over Europe. He himself translated *La République* into Latin in 1586, when it had already been translated into Italian, Spanish and German. His ideas seem to have met with similar interest in England, for when Bodin came to this country in 1579 private lectures were held both in London and Cambridge to explain his work.

. . . [The utopias of the Renaissance] are, in many respects, widely dissimilar. Thomas More abolishes property but retains family institutions and slavery; Campanella, though a staunch Catholic, wants to abolish marriage and the family; Andreae borrows many of his ideas from More and Campanella but puts his faith in a new religious reformation which would go deeper than that inspired by Luther; Bacon wants to preserve private property and a monarchal government but believes that the happiness of mankind can be achieved through scientific progress.

Glenn Negley and J. Max Patrick (essay date 1952)

SOURCE: "Utopias from 1500 to 1850," in *The Quest for Utopia: An Anthology of Imaginary Societies,* Henry Schuman, Inc., 1952, pp. 286-95.

[*In the following essay, the critics discuss the revival of utopianism during the Renaissance, focusing on themes of communism, religion, and natural science in utopian thought.*]

With the rise of humanism and naturalism, and with the general revolution in human thought at the time of the Renaissance, utopianism revived. The medieval ideal of a static, divinely sanctioned order persisted in the writings of Robert Crowley in the sixteenth century, and lingered as the ideal of one aspect of seventeenth-century utopianism, though in national rather than international application. The semiutopian ideal of the Holy Roman universal society persisted through the middle ages and revived in modified form in Tommaso Campanella's *Spanish Monarchy* and in the hopes for a united Christendom which centered about Philip II of Spain. In 1516, Thomas More started a tradition of humanist utopias, the chief of which were probably intended less as models for society than as norms by which to judge it. The revived study of the classics, a movement with which More himself was closely connected, also led to a group of Italian utopias.

These Italian utopias of the sixteenth century are of two types: the "ideal" and the "practical." The first type is universal in basis and application, and presents the *idea* or *ideal* of a state. The other is more specific: it is civic or national in both its nature and its application. The "practical" utopia is thus a model, applicable constitution or plan for society, of the type represented by Harrington's *Oceana* in the following century. An "ideal" utopia like Plato's *Republic* puts forward the philosophical or theoretical end of a state and society, in general, moretheoretic terms. During the Renaissance in all countries, the "practical" type predominated, probably because of the prevalence of naturalism. Natural philosophy taught the infallible goodness of natural law as the guide and purifying force of every society. If science was directed to study the laws of nature, and if the laws of nature were utilized to the ends of civil society, conclusions could be drawn which would contribute to the ordering of an ideal society which would be constructed in accordance with the dictates of the new experience. Natural philosophy thus led men to envisage the possibility of a model state governed by few and wise laws deduced from nature and yet dominant over her. Since it was believed that error was absent from nature, it would likewise be absent from this state; nor would anything there contradict the principles of philosophy.

The kind of model state which matured in the humanist, renaissance mind was fixed by the *Utopia* of Sir Thomas More, and by three Italian utopias, "The Imaginary Republic" by Ludovico Agostini, "The Learned World" by Antonio Francesco Doni, and *The Happy City* by Francesco Patrizi. All four, especially the Italian ones, are in the nature of academic exercises devoted to philosophical speculation or the instructive admiration of a utopian people. An account of one of them will illustrate this. The goal of the citizens in Patrizi's *Happy City* (Venice, 1553) is to get into tune with the Divine Idea and to drink supercelestial waters. The society is divided into six castes or orders. Physical necessities are provided by the three lowest orders, the peasants, artisans, and merchants. Since they are unable to give their souls to civic and contemplative virtues, they cannot attain happiness, and are, accordingly, denied citizenship and its privileges. The superior classes—warriors, governors, and priests—perform civic duties, but their chief aims are the speculative virtues and communion with the highest. However, there is no need to give further details here: the work is essentially a recasting of Plato's *Republic*.

In contrast with such "ideal" works, an example of a "practical" sixteenth-century utopia is to be found in "The Door Opened to the Republic of Evandria," which Ludovico Zuccolo included in his *Dialogues* (Venice, 1625). It is significant because of the light it throws on one origin of utopias. The practice of idealizing an existing city or state is common to all ages, but it was particularly strong in sixteenth-century Italy. Glorifications of Lucca, Florence, and Venice are not far to seek in that period. The transition to an imagined perfect society was an easy one. Zuccolo first described San Marino with admiration for the simple butcomfortable life of its citizens. They were poor, but enjoyed a sufficiency of this world's goods; and the result of their poverty was cooperativeness, plain living, freedom from covetousness; a lack of corrupting luxuries and vices; absence of strangers, visitors, and bankers; and consequent freedom from the harms which they might bring. Zuccolo then proceeded to describe a fantastic voyage to the exemplary Republic of Evandria. Its site is remote, and it is further protected by natural barriers. In it wickedness is banished, and a perfect society exists under an annually elected magistracy. Thus Zuccolo's utopia began in glorified reality and was carried to imaginative perfection. In contrast, More started from a consideration of the evils of England and then moved into a speculative dream of an ideal state which he held to be impossible of attainment.

The difference between utopias classified as "ideal" and those grouped as "practical" is one of degree and tendency, but such a difference is quite noticeable if the states of More and Patrizi are compared with those written in the seventeenth century. In general, the latter, influenced no doubt by the Reformation and by developments in natural science, were intended to be practical. Joseph Hall's *Discovery of a New World* is an exception, for it is an academic exercise in burlesque and satire. But the extraordinary utopian efflorescence in the two decades which followed produced in four different countries five accounts of imaginary societies. In varying degrees, all of them may be classified as "practical." Tommaso Campanella not only asserted the practicability of his *City of the Sun,* but participated in a Calabrian revolt to realize his end. I.D.M.'s *Antangil,* though strongly influenced by Plato and More, is obviously intended to be applicable to France in 1616. Bacon's *New Atlantis,* which appeared a decade later, heavily stresses the practical advantages of science and invention; and even Robert Burton's "poetical commonwealth of mine own" proves, on examination, to have realistic reference to the condition of England. Johann Valentin Andreae's Latin utopia, *Christianopolis,* like Campanella's *City of the Sun,* combines metaphysical speculation and immediate applicability.

Sufficient background in the history of utopianism has been given above to make possible a more rapid survey and classification of utopias written before 1850.

One of the main currents was that of communism and socialism. It is traceable back to early accounts of the Golden Age. Developed in the utopias of Plato, Iambulus, and Euhemerus, it recurred in the Middle Ages in such teachings as those of John Ball, which provided an ideological basis for peasant revolts. Thomas More based his Utopia on communism but moderated its power by his humanistic stress on education, natural virtues, and the institution of the family. Campanella went to an extreme and provided for community of property and women. After him, for a few decades, communist theory lingered in oral tradition, in poetry about the Golden Age, and in satire. However, in 1652, Gerrard Winstanley published a communist utopia, *The Law of Freedom in a Platform.* Since it is not included in the present anthology, some account of it is necessary. Winstanley was a leader of a tiny group known as the Diggers at the extreme political Left of the Puritan Revolution. As the result of mystical visions and voices he and his fellows attempted to cultivate some rather barren land in Surrey in defiance of those who had property rights over it. Morally their case had some strength, for, having helped to overthrow the despotism of Charles I, they sought to have a small share of England on which they could earn their living. However, when the religious miracle which was expected to fertilize the ground they had chosen failed to materialize, and when landowners and the state interfered with force, they abandoned their attempt. Winstanley's utopia was printed two years later in an effort to persuade Cromwell to set up a somewhat primitivistic communistic system in England.

Winstanley's theme is simple: the earth and its products should belong to all; therefore the land should be returned to its original owners, the people. He decides that the main work of reformation is to reform the clergy, the lawyers, and the law. After reviewing the injustices of economic tyranny, he stresses the favorite seventeenth-century theme of legal and constitutional right, and proves, to his own satisfaction, the laborer's right to the land. He attempts to answer the stock objections to communism, distinguishes between individualism and individuality, and between private and personal property, and halts short of advocating compulsory participation in communism. In his society each man produces for central storehouses from which he draws as his needs demand. The control of this system is under the aegis of clearly expressed laws, strictly enforced. After disposing of freedom to trade, religious freedom, and freedom of inheritance, as bogus types, Winstanley lays down the thesis that true freedom lies where a man receives his nourishment, and that it consists in the free enjoyment of the earth. His description of the governmental function arises out of this conception: "Government," he writes, "is a wise and free ordering of the earth and the manners of mankind by observation of particular laws or rules, so that all theinhabitants may live peaceably in plenty and freedom in the land where they are born and bred." His interpretation of history is a materialistic, economic one. He approaches the doctrine of the dictatorship of the proletariat by confining the vote to men of stern moral character and excluding "kingly" men from the franchise. He describes a pyramided structure of government with an all-powerful "preserver of the peace"— Parliament—at its head. It lacks an executive, but the lack is compensated by the provision of overlapping officials whose only function is to see that the laws are kept. Education is to be severe, comprehensive, and practical. Everyone will follow a trade or profession. Invention and the use of talent will be encouraged. Punishments will take the form of work under a taskmaster. A short civil ceremony will suffice for marriage or divorce. And the institution of the family will be maintained.

Though outwardly "progressive," Winstanley's utopia was retrograde in tendency. It would have resulted in a primitivistic agrarian society inconsistent with the economic development of England and the growth of that country as a great trading nation. But his communism had at least the merit that it was tempered by Christian ethics.

Communism in utopian writing next appeared in *The Australian Land Discovered* by Gabriel de Foigny and *The History of the Sevarites* by Denis Veiras, though it is to be doubted that either of them proposed the abolition of private property with any seriousness. Common ownership of productive goods was more earnestly advocated in the eighteenth century by Morelly in his *Code of Nature.* Francis Babeuf took over his theoretical teachings and attempted to promote them during the French Revolution. Neither of those men wrote a proper utopia, but their teachings probably influenced the author of *Equality or A History of Lith-*

conia, the first major utopia to be published in America. It was exceptional, for other socialists and communists, Fourier, Saint-Simon, Louis Blanc, Robert Owen, and Proudhon, failed to write proper utopias, but much of their thought is reflected in Étienne Cabet's *A Voyage to Icaria,* one of the most comprehensive communist utopias ever written.

Religious utopias are probably as numerous as communist ones in the period between 1600 and 1850. I.D.M.'s *Antangil,* the first French utopia, is dominated by a type of Puritanism, as are Andreae's *Christianopolis* and Samuel Gott's *Nova Solyma* (London, 1648).

Johann Valentin Andreae's *Christianopolis, the Description of a Christian Commonwealth and Administration* was written in Latin and published at Strassburg in 1619. It has not been included in the present volume because the utopias of I.D.M., Burton, Campanella, and Bacon sufficiently represent the ideal commonwealths of the early seventeenth century. Nevertheless the account merits some consideration.

Andreae (1586-1654) was born at Herrenberg, studied at Tübingen, and traveled widely in Europe. Religious discords in Geneva impressed him unfavorably, but he greatly admired the harmonious unity of customs and morals there. Having entered the Lutheran ministry, he made his congregation at Calw the starting point in an attempt to set up the ideal social system of which he had dreamed ever since his visit to Switzerland. This was the "practical" type of utopianism. His efforts began with the children but soon extended to the working classes at Calw. He organized cloth and dye workers in a mutual protective system supported by free contributions from his friends and parishioners. This association was so successful that it continued into the twentieth century. But Andreae's utopia is "ideal" in type.

Religion, education, morality, and science are the foundation stones of Caphar Salama, "the place of peace" which is the island site of Andreae's utopia. The allegorical content of the work is more considerable than that in Campanella's *City of the Sun,* with which Andreae was familiar. Setting sail in the good ship *Fantasy,* he was shipwrecked on the island which is a miniature of the whole world. Since he was a seeker of truth, he was accepted into the Christian city and well received by its four hundred inhabitants. In it production is carefully planned in advance. Supplies are placed in public storehouses from which the workers receive what they need without the use of money. Life is simple and untainted by luxuries. Although production and distribution are communistic, houses are inhabited by couples and meals are private. Great attention is paid to education, particularly to the advancement of science and its application to agriculture and industry.

Working hours are short, because the laborers are industrious and efficient. Leisure time is devoted primarily to the service of God, the avoidance of temptations, and growth in virtue. Government is by eight men and eight subordinates all full of the spirit of Christianity. "Never have I seen so great an amount of Christian perfection collected into one place." "Their first and highest exertion is to worship God with a pure and faithful soul; the second, to strive towards the highest and chastest morals; and the third, to develop the mental powers." They prize these qualities inmen: equality, the desire for peace, and contempt for riches, and, above all, culture of the soul. "The chief point with them is that Christians ought to be different from the world around, in morals as well as religion. . . . They declare that the Gospels require a government different from that of the world."

Thus Christianopolis is the City of God, the communion of practicing Christians throughout the world, symbolized in Andreae's theocratic community.

Samuel Gott's *Nova Solyma, the New Jerusalem* is a livelier work, descriptive of a far less ascetic religious commonwealth. It is couched in the form of a romance of intrigues and adventures. They integrate poorly with his holy community dedicated to God and the bourgeois virtues. Other Puritan works such as Richard Baxter's *A Holy Commonwealth* (1656) and John Eliot's *The Christian Commonwealth* (1659) describe theocracies, but are on the outskirts of Utopia. After 1660, few utopias are classifiable as dedicated primarily to Christianity. Joseph Glanvill's continuation of Bacon's *New Atlantis,* published at the end of his volume of *Essays* in 1676, centers upon religion but is better regarded as an exposition of the doctrines of the Cambridge Latitudinarians than as a proper utopia. However it is interesting to note that Glanvill apparently regarded the utopian genre as the most effective form in which to propound his ideas.

The Christian element in utopias written after 1660 undoubtedly declined, but not the interest in religion. More's Utopians had practiced a naturalistic religion. Following his precedent a series of deistic and libertine utopias appeared in the late seventeenth and eighteenth centuries. The utopias of Foigny and Veiras, Tyssot de Patot's *Voyage of Jâmes Massey* (1710), Mercier's *Memoirs of the year 2500* (1770), and G. A. Ellis's *New Britain* (1820), all devote chapters to natural religion and deistic speculations. These are also echoed by Cabet.

Natural science is also important in utopian thought. Bacon's concentration upon it was anticipated slightly by More, largely by Campanella, probably by Andreae, and mildly by Robert Burton (in the utopia which the latter included in the first and second edition of his *Anatomy of Melancholy*). Later editions of the last-mentioned work showed the influence of Baconian science. Likewise under the influence of Bacon, Gott paid some attention to scientific experimentation in his *Nova Solyma,* and Winstanley wrote what is probably his finest prose passage in praise of science. In 1660, *New Atlantis Continued* by R. H. was devoted to adulation of monarchy and glorification of the possibilities of science. Thenceforth nearly all utopias paid some attention to the importance of science in a perfected society. This element is particularly noticeable in the utopias of Mercier and Cabet.

Militarism is also a leading theme in utopias written before 1850. Plato set the precedent of devoting a whole class to the protection of society. Thomas More also paid great attention to the military aspects of his *Utopia,* not that he favored militarism as such, but that realism demanded its inclusion. It is startling to find that his highly moral Utopians, who would have despised bribery at home or any hiring of one free man by another, used both hired soldiers and bribery in wars. The author of *Antangil* may well have been a soldier, for militarism is one of his main preoccupations. The problems of war and peace, defense, military organization, and the like also receive special attention from James Harrington in the various utopias which he wrote in the middle of the seventeenth century; militarism is also stressed by Veiras, and by Foigny (who makes the wars of the Australians against natural and human enemies an integral part of his plot), and, indeed, by almost all the utopias up to 1850. Ellis, for example, in *New Britain,* is especially concerned with military problems and organization, though he does not allow them to be dominant in his society, as I.D.M. had done in *Antangil.*

The main theme of utopias from 1500 to 1850 was advocacy, explicit or implicit, of the fullest possible, efficient utilization of the available resources of men and materials in a given society. Conservatives found this a means of supporting established ideas, institutions, and ways of life. Radicals, intent upon such total utilization, advocated a revolution in ideas and institutions as necessary to their goal. In general, the conservatives, Bacon, for example, looked to science tempered by morals and religion as the chief means to this full exploitation of resources. Radicals like Cabet, looked less to science than to education and institutional reforms.

However, not all utopists regarded the material basis of society as primary in their utopias. Fénelon and Ellis, for example, saw the value of the simple life, uncomplicated by luxuries and their accompanying vices. This ascetic, somewhat primitivistic current in utopian thought derived largely from More and was greatly influenced by Rousseau.

Utopias from 1600 to 1850 may be roughly classified in their historical development, as follows. The imaginary states of I.D.M., Campanella, Andreae, Burton, and Bacon constituted what might be called the Utopian Efflorescence of the earlier seventeenth century. Although they vary greatly from each other, all these writers were influenced by Plato and More; all stress the application of modern science in society; all are optimistic in outlook and show the influence of the idea of progress, which previously had not been widespread. These utopias were written between 1600 and 1630. Then a current of utopian fantasy revived—a continuation of the tradition of fantastic voyages which dates back to Iambulus and Euhemerus, and which was frequently echoed in the Middle Ages in such works as *The Anticlaudian* of Alain de Lille and in the voyage of Astolfo to the moon in Ariosto's *Orlando Furioso.* The imaginary societies described by Rabelais and by Joseph Hall in his *Discovery of a New World* were in the same tradition. In 1638 it revived with *The Man in the Moon,* by Francis Godwin, which was rapidly followed by John Wilkins' *Discourse concerning a New World and Another Planet* (1640). Further fantastic celestial voyages and satirical accounts of imaginary commonwealths are contained in D'Ablancourt's translation of Lucian's *True History,* a work of the later period of ancient Greek civilization. Indeed, Lucian may be regarded as the father of this type of superterrestrial "science fiction." D'Ablancourt added a supplement of his own to the *True History* and published both about 1648. The tradition continued in Cyrano de Bergerac's *Comical History* (1656 and 1662), with its satirical accounts of societies on the moon and sun.

Meanwhile Puritan utopianism came to the fore. The tradition established by I.D.M. and Andreae branched into romance literature with Samuel Gott's *Nova Solyma* (1648). The Levellers of the Puritan Revolution had many utopian ideas but failed to write a work in this genre. However, Digger communism produced such a work in Winstanley's *Law of Freedom.* Meanwhile the Fifth Monarchist Puritans propounded semiutopian conceptions of a Kingdom of Christ shortly to be established on earth; and Baxter and Eliot approached the utopian type in *A Holy Commonwealth* and *The Christian Commonwealth,* both of which appeared in 1659. But as secularism began to prevail over Puritanism, less theocratic imaginary states were described: such were Samuel Hartlib's *Macaria* (1641), which was strongly influenced by Bacon; *The Poor Man's Advocate,* by Peter Chamberlen (1649); Robert Norwood's *Pathway unto England's Perfect Settlement* (1653); Peter Plockhoy's *Way to the Peace and Settlement of these Nations,* and similar works. Few of these completely satisfy the definition of a proper utopia, but all of them propound economic programs intended to realize something approaching a perfect society. Parallel to them were a host of political utopias and related works. These put forth model constitutions. Such were Marchamont Nedham's *Excellency of a Free*

State (1656), the anonymous *Chaos* (1659), William Sprigge's *Modest Plea for an Equal Commonwealth* (1659), the various utopias penned by James Harrington, especially his *Oceana* (1656), and a royalist work written in Latin by a Frenchman in England—*Syndromedia* by Antoine Le Grand (1669).

Boesky on utopias of the seventeenth century:

In the 1640s and 1650s, while Milton was earning a name for himself through the achievements of his "left hand," a prodigious number of utopias were being written and published in England. There were as many as two hundred sects in England in the middle of the century, and almost every sect had its utopia. . . .

English utopias written during the 1640s and 1650s reflect [a] new aesthetic of discipline and regulation while introducing a new kind of army—a civilian corps of trained and zealous workers, dedicated to the common goal of productivity. In Gabriel Plattes's *A Description of the Famous Kingdome of Macaria* . . . (1641), a Traveler presents "strange newes, and much knowledge" of the commonwealth of Macaria, governed by exacting "principall Lawes," a commonwealth in which self-regulation is projected onto the "treasure house" of the land. Macaria's citizens, trained in its central College of Experience, are presented as a regiment of workers, uniform in their zeal to conquer "want" by mining and plumbing the land.

Amy Boesky, "Milton's Heaven and Utopia," in
Studies in English Literature, 1500-1900,
Winter, 1996.

Cyrano de Bergerac's *Comical History* may be classified as the first of a series of French libertine utopias. After England had her Revolution, utopianism declined there, except for semiutopian schemes written largely under the influence of Harrington, of which the anonymous *Free State of Noland* (1696) is representative. But in France the ideological undermining of the *ancien régime* had still to take place, and a potent force in that direction were the libertine utopias by Cyrano, Veiras, Foigny, Claude Gilbert, and Tyssot de Patot. In general, the outlook of these writers was heterodox. Not infrequently blasphemous, they questioned the established orthodoxies of religion, morals, and politics in their period.

German utopianism lagged behind that of the rest of Europe. If Andreae's Latin work is excepted, the first German utopia was the anonymous *State of Ophir (Ophirischer Staat),* a comprehensive, pedestrian, earnest, prodigiously long work published in 1699. It has been largely neglected by scholars, and, like the Latin utopia, *Icaria* (1637), by Joannes Bisselius, deserves

further attention. . . .

In the eighteenth century, the fantastic voyage tradition continued and resulted in the semiutopian land of the Houyhnhnms in Swift's *Gulliver's Travels,* and in such works as Simon Berington's *Gaudentio di Lucca.* Ludvig Holberg followed the precedent of Swift in *The Voyages of Niels Klim* (1741); and the constitutional type of utopia, combined with a modified communism, recurred in the accounts of Spensonia by Thomas Spence about 1800. But for the most part, though rich in Rousseauistic and utopian socialist theories, the eighteenth century produced few utopias. *Memoirs of the Year 2500* by Sebastien Mercier, published in French in 1770, is therefore noteworthy. Its intrinsic value is slight, but its historical interest is great, for, in some measure, it forecasts the French Revolution. Moreover, it reflects the sentimentality, the optimism, and, to some extent, the Rousseauism of the eighteenth century; and it anticipates Romanticism. . . .

Frank E. Manuel and Fritzie P. Manuel (essay date 1979)

SOURCE: "The Utopian Propensity," in *Utopian Thought in the Western World,* Cambridge, Mass.: The Belknap Press of Harvard University Press, 1979, pp. 1-29.

[*In the following excerpt from their introduction to* Utopian Thought in the Western World, *the critics discuss several aspects of utopian literature, including: utopian literary forms, critical approaches to interpretation of utopian literature, the influence of New World exploration and scientific discovery on utopian thought, the cultural traditions that have influenced the western conception of utopia, and the characteristics of the utopian writer.*]

Anthropologists tell us that blessed isles and paradises are part of the dreamworld of savages everywhere. The dogged wanderings of the Guarani tribe in search of a "Land-without-Evil" have been tracked over the length and breadth of Brazil, and the contemporary cargo-cults of Asia and Africa have been investigated for their marvelous syncretism of Christian and native paradises. Neither pictorial nor discursive philosophico-religious utopias are exclusive to the Western world. Taoism, Theravada Buddhism, and medieval Muslim philosophy are impregnated with utopian elements. There are treatises on ideal states and stories about imaginary havens of delight among the Chinese, the Japanese, the Hindus, and the Arabs, but the profusion of Western utopias has not been equaled in any other culture. Perhaps the Chinese have been too worldly and practical, the Hindus too transcendental to recognize a tension between the Two Kingdoms and to resolve it in that myth of a heaven on earth which lies at the heart of utopian fantasy.

In the Beginning Was the Word

For some time before the publication in 1516 of the *De Optimo Reipublicae Statu deque Nova Insula Utopia Libellus Vere Aureus,* Thomas More and his friend Erasmus had been referring to it simply as the "Nusquama," from a good Latin adverb meaning "nowhere." But then the spirit of neologism possessed the future saint. He combined the Greek *ou,* used to express a general negative and transliterated into the Latin *u,* with the Greek *topos,* place or region, to build Utopia. In the playful printed matter prefixed to the body of the book the poet laureate of the island, in a brief self-congratulatory poem written in the Utopian tongue, claimed that his country deserved to be called "Eutopia" with an *eu,* which in Greek connoted a broad spectrum of positive attributes from good through ideal, prosperous, and perfect. Guillaume Budé, the great French humanist and a well-wisher of More's, added to the confusion by remarking in his complimentary Latin letter to the author that he had heard the place called "Udepotia," or "Neverland," from the Greek for "never." Finally, Germain de Brie, otherwise known as Brixius, author of the sarcastic *Antimorus,* heaped scorn on both the Greek of More's title and the many new words crowded into his Latin text. Through the centuries utopias have preserved the complexity of the original nomenclature.

In the sixteenth and seventeenth centuries, descriptive works that imitated the *Utopia* were called utopias, with a minuscule, and they adhered more or less to traditional literary devices that More himself had received from Lucian of Samosata, who in turn had inherited them from Hellenistic novels, many of them no longer extant. The invention of printing made readily available translations of tales of this character from one European language into another, and they came to constitute an ever-expanding corpus, in which stock formulas and concepts can be traced historically and their modifications charted. The principal elements are a shipwreck or chance landing on the shores of what turns out to be an ideal commonwealth, a return to Europe, and a report on what has been remarked. If arranged in chronological order these works, considered "proper utopias" by bibliographers, form a sequence in which the imitation of predecessors is patent.

How to classify the Morean utopia as a form of rhetoric and a way to knowledge was taken up as early as 1595 in Sir Philip Sidney's *Defence of Poesie.* There he coupled utopia with poetry and ranked them both above philosophy and history as more persuasive in leading men to virtue than a weighty philosophical argument: "But even in the most excellent determination of goodnesse, what *Philosophers counsaile* can so readily direct a Prince, as the feined *Cirus* in *Xeno-*phon, or a vertuous man in all fortunes as Aeneas in Virgill, or a whole Common-wealt, as the Way of Sir Thomas Moores Eutopia?" Courtier of Elizabeth and loyal member of the Church of England, Sidney discreetly avoided what might have been interpreted as unqualified commitment to the political ideal of a Papist executed for treason; but his praise of the genre was unaffected. "I say the Way, because where Sir Thomas Moore erred, it was the fault of the man and not of the Poet: for that Way of patterning a Common-wealth, was most absolute though hee perchaunce hath not so absolutely performed it." Sidney's pithy definition of poetry, "a speaking *Picture,* with this end to teach and delight," was applied equally to utopia. The term utopia speedily made its way into other European languages. By the early seventeenth century it was not uncommon for great writers—Cervantes, Shakespeare—to interpolate a utopian episode or allude to utopian conceits by name. Francis Bacon made a point of mocking utopias and labeling the *New Atlantis* a fable, but contemporary compendia-makers forced him into the utopian company of More and Campanella.

Before the sixteenth century was out, the adjectival form "utopian" was born, and when it was not a merely derogatory epithet, connoting a wild fancy or a chimerical notion, it could refer to an ideal psychological condition or to an idealizing capacity. The use of the word by John Donne, a descendant of More's, may be its subtlest early extension to imply a general emotional attitude. In a verse letter to Sir Henry Wotton, who had spent many years in the courts of Venice and Florence, the poet wrote:

> I thinke if men, which in these places live
> Durst looke for themselves, and themselves retrive,
> They would like strangers greet themselves, seeing then
> Utopian youth, growne old Italian.

By the seventeenth century utopia was no longer restricted to a speaking picture, a dramatic narrative portrayal of a way of life that is so essentially good and fulfills so many profound longings that it wins immediate, almost instinctive, approbation. It could embrace as well the underlying principles of an optimum society expounded and argued either by the author directly or by several interlocutors. Utopia also came to denote general programs and platforms for ideal societies, codes, and constitutions that dispensed with the fictional apparatus altogether. When the discursive, argumentative utopia assumed a place alongside the speaking picture, the line between a utopian system and political and social theory often became shadowy. In *A Voice in Rhama* (1647) Peter Chamberlen, an English royal physician and a Fifth Monarchy man—not so improbable a combination as might be imagined—wrote of his hope that the world would return to its "first simplicity" or to a "Christian utopia." John Milton, in his *Apology for Smectymnuus* (1642), and his friend Samuel Hartlib, who had been appointed an official "Projector" by Parliament, both used utopia in the sense of a model for an ideal commonwealth. In the Pansophic utopia of Campanella, Andreae, Comenius, and Leibniz, the boundaries of an ideal Christian republic were enlarged to encompass the whole world. While religious commentaries on what heavenly paradise would be like kept up a constant flow of images as they had for two thousand years, the conception of a millennium as a real society on earth covering a fixed period of time gave rise to speculations about what events would occur in that blessed epoch, what government would be instituted, and what social relationships would prevail. Whenever the vaguely oracular mode of prophecy was set aside in the seventeenth century, the millenarian utopia could respond to concrete, matter-of-fact questions. Fifth Monarchy men of England even committed themselves to a specific tariff policy for their millennium.

Toward the end of the eighteenth century, in a growingly de-Christianized Europe, even while the old isolated island and valley utopias and a newer type of awakened-dreamer utopia continued to be regurgitated, there came into greater prominence the branch of utopian thought that spurned any fictional backdrop, broke with the limitations of specific place, and addressed itself directly to the reformation of the entire species. The Frenchmen Morelly, Dom Deschamps, Restif de la Bretonne, and Condorcet wrote what in effect were constitutions for a new secular, global society, and conceived of themselves as universal lawgivers, as would the utopian socialists of the post-Revolutionary era. By the early nineteenth century innovative utopian thought had all but lost its enclosed space. The novels portraying encapsulated and protected pictorial utopias, while they have continued to be sold in millions of copies into our own time, were often in content residual and derivative, dependent upon revolutionary utopian theory that others had propounded. A utopian genius like Charles Fourier might still initiate his project with the description of a single phalanstery, and on occasion one detects the rudiments of a story among his papers, but his phalanstery was conceived as a cell in an international movement that he hoped would soon spread throughout the globe, with similar communities joined in a vast federation.

In these rationalist, systematic utopias whose province was the whole world, the means of reaching utopia was transformed from an adventure story or a rite de passage to Elysium into a question of political action: How do you change a present misery into a future happiness in this world? The method of reaching utopia and the speed of travel, usually peripheral in the novelistic form, were now central, and the prickly issues of revolution, evolution, the uses of violence, the mechanics of the propagation of a new faith, determinism and free will, the imperatives of blind historical destiny, and the requirements of human freedom became intrinsic to utopian thought. In the early utopia the mode of access did not alter the nature of the perfect society. In the discursive universal utopia, though the idea was rarely spelled out, the way of attaining the ideal city affected the nature of the city itself. The vision of perfection was henceforward either disfigured or enhanced by the path to utopia. When utopia became attached to global philosophies of history, practitioners of that form of knowledge were turned into unwitting utopians or anti-utopians as they prognosticated the ineluctable end toward which mankind was moving.

Utopia thus became laden with meanings as it moved through time: a literary genre, a constitution for a perfectly restructured polity, a state of mind, the religious or scientific foundations of a universal republic. Many French eighteenth-century works called by their authors *rêves, codes, robinsonades, voyages imaginaires* were patently utopias in the conventional sense. Utopia could always be used either positively or pejoratively. In philosophe circles, Grimm and Meister's literary newsletter applied the disdainful epithet *espèce d'utopie* to the flood of stories that, with constantly changing content, imitated Morean devices. In the positivist tradition of the nineteenth century Littré's French dictionary defined *utopie* as *chimère*, noted its early appearance in Rabelais's *Pantagruel*, and seized the opportunity to deliver a brief homily on the deceptions of utopian promises. Over the years a utopian vocabulary entered the French language—*utopie, utopique, utopiste, utopiens*—though not all terms were welcomed into the Academy. In English a utopian became a person who inhabits a utopia or one who would like to be in a utopia or has a utopian cast of temperament. Some men were utopographers, a seventeenth-century word for the writers or inventors of utopias. The researcher into the utopian propensity of mankind, though he is one of a long line going back to Aristotle, has no particular name, and must rest content with the plain appellation historian, though his subject has been dubbed utopology by a recent innovator.

Two further neologisms have proved to be of use to us in designating different aspects of the subject, and we have accepted them without slighting the time-sanctioned coverall of utopia. The term uchronia, no time, was invented in the late nineteenth century by the French philosopher Charles Renouvier to characterize a fictitious history of the past written on the supposition that a critical turning point had had a different outcome. There has beena sizable literature of such exercises since the end of the eighteenth century, none of it noteworthy. We took the label uchronia, rashly altered its spelling to euchronia, good time, and applied it to a major departure in Western utopia and utopian thought that occurred when good place, good state of consciousness, and good constitution were all translated to a good future time. The Germans have coined a word for the speaking-picture euchronia, the *Zukunftsroman.* The other neologism, eupsychia, was introduced by the psychologist Abraham Maslow to signify an ideal state of consciousness; though the idea had already been incorporated into utopia in the sixteenth century, we have had occasion to borrow its new name.

This abbreviated overview of historical semantics with its limited terminological armature may help to guide us through a broad and loose-jointed universe of utopian discourse.

The Shadowy Boundaries of Utopia

[If] the land of utopia were thrown open to every fantasy of an individual ideal situation the realm would be boundless. The personal daydream with its idiosyncratic fixations has to be excluded. The ideal condition should have some measure of generality, if not universality, or it becomes merely a narcissistic yearning. There are utopias so private that they border on schizophrenia. *The Description of a New World, called the Blazing World* (1666) by Margaret Cavendish, Duchess of Newcastle, has much in common with the delusions of Dr. Schreber analyzed by Sigmund Freud in a famous paper. Uncounted utopian worlds of this stripe, many of them highly systematized, are being conjured up every day, in and out of hospitals, though few of them are ever set in print. (The title of Giulio Clemente Scotti's *Lucii Cornelii Europaei Monarchia Solipsorum ad Leonem Allatium* [1645] suggests a solipsistic utopia, but the work turns out to be a utopian parody of the Jesuit order.) We have preferred to steer clear of solipsistic manifestations and continently restrict ourselves to those utopias that have won a measure of public acceptance and become at least folie à deux, the author and the printer. When, however, a solipsistic utopia is projected into a social utopia, it falls within the permissible sphere, especially if the creator of the psychic *monde idéal* happens to be Jean-Jacques Rousseau. It would require a bit of stretching to incorporate Diogenes the Cynic's concept of autarchy into utopia, though a fragment on an ideal primitive condition is imputed to him, and his notion of shamelessness has found a counterpart in Reformation andpresent-day eupsychias.

Nor should every political and economic prognostication be considered utopian. In mid-eighteenth-century England, a Tory gentleman outlined the future history of European wars in the twentieth century under the reign of a George VI [in *The Reign of George* VI]. He predicted Russia's penetration deep into Europe, the occupation of Scandinavia, and the defeat of France by England. Nothing in the life of the British Isles is portrayed as remarkably different from what it was under George III, except that the empire is administered from a Versailles-like capital called Stanley. The changes envisaged are not radical enough—they do not strike at the roots of existence—to be included in the utopian orbit. They are nothing but minor, false prophecy. A perennial question arises as to how to distinguish a program of reform or a five-year plan from a utopia. The reply that the difference lies in the extent of the proposed transformation begs the question, because one man's trivial revision is another man's upheaval. Utopia should probably exclude mere futurist projections of existing series, short-term predictions still fettered to the present. Final judgment in these instances has to be subjective, though perhaps some historical testimony or contemporary consensus can be invoked.

The facile extrapolations of a scientist futurology that looks only to tomorrow, or to the year 2000, and engages in immediate problem-solving are of a different order from the leap into a new state of being in which contemporary values in at least one area—the critical one for the utopian—are totally transformed or turned upside down. In the *Utopia* of Thomas More, who was anguished over greed and corruption in the Christian polity, such a transvaluation was symbolized in the conversion of gold specie into chamber pots and jewels into children's baubles, and was embodied in conceptions of work, pleasure, and property. And in the seventeenth century, when the new science, which had earlier been obliged to apologize for its existence, was glorified as the foundation stone of a world Christian society in Pansophic visions from Bacon through Leibniz, a real world in which science had either been feared or despised was metamorphosed by utopia. Condorcet's flights of imagination in his commentary on the *New Atlantis* and the recent projections of those who expect a self-alteration of species man in an extraterrestrial environment may have been regarded by these scientist-utopians as reasonable predictions. Many of their foretellings have in fact come true, and the developments they envisaged could be read as possible, if daring, extensions of contemporary knowledge. But their revolutionary character has produced the pattern for a human condition that is totally new by any standard.

We have deliberately separated utopian theory and invention from attempts to put them into practice. Studying the actual experience of those who sought to implement utopias would bring us too dangerously close to reality. There have been thinkers who, having given birth to an idea, proceeded to act it out, men who founded movements and organized schools, who formed conspiracies and hatched cabals, who led bands of followers to strange places. Some, like Thomas Müntzer and Tommaso Campanella and Gracchus Babeuf, paid dearly for their ventures; others, like Fourier, Owen, Comte, and Marx, ended up in constant bickering with their disciples. The fortunate ones, like Henri Saint-Simon, initiated their followers into the system and then had the good judgment to die. But usually there has been a functional division of labor between writers of utopias and the activist utopians who have established utopian communities or launched revolutions for the sake of seeing the glory of utopia with their own eyes. When we analyze popular millenarian or revolutionary movements, it is the content of the dreams, manifest or hidden, not the strategies for their realization, that primarily engages us. Were a new science to be founded—and we have no such pretension—it would be valid to distinguish between theoretical utopistics and applied utopistics. Utopian practice, if indeed it is not a contradiction in terms, has sometimes affected later theorists; but on the whole the ardor of a utopian innovator in the moment of creation is overwhelming and is not dampened by his knowledge of previous defeats.

Popular hope literature has not been excluded from this study on principle, or without awareness that a police or other judicial record, or a hospital casebook, or a prize essay contest in a provincial French academy, might reveal an unnoticed utopian thinker operating in his own world whose dreams could be more representative of large segments of the population than a formally printed utopia. The lines had to be drawn somewhere, and the task of capturing the utopian consciousness of great masses of people has been left to others, some of whom have already begun their explorations. A distinction has to be made between a collective utopia that exists in a passive state among a large segment of the population and a utopia expressly written for the purpose of instructing men and persuading them to some action. Doubtless the unwritten popular utopia of a country is constantly undergoing change, but access to the transformations would involve the development of new strategies that will have to await other historians. The complete speaking-picture or finished discursive utopia is usually the product of deliberate educative intent, and it is explicit and organized in its presentation. This may be both a virtue and a limitation.

The problem of the relations between the book utopia and other more popular manifestations of similar ideas has not been wholly resolved. There are times when both have been swept up by a wave and carried away in the sea of a common utopia. The utopia of the people has been mediated by members of the literate classes in Attic comedy, in Midrashic literature, in trial records of the Inquisition and interrogations of millenarians, in police spy reports, in court trials following riots and uprisings. The mutual interpenetration of popular utopian elements and literary documents appears obvious. If a group or a class is isolated, it will evolve a utopia

unique to itself; its archaeological reconstruction is another matter. But there is reason to be leery of the eighteenth-century *Bibliothèque bleue,* written for, but not by, "the people," as a mirror of the utopian *espérance* of the masses. Folktale and folksong may yield a more authenic picture, though the decipherment of their universal images demands skills beyond those of the professional historian and their message may be ahistorical.

This history is not in search of the utopian ideas most widely diffused in the population of the West at particular moments, one living head being counted as the repository of one utopian idea. Kant's reading of Rousseau's primitivist utopia is not equivalent to everyman's. Since for most ages the popular utopia is largely inaccessible, or the materials still remain to be assembled, the present work tends to dwell on the utopian thought of the literate classes in Western society. Through time they have changed in character and in numbers and so has the representativeness of their utopias. But the study of utopian thought in books composed by philosophers and litterateurs does not limit the significance of the enterprise to upper-class culture. Often the utopias of the "educated classes" have had a way of seeping into popular action programs and general social movements, so that in considering today's upper-class utopia we may be witnessing a preview of tomorrow's mass demands. (This is not always so; many major utopian conceptions remain literary.) Though the utopia is inspired by one man's experience of his society, he may well become the voice of whole silent segments of the population. He creates consciousness, as the chapbooks say. Virtually every one of the major slogans that expressed the hopes of French and English working-class movements of the first half of the nineteenth century was plucked from the gardens of the printed works of utopian writers.

The Critical Study of Utopia

Like the utopias themselves, the analytic and historical study of utopia has had precedents going all the way back to the Greeks. That proposals for "ideal states" demanded objective critical examination was first argued by Aristotle in Book II of the *Politics,* where he entered the lists against forms "designed by theorists" and took on seriatim Plato, Phaleas of Chalcedon, and Hippodamus of Miletus. If we forgo for the present a laborious tracing of Aristotle's successors and restrict ourselves to relatively modern times, the earliest known academic treatment of utopian thought is probably a stillborn Latin dissertation published in 1704 by the hapless Henricus ab Ahlefeld, whose fame has been obscured by cataloguers' attributing his work to Georg Pasch, the professor who approved the thesis. But it was not until Louis Reybaud's *Etudes sur les réformateurs ou socialistes modernes* (1840) that the *utopies sociales,* which he branded subversive, really received detailed consideration as a type. Simultaneously, on the other side of the Rhine, Robert von Mohl drew up a list of some twenty-five utopias from Plato down, baptized them *Staatsromane,* and bravely proposed to incorporate them into political science. Utopia became a subject of contention in world revolutionary movements when Marx in the *Communist Manifesto* and Engels in the *Anti-Dühring* conceived of their doctrine dialectically as at once an outgrowth of earlier utopian thought and its contradiction, and condemned utopias as outdated and historically superseded fantasies, though anyone ploughing through the *Marx-Engels Gesamtausgabe* is immediately aware of a constant preoccupation with utopians of the past.

Although utopianism attracted a few champions in the 1920s and 1930s, to many observers it was a corpse. The nails were hammered into the coffin with resounding blows struck by Marxists at one end and Fascist theorists at the other. The latter group, adapting the language of Georges Sorel, grandiloquently proclaimed the superiority of their own creative myths as "dynamic realities," spontaneous utterances of authentic desires, over the utopias, which they dismissed as hollow rationalist constructs. For a whole galaxy of other twentieth-century thinkers utopia was a *Schimpfwort:* Ortega y Gasset labeled it outrightly "the fallacious"; Karl Popper, no less contemptuous, was more verbose in denigrating utopian engineering; and for Arnold Toynbee utopia was a symptom of the descending stage of the civilization cycle.

But in a renewal of critical and historical study, a number of twentieth-century writers—particularly in the last three decades—have been considering the utopian propensity of man in a different spirit, making strenuous efforts to grasp its inner meaning as an aspect of human nature instead of sitting in pontifical judgment and either approving or condemning. Along with university seminars on utopian thought and international conferences among the learned in various parts of the world, an accumulation of theoretical works bears witness to the revival of interest in utopianism. Karl Mannheim's redefinition in his own private language of the idea of utopia and his typologizing of the whole body of political and social thought in *Ideologie und Utopie* (1929), though it hardly won universal acceptance among sociologists and political scientists, had been hailed in its day as the outline of a discipline that promised a new and more profound understanding of social life. Shortly after World War II, two French thinkers, both of whom died prematurely, devoted themselves to a fresh consideration of the uses of utopia. Raymond Ruyer's *L'Utopie et les utopies* (1950) delineated the "utopian mentality" in psychological terms and identified *le mode utopique* as "a mental exercise on lateral possibilities." Georges Duveau's plan for a full-scale sociology of utopia was left incomplete, but

his posthumously assembled essays [*Sociologie de l'utopie et aûtres "essais"*] constitute a serious effort at a rehabilitation of what he called the "realistic" eighteenth- and nineteenth-century utopias as guides for the world of tomorrow, in preference to Hegelian-Marxist historical determinism. In an entirely different intellectual atmosphere the writings of Martin Buber on utopian socialism were meant to serve a similar purpose in the reconstruction of modern society.

Even more ambitious undertakings on the conceptual level were the works of Ernst Bloch, Frederik Lodewijk Polak, and Roger Mucchielli. Bloch, a Weimar philosopher who migrated to the United States, moved to East Germany after World War II and to West Germany in 1967, had first propounded his ideas back in 1918 in *Geist der Utopie,* a work aimed at infusing positive meaning into the idea of utopia. At his death in 1977 he was the most famous contemporary commentator on the utopian propensity of Western man. The full development of his concepts of the *Noch-Nicht-Seins* and of the utopia of the concrete, with their amalgam of Marxism and expressionist flights of fancy, did not come until the 1940s and 1950s in the writing and publication of his three-volume chef d'oeuvre, *Das Prinzip Hoffnung.* Two volumes first appeared in East Germany, the third in West Germany. The wanderings of thisperennial heretic have inevitably left their traces in the changing ideational nuances of his works over six decades. In *The Image of the Future* (1955) Polak, who enjoyed the patronage of the Council of Europe, warned of grave dangers to Western culture should its "unique succession of powerful images of the future" become exhausted and not be replenished. Roger Mucchielli's *Le Mythe de la cité idéale* (1961) saw utopia as an enduring manifestation of the human spirit. We need not accept Mucchielli's rather complex typology of ideal cities, or his turgid definition of utopia as "a myth, awakened by a personal revolt against the human condition in general in the shape of existing circumstances, which, meeting the obstacle of impotence, evokes in the imagination an *other* or a nowhere, where all obstacles are removed." But his pointed critique of Ruyer's psychological reductionism that posits a single utopian mentality is persuasive.

In 1967, Jean Servier presented a brief synoptic view of the history of utopias in the West that nourished the dominant sociological and psychological interpretations with an adventurous psychoanalytic reading of some of the symbols in utopian literature. Melvin Lasky's *Utopia and Revolution* (1976) is the most ambitious recent attempt to relate theoretical and applied utopistics. Pierre Versins's *Encyclopédie de l'utopie, des voyages extraordinaires et de la science fiction* (1972), a thousand pages of summaries of utopian stories and projects arranged in alphabetical order, though amateurish in its execution, is testimony that concern with utopias of the past has moved from the anthological stage to the higher stage of the compendious lexicon. In 1978 Michael Winter published the first volume of a *Compendium Utopiarum* that promises to assemble as complete and meticulous a bibliography of "proper" utopias as the present state of the art allows. Critical literature on the nature of utopia in books and journals has now reached avalanche proportions, perhaps testimony that the analytic mode has submerged, at least for the time being, the creative utopian impulse. The concentrations is heavily German and Italian, and appears to be intimately related to attempts at a redefinition or revision of Marx. The theologizing of Marx and the multiplication of deviations only highlight his continued centrality in utopian thought and the poverty of contemporary Marxist philosophy.

Our Way to the Utopian Constellations

The historical longevity of certain mythic themes in utopia that evoke associations remote and deeply rooted in Western consciousness can help us to understand the fascination utopias have exerted over the minds of men. Anyone born into a culture is likely to imbibe a set of utopian fantasies even as he internalizes certain prohibitions at an early age. We do not know whether these utopian elements are part of a collective unconscious. The problem of conformities in the symbols of utopia is not unlike that of dream symbols. They may be ahistorical and acultural, though always found in a specific context, social and psychological. But even as we probe in this study for the continuities in Western utopian thought, we are acutely aware of the temporal and geographic fractures and demarcations that separate one utopian constellation from another.

Particularly rich utopian moments have been attached to political revolutions and the dictatorships that follow in their wake, such as the English Civil War or the Age of the French Revolution—periods, incidentally, in which de facto restrictions on printing disappear for a while and allow a host of new conceptions to surface. At such times all things seem possible, and the utopian appears no madder than other men. Religious schisms and intellectual revolutions like the emergence of the new science in the seventeenth century, or the dramatic introduction of new modes of production in the nineteenth, or the exploration of new space in the Americas, in the South Seas, or beyond the bounds of this sphere, have all sparked novel utopian ideas and led to the formation of startling new utopian constellations.

Despite the thesis in Victor Dupont's grand compendium on utopia and utopian thought in English literature—that there is a special affinity between the English national temperament and utopia [*L'Utopie et le roman utopique dans la littérature anglaise*]—the utopian propensity is common to the Western world. The

Italian architectural utopias of the Renaissance and the French social utopias of the eighteenth and nineteenth centuries were among the heights of utopian expression, and the Pansophic vision of the seventeenth century had a deep Germanic and Lutheran coloration. In a particular epoch the spirit of utopia may have been more active in one national culture than in others or a utopian form may have flourished in only one land; but utopia in general has not been geographically exclusive. The relative unity of Western culture has guaranteed the rapid diffusion of utopian ideas irrespective of the countries in which they originated. We consider Russian and American utopian thought before the late nineteenth century an overflow of European types— Prince M. M. Shcherbatov's *Journey to the Land of the Ophirs* (1796) and New England millenarian sermons are derivative. A long tradition identifies the colonies and the United States with utopia, but, curiously, those who were actually fashioning that utopia were dreaming about it in European terms. The writings of the Puritans with all their millenarian imagery and the later utopian proclamations of the victorious colonial insurgents are extensions of European idea systems. The seven books of Cotton Mather's *Magnalia Christi Americana: or, the Ecclesiastical History of New-England, from its first planting in the year 1620, unto the year of our Lord, 1698,* constitute a mammoth, self-adulatory utopia whose spiritual roots are in England, where it was first published in 1702. The Winthrops and the Mathers were putting utopia into practice, building a Christian utopia and a New Jerusalem in their commonwealth with imported thoughts and symbols, even as in the nineteenth century New England Transcendentalists would experiment with Fourierist ideas in Brook Farm. The absence of a sustained utopian tradition in Spain is peculiar, though free-floating utopian affect may have somehow attached itself to the figure of Don Quixote. The manuscript of an Enlightenment utopia, *Descripción de la Sinapia, península en la terra austral,* has recently been published, but it hardly modifies the generalization that Spain was relatively untouched by the utopian main current until the penetration of Marxist and anarchist thought. Danes, Swiss, Poles, Czechs, and members of other European nations have written utopias, though the overwhelming number of Western utopias—whatever their national origin—were first printed in Latin, English, French, Italian, or German.

Not all utopias can without straining be squeezed within the chronological benchmarks and attached to the ideational clusters that we shall outline, but one can seek out those constellations of utopias and utopian thought in each epoch that have embodied significant innovations and new content. Although virtually all utopias deal with major aspects of living, such as work, government, love and sexuality, knowledge, religion, beauty, the tone and quality of life, dying, each of these subjects has at one or another time preempted a central position in utopian consciousness and has inspired new forms. Works that spew forth worn-out themes, even when numerically weighty, have been neglected or underplayed here in favor of new departures. Nobody can really copy straight even when that is the intention, and hence there are minor intrusions of novelty in the most hackneyed utopian thought; these offshoots, however, are to be distinguished from authentic innovations, when the rather repetitive series is broken by a genius who establishes a new style. Though in most utopian thinkers the past is present, there are rare moments of disjuncture too acute to allow for the utopian past as a prime catalytic agent in a new creation. We have usually hurried over the pabulum of an age, the chewed cud of previous epochs, and looked for fresh invention.

The underlying pattern of this book involves identifying the major historical constellations of utopian thought in the Western world. Our task has been to explore the main lines of transmission, without enslavement to a chain of influences, and at the same time to mark and highlight innovations, fractures, and discontinuities, the formation of new clusters, without accepting every self-proclaimed discoverer in utopia at his word.

Mapping the Constellations

The fixing of a point of departure confronted us with our first problem. One possibility entailed going all the way back to the paradisaical fantasies of the Near East in the third millennium before Christ, another to Plato's presentation of both the *mythos* and the *logos* of an ideal city. But the unique character of utopia in the West was in our judgment best brought out by initiating the history in medias res, so to speak, with its baptism in the Age of the Renaissance. Utopia is a hybrid plant, born of the crossing of a paradisaical, other-worldly belief of Judeo-Christian religion with the Hellenic myth of an ideal city on earth. The naming took place in an enclave of sixteenth-century scholars excited about the prospect of a Hellenized Christianity. While we may loosely refer to ancient and medieval works with some utopian content as utopias, the Western utopia is for us a creation of the world of the Renaissance and the Reformation. Since that period, the history of utopia has been reasonably continuous. Works and parts of works that entered utopian consciousness from the ancient Judeo-Christian, Hellenic, and medieval worlds have been considered not in themselves but as the vital prehistory or underthought of modern utopia, that strange absorption in a heaven on earth, the desire for both worlds. In this context we have read the ancient works, in the first instance, not as they might be reconstituted in their native habitat by present-day scholars, but as they appeared to Renaissance Europeans who laid the foundations of the Christian utopia. After tracing the Judeo-Christian and Hellenic strands in the underthought of utopia, we ad-

vance directly to our first historical constellation, marking the principal figures in the age of birth and naming.

The period of the latter part of the fifteenth and the early sixteenth centuries recommended itself as a starting point because of the confluence of diverse intellectual and social forces whose relation to the creation of modern utopia was provocative, if not causal: the translation of Plato's *Republic* in the fifteenth century, to the accompaniment of a tumultuous debate on Italian soil among Byzantine émigrés over the admissibility of Plato's communist politics into Christian society; the printing within a century or so of a large part of the Greek and Latin corpus, which made available to the learned a thousand years of experience with the ancient rationalist problem of what an ideal condition in this world would be like; the overflow into print and into organized social movements of a stream of paradisaical, apocalyptic, and millenarian visions that had had a continuous existence since the Christian era and some roots going further back to the early cultures of the Near East; the discoveries of lands to the West, throwing open the windows of the utopian imagination to novel social and religious arrangements, as Alexander's push eastward had given rise to Hellenistic exotic novels.

A Renaissance utopian did not have to seek out esoterica buried in the Greek and Latin corpus. If he had access to Aristotle's *Politics,* Plato's *Republic* and *Laws,* and Cicero's *Offices,* what Aristotle called the study of the form of political association that was "the ideal for those who can count upon the material conditions of their life being, as nearly as possible, just what they would themselves wish" could be nourished with the fundamental texts inherited from antiquity that were necessary for a discursive utopia. The speaking-picture utopia had a storehouse of images in Homer, Hesiod, and Ovid, in Xenophon's historical romance, the *Cyropaedia,* in excerpts from Hellenistic novels incorporated as geography in Diodorus Siculus' *Library of History,* and in Plutarch's lives of Solon and Lycurgus. Aristophanes and Lucian provided materials in a lighter vein, but when they were read in a humorless, literal fashion the ideal cities and government projects they mocked could inspire earnest utopian disquisitions. Reports from explorers to the New World fitted in neatly with classical sources and medieval accounts like Sir John Mandeville's of exotic peoples living in a state of happiness. Paradisaical, apocalyptic, and millenarian fantasies had been kept alive throughout the Middle Ages in scores of heretical and some orthodox movements of reformation. The publication of the works of Joachim of Fiore spread more widely ideas about a third *status* on earth, the reign of the Holy Ghost, an age of peace and love. And medieval fabliaux preserved the delights of a cokaygne utopia, sustained by a collective gastronomic unconscious whose manifest images had surfaced in Attic comedy, the Midrash, and the Church Fathers.

The two ancient beliefs that molded and nurtured utopia—the Judeo-Christian faith in a paradise with the world and destined to endure beyond it, and the Hellenic myth of an ideal, beautiful city built by men for men without the assistance and often in defiance of the gods—were deeply embedded in the consciousness of Europeans. The utopia born in the Renaissance was of course designed for a society whose cities, jewels in a rural landscape, were assuming new dimensions to which both the Eastern paradise and the community of the small Greek city-state in pursuit of perfection were profoundly alien. There were also inherent contradictions between the two myths, which the Christian utopia of the sixteenth and seventeenth centuries attempted to gloss over. Moreover, neither the paradisaical nor the Hellenic myth was a monolith; the legacies transmitted were rich and varied, full of contrarieties. But though the powerful arguments of the Greek philosophers and the authority of the philosophical poets were in many respects profoundly different from the prophetic spirit of Judaic and Christian enthusiasm, there were times when they fortified each other. The Greek golden age and biblical paradise were recognized to have striking similarities, readily explained by the Church Fathers and Renaissance commentators as the classical poets' piracy from Moses. On rare occasions the Greco-Roman and the Judeo-Christian worlds shared a utopianized historical reign, like that of Cyrus, though the divergent perceptions of Xenophon and Isaiah are illustrative of the different tempers of their two societies, briefly joined in common celebration. But even when the Hellenic and the Judeo-Christian elements were uncongenial to each other, they coexisted in utopia, a synthesis often on the verge of falling apart.

The conception of a heaven on earth that underlies Western utopian thought presupposes an idea of perfection in another sphere and at the same time a measure of confidence in human capacity to fashion on earth what is recognized as a transient mortal state into a simulacrum of the transcendental. Judeo-Christianity and Hellenic culture provided Europe with two distinct versions of an otherworldly state which could be conjoined. But the relation of the utopian to the heavenly always remains problematic. Utopia may be conceived as a prologue or a foretaste of the absolute perfection still to be experienced; it then resembles the Days of the Messiah or the Reign of Christ on earth of traditional Judaism and Christianity, with the vital addition of human volition as an ingredient in the attainment of that wished-for state. Or the utopia, though originally implanted in a belief in the reality of a transcendental state, can break away from its source and attempt to survive wholly on its own creative self-assurance. Whether the persistence of the heavenly vision in a secularized world, if only in some disguised shape, is a necessary condition for the duration of utopia is one of the unresolved questions of Western culture. At that moment in time when utopia first came into existence faith in a Christian heavenly paradise was still unshaken and the assertion of human talent to invent, discover, and devise was as if reborn.

The utopian constellations of the period from the mid-fifteenth to the early eighteenth century, still united by their total commitment to Christianity, have a common driving purpose: the radical transformation of the nature and domain of the Christian world. The main line of this utopia runs roughly from Thomas More and Thomas Müntzer to the death of Leibniz. In Italy one has to reach back to Alberti and Filarete and Francesco di Giorgio Martini in the fifteenth century for the Renaissance rediscovery of the symbolic radial form of the ideal city, thereby spoiling the perfect symmetry of a simultaneous beginning everywhere in Europe but gaining the advantage of initiating the modern utopian world with the printed recovery of the corpus of classical antiquity.

The utopia that was born and bred in the Christian society of Europe has been divided into two separate constellations, one covering the period of its birth, the other its seventeenth-century flowering and final demise. The chronological beginning of the first constellation could conceivably have been pushed back to the Middle Ages. The rule of the Benedictines and subsequent regulations for the government of monastic institutions doubtless left prototypes for an ideal Christian existence on earth, and the passion for ordering the minutiae of every aspect of existence made its imprint upon later utopias, which often are reminiscent of monastic establishments. Ramón Lull's *Blanquerna*, a didactic romance written in Catalan between 1283 and 1285, and Pierre Dubois's *De recuperatione Terre Sancte* (ca. 1305-1307) might be considered embryonic Christian utopias, but they appear to have left no significant traces in Western utopian literature before the seventeenth century. The philosophical writings of Lull then joined the main current of utopian thought and and were assimilated by the Pansophisits. Campanella and Leibniz were aware of Lull's ideas when three centuries after his death they again tried to interest princes and popes in projects for Christian unity and militant propagation of the faith among the heathen in order to establish one heavenly community on earth, but both Lull and Dubois have to be regarded as precursors rather than initiators of a new mode.

Similarly, the second constellation of the Christian utopia could have been prolonged to include residual manifestations in the eighteenth and nineteenth centuries, examples of a surviving Christian utopian force in a de-Christianized Europe: the ideas behind the communal organization imposed upon the Paraguayan Indians by the Jesuits, the various forms of the Herrnhut communities founded by Count Ludwig von Zinzendorf, the intermittent recrudescence of millenarian conceptions among groups like the Shakers, the Catholic traditionalist political theory of Joseph de Maistre and Louis-Gabriel-Ambroise de Bonald, the mystical visions of Pierre-Simon Ballanche, and even the Christian anarchism of Tolstoy. But in our judgment the principal utopian concerns in the eighteenth and nineteenth centuries were secular, and Christian utopia was a feeble remnant. It is primarily in the sixteenth and seventeenth centuries, when nascent secular utopian and Christian other-worldly strains of thought interpenetrate, that the tension of the Christian utopia is at its highest. It does not matter that major utopias, such as More's little book, Campanella's *City of the Sun,* and Vairasse's *History of the Sevarambians,* portray pre-Christian or non-Christian societies; all are confronting the problems of Christianity in a world that is approaching the crisis of secularism. Utopian thought is a fair barometer of this spiritual contest.

Morton on the national characteristics that have influenced the English utopian tradition:

[A] reason for the richness of the English Utopia is the simple one that England is an island. For it is always easier to imagine anything in proportion as it resembles what we are or know, and it is as an island that we always think of Utopia. The fact that an island is self-contained, finite, and may be remote, gives it just the qualities we require to set our imagination to work. True we shall find utopias underground, under the sea, surrounded by mountains in the heart of Africa or Asia, even on another planet or perhaps remote in time rather than space, nevertheless the vast majority of utopias are still to be found on islands. . . .

In the beginning Utopia is an image of desire. Later it grows more complex and various, and may become an elaborate means of expressing social criticism and satire, but it will always be based on something that somebody actually wants. The history of Utopia, therefore, will reflect the conditions of life and the social aspirations of classes and individuals at different times. The specific character of the land is reported varyingly according to the taste of the individual writer, but behind these variations is a continued modification that follows the normal course of historical development: the English Utopia is, as it were, a mirror image, more or less distorted, of the historical England.

A. L. Morton, in his introduction to The English Utopia, *Lawrence & Wishart, 1952.*

Under the rubric of the Birth of Utopia we have treated three different geographic and temporal units. The Christian humanist utopia of More has been read in the spirit of northern humanism common to Erasmus and Rabelais, though here can also be discovered conceptions of work and honest pleasures and equality that have an enduring resonance and a complicated *fortuna* as More goes through scores of translations. The Italian Renaissance utopia of the *città felice* (from the title of Patrizi of Cherso's book), embodied both in words and in architectural drawings, is one of the rare moments when the idea of beauty permeates utopia and creates an aristocratic Christian fantasy that is conscious of two levels of social existence, symbolized perhaps by the two-layered city of Leonardo's sketches. As a celebration of radial form, the architectural utopia responds to a variety of military, symbolic, and hygienic needs that live together in close disharmony. Finally, in the Germanic world of the early sixteenth century the utopia of the common man, the *Gemeinermann,* rises out of the mystical and political sermons and the legend of Thomas Müntzer and the radical Anabaptists.

Christian utopian thought in the seventeenth century, which saw its apogee and decline, while forming one overall cluster, has been examined in its varied geographic manifestations. The protracted upheavals of the English Civil War allowed for a massive discharge of utopian fantasy. A few of the radical utopians acknowledged a distant relationship to Müntzer and the Anabaptists and referred to them with favor; for the most part, however, their thought, steeped in bibliolatry, has a distinctive national character, and its magnificent vituperative style was not for export. By contrast, the Pansophic dream of a universal Christian Republic that would be nourished by the new science is European in its contours (there were influential Comenians in England and in the American colonies), though if a principal locus were to be established it would be the Central European world, devastated by war. Pansophia is anything but a populist utopia; its propagators are learned men associated with universities and courts, most of their all-too-voluminous tracts and treatises are in Latin, and the scholars engaged in the enterprise look to ruling princes, rich burghers, the Pope, the Emperor, the Czar as the divine instruments for its implementation. The Pansophists of the Germanic world, Italy, and England are closely linked with one another and are the bearers of the last great Christian hope for a unified religious society of all men everywhere. A third utopia of the seventeenth century is relatively minor, as parochially French as the creations of the English Civil War are English. Both Huguenot and Catholic utopians of the latter part of the century, Vairasse as well as Fénelon, repudiated the luxury-ridden society of Versailles forged by the triumphant monarchy of Louis XIV and moved off to Sevarambia or La Bétique. Since they recounted daring exploits and wrote in French (readily translated into other vernacular tongues), they appealed to a far broader audience than the scholarly Pansophists.

The utopian constellations of the Enlightenment and of the French Revolutionary era lose the focus of the earlier centuries as their authors are pulled in different directions. Old hopes of the Christian utopia have been forsaken and there is not yet full commitment to the euchronian constellations that dominate the next epoch. The *patres majores* among the French philosophes, with their troubled ambivalence toward utopia, and even Rousseau's enigmatic *moi commun* and *monde idéal,* are transitional. The philosophes have to be left in utopian limbo, which is just where they belong. They were not emancipated enough from the classical doctrine of the cyclical vicissitudes of states and empires to be convinced of an endlessly dynamic future. There is no article on utopia in the *Encyclopédie,* and old utopians are treated with contempt. Nonetheless, the eighteenth century proliferated utopias of every type— Morean, Robinsonian, physiocratic, communistic, sexual. On the eve of the Revolution, disquisitions on sexuality, ideal architectural forms, property, and equality cropped up all over the place in a utopian format, signaling alternative paths for a return to nature, or, faute de mieux, to a quasi-natural state in the midst of civilization. A babel of utopias trumpeted in the Revolution. Its many tongues were the education of party chiefs, but however radically the visions may have differed from one another, in toto the eighteenth-century utopia was still framed in terms of an agrarian society.

Unfortunately, chronological models are rarely neat, and Turgot, Condorcet, and Mercier, the initiators in different styles of the new euchronia, in which good place gives way to good time, had the bad grace to be Enlightenment stalwarts, bred in its Parisian womb. In this instance nothing avails but to call the dialectical principle to the rescue: In the bosom of a utopia of agrarian calm felicity a utopia of endless, dynamic change in science and technology was born. This switch to euchronia was heralded with the awakened sleeper of Sébastien Mercier's *L'An 2440* and with the utopian projections in the Tenth Epoch of Condorcet's *Esquisse.* The vision of a future society of *progrès indéfini* predominates through the emergence of Marx on the utopian landscape. Paradoxically, un-Christian euchronia represented a resurgence of a strong millenarian, paradisaical, and apocalyptic current in secular form. The free rational choices of the Morean Utopian lawgiver or the Renaissance architect were abandoned to history: Utopia became less Hellenic and more Judeo-Christian. Older rhythms of thought from millenarianism and Joachimism were secularized, and translations of Judeo-Christian apocalyptic rhetoric into new terms became the stuff of the transformation.

Both in fertility of invention and penetrating insight into the human condition, the French thinkers from Saint-Simon through Fourier, Comte, and their schools were a luminous constellation of modern utopian thought: Work and love were brilliantly analyzed and their felicitous union was established as a prerequisite for an ideal society. Robert Owen and German originals like Wilhelm Weitling were lesser lights of the same species. Marx brought the triumph of euchronia to a European climax by incorporating French, German, and English elements into a unique synthesis, condensed in that banderole of the *Gotha Program Critique,* "From each according to his abilities, to each according to his needs." After Marx, there was a falling-off in utopian invention. The utopians of the earlier part of the nineteenth century were reacted against, assimilated, cribbed, echoed, regurgitated, and watered down in a variety of new forms, discursive and novelistic. The anarchist utopia is the most virulent of the utopian forces competitive to the Marxist; and the "Utopia Victoriana," typified by the works of Chernyshevskii, Morris, Bellamy, and Hertzka, is its most genteel dilution. Lenin treasured his executed brother's copy of Chernyshevskii's *What Is to Be Done?* but clearly Lenin's field of specialization was applied utopistics.

At a time when utopian formulas still enjoyed a great vogue, two intruders broke into heaven on earth: Darwin and Freud. Popular Darwinism and the new utopia of science and science fiction that flowed from it at once opened vast new vistas and closed others. The new utopia to counteract a Darwinian cosmic pessimism was epitomized by the noösphere of Teilhard de Chardin and the scientific utopia of Bernal, with its marvels of biological engineering and the projection of humanity into outer space as an ultimate destiny. Freud, the trenchant critic of "lullabies of heaven," was followed by an outcropping of Freudo-Marxists, who tried to soften the Freudian sermon on the eternity of aggression. Their works culminated in Marcuse's utopian "Ende der Utopie," with its exaltation of a new utopian value that he called sexual-aesthetic. The diffuse manner in which the utopian imagination has responded to the dystopian forces of Darwin and Freud represents a weakening and an attenuation of earlier ideas and imagery, and suggested the phrase "twilight of utopia" as descriptive of the most recent period.

The Pluralism of the Commentary

Utopias can be considered from a number of points of view: geographical, historical, psychological, sociological; as a form of belles-lettres; as philosophicomoral treatises; as a new mythology. Just as there have been monist theories that pretend to explicate all myths, so those who have psychologized, sociologized, or historicized utopias or treated them as a literary genre or a philosophical principle have had a tendency to constrict their significance within the limits of a single discipline. . . .

An easy, though restricted, access to utopia is through

its historical geography. The historian of "proper utopias" twirls a globe dotted with ideal societies on distant islands with specific geographic locations, in isolated valleys, remote mountain fastnesses, underground galleries, caverns in the bowels of the earth, inaccessible jungle clearings. Fortunate peoples inhabit floating platforms in space, the moon, the sun, Mars, Venus; they populate an infinity of worlds.

Much of Western utopia can be related to the acquisition of the known visible world by the peoples of the peninsula of Europe. This development cuts across the individual historical constellations. Imaginary societies are situated along the general path of actual conquests, discoveries, and explorations. In the wake of Alexander's drive to the heart of Asia, Euhemerus, a Hellenistic Greek, found a good order of society on Panchaïa, an island in the Indian Ocean. The trader Iambulus, probably a Syrian metic, abandoned to the sea by his Ethiopian captors as a sacrificial offering, told how his boat had drifted to Islands of the Sun somewhere near the east coast of Africa. Other Greek writers claimed acquaintance with the happy Hyperboreans and the men of Ultima Thule on the edge of the European continent. The Romans rarely stretched themselves far beyond the boundaries of the Greek romances; in their imperial triumph many Romans were too complacent and too self-satisfied to dream of ideal polities; for them, Rome itself was utopia. But after the fall of Rome and throughout the Middle Ages new lands were constantly being incorporated into the utopian *mappamundi* from the seas to the west of Europe and Africa. Saint Brendan's Fortunate Isle, the most famous of them, was a Christianized gift of Celtic fantasy. Often the creation of medieval utopias was incidental to a search for the eastern site of the terrestrial Garden of Eden or to a quest for the Holy Grail, in whose presence the knights would be overcome by feelings of ineffable joy. Eldad ha-Dani, a Jewish traveler of the late ninth century. came upon a perfect society on the other side of the River Sambatyon, where the ten lost tribes of Israel had migrated. And in the fourteenth century Sir John Mandeville was carried by his reveries to the mysterious East, to the Isle of Bragmans, where there was "neither thunder ne levening, hail ne snow, ne other tempests of ill weathers; ne hunger, ne pestilence, ne war, ne other tribulations."

Within a few decades after Europeans had broken through their continental shell in the fifteenth century and sailed off in ships to possess the world, Utopia itself was "discovered" by Raphael Hythloday, a Portuguese mariner who had purportedly participated in Amerigo Vespucci's expeditions and returned to recount his adventures to Thomas More. For two hundred years thereafter the imaginary encounters of literary voyagers with stranger peoples kept close pace with the real adventures of their seafaring counterparts in America and Asia. Sometimes the utopias prophet-ically preceded rather than followed historical landings of Europeans in new places: Toward the latter part of the seventeenth century, at a time when the South Sea islands and Australia were still unexplored, the utopians outstripped the sailors, and the Huguenots Gabriel de Foigny and Denis Vairasse situated kingdoms in the Mers Australes. For some, there was no longer enough wonderment attached to the coastline of the Americas. Happiness was where they were not, beyond the horizon. During the course of the next century ideal societies multiplied in a balmy region of the Pacific—in Tahiti and on the island of Nouvelle-Cythère—*rêves exotiques* bred by the real voyages of Captain James Cook and Louis Antoine de Bougainville in the same area. After 1800 the wilderness of the American West, opened to travelers, yielded up utopian worlds in hidden valleys and on the broad plains and plateaus. New territories were progressively annexed to utopia until the whole face of the earth was covered and men had to seek elsewhere.

The astronomical and mechanical studies of the seventeenth century had already encouraged the utopian imagination to soar into outer space, giving a strong impetus to explorations that had been begun rather gingerly by the Greeks and the Romans. The Neoplatonists Plutarch and Plotinus, through an ingenious and daring exegesis of Homer, had translated Elysium from the ends of the earth to the moon, and Lucian's mockery of the whole Greek corpus of utopian expeditions had kept the moon site prominent all through the Middle Ages. But extraterrestrial utopian societies really began to crowd one another only after 1600, when moon travel dependent upon breaking through the gravitational pull and attaining a state of weightlessness for most of the journey became a theoretical scientific possibility. Johannes Kepler's *Somnium, seu Opus Posthumum de Astronomia Lunari* (1634) placed a human on the moon to observe the earth, and John Wilkins' *Discovery of the New World in the Moon* (1638), a popular-science treatise on the mechanics of lunar voyages, though not a utopia, discussed the feasibility of living on the moon. The utopian excursions of Francis Godwin, Cyrano de Bergerac, and a host of others were not long delayed once the idea became a commonplace. The universe beyond the earth was peopled in man's fantasy for centuries before the giant step on the moon in 1969; and a proliferation of works of science fiction and predictive science in the twentieth century prefigured the event.

Since the fabrication of utopian societies and the expeditions to new lands ran parallel, it is not surprising that their two geographies, the imaginary and the real, were sometimes confused. Like the voyages of the Argonauts and of Sinbad the Sailor, utopian adventures never completely severed their ties to the phenomenal world. At times the utopia-writer lent such verisimilitude to the description of his fantasy land that fictional names, such as those of the East Indian islands in the Huguenot François Misson's *Voyage et avantures de François Leguat* (1708), found their way into serious geography books and remained there for centuries. The novel by the trader lambulus, preserved in the histories of Diodorus Siculus, was reprinted in Giovanni Battista Ramusio's mid-sixteenth-century collection of voyages (though he hedged a bit about its authenticity, suggesting that it was part truth, part fable), and it survived as an inspiration of Tommaso Campanella's *Città del Sole* (1602). A great utopia like Thomas More's exerted a more profound and subtle influence. It penetrated the consciousness of literate men and colored their whole view of reality. More's perception of things stamped the European mind so indelibly that the schema of Book II of the *Utopia* was adopted in scores of genuine, as well as imaginary, travel accounts, and became an accepted framework for circumstantial reporting on newly discovered lands.

Not content with inventing a fabulous universal geography, the Western imagination has waved a magic wand over many of the great historical societies, so that idealized depictions of Egypt, Sparta, Athens, Scythia, Persia, Rome, Israel have in a way become part of the utopian corpus. Plutarch's Lycurgan Sparta and Xenophon's Persia, long after the historical passing of these states, assumed separate existences as utopian polities worthy of imitation by all mankind. Egocentric eulogists have composed self-adulatory utopias, painting their own societies in colors so dazzling that those not possessed can hardly recognize even the outlines of actuality. The sixteenth- and seventeenth-century myth of Venice as the ideal commonwealth would boggle the minds of twentieth-century men were we not inured to the apotheosis of societies whose ugliness and depravity we have beheld with our own eyes. There is hardly a polity so vicious that it cannot be transformed into a paragon of virtue by the power of the imagination interweaving utopian and historical modes.

Every utopia, rooted as it is in time and place, is bound to reproduce the stage scenery of its particular world as well as its preoccupation with contemporary social problems. Here analogies to the dream and the psychotic fantasy may be telling. Observers of paranoid behavior report that though the disease remains relatively constant, the mysterious, all-seeing forces that watch and persecute their patients change with time and technology. They maybe spirits, telephones, radios, or television sets in successive periods. Utopias are not an illness; but to a large degree they avail themselves of the existing equipment of a society, perhaps its most advanced models, prettified and rearranged. Often a utopian foresees the later evolution and consequences of technological development already present in an embryonic state; he may have antennae sensitive to the future. His gadgets, however, rarely go beyond the mechanical potentialities of his age. Try as he may to invent something wholly new, he cannot make a world out of nothing.

If utopias are classified by the style of their furniture, sociological and historical, and the style is related to a contemporary social reality, the utopia can be studied as a reflection of the specific crises that it presumes to resolve. That utopia is tied to existing social conflicts and that the utopian often aligns himself with one side or the other has been profusely illustrated. In Hesiod one senses the state of decline after the heroic epoch of Hellas, in Plato the temper of growing luxuriousness in Athenian life and the impending demise of the polis. The utopias of Alberti, Filarete, and Patrizi communicate the spirit of a new Renaissance aristocracy of wealth as distinct from a rough, feudal nobility, and the elegant patricians of their ideal cities keep themselves aloof from both the swashbuckling condottieri and the plebeians on the lower levels of society. Thomas More, it is said, is reacting against the enclosure movement, but whether in the name of the new burghers of London or of nostalgic medieval agrarianism or the spiritual ideals of a Christian humanism remains debatable. The great seventeenth-century utopias strive to mend the political and religious schisms in the Christian world and to reconstitute a universal order on the basis of Christian virtues bolstered by the new science. Many eighteenth-century utopias with their ever-normal granaries and orderly physiocratic policies directed by a wise paternal legislator and a meritocracy in the spiritual and temporal realms point the way to ending the endemic hunger of the ancien régime and ridding society of its vestigial feudal institutions. Saint-Simon and Fourier had the perspicacity to respond to the economic and psychic dislocations of the new industrial society long before its griefs had become plainly visible. Marx sought to master the same forces at a maturer stage of capitalism and Hertzka at an even later stage, when the problems of industrialism were complicated by imperialist expansion. Present-day utopians are trying to cope with the anxieties and potentialities of what has been called postindustrial society. But since most epochs in the West have been turbulent, the proposition that the utopias they have produced are related to economic and social upheavals becomes truistic. To announce in tones of dramatic revelation that a utopia mirrors the misery of the working classes or the squeeze of the lesser nobility between the peasants and the royal power is to say something, but not enough. To identify elements in utopias of the seventeenth and eighteenth centuries as manifestations of *Frühkapitalismus,* a current fashion, is to mistake a rubric for a statement of content.

Identifying the sources of a utopia in historical reality can of course be done with more or with less sensitivity. Granted that the utopia-maker reflects the historical moment, in the rare instances where he has genius he reveals the inner depths, the essence, of that moment rather than mere externals. He has the capacity to achieve a measure of distance from the day-to-day controversies of the marketplace and to view the life of his society in the light of its manifold possibilities. Even though he may not be so insightful as a sublime poet, the utopian can capture the anguish of an epoch in a striking metaphor. In dissecting the urgent requirements of his times, he may also lay bare age-old, if not eternal, needs of man. Limiting an interpretation to the immediate environment of the utopian, tying him down too closely and mechanically to the precise circumstances and incidents that could have triggered his writing, fails to recognize that he may have something ahistorical to say about love, aggression, the nature of work, the fulfillment of personality. The truly great utopian is a Janus-like creature, time-bound and free of time, place-bound and free of place. His duality should be respected and appreciated.

Certain historical generations are peculiarly susceptible to utopian thinking and it is not uncommon to find the same young men possessed by a succession of utopias and stumbling from one utopian movement into another. English seekers of the Civil War, though primarily embarked on an individual quest for a way to God, became involved, as they wandered from sect to sect, with the social utopias related to each new doctrine. Rootless young Frenchmen of the generation of 1798, when they reached maturity under the Restoration, made the rounds from Saint-Simonism to Fourierism to Comtism (not always in that order). The spiritual migrations of the 1930s and the 1960s tell similar stories in the United States. Such concentrations represent far larger numbers than the interplay of an exclusive band of northern Christian humanists, or the Renaissance architects of the ideal city, or the Pansophists of the seventeenth century. And yet in their own small way the young Rhineland academics touched by the Rosicrucian hope of reforming the world underwent psychic experiences that were not dissimilar to those of the French Romantic utopians. A historical sociology of utopian movements or, better, affinity groups would have to go back to the Pythagoreans, the Essenes, the radical sectaries of the Middle Ages and the Reformation, if it were not to get bogged down in the parochial though rich nineteenth-century American experience with utopian communities. We have been preoccupied chiefly with the thought behind these movements, but some consideration of their character and organization throws light on the ideational substance.

Utopias have been powerful dynamic forces in the political arena, though not necessarily when first published. If their astute empirical diagnosis strikes a chord that has resonances among some classes of their society, they become famous; failing, they are forgotten, or may wait in some utopian limbo to be revived at a future date. The *fortuna* of the original document is an inseparable part of its meaning, and should be examined along with the changed content that new generations have constantly poured into the old utopia. A work can hardly escape fundamental transformation as its audience changes: More's Christian-humanist *declamatio* becomes a revolutionary manifesto; Marx's notebooks in which a young man is trying out his ideas are read as dogma a century later; Comenius' massive systematic manuscript, *General Consultation on an Improvement of All Things Human,* aimed at effectuating a radical universal reform, ends up as a mere historical curiosity, a scholar's felicitous discovery three hundred years after the author's death and of interest only to limited number of specialists. Of late, statistical records of the past compiled by government officials with one specific intent, when placed in another context have begun to speak a very different language to researchers. Similarly, utopian ideas assume new meanings as they are moved about from series to series. A commentator focusing on utopian sexual fantasies will not pluck the same meaning from an account of a Ranter assemblage during the English Civil War as did a contemporary presbyter. The observer of utopia over a period of hundreds of years is constrained to consider each event as having roots in the past and sending out tentacles to the future and to coevals scattered over a broad area. No important utopian event is encapsulated or autonomous, because future history has embraced it. A critical history, while it can never escape its own historicity, may succeed in combining a measure of distance with its empathy and antipathy.

The changing size of the reading public is part of the commentary that illuminates utopias. Thomas More's Latin *libellus* was originally accessible to a far smaller public than Edward Bellamy's *Looking Backward,* but it was large compared to Winstanley's Digger *Platform* or a Ranter sermon that made its way into the hostile report of Thomas Edwards' *Gangraena.* Marx's definition of the higher stage of communism in the *Critique of the Gotha Program* has surely been read by a far greater number of persons in contemporary China, where it is said to be discussed at peasant study sessions, than it was in the 1890s when it was published. And if we would pursue fragments of utopias that penetrate the rhetoric of popular movements, we enter a world of diffusion where solids have become gaseous and impossible to isolate. Confronted with a shifting readership and the utopian's mobile or ambivalent original purpose, the critical historian who reviews the whole process ought not to take too rigid a stance, for the same text tells many different things about utopian thought at widely dispersed times, and even among different classes of contemporaries.

The Utopian and His Creation

As a mental event, a utopia takes the form of a written

document and is usually composed by one man. On rare occasions a group of men may concert together to formulate a utopian program; for that moment, at least, they give the appearance of being of one mind and they share a common utopian experience. The utopian may, as politician, reformer, revolutionary, prophet, use bits and pieces of his own utopian structure. Others may cannibalize his utopia and incorporate it into their manifestoes for action, inscribe its slogans on their banners. But every subsequent usage of utopian rhetoric after the initial creation involves a tearing apart and perhaps even a total destruction of the original. A history of utopian thought may deal with the preliminaries in the life of the individual utopian, the dynamic internal psychic forces that climaxed in the recording of the utopian experience, and the communication, popularization, vulgarization, stereotyping, or rigidifying of the utopian event in the course of time. But in the process the mental event itself should not be diluted to the point where it is hardly distinguishable from the waters that flowed in and those that poured out; it remains a unique creation.

At a time when individual psychological analysis flourishes, one is tempted to turn to the person of the utopian for the illumination of his fantasy. Though a poet has related the utopian mode to youth and the attraction of ideal world systems may be most powerful in adolescence, there are many middle-aged utopian fantasts, and the utopian propensity is not restricted to any one stage of the life cycle. More wrote his utopia in his late thirties, Restif and Saint-Simon composed theirs when they were about forty. One version of Rousseau's utopia was a deathbed revelation and Diderot's *Supplément au voyage de Bougainville* was the daydream of an aging man. Since the illusory world serves some purpose in the psychic economy of its author, interpreters have undertaken to ferret out and relate the utopian's hidden drives to major elements of his imaginary society. The effort should not be scorned. For many, such as More, Comenius, Bacon, Jean-Jacques, Fourier, Marx, the data are richly available and the quest is rewarding; for others, the psychological perceptions that can be mustered are severely limited, since we may know nothing but the author's name, perhaps a nom de plume at that, or only a family name as with Morelly, whose *Code de la nature* was a significant utopian landmark and played a major part in the intellectual world of Babeuf. But paucity of materials does not discourage the convinced believer in the paramountcy of his psychological techniques. He can reconstruct a personality on the basis of psychological disclosures in the fantasy and then triumphantly interpret the fantasy in terms of its creator. An ideal visionary type, the perfect utopian, would probably both hate his father and come from a disinherited class. A bit of schizophrenia, a dose of megalomania, obsessiveness, and compulsiveness fit neatly into the stereotype. But the utopian personality that is more than an item in a cat-

alogue must also be gifted and stirred by a creative passion. The great utopias—and they are not numerous—are marked but not necessarily marred by the scars of their authors. Sometimes the wounds lie well concealed, as was More's hair-shirted and lacerated body beneath the inky cloak of the Holbein portrait.

There is a sense in which the mental act of creating a utopian world, or the principles for one, is psychologically a regressive phenomenon for an individual. In this respect the utopian is kindred to the religious, scientific, and artistic creators who flee to the desert, suffer psychic crises, become disoriented by the contradictions between accepted reality and the new insights of which they have a glimmer. In the first instance the utopian is overwhelmed by the evil complexities of existence. The great utopians have all borne witness to their anger at the world, their disgust with society, their acute suffering as their sensibilities are assailed from all sides. They withdraw from this world into a far simpler form of existence which they fantasy. The escape from everyday conflicts and disappointments has a childlike quality. And their way back from utopia, their return to the real world they had abandoned, is often characterized by devotion to a fixed idea with which they become obsessed. They clutch frantically at this overvalued idea that at once explains all evil and offers the universal remedy, and they build an impregnable fortification around it. The one idea becomes a fetish that they worship and defend with marvelous ingenuity. To outsiders they are monomaniacs. These reflections naturally apply only to the select number of authentic utopians who endure the travail of new birth, not to the hundreds of utopian imitators who crowd bibliographies as poetasters do histories of literature.

Utopians are almost always tragic or tragicomic figures who die unfulfilled; the future does not begin to conform to their fantasy. Then appear the disciples or curious readers who have not been shaken in their innermost being with anything like the intensity of the original utopian visionary, and they adapt, prune, distort, refine, render banal, make matter-of-fact the utopia, so that it reenters the world as a force for good or evil. Compromises with existence are effected; the ironclad formula is relaxed. To measure the pure utopian theory by the achievements of "applied utopistics" is fatuous, as is any attempt to make fathers responsible for the sins and barbarities of their putative sons. By definition, the utopian creation born of a yearning for return to a simple haven or of a descent into the lower depths of the unconscious cannot be put into practice.

One of the most prickly tasks for the commentator on utopia is to assess the commitment of a utopian author to his own work. Appraisals range from the mere jeu d'esprit through rhetorical *declamatio* as a didactic device, from the utopia as wish rather than anticipation to zealous conviction of the need for or expectation of the total implementation of the utopian principles on the morrow or at most the day after. When the utopian is torn by doubts, on the manifest or covert level, an evaluation becomes acutely problematic. Restif de la Bretonne, a type familiar enough to modern psychologists, wrote both expansively permissive and obsessively repressive utopias. Some utopians wear a mask of harlequin, as Fourier did on occasion, to attract attention with absurdities and scandalous utterances. Many who conceived of their utopias as popular forms of a Platonic idea would have been content with far less than complete realization in this world. Others, possessed by the spirit of religious ritualism, would not allow for the changing of an iota in their system lest the magical efficacy of the whole be impaired. Both proper and discursive utopias are literary texts in which ambivalence and ambiguity are very ofteninseparable from the thought itself. Obviously, once they have left their author's hands they lead lives of their own, and the most ironic or hyperbolic positions can subsequently be read as if they were biblical commandments, mathematical demonstrations, or the triumphs of academic discourse in which points are proved and disproved. This applies not only to Thomas More's work, where divergent contemporary commentaries are at last making the Christian humanist tone evident, but to many other utopias that to this day are interpreted in a doltishly straight-faced manner because the doubt of the author has been ignored. Searching for the utopian intent, almost always elusive, comes to occupy a significant part of this historical commentary.

Paradoxically, the great utopians have been great realists. They have an extraordinary comprehension of the time and place in which they are writing and deliver themselves of penetrating reflections on socioeconomic, scientific, or emotional conditions of their moment in history. They have discovered truths that other men have only vaguely sensed or have refused to recognize. The utopian often emerges as a man with a deeper understanding of the drift of his society than the hardheaded problem-solvers with their noses to the grindstone of the present, blind to potentiality. Perhaps the utopians stand out because of the tenacity with which they hold to their ideas. They have a penchant for focusing the full glare of their insight on a particular aspect of the world and leaving much unnoticed. But if they are fixated on one face of reality, this face they understand as other men have not. Their knowledge serves them as a springboard for a jump into a future which could be either a total negation of the present or so sharply lateral that others would at first glance consider it chimerical, fantastic, improbable—in a word, utopian. There is an almost inevitable inclination in a utilitarian society to value most those utopian visionaries whose "dreams came true," not the best criterion for judgment. The short-term prognosticator can be a bore. He is merely a meterologist, useful in planning an outing or a military invasion.

Eurich on utopian thought and the rise of science:

The great and eventually startling advances in scientific knowledge and the possibilities it offered for man's betterment were slow in building, slow in reaching even the learned men, much less the general public. Naturally then, the new ideas emerging did not immediately displace all other human visions of the happier state. Traditional notions are hard to abandon and, during this period of transition, some utopian writers clung tenaciously to the old values and saw improvement through the pursuit of virtue alone; they either deliberately omitted mention of scientific discovery or were ignorant of the new learning. . . .

In the first quarter of the 17th century, however, another group of utopists had come to the conclusion that the new age of mankind was to be the result of science and the new learning. While their visions did not instantly blot out all other views of utopia—we have seen the various solutions of their contemporaries—still their quick and creative adoption of scientific discoveries proved to be the main road to the future that we have traveled. Here are Andreae, Bacon, Campanella, and others who set the stage on which George Orwell and Aldous Huxley have drawn the curtains, leaving man controlled in the darkness of his own creation. In the period of scientific gestation, there was no thought of such a conclusion; the new utopia was flooded with the brilliant light of new knowledge.

Nell Eurich, "The Renaissance and Transition," in Science in Utopia: A Mighty Design, *Harvard University Press, 1967.*

Without taking leave of reality, utopians have performed symbolic acts to dramatize their break with the present. They have located their ideal societies at a distance in space—this was the normal device of the Morean utopia that required the rite of passage of an ocean voyage. King Utopus cut the isthmus that had once attached his newly conquered kingdom to the mainland as one would snip an umbilical cord. In the twentieth century Bernal required a light-year of flight to establish the necessary pathos of distancefor one of his artificial planets. Men have fallen into holes in the earth to get to the ideal center of things; they have crossed impassable mountain ranges to descend into pleasant valleys; they have broken the time barrier of the present through machines or through sleep; they have distinguished between evil prehistory and utopian history. The critical negation may be incorporated in a separate book and composed after the utopia proper. We now know that More's Book I postdated the composition of Book II; the whole is a study in contrasts. In other Morean utopias the negative and the positive are intermingled in the same account, as the strangers, or the utopians (who are sometimes all-knowing), play a counterpoint between Europe and the newly discovered island, or the present and the future. The movement back and forth between heaven and hell is precipitous, so that the reader is constantly made aware of the antithesis.

The utopians whose repudiation of the present is in the Greek tradition tend to seek a more rationalist and analytical way to expose what to Aristotle were the defects in existing forms. In the Judeo-Christian corpus the revulsion against the pervasiveness of religious sin is more emotive. But the logical argumentative character of the classical search for perfect forms may only disguise the force of the underlying negative affect. The medical metaphor of Plato, diagnosing his contemporary city as suffering from an inflammation, and the summary condemnation in his Seventh Epistle of "all the states which now exist" as "badly governed" dramatize the feeling that preceded or accompanied the analysis.

It would be deceptive to stress the utopia as negation of present reality to the neglect of curiosity, inventiveness, the exploratory drive that has led man on the most daring adventures. The two strains have had changing relative potencies at different epochs. There are times when the utopia of calm felicity dominates Western culture and the imagery of a return to the protective womb of paradise seems to suffuse the emotional atmosphere; then a Promethean element breaks through and utopian existence becomes the dramatic torch race of which Bacon wrote in *Wisdom of the Ancients*. Utopians are often intrepid, bold explorers whom many of their contemporaries consider wild because they neither repeat existing rhetoric with variations nor pursue familiar directions. If a utopia is merely or primarily reflective of existing reality it is trivial. On the other hand, when the imaginary world is cut off from all relationship with reality, it becomes a vaporous fairy tale, formless and pointless, like many *voyages imaginaires* and *songes* and *romans cabalistiques* of the eighteenth century and muchof contemporary science fiction, where the utopian elements are so feeble they are only sedatives, pastimes, narcotics. The great utopia startles and yet is recognized as conceivable. It is not a sleepy or bizarre vision but one that satisfies a hunger or stimulates the mind and the body to the recognition of a new potentiality.

THE CLASSICAL BACKGROUND

Lewis Mumford (essay date 1922)

SOURCE: A chapter from *The Story of Utopias*, Boni and Liveright, 1922. Reprint by The Viking Press, 1962, pp. 29-55.

[*In the following essay, Mumford discusses the origins of the concept of utopia in ancient Greece, focusing on Plato's conception of the ideal city in the* Republic.]

Before the great empires of Rome and Macedonia began to spread their camps through the length and breadth of the Mediterranean world, there was a time when the vision of an ideal city seems to have been uppermost in the minds of a good many men. Just as the wide expanse of unsettled territory in America caused the people of eighteenth century Europe to think of building a civilization in which the errors and vices and superstitions of the old world might be left behind, so the sparsely settled coasts of Italy, Sicily, and the Aegean Islands, and the shores of the Black Sea, must have given men the hope of being able to turn over a fresh page.

Those years between six hundred and three hundred B.C. were city-building years for the parent cities of Greece. The city of Miletus is supposed to have begotten some three hundred cities, and many of its fellows were possibly not less fruitful. Since new cities could be founded there was plenty of chance for variation and experiment; and those who dreamed of a more, generous social order could set their hands and wits to making a better start "from the bottom up."

Of all the plans and reconstruction programs that must have been put forward during these centuries, only a scant handful remains. Aristotle tells us about an ideal state designed by one, Phaleas, who believed like Mr. Bernard Shaw in a complete equality of property; and from Aristotle, too, we learn of another utopia which was described by the great architect, city planner, and sociologist—Hippodamus. Hippodamus was one of the first city planners known to history, and he achieved fame in the ancient world by designing cities on the somewhat monotonous checkerboard design we know so well in America. He realized, apparently, that a city was something more than a collection of houses, streets, markets, and temples; and so, whilst he was putting the physical town to rights, he concerned himself with the more basic problem of the social order. If it adds at all to our sense of reality in going through utopia, let me confess that it is ultimately through the inspiration and example of another Hippodamus—Patrick Geddes, the town planner for Jerusalem and many other cities—that this book about utopias came to be written. In many ways the distance between Geddes and Aristotle or Hippodamus seems much less than that which separates Geddes and Herbert Spencer.

When we look at the utopias that Phaleas and Hippodamus and Aristotle have left us, and compare them with the Republic of Plato, the differences between them melt into insignificance and their likenesses are apparent. It is for this reason that I shall confine our examination of the Greek utopia to that which Plato set forth in the Republic, and qualified and broadened in the The Laws, The Statesman, and Critias.

Plato's Republic dates roughly from the time of that long and disastrous war which Athens fought with Sparta. In the course of such a war, amid the bombast that patriotic citizens give way to, the people who keep their senses are bound to get pretty well acquainted with their enemy. If you will take the trouble to examine Plutarch's account of the Laws of Lycurgus and Mr. Alfred Zimmern's magnificent description of the Greek Commonwealth you will see how Sparta and Athens form the web and woof of the Republic—only it is an ideal Sparta and an ideal Athens that Plato has in mind.

It is well to remember that Plato wrote in the midst of defeat; a great part of his region, Attica, had been devastated and burned; and he must have felt that makeshift and reform were quite futile when a Peloponesian war could make the bottom drop out of his world. To Plato an ill-designed ship of state required more than the science of navigation to pull it through stormy waters: if it was in danger of perpetually foundering, it seemed high time to go back to the shipyards and inquire into the principles upon which it had been put together. . . .

In describing his ideal community Plato, like a trained workman, begins with his physical foundations. So far from putting his utoopia in a mythical island of Avilion, where falls not hail nor rain nor any snow, it is plain that Plato was referring repeatedly to the soil in which Athens was planted, and to the economic life which grew out of that soil. Since he was speaking to his own countrymen, he could let a good many things pass for common knowledge which we, as strangers, must look into more carefully in order to have a firmer sense of his utopian realities. Let it be understood that in discussing the physical side of the Republic, I am drawing from Aristotle as well as Plato, and from such modern Greek scholars as Messrs. Zimmern, Myres, and Murray.

Nowadays when we talk about a state we think of an expanse of territory, to begin with, so broad that we should in most cases be unable to see all its boundaries if we rose five miles above the ground on a clear day. Even if the country is a little one, like the Netherlands or Belgium, it is likely to have possessions that are thousands of miles away; and we think of these distant possessions and of the homeland as part and parcel of the state. there is scarcely any conceivable way in which a Dutchman in Rotterdam, let us say, possesses the Island of Java: he does not live on the island, he is not acquainted with the inhabitants, he does not share their ideas or customs. His interest in Java, if he has an interest at all, is an interest in sugar, coffee, taxes, or missions. His state is not a commonwealth in the sense that it is a common possession.

To the Greek of Plato's time, on the contrary, the commonwealth was something he actively shared with his fellow citizens. It was a definite parcel of land whose limits he could probably see from any convenient hilltop; and those who lived within those limits had common gods to worship, common theaters and gymnasia, and a multitude of common interests that could be satisfied only by their working together, playing together, thinking together. Plato could probably not have conceived of a community with civilized pretensions in which the population was distributed at the rate of ten per square mile; and if he visited such a territory he would surely have said that the people were barbarians—men whose way of living unfitted them for the graces and duties of citizenship.

Geographically speaking, then, the ideal commonwealth was a city-region; that is, a city which was surrounded by enough land to supply the greater part of the food needed by the inhabitants; and placed convenient to the sea.

Let us stand on a high hill and take a look at this city region; the sort of view that Plato himself might have obtained on some clear spring morning when he climbed to the top of the Acropolis and looked down on the sleeping city, with the green fields and sear upland pastures on one side, and the sun glinting on the distant waters of the sea a few miles away.

It is a mountainous region, this Greece, and within a short distance from mountain top to sea there was compressed as many different kinds of agricultural and industrial life as one could single out in going down the Hudson valley from the Adirondack Mountains to New York Harbor. As the basis for his ideal city, whether Plato knew it or not, he had an "ideal" section of land in his mind—what the geographer calls the "valley section." He could not have gotten the various groups which were to be combined in his city, had they been settled in the beginning on a section of land like the coastal plain of New Jersey. It was peculiarly in Greece that such a variety of occupations could come together within a small area, beginning at the summit of the valley section with the evergreen trees and the woodcutter, going down the slope to the hersman and his flock of goats at pasture, along the valley bottom to the cultivator and his crops, until at length one reaches the river's mouth where the fisher pushes out to sea in his boat and the trader comes in with goods from other lands.

The great civilizations of the world have been nourished in such valley sections. We think of the river Nile and Alexandria; the Tiber and Rome, the Seine and Paris; and so on. It is interesting that our first great utopia should have had an "ideal" section of territory as its base.

In the economic foundations of the Republic, we look in vain for a recognition of the labor problem. Now the labor problem is a fundamental difficulty in our modern life; and it seems on the surface that Plato is a little highbrow and remote in the ease with which he gets over it. When we look more closely into the matter, however, and see the way in which men got their living in the "morning lands"—as the Germans call them—we shall find that the reason Plato does not offer a solution is that he was not, indeed, confronted by a problem.

Given a valley section which has not been ruthlessly stript of trees; given the arts of agriculture and hering; given a climate without dangerous extremes of heat and cold; given the opportunity to found new colonies when the old city-region is over-populated—and it is only an exercise of ingenuity that a labor problem could be invented. A man might become a slave by military capture; he did not become a slave by being compelled, under threat of starvation, to tend a machine. The problem of getting a living was answered by nature as long as men were willing to put up with nature's conditions; and the groundwork of Plato's utopia, accordingly, is the simple agricultural life, the growing of wheat, barley, olives, and grapes, which had been fairly well mastered before he arrived on the scene. As long as the soil was not washed away and devitalized, the problem was not a hard one; and in order to solve it, Plato had only to provide that there should be enough territory to grow food on, and that the inhabitants must not let their wants exceed the bounties of nature.

Plato describes the foundations of his community with a few simple and masterly touches. Those who feel that there is something a little inhuman in his conception of the good life, when he is discussing the education and duties of the ruling classes, may well consider the picture that he paints for us here.

Plato's society arises out of the needs of mankind; because none of us is self-sufficing and all have many wants; and since there are many wants, many kinds of people must supply them. When all these helpers and partners and co-operators are gathered together in a city the body of inhabitants is termed a state; and so its members work and exchange goods with one antoher for their mutual advantage—the herdsman gets barley for his cheese and so on down to the complicated interchanges that occur in the city. What sort of physical life will arise out of this in the region that Plato describes?

Well, the people will "produce corn and wine and clothes and shoes and build houses for themselves. . . . They will work in summer commonly stript and barefoot, but in winter substantially clothed and shod. They will feed on barley and wheat, baking the wheat and kneading the flour, making noble puddings and loaves; these they will serve up on a mat of reeds or clean leaves; themselves reclining the while upon beds of yew or myrtle boughs. and they and their children will feast, drinking of the wine which they have made, wearing garlands on their heads, and having the praises of the gods on their lips, living in sweet society, and having a care that their families do not exceed their means; for they will have an eye to poverty or war."

So Socrates, in this dialogue on the Republic, describes to his hearers the essential physical elements of the good life. One of his hearers, Glaucon, asks him to elaborate it a little, for Socrates has limited himself to bare essentials. . . . Socreates answers that a good state would have the healthy constitution which he has just described; but that he has no objection to looking at an "inflamed constitution." What Socrates describes as an inflamed constitution is a mode of life which all the people of Western Europe and America at the present day—no matter what their religion, economic status, or political creed may be—believe in with almost a single mind; and so, although it is the opposite of Plato's ideal state, I go on to present it, for the light it throws on our own institutions and habits.

The unjust state comes into existence, says Plato through the mouth of Socrates, by the multiplication of wants and superfluities. As a result of increasing wants, we must enlarge our borders, for the original healthy state is too small. Now the city will fill up with a multitude of callings which go beyond those required by any natural want; there will be a host of parasites and "supers"; and our country, which was big enough to support the original inhabitants, will want a slice of our neighbor's land for pasture and tillage; and they will want a slice of ours if, like ourselves, they exceed the limits of necessity and give themselves up to the unlimited accumulation of wealth. "And then we shall go to war—that will be the next thing."

The sum of this criticism is that Plato saw clearly that an ideal community must have a common physical standard of living; and that boundless wealth or unlimited desires and gratifications had nothing to do with a good standard. The good was what was necessary; and what was necessary was not, essentially, many goods.

Like Aristotle, Plato wanted a mode of life which was neither impoverished nor luxurious: those who have read a little in Greek history will see that this Athenian ideal of the good life fell rather symbolically between Sparta and Corinth, between the cities which we associate respectively with a hard, military life and with a soft, super-sensuous aestheticism.

Should we moderate our wants or should we increase production? Plato had no difficulty in answering this question. He held that a reasonable man would moderate his wants; and that if he wished to live like a good farmer or a good philosopher he would not attempt to copy the expenditures of a vulgar gambler who has just made a corner in wheat, or a vulgar courtesan who has just made a conquest of the vulgar gambler who has made a corner in wheat. Wealth and poverty, said Plato, are the two causes of deterioration in the arts: both the workman and his works are likely to degenerate under the influence of either poverty or wealth, "for one is the parent of luxury and indolence, and the other of meanness and viciousness, and both of discontent."

Nor does Plato have one standard of living for his ruling classes and another for the common people. To each person he would give all the material things necessary for sustenance; and from each he would be prepared to strip all that was not essential. He realized that the possession of goods was not a means of getting happiness, but an effort to make up for a spiritually depauperate life: for Plato, happiness was what one could put into life and not what one could loot out of it: it was the happiness of the dancer rather than the happiness of the glutton. Plato pictured a community living a sane, continent, athletic, clear-eyed life; a community that would be always, so to say, within bounds. there is a horror of laxity and easy living in his Republic. His society was stripped for action. The fragrance that permeates his picture of the good life is not the heavy fragrance of rose-petals and incense falling upon languorous couches: it is the fragrance of the morning grass, and the scent of crushed mint or marjoram beneath the feet.

How big is Plato's community, how are the people divided, what are their relations? Now that we have discussed the layout of the land, and have inquired into the physical basis of this utopia, we are ready to turn our attention to the people; for it is out of the interaction of folk, work, and place that every community—good or bad, real of fancied—exists and perpetuates itself.

It follows almost inevitably from what we have said of Plato's environment, that his ideal community was not to be unlimited in population. Quite the contrary. Plato said that "the city may increase to any size which is consistent with its unity; that is the limit." The modern political scientist, who lives within a national state of millions of people, and who thinks of the greatness of states largely in terms of their population, has scoffed without mercy at the fact that Plato limited his community to an arbitrary number, 5,040, about the number that can be conveniently addressed by a single orator. As a matter of fact there is nothing ridiculous in Plato's definition: he was not speaking of a horde of barbarians: he was laying down the foundations for an active polity of citizens: and it is plain enough in all conscience that when you increase the number of people in a community you decrease the number of things that they can share in common. Plato could not anticipate the wireless telephone and the daily newspaper; still less would he have been likely to exaggerate the difference which these instrumentalities have made in the matters that most intimately concern us; and when he set bounds to the population his city would contain, he was anticipating by more than two thousand years the verdict of modern town planners like Mr. Raymond Unwin.

People are not the members of a community because they live under the same system of political government or dwell in the same country. They become genuine citizens to the extent that they share certain institutions and ways of life with similarly educated people. Plato was primarily concerned with providing conditions which would make a community hold together without being acted upon by any external force—as the national state is acted upon today by war or the threat of war. This concern seems to underlie every line of the Republic. In attacking his problem, the business of supplying the physical wants of the city seemed relatively unimportant; and even though Greece in the time of Plato traded widely with the whole Mediterranean region, Plato did not mistake commercial unity for civic unity. Hence in his scheme of things the work of the farmer and the merchant and the trader was subordinate. The important thing to consider was the general conditions under which all the individuals and groups in a community might live together harmoniously. This is a long cry from the utopias of the nineteenth century, which we will examine later; and that is why it is important to understand Plato's point of view and follow his argument.

To Plato, a good community was like a healthy body; a harmonious exercise of every function was the condition of its strength and vitality. Necessarily then a good community could not be simply a collection of individuals, each one of whom insists upon some private and particular happiness without respect to the welfare and interests of his fellows. Plato believed that goodness and happiness—for he would scarcely admit that there was any distinct line of cleavage between these qualities—consisted in living according to nature; that is to say, in knowing one's self, in finding one's bent, and in fuilfilling the particular work which one hd the capacity to perform. The secret of a good community, therefore, if we may translate Plato's language into modern political slang, is the principle of function.

Every kind of work, says Plato, requires a particular kind of aptitude and training. If we wish to have good shoes, our shoes must be made by a shoemaker and not by a weaver; and in like manner, every man has some particular calling to which his genius leads him, and he finds a happiness for himself and usefulness to his fellows when he is employed in that calling. The good life must result when each man has a function to perform, and when all the necessary functions are adjusted happily to each other. The state is like the physical body. "Health is the creation of a natural order and government in the parts of the body, and the creation of disease is the creation of a state of things in which they are at variance with the natural order." The supreme virtue in the commonwealth is justice; namely, the due apportionment of work or function under the rule of "a place for every man and every man in his place."

Has any such society ever come into existence? Do not too hastily answer No. The ideal in Plato's mind is carried out point for point in the organization of a modern symphony orchestra.

Now Plato was not unaware that there were other formulas for happiness. He expressly points out however that in founding the Republic he does not wish to make any single person or group happier beyond the rest; he desires rather that the whole city should be in the happiest condition. It would be easy enough "to array the husbandmen in rich and costly robes and to enjoin them to cultivate the ground only with a view to their pleasure," and so Plato might have conferred a spurious kind of felicity upon every individual. If this happened, however, there would be a brief period of ease and revelry before the whole works went to pot. In this Plato is a thoroughgoing realist: he is not looking for a short avenue of escape; he is ready to face the road with all its ups and downs, with its steep climbs as well as its wide vistas; and he does not think any the worse of life because he finds that its chief enjoyments rest in activity, and not, as the epicureans of all sorts have always believed, in a release from activity.

Plato arrives at his apportionment of functions by a method which is old-fashioned, and which anybody versed in modern psychology would regard as a "rationalization." Plato is trying to give a firm basis to the division of classes which he favored; and so he compares the community to a human being, possessed of the virtues of wisdom, valour, temperance, and justice. Each of these virtues Plato relates to a particular class of people.

Wisdom is appropriate to the rulers of the city. Thus arises the class of guardians.

Valour is the characteristic of the defenders of the city and hence a military class, called auxiliaries, appears.

Temperance, or agreement, is the virtue which relates to all classes.

Finally, there comes justice. "Justice is the ultimate cause and condition of all of them. . . . If a question should arise as to which of these four qualities contributed most by their presence to the excellence of the State whether the agreement of rulers and subjects or the preservation in the soldiers of the opinion which the law ordains about the true nature of dangers, or wisdom and watchfulness in the rulers would claim the palm, or whether this which I am about to mention," namely, "everyone doing his own work and not being a busybody—the question would not be easily determined." Nevertheless, it is plain that justice is the keystone of the Platonic utopia.

We must not misunderstand Plato's division of classes. Aristotle criticizes Plato in terms of a more simple system of democracy; but Plato did not mean to institute a fixed order; within his Republic the Napoleonic motto—*la carrière est ouvert aux talents*—was the guiding principle. What lay beneath Plato's argument was a belief which present-day studies in psychology seem likely to confirm; a belief that children come into the world with a bent already well marked in their physical and mental constitutions. Plato advocated, it is true, an aristocracy or government by the best people; but he did not believe in fake aristocracies that are perpetuated through hereditary wealth and position. Having determined that his city was to contain three classes, rulers, warriors, and workers, his capital difficulty still remained to be faced; how was each individual to find his way to the right class, and under what conditions would he best fulfill his functions there?

The answers to these questions bring us to the boldest and most original sections of the Republic: the part that has provoked the greatest amount of antagonism and aversion, because of its drastic departure from the rut of many established institutions—in particular, individual marriages and individual property.

In order to perpetuate his idea constitution Plato relies upon three methods: breeding, education, and a discipline for daily life. Let us consider the effect of these methods upon each of the classes.

We may dismiss the class of artisans and husbandmen very briefly. It is not quite clear whether Plato meant his system of marriage to extend to the members of this class. As for education, it is clear that he saw nothing to find fault within the system of apprenticeship whereby the smith or the potter or the farmer trained others to follow his calling; and so he had no reason for departing from methods which had proved, on the whole, very satisfactory. How satisfactory that system was, indeed, we have only to look at an Athenian ruin or vase or chalice to find out. Any improvements that might come about in these occupations would result from the Platonic rule of justice; and Plato followed his own injunction strictly enough to keep away from other people's business.

This of course seems an odd and hasty manner of treatment, as I said before, to those of us who live in a world where the affairs of industry and the tendencies of the labor movement are forever on the carpet. But Plato justifies his treatment by saying that "when shoemakers become bad, and are degenerate, and profess to be shoemakers when they are not, no great mischief happens to the state; but when the guardians of the law and the State are not so in reality, but only in appearance, you see how they entirely destroy the whole constitution, if they alone shall have the privilege of an affluent and happy life." Hence Plato concentrates his attack upon the point of greatest danger: while the shoemaker, as a rule, knows how to mind his own business, the statesman is for the most part unaware of the essential business which he has to mind; and tends to be negligent even when he has some dim notion as to what it may be—being all too ready to sacrifice it to golf or the favors of a beautiful woman. As we saw in Plato's original description of the State, the common folk would doubtless have a good many of the joys and delights traditional in the Greek cities; and doubtless, although Plato says nothing one way or the other, they would be permitted to own such property as might be needed for the conduct of their business or the enjoyment of their homes. The very fact that no definite rule was prescribed for them, makes us suspect that Plato was willing to let these things go on in the usual way.

The next class is known as the warriors, or auxiliaries. They are different in character from the guardians who rule the state; but frequently Plato refers to the guardians as a single class, including the auxiliaries; and it seems that they figured in his mind as the temporal arm of that class. At any rate, the auxiliaries as they are painted int he Critias, which was the dialogue in which Plato attempted to show his Republic in action, dwelt by themselves within a single enclosure; and had common meals and common temples of their own; and so we may surmise that their way of life was to be similar to that of the higher guardians, but that it was not capable of being pushed to the same pitch of development on the intellectual side. These warriors of Plato are, after all, not so very much unlike the regular or standing army in a modern State: they have a life of their own within the barracks, they are trained and drilled to great endurance, and they are taught to obey without question the Government. When you examine the naked business of the warriors and artisans, you discover that Plato is not, for all the difference in scale, so very far away from modern realities. Apart from the fact that women were permitted an equal place with men in the life of the camp and the gymnasium and the

academy, the real difference comes in the matter of breeding and selection. At last we approach the Governors, or the Guardians.

How does the Guardian achieve his position and power? Plato is a little chary of answering this question; he hints that it can only happen at the beginning if a person with the brains of a philosopher happens to be born with the authority of a king. Let us pass this by. How are the Guardians born and bred? This is the manner.

For the well-being of the state the Guardians have the power to administer medicinal lies. One of these is to be told to the youth when their education has reached a point at which iot becomes possible for the Guardians to determine their natural talents and aptitudes.

"Citizens, we shall say to them in our tale, you are brothers, yet God has framed you differently. Some of you have the power to command, and these he has composed of gold, wherefore also they have the greatest honor; others of silver, to be auxiliaries; others again who are to be husbandmen and craftsmen he has made of brass and iron; and the species will generally be preserved in the children. But as you are of the same original family, a golden parent will sometimes have a silver son, or a silver parent a golden son. And God proclaims to the rulers, as a first principle, that before all things they should watch over their offspring, and see what elements mingle in their nature, for if the son of a golden or silver parent has an admixture of brass and iron, then nature orders a transposition of the ranks; and the eye of the ruler must not be pitiful towards his child because he has to descend in the scale and will become a husbandman or artisan, just as there may be others sprung from the artisan class who are raised to honor, and become guardians and auxiliaries."

As the safeguard of this principle of natural selection of functions, Plato proposed a system of common marriage. "The wives of these guardians are to be common, and their children are also common, and no parent is to know his own child, nor any child his parent." Starting from the day of the hymeneal, the bridegroom who was then married will call all the male children who are born ten and seven months afterwards his sons, and the female children his daughters, and they will call him father. . . . And those who were born at the same time they will term brothers and sisters, and they are not to intermarry." One of the features of this system is that the best stocks—the strongest and wisest and most beautiful—are to be encouraged to reproduce themselves. But this is not worked out in detail. There is to be complete freedom of sexual selection among the guardians; and those who are most distinguished in their services are to have access to a great number of women; but beyond encouraging the guardians to be prolific, Plato did not apparently consider the possibilities of cross-breeding between the various classes.

On the whole, on may say that Plato puts it up to the Guardians to perpetuate themselves properly, and indicates that this is to be one of their main concerns. His good breeding was biological breeding, not social breeding. He recognized—as some of our modern eugenists have failed to—that good parents might throw poor stock, on occasion, and that abject parents might have remarkably good progeny. Even if the Guardians are to be encouraged to have good children, Plato provides that the children themselves must prove their goodness before they are in turn recognized as Guardians. As for the children of the baser sort—well, they were to be rigorously limited to the needs and resources of the community. Plato lived at a time when a great many children were born only to be murdered through "exposure" as it was called; and he had no qualms, apparently, about letting the Guardians send the children with a bad heredity into the discard. If his population could not grow properly in the sunlight without getting rid of the weeds, he was prepared to get rid of the weeds. People who were physically or spiritually too deformed to take part in the good life were to be eliminated. Plato, like a robust Athenian, was for killing or curing a disease; and he gave short shrift to the constitutional invalids.

But to breed Guardians is only one-half the problem. The other half comes under the heads of education and discipline; and when Plato discusses these things, he is not speaking, as a modern college president perhaps would, of book-learning alone; he is referring to all the activities that mold a person's life. He follows the older philosopher, Pythagoras, and anticipates the great organizer, Benedict, by laying down a rule of life for his guardians. He did not imagine that disinterested activities, spacious thoughts, and clear vision would arise in people who normally put their personal comfort and "happiness" above necessities of their office.

Let us recognize the depth of Plato's insight. It is plain that he did not despise what a modern psychologist would call "the normal biological career." For the great majority of people happiness consisted in learning a definite trade or profession, in doing one's daily work, in mating, and when the tension of the day relaxed, in getting enjoyment and recreation in the simple sensualities of eating, drinking, singing, love-making, and what not. This normal biological career is associated with a home, and with the limited horizons of a home; and a host of small loyalties and jealousies and interests are woven into the very texture of that life.

Each home, each small circle of relatives and friends, tends to be a miniature utopia; there is a limited community of goods, a tendency to adjust one's actions to the welfare of the little whole, and a habit of banding together against the world at large. But the good, contrary to the proverb, is frequently the enemy of the better; and the little utopia of the family is the enemy—indeed the principal enemy—of the beloved community. This fact is notorious. The picture of a trade union leader which Mr. John Galsworthy portrays in Strife, whose power to act firmly in behalf of his group is sapped by the demands made by family ties, could be matched in a thousand places. In order to have the freedom to act for the sake of a great institution, a person must be stript of a whole host of restraining ties and sentimentalities. Jesus commanded his followers to leave their families and abandon their worldly goods; and Plato, in order to preserve his ideal commonwealth, laid down a similar rule. For those who as guardians were to apply the science of government to public affairs, a private life, private duties, private interests, were all to be left behind.

As to the education of the Guardians, I have scarcely the space to treat the more formal part of it in detail; for among other things, as Jowett points out, the Republic is a treatise on education; and Plato presents a fairly elaborate plan. The two branches of Greek education, music and gymnastic, applied in the student's early years to the culture of the body and the culture of the mind; and both branches were to be followed in common by both sexes. Instruction during the early part of a child's life was to be communicated through play activities, as it is today in the City and Country School in New York; and only with manhood did the student approach his subjects in a more formal and systematic manner. In the course of this education the students were to be tested again and again with respect to their mental keenness and tenacity and fortitude; and only those who came through the fire purified and strengthened were to be admitted to the class of guardians.

The daily life of the Guardians is a rigorous, military regime. They live in common barracks, and in order to avoid paying attention to private affairs, instead of minding the good of the whole community, no one is allowed to "possess any substance privately, unless there be a great necessity for it"; next, Plato continues, none shall have any dwelling or storehouse into which whoever inclines may not enter; and as for necessaries, they shall be only such as brave and temperate warriors may require, and as they are supported by other citizens, they shall receive such a reward of their guardianship as to have neither an overplus nor a deficit at the end of the year. They shall have public meals, as in encampments, and live in common. They are to refrain from using gold and silver, as all the gold and silver they require is in their souls.

All these regulations, of course, are for the purpose of keeping the Guardians disinterested. Plato believed that the majority of people did not know how to mind public business; for it seemed to him that the ordering of a community's life required a measure of science which the common man could not possibly possess. Indeed, in a city of a thousand men he did not see the possibility of getting as many as fifty men who would be sufficiently well versed in what we should today call sociology to deal intelligently with public affairs—for there would scarcely be that many first-rate draughts players. At the same time, if the government is to be entrusted to a few, the few must be geniunely disinterested. If they possessed lands and houses and money in a private way they would become landlords and farmers instead of Guardians; they would be hateful masters instead of allies of the citizens; and so "hating and being hated, plotting and being plotted against, more afraid of the enemies within than the enemies without, they would drag themselves and the rest of the state to speedy destruction."

It remains to take a glance at the manhood and later life of the Guardians.

As young men, the Guardians belong to the auxiliaries; and since they are not permitted to perform any of the manual arts—for skill in any of the trades tended to make a man warped and one-sided, like the symbolic blacksmith god, Hephaestos—their physical edge was maintained by the unceasing discipline of the gymnasium and "military" expeditions. I put military in quotation marks, because a greater part of the warriors' time is spent not in war but in preparation for war; and it is plain that Plato looked upon war as an unnecessary evil, for it arose out of the unjust state; and therefore he must have resorted to warlike discipline for the educational values he found in it. From thirty-five to fifty the potential Guardians undertake practical activities, commanding armies and gaining experience of life. After fifty, those who are qualified devote themselves to philosophy: out of their experience and their inner reflection they figure the essential nature of the good community; and on occasion each guardian abandons divine philosophy for awhile, takes his turn at the helm of the state, and trains his successors.

What is the business of the Guardian? How does Plato's ideal statesman differ from Julius Caesar or Mr. Theodore Roosevelt?

The business of the Guardian is to manufacture libery. The petty laws, regulations, and reforms with which the ordinary statesman occupies himself had nothing to do, in Plato's mind, with the essential business of the ruler. So Plato expressly foregoes making laws to regulate marketing, the affairs of industry, graft, bribery, theft, and so forth; and he leaves these matters with the curt indication that men can be left to themselves to devise on a voluntary basis the rules of the game for the different occupations; and that it is not the business of the Guardian to meddle in such matters. In a well-founded state, a great number of minor maladjustments would simply fall out of existence; whilst in any other state, all the tinkering and reforming in the world is quite powerless to amend its organic defects. Those make-believe statesmen who try their hand at legislation and "are always fancying that by reforming they will make an end of the dishonesties and rascalities of mankind," do not know that in reality they are trying to cut away the heads of a hydra.

The real concern of the Guardians is with the essential constitution of the state. The means that they employ to perfect this constitution are breeding, vocational selection, and education. "If once a republic is set a-going, it proceeds happily, increasing as a circle. And whilst good education and nurture are preserved, they produce good geniuses; and good geniuses, partaking of such education, produce still better than the former, as well in other respects, as with reference to propagation, as in the case of other animals." All the activities of the Republic are to be patterned after the utopia which the Guardians see with their inward eye. So gradually the community becomes a living unity; and it exhibits the health of that which is organically sound.

What do we miss when we look around this utopia of Plato's? Contacts with the outside world? We may take them for granted. Downy beds, Corinthian girls, luxurious furniture? We can well spare them. The opportunity for a satisfactory intellectual and physical life? No: both of these are here.

What Plato has left out are the poets, dramatists, and painters. Literature and music, in order to contribute to the noble education of the Guardians, are both severely restricted in theme and in treatment. Plato has his limitations; and here is the principal one: Plato distrusted the emotional life, and whilst he was prepared to do full homage to man's obvious sensualities, he feared the emotions as a tight-rope walker fears the wind; for they threatened his balance. In one significant passage he classifies "love" with disease and drunkenness, as a vulgar misfortune; and though he was ready to permit the active expression of the emotions, as in the dance or the sexual act, he treated the mere play upon the feelings, without active participation, as a form of intemperance. Hence a great deal of music and dramatic mimicry was taboo. . . .

As we leave this little city of Plato's, nestling in the hills, and as the thin, didactic voice of Plato, who has been perpetually at our elbows, dies away from our ears—what impression do we finally carry away?

In the fields, men are perhaps ploying the land for the autumn sowing; on the terraces, a band of men, women, and children are plucking the olives carefully from the trees, one by one; in the gymnasium on the top of the Acropolis, men and youths are exercising, and as they practice with the javelin now and then it catches the sun and glints into our eye; apart from these groups, in a shaded walk that overlooks the city, a Guardian is pacing back and forth, talking in quick, earnest tones with his pupils.

These are occupations which, crudely or elaborately, men have always engaged in; and here in the Republic they engage in them still. What has changed? What has profoundly changed is not the things that men do, but the relations they bear to one another in doing them. In Plato's community, servitude and compulsion and avarice and indolence are gone. Men mind their business for the sake of living well, in just relations to the whole community of which they are a part. They live, in the strictest sense, according to nature; and because no one can enjoy a private privilege, each man can grow to his full stature and enter into every heritage of his citizenship. When Plato says no to the institutions and ways of life that men have blindly fostered, his eyes are open, and he is facing the light.

SOCIAL MYTHS:
UTOPIA AND THE SOCIAL CONTRACT

Northrop Frye (essay date 1965)

SOURCE: "Varieties of Literary Utopias," in *Utopias and Utopian Thought,* edited by Frank E. Manuel, Houghton Mifflin Company and the American Academy of Arts and Sciences, 1965, pp. 25-49.

[*In the following excerpt from an essay first published in the Spring, 1965 issue of* Daedalus, *Frye discusses common characteristics of utopian literature, emphasizing the importance of ritual, the Christian tradition, and education.*]

There Are two social conceptions which can be expressed only in terms of myth. One is the social contract, which presents an account of the origins of society. The other is the utopia, which presents an imaginative vision of the *telos* or end at which social life aims. These two myths both begin in an analysis of the present, the society that confronts the mythmaker, and they project this analysis in time or space. The contract projects it into the past, the utopia into the future or some distant place. To Hobbes, a contemporary of the Puritan Revolution, the most important social principle was the maintenance of *de facto* power; hence he constructs a myth of contract turning on the conception of society's surrender of that power. To Locke, a contemporary of the Whig Revolution, the most im-

portant social principle was the relation of *de facto* power to legitimate or *de jure* authority; hence he constructs a myth turning on society's delegation of power. The value of such a myth as theory depends on the depth and penetration of the social analysis which inspires it. The social contract, though a genuine myth which, in John Stuart Mill's phrase, passes a fiction off as a fact, is usually regarded as an integral part of social theory. The utopia, on the other hand, although its origin is much the same, belongs primarily to fiction. The reason is that the emphasis in the contract myth falls on the present facts of society which it is supposed to explain. And even to the extent that the contract myth is projected into the past, the past is the area where historical evidence lies; and so the myth preserves at least the gesture of making assertions that can be definitely verified or refuted.

The utopia is a *speculative* myth; it is designed to contain or provide a vision for one's social ideas, not to be a theory connecting social facts together. There have been one or two attempts to take utopian constructions literally by trying to set them up as actual communities, but the histories of these communities make melancholy reading. Life imitates literature up to a point, but hardly up to that point. The utopian writer looks at his own society first and tries to see what, for his purposes, its significant elements are. The utopia itself shows what society would be like if those elements were fully developed. Plato looked at his society and saw its structure as a hierarchy of priests, warriors, artisans, and servants—much the same structure that inspired the caste system of India. The *Republic* shows what a society would be like in which such a hierarchy functioned on the principle of justice, that is, each man doing his own work. More, thinking within a Christian framework of ideas, assumed that the significant elements of society were the natural virtues, justice, temperance, fortitude, prudence. The *Utopia* itself, in its second or constructive book, shows what a society would be like in which the natural virtues were allowed to assume their natural forms. Bacon, on the other hand, anticipates Marx by assuming that the most significant of social factors is technological productivity, and his *New Atlantis* constructs accordingly.

The procedure of constructing a utopia produces two literary qualities which are typical, almost invariable, in the genre. In the first place, the behavior of society is described *ritually*. A ritual is a significant social act, and the utopia-writer is concerned only with the typical actions which are significant of those social elements he is stressing. In utopian stories a frequent device is for someone, generally a first-person narrator, to enter the utopia and be shown around it by a sort of Intourist guide. The story is made up largely of a Socratic dialogue between guide and narrator, in which the narrator asks questions or thinks up objections and the guide answers them. One gets a little weary, in reading a series of such stories, of what seems a pervading smugness of tone. As a rule the guide is completely identified with his society and seldom admits to any discrepancy between the reality and the appearance of what he is describing. But we recognize that this is inevitable given the conventions employed. In the second place, rituals are apparently irrational acts which become *rational* when their significance is explained. In such utopias the guide explains the structure of the society and thereby the significance of the behavior being observed. Hence, the behavior of society is presented as rationally motivated. It is a common objection to utopias that they present human nature as governed more by reason than it is or can be. But this rational emphasis, again, is the result of using certain literary conventions. The utopian romance does not present society as governed by reason; it presents it as governed by ritual habit, or prescribed social behavior, which is explained rationally.

Every society, of course, imposes a good deal of prescribed social behavior on its citizens, much of it being followed unconsciously, anything completely accepted by convention and custom having in it a large automatic element. But even automatic ritual habits are explicable, and so every society can be seen or described to some extent as a product of conscious design. The symbol of conscious design in society is the city, with its abstract pattern of streets and buildings, and with the complex economic cycle of production, distribution, and consumption that it sets up. The utopia is primarily a vision of the orderly city and of a city-dominated society. Plato's Republic is a city-state, Athenian in culture and Spartan in discipline. It was inevitable that the utopia, as a literary genre, should be revived at the time of the Renaissance, the period in which the medieval social order was breaking down again into city-state units or nations governed from a capital city. Again, the utopia, in its typical form, contrasts, implicitly or explicitly, the writer's own society with the more desirable one he describes. The desirable society, or the utopia proper, is essentially the writer's own society with its unconscious ritual habits transposed into their conscious equivalents. The contrast in value between the two societies implies a satire on the writer's own society, and the basis for the satire is the unconsciousness or inconsistency in the social behavior he observes around him. More's *Utopia* begins with a satire on the chaos of sixteenth-century life in England and presents the Utopia itself as a contrast to it. Thus the typical utopia contains, if only by implication, a satire on the *anarchy* inherent in the writer's own society, and the utopia form flourishes best when anarchy seems most a social threat. Since More, utopias have appeared regularly but sporadically in literature, with a great increase around the close of the nineteenth century. This later vogue clearly had much to do with the distrust and dismay aroused by

extreme laissez-faire versions of capitalism, which were thought of as manifestations of anarchy.

Most utopia-writers follow either More (and Plato) in stressing the legal structure of their societies, or Bacon in stressing its technological power. The former type of utopia is closer to actual social and political theory; the latter overlaps with what is now called science fiction. Naturally, since the Industrial Revolution a serious utopia can hardly avoid introducing technological themes. And because technology is progressive, getting to the utopia has tended increasingly to be a journey in time rather than space, a vision of the future and not of a society located in some isolated spot on the globe (or outside it: journeys to the moon are a very old form of fiction, and some of them are utopian). The growth of science and technology brings with it a prodigious increase in the legal complications of existence. As soon as medical science identifies the source of a contagious disease in a germ, laws of quarantine go into effect; as soon as technology produces the automobile, an immense amount of legal apparatus is imported into life, and thousands of non-criminal citizens become involved in fines and police-court actions. This means a corresponding increase in the amount of ritual habit necessary to life, and a new ritual habit must be conscious, and so constraining, before it becomes automatic or unconscious. Science and technology, especially the latter, introduce into society the conception of directed social change, change with logical consequences attached to it. These consequences turn on the increase of ritual habit. And as long as ritual habit can still be seen as an imminent possibility, as something we may or may not acquire, there can be an emotional attitude toward it either of acceptance or repugnance. The direction of social change may be thought of as exhilarating, as in most theories of progress, or as horrible, as in pessimistic or apprehensive social theories. Or it may be thought that whether the direction of change is good or bad will depend on the attitude society takes toward it. If the attitude is active and resolute, it may be good; if helpless and ignorant, bad. . . .

Plato's *Republic* begins with an argument between Socrates and Thrasymachus over the nature of justice. Thrasymachus attempts, not very successfully, to show that justice is a verbal and rhetorical conception used for certain social purposes, and that existentially there is no such thing as justice. He has to use words to say this, and the words he uses are derived from, and unconsciously accept the assumptions of, a discussion started by Socrates. So Socrates has little difficulty in demonstrating that in the verbal pattern Thrasymachus is employing justice has its normal place, associated with all other good and real things. Others in the group are not satisfied that an existential situation can be so easily refuted by an essentialist argument, and they attempt to restate Thrasymachus' position. Socrates' argument remains essential to the end, but it takes the form of another kind of verbal pattern, a descriptive model of a state in which justice is the existential principle. The question then arises: what relation has this model to existing society?

If what seems the obvious answer is the right one, Plato's imaginary Republic is the ideal society that we do not live in but ought to be living in. Not many readers would so accept it, for Plato's state has in full measure the forbidding quality that wehave noted as a characteristic of utopias. Surely most people today would see in its rigorous autocracy, its unscrupulous use of lies for propaganda, its ruthlessly censored art, and its subordination of all the creative and productive life of the state to a fanatical military caste, all the evils that we call totalitarian. Granted all the Greek fascination with the myth of Lycurgus, the fact that Sparta defeated Athens is hardly enough to make us want to adopt so many of the features of that hideous community. Plato admits that dictatorial tyranny is very like his state-pattern entrusted to the wrong men. But to assume much of a difference between tyranny and Plato's state we should have to believe in the perfectibility of intellectuals, which neither history nor experience gives us much encouragement to do.

We notice, however, that as early as the Fifth Book Socrates has begun to deprecate the question of the practicability of establishing his Republic, on the ground that thought is one thing and action another. And, as the argument goes on there is an increasing emphasis on the analogy of the just state to the wise man's mind. The hierarchy of philosopher, guard, and artisan in the just state corresponds to the hierarchy of reason, will, and appetite in the disciplined individual. And the disciplined individual is the only free individual. The free man is free because his chaotic and lustful desires are hunted down and exterminated, or else compelled to express themselves in ways prescribed by the dictatorship of his reason. He is free because a powerful will is ready to spring into action to help reason do whatever it sees fit, acting as a kind of thought police suppressing every impulse not directly related to its immediate interests. It is true that what frees the individual seems to enslave society, and that something goes all wrong with human freedom when we take an analogy between individual and social order literally. But Plato is really arguing from his social model to the individual, not from the individual to society. The censorship of Homer and the other poets, for example, illustrates how the wise man uses literature, what he accepts and rejects of it in forming his own beliefs, rather than what society ought to do to literature. At the end of the Ninth Book we reach what is the end of the *Republic* for our purposes, as the Tenth Book raises issues beyond our present scope. There it is made clear that the *Republic* exists in the present, not in the future. It is not a dream to be realized in practice; it is

an informing power in the mind:

> I understand; you speak of that city of which we are the founders, and which exists in idea only; for I do not think thatthere is such an one anywhere on earth.

> In heaven, I replied, there is laid up a pattern of such a city, and he who desires may behold this, and beholding, govern himself accordingly. But whether there really is or ever will be such an one is of no importance to him; for he will act according to the laws of that city and of no other.

In Christianity the two myths that polarize social thought, the contract and the utopia, the myth of origin and the myth of *telos,* are given in their purely mythical or undisplaced forms. The myth of contract becomes the myth of creation, and of placing man in the garden of Eden, the ensuing fall being the result of a breach of the contract. Instead of the utopia we have the City of God, a utopian metaphor most elaborately developed in St. Augustine. To this city men, or some men, are admitted at the end of time, but of course human nature is entirely incapable of reaching it in its present state, much less of establishing it. Still, the attainment of the City of God in literature must be classified as a form of utopian fiction, its most famous literary treatment being the *Purgatorio* and *Paradiso* of Dante. The conception of the millennium, the Messianic kingdom to be established on earth, comes closer to the conventional idea of the utopia, but that again does not depend primarily on human effort.

The church, in this scheme of things, is not a utopian society, but it is a more highly ritualized community than ordinary society; and its relation to the latter has some analogies to the relation of Plato's Republic to the individual mind. That is, it acts as an informing power on society, drawing it closer to the pattern of the City of God. Most utopias are conceived as élite societies in which a small group is entrusted with essential responsibilities, and this élite is usually some analogy of a priesthood. For in Utopia, as in India, the priestly caste has reached the highest place. H. G. Wells divides society into the Poietic, or creative, the Kinetic, or executive, the Dull, and the Base. This reads like an uncharitable version of the four Indian castes—particularly uncharitable considering that the only essential doctrine in Wells' utopian religion is the rejection of original sin. Wells' writing in general illustrates the common principle that the belief that man is by nature good does not lead to a very good-natured view of man. In any case his "samurai" belong to the first group, in spite of their warrior name. The utopias of science fiction are generally controlled by scientists, who of course are another form of priestly élite.

Another highly ritualized society, the monastic community, though not intended as a utopia, has some utopian characteristics. Its members spend their whole time within it; individual life takes its pattern from the community; certain activities of the civilized good life, farming, gardening, reclaiming land, copying manuscripts, teaching, form part of its structure. The influence of the monastic community on utopian thought has been enormous. It is strong in More's *Utopia,* and much stronger in Campanella's *City of the Sun,* which is more explicitly conceived on the analogy of the church and monastery. The conception of the ideal society as a secularized reversal of the monastery, the vows of poverty, chastity, and obedience transposed into economic security, monogamous marriage, and personal independence, appears in Rabelais' scheme for the Abbey of Thélème. Something like this re-appears in many nineteenth-century Utopias, not only the literary ones but in the more explicitly political schemes of St. Simon, Fourier, and Comte, of whose writings it seems safe to say that they lack Rabelais' lightness of touch. The government of the monastery, with its mixture of the elective and the dictatorial principles, is still going strong as a social model in Carlyle's *Past and Present.* Utopian satire sometimes introduces celibate groups of fanatics by way of parody, as in *1984* and in Huxley's *Ape and Essence.*

It is obvious from what we have said that a Christian utopia, in the sense of an ideal state to be attained in human life, is impossible: if it were possible it would be the kingdom of heaven, and trying to realize it on earth would be the chief end of man. Hence More does not present his Utopia as a Christian state: it is a state, as we remarked earlier, in which the natural virtues are allowed to assume their natural forms. In that case, what is the point of the *Utopia,* which is certainly a Christian book? Some critics feel that More could have meant it only as a *jeu d'espirit* for an in-group of humanist intellectuals. But that conception makes it something more trivial than anything that More would write or Rabelais and Erasmus much appreciate. The second book of *Utopia* must have been intended quite as seriously as the trenchant social criticism of the first.

We note that the *Utopia,* again, takes the form of a dialogue between a first-person narrator and a guide. The guide is Hythloday, who has been to Utopia, and whose description of it takes up the second book. The narrator is More himself. In the first book the social attitudes of the two men are skillfully contrasted. More is a gradualist, a reformer; he feels that Hythloday should use his experience and knowledge in advising the princes of Europe on the principles of social justice. Hythloday has come back from Utopia a convinced communist and a revolutionary. All Europe's misery, blundering, and hypocrisy spring from its attachment to private property: unless this is renounced nothing good can be done, and as this renunciation is

unlikely he sees no hope for Europe. At the end More remarks that although he himself has not been converted to Hythloday's all-out utopianism, there are many things in Utopia that he would hope for rather than expect to see in his own society. The implication seems clear that the ideal state to More, as to Plato, is not a future ideal but a hypothetical one, an informing power and not a goal of action. For More, as for Plato, Utopia is the kind of model of justice and common sense which, once established in the mind, clarifies its standards and values. It does not lead to a desire to abolish sixteenth-century Europe and replace it with Utopia, but it enables one to see Europe, and to work within it, more clearly. As H. G. Wells says of his Utopia, it is good discipline to enter it occasionally.

There is however an element of paradox in More's construct that is absent from Plato's. More's state is not eutopia, the good place, but utopia, nowhere. It is achieved by the natural virtues without revelation, and its eclectic state religion, its toleration (in certain circumstances) of suicide and divorce, its married priesthood, and its epicurean philosophy all mean that it is not, like the Republic, the invisible city whose laws More himself, or his readers, would continually and constantly obey. It has often been pointed out that More died a martyr to some very un-Utopian causes. The point of the paradox is something like this: Europe has revelation, but the natural basis of its society is an extremely rickety structure; and if Europe pretends to greater wisdom than Utopia it ought to have at least something of the Utopian solidity and consistency in the wisdom it shares with Utopia. This paradoxical argument in More re-appears in Montaigne's essay on the cannibals, where it is demonstrated that cannibals have many virtues we have not, and if we disdain to be cannibals we should have at least something of those virtues. Similarly Gulliver returns from the society of rational horses to that of human beings feeling a passionate hatred not of the human race, as careless readers of Swift are apt to say, but of its pride, including its pride in not being horses.

In most utopias the state predominates over the individual: property is usually held in common and the characteristic features of individual life, leisure, privacy, and freedom of movement, are as a rule minimized. Most of this is, once more, simply the result of writing a utopia and accepting its conventions: the utopia is designed to describe a unified society, not individual varieties of existence. Still, the sense of the individual as submerged in a social mass is very strong. But as soon as we adopt the principle of *paradeigma* which Plato sets forth in his Ninth Book, the relation of society to individual is reversed. The ideal state now becomes an element in the liberal education of the individual free man, permitting him a greater liberty of mental perspective than he had before.

The Republic built up by Socrates and entered into by his hearers is derived from their ability to see society on two levels, a lower natural level and an upper ideal level. What gives them the ability to perceive this upper level is education. The vision of the *Republic* is inextricably bound up with a theory of education. The bodily senses perceive the "actual" or objective state of things; the soul, through education, perceives the intelligible world. And though not all utopia-writers are Platonists, nearly all of them make their utopias depend on education for their permanent establishment. It seems clear that the literary convention of an ideal state is really a by-product of a systematic view of education. That is, education, considered as a unified view of reality, grasps society by its intelligible rather than its actual form, and the utopia is a projection of the ability to see society, not as an aggregate of buildings and bodies, but as a structure of arts and sciences. The thought suggests itself that the paralysis in utopian imagination we have mentioned in our society may be connected with a confusion about both the objectives and the inner structure of our educational system.

It is a theory of education, in any case, that connects a utopian myth with a myth of contract. This is abundantly clear in Plato and later in Rousseau, whose *Emile* is the utopian and educational counterpart of his *Contrat social.* In the sixteenth century, Machiavelli's *Prince,* Castiglione's *Courtier,* and More's *Utopia* form a well-unified Renaissance trilogy, the first two providing a contract myth and an educational structure respectively, based on the two central facts of Renaissance society, the prince and the courtier. Other Renaissance works, such as Spenser's *Faerie Queene,* set forth a social ideal and so belong peripherally to the utopian tradition, but are based on an educational myth rather than a utopian one. For Spenser, as he says in his letter to Raleigh, the Classical model was not Plato's *Republic* but Xenophon's *Cyropaedia,* the ideal education of the ideal prince.

Both the contract myth and the utopia myth, we said, derive from an analysis of the mythmaker's own society, or at least if they do not they have little social point. The overtones of the contract myth, unless the writer is much more complacent than anyone I have read, are tragic. All contract theories, whatever their origin or direction, have to account for the necessity of a social condition far below what one could imagine as a desirable, or even possible, ideal. The contract myth thus incorporates an element of what in the corresponding religious myth appears as the fall of man. Tragedy is a form which proceeds toward an epiphany of law, or at least of something inevitable and ineluctable; and a contract myth is by definition a legal one. The *telos* myth is comic in direction: it moves toward the actualizing of something better.

Any serious utopia has to assume some kind of contract theory as the complement of itself, if only to explain what is wrong with the state of things the utopia is going to improve. But the vision of something better has to appeal to some contract behind the contract, something which existing society has lost, forfeited, rejected, or violated, and which the utopia itself is to restore. The ideal or desirable quality in the utopia has to be *recognized,* that is, seen as manifesting something that the reader can understand as a latent or potential element in his own society and his own thinking. Thus Plato's *Republic* takes off from a rather gloomy and cynical contract theory, adapted apparently from the sophists by Glaucon and Adeimantus for the pleasure of hearing Socrates refute it. But the vision of justice which Socrates substitutes for it restores a state of things earlier than anything this contract theory refers to. This antecedent state is associated with the Golden Age in the *Laws* and with the story of Atlantis in the two sequels to the *Republic,* the *Timaeus* and the *Critias.* In the Christian myth, of course, the pre-contract ideal state is that of paradise. We have now to try to isolate the paradisal or Golden Age element in the utopian myth, the seed which it brings to fruition.

The utopian writer looks at the ritual habits of his own society and tries to see what society would be like if these ritual habits were made more consistent and more inclusive. But it is possible to think of a good many ritual habits as not so much inconsistent as unnecessary or superstitious. Some social habits express the needs of society; others express its anxieties. And although we tend to attach more emotional importance to our anxieties than to our needs or genuine beliefs, many anxieties are largely or entirely unreal. Plato's conception of the role of women in his community, whatever one thinks of it, was an extraordinary imaginative break from the anxieties of Athens with its almost Oriental seclusion of married women. Every utopian writer has to struggle with the anxieties suggested to him by his own society, trying to distinguish the moral from the conventional, what would be really disastrous from what merely inspires a vague feeling of panic, uneasiness, or ridicule.

So far we have been considering the typical utopia, the rational city or world-state, and the utopian satire which is a product of a specifically modern fear, the Frankenstein myth of the enslavement of man by his own technology and by his perverse desire to build himself an ingenious trap merely for the pleasure of getting caught in it. But another kind of utopian satire is obviously possible, one in which social rituals are seen from the outside, not to make them more consistent but simply to demonstrate their inconsistency, their hypocrisy, or their unreality. Satire of this kind holds up a mirror to society which distorts it, but distorts it consistently. An early example is Bishop Hall's *Mundus Alter et Idem* (1605), much ridiculed by Milton, but perhaps more of an influence on him than he was willing to admit. A more famous one is *Gulliver's Travels,* especially the first part, the voyage to Lilliput. The Lilliputian society is essentially the society of Swift's England, with its rituals looked at satirically. In the voyage to Brobdingnag the ridicule of the gigantic society is softened down, in the portrayal of the king even minimized, the satirical emphasis being thrown on Gulliver's account of his own society. The shift of emphasis indicates the close connection between this kind of satire and utopian fiction, the connection being much closer in the last part, where the rational society of the Houyhnhnms is contrasted with the Yahoos.

In Butler's *Erewhon,* again, we have an early example of the contemporary or technological utopian satire: the Erewhonians are afraid of machines, and their philosophers have worked out elaborate arguments to prove that machines will eventually take over if not suppressed in time. We could in fact trace this theme back to *Gulliver's Travels* itself, where the flying island of Laputa demonstrates some of the perils in combining human mechanical ingenuity with human folly and greed. But most of *Erewhon* adheres to the earlier tradition of the mirror-satire. The Erewhonians, for example, treat disease as a crime and crime as a disease, but they do so with exactly the same rationalizations that the Victorians use in enforcing the opposite procedure.

Following out this line of thought, perhaps what ails ordinary society is not the inconsistency but the multiplicity of its ritual habits. If so, then the real social ideal would be a greatly simplified society, and the quickest way to utopia would be through providing the absolute minimum of social structure and organization. This conception of the ideal society as simplified, even primitive, is of far more literary importance than the utopia itself, which in literature is a relatively minor genre never quite detached from political theory. For the simplified society is the basis of the *pastoral* convention, one of the central conventions of literature at every stage of its development.

In Christianity the city is the form of the myth of *telos,* the New Jerusalem that is the end of the human pilgrimage. But there is no city in the Christian, or Judaeo-Christian, myth of origin: that has only a garden, and the two progenitors of what was clearly intended to be a simple and patriarchal society. In the story which follows, the story of Cain and Abel, Abel is a shepherd and Cain a farmer whose descendants build cities and develop the arts. The murder of Abel appears to symbolize the blotting out of an idealized pastoral society by a more complex civilization. In Classical mythology the original society appears as the Golden Age, to which we have referred more than once, again a peaceful and primitive society without the complications of later ones. In both our main literary traditions, there-

fore, the tendency to see the ideal society in terms of a lost simple paradise has a ready origin.

In the Renaissance, when society was so strongly urban and centripetal, focused on the capital city and on the court in the center of it, the pastoral established an alternative ideal which was not strictly utopian, and which we might distinguish by the term Arcadian. The characteristics of this ideal were simplicity and equality: it was a society of shepherds without distinction of class, engaged in a life that permitted the maximum of peace and of leisure. The arts appeared in this society spontaneously, as these shepherds were assumed to have natural musical and poetic gifts. In most utopias the relation of the sexes is hedged around with the strictest regulations, even taboos; in the pastoral, though the Courtly Love theme of frustrated devotion is prominent, it is assumed that making love is a major occupation, requiring much more time and attention than the sheep, and thus more important than the economic productivity of society.

The Arcadia has two ideal characteristics that the utopia hardly if ever has. In the first place, it puts an emphasis on the integration of man with his physical environment. The utopia is a city, and it expresses rather the human ascendancy over nature, the domination of the environment by abstract and conceptual mental patterns. In the pastoral, man is at peace with nature, which implies that he is also at peace with his own nature, the reasonable and the natural being associated. A pastoral society might become stupid or ignorant, but it could hardly go mad. In the second place, the pastoral, by simplifying human desires, throws more stress on the satisfaction of such desires as remain, especially, of course, sexual desire. Thus it can accommodate, as the typical utopia cannot, something of that outlawed and furtive social ideal known as the Land of Cockayne, the fairyland where all desires can be instantly gratified.

This last is an ideal halfway between the paradisal and the pastoral and is seldom taken seriously. The reason is that it does not derive from an analysis of the writer's present society, but is primarily a dream or wish-fulfillment fantasy. In the fourteenth-century poem called *The Land of Cockayne,* roast geese walk around advertising their edibility: the line of descent to the shmoos of "Li'l Abner" is clear enough. The same theme exists in a more reflective and sentimental form, where it tends to be an illusory or vanishing vision, often a childhood memory. This theme is common as a social cliché and in the popular literature which expresses social clichés: the cottage away from it all, happy days on the farm, the great open spaces of the west, and the like. A typical and well-known literary example is James Hilton's *Lost Horizon,* a neo-Kantian kingdom of both ends, so to speak, with its mixture of Oriental wisdom and American plumbing. But though the Land of Cockayne belongs to social mythology more than to the imaginative mythology of literature, it is a genuine ideal, and we shall meet other forms of it.

Spenser's *Faerie Queene,* already alluded to, is an example of the sort of courtier-literature common in the Renaissance, which had for its theme the idealizing of the court or the reigning monarch. This literature was not directly utopian, but its imaginative premises were allied to the utopia. That is, it assumed that for mankind the state of nature is the state of society and of civilization and that, whether man is in his nature good or bad, life can be improved by improving his institutions. The pastoral, though of no importance politically, nevertheless kept open the suggestion that the state of nature and the state of society were different, perhaps opposing states. The pastoral was allied to the spirit of satire which, as in Erasmus' *Praise of Folly* and Cornelius Agrippa's *Vanity of the Arts and Sciences,* called the whole value of civilization into question.

In the eighteenth century these two attitudes both assumed political importance, and met in a head-on collision. The eighteenth-century descendant of the pastoral myth was the conception of the "natural society" in Bolingbroke, and later in Rousseau. Here the natural state of man is thought of as distinct from and, so to speak, underlying the state of society. The state of nature is reasonable, the state of society full of anomalies and pointless inequalities. The conservative or traditional view opposed to this is, in Great Britain, most articulate in Burke, who, following Montesquieu, and in opposition to the principles of the French Revolution, asserted that the state of nature and the state of society were the same thing. The difference between the two views is primarily one of contract theory. For Burke the existing social order in any nation is that nation's real contract: for Rousseau it is essentially a corruption of its contract. The *telos* myths differ accordingly. For Burke improvement is possible only if we preserve the existing structure. This is not a utopian view, but it is not necessarily anti-utopian: it still keeps the utopian premise of the improvability of institutions. For Rousseau the *telos* myth becomes revolutionary: only an overthrow of the existing social order can manifest the natural and reasonable social order that it has disguised.

The fourth book of *Gulliver's Travels* is a pastoral satire representing the conservative opposition to the pastoral conception of a natural society. The Yahoo is the natural man, man as he would be if he were purely an animal, filthy, treacherous, and disgusting. Gulliver has more intelligence than the Yahoos, but what he learns from his sojourn with the Houyhnhnms is that his nature is essentially Yahoo nature. His intelligence, he discovers, is nothing he can take pride in, for hu-

man beings back home make "no other use of reason than to improve and multiply those vices whereof their brethren in this country had only the share that nature allotted them." The natural society, if it could be attained at all, could be attained only by some kind of animal like the Houyhnhnm, who possessed a genuine reason not needing the disciplines of state and church. The Houyhnhnms can live in a genuinely pastoral world; human beings have to put up with the curse of civilization.

The terms of this argument naturally changed after the Industrial Revolution, which introduced the conception of revolutionary process into society. This led to the present division of social attitudes mentioned above, between the Marxist utopia as distant end and the common American belief in the utopianizing tendency of the productive process, often taking the form of a belief that utopian standards of living can be reached in America alone. This belief, though rudely shaken by every disruptive historical event at least since the stock market crash of 1929, still inspires an obstinate and resilient confidence. The popular American view and the Communist one, superficially different as they are, have in common the assumption that to increase man's control over his environment is also to increase his control over his destiny. The refusal to accept this assumption is the principle of modern utopian satire. . . .

ORIGINS IN MYTHOLOGY

Robert C. Elliott (essay date 1970)

SOURCE: "Saturnalia, Satire, and Utopia," in *The Shape of Utopia: Studies in a Literary Genre,* The University of Chicago Press, 1970, pp. 3-24.

[*In the following essay, Elliott presents argues that "utopia is the secularization of the myth of the Golden Age," and that "utopia and satire are ancestrally linked in the celebration of Saturn."*]

Engels once spoke of Charles Fourier, the nineteenth century's complete utopian, as one of the greatest satirists of all time. The conjunction may seem odd; we normally think of utopia as associated with the ideal, satire with the actual, which (man and his institutions being what they are) usually proves to be the sordid, the foolish, the vicious. In fact, however, the two modes—utopia and satire—are linked in a complex network of genetic, historical, and formal relationships. Some of these I propose to trace.

First, a tangle of genetic lines which, in the way of these matters, lead to unexpected places. "All Uto-

"The Golden Age" by Lucas Cranach.

pias," writes Arthur Koestler, "are fed from the sources of mythology; the social engineer's blueprints are merely revised editions of the ancient text." Insofar as utopia incorporates man's longings for the good life, it is part of a complex of ideas that includes the Golden Age, the Earthly Paradise, the Fortunate Isles, the Islands of the Blest, the Happy Otherworld, and so on. The archetypal text, at least for the Western world, is that of Hesiod:

> *In the beginning, the immortals*
> > *Who have their homes on Olympos*
> *created the golden generation of mortal*
> > *people.*
> *These lived in Kronos' time, when he*
> > *was the king in heaven.*
> *They lived as if they were gods,*
> > *their hearts free from all sorrow,*
> *by themselves, and without hard work or pain;*
> > *no miserable*
> *old age came their way; their hands, their*
> > *feet,*
> > *did not alter.*
> *They took their pleasure in festivals,*
> > *and lived without troubles.*
> *When they died, it was as if they fell asleep.*
> > *All goods*
> *were theirs. The fruitful grainland*
> > *yielded its harvest to them*
> *of its own accord; this was great and*
> > *abundant,*
> > *while they at their pleasure*
> *quietly looked after their works,*
> > *in the midst of good things*
> *prosperous in flocks, on friendly terms*
> > *with the blessed immortals.*

For the fifth race of man, for us of the iron age, it was a good dream and it lasted, as Lionel Trilling has indicated, until it was dispossessed by the nightmare of Dostoevski's Underground Man.

Variations of Hesiod's story probably existed long before his time in folktales of a magical land of plenty where wine runs in rivers and pancakes grow on trees. At any rate the Greek comic writers picked up these themes as a handy way of satirizing the literature of the Golden Age, which even then (as ever since) was sadly stereotyped. An early example of the satire is this from Teleclides:

> First there was peace among all things like water covering one's hands. And the earth bore neither fear nor disease, but all needed things appeared of their own accord. For every stream flowed with wine, and barley cakes fought with wheat cakes to enter the mouths of men. . . . And fishes, coming to men's houses and baking themselves, would serve themselves upon the tables. . . . and roasted thrushes with milk cakes flew down one's gullet.

The references to peace and to freedom from fear and disease make the target of the parody clear enough; but parody or no, there is inevitable doubleness of effect—longing as well as laughter. Tales of Cockaigne turn up in the folklore of many lands, nearly always with similar effects. An English version from the early fourteenth century makes Cockaigne out to be fairer than Paradise. Here is an abbey built entirely of food, where geese fly roasted from the spit advertising their own succulence: "Geese, all hot, all hot!" Here are rivers of oil and milk and honey and wine along which lusty monks chase willing nuns. Here (with the negative emphasis necessary in these matters) is no strife, no pain, no death. These lines (in a modern version by A. L. Morton) emphasize the longing:

> *In Cockaigne we drink and eat*
> *Freely without care and sweat. . . .*
> *Under heaven no land like this*
> *Of such joy and endless bliss.*
>
> *There is many a sweet sight,*
> *All is day, there is no night,*
> *There is no quarreling nor strife,*
> *There is no death but endless life. . . .*
>
> *Every man takes what he will,*
> *As of right, to eat his fill.*
> *All is common to young and old,*
> *To stout and strong, to meek and bold.*

On the other hand, much of the poem is satirical; but satire is easily overwhelmed in such express outpouring of desire. One finds the same longing and the same laughter in "The Big Rock Candy Mountain," a song sung in the United States by men on the bum in the 1930s. Cockaigne knows no limitations of space or time: in its untrussed moments every age shares Sir Epicure Mammon's dream of "a perpetuitie / Of life, and lust." America's Rock Candy Mountain is an authentic part of Cockaigne's lush landscape.

The Golden Age and Cockaigne provide the elements out of which theintellectual concept of utopia develops. We can see this happening in the literature of ancient Greece; Plato's adoption of the gold, silver, brass, and iron imagery from Hesiod to make palatable the "noble lie" of *The Republic* is an emblem of the process. When belief in the historical reality of the Golden Age broke down, it became possible to bring many of the ideal elements of the myth into closer relation with the realities of man's existence. Philosophers transferred the notion of an ideal life in the irrecoverable past into utopian tales of what the world might—even should—be like; the myth, that is, provided sustenance for a conceivable reality. It has been the same ever since.

The Golden Age and utopia, the one a myth, the other

"The Land of the Cockaygne" by Pieter Breughel the Elder

a concept, are both projections of man's wishful fantasies, answering to the longings for the good life which have moved him since before history began. "Véritable rêve de paysan fatigué": so Maurice Croiset characterizes Hesiod's account of the Golden Age. Utopia comes ultimately from the same dream. Identity of origin, however, by no means implies identity of function. Plato, undertaking the Socratic search for the meaning of justice, is led to conceive an ideal social order—a utopia; but justice, the object of his search, would be USELESS, as David Hume emphatically put it, in a society like that of the Golden Age ["Of Justice," *The Philosophical Works,* ed. T. H. Green and T. H. Grose, 1964]. The contours and customs of these ideal lands are very different indeed. In Utopia, the work of the world goes on, rationalized, cleaned up—often to the point where sewers hardly smell— given dignity; the work is there, nevertheless, as a necessary condition of Utopia's existence. In Cockaigne, says the song, "they hung the jerk that invented work." Sebastian de Grazia makes the distinction thus [in *Of Time, Work, and Leisure,* 1962]: "Utopia is a possessor of culture; Cockaigne is possessed by the folk."

A dialogue of Lucian neatly points up the functional difference. Just before the annual celebration of the feast of the Saturnalia, Cronosolon complains to the tutelary god Cronus about his poverty. Look, he says, how many pestilent rich fellows there are these days, while I and others like me, skilled in the liberal arts, have only want and trouble for bedfellows. And you, Cronus, will not "order things anew, and make us equal."

"In common life," answers Cronus, "'tis no light matter to change the lots that Clotho and her sister Fates have laid upon you; but as touching the feast, I will set right your poverty." The point is this: for the period of the Saturnalia, Cronosolon and his fellows will enjoy the good things of life on the same footing as the rich. During this sacred time the Golden Age will come again to earth—that, after all, is the meaning of the festival. But this is a very different matter, Cronus points out, from changing the way things are in common life and making everybody equal; such affairs are in his son Zeus's jurisdiction, not in his. Clearly, if one does not believe in Zeus's good will, or even in his existence, these become matters for man alone.

Utopia is the application of man's reason and his will to the myth. For the Golden Age is given by the gods, like the millennium in Christian eschatology, independently of man's will. To be sure, heretical religious sects, intoxicated with dreams of millennial bliss, have tried to establish paradise on earth by fiat; some of the bizarre results are brilliantly documented in Norman Cohn's *Pursuit of the Millennium*. But Utopia is different: Utopia (in the sense we are concerned with here) is man's effort to work out imaginatively what happens—or what might happen—when the primal longings embodied in the myth confront the principle of reality. In this effort man no longer merely dreams of a divine state in some remote time; he assumes the role of creator himself.

Giamatti on Medieval and Renaissance conceptions of Paradise:

Throughout the Middle Ages, the Fathers and Doctors, saints, monks and martyrs argued endlessly about the location and nature of man's lost state of bliss. Where was it now? Who was there? What was it like and what did it mean? The answers were complex and various. But for richness, none of the arguments produced by medieval churchmen matched the legends and stories unceasingly repeated by medieval man. As Christianity had replaced the locus of the Golden Age with the place of the Fall, so the popular mind changed the name of the Fortunate Islands or land of the Hyperboreans to the Country of Prester John or land of Cocaigne. St. Brendan's voyage to an otherworld of delight was no less renowned than the vision of Tnugdal or the fabled travels of John Maundeville. Just as Pliny, Plutarch, and Strabo had said they knew where the place was located, so also the Middle Ages and Renaissance flourished with maps and treatises describing its position, now east, now west, now on an island, now behind or upon a mountain—but always remote, always inaccessible. Columbus thought he had found the blessed land across the wide waters, and he was certainly not the last man to search.

A. Bartlett Giamatti, in his introduction to The Earthly Paradise and the Renaissance Epic, *Princeton University Press, 1966.*

A characteristic of the Golden Age, whatever the version, is that it exists outside history, usually before history begins: *in illo tempore*. In Hesiod's account, it is true, men are timebound in the sense that they finally die—*Et in Arcadia ego*—but only after long lives joyously lived, without the sufferings of old age. Other variations of the paradise myth speak of a timeless, changeless, deathless existence, as in Hesiod's own description of the Islands of the Blest, where the heroes who fought at Troy and Thebes live in perpetual joy; or as in the Irish myth of the voyage of Bran which in a stroke or two superbly dramatizes the dis-

tinction between mythical time and the time of history. Bran and his men sail back to Ireland after having spent indeterminate ages in the Happy Otherworld. As they approach land, Bran calls out to a man on shore: "I am Bran, the son of Febal." The man responds: "We do not know such a one, though the Voyage of Bran is in our ancient stories." Then one of Bran's men leaps from the coracle to shore. "As soon as he touched the earth of Ireland, forthwith he was a heap of ashes, as though he had been in the earth for many hundred years." Paradise is necessarily transhistoric.

Planners of Utopia have often tried to approximate that condition, aiming at a static perfection which would rule out the vicissitudes of history and to some degree those of time. Sparta, Athens, and Rome would not now be lying in ruins, wrote Jerome Busleyden in the sixteenth century, if they had known and followed the laws expounded in Thomas More's great *Utopia*: "On the contrary, they would have been still unfallen, still fortunate and prosperous, leading a happy existence, mistresses of the world meanwhile." As with states, so with men: it is a rare utopia that does not broach the theme of immortality or greatly increased longevity in one form or another, from elixirs in Bacon's *New Atlantis* to application of evolutionary theory in twentieth-century utopias. The attempt of utopian writers to freeze history—the fight of utopia against history—has prompted severe criticism of the whole utopian enterprise; but the attempt has been merely one way in which man has tried to arrive imaginatively at the condition of paradise on earth.

Ritual has provided another approach to the same state. The annual feast commemorating the reign of Cronus (in his Roman form, Saturn) was avowedly a reenactment of the Golden Age—a return to the time when all men were equal and the good things of life were held in common. Out of his primal authority Cronus reserved a few days in the year, he says in one of Lucian's dialogues, so that "men may remember what life was like in my days." The happy anarchy of his rule was recollected in Roman law which held that during the Saturnalian festival war could not be begun nor could criminals be punished—for what was war and who were criminals in the Golden Age? Lucian's dialogues convey marvelously the atmosphere of the Saturnalia, but at the same time they are permeated by his characteristic skepticism. Most celebrants are likely to have had a different attitude, to have felt that, for the few days of celebration, they were reliving the myth, actually participating in the far-off age at the beginning of things which answered to their deepest longings. The Saturnalia were more than an excuse to get drunk and (like Horace's slave in the famous Satire) to say aloud what one thought of one's superiors; they were themselves an abrogation of time. In all imitations of archetypes, writes Mircea Eliade [in *The Myth of the Eternal Return,* 1955], "man is projected into the mythical epoch in which the archetypes were first revealed." Profane time and history are abolished in the act of celebration, for one "is always *contemporary with a myth,* during the time when one repeats it or imitates the gestures of the mythic personages." [*Myths, Dreams and Mysteries,* trans. Philip Mairet, 1960.] Thus the divine efficacies of the Saturnalia made present the joy that had been irrevocably lost from earth. Through the alchemy of ritual the age of iron was temporarily transmuted into gold.

The forms that the Saturnalia take allow us to see what the memory of a Golden Age really means. To reenact it is to experience the extravagant joy of overthrowing the restraints, the inhibitions and renunciations, which, as the price we pay for civilization, trammel us relentlessly in the real world. The theme of the Saturnalia is reversal—reversal of values, of social roles, of social norms. The real world is a world peopled normally by a few camels and many ants, in Lucian's image; under the dispensation of ritual it becomes a place where discrepancies disappear and all become equal. The Saturnalia are ruled over, not by a camel, but by a king chosen by lot; slaves sit down with their masters and are served by them; everyone speaks as he wills, eats and drinks as he pleases (as though Nature again produced lavishly for all), and enjoys a sexual liberty unthinkable at any other time. The Saturnalia mean release.

In some of the cognate festivals of Western Europe the release is spectacularly explosive. Consider the Feast of Fools as it was celebrated in Paris at New Year's in the fifteenth century. This is from a contemporary account:

> Priests and clerks may be seen wearing masks and monstrous visages at the hours of office. They dance in the choir dressed as women, panders, or minstrels. They sing wanton songs. They eat black puddings at the horn of the altar while the celebrant is saying mass. They play at dice there. They cense with stinking smoke from the soles of old shoes. They run and leap through the church, without a blush at their own shame. Finally they drive about the town and its theatres in shabby traps and carts; and rouse the laughter of their fellows and the bystanders in infamous performances, with indecent gestures and verses scurrilous and unchaste.
>
> [Translated by E. K. Chambers in *The Medieval Stage,* 1903]

Again, reversal and release. The words of the Magnificat—"He hath put down the mighty from their seats, and exalted them of low degree"—triggered the revelry of the Feast of Fools. It was an affair largely of the lower clergy (E. K. Chambers calls it an "ebullition of the natural lout beneath the cassock") who, like the lower orders at the Saturnalia, could on this occasion turn distinctions of rank and status upside down, sub-

ject the ceremonial forms which ordered their lives to wild burlesque, give way to verbal and sexual license in a great outburst of pent-up repression. All order is repressive, not least that of the Church. The Feast of Fools is an anarchic blow at order, like the paganfeast at Rome a reaching out for a state of "pure" freedom.

In these rites which temporarily turn society inside out, ridicule, mockery, burlesque—in short, satire, using the word in its broad sense—seem always to have important functions. A characteristic of saturnalian festivals everywhere is that during the license of the holiday the most sacred institutions may be subjected to mockery and sacrosanct individuals exposed to satire. To take an exotic example: among the Ashanti of West Africa, a people so sensitive to ridicule that it often drives them to suicide, there is (or was recently) a festival period set apart in which even the sacred chief was satirized. "Wait until Friday," said the chief, "when the people really begin to abuse me, and if you will come and do so too it will please me." The high-priest explained to R. S. Rattray, the inquiring anthropologist, that the forebears of the Ashanti had "ordained a time, once every year, when every man and woman, free man and slave, should have freedom to speak out just what was in their head, to tell their neighbors just what they thought of them . . . [and] also the king or chief. When a man has spoken freely thus, he will feel his soul cool and quieted" [*Ashanti,* 1923].

To speak out on these privileged occasions is almost always to make mocking verses—in Ashanti at the *Apo* ceremony:

> All is well today.
> We know that a Brong man eats rats,
> But we never knew that one of the royal blood
>   eats rats.
> But today we have seen our master, Ansah,
>   eating rats.
> Today all is well and we may say so, say so,
>   say so.
> At other times we may not say so, say so, say
>   so.

In Latin at the Feast of Fools:

> Gregis pastor Tityrus,
> asinorum dominus,
> noster est episcopus.
>
> eia, eia, eia,
> vocant nos ad gaudia
> Tityri cibaria.
> ad honorem Tityri,
> festum colant baculi
> satrapae et asini. . . .

This is David Crowne's translation:

We make Tityrus our pastor,
Of these asses lord and master,
Episcopal ecclesiaster.

Holy smoke! delicious scents
Lead us by our noses hence
Where the food's in evidence.

Granting Tityrus recognition,
Men of asinine condition
This feast of misrule do commission. . . .

The uninhibited words of carnival are everywhere akin. This is the language of satire before satire becomes literature; it is preliterary as well as subliterary. These utterances are ritual gestures, marked off from real life by the parenthesis of the holiday.

It seems clear that the mechanisms behind the *Apo* ceremony of the Ashanti are very like those that prompted the festival of the Sacaea in Babylon, the Cronia in Greece, the Saturnalia and the Kalends in Rome, the Feast of Fools in France, the Lord of Misrule in England, and many other comparable rites of reversal. Diverse as the cultures concerned certainly are, the rites themselves can be brought under a single classification by an observation of Freud [in *Group Psychology and the Analysis of the Ego*]: "In all renunciations and limitations imposed upon the ego a periodical infringement of the prohibition is the rule; this indeed is shown by the institution of festivals, which in origin are nothing less nor more than excesses provided by law and which owe their cheerful character to the release which they bring. The Saturnalia of the Romans and our modern carnival agree in this essential feature with the festivals of primitive people, which usually end in debaucheries of every kind and the transgression of what are at other times the most sacred commandments." The festivals provide permitted release from limitation and renunciation. In the Saturnalia that release is the sanctioned way to the Golden Age. Here is a clue to what the Golden Age actually is: a time or a condition in which limitation and renunciation do not exist. This is implicit in most accounts of the Golden Age and occasionally it is made explicit.

"O happy Golden Age," exults the chorus in Samuel Daniel's translation of the famous passage from Tasso's *Aminta;* the age was happy, however, not because of milk and honey and a bountifullyburgeoning earth, but because man's sexual instincts were still unrestrained, the "sweet delights of joyful amorous wights" not yet frustrated by

That idle name of wind,
That idol of deceit, that empty sound call'd
   Honor. . . .

Instead of Honor's restrictive laws, men followed

golden laws like these
Which Nature wrote. That's lawful which doth
   please.

Tasso catches here the essence of the myth.

Because all restraints are undesirable, saturnalian festivals take on their anarchic form: the slave mocks his master, the tribesman his chief; the priest burlesques the ceremony of his church. These are ritual gestures abrogating rule: the ritual satire a negative means to the positive end. In this way, it seems to me, the Golden Age comes together with satire in the saturnalian festival. But the Golden Age (or Cockaigne or other versions of the Earthly Paradise) is not utopia; as we have seen it belongs to Cronus, not to Zeus. Nor is the ritual "satire" of the festival equivalent to the literary art we know. These are the elements out of which individual artists were to create their much more sophisticated structures: Thomas More and William Morris their utopias, Horace and Alexander Pope their satires. The genetic relation of the two modes, however, derives from the sanctioned license of the holiday.

It is a mighty leap from the festivals, which have the structure of ritual, to the literature of satire and utopia. In between, as it were, lie intermediate artistic forms which contain in various combinations and proportions relatively unassimilated ritualistic and mythical elements. A splendid example is the middle-Irish tale *The Vision of MacConglinne* in which the stuff of magic and folklore is used for highly sophisticated ends. The *Vision* is an epic of food, a mock-epic rather, with all the ambivalence—the longings and the mockery—we associate with tales of Cockaigne. The half-starved poet of the story lets his imagination go wild: "Then in the harbour of the lake before me I saw a juicy little coracle of beef-fat, with its coating of tallow, with its thwarts of curds, with its prow of lard, with its stern of butter. . . . Then we rowed across the wide expanse of New-Milk lake, through seas of broth, past rivermouths of mead, over swelling boisterous waves of buttermilk, by perpetual pools of gravy."

Framing this vision of Cockaigne is a structure of satire astonishing in its variety and comprehensiveness. Although the author of the *Vision* reaches into Ireland's most primitive traditions to exploit the ancient belief in magically efficacious satire, he also uses irony and ridicule and literary parody with delicacy and great sophistication. His target is nothing less than the religious and literary forms of medieval Ireland. From the most sacred Christian doctrine to the almost equally sacred heroic saga, MacConglinne's mockery spares nothing. This is a Saturnalia outside the ritual frame, a ceremony of reversal shocking and hilarious in its effect. As Robin Flower says [in *The Irish Tradition*, 1947], the *Vision* "sums up and turns into gigantic ridicule the learning of the earlier time much in the same way as François Rabelais at once typified and transcended the learning of the later Middle Ages." A short step only separates *The Vision of MacConglinne,* which is compounded of primitive materials out of Cockaigne and ritual satire, from the art of Rabelais.

Some of these matters are pulled together and given point by a curious incident in the career of Francis Bacon, a man we are unlikely to think of in connection with Saturnalia, Cockaigne, and the like. In early December 1594, Bacon's mother, mindful of the holiday time to come, wrote in a letter: "I trust they will not mum nor mask nor sinfully revel at Gray's Inn." Revelry was much in the minds of those of Gray's Inn, however; and on 20 December, the twelve days of Christmas license were inaugurated by the Prince of Purpoole (in common life, Mr. Henry Holmes of Norfolk), the mock-king who with his court was to preside over the festivities. The first night's revels went well: the burlesque of court activities, the bawdy personal gibes, the parody of the administration of justice by the Crown in Council were all gaily received. Next night a performance of Shakespeare's *A Comedy of Errors* climaxed activities, but this time revelers got out of hand and the evening ended in wild confusion. Appalled by this blow to their prestige, members of Gray's Inn asked Francis Bacon to help write an entertainment that would recoup their lost honor. On the night of 3 January, Bacon's *Gesta Grayorum; or, The History of the High and Mighty Prince Henry, Prince of Purpoole, Arch Duke of Stapulia* was performed to great applause. A character in this resolutely sober interlude begs the Prince of Purpoole to bend his mind to the conquest of nature, to undertake the "searching out, inventing, and discovering of all whatsoever is hid in secret in the world." To this end, the Prince is advised to acquire a number of aids: an enormous library; a wonderful garden, complete with birds and beasts and fish so as to provide "in a small compass a model of universal nature"; a huge cabinet containing whatever rare objects the hand of man or "the shuffle of things" has produced; and a house fitted with all instruments so as to be a palace "fit for a philosopher's stone." In short, Bacon worked out in the *Gesta Grayorum* a first draft of Solomon's House, the heart of his utopia, *The New Atlantis.* Bacon's city of Bensalem is a notably chaste community, "The Virgin of the World." How remarkable it is that the conception of Solomon's House, that Cockaigne of the scientific imagination, should first have appeared in the context of a saturnalian festival.

Satire and the Golden Age are functionally linked in festival. They are associated in a different way, however, under the puzzlingly contradictory sign of the god Saturn himself. A curious doubleness has characterized Cronus-Saturn from the beginning. He has a strongly benevolent aspect insofar as he was the ruler in the Golden Age, the happiest time ever known on earth. Furthermore, after his imprisonment by Zeus, he was released, Hesiod says, to rule in the Isles of the Blest. To the Romans Saturn was the bringer of civilization to Italy, in addition to being god of agriculture and king of the Golden Age. But the other side of the myth is fearsome and dark: Cronus-Saturn castrated his father and ate his children. The sickle in the iconography of Saturn is an agricultural tool or the castrating weapon, depending upon which aspect of the myth is uppermost. He was the oldest of the gods—professionally old, Panofsky says—and when the gods came to be identified with the planets, he was associated with the slowest and most remote of all. This dark side of the myth may help account for the fact that in the Middle Ages and the Renaissance Saturn is simultaneously the beneficent ruler of a paradise on earth and a singularly malignant influence on human affairs. In Chaucer's *The Knight's Tale,* "pale Saturnus the colde" boasts of his powers:

> *Myn is the drenchyng in the see so wan;*
> *Myn is the prison in the derke cote;*
> *Myn is the stranglyng and hangyng by the*
>   *throte,*
> *The murmure and the cherles rebellyng,*
> *The groynynge, and the pryvee empoysonyng . . .*
> *My lookyng is the fader of pestilence.*
>   [11.2456-69]

Astrological lore regularly ascribes disasters like these, both public and personal, to Saturn. Lydgate in *The Fall of Princes* characterizes Saturn's influence in terms precisely like those above, then elsewhere in the same poem speaks of the time when Saturn, Noah, and Abraham were alive in a golden age of temperance and sobriety, when knights cherished chastity and heretics were properly punished. But Lydgate's *The Assembly of Gods* has Saturn dressed in frost and snow, holding a bloody falchion, wearing a necklace of icicles and a leaden crown.

During the Renaissance in England literary satire becomes associated with the malign aspect of the Saturn character. An etymological tangle may be in part responsible. Thomas Drant in 1566 suggests the possibility that the word "satyre" may be derived from Saturn:

> *Satyre of writhled waspyshe Saturne may be*
>   *namde*
> *The Satyrist must be a wasper in moode,*
> *Testie and wrothe with vice and hers, to see*
>   *both blamde*
> *But courteous and frendly to the good.*
> *As Saturne cuttes of tymes with equall scythe:*
> *So this man cuttes downe synne, so coy and*
>   *blythe.*

Whatever the explanation, the conventional tone for

English satire during the late sixteenth and early seventeenth centuries became that of cold, snarling invective. Satirists proudly speak of themselves as Saturnian men, melancholy because of his influence. Their obsessive concern with disease and death follows on the pattern of their astrological patron; in an aggressive way they are eager to claim for themselves his most malignant powers. Thus Renaissance satire flaunts its unpleasantly hectoring tone under the sanction of the god who in another aspect presided over the Golden Age.

When we turn from these genetic and tutelary ties to the formal relations between uptopia and satire, we are on firmer ground. Aristophanes managed the conjunction superbly. Under the rule of women in the *Ecclesiazusae,* for example, all citizens are to be equal and share in wealth and pleasure:

> *mankind should possess*
> *In common the instruments of happiness.*
> *Henceforth private property comes to an*
> *   end—*
> *It's all wrong for a man to have too much to*
> *   spend,*
> *While others moan, starving; another we see*
> *Has acres of land tilled prosperously,*
> *While this man has not enough earth for his*
> *   grave.*
> *You'll find men who haven't a single lean*
> *   slave*
> *While others have hundreds to run at their*
> *   call. . . .*
> *That's over: all things are owned henceforth*
> *   by all.*

Law courts are to be converted to banqueting halls; marriage to be abolished in favor of complete sexual freedom: "the whole city of girls are your wives now, and gratis!" In short, Praxagora, the leader of the female revolution, will rule over a hedonist's Utopia. At the same time, of course, satire pervades the play— some of it directed inward at Utopia itself (perhaps even at portions of Plato's *Republic*), but more at the follies of the real world outside. Aristophanes takes his women and their ideal state seriously. In a number of his plays—*Lysistrata, The Birds, The Clouds, Plutus*—he sets up utopian themes as a baseline from which the satire thrusts out: they form the positive term of the hilariously destructive attack.

Satire and utopia seem naturally compatible if we think of the structure of the formal verse satire, usually characterized by two main elements: the predominating negative part, which attacks folly or vice, and the understated positive part, which establishes a norm, a standard of excellence, against which folly and vice are judged. The literary utopia, on the other hand, reverses these proportions of negative and positive—as the Russian writer Eugene Zamyatin says, utopias have a plus sign—presentation of the ideal overweighing the prescriptive attack on the bad old days which Utopia has happily transcended. (It may still be true that in many utopias, Bellamy's *Looking Backward,* for example, the exposure of contemporary evils is the liveliest thing in the book.) But even without overt attack on contemporary society, utopia necessarily wears a Janus-face. The portrayal of an ideal commonwealth has a double function: it establishes a standard, a goal; and by virtue of its existence alone it casts a critical light on society as presently constituted. William Blake's *Songs of Innocence,* writes Northrop Frye, "satirize the state of experience, as the contrast which they present to it makes its hypocrisies more obviously shameful." The utopia of Rabelais's Abbey of Thélème is physically framed by negative and positive coordinates: upon the great gate of the Abbey are set fourteen verses, the first seven a lively satirical catalogue of those who may not enter, the second seven a welcome to the gay, the handsome, the pure, the honest— those who are to live a life governed by the quintessential utopian injunction: "Do what thou wilt." Pantagruel, we recall, was born in Utopia.

As the next essay shows in detail, it is in Thomas More's *Utopia* itself that the two modes satire and utopia are most clearly seen to be indivisible. They share the most elemental devices of structure. Many formal verse satires, for example, are framed by an encounter between a satirist and an adversary: in one of his satires, "Horace" walks in the Forum and gets entangled in talk with an intolerable bore, or in another he goes to his learned friend Trebatius for advice and the two argue; or in his third satire "Juvenal" walks to the outskirts of Rome with the disillusioned Umbricius, while the two discuss in graphic detail the horrors of metropolitan life. In each case the encounter sets the stage for a dialogue in which the satirist attacks some target against the resistance, or at least at the prompting, of the adversary. So it is in *Utopia*. The governing fiction of the work is that Thomas More, while he was on an embassy abroad (the historical man a character in his own fiction), meets a seafaring philosopher named Raphael Hythloday. The two talk throughout a long and memorable day in a garden in Antwerp. "More's" function is to draw Hythloday out and to appose him on certain issues, Hythloday's defense of the communism he found in the land of Utopia, for example. "More" is the adversary. Hythloday's role is to expose the corruption of contemporary society: "so God help me, I can perceive nothing but a certain conspiracy of rich men procuring their own commodities under the name and title of the commonwealth" and to set up against that corruption a norm: the picture of an ideal commonwealth, Utopia, "which alone of good right may take upon it the name." Hythloday is a satirist—a magnificent satirist, commanding the entire range of tones and rhetorical techniques available to his kind. He makes lavish use of his talent.

Just as satire is a necessary element of the work which gave the literary form "utopia" its name, so, I should think, the utopias of Lilliput, Brobdingnag, and Houyhnhnmland are essential to the satire of More's great follower, Jonathan Swift. I suspect that we distinguish between *Utopia* as "a utopia" and *Gulliver's Travels* as "a satire" primarily because of the difference in distribution of positive and negative elements in the two works. Both are necessary to both kinds.

To summarize: utopia is the secularization of the myth of the Golden Age, a myth incarnated in the festival of the Saturnalia. Satire is the secular form of ritual mockery, ridicule, invective—ritual gestures which are integrally part of the same festival. Thus utopia and satire are ancestrally linked in the celebration of Saturn, a god who reigns over the earthly paradise, but who also by reason of his concern with melancholy, disease, and death becomes the patron of snarling Renaissance satirists. The two modes are formally joined in More's eponymous work, and indeed the very notion of utopia necessarily entails a negative appraisal of present conditions. Satire and utopia are not really separable, the one a critique of the real world in the name of something better, the other a hopeful construct of a world that might be. The hope feeds the criticism, the criticism the hope. Writers of utopia have always known this: the one unanswerable argument for the utopian vision is a hard satirical look at the way things are today.

UTOPIAN IDEALS:
THE RENAISSANCE COUNTRY HOUSE

Lewis Mumford (essay date 1922)

SOURCE: An excerpt from *The Story of Utopias,* 1922. Reprint by The Viking Press, 1962, pp. 196-211.

[*In the following excerpt from his survey of utopian thought, Mumford discusses the place of social myth in utopianism, focusing on the Renaissance ideal of the Country House: "the chief pattern by means of which the mediaeval order was transformed into the modern order."*]

To understand the utopia of the Country House we must jump back a few centuries in history.

Anyone who has ranged through the European castles that were built before the fourteenth century will realize that they were no more built for comfort than is a modern battleship. They were essentially garrisons of armed men whose main occupation was theft, violence, and murder; and every feature of their environment reflected the necessities of their life. These castles would be found beetling a cliff or a steep hill; their walls and their buttresses would be made of huge, rough hewn stones; their living arrangements would resemble those of a barracks with an almost complete lack of what we now regard as the normal decencies and privacies, except possibly for the lord and his lady; and the life of these feudal bands was necessarily a crude and limited one.

Up to the fourteenth century in Western Europe the little fortified town, or the unfortified town that lay beneath the protection of a garrison on a hill, was the only other social unit that competed with the even more limited horizons of the peasant's village, or with the spacious claims for the Here and the Hereafter which were put forward by the Roman Church. To dream of huge metropolises and farflung armies and food brought from the ends of the earth would have been wilder in those days than anything More pictured in his Utopia.

During the fifteenth century in England, and in other parts of Europe the same thing seems to have happened sooner or later, this life of agriculture and warfare and petty trade was upset: the feudal power of the reigning nobles was concentrated in the hands of a supreme lord, the King; and the King and his archives and his court settled in the National Capital, instead of moving about from place to place in the troubled realm. The territories of the feudal lords ceased to be dispersed; their possessions were confined more and more within what were called national boundaries; and instead of remaining in their castles the great lords gave up their crude, barbaric ways, and went up to the capital to be civilized. In the course of time money took the place of direct tribute; instead of receiving wheat and eggs and labor, the lord came into possession of a rent which could be figured in pence and pounds; a rent which could be transferred to the new trading cities for the goods which the rest of the world had for sale. There is a fascinating picture of this change in W. J. Ashley's *Economic History*; and the old life itself is outlined, with a wealth of significant detail, in J.S. Fletcher's *Memorials of a Yorkshire Parish*.

At the same time that this change was taking place in the physical life of Western Europe, a corresponding change was taking place in the domain of culture. Digging about the ruins of Rome and other cities, the men of the late Middle Age discovered the remains of a great and opulent civilization; and exploring the manuscripts and printed books which were getting into general circulation, they found themselves face to face with strange conceptions of life, with habits of refinement, ease, and sensuous luxury which the hard life of the camp and the castle had never really permitted.

There followed a reaction against their old life which was little less than a revulsion; and in that reaction two great institutions fell out of fashion. Men ceased to build castles to protect themselves against physical dangers; and they left off entering monasteries in order to fortify their souls for the Hereafter. Both the spiritual and the temporal life began to shift to a new institution, the Country House. The idolum of the Country House drew together and coalesced; and as a familiar symbol of this change the colleges at Oxford which date from the Renascence can scarcely be distinguished in architectural detail from the palaces which the aristocracy were building in the same period; wuile our banks and our political edificed to this day bear almost universally the stamp of that Roman and Grecian litter which men discovered on the outskirts of the mediaeval city.

We do not know the Country House until we realize, to begin with, what its physical characteristics are like. There are a great many descriptions which the reader may consult if he does not happen to live in the neighborhood of a great Country House: but perhaps instead of examining the contemporary Country House it will be well to go back to its beginnings, and see how it was pictured in all its encrusted splendor at the first movement of the Renascence—in the setting which Rabelais, in one of the few downright serious passages in his great work, *Gargantua*, sought to provide for the good life.

Gargantua purposes to build a new Abbey which he calls the Abbey of Theleme. This Abbey is to be in every respect what the mediaeval Abbey was not. Hence to begin with, the Abbey, unlike the castle, is to lie in the midst of the open country; and unlike the monastery, it is to have no walls. Every member is to be furnished with a generous apartment, consisting of a principal room, a withdrawing room, a handsome closet, a wardrobe, and an oratory; and the house itself is to contain not merely libraries in every language, but fair and spacious galleries of paintings. Besides these lodgings there is to be a tilt-yard, a riding court, a theatre, or public playhouse, and a natatory or place to swim. By the river, for the Abbey is to be situated on the Loire, there is to be a Garden of Pleasure, and between two of the six towers of the hexagon, in which form the building is arranged, there are courts for tennis and other games. Add to this orchards full of fruit trees, parks abounding with venison, and an archery range, fill all the halls and chambers with rich tapestries, cover all the pavements and floors with green cloth—and the furnishing of the Abbey of Theleme is complete.

The costumes of the inmates are equally splendid and elaborate. In order to have the accoutrements of the ladies' and gentlemen's toilets more convenient, there was to be "about the wood of Theleme a row of houses to the extent of half a league, very neat and cleanly, wherein dwelt the goldsmiths, lapidaries, jewellers, embroiderers, tailors, gold drawers, velvet weavers, tapestry makers, and upholsterers. . . ." They were to be "furnished with matter and stuff from the hands of Lord Nausiclete, who every year brought them seven ships from the Perlas and Cannibal Islands, laden with ingots of gold, with raw silk, with pearls and precious stones."

The women who are admitted to Theleme must be fair, well-featured, and of sweet disposition; the men must be comely and well-conditioned. Everyone is to be admitted freely and allowed to depart freely; and instead of attempting to practice poverty, chastity, and obedience, the inmates may be honorably married, may be rich, and may live at liberty.

The liberty of Theleme is indeed complete; it is such a liberty as one enjoys at a Country House to this day, under the care of a tactful hostess; for everyone does nothing except follow his own free wiill and pleasure, rising out of his bed whenever he thinks good, and eating, drinking, and laboring when he has a mind to it. In all their rule and strictest tie of their order, as Rabelais puts it, there is but one clause to be observed—

"Do what you please."

When we turn our attention from Rabelais' conceit of an anti-monastic order, we discover that he has given us an excellent picture of the Country House, and of what I shall take the liberty of calling Country House culture. We see pretty much the same outlines in the introduction to Boccaccio's *Decameron*; it is elaborately described in terms of that most complete of Country Houses, Hampton Court, in Pope's *Rape of the Lock*; it is vividly pictured by Meredith in his portrait of *The Egoist*; and it is analyzed in Mr. H. G. Wells' cruel description of Bladesover in *Tono-Bungay*, as well as by Mr. Bernard Shaw in *Heartbreak House*. Whether Mr. W. H. Mallock holds the pattern of Country House culture up to us in *The New Republic* or Anton Chekhov penetrates its aimlessness and futility in *The Cherry Orchard*, The Country House is one of the recurrent themes of literature.

This Renascence idolum of the Country House, then, is powerful and complete: I know no other pattern which has imposed its standards and its practices with such coomplete success upon the greater part of European civilization. While the Country House was in the beginning an aristocratic institution, it has penetrated now to every stratum of society; and although we may not immediately see the connection; it is responsible, I believe, for the particular go and direction which the industrial revolution has taken. The Country House standards of consumption are responsible for our Acquisitive Society.

Perhaps the shortest way to suggest the character of Country House institutions is to say that they are the precise opposite of everything that Plato looked upon as desirable in a good community.

The Country House is concerned not with the happiness of the whole community but with the felicity of the governors. The conditions which underly this limited and partial good life are political power and economic wealth; and in order for the life to flourish, both of these must be obtained in almost limitless quantities. The chief principles that characterize this society are possession and passive enjoyment.

Now, in the Country House possession is based upon privilege and not upon work. The title to land which was historically obtained for the most part through force and fraud is the economic foundation of the Country House existence. In order to keep the artisans and laborers who surround the Country House at their work, it is necessary to keep them from having access to the land on their own account, provision always being made that the usufruct of the land shall go to the owner and not to the worker. This emphasis upon passive ownership points to the fact that in the Country House there is no active communion between the people and their environment. Such activities as remain in the Country House—the pursuit of game, for instance—rest upon imitating in play activities which once had a vital use or prepared for some vital function, as a child's playing with a doll is a preparation for motherhood. The Country House ideal is that of a completely functionless existence; or at best, an existence in which all the functions that properly belong to a civilized man shall be carried on by functionaries. Since this ideal cannot be realized in the actual world, for the reason that it is completely at odds with man's biological inheritancve, it is necessary in the Country House utopia to fill in by play and sport an otherwise desirable vacuity.

In the Country House literature and the fine arts undoubtedly flourish: but they flourish as the objects of appreciation rather than as the active, creative elements in the community's life; they flourish particularly in the fashion that Plato looked upon as a corrupting influence in the community. In the arts, a gourmandizing habit of mind—the habit of receiving things and being played upon by them—prevails; so that instead of the ability to share creative ecstasy, the chief canon of judgment is "taste," a certain capacity to discriminate among sensory stimuli, a capacity which is essentially just as hospitable to a decomposing cheese as to the very staff of life. The effect of this gourmandism in the arts can be detected in every element of the Country House from cellar to roof; for the result has been to emphasize the collection of good things rather than their creation, and htere is an aspect in which the Country House is little better than a robber's hoard or a hunter's cache—a miniature anticipation of the modern museums of natural history and art.

Observe the architecture of our Country House. If it has been built in England during the last three hundred years, the style is probably that bastard Greek or Roman which we call Renascence architecture; if the Country House was built in America during the last thirty years, it is as likely as not a Tudor residence with traces of castle fortification left here and there on the facade. On the walls there will be plenty of paintings; indeed a whole gallery maybe devoted to them. In all probability, however, the paintings have been created in other times by men long since dead, and in other countries: there may be a portrait by Rembrandt, a Persian miniature, a print by Hokusai. Some very fine element in the structure, a fireplace of a bit of panelling, may have been removed piece by piece from the original Country House in England, Italy, or France; even as many features of the original Country House were quarried, perhaps, from some mediaeval abbey. The very china that we use upon our tables nowadays is a Country House importation which took the place of pewter and earthenware; and wall paper is another importation. From feature to feature everything is derivative; everything, in the last analysis, has either been stolen or purchased from the original makers; and what has not been stolen or purchased has been basely copied.

The insatiability of the Country House to possess art is only equalled by its inability to create it. In the Country House, the arts are not married to the community, but are kept for its pleasure.

Let there be no confusion as to either the facts or the ideal we are examining. There is a vast difference between the fine mingling of traditions which is the very breath of the arts, as the lover of classic Greek statuary knows, and the rapacious imperialistic habit of looting the physical objects of art which has been the essence of the Country House method in modern times, even as it seems to have been a couple of thousand years ago in the Roman villa. A genuine culture will borrow steadily from other cultures; but it will go to them as the bee goes to the flower for pollen, and not as the beekeeper goes to the hive for honey. There is a creative borrowing and a possessive borrowing; and the Country House has in the main limited itself to possessive borrowing. The Country House ideal, in fact, is limitless possession: so the great Country House masters have five or six houses, perhaps, in their name, although they need but a single one to cover their heads.

Now the Country House idolum involves a dissociation between the Country House and the community in which it is placed. If you will take the trouble to examine mediaeval conditions, you will find that differences of rank and wealth did not make a very great difference between the life of the lord in his castle, and his retainers: if the common man could not claim to be as good as his lord, it is plain that the lord shared most of the common man's disabilities, and was, for all the exaggerations of chivalry, just as ignorant, just as illiterate, just as coarse. In the cities, too, the lowest workman in the guild shared the institutions of his masters: the churches, the guild pageants, and the morality plays were all part and parcel of the same culture.

The Country House changed this condition. Culture came to mean not a participation in the creative activities of one's own community, but the acquisition of the products of other communities; and it scarcely matters much whether these acquisitions were within the spiritual or the material domain. There had of course been the beginnings of such a split in mediaeval literature, with its vulgar Rabelaisian tales and its refined romances of the court; but with the integration of the Country House idolum, this divorcement was accentuated in every other activity of the community. One of the results of this split was that popular institutions were deprived of their contacts with the general world of culture, and languished away; or they were transformed, as the public schools of England were transformed into restricted upper class institutions. Far more important than this, perhaps, was the fact that each separate Country House was forced to obtain for its limited circle all the elements that were necessary to the good life in a whole community such as Plato described. . . .

Let us admit what is valid in the utopia of the Country House. enjoyment is a necessary element in achievement, and by its regard for the decent graces of life, for such things as an ease in manners and a fine flow of conversation and the clash of wits and a sensitiveness to beautiful things, the Country House was by all odds a humanizing influence. In so far as the Country House fostered a belief in contemplation and a desire for the arts apart from any uses that might be made of them by way of civic advertisement; in so far as it urged that all our pragmatic activities must be realized in things that are worth having or doing for themselves, the Country House was right, eminently right. It was no snobbery on the part of Russian soviet officialism when it opened up some of its Country Houses as rest houses for the peasants and workers, and then insisted that some of the airs of the Country House should be acquired there, to replace the rough usages of the stable, the dungpile, and the field. Ruskin and Samuel Butler were possibly right when they insisted that the perfect gentleman was a finer product than the perfect peasant or artisan: he is a finer product because he is essentially more alive. Even by its emphasis upon appreciation the Country House did no mean service; for it called attention to the fact that there were more permanent standards—standards which were common to the arts of Greece and China—than those which

were looked upon as sufficient in the local region. In sum, the Country House emphasized a human best, which was the sum of a dozen partial perfections; and so all that was crude and inadequate in the old regional cultures was brought to light and criticized. All these virtues I admit; and they hold just as good today as they ever did.

The fatal weakness of Country House culture comes out all the plainer for this admission. The Country House did not see that enjoyment rested upon achievement, and was indeed inseparable from achievement. The Country House strove to put achievement in one compartment and enjoyment in another; with the result that the craftsman who no longer had the capacity to enjoy the fine arts no longer had the ability to create them. The effect of an isolated routine of enjoyment is equally debilitating; for enjoyment, to the masters of the Country House came too easily, with a mere snap of the fingers, as it were, and the tendency of connoisseurship was to set novelty above intrinsic worth. Hence the succession of styles by which Country House decoration has become a thing for mockery: Chinese in one age, Indian in another, Persian in the next, with Egyptian, Middle African, and heaven knows what else destined to follow in due order. There is nothing to settle to, because there is no task to be done, and no problem to work out; and as soon as the first taste for a style gets exhausted it is speedily supplanted by another.

It would be impossible to calculate the extent to which the Country House has degraded our taste but I have little doubts as to the source of the degradation. The stylicism which has perverted the arts and has kept a congruent modern style from developing has been the work of Country House culture. I remember well the contempt with which a furniture manufacturer in the Chiltern Hills told me about the way in which he produced an original Sheraton: his knowledge of sound furniture design was subordinated to some other person's knowledge of "style" and the miscarriage of the man's innate craftsmanship made him so mordant on the subject that it seemed as though he had been rading Thorstein Veblen's *Theory of the Leisure Class*. It is the same through all the arts. A visit to the industrial sections of the Metropolitan Museum in New York will show how dismally the taste for novelty, which led the Sheratons and Chippendales to find "classic motifs" in one age, causes the designers of the present day to seek the motifs of Sheraton and Chippendale. So much for what happened to the arts when enjoyment and achievement are separated.

The industrial bearing of the Renascence ideal is of capital importance.

During the Middle Age the emphasis in industry was upon the production of tangible goods; the craft guilds set high standards in design and workmanship; and the aim of the worker, in most of the trades, was to get a living from his work, and not simply to get enough money to free himself from the necessity of working. This is a broad generalization, I need scarcely emphasize, and there is plenty of evidence of pecuniary interests under the best of conditions; but it seems fair to say that the dominant ideals of the older industrial order were industrial rather than commercial. In the trading ventures that the Country House promoted under its Drakes and Raleighs, ventures which were needed to bring them "Ships from the Perlas and Cannibal Islands," the emphasis shifted from workmanship to sale; and the notion of working and gambling to acquire multifarious goods took the place of that earlier ideal which Henry Adams so sympathetically described in Mt. St. Michel and Chartres. Thus the good life, as I have said elsewhere, was the Goods Life: it could be purchased. If the whole community no longer offered the conditions for this life, one might filch what one wanted from the general store, and try to monopolize for self or family all that was needed for a good life in the community.

What is the chief economic outcome of this idea? the chief outcome, I think, is to exaggerate the demand for goods, and to cause an enormously wasteful duplication of the apparatus of consumption. If the limit to one's possessions should be simply the extent of one's purse; if happiness is to be acquired through obtaining the comforts and luxuries of life; if a man who possesses a single house is considered fortunate, and a man who possesses five houses five times as fortunate; if there are no standards of living other than the insatiable one that has been set up in the Country House— well, then there is really no limit to the business of getting and spending, and our lives become the mean handiwork of coachman, cook, and groom. Our Country House will not merely be a house: there will be a chapel, an art gallery, a theater, a gymnasium, as Rabelais imagined. As the common possessions of the community dwindle, the private possessions of individuals are multiplied; and at last, there remains no other community than a multitude of anarchic individuals, each of whom is doing his best to create for himself a Country House, notwithstanding the fact that the net result of his endeavors—this is the drab tragedy and the final thing to be said against it—is perhaps nothing better than six inadequate rooms at the end of nowhere in a Philadelphia suburb.

The Country House, then, is the chief pattern by means of which the mediaeval order was transformed into the modern order. It does not matter very much whether the Country House is an estate on Long Island or a cottage in Motclair; whether it is a house in Golder's Green or a family manor in Devonshire: these are essentially affairs of scale, and the underlying identity is plain enough. The idolum of the Country House pre-vails even when quarters are taken up in the midst of the metropolis. More than ever the Country House today tries to make up by an abundance of physical goods for all that has been lost through its divorce from the underlying community; more than ever it attempts to be self-sufficient within the limits of suburbia. The automobile, the phonograph, and the radio-telephone have only served to increase this self-sufficiency; and I need not show at length how these instrumentalities have deepened the elements of acquisitiveness and passive, uncreative, mechanical enjoyment. . . .

UTOPIA AND MILLENARIANISM

Keith Thomas (essay date 1987)

SOURCE: "The Utopian Impulse in Seventeenth-Century England," in *Between Dream and Nature: Essays on Utopia and Dystopia,* edited by Dominic Baker-Smith and C. C. Barfoot, Rodopi, 1987, pp. 20-46.

[*In the following essay, Thomas discusses the utopian impulse in literature in relation to millenarianism during the sixteenth and seventeenth centuries.*]

At the beginning of the seventeenth century the prevailing orthodoxy in England was profoundly anti-utopian. Official religious teaching was that life was necessarily imperfect. Absolute felicity had been enjoyed by Adam and Eve and would be regained by some of their descendants in Heaven. In the meantime man was fallen, nature was harsh and this life could offer only a secondbest.

But the ideal of what constituted perfection was clear enough. Generations of Biblical commentators had built up an accepted picture of Eden as a place of pastoral innocence. Adam and Eve had lived among flowers, fruits and trees, naked and unashamed. They had enjoyed beauty, immortality and eternal youth. Nature had been fertile and temperate. There was work to do, for Adam had been set in the garden to dress it and keep it. But the work was "delightful" (*Paradise Lost* IV. 437). Adam and Eve had lived in an earthly paradise: a place of beauty, comfort and, in Milton's view at any rate, sexual fulfilment.

All this had been lost by the Fall. By rebelling against God, man forfeited his easy dominion over nature. The earth degenerated. Thorns and thistles grew up where there had once been only fruits and flowers. The soil became stony and less fertile, making arduous and painful labour necessary for its cultivation. Many animals grew fierce and dangerous. Man himself became inherently sinful. Social and political repression was now the only way of restraining his wicked impulses. Perfection was not to be obtained in this world and the prospects of any real alleviation of the human condition were doubtful.

In Heaven, however, paradise would be regained, though only by some (the idea that all would be saved was an unacceptable heresy). Contemporary descriptions of heaven tended to be vaguer than those of hell, whose pains and torments, foul smells and hideous sounds, dark lakes and sulphurous fires were evoked with relish. But the genera character of life in heaven was reasonably clear. It was not a place of sensual pleasure, as the Muslim heaven was said to be. Its delights were spiritual rather than physical. But there would be no disease and no death. Youth would not grow old and beauty would never fade. There would be "no wanton dancing, no idle sports", but there would be glorious singing of alleluias. The air would be full of delightful odours and "an unspeakable sweetness of all delectable things" would linger on the palate [Christopher Hooke, "A Sermon preached in Paules Church," London, 1603, sig. B2v; William Gearing, "A Prospect of Heaven," London, 1673, pp. 127, 246].

This hope of heaven was the only ideal prospect in the eyes of most people. Otherwise, images of perfection were nostalgic. For the educated the myth of Eden was paralleled by the classical notion of the golden age: a time of arcadian innocence and harmony, when human needs were satisfied without strife or painful labour. The golden age had gone for ever because both men and nature had degenerated. Some explorers of the New World were ready to believe that survivors of the golden age might yet be discovered in some tropical paradise. But no one suggested that this sort of earthly paradise could be regained in Europe. Literary tradition and conventional Christian teaching thus encouraged reflection on what the ideal human condition might be. But they discouraged any hope of achieving it in this life.

During the seventeenth century this pessimistic view was seriously challenged by two associated currents of thought, each of which held out the possibility that the lost perfection might be restored in the future, and in this life rather than the next.

The first of these currents of thought came out of the Christian tradition itself. Alongside the pessimistic view of history as a story of relentless deterioration, medieval theology had bequeathed rival and more optimistic ways of thinking. The Jewish Messianic tradition held out the prospect of a future age of peace, justice and plenty; *Revelation* forecast that Satan would be bound for a thousand years; and the twelfth-century prophet

Joachim of Fiore had predicted a coming age of spiritual renewal, a *renovatio mundi*. Though strenuously refuted by the orthodox, these associated traditions all suggested that perfection might be achieved once more before the end of the world; and in the sixteenth century the combined effect of unprecedented geographical discovery and dramatic religious upheaval was to foster the notion that such a new age might well be imminent.

This belief in an approaching milennium became particularly strong in England during and after the Civil War, when it was encouraged by a sequence of spectacularly unprecedented events, including the War itself, the collapse of the Anglican Church, the execution of Charles I and the abolition of the monarchy. The creation of a perfect state governed by an elect minority became the objective of one sect, the Fifth Monarchy Men, and the imminence of the millennium was proclaimed by many others, who confidently awaited an era which would be characterised by universal peace and the progressive revelation of all divine mysteries.

Closely associated with this millenarian hope was the belief of many of the heterodox Protestant sects which sprang up under the favourable conditions of the mid-century that spiritual perfection could be achieved in this life: divine illumination would offset the effects of original sin and a new dispensation of the Spirit would supersede the old moral Law. The Familists, the Ranters and the Quakers all made claims of this kind; and their belief in perfectibility and universal redemption was often associated with a more practical vision of reforms in the Church, education, medicine and the law.

The millenarians placed their faith in divine intervention. The restoration of Eden would be achieved by God, not man, even though man could play his part in forwarding God's objectives. For this reason, millenarianism is normally regarded as something different from the other optimistic current of thought in this period, utopianism. For a utopia envisages an ideal society created by human effort. It requires no prior transformation of man's nature, no change in the natural world, no spectacular supernatural occurrence. It is therefore usually distinguished from the millennium, which is achieved by an act of God. It is also different from nostalgic visions of Eden or arcadia, where problems disappear because men are innocent and nature obliging.

The literary utopia was a genre which had been extinct since classical times. It was revived by Thomas More and developed by Patrizi, Doni, Stiblinus and other humanist writers. In the early seventeenth century its most notable European instances were Campanella's

City of the Sun (1602; published 1623), the work of Calabrian friar, and Johann Valentin Andreae's *Christianopolis* (1619), a vision of a Christian community

---

Kateb on modern antiutopianism:

[Certain] attacks—most of them modern . . . have been made on utopianism. These attacks stem from the belief that the world sometime soon (unbearably soon) will have at its disposal—if it wishes to use them—the material presuppositions of a way of life commonly described as "utopian." Such a prospect, one would have thought, would be a cause for gladness. It has not been that, at all, but rather a signal for men of various persuasions and temperaments to devote themselves strenuously and in all sincerity to exposing both the insufficiency of utopian ideals and the unacceptability of arrangements thought necessary to the realization of those ideals. On the face of it, it would seem absurd that serious thinkers would seek to turn us away from what mankind, all through time, has cherished. The apparent absurdity becomes more acute, and more engaging, when it is seen that the motives of the antiutopians are, for the most part, unimpeachable by any humanitarian. How could it be that there are well-disposed men who, from their very benevolence, take fright at the thought of a general reign of benevolence? Surely what is involved is not cheap paradox on anyone's part, nore any spite or perversity; surely, there must be something else at work in the minds of these men. . . .

George Kateb, in his introduction to Utopia and Its Enemies, *The Free Press of Glencoe, 1963.*

---

composed by a Lutheran minister. Characteristically, the literary utopia describes an imaginary society which is, at least by implication, better than the one in which the author lives. This society is portrayed as actually in existence, usually in some remote location. Its workings are evoked in detail, with special attention to the political structure, the laws and religion, the system of education, the economy and the working habits and living conditions of the population. The activities of the citizens are regulated in meticulous detail; and the society exists in a timeless state of unchanging equilibrium.

The sixteenth-century literary utopia, however, was not a programme for action. No route from contemporary reality to the desired state of perfection was offered; indeed the practical implications of the model were wholly unclear. The vision of perfection held out by More or Doni was thus no more revolutionary in practice than were the concepts of paradise or heaven. For this reason there are modern writers like Karl Mannheim who scarcely mention More when discussing utopianism. For Mannheim "utopia" has to be revolutionary in its implications, by contrast with "ideology", which reinforces the status quo. Consolatory myths of heaven or paradise are ideology, because their effect is to reconcile people to the existing state of imperfection by proffering the hope of a better future in the next life. By contrast, a genuinely utopian vision will seek to inspire collective activity in an effort to change the world now.

On this definition, it was not the sixteenth but the seventeenth century which was the decisive period in the history of utopianism because only then did there emerge the action-oriented utopia, that is to say a model of a more perfect society intended for direct human implementation. This new utopian impulse took various forms, not all of them literary. What was common to them all was that they involved both a model, explicit or implicit, of what a perfect society would be like and a desire to put the mode into operation. Instead of aiming at pragmatic, piecemeal reform, the utopian was animated by a vision of the whole; and he set out to achieve goals which most of his contemporaries regarded as either impractical or undesirable or both.

There were, I suggest, at least eight different forms which the utopian impulse took during this period. The first, was the composition of literary utopias in the now traditional manner, but with an increasingly practical purpose in mind. The most notable of these works were Francis Bacon's *New Atlantis* (1624; published 1627) and its later continuations by "R.H." (1660) and Joseph Glanvill (1676); Robert Burton's "poetical commonwealth", prefaced to his *Anatomy of Melancholy* (1621); Gabriel Plattes's *A Description of the famous Kingdome of Macaria* (1641); *Nova Solyma* (1648), a philosophical romance in Latin by the lawyer, Samuel Gott; *Oceana* (1656), by the political theorist James Harrington; and the anonymous *Essay concerning Adepts* (1698), which describes a Christian community reminiscent of Andreae's *Christianopolis*. There were at least a dozen other loosely comparable writings, though few of them contain the detailed social specification characteristic of More's *Utopia* and in some of them the element of fantasy or romance predominates. In Francis Godwin's *The Man in the Moone* (1638), for example, the aeronaut hero stumbles on world where all live in "such love, peace and amity as it seemeth to be another paradise", but the work gives only a very brief account of this state of felicity and does not specify how it is achieved. Many such romances or imaginary voyages do not qualify as utopias proper because they presuppose either an unnaturally virtuous people or a race endowed with unusual physical properties, like the pygmies of Joshua Barnes's *Gerania* (1675) or the inhabitants of Gabriel de Foigny's *Terra Incognita Australis* (English translation, 1693), who are eight-foot tall hermaphrodites. But some romances include descriptions of ideal states which seem true members of the utopian genre.

At least one literary utopia has not been studied because it is still in manuscript. This is the language-reformer Francis Lodwick's *Description of a Country Not Named;* it depicts a society whose members speak a perfect language, follow a religion unchanged for a thousand years, possess a developed system of education, support learned philosophers who engage in experiments and maintain a clergy who do not bother with theological disputes but provide education and free medicine to the poor [British Library, Sloane MS 913, fols. 1-33]. Other seventeenth-century utopias have been lost, like "*Jamesanna* or the pattern of a perfect city, the which, in imitation of the *Utopia* of Thomas More, representeth the good qualities, customs, perfections that both every sovereign prince and all sorts of subjects should aspire unto", a composition which the writer James Maxwell listed in 1615 among his works "not as yet published" [*Admirable and Notable Prophesies,* London, 1615].

These literary utopias served diverse purposes; Lodwick's *Description of a Country not Named,* for example, was a vehicle for the author's views on biblical criticism, the age of the world and the descent of man. But many of them were intended to offer a programme for implementation. Plattes's *Macaria,* for instance, was a scheme for a welfare state based on the increased exploitation of productive resources. The author dedicated it to the House of Commons in 1641 in the hope that the House would "lay the cornerstone of the world's happiness before the final recess". He described his model as "easy to be effected, if al men be willing" and his aim as "to make England to be like to *Macaria*" [*Samuel Hartlib and the Advancement of Learning,* ed. Charles Webster, Cambridge, 1970]. Works of this programmatic kind have no real precedent in English literature.

A second form of seventeenth-century utopianism was the devising of elaborate schemes for ideal commonwealths, though without the fictional pretence that such a commonwealth already existed and without the imaginative exploration of what the texture of life in such a state might be. Both John Eliot and Richard Baxter published schemes for a theocracy or "holy commonwealth": "a divine platform of government taught by God himself", as Eliot put it [in *The Christian Commonwealth,* c. 1660]. In the same spirit, Gerrard Winstanley in his *The Law of Freedom in a Platform* (1652) offered a detailed code of laws for the immediate achievement of a communist state, a "Platform for the Government of the Earth without buying and selling". The most celebrated of such schemes was Thomas Hobbes's *Leviathan.* Hobbes denied that his aims were utopian: as he remarked, "the state of man can never be without some incommodity or other". Nevertheless, he presented his state as a solution to the most fundamental probems of human life and he freely admitted that it transcended anything which had ever historical-

ly existed. To many of his contemporaries his proposals seemed impossibly unrealistic.

Closely associated with such ideal commonwealths was the third type of utopianism, the making of new constitutions for the government of England. The Levellers were a radical group who emerged in the aftermath of the English Civil War. They drew up the first written constitution in English history, *The Agreement of the People,* which, in its successive versions, was meant to be subscribed by all members of the population as the basis of a new state. It was but one of many such schemes for political reconstruction put forward in the Civil War period, when there was a widespread feeling that all things were now possible. In 1653 Cromwell's Protectorate was inaugurated by the Instrument of Government, a written constitution produced by the army. This was the first time that English government had been founded on a written constitution; and the adoption of the Humble Petition and Advice, which amended that constitution in 1657, was the last. Of course, such constitutions were not utopian in the full sense, for they provided a framework only for the distribution of political power and did not purport to regulate all aspects of society. But in their attempt to make the future run along ideal lines they revealed a utopian aspiration; and their invariable omission of any provision for subsequent constitutional amendment indicated that, like the literary utopians, they envisaged that future as a state of unchanging equilibrium.

Fourthly, there were idealized descriptions of other societies which did exist, or had existed, and were now perceived as perfect models of political and social organization. In the seventeenth century the most popular historical subjects for such treatment were ancient Israel, the Roman republic, the free Anglo-Saxons and the Merric England which had existed before the Reformation. In contemporary Europe, there was Venice, which was praised for its mixed constitution and political stability: "Many make [it] the very mirror of policy", wrote Thomas Gataker in 1619 [in *Of the Nature and Use of Lots*], "and some suppose [it] to be a model of Plato's old platform". There were the United Provinces of the Netherlands, which afforded an example of hard work, political freedom, economic prosperity, care for the poor and religious toleration: in 1622 Thomas Scott thought there was no need for Plato's *Republic* or More's *Utopia,* since "the reality of their wishes and best conceptions" could be seen in action among the Dutch [*The Belgicke Pismire,* 1622]. Outside Europe there was China, which Sir William Temple regarded as superior to "all those imaginary schemes of the European wits, . . . the *Utopias* or *Oceanas* of our modern writers" ["Of Heroick Virtue", in *Miscellanea, II,* 4th edn., 1696].

Fifthly, there was the formation of secret or semi-secret societies, pledged to the reform of the world. Particularly celebrated were the Rosicrucians, alleged authors of two manifestos published in Germany in 1614 and 1615, though it is doubtful whether any such fraternity in fact existed. The brotherhood of the Rosy Cross was represented as a mystical elite whose alchemical researches, conducted in a spirit of Christian charity, would enable them to eliminate hunger and painful labour and to cure all diseases. Their object was the "Universal and General Reformation of the whole wide world" [Frances A. Yates, *The Rosicrucian Enlightenment*, 1972]. An English translation of the Rosicrucian manifestos was published in 1652 by Thomas Vaughan [*The Fame and Confession of the Fraternity of R: C: commonly, of the Rosie Cross.*] Ten years later John Heydon claimed [in *The Holy Guide*, 1662] that the Rosicrucian fraternity, "seraphically illuminated", was alive and well and living in a castle in the West of England, where they held the secret of long life, health, riches and virtue. Various hermetic and alchemical groups undoubtedly existed. We can perhaps detect their influence as late as 1698 in the anonymous utopia called *An Essay concerning Adepts,* which outlines the spiritual reformation necessary before men are fit to receive the secrets of the philosopher's stone.

A more influential group was the association formed in the late 1650s by the Prussian emigré Samuel Hartlib and the Scottish minister John Dury, and later joined by the Czech educationalist Jan Comenius. Hartlib and Dury were indebted to the example of Andreae, who had urged the formation of small Christian societies, and of Bacon, who had envisaged a universal college or international association of the learned. They later adopted Comenius's Pansophism, a scheme for a unified system of learning which traced its origins to the Neoplatonic belief in the universal harmony of nature. During the 1640s Hartlib became the centre of a small but active circle pledged to the dissemination of science, the reform of schools and universities, the improvement of technology, the achievement of full employment, the discovery of a universal language and the union of the churches. In 1649 the new Commonwealth appointed him "Agent for the Advancement of Universal Learning and the Public Good". His aim, he said later, was "the reformation of the whole world".

At various stages in his career, Hartlib hoped to found a Christian society, called Antilia and inspired by Andrea's *Christianopolis,* as a colony in Virginia or Bermuda. This dream of an ideal colonial society is our sixth form of utopianism. Obvious examples are the various efforts to create a Bible Commonwealth or New Jerusalem in Puritan New England. The covenant drawn up in 1636 by the founders of Dedham, Massachusetts, pledged its signatories to live "according to that most perfect rule, the foundation whereof is everlasting love" (significantly, it excluded "all such

as are contrary-minded"). Its historian describes Dedham "a highly conscious attempt to build the most perfect possible community" [Kenneth A. Lockridge, *A New England Town. The first Hundred Years. Dedham, Massachusetts, 1636-1736,* 1970]. Pennsylvania was even more utopian in conception. Its founder William Penn regarded it as a "holy experiment", intended it as "an example . . . to the nations" and named its capital Philadelphia, the city of brotherly love [*The Papers of William Penn, II* (1680-1684), ed. Richard S. Dunn and Mary Maples Dunn, 1982].

Seventhly, there were smaller communities deliberately created by idealistic individuals to enable their members to live a more perfect existence. They could be a refuge from a harsh world, like Nicholas Ferrar's household at Little Gidding in Huntingdonshire, which led a semi-monastic life until broken up in 1647. Or they could offer an example which it was hoped others would follow, like Winstanley's community of Diggers, cultivating the commons at St George's Hill, or the collective settlements of Pieter Cornelisz Plockhoy in London and Bristol.

Finally, there were what the seventeenth century called "projectors", ingenious people with an infinity of schemes of reform. These might range from plans to erect workhouses or introduce new crops to more ambitious programmes for a universal language, the reunion of the Christian churches and perpetual peace. Reformers as such should not be regarded as utopian if their reforms are limited in scope and are not meant to transform the whole of society. But the greater their readiness to regard their particular scheme as a panacea for all the world's problems the more do they deserve the label. The later seventeenth century was what Defoe called "the projecting age" and it was the projectors who provided the object of some of Swift's most scathing satire in *A Voyage to Laputa.*

I have listed eight forms of seventeenth-century utopianism. All of them presupposed that man was fallen and nature recalcitrant. All placed their faith in human effort. I have therefore contrasted them with the millenarian impulse, which relied on divine intervention and envisaged a miraculous transformation of both man and nature.

Yet we know that this distinction is spurious. For it was precisely when the millenarian current was running most strongly that theutopian faith in human effort was most buoyant. The advancement of idealistic schemes was encouraged by the feeling that the times were special and that God had great purposes afoot. The approaching prospect of a new age of perfect knowledge explains the educational preoccupations of Comenius, while the tireless activity of Hartlib and Dury is unintelligible if we overlook their millenarian conviction that time was on their side. In an atmosphere of eschatological expectation, particularly intense between 1640 and 1660, utopianism flourished most vigorously. It was because of their sense of living in a special time that, as a contemporary put it, "all sorts of people dreamed of an Utopia" [*Persecution Undecima*, 1681]. "The spirit of the whole Creation", Winstanley confidently wrote in the preface to his *Law of Freedom,* "is about the Reformation of the World".

Mannheim on the distinction between utopia and ideology:

A state of mind is utopian when it is incongruous with the state of reality within which it occurs.

This incongruence is always evident in the fact that such a state of mind in experience, in thought, and in practice, is oriented towards objects which do not exist in the actual situation. However, we should not regard as utopian every state of mind which is incongruous with and transcends the immediate situation (and in this sense, "departs from reality"). Only those orientations transcending reality will be referred to by us as utopian which, when they pass over into conduct, tend to shatter, either partially or wholly, the order of things prevailing at the time.

In limiting the meaning of the term "utopia" to that type of orientation which transcends reality and which at the same time breaks the bonds of the existing order, a distinction is set up between the utopian and the ideological states of mind.

Karl Mannheim, in Ideology and Utopia: An Introduction to the Sociology of Knowledge, *Harcourt, Brace & World, 1936.*

It is therefore not easy to separate the utopian impulse from the millenarian current which accompanied it. If we examine the content of seventeenth-century millenialism and compare it with seventeenth-century utopianism we find that the two were twins.

For how was the millennium envisaged? Of course, it varied according to the millenarian concerned. For the radical sectary, George Foster [in *The Pouring Forth of the Seventh and Last Viall,* 1650], the millennium was a time when the common people would be freed from bondage and the saints would "have all things in common". For the cultivated Richard Roach, the millennium would be marked by "wit and delightful conversation" [John Edwards, *A Compleat History or Survey of all the Dispensations and Methods of Religion,* 1699]. But the most common notion was that the millennium would see the restoration of mankind to Adam's state before the Fall. Writing at the very end of the seventeenth century, the Calvinist divine John

Edwards explained just what this would mean. The earth, he said, would be renewed and become more fertile. Better air would give men "bodily strength and vigour in an unusual degree" so that everyone would be "healthful and vivacious, brisk and sprightly". There would be a vast expansion in human knowledge: even little children would know more than did the wisest centenarians at present. Natural philosophy would be "improved to the utmost". Human longevity would be enhanced by an increased understanding of the workings of the body. The nature of all vegetables and minerals would be laid open by "exquisite experiments". Wild animals would become tame and gentle. There would be more people in the world and they would live longer. But this increase in population would cause no problems. Commerce by land and sea would be "mightily increased". A common language would enable all peoples "with ease and freedom [to] confer with one another; and compare their notions together, and thereby come to an entire agreement". In this era of universal peace and concord, all religious controversies would vanish and there would be an end to warfare. Life would be "attended with all outward conveniences, comforts and refreshments of what nature soever, together with inward peace, pleasure and satisfaction". And all these earthly conveniences would be as nothing to the spiritual blessings which the millennium would bring.

Edwards was emphatic that this felicity would be achieved, not by human effort, but by heaven: "The Supreme Arbitrator and Manager of the World can, of a sudden, dispel all difficulties and alter the course of the universe and frame men's minds as he pleaseth". Yet his conception of ultimate happiness bears a striking similarity to the objectives of utopians who did not rely on supernatural aid. In many respects the goals were the same; only the methods were different. It would, of course, be absurd to suggest that all seventeenth-century utopians were working in the same direction. There was no single utopian impulse and the values and aspirations of the different utopian thinkers varied enormously. Even so, it is not too fanciful to detect, under the obvious differences, some abiding preoccupations; and they are ones to which the account of the millennium given by Edwards and others bears a close affinity.

For what was the aim of the utopians if not the restoration to man of what he had enjoyed in Eden: dominion over nature; comfortable living; perfect knowledge; harmony and peace? In England it was Francis Bacon who first urged that man himself could undo the worst consequences of the Fall and inaugurate a new age of knowledge. Dominion over nature, forfeited through sin, could be patiently regained by the advancement of the arts and sciences; and the state of innocence could be recaptured by the practice of piety and religion. In the "Salomon's House" of his *New Atlantis,* Bacon provided the model of a scientific institute (or "college"), staffed by a semi-priestly elite dedicated to "the finding out of the true nature of all things, (whereby God might have the more glory in the workmanship of them, and men the more fruit in the use of them)".

This attempt to restore Paradise by a combination of science and Protestant piety was characteristic of an attitude which was widespread in early seventeenth-century Europe and which provided the intellectual inspiration for much later utopian activity. The Rosicrucians, for example, promised that by studying the book ofnature man could return to paradise. In their case the claim took on a hermetic, mystical character, with much talk of divine illumination, universal medicine and the philosopher's stone. The Pansophists also sought to restore Eden by a combination of piety and knowledge. They aimed at a Christian synthesis of all forms of truth. Comenius believed that he was living in an era of dawning enlightenment and envisaged an international fraternity of intellectuals who would write universal textbooks in a universal language, disseminating universal knowledge for "the improvement of all human affairs, in all persons and everywhere". The *Great Didactic* was "a scheme for readily and soundly teaching everybody everything" [John William Adamson, *Pioneers of Modern Education 1600-1700,* 1905].

The intellectual influence of Bacon and Comenius upon Samuel Hartlib's utopian projects in England during the Civil War period has been admirably demonstrated by Dr Charles Webster. Hartlib and his associates had schemes to achieve everything, from poor relief to the introduction of decimal currency. But their aims transcended merely material well-being: the accumulation and dissemination of knowledge would relieve man's estate; it would also bring him nearer to God.

In this way the utopian dreams of Bacon's *New Atlantis* bore practical fruit, though sometimes in bizarre form. In 1659, for example, the adventurer Thomas Bushell proposed to build Salomon's House in Wells, Somerset, by placing there "a select society of . . . philosophers" to study the mining of underground treasures which were popularly believed to be guarded by subterranean spirits. Staffed by "six exquisite, lucre-hating philosophers" and with convicted criminals and debtors as its labour force, this "matchless academy" would ensure that "thousands of poor subjects shall eat the bread of comfort; offenders be purged and freed; trade increased and customs augmented . . . new arts discovered for the universal good and honour of the nation". And when they died, the "six exquisite, lucre-hating philosophers" would have their statues erected in the city of Wells, "and . . . each . . . shall hold a significant character of their peculiar invention in their well-proportioned hands", just in the way that *New Atlantis* had recommended [J. W. Gough, *The Superlative Prodigall. A Life of Thomas Bushell,* 1932].

The first great utopian goal was thus the reorganisation and advancement of knowledge by an elite of Christian scientists and its propagation by a reformed educational system. The moral value of learning was widely accepted. Education was the means of undoing original sin: it aimed, said Milton, "to repair the ruins of our first parents by regaining to know God aright". The search for lost innocence thus underlay much of the educational activity of the period. Both Dury and Hartlib thought that the education of the young was the quickest route to the nation's reformation; and for Comenius the school was the solution to all problems.

The second goal was the regaining of dominion over nature by the controlled use of scientific discovery. *Macaria* set out a programme for the state-encouraged improvement of husbandry, fishing and trade; and many of Hartlib's projects were designed to use new technology to enlarge the means of subsistence. Medicine was a particularly important part of the work of regeneration. Some form of state medical service was proposed by Plattes, Lodwick, Hartlib and other English utopians, just as it had been envisaged by Campanella and Andreae. The essential point was that physical health was regarded as a necessary precondition for spiritual well-being.

This was connected with the third objective, which was the relief of hunger, poverty and unemployment. Here, too, the primary aim was a moral one. In their degraded state the poor were incapable of worshipping God or leading a moral life. An adequate standard of living should therefore be ensured for everyone. It was "to prevent the ill breeding, wicked life and bad end that many thousands have fallen into through idleness" that Thomas Lawson made his *Appeal to the parliament, concerning the Poor, that there may not be a beggar in England* (1660). In the same spirit Peter Chamberlen declared [in *The Poore Mans Advocate,* 1649] that all previous legislation for the poor had been useless. The houses of correction only degraded their inhabitants and made them desperate. Instead, the aim should be to "civilise" the poor by providing them with an honest livelihood.

There were two alternative methods of guaranteeing a reasonable living for everyone. The first was to ensure that all were engaged in productive labour. Those who had no work should be provided with it in workhouses, financed by the state or by a local authority or by a private patron or group of joint-stock investors. Life within these workhouses would be so regulated as to turn them into miniature godly communities. As a result, the poor would cease to be a burden to others and become a source of strength and piety. John Stratford, a Gloucestershire projector, claimed that the introduction of flax-growing would turn the idle poor into a profitable asset, living "according to God's ordinance by the sweat of their face in a more religious order".

[Joan Thirsk, *Economic Policy and Projects,* 1978]. The Quaker John Bellers believed that his "colleges of industry" would revive the spirit of primitive Christianity by providing a regular life, religious instruction and "easy honest labour" [A. Ruth Fry, *John Bellers 1654-1725, Quaker, Economist and Social Reformer,* 1935].

These proposals sound bland enough, but they were breath-taking in their ambition. No greater single transformation of seventeenth-century English society could be imagined than the conversion of the poor (whom Peter Chamberlen estimated as the majority of the population into a well-fed, hard-working and religious group. It is sometimes said that one of the distinguishing features of utopianism is that it envisages an improvement in the human condition without a prior change in human nature. But what is surely notable about the full-employment utopias of this period is that their authors believed that human nature, or at least its external symptoms, could be radically changed by social engineering.

The other method of eliminating poverty was equally ambitious. Instead of seeking to increase production, it aimed to limit consumption by forbidding luxury, enforcing greater social equality and eliminating superfluous wants. The literary utopias are particularly draconian in this respect, often prescribing uniform dress and living conditions and forbidding all forms of conspicuous display. If nothing was wasted on superfluities, declared the *Essay concerning Adepts,* there would be enough for everyone. No doubt it was hard for the rich to have to lay aside their gay attire and other luxuries, but what reason was there why they should "abound in superfluities, and others should want necessaries"? Rich garments, changes of fashion in clothes and all unnecessary expenditure should be "hinder'd by most severe penalties" [Philadept, *An Essay concerning Adepts,* 1698].

The idea that happiness could be achieved by the limitation of wants was an ancient one. What is particularly striking about these seventeenth-century proposals is less their readiness to envisage equality or even communism, remarkable though that is, than their implicit assumption that the economic process could somehow be stopped, demand checked and the desire for new fashions arrested. Absurdly unrealistic though such a belief may appear to us, it was widely held, and not only by utopians narrowly defined. In 1621 a Member of Parliament called for an act to establish "a settled fashion" in clothes and a few years earlier the Church of England's canons had expressed the wistful hope that, "in time", "newfangleness of apparel" would "die of itself". Not until the end of the century did economists recognize that to attempt to limit consumer demand was to fly in the face of an inexorable economic process. In the meantime the characteristic seventeenth-century utopia was based on the limitation of wants rather than the expansion of productive capacity.

Adequate living standards were only part of the utopian dream. The fourth great objective was the attainment of peace and harmony between men. For religious enthusiasts like George Foster it was only in the millennium that "the root of all malice, strife, hatred and war may be digged up and . . . universal love and freedom to sorts of people . . . brought in". But the utopians sought peace and harmony by human action. One method was by the elimination of lawyers. Like most contemporaries, the utopians were deeply hostile to the multiplication of lawyers and lawsuits which had been such a feature of the period. They romanticized the medieval past as a time when there had been few legal disputes and they regarded the growth of litigation and the rise of a legal profession as a sign of social ill-health. In virtually all the literary utopias, lawyers are non-existent. They were deemed unnecessary in *Christianopolis* and deprived of civil rights in *Oceana.* There was little room for them in Francis Godwin's *Man in the Moone,* in Antoine Le Grand's *Scydromedia* or in Francis Lodwick's *Country not Named.* Winstanley declared flatly that "there shall be no need of lawyers . . . for all shall walk and act righteously". Even Robert Burton, whose ideals were less radical than most, prescribed that as far as possible each man should plead his own cause and that the few lawyers who were needed should earn no fees but be paid out of public funds. More realistic contemporaries protested that the growth of litigation reflected the growing complexity of economic life rather than mere professional cupidity. But the utopians regarded litigation, quarrels and disputes as a symptom of imperfect human relationships; their aim was to eliminate them.

This was particularly true of the disputes caused by religion. It is a characteristic of virtually all the literary utopias that the societies they portray are free from religious debate and persecution. This happy state is achieved sometimes by toleration, as in *Oceana,* but more often by the prescription of a uniform state religion, relatively free of dogmatic content and confined to fundamentals on which all Christians could agree. In "Astreada", the ideal state of the anonymous *Antiquity Reviv'd* (1693), religious dogma is limited to what can be known with certainty. In Lodwick's utopia, the articles of faith are very few and the subjects must obey the rulers in all inessentials. In *Macaria* there are no religious disputes and the death penalty falls on anyone who tries to communicate new religious opinions to the common people. In the Duchess of Newcastle's *New Blazing World* (1666) the inhabitants follow a single religion and no dissent is permitted.

An ever greater cause of dissension than religious disputes within the state was religious controversy between states. Ever since the Reformation there had been ecumenical attempts to close the newly-opened gaps between the Christian churches and they were kept alive by millenarian expectations of an approaching age of peace and harmony. Hartlib's associate John Dury spent over fifty years in an unceasing attempt to bring together the Lutheran and Calvinist churches of Europe. Travelling through Germany and the Netherlands, negotiating with the Danes and the Swedes, the English, the Scots and the Swiss, Dury devoted his life to a fruitless quest for ecclesiastical reconciliation on the basis of religious fundamentals declared by a Protestant General Council. There were many in England who shared his objectives, from James I onwards. "Religious division", it has been perceptively remarked, "is the great anxiety of early modern Europe, as keen a stimulus to thought and guilt as class division in modern Europe" [Blair Worden, "Toleration and the Cromwellian Protectorate", in *Studies in Church History* 21, Oxford, 1984]. At the beginning of the eighteenth century John Bellers, author of the scheme for "colleges of industry", was still proposing that a General Council of all Christian states should settle principles on which they could agree.

The prospect of a single world religion had long been held out by millenarian and Joachimite prophets. The conversion of the Jews, for example, and their return to Jerusalem, were, on the basis of a passage in St Paul's epistle to the Romans, an accepted part of the cosmic drama, a recognized preliminary to the coming of Christ. For that reason mid seventeenth-century England was rich in prophets who offered themselves as would-be couriers, prepared to assemble the Jews together and lead them back to the Holy Land. Gott's *Nova Solyma* describes an ideal society created after the resettlement of the Jews in the Holy Land. The same millenarian concern underlay Cromwell's summoning of a conference in 1655 which pronounced that there was no legal objection to the return to England of the Jewish community which had been banished in the thirteenth century. Characteristically, Samuel Hartlib wanted "to make Christianity less offensive and more known unto the Jews".

Equally ecumenical in intention were the numerous schemes for a universal language which would restore to mankind the common tongue they had lost since Babel. Such a language, it was urged, would foster trade, spread true religion and achieve amity and understanding between peoples. Closely associated was the search for a "real character", that is to say a perfect language in which words corresponded exactly to things, in the way that the language of Adam had done and, it was believed, the characters of the Chinese still did. There could be no better way of eliminating all the controversies and misunderstandings which stemmed from linguistic confusion. The quest

for a universal language and a real character occupied many of the best minds of the period. It would be unforgettably satirized by Swift, who in *Laputa* depicts a scheme to shorten discourse by leaving out verbs and participles and, ultimately, by abolishing words altogether; instead, the inhabitants carry about a huge load of objects to which they point when wishing to carry on a conversation.

Linguistic unity and religious pacification were means to the final objective: the prevention of war between states and the unification of the human race: "oneness" or *concordia*. Projects for universal peace and concord had less influence in England than they did on the Continent, perhaps because England was less affected by the carnage of seventeenth-century warfare. Gabriel Plattes, the author of *Macaria,* declares in [*A Discovery of Infinite Treasure,* 1639] that "the whole world is all of one God's making, and, no question is or should be one body politic". Yet not even Hobbes put forward a plan for a world state, logical culmination of his thought though it would have been. Only the Quakers bothered with projects for international federation. William Penn propounded a scheme in 1693 for a European Parliament and John Bellers also put forward a plan for a European Senate which would settle all international disputes without bloodshed.

It was, therefore, always the same imperfections which the seventeenth-century utopians sought to remedy; and though they differed widely in the details of their proposals, their goals display a remarkable affinity: the advancement of knowledge, the control of nature, the relief of poverty, the elimination of disputes and the attainment of universal peace and harmony. These objectives underlay most of the literary utopias, just as they coloured the idealized accounts of other countries and inspired the activities of the projectors and colonists. The interest of these utopian goals is that they help to define the preoccupations of the age in which they originated: above all the obsession with harmony and the faith in the power of knowledge. Such preoccupations can be related to the social problems of the era, but they owe even more to the stylized preoccupations of biblical commentary. Peace and knowledge were the essential features of the New Jerusalem.

The dreams of the seventeenth century, therefore, were not those of the twentieth. There was very little concern with sexual fulfilment, for example, and no concept of utopia as a place of personal authenticity or self-realisation. On the contrary, most seventeenth-century utopias, far from encouraging human self-expression, showed an anxiety to regulate and control. "There will be rules made for every action a man can do", wrote Winstanley. The literary utopians wanted a regular time-table, a clearly defined hierarchy and a firm code of rewards and punishments. Their favourite models of social organization were the monastery, the workhouse, the college and the school.

This concern with the small institution reflected another tendency—the disposition to turn away from the unregenerate mass of mankind and to withdraw into a select community of reforming spirits. Hartlib, Dury, Plockhoy, Bellers and many others were attracted by what John Beale called "the design of beginning buildings of Christian societies in small models" [*The Diary and Correspondence of Dr. John Worthington,* ed. James Crossley, I 1847]. The small, godly community, thought John Evelyn, was "the most blessed life that virtuous persons could wish or aspire to in this miserable and uncertain pilgrimage". There was indeed a hermetic quality about much seventeenth-century utopianism, shown in the recurring tendency for little groups of select individuals to make private pacts in a belief that their illumination would enable them to reform the world.

After Charles II's restoration in 1660, hopes of such reform grew faint. England was no longer a *tabula rasa,* as she had seemed to be in the 1640s, and the prospect of radical reconstruction became remote. "The times of such a public universal happiness seem not yet to be at hand", concluded Hartlib [*Proceedings of the Massachusetts Historical Society, 1878,* 1879]. The utopians had never been more than a tiny minority and had long been denounced as dreamers, impractical visionaries. Works like *Christianopolis* or *New Atlantis* were "witty fictions", "mere chimeras", "airy castles", "romantic whimsies". Perfection was impossible in this world, went the chorus. Human nature could never be reformed and if one evil was eliminated another would spring up in its place. "Dream not of other worlds", said Milton's Angel to Adam.

This was the conservative refrain. As Mannheim says, it is the socially dominant group which determines what is or is not "unrealistic". When Parliament asked for control of Charles I's counsellors, the King denounced their demands as the "new Utopia of religion and government into which they endeavour to transform this kingdom". When the Levellers put forward proposals for a more democratic regime, they were told that "the dispute is not now of what is absolutely best if all were new, but of what is perfectly just as things now stand: it is not the Parliament's work to set up an Utopian commonwealth, or to force the people to practise abstractions, but to make them as happy as the present frame will bear" [*The Leveller Tracts 1647-1653,* eds William Haller and Godfrey Davies, 1964]. In 1639 Archbishop Ussher commented that John Dury would do better to come home, since England's own religious divisions made his efforts to unite the churches of Europe appear ridiculous.

The ultimate refutation of utopia is dystopia, the demonstration that utopian visions are not just impractical, but potentially sinister. "I am verily of opinion", wrote one seventeenth-century critic, "that fantastic eutopian commonwealths (which some witty men . . . have drawn unto us), introduced among men, would prove far more loathsome and be more fruitful of bad consequences than any of those of the basest alloy yet known . . . because they seem all to me rather suited to the private conceptions and humours of their architects than to the accommodation and benefit of men" [J. Philolaus, *A Serious Aviso to the Good People of this Nation, Concerning that Sort of Men, called Levellers,* 1649].

> A Heav'n on Earth they hope to gain,
>   But we do know full well,
> Could they their glorious ends attain,
>   This Kingdom must be Hell.

Yet the only seventeenth-century work which set out to prove this was published as early as 1605 and took as its target not the millenarian utopianism of the mid-seventeenth century, but the old peasant myth of the land of cockayne. Joseph Hall's *Mundus Alter et Idem* (c. 1606) is a satirical burlesque, mocking vice of every kind, but particularly concerned to show that limitless sensual gratification generates moral and physical deterioration. It was written by a man who believed it immoral to "dream of an utopicall perfection" or to hope for paradise in this inferior world; and it is the only dystopia of the period. [Richard A. McCabe, *Joseph Hall. A Study in Satire and Meditation,* 1982]. There were some writers who expressed the modern liberal objection to utopianism, namely its implicit authoritarianism and its certainty that its exponent knows what is right for others. But not until Jonathan Swift do we meet a full dystopian onslaught on the idealism of the mid seventeenth century: the reference in *Laputa* to a scheme devised forty years ago "of putting all arts, sciences, languages and mechanics upon a new foot" is surely an allusion to Hartlib and his circle. Yet even in Swift it is the impracticality of the projectors which is most effectively satirized. The notion that hopes of perfection are necessarily self-defeating is less convincingly established. Swift's Struldbruggs are a dreadful warning of what immortality would mean if unaccompanied by health and energy; but since the seventeenth-century medical reformers who sought to increase the expectation of life also hoped to prolong human vigour, the criticism was unfair.

As social philosophy, the defects of seventeenth-century utopianism seem obvious enough to us. Buttressed in most cases by a millenarian belief that God was on their side, the utopians were absurdly optimistic about the possibility of attaining their objectives. With charity, faith and industry, thought John Bellers, "then mountains of difficulty will vanish away, as mists before the sun". Moreover, their conception of felicity was still a largely static one. There was a dynamic element implicit in the belief that science would better the human condition by transforming man's relationship to nature, but even Bacon assumed that the achievement of science would be a finite matter. When peace, harmony and perfect knowledge had been secured, history would by implication stop. No one considered the possibility that if people were freed from pain and worry they would become bored, living a life of indifference or finding some new source of unhappiness. The practical meaning of such abstract goals as "peace" and "harmony" was never explored.

Yet we should not be too quick to condemn the utopians for a lack of realism. In the conditions of the mid-seventeenth century it really did seem possible that a gigantic reformation could take place. The old institutions had been torn down and were waiting to be replaced. Utopianism offered effective criticism because it provided an alternative model. "No wise man", thought Hartlib, "will lay his old habitation waste till he know what to erect instead thereof; hence it is that a new model is commonly firstprepared before the old one be removed". The aim, agreed Hartlib's friend John Pell, "is to propose to ourselves the perfectest ideas that we can imagine, then to seek the means tending thereto, as rationally as may be, and to prosecute it with indefatigable diligence; yet if the idea prove too high for us, to rest ourselves content with approximation" [John Pell, *An Idea of Mathematics,* in John Durie, *The Reformed Librarie-Keeper,* 1650].

However utopian, there was nothing "unrealistic" about such an approach; and it did not prove totally unsuccessful. The foundation of overseas colonies, the return of the Jews to England and the establishment of the Royal Society were all achievements which can be credited at least in part to the utopian impulse of the age. The tireless projecting of the Hartlib circle anticipated much of what we now take for granted: a national health service, free legal aid, universal education, public libraries, decimal coinage, a university of London. The utopian faith in the power of state planning to solve problems of health, education and poverty proved genuinely prophetic. The officials who manage the economy and oversee welfare in Robert Burton's "poetical commonwealth" prefigure the modern bureaucratic state.

What above all impresses about seventeenth-century English utopian speculation is its moral and religious seriousness. Because the forces of anti-utopian sentiment rested so heavily on the theology of original sin, it was only from within a religious context that a convincing alternative current of thought could arise. It was the millenarian belief in the imminence of a new golden world which encouraged the utopian impulse; and it was the stylized, Biblically-derived assumption that harmony and knowledge were essential features of that world which shaped the objectives of utopian activity. A truly secular utopia would have to wait for

another age.

FURTHER READING

Hertzler, Joyce Oramel. *The History of Utopian Thought.* New York: The Macmillan Company, 1923, 321 p.

In her preface, Oramel describes her book as "a study in the history of social thought . . . [that] attempts to give an hisorical cross-section of representative Utopian thought. But it is also a study in social idealism."

Kaufmann, M. *Utopias; or, Schemes of Social Improvement.* 1879. Reprint. Folcroft Library Editions, 1972, 267 p.

Examines the history of socialism and includes discussion of the leaders of Renaissance utopian thought. Aims to "present the several schemes for social improvement in the light of contemporary history, to show how far they reflect the spirit of the times, and what were the causes in the condition of the people which gave rise to the Utopian speculations they contain."

Lasky, Melvin J. *Utopia and Revolution: On the Origins of a Metaphor, or Some Illustrations of the Problem of Political Temperament and Intellectual Climate and How Ideas, Ideals, and Ideologies Have Been Historically Related.* Chicago: The University of Chicago Press, 1976, 726 p.

Includes the following chapters: "The Utopian Longing," "The Revolutionary Commitment," "The Heretic's True Cause," "Martyrs of Reason and Passion," "The Birth of a Metaphor," "The Metaphysics of Doomsday," "The Novelty of Revolution" "The Great Intelligencers," "The Politics of Paradise," and "The English Ideology."

Liljegren, S. B., ed. *Studies on the Origin and Early Tradition of English Utopian Fiction.* Uppsala: A. B. Lundequistska Bokhandeln, 1961, 151 p.

Includes the following chapters: "The Earthly Paradise and the Insulae Fortunatae," "The Geographical Discoveries," "The Narratives of Travel and of Adventure," "Panegyrics on England," "The Utopia," and "Bacon, Hartlib, and Harrington."

Masso, Gildo. Education in Utopias. New York: Teachers College, Columbia University, 1927, 201 p.

In his Foreword, the author comments: "The study that follows has four purposes:— (1) to show the place of education in utopias; (2) to present the educational views of the authors of utopias; (3) to discuss the utopian educational agencies; and (4) to determine to what extent there is any realization of utopian theories in present-day practices or any promise of such realization in the future."

Walsh, Chad. *From Utopia to Nightmare.* New York: Harper & Row, 1962, 191 p.

Examines what Walsh perceives to be "the gradual decline in our times of the utopian novel and its displacement by the 'dystopia' or 'inverted utopia'."

Johann Valentin Andreae

1586-1654

German prose writer, poet, theologian.

INTRODUCTION

An influential Lutheran theologian, a prolific writer, and a champion of the practical application of Christian principles, Johann Valentin Andreae best expressed his passion for educational and social reform in his utopian work *Christianopolis* (1619). Although influenced by Tommaso Campanella's *City of the Sun* (1602) and Sir Thomas More's *Utopia* (1516), Andreae's utopian vision is unique in its synthesis of science and Christian ideals as elements of social order. The emphasis in *Christianopolis* on the creation of an enlightened system of learning reflected Andreae's concern about the oppressive educational practices of his time, and the presentation of a city structure geared towards the orderly production of food and goods presaged modern urban planning techniques. Because the work was not translated from the Latin original until the eighteenth century, *Christianopolis* received less recognition than the works of More and Campanella. *Christianopolis*, however, was widely read by Andreae's intellectual contemporaries and is believed to have influenced Sir Francis Bacon's *New Atlantis* (1627). Modern scholars praise Andreae's prose style and consider the *Christianopolis* to be a vivid example of seventeenth century utopian philosophy.

Biographical Information

Born 17 August 1586, Andreae was descended from a tradition of influential theologians. His grandfather, Jakob Andreae, was instrumental in forming a strong Lutheran unity based on Reformation orthodox principles rather than sectarianism, and his father, Johannes Andreae, served as a pastor in the Lutheran church. Influenced by their orthodox values, Andreae would later use Lutheran principles as the basis of his ideal state in *Christianopolis*. His father's involvement in alchemy and his mother's knowledge of pharmaceuticals contributed to Andreae's fascination with alchemy and pharmacology. Upon her husband's death in 1601, Maria Andreae sought employment to support her seven children, and her distinguished work in pharmaceuticals led to a post as court apothecary. Determined to educate her sons in the tradition of Reformation Lutheran theology, she moved the family to Tub-

ingën where Johann Valentin attended university. He received an extensive classical education in literature, science, and mathematics, earning a baccalaureate in 1603 and a master of arts in 1605. Late in his universtiy career Andreae wrote his first creative works, the comedies "Hyacinthus" (1605) and "Esther" (1605). Although not published until 1616, Andreae's prose piece *Chymische Hochzeit Christiani Rosencreuz anno 1459* (*The Chemical Wedding of Christian Rosenkreutz in the year 1459*) was also written in his final year of school. Upon graduation he travelled extensively in Germany and Europe between tutoring assignments for the nobility. Particularly impressed with the strict Calvinist discipline and social order in Geneva, Andreae wrote: "While I was at Geneva, I noted something of a great moment which I will remember with nostalgia till the end of my days. Not only does this city enjoy a truly free political constitution; it has besides, as its particular ornament and means of discipline, the guidance of social life." Andreae particularly admired the moral supervision of the citizenry by the government, which he believed was the cornerstone for the apparently high level of social order in the city. Eventually Geneva would serve as a model for the vision of moral societal order expressed in the *Christianopolis*. Andreae returned to Tubingën to continue his religious studies, and in 1614 he became a deacon and began to develop friendships with leading intellectuals, several of whom were then circulating Campanella's ideas. The years 1614 through 1620 were the most prolific of Andreae's literary career. All of his important works were published during this time, including *Chymische Hochzeit*, the satirical play *Turbo* (1616), *Christiano polis*, and a volume of original poetry and translations entitled *Geistliche Kurtzweil* (1619). These works, along with several theological treatises, expressed Andreae's philosophical views on ideal societies, Christian principles, active good works, and the practice of alchemy as applied to evangelical truths. Andreae also published a series of pamphlets which, along with *Chymische Hochzeit*, are considered by some to have been the founding tracts for the Rosicrucian movement, although Andreae's role as the founder of the sect is disputed by modern scholars. In 1620 Andreae moved to Calw to take a position as chief pastor, a post he held for nineteen years. While at Calw, he practiced his philosophy of social and educational reform while speaking out against the suffering associated with the Thirty Year's War. Although he continued to publish during his years at Calw, including the philosophical work *Thephilus* (written 1623, published 1649), his output declined due to the increasing burden of his ministerial duties and harsh wartime conditions. In 1634 Bavarian and Croatian troops destroyed Calw, including Andreae's personal library of 3,000 volumes. This calamity effectively halted Andreae's literary pursuits for several years. He served in several influential posts for the rest of his career, including court chaplain in Wurttemberg and abbot of Bebenhausen. Although he continued to write, his energies during these later years were devoted to ministerial duties and the personal fulfillment of his views concerning the importance of an active Christian life. Andreae died 27 June 1654 in retirement at Stuttgart, leaving a legacy of generosity and public work that would influence the course of church history in Wurttemberg for the next two hundred years.

Major Works

Andreae's major works illustrate the application of Christian values—most importantly love and generosity—as predominant elements of order in a society. In his play *Turbo*, Andreae's protagonist becomes disillusioned with sterile, secular philosophies and turns instead to the teachings of Christ for guidance. Like many of his contemporaries, Andreae strongly believed in the promise of scientific inquiry and its benefits to society, and in *Turbo*, the propagators of "false science," particularly the alchemists, are criticized. The

marriage of science and Christian virtue was further explored in the *Chymische Hochzeit*, published anonymously that same year. Full of Christian Resurrection symbolism, the *Chymische Hochzeit* satirizes the practice of alchemy. In his best known work, the *Christianopolis*, Andreae turned from satire to the creation of a utopia that embodied his moral philosophies. Based on the strict Christian moral structure Andreae witnessed in Geneva, the citizens of Christianopolis are ruled by spiritual authority. The protagonist, Cosmoxenus Christianus, is introduced to all facets of a society in which spiritual fulfillment and intellectual activity constitute the primary goals of each individual. Scientific pursuits are the highest intellectual calling and are linked to the achievement of spiritual perfection, although intellectual activity is never separated from physical labor: scientists are also artisans, a union that reflects Andreae's belief in the practical application of learning and discovery. Educational reform objectives are outlined, with educators culled from the leading intellectuals of society and teachers and students conducting their studies in pleasant surroundings. Andreae presents the structure of his city as a series of regions devoted to different means of production, a delineation that prompted the urban planner Lewis Mumford to comment: "The separation of the city into zones, the distinction between heavy industries and light industries, the grouping of similar industrial establishments, the provision of an agricultural zone adjacent to the city—in all this our garden cities are but belated reproductions of Christianopolis . . . ." While many elements of Andreae's utopia share similarities with the utopian constructions of Campanella and More, Andreae's work is unique among utopian fiction in its emphasis on strict Christian morality and the spiritual transformation of the protagonist, who enters Christianopolis corrupted by worldly concerns and is converted to Christian idealism by the work's end. Critics have noted that the active engagement and epiphany of the main character in the work reflects Andreae's belief in the necessity of tangible action toward the achievement of social enlightenment.

Critical Reception

Modern scholars lament the circumstances which led to the *Christianopolis'* relative obscurity in the canon of utopian literature. Although widely read among intellectuals in Andreae's time, the work was not translated until the eighteenth century, well after More and Campanella became recognized as the leading utopian philosophers. Critics praise the concreteness of Andreae's utopian vision, a clarity often lacking in his contemporaries' work, and have commented on the realism that pervades the work despite its obvious allegorical conceits—a realism grounded in Andreae's practical experiences with social reform. Andreae's vivid writing style is also cited by scholars as both entertaining and concise in comparison to other Utopian writers of his time. Marie Louise Berneri has perceived *Christianopolis* as a precursor to the nineteenth century reformist utopias, pointing to the work's utilitarian language and orderly presentation of details, which contrasts with the "unreal dreams of More and Campanella." As an expression of contemporary seventeenth century intellectual thought and the exploration of spiritual fulfillment and societal goals, the *Christianopolis* is considered a vital and much neglected contribution to utopian literature.

PRINCIPAL WORKS

Collectaneorum mathematicorum decades XI (nonfiction) 1614

Vom Besten und Edelsten Beruff (poetry) 1615

Chymische Hochzeit Christiani Rosenkreutz anno 1459 [*The Chemical Wedding of Christian Rosenkreutz in the Year 1459*] (prose) 1616

Turbo (drama) 1616

Menippus Inanitatum Nostratuum Speculum (satire) 1617

**Christenburg, ein schön geistlich Gedicht* (poetry) 1619

Christianopolis (utopian fiction) 1619

Geistliche Kurtzweil (poetry) 1619

Mythologiae Christianae sive virtutum and vitiorum vitae humanae imaginum libri tres (vignettes) 1619

Theophilus (philosophy/theology) 1623

Dichtungen (poetry) 1786

Vita ab ipso conscripta (autobiography) 1799

*Published in 1649
**First published in 1836.

CRITICISM

Felix Emil Held (essay date 1916)

SOURCE: "More's *Utopia*, Campanella's *Civitas Solis*, and the *Christianopolis*," in *Christianopolis: An Ideal State of the Seventeenth Century*, translated by Felix Emil Held, Oxford University Press, 1916, pp. 16-40.

[*In the following excerpt, Held compares* Christianopolis *with other seminal Utopian works, and describes Andreae's conception of the Utopian state.*]

[The] chief differences between the works of More and Campanella as compared with Andreae, are not to

be superficially sought in [external characteristics]. . . . The plan and conception of the three seem to be essentially different.

More was closely in touch with political conditions in England and on the Continent. Political reform and his favorite principle of communism are the nucleus of his *Utopia,* and in direct connection with this principle is the problem of the source of supply for the necessities of life. Hence More makes agriculture the chief occupation, and states that while there are various trades and crafts, agriculture is known to all; and all have training therein, in school and in the fields.

The *Utopia* is written in two books, the first of which consists of a discussion carried on by three persons, as to what constitutes the best form of government, and what practices are undesirable. Two abuses are especially censured—exorbitant taxes intended to swell the coffers of wasteful monarchs, and monopoly of land and property granted to privileged classes. So there are rehearsed the various methods of collecting money from the general public—methods common in England in More's own time. And the Genoese captain is quoted as saying, "To speak my real sentiments plainly, I must freely own that as long as there is any property, and while money is the standard of all other things, I cannot think that a nation can be governed either justly or happily." This leads directly to a description of the government of Utopia, where "people are governed better than anywhere else." And at the close, as a summary of the whole, four pages are devoted to a rehearsal of the reasons for the happiness of the Utopians, the trend of which is the following: "Thus I have described to you, as particularly as I could, the constitution of that commonwealth, which is the only commonwealth deserving the name. In all other places it is noticeable that while people talk of common wealth, everyone seeks his own wealth. But in Utopia there is no unequal distribution; and though no man has anything, yet they are all rich." It is not difficult to see the chief point in More's mind.

Just what is the model for the *Civitas* is not very clear. Of the various interpretations, Gussmann agrees with Sudre when the latter says: "The monastery is the model for his (Campanella's) social organization. The priestly power and the church hierarchy are the foundation for the government of his new society. The sun-cities are groups of cloisters in which men and women live under a strict system of government" [*Reipublicae Christianopolitanae Descriptio*].

It must be admitted that parallels are not wanting. The head authority (Metaphysicus), as has been said, the judge in matters of both church and state, represents the pope, he with his three subordinate rulers appointing the rest. While political freedom and religious toleration are repeatedly mentioned, both are restricted by law and custom. Occasionally one even finds a phrase or sentence which smacks decidedly of the cloister—as when describing the common dining-room, "On one side sit the women and on the other the men; and, as in the refectories of the monks, there is no noise."

As in the *Utopia,* common ownership of property is an important feature. But carrying the point to a greater extreme, Campanella would make women part of the *"Gemeingut"* of the state. And his point of view is very clear. In the *Civitas* the individual exists for the state, not the state for its citizens. Hence, that the state may be of a high standard physically and intellectually, that it may be able to defend itself against possible attack, that therace may continue to be powerful, he has those in authority mate men and women, even as cattle are bred, considering only physical and temperamental characteristics, and thus assuring a stalwart offspring; for sexual love, as we have it between husband and wife, is not known. Should a man and a woman be inspired with a natural feeling of love, "it is permitted them to converse, joke, crown each other with wreaths and garlands, and even to write verses in one another's honor." But in general "they know in their love nothing other than feelings of friendliness."

While at the Dominican monastery of Stilo, Campanella—then about seventeen years of age—met an old rabbi to whom he felt strangely attracted. During the week they spent together, Campanella was instructed in the mysteries of the occult sciences—alchemy, astrology, and magic. Of these astrology exerts the strongest influence in the *Civitas* of Campanella. On the walls of the temple, representations of the stars are to be seen; and verses describing their size, courses, and secret influences are added. Another set of verses explains the homes of trees and plants, their chief characteristics and *their relation to the stars.* Trees are planted by the gardeners, cattle are bred by their caretakers,—even men and women are allowed to mate, only *when certain heavenly bodies are in conjunction.* Inventions and scientific discoveries are made, calamities are averted,—in fact "we do all things under the influence of the heavens." As More's *Utopia* closes with a lengthy summary, which is to a great extent an elaboration of the principles of communism, so the closing pages of the *Civitas* are a tribute to the accomplishments of astrology—beginning with an exclamation on the part of the sea-captain, "O, if you but knew what they have learned from astrology . . . !"

The question is raised by Voigt [in *Die Sozialen Utopien*] whether the **Descriptio** is to be considered at all seriously, or whether Andreae intended that it should be taken in a purely allegorical sense. In support of the latter hypothesis, Voigt quotes a fable of Andreae's in which Truth, wandering about nakedly, and complaining of ill-treatment at the hands of those whom she would like to assist, is given this advice by Aesop:

"Clothe your form in fable and fairy-tale, and you will be able to do your duty by God and man" [in **Apologorum Christianorum Manip**, VI, No. 29]. Voigt continues: "If Andreae was here thinking of his **Descriptio,** then we cannot class the latter with those utopias which were intended to represent a practical execution of an ideal; but we must rather look upon it as a mere poetic expression of his wishes."

Andreae learned early that the safest and most certain way to fix an argument and to secure the acceptance of a doctrine, is to give it a touch of poetic fancy. In commenting on this characteristic, Herder says: "All that Andreae writes takes the form of the fable—the expression in clever garb (*Einkleidung*); he speaks truths to which we hardly venture to give utterance now, after a hundred years' advancement. He speaks them with as much love and honesty, as brevity and sagacity; so that even yet he stands new and fresh in this quarreling, heretical century, and blooms in delicate fragrance like a rose among thorns [in Glöckler's *Johann Valentin Andreae: ein Lebensbild*]. We need only refer to the **Fama Fraternitatis,** the **Confessio, Die Christenburg,** or the **Chymische Hochzeit.** Is this sufficient reason for concluding that Andreae was not serious, nor hoped to outline a plan according to which a real social community and city government could exist? Or shall we think that Bacon was not in earnest with his utopia, when he called it "The *Fable* of the New Atlantis"? In explaining his purpose in the use of satire in the **Menippus,** Andreae says: "I call upon God to witness that I have not persecuted anyone, nor made sport at the expense of another, wantonly; but the cause of Christianity lay near my heart, and I desired to advance that cause by all means. As I could not do this directly, I tried a roundabout method—not, as it seemed to some, for the love of satire as many pious people do; but that I might accomplish something by means of jest and biting wit, and inspire love for Christianity" [**Vita**]. Shall we regard More less seriously because his *Utopia* is an ill-concealed satire on the conditions existing in his own country? This view would seem to be just as unwarranted as that of Mohl when he, going quite to the other extreme, accuses Andreae of a substitution of the *"prosaic* realities of an orthodox-protestant country" for Campanella's more imaginative efforts, and denies a sufficient tact and spirit (*Geist*) on Andreae's part to handle the subject [*Geschichte u. Literatur d. Staatswissenschaft*]. As a matter of fact, the two decades he spent at Calw as Dekan and Spezialsuperintendent, represented a continuous effort, in spite of the most discouraging conditions, to put into execution the ideals which he had long cherished and which he had stated in his utopia. His efforts were not successful. The Thirty Years' War sapped the life and strength of the community, but his perseverance and his renewed efforts, after each interference, to realize the very principles taught in the **Descriptio,** give evidence of the place the latter held in his own opinion. There is reason to believe that More, Campanella, and Bacon, as well as Andreae, looked upon their respective utopias as the embodiment of the teachings they desired to give to the world.

In his autobiography Andreae gives the following very interesting and suggestive description of the impression made upon him by conditions at Geneva—which city he visited on his journey of 1610. "When I was in Geneva, I made a notable discovery, the remembrance of which and longing for which will die only with my life. Not alone is there in existence an absolutely free commonwealth, but as an especial object of pride (*ornamentum*) a censorship of morals (*disciplina*) in accordance with which investigations are made each week into the morals and even into the slightest transgressions of the citizens—first by the supervisors of the wards, then by the aldermen, and finally by the magistrate, according as the case demands. As a result, all cursing, gambling, luxury, quarreling, hatred, conceit, deceit, extravagance, and the like, to say nothing of greater sins, are prevented. What a glorious adornment—such purity of morals—for the Christian religion! With out bitterest tears we must lament that this is lacking and almost entirely neglected with us; and all right-minded men must exert themselves to see that such is called back to life" [*Vita*]. One cannot help feeling that this "ideal state" of affairs—as it seemed to him—was the germ which gave incentive to his efforts of succeeding years. And there can be little doubt that his ideas of a utopia date from this time, especially as his *Descriptio* paints just such a picture of moral purity as here described.

The introduction of the *Christianopolis* is by no means its least interesting or suggestive division. Andreae sees two classes of persons in the world, one class composed of those who constantly admire and defend conditions as they exist; the other, of those who bear patiently the burdens which are heaped upon them, but who continually sigh for an improvement of society. The one in its misguided zeal keeps stirring up trouble and confusion, but accomplishes nothing; the other by sense and modesty acts as a conservative balance. Some have thought that God purposely permits the one class to be covered by mental darkness, that those who see the light from above may, when matters arrive at too evil a stage, overturn the corrupt system. And this is actually what was done by Dr. Luther, when his pleadings for reform were not heeded. In the meantime another darkness has fallen upon Christians; the success of the former reformation is not complete. There is need of another "general reformation" which shall accomplish what was missed before. The Devil is trying to persuade even Christians that no further efforts are necessary. But greed, extravagance, envy, laziness, and a whole catalogue of sins have again crept into the lives of men. Some still retain the light of the new religion, a proper conception of learning and art, of the

rules of daily life; but these are surrounded by tyrants, sophists, and hypocrites. Recently when a so-called "*Brüderschaft*" [a reference to the Rosicrucian brotherhood] was suggested, whose teachings were exactly the reform the world needs,—what a disturbance was created among those who feared the overthrow of their power, and an abolishment of their deceitful performances, juggleries, and sophistries. And when it was discovered that the "*Fraternitas*" was secret and could not include the world in general, and when people became confused as to its real meaning, then one praiseworthy man called out, "Why do we wait for the coming of such a fraternity? Let us rather make a trial ourselves of that which seems good to us." Whereupon Andreae suggests the possibility of persons forming together a community where the principles of right living and freedom may be practiced, unhampered by the enemy. "An example of this rest and safety" is to be found in the lives of the inhabitants of Christianopolis now to be described,—not merely as they ought to be, but as they actually live. No one is compelled to come to this place; but all who desire to do so, if found to be of proper character, are welcome. This invitation is repeated at the close of the work when the pilgrim returns to his native land, and at parting from the inhabitants of the island, asks permission to return and bring along his friends.

A beautiful opening chapter, which probably is partly responsible for the opinions of some, that the *Christianopolis* is a mere allegory, introduces the hero, a stranger in the realm of the authorities of tyranny, false art, and hypocrisy, as about to set out anew upon the "*Mare Academicum*" in search of enlightenment and a peaceful abode. The weather, fair and favorable at first, soon begins to darken; and the ship, "*Phantasia*," is beaten about by the storms of envy and slander, driven into the sea of darkness, and finally wrecked.

Caphar Salama is the island upon which one of the survivors of the wreck is thrown. Before he can be taken up into the city, he is subjected to a close examination by each of three officials. This is an entirely new feature in utopias, and serves among other things to give the impression of a more complete and finished production. Later utopias make use of and expand this point. The first examination is preliminary, and a satisfactory conclusion of the same is necessary before the visitor may be fed or refreshed. This is a guard against the admittance of tramps and professional beggars. The second examiner is without peer in shrewdness and ability to read character. It is his duty to obtain information regarding the stranger's family, history, manner of life, health,and so forth. He makes no pretensions toward learning, but leaves this field to the third. This examination proves to be the most embarrassing of all. The visitor, though by self-confession a scholar, finds himself irretrievably beyond his depths in the discussions of language, art, science, investigation, natural history, as also in that of charity, church, and theology. He is now given an escort of three men who accompany him upon a tour of inspection and instruct him in all matters. An examination into the facts thus obtained and an analysis of material used will help give an idea of Andreae's conception of an ideal state, and will be a second proof of the comparative lack of dependence, in essentials, upon More and Campanella.

The most important and the most oft-recurring theme in the **Christianopolis** is that of education and training of the youth, and it is this which contains most of Andreae's personality. The teaching profession is highly honored, and rightly. For instructors are not chosen from the lower classes—men who have not the ability to be useful in other lines, and who are therefore willing to teach for little pay—but they are selected on account of being remarkable for character and information. The teachers are of reasonable age, clean in life, upright, industrious, and gentlemen in every way. They are equipped with skill, shrewdness, and sense, and the ability to apply these virtues. For the citizens of Christianopolis realize that to intrust their sons and daughters to worthless or careless instruction, is to ruin the individual and the state as well. "For certain it is that no ones serves youth well except he likewise be able to care for the state; and he who proves himself of value to youth, has already benefited the state." Boys and girls are sent to the boarding school at six years of age. Parents do not hesitate to send their children from home, for they have the best possible care and attention. Education is threefold: worship of God with a pure soul, practice of a moral life, intellectual development. Boys recite in the morning, girls in the afternoon. The other half of the day is spent in mechanical occupation and household science and art. Their physical training consists of running, wrestling, riding, fencing, throwing, and the like.

Intermediate education is given in institutions of fine arts, classed as schools of grammar, rhetoric, and languages. Foreign—modern and ancient—languages are studied and learned much more rapidly than in other countries. The chief object is not so much the attainment of learning as a means of boastfulness, but the ability to hold intercourse with other peoples, "both the living and the dead." This is a chapter out of Andreae's life. With all his study of science, mathematics, and theology at Tübingen, he was deeply interested in foreign languages, ancient and modern; so that before he was out of university, he was master of seven or eight. He gives as one object of his trip through France in 1610, the chance it would give to perfect himself in French. Prys [in *Der Staatsroman*] is hardly justified in comparing the **Christianopolis** with *Civitas Solis* on the basis of lack of appreciation of the value of languages. On the contrary, in Andreae's state it is required that all pupils perfect themselves in languag-

es, as has already been seen. However, it is considered a serious mistake to neglect the mother tongue. For in this a student will express himself most naturally, and natural development of the mind and soul are especially to be desired. In rhetoric and oratory the same argument carries weight. While eloquent speakers and forceful writers are trained, *mere polish* and beauty of address are scorned.

Advanced studies are pursued in seven other auditoria or lecture halls. Dialectics, metaphysics, and theosophy may be studied in the second. The practical application of a good method is the aim of dialectics. Observation of the True, the Good, and the Beautiful, of unity and harmony, is the essence of metaphysics. Theosophy is the highest form of this group. "Where nature ends, theosophy begins; it is the last resort, the finding in God what cannot be obtained by physical experiment." And only a few, comparatively, attain this. What fools men are who try to prove through Aristotle what God alone can fathom! Here Andreae proves that he is neither a sophist nor an unreasoning believer in astrology or alchemy. His philosophy of life is suggested in a number of instances throughout this and other works: Gain all possible information by sensible and reliable experiment and investigation; but thereafter leave the impossible, and *accept* nature and God.

The third auditorium is that of mathematics. Arithmetic, algebra, geometry, surveying, and mystic numbers are important as affording good mental training and also for their practical use when applied to the experiences of everyday life. Under the term "secret and mystic numbers" are not meant the cabalistic and deceiving combinations of jugglers, but rather the proportions of higher mathematics, then but dimly understood. "Harmony," "symmetry," "measurements of calculation" are favorite terms with Andreae to suggest the divine plan of the universe. He distinctly states here and elsewhere that faith in God, and not in *superhuman* endeavor, must be the test of our efforts. "Into these matters which seem to give forth such brilliant light let us not pry, unless the light of Christ leads the way and calls us into the sealed secret."

Music is treated scientifically and artistically. This is the fourth division. A knowledge of mathematics is an essential requisite. Combination of tones—harmony— is practiced, and produces almost unbelievable results. Musical instruments are manufactured and kept on hand—all possible kinds and of the finest quality. Hardly a citizen can be found who does not play one or the other of them. The voice is not neglected. But vocal music is restricted almost entirely to sacred song. The chorus is splendid, and passes singing through the streets of the city each week.

Astronomy and astrology are the departments of the

fifth auditorium, and these are treated in close relationship to each other. It is of importance to observe the heavens and the heavenly bodies; for man is directly dependent upon them for light, heat, rain, and so forth. He would be a fool, according to Andreae, who would deny the practical use of such a science; but there is so much difference of opinion and quarreling among scientists as to the mystical effect of the planets upon human beings, that the inhabitants of Christianopolis think it safer to look toward the spiritual heavens than upon the visible, for prophetic information. One brief sentence will serve to explain. "Experience strengthens faith, but reason is ever in doubt and confusion." Andreae is here entirely consistent with his views as expressed in other writings and, though he lived in an age when the wisest were strongly affected, is singularly free from contamination with the extreme teachings of astrology and alchemy.

Natural history, secular and church history furnish the subject-matter for the teachings of the sixth lecture hall. "It is needless to tell why they are so interested in natural history, since the very necessity of the science demands it. For through it we arrive at a general, as well as a specific, exact knowledge of the world; and investigate the movements, characteristics, behavior, and passions of creatures; what are the elements, form, measure, place, and time of things; how the heavens are moved, the elements are mixed, how things grow, what metals are useful. . . ." Natural history accompanies the science of human history—the relation of the experiences of man.

Ethics, political science, and Christian humility are in the seventh auditorium. Theology, gift of prophecy, and sanctification are in the eighth. Three principles stand out in the political and public life of Christianopolis: preserving the peace, equality of citizens, and contempt for large possessions. The practice of these principles guards the state and its citizens against the three greatest evils: war, slavery, and corruption in public affairs. The school of prophecy is intended not to teach the ability to prophesy, as has deceived so many, but to observe the harmony and truth of the prophetic spirit, as well as to be able to interpret the workings of the holy spirit and recognize inspiration from above.

The library, the armory, and the college must yet be mentioned as important features of the town. The two former are in the central keep, and are opposite each other. The one is a storehouse of learning. Ancient books, lost to Europeans, are to be found here. Most of the citizens, however, care for only a few reliable books (including, of course, the Bible), and prefer to get knowledge directly from the "book of nature." The armory might better be called a museum. While cannon and guns are on hand in great numbers and ready for use in case of need, they are looked upon with

horror, and the necessity for their usefulness is considered an invention of the Devil.

"Now it were time that we should approach the very center of the city, which you might well call its soul and life, . . . Here religion, justice, and learning have their abode, and theirs is the control of the city. They have eloquence associated with them as their interpreter. Never have I seen such an amount of human perfection collected in one place, a fact which you will all acknowledge as soon as you have heard the description.

The art of painting is very highly prized. Like Campanella, Andreae has his city thoroughly fitted out with paintings. Even the private rooms of the school children are appropriately adorned. Furthermore, taking a decided step forward, Andreae causes painting to be taught to the youth as an auxiliary to his education. The pupils improve their time with the brush, as one form of recreation, while among us, time is wasted in cards, dice, and so forth. To this, architectural drawing is added, and all necessary instruments are supplied. It should be noted that in the *Civitas* of Campanella the *observation* of pictures *is* the education; and it is distinctly stated that pupils learn "as in play and without any effort on their part." This is, in the extreme, a dangerous method. Education, by means of sugar-coated and predigested capsules of knowledge, is too much the tendency in our own day. Andreae could give us a wholesome warning. His young people, it is true, use pictures for illustration, but they *make their own* illustrative material, and learn by trial and experiment.

The introduction of experimental investigation and inductive teaching in utopias, practically begins with Andreae; and this is the foundation of his chapters on science and invention. Among these are descriptions of the laboratory, the drug shop, anatomy, the theater of physics, the study of nature, and medicine.

Religion is the leaven of Caphar Salama, for its colony is a practical Christian city. There is no hypocrisy nor compulsion. The inhabitants are here by choice, and live voluntarily according to the principles of the Christian religion. Freedom, the keynote of government, is also the essence of the religious life. Religion has taken up her abode here to escape persecution. Though Andreae's worst experiences came later than 1619, persecution and the horrors of a religious war were not unknown to this time. And the name of his "place of refuge" . . . is typical of his own lifelong desire for a home of religious peace and rest.

Two plates of bronze, one giving at some length the confession of faith, and the other setting forth the aims and rules of daily life, are publicly posted—not merely that visitors may become acquainted with their creed, but that the latter may be ever before the inhabitants.

Herein they pledge themselves to a pure, temperate, and active life, subject only to the commands of Christ and His representatives. As will be naturally supposed, prayer takes an important place—at the tables, in school, and in all meetings; a fact which gives occasion for Mohl's ironical remark already referred to, namely, that Andreae merely adds "prayer meetings," and for the rest, copies Campanella directly.

With such principles of education and religion, the government and social and family life of Christianopolis will be readily understood. The officials are not feared but respected. Their offices are performed in kindness and co-operation. A direct influence of the government of Geneva (as quoted above from Andreae's *Vita*) is found in the description of the office of chief judge. This individual makes it his business, and it is also his pride, to guard against the temptations that come to the citizens, and to help them to resist the same. Lawsuits do not occur, as property rights are not involved. The jurists are teachers of political science and Roman law. They are the official scribes of the community. The senators are truly old, wise men. They study carefully the history of the past and look ahead to plan and meet emergencies.

The family is the unit of social life. Chastity is the highest virtue, and transgressions are abhorred and punished. Marriage is a sacred institution. There being no property endowment, the emphasis is laid upon character and personal worth. Moderation in the relations between husband and wife is practiced—there is such a thing as chastity even in married life. "The crown of woman is motherhood, in the discharge of which duty she takes precedence of all heroes of the world." If one compares the delicacy of Andreae's chapters relating to woman, with the almost bestial principles of the purely physical marriage in the *Civitas,* an idea of the difference in ethical tone which pervades the two works will be obtained. It is not the liberal and modern "eugenic" view of *Civitas Solis,* readjusted to the "prosaic monotony of an orthodox-protestant town," but fundamental differences in the spiritual make-up of the two men. Though nowhere as noticeable as in these chapters, yet the difference of standards and fineness of feeling are evident throughout.

If, in looking over the content of the ***Christianopolis,*** those features are selected upon which Andreae lays most stress, and which for him form the essential parts of an ideal state, and condense them into groups, the following will appear: education, science, and investigation; religion, music, and art; government and social connections. A comparison of the above headings with the emphasized factors in the *Utopia* and the *Civitas Solis,* and also the method of treatment of these items, will show, 1) that between the **Christianopolis** and the *Utopia* there is slight or partial agreement only in some matters of social laws, government, and religion, though even in these fields the differences are greater than the likenesses; 2) that the *Civitas* lays emphasis upon objective methods of teaching, failure of the Aristotelian method, scientific investigation of nature, mathematics, and the value of painting. To say, however . . . that this coincidence necessarily means a copy, is absurd. For these principles of education were a part of Andreae's system long before he saw any of Campanella's manuscript. This will be evident from an inspection of the **Fama** and the **Confessio,** which were in print respectively in 1614 and 1616, and the former of which was circulated in manuscript form as early as 1610. The introduction of the **Fama** contains this prophecy: "The blessed dawn will soon appear, which, after the passing of the gloomy night of moonshine or the scanty glimmerings of the sparks of heavenly wisdom which may still linger with men as presagers of the sunshine, will usher in the pure day, with which all heavenly treasures will become known. This will be the genuine carbuncle, of which we have learned that it will give forth light in darkness—a welcome medicine to take away all ills and anxieties of men." Otherparts of these earlier works will be used on later occassions. Besides showing Andreae's early interest in the "wisdom which should reveal all invisible things in the world-secret" (knowledge by experimental investigation), this section is also important because it shows that even in 1610 the philosopher's stone as such was for him a myth and merely symbolical of enlightenment.

In defense of the originality of the ***Descriptio*** (not considering minor likenesses in form and detail) it may then be briefly stated:

1) Andreae's notion of a utopia dates from his visit to Geneva, and his seriousness in the matter of a realization of such an ideal state is proved by his own personal efforts in the communities in which he lived.

2) The principles inculcated are not duplicated in preceding utopias—his conception of an ideal state is a new one; and the system of education as outlined, a marked improvement over all preceding, and, as far as utopias are concerned, is strictly his own.

3) In matters of science and education where the ***Christianopolis*** and the *Civitas* have important points in common, there is no proof of copying, as the same principles are found in Andreae's earlier works, especially the **Fama,** which antedates the *Civitas.*

4) As a final argument it may be said with Gussmann [***Christianopolis,*** VII, 1886]: "It would indeed speak but badly for Andreae's historical greatness, if his work, which fits so exactly into the frame of his other writings, and which is so thoroughly filled with his own peculiar soul (*Geist*), were nothing more than a dry recasting, the trivial bowdlerization (*Verballhornung*)

of the work of another."

Lewis Mumford (essay date 1922)

SOURCE: An excerpt from *The Story of Utopias,* Boni and Liveright, Inc., 1922, pp. 81-99.

[*In the following excerpt from his critical study* The Story of Utopias, *Mumford analyzes Andreae's Utopian vision in the* Christianopolis *with an emphasis on the structure of the city, industry, and society.*]

[The] man who next conducts us into Utopia is a Humanist scholar. After the manner of his time, he answers to the latinized name, Johann Valentin Andreæ. He is a traveller, a social reformer, and above all things a preacher; and so the vision he imparts to us of Christianopolis seems occasionally to flicker into blackness whilst he moralizes for us and tells us to the point of tedium what his views are concerning the life of man, and in particular the conceptions of Christianity which his countrymen, the Germans, are debating about. Sometimes, when we are on the point of coming to grips with his utopia, he will annoy us by going off on a long tirade about the wickedness of the world and the necessity for fastening one's gaze upon the life hereafter—for Protestantism seems just as other-worldly as Catholicism. It is the Humanist Andreæ rather than the Lutheran Andreæ who paints the picture of a Christian city. While Andreæ sticks to Christianopolis his insight is deep, his views are sound, and his proposals are rational; and more than once he will amaze us by putting forward ideas which seem to leap three hundred years ahead of his time and environment.

It is impossible to get rid of the personal flavor of Andreæ: his fine intelligence and his candor make our contacts with Christianopolis quite different from the dreary guidebook sketches which some of the later utopians will inflict upon us. The two other utopians who wrote in the same half century as Andreæ—Francis Bacon and Tommaso Campanella—are quite second-rate in comparison; Bacon with his positively nauseating foppishness about details in dress and his superstitious regard for forms and ceremonials, and Campanella, the lonely monk whose City of the Sun seems a marriage of Plato's Republic and the Court of Montezuma. When Bacon talks about science, he talks like a court costumer who is in the habit of describing the stage properties for a masque; and it is hard to tell whether he is more interested in the experiments performed by the scientists of the New Atlantis or the sort of clothes they wear while engaged in them. There is nothing of the snob or the dilettante about Andreæ: His eye fastens itself upon essentials, and he never leaves them except when—for he is necessarily a man of his age—he turns his gaze piously to heaven.

This teeming, struggling European world that Andreæ

turns his back upon he knows quite well; for he has lived in Herrenburg, Koenigsbrunn, Tuebingen, Strassburg, Heidelberg, Frankfurt, Geneva, Vaihingen, and Calw; and he is in correspondence with learned men abroad, in particular with Samuel Hartlib, who lives in England, and with John Amos Comenius. Like the Chancellor in Christianopolis, he longs for an "abode situated below the sky, but at the same time above the dregs of this known world." Quite simply, he finds himself wrecked on the shore of an island dominated by the city of Christianopolis. After being examined as to his ideas of life and morals, his person, and his culture, he is admitted to the community.

This island is a whole world in miniature. As in the Republic, the unit once more is the valley section, for the "island is rich in grain and pasture fields, watered with rivers and brooks, adorned with woods and vineyards, full of animals."

In outward appearance, Christianopolis does not differ very much from the pictures of the cities one finds in seventeenth century travel books, except for a unity and orderliness that these cities sometimes lack. "Its shape is a square whose side is 700 feet, well fortified with four towers and a wall. . . . It looks therefore towards the four quarters of the earth. Of buildings there are two rows, or if you count the seat of the government and the storehouses, four; there is only one public street, and only one marketplace, but this one is of a very high order." In the middle of the city there is a circular temple, a hundred feet in diameter; all the buildings are three stories; and public balconies lead to them. Provision against fire is made by building the houses of burnt stone and separating them by fireproof walls. In general, "things look much the same all around, not extravagant nor yet unclean; fresh air and ventilation are provided throughout. About four hundred citizens live here in religious faith and peace of the highest order." The whole city is divided into three parts, one to supply food, one for drill and exercise, and one for looks. The remainder of the island serves the purposes of agriculture, and for workshops.

When we look back upon the Republic, with its external organization so plainly modeled upon military Sparta, we see the camp and the soldier giving the pattern to the life of the whole community. In Utopia, the fundamental unit was the farmstead and the family; and family discipline, which arises naturally enough in rural conditions, was transferred to the city. In Christianopolis, the workshop and the worker set the lines upon which the community is developed; and whatever else this society may be, it is a "republic of workers, living in equality, desiring peace, and renouncing riches." If Utopia exhibits the communism of the family, Christianopolis presents the communism of the guild.

Industrially speaking, there are three sections in Christianopolis. One of them is devoted to agriculture and animal husbandry. Each of these departments has appropriate buildings, and directly opposite them is a rather large tower which connects them with the city buildings; under the tower a broad vaulted entrance leads into the city, and a smaller one to the individual houses. The dome of this tower roofs what we should call a guildhall, and here the citizens of the quarter come together as often as required to "act on sacred as well as civil matters." It is plain that these workers are not sheep led by wise shepherds, as in the Republic, but the members of autonomous, self-regulating groups.

The next quarter contains the mills, bake-shops, meat-shops, and factories for making whatever is done with machinery apart from fire. As Christianopolis welcomes originality in invention, there are a variety of enterprises within this domain; among them, paper manufacturing plants, saw mills, and establishments for grinding and polishing arms and tools. There are common kitchens and wash houses, too; for, as we shall see presently, life in this ideal city corresponds to what we experience today in New York, London, and many another modern industrial city.

The third quarter is given over to the metallurgical industries, as well as to those like the glass, brick, and earthenware industries which require constant fire. It is necessary to point out that in planning the industrial quarters of Christianopolis, these seventeenth century Utopians have anticipated the best practice that has been worked out today, after a century of disorderly building. The separation of the city into zones, the distinction between "heavy" industries and "light" industries, the grouping of similar industrial establishments, the provision of an agricultural zone adjacent to the city—in all this our garden cities are but belated reproductions of Christianopolis.

Moreover, in Christianopolis, there is a conscious application of science to industrial processes; one might almost say that these artisans believed in efficiency engineering; for "here in truth you see a testing of nature herself. The men are not driven to a work with which they are unfamiliar, like pack-animals to their task, but they have been trained before in an accurate knowledge of scientific matters," on the theory that "unless you analyze matter by experiment, unless you improve the deficiencies of knowledge by more capable instruments, you are worthless." The dependence of industrial improvement upon deliberate scientific research may be a new discovery for the practical man, but it is an old story in Utopia.

What is the character of this artisan democracy? The answer to this is summed up in one of those sayings that Andreæ, in the midst of his energetic exposition, drops by the way.

"To be wise and to work are not incompatible, if there is moderation."

So it follows that "their artisans are almost entirely educated men. For that which other people think is the proper characteristic of a few (and yet if you consider the stuffing of inexperience by learning, the characteristic of too many already) this, the inhabitants argue, should be attained by all individuals. They say that neither the substance of letters is such, nor yet the difficulty of work, that one man, if given enough time, cannot master both."

"Their work, or as they prefer to hear it called, 'the employment of their hands,' is conducted in a certain prescribed way, and all things are brought into a public booth. From here every workman receives out of the stock on hand whatever is necessary for the work of the coming week. For the whole city is, as it were, one single workshop, but of all different sorts and crafts. The ones in charge of these duties are stationed in the small towers at the corners of the wall; they know ahead of time what is to be made, in what quantity, and of what form, and they inform the mechanics of these items. If the supply of material in the work booth is sufficient, the workmen are permitted to indulge and give free play to their inventive genius. No one has any money, nor is there any use for any private money; yet the republic has its own treasury. And in this respect the inhabitants are especially blessed, because no one can be superior to the other in the amount of riches owned, since the advantage is rather one of power and genius, and the highest respect that of morals and piety. They have very few working hours, yet no less is accomplished than in other places, as it is considered disgraceful by all that one should take more rest and leisure time than is allowed."

In addition to the special trades, there are "public duties to which all citizens have obligation, such as watching, guarding, harvesting of grain and wine, working roads, erecting buildings, draining ground; also certain duties of assisting in the factories which are imposed upon all in turn according to age and sex, but not very often nor for a long time. For even though certain experienced men are put in charge of all the duties, yet when men are asked for, no one refuses the state his services and strength. For what we are in our homes, they are in their city, which they not undeservedly think a home. And for this reason it is no disgrace to perform any public function. . . . Hence all work, even that which is considered rather irksome, is accomplished in good time, and without much difficulty, since the promptness of the great number of workmen permits them easily to collect or distribute the great mass of things."

In this Christianopolis, as Mr. Bertrand Russell would put it, the creative rather than the possessive impulses are uppermost. Work is the main condition of existence, and this good community faces it. It is a pretty contrast to the attitude of the leisured classes who, as Andreæ says, with an entirely mistaken sense of delicacy shrink from touching earth, water, stones, coal, and things of that sort, but think it grand to have in their possession to delight them "horses, dogs, harlots and other similar creatures."

The place of commerce in this scheme of life is simple. It does not exist for the sake of individual gain. Hence no one engages in commerce on his own hook, for such matters are put in the hands of "those selected to attend to them," and the aim of commerce is not to gain money but to increase the variety of things at the disposal of the local community; so that—and again Andreæ steps in for emphasis—"we may see the peculiar production of each land, and so communicate with each other that we may seem to have the advantages of the universe in one place, as it were."

The constitution of the family in Christianopolis follows pretty definitely upon the lines dictated by urban occupations; for Andreæ is a city man, and since he does not despise the advantages city life can give, he does not shrink from their consequences. One of these consequences is, surely, the restriction of domesticity, or rather, the projection in the city at large of the functions that in a farmstead would be carried on within the bosom of the family.

When a lad is twenty-four and a lass is eighteen, they are permitted to marry, with the benefit of Christian rites and services, and a decorous avoidance of drunkenness and gluttony after the ceremony. Marriage is a simple matter. There are no dowries to consider, no professional anxieties to face, no housing shortage to keep one from finding a home, and above all, perhaps, no landlord to propitiate with money, since all houses are owned by the city and are granted and assigned to individuals for their use. Virtue and beauty are the only qualities that govern a marriage in Christianopolis. Furniture is provided with the house out of the public store. If in Utopia the families are grouped together in a patriarchal household, such as More himself maintained at Chelsea, in Christianopolis they consist of isolated couples, four, at most six people in all, a woman, a man, and such children as are not yet of school age.

Let us visit a young couple in Christianopolis. We reach the house by way of a street, twenty feet broad, faced by houses with a wide frontage on the street, some forty feet in length, and of from fifteen to twenty-five feet in depth. In our crowded towns, today, where people pay for land by the front foot, the frontage is narrow and the houses are deep; and as a result there is a dreadful insufficiency of light and air; but in Christianopolis, as in some of the older European towns,

the houses are built to get a maximum of air and sunlight. If it is raining when we make our visit, a covered walk, five feet wide, supported by columns twelve feet high, will shelter us from the rain.

Our friends live, we shall say, in one of the average apartments; so they have three rooms, a bathroom, a sleeping apartment, and a kitchen. "The middle part within the tower has a little open space with a wide window, where wood and the heavier things are raised aloft by pulleys"—in short, a dumbwaiter. Looking out from the window in the rear, we face a well-kept garden; and if our host is inclined to give us wine, he may let us take our pick from among the cobwebs of a small private cellar in the basement, where such things are kept. If it is a cold day, the furnace is going; or if we happen to make our visit in the summer time, the awnings are drawn.

Our host makes apologies, perhaps, for a litter of wood and shavings that occupies a corner of the kitchen, for he has just been putting up a few shelves in his spare time, and has borrowed a kit of tools from the public supply house. (Since he is not a carpenter, he has no need for these tools the rest of the year; and other people can have their turn at them.) Coming from Utopia, one of the things that strikes us is the absence of domestic attendance; and when we ask our hostess about it, she tells us that she will not have anyone to wait upon her until she is confined.

"But isn't there a lot of work for you to do all by yourself?" we shall ask.

"Not for anybody with a college training," she will answer. "You see that our furnishings are quite simple; and since there are no gimcracks to be dusted, no polished tables to be oiled, no carpets to be swept, and nothing in our apartment that is just for show to prove that we can afford to live better than our neighbors, the work is scarcely more than enough to keep one in good health and temper. Of course, cooking meals is always something of a nuisance; and washing up is worse. But my husband and I share the work together, in everything but sewing and washing clothes, and you would be surprised how quickly everything gets done. Work is usually galling when somebody else is taking his ease while one is doing it; but where husband and wife share alike, as in Christianopolis, there is really nothing to it. If you'll stay to dinner, you'll find out how easily it goes. Since you haven't brought your rations, my husband will get some cooked meats in the public kitchen, and that will do for all of us."

"No one need be surprised at the rather cramped quarters," Andreæ hastens to interject. "People who house vanity . . . can never live spaciously enough. They burden others and are burdened themselves, and no one measures their necessities, nay even their comforts, easily otherwise than by an unbearable and un-movable mass. Oh, only those persons are rich who have all of which they have real need, who admit nothing else, merely because it is possible to have it in abundance."

Carried to its extreme, you will find this philosophy put once for all in Thoreau's Walden. We have got our bearings in Utopia, I believe, when we have deter-mined what a life abundant consists of, and what will suffice for it.

Suppose that our friends have children. During the early years of their life they are in the care of their mother. When they have completed their sixth year, the chil-dren are given over to the care of the community, and both sexes continue in school through the stages of childhood, youth, and early maturity. "No parent gives closer or more careful attention to his children than is given here, for the most upright preceptors, men as well as women, are placed over them. Moreover," the parents "can visit their children, even unseen by them, as often as they have leisure. As this is an institution for the public good, it is managed agreeably as a com-mon charge for all the citizens. They see to it that the food is appetizing and whole some, that the couches and beds are clean and comfortable, and that the clothes and attire of the whole body are clean. . . . If diseases of the skin or body are contracted, the individuals are cared for in good time; and to avoid the spreading of infection, they are quarantined."

There is scarcely need to examine the program of study except in its broad outlines. It is enough to observe that "the young men have their study period in the morning, the girls in the afternoon, and matrons as well as learned men are their instructors. . . . The rest of their time is devoted to manual training and domes-tic art and science, as each one's occupation is as-signed to his natural inclination. When they have va-cant time they are permitted to engage in honorable physical exercises either in the open spaces of the town or in the field."

Two points, however, deserve our attention. The first is that the school is run as a miniature republic. The second is the calibre of the instructors. "The instruc-tors," says our zealous humanist, "are not men from the dregs of human society nor such as are useless for other occupations, but the choice of all the citizens, persons whose standing in the Republic is known and who very often have access to the highest positions of the state." . . .

It remains to record the further stages of learning. The halls of the central citadel are divided into twelve departments, and except for the armory, the archives, the printing establishment, and the treasury, these halls are devoted entirely to the arts and sciences.

There is, to begin with, a laboratory of physical sci-ence. "Here the properties of metals, minerals, and vegetables, and even the life of animals, are examined, purified, increased, and united for the use of the hu-man race and in the interests of health. . . . Here men learn to regulate fire, make use of air, value the water, and test the earth."

Next to this laboratory is a Drug Supply House, where a pharmacy is scientifically developed, for the curing of physical disease, and adjoining this is a school of medicine, or as Andreæ reports, "a place given over to anatomy. . . . The value of ascertaining the location of the organs and of assisting the struggles of nature no one would deny, unless he be as ignorant of himself as are the barbarians. . . . The inhabitants of Christian-opolis teach their youth the operations of life and the various organs, from the parts of the physical body."

We come now then to a Natural Science laboratory which is in effect a Museum of Natural History, an institution founded in Utopia a century and a half before a partial and inadequate substitute—a mere extension of the curio chamber of a Country House—waspre-sented to an admiring world as the British Museum. "This," as Andreæ says, "cannot be too elegantly de-scribed," and I heartily agree with him; for he paints the picture of a museum which the American Museum at New York or South Kensington in London has only begun to realize within the last decade or two of their existence.

"Natural history is here seen painted on the walls in detail, and with greatest skill. The phenomena of the sky, views of the earth in different regions, the differ-ent races of men, representations of animals, the forms of growing things, classes of stones and gems, are not only on hand and named, but they even teach and make known their nature and qualities. . . . Truly is not recognition of things of the earth much easier of com-petent demonstration if illustrative materials are at hand and if there is some guide to the memory? For instruc-tion enters altogether more easily through the eyes than through the ears, and much more pleasantly in the presence of refinement than among the base. They are deceived who think it is impossible to teach except in dark caves and with a gloomy brow. A liberal minded man is never so keen as when he has his instructors on confidential terms."

Going farther, we find a mathematics laboratory and a department of mathematical instruments. The first is "remarkable for its diagrams of the heavens, as the hall of physics for its diagrams of the earth. . . . A chart of the star-studded heavens and a reproduction of the whole shining host above were shown," . . . and also "different illustrations representing tools and ma-chines, small models, figures of geometry; instruments of the mechanical arts, drawn, named, and explained."

I cannot help expressing my admiration here for the concrete imagination of this remarkable scholar: he deliberately anticipated, not in the vague, allegorical form that Bacon does, but as lucidly as an architect or a museum curator, the sort of institute which South Kensington, with its Departments of Physical and Natural Science, or perhaps the Smithsonian in America, has just begun to resemble. If our museums had begun with the ideal Andreæ had in mind, instead of with the miscellaneous rubbish which was the nucleus of their collections—and still remains the nucleus in many of the less advanced institutions—the presentation of the sciences would be a more adequate thing than it is.

Does Andreæ leave the fine arts out of his picture? By no means. "Opposite the pharmacy is a very roomy shop for pictorial art, an art in which the city takes the greatest delight. For the city, besides being decorated all over with pictures representing thevarious phases of the earth, makes use of them especially in the instruction of youth and for rendering learning more easy. . . . Besides, pictures and statutes of famous men are to be seen everywhere, an incentive of no mean value to the young for striving to imitate their virtue. . . . At the same time also, the beauty of forms is so pleasing to them that they embrace with a whole heart the inner beauty of virtue itself."

At the summit of art and science we naturally find in Christianopolis the temple of religion. Alas! the hand of Calvin has been busy in Christianopolis—recollect that Andreæ once lived in Geneva and admired its ordinances—and attendance at prayers is compulsory. In order to get an idea of this great circular temple, three hundred sixteen feet in circumference and seventy feet high, we must think of a colossal moving picture theater in a modern metropolis. The comparison is not essentially sacrilegious; and I believe that those who will take the trouble to look below the surface will find without difficulty the common denominator between the profane and the ecclesiastical institution. (Attendance at motion pictures, I must quickly add for the benefit of the future historian, has not yet been made compulsory in the modern metropolis.)

One-half of the temple is where the public gatherings take place; and the other is reserved for the distribution of the sacraments and for music. "At the same time, the sacred comedies, by which they set so much store, and are entertained every three months, are shown in the temple."

We have discussed folk, work, and place in Christianopolis; and we have dealt in an admittedly sketchy fashion with culture and art. We must now turn attention to the polity; and here we must note that Andreæ's description shifts for once to an allegorical plane, and departs not a little from the realism of his treatment of science and the arts.

At the bottom of the polity there are glimpses of a local industrial association, meeting in the common halls that are provided in the towers of each of the industrial quarters; and we gather that to represent the city at large twenty-four councilmen are chosen, while as the executive department there is a triumvirate consisting of a Minister, a Judge, and a Director of Learning, each of whom is married, for metaphorical point, to Conscience, Understanding, and Truth, respectively. "Each one of the leaders does his own duty, yet not without the knowledge of others; all consult together in matters that concern the safety of the state."

In the censorship of books, Christianopolis reminds us of the Republic; in the exclusion of lawyers it calls up nearly every other utopia; and in its attitude towards crime it has a temperance and leniency that is all its own, for "the judges of this Christian city observe this custom especially, that they punish most severely those misdeeds which are directed straight against God, less severely those which injure men, and lightest of all those who harm only property. As the Christian citizens are always chary of spilling blood, they do not willingly agree upon the death sentence as a form of punishment. . . . For anyone can destroy a man but only the best can reform."

How shall we sum up this government? Let Andreæ speak his own words; for he has reached the innermost shrine of Christianopolis and perceives the center of activity in the state.

"Here religion, justice, and learning have their abode, and theirs is the control of the city . . . I often wonder what people mean who separate and disjoint their best powers, the joining of which might render them blessed as far as may be on earth. There are those who would be considered religious, who throw off all things human; there are some who are pleased to rule, though without any religion at all; learning makes a great noise, flattering now this one, now that, yet applauding itself most. What finally may the tongue do except provoke God, confuse men, and destroy itself? So there would seem to be a need of co-operation which only Christianity can give—Christianity which conciliates God with men and unites men together, so that they have pious thoughts, do good deeds, know the truth, and finally die happily to live eternally."

There are some who might object to this statement on the ground that it smacked too heartily of supernatural religion; but it remains just as valid if we translate it into terms whose theological reactions have been neutralized. To have a sense of values, to know the world in which they are set, and to be able to distribute them—this is our modern version of Andreæ's conception of religion, learning, and justice. A little search might uncover another expression of the Humanist ideal as complete and magnificent as this; but I doubt if it would find a better one. In essence, this blunt and forthright German scholar is standing shoulder to shoulder with Plato: his Christianopolis is as enduring as the best nature of men.

Marie Louise Berneri (essay date 1950)

SOURCE: "Valentin Andreae: *Christianopolis*," in *Journey Through Utopia*, 1950. Reprint by The Beacon Press, 1951, pp. 103-26.

[*In the following essay, Berneri provides an overview of the main characteristics of Andreae's* Christianopolis, *with a focus on the areas of work, education, and marriage.*]

Andreae's **Christianopolis** was published in 1619, only seventeen years after Campanella wrote his *City of the Sun,* yet it bears a much closer resemblance to the reformist utopias of the 19th century than to that of the Calabrian monk. Johann Valentin Andreae, the German scholar and humanist, has much in common with the cotton manufacturer and great reformer, Robert Owen, and it is perhaps for this reason that his ideal city seems more familiar than the unreal dreams of More and Campanella. Andreae does not write with the imagination and originality of a visionary; he discusses questions which he must have known intimately and for which he offers immediate solutions. And like most reformers he is not exempt from proselytism. His book is written in the form of a letter addressed to those who would wish to take refuge in his ideal city, and reads more like a recruiting tract than a story meant purely for edification or amusement.

Andreae was born in 1586; an extensive education and wide travels made him thoroughly acquainted with the thought and writings of the Renaissance. The revolution in knowledge had been accomplished; the Aristotelian method was vanquished but the task of replacing it by a new method of education was still to be completed. Andreae devoted most of his life to this work, and already, when he was at the University, he planned a reform of the educational system, and later published several pedagogical works which were received with great interest. As a teacher he was able to put some of his ideas into practice and produced the first plan for a well-regulated gymnasium.

His interests, however, spread outside education, to more general schemes of social reform, which again he tried to put into practice. Professor [Felix Emil] Held, whose translation of **Christianopolis** is prefaced by a very interesting study of Andreae's work and influence, tells us how, when Andreae became Dekan and Spezialsuperintendent at Calw on the Nagold, he tried to establish a social system such as he had described in **Christianopolis**: "He made his own congregation the starting point of his activities, and the children his material. Thence his efforts spread to the working classes in the city, whether in his church or not. He founded a mutual protective association among the workmen in the cloth-factories and dye-works, and supported it from voluntary subscriptions of his parishioners and friends."

It is probably thanks to Andreae's direct experience in social reforms that his utopia has a concreteness that is absent from those which inspired him. His scheme of education, carefully described in **Christianopolis,** had a great influence on Comenius, who acknowledged himself a pupil of Andreae, and on English writers such as Hartlib, Drury, Milton and others, who were similarly interested in educational reform. He also influenced Samuel Gott, whose utopia, *Nova Solyma,* closely resembles Andreae's. The book did not, however, achieve the fame of More's or Campanella's works; a German translation did not appear until 1741 and it was not translated into English until 1916. Little did Robert Boyle who, in a letter to Samuel Hartlib written in 1647, expressed the wish that an English version might be made of **Christianopolis,** suspect that it would only appear three hundred years later, and in New York.

The neglect of this work might be attributed partly to the troubled times in which it appeared and partly to its style, but a further contributory cause may well have been the accusation of some writers that it was merely a copy of More's *Utopia* and Campanella's *City of the Sun.* Andreae was acquainted with both works, and his ideal city bears many resemblances to that of Campanella. But these are mostly superficial, and his scheme of education, which occupies the greater part of the book, is entirely original. Contrary to the previous utopias, the influence of Greek writers hardly makes itself felt in Andreae. On the other hand, the influence of the mediaeval city is very strong. The conception of brotherhood, the respect for Craftsmanship, the attitude towards work and trade, the importance given to the craft and the family, all remind us of the guilds which had been so flourishing in the German towns of the Middle Ages.

There is also a completely new influence in Andreae's ideal commonwealth, that of the city of Geneva, which he had visited during his youth and which had made a very strong impression on him. He had been filled with admiration by the high moral standard of the Genevan people and he says, in his autobiography: "If differences in religion had not restrained me, the harmonious unity of their customs and morals would have bound me to the place for ever."

Andreae did not subscribe to the teachings of Calvin

but wholeheartedly supported the severity of morals he had introduced in Geneva, and he would have liked to see a new reformation in the Lutheran Church carried out in the spirit of Iron Calvin. Another passage from his *Vita* showed how much he owed to his visit to Geneva:

"When I was in Geneva, I made a notable discovery, the remembrance of which and longing for which will die only with my life. Not alone is there in existence an absolutely free commonwealth, but as an object of pride a censorship of morals in accordance with which investigations are made each week into the morals and even into the slightest transgressions of the citizens— first by the supervisors of the wards, then by the aldermen, and finally by the magistrate, according as the case demands. As a result, all cursing, gambling, luxury, quarrelling, hatred, conceit, deceit, extravagance, and the like, to say nothing of greater sins, are prevented. What a glorious adornment—such purity of morals, for the Christian religion! With our bitterest tears we must lament that this is lacking and almost entirely neglected with us; and all right-minded men must exert themselves to see that such is called back to life."

We shall see later how another Utopian, the unfrocked monk, Gabriel de Foigny, was to fare in the city which aroused such admiration in Andreae. This "free commonwealth," in which "investigations are made each week into the morals of the citizens," must have already been somewhat bleak at the time of Andreae's visit. The means by which "purity of morals" was achieved in Geneva give us an idea of what Andreae's utopia might have been like, had it not remained in the imagination of its author. In 1562, an historian tells us, twelve men were burnt alive for witchcraft, a woman was drowned in the Rhone for having committed adultery, and a bourgeois of Geneva was condemned to death for the same offence. A certain Jacques Chapellaz, who confessed that he had cursed God and said that he had eaten the devil but could not swallow his horns, and who had already been punished for a previous similar offence, was condemned to have his tongue cut out.

If the spirit of the Renaissance makes itself strongly felt in Andreae's views concerning education, it is the mentality of the religious reformers which guides his moral outlook. The freedom of the inhabitants of Christianopolis, like that of the inhabitants of Geneva, does not include the right to ignore God. Calvin's ordinances of the year 1609 and 1617 made it compulsory for all inhabitants of Geneva to attend sermons regularly and we find the same compulsion in Andreae's ideal city. The censorship of books is also there, as well as the house inspectors; adultery is severely punished; and though the German reformer has some very humane things to say about the death penalty and the

wickedness of men who punish rather than reform, his statement that crimes against God are to be punished more severely than any other has an ominous sound.

One would feel more attracted to *Christianopolis* if Andreae's religious principles had allowed him more understanding for human feelings, and if man's nature were allowed to express itself without being suspected of falling, at every moment, into the snares of Satan. But we are reminded at every other line of the wickedness of man. "Everyone," Andreae warns us, "carries with him domestic, rustic, or even paternal and inborn evil and wickedness, and communicates these to his comrades, with so poisonous a contagion that it spares not even those who ought to be consecrated entirely to God, but winds its way with varying wickedness, deceit, and rudeness, and takes possession of them so entirely that they cannot throw it off throughout their whole lives, and among the most honourable offices. . . ."

In order to keep Satan away Andreae accompanies his descriptions of the manners and customs of the inhabitants of Christianopolis with long sermons, of which one can truly say that "to have read one is to have read them all." There are few subjects which do not provide him with an opportunity to preach and in his godly city even dishes are seasoned with pious thoughts. These exhortations take so much space in the book that one may be forgiven for quoting one of them on Andreae's favourite theme of "light." Street lighting offers him an admirable excuse and, after stating very briefly that the inhabitants of Christianopolis "do not allow the night to be dark, but brighten it up with lighted lanterns, the object being to provide for the safety of the city and to put a stop to useless wandering about, but also to render the night watches less unpleasant," he continues with this long tirade on the symbolic significance of light:

They would strive in this way to resist the dark kingdom of Satan and his questionable pastimes; and they wish to remind themselves of the everlasting light. What Antichrist expects from the great number of wax candles, let him see for himself; but let us not shrink back from any system which lessens the fear of a man working at night in the darkness, and which removes the veil which our flesh is so anxious to draw over license and dissoluteness . . . Oh, if we would but turn more to light, there would not be such an opportunity for every sort of meanness, nor such great number of swindlers! Would that the light of our hearts were burning more frequently, and that we would not so often endeavour to deceive the all-seeing eye of God! Now that the darkness serves as excuse for the world and opens it for all sorts of baseness, while it spreads blindness over those things of which it is ashamed, what will be the situation when at the return of Christ, the Sun, every fog will be dispelled and the World's corruptness which it guards with so many covers, shall appear, when the wantonness of the heart, the hypocrisy of the lips, the deceitful deeds of the hands and its much other filth shall be a disgrace to itself and a mockery to the blessed?

The whole personality of Andreae seems to be expressed in this passage. His goodness and consideration for his fellow men, as well as his practical sense, asked that the city should be lighted to provide for safety and to render night watches less tiresome, but his moral and religious feelings made him go beyond these practical considerations. Throughout his utopia one feels that his love of men inclined him to trust them as sensible beings capable of going about their lives in a reliable and honest way, but his religion told him that man is wicked and has to be carefully guided, preached to and, if necessary, threatened, to be kept away from sin. That is why his ideal city is a curious combination of free guilds and religious tyranny, of personal responsibility and of complete submission to religion.

It would be perhaps more exact to describe **Christianopolis** as an ideal community than as an ideal commonwealth. Though the island on which it is situated is described as a world in miniature and the city contains all the elements of a state, Andreae did not conceive it as being inhabited by people who happened to be there but by those who have come together, through a community of ideals and principles. It appears, from Andreae's introduction to **Christianopolis**, that he had attempted to form a secret society for the purpose of carrying out the religious reform which stood so near to his heart. This *Brüderschaft* (generally described as a Rosicrucian brotherhood) was intended for a small élite and did not answer the desire of the people who wanted to find a haven of rest and safety in the midst of the horrors and confusion of the times. It was to fulfil their wish that the greater community of Christianopolis was described.

Whether this Rosicrucian brotherhood was purely a mythical organisation and whether we must believe Andreae's reasons for presenting the plan of an ideal city are matters for speculation. If we accept Andreae literally, **Christianopolis** was meant as a pattern for a community which could come into existence as soon as a sufficient number of people have gathered together for this purpose. This is how, two centuries later, Owen and Fourier were to conceive the formation of their ideal communities. Yet Andreae begins his narrative with a purely allegorical chapter which has led many to believe that his book was only a fable. Here is the passage, which does not lack poetical beauty:

> While wandering as a stranger on the earth, suffering much in patience from tyranny, sophistry and hypocrisy, seeking a man, and not finding what I so anxiously sought, I decided to launch out once more

upon the Academic Sea though the latter had very often been hurtful to me. And so ascending the good ship, Phantasy, I left the port together with many others and exposed my life and person to the thousand dangers that go with desire for knowledge. For a short space of time conditions favoured our voyage; then adverse storms of envy and calumny stirred up the Ethiopian Sea against us and removed all hope of calm weather. The efforts of the skipper and the oarsmen were exerted to the limit, our own stubborn love of life would not give up, and even the vessel resisted the rocks; but the force of the sea always proved stronger. Finally when all hope was lost and we, rather of necessity than on account of bravery of soul, had prepared to die, the ship collapsed and we sank. Some were swallowed up by the sea, some were scattered to great distances, while some who could swim or who found planks to float upon, were carried to different islands scattered throughout this sea. Very few escaped death, and I alone, without a single comrade, was at length driven to a very minute islet, a mere piece of turf, it seemed.

The traveller lands on the island, Caphar Salama, which was "rich in grain and pasture fields, watered with rivers and brooks, adorned with woods and vineyards, full of animals, just as if it were a whole world in miniature."

Before being admitted into the city the traveller is interrogated by three examiners. Andreae is the first to make the entrance to his utopia dependent on an examination, and we can be grateful that immigration officers nowadays are not as thorough as those of Christianopolis. The first examiner satisfies himself that the traveller is not a quack, or a beggar, or a stage player. The second investigates his moral character and temperament, and the third wants to know, amongst other things, what progress he has made "in the observation of the heavens and the earth, in the close examination of nature, in instruments of the arts, in the history and origin of languages, the harmony of all the world . . ." The traveller is not very well prepared for answering these questions, but as he brings "an unsullied slate, washed clean, as it were, by the sea itself," he is admitted into the city.

The city is small but compact, and built as a unit in which each section serves a specific function. It betrays that love of perfect symmetry which characterises the architecture of the Renaissance:

> Its shape is a square, whose side is seven hundred feet, well fortified with four towers and a wall. It looks, therefore, toward the four quarters of the earth. . . . Of buildings there are two rows, or if you count the seat of government and the store-storehouses, four; there is only one public street, and only one market-place, but this one is of a very high order. If you measure the buildings, you will find from the innermost street, being twenty feet in

width, the numbers increase by fives even up to one hundred. At this point there is a circular temple, a hundred feet in diameter. . . . All buildings are in three stories, and public balconies lead to these . . . All buildings are made of burnt stone and are separated by fireproof walls so that a fire could not do very severe damage . . . Things look much the same all around, not extravagant nor yet unclean; fresh air and ventilation are provided throughout. About four hundred citizens live here in religious faith and peace of the highest order. Outside the walls is a moat stocked with fish, that even in times of peace it may have its uses. The open and otherwise unused spaces contain wild animals, kept, however, not for purposes of entertainment but for practical use. The whole city is divided into three parts, one to supply food, one for drill and exercise, and one for books. The remainder of the island serves purposes of agriculture and for workshops.

The organisation of Christianopolis is not based on the patriarchal family as in Amaurot, or on the monastic community as in the City of the Sun. The city is divided into sections according to the work carried out in each of them. On the periphery we find those devoted to the production and storing of food, as well as that for heavy industry. The section of the corporation which faces east is the farm quarter; it is divided into two parts, agriculture proper on the one side, and animal husbandry on the other. The section which faces south is occupied by mills and bakeries, that which faces north by the meat shops and supply stores, and finally, the section on the west is given over to the forge.

Inside the city craftsmen are also divided into four sections: "For even as the city is four-cornered, so also the inhabitants deal with four materials: metals, stones, woods and the things that are needed for weaving; but with this difference, that the occupations which require more skill and innate ability are assigned to the inner square, while those which admit of more ease in working, to the outer or greater square."

This functional town-planning is being followed by our modern architects and has aroused the admiration of an authority on cities, Lewis Mumford: ". . . In planning the industrial quarters of Christianopolis, these seventeenth century Utopians have anticipated the best practice that has been worked out to-day, after a century of disorderly building. The separation of the city into zones, the distinction between heavy industries and light industries, the grouping of similar industrial establishments, the provision of an agricultural zone adjacent to the city, in all this our garden cities are but belated reproductions of Christianopolis."

For all its modernism, however, Christianopolis is based, to a certain extent, on the mediaeval city which Kropotkin describes as being "usually divided into four quarters, or into five to seven sections radiating from the centre; each quarter corresponding to a certain trade or profession which prevailed in it, but nevertheless containing inhabitants of different social positions and occupations."

The local administration of the city is based on this division according to occupation. In the east section, that is the farm quarter, a tower dominates the buildings and under the dome of this tower "the citizens of that side of the town may come together, as often as the ordinances require, and act on sacred as well as on civil matters." Thus we see that the "guild" is based on the work performed and on the place where the worker lives.

The government is carried out by a triumvirate because, "though a monarchy has many advantages yet they prefer to preserve this dignity for Christ, and they distrust, not without cause, the self-control of human beings." The central part of the state is governed by eight men, each of whom lives in one of the larger towers and has under him eight other subordinates, distributed through the smaller towers. There are a further twenty-four councillors elected by the citizens. The members of the triumvirate, the officials and the councillors, owe their position not to their birth or wealth but to their higher virtues, their experience in public affairs, and the love and respect they inspire. The state is ruled by religion, and a double tablet, inscribed in letters of gold, sets down their confession of faith and the aims and rules of daily life, for these are "a people of Christ, whose religion agrees with that of the apostles and the state administration with the law of God."

In this Christian Republic there is no private property. Everyone receives whatever he needs from the community: "No one has any money, nor is there any use for any private money; yet the republic has its own treasury. And in this respect the inhabitants are especially blessed because no one can be superior to the other in the amount of riches owned, since the advantage is rather one of power and genius, and the highest respect, that of morals and piety."

Work occupies an honoured place in Christianopolis, and though Andreae echoes Campanella in abolishing slavery and condemning the injustice that working people should support idlers, he goes further by showing how even unpleasant work can cease to be a burden if it is carried out in an atmosphere of equality and freedom:

> They have very few working hours, yet no less is accomplished than in other places as it is considered disgraceful by all that one should take more rest and leisure time than is allowed. Since in other places it is true that ten working men with difficulty support one idler, it will not be difficult to believe

that with all these men working there is some time of leisure left for individuals. And yet they all together attend to their labours in such a way that they seem to benefit rather than harm their physical bodies. Where there is no slavery, there is nothing irksome in the human body which weighs down or weakens.

And elsewhere he attacks the prejudice attached to manual labour:

There are also public duties, to which all citizens have obligation, such as watching, guarding, harvesting of grain and wine, working roads, erecting buildings, draining ground, also certain duties of assisting in the factories, which are imposed on all in turn according to age and sex, but not very often nor for a long time. For even though certain experienced men are put in charge of all the duties, yet when men are asked for, no one refuses the state his services and strength. For what we are in our homes, they are in their city, which they not undeservedly think a home. And for this reason it is no disgrace to perform any public function, so long as it be not indecent. Hence all work, even that which seems rather irksome, is accomplished in good time and without much difficulty, since the promptness of the great number of workmen permits them easily to collect or distribute the greatest mass of things. Who does not believe, since we are willing, all of us, to rejoice in and enjoy privileges and conveniences of a community, that the care and the work are ordinarily imposed upon a few, while continual idleness and gluttony are made permissible to the many? On the contrary, who denies that every citizen, in his own place and order, owes his best efforts to the republic, not merely with his tongue but also with hands and shoulder? With an entirely mistaken sense of delicacy do the carnal-minded shrink from touching earth, water, stones, coal and things of that sort; but they think it grand to have in their possession to delight them, horses, dogs, harlots and similar creatures.

While More thought that some trades had a degrading effect on those who carried them out, Andreae says that in Christianopolis: "Men that have to do the heavy work do not become wild and rough, but remain kindly, the guards are not gluttons, but are temperate, not evil-smelling but cleanly washed . . . A district on the north is devoted to the slaughter houses . . . this part has no suggestion of the bestial about it. And yet in other places men become coarse from the daily custom of shedding blood, or the handling of meats, fats, hides, and the like."

He also shows that work is not a penance if it is accompanied by sufficient leisure: "While among us one is worn out by the fatigue of an effort, with them the powers are reinforced by a perfect balance of work and leisure so that they never approach a piece of work

without alacrity."

Unlike Plato, he does not think that manual and intellectual work should be separated, but rather that each individual should engage in both:

. . . their artisans are almost entirely educated men. For that which other people think is the proper characteristic of a few (and yet, if you consider the stuffing of inexperience as learning, the characteristic of too many men already) this the inhabitants argue should be attained by all individuals. They say neither the subtleness of letters is such, nor yet the difficulty of work, that one man, if given enough, cannot master both.

His views on the application of science to industry are interesting. Science will not merely benefit production; it will also permit the workers to understand what they are doing and thereby increase their interest in their work:

In the section given over to the forge . . . on the one side are seven workshops fitted out for heating, hammering, welting, and moulding metals; while on the other side are seven others assigned to the buildings of those workmen who make salt, glass, brick, earthenware, and to all industries which require constant fire. Here in truth you see a testing of nature herself; everything that the earth contains in her bowels is subjected to the laws and instruments of science. The men are not driven to a work with which they are unfamiliar, like pack-animals to their task, but they have been trained long before in an accurate knowledge of scientific matters, and find their delight in the inner parts of nature. If a person does not here listen to the reason and look into the most minute elements of the microcosm, they think that nothing has been proved. Unless you analyse matter by experiment, unless you improve the deficiencies of knowledge by more capable instruments, you are worthless. . . . Here one may welcome and listen to true and genuine chemistry, free and active; whereas in other places false chemistry steals upon and imposes on one behind one's back. For true chemistry is accustomed to examine the work, to assist with all sorts of tests, and to make use of experiments. Or, to be brief, here is practical science.

This is how, in Christianopolis, production is carried out for use instead of profit:

Their work, or as they prefer to hear it called, "the employment of their hands," is conducted in a certain prescribed way, and all the things made are brought into a public booth. From here every workman receives out of the store on hand, whatever is necessary for the work of the coming week. For the whole city is, as it were, one single workshop, but of all different sorts of crafts. The ones in charge of these duties are stationed in the smaller towers at the corners of the wall; they know ahead of time what is to be made, in what quantity, and of what form, and they inform the mechanics of these items. If the supply of material in the work booth is sufficient, the workmen are permitted to indulge and give play to their inventive genius.

If the inhabitants of Christianopolis are wise enough not to produce more than they can use they also guard themselves against unnecessary wants. The families, being small, do not need big houses, but live in small flats; they do not require servants except on rare occasions, and, being all equals, they do not wish to impress one another by unnecessary luxury:

Almost all the houses are built after one model; they are well kept and especially free from anything unclean. There are three rooms in the average house, a bathroom, a sleeping apartment, and a kitchen. And the latter two are generally separated by a board partition. The middle part within the towers has a little open space with a wide window, where wood and heavier things are raised aloft by pulleys . . . The houses are kept up at the expense of the state, and provision is made by the carefulness of inspectors that nothing is thoughtlessly destroyed or changed.

No one need be surprised at the rather cramped quarters; for their being only a very few persons, there is also need for only a very little furniture. Other people who house vanity, extravagance, and a family of that sort, and who keep up baggage of iniquity, can never live spaciously enough. They burden others and are burdened themselves, and no one measures their necessities, nay even their comforts, easily otherwise than by an unbearable and unmovable mass.

Now it will be easy to guess what the furnishings are. There are none except the most necessary, and even then scant. . . . There are the necessary dishes for the table and enough cooking utensils. For why should you want great numbers of things when all that you may reasonably desire can always be obtained at the public store-house?

They have only two suits of clothes, one for their work, one for the holidays, and for all classes they are made alike. Sex and age are shown by the form of the dress. The cloth is made of linen or wool respectively for summer or winter, and the colour for all is white or ashen grey, none have fancy, tailored goods.

Since grown children are brought up elsewhere, in most instances a family consists of four or five, less frequently six individuals, father, mother, and one or two children. Servingmen and servingwomen are a rare thing, nor very noticeable, except in the case of those attending the sick, those in confinement, or babies. The husband and wife perform together the ordinary duties of the home, and the rest is taken care of in the public workshop.

Contrary to most utopias, there are no common meals in Christianopolis, but this does not lead to inequalities, for a comprehensive rationing system is applied:

Their meals are private to all, but the food is obtained from the public storehouse. And because it is almost impossible to avoid unpleasantness and confusion when the number of those partaking of a meal is so great, they prefer that individuals shall eat together privately in their own homes. Even as the food is distributed according to the nature of the year, so also it is apportioned weekly according to the number of families. But provision of wine is made for a half year, or if conditions admit, of still longer period. They get their fresh meat from the meat shop, and they take away as much as is assigned to them. Fish, as also game, and all sorts of birds are distributed to them according to each one's proportion, the time and age being taken into consideration. There are ordinarily four dishes, and these after being carefully washed are prepared by the women, and are seasoned with wise and pious words. Whoever wishes to have a guest may do so, and the parties concerned, join their dishes accordingly, or if it be a foreigner, they ask from the public supplies that may be necessary.

In previous utopias one of the reasons for abolishing private meals was obviously to free the women for what were considered more worthy occupations such as, for example, military training. From Plato to Campanella, the utopian woman had been amazonian. Andreae gives her a purely feminine role, but he is not altogether Victorian. He would have women keep their place, and refuses them the "vote," but he provides girls with the same college education as boys:

The married women make use of the knowledge which they acquire while in college. For whatsoever human industry accomplishes by working with silk, wool, or flax, this is the material for woman's arts and is at her disposal. So they learn to sew, to spin, to embroider, to weave, and to decorate their work invarious ways. Tapestry is their handiwork, clothes their regular work, washing their duty. In addition to this they care for the house and the kitchen and have them clean. Whatever scholarship they have, being mentally gifted, they improve diligently, not only to know something themselves, but that they may sometimes also teach. In the church and in the council they have no voice, yet none the less do they mould the piety and morals, none the less do they shine with the gifts of heaven. God has denied this sex nothing, if it is pious, of which the eternally blessed Mary is a most glorious example. If we read the histories, we shall find that no virtue has been inaccessible to women, and there is none in which they have not excelled. However rarely do

many of them comprehend the value of silence. . . .
Women have no adornments except that mentioned
by Peter; no dominion except over household
matters; no permission to do servants' work (a thing
that will surprise you), unless disease or some
accident demands it. No woman is ashamed of her
household duties, nor does she tire of attending to
the wants of her husband. Likewise no husband of
whatsoever employment thinks himself above
honourable labours. For to be wise and to work are
not incompatible if there is moderation.

His views on marriage are also much more conservative than those of earlier utopians. It is not carried out
according to eugenic principles, but according to inclination, if this does not meet with the disapproval of
the family and the state:

> It is nowhere safer to get married than here. For as
> the unusualness of the dowry and the uncertainty of
> daily bread are lacking, it remains only that the
> value of virtues and sometimes of beauty be made.
> It is permitted a youth of twenty-four years to marry
> a girl not under eighteen, but not without the
> consent of the parents, consultation of the relatives,
> approbation of the laws, and benediction of God.
> There is with them the greatest reverence of
> relationship of blood. The factors considered in
> joining in marriage are for the most part conformity
> of natures and propriety; but also a thing that is
> elsewhere so rare, recommendation of piety. The
> greatest fault is considered to be impurity and the
> laws against such offenders are severe. But by
> removing opportunities they easily eliminate the sins.
> The marriages have almost no expense or noise;
> they do not at all expect worldly foolishness and
> senselessness . . . without any drunkenness, which
> usually initiates all sacred functions elsewhere, but
> not without a hymn and Christian congratulations,
> they are married. There is no dowry at all except
> the promises of Christ, the example of parents, the
> knowledge acquired by both, and the joy of peace.
> Furniture is provided together with the house out of
> the public store. In this summary fashion they ren-
> der most safe and speedy, our cross, punishment,
> torment, purgatory, and however else we are ac-
> customed to call inauspicious marriages.

The purpose of marriage is that of reproduction, and
Andreae, unlike Campanella, does not admit of sexual
relationships for pleasure alone:

> They have the greatest desire for conjugal chastity,
> and they set a premium upon it, that they may
> not injure or weaken themselves by too frequent
> intercourse. To beget children is quite proper; but
> passion of licence is a disgrace. Others live together
> like beasts; yet even the cattle have characteristics
> which put such persons to shame, who might better
> with mutual love and mutual aid first care for heaven
> and later for things of the earth. So the citizens of
> Christianopolis believe that there may be to a certain
> extent fornication and pollution even in marriage.

> Oh, the carnal-minded who are not ashamed to make
> sin out of lawful as well as unlawful practices!

Religion is the keynote of education, as it is of marriage. Children are not brought up to become the soldiers of the state, but good Christians. As the family
and the state are one with religion there is no need for
segregating the children from their parents; as all citizens are equal, the system of education is the same for
all children, boys and girls.

Ideas on education had made enormous progress during the Renaissance, and there had been, particularly
in Italy, many academies and colleges where the sons
and daughters of the aristocracy and of the wealthy
received a thorough and liberal education. Andreae did
not concern himself, however, with the education of a
small, privileged minority, the sons of princes and rich
merchants who could afford tutors or private schools.
For this reason his education has none of the glamour
of that received by the fortunate Thelemites, but it has
the advantage of being accessible to all.

The great majority of the schools of his time had not
been influenced to any great extent by the ideas of the
Renaissance, and radical changes were needed not only
in the methods of education, but also in the schools
themselves and the teaching profession. Conditions at
the time of Andreae were still the same as those Erasmus denounced with such vehemence in his *Praise of
Folly*:

> The Grammarians . . . being ever hunger-starv'd,
> and slovens in their Schools—Schools, did I say?
> Nay, rather Cloisters, Bridwells or Slaughter-
> houses—grown old among a company of boyes, deaf
> with their noise, and pin'd away with stench and
> nastiness. And yet by my courtesie it is that they
> think themselves the most excellent of all men; so
> greatly do they please themselves in frighting a
> company of fearful boyes, with a thundering voice
> and big looks, tormenting them with Ferules, Rods,
> and Whips; and, laying about 'em without fear or
> wit, imitate the Ass in the Lion's skin.

In Christianopolis the school is roomy and beautiful,
"all is open, sunny, and happy, so that with the sight
of pictures, even, they attract the children, fashion the
minds of the boys and girls, and advise the youths.
They are not baked in summer nor frozen in winter;
they are not disturbed by noise nor frightened because
of loneliness. Whatever is elsewhere given over to
luxury and leisure of palaces, is here devoted to honourable recreation and pursuits, an investment that is
nowhere more satisfactory or better paying."

Next to the appearance of the school, the greatest care
must be given to the choice of masters:

> Their instructors are not men from the dregs of

human society nor such as are useless for other occupations, but the choice of all the citizens, persons whose standing in the republic is known and who very often have access to the highest positions in the state. The teachers who are well advanced in years and are specially remarkable for their pursuit of four virtues: dignity, integrity, activity and generosity, must spur their charges on as free agents with kindness, courteous treatment, and a liberal discipline rather than with threats, blows and like sternness.

All the children of both sexes are taken into training. When they have completed their sixth year, their parents give them over to the state. They eat and sleep at the school but parents "can visit their children, even unseen by them, as often as they have leisure." The living quarters are arranged with the same attention as the school itself to create "hygienic" conditions. "They see to it carefully that the food is appetising and wholesome, that the couches and beds are clean and comfortable, and that the clothes and attire of the whole body are clean. The pupils wash often and use linen towels for drying. The hair is also combed to prevent anything unclean from collecting. If diseases of the skin or body are contracted, the individuals in question are cared for in goodtime; and to avoid the spreading of infection, they are quarantined."

Education in Christianopolis is directed towards three aims and the first is, naturally, "to worship God with a pure and faithful soul"; the second, to strive toward the best and most chaste morals; the third, to cultivate the mental powers. It is clear that Andreae does not conceive of education as the acquisition of knowledge in the narrow sense we give it to-day. He is more concerned with forming the mind and personality of the child and with developing his faculties than with increasing the volume of his learning.

Boys and girls follow the same courses, though not simultaneously; the boys have their study periods in the morning, the girls in the afternoon. The rest of their time is devoted to manual training, domestic art and science. Matrons as well as learned men act as instructors.

The school is divided into eight halls, which correspond to the eight departments of education. The first is the school of arts, divided into three sections according to the age of the pupils. The youngest students begin with grammar and languages, and learn to name "all sorts of things and actions in three languages, Hebrew, Greek and Latin," but Andreae reassures us by saying that they are careful not to overload delicate and fragile creatures, and that liberal recreation is allowed.

The more mature students are taught oratory, that is, to refute all sorts of arguments in accordance with the rules of the art. Though they learn how to adorn their speeches "with little flowers of elegance," more stress is laid upon natural force than artificial form. Those who are old enough also learn modern languages "not merely for the sake of knowing more, but that they may be able to communicate with many peoples of the earth—the dead as well as the living, and that they may not be compelled to put faith in every supposed scholar." But the study of languages should not be valued beyond its uses; the important thing is what one has to say and that can be expressed just as well in one's native tongue: "If righteousness and honesty are at hand, it matters little in what tongue they are spoken, if they are absent, it is of no advantage whether one goes astray speaking Greek or Latin."

The students who have already made some progress enter the second department, where they attend lectures on logic, metaphysics and theosophy. Logic must be used as a means and not as an end in itself: "No skilled workman boasts of his sun-dial pin or his plumbline alone, unless there is something of his own work on hand to exhibit."

In their study of metaphysics and theosophy all concern for concrete things, for investigation and invention, is left behind and knowledge is acquired by "consulting the divine sun and ascending to the known God."

In the third hall we come back to the less esoteric sciences of arithmetic, geometry and algebra, which develop mental faculties and help to solve practical matters with remarkable diligence. Here is also taught the science of mystic numbers which played such an important role in the philosophy of the Renaissance. To the planners of the Renaissance it seemed impossible that God, the arch-planner, should not have organised the world according to harmonious rules and measurements. "Surely," says Andreae, "that supreme Architect did not make this mighty mechanism haphazard, but He completed it most wisely by measures, numbers, and proportions, and He added to it the elements of time, distinguished by a wonderful harmony." This admirable plan cannot be discovered with "compasses from human philosophy" but only through God's revelation, which is not always easy to detect. The same caution must be used in the divination of the future; Andreae does not deny the value of prophecies, but warns that "God has reserved the future for Himself, revealing it to a very limited number of individuals and then only at the greatest intervals."

To enter the fourth department, that of music, one must have a knowledge of arithmetic and geometry. Music in Christianopolis, he says, aspires to that of heaven and does not encourage "the madness of dancing, the frivolity of vulgar songs, the wickedness of roisters. All of these things have been long ago driven out of this republic and are now unheard." Their instruments, of which they have a great number and variety and which are skilfully used by practically everyone, are attuned to the instruments of God, and their chorus, which is also devoted only to solemn music, passes through the city once every week, in addition to the holidays.

The fifth department is devoted to astronomy and astrology, which are "deserving of humankind as any other art." It is unworthy of man "to look at the sky no more observantly than any beast," and those who do not know the value of astrology in human affairs, or foolishly deny it, should be condemned to dig in the earth, cultivate and work the fields, for as long a time as possible, in unfavourable weather! But astrology is far from playing here the capital role it plays in *The City of the Sun*. The inhabitants of Christianopolis say that it is an uncertain thing to make everything dependent on the stars "on the first moment of existence and birth, and from this moment to accept judgement of life or death. And so they emphasise rather this as to how they may rule the stars, and by faith shake off the yoke if any exists."

In the sixth hall are taught natural philosophy, secular and church history. The knowledge of the worlds and their creatures must be accompanied by that of the events of human tragedy. Andreae stresses the need for historical truth, but also warns against those who merely look on the wickedness of mankind, on the monstrous deeds, the hideousness of wars, the horrors of massacres, and ignore the germs of virtue, the dignity of the human soul, the abundance of peace and restful quiet. "There are scholars who are bold enough to be unacquainted with such facts and who rank them with fables; they are very worthy themselves to be told of in fable."

We have seen that the whole of Andreae's scheme of education is as much concerned with giving a moral education as with dispensing knowledge. In spite of this the seventh department is reserved to ethics, which includes the study of all human virtues not only in theory, but also in practice, as well as the art of government and Christian charity. The three qualities of man most valued are: equality, the desire for peace, and the contempt for riches.

The last school is devoted to theology, which teaches the "strength, elegance, efficacity, and depth" of the Holy Scriptures, and practical theology, which instructs them on how to pray and meditate. They have also a school of prophecy, not to give instruction in soothsaying, but to test those who have been favoured with the gift of prophesying, and to observe the harmony and truth of the prophetic spirit.

Besides the eight halls already described there are two rooms assigned to the study of medicine and two to jurisprudence. The study of the latter is purely academic, as there is no need for lawyers in Christianopolis. For some reason, however, lawyers and notaries have not disappeared, and Andreae informs us that, so that they may not be idle, if anything has to be copied it is entrusted to these men.

There is nothing surprising in the importance attached by Andreae to chemistry, natural sciences, anatomy, mathematics and astronomy; they were sciences that a man of the Renaissance would not dream of neglecting any more than a Greek would have left music or gymnastics out of a system of education. What is surprising, however, is the modern and rational attitude displayed in the method of teaching. His laboratories were not reserved for great savants like Bacon's House of Salomon; they were available to students, and if they were made as attractive as possible it was not for "show" but because "instruction enters altogether more easily through the eyes than through the ears, and much more pleasantly in the presence of refinement than among the base. They are deceived who think that it is impossible to teach except in dark caves and with gloomy brow."

Andreae is also the first to include the teaching of pictorial arts in his utopian scheme of education. The city has its studio, "a very roomy shop for pictorial art," and not merely are painting, drawing and sculpture used to decorate the city with beautiful and useful paintings and statues, but the teaching of art is encouraged, for, those who "practice with the brush, wherever they enter, bring along their experienced eyes, their hands adapted to imitation, and what is of greater importance, a judgement equal to and already trained for things, not unfruitful or mean." However, even when using a brush one may be caught in Satan's snares and the artists of Christianopolis "are seriously commanded to observe purity," so that they will not poison the eyes of the innocent with impure pictures.

Next to the work of educational reform, Andreae was interested in the formation of a "college" or society which would unite all men of learning and provide them with the necessary means to carry out their researches. Already in the *Fama,* published in 1614, and circularised in manuscript form as early as 1610, he outlined a plan for scientific investigation and had given the model for a college or society of fellows which would institute a "general reformation" of the whole civilised world. Professor Held in his introduction to *Christianopolis* has shown how Andreae's ideas influenced those writers and philosophers who laid the foundations of the Royal Society in London. It is probable also that Bacon was acquainted with Andreae's works and that they influenced his invention of the House of Salomon.

In *Christianopolis* the College is described rather briefly, and it is not clear whether it is composed of all those who wish to carry out studies or researches, or whether it is limited to a chosen few:

> Now is the time when we approach the innermost shrine of the city which you would rightly call the centre of activity of the state . . . Here religion, justice, and learning have their abode, and theirs is the control of the city, and eloquence has been given them as an interpreter. Never have I seen so great an amount of human perfection collected into one place. . . .

If we are left rather vague as to the exact attributes of the college, we are given on the other hand a detailed and concrete description of the library, armoury, laboratories and botanic gardens, which belong to it.

In the laboratory dedicated to chemical science "the properties of metals, minerals, and vegetables, and even the life of animals are examined, purified, increased, and united, for the use of the human race and in the interests of health . . . here men learn to regulate fire, make use of the air, value the water, and test the earth."

There is a pharmacy where one can find a carefully selected collection of all that can be found in nature "not only for the cause of health, but also with a view toward the advancement of education in general." They have also a place given over to anatomy, where animals are dissected, for: "The inhabitants of Christianopolis teach their youth the operations of life and the various organs, from the parts of the physical body. They show them the wonderful structure of the bones, for which purpose they have not a few skeletons and of the required variety. Meantime they also show the anatomy of the human body, but more rarely because the rather sensitive human mind recoils from a contemplation of our own suffering."

The greatest care is devoted to the Natural Science laboratory. Here we find, as in *The City of the Sun*, that natural history is painted on the walls in detail and with the greatest skill. "The phenomena in the sky, views of the earth in different regions, the different races of men, representations of animals, forms of growing things, classes of stones and gems are not only on hand and named, but they even teach and make known their nature and qualities." But the laboratory does not merely contain pictorial representations; it is also a well-ordered museum where all the specimens of nature that can be beneficial or injurious to man's body are kept, and a competent demonstrator explains their uses and properties. The citizens of Christianopolis condemn those who acquire their knowledge merely from books and "hesitate when placed face to face with some little herb."

Mathematics of course play an important part, and there

is an "excavated" workshop for astronomical instruments and a hall of mathematics, "remarkable for its diagrams of the heavens, as the hall of physics is for its diagrams of the earth."

While war or the preparations for war play such an important part in the utopias considered previously, they are mentioned extremely briefly in *Christianopolis*:

> Of the Armoury . . . they have a still more critical opinion. For while the world especially glories in war—engines, catapults and other machines and weapons of war, these people look with horror upon all kinds of deadly and death-dealing instruments, collected in such numbers; and they show them to visitors not without disapproval of human cruelty . . . However, they do bear arms, though unwillingly, for keeping off some greater evil, and they distribute them privately among the individual citizens, that they may serve in the homes in the case of sudden emergency.

Before we leave Christianopolis we shall quote these passages which express well the idealist character of Andreae's community:

> You will want to know of what advantage it is for one of regular morals and excelling talent to live in this city when you hear nothing of rewards. Well, he of the Christian city solves this difficulty very easily; for it is glory and gain enough for him to please God. . . . The pleasure of the consciousness of having done right, the dignity of a nature that has overcome darkness, the greatness of domination over the passions, and above all, the unspeakable joy of the companionship of the saints, take possession of a refined soul far too deeply than that the renouncing of worldly pleasures should be feared.

> In the same way we may say of penalties, there is no use of these in a place that contains the very sanctuary of God and a chosen state, in which Christian liberty can bear not even commands, much less threats, but is borne voluntarily toward Christ. Yet it must be confessed that human flesh cannot be completely conquered anywhere. And so if it does not profit by repeated warnings (and in case of need, serious corrections) severer scourges must be used to subdue it. For this purpose fit remedies are on hand, not of one sort only, but chosen to suit different individuals. For truly, if one withdraws the sustenance from one's carnal appetites, or substitutes the cudgel for the tickle of lust, much may be remedied. It is the art of arts to guard against permitting sin to become easy for anyone. On the other hand, how wicked it is to vent one's wrath against those towards whose ruin you hurl stones. At any rate, the judges of the Christian City observe this question especially, that they punish most severely those misdeeds which are directed straight against God, less severely those which injure men,

and lightest of all those which harm only property. How differently the world does, punishing a petty thief much more harshly than a blasphemer or an adulterer. As the Christian citizens are always chary of spilling blood, they do not willingly agree upon the death sentence as a form of punishment; whereas the world, ever prodigal even of a brother's blood, pronounces wantonly the first sentence which occurs to it, feeling safe in this subterfuge that it has not personally employed sword, rope, wheel and fire, but only through a servant of the law. Christ be my witness, it is certainly handsome logic on the part of a government to make thieves of dissolute characters, adulterers of the intemperate, homicides of loafers, witches of courtesans, in order that it may have someone with whose blood to make expiation to God! It is far more humane to tear out the first elements and roots of vice than to lop off the mature stalks. For anyone can destroy a man, but only the best one can reform.

Ernst Bloch (essay date 1959)

SOURCE: "Andreae's *Chemical Wedding of Christian Rosenkreutz anno 1459*," in *The Principle of Hope,* Neville Plaice, Stephen Plaice, and Paul Knight, trans., Basil Blackwell, 1986, pp. 634-39.

[*In this excerpt from* The Principle of Hope, *originally published in German as* Das Prinzip Hoffnung *in 1959, Bloch examines the allegorical significance of Andreae's* Chemical Wedding *and the* Christianopolis.]

The *Chemical Wedding of Christian Rosenkreutz anno 1459* appeared in 1616, it aims at a broader 'refinement' than that of base metal into gold. The author of this anonymously published work is almost certainly Johann Valentin Andreae, Swabian poet, churchman, theosophist, utopian. The work sharply criticizes the bad gold-cookers, in places it can even be interpreted as mocking the whole hermetic craft. But more striking than the undeniable presence of an element of satire is the solemn *significance* which the *Chemical Wedding* gives to the path of gold and to the allegorical knight who takes it. In two earlier works, the *Fama Fraternitatis* and the *Confessio Fraternitatis,* Andreae had already invented and introduced Rosenkreutz, a founder of an order. Born in 1388, the latter travels to the East as a young man, is there initiated into the occult sciences and into a 'reformation', of which the transformation of metals is only the beginning. The *Chemical Wedding* shows the same Rosenkreutz as an old man, engaged in a new journey, on the eve of Easter Day, to the royal castle where a wedding is to be celebrated. He is admitted to the mysterious castle, undergoes a kind of ordeal of fire and water, then afterwards, adorned with the Golden Fleece, attends the seven-day wedding celebration as chief guest, has a vision of death and afterwards the resurrection of the royal couple. The guests are dubbed Knights of the Golden Stone, but Christian Rosenkreutz, having forced his way into a chamber where he found Lady Venus asleep, is induced, as the wedding is in full swing, to remain in the castle as a doorkeeper or as Peter. 'Alchymia' gives away the bride at the wedding, she is the 'parergon to the ergon of the seven days'. On the whole the alchemical meaning in Andreae's allegory is clear, but not as one which refers exclusively to metallurgy. If it is confined to the latter, then the *Chemical Wedding* bears no or only very little relation to gold-cooking. If, however, alchemy is conceived as giving away the bride of a transformation of the world or 'general reformation', then it is understandable that contemporary believers saw in the novel, even if it is typically a fragment, the most sublime allegory of the 'work of perfection', of the extraction of philosophical gold. A Rosicrucian by the name of Brotoffer published an interpretation in 1617: 'Elucidarius major or Synopsis of the Chemical Wedding F.R.C., in which praeparatio lapidis aurei is very neatly described.' This interpretation openly explains the seven days of the wedding as the seven stages of the alchemical process, spiritually brought to light: as destillatio, solutio, purefactio, nigredo, albedo, fermentatio, and projectio medicinae (tincture of gold). It is even correct that the *Chemical Wedding* was not only intended as allegory but as symbolism in the comprehensively final sense, i.e. as metaphorical reference to an ultimate Unitas, to the fermenting golden Pan. So, in alchemy of *this* kind, this was supposed to be the solemn *significance* announced above: that of an *Easter Day* to be fantastically created against ice and barriers. The bourgeois impulse towards the 'Freedom of the Christian Man' [Luther's 'Freiheit des Christenmenschen'] that did not arrive nowadopted such strange paths and naturally-adorned disguises in the so-called hermetic societies of the German Baroque and their stated symbolism. A reveille was intended which was to resound through the *whole earthly layer,* an 'Awake, frozen Christian', through lead, creation, society and the remaining Alteritas. *The preparation of gold and the promotion of humanity* are jumbled together in Rosicrucianism from then on, constitute the peculiar quality of its mixed fantasy. In 1622 the since famous Society of Rosicrucians was founded in The Hague, though the name of the order itself is older than the Fama and Confessio which Andreae produced about it. Paracelsus cites a Rosicrucian lodge in Basle in 1530, not wholly unequivocal manuscripts from the beginning of the twelfth century tell of lodges of this name in Germany. Not content with this, Rosicrucians from the time of Andreae, and even from that of the Magic Flute, claimed to have preserved that 'veram sapientiam' for thousands of years 'quae olim ab Aegyptiis et Persiis magia, hodie vero a venerabili fraternitate Roseae Crucis Pansophia recte vocatur'. But however old the name Rosicrucian is and however far the emblem may go back into utopianizing or utopianized myths: only

Andreae with his **Chemical Wedding** gave it the sense, claimed to be rising or humane, of 'higher alchemy'. We must continue even further, into the peculiar connection which exists, through Andreae's link of a 'general reformation', between something as superstitious as alchemy and something as sunlike and crystal-clear as the Enlightenment, this battle of light against superstition. For the pathos of light itself, as the 'birth', as the advancing 'process' of light (gold), comes from alchemy: 'Enlightenment' itself is originally an alchemical concept, just like 'process' and its 'result'. Conversely the strange connection of freemasonry, and even the Enlightenment with occultism arises from this, of course; even Andreae mixed his fraternities with magic rites. The golden dream of a societas humana thus found its philanthropic alchemical conventicles in Germany, but also in the strangely theosophical England throughout the whole of the seventeenth and eighteenth century. There was a secret society called Antilia, another called Makaria, a 'brotherhood of the celestial wheel for the restoration of hermetic medicine and philosophy'. There was, with a mixed social-cosmological dream, the collegium lucis which was founded by no less a person than Comenius, the disciple of Andreae; and all these sections set up the Rosy Cross or the 'higher alchemy'. They all wanted to turn the course *of society and of nature* towards the original state of paradise, where social equality and unfallen or golden nature were one and the same.

The dream of these alchemical sects thus remained general reformation throughout, in the sense of the restoration of the original state of paradise, and above all of leading the fallen world over to Christ; which is why the Rosicrucians were also continually compared with the Anabaptists by their enemies at the time. Gold-cooking became chiliastic or, as a hostile tract denounced it at the time: 'Turning the whole world upside down before the Day of Judgement into an earthly paradise such as Adam occupied before the Fall, and the restitution of all the arts and wisdom possessed by Adam, after the Fall, Enoch and Solomon.' *Alchemy and chiliasm together* thus entered the hermetic sects, with the transformation of metals as a prelude to the 'true' homunculus or to the birth of the new man. A late after-image of this is still to be found in Goethe's fragment 'The Mysteries', concerning the dream of a chemical kingdom. The wanderer, 'exhausted by the day's long journeying / He undertook upon impulse sublime', here sees a mysterious image on the monastery gate, sees the cross entwined with roses, 'and light celestial clouds of silver float, / To soar into the sky with cross and roses'. Thirteen chairs are standing in the monastery hall, at their heads hang thirteen shields with unmistakably alchemical allegories: 'And here he sees a fiery dragon pause / To quench his raging thirst in wild flames; / And here an arm caught in a bear's

fierce jaws, / From which the blood is pouring in hot streams.' The images on the shields signify in this order thirteen stages of turning to gold, and thus they are the ancestral hall which the old man in the monastery tells the wanderer about. But then the wise man, who has such diverse ancestors behind him, is called Humanus in Goethe's strange poem; and this very name has also been claimed in the Rosicrucianism of Andreae to be the final name and content which rises from the transformation of metals and the world. Cross and rose, the first the symbol of pain and of dissolution, the second the symbol of love and life, thus united allegorically in the 'work of perfection'. 'And a French philosopher', as Gottfried Arnold's history of heretics of 1741 relates, in the chapter on the Rosicrucians, 'has sought the secret of making gold in the name itself and suggested that rose comes from ros or dew, and crux means lux for them, which things the alchemists used most.' Thus again and again Rosicrucianism opened out into a kind of second storey of alchemy; the philosopher's stone in the Chemical Wedding was at the same time Christ the cornerstone. For lead and man and for the whole world: 'Vita Christi, mors Adami, Mors Christi, vita Adami', [Life of Christ, death of Adam, Death of Christ, life of Adam] ran the epitaph of the Rosicrucian and friend of Jakob Böhme, Abraham von Franckenberg. Or as the same Franckenberg, in connection with the Chemical Wedding, had taught: alchemy was 'renewal of the celestial lights, ages, men, animals, trees, plants, metals and all things in the world'. Moreover this kind of thing was levelled at any constraint or spellbinding by the *existing celestial lights,* and therefore, despite some cross-connections, at the mythology of fate at that time: astrology. Some cross-connections did exist of course, all metals bore planetary symbols and vice versa, the position of the planets was always taken into account when cooking gold. Nevertheless, the superstition of alchemy has always reserved to itself something distinctive from, even contrary to that of astrology, simply the act of intervention, combination, the changing process; all this was to be levelled precisely at the 'frozen heavens'. At the horoscope of the beginning, which also claims right at the beginning to be an epitaph as well, an unchangeable, inescapable one. The planetary symbols themselves, in metals and in the heavens, were to be 'chemically surmounted', namely by the sun or by gold. That is why Franckenberg's *Oculus siderius* of 1643 boils down to this: 'Since we have been stuck long enough in the circumscribed cage or whitewashed imaginary vault of the frozen heavens and have fooled one another with all kinds of fantastic visions and constellations, we now need to rub the sleep of seven ages out of our eyes at once.' The hidden alchemy at work in Thomas More and his liberal utopia has already been referred to, as the 'mythology of liberation.' This was in contrast to astrology, the characteristic guiding system in Campanella's authoritarian utopia; astrology is solely magic that descends from above, it does not, like alchemy,

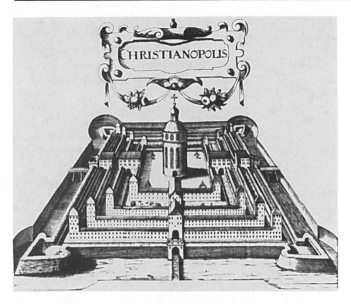

Illustration from Andreae's Reipublicae Christianopolitanae Descriptio, *1619.*

ascend from below into something better. Turning to gold as a whole was and remained for Andreae and his successors the transformation of the world, and metallurgy a mere vicarious test of this 'technology'. In the end, out of the really divined Pan, the world was to be rebuilt, by means of 'pansophy' and humanity.

The paths to this were clearly confused, and in a more familiar region they became conspicuously short. In 1619, three years after the anonymous *Chemical Wedding,* Andreae also published a social utopia: *Reipublicae Christianopolis descriptio.* Outside the background we have just seen, it is not particularly important and is not independent in any case; that is also why we can talk about it only now, in connection with the Rosicrucians. The golden order has here become a kind of thoroughly Christianized city of artisans and schools, an island-city with a circular temple in the middle, with a market-, gymnastics- and pleasure-zone around it, with fields and workshops on the outskirts of the city. Admittedly there is no mention of alchemy even in the curriculum of the utopian school, even the undoubted dispersion of the city is surrounded by a kind of planetary circle, almost in the manner of the somewhat later *Civitas solis* of Campanella. Nevertheless, an alchemical consciousness, opposed to the astrological one, is at work on this social utopia, as was already the case in that of More; for Christianopolis rises in an emphatically antithetical manner, as if processed out, from 'the dross of the topsy-turvy, completely corrupt world'. And the science of its wise men, divided into three stages, is not static and self-enclosed, as in Campanella, but the final lesson in the top class is called: 'Prophecy of the final status', 'prophetic theology'. With this the arc towards the 'general reformation' is described once again, towards Rosicrucianism, which combined superstition with light, 'pansophy' with

the Day of Judgement in such a strange way. And in the end the most important disciple of Andreae: *Comenius,* the founder of visual instruction, but also of an 'Ecclesia philadelphica', also summarized the intention of Rosicrucian alchemy. Exactly like Andreae, Comenius also speaks ironically and not just enthusiastically about it, but even the irony shares the superstition-faith which it mocks. In *The Labyrinth of the World and the Paradise of the Heart,* 1631, the following is related of the Rosicrucians 'to the sound of trumpets': 'Making gold is the least among a hundred other things they can do; for since the whole of nature is an open book to them, they are capable of giving a particular form to every single thing at will and of knowing everything that happens within the whole circumference of the old world and in the new world, especially as they can speak to one another at a distance of a thousand miles. Then they possess the philosopher's stone, with the aid of which they cure all diseases and confer long life . . . and after they have kept themselves hidden for so many centuries and have worked quietly at the perfection of philosophy, they are willing, especially now everything is in order and in their opinion a powerful upheaval is in store for the world, not to remain hidden away any longer but to come out into the open, and are ready to communicate their most precious secrets to anyone who is worthy of them'. The 'precious secrets' are here always the same as the secret ways to turn the topsy-turvy world the right way up, so that the gold emerges from it. That very gold which for the very symbolic economic-technological enthusiasts of that time, apart from what it actually is, was also the solar symbol for what had blossomed out, was rounded, and luminous.

John Warwick Montgomery (essay date 1973)

SOURCE: "Andreae's Life from the Sources," in *Cross and Crucible: Johann Valentin Andreae (1586-1654), Phoenix of the Theologians. Vol. I,* Martinus Nijhoff, 1973, pp. 24-111.

[*In the following excerpt from his* Cross and Crucible, *Montgomery emphasizes the continuity of Andreae's Christian philosophy throughout his life and dismisses "the questionable efforts on the part of some (both 'occultists' on the left and 'orthodoxists' on the right) to drive a wedge between Andreae's allegedly 'radical' youth and 'conservative' manhood."*]

While preparing himself for ordination, Andreae lived at the famous Tübinger Stift, whose roster of famous *stipendiarii* over the centuries has included Kepler, Schelling, and Hegel. The Stift must have reinforced for Andreae the orthodox Lutheranism of his University years, for the theological tone had been set by Jakob Andreae, Heerbrand, Hafenreffer, Stephan Gerlach, J. Heilbrunner, Polycarp Leyser, and Aegidius Hunnius. Probably the social-service nature of the Stift influenced Andreae's later concern for the well-being and support of students; certainly for him the Stift experience was a positive one, for he was instrumental in its survival through the black period of the Thirty Years' War. At the Stift he formed friendships with David Hafenreffer, Matthias' son; and with Johann Jakob Heinlin and Wilhelm Schickhardt, both of them students of theology and mathematics who in future years maintained contact with him by correspondence. Through Besold he entered into friendship with Wilhelm Wense, who would shortly become acquainted with Campanella in Italy, and who would later be named by Andreae as a prime stimulant to Andreae's "Socictas Christiana"; and Wense put Andreae in touch with Tobias Adami, who as early as 1613 began to introduce Campanella's ideas into German circles, and who also became a supporter of the "Societas Christiana." Some writers, by misusing these facts and misapplying Andreae's genuine appreciation for certain aspects of Campanella's work, have claimed that Andreae's *Christianopolis* is but a pale reflection of Campanella's *Civitas solis,* or that Campanella, via Andreae, lies at the root of Rosicrucianism—claims that simply will not stand up under careful historical and literary scrutiny.

Andreae, then, made new friends at the Stift; also, he profited from his stay there by taking part in a "Collegium mathematicum," which led to the writing of one of his first published works, the ***Collectaneorum mathematicorum decades XI*** [1614], that well displays his wide scientific interests and the harmony of science and faith characteristic of his ***Chymische Hochzeit.*** At this time he prepared his ***Doctrinae christianae summa: ex Hafenrefferi Locis communibus contracta*** [1614], which shows beyond all doubt that he had drunk deeply at the founts of Hafenreffer's orthodox Lutheranism. He spent much time in the reading of theological classics; he concentrated especially, he tells us, on the "consummatissima theologia" of Luther himself, and on the "solid food" of the fathers—Jerome and Augustine. Significantly, these theological works he read had been part of his father's library: through the years of education and travel, when a new world of learning had opened for Andreae, the "old, old Story" of Christian truth never lost its central place in his life.

On February 25, 1614, Johann Valentin Andreae was ordained to the holy ministry, having received his first ecclesiastical call—to the position of "deacon" (in present-day terminology roughly equivalent to "assistant pastor") of the church in Vaihingen/Enz, a little town fourteen miles northwest of Stuttgart. The remainder of his life would be spent in the active pastorate. It is impossible to present here a full account of those years of Christian service . . . but an attempt will be made to point up the highlights of his career and to show its essential unity with his early years—over

against the questionable efforts on the part of some (both "occultists" on the left and "orthodoxists" on the right) to drive a wedge between Andreae's allegedly "radical" youth and "conservative" manhood. In contrast to such a dichotomy, we shall find in the pastorate the same Andreae as we found at Tübingen, Strasbourg, Geneva, Rome, and Augsburg: a believing Christian of strong Lutheran persuasion, compelled by inner necessity to make the Gospel relevant both to the intellectual and to the social challenges of his day.

In the last year of his life, Andreae epigrammatically outlined his pastoral career in a letter to Duke Augustus of Brunswick-Lüneburg:

> Anno
> 1614. conduxit ad Laboratorium
>   Vaihingam.
> 1620. produxit ad Directorium
>   Calvam.
> 1639. pellexit ad Oratorium
>   Studtgardiam.
> 1650. depressit ad Purgatorium
>   Bebenhusam.
> 1654. eduxit ad Refrigerium
>   Adelbergam.
> Dominus porro provideat.

Let us briefly consider in turn each of these phases of Andreae's ministerial life.

Vaihingen: the "Laboratorium"

One would think that the picturesque town of Vaihingen, situated between the Black Forest and Heidelberg's romantic Neckar river, should have provided Andreae with a peaceful respite after his hectic but exciting period of wanderings. However, he rightly refers to his six year Vaihingen pastorate as a "workroom." From April 2, 1614, when he made his first entry in the ecclesiastical "Toten-Register," to February 18, 1620, when he performed this duty at Vaihingen for the last time, his days were filled with labor and with accomplishment—and also with love. Only a few months after his arrival at Vaihingen we find him writing to his friend of student days, Johann Bernhard Unfrid, *candidatus juris* of Tübingen, about "the girl who is going to unite herself to me in the everlasting bonds of love." He invites Unfrid to the forthcoming August wedding which is to take place at Poppenweiler, and (as if the hurried script did not already indicate it), he signs himself "occupatus." August 2 was the wedding day, and the bonds of love did indeed become perpetual: Agnes Elisabeth, née Grüninger, would remain his companion for life; she survived her husband by five years.

In Andreae's "Breviarium Vitae" the entry following that for his wedding reads: "Hinc prognati Liberi ac

Libri." This same coupling together of physical and literary progeny occurs in Andreae's *Indiculus librorum* [1642?], so the juxtaposition can hardly have been merely a conceit: for Andreae, scholarly productivity as well as the joy of parenthood was bound up with a loving and stable marriage. Many have wondered why Andreae published the *Chymische Hochzeit* when he did (in 1616)—so many years after he had originally drafted it (1605); could his early months of marriage, when he experienced personally the closest human analogy to the union of Christ and His Church have moved him to give to the world his striking allegory of the ineffable marriage of heaven and earth that centers in the Person and Work of Jesus Christ? There is every reason to think so.

Three of Andreae's nine children were born in Vaihingen: Maria (1616-1681), who eventually married a citizen of Calw when her father had his pastorate there; Concordia, who was born June 29, 1617 and died a month later, on July 28; and Agnes Elisabeth, who died at birth on September 19, 1618. That Andreae was still maintaining close contact with his friends of Tübingen days is evident from the fact that Besold, Hoelzel, and Wense served as respective god-parents of these three children. In the matter of "libri," the Vaihingen period was the most intensively productive in Andreae's life: an examination of the chronological Bibliography of his printed works will show that over twenty separate writings came from his pen during that time, and that they represent a remarkable breadth of subject matter, including theology, political philosophy, social criticism and satire, and belles-lettres. These works reflect Andreae's spiritual outlook at the time he offered his *Chymische Hochzeit* to the general public, and thus the more prominent of them deserve at least cursory mention here—particularly when we remember that the *Chymical Wedding* may have undergone revision between the time of original composition and that of publication.

Andreae never wrote a non-theological work, for his faith illumined every subject he took in hand. Yet some of his writings are more strictly theological than others. During the Vaihingen period three such works stand out with special prominence; one is of an editorial nature, the other two are original compositions. In 1615, Andreae published a summary of Johann Arndt's famous devotional work, *True Christianity*. Andreae's high opinion of Arndt is evident from the fact that in 1621 he published still another anthology of *True Christianity,* and in 1644 he included both of these digests in his *Summa doctrinae christianae trigemina* along with his editions of Hafenreffer and Schaefer. In the letter of dedication to Duke Augustus which he prepared in conjunction with his autobiography, Andreae includes Arndt among six "blessed athletes and faithful shepherds of God's flock" (the others: Luther, Brenz, Jakob Andreae, Hafenreffer, and Johann Ger-

hard); these are clearly the theologians whom he regards most highly. It is not difficult to see why Arndt appealed to Andreae—and why his name later appears first in Andreae's list of the supporters of his "Societas Christiana" of 1618-1619: Arndt was firmly committed to orthodox Lutheranism (he had studied under Pappus at Strasbourg and had given his allegiance to the *Formula of Concord*); he had a definite interest in the interpretation of alchemy from a Reformation standpoint (he wrote a short commentary on Khunrath's *Amphitheatrum*); and his entire career was spent in an effort to make the truths of Lutheran theology live in the personal experience of believers. This passion to "existentialize" the Christian message, over against the tendencies toward "dead orthodoxy" in his time (comparison with Søren Kierkegaard in nineteenth century Denmark is irresistible) touched Andreae deeply, for Arndt's concern for a living, "true" Christianity was Andreae's own concern as well. "L'insistance qu'il [Arndt] mettait sur l'union mystique" would certainly have appealed to the author of the *Chymical Wedding*; and when, in 1619, Andreae dedicates his *Christianopolis* to Arndt, he is saying that in his opinion, Arndt's vital Christianity holds the key to an ideal Christian society.

In 1616—a year after the publication of Andreae's anthology of Arndt and the same year the *Chymical Wedding* was given to the public—there appeared Andreae's *Theca gladii spiritus*. This small volume was issued anonymously by the publishing house of Lazarus Zetzner in Strasbourg, and, in common with the first printing of the *Chymische Hochzeit* by that firm, the book carries the Zetzner mark on the title page and Conrad Scher's printer's device as a colophon. Because the book contains prefatory remarks about and some memorial verses for Andreae's friend Tobias Hess, who had died two years before, it has frequently been attributed to Hess; however, as Andreae expressly states in his autobiography, he himself wrote the work and had it published in common format with Besold's *Axiomata philosophico-theologica* (1616), which Besold dedicated to him. The outward similarity of these companion volumes (each contains numbered aphorisms—847 in Besold's book, 800 in Andreae's) has seemed to support the contention of Kienast that during the period when Andreae wrote and published the *Chymical Wedding* he had fully absorbed Besold's occult-mystical approach to life. But in reality, the similarity between the two books ends with their external format and structure. The titles of the works reveal their essential difference: Besold writes first as a philosopher, and only secondarily as a theologue; Andreae, however, humbly prepares a sheath for "the sword of the Spirit": an allusion to Eph. 6:17, where the Apostle identifies that sword as nothing less than the Word of God—meaning, as axiom 771 puts it: "divina dicta sumite." An examination of the respective contents of the two books confirms this fundamental distinction: Besold, though he presents many Biblical references and allusions, prefers to display his wide learning through citations to secular authors; Andreae, however, mentions non-Biblical writers only once in his eight hundred axioms (no. 372: Abbots Joachim of Flora and Tritheim). Besold, while he makes quite clear in his axioms that he is a Christian believer (and feels it necessary to add a postscript stating that the book really presupposes his orthodoxy!) continually strives to find philosophico-mystical depths and extensions of Christian faith; Andreae, quite to the contrary, totally subordinates man to God-in-Christ, as his axioms 759 and 760 well show:

> Philosophus ratione, conscientiâ, amicitiâ, coronâ, sceptro, sigillo, rex mortalitatis est.

> Nemo in hoc magno universo magnus, felix, bonus, sapiens, dives,dominans, liber, nisi Christianus; Christi sui, filius, frater, amicus, divinae possessionis cohaeres, angelorum nunc cura, aliquandò judex, Sacrosanctae Trinitatis delitium.

True, between axioms 777 and 778, Andreae inserts a Zodiac table—but it is a *"Zodiac of the Christian who is a Pilgrim in this World"* ("Zodicus Christiani Cosmoxeni"), in which each of the twelve signs is made to convey an aspect of Christian doctrine or practice; just as Andreae in the **Chymical Wedding** employs alchemy as a pointer to evangelical truth, so here he brings astrological motifs into captivity to Christ. No better illustration of the totally dissimilar thrusts of Besold's *Axiomata* and Andreae's **Theca** exists than the final aphorism in each book. Besold's obscure and mystical axiom reads:

> Cabbalisticum est: Angelus omnia secum habet; Angelico ac spirituali modo. Imò totam mundi machinam in se complicat, & est quasi omnia inferiora.

Andreae, however, concludes with the simple yet profound assertions:

> Scientia inflat: Charitas aliis prodest.
> *Nil Christo triste recepto.*

The year 1618 saw the appearance of another independent theological work by Andreae—but a work which, both by its title and by its content, shows Arndt's influence on him. The **Veri Christianismi solidaeque philosophiae libertas**, which contains a moving "encomium to Jesus Christ," sets forth, in a manner reminiscent of Luther's *Christian Liberty,* the freedom which comes from a personal, living union with Jesus Christ. Here, as in his comments on his Geneva experience, one sees that for Andreae "freedom" is never "from" but always "for"—freedom to live the kind of morally upright life that is capable of producing an ethically transformed society.

As a bridge between theology and belles-lettres during the Vaihingen period, we encounter Andreae's **Herculis christiani luctae** XXIV of 1615, and his Christian poetry. The **Hercules,** written in memory of Andreae's close friend Tobias Hess who had died the previous year, allegorically employs and freely develops the struggles of the most popular classical Hero to point up the temptations of the Christian life and the means of overcoming them. To take but one example from this exceedingly clever work: the Christian Hercules' twelfth labor requires him to overcome the giant Antaeus, whom Andreae takes to represent human wisdom. The classical Hero, on observing that every time Antaeus fell on the earth he gained new strength, killed him by holding him aloft in the air. Likewise the only way for a Christian to deal with human wisdom, says Andreae, is to hold it up to the "liberum Divinae lucis aërem," for all so-called human remedies only add to the monster's strength. Thus throughout his book Andreae witnesses to eternal truth through the motifs of classical literature.

Andreae's poetry likewise employs literary technique to illumine the Christian message. His earliest published verses appeared in 1615 in his **Vom Besten und Edelsten Beruff. Des wahren Diensts Gottes,** which included five "geistliche Lieder." The allegorical-epic poem **Christenburg** was probably composed in 1619, though it may date back as far as the year 1615; it was not published until 1836. Two of its most striking sections are the "Summarische Bekandtnuss unnd Glaub Eines Christen" (setting forth, in obvious reliance upon the Catechisms of Luther and Brenz, Baptism, the Creed, the Lord's Prayer, the Eucharist, the Law, and the Office of the Keys) and the sanctificatory verses under the rubric, "Von dem Wahren Creutz der Christen." In 1619, Andreae published his **Geistliche Kurtzweil,** a collection containing both original poetry and poems in translation. Perhaps the most interesting original selection in the **Kurtzweil** is Andreae's **"Das Gute Leben eines recht-schaffenen Dieners Gottes,"** which so moved Herder that he included it in one of his own works, and which modern editors have not inappropriately titled **"Alte Reime von der praktischen Theologie"** and **"Eine Pastoraltheologie in Versen."** In some 640 lines it discusses the pastor's calling:

> Da müsst ihr glauben, wissen, tun,
> Leiden lassen, fürchten und hon . . .

As the **Chymische Hochzeit** shows how Andreae put alchemical science into the service of the Gospel, so his poetry shows how he brought the Muse into its service also. And the absence in Andreae's thinking of the baleful separation of the "two cultures" of art and science is illustrated by the several poetical interludes in the **Hochzeit** itself.

During the Vaihingen years Andreae wrote a number of belletristic works of timeless value, though they have, in general, been forgotten in modern times. Four of these are social satires, and on the basis of them Andreae has been called "the Christian Lucian."A closer parallel is with Erasmus' *Praise of Folly,* and certainly Andreae's satires reach the literary level of Erasmus' work—and, in their powerful theological dynamism, they may be said to surpass the *Praise of Folly,* with its tendencies toward dilettantism. Andreae's *Turbo* [1616] is a comedy which—while displaying an extraordinary erudition that moves effortlessly from Hesiod to Rabelais and from Slovanic to Spanish—lampoons the pretentions of the pseudo-intellectuals of the day and the educational institutions they create in their own image; the large cast of characters includes, *inter alios,* a rhetorician, a mathematician, a political scientist, a historian, a linguist, a traveller, musicians, students, an alchemist, and numerous personified virtues. The hero, "Turbo"—who on one level represents the playwright himself—encounters all varieties of intellectual presumption, and though in consequence "suam dolet vitam, à Sapientia ad quietem tandem ducitur." By leading Turbo to a personal knowledge of God, Sapientia brings him in the last scene to pray:

> Creator Deus, Benefactor Christe, Illuminator Spiritus, quas tibi grates referam, qui, quae abscondita hactenus, & abstrusissima credidi bona, in Cor hoc meum seminâsti, & jam aperire se, excrescere, & fructum ferre voluisti. Accipe hoc ipsum cor, quod tibi humiliter offero.

This play has rightly been regarded as a forerunner of Goethe's *Faust,* but it should be clearly noted that whereas *Faust,* whose author had moved beyond confessional Christianity, centers attention on man (either as a Prometheus in Part One or as one who achieves personal enlightenment in Part Two), the *Turbo,* written by a convinced Lutheran believer, offers an uncompromisingly theocentric answer to the human dilemma. The *Turbo* deserves theatrical production and would have real impact in our own time—when anthropocentric erudition is so often mistaken for theocentric wisdom, and when so many suffer from the *Angst* which the comedy's leading character typifies.

Andreae's *Menippus,* the first edition of which appeared in 1617 and the second the following year, consists of one hundred short satires and several satirical appendixes; it is subtitled, "inanitatum nostratium speculum," and it deals with all manner of folly—secular and religious. The literary technique employed is Andreae's favorite one, the dialogue (which—let it be noted—aligns him closely with the theological atmosphere of our day). Herder's translation of selections from the *Menippus* is but one indication of the timeless quality of the book. The closing affirmation of the one hundredth satire is both Andreae's answer to the follies he has so mercilessly exposed, and perhaps the most succinct statement of the heart of his world-view to be found anywhere in his writings:

> At nos, mi frater, quibus & haec displicent, & imposturae multae patent, vitam studiaque ita instituamus, ut religio nobis nulla sit nisi pietas Jesu, leges nullae quàm charitas Jesu, medicina nulla praeter abstinentiam Jesu, eruditio nulla post simplicitatem Jesu, mores nulli ubi non humilitas Jesu, exercitium nullum ultra Crecem Jesu, Societas nulla extra Fraternitatem Jesu, finis nullus praeterquam aeterna cohabitatio Jesu: ita Jesus nobis omnia erit in omnibus, quo in uno acquiescemus.

Along much the same line is Andreae's *Peregrini in Patria errores* [1618], with a title-page quotation from the last verse of Psalm 119: "I have gone astray like a lost sheep." Here Andreae describes the "lostness" which man, apart from Christ, always experiences in the world. The remedy is set forth in the *Civis christianus* of the next year, whose theme is clearly indicated by its title-page motto—the concluding verse of Jesus' parable of the lost sheep who is sought and found by its shepherd: "I say unto you, that likewise joy shall be in heaven over one sinner that repenteth, more than over ninety and nine just persons, which need no repentance" (Luke 15:7).

Sixteen-nineteen also saw the publication of Andreae's *Mythologiae christianae sive virtutum & vitiorum vitae humanae imaginum libri tres,* where he employs the mythical technique of the *Chymische Hochzeit* to produce numerous vignettes of human folly and the divinely revealed correctives for it. Here Andreae reveals himself as the very opposite of the Bultmannian "demythologizer" of the twentieth century; for Andreae, myth is not an obstruction to faith, but one of the best vehicles for conveying it! In the *Mythologia* Andreae shows acquaintance with an impressive number of Italian writers: Petrarch, Machiavelli, Giovanni Pico della Mirandola, Scipione Gentili, Girolamo Cardano, Bernardino Ochino, Boccalini, and Campanella. Like his contemporary, the great Lutheran baroque musician Michael Praetorius, who has left a permanent legacy in his work on organ construction and in his magnificent chorale preludes, Andreae apparently believed that "Germany and Lutheranism needed the relaxing influence of the Italians." So impressed was Herder by the *Mythologia* that in the late eighteenth century he prefaced a free translation of selections from it [*Dichtongen,* 1786] with the comment: "Valentin Andreä gehört so eigentlich für unsre Zeit, dass ich in Vielem, Vielem ihr jetzt einen Andreä wünschte."

Andreae's most famous writing likewise appeared in 1619: his utopia, the *Christianopolis,* appropriately dedicated to Johann Arndt. It would be impossible here to do the work justice; nor is a general analysis necessary, since the **Christianopolis** is the one work of Andreae already provided with a modern English translation, accompanied by an exceedingly valuable critical introduction. The pity is that this preeminent Christian conception of an ideal society remains less well known than the *Utopia* of Sir Thomas More, which is inferior to it in many ways. The **Christianopolis** beautifully sets forth the social ideal of Protestantism at its best: a wedding of learning and social justice centering on, and receiving its dynamic from, the free grace of God in Jesus Christ. As for the other major works of the Vaihingen period—the *Invitatio fraternitatis Christi,* the *Turris Babel,* and the *De curiositatis pernicie syntagma*—these are intimately connected with the Rosicrucian question and with Andreae's plan for a "Societas Christiana". . . .

Andreae's literary accomplishments during the six years of Vaihingen pastorate might give the impression that he sorely neglected his ministerial role in relation to his immediate flock. Nothing could be further from the truth. In actuality, he made such a spiritual and civic impact upon the community that he is still remembered as one of its foremost citizens: legends have grown up about him and in the 1950's a stained-glass window to his memory was placed in the Vaihingen *Rathaus.* His posthumous fame in the town is based chiefly upon the fact that he was instrumental in the rebuilding of the community after two devastating conflagrations to which the town was subjected during the Thirty Years' War. He himself prepared and published careful accounts of these destructions of November 1, 1617 and October 9, 1618, and later incorporated the substance of them into his autobiography [*Vita,* 1849]. The accounts contain digests of the sermons he preached to a populace sick with shock after these dual calamities within a year of each other. He beautifully combines Law and Gospel (did not Luther define the true "doctor of theology" as one who could do so?) by underscoring God's judgment on sin and His grace to those who rely on him for mercy. A persistent tradition in Vaihingen says that the first sermon, following a conflagration that destroyed most of the town but missed the parsonage, was a discourse on just punishment for the excessive consumption of alcohol by the citizenry; and that the sermon which followed hard on a second burning that *did* destroy Andreae's home and valuable personal library had as its theme a warning against becoming too attached to one's own possessions! Though the story requires some modification from a strictly historical standpoint, it accomplishes the feat of the true legend by capturing in epitomal form the essence of a man's character: Andreae was indeed a person who consistently strove to bring men to actualize the Christian faith in their ethical conduct—and at the same time he was concerned, as a physician of souls, that "having preached to others," he might not himself become "a castaway."

Andreae's appreciation for the "true" Christianity of Arndt—which shows itself in literary terms at the beginning of his Vaihingen experience—is manifested in the warmth and suppleness of his heart during the practical trials and agonies of that wartime pastorate.

Lasky on the place of Christianopolis in European utopian thought:

This so-called German utopia of Andreae, influenced as it was by Thomas More and influencing in turn Francis Bacon, completes in a strikingly circular way the first century of European utopianism. Christianopolis was conspicuously more religious in its essential spiritual conception than the regime of King Utopus, but both were equally involved in the dilemmas and complexities of the utopian political impulse. The private hope of imaginative escape is balanced by the ethical injunction to help transform an evil world; the motives of hate and anger against glaring iniquities are mixed with the tenderest feelings for all mankind; the patient promise of gentle progress is overshadowed by a prophetic rage for action this day. These are all themes which begin to dominate the revolutionary temperament as early as the seventeenth century, and there are notable pages in Andreae's work which document the shaping of attitudes among a generation's representative minds.

There is, in the first place, a new semi-secular rhythm to the utopian movement which tends more and more to displace the simpler older swing from the lostness of paradise to its restoration....

In this perspective, Andreae can be seen to have transcended some of the traditional limitations of Christian prophets of paradise and to have placed himself in the ranks of a new intellectual movement which tried to put the divine apocalypse at the service of human progress and refused to allow its nostalgia for a past Eden to preclude its present commitment to a better future.

Melvin Lasky, "Andreae's German Utopia," in Utopia and Revolution, *The University of Chicago Press, 1976.*

Frank E. Manuel and Fritzie P. Manuel (essay date 1979)

SOURCE: "Andreae, Pastor of Christianopolis," in *Utopian Thought in the Western World,* Cambridge, Mass.: The Belknap Press of Harvard University, 1979, pp. 289-308.

[*Below, the critics provide an overview of the* Christianopolis *and compare Andreae's ideas with the utopian philosophies of* More, Bacon, *and* Campanella.]

Of his hundred-odd writings the **Christianopolis** was the one work through which Andreae entered general histories of utopian thought. In this portrait of an ideal Christian society science and orthodox Lutheran religion are completely integrated; while knowledge of Christ is the highest good, physical science becomes a major human preoccupation that has been sanctified. As early as Robert Burton's *Anatomy of Melancholy,* **Christianopolis** was classified with More's *Utopia,* Bacon's *New Atlantis,* and Campanella's *City of the Sun* as a utopia. In his funeral oration for Wilhelm Wense, Andreae had called the **Christianopolis** the literary pendant to the Societas Christiana. It became one of the recognized progenitors of the Comenian Pansophia and a foundation of Leibniz' universal projects. Since it was composed in Latin and was not translated into German until the eighteenth century, its direct influence was generally restricted to the learned world; but there it was often imitated, extending its imagery over a broader field as the ideas appeared secondhand in the vernacular.

Andreae's utopian masterpiece is written in his satiric, imagistic, Erasmian, often cryptic style, more apt for the description of spiritual experience than for arguing the fine points of theology. The **Christianopolis** departs in significant ways from its utopian contemporaries. It is fervently Christocentric, and the observer who is the protagonist is not a wooden robot; he is psychically transformed by the experience of the holy city. **Christianopolis** is the history of an adept in an ideal Lutheran community, and the alterations of his inner being, his exaltation through the sight of the meticulously ordered Christian city, is the heart of the work. By contrast, nothing much happens to Bacon's sailors shipwrecked on New Atlantis; though they feel amazement and gratitude for the kind treatment they receive, they do not undergo a spiritual conversion. As for the Genoese captain who has seen the glories of Campanella's City of the Sun, he is nothing but a figurehead, in haste to sail away once his tale has been recounted.

The hero of **Christianopolis** is Cosmoxenus Christianus, a stranger, a pilgrim who suffers from the corrupt uses of the world; the allegory is not disguised. Raphael Hythlodaeus, the hero of More's *Utopia,* is presented as a member of Vespucci's expedition functioning on a realistic level, and More's artifice throughout is to preserve verisimilitude. Andreae's pilgrim embarks on the ship named Fantasy; after it is wrecked, he is washed ashore on Caphar Salama (named for the place where Judas Maccabaeus conquered Nicanor's forces), an island whose inhabitants live in community under a spiritual rule. Caphar Salama is described in fifty chapters covering all aspects of the society under as many headings. The guardians of Christianopolis first submit the outsider to a moral examination, which he passes. Immersion in the sea, represented as a baptism, has

prepared him for a new life. In stages he is shown the city. First there is a review of the material order, the things that concern the historians of mechanical utopias—agriculture, artisans' work, public projects. Then Cosmoxenus ascends to the innermost shrine of the city, where the institutions of justice, religion, and education are located. On entering the holier region he is confronted by twelve articles inscribed in gold. They are Christological, orthodox in their formulas on the ministry of the word, free forgiveness of sin, general resurrection of the flesh. Part of the credo testifies: "We believe in an eternal life by which we shall obtain perfect light, ability, quiet knowledge, plenty and joy; by which also the malice of Satan, the impurity of the world, the corruption of men shall be checked, by which it shall be well with the good, and evil with the evildoers, and the visible glory of the Holy Trinity shall be ours forever." [**Christianopolis,** translated by Felix Emil Held. (All quotations in this essay are from the Held translation unless otherwise noted.)] To Andreae, Satan was as palpable as he had been for Luther, and men had to give him combat through word and deed. In few other utopias are explicit creedal utterances so prominently featured. More's Utopians require only a belief in God, the immortality of the soul, and rewards and punishments in the next world; religion is reasonably tolerant of deviations. Bacon's Atlantens have become Christian through a miraculous epiphany, but not much is made of the whole matter beyond observance of certain Christian restraints on behavior. Christianopolis not only has a detailed creed, but some articles are believed *toto corde,* "with all our heart"—a pietistic intensity has suffused religious belief.

Andreae's man has been restored to the dignity forfeited by Adam's transgression, and through the Holy Spirit he has entered upon a new relationship with nature. Article VIII reads: "erudimur supra naturam, armamur contra naturam, conciliamur cum naturam." In the interrogation to which Cosmoxenus submitted before entering Christianopolis, one of the failings to which he confessed was that "by . . . inexcusable folly" he had neglected the countenance of nature. In another passage, Andreae reflected: "For what a narrow thing is human knowledge if it walks about as a stranger in the most wholesome creations and does not know what advantage this or that thing bears to man, yet meanwhile wanders about in the unpleasant crackle of abstractions and rules, none the less boasting of this as a science of the highest order!"

The mood of Christianopolitan society conforms to the Morean rule about "honest allowable pleasures," not quite monastic in its austerity, but hardly indulging in superfluities. "Oh," says the narrator, "only those persons are rich who have all of which they have real need, who admit nothing merely because it is possible to have it in abundance!" The evils of disorder, hunger, misery, and war prevalent in the outside world are lamented as impediments to spiritual fulfillment. The ideal secular institutions of Christianopolis, the educational system that fosters excellence and the utopian mechanics proper governing production and consumption, are not ends in themselves, but merely a preparation for the spiritual feast, the theosophical stretching of the soul. They are preliminaries that insure against the loss of spiritually creative members of the community through want and neglect. In a specially appointed place in Christianopolis where the qualified inhabitants convene for lectures on metaphysical science, the chosen ones acquire a mystic vision of God in the Christian Neoplatonic tradition. Rapture makes them oblivious of all earthly concerns—"they find themselves again." Though this is not an enduring or continuing state, they return to earthly matters ennobled by the experience. Differences are recognized in the capacity of various men for such an exalted spiritual achievement. The highest stage of theosophy, a science reserved for a select group capable of receiving God's direct illumination, begins where the knowledge of nature ends. It is secret and is communicated through the vision of the Cross. Andreae has drawn on the rich German mystical tradition, into which images from the new science have been infused, as a way of finding union with God. More's Christian humanist utopia allowed for an elite, but they were far closer to all other men than the awesome scientist-priests of Bacon and Campanella or the spiritual directors of Christianopolis.

In a passage leveled against excessive emphasis upon sterile logic, Andreae defined the intellectual temper of the island in language at once theological and scientific: "They incite their talented men to recognize what reason has been entrusted to them and to test their own judgment of things lest they find it necessary to seek everything outside of themselves and to bring in theories from without. For man has within him a great treasure of judging if he prefers to dig it up instead of burying it with mounds and weight of precepts." The inhabitants of Christianopolis turn to modern mathematics and geometry for sharpening their wits, rather than to Aristotelian logic. Both the Baconian empirical science and mathematics were integrated into the Christian science; but such knowledge was not autonomous or sufficient unto itself.

> Surely that supreme Architect did not make this mighty mechanism haphazard, but He completed it most wisely by measures, numbers and proportions and He added to it the element of time, distinguished by a wonderful harmony. His mysteries has He placed especially in His workshops and typical buildings, that with the key of David we may reveal the length, breadth, and depth of divinity, find and note down the Messiah present in all things, who unites all in a wonderful harmony and conducts all wisely and powerfully, and that we may take our delight in adoring the name of Jesus.

The secret brotherhood, the elect alone, learn of the mystic numbers and proportions of things. Despite the generally communal spirit of the society, the esoteric character of the highest knowledge in Christianopolis excludes the "rabble," and even the most illuminated must accept the existence of bounds to their knowledge of God and His ways, an idea of human limitations Andreae shared with Francis Bacon. Millenarian prophecy is rejected.

> In this *Cabala* it is advisable to be rather circumspect, since we have considerable difficulty in present matters, grope in events of the past, and since God has reserved the future for Himself, revealing it to a very limited number of individuals and then only at the greatest intervals. Let us then love the secrets of God which are made plain to us and let us not, with the rabble, throw away that which is above us nor consider divine things on an equal basis with human; since God is good in all things, but in Hisown, even admirable.

In Christianopolis there is a negative attitude toward the traditional Aristotelian classics of philosophy and even a certain ambivalence about the printing press because it has propagated so much irreligion and absurdity, but there is no such denigration of the chemical laboratory. Here true nature, God's world, is revealed without falsification. Only direct exploration of nature yields truth; everything the ancients wrote about nature is prima facie suspect since they were heathens. "Whatever has been dug out and extracted from the bowels of nature by the industry of the ancients, is here subjected to close examination, that we may know whether nature has been truly and faithfully opened to us." While Luther in his table talk may have denigrated astronomy in general (and perhaps Copernicus in particular), he had not been opposed to alchemical inquiries. The new astronomy could run up against the literal, precise Lutheran interpretation of scriptural text, but alchemical chemistry and mathematics were not exposed to such risks since their content was by no stretch of the most punctilious scholar's imagination covered in the Bible. It has even been surmised that the Lutheran dogma of the real presence in the Eucharist could lead to a veneration of the world of nature in all its chemical complexity. The pharmacy in Christianopolis is a veritable microcosm of the whole of nature. "Whatsoever the elements offer, whatever art improves, whatever all creatures furnish, it is all brought to this place, not only for the cause of health, but also with a view toward the advancement of education in general." Pharmacology and chemistry have become the exemplar sciences, whose teachings can by analogy be extended to public affairs. "For how can the division of human matters be accomplished more easily than where one observes the most skillful classification, together with the greatest variety!"

The *laboratorium* in the center of the city is described

with meticulous detail. "Here the powers of metals, minerals, vegetables, and also animals are investigated, refined, increased, and combined for the use of the human race and the improvement of health. Here sky is married to earth, and the divine mysteries impressed upon the earth are discovered; here one learns to master fire, make use of air, measure water, and analyze earth. Here the ape of nature has wherewith it may play, while it emulates her principles, and through the traces of the great machine forms something minute and most elegant."

The evils of the world, the brevity of life, the weariness and plagues of existence are taken for granted; but men need not be broken by them. Andreae propounds no progressionist doctrine of science in the Condorcet manner, nor does he foresee a great prolongation of human life, the Baconian goal. The traditional allotted span would be sufficient, if it were not misspent in debauchery and avoidable suffering. Both Bacon and Andreae lay emphasis on the chemical and biological sciences as the clue to whatever transformations are to occur on earth. Galilean mathematical science, though respected, had not yet been conceived as applicable to human behavior. In Christianopolis the anatomy of animals is studied in order to be able to assist the struggles of nature, and Andreae is distressed that men outside the utopian island do not understand the internal operations of their own bodies.

Most sections of the ***Christianopolis*** are devoted to an account of the basic, everyday requirements of a society in which material necessities are readily provided for in a communal order. Houses are not privately owned, and cooked food is obtained from a central storehouse, though consumed at home to avoid the tumult of public mess halls. Work is freed from the biblical curse and is reconceptualized as an expression of man's divinity, an act of creation imitative of God the Creator. Necessity is no longer the whip that forces men to labor: They do not have to be driven to work like pack animals to their tasks. Having been trained in accurate knowledge of the science that underlies their work, they find delight in manipulating the innermost parts of nature. Science, work, and techniques have been interrelated. If a person in Christianopolis does not investigate the minutest elements of the world, filling in gaps in knowledge by devising more precise instruments, he is considered worthless. The worker-scientist-artisans, the predominant class, labor "in order that the human soul may have some means by which it and the highest prerogative of the mind may unfold themselves through different sorts of machinery, or by which, rather, the little spark of divinity remaining in us, may shine brightly in any material offered."

The combination of the artisan and the scientist in one person was the natural consequence of a realization that the artisans were the repositories of scientific knowledge, of the Baconian test of science as knowledge that results in practical works, and of the new spiritual valuation of manual labor. There is mockery of the "carnal-minded" who avoid science because, with aristocratic affectation, they shrink from touching earth, water, coal, and other material objects required in scientific experiments, while they boast of their possession of horses, dogs, and harlots. The whole state of Christianopolis can be considered one great workshop of educated artisans skilled in different sorts of crafts, who work short hours. Since there is no slavery or forced labor their work is not irksome to the human body. There is a great variety of products to be freely exchanged, since pecuniary gain is not a motive of production. Everything is clean and neatly arranged as befits a proper appreciation of the gifts of God. A minister, a judge, and a director of learning, combining in their persons religion, justice, and science, take care of public administration, and a state economist has supervision over the division of work tasks and produce. "For though no one in the whole island ever goes hungry, yet by the grace of God or the generosity of nature, there is always abundance, since gluttony and drunkenness are entirely unknown."

But concentration on the utopian earthly order was not an end in itself. In a subtle, paradoxical sense the perfect order of this world achieved in Christianopolis becomes a means to freedom from earthliness. The director of learning had a way of at once valuing and transcending the knowledge of material things. "For he insisted that a close examination of the earth would bring about a proper appreciation of the heavens, and when the value of the heavens had been found, there would be a contempt of the earth."

Andreae does not rely on the mere mechanics of a social utopia to bring about the general reformation of mankind. They are a part of the propitious setting for a Christian renewal; but only after men have undergone an inner transformation can they realize a terrestrial Christianopolis that will be both a simulacrum and a foretaste of the heavenly city. Universal brotherhood, godliness in men's hearts, must precede the establishment of Christianopolis. There is no authoritarian legislator as in More's *Utopia*; his function is replaced by the experience of religious and scientific conversion. The pursuit of science is recognized as the occupation most worthy of man and most acceptable to God because of its religious character.

Spiritual regeneration in Christianopolis takes place within the limitations of fallen man. The origin of life, like death, is putrid. Ultimate blessedness is not of this world; it is only of the resurrected body purified and refined in heaven. In this world science raises fallen man and restores him to a state that approximates the prelapsarian condition—an apology for science that-would be reborn with Wilkins and Glanvill in the Royal Society and would survive as a secularized image as late as Saint-Simon. While Plato's spirited guardians exercised their bodies and listened to prescribed music, and More's Utopians at leisure were humanist scholars who learned moral truths from ancient literature, by the seventeenth century scientific activity became the principal preoccupation of the elite in *The City of the Sun,* the *New Atlantis,* and **Christianopolis**. At a time when Italian cardinals still refused to look into Galileo's glass, Andreae's community was equipped with "the very valuable telescope recently invented," with models of the heavens, tools, instruments for astronomical study and observation of the "spots on the stars." Galileo and Kepler were known, as were Bruno's "short cuts in memorizing." There is no battle of the two cultures, and Andreae takes the stand that a man ignorant of science and mathematics is only half-educated. In **Christianopolis** a marked contempt for contemporary scholars ignorant of science obtrudes and echoes Kepler's *Nova Astronomia:* "If like strangers in a foreign land they shall bring to humanity no assistance or counsel or judgment or device, then I think they deserve to be contemned and classed with the tenders of sheep, cattle, and hogs." But though science plays an important role in this and other utopias, most of the inhabitants are still primarily engaged in agricultural pursuits affected neither by the new science nor by technological innovation. In Christianopolis "the agriculture of the patriarchs is reproduced, the results being the more satisfactory the closer the work is to God and the more attentive to natural simplicity." What Andreae imagined the agriculture of Abraham and Isaac to have been is not disclosed.

The educational reforms of Comenius are presaged in Andreae's ideal city, even as the pictures of scientific matter writ large on the walls of Campanella's City of the Sun were repeated in Comenius *Orbis Sensualium Pictus.* The goals of education were first to teach the worship of God, then to instill the virtue of chastity, finally to develop intellectual prowess. As in the City of the Sun, competitiveness and striving were encouraged; the pupils had to exert themselves to learn. Schools were airy, sunny, and decorated with pictures. Teachers were directed to acquire a sense of the individual psychological character of the children in their charge, and praise or disgrace were the instrumentalities that replaced the scourge, now restricted to exceptional cases. As corporal punishment of children was virtually banished among advanced utopian thinkers from Andreae and Comenius through Rousseau and Fourier, shaming was substituted—the replacement of physical by psychic pain as a desperate last resort. Teachers in contemporary schools, who were the dregs of society, were attacked by Andreae for raining blows upon their pupils instead of displaying generosity and kindness. Andreae may have been drawing on personal experience when he wrote that those who had suffered

indignities at the hands of schoolmasters bore witness with bodies enfeebled for the rest of their lives. The training of girls did not exclude learning, though much of their effort was devoted to domestic art and science; girls as well as boys studied Hebrew, Greek, and Latin. Andreae would not drop ancient languages from the curriculum, but he voiced the Lutheran argument against excessive emphasis upon this branch of knowledge: God understands the vernacular well enough. The summit of happiness was to be able, with one and the same effort, to preserve the safety of the republic and secure the future life, and education was the key to both. "The children which we bear here, we may find to our satisfaction have been born for the heavens as much as for the earth." An idea has been introduced that will have great potency in secularized versions of utopia. "Happy and very wise are those who anticipate here on earth the firstlings of a life which they hope will be everlasting."

Christian renovation was dependent upon the integration into a whole of the benign efforts of men, which were now divided into autonomous parts. Upon his penetration of the innermost shrine of Christianopolis, Cosmoxenus learned that the truly religious man would not sever connections with things human and adopt a theology directed only toward the divine. Nor would he exercise power and rule without the check of Christianity. Nor would he imitate those learned men who, instead of seeking truth for the sake of God and men, were motivated primarily by vanity and self-love. In the real world there was discord because of the separation of divinity, sovereign rule, and knowledge into compartments; in the ideal city there was *concordia.* "Christianity . . . conciliates God with men and unites men together, so that they piously believe, do good deeds, know the truth, and finally die happily to live eternally." [Quoted in John Warwick Montgomery's *Cross and Crucible: Johann Valentin Andreae.*]

Dynastic wars made more vicious by religious differences had brought about a world in disintegration. Andreae's brotherhood of the learned and the use to propagate a belief in the new unity. Where Wallenstein's Christian societies he founded were the instrumentalities he hoped to troops struck, men were reduced to an animalian state without rule, godliness, or knowledge. The Continental wars of the seventeenth century awakened men of virtually every religion in Europe to the disaster of the major Christian schism, and the English Civil War soon revealed the fragmentation of religion into literally hundreds of rival sects. The Christian utopia of Andreae answered to an anguished longing for a restored unity, without which there could be no renovation as Christian energies spent themselves in bloody internecine strife. A gulf separates More's utopia, composed on the eve of the Reformation, from the seventeenth-century religious utopias, whose main purpose was to put the pieces together again into a new whole.

Hugh Powell (essay date 1988)

SOURCE: "Johann Valentin Andreae: A Practising Idealist of the Seventeenth Century," in *German Life and Letters,* Vol. 41, No. 4, July, 1988, pp. 363-70.

[*In the following essay, Powell gives a brief overview of Andreae's life and discusses his satiric drama* Turbo.]

In our universities students are encouraged to see [Johann Gottfried von] Herder as mentor of the 'Sturm and Drang' and inaugurator of the classical age in German literature. What they are generally not told is that, in addition to reviving old folk-songs and ballads, Herder was also active in rescuing from oblivion writers of the century immediately preceding his own— amongst them Johann Valentin Andreae and Jacob Balde. Although Herder's position as exalted official of the Lutheran church tends to be minimized in surveys of literature, it is not irrelevant in the context of the present essay. Andreae was also a Lutheran clergyman and ultimately appointed to high office in the church. Balde, on the other hand, was a Jesuit, and when Herder published renderings of some of Balde's poems under the title of *Terpsichore* (1795-6), he considered it expedient to withhold the poet's name until the third and final volume. The principles inspiring both Lutheran dignitary and Jesuit, and their criticism of contemporary social and ecclesiastical *mores* were hailed by Herder who found a kindred soul in Andreae and solace in the study of Balde's poetry. He was so taken with the former ('einer der angesehensten, gelehrtesten, frömmsten, verdientesten Theologen unsrer Kirch') [*Briefe, das Studium der Theologie betreffend, IV*], that he planned a memorial essay and told Lessing about this (15 January 1781). Possibly the project was pushed aside by others more pressing although, in addition to reprinting various poems of Andreae and retelling some of his parables, he did write an appraisal of his hero as preface to a translation by K. G. Sonntagof a selection of Andreae's Latin writings under the title *Dichtungen zur Beherzigung unsers Zeitalters* (1786). Hitherto the scholarly attention paid to Andreae has been directed mainly to his connection with the emergence of the Rosicrucians or to his work as theologian and pedagogue, including the utopian story ***Christianapolis,*** but there are other aspects of this indefatigable man that deserve more scrutiny and recognition than have been accorded them.

Just over a century ago in an enlightening essay [appearing in *Goethe Jahrbuch,* Vol. 4, 1883], Erich Schmidt saw Andreae's Latin drama **Turbo** (1616) as a link in the chain connecting the historical Faust to Goethe's tragedy. Penetrating and sensitively present-

ed as that great scholar's argument is, there are some features in the play he did not dwell on, presumably because they were not thought to be strictly germane to the burden of his thesis. I am alluding to the four *entr'actes* in **Turbo** which underscore Andreae's opinion of contemporary ideas and practices as recorded in his other pedagogical works. But first an outline of the events within the five acts.

Turbo is a student who, after submitting for ten years to sterile logic and specious syllogistic reasoning in the lecture hall, has become totally disenchanted with his training. His quest is for ultimate wisdom with the serenity that would accompany it. Breaking away from the network of Scholasticism he takes advice in turn from a rhetorician, mathematician, politician and finally from a much travelled man of the world, all of whom urge him to widen his horizon. With Harlequin as his companion he goes to Paris to acquire the art of cultivated living. Back in Germany he falls into the clutches of an alchemist who relieves him of his fortune while persuading him that he is on the verge of discovering the key to the innermost secrets of Nature. When the alchemist is exposed as a fraud, Turbo sinks into deep despair. He is now visited by a company of allegorical figures personifying Truth, Wisdom, Simplicity and so on, who exhort him to lead a life according to the teaching of Christ, if he wishes to find ultimate wisdom. Turbo admits his errors and declares himself ready to accept this advice. So much for the main action.

Of the *entr'actes* the first, entitled *Disputatio,* is a parody of old fashioned learning processes in the universities which are based on pseudo-Aristotelian logic, merely confirming what had been authoritative in medieval thought. In this first interlude the attack on the sterility and spuriousness of academic disputationsis direct and uncompromising. The propositions listed are absurd and the manipulation of terms ludicrously unsubtle. Andreae was one of a number of intrepid spirits who deplored the futility of such academic philosphy. The antiquated mode of study in so many German universities was one important reason numerous students were advised to go abroad to advance their knowledge. . . . The second interlude presents officers of a closed society interviewing six candidates for membership. The principal criteria required are small-mindedness, egoism, cupidity and unconcern for those in need. Since all applicants maintain they display these characteristics each in his own way, they are admitted to the society. Hermaphroditus, the 'causa productus' of the third interlude, is announced as 'Fortunae gratia Princeps Gomorrhicus, Imperator impudicissimus, cogitantes nostrorum numerum hoc accommodo seculo adaugere bonorumque potentiam frangere'. In the presence of five trusty henchmen the principles of his régime in this world are reviewed, his goal being to undermine the ethical base of Christian society in its individual forms: church, state, community, civil service and military. Cynicism, hypocrisy and deceit are the tactics advocated by this Prince of Darkness and Antichrist. The choice of the name Hermaphroditus is to be linked to its usage since Luther for the Pope, and we recall that in the propaganda literature of the Reformation the Pope was often identified with the Devil. The final interlude introduces Peregrinus, who has been sent from the Elysian Fields back to earth with a message for mankind. In an encounter with Harlequin he draws a dismal picture of the role towering figures of antiquity have to play in the underworld. Their great intellectual and artistic gifts are of no account in Elysium, where they have to perform the simplest menial tasks. In brief, the message Peregrinus brings is that the values cultivated and extolled on earth do not transcend life here; it is an instance of the vanitas-theme that permeates seventeenth-century culture.

The subjects of these interludes: the diehard Schoolmen in the universities; the selfishness, meanness and greed in society; the papal see and its servants; the cult of false values in this world, all are targets of Andreae's repeated attacks throughout his works. As a clergyman the mission he adopted was a renewal of the original spirit of the Reformation and in this respect he was a follower of Johann Arndt, the author of *Vier Bücher vom wahren Christentum*. Because he demanded a stop to quibbling over inconsequential points of dogma (which had become characteristic of a degenerate Lutheran orthodoxy), and because he called for more application of the teachings of Christ in daily life, Arndt was vilified by his associates; so was Andreae. In other respects, too, Andreae considered his Church to be in a parlous state, but his suggestions for reforming it aroused the vicious enmity of many colleagues in high places who saw their image and position threatened. He was also disturbed by the clergy's neglect of their pastoral duties when these were sorely needed during the deprivations of the war. This and other unwelcome opinions were expressed publicly as well as privately, as he recorded in the dedication of his autobiography to Duke August of Wolfenbüttel.

The fourth act of the drama is devoted mainly to Turbo's involvement with the alchemist Beger and indicates the severity of Andreae's attack on what he saw as a bogus science cultivated by charlatans. Another token of this is the choice of name which is an anagram of Geber, as the eighth-century Arab practitioner Dschabir Ibn Haijan, father of European alchemy, was known. The author, then, was not only taking to task contemporary alchemists, but also taking aim at the source of what he saw as so much fond illusion, wishful thinking and downright deception. Indeed, one may see in this little known play a counterpart of Ben Jonson's *Alchemist* which was first produced in London the year before work on *Turbo* started. Of his elder

brother Jakob, also a clergyman, he said [in his *Vita ab ipso conscripta*] he had devoted much of his time to 'nichtigen chymischen Versuchen.' In 1616, the same year as the play first appeared, a book was published anonymously which Andreae was to acknowledge as his own. Its title began *Chymische Hochzeit Christiani Rosencreutz* . . . and in his autobiography he called it 'ein unbedeutendes Werkchen' which demonstrated 'die unnützen Bemühungen der Neugierigen.' Elsewhere in his writings the term *curiosus* or *curiositas* occurs frequently, implying a kind of inquisitiveness that was apt to lead to magic, sorcery and other occult practices and consequently suspect on moral and religious grounds. His tract of 1620 *De curiositatis pernicie* . . . specifically attacked alchemy, magic, prophesying and, furthermore, the search for perpetual motion. A dialogue of his bearing the title *Institutio magica pro Curiosis* shows an individual wishing to be coached in magic being instead deftly led towards Christian wisdom. Andreae the dedicated Lutheran theologian, it must be emphasized, was not opposed to the search for 'truth', but for him there were illicit paths which, if followed, necessarily led the enquirer astray. This is what Turbo the erring student is bluntly told by the allegorical figures Wisdom and Truth at the end of the play; in his case alchemy was a particularly pernicious *ignis fatuus*.

It was wholly in accordance with Andreae's progressive mind that he should show interest in mathematics and mechanics. His teacher in these subjects had been David Mästlin (who had also taught Kepler) and at the age of twenty-eight Andreae the student of theology, published *Collectaneorum Mathematicorum Decades XI. centum et decem tabulis aeneis* (1614). His interest in mechanics as well as optics and architecture is demonstrated by these engravings and comes to light in the fourth act of *Turbo* when Haspellus, an engineer accustomed more to ridicule than to recognition, is mocked when presenting his credentials to a couple of men about town. The flowering of interest in architecture, military technology, landscaping, waterworks and fountains inspiring this incident was late in migrating from Italy to the German territories and in some disciplines, notably astronomy and medicine, stubborn reluctance to accept new ideas, discoveries, techniques was shown by some. The scepticism encountered by the engineer Haspellus is symptomatic of such recalcitrance and the incident itself a record of Andreae's disapproval of it. What is more, the significance of the encounter is enhanced by its insertion between Turbo's supposed triumph as an alchemist and his discovery that he is the victim of colossal deceit at the hands of an impostor to whom he had given his whole trust and fortune. The message is thus brought into clear relief: too many people clung to old illusions and false values while ignoring manifestations of the new (scil.) genuine science.

Harlequin in Andreae's play is a lively and occasionally provocative, though consistently loyal companion of Turbo whom he will criticize but also defend against all comers, by word and deed. He has attended classes with Turbo and submitted to the discipline of Scholastic logic; he quotes from Virgil and Horace, reasons aloud, now and then directing his thoughts to the audience. His judgements are apt to be shrewd. In short, Harlequin is no fool, but if he reminds us of Shakespeare's clowns, he is far from being their equal in imagination and wit. He introduces himself thus: 'Ego Harlequinus, sum Turbonis Minister, turbarum socius, turbinum executor'. He is, then, associated with disorder and confusion and he delights in wordplay. Now as a scholar well versed in the classics Andreae was familiar with the comic figure in Terence and Plautus. Furthermore, when travelling in Italy he had opportunity enough to see performances of the *Commedia dell'arte* including Arlecchino and Colombina. Another memorable experience will have been performances of English actors, for in his autobiography we read that as early as 1602-3 when he was sixteen or seventeen, he tried his hand at writing plays, one being called **Esther** and the other **Hyacinth,** both composed 'ad aemulationem histrionum anglicorum' [**Vita**]. The question arises: how and where did Andreae see performances by actors from England?

It is well known that the presence on the European continent of players from Elizabethan England is documented from the late sixteenth century. They were as far south as Austria by 1608 when Archduchess Magdalena wrote to her brother Ferdinand that at Fasching she had seen in Graz 'Engelländer . . . guete Comedianten' and that they played amongst other things 'Dockhtor Faustus', i.e. twenty years after Marlowe's play was first published. A testimonial to their professional skill was offered by G. F. Gumpelzhaimer who praised the English actors [in *Gymnasma de exercitiis academicorum,* 1621], 'qui tum in inventionibus, tum actionibus omnes post se relinquunt.' Andreae's knowledge of the skill and technique of the visiting players was, however, probably not based entirely on hearsay, for events near his home when he was seventeen suggest direct acquaintance.

Frederick I Duke of Württemberg had for some time coveted the Order of the Garter. Towards the end of her life Elizabeth had given the royal assent to the award, but the Lutheran prince had to wait another six years before her successor James I dispatched his ambassadors to Stuttgart for the formal induction in 1603. To judge by a contemporary account from the pen of a Tübingen professor [Erhardus Cellius], it was a brilliant occasion. The ambassadors and their retinue were supported by a company of actors and musicians from Britain, the concerts and dramatic performances being continued outside the capital city when the visitors were taken on a sightseeing tour of the Duchy

that included Tübingen. Amid all the fanfare and excitement it would have been virtually impossible for the intellectually alert youth Andreae, who was in the neighbourhood, not to have witnessed and savoured something of the talent of the foreign guests. Turbo's companion Harlequin who, as observed above, was no fool, together with the mingling of serious and comic elements in the play, reminds us of Elizabethan drama. That the young man's earliest attempts at writing should have embodied impressions gained from recent presentations by the English actors is not difficult to accept. Hence his reference to the lost plays **Esther** and **Hyacinth** 'ad aemulationem histrionum anglicorum'.

An astonishing feature of Andreae's life is the prodigious, endless activity of the man, despite a constitution which was less than robust, and notwithstanding sustained personal attacks on him. As pastor in the Swabian town of Calw he was responsible for the spiritual and moral welfare of the inhabitants, but he also assumed the task of administering to their physical needs during times of economic distress, famine, plague and war. Many pages of his **Vita** amount to a catalogue of misfortunes which, however, failed to destroy his will to persevere. In Württemberg as elsewhere the 'Kipper' and 'Wipper' left misery and deprivation behind them. He himself lost 800 gulden to the profiteers, and this appears to have strengthened his sympathy with those impoverished by them, for in the 1620s he repeatedly organized help, including free meals for children and relief for the sick and aged. Andreae estimated that between 1626 and 1631 he and his helpers fed over 1,000,000 starving people. In the face of opposition from the 'Magistrat' he solicited funds to train destitute individuals for a craft, but some sympathizers did support his efforts morally and financially—and he names them. When his parish was overrun by imperial troops, he had to contend not only with them but also with those citizens who trimmed their sails to the prevailing wind, doing whatever they could to hinder him in his pastoral duties. Whenever his health broke, he managed to recover where others around him succumbed. He cites figures of deaths from disease and malnutrition and of the obsequies he presided over. Being without a deacon for four months, he reports he buried singlehanded 430 bodies and made 85 funeral orations. An assistant who was ultimately appointed died a month later and his successor followed him to the grave a few days after arrival. Andreae lost twelve relatives in one year, the mortality rate among his own children being utterly devastating. This aspect of his life is worthy of recall as evidence that the man practised what he found wanting in so many of the clergy of his day.

The moral lethargy confronting him whichever way he turned was so exasperating and frustrating that we find him moving to this conclusion: 'so ersehe ich, da es schon Wohlwollen ist, wenn man einem nicht übel will, daß die meisten eigentlich gar keinen Willen haben, und nicht haben können, und da Zwischenzeiten und Wechsel das meiste ändern'. Andreae was made of different stuff. An inner compulsion drove him on errands of mercy and to projects to further the spiritual and physical welfare of his flock. The years 1627-28 witnessed the renovation of the hospital chapel and the extension of the church building in Calw to accommodate another 1,000 persons. Andreae supervised these operations and, although (possibly because) the work was financed by contributions from the citizens without support from the state, the enterprise, he tells us, excited envious criticism in some quarters. The moral, religious and political anarchy surrounding him and the trials besetting him personally were enough to threaten his will to live. Since, however, he survived the repeated and deadly onslaughts of the plague while ministering to the dying, and at the age of 51 an attack by robbers who broke one of his ribs, he saw as God's will that he be spared to persevere in his calling. The year 1635 he named his 'Kerkerjahr' when the vicissitudes of war forced him to move from one lodging to another until he built himself a 'Hüttchen'. The previous year a fire had destroyed his home with precious works of art 'von den größten Meistern' (Johann Imhoff the Elder had given him a Madonna portrait by Dürer and Eberhard von Rappoltstein a Conversion of St. Paul by Holbein). The bitter loss of such treasures did not deter him from continuing his efforts on behalf of the destitute and bereaved; indeed, his appeals during one period brought in 4,532 gulden from the citizens, to which he added 1,000 of his own. Substantial success in abolishing abuses such as simony in the church eluded Andreae and this made him look forward to complete retirement. This he never achieved for in 1650 at the age of 64 he was appointed Abbot of Bebenhausen and the following year 'Generalsuperintendent'. In Bebenhausen occasional visits by distinguished persons rendered tolerable a life of hopes deferred, and the work there was lighter than in Stuttgart where as 'Hofprediger' he had preached 1,040 sermons in ten years.

The depression of his last years was brought on mainly by the loss of old friends and family members, failing health and difficult relations with colleagues. The failure of two attempts to go to Wolfenbüttel in response to the repeated invitations of Duke August was a bitter disappointment. The visit planned for the spring of 1646 had to be cancelled because of a fall from his horse. Five years later when he was about to leave for Wolfenbüttel, sickness laid him low rendering him incapable of using the sedan the Duke had sent expressly for the journey. So Andreae was destined never to see his most magnanimous benefactor. The connection between the two scholars was first made in 1630 through the mediation of Andreae's good friend Wilhelm Wense, and by 1643 a weekly correspondence had developed, the Duke's consort Sophia Elisabeth and three of their four children also writing occasionally. The Duke's benevolence was such that, on Andreae's testimony it would be difficult to overestimate its effect on the last decade of his life. Apparently it saved his protégé from a poverty-stricken existence in his later years, for on several occasions he accepted money and valuable gifts, the most substantial being a stipend of 400 Thaler when Duke August made him a member of his 'Kirchenrat' in recognition of Andreae's service to the Lutheran church and alsoin return for his dedication to the Duke of *Rei Christianae et Litterariae Subsidia*. In the last year of his life he complained that his stipend from the state was in arrears and attributed this to the malice of administrators. Meanwhile his health had deteriorated too. The digestive troubles, he believed, were caused by a sedentary life, but in his youth he had endeavoured to counterbalance this by indulging in his favourite exercise: 'Mir gefiel die körperliche Übung, auf ein Pferd zu springen, und ein Rad zu schlagen'. Love of horseriding occasioned the pathetic comment that when imperial troops occupied the town of Calw in 1635, he was so busy ministering to the sick and homeless that he had not been on horseback for over a year. By then he was in his fiftieth year. As a young man in Italy he had seen a form of exercise that fascinated him: the wooden vaulting horse. On his return to Tübingen he introduced it to his friends 'wobei eine große Menge adelicher Jünglinge sich einfand, daß mir dieses Spiel enträglicher wurde, als jedes ernsthafte Studium'. 'Voltigieren' or 'Ro springen' was not unknown elsewhere in Germany, but the advantage of the sawbuck was that it could be used indoors.

Gottfried Keller wrote these words [in the sixth chapter of the *Sinngedicht*]:

> in den Aufzeichnungen des lutherischen Theologen und Gottesmannes Johannes Valentin Andreae rauchte und schwelte der Dreißigjährige Krieg. Ihn bildeten Not und Leiden, hohe Gelahrtheit, Gottvertrauen und der Fleiß der Widersacher so trefflich durch und aus.

A polyhistor then, but a Humanist who was demonstrably humane; a compassionate social worker, but with an intolerance of any deviation from Lutheran orthodoxy as his most visible foible today; a man interested in mathematics and mechanics with a discriminating taste in fine art and a delight in physical skills and exercise; in fact someone bringing to mind the ideal of *uomo universale*. Yet with all his intellectual and artistic interests and accomplishments Andreae insisted on tending his flock, thus fulfilling his role of pastor in the real sense of the word.

FURTHER READING

Biography

Montgomery, John Warwick. *Cross and Crucible: Johann Valentin Andreae (1586-1654): Phoenix of the Theologians.* The Hague: Martinus Nijhoff, 1973, 255 p.

> Complete study of Andreae's life, career, and philosophical views.

Criticism

Tod, Ian and Wheeler, Michael. "Citadels of Science." In *Utopia,* pp. 51-3. New York: Harmony Books, 1978.

> Briefly discusses the important characteristics of Andreae's utopian vision in the *Christianopolis.*

Walsh, Chad. "Plato and Company." In *From Utopia to Nightmare,* pp. 45-6. New York: Harper & Row Publishers, 1962.

> Presents brief overview of the social structure of *Christianopolis.*

New Atlantis

Sir Francis Bacon

Utopian fiction.

INTRODUCTION

Considered a paradigm of Renaissance scientific and utopian literature, Bacon's *New Atlantis* (1624) pioneered new methodological standards by systematizing the process of scientific enquiry and discovery. The work is the foundation of Bacon's reputation as the father of modern science in England and as a herald of the modern scientific and philosophical worldview. Bacon has also been distinguished by scholars and scientists throughout the centuries for his important contributions to politics, law, and literature as well as philosophy and science. Thomas Jefferson characterized him as one of the three greatest men the world had ever known. Though scientists and political theorists today reject many of Bacon's findings, they are indebted to his *New Atlantis* and other scientific writings for offering a model for modern research and development.

Biographical Information

Bacon apparently intended the *New Atlantis* as the culmination of his philosophical vision, or "Instauratio Magna" (Great Instauration), a lifelong project that proposed to classify and interpret all knowledge by restoring what the writer saw as humankind's primeval mastery of the natural world. Bacon envisioned the "new Atlantis," Bensalem, as a society governed by the principles of learning entailed by this grand scheme. Bacon's secretary, William Rawley, who edited and published the *New Atlantis* after Bacon's death, claims that Bacon meant to write a concluding account of Atlantis's laws but was distracted by the composition of his natural histories. Throughout his political career Bacon had attempted to promote his grand scheme. He became a member of the English Parliament in 1584 and held many subsequent positions as a courtier. He wrote many legal and political tracts, and published his philosophical magnum opus *Summi Angliae Cancellarii Instauratio magna (Novum Organum)* in 1620. Bacon reached his highest point in office when he was appointed Viscount Saint Albans in 1621. That year, however, also marked Bacon's political downfall. Accused of accepting bribes from a client in a lawsuit, Bacon was tried, convicted, imprisoned in the Tower of London, and fined £40,000 by the House of Lords. Although he in fact paid no fine, remaining in prison only three or four days and receiving a general pardon later that year, Bacon's political career was finished. Furthermore, he was forced to leave office without having gained the respect of either monarch he served so faithfully: neither of the two monarchs under whom he served—Elizabeth and James I—ever seemed interested in Bacon's suggestions concerning statecraft. Nevertheless, he continued working with great energy, publishing the *New Atlantis* in 1621. In 1623 he published *De Dignitate & Augmentis Scientarium,* a Latin translation of *Of the Proficience and Advancement of Learning* (1605), a work which illustrated the first part of his grand scheme; two years later, the final edition of his *Essays* (1625) appeared. Less than one year after Bacon's death in 1626, Rawley published his unfinished *New Atlantis* in the *Sylva Sylarum: or A Naturall Historie In Ten Centuries.*

Plot and Major Characters

In the *New Atlantis* a fictitious merchant sea captain recounts his experiences on an island called Bensalem, from which he has returned to describe that enlightened society. A sustained gale propelled his ship for many days until, its provisions exhausted, it entered Bensalem's harbor. The natives' enigmatic welcome—remote yet comforting—was a sign of things to come: at every stage of the crew's apparent assimilation the island society surrounded them with prohibitions and secrets. Visitors to Bensalem are few, and those who have touched its shores have almost never returned to their homes; just thirteen have done so in nineteen hundred years. The attractiveness of the island made the sailors "forget all that was dear" in their own countries, ensuring that they would not return home to spread the news of Bensalem's location and riches. The captain alone was allowed to hear of the most important Bensalemite institution, the research and development laboratories of Salomon's House, though the information he received from a "Father" of the house is a list of wonders rather than a revelation of natural laws. Salomon's House is devoted to the "enlarging of the bounds of Human Empire, to the effecting of all things possible," including the resuscitation of what might "seem dead in appearance." Its researches focus on discovering the means of making anything into anything else, either materially or by means of illusions that are generated in "perspective houses" and "houses of deceits of the senses." Spy missions to the outside world collect additional information about scientific innovations. The Salomonic priesthood withholds some inventions from the state; those it publishes are made known "without all affectation of strangeness" so as not to "induce admiration" by making their operations "seem more miraculous." Hymns are sung daily, in prayer to God for guidance in new inquiries and applications. The priesthood's extraordinary secrecy, power to alter the world, and ability to alter perceptions of its accomplishments are mitigated—and yet concealed—by its private religiosity and the benevolent appearance of its wonders. The occurrence of miracles is accepted, but these must be certified by the scientific priests. It was a Father of the House of Salomon who interpreted the revelation of Christianity to the Bensalemites when a column of light topped with a cross appeared in the sea near the coast. Unable to approach it nearer than sixty yards, the people were dumbfounded until a representative of Salomon's House, the institution serving as "the very eye" of the kingdom, certified the wonder as a genuine miracle. Without the authoritative word of a member of the pious scientific elect, the Bensalemites would not have been able to distinguish this miracle from an illusion.

Major Themes

Conflict between tradition and innovation is a central theme in Bacon's writings. In his *New Atlantis* the conundrum presents itself when he develops an empirical method of inductive scientific research and enquiry without abandoning assumptions that today would be considered archaic or occult. Bacon believes that human perception can be reconfigured by implementing a system of "new learning" that merges theology and empiricism. This, he argues, will enable a person to determine "the Knowledge of Causes, and Secrett Motions of Things; And the Enlarging of the bounds of Humane Empire, to the Effecting of all Things possible." Most modern scientists and scientific thinkers hold that Bacon's epistemological focus is incompatible with modern scientific methodology. For Bacon, however—as Bensalem's scientific certification of miracles makes clear—religion justifies, but does not influence, science and affairs of state. He concludes that neither science nor religion alone is sufficient for Bensalem's peace and prosperity, but that properly conducted scientific research is, in fact, consistent with religious propriety and social stability; or, as Judah Bierman explains in her 1963 essay "Science and Society in the *New Atlantis* and other Renaissance Utopias," "that science will not make atheists and communists of the citizens."

Critical Reception

The effect of Bacon's message—especially as expressed in the *New Atlantis*—was immediate. His ideas were well-received by many of his contemporaries, especially Ben Jonson, the first (though unofficial) poet laureate of England and a prominent writer of the Elizabethan Age, whose praise influenced seventeenth-century attitudes toward Bacon's scientific works and enhanced his reputation. Detractors, however, considered the *New Atlantis* to be awkwardly written, enigmatic, and painfully didactic. Bacon's ideas of progress spread quickly, first in England in the later seventeenth and eighteenth centuries, then in Europe, and then throughout the world in the nineteenth and twentieth centuries. Shortly after Bacon's death, institutions based on Salomon's House appeared throughout Europe. In 1645 the Invisible College for the discussion of natural philosophy was established, an institution from which the Royal Society of London developed. Modern scientists, however, find Bacon's method flawed in several ways: Bertrand Russell, a twentieth-century British philosopher and mathematician, for example, stated that "Bacon's inductive method is faulty through insufficient emphasis on hypothesis. He hoped that mere orderly arrangement of data would make the right hypothesis obvious, but this is seldom the case. . . . Usually some hypothesis is a necessary preliminary to the collection of facts, since selection of facts demands some way of determining relevance. Without something of this kind, the mere multiplicity of facts is baffling." Inadequate for the development of natural science, Bacon's philosophy and his deep thirst for knowledge nevertheless faithfully reflect the expansive spirit of the seventeenth century.

CRITICISM

William Rawley (essay date 1627)

SOURCE: In *The Works of Francis Bacon, Vol. V,* James Spedding, Robert Leslie Ellis, and Douglas Denon Heath, eds., Brown and Taggard, 1862, p. 348.

[*Rawley, Bacon's secretary, published the unfinished* New Atlantis *in 1627 at the end of the volume containing Bacon's* Sylva Sylarum. *In the following note to the reader, Rawley states Bacon's purpose in writing the* New Atlantis.]

This fable my Lord devised, to the end that he might exhibit therein a model or description of a college instituted for the interpreting of nature and the producing of great and marvellous works for the benefit of men, under the name of Salomon's House, or the College of the Six Days' Works. And even so far his Lordship hath proceeded, as to finish that part. Certainly the model is more vast and high than can possibly be imitated in all things; notwithstanding most things therein are within men's power to effect. His Lordship thought also in this present fable to have composed a frame of Laws, or of the best state or mould of a commonwealth; but foreseeing it would be a long work, his desire of collecting the Natural History diverted him, which he preferred many degrees before it.

This work of the *New Atlantis* (as much as concerneth the English edition) his Lordship designed for this place; in regard it hath so near affinity (in one part of it) with the preceding Natural History.

James Spedding (essay date 1862)

SOURCE: "Preface to *The New Atlantis,*" in *The Works of Francis Bacon, Vol. V,* James Spedding, Robert Leslie Ellis, and Douglas Denon Heath, eds., Brown and Taggard, 1862, pp. 349-53.

[*In the following excerpt, Spedding correlates Bacon's* New Atlantis *with several of his concurrent works, and describes how Bacon's desire to complete a natural history forestalled the work's completion.*]

The *New Atlantis* seems to have been written in 1624, and, though not finished, to have been intended for publication as it stands. It was published accordingly by Dr. Rawley in 1627, at the end of the volume containing the *Sylva Sylvarum;* for which place Bacon had himself designed it, the subjects of the two being so near akin; the one representing his idea of what should be the end of the work which in the other he supposed himself to be beginning. For the story of Solomon's House is nothing more than a vision of the practical results which he anticipated from the study of natural history diligently and systematically carried on through successive generations.

In this part of it, the work may probably be considered as complete. Of the state of Solomon's House he has told us all that he was as yet qualified to tell. His own attempts to "interpret nature" suggested the apparatus which was necessary for success: he had but to furnish Solomon's House with the instruments and preparations which he had himself felt the want of. The difficulties which had baffled his single efforts to provide that apparatus for himself suggested the constitution and regulations of a society formed to overcome them: he had but to furnish Solomon's House with the helps in head and hand which he had himself wished for. His own intellectual aspirations suggested the result: he had but to set down as known all that he himself most longed to know. But here he was obliged to stop. He could not describe the *process* of a perfect philosophical investigation; because it must of course have proceeded by the method of the *Novum Organum,* which was not yet expounded. Nor could he give a particular example of the result of such investigation, in the shape of a Form or an Axiom; for that presupposed the completion, not only of the *Novum Organum,* but (at least in some one subject) of the Natural History also; and no portion of the Natural History complete enough for the purpose was as yet producible. Here therefore he stopped; and it would almost seem that the nature of the difficulty which stood in his way had reminded him of the course he ought to take; for just at this point (as we learn from Dr. Rawley) he did in fact leave his fable and return to his work. He had begun it with the intention of exhibiting a model political constitution, as well as a model college of natural philosophy; but "his desire of collecting the natural history diverted him, which he preferred many degrees before it." And in this, according to his own view of the matter, he was no doubt right; for though there are few people now who would not gladly give all the *Sylva Sylvarum,* had there been ten times as much of it, in exchange for an account of the laws, institutions, and administrative arrangements of Bensalem, it was not so with Bacon; who being deeper read in the phenomena of the human heart than in those of the material world, probably thought the perfect knowledge of nature an easier thing than the perfect government of men,—easier and not so far off; and therefore preferred to work where there was fairest hope of fruit.

To us, who can no longer hope for the fruits which Bacon expected, the *New Atlantis* is chiefly interesting as a record of his own feelings. Perhaps there is no single work of his which has so much of himself in it. The description of Solomon's House is the description of the vision in which he lived,—the vision not of an ideal world released from the natural conditions to which ours is subject, but of our own world as it might be made if we did our duty by it; of a state of things which he believed would one day be actually seen upon this earth such as it is by men such as we are; and the coming of which he believed that his own labours were sensibly hastening. The account of the manners and customs of the people of Bensalem is an account of his own taste in humanity; for a man's ideal, though not necessarily a description of what he is, is almost always an indication of what he would be; and in the sober piety, the serious cheerfulness, the tender and gracious courtesy, the open-handed hospitality, the fidelity in public and chastity in private life, the grave and graceful manners, the order, decency, and earnest industry, which prevail among these people, we recognise an image of himself made perfect,—of that condition of the human sould which he loved in others, and aspired towards in himself. Even the dresses, the household arrangements, the order of their feasts and solemnities, their very gestures of welcome and salutation, have an interest and significance independent of the fiction, as so many records of Bacon's personal taste in such matters. Nor ought the stories which the Governor of the House of Strangers tells about the state of navigation and population in the early post-diluvian ages, to be regarded merely as romances invented to vary and enrich the narrative, but rather as belonging to a class of serious speculations to which Bacon's mind was prone. As in his visions of the future, embodied in the achievements of Solomon's House, there is nothing which he did not conceive to be really practicable by the means which he supposes to be used; so in his speculations concerning the past, embodied in the traditions of Bensalem, I doubt whether there be any (setting aside, of course, the particular history of the fabulous island) which he did not believe to be historically probable. Whether it were that the progress of the human race in knowledge and art seemed to him too small to be accounted for otherwise than by supposing occasional tempests of destruction, in which all that had been gathered was swept away,— or that the vicissitudes which had actually taken place during the short periods of which we know something had suggested to him the probability of similar accidents during those long tracts of time of which we know nothing,—or merely that the imagination is prone by nature to people darkness with shadows,—certain it is that the tendency was strong in Bacon to credit the past with wonders; to suppose that the world had brought forth greater things than it remembered, had seen periods of high civilisation buried in oblivion, great powers and peoples swept away and extinguished.

In the year 1607, he avowed before the House of Commons a belief that in some forgotten period of her history (possibly during the Heptarchy) England had been far better peopled than she was then. In 1609, when he published the *De Sapientiâ Veterum,* he inclined to believe that an age of higher intellectual development than any the world then knew of had flourished and passed out of memory long before Homer and Hesiod wrote; and this upon the clearest and most deliberate review of all the obvious objections; and more decidedly than he had done four years before when he published the *Advancement of Learning*. And I have little doubt that when he wrote the *New Atlantis* he thought it not improbable that the state of navigation in the world 3000 years before was really such as the Governor of the House of Strangers describes; that some such naval expeditions as those of Coya and Tyrambel may really have taken place; and that the early civilisation of the Great Atlantis may really have been drowned by a deluge and left to begin its career again from a state of mere barbarism.

Among the few works of fiction which Bacon attempted, the *New Atlantis* is much the most considerable; which gives an additional interest to it, and makes one the more regret that it was not finished according to the original design. Had it proceeded to the end in a manner worthy of the beginning, it would have stood, as a work of art, among the most perfect compositions of its kind.

Joyce Oramel Hertzler (essay date 1923)

SOURCE: "The Early Modern Utopias," in The Utopiansm of Frances, Bacon's 'New Atlantis,'" in *The History of Utopian Thought,* The Macmillan Company, 1923, pp. 121-80.

[In the following excerpt, Hertzler examines several utopian aspects of the New Atlantis *and comments on how the nature of Bacon's thinking best applies to social science.]*

There was a paucity of Utopian literature for nearly a century following the appearance of More's *Utopia*. This silence was broken in England by Francis Bacon, Baron of Verulam, with his ingenious fragment, the *New Atlantis*. He never finished this work but enough remains to show what the nature of his thinking was, and illustrates the application of his best thought to social science.

Francis Bacon was born in 1561 at London, the son of Sir Nicholas Bacon, who was Lord Keeper of the Great Seal. Like More, he was intended for orders, but instead was educated as a lawyer. Unlike More, he attended Trinity College, instead of Oxford. He himself

Voltaire comments on Bacon's writings and ideas:

The best and most remarkable of [Bacon's] works is the one which is the least read today and the least useful: I refer to his *Novum Scientiarum Organum*. It is the scaffolding by means of which modern scientific thought has been built, and when that edifice had been raised, at least in part, the scaffolding ceased to be of any use.

Chancellor Bacon did not yet understand nature, but he knew and pointed out the roads leading to it. He had very early scorned what the Universities called Philosophy, and he did everything in his power to prevent these institutions, set up for the perfection of human reason, from continuing to spoil it with their *quiddities,* their *abhorrence of a vacuum,* their *substantial forms* and all the inappropriate expressions which not only ignorance made respectable, but which a ridiculous confusion with religion had made almost sacred.

He is the father of experimental philosophy. It is true that some amazing secrets had been discovered before his time. Men had invented the compass, printing, engraving, oil-painting, mirrors, the art of restoring to some extent sight to the aged by glasses, called spectacles, gunpowder, etc. . . .

[However,] nobody before Chancellor Bacon had grasped experimental science, and of all the practical applications made since, scarcely one is not foreshadowed in his book. He had made several himself; he made a kind of pneumatic machine by means of which he guessed at the elasticity of the air, and he circled all round the discovery of its weight, indeed he almost had it, but the truth was seized upon by Torricelli. Not long afterwards experimental physics was suddenly taken up simultaneously in almost all parts of Europe. It was a hidden treasure the existence of which Bacon had suspected and which all the scientists, encouraged by his promise, strove to dig out. . . .

Voltaire, in his Lettres anglaises ou
philosophiques, *1734.*

was one of More's successors as Lord Chancellor of England. His life was a peculiar combination of pusillanimity and grandeur. As a man in high office he stooped to the meanest of things and was guilty of all kinds of irregularities and unscrupulous actions in his dealings. He practiced deceit and dissimulation whenever it could be made to pay, passing at the same time as an honest and outspoken man. Similarly in his management of men he was a pitiable failure. But his unfortunate and two-faced political life came to an abrupt end in 1621, when after being accused of accepting bribes and committing other dishonesties, he admitted the charges, and was dismissed from his office of Lord Chancellor. He was sentenced to a fine of

£40,000 and life imprisonment, but the King relieved him of punishment. Thus driven from London in disgrace he retired to his own country home at St. Albans. Here he devoted the rest of his life to literature, philosophical speculation and science. In the achievements he accomplished in his retirement, he showed himself to be truly great; few have been greater. The *New Atlantis* was a product of this final period of retribution and contemplation having been written in 1622. It is thus the product of an old man, written at the end of his life, while the *Utopia* was written by a younger man, before he had undergone the strains and disillusionings of high public life. He died in 1626, at the age of sixty-five years.

Bacon doubtless stands next to Shakespeare, his contemporary, in the empire of human intellect of sixteenth century England. In mind Bacon was a typical product of the European Renaissance. His intellectual interests embraced every topic of the time, and his writings touched almost every subject of study. He was at once historian, essayist, legal writer, logician, philosophical speculator, and writer on almost every known branch of science, and to each he brought the same eager curiosity and efficient insight.

The *New Atlantis* was a great by-product of Bacon's studies in connection with the preparation of his *Novum Organum,* which embodied his scientific methods. He received the vision of a *New Atlantis,* a land of freedom and justice, in which were established institutions and principles which would carry into effect the system treated in *Novum Organum.* While Thomas More was a representative of the Humanistic Period of the Renaissance with its emphasis on pantheism and recognition of equal social rights for all reasoning men, Bacon was a representative of the Natural Science period when thinkers had come to believe that man's ultimate regeneration and perfectibility depended primarily not on reform of laws of property or on social revolution, but on the progress of science and the regulation of human life by the scientific spirit. "Bacon's *New Atlantis* proclaimed with almost romantic enthusiasm that scientific method alone was the ladder by which man was to ascend to perfect living." Its new program to attain Utopia was the rebuilding of society in the light of knowledge and discovery. Bacon shared and expressed the confidence of his time that wonderful things were to be revealed; and that nothing was impossible to man provided he hit upon the right key to nature's secrets. Just as every age that feels itself upon the threshold of a new world epoch writes Utopias, so Bacon wrote the *New Atlantis,* giving expression in it to his optimism about the future of a distinctly secular science. Through experimental science men gained dominion over things, "for nature is only governed by obeying her." Or in the words of Durant [in *Philosophy and the Social Problem,* 1917] "I accept it (i. e., nature), says Bacon, but only as raw material. We will listen to nature, but only that we may learn what language she understands. We stoop to conquer." He was convinced that the possession of exceptional intellectual power properly applied, would revolutionize man's relation with nature and reveal to him her hidden secrets.

While Bacon's utopianism centers about the influence of science and knowledge, there are a few other elements which first demand our attention. From the spirit of the work we gather that the end of government is the welfare of the people. The King should rule by virtue of his ability and his disposition to rule for the commonwealth. The state should be to a large extent self-sufficient, echoing the mercantilistic doctrines current at his time. Foreign influence must be carefully watched lest the inhabitants of the state be corrupted.

The family is for him the unit of society and upon it is built the whole social fabric and he consequently glorified its office. Its importance is emphasized by special ceremonies. One of these is the Feast of the Family which is instituted and paid for by the State, and celebrated in honor of him whose family counts at least thirty living members above three years of age. The head of the family from thenceforth wears a medal presented by the king. The feast is largely religious in character consisting partly of invocation hymns, prayer and benediction. It is also made an occassion for settling all petty disputes between members, to impress lessons of morality, piety, patriotism and obedience. It emphasizes three strong points from the social point of view. First, the principle of family unity is dwelt upon. It shall not be a family which breaks up for lack of cohesion or proper authority. At the ceremony one of the sons is chosen who shall henceforth live with the father in the latter's house, and so hold the family together by taking the father's place in case of his death. Second, the idea of raising a large family is emphasized, for no man is so honored throughout the state as such a "family-father." The world had not yet been disturbed by a doctrine of diminishing returns and a Malthusian theory of population. Third, unlike the conditions in all earlier secular utopias, there were no common tables, except for pupils in the boarding schools. The family met daily around its private board thereby tightening the family tie.

In his discussion of the marriage relation, Bacon indulges in bitter satire on the social ethics of his age. He accuses them of making marriage merely a remedy for unlawful concupiscence. Marriage in Europe was "but a very bargain, wherein is sought alliance or portion, or reputation with some desire (almost indifferent) of issue." Nor did marriage seem to change matters for the better so much among men. "The haunting of those dissolute places, or resort to courtezans, are no more punished in married men than in bachelors. And the depraved custom of change, and the delight in meretricious embracements (where sin is turned into art) maketh marriage a dull thing, and a kind of imposition or tax."

Bacon would have marriage be the faithful nuptial union of one man and one woman, chaste and clean for "their usual saying is that whosoever is unchaste cannot reverence himself"; the purpose of marriage being to supply a strong intelligent offspring to the State. Any union threatening social welfare was forbidden or frowned upon by social disfavor. Bacon objected to More's method of examining and selecting partners, "where the married couple are permitted before they contract, to see one another naked." Bacon said, "This they dislike, for they think it a scorn to give a refusal after so familiar knowledge; but because of hidden defects in men and women's bodies, they have a more civil way; for they have near every town a couple of pools (which they call Adam and Eve's pools), where it is permitted to one of the friends of the man, and another of the friends of the woman, to see them severally bathe naked." Thus, in a rude way did More and Bacon grope after the eugenic ideal.

The utopianistic element of greatest value and that factor of the *New Atlantis* which has been primarily responsible for its fame, is the picture drawn and the description given of a great "college called Salomon's Home, a self-perpetuating group of learned and capable men endowed and working together for the common end of being—"the noblest foundation that ever was upon the earth, and the lantern of this kingdom,"— the end of the attainment of knowledge by experiment, research and travel, the enriching of the world's store of information by the process of investigating into nature and the ways of men, and discovering the truths and principles which make for progress and happiness. Bacon sought to describe an imaginary college, which should be instituted for the purpose of interpreting nature, and of producing great and marvelous works for the benefit of men. Bacon has the governor of Salomon's House describe its functions as follows: "The end of our foundation is the knowledge of causes and secret motions of things and the enlarging of the bounds of human empire, to the effecting of all things possible." Here we find the personal conviction and ideals of Bacon, the Renaissance scholar. He saw an ideal of comfort for human life, made possible through the systematic use of the knowledge and control of nature through science. He and his contemporaries felt that all social injuries would be healed by raising human society, by means of the scientific advancement of external civilization, beyond all cares and all the needs which vex it. What transformations were possible when invention, research and experiment became intelligently exercised arts! This reaction toward natural ethics was perfectly understandable, since it came at a time when the authoritarian sanctions of supernatural religion were becoming impotent and falling into the discard. Men felt that only by speculation and research could the evils of society be overcome. For them, to use the words of Turgenev, "Nature is not a temple, but a workshop," the raw material out of which Utopians were constructed.

Of course, there is much that is fantastic about Bacon's imaginings. There are caves sunk 600 fathoms deep in which "refrigerations and conservations of bodies" are perfected, and new metals artifically contrived. There are towers half a mile high used for purposes of meteorological observation. By means of unsuspected chemical discoveries, by special changes as baths and air cures diseases are banished and life prolonged. New flowers and fruits are brought into being in the orchards to add to the welfare of man. "And many of them we so order, as that they become of medicinal use." Vivisection is practiced on beasts and birds so that opportunities may be at hand to test the effects of poison and new operations in surgery, and to widen the knowledge of physiology. There is an establishment where tricks that deceive the senses like feats of juggling, or spiritualistic manifestations, or ghostly apparitions, are practiced to the highest perfection and then explained to serious students who go out into the world, and by their instruction prevent the simple-minded from being deceived by quacks and imposters. They make divinations of diseases, plagues, earthquakes, temperature and divers other things, and give counsel as to what the people shall do for the prevention and remedy of them. And in short, the whole purpose of the college itself directed toward improving the material state of society.

The House of Salomon is conducted by a great hierarchy of fellows, or endowed students, the real aristocracy of the island. These make experiments, devise philosophic inventions, conduct researches, and do anything to aid in the truly philanthropic welfare of the race. A number of these fellows are sent abroad every twelve years to study the affairs, improvements and sciences of other countries, remaining there until relieved by the next twelve, when they return home bringing back books, patterns and instruments and ideas of all kinds to make available the information they have collected. Bacon as one of the inhabitants says, "Thus you see we maintain a trade, not for gold, silver or jewels, nor for silks, nor for spices, nor any other commodity of matter; but only for God's first creature, which was light; to have light, I say, of the growth of all parts of the world." This illuminating sentence sets forth the spirit and the high purpose of the writer. Generally the inventors of great things were to be honored by having statues erected to their honor in the House, and a liberal and honorable reward was given them.

Bacon's society was established, not upon a communism of wealth, but upon a communism of knowledge, and it was a communism which meant the largest possible participation of all members in the benefits of society. And yet it was a communism something like that of Plato wherein the virtue flowed from the philosophic few to the untutored many.

In the "New Atlantis" Bacon illustrated the possibility of the influence of the social will consciously ordering social progress. Any people or any nation, by putting aside a substantial part of its material resources to the equipment of scientific work, research, exploration, and philosophic speculation could direct its progress as it wished. Ignorance, dark, prejudiced ignorance was the source of social evils, and human suffering. Society's hope lay in the reorganization for social purposes of the processes of discovery and interpretation of nature. Having discovered the truth, men would be free. Moreover Bacon felt that this was a progressive process; men shall always become free. Quoting Lee, "He refused to believe that any limits were set beyond which human intellect when clarified and purified could not penetrate. He argued that, however far we may think we have advanced in knowledge or science, there is always more beyond, and that the tracts lying beyond our present gaze will in due course of time come within the range of a purified intellectual vision. There were no bounds to what human thought might accomplish. To other children of the Renaissance the same sanguine faith had come, but none gave such emphatic voice to it as Bacon."

Another utopianistic truth stands out as we read the *New Atlantis* and that is that there is nothing that we may not do, if we but will it strong enough; but it must be a willing of means as well as ends. Tenacity of purpose supported by a careful organization of the arts and sciences and tempered by a superb patience will make all things possible.

There is one thing, however, which Bacon and the men of his time did not realize as clearly as we now do, and that is that science and knowledge unaided cannot solve our social problems. During the last four centuries we have invented and invented, only to widen the hiatus between classes. The scientist must also be a social philosopher and view his own work as part of the universal whole, and seek to make his work redound to human welfare and social progress in general. Science for science's sake must become anathema. The results of a humanized science are fittingly described by Durant: "Before it can be of real service to life, science must be enlightened by some consideration and fitting together of human ends: without philosophy as its eye-piece, science is but the traditional child who has taken apart the traditional watch, with none but the traditional results."

Harry W. Laidler on Bacon's social philosophy:

Bacon's great defect was his refusal to see that the development of science, while necessary to any ideal society, was not sufficient. He failed to realize that the people of a nation must not only produce, but also must learn the art of social co-operation, and determine how every new invention and discovery may be applied to the broadest possible social ends. The history of civilization has since shown that science may not only be used as a great constructive force, but also as a great destroyer, unless guided by a correct social philosophy.

Harry W. Laidler, in Social-Economic Movements, *Thomas Y. Crowell Company, 1944.*

Moody E. Prior (essay date 1949)

SOURCE: "Bacon's Man of Science," in *Journal of the History of Ideas,* Vol. XV, No. 3, June, 1949, pp. 348-70.

[*In the excerpt below, Prior summarizes Bacon's view of the ideal man of science.*]

The dominating motive of Bacon's intellectual life was the complete reformation of learning, and he labored under the conviction that he was, almost single-handed, promoting a revolution in knowledge to the end that man might win a new empire over things. In those of his writings which he regarded as the parts of his grandiose plan, he gave frequent expression to his new conception of the proper goals of human knowledge and proposed new methods by which they were to be attained. And clearly implicit in this new approach to learning was an alteration in the conception of the learned man. Since the new aim and the method were to make unprecedented demands on the knower, it became necessary for Bacon to conceive a new scientist as well as a new science. This is not immediately apparent because it was to the development of his aims and methods that Bacon gave primary attention in his writings. Incomplete as his system remains, the outlines of his plan are clear and explicit, and portions are developed in detail; but the details of his picture of the new man of science are scattered, and the image has to be pieced together. From the writings of such later men as the early members of the Royal Society, for whom Bacon was a patron saint, the common elements of an image of the new scientist are clearly discernible; but though it was largely from Bacon that they caught the lineaments of the ideal which inspired them, the later portrait appears generalized and simplified when compared to the original. Every detail of the character of Bacon's new scientist is rooted in the goals which he set up and the methods he proposed. All of

Bacon's objection to the learning of the past, all his hopes for the future, and all his philosophical aims are reflected in the image which he seems to have clearly visualized of the new scientist who was to be the instrument of the new learning as well as its product.

The intellectual, psychological and ethical qualities which Bacon demanded of his new scientist form an organic concept, but it is possible to distinguish certain qualities which are associated very closely with the requirements of the method and certain others which are necessarily bound up with the proper aims of learning and the rôle which they impose on the scientist. The immediate purpose of Bacon's methodological principles was nothing less than truth and certainty, and the goal he proposed was nothing less than the profound improvement of man's lot. The spirit and tone of his writings is therefore strongly optimistic. But Bacon did not ground his hopes on any extravagant estimate of man's powers. The hard realism of his mind, so clearly manifested in his comments on worldly affairs, is also revealed in his adoption of a very critical attitude toward the limited capacities by means of which man perceives and comes to a knowledge of his universe. Bacon's method, therefore, is founded on a review not only of the errors and defects in learning but of the deficiencies of the knower. If the past was to be swept aside, the mind wiped clear, and a new way charted, the positive program could begin only after all established illusions about man himself had been anatomized and taken into account.

For a rigorous critique of the failings in man which stood in the way of attaining certainty Bacon had not far to seek. The Sceptics of antiquity had systematically analyzed the defects in man's capacity to perceive and judge of reality, and had concluded on the basis of this analysis that nothing can be known. Strengthened by new illustrations and revitalized by literary embellishment, notably in the writings of Montaigne, this ancient school enjoyed a vigorous revival during the sixteenth century. But neither in motives nor conclusions were the ancient Sceptics or the new essentially akin to Bacon. Bacon—like others among the philosophers of the new developments in natural science— found the sceptical critique of man powerfully stimulating; moreover, he recognized it as something to be acknowledged and met before a way to truth could be recommended. Bacon's awareness of the force of the sceptical arguments is everywhere apparent, but it is in the famous discussion of the Idols in ***Novum Organum*** that the influence is most direct. Incorporated into a novel analysis and surrounded by many important original extensions can be discovered all of the sceptical "modes." The sceptical deductions and conclusions are, however, missing. Bacon simultaneously accepted scepticism as a critique and rejected it as a philosophy of knowledge: he represented himself as one who maintained not that nothing can be known, but that nothing can be known except in a certain way.

This way—the new method—was thus to provide correctives for the limitations of the knower. The critique of the Sceptics Bacon acknowledged, but despair in consequence of it he regarded as merely the result of neglecting the aid available: "The doctrine of those who have denied that certainty could be attained at all, has some agreement with my way of proceeding at the first setting out; but they end in being infinitely separated and opposed. For the holders of that doctrine assert simply that nothing can be known; I also assert that not much can be known in nature by the way which is now in use. But then they go on to destroy the authority of the senses and understanding; whereas I proceed to devise and supply helps for the same." Scepticism becomes therefore not a philosophy of knowledge but a principle of method: "that which I meditate and propound is not *Acatalepsia* but *Eucatalepsia;* not the denial of the capacity to understand, but provision for understanding truly."

For the defects of the senses Bacon proposed as correctives the use of instruments and, most important of all, experiments. The correction of the defects of the understanding, however, demanded more subtle forms of control. Scepticism as a method called for calmness of spirit equal to the demands of systematic doubt—of unwillingness to assent or deny prematurely. But this was an attitude very different from the *ataraxia* and *epoche* of the ancient Sceptics, which it resembles superficially, just as it had little in common with the ultimate triumph over passion of the Stoics. And it was necessarily opposed to the dogmatism of the system-builders and to the agitation encouraged by the disputations methods of the schools. Bacon described it as an attitude that mediated between the extremes of dogmatism and scepticism, "between the presumption of pronouncing on everything and the despair of comprehending anything." And its ultimate destination was truth: "Another error is an impatience of doubt, and haste to assertion without due and mature suspension of judgment . . . if a man will begin with certainties, he shall end in doubts; but if he will be content to begin with doubts, he shall end in certainties."

This restraint of the intellect—the chronic doubt and suspension of mind which were the necessary temperamental consequences of scepticism used as method—failed to meet the sceptical argument that certainty was unattainable because life was short and art was long, the depth of nature profound and infinite, and the span of man's life finite and subject to the cycles of time. Bacon understood the discouraging potency of these arguments: "But by far the greatest obstacle to the progress of science and to the undertaking of new tasks and provinces therein, is found in this—that men despair and think things impossible. For wise and serious men are wont in these matters to be altogether distrust-

ful; considering with themselves the obscurity of nature, the shortness of life, the deceitfulness of the senses, the weakness of the judgment, the difficulty of experiment and the like; and so supposing that in the revolution of time and of the ages of the world the sciences have ebbs and flows; that at one season they grow and flourish, at another wither and decay, yet in such sort that when they have reached a certain point and condition they can advance no further." Bacon's answer to this melancholy wisdom of the ages was to substitute for it a radical, progressive attitude toward truth and knowledge. One error in the old sceptical view lay in approaching the problem of knowledge in terms of the limits of a single life and to despair because the goal was so clearly out of reach. Bacon was indifferent to this despair because he placed certainty as the limit toward which a properly organized search for knowledge continuously moved. "I propose," he wrote in the Preface to **Novum Organum,** "to establish progressive stages of certainty." The fullness of knowledge lay in the fullness of time, and time was generative in a progressive way: "let great authors have their due, as time which is the author of authors be not deprived of his due, which is further and further to discover truth." For Bacon, "truth is the daughter of time." Truth will therefore appear impossible only when viewed from the conventional perspective as something to be encompassed by individual men through the exercise of their powers of understanding: "touching impossibility, I take those things are to be held possible which may be done by some persons, though not by everyone; and which may be done by many, though not by any one; and which may be done in succession of ages, though not within the hourglass of one man's life; and which may be done by public designation, though not by private endeavour." Thus while granting a premise that traditionally led to despair, Bacon's progressive view of knowledge encouraged an optimistic outlook in the scientist, not only because the new method promised accelerating results but because fulfilment was continuous. Bacon sometimes seems naïve in his hopes that through collaborative effort on the right principles a complete history of nature might be a finite task whose end could be foreseen, but it is difficult to determine at times whether the source of his enthusiasm lies there or in the possibility of continuous progress: "There is therefore much ground for hoping that there are still laid up in the womb of nature many secrets of excellent use, having no affinity or parallelism with anything that is now known, but lying entirely out of the beat of the imagination, which have not yet been found. They too no doubt will some time or other, in the course and revolution of many ages, come to light of themselves, just as the others did; only by the method which we are now treating they can be speedily and suddenly and simultaneously presented and anticipated."

In this progressive view of the problem of knowledge

and certainty there was, moreover, a further conse-quence for the character of the Baconian scientist more profound than chronic optimism. For him there could never be the gratification of bringing all truth into a single order through the strength of the intellect. This, Bacon insisted, was an illusion of the dogmatist, who, out of arrogant pride in the operation of his intellect, substituted the patterns of his mind mistakenly for the complexities of the universe. Real confidence and hope lay only in the realization that the true goal was distant and that it required not one man but many, not one lifetime but generations of men working with a com-mon purpose. In the optimism which grew out of a progressive and collective view of knowledge and truth the Baconian scientist buried his pride.

This subduing of the pride of intellect has a direct bearing on Bacon's views concerning the proper end of knowledge. The failure of learning, Bacon main-tained, had resulted from "the mistaking or misplacing of the last or furthest end of knowledge," and the hope for the future of learning lay in the realization of its proper goal: "It is not possible to run a course aright when the goal itself has not been rightly placed. Now the true and lawful goal of the sciences is none other than this: that human life be endowed with new dis-coveries and powers." If knowledge was to dedicate itself to "the glory of the Creator and the relief of man's estate," it must be directed toward a deep un-derstanding of the behavior of nature and the applica-tion of this knowledge to the systematic development and improvement of the arts. The difference between civilization and barbarism, Bacon maintained—reply-ing at the same time to various old and current theo-ries—"comes not from the soil, not from climate, not from race, but from the arts." And "the empire of man over things depends wholly on the arts and sciences. For we cannot command nature except by obeying her."

In the light of this aim, many conventional and appar-ently normal motives to study lose their importance for Bacon and in effect become base or misleading: "For men have entered into a desire of learning and knowl-edge, sometimes upon a natural curiosity and inquisi-tive appetite; sometimes to entertain their minds with variety and delight; sometimes for ornament and rep-utation; andsometimes to enable them to victory of wit and contradiction; and most times for lucre and profes-sion; and seldom sincerely to give a true account of their gift of reason, to the benefit and use of men." Some of these common and traditionally admired motives may be, Bacon conceded, "more worthy than others"; they are nevertheless "all inferior and degen-erate." Moreover, their setting aside involves a radical departure from traditional standards for the character and conduct of a learned man. The traditional ideal of contemplation as the perfect activity and final good of rational man is abandoned—and so apparently must be its modern analogue, disinterested curiosity. Bacon's

scientist is disinterested only in preferring the common good to private good, and Bacon finds it necessary to reject the Aristotelian and scholastic ideal of the con-templative life: "It [the common good] decides the question touching the preferment of the contemplative or active life and decides it against Aristotle. For all the reasons which he brings for the contemplative re-spect private good, and the pleasure and dignity of a man's self; in which respects no question the contem-plative life has the pre-eminence. . . . But men must know that in this theatre of man's life it is reserved only for God and the Angels to be lookers on." The contemplative ideal, by exalting the "pleasure and dig-nity of a man's self," preverts the end of learning by depriving it of its power. Only a change in emphasis can restore to learning its true character: "this is that which will indeed dignify and exalt knowledge, if contemplation and action may be more nearly and strait-ly conjoined and united together than they have been."

The inspiration for true learning was for Bacon not the pleasure of study and the excitement of discovery, but the needs of mankind. Though many assertions made during his divided life by this remarkable man have been looked at with suspicion, it is impossible to ques-tion the sincerity of his expressed compassion for the lot of man. In his celebrated letter to Burghley, which contains the first recorded statement of his intellectual ambitions, he concludes: "This, whether it be curiosi-ty, or vain glory, or nature, or (if one take it favour-ably) *philanthropia,* is so fixed in my mind as it can-not be removed." Bacon may have listed the inferior motives because he did not wish to expose his earnest-ness and sincerity too clearly before the worldly min-ister, but later expressions of this theme appear with no concessions. The superior ethical motive became inseparable from the intellectually superior end, as though Bacon had realized that no motive other than "philanthropia" could ever guarantee that science would hold to the proper end of learning and consequently employ correct methods. If learning was to become the mastery of nature for the uses of life, it could be guid-ed only by men who were continually inspired by compassion for the lot of man. At the conclusion of the "Proemium" to the ***Magna Instauratio*** Bacon thus explains his haste in publishing: "The cause of which haste was not ambition for himself, but solicitude for the work; that in case of his death there might remain some outline and project of that which he had con-ceived, and some evidence likewise of his honest mind and inclination towards the benefit of the human race. Certain it is that all other ambition whatsoever seemed poor in his eyes compared with the work which he had in hand, seeing that the matter at issue is either noth-ing, or a thing so great that it may well be content with its own merit, without seeking other recompence." Even in his most worldly practical discourses, Bacon dis-credited as inferior the actions that stem from self-love ("Of Wisdom for a Man's Self"), and proclaimed "philanthropia" as the noblest of man's capacities ("Of Goodness and Goodness of Nature"). Philanthropia was the seed from which the new science must grow, and so the new man of learning must of necessity be touched by the needs of others. How deeply Bacon's own feelings ran can be seen by the following lines from the Preface to *The Great Instauration*:

> Wherefore, seeing that these things do not depend upon myself, at the outset of the work I most humbly and fervently pray to God the Father, God the Son, and God the Holy Ghost, that remembering the sorrows of mankind and the pilgrimage of this our life wherein we wear out our days few and evil, they will vouchsafe through my hands to endow the human family with new mercies.

Compassion is the invariable mark of Bacon's true scientist. Of the personage who addresses the gathering of learned men in *Redargutio Philosophiarum* he writes: "aspectus . . . admodum placidi et sereni; nisi quod oris compositio erat tanquam miserantis." And in the description of one of the Fathers of Salomon's House in *New Atlantis,* almost the first detail has to do with compassion: "The day being come, he made his entry. He was a man of middle stature and age, comely of person, and had an aspect as if he pitied men."

The identification of scientific truth with use and therefore with charity, with power and therefore with pity, is fundamental to Bacon's conception of true learning. There are, however, several puzzling passages in Bacon's writings which seem to contradict this frequently expressed position, as though Bacon had temporarily forgotten, in a moment of personal enthusiasm, his formal rejection of the traditional ideal of contemplation; for instance, the following from the *Novum Organum*:

> Again, if men have thought so much of some one particular discovery to regard him as more than man who has been able by some benefit to make the whole human race his debtor, how much higher a thing to discover that by means of which all things else shall be discovered with ease! And yet (to speak the whole truth), as the uses of light are infinite, in enabling us to walk, to ply our arts, to read, to recognize one another; and nevertheless the very beholding of the light is itself a more excellent and fairer thing than all the uses of it;—so assuredly the very contemplation of things, as they are, without superstition and imposture, error or confusion, is itself more worthy than all the fruit of invention.

This statement is particularly surprising in the *Novum Organum*. The very aim of this work—the discovery of "that by means of which all things else shall be discovered with ease"—appears to have been assigned inferior status to the pure contemplation of truth which Bacon elsewhere so clearly rejects. It is true that in the same work Bacon raises this very question: "Again it will be thought, no doubt, that the goal and mark of knowledge, which I myself set up . . . is not the true or the best; for that the contemplation of truth is a thing worthier and loftier than all utility and magnitude of works." In resolving the problem Bacon distinguishes between true knowledge and fanciful philosophical systems, and concludes: "Truth therefore and utility are here the very same things: and works themselves are of greater value as pledges of truth than as contributing to thecomforts of life." The difficulty cannot be completely explained in this way, particularly as there are other instances in Bacon of apparent discrepancies of the same sort. For example, the extended analysis of the defects of learning in *The Advancement of Learning* is followed by a briefer section extolling the virtues of learning, and the theme of this section is announced by examples of the attributes and acts of God and the angels, concluding: "So in the distribution of days, we see the day wherein God did rest and contemplate his own works, was blessed above all the days wherein he did effect and accomplish them." This may be construed as a hyperbole symbolic of the beauty of truth, since contemplation is proper to God and the angels; but such an explanation does not account for the curious interpretation of the Cain and Abel story which shortly follows: ". . . in the two simplest and most primitive trades of life, that of the shepherd (who by reason of his leisure, rest in a place, and living in view of heaven, is a lively image of a contemplative life,) and that of a husbandman, where we see again the favour and election of God went to the shepherd and not to the tiller of the ground." The Essay **"Of Truth"** seems in some respects to be a development of these themes: ". . . truth, which only doth judge itself, teacheth that the inquiry of truth, which is the love-making or wooing of it, the knowledge of truth, which is the presence of it, and the belief of truth, which is the enjoying of it, is the sovereign good of human nature." This portion of the essay is climaxed by a translation of Lucretius' eulogy of the pleasures of truth, which concludes, along with Bacon's parenthetical insertion, "*but no pleasure is comparable to the standing upon the vantage ground of Truth* (a hill not to be commanded and where the air is always clear and serene) *and to see the errors, and wanderings, and mists, and tempests in the vale below.*"

In their context, however, most of these expressions of the pure delight in knowledge are undercut by qualifications which diminish their emphasis and by rhetorical overtones which weaken their force. In reading Bacon's comments on the story of Abel's sacrifice, for instance, it is difficult to erase the effect of the extended analysis of the "peccant humours" of learning which precedes it and which concludes only a few paragraphs before on a strong note of utility. "The end ought to be . . . to preserve and augment whatsoever is solid and fruitful; that knowledge may not be as a curtesan, for pleasure and vanity only, or as a bond-woman, to acquire and gain to her master's use, but as a spouse, for generation, fruit, and comfort." ***The Advancement of Learning*** is in some respects a rebuttal of the contemporary attacks on learning, and from this perspective the gloss on Abel's sacrifice makes the distinction, common to Bacon, between the life devoted to learning and the life of public affairs. Bacon had noted immediately before this Biblical example that in the hierarchy of the angels, "the angels of knowledge and illumination are placed before the angels of office and domination"; but what is perhaps more significant is that Bacon assigns to contemplation a second place even among angels: "the first place or degree is given to the angels of love, which are termed Seraphim, the second to the angels of light, which are termed Cherubim, and the third and so following places to thrones, principalities, and the rest, which are all angels of power and ministry." First comes charity. And this is the resolution of the essay **"Of Truth."** The preoccupation with truth is there pronounced "the sovereign good of human nature" and God's pure love of truth is expressed through the symbolism of the initial creation of light; but when Bacon concludes his quotation from Lucretius, which climaxes this exaltation of pure contemplation, he adds: "so always that this prospect be with pity and not with swelling or pride. Certainly it is heaven upon earth to have a man's mind move in charity, rest in providence, and turn upon the poles of truth." Learning can be freed from the distortions of pride only through charity, which projects itself through pity for the lot of men, in which case learning cannot properly be detached from use.

Bacon never lost the sense of excitement and the feeling of superiority which accompany the pursuits and discoveries of the mind. He recognized, moreover, that the pursuit of any enterprise for its own sake is a characteristic chiefly of learned men: ". . . only learned men love business as an action according to nature, as agreeable to health of mind as exercise is to health of body, taking pleasure in the action itself, and not in the purchase: so that of all men they are the most indefatigable." Moreover, although he defined the proper end and final product of learning as the improvement of life through the improvement of the arts, he realized that this great end was, paradoxically, more likely to be advanced by the contemplative type of mind rather than the mechanical and inventive: "For the mechanic, not troubling himself with the investigation of truth, confines his attention to those things which bear upon his particular works, and will not either raise his mind or stretch out his hand for anything else. But then only will there be good ground of hope for the further advance of knowledge, when there shall be received and gathered together into natural history a variety of experiments, which are of no use in themselves, but simply serve to discover causes and axioms; which I call

'*Experimenta lucifera,*' experiments of *light,* to distinguish them from those which I call '*fructifera,*' experiments of *fruit.*" Light, in fact, is one of Bacon's favorite symbols, associated at its highest with the attributes of God in the first act of the creation. But though Bacon realized that it is natural to the learned man to rest in the delight of the pursuit and contemplation of knowledge, and though his own enthusiasm emerges at times in expressions of this delight, he recognized it as a serious danger having the power to corrupt the man whom it seduces. If the prime need and sole hope of mankind lay in gaining empire over things, contemplation could not be held up as the perfect human activity: truth could not be a final end in itself, nor mere curiosity the chief motive to learning. Contemplation, Bacon said, is proper as an end only to God, expressing thereby at once the nobility and grandeur of the activity and its inappropriateness to mere man. Among mortals, only Adam was privileged to savor this delight in an inferior form:

> After the creation was finished, it is set down unto us that man was placed in the garden to work therein; which work so appointed to him could be no other than work of contemplation; that is, when the end of work is but for exercise and experiment, not for necessity; for there being then no reluctation of creature nor sweat of the brow, man's employment must of consequence have been matter of delight in the experiment, and not matter of labour for the use.

But this was the pre-lapsarian Adam, who had no need to gain empire over things.

The story of the Fall exercised a strong fascination for Bacon and he alludes to it frequently, particularly in relation to the problem of knowledge and man's welfare. He nowhere questions its literal validity; nevertheless, he approaches it in much the same spirit as inspired his extraordinaryinterpretations of classical myths as symbols or "emblems" prefiguring truths which, when expounded properly, invariably show remarkable parallels to Bacon's favorite notions. Biblical myths he found useful in the same way. In putting the Cain-Abel story to the service of his preference for contemplative activity over the life of practical affairs he says parenthetically, "the Scriptures have infinite mysteries, not violating at all the truth of the story or letter." He might with equal appropriateness have asserted this principle in connection with his numerous allusions to and glosses on the myth of the Fall.

Bacon had almost inescapably to take cognizance of this Biblical episode, if only because it had come to mean that men can know too much and that God had set limits to man's restless Faustian search for knowledge. Early in ***The Advancement of Learning*** he challenges the popular notion that "the aspiring to over-

Portrait by Paul van Somer

in consequence of the first transgression and thus incapable of improving his lot by a dependence on his own powers. For the new scientist, however, optimism concerning man's ability to gain empire over things and command nature was required as an act of faith. Bacon accordingly endowed the Biblical story with new implications which inspired incentive to effort in this direction. Paradise could be regained. Bacon speaks of the true end of learning as "a restitution and reinvesting (in great part) of man to sovereignty and power (for whensoever he shall be able to call the creatures by their true names he shall again command them) which he had in the first state of creation." Bacon did not minimize the several ruinous consequences presumed to have been produced by the Fall, but he insisted that man was not without resources: "For man by the Fall fell at the same time from his state of innocency and from his dominion over nature. Both of these losses, however, can even in this life be in some part repaired; the former by religion and faith, the latter by the arts and sciences." To these Bacon added a third resource: in *De Augmentis Scientiarum* Bacon considered poetry as a means of compensating for some absent beauty and order in the world.

> For if the matter be attentively considered, a sound argument may be drawn from Poesy, to show that there is agreeable to the spirit of man a more ample greatness, a more perfect order, and a more beautiful variety than it can any where (since the Fall) find in nature. . . . Whence it [poesy] may be fairly thought to partake somewhat of a divine nature; because it raises the mind and carries it aloft, accommodating the show of things to the desires of the mind, not (like reason and history) buckling and bowing down the mind to the nature of things.

The original paradise was not to be restored in its pristine entirety or through any singly directed effort, but was to be achieved in parts; religion, poetry, science was each in its own way responsible for a particular alleviation of man's post-lapsarian deficiencies. Whether Bacon thought the Biblical paradise historically real or merely symbolic, the important element in his preoccupations with it is his conviction that it was within man's powers to make great amends in this life for the deficiencies which oppressed mankind. He accepted the Christian religion as the instrument through which men can come by a knowledge of God's will and law. He found in the continuing accomplishments of poetry adequate means to satisfy man's thirst for ideal beauty and order. The overwhelming lack in the conditions for man's earthly felicity was in the area of science and the arts. Bacon tells us in the Prœmium to *Instauratio Magna* that "he thought all trial should be made, whether that commerce between the mind of man and the nature of things, which is more precious than anything on earth, or at least than anything that is of the earth, might by any means be restored to its perfect and original condition, or if that may not be,

much knowledge was the original temptation whereupon ensued the fall of man." Bacon's interpretation of the Fall imposes no limits on the pursuit of natural knowledge: "it was not the pure knowledge of nature and universality, a knowledge by the light whereof man did give names unto other creatures in Paradise, as they were brought before him, according unto their properties, which gave the occasion to the Fall; but it was the proud knowledge of good and evil, with an intent in man to give law unto himself and to depend no more upon God's commandments, which was the form of the temptation." The danger was not in the quantity: "it is merely the quality of knowledge, which be it in quantity more or less, if it be taken without the true corrective thereof, hath in it some nature of venom or malignity, and some effects of that venom, which is ventosity or swelling."

Thus understood, the story of the Fall became a support of Bacon's aims and hopes. But the myth carried further traditional implications at odds with these, for it represented man, as well as nature, ruinously changed yet reduced to a better condition than that in which it now is." This restitution was not beyond the powers of man, though the inadequacy of former and prevailing means and aims stood in the way: "For creation was not by the curse made altogether and forever a rebel, but in virtue of that charter 'In the sweat of thy face shalt thou eat bread,' it is now by various labours (not certainly by disputations or idle magical ceremonies, but by various labours) at length and in some measure subdued to the supplying of man with bread; that is, to the uses of human life." Milton's "paradise within" was not enough for Bacon. He seemed too acutely aware of "the miseries of the human race and this pilgrimage of our life in which we wear out our evil days and few." The scientist had a rôle equal to that of the poet or the servant of God—in fact, Bacon came to think of him as though he were a servant of God and a dedicated soul.

It is everywhere apparent in Bacon that the virtues of the man of science are not wholly intellectual, any more than are his possible shortcomings. In Bacon's conception of the scientist there is a pronounced ethical element. The world of science has its sinners as well as its elect. Bacon attacks on practical methodological grounds the reliance on the pure intellect, because reason sets aside reality and imposes schemes created out of its own inner order upon the complex world of nature; but to this methodological error he regularly assigns the moral taint of pride. In a curious passage in the ***Natural and Experimental History*** he describes this prevailing evil of the learned world as the consequence of a kind of second Fall of man:

> For we copy the sin of our first parents while we suffer for it. They wished to be like God, but their posterity wish to be even greater. For we create worlds, we direct and domineer over nature, we will have it that all things *are* as in our folly we think they should be, not as seems fittest to the Divine wisdom, or as they are found to be in fact; and I know not whether we more distort the facts of nature or our own wits; but we clearly impress the stamp of our own image on the creatures and works of God, instead of carefully examining and recognising in them the stamp of the Creator himself. Wherefore our dominion over creatures is a second time forfeited, not undeservedly; and whereas after the fall of man some power over the resistance of creatures was still left to him—the power of subduing and managing them by true and solid arts—yet this too through our insolence, and because we desire to be like God and to follow the dictates of our own reason, we in great part lose.

If the fatal sin against the canons of true science is pride, the all-embracing virtue is charity. In the exercise of this virtue man might wish to be like God without error: "In aspiring to the throne of power the angels transgressed and fell, in presuming to come

within the oracle of knowledge man transgressed and fell; but in pursuit towards the similitude of God's goodness or love (which is one thing, for love is nothing else but goodness put in motion or applied) neither man or spirit ever hath transgressed, or shall transgress."

There is an obvious similarity between Bacon's notions about the deadly sin and cardinal virtue in science and the moral ideals of man in the Christian tradition. But the distinction between the ethical virtues and vices of a scientist is not insisted upon in Bacon because it is essentially religious and Christian. Christianity may be the source, but it is not the sanction. The grounds of Bacon's analysis are naturalistic and humanistic, and he derives them out of the aims of true learning and the demands of good method. It is a question of success and failure in the discovery of useful knowledge. The scientist must cultivate charity and shun pride not in consequence of being a Christian but in consequence of being a scientist. Bacon, it is true, represents his scientist as a religious man. To some extent he does so to defend the new learning against the charge that it leads to atheism. Bacon concedes that "a little natural philosophy inclineth the mind to atheism, but a further proceeding bringeth the mind back to religion." Bacon claims also that learning does a service to religion, since the deep investigation into God's works inspires admiration for His glory, and leads to "meditation of the omnipotency of God." Bacon may have written thus in all sincerity. But these considerations play a relatively minor rôle in his preoccupation with science and his apologetics for the new learning: compare, for instance, the trifling and inconspicuous place which the argument from design occupies in Bacon's thought with its ubiquity and extensive development among the English scientists of the next generation. Bacon separated completely the realms of religion and of natural knowledge in the interest of establishing a science free of superstition and presumably a religion free of sophistry. The basis of religion was for him the knowledge of God's will and law, matters which lay beyond man and hence were knowable only through divine revelation. Bacon urged therefore "that we do not presume by the contemplation of nature to attain to the mysteries of God," that the pursuit of natural knowledge be kept clear of religion, and that men "do not unwisely mingle or confound these learnings together." Religion in scientific matters was recommended largely indirectly as a corrective: against the fear that through science unknown power may be granted without adequate restraints, he advised "that all knowledge is to be limited by religion and is to be referred to use and action," and against the danger of "the debasement of arts and sciences to purposes of wickedness, luxury, and the like," he expressed the pious hope that "the exercise thereof will be governed by sound reason and true religion." But when viewed from the center of Bacon's thought, this strain seems like conventional embroidery. In the pursuit of the true end of learning with the proper methods, Bacon's man of science had to possess and exercise qualities which by their nature rendered such admonitions superfluous. As long as he functioned as a good scientist he had of necessity to be incorruptible and a good man. Bacon often leaves the impression that the career of science is something of a religion in its selflessness and sense of dedication, and he at times spoke of the future scientists as though they were a priesthood. And always he speaks of the pursuit of natural knowledge as though it were the noblest of human activities.

This idealization of the seeker of truth in the pursuit of the secrets of nature may be set in relief by comparing it with Bacon's analysis of other sorts of notable activity, especially as these are presented in the *Essays*. This is not to imply the conventional view of the *Essays* as largely cynical and worldly commentaries on success in the great world of affairs. The *Essays* are of a piece with everything Bacon wrote. He recognizes in them certain capacities and inclinations in man which endow human actions with nobility and dignity. One is the inclination to knowledge, and he terms the pursuit and contemplation of truth as "the sovereign good of human nature" (**"Of Truth"**). The other is "philanthropia," "the affecting of the weal of man," which he believes is "implanted deeply in the nature of man," and which "of all virtues and dignities of the mind is the greatest." (**"Of Goodness and Goodness of Nature"**). These are the poles between which human activity is measured. Their relation to the prime virtues essential to Bacon's scientist is at once apparent. Since the essays deal largely with the actions and ornaments of men in public life, "philanthropia" is the measure directly or tacitly applied for the most part. Thus, selfishness is despised: "it is a poor centre of a man's actions, himself," "it is a depraved thing" (**"Of Wisdom for a Man's Self"**). In public life, "merit is the end of man's motion" and "power to do good is the true and lawful end of aspiring" (**"Of Great Place"**). Riches "are for spending, and spending for honour and good actions" (**"Of Riches"**). Thus, activities or passions which are inimical with the proper aims of life and their realization, Bacon treats with suspicion or contempt (**"Of Love," "Of Revenge"**). Where they are indifferent to these ends, Bacon tends to analyze without resolving the issues (**"Of Marriage"**). Where they may be an aid, he treats them with respect (**"Of Friendship"**). The worldly and at times cynical tone of the *Essays* arises from the fact that when Bacon concerns himself with the operational aspects of public life—as always realistically and dispassionately, in the spirit of Machiavelli, whom he admired for treating of men as they are and not as they ought to be—he finds himself in an area where man's conduct becomes less than noble. However lofty one's aims, when it is a question of gaining power or of knowing what to do "if you would work any man" in the exercise of it,

there is no escaping the ruthless and grimy world of **"Of Negotiating."** In the best hands the instruments of power have an evil aspect. The rising to great place is "sometimes base, and by indignities men come to dignities." Power can corrupt because the means are corrupting. But the seeking of power over nature is not corrupting because the ends and means which make for success are of necessity corrective of the defects of men and require the exercise of his noblest inclinations. Bacon's expressed preference is always for the life of true learning against the life of power; in the traditions of ancient times, he notes, lawgivers and statesmen have been honored by titles of worthies and demigods, but inventors of new arts have been consecrated among the gods themselves; God preferred Abel's sacrifice to that of Cain; the angels of power and ministry rank below those of knowledge and illumination. Bacon could never have had any grave doubts on this matter during a life of divided purpose between the ambitions of the great scholar and the great man. "The commandment of knowledge," he wrote, "is yet higher than the commandment over the will." At the collapse of his fortunes he knew that he had betrayed his calling as one of the elect and had misspent that one talent which is death to hide. This sense of tragic futility he summed up in a prayer which he composed after his indictment: "Besides my innumerable sins, I confess before thee, that I am debtor to thee for the gracious talent of thy gifts and graces, which I have neither put into a napkin, nor put it (as I ought) to exchangers, where it might have made best profit; but misspent it in things for which I was least fit; so that I may truly say, my soul hath been a stranger in the course of my pilgrimage."

When viewed as a whole, Bacon's ideal of the scientist establishes a new ideal of man, different from the ideal of the patriot, the saint, the gentleman courtier and prince of the Renaissance, and even the citizen of the perfect state. The good man is one who possesses or is capable of exercising the intellectual and ethical virtues demanded by the aims and methods requisite for the discovery of truth in the study of nature, and the good life is the dedication to the improvement through this means of man's lot on earth.

For this man, Bacon envisioned a new rôle in society and a society vastly improved by his dominant rôle in it. The character with which Bacon endowed him rendered him superior to others, and hence Bacon saw him as occupying a superior position in society. His scientist would be a member of an élite class, though not by virtue of birth, or political status, or the possession of an aloof intellectual supremacy. Bacon found it necessary to combat certain conventional notions of social superiority in order that members of the gentry and aristocracy might not be deterred from devoting themselves to such studies under the mistaken notion that certain activities were base. Science required experiments, and therefore the work of artisans and crafts-men was to be cultivated. Moreover, Bacon was impressed by the fact that in the mechanical arts important inventions and discoveries were followed by progressive improvements, whereas in pure learning impressive achievements seemed to end in themselves. He came to respect the qualities which were associated with the mechanical arts, and made a point of calling attention to his own activities in this direction with pride: "For myself, most excellent king, I may truly say that both this present work, and in those I intend to publish hereafter, I often advisedly and deliberately throw aside the dignity of my name and wit (if any such thing be) in my endeavour to advance human interests; and being one that should properly perhaps be an architect in philosophy and the sciences, I turn common labourer, hodman, anything that is wanted; taking upon myself the burden and execution of many things which must needs be done, and which others through an inborn pride shrink from and decline." These views accord with both the humility and the realism which Bacon required of his scientist, but they do not imply that he required of his scientist the psychology of a glorified menial humbly content with his useful-drudgery. Though he despised the arrogance which he associated with older ideals of the learned man, when he came to present the picture of the scientist in *New Atlantis* in an imagined perfect setting, he pictured him surrounded by the pomp and reverence usually associated with kings and prelates. The visit of one of the Fathers of Salomon's House is preceded by awesome heraldings of his arrival, and he comes handsomely accoutered, and impressively carried about "in a rich chariot without wheels litter-wise; with two horses at either end, richly trapped in blue velvet embroidered; and two footmen on each side in the like attire." His impressive train is reported, nevertheless, to lack some of the accompaniments of purely regal processions, out of a desire "to avoid all tumult and trouble." His behavior suggests the high priest: "He held up his bare hand as he went, as blessing the people, but in silence." The mariners in the story recount among the remarkable features of Bensalem the courteous refusal of the local dignitaries to accept the usual marks of obeisance, yet Bacon's narrator reports of their visit to the Father of Salomon's House: "When we came in, as we were taught, we bowed low at our first entrance; and when we were come near his chair, he stood up, holding forth his hand ungloved and in a posture of blessing; and we everyone of us stooped down, and kissed the hem of his tippet." In Bensalem the scientists are a consecrated priesthood, and it seems less correct to say of them that they were religious men than that they constituted a religious cult in themselves: "We have certain hymns and services, which we say daily, of laud and thanks to God for his marvellous works: and forms of prayers, imploring his aid and blessing for the illumination of our labours, and the turning of them into good and holy uses."

The loyalties of such men would not be bound by conventional standards. They could have no compelling class affiliations, since useful information could come from the most humble sources. What is more important, such scientists would not be confined by national boundaries. This point is effectively presented in *New Atlantis*. The citizens of Bensalem are forbidden by royal decree from travel outside their kingdom, but this restraint does not apply to certain fellows of Salomon's House, who are termed Merchants of Light. At regular intervals they are sent out to all parts of the globe to gather information on the advances in the arts and sciences: "But thus you see we maintain a trade, not for gold, silver, or jewels; nor for silks; nor for spices; nor any other commodities of matter; but only for God's first creature, which was *Light*; to have *light* (I say) of the growth of all parts of the world." One must not minimize the importance of this theme because of the utopian setting. Bacon's utopia, at least with reference to Salomon's House, comes much closer to being a picture of what the author believed to be possible—as distinct from what he believed to be ideally desirable—than is the case with most ideal commonwealths. In a more straight-forward context he had made his views on this point quite clear: "Further, it will not be amiss to distinguish the three kinds and as it were grades of ambition in mankind. The first is of those who desire to extend their own power in their native country; which kind is vulgar and degenerate. The second is of those who labour to extend the power of their country and its dominion among men. This certainly has more dignity, though not less covetousness. But if a man endeavour to establish and extend the power and dominion of the human race over the universe, his ambition (if ambition it can be called) is without doubt a more wholesome thing and more noble than the other two." The humanitarian impulse of the scientist could not be confined to local loyalties and limits, and true knowledge, by its nature, transcended time and space: " . . . if the invention of the ship was thought so noble, which carrieth riches and commodities from place to place, and consociateth the most remote regions in participation of their fruits, how much more are letters to be magnified, which as ships pass through the vast seas of time, and make ages so distant to participate of the wisdom, illuminations, and inventions, the one of the other?" The scientist was of no country, as scientist; he was a member of an international free-masonry.

That there were dangers in the extension of man's dominion over nature, Bacon was aware. Had his scientist no responsibility to these? Bacon's answer to this question was usually evasive. Certainly it was possible that the new learning might be put to base uses, but are not all good things perverted by evil and foolish men from their proper ends, and is that sufficient reason for discouraging the good things themselves? It was also true that the new knowledge might "open a fountain, such as it is not easy to discern where the issues thereof will take and fall," and that it would make available vast resources to all men; Bacon consoled himself in the hope that the new knowledge and power would be beneficently employed by the exercise of right reason and religion. But Bacon knew too well the psychology of power to feel greatly comforted by his own casual reassurances. All men were not scientists. Bacon's failure to confront this important question with his customary resoluteness and realism suggests the real measure of his fear. It was only in the utopian setting of *New Atlantis* that he faced the issue squarely and carried the implications of his fears to their logical conclusion: "And this we do also. We have consultations, which of the inventions and experiences which we have discovered shall be published, and which not: and take all an oath of secrecy, for the concealing of those which we think fit to keep secret: though some of those we do reveal sometimes to the state and some not." This brief passage says in effect that just as in the interest of mankind scientists must constitute themselves an international free-masonry or priesthood, in the same interest they must set themselves above the state. To appreciate how remarkable is the appearance of this idea in Bacon, it is only necessary to recall that in defense of the royal prerogative he had opposed Coke in the theory of common law, and that in the essay "Of Judicature" he had described the judges as lions, but as lions under the throne. Bacon had stated with unmistakable clarity his conviction that science—though not necessarily the scientist—must in his own day be separated from religion. The brief passage from *New Atlantis* indicates that Bacon had more than a premonition of the necessity for separating science from politics in future times when the character of scientific discovery and the vital rôle of the scientist in a technological civilization would place in strong relief the foolish and vicious possibilities in the use of the new knowledge by society and its exploitation by political power.

This fact is illustrative of the direct way in which Bacon's conception of the new man of science reflects in detail every facet of his thought—his criticism of knowledge, his plans for its reform, his hopes for the human race. Herein lies its richness and complexity. Among the seventeenth-century writers on science whom Bacon most directly influenced, the portrait of the man of science has already undergone some simplification. They call attention to the scientist's slowness to assent, to his freedom from contention, and to his devotion to truth rather than victory, and they emphasize, to a much greater degree than Bacon, the Christian piety to which the scientist is disposed by virtue of his science. But even when some eloquent apologist [e.g., Glanvill in *Scepsis scientifica,* 1665] presents the scientists as a new race of Olympians, certain of Bacon's more interesting and impressive overtones are lacking. In more modern times the ideal

of the scientist has become almost exclusively identified with the exact and disinterested pursuit of scientific truth independent of all other considerations. And there have been hopes that on the demonstration through science that man is capable of this virtue, a new ethics for a modern society might be constructed. It is only in very recent times that this latest ideal has been brought into question through unusual developments in science itself and through new developments in political theory.

Comparisons with Bacon suggest themselves, but it is at the moment hazardous to indulge in them. The changing conception of the scientist is one of the unwritten pages in the history of science. When it is written, the chief irony in it may be that Bacon, who has been described as a cynic and a Machiavellian and who has been condemned for having destroyed the connection between science and religion and thus deprived science of its ethical foundations, should have created in the first clearly realized image of the scientist a figure more impressive in some respects than its successors and possibly too flattering to human nature.

Hegel remarks on Bacon's methodical approach to science:

[What] is noteworthy is that Bacon applied himself to the sciences in a practical manner, apprehending phenomena in a reflective fashion and considering first "their utility." He pursued this course methodically; he did not put forward mere opinions or sentiments and did not express his views on the sciences in the way a fine gentleman would, but proceeded meticulously and established a method for scientific cognition and general principles for cognitive procedure. The methodical character of the approach that he introduced is just what makes him noteworthy in the history of the sciences and of philosophy, and it was through this principle of methodical cognition that he had great influence. . . .

Georg Wilhelm Friedrich Hegel, in his Lectures on the History of Philosophy, *3 Vols., 1833.*

A. L. Morton (essay date 1952)

SOURCE: "Revolution and Counter-Revolution," in *The English Utopia,* 1952. Reprinted by Seven Seas Publishers, 1968, pp. 78-111.

[*In the following excerpt, originally published in 1952, Morton relates the Utopian ideas of the* New Atlantis *to political issues occasioned by the rise of the bourgeoisie.*]

> *Ireton:* All the main thing that I speak for, is because I would have an eye to property. I hope we do not

come here to contend for victory—but let every man consider with himself that he do not go that way to take away all property. For here is the most fundamental part of the constitution of the kingdom, which if you take away, you take away all by that.
. . .

Rainborough: Sir, I see that it is impossible to have liberty but all property must be taken away. If it be laid down for a rule, and you will say it, it must be so. But I would fain know what the soldier hath fought for all this while? He hath fought to enslave himself, to give power to men of riches.

Debate of the General Council of the Army.
Putney, October 29th, 1647.

At no other time is there such a wealth of Utopian speculation in England as in the seventeenth century. And at no time is this speculation at once so bold and practical and so dry and narrow. In this age of revolution Utopia comes closest to immediate politics and the every day problems of government, and in doing so it loses as well as gains. More, as we have seen, was concerned with the relation of wealth and poverty, with the abolition of classes, and, ultimately, with the questions of human happiness and social justice. The typical Utopian writers of the seventeenth century are concerned with political questions in the narrow sense, with the framing of a model constitution and with its working machinery, with the formation and character of governments and the perfection of parliamentary representation. They are concerned, in short, not so much with justice as with power.

As a result, there is a complete change in temper and style. We find nothing to correspond to More's breadth of vision, his pity and anger, his doubts and the wry humour with which these doubts are expressed. Everything now is dry, precise and lawyerlike. There is a cool confidence, a bright, hard certainty that here, in Macaria or Oceana, is the one true light, that here is a practical programme that need only be adopted to carry the revolution to its full perfection. And, to a very large extent, this confidence was justified, for the problem which had baffled and tormented More had been solved, the bourgeoisie had won power, had the means of making their desires effective. Hence, as this chapter will try to show, there was a close relationship between the Utopian writings and the active framing of constitutions which went on throughout the Commonwealth period.

This change in the climate of Utopia corresponds exactly to the change in the English political climate. We have seen something of the beginnings of the development of capitalism; of the growth and decline of classes, the transfer of wealth and the peculiar relations

which existed between the bourgeoisie and the House of Tudor. The Tudor absolutism gave the men of the new wealth the necessary shelter and breathing space in which to grow strong: ample advantage was taken of this opportunity, till, by the end of the century, the protection had ceased to be a necessity and the protector had become a burden. In alliance with the crown the bourgeoisie had decimated the peasantry, humbled the church, crushed Spain, traversed oceans and explored new continents. Now, appearing for the first time in history as an independent force, they attacked the monarchy itself, deposed and beheaded a king and established a republic. For a brief space Utopia ceased to be a fiction but was felt by thousands to be just round the corner. If there were any limits to the power of this brave new class, they were not immediately apparent.

Before the confident morning of the revolution there was a rather bleak dawn period, the generation in which the alliance between crown and bourgeoisie was breaking, when the tension of events created bewilderment, weariness and disillusion. It was the period of Shakespeare's tragedies, the age when the bounding extravagance of *Tamburlaine* had given place to the extravagant psychological horrors of Webster. To this period belongs Francis Bacon's *New Atlantis,* and in the history of the English Utopia Bacon is the link connecting More with the utopian writers of the revolutionary period.

Like More, Bacon was a member of a family which was prominent in the service of the crown, was trained as a lawyer but combined the profession of law with a continuing passion for philosophy, became Lord Chancellor of England, and, at the height of his fortune, was disgraced and driven from office. Here, however, the parallel ends, for few men have ever been more dissimilar in their interests or character. There is perhaps no great English writer whose personality is less attractive than Bacon's, and all the elaborate apologias of his many admirers and the power and magnificence of his prose only increase the distaste we feel in the presence of the man. Never was such a subtle and splendid intellect employed to serve meaner or more trivial ends, and neither pride nor gratitude nor loyalty to friends were allowed to brake his climb to wealth and influence. Grasping timidity and profuse display seemed continually to deny the austere impersonality of the philosopher's creed.

Yet this is only a part of the truth about Bacon: it would be quite wrong, I believe, to imagine that the philosophy was not both sincere and profoundly felt. Partly, it may be, the very subtlety of the intellect deceived itself, but more than that, Bacon's character expresses in a new form the essential contradiction within Humanism, the contradiction that lies at the very heart of the bourgeois revolution. Humanism fought to liberate mankind from superstition and ignorance, but also to liberate capitalist production from the restraints of feudal economy: the bourgeois revolution was waged for the ultimate advantage of mankind as a whole but also to secure for a new exploiting class power to rob and to become rich, and in this revolution meanness and nobility, cruel oppression and generosity are inextricably tangled. The pursuit of truth and the pursuit of wealth often seemed the same thing, and whatever Bacon's faults may have been, about the pursuit of truth he was always passionately in earnest.

And truth for Bacon meant power, not indeed political power, since he was a loyal servant of the crown and well content with the existing order, but power over nature through the understanding of natural law. This is the core of all his work, and not least of the *New Atlantis,* which, under cover of describing a utopian commonwealth is really a prospectus for a state-endowed college of experimental science. It was the work of his old age, written when, over sixty, he was dismissed and ruined, but still hoping against all reason that he might be restored to power. It was a fragment only, begun and laid aside unfinished, and never published in his life-time. He began it in the hope that James I would adopt and subsidise his proposals: its incomplete state is the proof of the final abandonment of his hopes, and therefore of his interest in the work, since that interest was confined solely to its possible practical outcome.

Bacon, unlike More, was not concerned with social justice. He, too, was a Humanist, but by the beginning of the seventeenth century Humanism had run cold: the difference between *Utopia* and *New Atlantis* is not so much a difference of content as a difference of purpose, a shift of interest and a lowering of temperature. The earlier Humanists believed in reason and in the possibility of the attainment of happiness by the unfettered exercise of reason. Bacon and his contemporaries, while not denying the power of reason had gradually shifted the weight of emphasis away from reason to experiment. As Bacon wrote:

> Our method is continually to dwell among things soberly . . . to establish for ever a true and legitimate union between the experimental and rational faculty.

And elsewhere:

> For the wit and mind of man, if it work upon matter, which is the contemplation of the creatures of God, worketh according to the stuff and is limited thereby; but if it work upon itself, as the spider worketh its web, then it is endless, and brings forth indeed cobwebs of learning, admirable for the fineness of the thread and work, but of no substance or profit.

Bacon stood at the beginning of the first period of

materialism, in which it was confidently believed that the whole universe, from the solar system to the mind of man, was a vast and complex machine and could be mastered absolutely by a sufficient understanding of the laws of mechanics. He saw it as his task to use his prestige and his incomparable control over language to urge upon his contemporaries the undertaking of this final assault upon the mysteries of nature. As Basil Willey says in his admirable book, *The Seventeenth Century Background:*

> Bacon's rôle was to indicate with fine magniloquence the path by which alone 'science' could advance. This he did, while other men, such as Galileo, Harvey or Gilbert, in whom he took comparatively little interest, were achieving great discoveries on the principles which he taught. Bacon's great service to 'science' was that he gave it an incomparable advertisement.

The information which we are given about the social and economic and political organisation of Bensalem, the utopian island of *New Atlantis,* is naturally, therefore, meagre and indirect, since Bacon only intends the fiction to provide an interesting background for the pamphlet. But one cannot but be struck with the remarkable decline from the standpoint reached in *Utopia,* and, since Bacon had obviously read More's book, this may be taken as an implied criticism in the points where they differ. Bensalem is a monarchy of an orthodox type, with the inevitable fixed constitution handeddown from the founder-king Salomona. It has private property and classes, as we have to infer from a passage which says that on certain ceremonial occasions.

> if any of the family be distressed or decayed, order is taken for their relief, and competent means to live.

That is to say, that while the necessities of the poor are provided for, this is done as a charity and not as of right, and the need for such charity appears normally to arise. Correspondingly there are marked social gradations and inequalities, and the officials and leading citizens are distinguished by magnificent clothes and lavish display and have numbers of personal servants. There is a strongly patriarchal family, quite unmarked by any trace of the communism with which More tempered family life, and great power is enjoyed by the heads of these families and by the old generally.

Chance voyagers, like the narrator of the story, were welcomed in Bensalem and received hospitably, but intercourse with foreign lands was discouraged because King Salomona,

> recalling into his memory the happy and flourishing estate wherein his land then was, so as it might be

a thousand ways altered to the worse, but scarce any one way to the better; thought nothing wanted to his noble and heroical intentions, but only, as far as human foresight might reach, to give perpetuity to that which was in his time so happily established; therefore . . . he did ordain the interdicts and prohibitions which we have touching the entrance of strangers.

At the same time, as was fitting for a people given up to the search for knowledge, every effort was made to discover and import all that was known in other lands, and with this object secret missions were sent out at regular intervals to visit all civilised lands and bring back reports.

To Salomona, also, was credited the establishment of Salomon's (or Solomon's) House, whose 'fellows' were the object almost of veneration among the Bensalemites. Here we come to Bacon's real point: *New Atlantis,* like Bensalem itself, exists only for the sake of it. And in nothing more than in his ideas about education does Bacon differ from More. For More, as we have seen, education was a social and co-operative pursuit, with its object the increasing of the happiness and the enrichment of the personalities of the whole people: for Bacon it was the affair of a body of specialists, lavishly endowed by the state and carrying on their work in complete isolation from the masses (we are told that the visit of one of the fathers of Salomon's House to the capital city was the first for a dozen years). Its object was not happiness but power:

> The end of our foundation is the knowledge of causes and secret motions of things and the enlarging of the bounds of human empire, to the effecting of all things possible.

There is a kind of holy simplicity in this unbounded belief in man's powers that is the most attractive side of Bacon and which makes him the truly representative man of his time, but this samesimplicity limits his objectives to the quantitative and the empirical. There is little in Bacon of the desire to pass beyond catalogue to synthesis, and he was a superb generaliser with a deep distrust of generalisation.

For this reason the methods of Salomon's House were purely experimental, and to the cataloguing of experiments Bacon devotes the ten happiest pages of *New Atlantis,* describing a great variety of metallurgical, biological, astronomical and chemical marvels, as well as the practical application of science to the making of new substances and fabrics, to medicine and even to engineering:

> We imitate also the flights of birds: for we have some degree of flying in the air: we have ships and boats for going under water. . . . We have divers

curious clocks and other like motions of return, and some perpetual motions. We imitate also the motions of living things by images of men, beasts, birds, fishes and serpents.

Bacon hoped to interest King James, who prided himself upon his virtuosity and delighted to be called the modern Solomon, in his scheme, and, no doubt, dreamed that the foundation of such a college of science might lead to his return to public life and favour. In this he was disappointed, for James had little interest in science for its own sake and already the political struggle was curtailing the resources of the crown. It was not till 1645, under the rule of the Long Parliament, that Bacon's scheme assumed a modest practical form as the "College of Philosophy". Its founders, Samuel Hartlib, author of the utopian essay *Macaria,* and the Czech scholar Comenius, both admitted that their scheme was inspired by *New Atlantis.* Similarly, when the College of Philosophy developed into the Royal Society in 1662, Sprat, Boyle, Glanville and others declared that this was only the carrying into effect of Bacon's outline of Salomon's House. Later still, it was among the main influences which determined the form to be taken by the work of the French Encyclopedists. Diderot, in the Prospectus, stated specifically:

> If we have come at it successfully, we shall owe most to the Chancellor Bacon, who threw out the plan of an universal dictionary of sciences and arts, at a time when, so to say, neither arts nor sciences existed. That extraordinary genius, when it was impossible to write a history of what was known, wrote one of what it was necessary to learn.

New Atlantis, therefore, belongs to the history of science as much as to the history of Utopia or to the history of politics. Nevertheless, the development of science and industrial technique was an essential part of the advance of the bourgeoisie, and, as I have said, Bacon's preoccupation with applied science as a form of *power* links him with the extremely political utopian writers of the Commonwealth. . . .

Robert P. Adams (essay date 1954)

SOURCE: "The Social Responsibilities of Science in *Utopia, New Atlantis* and After," in *Journal of the History of Ideas,* Vol. X, No. 3, June, 1954, pp. 374-98.

[*In the following excerpt, Adams looks at the* New Atlantis *as a "plan for the perfection of science and the advancement of human welfare."*]

In what follows I accept [James] Spedding's conclusion that while the *New Atlantis* is incomplete, it seems intended for publication as it stands, that in it Bacon included "as if already known, the things he most wanted to know," and that most probably "the unfinished portions would have dealth with the method of scientific investigation rather than with the general problems of society."

In the *New Atlantis* the "very eye of the kingdom" of Bensalem is Salomon's House, or the College of the Six Day's Works, an elaborately equipped institute for cooperative pure and applied scientific research, intended "for the finding out of the true nature of all things (whereby God might have the more glory in the workmanship of them, and men the more fruit in the use of them)." Although this College is said to be "dedicated to the study of the Works and Creatures of God," the book contains no discussion of scientific and religious principles as being interfused. We may, however, observe the ideas suggested by the actions of the leading Atlantic characters. Typically a man of science, after a hard day's work in his laboratory, joined his fellows in "certain hymns and services . . . of laudand thanks to God for his marvellous works . . . imploring his aid and blessing for the illumination of our labours and the turning of them into good and holy works." Here may be seen the kind of separation of science from religion that Bacon thought good. As Professor [Basil] Willey said, while Bacon argued that science "leads us directly to God in the end," he desired to separate "religious truth and scientific truth . . . in the interests of science, not of religion. He wished to keep science pure from religion."

The relationship of science to social progress is touched upon at many points in the *New Atlantis*. As we have seen, the invariable Utopian practice was to restrict production of material goods and services to what both natural philosophy and history had shown to be naturally "necessary" for personal health, pleasure, and sanity and, in the larger view, to what had been found essential to maintain the health and integrity of the commonwealth. The Utopian criteria were essentially pragmatic: no pleasure which was not definitely known to be socially baneful was prohibited, "For they be much enclyned to this opinion: to thinke no kynde of pleasure forbidden, wherof cummeth no harme." In striking contrast, in the *New Atlantis* the boldest emphasis is laid on the idea that the main purpose of applied science is to bring forth endless, ever-increasing torrents of usable inventions and luxuries, or "fruits," for the delight of a supposedly insatiable public, perpetually in raptures over the latest, most novel productions of the laboratories and factories. For the improvement of foods and beverages, for instance, no limits are implied except perhaps those the natural flesh is heir to. Hence the plans (puzzling to some of Bacon's editors) for ceaseless scientific multiplication of the varieties of pleasant drinks, of perfumes and pre-

cious stones, of delicious fruits and sweetmeats, of beasts and of birds. In the *New Atlantis* we find therefore a notable early appearance of man considered, not (as with More and as with Hamlet before his disillusionment) as most noble in reason and godlike apprehension, but as a "consumer"—as a sort of belly capable of almost infinite distention.

No doubt Macaulay's antithesis was over-simple; at any rate his praise of Bacon seems inexact. He asserted [in *Critical & Historical Essays,* ed. A. Grieve, 1910] that "The aim of the Platonic philosophy was to raise us far above vulgar wants. The aim of the Baconian philosophy was to supply our vulgar wants." Clearly in the Utopian state great care was taken to meet men's actual needs. Indeed, as a really thorough-going Elizabethan materialist put it, "If sack and sugar be a fault, God help the wicked!" Bacon elsewhere recognized claims of divine and moral philosophy, and perhaps it is true, as some have conjectured, that if the *New Atlantis* had been completed, its "tendency would . . . have appeared less materialistic."

Nevertheless, one of Bacon's distinctive contributions to the idea of utopian progress, as foreshadowed in the *New Atlantis,* is the concept that science can be responsible for human happiness, not merely through providing the necessary things with which the Utopians, like Thoreau at Walden, sought to satisfy their vulgar wants and to gain leisure for peculiarly human joys such as those born of "the free liberty of the mind and garnishing of the same." In the *New Atlantis* man's vulgar wants are becoming insatiable, and applied science therefore is turned to increasing without fixed limits the material goods and sensual luxuries available to the people. Yet human history, as the humanist Hythlodaye is aware, and as portrayed in the Scriptures which are known in Bacon's island of Bensalem, proves that such devotion to luxury has regularly tended to generate social corruption and disintegration. . . .

Only one point relating to scientific progress in warfare needs to be mentioned. The Utopians depend mainly on their strong natural defensive position, and are not said to be particularly superior to their neighbors in offensive weapons themselves. While they abhor war as most "beastly" (i.e. contrary to man's uncorrupted "nature"), they take such minimum measures as are deemed necessary for defence, but always they draw their decisive strength from trained men and minds joined by a bond of natural devotion to each other and to the commonwealth. On the other hand, the scientists of Salomon's House, just as they labor incessantly to perfect all knowledge, so they strive to discover all possible poisons, new weapons, and improved techniques of warfare. This implies no scientific or national ill-will toward states near to Bensalem, but represents simply another form of taking all knowledge for one's province—in short, another facet of the Baconian idea of progress. . . .

Sidney Warhaft (essay date 1958)

SOURCE: "Science Against Man in Bacon," in *Bucknell Review,* Vol. VII, No. 3, March, 1958, pp. 158-73.

[*In the excerpt below, Warhaft points out the limitations and dangers implied by Bacon's method for a scientific utopia, arguing that he lacks the "cultivation of the entire person," as well as "a thorough, energetic, and systematic development of the potentialities of the human as an essentially social and moral being." For these reasons, Warhaft concludes that the* New Atlantis' *utopian ends are not necessarily met, and submits that his model may have contributed to the imperfections of contemporary society.*]

Somewhere in New Atlantis amid the caves, towers, lakes, wells, chambers, baths, orchards, enclosures, breweries, dispensatories, and furnaces—somewhere, somehow, in the midst of all this Baconian plenty,

lives man. Religious, moral, compassionate, and content, man owes his place in this best of all impossible worlds to the aims and means of the inductive method. As Bacon had promised, his life is endowed with discoveries and powers, and his estate is relieved by many singular commodities. Having for centuries scrupulously pursued the furthest end of knowledge, he seems now to be able justifiably to claim to have given a true account of the gift of reason to human benefit and use.

But the rosy appearance is deceptive: Bacon was hardly the shining glorifier of humanism that Geoffrey Bullough [in *Seventeenth-Century Studies Presented to Sir Herbert Grierson,* 1948], for one, has made him out to be. Indeed, despite the enthusiasm of almost every editor of the *New Atlantis* (including Robert Ellis and A. B. Gough) and of many a commentator from the seventeenth century to the present day (from Cowley and Sprat to H. Minkowski and G. S. Gordon), the human condition in Bensalem is after all neither so enviable nor so inevitable as at first it seems. Certainly it is by no means the logical product of his philosophy that Bacon thought it to be. In fact, given the ideas, goals, and methods on which the human condition is ostensibly based, it could easily have turned out far otherwise—it could, for instance, have turned out as it is today. For the modern age of anxiety, rather than New Atlantis, is in many ways the logical result of the Great Instauration: the growth of many of the modern ills can be traced back, however, deviously, to this system or at least to the movement of which it is a significant part. To be sure, many advantages also have been developed, directly or indirectly, through this system. However, what was needed, in Bacon's day as in ours, was not only some kind of organized attack upon nature but also an accompanying cultivation of the entire person, a thorough, energetic, and systematic development of the potentialities of the human as an essentially social and moral being. It is this need, says [John] Dewey, which constitutes the specific problem of philosophical reconstruction at the present time (although one does not have to subscribe to his solution, or at least the application of his solution by his followers). That this reconstruction has been so long delayed may be charged in part at least to certain limitations and dangers implicit in Bacon's method.

I

The striking piety of the people of New Atlantis is undoubtedly Bacon's means of trying to satisfy the zeal and jealousy of divines, critics whom Bacon sought all his life to convince of the worth and innocence of his organon. His first and repeated adviso on the problem of the relationship between religion and natural philosophy was that the two fields should be separated for their mutual good: "The prejudice hath been infinite that both divine and human knowledge hath received by the intermingling and tempering of the one with the other." But physical investigation was nevertheless to remain limited by religion. Not that this caution was absolutely necessary, for it is an "assured truth" that the study of nature leads inescapably to a knowledge of God's bounty and glory. Thus it becomes impossible for any man to "search too far or be too well studied in the book of God's word or in the book of God's works; divinity or philosophy." In fact, nature is almost as effective as the Scriptures in opening the Christian path to a lost sheep: "Natural philosophy is, next to the divine word, the most certain remedy of superstition, and the most wholesome food of faith." Finally, examination of second causes (nature) is actually worship of God—and with His authorization: "For he did not err who said, 'Ye err in that ye know not the Scriptures and the power of God,' thus coupling and blending in an indissoluble bond information concerning his will and meditation concerning his power."

All this is dramatically illustrated in New Atlantis. Here is living demonstration that, even if philosophy were not the faithful handmaid she is, Christianity would still remain supreme "over the sense . . . and the investigation of truth in nature." Thus science is sanctioned by both its innocence and effectiveness, and is shown to be "an excellent defense against both extremes of religion, superstition and infidelity." As Bensalem clearly illustrates, not only is the faith strong enough to stand up against man's puny questions, but it has nothing to fear and everything to gain from the inductive method. Was it not to a Father of Salomon's House only that the Scriptures could be entrusted?

The charity, humility, and virtue of the islanders also seem to follow from Bacon's counsels. These people are reverent and humane, and the Father of Salomon's House, like the speaker in *Redargutio philosophiarum*, has "an aspect as if he pitied men," because in Bacon's system the attainment of the power of knowledge without pity and *philanthropia* is unthinkable. Just as he insists in his essay **"Of Truth"** that the contemplation of truth must "always . . . be with pity," so he often held that the fruits of natural philosophy are to be devoted to the good of mankind with true benevolence and affection. Like Paul, he "notably disavowed both power and knowledge such as is not dedicated to goodness or love." Fortunately for mankind and science, however, the study of nature not only requires humility and virtue on the part of the investigator but also helps instil these attributes in him. Constant work among things not only leads to religion but is itself practice in humility, because thereby all wits are levelled and man must learn to obey nature in order to command her. Thus physical truth and human good are almost identical, since the scientist "doth ever intermix the correction and amendment of his mind with the use and employment thereof. . . . Certain it is that *veritas* and *bonitas* differ but as the seal and the print;

for truth prints goodness. . . . " Moreover, the discovery and contemplation of the laws of second causes are God-like. Also God-like is the true end of the scientist's efforts, the use or application of the laws of nature for the benefit of mankind. In fact, only in this way, through "goodness put in motion or applied," may man hope or dare to emulate God.

None of this becomes particularly explicit in the *New Atlantis*, although it is all everywhere implied. Certainly the Bensalemites have not been corrupted by the methods and attainments of Salomon's House; the contrary would seem to be true. Even the Jews, those favorite children of scorn in Renaissance England, are in this kingdom "of a far differing disposition from the Jews in other parts"—the implication being that such is the beneficent effect of "the knowledge of Causes, and the secret motions of things." The other citizens seem also to have been moulded by this benign influence, for even though their fine character is mostly traceable to their faith (which of course is itself directly connected to the experimental philosophy), they appear to have been virtuous *before* they received the revelation of God's word. Thus man adds a cubit here and there to his spiritual and moral statute as a necessary concomitant to the enlarging of the bounds of human empire.

II

But we must not stay too long in the light of this vision; let us now pass on to the darker reality behind.

The first objection to Bacon's position is that there is nothing inexorable about that part of his logic, eloquent as it is, which seems to establish a rapprochement between religion and science after he has decreed their divorce. There is nothing in the *New Atlantis* or in any other of his writings to substantiate the idea that the study of nature is a kind of faith or at least an inescapable sacred duty. From the religious point of view, the suggestion that science provides "that knowledge or rudiment of knowledge concerning God, which may be obtained by the contemplation of his creatures" is surely suspect. This, to invert Bacon's phrase, is seeking the living among the dead and raising the profane investigator and his functions to a sacrilegious height. And in fact Bacon is indictable on both charges.

In the first place, although his purpose required, as Basil Willey has shown [in *The Seventeenth-Century Background,* 1934], that nature should be established as divine instead of Satanic, those who know beyond question that nature has been and remains corrupted by the Fall would not be sympathetic to the requirement, nor, consequently, to the invitation to return to our original innocence through scientific research. There is danger as well as impiety in such ideas, for they involve the strong possibility that religion will be, if not destroyed, put on a physical basis and its commandments, Bacon's own warnings notwithstanding, drawn from the laws of nature. In the second place, and for much the same reasons, it is impossible to accept Bacon's innumerable suggestions that science is a sacred activity, that entrance into the kingdom of nature is "not much other than the entrance into the kingdom of heaven, whereinto none may enter except as a little child," that inventors are god-like, and that scientists are a kind of elect or priesthood—much like the magnificent Father in Bensalem who, as he made his way through the populace, "held up his bare hand . . . , as blessing the people." This need and desire, incidentally, to display a divine *imprimatur* on his views are strikingly exposed by Bacon's indulgence in an anachronism in the **New Atlantis**. The College of Six Days Work or Salomon's House seems to have been so named some three hundred years *before* the Scriptures from which these names are drawn were revealed to the community. The discrepancy is a small one, but the motivation behind it is significant. And of course it does not excuse or vindicate its author in any way. Illogical or not, the assurance of salvation through a science underwritten by an elite of sanctified Baconians falls rather short of a valid ideal.

But it is the natural separation of the two domains—despite Bacon's remarks to the contrary—which engenders the greatest mischief. For such a divorce tends, by weakening the authority of religion, not only to distract attention from what the pious consider man's main concern on earth, salvation, but also, by removing religion from reality, to release the world from all spiritual guides and checks. When religion is relegated at best to the "talkative arts," to words as opposed to the matter of the world, its impotency must follow soon after. As Douglas Bush put it [in *English Literature in the Earlier Seventeenth Century,* 1945], by excluding faith from science Bacon "virtually denied the validity of a religious view of the world. If religion was outside the sphere of knowledge, it was outside the sphere of reality. . . . To machinery and material progress he sacrificed, in a large and noble way, to be sure, that scale of spiritual and ethical values which the best minds of antiquity, the Middle Ages, and the Renaissance had striven to make prevail."

There can be no doubt that Bacon made the separation of the two realms in the interests of philosophy and not of faith. In fact, the whole emphasis of his life and works insists on the incompatibility of the two spheres of knowledge and the essential superiority of nature to revelation. One of his characteristic objections, delivered under the guise of saving religion, underlines this incompatibility and assumption of superiority: some moderns, he complains, have frivolously and impiously attempted to found a system of natural philosophy on the Scriptures. The inhibition and repression of this offence, he says, are essential "because from this unwholesome mixture of things human and divine there arise not only a fantastic philosophy but also an heretical religion. Very meet it is therefore that we be sober-minded, and give to faith that only which is faith's"—and so, we must add, be free to render unto Caesar that which is now completely Caesar's. And "that only which is faith's" releases a great deal unto Caesar.

That the citizens of New Atlantis have not suffered the less attractive consequences of Bacon's split can best be accounted for simply by the fact that their fortune is Bacon's hostage. But the religion of the Fathers of Salomon's House reveals nevertheless that the retreat of a personal god of love from the world is already under way. Their prayers, if nothing else, disclose that God is to them little more than an overseer of nature, a not-altogether deaf functionary concerned mainly with directing their investigations and assuring their usefulness. Aside from paying homage to God constantly through their natural research, the fathers get together daily for "certain hymns and services . . . of laud and thanks to God for his marvelous works: . . . imploring his aid and blessing. . . ." Earlier, the Father to whom Bartholomew gave the Scriptures petitioned God for their release in this manner: "Thou hast vouchsafed of thy grace to those of our order, to know thy works of creation, and the secrets of them; and to discern . . . between divine miracles, works of nature, works of art, and impostures and illusions of all sorts. I do here acknowledge and testify before this people, that the thing which we now see before our eyes is thy Finger and a true Miracle; . . . we most humbly beseech thee to prosper this great sign, and to give us the interpretation and use of it in mercy." God is here well on His way to being a kind of supernatural guarantor of all the progress made in the kingdom of man, apparently answerable only to the clear-seeing philosopher. His major characteristics would now appear to be efficiency and liberality, and His major function the revelation, almost will-He nill-He, of the laws governing His works to His grateful, inquisitive, puissant ministers. It was only a matter of time before, having yielded up to them the secrets of His universe, He was, as Fontenelle suggested to the Duchess, to withdraw altogether, leaving behind Him nothing for mankind but the ambiguous grin of His creation.

From a more secular point of view, Bacon's solution to the problem of religion in Bensalem may appear questionable for other reasons. The non-religious critic could also, of course, argue that nothing in Bacon's works necessitates the piety of the New Atlantans, but his major objection would be that Bacon did not reject religion sufficiently and consequently compromised his aim of universal knowledge: the wonder of Bensalem is that the Fathers there managed to accomplish as much as they did. By not freeing science completely from the authority and tendentiousness of religion, the argument goes, Bacon helped distort and impede his ideal for centuries. Clearly he was too often too anxious to protect himself, or at least his beloved method, even though such protection was in the end to count seriously against it. For Bacon to maintain, from whatever compulsion, that nature is good, even divine, like some sacred virgin waiting invitingly to be possessed, is to falsify the facts. To hold that nature is anything but neutral is to place an unnecessary and disturbing burden on the investigator. For this way leads to obscurantism, to the very kind of *ne plus ultra* Bacon himself resented, in matters most intimately concerning man. To be sure, Bacon was also attracted to the rational investigation of spiritual problems as part of things as they are, and he advocated such an investigation as strongly as he dared. Even though sacred theology or divinity, he said, "is grounded only upon the word and oracle of God, and not upon the light of nature . . . , there hath not been . . . sufficiently enquired and handled the true limits and use of reason in spiritual things, as a kind of divine dialectic." But he did not dare enough, and his final pronouncement on this problem cut off sharply all discussion on fundamental aspects of the soul and of the divine being. "So then the doctrine of religion, as well moral as mystical, is not to be attained but by inspiration and revelation from God." Thus was Bacon too much a child of the Renaissance to accept the secular view, and too much the father of modern times to refuse it.

III

Just as Bacon split the domain of faith, so he divided the study of ethics into the forbidden and the allowed and then turned over the whole area to the forbidden. On the one hand, he repeated again and again that ethics was deficient and that a "Georgics of the mind," based on the inductive method, was an undertaking devoutly to be recommended. The old philosophers, he complained, have achieved little in this field; if they "had cast their eyes abroad upon nature, . . . they would have saved and abridged much of their long and wandering discourses of pleasure, virtue, duty, and religion." But, on the other hand, the promising idea that we should examine our nature as it really is and derive a system of ethics from "what men do, and not what they ought to do," Bacon undermined completely by giving in to current views and pressures and finally placing moral philosophy under divinity and therefore out of reach. Thus, arriving at the point of fixing of good and obliterating of evil in the individual—surely the core, as he himself has implied, of any study of man's conduct—he stops short and says: "But this part seemeth sacred and religious, and justly; for all good Moral Philosophy . . . is but an handmaid to religion."

Thus the people of Bensalem are not absolutely fated or forced by the Baconian method to be charitable, humble, and virtuous. They are not good because they are vitally aware of the problems of good and evil, or because they have learned sound moral lessons from nature: they are good because they are religious, and because Bacon has fashioned them that way. They have not studied mankind according to their master's method—even if they had they would have been no wiser or better. For Bacon's application of his method to human virtue dwindles disappointingly away into a handful of precepts differing from a myriad of other precepts only in Bacon's mastery over phrasing. To be good and virtuous, he says, all that is needed "is the electing and propounding unto a man's self good and virtuous ends of his life, such as may be in a reasonable sort within his compass to attain. . . . And . . . it will follow that he shall mould himself into all virtue at once. And this is indeed like the work of nature." On this basis, the inhabitants of New Atlantis can justifiably echo Bacon's own complaint against his predecessors in the field: they both have "made good and fair exemplars and copies . . . of Good, Virtue, Duty, Felicity; . . . but how to attain these excellent marks, and how to frame and subdue the will of man to become true and conformable to these pursuits, they pass over altogether or slightly and unprofitably." Thus Bacon's needs once again blinded him to the logical implications of his position. He was forced to make the islanders compassionate and virtuous simply in order to show that the *Great Insturation* held no perils for established morality; and he would like us to believe that they have attained their goodness by creeping up the chain of nature to the foot of Jupiter's chair with the help of experiments and axioms. The sad fact is that they have little basis for their humanity besides their creator's will and good wishes.

For although Bacon regularly preached the three virtues of faith, hope, and charity, to him the greatest of these was hope. He believed with a constant intensity in the ideal of natural progress and in the beneficent effect of such progress to the end even of restoring to man some of the glory that was his before the Fall. The assurance, or the thesis, runs throughout his works that "the glory of inventions is that they raise human nature, without hurting anyone." To him the true end of the knowledge gained from the interpretation of nature "is a restitution and reinvesting (in great part) of man to the sovereignty and power which he had in his first state of creation. . . . It is a discovery of all operations and possibilities of operations from immortality (if it were possible) to the meanest mechanical practice." The realization of this vision of restitution of man's original powers, his New Atlantis, consequently becomes a kind of paradise regained, a new Eden filled with prelapsarian Adams enjoying the kingdom of Christ without the renunciation of the world. Truly here is demonstrated that those who have humbled themselves have been exalted.

But Bacon was clearly fooling himself or his readers. He surely was aware that what he called "the sorrows of mankind and the pilgrimage of this life wherein we wear out days few and evil" are not remedied by inventions, or at least not by inventions alone. He also was surely aware that there was at least a psychological reason in the old myth of the Fall and therefore that to restore dominion without *absolutely insuring* innocence was a very dangerous proceeding indeed. For this is where his hope took him: to a universe of benefits and discoveries wrested from external nature without a parallel guarantee of spiritual and moral safeguards and advancement. His first reaction to the suggestion that his method involved grave perils to man was one of impatient question-begging: "If the debasement of arts and sciences to purposes of wickedness, luxury, and the like, be made a ground of objection, let no one be moved thereby. For the same may be said of all earthly goods; to wit, courage, strength, beauty, wealth, light itself, and the rest." True, he was not completely blinded by his own zealous meliorism, for as we have seen he frequently insisted that "knowledge is of the number of those things which are to be accepted of with caution" and to be limited by charity and religion. But his counsel (which never amounted to much more than eloquent exhortation) quickly paled in the light of his optimism. Confronted with the danger of inhuman exploitation of the power-of knowledge, his hopefulness triumphed to give expression to an incredibly naive belief: "Only let the human race recover that right over nature which belongs to it by divine bequest, and let power be given it; the exercise thereof will be governed by sound reason and true religion." It is difficult not to question Bacon's sincerity or at least his common sense here.

Since this hope is clearly the basis of **New Atlantis,** the work obviously embodies (perhaps not entirely consciously) an impossible ideal because, as Bacon well knew, men are rarely improved by the acquisition of power. It is true that the Fathers of his utopia maintain complete control over their inventions and that they apparently have the power, superior to that of the state in which they operate, to withhold whatever findings they consider wrong to reveal: "We have consultations, which of the inventions and experiences which we have discovered shall be published, and which not: and take all an oath of secrecy, for the concealing of those which we think fit to keep secret: though some of those we do reveal sometimes to the state, and some not." But how is this benevolent dictatorship of the scientist maintained? By what standards are works judged "fit to keep secret" or not? What guarantees do the state and its citizens have, first, that those inventions which are published will not be abused, and, second, that the scientists themselves are completely trustworthy, both in their intentions and decisions? And just how is an uncharitable investigator of physical science to be avoided or, if not avoided, disqualified?

R[obert] P. Adams [in "The Social Responsibilities of Science in *Utopia, New Atlantis* and After," *JHI,* 1949] is undoubtedly right in saying that in this work "we find no . . . profound awareness of man's capacity for good or evil . . . , but rather an expression of almost unbounded faith in human rationality, human goodness, and in the beneficence of scientific power over nature." Yet history, Scriptures (the very same Scriptures followed so faithfully in Bensalem), the literature of both ancients and moderns, all his training, education, and experience must have indicated to Bacon that such faith was baseless and dangerous on all three counts. Not that he needed to be told. Even if his life did not reflect such knowledge, surely those disingenuous observations of what life is really like, his essays, reveal that he understood very clearly indeed that "by indignities men come to dignities." As a result, with the advent of power and wealth in New Atlantis, he erred unforgivably in not providing against the human weakness that La Rochefoucauld was later to formulate into a maxim, namely, that we need greater virtues to endure good than evil fortune. His offense is in fact increased by the possibility that he himself provided La Rochefoucauld with the basis for the maxim in his own fine observation that "Prosperity does best discover vice, but adversity does best discover virtue."

IV

Bacon not only failed to make proper provision for the nurture and cultivation of the moral life but he even endangered the moral life further by opening the way (as he had for religion) for its being placed on a natural basis. To those who believe that nature is red in tooth and claw rather than benign and sacred, might easily becomes right under the new philosophy and man retains his ethical stature only on all fours; to those who see nature merely as a cold collection of mechanisms, man becomes one mechanism among many, deriving his standards of conduct from his functional efficiency. That the first danger was a real one was witnessed a few years later by Hobbes's unsentimental application of the Baconian system to human values in the *Leviathan* and elsewhere. Bacon himself sometimes yielded to the second tendency. If the moral philosophers, he argued, had spent more time examining the natural bases of good and evil before accepting "popular and received notions of virtue and vice, . . . they had given, in my opinion, a great light to that which followed; and especially if they had consulted with nature, they had made their doctrines less prolix and more profound." Since they had entirely neglected this approach, Bacon took it upon himself to "resume and open in a more clear manner" the sources of morality. As iron must follow certain laws in its attraction to the lodestone, he suggests, so man must follow similar laws in "communicative" or public good: "it was the same God that gave the Christian law to men, who gave those laws of nature to inanimate creatures."

Elsewhere he recommends that we be virtuous "like the work of nature" and proceeds to draw an extended analogy between gold and memory to show how virtue might properly be discovered and examined.

Moreover, if, as he periodically insisted, natural philosophy is the mother of all science and the foundation of learning, the study of man can, as it occasionally has, become the mere collection of phenomena freed from the trammels of ethical evaluation. And from here it is only a matter of time before *what is* is confused with what is right. Some of Bacon's own pronouncements in fact seem founded on such a confusion. For instance, believing there is "nothing in practice, whereof there is no theory and doctrine," he can, with complete aplomb, devote thirty unemotional pages to the problem of worldly success or "wisdom for oneself"—an advanced course in the Dynamics of Applied Materialism or Machiavellian Physics, a course entitled by Bacon himself "Architect of Fortune, or the Knowledge of Advancement in Life." Because ambition and interest, greed and selfishness exist, it follows that they must be catered to, thoroughly studied and scientifically satisfied. It was indeed a rare good fortune for New Atlantis that it had been isolated so completely and so long from the less savory subjects of investigation and from the more shoddy proclivities of the rest of mankind.

v

But the inhabitants are not so lucky from the intellectual and esthetic points of view. For, in setting up his method, Bacon cast such doubt on all the values derived from the senses, the understanding, and the imagination, that he opened the way wide to a cultural wilderness as empty as that in which Huxley's Savage finally hanged himself. By denying the ability of the mind and senses to find out truth for themselves without mechanical and methodological helps, he contributed much to making man unsure of himself as man and of his legitimate place in this world. Under such conditions reality and truth become a matter either of belief or of the certainty of mere things, existing only by grace of law revealed or induced. If the mind is "an enchanted glass, full of superstition and imposture," if man is plagued by "dulness, incompetency, and deceptions, of the senses," if there is "no soundness in our notions whether logical or physical," and if truth is gauged simply by fruits and works, then the whole realm of the subjective—feeling, intuition, wish, desire, fantasy—everything that makes up the inner self, has to be abandoned. Imagination especially, because it makes "unlawful matches and divorces of things" and is not tied to the laws of matter, disappears into the questionable shadows of fancies and vanities. As for the major product of the imagination, poetry, it too is suspect and becomes at best a kind of didactic tool, a "Feigned History" used "to give some shadow of satisfaction to the mind of man in those points wherein the nature of things doth deny it." In Bensalem there is excellent poetry, says Bacon, but this "excellence" seems to invest little more than occasional hymns and rhymed religion. As for the other arts, they get no mention whatsoever in brave New Atlantis, and in Bacon's other works they receive short and derogatory notice. Thus the puritanical tyranny of things forces the abandonment of one whole side of life in the interests of usefulness and certainty, and the artist is cut off by "inclosures of particularity" from the only truth and reality that matter to him. To achieve the "real truth" one must not "devise mimic and fabulous worlds of [his] own, but to examine and dissect the nature of this very world; must go to facts themselves for everything."

Bacon's method encouraged the displacement of the human in every department of life. Despite his protestations to the contrary, his new organon was not intended essentially for man—it was a cold ideal in which man tended to appear not as a complete person but as an idea or kind of mathematical point around which all else revolved. It is all for man, just as *Das Kapital* was all for man, but in the one as in the other the concern over technics and the system far overshadows all those human considerations for which the system is ostensibly erected. Moody E. Prior has argued in a perceptive article ["Bacon's Man of Science," JHI, XV, 3 (June 1954)] that it is impossible to question the sincerity of Bacon's expressed compassion for the lot of man, and Robert Ellis declared long ago that "a deep sense of the misery of mankind is visible throughout his writings." But Bacon nowhere indicates precisely what he considers the lot of man to be, and one must conclude that much of his emphasis on compassion and charity is traceable to his need to protect and justify his method rather than to help man. The charity of the Baconian scientist is important not because he is a man who owes it to himself or to man or to his God to be charitable, but because he is a scientist who owes it to his philosophy. And under what compulsion his charity must somehow get itself transferred from natural to human interests is not clear. In reality, compassion is in great part only a tool much like any other, necessary to improve not so much man as his estate; and somewhere in the application of this tool, man gets lost.

Lest these strictures seem unfair, we might compare the vision of the good life in *New Atlantis* with that in almost any utopia from Plato's and Sir Thomas More's to *Erewhon*. Or we might contrast Bacon's views with Petrarch's (or Ascham's, or Erasmus's, or Milton's) on nature and man. "What does it advantage us," Petrarch asks, "to be familiar with the nature of animals, birds, fishes, reptiles, while we are ignorant of the nature of the race of man to which we belong, and we do not know or care when we come or whither we go?" Against such a background the source of most of the deficiencies in the new organon stands out clearly—namely, that Bacon has shifted the center of interest from man to the world, from the human being to external nature. In the process man becomes a many-splintered thing. His religion is divided and distinguished from the world in which he lives, and, together with his soul, is spirited away out of reach. His finest efforts in art, humane letters, and philosophy are set apart from "real truth" as shadowy, barren, and useless. His personal inner world is also made unreal, while the actual world about him is transformed into a fertile field which, with proper exploitation, may be made to yield endless and exciting forms of luxury and power. His happiness and his level of civilization are measured in terms of technics and things, of material progress, novelty, and comfort. And he himself, as Robert P. Adams has convincingly demonstrated becomes, like the New Atlantan, a creature "supposedly insatiable" and perpetually in raptures before the "ever-increasing torrents of usable inventions," a consumer, "a sort of belly capable of almost infinite distention." The beacon of the Instauration, turned as it is toward nature, casts a long, dark shadow on man.

Much of what we find, directly or through implication, in the **New Atlantis** has been realized in one way or another in our time. [Alfred North] Whitehead [*Science and the Modern World*, 1925] has observed that "when you have made all the requisite deductions, Bacon remains as one of the great builders who constructed the mind of the modern world." Others have called Bacon "the great forerunner of the spirit of modern life," the *buccinator novi temporis*, the herald, the prophet, and the bell-ringer of the twentieth century. But if we owe much to Bacon for the method and inventions of our age, so too do we owe him much for our world of telegrams and anger. In this light Pope's statement that Bacon was the "wisest, brightest, meanest of mankind" takes on a new dimension. For if this man was the father of the modern spirit of delight in the "hypermagical ultraomnipotence" of science, he was also the spiritual progenitor of e. e. cummings' modern invitation, bitter ambiguity and all,

> . . . listen: there's a hell
> of a good universe next door; let's go

A. Wigfall Green (essay date 1966)

SOURCE: "Scientific Utopia: *New Atlantis*," in *Sir Francis Bacon,* Twayne Publishers, Inc., 1966, pp. 170-78.

[*In the following excerpt, Green briefly reviews the probable sources and the content of the* New Atlantis.]

The **New Atlantis,** the most imaginative of Bacon's works, is a "fable"—as Dr. William Rawley referred to it when he published the unfinished work in 1627—intended to be used as a model of a college for the interpretation of nature "and the producing of great and marvellous works for the benefit of men under the name of Salomon's House, or the College of the Six Days' Works." Rawley says in his address to the reader that "the model is more vast and high than can possibly be imitated in all things; notwithstanding most things therein are within men's power to effect." Bacon was creating a pattern "of the best state," for which he had planned to compose "a frame of laws."

The ideal commonwealth is probably as ancient as the longing of man for a life better than the one he is experiencing. From the antique treasures of Greece, probably by way of Turkey and Italy, the *Republic* of Plato came to England and there, as part of the intellectual and spiritual reawakening of the Renaissance, inspired Sir Thomas More to design his *Utopia,* the reveille of the English Renaissance, and Bacon to write **New Atlantis,** the tattoo of that great movement. Before looking at Bacon's work in detail, a survey of people and works that influenced him gives additional insight to his work.

Sources and Similarities

Like More and Bacon, Plato was an aristocrat and was thoroughly trained in law and in political theory. Descendant of Solon and student with Socrates for eleven years, Plato pursued metaphysics in Egypt. More was attracted by Plato's *Republic* and also by St. Augustine's *City of God,* upon which he lectured in London. (His ardor for Pico della Mirandola also kindled him to write a biography and to edit some of Pico's works.) More, like Plato and Bacon of excellent family, was the son of a justice of the King's Bench; and, again like Bacon, he left the university to study law at the Inns of Court. More was only fourteen when America was discovered; and, shortly before the publication of *Utopia* ("nowhere"), some of the letters of Amerigo Vespucci appeared in Florence. The chief character of More's *Utopia* is Raphael Hythloday, a given name having rich cultural connotation and a family name meaning in the Greek "learned in trifles." Hythloday is supposed to have made three visits to America with Vespucci. Confessedly influenced by Plato's *Republic,* Raphael says that the present ideals of conduct are no farther from what he has read in Plato or seen among the Utopias than from the doctrines of Christ. After Raphael had introduced the study of Greek to the Utopians, they promptly mastered Plato and many other Greek authors. Written in Latin, *Utopia* was published in Louvain in 1516, and was translated into English and published by Ralph Robynson in 1551.

Francis Bacon, son of the lord keeper of the great seal, entered Cambridge University at twelve and Gray's

Inn at fourteen. He began the **New Atlantis,** it must be conjectured, about 1612 and probably not about 1624, as sometimes has been said. Like More's *Utopia,* the **New Atlantis** has its origin in Plato's *Republic,* but Bacon's work is more heterogeneous than the others: Early in the work he introduces his interest in the drama and confirms the platitude that "Art becomes more delightful when strangeness is added to beauty"; to poetic touches from the Old Testament he adds much Hebraic and Oriental culture, and from these he gets or creates exotic names; and his theories of government and legal systems gradually yield to an even greater interest, experimental science: he begins with a rhetorical crescendo, about the waves from Peru to China, but ends with a practical diminuendo about a desire for a catalogue of artificial minerals and cements.

Taine on Bacon's approach to science:

For [Bacon], the object of science is always the establishment of an art, that is, the production of something of practical utility; when he wished to describe the efficacious nature of his philosophy by a tale, he delineated in the *New Atlantis,* with a poet's boldness and the precision of a seer, almost employing the very terms in use now, modern applications, and the prsent organisation of the sciences, academies, observatories, air-balloons, submarine vessels, the improvement of land, the transmutation of species, regenerations, the discovery of remedies, the preservation of food. The end of our foundation, says his principal personage, is the knowledge of causes and secret motions of things, and the enlarging of the bounds of human empire, to the effecting of all things possible. And this "possible" is infinite.

H.A. Taine, in his History of English Literature, *translated by H. Van Laun, 1873.*

The dreams of each of the three Utopians who would create an ideal state were transformed to nightmares: Dionysius placed in jeopardy the life of Plato because of his unrestrained criticism of government; More was beheaded for refusing to take an oath recognizing royal supremacy in spiritual matters; and Bacon, impeached, died in loneliness. But each of the dreamers and his friends realized that an ideal state is largely theoretical: Socrates says that he and his companions were constructing only "in theory the pattern of a perfect state"; More closed his work by saying that "many things be in the Utopian wealpublique which . . . I may rather wish for than hope for"; and Bacon's chaplain says the "fable my lord devised was but 'a model'" of an institution for interpreting Nature and that "the model is more vast and high than can possibly be imitated in all things."

For this reason, locale is vague in the three republics, although each author did desire to apply allor a part of his work to his own nation. Plato probably had in mind Atlantis, the mythical continent and the setting also of Bacon's work. Nowhere does it exist on earth, Plato says, but in heaven there may be a pattern of his republic. More had England in mind but the name of his work comes from the Greek negative *ou* plus *topos,* meaning not a place. The opening and the aim of the three great utopias are also similar: the dialogists of the *Republic* first meet at a seaport; in *Utopia,* Raphael describes the ideal island; and in the **New Atlantis** the port of embarkation is in Peru. In each of the three lands, man can attain truth and be accorded justice and live in accordance with the laws of Nature.

The governing class is similar in each work: in the *Republic,* guardians of the state; in the *Utopia,* magistrates or fathers; and in the **New Atlantis,** the head of the family or unit, respectively, the father or the tirsan. Moreover, in the *Republic,* each person has his own work; in the *Utopia,* each a craft; and in the **New Atlantis,** each a science or a trade. But property is held in common by the citizenry: Plato opens to the public the storehouses of the elders; More and Bacon provide the public with all food and clothing needed.

Precious metals are held in contempt in all three ideal commonwealths: Socrates says in the *Republic* that the inhabitants must not pollute "the divine gold and silver of their souls by mixture with the possession of these metals"; More says of gold and silver that no person must "more esteem it than the very nature of the thing deserveth," and he makes iron the standard of value; Bacon's citizens engage in trade not for gold or silver but for light.

Plato does not directly limit the size of his city; it may be "small or great or of moderate extent." But, through limitation of propagation, he determines size, as well as excellence of his community: those men who have distinguished themselves physically and mentally may unite with the women of the state more freely than may the inferior. Women and children are the property of the state. More and Bacon permit a choice of mate, and each is interested in eugenics to the extent that the prospective mate may be seen in the nude. In the three ideal states, relationship between the sexes is considered to be natural and necessary.

As respects physical, intellectual, and spiritual development, music and gymnastics, producing harmony and providing the foundation of education in Plato's state, are coupled with physics, mathematics, geometry, and astronomy. The Utopians study music, logic, arithmetic, geometry, astronomy, and philosophy. The New Atlanteans may choose for study any of the various arts and sciences. Plato prescribes the worship of the good, or God. King Utopus permits every man to believe what he will; the citizens of the **New Atlantis** worship

God, the ruler of Nature.

Other similarities between the three ideal commonwealths and examples of Bacon's indebtedness to the earlier works are too numerous for inclusion. But there are things that Bacon thought and wrote which form a backdrop for the *New Atlantis*. At Christmas of 1594 his *Gesta Grayorum* was staged at Gray's Inn. In the masque six counselors offer advice to the prince. The first advisesengagement in warfare, thus forming the background for *An Holy War and Considerations Touching a War with Spain* dedicated "To the Prince." The advice of the other counselors provides background for the *New Atlantis:* the second, for instance, advocates "the conquest of the works of Nature" and "the searching out, inventing, and discovering of all whatsoever is hid and secret in the world" and also the erection of four monuments: a "most perfect and general library," a vast garden with flora from all the world and rare beasts, birds, and fishes, a great cabinet in which will be preserved the rare things which man has made or Nature has produced, and last a "still-house" equipped with "instruments, furnaces, and vessels." The third counselor advises the prince to rear buildings and foundations and to create new "orders, ordinances, and societies"; but he is not, he says, interested in "dead buildings" so much as in "foundations, institutions, and creations." The fourth advocates following "the order of Nature" and "first to make the most of that you possess." The fifth urges an examination of laws and justice and that the prince "purge out multiplicity of laws, clear the incertainty of them, repeal those that are snaring, and press the execution of those that are wholesome and necessary," but the prince, he says, must not trust the "laws for correcting the times"; instead, he must "give all strength to good education" and "see to the government of your universities and all seminaries of youth."

Also forming a part of the background of the *New Atlantis* is Bacon's *Transportata* under date of July 26, 1608, a part of which appears also in the second book of the *Advancement of Learning*. In the former he shows interest in "an History mechanique," but first he has to decide upon materials and instruments requisite, and the method of operating each instrument. Then the work itself is to come. To aid in the research, he must look to the various preparatory schools and to Trinity and St. John's colleges at Cambridge and to Magdalen at Oxford. He considers pensions for those engaged in research, the foundation of a college for inventors, galleries with statues of inventors of the past and spaces for statues of inventors to come, and the need for "a Library and an Inginary." Workhouses, vaults, and furnaces are to be constructed. Allowances are to be granted for travel and experimentation. Collaboration with universities abroad would be desirable, and consideration must be given to maintaining secrecy as well as to publication of the results of investigation.

Setting and Structure

A haven for the person who would penetrate the mysteries of nature, New Atlantis is called *Bensalem* in the native tongue—possibly no more than a blend of *Bethlehem* and *Jerusalem,* or *Ben* and *Salem,* the Good Jerusalem. The "lanthorn of this kingdom" is Solomon's House, an "Order or Society . . . dedicated to the study of the Works and Creatures of God," otherwise called The College of Six Days' Works. King Utopus gave his name to Utopia because Brutus gave his name to Britain; in the same way King Solamona, or Solomon (the name is spelled in various ways), who reigned "about nineteen hundred years ago," gave his name to the society. The College of the Six Days' Works was probably named not only from the fourth commandment but also from the College of God's Gift, founded by the famous actor Edward Alleyn. Bacon had examined the charter for Alleyn's projected college and had endeavored to have the money involved placed with theuniversities and not used for the founding of a new college. Bacon also seems to have had in mind as the site of his college Twickenham Park, which he had sold when much younger. He left instructions that it be repurchased as a place for carrying on research, for he had found it a good place for arriving at philosophical conclusions.

The location of New Atlantis is vague, and was perhaps vague to Bacon. The sailors left Peru for China and Japan; easterly winds favored them for five months, but for many days westerly winds impeded progress. These winds, though, were followed by "strong and great winds from the south, with a point east." The direction, therefore, was northwesterly; and New Atlantis must be in the neighborhood of Hawaii, certainly north and east of Australia. Atlantis seems to be associated with America, and the uncivilized state of the American Indians may be attributed to the fact that, when Atlantis was inundated about three thousand years ago, only some "wild inhabitants of the wood escaped" drowning. The natives of the New Atlantis know Hebrew, Greek, Latin, and Spanish. For the most part they speak Spanish.

Two decades after the ascension of Christ, the natives of the one city, Renfusa, found at sea an ark containing a book comprised of the Old and New Testaments and the Apocalypse, and other books of the New Testament then unwritten. They found also a letter which said that the Father and the Lord Jesus had sent them peace. Although Christian, the natives allow the Jews of the island to worship according to their own religion.

The first person, singular and plural, is used for the narration of the adventurers. The sailors are lost in the "greatest wilderness of waters in the world," but they arrive on land and are hospitably received in the Strangers' House. While the sick are being healed as though divinely, the governor of the Strangers' House tells them the history and the social organization of the island.

On the island the family unifies society. A man with thirty descendants, all more than three years old, is honored at a feast. Bacon, almost in love with the enameled beauty of his own rhetoric, describes a feast in which "The herald and children are clothed with mantles of sea-water green sattin; but the herald's mantle is streamed with gold, and hath a train." A father of Solomon's House wore gloves "that were curious, and set with stone, and shoes of peach-coloured velvet." Finally the visitors meet the head of Solomon's House, seated on "a low throne richly adorned" and over his head "a rich cloth of state . . . of blue satin embroidered." He promises first to tell the aim of the foundation; then about the preparations and instruments; third, the nature of the employment of fellows; and, fourth, the ordinances and rites.

First, the objective of the foundation, he says, "is the knowledge of causes, and secret motions of things, and the enlarging of the bounds of human empire, to the effecting of all things possible." Second, the "preparations and instruments" include caves, some three miles deep, for coagulation and preservation of bodies; holes in the earth for the burial of cements and for making the earth fruitful; high towers for refrigeration, for the observation of meteors, and for the residences for hermits who make the observations; great lakes, salt and fresh, for fish and fowl, and pools for converting salt water to fresh and fresh to salt, and cataracts for "many motions" and for driving engines for increasing winds. There are also artificial wells and fountains and a water of paradise for prolonging life; houses for imitating and demonstrating meteors and snow and rain, and for generating bodies, such as frogs and flies. Through grafting, wild trees are converted into fruit trees, and fruits and flowers are produced later or earlier than they would be normally. Enclosures exist for beasts and birds upon which various medicines are tried and the bodies of which are dissected to throw light upon the body of man; breweries, in which drinks are brewed of herbs and various meats; shops, for dispensing medicines; divers mechanical arts and excellent dyes; furnaces imitating the heat of heavenly bodies; houses for demonstration of lights, including "delusions and deceits of the sight." Other inventions are microscopes for examining urine and blood; sound-houses and musical instruments previously unknown and echoes and instruments for increasing the voice and for conveying sounds in pipes for some distance; perfume houses; instruments of warfare; fireworks; machines which imitate birds and fly in the air; ships for going under water and swimming-girdles. A house

also has been created for solving problems in mathematics, geometry, and astronomy.

Third, as for employments: twelve men travel to collect books and patterns of experiments; three men collect the experiments from the books; three collect experiments in the mechanical arts and liberal sciences; three try new experiments; three draw experiments into titles and tables; three study experiments of their colleagues and try to develop things of use to man; three direct new experiments; three more execute the experiments and report on them; and three raise discoveries into axioms and greater observations. In addition, there are novices and apprentices, and servants and attendants, men and women.

White describes how the nomenclature of the *New Atlantis* contributes to the work's universality:

The names are not, like those of More, references to remoteness and improbability. Some are historical names, or quasi-historical names. The institution of Solomon's House is founded by King Solamona, the wisest of Bensalem's kings and the counterpart of Solomon. The merchant is called Joabin, implying the plural of Joab, executed by Solomon, but in the *New Atlantis* serving as a herald for the Father of Solomon's House. Other names can be understood not in terms of historical roles but as translations: the name of Bensalem itself, as has been noted, is Hebrew, and I have mentioned the meaning. The name of the other historic Bensalem king, besides Solamona, is Altabin, which is presumably Latin, and means "twice lofty." And the name of the city to which the miracle is brought is Renfusa, which is Greek, and means "of the nature of sheep." The impression of the universality of this society is heightened not only by the kind of names, derived from distinct languages, but by the deliberate confusion of symbols: both the first officer we meet and the Governor of Strangers' House wear "turbans," though smaller than the Turkish, while the Father of Solomon's House wears a hat like a Spanish montera, and walks upon carpets, "like the Persian but far finer." Joabin, a Jew, espouses certain Moslem doctrines, and mingled in with a presumably Persian feast are doctrine and symbolism derived from the myths of Isis. These examples should, I believe, suffice to show the eclectic character of the symbols and the kind of devices used to designate the universal utopia. . . .

Howard B. White, in Peace Among the Willows: The Political Philosophy of Francis Bacon, *Martinus Nijhoff, 1968.*

Fourth, patterns of rare and excellent inventions are placed in long galleries as are the statues of all principal inventors. In addition to these "ordinances," there are "rites," like the singing daily of thanks to God.

Visits are made to the principal cities, where profitable inventions are made public and where the citizens are warned of tempests, earthquakes, and floods and are given the means to prevent or to remedy various diseases and plagues.

After this explanation the head of Solomon's House withdrew, leaving behind the blessing of God. The list of thirty-three desiderata appended to the unfinished *New Atlantis* includes the alteration of features, the making of new species, and the force of the imagination upon the body or upon another body.

Influence of the New Atlantis

The foundation of the Invisible College in 1645 was inspired by the *New Atlantis,* and the Royal Society developed from this Invisible College. Joseph Glanvill said in an address before the Royal Society that "Solomon's House in the *New Atlantis* was a prophetic scheme of the Royal Society," a statement confirmed by Disraeli. In writing to the president of the Royal Society, the diarist John Evelyn stated: "Solomon built the first temple, and what forbids us to hope that as great a prince may build Solomon's House. . . . Nothing in that august and noble model" is impossible or "beyond the power of nature and learned industry." Thomas Sprat in his history of the Royal Society says that the Dutch of The Hague may soon copy a town of the *New Atlantis*.

The style of the *New Atlantis* is flamboyant in some places and more than plain in others; the rhetoric is often antique and haunting and wistful—like the face of the father of Solomon's House, which looks as if it "pitied men."

J. Weinberger (essay date 1976)

SOURCE: "Science and Rule in Bacon's Utopia: An Introduction to the Reading of the *New Atlantis,*" in *The American Political Science Review,* Vol. LXX, No. 3, September, 1976, pp. 865-85.

[*Here, Weinberger provides a comprehensive overview of the* New Atlantis, *examining the roots of modernity in order to provide a more complete understanding of the vision behind Bacon's seemingly anomalous, strictly scientific, approach toward the development of a modern utopia.*]

Modern utopian thought springs from the promise of modern science. It is the political expression of the claim of science to relieve man's estate and to enlarge the bounds of human empire. The modern utopianism of modern science is nowhere more succinctly presented than in the claim Hobbes made for his novel political science. When founded on the principles of the new science with its "clear and exact method," the study of morals and politics would disclose a "true and certain rule of action by which we might know whether that which we undertake be just or unjust." For Hobbes, the final victory of science over nature depended on the conquest of the problem of human nature, which Hobbes thought to be the problem of political rule. The aim of the new science of politics was to abolish the grounds of political controversy and thus to dissolve the problematic character of political discourse and life. The question of rule was reduced to the simple recognition of positive law; the new political science would guarantee that the precepts of natural law would be contained in the conventional precepts of civil law.

The claim of the new science obscured the distinction between theoretical and practical speech, for the perfection of speech about man and nature was to facilitate the perfection of practical life. As determined by Hobbes's application of scientific method to politics, modern scientific discourse about politics is inherently utopian. The development of modern utopianism is not simply the development of a particular mode of political thinking, but is, rather, "a perfect paradigm of the course of modernity." Thus unlike Plato's *Republic* and More's *Utopia,* modern utopia has "ceased to be ironical and has become oppositional." Whereas premodern utopia articulated human perfection by reflecting on the inherent delimitation of human nature, modern utopia illuminates present human defect from the standpoint of a future achievable human perfection. In modernity the literal meaning of utopia has been reversed; it no longer points to no place but, rather, lights the path to every place.

Bacon's *New Atlantis* is anomalous when seen in the light of the course of modernity. For the *New Atlantis* depicts a society formed by the rule of science, but it presents no explicit teaching about natural right or political rule. We wonder, then, why the political utopianism of modern science was not simply coeval with the origins of modern science. Though Hobbes was the first to proclaim the birth of political science, he was neither the first pioneer of science nor the first to proclaim modern teachings about morality and politics. According to Rawley [in his prefatory note to the *New Atlantis,* 1862] it was Bacon's intention to include an account of the best regime in the *New Atlantis,* but the labor required and the enticement of natural history diverted his attention. If Rawley is correct, the *New Atlantis* is incomplete simply because it lacks a political teaching. We might conclude, then, that the novelty of Hobbes's political science consists simply in his being the first to apply the new science of nature to the human things. If Rawley is not correct, Bacon's motives were more complex, and the *New Atlantis* would present the promise of science in conjunction with a circumspect prudence toward any teaching about political rule. The *New Atlantis* would then be *both* oppositional and ironical, and for Bacon the relationship between science and political rule would be problematic. It might then be the case that the post-Baconian link between modern science and a certain, demonstrable political science sprang from the necessity to modify Bacon's teaching about science for the sake of moral and political perfection. The question of the *New Atlantis* is the question of its completeness, and the question of its completeness points to the roots of modernity. To study the *New Atlantis* is to study the coherence of the utopian promise of modern science.

The New Atlantis and the Coherence
of Bacon's Corpus

Bacon's *New Atlantis* appears to be a strange choice of texts for an inquiry into the utopian character of modern scientific discourse about politics. It could be argued that since Bacon's works antedate Hobbes's political science, it is no wonder that the *New Atlantis* is not a serious reflection about politics at all. According to the traditional account, the *New Atlantis* is incomplete because it does not contain a teaching about government or political rule. This traditional account still obtains: most scholars accept the *New Atlantis* as a part of the plan of the *Great Instauration* because they take it to be a primitive description of a scientific academy and because it does *not* contain a thematic account of government. This must mean that there is no commonly accepted "most important" political treatise by Bacon because he wrote no political treatise. Particular advice about particular problems offered to particular men may be interesting, but especially in Bacon's case, they do not seem to constitute a coherent and comprehensive account of man's political nature. Bacon's political writings consist of several of the **Essays** : **"Of Nobility"**, **"Of Seditions and Troubles"**, **"Of Empire"**, **"Of Counsel"**, **"Of the True Greatness of Kingdoms and Estates"**, **"Of Faction"**; the fragment **"Of The True Greatness of Britain"**, and fragments, letters and speeches touching holy war, British domestic policy, and policy toward Spain. These writings treat some matters of political negotiation and policy and focus mainly on the enlarging of British political influence in the world. But they do not make up a treatise on the fundamental considerations of political philosophy: the nature of the best regime, the ends of political life, and the nature and relations between the virtues of justice, moderation, wisdom and courage.

The lack of a political teaching in Bacon's works reflects a serious disunity in Bacon's teaching as a whole. Common knowledge justly reveres Bacon for his role in the birth of modern natural science. But if Bacon's importance is as a founder of modern science, his teaching can be but an interesting historical relic, for modern science doubtless has far surpassed its crude genesis with respect to method and content. The modern reader of Bacon's writings on natural history must find them to be quaint, and so only decent charity prevents them from being considered ridiculous. If the modern reader turns to Bacon's writings about method, he will find that they are incomplete and encumbered by metaphysical concerns now considered to have no place in the progress of scientific discovery. Indeed, these metaphysical concerns were so damaging as to blind Bacon to the crucial importance of mathematics for the interpretation and conquest of nature. If the modern reader is interested in the historical relics of modernity at all, he will be better served by turning his attention to Descartes and the origins of mathematical physics than to Bacon, who failed to recognize the importance of Copernicus and Galileo.

If Bacon's writings are useless to one concerned with the method and content of modern science, the importance of his teaching about science must be his recommendation of practically useful science as the horizon for man's self-improvement. But surely this recommendation is a self-evident commonplace. The importance of this recommendation is again merely historical; its importance is visible from a contrast to its historical context that was unenlightened and darkened by the obscurities of prescientific thinking. Thus Bacon's importance is as a pioneer. But in the light of the urgent task of penetrating and conquering nature— Bacon's own view of the human project—pioneers deserve reverence but not serious reflection. Reverence does not necessarily deflect our time and energy from the scientific project; serious reflection most certainly does. It seems that on the basis of Bacon's only serious teaching, serious reflection on that teaching must be less than serious.

We are faced with a disconcerting alternative. Either Bacon's works are not important, or they are imperative for the serious student because the scientific project is problematic. Of course, by itself the latter possibility does not justify a reading of Bacon. Rather, we can profitably turn to Bacon if the scientific project is or may be problematic and if Bacon's teaching illuminates *how* it may be problematic. This means that Bacon's teaching about science is important only if it is a part of a comprehensive teaching about science, human ends, and human perfection. But Bacon's writings do not appear to provide such a comprehensive teaching. Bacon's most famous writings about man's morals and manners are the *Essays* and the *New Atlantis*. But while the *Essays* treat manners, morals, and, in a cursory way, politics, they do not treat these subjects in relation to the project of a new science. The *New Atlantis* is incomplete, and, according to the traditional account, it is incomplete because it lacks a teaching about the "best state or mould of a commonwealth." The *New Atlantis* is incomplete because it fails to combine an account of the organization of the project of science with an account of the political rule necessary for the best form of human life.

A unified and comprehensive account of man and science appears to be lacking even in those works that treat the virtue of science thematically. In the *Advancement of Learning,* Bacon argues that piety requires the dignity of natural philosophy to be separated from the proscribed articulation of human ends and perfection. In concert with this piety, Bacon only hints at the virtue of knowledge as man's conquest of nature and argues that knowledge is useful for various human virtues without questioning the nature or status of those virtues as virtues. When Bacon discusses the human good, he makes several dogmatic assertions of the superiority of the "communicative good" over the "private and particular good" and the "active good" over the "passive good." But in these very brief assertions, Bacon gives no systematic description of the nature or content of the human good and the human virtues, and, what is more important, he makes no mention of the human good and the human virtues in connection with the virtue of knowledge in general or natural science in particular.

In the *Wisdom of the Ancients, Masculine Birth of Time, Thoughts and Conclusions,* and the *Great Instauration,* Bacon declares the end of knowledge to be the human mastery of nature by means of practical natural science, but in none of these works is the nature of man as conqueror explicitly articulated. It seems that Bacon's works provide no complete and comprehensive account of science and human perfection. If modern utopianism is the political expression of the claim of science to determine the horizon of human possibilities, Bacon's writings hardly seem to be such an expression. Not only does the *New Atlantis* seem to lack a political teaching, but Bacon's works as a whole appear to provide no unified basis from which we might infer such a teaching.

But the preceding argument may be much too hasty. If we are to search for the meeting of Bacon's teachings about science and man, we must proceed by taking our bearings from Bacon's own words, and there is a Baconian work that presents an explicit organization of his scientific project. Bacon's sole organizational work must be the start of any attempt to penetrate the comprehensive, unified whole of his teaching.

The *Great Instauration* announces Bacon's plan for the complete reformation of human science and knowledge, which will "lay the foundation, not of any sect or doctrine, but of human power and utility" in order to "command nature in action." Bacon's intention was to insure the harmony of theory and practice, of the "intellectual and terrestrial globes," which will guarantee man's power over nature. Elsewhere Bacon argues that the noblest end of science is the preservation and

restoration of the corruptible things. The *Great Instauration* is Bacon's public announcement of the whole of his project, and the conventional demands of piety prevent explicit identification of the commanding of nature with the conquest of nature's corruptibility. But since Bacon does hold the end of science to be the conquest of nature's corruptibility, and since the fullest commanding of nature must include overcoming natural decay, it is this highest conquest that in fact governs the plan of the *Great Instauration*.

A first glance at the *Great Instauration,* however, disappoints our hope of discovering a unified and comprehensive consideration of science and human perfection. For the most obtrusive characteristic of Bacon's great instauration is its incompleteness, an incompleteness acknowledged by Bacon himself. Part one is to be a division of the sciences, but it is declared to be wanting, although "some account of them will be found in the second Book of the 'Proficience and Advancement of Learning.'" Part two is to present the new inductive method or the "art itself of interpreting nature" and is provided in the *Novum Organum,* but only as "a summary digested into aphorisms." Part three is to be a foundational natural history, or the actual "first food" or factual material on which the new method will work. Although this part of the instauration is the most filled out, it is incomplete according to Bacon's description of its particulars in the *Great Instauration*. Part four is to "set forth examples of inquiry and invention" according to his method and is missing except for a very small fragment. Part five is to present Bacon's own provisional discoveries not "according to the true rules and methods of interpretation, but by the ordinary use of the understanding in inquiring and discovering." Like part four, part five is missing except for a very small fragment. Part six is to disclose and set forth the "developed and established" new philosophy that will be the "real business and fortune of the human race, and all power of operation." But as a formally identified part of the plan, part six is missing altogether.

In view of the incompleteness of the project outlined in the *Great Instauration,* a unified and comprehensive consideration of the crucial questions of science and man seems to be lacking. This lack is all the more important since Bacon's discussion of scientific method is admittedly incomplete and but a "summary digestion." This confirms our earlier observation that it would be less than profitable to return to Bacon for any serious consideration of scientific method as we know it today. Again we find that the important theme is the way of the new science in the light of human ends and perfection. It is all the more dismaying, then, that there is no completed part of the plan that would present a thematic account of the virtue of the new science as a part of a comprehensive teaching about human ends and perfection. Although the *Great In-*

stauration projects such an account as part six, Bacon thwarts our search by failing to identify even a part or hint of its completion. At best the **Great Instauration** repeats and directs us to the dogmatic and incomplete remarks about the human and scientific virtues in the **Advancement of Learning**. It would appear that Bacon tells us nothing important about scientific method and tells us nothing about the crucial problem of the virtue or value of science itself. Small wonder it is that, in the absence of a substantial consideration of the latter problem, most scholars approach Bacon with an interest in the teaching about method. Small wonder it is also, then, that these scholars are hard pressed to demonstrate the importance of Bacon as anything other than a quaint relic of an age which was but the infancy of scientific enlightenment.

But perhaps the massive incompleteness of the great instauration as outlined in the work of that name is more apparent than real, and so perhaps the crucial question of the value of science constitutes a completed part of the plan. The plan of the **Great Instauration** presents a general picture of the end and method of the new science, rather than the step by step proceeding of the new science to its end. This cannot be otherwise, for parts three, five and six must be incomplete simply because of Bacon's personal mortality. Since part four is "in fact nothing more than an application of the second part in detail and at large," the first and second parts, which are provided, present the thematic core of the plan, for the coherence and intelligibility of the plan does *not* depend on its being complete or immediately completable. Bacon makes this point in a subtle way when he explains the incompletability of part six. Bacon says that part six would "disclose and set forth that philosophy by which the legitimate, chaste, and severe course of inquiry which I have explained and provided is at length developed and established." In the light of Bacon's remarks in the preface and in the descriptions of parts three and five, it goes without saying that part six must be beyond hope of completion for Bacon. Bacon's personal mortality prevents his giving a full account of the completely developed penetration, understanding, and conquest of nature. But Bacon does *not* say that the picture of the end of science, the condition where "human knowledge and power do really meet in one," is inconceivable. Rather, he says that the fortune of the human race, which will give issue to Bacon's beginning, cannot *easily* be conceived or imagined. This means, of course, that with difficulty man's fortune can be conceived or imagined. The human possibilities illuminated by the new science of nature can be articulated before the step-by-step way of the new science is fully presented or completed. By the implication of his own words, Bacon's claim that part six is simply incompletable is less than strictly true.

Since part six can be completed before the perfection

of method and before the specific content of the new science is completed, then if it exists, it must be a description of human life liberated or being liberated in the way that the new science promises to liberate. If part six exists, it must be a description of human life liberated "to some degree" from the "necessities and miseries of humanity," and that degree will be measured by the preservation of the corruptible things. We must look to Bacon's corpus to see if such a description exists, and the writing that is the obvious candidate is the **New Atlantis**. The **New Atlantis** presents the picture of a society of men dedicated to the pursuit of science and so to the end governing the pursuit of science. Other than the description of the scientific institution, the longest description of the society visited by the sailors is the description of the festival celebrating the procreation and preservation of the human body, surely the most important of the corruptible things.

However much the preceding argument may be true, it does not alter the obvious fact that the **New Atlantis** is incomplete. The work that would treat the virtue of science in the light of human ends and perfection is incomplete, and so all we have discovered is that the incompleteness of the **New Atlantis** reflects the crucial disunity of Bacon's teaching as a whole. But lest we give up the chase in disgust, we must be reminded of Bacon's remark in the description of part six. The imagining and conceiving of man's scientific fortune is possible but difficult. The pressing task must be to explore the way of this difficulty and the reason for it.

The New Atlantis and the Whole of Bacon's Teaching

Next to the title, obvious incompleteness is the most obtrusive characteristic of the **New Atlantis**. But what is omitted because of the formal incompleteness? According to the traditional account, the **New Atlantis** is incomplete because it does not contain a teaching about government or political rule. We noted that the traditional account still obtains, but if we have been correct so far, the very worth of Bacon's teaching depends on the falsity of this account. Since a comprehensive account of the human good must include an account of government, the question of the traditional view of the incompleteness of the **New Atlantis** becomes the most important question guiding any approach to Bacon's teaching.

A first glance at the **New Atlantis** both supports and subverts the traditional account. On the one hand, the **New Atlantis** is not simply silent about government. We learn that Bensalem is a monarchy, and much of the **New Atlantis** is an account of the origin of Bensalemite law and a description of its customs. On the other hand, this apparently sketchy information would hardly seem to be a comprehensive account of the best form of commonwealth. If we are to discern how the *New Atlantis* is a comprehensive description of human perfection facilitated by science, we must discern how the sketchy political information could possibly be a whole or complete part of a complete teaching about the true, scientific human good. A reconsideration of the place of the *New Atlantis* in the plan of Bacon's great instauration provides the necessary clue for this discernment.

If we are correct to view the *New Atlantis* as the image or pattern of human life where knowledge and power do really meet in one, then it must be the end that governs the articulation of parts one and two of the *Great Instauration*. The need for the new method and the announcement of the sufficient and deficient sciences is governed by human possibilities that determine the fortune of the human race, for it is this fortune that will give issue to Bacon's account of beginnings. There must be a harmony between the content of the *New Atlantis* and the content of parts one and two of the *Great Instauration*. If there is a particular way in which these parts are incomplete, it must be reflected in the incompleteness of the *New Atlantis*. Thus if there is a particular way in which the *Novum Organum* and the division of the sciences are incomplete, it will provide a positive determination of just how the *New Atlantis* is incomplete. But if we find such a positive determination, is it not the discovery of fool's gold? Would not such a positive determination simply confirm the worthlessness of Bacon's work? We must hope that the positive determination of incompleteness provides the determination of the completeness of Bacon's teaching.

The positive determination of incompleteness is not to be found in the incompleteness of the *Novum Organum,* which presents the new inductive method in but a "summary" form "digested into aphorisms." In the light of Bacon's remarks about his personal mortality and hopes for the completion of his project, it is clear that the account of method need not be fully articulated in order for the plan of his instauration to be complete as an outline of proper directions and ends. This does not apply to the division of the sciences, however, because the particularization of the deficient and sufficient sciences is determined by the human possibilities that constitute man's fortune. The exact determination of the means to the perfection of these sciences, the actual fulfillment of their content, can and must wait for the labor of others. The positive determination of the incompleteness of the *New Atlantis* depends on the determination of the incompleteness of the division of the sciences.

In the *Great Instauration,* Bacon openly informs the reader that the division of the sciences is incomplete. The heading of the first part of the *Great Instauration* declares that the first part is "wanting," although "some

account of them will be found in the Second Book of the 'Proficience and Advancement of Learning, Divine and Human.'" But in the dedication of *An Advertisement Touching An Holy War,* Bacon asserts that the expanded, Latin version of his "book of Advancement of Learning" will "serve in lieu of the first part of the Instauration and acquit [his] promise in that part." This contradiction is important for two reasons. First, the translation and expansion of the *Advancement of Learning,* the *De Augmentis,* does not significantly change the determination of the sciences judged to be lacking or insufficient. Second, it is very curious that Bacon did not announce the completeness of part one in the *De Augmentis* itself. Rather, he chose to make this important announcement in a fragment that is apparently unrelated to the division of the sciences. Bacon was certainly aware of the importance of the announcement; although he did not include it in the *De Augmentis,* he instructed Rawley to translate and publish the *Advertisement* even though it was to remain as an incomplete fragment. Bacon's strange indirectness can be understood only by understanding how the claim of the *Great Instauration* and the claim of the *Advertisement* can be consistent. That is, Bacon's strange indirectness can be understood only by discerning how the division of the sciences, and so also the *New Atlantis,* can be both complete and incomplete. It appears that we have begun to find our clue: however we find the division of the sciences to be incomplete, we must be prepared to discover that that incompleteness is a positive part of a whole or complete teaching about man's scientific fortune.

Bacon provides an explicit standard of completeness for part one in his description of that part in the *Great Instauration*. He says that in the division of the sciences it is his intention "not merely to set down a simple title or a concise argument of that which is wanting." but "(provided it be a matter of any worth) to take care to subjoin either directions for the execution of such a work, or else a portion of the work itself executed by myself as a sample of the whole: thus giving assistance in every case by work or by counsel." In the *Novum Organum,* Bacon asserts that his .new method is "certainly meant" to apply to natural philosophy, logic, ethics, and politics. Of these important sciences, only politics is listed merely by mention of "simple title" in the *Advancement of Learning*. In the division of the sciences in the *Advancement of Learning,* the study of government is the third part of civil knowledge, the first two parts of which are knowledge of conversation and knowledge of negotiation. Knowledge of conversation is declared to be not deficient and is, therefore, not discussed. However, the two parts of knowledge of negotiation or business, wisdom of counsel and wisdom of pressing a man's own fortune, are explicated in great detail. At one point Bacon provides so many examples that he apologizes for dwelling longer than is "agreeable to the proportion of an example." Thus in the contexts both of the division in general and of civil knowledge in particular, the mention or division of the science of government stands out by its conspicuous violation of Bacon's announced standard of completeness.

The reason for Bacon's silence is not because the science of politics is complete or sufficient, for we know that the new method must be applied to it. Rather, Bacon states explicitly that the study of government or political science is a subject "secret and retired." The reason for this secrecy is that political science is either too hard or not fit to utter. It is easy to see why that which is not fit to be uttered must be unuttered, for to speak what must not be spoken is to cause damage or alarm. But why should the difficult be unuttered? There can be but one reason: if the speaking of the difficult is forbidden, it is because as spoken it will cause damage or alarm. The argument from difficulty is assimilated to the argument from unfitness since both are problematic because of possible damage or alarm.

In the *De Augmentis,* the secrecy of political science is demonstrated with even greater emphasis. In the *De Augmentis,* Bacon underscores the secrecy of political science by distinguishing between those parts of civil knowledge which do not belong to the secrets of empire. Just as in the *Advancement of Learning,* political science is the third of three parts of civil knowledge. The first, knowledge of conversation, is sufficient. The second, knowledge of negotiation, is deficient and so many examples of such a doctrine are given. Unlike the *Advancement of Learning,* however, the *De Augmentis* emphasizes the secrecy of the third part, political science, by distinguishing between those parts of political science which are deficient and which can be treated, for which he gives examples "according to his custom," and those parts of political science which cannot be mentioned and so which cannot be divided. The reason Bacon gives for his silence is deference to King James who is "such a master" in the art of government and to whom the *De Augmentis* and the *Advancement of Learning* were dedicated. But certainly in comparison to the *Advancement of Learning,* Bacon's stance toward the King in the *De Augmentis* is less than deferential. Brevity is not the same as silence, and even so, Bacon is not brief in his examples of the mentionable parts of political science. Again, with greater emphasis laced with audacity, Bacon argues that the reason for his silence is the secret nature of political science.

Bacon's clues disclose how the division of the sciences is incomplete. The division of the sciences articulates the "intellectual globe" that must become harmonious with the "terrestrial globe" for the issue of man's true fortune. But although the new harmony between the intellectual and terrestrial globes must include a teaching about government or politics, any compre-

hensive pattern or plan of these globes, i.e., man's scientific fortune, must be outwardly incomplete because of the unmentionableness of dangerous political science. Since the *New Atlantis* is the image or pattern of man's scientific fortune, the division of the sciences and the *New Atlantis* stand together in a relationship of mutual dependence. Although the *New Atlantis* must be of highest importance as the outline of the human possibilities governing the particularization of the deficient sciences, the division of the sciences must be articulated and followed if true human fortune is to be given issue. Thus the image or pattern illuminated by the *New Atlantis* must be congruous with the principles of the division, and for this reason we must conclude that the *New Atlantis* is incomplete because of the unmentionableness of dangerous political science.

Bacon's clues disclose how the division of the sciences and the *New Atlantis* are incomplete, but they also insist that the division of the sciences is complete, that the duty of part one has been "acquitted," and so they insist that the *New Atlantis* is complete. This means that both the division of the sciences and the *New Atlantis* must contain a teaching about government, but that it must be presented in an informal and indirect way that conforms to the retiredness and secrecy of political science. The *New Atlantis* is incomplete because it presents an image or pattern of scientific perfection that lacks a formal, direct, and open account of political science. The *New Atlantis* is complete because it presents an image or pattern of scientific perfection that includes an informal, indirect, and secret teaching about government that is dangerous and problematic. Our attempt to reach the core of Bacon's teaching directs us to his teaching about human perfection based on man's rule over nature. But before we can investigate that human utility, we are silently taught that in spite of man's rule over nature and the conquest of nature's corruptibility, the rule of men over men is problematic.

Bacon's articulate silence was governed by an extraordinarily circumspect prudence. This prudence is disclosed by reexamining the way we have come. In the *De Augmentis,* Bacon remarks that if his "leisure time shall hereafter produce anything concerning political knowledge, the work will perchance be either abortive or posthumous." In the meantime he presents those parts of civil knowledge "which do not belong to the secrets of empire" so that all the sciences being "ranged as it were in their proper seats," the seat of political science will not be left vacant. In this description Bacon is unclear as to whether the alternative "abortive or posthumous" is meant to be inclusive or exclusive. On the one hand, it would seem that Bacon's description is inclusive, that is, that the political teaching will be either abortive or posthumous and possibly both. For the *New Atlantis* is both abortive and posthumous. On the other hand, it would seem that Bacon's description is exclusive, for the division of the sciences, which must mirror the *New Atlantis,* is abortive but nonposthumous. Thus the description of his political teaching is both inclusive and exclusive. Although the *New Atlantis* must mirror the division of the sciences, and vice versa, the *New Atlantis* is the head of Bacon's teaching about man's scientific fortune because it presents an image or pattern of human life as it is lived according to the perfection of natural science. According to our way of discovery, guided by Bacon himself, the combination of the abortive and nonposthumous with the abortive and posthumous illuminates the complete and the posthumous. The combination of the division of the sciences with the *New Atlantis* makes available Bacon's complete teaching by means of the clue given in a political work. *An Advertisement Touching An Holy War*. The latter work is the key, but the door that it opens was presented only after Bacon's death. Bacon's extraordinary prudence underscores the serious importance of its cause: the completeness provided by Bacon's silent or secret political teaching is the completeness of Bacon's most important teaching—the teaching about the human ends and perfection that illuminate the new science of nature and that are facilitated by the new science.

We are now prepared to see how the sketchy political information in the *New Atlantis* completes a whole part of a comprehensive teaching about the true, scientific human good. The danger of political science is the danger of Bacon's comprehensive teaching about science and man. The serious reader of Bacon must be open to the possibility that Bacon's political teaching is the core of his teaching about the human possibilities freed by the new science of nature. Since the noblest end of the new science is the preservation and resurrection of the human body, the most important of the corruptible things, the limit of that preservation and resurrection may consist in the relations between human bodies rather than in the nature of any or all particular human bodies. But if political science and so the full understanding of the possible relations between human bodies is so dangerous as to require Bacon's circumspect prudence, the serious reader of Bacon must be open to the possibility that the human possibilities freed by the new science are morally problematic in their very perfection. The ground on which Bacon's teaching about science and man comes together is hispolitical science, and we know now why this ground must be elusive. But this elusiveness is ultimately important because of the coexistence of Bacon's explicit optimism and zeal for the conquests of science and the prudent, articulate silence of his central political teaching. Whatever the moral problems and dangers of the new science may be, Bacon intends for mankind to embrace them as a part of man's necessary fortune. Bacon intends for mankind as a whole to embrace a fortune that can be seen in its entirety only by those men who are the most courageous and reso-

lute.

If the combined completeness and incompleteness of the *New Atlantis* issue in a dangerous teaching about government, just how is the *New Atlantis* complete and incomplete, and what does the *New Atlantis* reveal about the dangerous political problem of man's scientific fortune? The title and final line declaring formal incompleteness are the most obtrusive parts of the *New Atlantis*. "New Atlantis" is not an obvious title. "Bensalem," "Renfusa," or "Salomon's House" would all be more plausible titles, for Atlantis is mentioned only as the country defeated by the ancient Bensalemites and destroyed by natural catastrophe. The title calls our attention to another important account of the ancient Atlantis in a way that suggests the reformation or perfection of the ancient Atlantis. The other account, to which Bacon explicitly refers, is that of Plato. Since Bacon's title is less than obvious, the connection between the ancient Atlantis and Bensalem is obscure. But the less than obvious title openly directs our attention to Plato's account in the *Timaeus* and *Critias,* and so to the ends of the old and new stories. For like Bacon's story, the *Critias* is incomplete. Plato's dialogue breaks off just as Zeus, angered by the prideful insolence of Atlantis, prepares to announce his intended chastisement of Atlantis to the assembly of the gods. Thus we are uniformed of Zeus' punishing that was to moderate and harmonize the Atlantians. That Bacon repeats the incompleteness of the *Critias* appears strange in the light of the title. Since the title suggests the reformation or perfection of the ancient Atlantis, one would expect the opposite of what in the *Critias* insures the imperfection or defectiveness of Atlantis. One would expect the *New Atlantis* to be finished so as to illuminate the true perfection of Atlantis.

In comparison to the *Critias,* however, the *New Atlantis* is a finished story. Whereas the speech of Zeus that would describe the defect and future perfection of Atlantis is omitted, the speech of the Father of Salomon's House that describes the "true state of Salomon's House," the "noblest foundation" ever upon the earth and the "lanthorn" of Bensalem, is provided to reveal the perfection of the new Atlantis for "the good of other nations." So although the story is declared to be incomplete, it is not transparently clear in what the incompleteness of the *New Atlantis* consists, how the title is related to the final line, and how the new Atlantis is related to the old. As directed by Bacon's circumspect prudence, we know that to penetrate the *New Atlantis* is to penetrate the unity or completeness of Bacon's comprehensive teaching about science and man, and we know that the core of that teaching may be a teaching about political science. We can determine the latter possibility only by working through the *New Atlantis* to see if the directions and content of a political teaching can be found. But whatever the directions and content may be, we can pursue them only by careful attention to Bacon's prudent and circumspect way. In the *New Atlantis*. Bacon teaches by what he does not say as guided by what he does say, and by the careful combination of his articulate silence with an indirect but available structure of allusions.

Arrival in Bensalem

The story narrated in the *New Atlantis* consists of two overlapping major themes. The first major theme depicts the changing character of the sailors who visit Bensalem and who ultimately become the announcers of Bensalem's virtues. This first theme is itself twofold: its first section tells of the plight of the sailors, who are at the mercy of nature's necessity and chance and who consider themselves to be unfree; the second section tells of the sailors' experiences after they come to regard themselves as free men. The second major theme of the story depicts the revelation of Bensalem to the sailors. It is composed of four sections. The first section portrays the way the sailors are received by the Bensalemites; the second section presents a history of Bensalem that explains its Christianity and laws of secrecy; the third section describes the current practices that extol and control Bensalemite erotic behavior; and the fourth section presents a description of the House of Salomon by the Father. The two major themes overlap and intersect. The cut between the two sections of the first major theme is also the cut between the second and third sections of the second major theme. This shared cut is the sailors' declaration of their liberation. Taken together, the two major themes combine to form a third major theme that springs from the story as a whole. This third theme presents the revelation of Bensalem to the rest of the world, and since the intersection of the first two constituent themes is the sailors' declaration of their liberation, we must wonder whether and why liberation is necessary for their becoming the announcers of Bensalem.

Although the liberation of the sailors and the revelation to them of Bensalem come together to form the universal revelation of Bensalem, the two revelations are not identical. The difference between them consists precisely in the degree or fullness of revelation. Although the sailors, through the narrator, tell all that they know, the Bensalemites do not tell all that *they* know. The sailors are not told all there is to know of Bensalem's laws of secrecy, and this must seem strange in the light of the central deed of the story. This deed is the unveiling of Bensalem and its exposure to the rest of the world, which eliminates the need for the laws of secrecy. The universal revelation that subverts the reason for secrecy is itself limited by secrecy. Thus, only a careful study of the story will provide a complete revelation that unveils the secrecy inherent in the revelation of Bensalem to the sailors and the world. Only a comprehensive understanding of this secrecy

illuminates the true nature of the sailors' liberation and the liberation of their worldwide audience.

The sailors are speakers of Spanish and English and are, therefore, representatives of the early European masters of exploration. The narrator begins by relating how the men became subject to the vicissitudes of wind and sea, which they take to be the product of God's providence. Their predicament is not their fault, for they have taken care to make "good spare of their victuals." In response to God's inhospitable providence, the men display lax or superficial piety and pray only when their bodies are in danger. No mention of prayer is made in describing their departure; we are not told if a priest is on board, and the men pray only for survival, not for the forgiveness of sin. The prayer, beseeching God, who "showeth His wonders in the deep," makes obvious reference to Psalms 107:23-32, where God rains great storms to terrify men in ships only to redeem them and bring them to their "desired haven." A close look reveals that Bacon reverses the Psalmist's story. Though strong winds afflict the sailors, it is these same strong winds, not calm, that bring them to a haven that is at first not desired. While the men of the psalm do nothing to help themselves, and "reel and stagger" and come to their "wits' end," Bacon's sailors do all in their power to save themselves, turning to prayer only as a last resort. Although the sailors refer to God as creator, His creating is mentioned in the context of scarcity of victual and hostility of sea. Comparison of Bacon's "psalm" to that of the psalmist underscores the superficial piety of the sailors and suggests a contrast between their own prudent responsibility and the irresponsibility of divine providence. At this point in the narrative, the sailors are ignorant of the House of Salomon and hence are ignorant of the possible Bensalemite control of wind and sea. Bacon's change in the psalm, then, suggests the possibility that the providence displayed in the *New Atlantis* replaces the providence of an irresponsible and hostile creator. Thus in the beginning, the sailors' ignorance of Bensalemite science causes them to seek final refuge in the bonds of heavenly grace; this ignorance and their gradual enlightenment provide the background for their liberation.

In contrast to what has become of Plato's Atlantis, Bensalem is an island naturally open to ships, although access to the port and city is strictly controlled by law. The Bensalemites are "humane" but prudent: the "man of place" or high rank claims to worry only about disease but stays "a flightshot" away. The accounts of the first encounters and of the sailors' going ashore are characterized by unusual procedures and events. The sailors learn gradually that tips are scorned in Bensalem as double payment. The Bensalemites are very concerned with the precise limitation of rewards and with the prevention of "extras" or petty bribes. A second kind of tip, the sailors' promise of God's "reward" to the Bensalemite officer, while not scorned, is met with silence—a strange reaction for a Christian man. The oath required of the sailors illuminates this strange reaction. Before the sailors are allowed to come ashore, they must swear "by the merits" of Jesus that they are not pirates and have not shed blood "lawfully or unlawfully" within forty days. The conditions of the oath refer merely to the tainting of recent bloodshed and make no distinction between lawful and unlawful killing. With respect to righteousness, this is a contradiction of the Old Law, which makes a distinction between lawful and unlawful killing. Taken together, the oath and the "psalm" hint that Bensalemite law provides a grace superior to that of Christ, that Bensalemite law surpasses both the Old and New Laws, but in a way that would count recent killing worse than old murder. Bensalem acknowledges the human lust for blood, and its law permits an oath that obscures the difference between killing and murder.

The men go ashore and are confined for three days while their sick are cured by the marvelous medicine of Bensalem. During their confinement the narrator addresses the sailors, likening their situation to that of Jonah and suggesting that they behave with restraint because their hospitable confinement may be a pretext for careful scrutiny by the Bensalemites. The differences between the sailors plight and that of Jonah are obvious. Jonah fled from divine command, while the sailors travel for exploration or money or both. God sent a tempest to buffer Jonah, while strong winds of suspicious origin firmly guide the sailors to their destiny. Jonah subjected himself to bodily harm, while the sailors appear solely concerned to avoid bodily harm. Jonah brought tidings of destruction and learned a lesson in pity, while the sailors bring no such tidings but do learn something of pity. While Jonah obeys divine command, the sailors obey only Bensalemite command. It is in this context that the sailors first mention the well-being of the soul, although the reason for their concern is explicitly utilitarian, and weal of body is mentioned in the same breath with weal of the soul. Thus, comparison of Bacon's Jonah with the biblical Jonah again suggests that Bensalem offers a grace that surpasses the power of divine grace to save or preserve body and soul. Like Jonah, the sailors learn something about pity, but, since the grounds of that pity may be a new kind of grace, we must wonder whether in Bensalem a new kind of pity will replace divine pity.

The sequel to the narrator's speech illuminates the unseemliness that lies beneath the outward hospitality of Bensalemite ways. The narrator's suspicions are confirmed. With the next visit of a Bensalemite official we learn that the sailors still fear for their lives but that this fear is dampened by the speech and offer of the official. The sailors are informed that they may be told some things they will not be unwilling to hear. Providing they do not go beyond one "Karan" from

the city walls without special leave, the state will allow them to stay for six weeks or more, and if they have any request, they must not fear to ask it of the Bensalemites because their countenances will not be "made to fall." All this is possible because the Strangers' House is rich; it has been thirty-seven years since any strangers have visited.

The official's remark that the sailors may be told some things that will be happily heard indicates other things that would be unhappily heard. This points to the possible grounds of Bensalemite inhospitality and the narrator's earlier concern. The offer to stay comes after the three days of confinement. Since the Bensalemites study ways to control wind and sea, there may be another reason for the wealthiness of the Strangers' House. The Strangers' House could be rich simply because the Bensalemites have chosen not to spend their wealth on men they have previously brought to the island. The governor of course speaks only of a lack of visitors, but the power of Bensalemite science to draw "visitors" to its shores and the necessary laws of secrecy illuminate the harsh reality feared by the narrator. For when the governor-priest later explicates King Solamona's laws of secrecy, he remarks that no strangers have been detained against their will and that the sailors must think that anything reported by returning strangers would be "taken where they came but for a dream." In the sequel, however, it is said that the missions of the Fellows of Salomon's House (the scientific institution) are strictly governed by the laws of secrecy. This of course reflects the reason for the laws of secrecy: protection from corruption or attack by foreigners who might change or despoil the island. Surely, then, the laws of secrecy assume the credulousness of non-Bensalemite peoples. The final revelation of the House of Salomon, meant as it is "for the good of other nations," also presupposes such credulousness. The conclusion that must be drawn is obvious. Until the visit of the sailors, no strangers left Bensalem, and those who were unwilling to stay must have been imprisoned or killed.

The Bensalemites are outwardly moderate, humane, and Christian, but a close examination of their oath and their laws suggests the subversion of divine law and the extreme opposite of hospitality. In this light, the seemingly commonplace and polite offer that gilds the Bensalemites' ambiguous hospitality must be viewed with circumspection. The offer is an open offer: the official says that *any* request will be met. Bacon modestly fails to mention the most notorious need of disembarking sailors, but we may now wonder if the offer goes beyond the healthy lust of seamen. The offer can be fully understood only in the light of Joabin's later mention of "Lot's Offer," but at this point we know that although all things may not be told, all things may be requested. If the Bensalemites' policy toward unwanted visitors may require murder unrestrained by divine or civil law, we may wonder whether for some wanted visitors, no request by such visitors will be too base.

The first part of the *New Atlantis* shows that the Bensalemite hospitality offered to the unliberated sailors suggests a combination of restraint and excess. The sailors are capable of great restraint: for the sake of their bodies and souls they restrain their use of victuals, restrain their "vices and unworthiness," and accept the travel limitation in spite of the inflammation of their hearts. Yet even this restraint is not at first as extensive as Bensalemite restraint, for they only gradually conform to the Bensalemite scorn of tips. But Bensalemite restraint, like Bensalemite Christiantity and humanity, is beclouded by the harshness and baseness suggested by ambiguous hospitality. This hospitality hints at the coherence of moral opposites but not in a formally open way, and the secrecy of the *New Atlantis* illuminates the obscure grounds of the explicit secrecy of Bensalem. Bacon directs our attention to the possibility that the imperatives governing the choice and reception of visitors as the announcers of science necessitate the opposites of Bensalem's outward hospitality and restraint. The propagation of Bensalemite perfection is not immune from the possible problem of immoral means for moral ends. The important question is whether this problem is the sole root of Bensalem's secrecy. If it is, the *New Atlantis* must appear to be incomplete because of a problem that is overcome with the perfection of science. If it is not, thc *New Atlantis* must appear to be incomplete because of a problem at the heart of man's scientific fortune.

Bensalem's Past: The Histories

Since the sailors are ignorant of Bensalem while the Bensalemites know about the sailors, the sailors are permitted to ask questions about Bensalem and its people. The questions prompt the governor-priest to relate the religious and institutional histories of Bensalem, which illuminate the nature of Bensalemite secrecy and the nature of the sailors' liberation.

The first question asks about the nature of Bensalem's conversion to Christianity. The answer relates an instance of the miracle of revelation but is actually a subversion of divine revelation. For the implication of the wise man's prayer is that scientific speech must be the vehicle for divine miracles. Miracles must be "acknowledged" and "testified" for people by a man with the requisite scientific knowledge. Without this acknowledgment it would be impossible to discern true miracles from art, natural phenomena, fraud, or illusion. In the Bible, however, discursive speech is distinguished frommiracles or signs: the miracles of God are meant to circumvent the need for speech. There is, therefore, no biblical distinction between true and false miracles but only between true and false speech, be-

tween true and false prophecy. Bacon, however, assimilates the veracity of prophecy to the veracity of miracles, and the result of this assimilation is the debunking of both. In the *Advancement of Learning*. Bacon implies that there can be no standard for verifying miracles as distinct from natural oddities because both are by nature rare. Thus there can be no certain distinction between true miracles and tales or impostures. Insofar as Bensalem holds the wise man of Salomon's House to be the necessary judge of miracles, it invokes a natural scientific standard that is necessary and yet inapplicable. The Bensalemite test for veracious miracles debunks the status of miracles altogether. Bacon includes in this debunking not just the miraculous transmission of previously revealed divine speech, but also an original miracle of divine revelation. Without trustworthy divine revelation, the shepherding of Christ or divine providence is impossible. Bensalem's saving and liberation of the sailors has nothing to do with God's claim to save and to liberate.

It is in the context of the debunking history of revelation that the names of the *New Atlantis* are revealed. The island is called "Bensalem," and the city on the eastern coast is called "Renfusa." Bensalem is a word of obvious Hebrew origin and is fashioned from the words "ben" and "šalem." The compound would be rendered "son or offspring of completeness, safety and peace." Bensalem, then, is the offspring of completeness as the product of science and scientific rule: Bensalem is the product of the completion or perfection of human knowledge and so represents the harmony of the possible intellectual and terrestrial globes. In spite of the formal incompleteness of the story, the name of the island explicitly suggests completeness and perfection. Bensalem is a complete and perfected model of the end of Bacon's great instauration. The island's name is revealed just before the veracity and hence the worth of divine revelation is debunked. Bensalem's perfection is independent of divine shepherding or providence. All the more important, then, is the name of the city, which is probably the port visited by the sailors. "Renfusa" is a combination of the Greek words [*ren*] and [*fusis*] which would be rendered "sheeplike" or "sheep-natured." Since sheep are in need of a shepherd, it is clear that the shepherd of the Bensalemites is not the debunked shepherd of divine revelation, but, rather, the independent perfection of science and scientific rule. The ambiguous relation of the shepherd to his flock is, therefore, not to be overlooked. If the history of Bensalem replaces the history of providence, it must be asked how and to what degree the Bensalemites are, in fact, sheep. The answer to this query more fully illuminates the saving and liberation of the sailors.

The speech about Bensalem's history repeats the replacement of divine providence by Bensalemite rule and reveals a problem inherent in that rule; it illuminates the relation between sheep and shepherd. The history follows the account of Bensalem's Christianization and provides a partial answer to the sailors' query about Bensalem's secrecy. The first part explains why the rest of the world has no intercourse with Bensalem, and the second part explains why the Bensalemites remain hidden from the world in spite of Bensalem's intercourse with the rest of the world. The civil history of Bensalem is the history of the coming of scientific rule. It must be noted at the outset that a history of Bensalem is a history of the perfection of science and as such is the perfection of human history. Thus Bacon's remarks about civil history in the division of the sciences are of great importance for understanding the civil history of Bensalem.

In the *Advancement of Learning*, Bacon likens the three kinds of civil history to three kinds of pictures or images: unfinished, perfect, and defaced. Thus there are three kinds of civil history: memorials, perfect histories, and antiquities. Perfect histories are either of times, lives, or actions. The history of times, which is the most complete kind of civil history, is distributed by God's providence and is divided into the antiquities of the world, the history of Greece and Rome, and modern history. Although the history of times and divine providence are linked, Bacon makes no mention of the history of God's works—the Bible—in his discussion of the history of times. Rather, he treats the two parts of the Bible, the history of prophecy and the history of providence, as parts of a separate discussion of ecclesiastical history. But in the first part of the *Advancement of Learning*, Bacon argues that ecclesiastical history often errs because miracles are too often given easy credit by "the people" only later to be esteemed old wives' tales or impostures. But at this crucial point in the *Advancement of Learning*, Bacon gives no hint as to what the criteria for judging the veracity of miracles may be. Rather, he contrasts his silence on this point to the mention of the standard of veracity in natural history: rareness and seeming incredibility. The standard of natural history only emphasizes his silence, for this standard cannot be used to discriminate between miracles because miracles are by definition rare and seemingly incredible. The unstated implication must be that there are no criteria for judging the veracity of miracles and that proper acceptance of miracles is simply indistinguishable from ignorance, superstitious simplicity, and politic toleration. In this respect, the *New Atlantis* is in perfect accord with the teaching of the division of the sciences.

Since the veracity of the Bible depends on the miracle of revelation, and since the demonstrable veracity of miracles is debunked, the Bible can prudently be taken only as a human document with human limitations. Since it is neither the history of Greece and Rome nor modern history, and since it purports to divide times and declare the end of days, the Bible can at best be the remaining kind of the civil history of times: it can at best be the antiquity of God's providence. But since antiquities are "defaced" and "subject to the shipwrecks of time," the Scriptures must be defective history rather than perfect history. With circumspect prudence, Bacon argues that the history of God's providence is simply a defective and incomplete part of civil history. If there is an end of days, it can be declared only by a completed, perfect, universal history of times that is *not* the history of God's works.

Bacon argues that a perfected or completed history of times *is* possible in a proper history of Great Britain, which is "after the manner of the sacred history" because both relate the uniting of separated kingdoms. Bacon implies that completed or perfected modern history will replace the sacred history in dividing times and declaring the end of days. Modern history in the form of a proper history of Great Britain will distribute the history of times and proclaim the end of days, which means that the proper history of Great Britain will declare completed or perfected human nature.

In his mention of the sacred history, Bacon refers only to the "story of the Ten Tribes and of the Two Tribes as twins together." In the context that points to the inherent limitation of sacred history, Bacon limits the sacred history to the period from the Exodus to the united Davidic monarchy. He makes no mention of the second empire or monarchy, the empire of Jesus Christ. It is, then, not immediately clear how perfectible modern history replaces the history of divine providence. While modern or perfected history replaces the claim of Christ to save, it is not clear whether the modern replacement of providence takes account of the difference between David and Jesus. From the standpoint of pious Christianity, which characterizes the outward appearance of Bensalemite society, this distinction is of paramount importance. The difference between the old and new covenants consists in the saving grace of Jesus whose divine and human perfection contrasts with the defects of the first of the House of David. Bacon's silence with respect to this crucial difference is striking. It suggests that the difference is of no importance and points to the possibility that perfected modern history, which proclaims perfected human nature, preserves the fundamental characteristic of Davidic-Solomonic hegemony. As any schoolboy knows, the rule of David and his successors was characterized by the sexual excesses and sins of David and the prophecy of Nathan. Thus if perfected modern history preserves the fundamental characteristic of Davidic hegemony, the human perfection it announces will be characterized by Davidic excess. Bacon's discussion of perfected civil history tells us what to note in his example of perfected civil history; if the example excludes the distinction between David and Jesus, we must wonder about the nature of scientific human perfection or completeness.

Bacon argues that the perfection of science will be coeval with the "circling of the earth, as the heavenly bodies do." That is, the perfection of science will be coeval with the circumnavigation of the terrestrial globe. Bensalem, of course, represents the possibility of such circumnavigation, and the sailors have been shown to represent the European masters of exploration, the Spanish and the English. The narrator writes in English, and we wonder if this does not reflect Spanish subservience to English exploration. Thus the sailing of the men to Bensalem represents the future way of Great Britain to the perfection of science and hence to the fulfillment and perfection of human destiny. The history of Britain's future is, therefore, the history of Bensalem, which ends in the true end of days. It declares the perfection of man, which, as perfect, distributes the history of times and ends the history of times. Thus the history of Bensalem and the history of England converge. It is all the more important, therefore, to note whether the history of Bensalem as perfected history, or the culmination of man's scientific fortune, admits the crucial distinction between David and Jesus.

The history related by the governor-priest tells the stories of Altabin's triumph over the insolent Atlantians, the institution by king Solamona of Salomon's House, and the institution of the Bensalemite laws of secrecy. As we should expect, the civil history of Bensalem contains the history of the coming of science. From the clues provided by the governor-priest, the chronology of Bensalemite history can be reconstructed, as well as the date of the sailors' voyage. If the "six score years" since navigation has begun to increase be reckoned from the obvious beginning of European navigation, 1492, the sailor's voyage takes place in 1612. The time referred to as "three thousand years ago" would, then, be 1388 B.C., 458 years before the biblical Solomon completed the temple in 930 B.C., and the date of king Solamona's reign, which brought Salomon's House, would be 288 B.C. The first mention of Bensalem's past is before the acme of Davidic greatness, and the event heralding the completion of Bensalemite greatness—Solamona's institution of the scientific academy—is 642 years after the acme of Davidic greatness. Thus the history and perfection of Bensalem as the model for human perfection is chronologically within the era of David's sin and Nathan's prophecy. Bensalem's perfection predates the coming of Christ; in spite of the Bensalemite replacing of Christ's saving and Christ's kingdom, the replacement of Bensalemite (English) history for sacred history excludes the distinction between Jesus and David. Although we can identify pre-Davidic beginnings of Bensalem, we cannot find a post-Davidic past and so an event that would obviate the prophecy of Nathan. Thus Bacon's remarks about history and his example of perfected history come together; the distinction between Jesus and David is no part of the human perfection that replaces the promise of sacred history.

Unless the advent of Solamona's reign explicitly obviates the prophecy of Nathan, we can expect the characteristics of Bensalem's Davidic past to be manifest in its post-Christian but "Davidic" present, which is England's and mankind's future. This important possibility can be finally accepted only after an examination of Bensalem's present and the speech of Joabin. It should be noted, however, in addition to the obvious implication of Joabin's name, that the unit of measure in Bensalem is the "Karan," a Hebrew word that can mean a ruler of the House of David and a horn.

Bacon's account of Bensalem's early encounter with the Atlantians (Coyans) makes explicit reference to Plato's account of Atlantis and Athens in the *Timaeus* and *Critias*. Important differences and distortions separate the two accounts, however, and suggest a Baconian revision of Plato's teaching about nature's necessity, and excess and moderation. Plato teaches that the Athenians defeated the technically advanced but insolent, prideful, and tyrannous Atlantians, and that they magnanimously freed those who dwelled within the bounds of Heracles despite their failure to aid in their own liberation. Bacon hides the magnanimity of the Athenians by declaring his uncertainty about the identity of the Greeks who, along with the Bensalemites, defeated the invading Atlantians. Rather, he contrasts the ruthlessness of the Athenians (or whoever it was), who destroyed every ship and man of the invading Atlantians (Tyrambelians), with the extraordinary humanity and clemency of Altabin, the king of the Bensalemites at the time.

In Plato's account, at a later time from the conflict, earthquakes and floods destroyed the entire body of Athenian warriors and caused the entire island of Atlantis to be swallowed by the sea. The deed no longer lives in Athenian memory because Athens, along with the rest of the world except for the Egyptians, was subject to "many and diverse destructions of mankind, of which the greatest are by fire and water, and lesser by countless other means." In Plato's account, Egyptian antiquity depends upon the combination of memory and piety, for although they are immune from rain and fire because of the fortuitous presence of the Nile, they are not immune from earthquakes. In Plato's account, then, both the moderate and the insolent were destroyed by nature's ravages; the distinction between them was preserved only in the mnemonic speech of the pious Egyptians. In Bacon's account, while Atlantis and the rest of the world are destroyed by "accidents of time," which consist of violent natural destruction or slow natural decay, the Bensalemites are saved from such destruction by the coming of science. Nature's power to destroy wholly is overcome; no one suffers the total annihilation of Plato's Atlantis. Thus, for Bacon, Bensalem combines the deeds of the Athenians (Greeks) and the surviving antiquity of Egypt. The difference between Egypt and Bensalem consists in the difference between piety and natural science. As might be guessed by now, this difference is, for Bacon, simply the difference between nature's chance and the scientific conquest of nature. He is careful to note that "that whole tract is little subject to earthquakes."

For Plato, the distinction between moderate and immoderate deeds can be permanent only in speech, for with respect to the rewards of deeds as such, the moderate and the immoderate are ultimately linked by the indiscriminate chastisement of natural catastrophe and decay. But since Plato teaches that it is not speeches that are permanent and enduring, but rather the intelligible things or *ideas* disclosed by speeches, the enduringly moderate or moderate in itself is in fact twice removed from particular moderate or immoderate deeds. For Plato, the search for the eternal *ideas* of the human virtues discloses the distinction between theory and practice. The articulation of the eternal *ideas* of the virtues explains the intelligibility of particular deeds as moderate or immoderate, but discloses the indeterminateness of particular deeds as singularly moderate or immoderate. For Bacon, the scientific overcoming of the distinction between speeches and deeds, between theory and practice, consists in the overcoming or conquest of natural catastrophe and decay and results in the permanence of speeches and deeds. As shown by the contrast of Plato's Athens and Atlantis to Bacon's Atlantis and Bensalem, the scientific conquest of natural catastrophe and decay facilitates the permanent and certain distinction between moderate and immoderate deeds. But Bacon has distorted the Platonic account of Atlantis, and our first comparison of the two accounts must be revised. The revision discloses astonishing results.

According to Bacon's distortion, the Athenians were no less ruthless than the Atlantians; the barbarism of the Athenians is contrasted with the extraordinary humanity of Altabin. Yet the Bensalemite overcoming of natural castastrophe and decay as well as necessity and chance, the creation of the perfected combination of Athens and Egypt, is the work of Solamona rather than Altabin. It is Solamona who brought science to Bensalem and is said to be its lawgiver; it was his intention to perfect the prescientific humanity of Altabin that was subject to natural decay. Yet Solamona's laws are laws of secrecy that contain the harsh reality of the most extreme inhospitality and inhumanity. Thus the humanity and hospitality of Altabin contrast with the potential inhumanity and inhospitality of Solamona's reign and laws that complete the humanity of Altabin. The humanity perfected by scientific conquest is a problematic humanity. It is in this light that Bacon's distortion of Plato is intelligible. If the deeds preserved by the memory of Egypt reveal no distinction between the moderate and the immoderate, the replacement of Egypt by Bensalem makes eternal the link between the moderate and the immoderate.

But we must not contrast Bacon's version of Plato's Athens with his description of Altabin's Bensalem. In terms of moral virtue, Plato's Athens and Altabin's Bensalem considered together contrast with Bacon's distorted Athens and Solamona's Bensalem considered together. The proper comparison is between Plato's moderate Athens and the humane Altabin, on the one hand, and Bacon's immoderate Athens and Solamona's Bensalem, on the other hand. Bensalem is a new Atlantis; Bacon's distorted Athens and Bensalem are alike in their immoderation and different only in their different susceptibility to natural catastrophe and decay. Bacon's Bensalem perfects and immortalizes the immoderation of Bacon's distorted Athens, but this means that Bensalem immortalizes the insolent pride of the old Atlantis.

For Plato, the distinction between the moderate and the immoderate is indeterminate with respect to particular human deeds. But while the distinction between the moderate and the immoderate is problematic in deed, the distinction as such is intelligible and is disclosed by the link between ephemeral speeches and the eternal things. Thus while there is no divine speech about justice or moderation, there is human speech that pursues the divine and illuminates the eternal grounds of justice and moderation. Although there can be no certain, demonstrable determination of particular moderate deeds, the theoretical pursuit of the moderate as such moderates the lure of those practical goods for the sake of which men commonly behave in moderate or immoderate ways. The common fate of Athens and Atlantis is not disheartening because human virtue is not determined by the strict superiority of one particular deed over another. Rather, the rough, indeterminate practical distinction between moderate and immoderate deeds, expressed by right opinion, is grounded on the distinction between theory and practice and the consequent superiority of the theoretical to the practical life.

For Bacon, the scientific conquest of natural catastrophe and decay permits practical life to endure. But the subtle contrast Bacon presents between the old and the new Atlantis suggests that the immortalization of practical life makes eternal the link between moderate and immoderate deeds, and we must wonder if this does not subvert the ground of any possible moderation. For Bacon, like Plato, there is no divine speech about justice and moderation. But unlike Plato, Bacon gives an account of the new Atlantis that is incomplete because of the dangerous, unmentionable product of the new science that will perfect human practice by facilitating the preservation and restoration of the corruptible things. While these suppositions spring from an interpretation of Bensalem's past, they are confirmed by the revelation of Bensalem's present, upon which the meaning of Bensalem's history and the whole of the ***New Atlantis*** depend.

Bensalem's Present: The Feast and Joabin's Speech

The cut between Bensalem's past and present corresponds to the cut between the two sections that illustrate the sailors' changes of heart and mind. It is at the juncture between Bensalem's past and present that the the sailors exhibit restraint that springs from desire rather than fear and declare their liberation. The historical speeches that proclaim the replacement of divine providence by Bensalem's promise and the laws of secrecy provide the background for the sailors' newfound freedom. Their freedom consists, therefore, in freedom from the limitations on bodily weal that they have known, and in corresponding freedom from the bonds of divine grace or providence. The speeches about Bensalem's present illuminate the relation between Bensalem's past and present, which in turn reveals the true nature of the sailors' new restraint and freedom.

The revelation of Bensalem's present consists of two parts: the first is a description of the sum of Bensalem's promise, and the second describes the regulation of that promise. The feast of the Tirsan (any father of thirty living descendants) is sponsored by the Bensalemite regime and honors the promise of the regime, the preservation and generation of the human body, which shows Bensalem to be "compounded of all goodness." Because of the Bensalemite priority of body over soul, the state of the soul is not the primary consideration in the feast of the Tirsan. Rather, it is "granted to any man that shall live to see thirty persons descended of his body alive together, and all above three years old." At the same time that the festival honors the ultimate priority of body over soul, it reveals the stringent moral restraints imposed by the Bensalemite regime. The regime guarantees, with the power of law, the orders of the Tirsan on the moral seemliness of his favored family. As we learn from Joabin, Bensalem is the "virgin of the world" who sees as the sum of all goodness the preservation and generation of the human body. The feast honors the end of Bensalemite restraint and humanity: the preservation of the human body and the most intense pleasure that accompanies the procreation of human bodies. In the action of the story, the sailors, who restrain body and soul for the sake of the weal of their bodies, show themselves to be open to the promise of Bensalem. While the humane restraint of the Bensalemites appears to reflect the humanity and restraint of Altabin and Solamona, the sequel to the description of the feast reveals the restraint and humanity of Bensalem to be problematic. This problematic restraint and humanity is confirmed by reflection on the relation of the Bensalemite past to the Bensalemite present.

The speech of Joabin explicates the full meaning of the feast. He is asked about marriage laws and customs because the relation of the feast to the narrator makes him wonder about "nuptial copulation" from which proceeds the "propagation of families." Joabin's remarks consist of a long speech about European and Bensalemite marriage and a short mention of the "Adam and Eve's pools."

Joabin first characterizes European and Bensalemite marriage practices. Whereas Bensalem is the most chaste of nations, "free from all pollution and foulness," and the "virgin of the world," European marriage practices are foul and debauched. In Europe, marriage is "ordained a remedy for unlawful concupiscence," but since Europeans have at hand "a remedy more agreeable to their corrupt will, marriage is almost expulsed." For "the depraved custom of change, and the delight in meretricious embracements (where sin is turned into an art) maketh marriage a dull thing and a kind of imposition or tax." The Europeans liken marriage to prostitution when they argue that prostitution, like marriage, should be tolerated because it prevents "greater evils; as advoutries, deflowering of virgins, unnatural lust, and the like." But Joabin says that the Bensalemites hold this argument to be a preposterous wisdom, and they call it "Lot's Offer; who to save his guests from abusing, offeredhis daughters. . . ."

After a brief interruption by the narrator, Joabin describes the laws that regulate Bensalemite nuptial copulation. There is no polygamy; there is a month wait between first interview and marriage or contract for marriage; marriage without parental consent is "mulcted in the inheritors," (i.e., the children are penalized); and finally, "because of the many hidden defects in men and women's bodies," before a contract is made, one friend of the potential bride and one friend of the potential groom are permitted to see the bride and groom "severally bathe naked" in the Adam and Eve's pools that are situated near every town.

Joabin's speech is the most important in the *New Atlantis*. Joabin as speaker is of crucial importance: except for the wise man who judged the miracle, Joabin is the only post-Solamonic character described as wise. The Father of Salomon's House, who makes the final speech revealing the "true state" of Salomon's House is *not* described as wise. Not only is Joabin said to be wise, but he is also said to be "learned, . . . of great policy, and excellently seen in the laws and customs of Bensalem." Joabin is, therefore, wise in the study of government or rule, and as such he speaks of the Jewish dreams "from tradition" rather than from conviction of truth. Joabin knows the Jewish dreams as dreams; as a man wise in general and wise in policy, he transcends the myths of Bensalem. It is as a man wise in general and wise in policy that Joabin exhibits the only comprehensive wisdom in the *New Atlantis*. In terms of explicit description, Joabin's wisdom surpasses even that of the large-hearted founder and lawgiver Solamona. It is all the more important, then, that Joabin's speech illuminates the fundamental problem of Bensalem's promise.

As Bacon has Joabin present it, the Bensalemite characterization of European marriage and prostitution as "Lot's Offer" is subtly inappropriate. Joabin argues that the European practice is to offer daughters (prostitutes or wives) to save other daughters, the potential victims of unnatural lust and rape. But Lot offered his virgin daughters to save male strangers, an act of extraordinary hospitality. If Joabin's characterization is meant to contrast European and Bensalemite practices—and this is Bacon's intention since the context is an explicit contrast of Bensalem to Europe—Bacon has Joabin express Bensalemite abhorrence of the offering of daughters to save daughters, but has him indirectly approve the offering of daughters for the sake of visiting strangers. The example of "Lot's Offer" points to the Bensalemite offer to the sailors and to Bacon's modest but conspicuous silence regarding the sailors' sexual desires. By means of subtle allusion and conspicuous silence, Bacon causes Joabin's speech to suggest the Bensalemite secrecy that hides the immoral means necessary for the propagation and rule of science. Just as restraint is necessary for the propagation and rule of science, so too are laws of secrecy that mask the unrestraint of "unlawful lust" necessary for the proper treatment of necessary strangers.

We are reminded of the harsh alternative to Bensalemite hospitality when the narrator says that Joabin's speech reminds him of his sin as Elias reminded the widow of Sarepta. Bacon causes the narrator to ignore the widow's fear that Elias had come to kill her son. The laws of secrecy hide Bensalem from the world in more than the obvious way; they mask Bensalem's hospitality and humanity, which can include basely open offers and the inhumane opposite of hospitality. Joabin's speech, which reflects the present practice of the "son of completeness" or perfection, illuminates the immoral means that are necessary for the promise of Bensalem's perfection. The speech reveals the secrecy necessary to overcome the temporal gap between Bensalem as a completed model and the task illuminated by the sailors' odyssey, the way of science to the actual lived reality of the image or model of scientific perfection.

The institution of the Adam and Eve's pools is an important part of Bensalem, which, as the offspring of completeness, is the model of scientific perfection. The institution of the Adam and Eve's pools regulates nuptial copulation by preventing the dissatisfaction with one's own partner made possible by the discovery of the "many hidden defects in men and women's bodies." The noblest end of science is the preservation of the human body. The pools regulate the act of generation and the most intense pleasure preserved by the conquest of bodily decay, they regulate the pleasure that informs the very end of science itself. Joabin's speech also exhibits a second crucial silence or secrecy; his remarks are interrupted at the point where obvious queries about this astonishing institution would naturally arise. Although we know that desire for bodies other than one's own mate's is a potential problem in Bensalem—this is the very reason for the institution of the pools—Bacon causes Joabin to make no mention of possible licentious desire provoked by that which is most conducive to the breakdown of restraint. Thus Bacon ignores the obvious possibility that a friend of a suitor might make a false report of bodily defect because he desired the intended partner for himself, for Bacon is silent about the sex and marital status of the friends. Thus, although Bacon acknowledges the desire for a more perfect or beautiful body and informs us that this desire must be regulated, he describes Bensalem as having an institution that ignores the very erotic desire it is designed to regulate. By causing Joabin to be silent because of a crucial interruption, Bacon describes an institution designed to control Bensalem's erotic behavior that in fact reinforces the licentious possibilities of choosiness, the love of one's own, and the desire for more. Although the institution is meant to keep the rooster in the coop, it exacerbates the possibilities of adultery and cuckoldry.

Bacon's indirect description of Bensalem's erotic practice is important in the light of what must by now be obvious. The only man said to be wise in general and wise in policy, who articulates the astonishing Bensalemite erotic practice, is named *Joabin*. Not only was Joab David's strong lieutenant in his rise to power, but he is known as one of the most ruthless men in the Old Testament. It was Joab who committed murder, who slew David's son, and who carried out the treachery against Uriah the Hittite. It was Joab, then, who assisted in adultery and cuckoldry; he was David's horns in matters that deal with horns. In the light of Bacon's indirect description it is again obvious that the institution and practice of the Adam and Eve's pools, revealed to us by Joabin, are imitations of the sin of David, which arose from the viewing of a friend's wife bathing. In the speech of Joabin, Bacon teaches by means of a subtle structure of allusion and conspicuous silence. With Joabin's speech, Bacon confirms the web of indirect suggestions of a problematic Bensalemite humanity and perfection that leads up to the speech. The speech of Joabin links Bensalem's past and present so as to disclose the dangerous truth about the perfection of science and man's scientific fortune. We noted earlier that unless the coming of Solamona obviated the prophecy of Nathan, unless it eliminated the defect of excessive desire, the defective characteristics of Bensalem's Davidic past would be present in its Davidic present and, hence, in England's and mankind's scientific future. Both the speech and name of Joabin, far from signaling the obviation of Nathan's prophecy, point to the repetition of Davidic excess. Bacon identifies Joabin with Joab and so identifies the ruthless Joab and the problem of excessive desire with the man of comprehensive wisdom. But "Joabin" is simply the plural form of "Joab"; Joabin's name and speech are not only of Joabin, not only of a wise man, but of all other and future men of comprehensive wisdom.

If the Davidic characteristics of Bensalem's past are inherent in Bensalem's present and future, the possibility of insolent excess is inherent in the promise of science. The grounds of that excess, which knows only the limits of barbarism, are the desires of one human body for another. One justly wonders, then, about the final disposition of unnecessary and undesired strangers. The contrast wrought by the institution of science in the history of Bensalem *is*, then, between the simple magnanimity and humanity of Athens and Altabin on the one hand, and the problematic magnanimity and humanity of the distorted Athens and Bensalem, or the new Atlantis, on the other hand. The speech of Joabin completes a picture that shows the true depth of Bensalem's problematic humanity to consist in the grotesque possibilities of excessive desire. Bacon's point is that since science requires restraint for most men, the full range of possibilities promised by science cannot be revealed in its entirety. Bensalem is not on the surface a nation of barbarous cannibals: on the contrary, the Bensalemites are sheep—"Tirsan" is a Persian word (tarsān) meaning timid or fearful—and they are shepherded by the rule of science. It is all the more important, therefore, to wonder in what or in whom the ultimate *rule* of science consists.

Joabin's speech explicates the secrecy which is a means of science to its end and which is abolished by the central deed of the story, the revelation of Bensalemite science to the world. But Joabin's speech also explicates the more profound secrecy which is inherent in the end and perfection of science and which is not abolished by the universal revelation of science. This latter secrecy necessitates Bacon's prudent, circumspect, and indirect way of teaching. It is only by following Bacon's way that we can see how the *New Atlantis* contains a teaching about political science, and so that we can see how the *New Atlantis* and the whole of Bacon's teaching are complete.

Conclusion

The last section of the story presents the magnificent return of a Father of Salomon's House, his revelation to the narrator of the "true state of Salomon's House," and the final deed of the story, the Father's giving of a "great largess" or tip to the narrator and his fellows. The Father's speech about the "true state" of Salomon's House reveals that it is dedicated to the study of the things above, the things below, and the

things in between, which constitute the visible whole. The study of the things above, however, does not include the study of the celestial heaven. The visible whole, the conquest of which is the "enlarging of the bounds of Human Empire," is limited to the realm inhabitable by the human body. The celestial heaven is excluded from the visible whole studied by the new science because of man's limited ability to fly. In the light of the eternal promise of science, the celestial heaven can be no image of the delimitation of human nature; the celestial heaven is ignored because it contributes in no way to the eternal, intelligible whole that is illuminated and constituted by science and human power.

Perhaps a more important study omitted from the House of Salomon is the study of policy or government. The House of Salomon studies natural philosophy and logic, it studies all varieties of bodies that are useful for the preservation and perfection of human bodies, but it does not study the relations between human (ensouled) bodies. In accordance with the secret and retired nature of government, the regime of Bensalem is hidden from view. It is not completely hidden, however. We learn that Bensalem is a monarchy, and we see its laws and deeds that regulate secrecy and erotic affairs. While the men of Salomon's House decide matters of secrecy, they do so without the science that governs the practice of secrecy. Their practice of secrecy points to someone learned in political science who would adjudicate their decisions. Thus, wherever the Bensalemite regime is located, it is clear that the wisdom that guides its rule does not spring from the House of Salomon. The Bensalemite regime must perpetuate secrecy, even toward the fellows and Fathers of Salomon's House, because of the problem of human eros. It must be wondered whether the Father himself is not a servant of the one who truly rules because the true ruler alone understands the full range of human possibilities illuminated by the new science. Bacon's mention of the Father's pity would, then, be doubly ironic. At the same time that its ambiguity reflects the scorn and compassion the Father feels for his sheep, it reflects the sheepishness of the Father himself.

Consideration of the possible source of wise Bensalemite rule obviously leads to a consideration of Joabin's comprehensive wisdom. If the true rule of science springs from a comprehensive understanding of science and man, then Joabin's comprehensive wisdom must be the source of the true rule of science. But Joabin's comprehensive wisdom also illuminates the fundamental and enduring problems of scientific rule. Joabin's wisdom, which reflects the harmony of speech and deed and the full range of human possibilities engendered by that harmony, illustrates the problem inherent in the very end or perfection of science itself.

Elisabeth Hansot on *The New Atlantis*:

The New Atlantis is a curiously ambivalent utopia. It is isolated in space, as were the classical utopias, but its ideal activity depends on time, on the "succession of ages," for its achievement. The objects of knowledge may be independent of man, but the process of knowing is not, like the Platonic contemplation of the forms, independent of the efforts of other men. Bacon's utopian ideal was a new proposal for the acquisition and organization of knowledge; by implication it was also a criticism of the way men studied the natural world in seventeenth-century Europe. Yet, the New Atlantis cannot be said to be a standard by which to judge society, for apart from the reform of science it offers no systematic comment on the existing social organization. To the contrary, Bacon's care in separating the House of Salomon from Bensalem indicates a desire to reassure his reader that the effects of scientific knowledge will not change the nature of a godly society. Rather, the aids science can offer, "the divinations of diseases, plagues, . . . scarcity, tempests, [and] earthquakes . . . ," serve to secure that society all the more certainly from accident and disease.

Elisabeth Hansot, in Perfection and Progress: Two Modes of Utopian Thought, *The MIT Press, 1974.*

The teaching about scientific rule is located in Joabin's wisdom, but that very teaching necessitates the outward incompleteness of the story. The completeness of the *New Atlantis* consists in a teaching about scientific rule that must appear to be missing. Bacon argues that the conquests of science will facilitate the subduing and overcoming "to some degree" of the "necessities and miseries" of humanity, and it is only in Joabin's political wisdom that the limit of this overcoming is to be found. The limit of the overcoming of necessity and misery does not consist in the delimitation of the human body as such; for the new science, the corruptibility of man's body is simply the jealous act of a conquerable God. Rather, the limits of the overcoming of human necessity and misery, as disclosed by Joabin's wisdom and Bensalemite rule, consist in the problematic relationships between human bodies whose desires are not limited merely to self-preservation.

The new Atlantis promises to preserve and restore the most important of the corruptible things, the human body, and so promises to preserve and restore the desires and pleasures of the human body. But as Bacon teaches in the *New Atlantis,* the preservation and restoration of desire must include the desire for more. The new science promises that human desire will be freed from the limits of the corruptible body and so from the disproportion between body and soul. The

new science suggests the possibility in lived reality of what would, before the new science, be possible only in speech or imagination. The new Atlantis promises to all men what most men desire, but the teaching of the *New Atlantis* shows that the perfection of science contains possible grotesque extremes that may threaten the felicity of some or even most men. The extraordinary restraint of the sheeplike Bensalemites is necessary for the conquests of science. But if the promise of science encourages and opens the way for human conquest, it does nothing to restrain the horizons of those men who are by nature conquerors.

The combination of Bacon's open recommendation of scientific conquest with his knowledge of the fundamental moral problem of this conquest was sufficient to require his prudent, circumspect, and indirect way of teaching. But the most profound and perhaps shocking reason for the apparent incompleteness or secrecy of the *New Atlantis* is its indirect teaching about those who contemplate the virtues of the new conquest and conquerors. For the wise speech that illuminates the possibilities and limits of human virtue comes from a source that represents the transgressing of those limits. The new science perfects practical life in a way that is problematic with respect to excess and moderation, but for Bacon, the nature of the theoretical life can be no basis for a defense of moderation. The very superiority of the new science consists in overcoming the distinction between theory and practice, and the *New Atlantis* teaches us that comprehensive wisdom is itself problematic precisely with respect to the possibilities of excess and moderation. The *New Atlantis* discloses that the perfection of human speech and deed, which depends on restraint and perfects humanity, points directly to human speech and deed that know no restraint and no humanity. The full meaning of the promise of science is disclosed by the man who is wise in general and wise in policy: comprehensive wisdom about the meaning of science and human ends is coextensive with comprehensive political wisdom. The deepest problem of Bensalemite (scientific) rule springs from its connection to the morally unstable knowledge about conquest and moderation that illuminates the whole of which man is the constitutive part.

The comprehensively wise Joabin encompasses, in speech and potential deed, the moderation and immoderation inherent in the end of science. The speech and deed of the Baconian wise man or self-knower reveal the necessary coexistence of the moderate and the immoderate within the comprehensive good articulated by science. The speech and deed of the wise man point at one and the same time to the unified grounds of restraint and excess, moderation and immoderation. The political rule that springs from the wisest human speech and deed is necessary because of therestraint necessary for science and the regulation of human eros, and yet that speech and deed together articulate and manifest the most extreme human possibilities. The rule of science must always be unstable with respect to restraint and excess; the ironic final deed of the story is an act of double payment, an admitted excess in Bensalem.

Joabin reminds us not of Socrates, but rather of Timaeus as described by Socrates. Timaeus provided the cosmogony and cosmology that preceded the account of the best city in motion, the story of Athens and Atlantis. Like Timaeus, Joabin combines the excellence of policy and philosophy. Like Timaeus' speech, Joabin's wise speech, which must be the final product of Bacon's great instauration, takes its bearings from the somatic and visible since, for Bacon, the only difference between image and lived reality is a temporal difference. Thus Bacon, like Timaeus, views man and the cosmic whole from the standpoint of the somatic and the visible. Also like Timaeus this standpoint entails the problem of the inability of the ensouled human body to be or to imitate the body of the visible whole. However, unlike Timaeus' speech, which is admittedly mythic and less than true, Bacon's speech is meant truly to illuminate lived reality. The question that arises, then, is how, for Bacon, the combination of the scientific measures of body and soul coupled with the new unconcern for astronomy and the celestial heaven produces a true science of bodies in motion.

Whereas for Plato, who is Bacon's target in the *New Atlantis,* the distinction between moderate and immoderate deeds cannot be strictly demonstrated, and so is rough or indeterminate in practical life, the contemplation of the distinction between theory and practice—the contemplation of a theoretical problem—provides the sole stable ground for moderation. Thus it is the speech of the man who pursues wisdom that illuminates and buttresses the meaning of moderation. For Bacon, the speech of the man whose wisdom pursues the conquest of nature discloses the link between moderation and immoderation and subverts the stable ground of any possible moderation. Bacon teaches that comprehensive wisdom is located in political science and that political science discloses the immoderation of any moderate speech to be linked to the immoderation of any moderate deed. His teaching is breathtaking because of its audacious resoluteness. Bacon recommends that men embrace the scientific conquest of natural necessity and chance, and so urges them to embrace the necessary possibility of the most extreme moral chance. The prudent dress of Bacon's utopia is necessitated by the restraint required by science and its open promise to the many. To know and embrace the full range of scientific possibilities requires a stouter and more resolute soul. [Friedrich] Nietzsche declared of Bacon [in his *Ecce Homo*, 1908]:

> the strength required for the vision of the most powerful reality is not only compatible with the most powerful strength for action, for monstrous

action, for crime—it even presupposes it. We are very far from knowing enough about Lord Bacon, the first realist in every great sense of that word, to know everything he did, wanted, and experienced in himself.

It would be a slight to both Nietzsche and Bacon to think that this remark refers to the petty transgression of bribery.

The *New Atlantis* is at once the core and the prolegomenon to the whole of Bacon's teaching. Bacon's prudent way requires that once the reader discovers the completeness of the *New Atlantis,* he must turn to the whole of Bacon's teaching in the light of the *New Atlantis.* For the completeness of the *New Atlantis* is the key to the unity of Bacon's teaching about science and man. The fundamental Baconian theme is the virtue of science as the highest human activity, and this theme consists in a teaching about the nature and virtue of the conquests facilitated by science. Bacon's fundamental teaching raises the questions related to the question of conquest: the questions of self-knowledge, the relationship of the active to the contemplative life, and, ultimately, the nature of and relations between the virtues of wisdom, courage, justice, and moderation. But these questions are encompassed by the question of the best regime and the ends of political life. The *New Atlantis* and Bacon's teaching as a whole are complete because they present a new, audacious, and morally problematic stance toward the traditional questions of political philosophy.

J.C. Davis (essay date 1981)

SOURCE: "Sir Francis Bacon and the Ideal Society," in *Utopia and the Ideal Society: A Study of English Utopian Writing 1516-1700,* Cambridge University Press, 1981, pp. 105-37.

[*In the following excerpt, Davis closely examines the structure and content of the* New Atlantis *with a view to clarifying "the scope and the crucial limitations of Bacon's approach to his ideal society."*]

'Ambivalence' has been seen as one of the central characteristics of the social thought of Sir Francis Bacon. He is the 'preemptory royalist' who helped to provide an intellectual basis for 'the English Revolution'; the scientific modernist consigning all past philosophy to oblivion yet unable to shake off the mental habits of the scholastic, the jargon of the alchemist and magician; the analyst of the imperfections of the human mind, carefully planning the retrieval of its dominion over nature; a constructer of self-consuming artefacts; pessimistic and optimistic, conservative and radical, timid and bold, a schemer tainted with corruption and yet possessed of a kind of integrity; Bacon, it appears, was all these things. So, likewise, his *New Atlantis* contains a central ambiguity: a society dominated by scientists who have the duty and the right to decide what information shall be made available to the state, but yet cannot be trusted not to lie and distort. The *New Atlantis* has the assured tone of Bacon's most confident works and yet he never completed it. His preoccupation with ideal-society images and with utopian notions remained so extremely ambivalent that it enables us to see at once the limitations of our ideal-society types, the way in which in practice they may overlap, the use to which they can be turned in analysing the complexities of his social thought, and the exigeant nature of the commitments imposed by the choice of a particular mode of ideal society.

Although the *New Atlantis* is well known as a 'utopia', it will be necessary to describe the work in considerable detail. There are two reasons for this somewhat arduous procedure. The first is that most commentaries have been unbalanced in their emphasis on the 'scientific' aspects of Bacon's ideal society. A detailed consideration of the work will show that Bacon's visualisation of an ideal society was not merely intended to serve as a backdrop to an imaginative description of his scientific schemes. The second reason is that only through a detailed consideration of the *New Atlantis* can both the scope and the crucial limitations of Bacon's approach to his ideal society be made clear.

Like More's *Utopia*, the *New Atlantis* may usefully, but somewhat arbitrarily, be seen in form as a drama. This approach has been used here because, although in some ways unwieldly, it does enable the work to be broken down into clear phases. Seen as a drama, the work may be divided into a Prologue and two Acts, as follows:

I. *Prologue*—the voyage to New Atlantis
II. *Act One*—New Atlantis and the outside world
  i. Scene one—initial reception
  ii. Scene two—the visit of a person of place, conditions of entry fulfilled
  iii. Scene three—the Stranger's House
  iv. Scene four—the narrator's address to his fellow travellers
  v. Scene five—the first interview with the governor of the Stranger's House
  vi. Scene six—the second interview
  vii. Scene seven—the third interview
III. *Act Two*—New Atlantis described
  i. Scene one—the Feast of the Family
  ii. Scene two—Joabim the Jew
  iii. Scene three—the arrival of the Fellow of Salomon's House in Bensalem
  iv. Scene four—interview with the Fellow of Salomon's House

In the Prologue the narrator describes how he and his fifty companions arrived at the island of New Atlantis. Having sailed from Peru for China and Japan, they had encountered such contrary winds for so long a period that they had consumed their twelve months' supply of victuals without sighting land and gave themselves up for lost. In despair they prayed to God 'that as in the beginning he discovered the face of the deep and brought forth dry land, so he would now discover land to us that we mought not perish'. On the following day they made landfall, and it is not without significance that Bacon emphasises that it was 'a kind of miracle' that had secured their delivery.

With the mariners' arrival at New Atlantis, the Prologue ends and the first Act begins. The theme of Act One is that of the New Atlantans' relations with the outside world. The paradox throughout is that the New Atlantans have knowledge of the affairs, learning and nature of the rest of the world, while the rest of the world remains in ignorance of them. They know without being known. In the first four scenes the difficulties and preconditions of access to New Atlantis are emphasised. 'A kind of miracle' is required to arrive there. Only in necessity, through sickness and lack of victuals, is humanitarian consideration given to the possibility of the mariners coming ashore. Before doing so, they must attest to the Christian faith, and abjure themselves of piracy and acts of violence. On disembarking, they are confined for three days under close scrutiny. Even when this confinement is relaxed, they are not allowed to travel over a mile and a half (a karan) from the city walls of Bensalem and their stay is subject to licence. These tests and restrictions on entry testify to the closed community nature of New Atlantis; only a certain type of individual is acceptable there.

The three remaining 'scenes' of the first 'Act' all take place within the Strangers' House in the form of interviews between the governor of the Strangers' House and a number of travellers. In the first of these, the governor, who was also a Christian priest, informed a delegation of six of the travellers that, their period of confinement having ended, the state had given them a license to stay for a further six weeks and that extensions of this might be permitted. In the meantime, they were to enjoy the facilities of the Strangers' House which was richly endowed, as it was thirty-seven years since its facilities had last been used. They were to be permitted to trade merchandise either for silver and gold or in barter for other goods, but they were still forbidden to travel over a mile and a half from the city wall without special leave.

Next morning, the governor visited them again. This time he talked with ten of the travellers; 'the rest were of the meaner sort, or else gone abroad'. His theme was a paradox of knowing without being known: 'by meanes of our solitary situation; and of the Lawes of Secrecy, which we have for our Travellers; and our rare Admission of Strangers; we know well most part of the Habitable World, and are ourselves unknowne'. Within this context, priority was given to the question of how the Christian faith had been made known to the New Atlantans. The answer was by a miracle. Twenty years after the ascension of Christ, a pillar of light had been seen over the sea off the east coast of the island. On top of it stood a great cross of light. Boats were sent out but some mysterious force prevented them from approaching closer to the column than a distance of sixty yards. In one of the boats was a Fellow of Salomon's House, who offered prayer to the 'Lord God of Heaven and earth'. In this prayer, he noted that one function of his 'order' was 'to discern (as far as appertaineth to the generations of men) between divine miracles, works of nature, works of art, and impostures and illusions of all sorts'. And, in accordance with that function, he acknowledged what was happening before them to be 'a true miracle' and begged God to grant them the interpretation of the miracle. At this, his boat was allowed to approach. The pillar and the cross disappeared, leaving 'a small Arke, or Chest of Cedar, dry and not wett at all with water, though it swam'. When taken from the water, the ark opened to reveal a book and a letter. The book contained the Old and New Testaments, including those 'Bookes of the New Testament, which were not yet written'. The letter was from one Bartholomew who revealed that he had been commanded by God to launch the ark and its contents. Although there were Hebrews, Persians and Indians in New Atlantis, as well as the native population, they were all able to read the works in their own tongue.

A number of points are worth noting about this account. The first is the priority and emphasis accorded to it by Bacon. The most important aspect of the New Atlantans' relations with the outside world, and, in particular, with their European visitors, is their common Christian faith. This is the first issue that the visitors raise in their dialogue with the governor of the Strangers' House, and he comments on the appropriateness of their priority. It reflects both the seriousness with which Bacon held his own Christian faith and his belief in the Christian religion as a good guarantee of social order.

The second point worth noting is the miraculous course of the conversion of New Atlantis. It is beyond doubt, irrational and complete. Faith, not reason, is the only means by which it can be interpreted. And this, of course, is a typical reflection of Bacon's distinction between faith as a means of knowing God and reason as a means of interpreting nature. But like Bacon himself, the Fellows of Salomon's House take all learning, and not merely what we would describe as natural science, for their province. Hence their duty of discerning 'between divine miracles, works of nature, works of art, and impostures and illusions of all sorts', and the Fellow's ability to certify this particular event a miracle. This ability is dependent upon his recognition of the peculiar basis of knowledge of the divine.

On the following day the travellers were once more visited by the governor who was again charged to explain how the New Atlantans could know so much of Europe whilst remaining unknown to Europeans. This interview, or 'scene', is taken up with an historical explanation of the seclusion enjoyed by the island. The governor first explained why other nations had no communications with New Atlantis. Three thousand years before, the island had been part of a worldwide network of traffic on a scale far greater than existed at the end of the sixteenth century. Their nearest great neighbour, Atlantis, on the American mainland, had launched two expeditions: one to the Mediterranean, from which no one had returned, and the other to the South Seas and the island of New Atlantis, where they were decisively outmaneuvered by King Altabin. Less than a century after these events, Atlantis was visited by divine retribution for these 'proud enterprises' and destroyed in a great flood. As a result, the natives of America, descendants of the Atlantans, remained a primitive people. In addition, the basis of commercial relations between New Atlantis and their closest neighbour, America, had collapsed. At about the same time, there had been a great decline in navigation elsewhere. Partly this was caused by war, partly 'by a naturall Revolution of Time' (from which, apparently, New Atlantis was immune), and partly by the development of vessels unsuitable for long voyages.

The problem remained as to why New Atlantans had accepted this isolation, for their shipping capacity and navigational skill had remained unimpaired. The answer, according to the governor of the Strangers' House, lay in decisions taken by King Solamona who had reigned about 1900 years before. Solamona viewed his country as self-sufficient. The island was large, fertile, and offered sufficient opportunities for its shipping in coastal trade, fishing and traffic to some nearby islands.

> And recalling into his memory, the happy and flourishing Estate, wherein this land then was; So as it mought bee a thousand wayes altered to the worse, but scarce any one way to the better; thought nothing wanted to his Noble and Heroicale Intentions, but onley (as farr as Humane foresight mought reach) to give perpetuitie to that which was in his time so happily established.

Thus, unlike Utopus, Solamona was no great state maker. He found a society which had every appearance of felicity, and sought to perpetuate that happy state by securing it from 'Novelties, and a Commixture of Manners'. Accordingly, he stopped the free entrance of strangers and the free exit of New Atlantans and made his policy of seclusion part of the 'Fundamentall Lawes' of his kingdom.

The governor contrasted the isolationist policy of New Atlantis with that of China. The former still admitted of humanity to strangers. Unlike the Chinese, the New Atlantans detained no one against their will, although they sought to make continued residence as attractive as possible, and, in fact, only thirteen visitors had ever chosen to leave. Finally the Chinese were freely allowed to travel abroad, but this was forbidden to the New Atlantans, with only one exception. 'Now for our travelling from hence into parts abroad, our Lawgiver thought fit altogether to restrain it . . . But this restraint of ours hath only one exception, which is admirable; preserving the good which cometh by communicating with strangers, and avoiding the hurt.'

The exception completes the explanation of the paradox of the isolation of New Atlantis, and, with it, what I have called Act One. It explains how the New Atlantans, unknown to others, know them so well. It also introduces what most commentators have seen as the key feature of Bacon's idealsociety, Salomon's House or the College of the Six Days' Work:

> amongst the Excellent Acts of that King, one above all hath the preheminence. It was the Erection, and Instillation of an Order, or Society, which wee call Salomon's House; The Noblest Foundation, (as wee thinke), that ever was upon the Earth; and the Lanthorne of this Kingdome. It is dedicated to the Study of the Works, and Creatures of God.

Every twelve years, two ships were sent out from New Atlantis, each carrying a mission of three Fellows of Salomon's House. They were commissioned to investigate assigned countries, 'And especially of the Sciences, Arts, Manufactures, and Inventions of all the World; and withall to bring unto us, Bookes, Instruments, and Patterns, in every kinde.' The ships returned immediately after landing the Fellows, who continued *incognito* their intellectual, technical and cultural espionage until the next expedition came twelve years later and picked them up. So the explanation of the paradox is complete. New Atlantis possessed full knowledge of the outside world without being corrupted by it. Of course, this place a heavy burden on the integrity of the Fellows of Salomon's House. For twelve long years, as they search for knowledge to take back with them, they are exposed to the corrupting influences of the world outside. Bacon did not discuss the point. He would appear to have assumed that they were capable of sustaining the burden. This silent assumption, as we shall see, is not without its significance.

With the opening of the second 'Act' the scene shifts

from inside the Strangers' House to the society outside. The period of confinement had ended and the visitors now wandered freely in Bensalem and became acquainted with residents of the city, though 'not of the meanest Quality'. As the scene shifts so the topic of concern changes from the relationship between New Atlantis and the outside world to the society of New Atlantis itself: 'continually we mett with many things, right worthy of observation & Relation: As indeed, if ther be a mirrour in the World, worthy to hold Mens Eyes, it is that Countrey.' The Act falls into four scenes: the Feast of the Family, the dialogue with Joabim the Jew, the arrival of the Fellow of Salomon's House, and, finally, his discourse on the work of that institution.

One day, two of the visitors were invited to a celebration of the Feast of the Family. 'A most natural, pious and reverned custom it is, showing that nation to be compounded of all goodness.' Any man living to see thirty persons descended from his body, alive and over three years old, might hold this feast at the cost of the state. Two days before the Feast, the father, or Tirsan as he was now to be known, with three friends and the assistance of the governor of the city or place, held council with all the members of the family. At this meeting, quarrels were settled, the distressed were relieved, the vicious reproved and disciplined and marriage plans arranged. The governor was prepared to use his public authority to enforce the decrees of the Tirsan, though this was seldom necessary, 'such reverence and obedience they give, to the Order of Nature'. Discipline and harmony having been established, the Tirsan chose one man from amongst his sons to live with him and this individual was known thereafter as the Son of Vine. The Feast day itself began with divine service which was followed by a procession honouring the Tirsan. In the course of this, heralds arrived bringing a royal charter conveying privileges and rewards to him: 'the King is Debter to no Man, but for Propagation of his subjects'. Then followed a ceremonial feast in which the Tirsan was waited upon by his family, sharing his magnificence only with such of his children as happen to be Fellows of Salomon's House. This celebration of propagation, fecundity and longevity involves a sharp contrast with what we know of the evanescent nucleated kinship group of Bacon's own day. Still more significant, perhaps, is the disciplinary and conflict-resolving function accorded to the patriarchal family, for, apart from this reference, there is no discussion of how conflict and social disorder are dealt with in New Atlantis. Bacon shared, somewhat incipiently, the patriarchalist attitudes common in his day. The Feast itself was accompanied by a hymn celebrating Adam, Noah and Abraham. 'whereof the former two peopled the world, and the last was the Father of the Faithful'. Elsewhere in his works, Bacon employed the patriarchalist's parallels between the authority of father over family, king over country and God over creation. He was also of the opinion that parricide was a form of treason and should be treated as such at law.

The second scene of this second Act continues the examination of the New Atlantan family. In it, the narrator makes the makes the acquaintance of Joabim, who was a Jewish Merchant.

> For they have some few Strips of Jewes, yet remaining amongst them, whom they leave to their owne Religion. Which they may better doe, because they are of a farre differing disposition from the Jewes in other Parts. For whereas they hate the *Name* of Christ; And have a secret inbred rancour against the People amongst whom they live; These (contrariwise) give unto our Saviour many high Attributes, and love the Nation of Bensalem, extreamely.

Joabim, for example, acknowledged Christ's virgin birth and that he was more than a man and is now God's ruler of the seraphims. He saw the laws of Bensalem as Mosaic in origin. This moderate semitism was necessary to enable Jews to meet Bacon's tests on entry to his ideal society, and also to provide against conflict between Christian and Jew, but more broadly significant is the connection between this image of a Christianised Jewry in an ideal society and the notion of the conversion of the Jews as a precursor of the latter day glory and, accompanying it, the Great Instauration, or restoration of man's pristine dominion over nature. We shall see this juxtaposition of themes most fully developed in Samuel Gott's *Nova Solyma*.

Bensalem, according to Joabim, is 'the Virgin of the World': 'there is not under the Heavens, so chast a Nation, as this of Bensalem. Nor so free from all pollution or foulenesse.' There are 'no Stewes, no dissolute Houses, no Curtisans, nor anything of that kind'. Homosexuality is unknown. By contrast, Joabim noted, in Europe single men were impure; marriage was 'but an office', most frequently merely a commercial bargain; the married were indifferent to the procreation of children; adultery was common. Not only is this critical analysis of sexual mores and marriage the single aspect of European life discussed in the work, but, apart from Salomon's House, marriage and the family are the only features of New Atlantan society dealt with in any detail. In New Atlantis polygamy was forbidden. No couple could marry or make a contract until one month after their first meeting. Curiously, in relation to Bacon's emphasis on patriarchal authority elsewhere, marriage without parental consent was not void, but the children of such marriages were not allowed to inherit above one-third of their parents' inheritance. The New Atlantans had explicitly rejected More's utopian device for direct naked viewing of the betrothed, as possibly hurtful to anyone spurned. Instead, because of 'many hidden defects in men and women's bodies', they had instituted a more indirect system of examination on a non-obligatory basis.

The third scene described the entry into Bensalem of one of the Fellows of Salomon's House. Joabim had secured a good vantage point for the narrator who describes in detail the magnificence and pomp with which the Fellow's entry was made. The latter sought 'to avoid all tumult and trouble' but, perhaps because this was the first view of a Fellow to Bensalem in the last dozen years, there was an elaborate procession in which all the officers of the City Companies appeared. The discipline of the people lining the streets was carefully noted. 'The street was wonderfully well kept; so that ther was never any Army had their men stand in better Battle-Array, then the People stood. The windowes likewise were not crowded, but every one stood in them as if they had been placed.' So the importance and prestige of the Fellows of Salomon's House and the good order of the people were underlined.

The fourth and final scene takes the form of a meeting between the narrator and the Fellow of Salomon's House and the Fellow's discourse describing the work of the foundation. Once more Bacon emphasised the status of the Fellow.

> He was sat upon a low throne richly adorned, and a rich cloth of state over his head, of blue satin embroidered. He was alone save that he had two pages of honour, on either hand one, finely attired in white. His undergarments were the like that we saw him wear in the chariot; but instead of his gown, he had on him a mantle with a cape, of the same fine black fastened about him. When we came in, as we were taught, we bowed low at our first entrance; and when we were come near his chair, he stood up holding forth his hand ungloved, and in posture of blessing; and we, everyone of us stooped down, and kissed the hem of his tippet.

The Fellow, speaking in Spanish, informed the narrator that he was going to give him his 'greatest Jewell', a description of Salomon's House and its works. The description is broken into four sections. First, 'The End of our Foundation is the knowledge of Causes, and Secrett Motions of Things: and the Enlarging of the bounds of Humane Empire, to the Effecting of all Things Possible.' Then follows a very long section detailing the foundation's arrangements for the study of natural phenomena. Included in this most familiar part of the **New Atlantis** are mines, towers, zoological and botanical gardens, lakes, furnaces, perspective and sound houses, engineering shops, a 'Mathematicall House' and 'Houses of Deceits of the senses'. Most of the effort here appears to be employed in the compilation of what Bacon would have described as a natural history. Such discoveries as had immediate application were put into use throughout the kingdom, but the emphasis is upon the collection of data. Objectivity and scrupulousness are at a premium: 'wee doe hate all Impostures and Lies: Insomuch as wee have severely forbidden it to all our Fellowes under paine of Ignominy and Fines, that they doe not shew any Naturall Worke or Thing, Adorned or Swelling; but onely Pure as it is, and without all Affectation of Strangenesse'. The third section of the Fellow's discourse deals with the 'Employments and offices of our Fellows'. Their duties were arranged so that data was collected, used to furnish axiomatic conclusions and so to direct further investigation. Twelve of the Fellows were engaged on overseas expeditions and the rest of them were divided into groups of three. The 'Depredatours' collected experiments from books and the 'Mystery-Men' collected them from mechanical arts, liberal sciences and elsewhere. Another trio, the 'Pioneers or Miners', performed new experiments, while the 'Compilers' drew the information so far gathered into convenient form. Out of this collection, three fellows called 'Benefactors' culled anything of immediate use in practice or theory. As a result of continual reviews of the current state of knowledge, three fellows, known as 'Lamps', were able to direct new experiments, which were carried out and reported on by the 'Inoculators'. Finally three 'Interpretators of Nature' induced from all this information 'greater observations, axioms, and aphorisms'. In addition the college housed novices and apprentices and a great number of servants. The disposition of the knowledge acquired in this way appears to be quite firmly in the hands of the Fellows. 'We have consultations, which of the inventions and experiences which we have discovered shall be published, and which not: and take all an oath of secrecy, for the concealing of those which we think fit to keep secret: though some of those we do reveal sometimes to the state, and some not.' Bacon was well aware that technical skill and knowledge could be put to evil, as well as good, uses. Here he chose to place the moral responsibility in the hands of the men of learning rather than in those of the state.

The fourth and final section of the Fellow's discourse deals rather sketchily with what are described as the 'Ordinances and Rites' of Salomon's House. They had a museum consisting of two galleries. One contained patterns and samples of the best inventions known to them. The other housed statues of discoverers, like Columbus, and of the inventors of such things as music, gunpowder, letters, observations in astronomy, printing, glass, metal and bread. Every day the Fellows gave thanks to God for his 'Marveillous Works' and implored his aid in illuminating their labours and turning them to use. Periodically, they undertook tours to inform the cities of New Atlantis of new and profitable discoveries, and also to assist them with preparations against illness and natural disaster. Judging from the fact that Bensalem had not seen any of the Fellows for twelve years, Bacon did not intend this education function of the foundation to be taken too seriously. So,

with the Fellow's blessing and a gift of a thousand ducats, the interview and the description of New Atlantis ends.

About a third of the book is thus taken up with the treatment of relations between New Atlantis and the outside world. The same space is required for a description of the work of Salomon's House. The rest is given over to a discussion of the family and marriage, and to general support material. It is, perhaps, a testament to Bacon's literary skill that we first read the New Atlantis without realising how little he has in fact told us about his ideal society and its institutions. There is no description of the island itself, so that we have no idea of its size, population or the number of cities on it. It was a monarchy but beyond that we know virtually nothing of its governmental institutions. Bacon clearly believed that factional politics was inevitable in an aristocratic society, but he offered no explanation of the elimination, or otherwise, of faction in New Atlantis. There were social gradations in the ideal society but what they were and whether there was an hereditary nobility we do not know. Similarly we are not told how the island was defended, nor what its military organisation was. There is no mention of any judicial organisation beyond the exceptional jurisdiction exercised over a limited field by the Tirsan. Production and distribution of goods, land settlement, provision for the poor; none of these topics, all of which Bacon showed interest in elsewhere, are dealt with in the New Atlantis. In the 1590s Bacon had written, 'Trust not to your laws for correcting the times, but give all strength to good education; see to the government of your universities and of all seminaries of youth, and to the private order of families, maintaining due obedience of children towards their parents, and reverence of the younger sort towards the ancient.' The Feast of the Family is in part, at least, an arrangement to comply with the second part of this advice, but nothing is known of the educational institutions or arrangements of the New Atlantans. Finally, what religious settlement existed in the ideal society? We know that there were priests and that Jews were tolerated but, apart from this, nothing. Are the Fellows of Salomon's House, who clearly played an important part in the religious life of New Atlantis, also priests? Bacon provided no answer. Perhaps most astonishing of all is our lack of knowledge of the House of Salomon. Bacon described in great detail the *work* of the foundation but said very little about its *organisation*. How were Fellows recruited? What were their conditions of service? How were they controlled and allocated their work? How was the foundation financed and what determined its relationship with society at large? That we know so little about the institution on which Bacon lavished most attention in his short fiction must form a key to any valid interpretation of the work as a whole.

The fact that Bacon left so many questions unanswered obviously makes it difficult to characterise the work. A number of apparently utopian elements appear in his description of the ideal society of New Atlantis. Amongst the institutions mentioned or implied are the Strangers' House, the Infirmary, Salomon's House, the City Companies and the municipal government. The difficulty is that many of these are merely mentioned and we are given very little, if any, idea of their organisation, purpose and rôle in relation to the rest of society. The same may be said of the handful of officials referred to. Mention is made of 'Fundamentall Lawes' but, beyond restrictions on the entry of foreigners, no details are given. There is, as we have seen, a disciplinary and conflict-resolving function allocated to fathers preparing for the Feast of the Family, but, given infant mortality rates and life expectancy, this can hardly have been expected to provide the basis for a general social order. Apart from this, the only general regulations that appear are the inheritance restrictions on the offspring of marriages without parental consent, the injunction against this, and one against deception by the Fellows of Salomon's House. It may be this very lack of institutional and legal completeness, verging on confusion, which has led some commentators [e.g., Joseph Anthony Mazzeo in his *Renaissance and Revolution: The Remaking of European Thought,* 1967] to characterise the New Atlantis as a realisable ideal.

The crucial problem, however, is the nature of that ideal. For, while there are elements of discipline by regulation and bits and pieces of what might be an institutional and bureaucratic apparatus, the description of New Atlantis is too superficial for it to be labelled utopian in the sense already elaborated. There are, moreover, hints that we are dealing with a community of self-regulating individuals, with a community of moral paragons, a perfect moral commonwealth [see V. Dupont's *L'Utopie et le Roman Utopique dans la Littérature Anglaise,* 1941]: 'we were come', the mariners decided, 'into a land of angels, which did appear to us daily and prevent us with comforts, which we thought not of much less expected'; 'we were apt enough to think there was somewhat supernatural in this island; but yet rather as angelical than magical'; 'there is not under the Heavens, so chast a Nation, as this of Bensalem. Nor so free from all pollution or foulenesse. It is the Virgin of the World.' The basis of this unrivalled chastity are the New Atlantans' twin maxims: 'That whosoever is unchaste cannot reverence himself'; and, 'That the Reverence of a Mans selfe, is next Religion, the chiefest Bridle of all Vices'. In the Tirsan's preparations for the Feast of the Family, provision was made for the city governor to give substance to his authority, but this was seldom needed, 'such reverence and obedience they give, to the Order of Nature'. New arrivals were carefully screened to maintain this general sense of moral responsibility. There is a sense in which, as Harold Osborne remarked

[in his *Bacon 'New Atlantis',* 1937], the social institutions of New Atlantis were rather expressions of the character of the people than formative of it.

But this is not the complete picture, for, while such emphasis was placed upon *self*-respect, *self*-control, internalised moral authority, nevertheless, some, admittedly very limited, social discipline and regulation was envisaged. The laws which limited the rights of those who defy patriarchal authority and marry without parental consent assumed that such defiance would and did take place. There is no nation on earth as chaste as Bensalem and yet it remains a function of the Tirsan to suppress vice in his family. Throughout the *New Atlantis* run contradictory suggestions of moral perfection and moral failure, suppression unnecessary and suppression in operation. In other words, the *leitmotif* pervading the work is the unresolved tension between perfect moral commonwealth and utopian ideals.

It has been shown that implicit in Bacon's vision of a new learning was an alteration in the conception of the learned man. The virtues of this ideal were not purely intellectual. Indeed Bacon attacked reliance on pure intellect. As the fatal sin remains pride, so the key virtue is charity. 'The identification of scientific truth with use and therefore with charity, with power and therefore with pity, is fundamental to Bacon's conception of true learning.' 'Bacon often leaves the impression that the career of science is something of a religion in its selflessness and sense of dedication, and he at times spoke of the future scientists as though they were a priesthood' [Moody E. Prior, "Bacon's Man of Science," 1968]. This saint-like image of the man of learning is clearly apparent in Bacon's treatment of the Fellows of Salomon's House and the relationship between them and society at large. The Fellow who paraded through the streets of Bensalem had 'an Aspect as if he pittied them' and while he arrived in great state he was careful to 'avoid all tumult and trouble'. 'He held up his bare hand as he went, as blessing the people, but in silence.' The Fellows of Salomon's House appear asa species of moral superman. While their fellow citizens are carefully shielded from the corrupting influences of the outside world, they, as we have seen, are deemed capable of withstanding them on their twelve year long expeditions of enquiry. Again, Bacon was well aware of the corrupting influence of power, but his learned paragons exercise it in high degree without deleterious effects. The philosophers in New Atlantis may not rule in any clearly expressed sense, but, as Mazzeo has pointed out [in his *Renaissance and Revolution,* 1967], they retain the power of technological innovation and with it the capacity to alter the conditions of life, if not the structure of society. Their collective moral responsibility even extends to deciding what knowledge shall be passed on to society at large. In New Atlantis the philosophers exercised a benevolent censorship even against the state, and Bacon appears to have assumed away the wider problems of political control under cover of the perfect moral character of the scientist. One is almost tempted to describe the result as a perfect moral commonwealth under the guidance of a benevolent, but unrestrained, moral élite, the Fellows of Salomon's House. Bacon's image of them has been described by one authority [Prior] as 'possibly too flattering to human nature'.

But even here Bacon hesitated and drew back. The optimism of the *New Atlantis* is not entirely 'unguarded', Bacon's faith in human rationality, human goodness not quite 'unbounded'. He admitted that the Fellows of Salomon's House might be tempted to lie about and to distort what they had learned; that their integrity was vulnerable. It was necessary to legislate accordingly. 'But wee doe hate all Impostures and Lies: Insomuch as wee have severely forbidden it to all our Fellowes under paine of Ignomiry and Fines, that they doe not shew any Naturall Worke or Thing, Adorned or Swelling; but onely Pure as it is, and without all Affectation of Strangenesse.' Once, however, Bacon had admitted the moral fallibility of the Fellows in one thing (particularly in such an important thing as this) then he had raised the question of it in all things. If the Fellows could be motivated to deceive and distort, why could they not be tempted to exploit?

Bacon left so many loose ends in the *New Atlantis* that it is tempting to return to the explanation that it was 'A Worke unfinished', half thought out, hastily executed, never intended for publication. Unfortunately there are difficulties here too. Partly these arise from the vexed question of when the work was written. Here the commentators are in considerable disarray. They fall basically into two groups: those who see it as a product of Bacon's last years, after his fall from office, and those who would attribute it to an earlier period of his life. An intelligent compromise suggestion [by Mazzeo] has been that Bacon first drafted the work in the period 1614-17 and revised it for publication in, or about, 1623. Clearly, if the *New Atlantis* was subject to a process of revision it becomes impossible to explain away its inconsistencies, its unresolved problems, in terms of the author's haste or his unwillingness to put his work before an audience. Whatever the date at which the *New Atlantis* was written, and it is doubtful whether this can be established with any precision, the significant point is that the cardinal ideas of the work had engaged Bacon's mind for a period of over thirty years of his life. In 1594, for the Christmas revels at Grays Inn, he composed a number of speeches as part of a masque in which counsellors addressed a mock monarch. The second counsellor advised the study of philosophy and commended four principal works or monuments. The first was 'the collecting of a most perfect and general library, wherein whatsoever the wit of man hath heretofore committed to books of

worth be they ancient or modern, printed or manuscript, European or other parts, of one or other language, may be made contributory to your wisdom'. Second, came a garden of all plants, a collection of all rare beasts and birds, and two lakes, one of salt water and the other of fresh: 'in small compass a model of universal nature made private'. Next was 'a goodly huge cabinet, wherein whatsoever the hand of many by exquisite art or engine hath made rare in stuff, form or motion; whatsoever singularly chance and the shuffle of things hath produced; whatsoever Nature hath wrought in things that want life and may be kept; shall be sorted and included'. The last of the four works was the construction of 'such a stillhouse, so furnished with mills, instruments, furnaces, and vessels, as may be a palace fit for a philosopher's stone'. The parallels between these four works or monuments and the 'Preparations and Instruments' of Salomon's House are too obvious to require much comment. Even more significant in this context is that, along with this, in the address of the Fifth Counsellor, Bacon coupled an appeal for governmental perfection, for 'Virtue and a gracious Government'. The prince was urged to seek inward peace; to visit all parts of his dominions, setting wrongs right; to check the faults of his great servants; to advance men of virtue and to repress faction; to reform the law, purging it of multiplicity and obscurity, and ensuring its execution; to back up the authority of the laws with good education in universities, schools and the home; and, finally, to seek prosperity. Thus, as early as 1594, the institutional advancement of learning and the notion of political perfection were linked by Bacon in a single design. The civil model of New Atlantis, as well as the intellectual, was prefigured. In July 1608 Bacon spent seven days on a detailed review of his affairs. Again, the twin projects of a new type of learned institution and political reform were in his mind at the same time. In his notes for 26 July, he wrote, 'Foundac. of a college for Inventors. 2 Galeries W[th.] statuas or bases for Inventors to come. And a Library and an Inginary.' He went on to make sketchy remarks about the rules, allowances, and secrecy necessary in connection with such an establishment. Two days later he was making notes of a scheme for the drafting of new laws and the amendment of old, towards the compilation of an ideal code of law.

Whenever the *New Atlantis,* as we know it now, was written, the point that needs to be repeated is that what Rawley [in his prefare to *New Atlantis,* 1624] considered to be the two cardinal features of the work, the scientific institution and the ideal society, were linked in Bacon's thought and writing over a period of at least thirty years. Given the longevity of the idea in Bacon's mind, it becomes difficult to accept the suggestion that the inconsistency and lack of development in the *New Atlantis* are entirely attributable to lack of thought, care and time. Moreover, if one relates this issue to the way in which he dealt with different types of ideal-society notions in his works, one becomes aware of a profound unwillingness, on Bacon's part, to be committed to any form of ideal society. Four of our ideal society types—the millennium, arcadia, the perfect moral commonwealth and utopia—impinged upon Bacon's thought and the impact of the last two was particularly strong. Yet in the end he remained aloof, detached from all of them. He was torn between an impulse to idealise and a scepticism about, if not a distaste for, the ideal. Whenever he committed himself to one of the ideal-society modes available to him, Bacon encountered amongst its exigencies features unacceptable to him and this was particularly so with the utopian mode. It is this which provides the most probable explanation of the problems of the *New Atlantis.*

Bacon's chiliastic references were tantalisingly scant and perfunctory. He used Daniel's prophecy, that learning would increase in the autumn of the world, to bolster an optimistic view of intellectual progress, and commented on the predictability of religious controversy in these 'latter days'. As we have seen in the *New Atlantis,* he played with the juxtaposition of a Christianised Jewry, a Great Instauration, and, by inference, a latter-day glory. These were hardly more than early-seventeenth-century conventionalities. Nowhere does Bacon set out systematically to examine millenarian ideas and their implications. Much more important and central to his thought was an arcadian strain arising out of his view of the ethico-religious end of the advancement of learning. As 'the proud knowledge of good and evil' had brought about the fall of man, so, Bacon argued, 'the pure knowledge of nature and universality' would lead to man's recovery of his original command over the creation. Thus, 'natural philosophy proposes to itself; as its noblest work of all nothing less than the restitution and renovation of things corruptible'.

> And therefore it is not the pleasure of curiosity, nor the quiet of resolution, nor the raising of the spirit, nor victory of wit, nor faculty of speech, nor lucre of profession, nor ambition of honour or fame, nor inablement for business, that are the true ends of knowledge; some of these being more worthy than other, though all inferior and degenerate: but it is a restitution and reinvesting (in great part) of man to the sovereignty and power . . . which he had in his first state of creation.

It was Bacon's truly astonishing claim that it was the business of learning to undo the consequences of the fall of man. He was not always prepared to see this as a possibility of *complete* recovery. In *Valerius Terminus* he wrote,

> It is true, that in two points the curse is preremptory, and not to be removed; the one that vanity must be

the end in all human effects, eternity being resumed, though the revolutions and periods may be delayed. The other that the consent of the creature being now turned into reluctation, this power cannot be otherwise exercised and administered but with labour . . .

Later, in more optimistic vein, Bacon argued that, as a result of the fall, man lost both his innocence and his dominion of the creation, but that he might recover 'the former by religion and faith, the latter by arts and sciences'. Labour would remain indispensable to progress in the arts and sciences but the inevitability of vanity was not mentioned. This recovery of human innocence and command of nature could clearly lead to an arcadian view of the ideal society as the Garden of Eden regained. At least one commentator [Paolo Rossi in *Francis Bacon: From Magic to Science,* 1968] has seen the *New Atlantis* in this light as an evocation of 'the happy existence of mankind before the Flood'. Unfortunately there is little to justify this and little of the Arcadian in Bacon's social thought. He never examined in any systematic way what the recovery of a pre-lapsarian state would mean in terms of men's mastery over themselves and over each other. At times he even permitted himself to doubt whether man could attain to knowledge of the highest laws of nature and hence to complete command over the natural universe.

On the other hand, Bacon frequently used the language and forms of the perfect moral commonwealth tradition. A good illustration of this may be found in the New Year letter he wrote to James I in January 1618.

> I do many times with gladness and for a remedy of my other labours, revolve in my mind the great happiness which God (of his singular goodness) hath accumulated upon your Majesty every way; and how complete the same would be, if the state of your means were once rectified, and well ordered. Your people militar and obedient; fit for war, used to peace. Your Church illightened with good preachers, as a heaven of stars. Your judges learned, and learning from you; just, and just by your example. Your nobility in a right distance between crown and people; no oppressors of the people, no overshadowers of the crown. Your Council full of tribute of care, faith, and freedom. Your gentlemen and justices of the peace willing to apply your royal mandates to the nature of their several countries, but ready to obey. Your servants in awe of your wisdom, in hope of your goodness. The fields growing every day by the improvement and recovery of grounds, from the desert to the garden. The city grown from wood to brick. Your sea-walls or *pomoerium* of your island surveyed and in edifying. Your merchants embracing the whole compass of the world, east, west, north and south. The times give you peace, and yet offer you opportunities of action abroad. And lastly, your excellent royal issue entaileth these blessings and favours of God to

descend to all posterity.

Of course, there is a strong element of flattery in this, but the approach employed is significant. Moreover, the flattery motive cannot have been a serious factor in shaping the description of Elizabeth I's reign which Bacon published in *The Advancement of Learning* two years after her death. Here again 'the conjunction of learning in the prince with felicity in the people' is the theme. Elizabeth's rule, according to Bacon, was marked by a period of constant peace and security, when the truth of religion was established, justice administered well, the prerogative used with discretion, learning flourished, both crown and subject enjoyed a 'convenient estate and means', and obedience became habitual. The idea that a happy and harmonious society could be achieved by the conscientious pursuit of civil morality by rulers, officials and subjects is quite clear here, as it is in Bacon's long letter of advice to George Villiers, when first he became favourite of James I.

Bacon's defence of learning hung in part on the conviction that learning could play a key rôle in the attainment of civil morality and social harmony. The learned man was a man equipped for conscientious morality and self-improvement. 'For the unlearned man knows not what it is to descend into himself or to call himself to account, nor the pleasure of that *suavissima vita, indies sentire se fieri meliorem.*' Men are governed by two faculties, force and reason: 'the one is brute the other divine.' Learning, by fostering the rational in man, as opposed to the brute, makes him amenable to government. 'And it is without all controversy that learning doth make the minds of men gentle, generous, maniable, and plaint to government; whereas ignorance makes them churlish, thwart and mutinous: and the evidence of time doth clear this assertion, considering that the most barbarous, rude, and unlearned times have been the most subject to tumults, seditions and changes.' Though learned men, contemplative rather than active, may lack experience of '*ragioni di stato*', 'yet on the other side, to recompense that, they are perfect in those same plain grounds of religion, justice, honour, and moral virtue; which if they be well and watchfully pursued, there will seldom be use of those other, no more than of physic in a sound or well-dieted body'. Indeed, it was no more difficult for the learned man to pursue true virtue than it was for the politician to adhere to reason of state. If learned men had any fault, in this respect, it was that 'they contend sometimes too far to bring things to perfection, and to reduce the corruption of manners to honesty or precepts or examples of too great height'.

The perfect moral commonwealth element in Bacon's thinking was then closely associated with his conception of the man of learning, and, as we have seen, this carries over into the *New Atlantis*. But, as before, Bacon

could not go the whole way. He did not commit himself. Even while speaking of the moral appeal and potency of learning, he had to admit the tenuousness of its hold:

> the nature and condition of men; who are full of savage and unreclaimed desires, of profit, of lust, of revenge, which as long as they give ear to precepts, to laws, to religion, sweetly touched with eloquence and persuasions of books, of sermons, of harangues, so long is society and peace maintained; but, if these instruments be silent, or that sedition and tumult make them not audible, all things dissolve into anarchy and confusion.

There were limits to men's capacity for self-control and self-discipline. 'Nature is often hidden; sometimes overcome; seldom extinguished'; 'let not a man trust his victory over his nature too far; for nature will lay buried a great time, and yet revive upon the occasion or temptation'. By the same token, even the best of monarchs could be 'depraved by the long habit of ruling'. So man's vulnerability to temptation and to the corrupting influence of power remained, crippling Bacon's willingness to commit himself to the vision of a perfect moral commonwealth. In his advice to James I on the disposal of Sutton's estate, he pointed out that the will to morality, good intentions, were not enough. Without 'such ordinances and institutions as may preserve the same from turning corrupt, or at least from becoming unsavoury and of little use', they were doomed to disappointment. Bacon was lifting his eyes from the vision of a society of conscientiously self-disciplined men of good will, a perfect moral commonwealth, to the legal and institutional guarantees of the performance of social good, that is towards utopia.

Bacon's interest in institutional methods of co-ordinating and controlling the behaviour of men is clearly apparent in his critical approach to past philosophy. It suffered from self-indulgent individualism: 'one catches at one thing, another at another; each has his own favourite fancy; pure and open light there is none; every one philosophises out of the cells of his own imagination, as out of Plato's cave'. To remedy this situation Bacon provided his elaborate programme and method on the assumption that 'the mind itself be from the very outset not left to take its course, but guided at every step, and the business be done as if by machinery'. The co-ordination of individual men's efforts was a key feature of his scientific method. And it was the method itself which was to provide the unifying force to which each worker must submit himself. In *Valerius Terminus* he suggested that knowledge should be administered as the king of Spain administered his dominions, with men absorbed in specialised or regional duties but subject to central control and direction. In the *New Atlantis* we find the work of the Fellows of Salomon's House organised on this kind of pattern. When he considered the advancement of learning, Bacon accorded a place of priority to the institutional framework—'foundations and buildings, endowments with revenues, endowments with franchises and privileges, institutions and ordinances for government'—without which progress was impossible. Again, this concern with academic institutions is to be found clearly reflected in the New Atlantis and Salomon's House. On the other hand, apart from some remarks on government by commission, Bacon showed little general interest in governmental institutions. He did not feel that any particular form of government was possessed of divine sanction. God allowed civil government (as he allowed ecclesiastical government)

> to be varied according to time and place and accidents, which nevertheless his high and divine providence doth order and dispose. For all civil governments are restrained from God unto the general grounds of justice and manners, but that policies and forms of them are left free. So that monarchies and kingdoms, senates and seignories, popular states or communalities, are all lawful, and where they are planted ought to be maintained inviolate.

In his discussion **"Of the True Greatness of Kingdoms and Estates"**, he followed Machiavelli in identifying greatness with capacity for war, but the key factors were population and spirit, not organisation or institutions.

It might be expected that Bacon, as a professional lawyer, would have had a dynamic view of law as a means of moulding the will and behaviour of men. Certainly there were occasions when he expressed the opinion that the law could be used more vigorously. The education of youth was a topic upon which, as Bacon saw it, philosophy spoke too much and laws too little. What he most admired in Henry VII was his ability as a lawmaker, an aspect of statesmanship which he found too often neglected by historians. In discussing duelling, Bacon utilised the concept of law as a means of combatting the defects of man's nature. 'Revenge is a kind of wild justice; which the more man's nature runs to, the more ought law to weed it out.' Perhaps the clearest discussion Bacon produced of the legislator's approach to a specific social problem was his essay **'Of Usury'**. Whilst usury had deplorable social effects, it had to be permitted because of the harshness of men's hearts, since without it they would not lend to those in need. The latter fell into two categories: those seeking relief from destruction, and those seeking commercial capital. Bacon therefore proposed that anyone might lend to the poor at a maximum rate of five per cent interest, while the supply of commercial capital should be at higher rates and subject to licence. Astonishingly enough, for a man who was to be Lord Chancellor of England, Bacon showed no recognition

of the practical and legal difficulties involved in a proposal of this kind. Yet he had complained, as early as the mid 1590s, of the multiplication of ineffective laws. Moreover, this pessimism about law's potential for the production of clear-cut solutions to problems was much more typical of him. Law, he argued, might solve old problems but, in the very process of doing so, it tended to create new ones. 'For new laws are like the apothecaries' drugs; though they remedy the disease, yet they trouble the body . . . ' He saw no capacity in the law for eliminating envy, greed, ambition, faction, anger or the depredations of cunning and corrupt men. The baser side of human nature would find a way round institutional and legal obstacles for the working of its ill-will.

Although Bacon maintained a lifelong interest in the compilation and amendment of English law it would hardly be correct to describe him as a law reformer. He was concerned rather with the clarity and expression of the law rather than with its substance: 'what I shall propound is not to the matter of the laws, but to the manner of their registry, expression and tradition: so that it giveth them rather light than any new nature'; 'the entire body and substance of law shall remain, only discharged of idle and unprofitable or hurtful matter; and illustrated by order and other helps, towards the better understanding of it, and judgement thereupon'. Thus, his approach to legal science, like his approach to natural science, could be inductive. His criticism of contemporary lawyers—'they write according to the states where they live, what is received law, and not what ought to be law'—is almost a parody of his own professional attitude.

Far more important than law itself in moving the will of men and influencing their behaviour was custom. It was 'the principal magistrate of man's life'.

> Men's thoughts are much according to their inclination; their discourse and speeches according to their learning and infused opinions: but their deeds are after as they have been accustomed. And therefore as Machiavel well noteth (though in an evil-favoured instance,) there is no trusting to the force of nature or to the bravery of words, except it be corroborate by custom . . . insomuch as a man would wonder to hear men profess, protest, engage, give great words, and then do just as they have done before; as if they were dead images, and engines moved only by the wheels of custom.

Custom alone was capable of altering and subduing men's natures, and, when socially endorsed, it was particularly strong: 'if the force of custom simple and separate be great, the force of custom copulate and conjoined and collegiate is far greater. For there example teacheth, company comforteth, emulation quickeneth, glory raiseth . . . Certainly the great multiplication of virtues upon human nature resteth upon societies well ordained and disciplined.

Herein, of course, lay the problem. Custom alone moulded the behaviour of men but how were good customs to be obtained and bad customs suppressed? Thought, persuasion, law were not enough. Bacon knew well enough that the problem was not to find models for the behaviour of men, but to find means of making men adhere to a good pattern of behaviour. In discussing the science of 'the Appetite and Will of Man', he wrote:

> In the handling of this science, those which have written seem to me to have done as if a man that professeth to teach to write did only exhibit fair copies of alphabets and letters joined, without giving any precepts or directions for the carriage of the hand and framing of the letters. So have they made good and fair exemplars and copies, carrying the draughts and portraitures of Good, Virtue, Duty, Felicity; propounding them well described as the true objects and scopes of man's will and desires; but how to attain these excellent marks, and how to frame and subdue the will of man to become true and comfortable to these pursuits, they pass it over altogether, or slightly and unprofitably.

In the second Book of *The Advancement of Learning,* Bacon pointed again and again to the failure of moral philosophy. Virtue was known but how to be virtuous was not; or, at most, men had made the question a topic of conversation but not of scholarship. Of the determinants of men's behaviour two areas—nature and fortune—were beyond our command. It was necessary, if ever a science of moral philosophy were to be developed, for the distinctions of nature and fortune to be listed and examined in effects. The ancients had made observations of this type 'and yet nevertheless this kind of observations wandereth in words but is not fixed in inquiry. For the distinctions are found (many of them), but we conclude no precepts upon them . . . 'There remained a third area of investigation: 'those points which are within our own command, and have force and operation upon the mind to affect the will and appetite and to alter manners: wherein they ought to have handled *custom, exercise, habit, education, example, imitation, emulation, company, friends, praise, reproof, exhortation, fame, laws, books, studies*'. Unfortunately Bacon restricted himself to a discussion of custom and habit, and this was merely a brief survey of a few commonplace precepts. There was, however,

> a kind of Culture of the Mind that seemeth yet more accurate and elaborate than the rest, and is built upon this ground; that the minds of all men are at some times in a state more perfect, and at other times in a state more depraved. The purpose therefore of this practice is to fix and cherish the good hours of the mind and to obliterated and take forth the evil.

He concluded, somewhat lamely, that the best means towards this end were 'the electing and propounding unto a man's self good and virtuous ends of his life, such as may be in a reasonable sort within his compass to attain'. Finally, when it came to civil knowledge, Bacon declared that a knowledge of the means of moving men to conscientious behaviour was quite unnecessary: 'moral philosophy propoundeth to itself the framing of internal goodness; but civil knowledge requireth only an external goodness'. The sum of civil behaviour was 'to retain a man's own dignity without intruding upon the liberty of others'. For the rest, Bacon concerned himself with the means to individual success and promised to treat government and law in a collection of aphorisms. Like much of his work, his discussion here of moral philosophy and civil knowledge was more valuable as criticism than for any positive contribution. He did little to make up for the neglect he found in others.

The nearest Bacon came to a systematic discussion of the means whereby the will of man might be moved and moulded was in a work on quite another topic. *A Letter and Discourse to Sir Henry Savill, Touching Helps for the Intellectual Powers* was written early in Bacon's career. In it, Bacon was concerned to show how capable of improvement the mental faculties of men were. His argument was that, of all creatures, man was 'the most susceptible of help, improvement, impression and alteration', and that, as this was true of his body, appetite and affection so it held good also of his power of wit and reason. Thus his discussion of the means of influencing the will of man was a mere preliminary to demonstrating how his intellectual, as opposed to moral, capacities might be improved. 'And as to the will of man', he wrote, 'it is that which is most maniable and obedient; as that which admitteth most medecines to cure and alter it.' The premier of these was religion; the 'most sovereign of all', 'able to change and transform it in the deepest most inward inclinations and motions'. (This was, of course, a priority reflected in the insistence on Christian faith as a precondition of entry to New Atlantis.) Next came 'Opinion and Apprehension; whether it be infused by tradition and institution, or wrought in by disputation and persuasion'. Third, was example; fourth, 'when one affection is healed and corrected by another; as when cowardice is remedied by shame and dishonour, or sluggishness and backwardness by indignation and emulation; and so of the like'. Lastly, 'when all these means, or any of them, have new framed or formed human will, then doth custom and habit corroborate and confirm all the rest'. These 'medicines' produced two kinds of cure: a true cure and a 'palliation'. The latter was 'more plentiful in the courts of princes, and in all politic traffic, where it is ordinary to find not only profound dissimulations and suffocating the affections that no note or mark appear of them outwardly, but also lively simulations and affectations, carrying the tokens of passions which are not'.

What is revealing about this is that, even here, Bacon does not see the state, its legal and institutional apparatus, as a means of influencing and changing conduct on a mass basis. Moulding the wills of men remained a question of individual influence, individual decision and individual will rather than collective influence, collective decision and collective will. The question then arises why, with these views as basic, Bacon's ideal society was not a straightforward perfect moral commonwealth. The answer lies, perhaps, in Bacon's profound pessimism about man—a pessimism which left him, as we have seen, with a nervous hesitation over the invulnerability of his moral supermen, the Fellows of Salomon's House. Men were imbued with a 'natural though corrupt' love of lies. Their rulers were corrupt, their treaties acts of deceit. The people were a brute rabble, 'always swelling with malice towards their rulers, and hatching revolutions'. 'There is in human nature generally more of the fool than of the wise; and therefore those faculties by which the foolish part of men's minds is taken are most potent.' Holiness of life so far exceeded the strength of human nature that it had to be regarded as a miracle. Paradoxically, for a defender of learning and the contemplative life, Bacon held a deeply pessimistic view of the human mind and senses. In the *Novum Organon* he referred to the 'dulness, incompetency and deceptions of the senses'. Elsewhere, he found the mind of man 'far from the nature of a clear and equal glass, wherein the beams of things should reflect according to their true incidence; nay, it is rather like an enchanted glass, full of superstition and imposture, if it be not delivered and reduced'. It was against the shortcomings of the mind that Bacon warned men in histheory of the Idols of the Mind. When these were added to the 'incapacity of the mind and the vanity and malignity of the affections', nothing was left but 'impotency and confusion'. Consequently, the mind could not be left to itself but had to operate under the continuous guidance of method. Only induction, sieved through exclusions, could lead man out of the darkness of his mind into the light of nature.

This pessimistic view of the nature and mind of man was instrumental in preventing Bacon from visualising a perfect moral commonwealth. More than this, it nourished a basic political conservatism which inhibited him from committing himself to any form of ideal society. In so far as Bacon applied his system of induction to the kingdom of politics and law, as well as to the kingdom of nature, he was bound to end up a moderate conservative. Hence his approach to ecclesiastical affairs was essentially that of a *politique*. He could see good and bad in both bishops and puritans. No system of church government was divinely ordained. Altering the established system could only be dangerous. Similarly, as he repeatedly said, he sought no

innovation in English law but merely 'the better to establish and settle a certain sense of law which doth now too much waver in incertainty'. In his great essay, **"Of Innovations"**, Bacon put forward a credo prefiguring the moderate conservatism of Edmund Burke. Innovations, he argued, are always misshapen but time itself is an innovator. It is necessary, therefore, for man to innovate according to time's pattern. 'It were good therefore that men in their innovations would follow the example of time itself; which indeed innovateth greatly, but quietly and in degrees scarce to be perceived.' In states experiments should be avoided, 'except the necessity be urgent, or the utility be evident'.

The conservative view of politics, the pragmatic attitude to change, are amongst the most consistent features of Bacon's thought. Elsewhere, he is hesitant, uncertain, ambivalent. He occupied a 'curiously anomalous position as a herald of the new scientific age who is also an incorrigible addict of modes of thinking which his expressed programme would replace: allegory, myth, iconographical symbolism, alchemy'. He was optimistic about the future of learning while retaining a pessimistic view of man's capacities as learner. His view of history hovered uncertainly between his inductive approach to history as a branch of knowledge, his dalliance with conventional cyclical theories, and his concern with history as the fall of man and the recovery in which his scientific method was to be instrumental. That Bacon was frequently lacking in precision of thought can hardly be gainsaid. It was almost a part of his intellectual milieu. But the problem goes deeper than this. Bacon, as Anne Righter [in "Francis Bacon," 1968] has argued, was caught in a dilemma 'between the desire for truth and the distrust of certainty, the need to generalize and abridge and the fear of violating the individuality of facts'. He was the victim of a double impulse, 'a need to discover and establish truth on the one hand, and to prevent thought from settling and assuming a fixed form on the other'. In a similar way, he acknowledged, but could never accept, the separation of the ideal and the actual.

Bacon's scientific certainty, his optimistic faith in a method capable of coping with man's fallibility, led him to visualise a society exploiting those methods. But when it came to idealising that society in other respects he was caught in a dilemma. Possessed of the pessimism about man of the utopian and the pessimism about institutional innovation of the perfect moral commonwealth theorist, he was caught in the tentacles of his own conservatism and could not commit himself to either view of a society purged, changed and perfected.

Bacon wished to visualise an ideal society in which science was esteemed, scientists were of crucial importance and scientific results were effectively harnessed for social benefit. In the *New Atlantis* he tried to adapt the mode of Sir Thomas More to this purpose and found himself trapped. For, in choosing the utopian mode, he was committing himself to the assumption of deficiencies in both man and nature. The latter, deficiencies in nature, were acceptable because science existed to remedy them. Indeed there would be no science in arcadia. The central problem lay in the utopian's assumption of human weakness and wickedness, for this meant that Bacon must assume the fallibility and corruptibility of his scientists. It followed therefore that, to prevent them from using their power to disorder society, he must restrain and control them and in so doing he risked destroying scientific freedom and with it the basis of the ideality of his society. Trapped in the exigencies of the utopian mode, Bacon exposes at once the problem and the impossibility of a scientific utopia. If science is to progress to the achieving of all things possible, minds, and to some extent actions, must be free of censorship and control. But scientific knowledge is power. It can, as Bacon knew, alter the material conditions of society and hence the structure of society itself. If we trust the scientist not only to pursue knowledge but to exercise his resultant power over society in a benevolent and enlightened way, then why may we not trust all men, particularly those not exposed to the temptations of scientific power? Why may we not, in other words, visualise a scientific perfect moral commonwealth? If, like the utopian, we cannot trust human nature, in scientists as well as others, how are we to have control without inhibiting freedom of enquiry? Bacon's failure to complete an ideal-society vision—his inability to assume either the automatic integrity of the scientist or to accept the stifling of free enquiry—is a great failure because it raises these still-unresolved issues at the moment of the conception of modern science.

Like More in Book I of the *Utopia,* Bacon faced the problem of the extent to which one is obliged to share true knowledge with those in power. More's problem here was solved in a perfect society because the knowledge he emphasised was moral knowledge which could be made consistent with, if it were not essential to, a stable and unchanging society. But Bacon's problem was not solved there because the knowledge he gave primacy to was technological knowledge. Behind it lay unanswered moral questions. Within it lay a capacity to produce instability and unknown social change.

Charles Whitney (essay date 1986)

SOURCE: "Reading Bacon: The Pathos of Novelty," in *Francis Bacon and Modernity,* Yale University Press, 1986, pp. 173-204.

[In the excerpt below, Whitney analyzes several aspects of the society described in the New Atlantis, *concluding that Bacon's description of the interaction between tradition and discovery within a utopia reflects issues of power and authority in both Bacon's time and the present.]*

[F]reudian processes are pertinent to Bacon's *New Atlantis,* where modern consciousness is symbolized by the island of Bensalem, "a land unknown." The *New Atlantis* is different. Surprisingly, because it is a fable, this utopia's relationship to reality is easier to grasp than that of [other] nonfiction works of Bacon. . . . For since Bacon's special problem is the relation of text-bound to text-free truth, an explicitly fictional story offers a relief. The *New Atlantis*'s fictionality and representational simplicity center on the proposition that one civilization in the world never needed cultural and social instauration, because it discovered the secret of scientific instauration long ago. This civilization aims not to match itself to its true identity using a series of figurations and surmises that are inaccurate in as yet indeterminate ways; rather, it becomes for its readers such a surmise. The island of Bensalem is isolated from the rest of the world, but in striking contrast to More's Utopia, Bensalem has a history that relates it to the rest of the world, indeed makes it the flower and realization of human history. For while the world experienced catastrophic wars and natural disasters that ruined the high level of civilization that prevailed three thousand years ago (and that has yet to be matched even in the European Renaissance), Bensalem escaped through luck, compassion toward enemies, and wisdom. The wise King Solamona established a program of scientific discovery based in the laboratory complex Solomon's House, and controlled and limited the contact between Bensalem and the rest of the world (which in its reduced state could probably offer only corruption anyway).

The *New Atlantis* represents and end run around the originary utopias of Western political philosophy, Plato's *Republic* and *Critias,* back to the greater time of which Plato and the readers of the *New Atlantis* are remnants. The problem that preoccupied or limited so many political theorists from Plato to Machiavelli to Bodin—how to overcome the flux of historical change and achieve stability, or how to achieve development in the face of historical degeneration—is answered in the fictional portrait of a society that has achieved its strength partly by ignoring the ages of civil and moral philosophy, instead preserving continuity with the ages before that, when natural philosophy dominated.

For all its conservatism, Bensalem's success is far from being the fulfillment and realization of Europe's long history. Its goals of preservation, isolation, and discovery come from a "revolutionary" urge (in the sense defined here) to achieve liberation from the compromising tension between tradition and innovation in the timeless presence of the moment of discovery ever repeated. Central planning buffers peaceful Bensalem from the shock of the new that must be constantly generated from the research complexes, and turns innovation to uses at once constructive and conservative; the continual production of new knowledge, Bacon asserts in the *New Atlantis* just as he asserts in his interpretation of the Orpheus myth, can neutralize history and so overcome its natural cycles of florescence and decline. Successful resistance to historical process through continuous discovery is thus really triumph over the necessity of having an historical consciousness, which must struggle with the fact that present conditions are different from past ones, and yet exist in a living relationship with them.

This modern goal of narrowing and intensifying consciousness finds reflection also in Bensalem's curious international relations. As Bacon attempts to manipulate the traditional and familiar from an autonomous vantage point in the present, and as he attempts to make the scientist's encounter with nature supremely disinterested, so the researchers of Bensalem send out spies to the rest of the world to gather information for their scientific programs. "We know, and are ourselves unknown" could be their motto, for the Bensalemites have become the world's intellectual imperialists. As Bacon aims to dominate and control the past for present use, so conditions for Europe's economic and political exploitation of the world find precedent in Bensalem's relationship to its intellectual "colonies"—the rest of the world. The dangers to the mother country of such a relationship are suggested by the ominous echo of "We know, and are ourselves unknown" in the Delphic oracle's ancient premise for civil and moral wisdom, "Know thyself." Such knowledge requires the introspection that is invigorated by a sense of ourselves in others' eyes. But Bacon's stance prevents such insights.

If a measure of a classic is that it continues to be timely, Bensalem's modernity, its resistance to historical process partly through its one-way commerce in ideas, also offers parallel, if not precedent, for neocolonial industrial development today, that is, the kind of "modernization" programs that benefit a tiny segment of third-world populations and preserve a one-way flow of profit and the sovereignty of transnational capital over nations. And as we can imagine the horror with which the good subjects of Bensalem contemplate a more balanced commerce in powerful knowledge, so we see the malevolence many good citizens of the United States today direct at third-world struggles to be free of neo-colonialism. Possibly our sophisticated colonizers have yet to enjoy the kind of introspection Bacon's Bensalem also denies to itself.

On the personal level Bacon, whom one historian [David Mathew, in his *James I,* 1972] has called "the one solitary figure of the Jacobean world," admits to

this kind of blindness: "My soul hath been a stranger to me in the course of my pilgrimage." Poignant, but Bacon kept this line from the Psalms handy, using it at appropriate moments over years. Such self-fashioning makes him vulnerable to Walter Savage Landor's stereotyping in an imaginary conversation between Bacon and Richard Hooker [*Imaginary Conversations* in *The Collected Works of Walter Savage Landor,* 1969].

> *Bacon.* But we who care nothing for chants and cadences, and have no time to catch at pleasures, push forward over stones and sands straightway to our objects. I have persuaded men, and shall persuade them for ages, that I possess a wide range of thought unexplored by others, and first thrown open by me. . . . Few [subjects] that occurred to me have I myself left untouched or untried: one however hath almost escaped me, and surely one worth the trouble.
>
> *Hooker.* Pray my Lord, if I am guilty of no indiscretion, what may it be?
>
> *Bacon.* Francis Bacon.

The *New Atlantis* is much less a narration of events than it is a narration of procedures, culminating in that of Solomon's House's scientific procedures. Before that culmination comes the detailed description of the ritual called the Feast of the Family, which epitomizes the society of Bensalem and itself is full of symbols celebrating nature and scientific discovery. At its worst the Baconian search for truth is a furious, compulsive, and ascetic "ritual" (as Karl Popper [in *The Logic of Scientific Discovery,* 1959] calls induction by negation) of life-negation. Bacon's utopia and the community of truth-seeking intellectuals at its core thus represent the blind or the secret will to domination and control that ideologies of both reform and revolution can harbor. At its best, Bacon's utopia represents an affirmative and healing ritual of life that attempts to encompass both reformative and revolutionary possibilities for human realization.

If a utopia governed by reason is like a family of many generations gathered lovingly to share their abundance and do honor to their progenitors in a ritual celebration at once magnificent and intimate, the attainment of knowledge as power, Bacon says in the *Instauratio Magna,* is like the bridal song or epithalamium sung at that marriage of the mind and the universe.

> The explanation . . . of the true relation between the nature of things and the nature of the mind is as the strewing and decorating of the bridal chamber of the mind and the universe, the divine goodness assisting, out of which marriage let us hope (and be this the prayer of the bridal song [epithalamium]) there may spring helps to man, and a line and race of inventions that may in some degree subdue and overcome the necessities and miseries of humanity.

The metaphor of marriage is used elsewhere by Bacon to describe the goal of his science: he wishes to correct "an unkind and ill-starred divorce": he hopes that "knowledge may not be as a courtesan, for pleasure and vanity only, or as a bond-woman, to acquire and gain to her master's use; but as a spouse, for generation, fruit, and comfort." Mind is groom, universe bride, but the objectification of the feminine implied by these metaphors does not necessarily invalidate the use of the marriage ritual as a metaphor for discovery or promise of fulfillment. With its allegory of a (male) deity's marriage to his congregation of worshippers, the Bible's epithalmium, the Song of Solomon, provides the reformative background for Bacon's ideal of redemptive intellectual marriage (with erotic anticipation in the Song of Solomon being divided about evenly). Spenser's poem *Epithalamion* assimilates this biblical background and displays a complex orderliness that parallels the kind of systematic knowledge Bacon hopes for. The twenty-three stanzas plus one envoy and the 366 long lines suggest that *Epithalamion* is a microcosm of all time, a metaphorical attempt to enclose time in a human ritual lasting twenty-four hours and representing a harmonious cosmos.

Of the ritual element of poetry in general, Northrop [in *Anatomy of Criticism,* 1957] says,

> Poetry imitates human action as total ritual, and so imitates the action of an omnipotent human society that contains all the powers of nature within itself. . . . The impetus of the magical element in ritual is clearly toward a universe in which a stupid and indifferent nature is no longer the container of a human society, but is contained by that society, and must rain or shine at the pleasure of man.

Bacon's (and perhaps Frye's) rituals are orderly rather than carnivalesque. The *New Atlantis* solemnly celebrates the knowledge that may be all people's power, but this popular power unfortunately finds inadequate correlatives in the narrative. For the general population of Bensalem is not part of the economy of knowledge production, nor do the fragments of ethnography in the *New Atlantis* show how the dissemination and application of knowledge has sustained the utopia. Since humanity's earthly goal is laboring to produce and then enjoying the knowledge that is power, most of the people in Bensalem must be working and living in varying degrees of alienation. And they represent the scientific ideology of their rulers in their allegorical feast. The wife of the patriarch, for instance, must sit alone, concealed in a special loft. She represents, probably, Nature, the feminine object of scientific study (whose "summary law" can never be disclosed), cheerfully validating the benevolent system that alienates her. Clearly Bacon understands how custom and belief can make authority seem legitimate, like his ancient Greek myth-makers grasping intuitively and experien-

tially what Gramsci and Althusser have studied more systematically.

It has recently been suggested, however, that the feasting family is a model for "incorporated families," royally chartered family businesses that became important in early English capitalism. In this reading the family *would* play an active part in technical innovation (the *New Atlantis,* after all, is unfinished). Bacon may then have been working toward suggesting a closer relationship between the sons of science and the ordinary citizens, whether or not he would have envisioned the extended families as in some ways free of the patterns of exploitation in which incorporated families actually participated.

But if scientists are clearly privileged in utopia, scientific language is not necessarily privileged in Bacon's utopian discourse. We have seen how Bacon demotes rhetoric in favor of inductive logic, excluding the former from the new science and assigning it to a popular rather than a learned audience. But if isolation of the discourse of science from the rest of discourse creates a new class of elite speakers and writers, this isolation may also have the effect (everywhere except in utopia) of separating, and demoting, the producers of knowledge from the institutional processes that maintain them. Since they lack control of management, the producers cannot really represent an elite. For instance, scientists need not understand the theological nuances of *instauratio,* but if they need funding from a theologically learned king, they certainly could use an agent who understands these matters. The Feast of the Family, which offers an allegorical version of scientific investigation preceding the literal version to follow in the description of Solomon's House, would represent an aristocratic, allegorical use of language in comparison with the bourgeois clarity of scientific language: the figured speaking would have a status that the plain speaking does not. Is the otherness of nature's secrets best preserved by a social other, as in pastoral and georgic, a technocratic group admired for its honest diligence? This question shows the degree to which the paradoxes of modernity (here of traditional and innovative language) can represent social conflict. In Bacon the ideologist and the scientist contend.

In the *New Atlantis* Bacon offers biblical sanctions for his ambivalent ideal of dominion: the wise and devout (for a time) rule of the Bible's King Solomon. Intellectual and technological dominion in the *New Atlantis* appears with biblical sanction: Solomon's Temple of worship has become Solomon's House of truth, which builds a model of the universe in the mind. Solomon himself hoped that the dominion of Israel and the dominion of the Hebrews over themselves would be achieved through faith in the dominion and omniscience of God over all. Thus his people's penitent recognition of their own sins would make prayerful appeals to

Solomon's Temple effective:

> If there be in the land famine, if there be pestilence, blasting, mildew, locust, or if there be caterpillar; if their enemy besiege them in the land of the cities; whatsoever plague, whatsoever sickness there be; What prayer and supplication soever be made by any man, or by all the people Israel, which shall know every man the plague of his own heart, and spread forth his hands toward this house: Then hear thou in heaven thy dwelling place, and forgive, and do, and give to every man according to his ways, whose heart thou knowest; (for thou, even thou only, knowest the hearts of all the children of men).
>
> [I Kings 8:37-39]

Like that of Solomon's Temple, the magic of Solomon's House can only work if the "petitioners," that is, the scientists, have insight into and control over selfishness and pride, and the competition and inequity pride breeds.

But it is not really so much the self-knowledge of the righteous that Bacon's new Temple recapitulates as the omniscience and omnipotence of God that Solomon himself so deeply admires in the prayer above, that he emulates as God's anointed ruler, and that finally results in his ruin amid strange gods. Thus the high point of the *New Atlantis,* the description of the wondrous achievements of Solomon's House, where hieratic garb and ritual adorn the priestlike members who work secretly to benefit men, hearkens back to its literary original, the description of Solomon's Temple. There the Temple is lavishly adorned with the symbols of divine power and dominion and of the wondrous order of the universe conceived, made, understood, and owned exclusively and totally by God. But now text threatens to undercut context rather than vice versa: it casts a shadow back on its precursor, and suggests that the Bible's vision of power and order itself remains necessarily blind to its full nature. We know, for instance, as Bacon did not, that the Bible in its glorification of God suppresses its enormous debt to prior religions' beliefs, practices, and revelations. Paul Ricoeur calls this suppression another kind of demythologization, the vast and necessarily covert and unauthorized demythologizing project of the Bible in its imagining of an exclusive god. This great Judaic demythologization aims, like that of the classical Greek philosophers, to free humanity's encounter with transcendence from the glittering veils of polytheism and ritual. Bacon's reliance on Solomon'sTemple thus represents not simply a brilliant and somewhat opportunistic appropriation of a sacred symbol but to some degree a validation and continuation of complex power relationships between text and predecessor. With the Bible as with Bacon, such relationships function in illuminating complex ideological roles. . . .

Bacon's account of how tradition and discovery inter-

act in utopia reveals issues of authority and dominion in Bacon's own cultural and social world and in our own. The *New Atlantis* . . . [points] to struggles between rhetoric and reason, representation and truth, and tradition and innovation. But [it] may also lead through these to questions about authority and legitimation, to an awareness of how struggles between text and context in the creation of meaning illuminate the operation of power in society.

Paolo Rossi's article "Baconianism" in the *Dictionary of the History of Ideas* is one of the strongest pieces ever written on Bacon. The institutionalizing dictionary format is significant. Rossi defines and defends Bacon's place in a canon of modern thinkers. He views modernity as a project and concludes, "The liberation of man—and in this too [Bacon] is modern—can be painfully achieved (by ways far more complicated than he was able to imagine) only through the labor, the works, the well-being of the whole of humanity." The necessarily abstract form of this conclusion may make it suitable for fervent or apathetic adoption by neoconservatives, liberals, and radicals alike. The conclusion is part of Rossi's response to Horkheimer's and Adorno's criticism of Bacon in *Dialectic of Enlightenment* for his instrumentalization of nature and language and for his multifarious will to power. Despite the onesidedness of much of this criticism, acknowledging its strengths, learning from it, and continuing to read in a resolutely critical spirit can contribute to the meaningfulness of Rossi's conclusions. My reading of Bacon as a modern has attempted to do this. Bacon's two mutually qualifying discourses on change form a vitally antithetical modern discourse. Combined with Bacon's own critical bent and his concern for the roles learning plays in society, this modernity criticizes from within and points beyond its constituent ideologies, which are in many ways still the ones that inform our life.

Charles C. Whitney (essay date 1990)

SOURCE: "Merchants of Light: Science As Colonization in the *New Atlantis,*" in *Francis Bacon's Legacy of Texts,* edited by William A. Sessions, AMS Press, 1990, pp. 255-68.

[*Here, Whitney describes how Bacon's narrow focus in the* New Atlantis *foreshadows the many benefits of inductive science, despite his failure explicitly to address contemporary social problems.*]

Surely Robert C. Elliott's remark [in *English Literary History* 30, 1963] about the diversity of ideological response to Thomas More's land of Utopia could not find a counterpart with respect to Bacon's utopia in the *New Atlantis:* "Many claim it: Catholics and Protestants, medievalists and moderns, socialists and communists; and a well-known historian has recently turned it over to the Nazis." Where More's *Utopia* addresses a range of contemporary social problems in ways that have encouraged interpreters of later ages to do the same, the *New Atlantis,* especially in hindsight, seems much more narrowly focused on a single subject, the spectacular foreshadowing of inductive science and its benefits, a foreshadowing that, precisely, avoids or cannot foresee many complex issues that might and do arise in science-oriented societies.

The relative marginality of social reference in the *New Atlantis* is underscored by the silent deletion, in the official University-of-Chicago-endorsed Great Books of the Western World Edition (edited by Robert M. Hutchins et al.), of the only two passages in the work where a subject of Bacon's utopian kingdom is allowed to comment upon conditions in contemporary Europe. Yes, the character Joabin's comments concern sex; perhaps this weird textual mutilation by those whose apologists today are our greatest priests of the textual masterpiece results from the same stodgy presumptiveness that marks the elitist offensive of those best-selling apologies. Certainly our latter-day editorial Guardians' elimination of an entire discursive dimension of contemporary historical reference from the *New Atlantis* represents a kind of covert ideological response. For one thing, the deletion has the effect of nudging our attention further away from historical contingency and toward celebration and legitimation of Western culture's destined progress toward domination through science. But may that nudge, unwelcome though it is, actually respond to an ideological thrust of the *New Atlantis* itself?

My own overtly ideological approach aims, to use Elliott's words, more to "turn over" Bacon's *New Atlantis* than to "claim" it. My assumption is that, though Bacon does not address contemporary social problems as explicitly as More does, his goal of demonstrating the benefits of science leads him to construct what is, in effect, a political allegory. A socially symbolic meaning, in many specifics unintended, thus supplements the main argument about science.

On the literal level, Bacon's island utopia, Bensalem, seems to be sustained by a covert form of colonization. Bacon's fantasy ideal is of a nation that enjoys maximum power and security by exploiting trading partners that do not even so much as know of its existence. This secret dependency enables the development of science in Bensalem through the importation of necessary information or raw facts. Within Bensalem itself, the scientific atmosphere produces a public docility reflecting an internalization of authority by the individual subjects of Bensalem.

Allegorically, Bensalem's curious non-empire offers in the first place an ideal colonialist solution to the challenge of empire facing Britain in the early seventeenth century in the wake of the triumph and the horror of the Spanish experience. It relates, for instance, to problems of English colonial administration in Ireland and Virginia. But relationships similar to that between colony and home country can work in several dimensions. Bensalem and its trade can be viewed as a prospective model of Britain and its empire, or Bensalem can be seen as a British colony planted among aliens; it can provide the British answer to Spain or represent a general European colonial endeavor far "nobler" than mere national aspirations. But the colonial relationship between Bensalem and its trading "partners" is also an apt analogy for an ideally exploitative class relationship between scientists and the artisans and mechanics whose inventive skills and useful devices Bacon would harness. As for the internalization of authority by individual subjects within the society of Bensalem itself, it can represent a solution to many social ills in England, as well as threats to royal prerogatives.

Secondary and tertiary resonances of meaning, further, could relate to the mercantile aspirations of later seventeenth-century Baconians, such as Joseph Glanvill, and to so-called neo-colonialism today, when (a now post-industrial) trade in information has become dominant. On the whole, the *New Atlantis* offers a vision of science linked inseparably to external and even internal colonialism. The implication of the *New Atlantis* is that European colonialism in the form of explicitly racist exploitation abroad and disciplinary technologies at home is a reality that finds an ideological counterpart in Bacon's far-sighted and influential vision of scientific freedom and power.

I

Trade and colonization are important themes in the *New Atlantis*. Three thousand years before the lost sailors miraculously happen upon it, Bensalem had resisted invasion by the Atlanteans of America. Then there was considerable trade, later lapsed and forbidden, between Bensalem and all the world. It ended nineteen hundred years previously by order of King Solamona, who intended to preserve his country's superior culture from contamination. At the moment of the narrative, there is mainly the trade in information vigorously prosecuted by Merchants of Light.

King Solamona founded Solomon's House to pursue "the knowledge of Causes and secret motions of things, and enlarging of the bounds of Human Empire, to the effecting of all things possible." Programs are overseen by thirty-six scientists assigned to different steps of the inductive process of investigation recommended by Bacon. Some scientists search for facts, some experiment, some frame axioms, and some look for applications. There are twelve fact-gathering Merchants of Light, who travel abroad looking for useful knowledge wherever they can find it. Such merchants of Light comprise over half of the twenty-one fact-gatherers and fully one-third of all scientists in Bensalem. Since twelve is to twenty-one as (approximately) twenty-one is to thirty-six, the numbers of scientists may have a symbolic meaning by exemplifying the Pythagorean golden mean. In any case, the large number of Merchants of Light is obviously significant for the operation of the industrial laboratories of Bensalem.

In fact, the Governor of the Strangers' House tells his guests that Merchants of Light

> give us knowledge of the affairs and state of those countries to which they were designed [i.e. assigned], and especially of the sciences, arts, manufactures, and inventions of all the world; and withal . . . bring unto us books, instruments, and patterns of every kind . . .

(III, 146)

When leaving Bensalem the Merchants bring:

> store of victuals, and good quantity of treasure . . . for the buying of such things and rewarding of such persons as they should think fit . . . But thus you see we maintain a trade, not for gold, silver, or jewels; nor for silk; nor for spices; nor any other commodity of matter; but only for God's first creature, which was *Light:* to have *light* (I say) of the growth of all parts of the world.

(III, 146-47)

This light, or knowledge in its raw form, is brought home to be processed into the finished products of scientific principle and invention. By the proportions given, the light of information gathered must account for about one-third of the gross national product of Bensalem's laboratories. Bensalem is clearly a technologically developed nation that depends upon imports of "raw material" from less developed ones.

There is no recognition in the **New Atlantis** that this arrangement does not actually achieve King Solamona's goal: the bounds not of human empire but only of Bensalem's "empire" are enlarged thereby. This is because the Merchants of Light operate secretly, in disguise—they "color themselves under the names of other nations" (III, 146). The vast joke on the world is that Bensalem and its labs are unknown to it. The result of Solamona's interdiction of trade was that the world gradually lost track of Bensalem. The few sailors who happened upon it naturally decided to stay, because things were so pleasant, or else were not believed when they went home; "We know . . . and are ourselves unknown" says the Governor of the Strangers' House. Secrecy, one infers, must insure ridiculously low prices for "light," since the sellers do not know the use value of their products. Secrecy must also compensate

for the vulnerability arising from technologically advanced Bensalem's substantial dependence on the labor and the ingenuity of less developed nations.

Thus, it is not just that Solomon's House does not fulfill its goal; even its limited success actually depends upon the continuing relative backwardness of the world beyond Bensalem and on a necessary technological distance measured between the raw material of fact and the "manufactured" generalization. Foreign backwardness produces not only lower prices but would preclude the advanced technological development by rivals that could threaten Bensalem's security. In short, Bacon has made scientific success dependent upon a kind of invisible exploitation.

A question of scientific freedom also stems from this relationship, since Bacon conceives of the relationship as scientists' exclusive control of information. The members of Solomon's House take an oath of secrecy and have discretion over what information becomes public; this "very eye of this kingdom" sees all the world in a panoptical gaze, yet no eye can penetrate it. As a result, scientific freedom itself becomes possible through and only through exploitation of those who are excluded from the benefits of science; knowledge is a local effect of general ignorance.

The absolute difference between knower and known that insures the freedom and sovereignty of Bensalem's science goes along with a distinctly colonialist trait incubated within the happy Pale: racism. Among Bensalem's subjects are the "strips" or small communities of most of the world's peoples. They live there freely and harmoniously—only because they have been weaned from their inferior ways by the science-based civilization of Bensalem. This becomes clear when we mark how even Joabin's criticism of Europe for its sexual depravity is less harsh than the caricatures with which the Governor of the Stranger's House, the speaker himself, or Joabin dismiss other groups. American Indians are "simple and savage," "rude and ignorant," "poor remnants of the human seed"; the Chinese are "a curious, ignorant, fearful, foolish nation"; Jews "hate the name of Christ, and have a secret inbred rancour against the people amongst whom they live." We also hear of "the Spirit of Fornication," "a little foul ugly Aethiop." On the one hand, the **New Atlantis,** most prominently Bacon's sympathetic portrait of the Jew, Joabin, stands for religious and ethnic toleration; strangers are received with the greatest courtesy and hospitality. But in its weak pluralism, differences can only exist within a larger homogeneity: there are "good" ethnics (the ones who live in Bensalem) and "bad" ones (all the others). Isolation breeds contempt: as Bensalemites gain scientific knowledge, they demonize those whom they themselves exclude from this knowledge. Here scientific progress breeds colonialist attitudes; toleration is a local function of the belief in foreigners' general depravity.

Bensalem itself is a hierarchical and traditional society, with a King, powerful and aloof scientists, grave pomp of ceremony and dress, social orders or classes (e.g., the Governor of the Strangers' House speaks of "the vulgar sort of mariners"), and poverty, which is to be relieved both by family and state. Presumably there is no large, displaced, discontented, "masterless" population as in Bacon's contemporary England, and no endemic, widespread, and ever-increasing poverty as in England—but Bacon is as noted before quite gingerly on specifics. Christianity is general, other faiths tolerated. Judging by the description of the Feast of the Family, extended, patriarchal, and authoritarian families seem to be the major social and economic unit. Perhaps in Bensalem science is also an ideological tool that, for instance, fixed patriarchal gender relations in strictly licit and heterosexual form. As Bacon's scientific gender imagery suggests elsewhere, women actually embody nature as the objects of scrutiny of what Bacon called "masculine" science. If so, the living of this very symbolic imagery would insure the matchless "chasteness" of Bensalem: if nuptial male desire is a figure for authentic scientific inquiry, then prostitution, adultery, and homosexuality, which we are told do not exist in Bensalem, are very bad sciences indeed.

In any case, and whether or not it includes actual training in science for the general population, the scientific atmosphere of Bensalem apparently encourages a disciplined internalization of authority, a willing acceptance of hierarchy and order. "Reverence of a man's self is, next religion, the chiefest bridle of all vices," says Joabin. People are courteous, obedient, and industrious, gravely ritualistic and orderly in their celebrations and assemblies. A work ethic seems to leave little time for getting into trouble, as does the willingness to be forever being called away on business. Science is clearly a force for social stability rather than change.

II

As a genre, the Renaissance utopia is related to the travel accounts and to the colonialist aspirations of the age of exploration. Michael Drayton's poem "To the Virginian Voyage" (which clearly precedes the hardships actually encountered after 1607) expresses a typical combination of colonialist hopes motivating explorers from Columbus and Vespucci on: political domination, exploitation of natural resources, and utopian community in an earthly paradise:

> To get the pearl and gold,
>   And ours to hold
> Virginia
> Earth's only paradise . . .
>   (11. 21-25).

More specifically, the *New Atlantis* represents an Englishman's thinking about colonization in the context of the Spanish example, and it also suggests how a figure of colonization can apply to other relationships of power.

The name "Solomon" powerfully links Bacon's story to Spanish colonization and to fabulous legends of a rich Southern Pacific land, an Australia or Ophir. Richard Hakluyt's compendium of travel accounts includes that of the Spanish captive Lopez Váz on the Solomon Islands discovered by Mendaña in 1568: they are called "the Isles of Salomon" after "those from whence Salomon fetched Gold to adorn the Temple of Jerusalem." Many contemporaries of Bacon also knew the widely circulated memorial of a later explorer of the Solomons, Ferdinand Quirós, who wanted to found an egalitarian "New Jerusalem" there—an apt model for Bacon's own South Sea, Christian, Solomonic utopia, trading however not gold, but "light." Quirós, like other Spaniards going west, sailed from Peru, and so the beginning of the *New Atlantis,* which is narrated by a Spanish colonist or trader who gets lost in the South Pacific, stresses the parallel to Spanish aspirations: "We sailed from Peru (where we had continued by the space of one whole year) for China and Japan by the South Sea."

Bacon had few illusions about the utopian possibilities of empire itself: "a thing rare and hard to keep." The non-empire of Bensalem may reflect Bacon's ambivalent and ambiguous attitudes about foreign domination expressed near the time when he wrote the *New Atlantis* or at least put it into its present form in about 1623. Undertaking an empire is the subject of a list of antitheses for and against in the *De Dignitate et Augmentis Scientiarum* (1623); in the essay **"Of the Vicissitudes of Things"** (1625) empires rise and fall according to historical cycles, and enervate the wealth and spirit of subject nations. In a letter of advice to the Duke of Buckingham (a bit earlier, 1616), Bacon is skeptical about empire, saying that subjects cannot be compelled to fight outside Britain. Whereas Bacon admires the ability of the Spanish to govern so much territory with so few native Spaniards, in *An Advertisement Touching a Holy War* (1629), he is repelled by their methods. Finally, in a famous passage in the *Novum Organum* (1620) Bacon opposes the aspiration to political empire to that of "extending the bounds of human empire" through science.

Bacon's work on the merits of a "holy" war against the Turks is actually reported to have been written just before Bacon took up the *New Atlantis;* immediately before that piece, Bacon supposedly wrote a set of recommendations about war with Spain that addressed the threat of Spain's colonial empire. Bacon thus moves from considering war against Spain to war in common with Spain to the *New Atlantis,* where a Spaniard reports on the visit to a peace-loving utopia—and then Bacon finally prepares a Latin translation of the *New Atlantis* so Spaniards and other Europeans could read it. In this moderation of sentiment science becomes not just the basis of some alternative, non-imperial and distinctively British empire to oppose the Spanish, but the basis of some more general European colonial project.

Bacon's positive views on colonization provide a promising way to understand this non-empire. After initial skepticism, Bacon became an investor not only in the Virginia Company but the Northwest Passage, Newfoundland, and East India Companies, and produced **"Of Plantations,"** which distills the experience of the Virginia colonists. He also wrote to both Elizabeth and James concerning Irish colonization. Although Bacon did not view English colonization as a utopian project, he recognized the importance of propaganda for inducing prospective colonists. And, like other Englishmen, he regarded English colonization as an expression of divine providence. He displays a consistently optimistic and peaceful view of colonial possibilities that is sharply crossed by actual events, such as the Indian massacre of 1622 in Virginia that resulted in a policy of "total war" against them.

There are contradictions in Bacon's position on colonization (contradictions typical of colonial discourse) that parallel the Bensalmites' self-deception about a "human empire" that means "our empire." Rather than "solve" these contradictions in a wish-fulfilling solution, the scientifically ordered world of Bensalem simply renders them harmless to the colonizers. A seemingly straightforward sentiment in **"Of Plantations"** embodies one such contradiction:

> I like a plantation in a pure soil; that is, where people are not displanted to the end to plant in others. For else it is rather an extirpation, than a plantation.

> (VI, 457)

Despite mythology dear to the hearts of colonizers for centuries after Bacon wrote, the New World could not represent in any sense "pure," that is, "virgin" soil (nor of course did Ireland); nor is it possible to determine from a standpoint outside a given culture in what sense an area is part of a native social world. Bacon's is a well-meaning sentiment that easily leads (and led) to misunderstanding and disaster.

Bacon speaks of the Irish in the same way that American Indians were commonly spoken of. In 1602, after an extended and bloody rebellion, they are "wild and barbarous"; by 1617 colonization directed by King James has supposedly brought them "from savage and barbarous customs to humanity and civility," their country "reclaimed from desolation and desert." Of

course, this new estimate could not survive many more years until oppression produced new rebellions to be characterized by English opinion as Bacon and others had formerly done. Yet in 1608-09 Bacon recommended to James new colonial efforts in Ireland on the ground that they "shall need no sacrifice expiatory in blood." This naive idealism—or diplomatic doublespeak—is elaborated in the comparison Bacon makes between the Irish plantation, scientific discovery, and divine creation through the concept of a new beginning. As in arts and sciences the first inventor, as in works of God the creation, and as in nature the birth, "so in Kingdoms the plantation is of more dignity and merit than all that followeth." This merit of beginning anew in Ireland, Bacon argues, would take advantage of God's providence in laying Ireland open to the English, enable emigration of English poor, prevent invasions launched from Ireland, and enrich Britain by developing the natural resources of this "unpolished" territory. The assumption behind the idea of a new beginning is, again, that, with perfect purity and integrity, an original seed of civilization can be benevolently planted behind paling impervious to a savage chaos beyond it. For here, like the earth "without form, and void" at the creation, the Irish apparently have no qualities or interests apart from those that may be imputed by the colonizers. As with the contrast between the civilized races of Bensalem and their barbarous counterparts elsewhere, the contrast here beween the light and the darkness in English colonial aspirations is complete.

Moreover, Bacon's image of the new plantation is not far from his image of Solomon's House. It also is a beneficiary of divine providence which, securely secreted from danger, knows all and has total discretion over the use of ideas and goods it develops from the "natural resources" outside it in intellectually colonized areas. The colonial introduction of laws and government to Ireland, Bacon finally tells James, recalls Orpheus's taming of stones and woods. A short time later in *The Wisdom of the Ancients* (1609) Bacon would contrast this mythological motif to Orpheus's attempted retrieval of Eurydice from Hades. There the former motif represents "civil and moral" knowledge, the latter the far nobler scientific knowledge that could render the former partly obsolete. Perhaps then the science of the *New Atlantis* could be thought of as representing a way around the harsh realities, or at least the inevitable uncertainties, of civil and moral knowledge as applied to English colonization. Similarly, speaking against too much exotic and luxurious trade with the East Indies, Bacon tells the Duke of Buckingham that England's fisheries are her true "Indian wealth." Beyond even fisheries is the trade of the *New Atlantis,* "not for gold, silver, or jewels; nor for silk; nor for spices . . . but only for God's first creature, which was *Light* . . .". Through science, Bensalem can exploit its neighbors and at the same time avoid turmoil, insecurity, and bloodshed. Is it possible a scientifically advanced England, or even Europe, could launch such a colonial enterprise?

In 1668, when world leadership in trade was tipping from Holland to England, Joseph Glanvill published a survey of new knowledge called *Plus Ultra* (a phrase with considerable imperial connotations of its own). Glanvill hails Bacon as the originator of experimental philosophy and inspirer of the Royal Society. In a following passage Glanvill seems to envision precisely the kind of advantageous terms of trade resulting from exclusive scientific and technological development that Bacon had imagined in the *New Atlantis*. As in Bacon's work, Glanvill's ideal of human empire over nature slides smoothly to that of trade empire.

> Another section of the usefulness of experimental philosophy, as to the empire of man over inferior creatures . . . the goods of mankind may be much increased by the naturalist's insight into trades . . . the naturalist may much advantage men, by exciting and assisting their curiosity to discover, take notice, and make use of the home-bred riches and advantages of particular countries, and to increase their number, by the transferring thither those of others . . . a ground of expecting considerable things from experimental philosophy is given by those things which have been found out by illiterate tradesmen, or lighted on by chance . . . (104-05).

Bacon called Merchants of Light those who engrossed experimental philosophy by "transferring thither" the "home-bred riches and advantages" of other countries, and by spying on "illiterate tradesmen."

Glanvill's tradesmen are local as well as foreign; and Bacon had often emphasized that the intellectual elite needs to humble itself to the level of the artisan in order to develop technological know-how. Indeed, in this respect the Merchants of Light represent not a colonial trade but an ideal relationship between artisan and scientist. This explains why Bacon seems to make Bensalem so dependent on trade in information; after all one would expect that after a time its very sophistication would render this trade with ordinary artisans obsolete. But Bacon responds to his contemporary situation in which scholars disdained the intellectual content of the work of mechanics and artisans. The relationship the author of the *New Atlantis* would like to see is on a colonial model. The secrets of lower-class artisans, cheerful no doubt in their humble labors and modest rewards, may be exploited at will by a learned elite who find profit in those labors and comfort in the laborers' continuing humility.

The domestic character of Bensalem thus offers a fantasy solution for the existing inefficiency, poverty, unrest, and opposition to royal authority. Manuel and Manuel [in *Utopian Thought in the Western World*,

1979] trace Solomon's House back to Sir Humphrey Gilbert's proposal for Queen Elizabeth's Academy, designed to train a civil service elite in a more efficient and practical manner than the schools did. A.F.C. Wallace [in *The Social Context of Innovation: Bureaucrats, Families and Heroes in the Early Industrial Revolution, as Forseen in Bacon's New Atlantis*, 1982] points out the similarity between Solomon's House and such vast complexes as the Royal Office of Ordance's navy yards, and finds in the patriarchal extended family of Bensalem a model of the royal-monopoly-protected family business increasingly important to the English economy after Bacon wrote. As Solicitor General and Lord Chancellor, Bacon fought to preserve the royal prerogative of granting patents and monopolies, which provided the King with much-needed revenue out of the ingenuity of his subjects. Bacon was engaged in a bitter Parliamentary fight over the important silk and gold thread monopoly just before he was impeached—an event that must have delighted the commercial interests who opposed monopolies.

In the *New Atlantis* Bacon generally wishes to demonstrate to conservative, potentially sympathetic readers that science may not be disruptive, but may eliminate sedition and even increase both authority and national wealth. Bensalem's common people fill the prescription Bacon offered in the essays **"Of Seditions and Troubles"** and **"Of the True Greatness of Kingdoms and Estates:"** hard-working and self-sustaining, more frugal than affluent. Their farms seem secure from threats like that of enclosure for pasture, as Bacon argued England's should be—here against what came to be royal policy. While Bacon thought the common people were changeable and even rebelliously depraved—certainly not fit for self-rule—he did not fear them unless, as in Bacon's contemporary England, they suffered greatly and, worse, became subject to the inflammation of what Bacon considered could be only opportunists. Thus, whereas science provided material relief for the people of Bensalem, science and religion would provide an atmosphere in which authority could be internalized in a work ethic, obedience, restraint, and racism. With such internalization, there would be less need in England for displays and exercise of physical power. Toleration could increase; substantial existing fears about popular assembly and riotous, blasphemous popular festivals would be needless if festivals were themselves orderly and expressed not misrule but acquiescence. Bensalem thus offers a glimpse of Michel Foucault's modern "disciplinary technologies" [in *Discipline and Punish: The Birth of the Prison,* 1977] in operation, internal codes that characterize the modern age, and that render a degree of physical force and theatrical display of power obsolete. These have supposedly enabled modern democracies to arise often without overturning existing power structures, that is, by getting people to want what the powerful want them to, or what some more impersonal structure of power requires.

Not until the Restoration was the new science firmly in the hands of a social and economic elite, and able fully to protect the stability of social relations, as Bacon apparently wished. During the Interregnum radical thinkers who advocated a more egalitarian science pushed men like Robert Boyle and Thomas Sprat to more conservative positions in which science was called upon, as John Jacob says [in *Politics and Culture in Early Modern Europe: Essays in Honor of H.G. Koenigsberger,* Phyllis Mack and Margaret C. Jacob, eds., 1986], to preserve the "existing hierarchical structure of society against subversion at the hands of the people." Bacon's English Orpheus of government who can tame the savage Irishman, and his yet greater scientific Orpheus who can tame nature and all people, both find a Restoration echo in Christopher Wren's *Pantalia.* There the "Orphean Charm" of science provides not only an outlet for distracting passions and a distraction from the miseries and injustices of society, but a discipline that makes "obedience" "not only the public but the private felicity of every subject."

Finally, the non-empire of Bensalem finds a startling counterpart today in what many call neo-colonial economic empires that have outlived the colonial ones. Post-industrial capitalist society depends on the production of information rather than goods and on the control of information by the technologically sophisticated global reach of transnational corporations, banks, aid agencies, and weapons. Like Bensalem, these entities can preserve traditional relationships of power through the promotion of "information dependency," computerized invasions of privacy, and increasing privatization of information ownership. Commands flow out from developed countries—the product designs and the plans for computerized assembly—to so-called "developing" countries for production, often under miserable conditions. World-views flow out; eighty per cent of the world's information originates from five Western news agencies. The capital-backed power of U.S. mass culture penetrates into the most distant corner of the earth. On the other hand, there is a reverse net flow of profitable information from undeveloped countries: contemporary Merchants of Lights such as satellites can transmit information about mineral deposits in an underdeveloped region of the world, deposits unknown to the people living near them, so that private companies may secure profitable mineral rights cheaply. The spread of computer technology today itself allegedly brings nations into an order of information dependency.

In fact, the post-industrial information order may be one of the truest realizations of Bacon's dictum "knowledge is power" and, in particular, of the unbalanced trade in information that sustains his utopian island. The most general ideological meaning to be found in this trade involves what must have been a moment when Bacon was able to think beyond the limits of mercantile economics toward capitalism. According to mercantilist principles, as Bacon states in the essay **"Of Seditions and Troubles,"** "the increase of any estate must be upon the foreigner (for whatsoever is somewhere gotten is somewhere lost)." Yet when Merchants of Light take from the foreigner, the loser still keeps; such can be the nature of information. Here is another sense in which the *New Atlantis* offers a wish-fulfilling solution to what was seen as a fact of economic life, the malignant ratio of mercantilist trade. But this fantasy solution also suggests the pleasant and at times self-serving ideology of capitalism as an alternative to that malignant ratio: the seller can receive a "fair" (i.e., "market") price for goods and services, and then wealth can actually be created through manufacturing by means of those goods plus new technology. Thus, in a foreshadowing of this ideology, Solomon's House creates, rather than transfers, goods and knowledge, after paying (when necessary) for materials.

Denise Albanese (essay date 1990)

SOURCE: "The *New Atlantis* and the Uses of Utopia," in *ELH,* Vol. 57, No. 3, Fall, 1990, pp. 503-28.

[*In the following excerpt, Albanese describes several utopian aspects of the* New Atlantis.]

In 1608 Bacon prepared a brief for King James to encourage the "plantation" of Ireland. In its course, he draws a comparison between its proposed structure of governance and that designed for Virginia,whose settlement had been fitfully pursued: "The second [proposition] is that your Majesty would make a correspondency between the commission there [in Ireland], and a council of plantation here [in London]. Wherein I warrant myself by the precedent of the like council of plantation for Virginia; an enterprise in my opinion differing as much from this, as Amadis de Gaul differs from Caesar's Commentaries." The advice here is pragmatic and direct—but takes a strange detour by likening Jacobean imperialism to written, indeed, literary texts. As the reference to Caesar suggests, Ireland is "another Britain," and the British may take Caesar's part in a war represented as discursive strategy, whose impetus, and hence ontology, are linear.

Amadis de Gaule in this context seems to define itself by opposition. A massive romance written in Spain by at least five different authors, then amplified in France before appearing in England, it suggests a range of alternative values: not the tight focus of Roman *imperium* but the ambition of early Renaissance colonialism, not linearity but narrative brachiolation, not chronicle but romance. And thus Virginia, too, is defined by opposition: it is a complicated text already inscribed by the hand of European incursion, but not yet entirely the site of conquest. Instead, it becomes, in Bacon's analogy, a stage for imaginative transformation, for fantasy, for fiction.

As Bacon's comparisons indicate, social and political enterprises can be recast by means of fictions. To impose fictional form on the world of actual practices is to render those practices at once formal and ideal, and thus to cloak them in a coherence the more useful for literature's complex and oblique relationship to the production of ideology. Although the domain claimed for poetry by Renaissance theorists is the aesthetic and the didactic, in such cases as this its form can be invoked pre-emptively, even authoritatively, to legitimate hegemonic practices. This is precisely the agenda of Bacon's **"Discourse"**: written to persuade the king that Ireland can be subjugated to English needs, it produces the literary both as a warrant for settlement and as a blind for the real acts of violence such settlement necessitates. In the lines I have initially quoted, Virginia, too, figures as a fiction, as the romantic narrative of colonialist ease, to whose plot one more episode, one more encounter, can always be added. The open-ended form of romance at once authorizes and mystifies the work of domination Bacon proposes, and provides aesthetic distance from the world of colonialist practices. This disavowal of the need for closure, this pre-emptive use of fictional form, permeates the ***New Atlantis:*** it is an ideological move that enables the scientific to be produced under the ostensible sign of the literary, and results in an act of discursive colonization that tropes the cultural agendas of Jacobean imperialism to which I have initially alluded.

Of all Bacon's texts, the ***New Atlantis*** can most readily be categorized as fictional. Despite its romantic aspects, however, it seeks alignment with More's *Utopia* rather than with *Amadis de Gaule,* which is to say with a political fiction that it also politic in its fictionality. *Utopia* maintains a difficult balance between revolutionary ideality and practical impossibility, simultaneously affirming and denying its radical agenda. More's text operates by invoking specific historical conditions in order to resolve the cultural anxieties attendant upon those conditions; at the same time, it engages ideological premises without overtly displaying its own ideological legitimation. Hence the paradox of More's *serio ludere.* In discussing Louis Marin's elaboration in *Utopics* upon the bipolarity of More, Fredric Jameson has noted the tendency of the text hallmarked as "utopian" to concede—indeed, to thematize—the conditions of its own emergence: "All genuine Utopias betray a complicated apparatus which is designed to 'neutralize' the topical allusion at the same time that it produces and reinforces it."

Thus defined, the utopian fiction problematizes the culture out of which it emerges, throws the forms of power it ascribes to that problematized culture off balance. What has been called More's communism, for an obvious instance, undermines the ground of the Henrician state, and thereby makes obsolete prior systems of material worth or social privilege. But it is a revolution on paper, contained within (and by) the purview of the text. To put it less starkly, the manifold nodes of impossibility/opposition Marin details within More's text guarantee that formalism prevails in its engagement with ideology. This formalism (which may conceivably be inscribed within Renaissance humanism proper) eschews hortatory social agendas by offsetting critique with textual play, by loosening the bounds of representation.

Yet its unexhausted capacity to reconfigure specific historical situations means that utopian form can be directed away from the production of paradox. In that case, the equipoise it maintains between the acknowledgement (which is also relief) of circumstantial anxiety, and the recognition that the social remedies it proposes for that anxiety are impossible, which is to say beyond its ken, can mutate into a simulacrum of utopian form. It sees the ideal it proposes as obtainable, and that ultimately sees texts as social machines in a way radically different from Renaissance notions of *dulce et utile.* A text "mutated" in this way would bear the apparent (formal) signs of the utopia, but would abandon the discursive stasis that the *Utopia* possesses, and presents as a condition of its own existence. If the ideal a utopian text embodies can be, not just apprehended as a formalized solution, but achieved as social practice, the mechanism for change from the present imperfect to the future perfect must inhere in the narrative. Certainly most of Bacon's writings concerned to propagandize the scientific offer themselves as operants of the type I have sketched: their efforts to repair the defects of the Fall may well bespeak profound (and maybe pre-revolutionary) nostalgia, but within the Baconian program they are also a call to arms—or at least to research.

This, too, is the case with the ***New Atlantis***. Insofar as it promotes Baconian philosophy, and thus works to produce in actual practice what it summons in the representational, the text reconfigures its own medium, invokes the literary only to present itself as utopian (a better word might be progressive) social agenda rather than as *Utopian* text. In introducing such philosophical inquiry as the ground upon which society is to be erected, the narrative—which depends upon the cultural role of literature, the legacy of humanism and, indeed, of More, for its force—seeks to replace the self-conscious fiction with the empirical structures of the emergent science. The ***New Atlantis*** belies the *Utopia* even as it invites juxtaposition with it: unlike More's, Bacon's text is ready, as the Virginian colony is, to take on all voyagers, to convert all readers.

I have suggested colonialism is more than a thematized element within the *New Atlantis:* it is a defining move in the emergence of modern scientific practice from within late Renaissance culture. The process of resorption and transformation the text performs with regard to its humanist authority becomes a discursive reproduction of European practice in the New World. The connection between the so-called New Science and the New World is repeatedly urged in the sixteenth and seventeenth centuries, not only within the Baconian program but within Continental natural philosophy as well. Both expeditions to America and scientific programs propagandize themselves as voyages out, into uncharted territory, where the sense of excitement that attaches to new ventures covers over the work of domination that underwrites exploration of the globe and of nature both. The importance accorded to novelty, and the closeness of the scientific enterprise to the colonial one, is attested to by the frontispiece to the *Great Instauration*. In the foreground of the engraving, a lone ship sails out through the Pillars of Hercules, the boundaries of the known world and hence symbolic of known experience. The eye is thus invited to focus on a moment of transition, poised between the old and the new and informed by both; this ship so engrosses the attention that another ship at the far left, about to slip from the field of representation, can barely be discerned. This other ship's position on the page marks, in turn, the position within late Renaissance culture, and its dominant forms of meaning, of the Baconian enterprise. It reproduces a moment of cultural liminality: a movement, discursively posited rather than physically apprehended, at the horizon of experience. Beyond that horizon, experience itself becomes novel—becomes, indeed, experiment. The distant ship is thus the palimpsest of prior texts as they make themselves felt in the *New Atlantis*.

The analogies between frontispiece and text, colonialism and natural philosophy, insist, at base, upon culture as production and as representation, and upon the need to see unprecedented experiences, and to devise unprecedented structures of knowledge, in terms of prior apprehensible form. Further, these analogies insist on the "literariness" of that form: a vexed concept, given that the idea of literature as profession and as cultural production is itself emergent in the late Renaissance, but one which, nevertheless, pervades the travel accounts as it does Bacon's discussions of colonialism. In his texts, and most especially in the *New Atlantis,* colonialism becomes both *topos* and trope, a culturally available validation of the novelty proclaimed by his philosophical program. But the relationship is not linear, since the *New Atlantis* recasts the work of colonization parodically, through an inversion governed by its utopianism. It recounts a voyage to an unknown land where, as with More's ideal citizens, the natives are presented as superior to the newcomers in religion, governance, and knowledge. Bensalemite knowledge,

based on a fetishized factuality, excludes the artifice of fiction from its ken. Yet Bacon's text promotes this system through utopian narrative, and thereby alienates that narrative in effect from its originary positioning. With the *New Atlantis* the discursive terrain of humanism, dominated as it is by *litterae,* by literature, is appropriated by the emergent ideology of science.

Through the warrant of its colonized utopianism, the *New Atlantis* also reproduces the culture of Jacobean England, transformed to fit the ideological contours of the scientific. Just as the encounter with previously unknown civilizations in the Americas necessitated rethinking the stipulated plenitude of the European world, so too does the imagined existence of the Bensalemites provoke a re-examination of English seventeenth-century society. The space both created and cleared by the premise of a utopianism based on natural philosophy changes the ground of authority: religious, civil, and, ultimately, monarchical power are occluded and displaced by the inquisitional, by the power to probe nature. The redrawn lines of authority derive from the specific character of the Baconian enterprise, in which the capacity to see accurately is the mark of social and moral eminence. This ability to survey nature constitutes the dynamism that unbalances the utopian, and that determines both Baconian praxis and the narrative agenda of the *New Atlantis*. In this text, seeing is more than believing: it is knowing, and that knowledge, co-extensive with the act of reading and generated by it, brings the Baconian ideal into the arena of potentiality. If, as I have initially suggested, fictions provide the means by which cultures engage in a complex and ideologically-laden form of self-fashioning, then the *New Atlantis* attests proleptically, if not teleologically, to the moment when cultural fictions give precedence to science.

I have indicated that the romantic open-endedness which sees Virginia as *Amadis de Gaule* has a bearing upon the realm of material practices. But it is not only written forms that indicate Bacon's stake in the structures of desire in which the New World was enmeshed. In 1609, he became a shareholder in the Virginia Compnay, and a member of its London-based council. If at times the New World was to bear the freight of romance, Bacon was also one of those who saw the fiction's economic potential.

II

A brief rehearsal of the *New Atlantis* makes clear the pertinence of an imperialism constelled with empiricism. Spanish sailors attempt to sail for China and Japan, recapitulating the voyage, and in some sense the fortuitous miscarriage, of Columbus. When they lose their course, as he did, they find Bensalem, the "New Atlantis," instead. Once there, they are made familiar with the habits of the Bensalemites, most especially its College of the Six Days' Works (also known as Salomon's House); this institution, designed to promote the acquisition of philosophical knowledge, is the textual realization of the academy that Bacon wished James I to patronize. After describing the college, the narrative breaks off, "unperfected."

The nationality of the sailors, and the miscarried itinerary they pursue, inevitably suggest that part of the *New Atlantis*'s philosophical agenda is best accomplished by recasting the discovery of the New World. Yet no sooner is the identification of New Atlantis with America made than it begins to rest uneasily. The New World is not truly "new" at all, being but "the great Atlantis (that you call America)" (3:141) rediscovered; further, its very novelty as discovery is called into question, since Atlantis/America was known to all the ancients, and continued to be known by the Bensalemites, their closest neighbors and the purported contemporaries of Bacon's English audience. Indeed, the inhabitants of America have not always been so uncouth as European explorers had found them, as the governor in charge of the newcomers explains:

> The great Atlantis was utterly lost and destroyed: not by a great earthquake . . . but by a particular deluge or inundation. . . . But it is true that the same inundation was not deep; not past forty foot, in most places from the ground: so that although it destroyed man and beast generally, yet some few wild inhabitants of the wood escaped. . . . So as marvel you not at the thin population of America, nor at the rudeness and ignorance of the people; for you must account your inhabitants of America as a young people; younger a thousand years, at the least, than the rest of the world. . . . For the poor remnant of human seed which remained in their mountains peopled the country again slowly, by little and little; and being simple and savage people, (not like Noah and his sons, which was the chief family of the earth,) they were not able to leave letters, arts, and civility to their posterity.

(3:142-43)

This passage manifests an exceedingly complex reaction to the discursive challenge of the New World: its condescension towards American natives affirms an enabling, Eurocentric racial hierarchy, while the account itself shifts authority from European to the New Atlantan. The Bensalemite governor's disquisition is both authoritative in tone and comprehensive in scope, providing a corrective to ancient mythology, integrating the New World into the biblical by means of allusion, and locating the development of its culture in the schema of universal history. What renders this Bensalemite's narrative of origins so effective within the larger framework is the evident superiority of his own society—not just compared to the natives of America, but also to the Spaniards. The easy assurance of the governor's cultural determinism reverses the logic of

colonial discourse practiced by the Spaniards and the English alike: as the denizen of a new America, that governor should be the object of this possessive scrutiny, rather than its commanding subject. Here, the closeness of America to Bensalem—by the force of the geography in the text as well as of the historical models that inform it—is the sign of opposition. The reversal is key to understanding the inflection given to colonialist domination within the text: the oppression of otherness which is elsewhere the focus of colonization is here transformed into a visual interrogation, and transferred to a native population phantasmatically more suave than the Europeans who "discover" them.

From the moment of the first encounter, it is, instead, the Spaniards who are scrutinized, contained and regulated by their apparently benign hosts. When they first try to come ashore, the sailors are warded away: "straightways we saw divers of the people, with bastons in their hands, as it were forbidding us to land." When they are finally brought ashore they are kept at close quarters by an officer: "lifting up his cane a little, (as they do when they give any charge or command,) [he] said to us 'Ye are to know that the custom of the land requireth [that] you are to keep within door for three days'"; and even when this ban is lifted, they can never go more than a mile and a half from the city. They are also told of "laws of secrecy concerning strangers" that will render any discursive exchange but fragmentary, and always controlled by the Bensalemites, who because of secret envoys to Europe know more of Europe than the Spaniards can ever know of them. The seamen are aware of the constraints under which they have been put, and attempt to discern the reason behind them: they know they are the objects of a detached scrutiny, a desire to penetrate appearances, that has turnedinto a form of surveillance: "For they have by commandment (though in form of courtesy) cloistered us within these walls for three days: who knoweth whether it be not to take some taste of our manners and conditions? and if they find them bad, to banish us straightways; if good, to give us further time. For these men that they have given us for attendance may withal have an eye upon us." The Spaniards, surveyors of the New World, have become the surveyed.

III

What do the Bensalemites watch for? And by what warrant? To answer those questions requires us to understand the structures of knowledge and authority summoned by the text's version of the utopian agenda, to comprehend, in short, the rhetorical distance traveled between Bacon's Jacobean England and its fictional counterpart. The fiction that a voyage of discovery is being reproduced is aligned both in form and practice with Bacon's scientific program, a point to which I shall later return. More immediately, the fiction takes the constituent elements of the Jacobean social realm and intercalates them within the new-found one by mapping out analogous institutions in Bensalem. Forms and observances are subtly transmuted, distilled through the operation of a fictional matrix into components informed by the social and political practices of the Jacobean state, and yet ideologically congruent with the investigation of nature propagandized by the text. The received coexists with the projective, and the resultant version of Bensalemite society is at once familiar and radically estranged.

Consider the Bensalemites' Christianity. It first serves in the text as yet another instance of reversed colonialism, with the natives' conversion an already accomplished fact—and at that by revelation, the very antithesis of the laborious and linguistically incoherent mission of salvation usual in the period. Even before the Papal edict of 1622, which mandated the *Congregatio de propaganda fidei*—and which thus expanded Catholic dominion into the New World as a counterbalance to the burgeoning Protestantism of the Old—the Spaniards had invoked the Church as warrant for their colonization of America. And as the title of Samuel Purchas's 1625 collection *Purchas His Pilgrimes* suggests, the English, too, connected the annexation of territory with the conversion of souls: to refer to explorers as "pilgrims," and their journeys pilgrimages, binds piety to empire, and casts sanctity upon endeavors whose most significant products were material.

The work performed by Christianity in Bacon's text corresponds to its deployment in the New World within late Renaissance culture. But instead of a mandate for physical colonization, Christianity becomes the code for an intellectual imperialism: a desire to take and absorb and control is legitimated by the sign of the cross. Hence its presence at the close of the Bensalemites' first message to the Spanish sailors; despite the peremptoriness of that message—the Spaniards profess themselves troubled because they are summarily warned off, and forbidden to land—the sign of the cross is "a great rejoicing, and as it were a certain presage of good" (3:130). The cruciform sign overrides all ambiguity. Like the vision of Constantine, its presence signifies ultimate favor, indeed, the power to conquer.

In Bensalem, it is the phenomenal world of nature, rather than the natural world of savages, that stands as the object of conquest. The cross equates Bensalem's suavity and moral superiority with its domination of nature; it then follows as evidence of that superiority that their Christianity forecasts their scientific accomplishment. Such a basis of affirmation is circular: the conventional European definition of moral superiority presupposes Christianity, and thus Christianity cannot yet be adduced as support for a goodness that, when the sailors first read the communication, remains to be proven. The text allows simultaneity to stand in for

causality, and thus argues for a natural philosophy endowed with conventional religious values by textually juxtaposing the two elements.

Such rifts can only be seen retrospectively; still, throughout the *New Atlantis* the pious philosophy of nature is an elusive production. At no time does this become more apparent than when the Spaniards are told how the Bensalemites have come to Christianity independent of apostolic mission or latter-day conversion. This moment also provides evidence of the structures of governance controlling the text, and of the inextricability of the spectacular and the authoritarian in the seventeenth century. When the governor of the Stranger's House relates the origins of Bensalemite religion, his utterance is highly marked with the signs of its own artificiality; to put it simply, he tells a tale. The coming of Christianity to Bensalem thus stands as strongly differentiated from other kinds of information imparted to the Spaniards: the governor's recitative has a formulaic beginning—"it came to pass"—and a cadenced ending—"and thus was this land saved from infidelity." All that lies between these two phrases stands in support of the mass conversion as narrative (and hence as cultural) exception, by reminding the seamen again and again of its very constructedness. The scene of revelation is carefully set, and subsequent details are ordered to culminate in the surprise of the revelation itself. The Spaniards are thereby made witness to what is, crudely speaking, a dramatic event, whose denouement resolves the suspense created by the artifice of the narrative.

But the analogy to drama goes even deeper, for the scene of revelation itself contains a "spectacle." A "pillar of light," surmounted by the (transcendental) cross, appears at sea; the inhabitants of the coastal city Renfusa gather around, become its audience—but they cannot reach it in their boats, which stand "all about as in a theatre." Nevertheless, one ship is allowed to approach, and it contains a Father of the House of Salomon, the philosophical institution that is the glory of Bensalem. When he rows to the pillar, he finds a watertight cedar chest that opens of its own accord. The chest is the engine of revelation, for it contains Scripture, other religious writings unknown to Europe, and a letter ordaining that the landing-place of the ark would be granted salvation. The people of Renfusa see the action clearly, but they, like any group of spectators, like any audience at a play, are constrained from entering the stage, from crossing over the formal boundary that demarcates spectacle from experience, the seen from the lived-through. The appearance of the pillar of light, which is the discovery of the Scripture, defines the Renfusans as a chosen community, yet it excludes them from direct participation and apprehension; save that their knowledge is optical rather than auditory, their knowledge of revelation is but little different from the Spaniards'. The Renfusans are marginalized even as they are blessed.

The Salomonic Father, however, is not marginal to the spectacle but, rather, part of it; his escape from the general paralysis indicates such boundaries as separate audience from performance can be crossed as a prerogative of power. The Father's actions valorize the inquisitional, insofar as he sets forth to investigate what at first sight is but an exceptional phenomenon of nature. The text at this juncture proclaims the Father's philosophical college "the very eye of [the] kingdom," and thereby banishes any presumed opposition between the scrutinizing practices of the Baconian scientist and the capacity for moral enlightenment. His pious initiative defines the centrality of the college to the spiritual life of Bensalem; for the moment, however, his singularity overrides his corporate identity. He alone of the crowd truly views the spectacle of the cross correctly, truly ascribes it the proper divine significance in spite of its ambiguity. He alone knows that he participates in an act of divine revelation: "I do here acknowledge and testify before this people, that the thing which we now see before our eyes is thy Finger and a true Miracle." He is central participant in the scene of revelation because he helps to produce it, because his presence at the event is part of its reason for being. By comparison, his countrymen are but mere consumers. As Stephen Orgel has similarly argued [in *The Illusion of Power: Political Theater in the English Renaissance,* 1975] concerning the monarch of the Jacobean masque, the Father is uniquely capable of mobilizing the spectacle, because he alone provides it the principle of intelligibility.

The Collegian's exceptional percipience raises questions about the site of authority in Bacon's Atlantan society: if the Father presides at a moment of such fundamental importance, who can be set over him? But preliminary to this question is the issue of the spectacle's intelligibility: what cultural work does it perform, and for whom? At first reading, the spectacle seems principally to insist that Bensalem is exceptional precisely because its Christianity is revealed, immediate, rather than discursive; this is certainly the point of the tale as told to the Spaniards. Yet the Salomonic Father prays to a "Lord God of Heaven and Earth" and knows the ends of miracles from books before he has ever set eyes on Scripture. The college of which he is a member is named after an Old Testament king at its founding, but that founding antedates the miracle at Renfusa. The Bensalemites do not live under the Old Covenant, for the Hebrews settled among them are classed with the Indians and the Persians; for all that, they seem to have prior knowledge of the basis of Christianity. Since More's foundational text had shown it possible to represent a society distinct from (if not alien to) received Christian doctrine, the *New Atlantis* is not forced into orthodoxy through the tacit coercion of precedent.

On the contrary. The scene of revelation is an act of mystification predicated upon the explanatory power of aesthetic modes in the Renaissance. The dramatic markers invoked to set off revelation from the fabric of the quotidian underscore it as exceptional—but the nature of that exception derives just as much from the differing epistemological claims it makes as from any sense of the Bensalemites' favored status with respect to the divine. Seen against the broader context of seventeenth-century culture, the tale of revelation responds to pervasive cultural anxieties about the congruence of piety and the interrogation of nature, which amounted to human attempts to compass the province of the divine. The Renfusan set-piece explains by declining to explain; instead, it asserts, through the symbolic presence of its literary construction, the transcendent legitimacy of what it represents, to beguile opposition by the operation of the aesthetic. As with Bacon's reference to *Amadis de Gaule,* real historical circumstance is domesticated by the shaping and ordering of literary form. The illusion of theatrical participation is sustained by immediate events in the narrative, since the governor who recounts the tale disappears after the performance to maintain its exceptional effect—and also to circumvent further inquiry. That the tale succeeds at its job of dispersing anxiety is borne out within the *New Atlantis*: the references to crosses and oblations, to piety and Christianity, which crowd the earlier pages of Bacon's text virtually disappear thereafter.

The scene at Renfusa is proclaimed a "true miracle" for the benefit of the populace; but when it is represented for the benefit of the Spanish seamen it become illusory, shifting, difficult to locate in any fixed system of meaning. Although Renfusan theological grace appears but seconded by its philosophical pre-eminence, it is that pre-eminence that underwrites its superiority to European culture. When it is compartmentalized in this way, Christianity becomes contingent rather than necessary: from there, it is the more readily recast as a free-floating legitimation, a potential accompaniment to an institutionalized meritocracy, rather than the ineluctable justification of kingship. That such a meritocracy, founded on the prerogatives of natural philosophy rather than on inherited divine right, could be thought into being is borne out by the representation of authority in the *New Atlantis*. In Bensalem, it is the College of the Six Days' Works, the institution whose Father figures so centrally at Renfusa, that provides both the material and the symbolic ground for New Atlantan society.

IV

In striking comparison to its humanist model, the *New Atlantis* never elucidates its civil hierarchy, never gives articulation to its structure of power. Rather, the text uses the words "state" and "kingdom" interchangeably, although the two words summon up images of government that pull (and would come to pull the more) in divergent directions: one is corporate, if faceless, the other incorporated by a titled head, known to all. It is possible to read this silence about the authority at the heart of Bensalem as an affirmation of social and political conservatism, the more likely because the text that contains it is the product of a Jacobean bureaucrat in search of patronage for his philosophical program. In this case, the insertion of the Baconian agenda into an imagined social milieu much like that of early seventeenth-century England becomes a matter of tactics, of strategies of accommodation to the status quo, rather than a radical departure from received culture like the *Utopia*.

Yet Bacon's text also licenses such a departure. To be sure, Bensalemite society bears signs of congruence with its Jacobean correspondent, and the resemblance domesticates the Baconian program to the contours of seventeenth-century actuality. But to say as much is to suggest that the *New Atlantis* conforms to some, at least, of the expectations of utopian form, as I have already suggested. What is more remarkable is the manner in which the unarticulated, because unquestioned, can be transformed into the unnecessary: the structures of control emanating from the monarch presumed to govern Bensalemite society may as well not exist, since by the de facto weight of the narrative the text invests authority in the alternative of the scientific. In the space opened up by that alternative resides the possibility of reading otherwise, and hence of imagining a society not strictly tied to Stuart absolutism, or to any other avatar of monarchy.

Authority is figured within the *New Atlantis* in ways whose complexities suggest the potential for new social formations. While the Spaniards meet several men of rank in the course of their visit, none can be clearly placed within a structure of governance; nor does the narrative accord weight to civil hierarchies. Instead, the role of authority is nearly always filled by the Fathers of the House of Salomon. Besides the twin displays of piety and acumen provided the sailors by the tale of conversion, there is the advent of the Father who controls the subsequent flow of information within the *New Atlantis* by introducing the sailors to the works of his college, and by giving them permission to reveal what they have learned when they return. He is at once source and patron, only begetter of the utopian narrative; his disclosures concerning the work of the college, and his permission to make those disclosures public, license the Spaniards to speak of their unprecedented experiences, and thus to serve, later on, the text's propagandistic intent. The very mode of his arrival proclaims his importance to the text: he enters dressed in solemn black, bedecked with jewels, and carried by horses in a wheelless chariot set with precious stones. He has many attendants, and all the cit-

izenry turn out to greet him, as if he were a monarch on progress; as he passes, he blesses them silently. The pageantry makes clear that he draws all forms of authority to the House of Salomon, either directly or indirectly. In the *New Atlantis,* narrative authority bears the weight of public responsibility. In representing the emergent structures of modern science as the basis of ideality, the text localizes those emergent structures in the Father, and codes him as the de facto ruler of his land.

By indirection, the Father's narrative importance marginalizes the operations of kingship within Bensalem. Monarchy is in fact displaced to an antiquarian concern, since the only monarch of whom the Spaniards are told lived two millennia previously. Although that monarch, Solamona, is profoundly venerated as the founder of both Bensalem and its college, he cannot be connected to either successor or descendant simultaneous with the arrival of the Spaniards. The history of his accomplishments bears great resemblance to the myths of origin so useful to Tudor and Stuart rulers in legitimating rule through the invocation of impeccable (if fictional) antecedents: yet in the *New Atlantis* there is no evident textual ruler to mobilize such forces in the first place.

There is, however, a clear address to Bacon's historical sovereign. The orthographic similarities between Solamona and Solomon demand that the mythic benevolent king of Bensalem be connected with James I, who was often figured as the Old Testament ruler, in Bacon's writings and elsewhere. When viewed in light of James's well-known avoidance of the public manifestations of kingship, the Bensalemite hierarchy seems designed to provide a blessed blind. It precisely avoids the precariousness of display unwittingly manifested in James's own *Basilikon Doron,* since in the Bensalemite model a king who never presents himself, and who in turn is never represented, cannot be held to account for misseeming. Only approved icons of kingship may be passed around, like the seals on the charters granted during the Feast of the Family; the body which provides the stamp of that image is withdrawn from circulation. Under this dispensation, the king is represented by his ceremonial and instrumental extensions, by the institutions and agencies whose very participation in the symbolic forms associated with kingship guarantee, so it would seem, the perdurability of kingship, the omnipresence of monarchical control. The Bensalemite monarch's public and ceremonial functions are apparently displaced in this way, both onto the college, composed of one group of "Fathers," and also onto domestic life itself, where the father of every family re-enacts the moment of coronation in his own domain on the Feast of the Family.

But it is possible for this displaced authority to do other cultural work, for the occultation of any current ruler of Bensalem to be as significant to Baconian ideology as an obeisance in the direction of his Jacobean prototype. If, as Jonathan Goldberg has written in his account of Jacobean literary politics [*James I and The Politics of Literature,* 1983], "Sovereignty is a matter of sight," then the **New Atlantis** reconfigures the scopic regime of monarchy for its own purposes: by removing the king from the sight of his subjects, dispersing his gaze, and hence calling his existence into doubt, the **New Atlantis** inserts the philosopher of nature into the space of authority, through the process of ocular reassignment. Apart from the traces of the royal image that can be discerned on such ceremonial occasions as the aforementioned Feast of the Family, the king's disappearance from the discursive field precisely coincides with the eminence of the House of Salomon, as the scene of revelation has already indicated. These men are the "eyes" of their kingdom, the royal intelligencers Bacon advocates in **The Great Instauration,** whose very omnivoyance makes them as potentially destabilizing to monarchical hegemony as useful to its maintenance. In the text at hand, the organization is the "lanthorn" of the realm—a source of visionary illumination, to be sure, but one which suggests the comparative obscurity of the king, as well as the benightedness of the rest of the realm.

The need for vigilant observation is a persistent *topos* in Renaissance ideal societies; from the relentless communality of More to the monastical rigor manifested in Tommaso Campanella's *Città del Sole,* virtue is most reliable when cloistered within community. The Baconian text, however, takes the mutuality of supervision characteristic of More's text and places it at the control not of a moral hierarchy but of an overtly political one. The dismantling of horizontal relations, symbolized above all by the objectification of nature that Baconian science is predicated upon, has its necessary counterpart in this reaffirmation of social hierarchy on what is, after all, still alien ground. By the inevitable warrant of history—which is to say, under the conditions which determine the emergence of the modern ideology of science—the king as authorizing principle sits at the head of that hierarchy; but his presence cannot be detected easily, and the government seems to work efficiently without him.

The occulted, disembodied monarch of Bensalem can then be read in two ways: as imaginative reconfiguration of the Jacobean monarchy, and as model for a subsequent co-existence between scientific investigation and the dismantling of Stuart absolutism. The text forces us to recognize that the Bensalemite monarchy contains the possibility not just of its own effacement, but of its own erasure from the system of social and political order. The apparent vacancy at the monarchical center of the **New Atlantis** embeds within it an alternative text, susceptible of a different reading in light of the agenda of the English Revolution, and of

social reformers during the period interested in the Baconian program. The removal of natural philosophy from the possible disposal of royalist prerogative is sustained by the structure of the **New Atlantis,** with its kingship most potent in the mythology of the past, and with the hegemonic presuppositions of the House of Salomon obscured by the scattered signs of conventional authority.

It would, of course, be facile to argue that Bacon's text enabled the English to unthink kingship, to posit it, in short, as a prelude to regicide. But the **New Atlantis** influential as it was in the period after its publication, must be seen as a constituent of post-Jacobean culture, whose productions were as various—and yet as interconnected—as the Invisible College and the Commonwealth. And if Bacon's text operates as a mechanism for installing its audience within the structures of science it produces, its philosophical agenda cannot be separated from its construction of power. It then remains to be seen how the **New Atlantis** introduces such process into the fixity of its utopian form, how it reforms humanist literary politics into the mechanism of modernity.

v

In whatever way the **New Atlantis** produces revolutionary readings through its abeyant dismantling of monarchical hegemony, the issue of authority within and without the text, and of the means by which the text opens up the space for difference, cannot be resolved solely by address to the thematized structures of governance bequeathed by English history. If, as I have suggested earlier in this analysis, the utopia is a form which plays upon, yet neutralizes, the pertinent conditions of its historical emergence, it then follows that treatment of the form itself is a matter of authority, testament to the pervasiveness of humanist texts as a cultural model for an emergent discourse.

Still, the **New Atlantis** is as much a reassignment of More's utopian form, and of its relationship to the culture out of which it emanates, as it is a testament to the availability of humanist texts. The closeness of many Bensalemite social practices to those inscribed within Jacobean society, even as regards the problematic representation of monarchy, runs counter to the distance the second book of the *Utopia* maintains from the concrete historical circumstances presented in the first. What I have earlier termed utopian equipoise in More is given up by Bacon in his writing of differentiation, which makes the text at once the colonizer of pre-existent form and the producer of ideological novelty—the regime of science—from within that form. In brief, what was once humanist paradox, imbued with the stuff of Renaissance courtly politics yet impracticable as radical agenda, has in Bacon's text become propaganda.

The discursive colonialism of the *New Atlantis* towards its humanist prototype is an important move in the all-but-silent prehistory of disciplinary formation: the emergence of "modern science," and the concomitant ideologies of culture that deem the humanities the antithesis of science, depend upon and emanate from this othering of literary representation by the scientific in the late Renaissance. The pertinence of colonization as a model for this process—which is to say the pertinence of such historically specific structures of domination and alienation—is determined by the moment of emergence. The *New Atlantis* was written, and indeed could only have been written, at a particular juncture in Jacobean culture: at that juncture, the fact of the New World was no longer novel, but the issue of how to control it, imaginatively as well as materially, had become critical. The sheer amount of writing generated about the Virginia Company's ventures alone was evidence of inadequate discursive mastery; thus Tobias Matthew, Archbishop of York, wrote in 1609 to the Earl of Somerset: "Of Virginia there are so many tractates, divine, human, historical, political, or call them as you please, as no further intelligence I dare desire."

Obviously, the New World looms large in much Renaissance writing besides Bacon's—in More's *Utopia,* for instance, its most proximate text. But in More's realm the comprehensiveness of description is a measure, not of the need to master and assimilate the unprecedented experience of the Americas, but of the tightness of social control within the geography of the imaginary. The text presents a wholly-realized society to make the invariance of that society concrete, to reify the stasis that is a precondition of Utopian ideality; thus control is writ large across Utopian life. For More, the New World is not a site for further exploration, but an informing presence whose newness "explains" the desire to create society anew, an impetus to formal and cultural innovation.

Bacon's advocacy of a revisionary philosophy of nature, on the other hand, shifts the focus of his utopian text from the formalized study of human society to the systematized knowledge of an alien natural world. Such a shift in positioning—which is perhaps more importantly a shift in object, in semiosis—brings with it a dynamism not operant in More's text. There, the reconstituted, completed social institutions of Utopia focus on the processing of a unanimous subjectivity, bespeaking the agenda of humanism even as those institutions appear to hark back to medieval monasticism. The Baconian text, however, stages inquisitional structures almost proleptically, as advance notice of a system whose material emergence its representational practices then make possible. In the way that the *New Atlantis* emphatically polarizes the flow of knowledge typical of colonialism, from the inhabitants to the seamen, from those granted power from the interrogation of nature to those comparatively unempowered, it turns the unempowered into objects of scrutiny themselves, into displaced versions of the nature presumed (and narrated) to be the primary site of investigation. Insofar as the reader is positioned likewise, the *New Atlantis* reconfigures the bemused idyll of More's *Utopia* into a narrative that privileges process and change.

This bend away from utopian convention is coterminous with an assimilation of narrative practice to the emergent structure of empiricism, an assimilation signaled at the outset of the text. The *New Atlantis* begins with lost sailors, desperate not because of storms but rather because of a strong wind which has carried them off course, leaving them in becalmed waters. Then the Spaniards spot "thick clouds" which put them "in some hope of land"; shortly thereafter, they arrive at Bensalem, and the process of their education commences. Such a beginning may well be termed uneventful, since it apparently seeks to avoid the impetus to travel narrative lent by storm and destruction, or for that matter the potential importance of a thematized break to signal the beginning of a text. Its eventuality, however, is not to be located in prior literary practice, but in the historical space that connects the New World with the New Science. The clouds the sailors see, and take as a sign that they are near land, are habituated observations that belong with the necessary skills of the seaman, and here provide textual emphasis for the correspondence between exploration and investigation. The sailors' acquaintance with natural phenomena effectively prefigures them as agents of such philosophical inquiry as that carried out by the Fathers of the House of Salomon. As Columbus writes in 1501: "the life of sailors . . . leads those who follow it to wish to know the secrets of this world."

Within the *New Atlantis,* such "secrets" are coded as a sign of initiation. While the Spaniards demonstrate their competence in the rudimentary decipherment of clouds, it is not until they submit themselves to a superior (because systematized) order of knowledge that they gain access to what the world, unless through the college, keeps to itself. The means of access put a spin on the epistemology of sight, enlist it to serve the emergent ideology of science: what is known through seeing is reconfigured as more real, and Hythlodaean tale-telling is replaced by an optical warrant whose signs are themselves available to be seen, read, and hence believed. The *New Atlantis* is advanced—propagated—by the agency of vision, just as authority within the kingdom of Bensalem inheres in its collective "eyes." But there is more than analogy at work here: the dispersal of kingly authority initiated by the text's bequeathing his specular prerogative to Salomon's House has its sign in the narrative obsession with speculation as spectacle, with knowledge as a form of display. Within the ideology of science, the eye is the sign of knowledge; it follows that a text designed to naturalize that knowledge would depend upon what is represented as seen in order to legitimate itself. Observations construct the world of the text as the enactment of the inquiry it espouses: insofar as the *New Atlantis* traces out its own agenda, it is through the accumulation of scrupulous detail. These details say less about the utopian valence of Bensalem than about the way that it comes to be known to the Spaniards—and by extension the way that the text itself is directed to the realm of material, historical practice.

This positing of the visual as the arbiter of both representation and practice within the *New Atlantis* accounts for the multitude of parenthetical phrases within the text. Sometimes, the phrases bracketed off from the main narrative in this way amplify upon an observation: they interrupt its forward impetus in order to scrutinize an object: "he drew forth a little scroll of parchment (somewhat yellower than our parchment, and shining like the leaves of writing tables, but otherwise soft and flexible)." At others, however, the enclosed elements call attention to the tenuous phenomenological basis of narrative convention. The parenthetical information betrays the assumptions of omniscience as it focuses on the perceived, and therefore tentatively known, significance of event or act: "there came towards us a person (as it seemed) of place"; "whereupon one of those that were with him, being (as it seemed) a notary"; "in his hand a fruit of that country. . . . He used it (as it seemeth) for a preservative against infection": "he smiling said, 'He must not be twice paid for one labour': meaning (as I take it) that he had salary sufficient of the state for his service. For (as I after learned) they call an officer that taketh rewards, *twice paid*."

This anxious display of warrant makes authority within the text an index of emergence. The parenthetical eruptions not only put under suspicion the local issue of representation as omniscience, of the literary as epistemology; through their obsessive interest in establishing an ocular, verisimilar basis for the text's knowing what it does, they also signal the shift away from literature as hegemonic practice in English Renaissance culture. By foregrounding a pragmatics of narrative information, they question the perfection bestowed by Sir Philip Sidney on poetry in the construction of humanist dominance—a point that can be extended to the ideality of utopian formations as well. Instead of either gilded improbabilities or internally conflicted ideals, The *New Atlantis* presents narrative as potential fact, and the work of reading the exercise of an acumen newly harnessed to the production of scientific knowledge. Bacon's text needs to be processed as the Collegians process the material of nature: to be scrutinized, sifted, and disposed of according to a nascent taxonomic hierarchy, where only that which can be accounted for by means of physical apprehension or its narrative embodiment is accorded

significance. The interpretation of any such data within the utopian frame of the text is steadfastly resisted, for there is always more to be known, and that superfluity denies formal closure. Such open-endedness lends Bacon's text the dynamism that I have mentioned earlier. But that dynamism is antithetical to utopian form, which imposes the fiction of coherence on the landscape of ideality, much like the coherence posited upon the natural world by hypothetical formulations in contemporary Continental science. In a narrative constructed by the all-consuming eye, however—and here I enlarge the term "narrative" to include Bacon's nonutopian texts—there is no room for unifying fictions, no cessation of the activity of processing, no apparent imposition of hypothetical form on the body of nature deconstituted by corrosive scrutiny.

The *New Atlantis* is literally an incomplete text: the last page concludes with the editorial note "the rest was not perfected," introduced at the place in the text after the Spaniards have been granted permission to disseminate information about Bensalem as a gesture of good will. There is a correspondence between this gesture towards dissemination and the cessation of narrative impetus: the fractional state of the text can be recuperated to the way the text dictates practice. To argue such a correspondence may appear to run the risk of overstaking a claim on the accidental. However, when all of Bacon's texts are to one degree or another "unperfected"—from the twice-revised and-augmented *Essays* to the *Great Instauration* and all the components nested within it—it becomes fair to consider the textual and ideological functions of imperfection in the Baconian program.

On one level, of course, the incompleteness of any Baconian text is a testament to its messianism. As the frontispiece of the *Great Instauration* evinces, the recasting of knowledge undertaken by Bacon must be understood through structures of liminality that represent the moment of change rather than its accomplishment. But this claim, in turn, demands to be inserted into the specific textual framework of the *New Atlantis*. "Perfection," properly, is completion; it also signifies that which is perfect, the ideal—the utopian. The *New Atlantis* cannot be "complete" in this specifically utopian, specifically textual sense, since it generates a model of continuous activity that in later history converges on the possibility of progress; it becomes a prime component of scientific ideology full blown, whose domination of the natural world Bacon's text seeks to authorize, even to inaugurate, by the means of its narration. The admonition to publicity on the last page of the text indicates that the work of science is durably configured by the Baconian text as open-ended, as an ever-deepening knowledge of the secrets of this world to be shared among initiates. At some point, the eye will have seen enough because the eye will have seen all: but the possibility of such transparency depends upon reiteration and repeatability, upon the sense of a shared and duplicated agenda that still characterizes the production of modern science. Like the endless romance of the New World in early Stuart England, the ideology of science is always in need of inscription.

John Michael Archer (essay date 1993)

SOURCE: "Surveillance and Enlightenment: Toward Bacon's *New Atlantis*," in *Sovereignty and Intelligence: Spying and Court Culture in the English Renaissance,* Stanford University Press, 1993, pp. 121-51.

[*In the following excerpt, Archer examines the aspect of political power in the* New Atlantis, *concluding that Bacon's "representation of the sciences of nature implies the unwritten methodology of the sciences of human control within the modern state."*]

In the **Essays,** Bacon had been largely concerned with the constitution of what he calls "a man's self"; in the **New Atlantis,** the production of a new self by means of a reconceptualization of the relationship between knowledge and power is part of Bacon's narrative method. Timothy Reiss [in *The Discourse of Modernism,* 1982] has pointed out "the use throughout the fiction of the first person, both singular and plural" by which "the new scientist *imposes* the discursive *I* upon the world outside him." Bacon's European explorers, however, are in a more complex relation to the land they stumble upon than this statement might suggest. As John C. Briggs [in *Francis Bacon and the Rhetoric of Nature,* 1989] observes, "the sailors who find it are also utterly lost, with no idea of what they have found until they land." They come across a civilization "beyond both the old world and the new," one that has already explored, and in an intellectual sense colonized, their own.

The colonialism that accompanied and sustained the development of the European nation-state generated many narratives of imposition and appropriation, but Bacon's story presents us with colonialism's mirror image. The dominant first person of this narrative is best represented by the relentless "we have" of the Father of Salomon's House in his catalogue of Bensalemite discoveries in natural science. It is this "we," the first-person pronoun of the other, that Bacon holds out to his readers, who are invited to find (or lose) themselves in the new machine for the production of knowledge that he describes: "if there be a mirror in the world worthy to hold men's eyes, it is that country."

The **New Atlantis** suggests a world of specialized knowledge that is always just beyond the reader's grasp. "From its opening page," as Briggs remarks, "the nar-

Title page of Sylva Sylvarum, *the volume that contains the first publication of the* New Atlantis, *1627.*

rative is a highly coherent play of light and shadow that intimates the paradoxical power of the new universal science and its wisdom of persuasion." The narrator claims plainly to discern an island that is shrouded in darkness; its inhabitants open themselves to their visitors yet maintain a closed society; and as we shall see, they seek to reveal the secrets of nature by spying on the discoveries of others. The illusion of this chiaroscuro reality, I would add, is created by the seemingly random accretion of fictitious detail. Bacon creates information by describing familiar substances while varying accidental attributes such as color. The reader shares the mariners' astonishment "to hear so strange things so probably told." The Bensalemites ward off infection with a fruit "like an orange but of colour between orange-tawney and scarlet," their parchment is shiny and flexible, and their building materials are "of somewhat a bluer colour than our brick." Bacon's fiction proceeds through the accumulation of putative fact: it opens with a set of fictitious directions and breaks off with the equally fictitious (but supposedly more feasible) scientific achievements of Salomon's

House.

Bacon masterfully creates an impression of strangeness while reproducing the conventional symbols of authority. The supposedly alien sign system that the Europeans confront when they sail into the harbor of Bensalem is really quite familiar to them, and to the reader. Among all the gestures and "signs," we have "a tipstaff of a yellow cane, tipped at both ends with blue," a robe with wide sleeves, and the supreme sign of the Cross. The scroll the voyagers are handed by the islanders may be made out of an unfamiliar material, but it is written upon in the languages of the Mediterranean world. By varying the accidentals in this way, Bacon creates fictitious knowledge about a fictitious power in a manner that imitates the powers and knowledges of Europe.

This mimesis also consists in a partial revelation of the potential of Europe's developing structures of authority. When the sailors offer money to one of the members of the welcoming party, "he smiling said, he must not be twice paid for one labour, meaning (as I take it) that he had salary sufficient to the state for his service." Bensalem possesses an adequately paid bureaucracy, something with which the strangers, accustomed to giving gratuities to the servants of monarchs, are practically unfamiliar. Bacon himself, of course, had been caught in the ambiguities of this system, which led to his downfall in 1621 and the enforced leisure during which he wrote the *New Atlantis* shortly afterward.

The regular and sufficient payment of government officials was to become an important part of the growth of the modern state, a development that was also accompanied by proposals for the creation of a medical bureaucracy. Charles Webster, in his book *The Great Instauration,* has noted the "definite medical bias" of both the *New Atlantis* and *Sylva Sylvarum,* the treatise with which it waspublished through eight editions between 1626 and 1658: "The general public were probably more familiar with these works than with any of Bacon's more philosophical writings." Medicalization was featured in a number of other utopian writings from England and the Continent before and during this period; state laboratories were envisioned and physicians "were characterized as devout public servants, or as 'ministers of nature.'" These humanitarian schemes were also programs for a new disposition of political power in its relations with its subjects. Bacon's mariners are told by a representative of the governor: "My lord would have you know that it is not of pride or greatness that he cometh not aboard your ship; but for that in your answer you declare that you have many sick amongst you, he was warned by our Conservator of Health of the city that he should keep a distance." Here the Europeans are introduced to a new form of political authority, one that holds aloof in the interests of public health rather than greatness of place.

If the *New Atlantis* mirrors the transition to new forms of power, the old forms are nevertheless not completely cast off. The Europeans must swear that they are not pirates, "whereupon one . . . being (as it seemed) a notary, made an entry of this act." Foucault writes [in *Discipline and Punish,* 1977] that the surveillance of individuals entails their placement in a network of writing, "a whole mass of documents that capture and fix them." The strangers in Bacon's fiction are subjected to the beginnings of such "small techniques of notation, of registration, of constituting files." But the narrator is unsure what to make of them, and hesitantly applies the old name of "notary" to their agent. This official also possesses the medical function of fumigating the European vessel with the orange-like fruit. He is the one who refuses to be "twice paid" because his government salary is sufficient.

The depiction of those public functionaries in Bensalem who possess a more exalted rank reveals the remnants of Europe's established power structures in Bacon's fiction more clearly. In the *New Atlantis,* power often makes itself spectacularly visible in addition to rendering its subjects visible. Bacon's delight in the costumes of various great men, for instance, culminates in the detailed set piece devoted to the accoutrements of the Father of Salomon's House, certainly the most visible figure of authority in Bensalem—when he chooses, that is, to make a public appearance. Stephen Greenblatt has pointed out the Tudor fascination with "detail, in knowing precisely what kinds of cloth were used, what color, what cut" in the conventional description of the entry or pageant. There is none of this, he remarks, in *Utopia.* More's work, written more than a century before Bacon's, is more accurately prophetic of the abstract program of power sketched by Foucault. In Utopia everyone is watched by everyone else; those in authority may dress the same as other citizens, but during meals they keep watch over their charges from the highest table in the dining hall. On the other hand, Bacon's fable is closer to the transitional state of historical reality in his own time. More foresaw the ideal program of power described retrospectively by Foucault, but Bacon's Bensalem captures something of the imperfect fulfillment of this schematic program in the nation-state during the Enlightenment and its aftermath. No state has ever thrown the trappings of power completely aside.

Two institutions stand at the threshold of Bacon's Bensalem, the Strangers' House and Salomon's House. The first is a benign combination of prison and hospital. It is spacious and well-appointed, and the Europeans marvel at the "parent-like usage" they receive there. They do not resist the paternalism of their new way of life, even though they are required to remain within the house for three days, and may not go beyond a mile and a half outside the city's walls without leave after this period. The narrator, indeed, enjoins his fellows:

> let us look up to God, and every man reform his own ways. . . . For they have by commandment (though in form of courtesy) cloistered us within these walls for three days: who knoweth whether it be not to take some taste of our manners and conditions? and if they find them bad, to banish us straightways; if good, to give us further time. For these men they have given us for attendance may withal have an eye upon us.

(3. 135)

It is clear that it does not matter whether the six attendants are filing reports on the new comers or not, for the sailors have already begun to internalize the generalized surveillance to which they are being subjected.

If the gaze of surveillance is inward-turning in the Strangers' House, it is directed toward the outside world by means of Salomon's House, "the very eye of this kingdom." In the first account of this foundation, we discover that there are six Brethren (compare the six servants) "whose errand was only to give us knowledge of the affairs and state of those countries to which they were designed, and especially of the sciences, arts, manufactures, and inventions of all the world; and withal to bring unto us books, instruments, and patterns in every kind." Later we are told that there are twelve "Merchants of Light" with this function, "that sail into foreign countries, under the names of other nations (for our own we conceal)." Although the Bensalemites are "especially" interested in science and technology, their intellectual imperialism is accompanied, and to some extent preceded, by political information gathering on "affairs and state."

The Fathers' mastery of global knowledge has given Salomon's House control over the affairs and state of Bensalem; without the account of "the best state or mould of a commonwealth" that Bacon's secretary William Rawley claimed his master intended to append to the *New Atlantis,* we are driven to assume that it is the defacto government of the island. It secretly inquires into the affairs of other nations, and at home its members, the Fathers, travel about in pomp, using their expertise to warn people about plagues and natural disasters, and distributing "great largesses where they come upon all occasions." They also freely decide "which of the inventions and experiences which we have discovered shall be published, and which not . . . though some of these we do reveal sometimes to the state, and some not." The sovereign has withdrawn into the background in the ancient figure of King Salomona, and the sovereignty he has left behind is divided between the discipline of fathers over their households and the knowledge of the Fathers of Salomon's House.

The remoteness of earthly sovereigns, even in their manifest glory, is a frequent complaint of Montaigne and other writers. The doctrine of state secrets and *arcana imperii,* as Jonathan Goldberg has shown, [in *James I,* 1983] was a traditional way in which power and knowledge were coupled in the reign of James I. In **"Of Empire,"** Bacon observes: "This is one reason also of that effect which the Scripture speaketh of, *That the king's heart is inscrutable* . . . Hence it comes likewise, that princes many times make themselves desires, and set their hearts upon toys; sometimes upon a building; sometimes upon erecting of an order." The King Salomona who built the order of Salomon's House, however, "had a *large heart,* inscrutable for good." In the same fashion, the passage from **"In Praise of Knowledge"** about the inability of the spials and seamen of monarchs to gain access to the sovereignty of knowledge is revised by the fictional success of Salomona's Merchants of Light in their voyages of discovery. Goldberg notices the explicit association of James with the biblical Solomon in Stuart propaganda, and suggests that the Banqueting House of 1619 was echoed in Bacon's Salomon's House. Nevertheless, the personal sovereign plays a severely limited role in the *New Atlantis* (we never catch a glimpse of him in the portion that Bacon completed), and his sovereignty is subsumed in the sovereignty of knowledge that his explorers provide. The reigning monarch is important chiefly as a sponsor of the patriarchal authority celebrated in a social ritual called the Feast of the Family. The almost mythical Salomona is the principal figure of the sovereign, and his greatest act was to found the institution that has taken over most of the functions and privileges of royal power. For this reason, I would argue that in the *New Atlantis* Bacon was moving away from the glorification of James's absolutism, or putative absolutism, and toward an idealization of the disembodied sovereignty of the remote state.

The Europeans marvel at the disembodied, indeed almost divine, operation of Bensalem's sovereign power in response to the governor's mention of his island's "laws of secrecy," and his assertion that "we know well most part of the habitable world, and are ourselves unknown": "That they should have knowledge of the languages, books, affairs of those that lie such a distance from them, it was a thing we could not tell what to make of, for that it seemed to us a condition and propriety of divine powers and beings to be hidden and unseen to others and yet to have others open and as in a light to them." When the governor objects that this "imported as if we thought this a land of magicians, that sent forth spirits of the air into all parts, to bring them news and intelligence of other countries," the mariners reply that they think of his island "rather as angelical than magical." Here the novel power of the disciplinary state is inscribed within older ideas about the angelic intelligence of the remote sovereign and the all-seeing eye of a hidden God. The frankly political version of this principle is found in Bacon's *Henry VII,* where we learn that "they may observe best who are themselves observed least." In the *New Atlantis,* however, power's self-concealment remains almost divine, despite the governor's misgivings about magic. Salomon's House is also called the College of Six Days' Works in memory of the biblical creation narrative, and the governor feels that it was probably named after the King of the Hebrews rather than its founder, King Salomona. "It is dedicated," he says, "to the study of the Works and Creatures of God."

The voyage to Bensalem, and its inhabitants' own circulation throughout the world, are part of a wider political theology of knowledge and power in Bacon's works. The *New Atlantis* brings to a head the apocalyptic rhetoric that Bacon often used when urging the importance of science. The principal formulation of the Baconian maxim "knowledge itself is power" occurs in his essay on heresy in *Meditationes Sacrae*, where it is God's power and God's knowledge that are said to be the same. In *Valerius Terminus* (1603), the earliest version of what became the *Instauratio Magna,* he cites Daniel 12:4, "where speaking of the latter times it is said, *Many shall pass to and fro, and science shall be increased;* as if the opening of the world by navigation and commerce and the further discovery of knowledge should meet in one time or age." Bacon gives this prophecy the same interpretation in *Redargutio Philosopharum,* another early tract, and in *Novum Organon* (1621), written a few years before the *New Atlantis*. A version of the biblical phrase also appears on the frontispiece to the *Instauratio,* accompanied by the famous illustration of a ship passing through the pillars of Hercules.

All the same, knowledge gathering cannot be reduced to a symptom of millenarianism in Bacon's work any more than his science can. The millenarian attitude made available to Bacon a predictive mode of writing that enabled him to forecast some of the elements associated with the development of the modern state. This is particularly true of the *New Atlantis,* where social organization and social surveillance are inseparable from the achievements of science. Bacon's sailors witness marvels in both realsm. He had always insisted that pure or "luciferous" science should precede applied or "fructiferous" technology, but in his utopia he allows his readers to catch a glimpse of the great instauration's projected fruits. In the social sphere, these fruits take the form of well-run patriarchal families whose success in producing offspring is represented by the artificial bunches of grapes carried in procession during the Feast of the Family. These grapes bring another biblical passage to mind: the thirteenth chapter of Numbers, in which the spies that Moses has sent into Canaan to report on its fruitfulness return with a magnificent cluster. The Europeans in Bensalem are themselves spies of a sort, the first explorers of a new Promised Land. Yet they are also the willing victims of Bensalemite surveillance. Bensalem has concealed itself from the world by absorbing strangers; like the Canaan described by Moses's spies, it is "a land that eateth up the inhabitants thereof."

The New Atlantis has retained a hierarchical social organization, and it still glories in the manifestation of power through pageantry and costume. The viewers of its pageantry, however, are expected to comport themselves with the discipline of an army, and large gatherings seem on the way to becoming opportunities for surveillance by power as well as occasions for its display. The Feast of the Family is the crowning example of this trend. The male head of a sufficiently large clan holds court upon the dais or "half-pace" that occupies one end of a big room. "Against the wall, in the middle of the half-pace, is a chair placed for him, with a table and carpet before it." His descendants stand about him, ranked "in order of their years without difference of sex." At this point in the ceremony seniority overrides the gender hierarchy. Both the family members and their guests are neatly arranged, "the room being always full of company, but well kept and without disorder." A few days before this public ritual the Father has examined the state of his family in private, settling disagreements among its members and censuring the wicked. "So likewise direction is given touching marriages and the courses of life which any of them should take, with diverse other the like orders and advices." The public gathering is the ceremonial counterpart of this *in camera* examination.

From the start of the account we are repeatedly reminded of the participation of women in the examination and its ceremony. The Father enters the room at the head of a procession, "with all his generation or lineage, the males before him, and the females following him," but when the room is full and the children are ranked according to age, the gender hierarchy appears to subside somewhat, so that the Father and the spectators alike can be presented with the seemingly neutral spectacle of a living, visible genealogy. Yet it is the Father who is credited by the state with the power of procreation and the production of new citizens, "for they say the king is debtor to no man, but for propagation of his subjects." If women predominate in a particular family, the ritual's ornamental cluster of grapes is green rather than purple, and is topped by a crescent moon rather than a sun. During the meal, the Father is served by his sons, "and the women only stand about him, leaning against the wall." Most important, it is the Father who is placed on display as the visible manifestation of power. He sits on the dais beneath an embroidered canopy that "is ever of the work of some of the daughters of the family."

The Feast of the Family, in which the fructiferous powers of nature are ultimately attributed to the patriarch, mirrors Salomon's House and its patriarchal domination of the natural world. Yet the new program of power that informs so much else in the *New Atlantis* makes its appearance in an unexpected form here. We are told in passing that "if there be a mother from whose body the whole lineage is descended, there is a traverse placed in a loft above on the right hand of the chair, with a privy door, and a carved window of glass, leaded with gold and blue; where she sitteth, but is not seen." The mother is carefully included in the ritual of power upon the dais, but her concealment means that she is excluded from any direct share in it according to the old scheme of things. Yet she is placed above the Father, a reversal of the spatially conceived hierarchy that also gives her a better vantage point from which to survey the entire ceremony. She is not part of the procession, and she enters her compartment invisibly through her "privy door." She sits in front of a window, not in order that she may be seen, but so that she may view the proceedings while remaining concealed. The window is "leaded with gold and blue," and yellow and blue, the colors of the tipstaff at the beginning of the *New Atlantis,* evidently signify authority in Bensalem. Is it not "a condition and propriety of divine powers and beings, to be hidden and unseen to others and yet to have others open and as in a light to them?" The mother, though excluded from the open display of power, is in the same position in relation to her family that Bensalem is to the rest of the world.

The *New Atlantis* embodies a conflict in the historical relationship between knowledge and power: Bacon was caught up in a contradiction between the historical conditions that made his program possible and those it was intended to create. He continued to associate women with surveillance even as he sought to exclude them from the "masculine birth of time" that is its correlate in scientific methodology. Bacon's mother, Anne, had been a strong and vigilant presence in his life, and thereis surely something here of what Coppélia Kahn [in *Rewriting the Renaissance*, ed. Margaret W. Fergusun et al., 1986] calls the "maternal subtext" in Renaissance writing by men, "the imprint of mothering on the male psyche." By extension, the hidden mother may also represent the fructiferous power that Bacon envied in a nature traditionally personified as a woman—the quotation from **"In Praise of Knowledge"** that opens *Dialectic of Enlightenment* proposes "the happy match between the mind of man and the nature of things." But another, more remote woman may have served as the principal model for the mother in the Feast of the Family. We must recall Alice Jardine's feminist revision of critical theory's account of the origins and consequences of modernity. Her definition of male paranoia as a response to the watching mother, "a woman who *knows*," locates the initial moment of this response "in the European transition from the Middle Ages to the Renaissance." Psychological explanations of the presence of the mother in the Feast of the Family reinforce a political one, for her position in the background, seeing but unseen, is also like the repressed memory of the feminized image of sixteenth-century English sovereignty.

Queen Elizabeth had wisely avoided "looking to her estate through too few windows." When she attended cathedral services among the people who composed the church of which she was the head, the queen was often accommodated in a manner that Bacon could well have been recalling a few decades later when he wrote the *New Atlantis*. "The Queene's Majestie to come to the body of the churche, and soe to enter in at the weste dore of the quier, and so uppe to her travase by the communion table," we read in a description of her reception at Westminster in 1597. At St. Paul's in 1588, "shee was, under a rich canopie, brought through the long west isle to her travers in the quire, the clergie singing the Letanie: which being ended, she was brought to a closet of purpose made out of the north wall of the church." Despite her dependence upon the regime of pomp and display that is also evident in these passages, there were already strong elements of surveilling power in Elizabeth's rule. These elements helped make possible Bacon's creation of both Salomon's House and the hidden mother in the traverse.

A final example of Bacon's involvement in Elizabethan surveillance will cast light on the origins of the scientific method that the *New Atlantis* was intended to promote. During the summer of 1594 Bacon served as inquisitor in an intense series of examinations in the Tower of London. The subjects were various men accused of a plot to assassinate the queen, and the method used in questioning them was called "examination upon interrogatories." Suspects who had implicated each other in earlier testimony were rigorously re-questioned, until—in James Spedding's words—"at last by successive siftings the several witnesses (each being carefully kept in the dark as to the others' tale) find themselves involved in irreconcilable contradictions." The *Novum Organon* (1620) advocates the extraction of hidden knowledge about nature from the senses in a similar manner. Bacon describes a form of inductive reasoning that analyzes experience by "submitting to examination those things which the common logic takes on trust." "The information of the senses itself I sift and examine in many ways," he continues, "For certain it is that the senses deceive; but then at the same time they supply the means of discovering their own errors." The senses are like prisoners examined upon interrogatories or the foreign inventors covertly monitored by Bensalem's Merchants of Light. Bacon's induction, which was an active—indeed, in some ways a deductive—operation rather than a passive openness to facts, owes much to his intelligence background and juridical experience in the nascent Elizabethan state.

"On the threshold of the classical age," Foucault remarked, "Bacon, lawyer and statesman, tried to develop a methodology of investigation for the empirical sciences. What Great Observer will produce the methodology of examination for the human sciences?" He goes on, however, to ask if such a methodology is even possible, for "the great investigation that gave rise to the sciences of nature has become detached from its politico-juridical model; the examination, on the other hand, is still caught up in disciplinary technology." We must read Francis Bacon through Horkheimer and Adorno as well as Foucault and Elias if we wish to complete the critique of the movement Bacon helped inaugurate. A new regime of state power was at stake along with the disciplinary power of surveillance, as Horkheimer and Adorno remind us:

> Bacon dreamed of the many things "which kings with their treasure cannot buy, nor with their force command," of which "their spials and intelligencers can give no news." As he wished, they fell to the burghers, the enlightened heirs of those kings. . . . Today, when Bacon's utopian vision that we should "command nature by action"—that is, in practice—has been realized on a tellurian scale, the nature of the thralldom that he ascribed to unsubjected nature is clear. It was domination itself.

Thus, in the **New Atlantis** the representation of the sciences of nature implies the unwritten methodology of the sciences of human control within the modern state. Yet in Bacon's final work we see the operation of the dialectic of enlightenment as well, whereby "the capacity of representation is the vehicle of progress and regression at one and the same time"—regression not so much to the repressed maternal realm of nature and myth as to the Elizabethan image of sovereignty contained in Bacon's influential program for an impersonal, technocratic, and surveilling state.

FURTHER READING

Biography

Fuller, Jean Overton. *Francis Bacon: A Biography.* London: East-West Publications, 1981, 384 p.
　　Chronicles Bacon's life and works from his infancy to his death.

Green, A. Wigfall. *Sir Francis Bacon: His Life and Works.* Denver: Alan Swallow, 1952, 296 p.
　　Describes how the "broadened intellectual vision resulting from the Renaissance" affected Bacon's quest for knowledge as a visionary, scientist, statesman, and philosopher.

Criticism

Achinstein, Sharon. "How To Be a Progressive without Looking Like One: History and Knowledge in Bacon's *New Atlantis.*" *CLIO* 17, No. 3 (Spring 1988): 249-64
　　Describes how "Bacon's *New Atlantis* presents the conflict between innovation and tradition as it focuses on the question of new knowledge."

Bierman, Judah. "Science and Society in the *New Atlantis* and Other Renaissance Utopias." *PMLA* 78, No. 5 (December 1963): 492-500.
　　Contrasts Bensalem's scientific structure in the *New Atlantis* with similar structures in other Renaissance utopias in order to clarify Bacon's impression of an operable scientific community, an image, the critic claims, which is not apparent in Bacon's previous works

————. "The *New Atlantis*, Bacon's Utopia of Science." *Papers on Language and Literature* 111, No. 2 (Spring 1967): 99-110.
　　Analyzes Bacon's use of dialogue in his depiction of the founding and Christianization of Bensalem in the *New Atlantis* so that one may uncover "his most radical proposals for a utopia of science."

Kaufmann, M. "Bacon's *New Atlantis* and Campanella's *City of the Sun.*" In *Utopias; or, Schemes of Social Improvement,* pp. 14-30. London: C. Kegan Paul & Co., 1879.
　　Contrasts the social improvements suggested by Bacon with those envisioned by Tommaso Campanella in his utopia of 1637.

Laidler, Harry Wellington. "Bacon's *New Atlantis.*" In *Comparative Survey of Socialism, Communism, Co-operation, Utopianism; and Other Systems of Reform and Reconstruction,* edited by Seba Eldridge, pp. 30-33. New York: Thomas Y. Crowell Company, 1944.
　　Contrasts Thomas More's egalitarian utopian ideals with the scientific ideals expressed by Bacon in his *New Atlantis.* The critic claims that Bacon's overemphasis of science in the work is a serious shortcoming for his social philosophy.

McCutcheon, Elizabeth. "Bacon and the Cherubim: An Iconographical Reading of the *New Atlantis.*" *English Literary Renaissance* 2, No. 3 (Autumn 1972): 334-55.
　　Examines the cherubim imagery in the *New Atlantis* to portray Bacon "as both artist and thinker, . . . [and] superlative myth-maker" who "transforms image after image in a deeply felt way that unifies means with end, light and truth with life and love."

Renaker, David. "A Miracle of Engineering: The Conversion of Bensalem in Francis Bacon's *New Atlantis.*" *Studies in Philology* 87, No. 2 (Spring 1990): 181-93.

Argues that the miraculous Christianization of Bensalem in the *New Atlantis* was necessary if Bacon intended the work to procure the non-violent rise of a Christian-based modern scientific society within a predominantly Protestant Europe.

Vickers, Brian. "Judgements of Bacon's Style." In *Francis Bacon and Renaissance Prose*, pp. 232-61. London: Cambridge at the University Press, 1968.

Traces the fluctuating attitudes toward Bacon's writing style between the seventeenth and twentieth centuries. Notable critics include Ben Jonson, Jonathan Swift, David Hume, Jeremy Bentham, William Blake, Charles Dickens, and George Eliot.

Wheeler, Harvey. "Francis Bacon's *New Atlantis*: The 'Mould' of a Lawfinding Commonwealth." In *Francis Bacon's Legacy of Texts: The Art of Discovery Grows with Discovery*, edited by William A. Sessions, pp. 291-310. New York: AMS press, 1990.

Depicts the society of Bensalem in the *New Atlantis* as a revolutionary yet practical model for the reformation of England in Bacon's own time.

Wiener, Harvey S. "Science or Providence: Toward Knowledge in Bacon's *New Atlantis.*" *Enlightenment Essays* 111, No. 2 (Summer 1972): 85-92.

Examines how Bacon links theology and science with the apprehension of knowledge and truth in his *New Atlantis.*

Additional coverage of Bacon's life and career is contained in the following sources published by Gale Research: *Concise Dictionary of British Literary Biography; Dictionary of Literary Biography,* **Vol. 151;** and *Literature Criticism From 1400-1800,* **Vol. 18.**

Tomasso Campanella

1568-1639

Italian philosopher and poet. The following entry contains discussion of Campanella's life and works published from 1922 through 1992.

INTRODUCTION

An important philosopher of the late Italian Renaissance, Campanella proclaimed himself to be the prophet of a new age that combined the best ideas of the old world with those of a new, modern society. His utopian vision is most clearly conveyed in his *La Citta del sole* (1623; *City of the Sun*), his most famous work. A man of action as well as of words, Campanella attacked both the Church establishment and the Spanish monarchy: he was involved in planning a revolt against Spain—which was unsuccessful—and was repeatedly imprisoned for his heretical beliefs. Contributing numerous volumes of philosophical and political writings, Campanella is also recognized as a courageous and rebellious individual, often hailed as one of the first great reformers of the modern age.

Biographical Information

The son of an illiterate shoemaker, Campanella was born Giovanni Domenico in Stilo, Calabria, on September 5, 1568. At a young age he displayed remarkable intellectual abilities. He joined the Dominican order at fourteen years old to study the philosophy of Aristotle. To his superiors' dismay, Campanella soon displayed Anti-Aristotelian tendencies, preferring a more intuitive and less analytical natural philosophy. In 1588 Campanella was sent to the theological house of studies at Cosenza where he first encountered the writings of Bernardino Telesio, a natural philosopher who also objected to Aristotle's teachings. He read Telesio's *De rerum natura juxta propria principia* (1565, 1586), and was thrilled to discover a kindred spirit. Telesio died before the two could meet, but his writings continued to inspire Campanella, becoming the cornerstone of his own philosophy. In 1589 Campanella completed his first significant work in just seven months' time, *Philosophia sensibus demonstrata*, in which he attempted to vindicate Telesio from the attacks of his detractors, especially Giocomo Antonio Marta. Around that time Campanella encountered a Jewish rabbi, Abraham, from whom he acquired strong interests in astrology and magic. As these interests (as well as his anti-Aristotelianism) were contrary to Dominican teachings and traditional Thomistic doctrines, Campanella was arrested, charged with heresy, and tried. He was instructed to reject Telesian doctrine and was ordered back to Calabria in 1592. Ignoring his sentence, Campanella went to Padua where he encountered Galileo and Paolo Sarpi. For almost a year Campanella continued to develop his thinking along Telesian lines in works like *Apologia pro Telesio* (c. 1593-94) and *Nova physiologia iuxta propria principia* (c. 1593-94). He was again arrested in 1594 by the order of the Holy Office in Padua who seized all of his manuscripts. Campanella was accused of many offenses, including being critical of Church doctrine, and was severely beaten and tortured. In his own defense he wrote several volumes including *Defensio Telesianorum,* all of which, unfortunately, have been lost. Released in December 1597 Campanella returned to his native Stilo on condition that he confine himself to the monastery in Calabria. The socio-political upheavals of the time and Campanella's belief in astrology and prophecies, however, compelled him otherwise. Convinced that great changes were at hand and that he was both a prophet and a leader of the millennium, Campanella helped instigate a revolt in Calabria against the Spanish monarchy. Unsuccessful in his attempt to replace the existing form of government with a utopian republic founded on religion and natural magic, he was subsequently arrested in 1599, but feigned madness to avoid being put to death. He spent the next twenty-seven years in prison, eight of which were spent in a windowless dungeon. During this period Campanella penned what is often considered his most significant prose and poetry, including *City of the Sun, Monarchia di Spagna* (1620), *Metaphysics* (1638), and *Theologia* (c. 1613). He also wrote letters appealing to the Pope, cardinals, or to anyone who could help him gain his freedom. Successful in these efforts he was released by the Spanish authorities in 1626. He was arrested less than one month later, however, by the Holy Office because of his philosophical opinions, and remained in prison until January, 1629. After spending nearly thirty years in prison and being continuously kept under observation by both the Papal and Spanish authorities, Campanella left Italy for France in 1634, where he was received with favor by Cardinal Richelieu and King Louis XIII. During his last years, as throughout his life, Campanella engaged in political and literary activities: he attempted to influence French politics by initiating anti-Spanish campaigns and prepared the final editions of his works. Campanella died on May 21, 1639 in France at a Dominican monastery in Rue St. Honoré.

Major Works

Throughout his life, Campanella wrote more than one hundred volumes ranging from metaphysics and theology to political theory and utopian fiction. His philosophical writings include *Philosophia sensibus demonstrata, De sense rerum et magia,* and *De gentilismo non retinendo* (1636), and contain strong anti-Aristotelian notions influenced by the new empirical ideas of Telesio and Galileo. This new mode of thinking is clearly evident in the *City of the Sun* as Campanella combines elements of abstract and rational modes to form the philosophical foundation of his ideal society. Moreover, his *Monarchia del Messia* (c. 1605) and *Atheismus triumphatus* (c. 1605-7) confim his theocratic convictions toward governing the new society, while his *Monarchia di Spanga* and *Ecloga in Principis Galliarum delphini admirandam nativitatem* (1639) provide the means to realize his utopian ends. Campanella's poetry also reveals both his optimism in his role as a prophet of the new age and his frustration at his inability to fulfill the mission. "I live as I write" wrote Campanella in a letter to Cardinal Antonio Barberini. Considered in their totality, the scope and complexity of Campanella's writings indeed reflect his turbulent yet courageous life.

Critical Reception

Reaction to Campanella's ideas varied from repeated imprisonment and torture to a milder form of censure from his contemporaries Gaspar Schopp and Samuel Sorbière, the latter once referring to Campanella as a "most inefficient and ignorant monk." Campanella's supporters such as Tobias Adami and Gabriel Naudé, however, lauded his extraordinary intelligence. During his own lifetime, both Campanella's admirers and detractors lacked objective critical analysis, while critics in the eighteenth through the twentieth century grappled with determining the extent his anti-Aristotelianism. Many recent critics are concerned with Campanella's political writings and with examining the apparent contradiction between his overtly stated antipathy to Machiavelli and the strategic opportunism of his political theories. This focus also sparked an interest in examining the *City of the Sun* in relation to the whole tradition of utopian writing. The majority of recent criticism, however, focuses on the historical elements of Campanella's philosophy, interpreting his paradoxical thought as reflecting the social and political climate of the late Italian Renaissance.

PRINCIPAL WORKS

Philosophia sensibus demonstrata [Experimental Philosophy] (philosophy) 1589

De sense rerum et magia (philosophy) c.1591

* *Apologia pro Telesio* (philosophy) c.1593-94

* *Nova Physiologia iuxta propria principia* (philosophy) c.1593-94

Monarchia del Messia (political treatise) c.1605

Atheismus triumphatus [Atheism Conquered] (prose) c.1605-7

Quaestiones physiologicae, ethicae et politicae (prose) c.1613

†*Theologia* (prose) c.1613

‡*Quod reminiscentur [On Converting the Heathen]* (prose) c. 1616

Del senso delle cose e della magia [On the Sense and Feeling in All Things and on Magic] (philosophy) 1620

Monarchia di Spagna [A Discourse Touching the Spanish Monarchy] (political treatise) 1620

Scelta d'alcune Poesie filosofiche (poetry) 1622

Apologia pro Galileo [The Defense of Galileo] (prose) 1622

La Città del sole [City of the Sun] (utopian fiction) 1623

De gentilismo non retinendo [On the Gentilism that must not be adhered to] (prose) 1636

Metaphysics (philosophy) 1638

Poetica (poetry) 1638

Ecloga in Principis Galliarum delphini admirandam

nativitem (political treatise) 1639

§ *Lettere* (letters) c.1601-39

* Date of composition. Date of first publication is unknown.
†Published in 1936.
‡Published in 1939.
§Published in 1925.

CRITICISM

Lewis Mumford (essay date 1922)

SOURCE: An excerpt from *The Story of Utopias*, Boni and Liveright, 1922, pp. 103-08.

[*In the following excerpt from his critical study of utopian thought, Mumford characterizes Campanella's* City of the Sun *as a "utopia of means," largely concerned with mechanical inventions and the material perfection of society.*]

A Genoese sea-captain is the guest of a Grand Master of the Knights Hospitaller. This sea-captain tells him of a great country under the equator, dominated by the City of the Sun. The outward appearance of this country is a little strange—the city with its seven rings named after the seven planets, and its four gates that lead to the four quarters of the earth, and the hill that is topt by a grand temple, and the walls covered with laws and alphabets and paintings of natural phenomena, and the Rulers—Power, Wisdom, and Love—with the learned doctors, Astrologus, Cosmographus, Arithmeticus, and their like: it is an apparition such as never yet was seen on land or sea. Small wonder, for this City of the Sun existed only in the exotic brain of a Calabrian monk, Tommaso Campanella, whose Utopia existed in manuscript before Andreae wrote his Christianopolis.

We shall not stay long in the City of the Sun. After we have become familiar with the outward color and form of the landscape, we discover, alas! that it is not a foreign country we are exploring, but a sort of picture puzzle put together out of fragments from Plato and More. As in the Republic, there is a complete community of property, a community of wives, and an equality of the sexes; as in Utopia, the younger people wait upon the elders; as in Christianopolis, science is imparted, or at least hinted at, by demonstration. When one subtracts what these other Utopian countries have contributed, very little indeed remains.

But we must not neglect to observe two significant passages. One of them is the recognition of the part that invention might play in the ideal commonwealth. The people of the City of the Sun have wagons that are driven by the wind, and boats "which go over the waters without rowers or the force of the wind, but by

a marvelous contrivance." There is a very clear anticipation of the mechanical improvements which began to multiply so rapidly in the eighteenth century. At the tale end of the sea-captain's recital, the Grand Master exclaims: "Oh, if you knew what our astrologers say of the coming age, that has in it more history within a hundred years than all the world had in four thousand years before! Of the wonderful invention of printing and guns, and the use of the magnet. . . . " With the mechanical arts in full development, labor in the City of the Sun has become dignified: it is not the custom to keep slaves. Since everyone takes his part in the common work, there is not more than four hours' work to be done per day. "They are rich because they want nothing; poor because they possess nothing; and consequently they are not slaves to circumstances, but circumstances serve them."

The other point upon which Campanella's observation is remarkably keen is his explanation of the relation of private property and the private household to the commonwealth. Thus:

> They say that all private property is acquired and improved for the reason that each one of us by himself has his own home and wife and children. From this self-love springs. For when we raise a son to riches and dignities, and leave an heir to much wealth, we become either ready to grasp at the property of the state, if in any case fear should be removed from the power which belongs to riches and rank; or avaricious, crafty, and hypocritical, if any is of slender purse, little strength, and mean ancestry. But when we have taken away self-love, there remains only love for the state.

How shall the common Utopia keep from being neglected through each one's concern for his little private utopia?

This is the critical problem that our utopians have all to face; and Campanella loyally follows Plato in his solution. it is perhaps inevitable that each utopian's personal experience of life should enter into his solution, and overwhelmingly give it color; and here the limitations of our utopians are plain. More and Andreae are married men, and they stand for the individual family. Plato and Campanella were bachelors, and they proposed that men should live like monks or soldiers. Perhaps these two camps are not so far away as they would seem. If we follow the exposition of that excellent anthropologist, Professor Edward Westermarck, we shall be fairly well convinced, I believe, that marriage is a biological institution, and thorough promiscuity is, to say the least, an unusual form of mating. Plato perhaps recognized this when he left us in doubt as to whether a community of wives would be practiced by his artisans and husbandmen. So he perhaps paves the way for a solution by which the normal life for the great majority of men would be marriage, with its individual concerns and loyalties, whilst for the active, creative elements in the community a less secluded form of mating would be practiced. The painter, Van Gogh, has given us a kernel to chew on when he says that the sexual life of the artist must be either that of the monk or the soldier, for otherwise he is distracted from his creative work. . . .

Campanella with his dream of powerful mechanical inventions, in which he had been anticipated by Leonardo, and Bacon with his sketch of scientific institutes—with these two utopians we stand at the entrance to the utopia of means; that is to say, the place in which all that materially contributes to the good life has been perfected. The earlier utopias were concerned to establish the things which men should aim for in life. The utopias of the later Renascence took these aims for granted and discussed how man's scope of action might be broadened. In this the utopians only reflected the temper of their time; and did not attempt to remold it. As a result of our preoccupation with the means, we in the Western World live in an inventor's paradise. Scientific knowledge and mechanical power we have to burn; more knowledge and more power than Bacon or Campanella could possibly have dreamed of. But today we face again the riddle that Plato, More, and Andreae sought to answer: what are men to do with their knowledge and power? . . .

Marie Louise Berneri (essay date 1950)

SOURCE: "Tommaso Campanella: *The City of the Sun,*" in *Journey Through Utopia,* 1950. Reprint by The Beacon Press, 1951, p. 88-102.

[*In the following excerpt, Berneri provides an overview of Campanella's philosophical ideas, political activities, and lengthy imprisonment, and notes that* "The City of the Sun *is in fact closely related to Campanella's unsuccessful attempt to create a Republic of Calabria.*"]

There is none of More's literary elegance and fine irony in Campanella's *City of the Sun,* for unlike him he did not write in the pleasant circle of refined humanists but with his mind and limbs still aching from the tortures of the Inquisition.

Giovan Domenico Campanella was born in 1568, at Stilo, in Calabria, that province of Italy which even today remains a mystery to the Italians themselves and stubbornly refuses to become assimilated into Europe. He came from a poor family, and his father, when called as a witness at one of the trials of his famous son, testified with a touching simplicity: "I had heard that my son had written a book in Naples and everybody told me how fortunate I was; now they all tell me how unlucky I am; as for me I can neither read nor write."

Campanella was put in a monastery when he was still a child; when he was fourteen years old he entered the order of the Dominicans and it was then that he took the name of Tommaso. He said later that he chose a monastic life more to satisfy his desire for study than from the call of religion. He soon showed an independent spirit and attacked the scholastic method and doctrines. When he was eighteen he became acquainted with the works of Bernardino Telesio, the great philosopher of the Renaissance, and felt such enthusiasm for his ideas that he left the monastery to visit him at Cosenza, but he arrived just after Telesio's death. Shortly afterwards, when he was staying at the monastery of Altomonte, he met a Rabbi who made a profound impression on him by his prophetic gifts and his knowledge of astrology. It was probably through this acquaintance that Campanella acquired a passion for astrology and prophecy which never left him. The curious combination of rationalist and scientific ideas and of a superstitious belief in supernatural phenomena, which characterises many thinkers of the Renaissance, manifests itselt in a remarkably acute form throughout Campanella's writings.

His philosophical ideas very soon attracted the attention of the religious authorities. At the end of the 15th century, Italy no longer enjoyed that tolerance for new ideas which had characterised the early period of the Renaissance. The Reformation had robbcd the Catholic Church of its power over a great part of Western Europe, and a state of siege had been declared in the countries which had remained under its domination. Italy was in the grip of the counter-reformation and no one, from the Pope to the most obscure monk, escaped thewatchful eye of the Inquisition. In 1590 Campanella was summoned to appear before a Dominican tribunal for his writings in defence of Telesio. Three years later, while he was staying in a Dominican monastery at Bologna, he was robbed of all his manuscripts by the Pope's secret police. Campanella, suspecting the Vatican, applied to them for the return of his manuscripts but they denied all knowledge of the affair. He found them, however, thirty years later in the archives of the Holy See. In 1594 Campanella was accused of heresy for his ideas concerning universal animation, and sent for trial before the Roman Inquisition, which was unable to prove the charge, but ordered him to remain in Rome under close watch. In 1597 he returned to Naples, where he clashed once again with the religious authorities, and was obliged to retire to the monastery at Stilo.

There was a widespread belief at that time that the end of the century would bring profound changes, and even that the world might come to an end. Campanella was very much affected by these rumours, and he saw, in the unrest of Naples under Spanish rule, in events such as floods, earthquakes and the appearance of comets, a confirmation that social convulsions were imminent. A strange and powerful dream arose in his mind. He believed that the coming changes would lead to a complete reformation of society, and that the moment had come for the creation of an Universal Republic. His native Calabria, under his leadership, would be the starting-point for this movement. Until now Campanella had fought against the old ideas in his writings alone but the philosopher was now to become a man of action.

Campanella believed that a threefold reformation should take place. On the social plane, by improving the conditions of the people; politically, by making Spain the leader of an unification of the world; and in the sphere of religion by a reformation of the Church. But Campanella did not conceive a reformation in the sense of Calvin or Luther, who wanted to detach themselves from the domination of the Church of Rome and thereby encouraged national aspirations. Campanella was a staunch Catholic, and he wanted to unite the world under the standard of the Catholic faith. He attributed the defeats of the Catholic Church to her adherence to the old scholastic doctrines, and thought that she would neither regain nor increase her power through religious persecutions, but only in the acceptance of the new philosophical ideas. He sought to modernise the Church rather than to reform it.

The Republic of Calabria which he planned to institute would serve as an example as well as a starting-point for the creation of an universal Republic. Campanella was not, as he has sometimes been described, an Italian patriot. If he plotted against Spain, it was in order to achieve this Holy Universal Republic under the spiritual leadership of the Catholic Church, and, though he rebelled against the Spanish authorities, he believed that Spain was the only Power capable of bringing the Universal Republic into being.

In the church of the convent at Stilo he preached that the moment had come for revolt, and he persuaded some political exiles who had taken refuge in the monastery, and a number of the friars themselves, that the Holy Universal Republic would take place before the end of the world, and that it was necessary to find "propagandists" and "men of the deed" to achieve it. The friars with their tongues, the people with arms, would start a movement to create new laws and institutions for a better world. Some of the reforms and laws which he advocated at the time were later incorporated in the *City of the Sun*.

The plot was discovered and Campanella and his associates were arrested. On the 8th November, 1599, they were taken to Naples, by sea, and some of Campanella's companions were quartered on the galleys, in full view of the people of Naples, who had assembled in the harbour to see their arrival.

A charge of heresy was added to that of conspiring against Spain, and out of the hundred and forty men who had been arrested (of whom 14 were friars), ten were sentenced to death. For five months Campanella was kept in a humid and dark cell, with chains on his legs. He was submitted to terrible tortures, and eventually some kind of a confession was extracted from him, which allowed the Inquisition to proceed with the charge of heresy. But a few weeks before his trial was due to begin he set fire to his cell, and began to talk and behave as if he had lost his reason. Whether he was simulating madness, as most historians are inclined to believe, or whether the tortures had really affected his mind, will never be known.

On the 10th May, 1600, the trial for heresy began again, and his madness did not protect him from being tortured once more, with greater cruelty than before and, on one occasion, for twenty-four hours without a break. The record of Campanella's ravings and cries, faithfully noted by an officer of the Inquisition, has been preserved and constitutes a truly terrifying document. This time he refused to answer any questions, and continued to behave as if he were insane. The Inquisition suspected him of simulating madness, but they had to abide by their own tests, and they could not condemn him to death because it would have meant damning his soul. After a trial which lasted a whole year he was condemned to life imprisonment.

It was just after this trial, in 1602, that Campanella wrote his *City of the Sun*. It is generally believed that this work was written at a later date, in Latin, and the circumstances in which it was first composed having been generally overlooked, it has been described as an "exotic" and "eccentric" dream, completely divorced from reality. *The City of the Sun* is in fact closely related to Campanella's unsuccessful attempt to create a Republic of Calabria. The tortures and trials had not succeeded in crushing his spirit, and he may have written it as an act of defiance, or simply to explain what would have been carried out had he been successful. It is also possible that he hoped to escape, and that he sought in this way to gain support for a renewed attempt. He himself said later that he tried to gain an ascendancy over his guardians by some magic practices which impressed them greatly. They helped to smuggle his manuscripts out of prison, and might have helped him to escape had he not been transferred to another fortress. Campanella seems to have had a considerable popular following at the time, and the sonnets, which he wrote in his cell, were recited all over Naples. The fact that he wrote *The City of the Sun* in Italian, and not in Latin, indicated that he did not consider it an academic work but wanted it to be as widely read as possible.

It has often been pointed out that Campanella has taken very little trouble to give an appearance of reality to his ideal city, and it is true that we are told practically nothing as to where it is situated or how the seaman who tells the story reached it. This is understandable if one considers that he had preached and agitated, plotted and faced torture, in order to create an ideal republic in his native Calabria. He did not wish his readers to consider his work as one of fiction and to imagine the ideal city in some distant and foreign country, but to think of it as around them and themselves as its citizens. That Campanella did not lack imagination and poetical gifts is shown by the many sonnets and poems he wrote throughout his life, yet *The City of the Sun* is as arid and uninspiring as a political blue-print, which in fact, it was meant to be.

Campanella remained a prisoner in Naples, until September, 1626, when he was freed through the intervention of the Italian Council in Madrid. After being at liberty for a month, he was arrested again, this time by order of the Pope, and was kept prisoner in the Vatican for three years. After his release he enjoyed a period of relative quiet until 1633, when the Spaniards began to persecute him anew because they held him responsible for the pro-French policy of the Pope, Urban VIII. These suspicions were probably justified, for Campanella had abandoned the hope that Spain would unify the world as he had dreamt, and believed that France should take her place. In 1636 he was obliged to flee to Paris, where he lived under the protection of Richelieu and Louis XIII, and where he was able to publish his works and lecture at the Sorbonne in spite of protests from the Vatican. He died on the 21st May, 1639, in a monastery.

Campanella has achieved fame through his tragic life and his *City of the Sun* rather than by his philosophical works, which, however, occupy an important, if not a foremost, place in the philosophy of the later Renaissance. In his own Calabria his memory still lives among the people, and it is said that he appears in dreams to reveal hidden treasurers, a legend which would not have displeased the philosopher who liked sometimes to be thought a magician and a prophet.

Campanella composed most of his writings in prison, sometimes under really inhuman conditions, and he said later that he had fought death by work. Many of his manuscripts were confiscated and some of them destroyed by his jailers, and this partly explains why there are so many versions of most of his works. Some of them were composed as many as five times. *The City of the Sun* was written a second time in Italian in 1611, and for the first time in Latin in 1613-14. He wrote it for a fourth time in Latin, in a revised version, in 1630-31. The Latin versions differ considerably from the Italian, not only in style, which is more polished in the later versions, but also because his ideas altered a great deal during his imprisonment. As the years pass his ideal city becomes more and more authoritarian, and conforms more to the ideas of the Church. For example, the community of goods and of women is not abolished, but the Fathers of the Church are quoted to justify it, and sexual freedom becomes severely restricted. Astrology occupies a less important place in the later versions, probably in view of the war the Vatican was waging against astrologers.

Campanella was never a revolutionary; he was a reformer with a rebellious spirit and when that spirit of rebellion left him he became a conformist. During his youth and the first years of imprisonment he fought for the new philosophical ideas and for a better system of society, but as the years of imprisonment went by he sought to regain his freedom by trying to make his ideas acceptable to the authorities, and at the end of his life he aspired to become a cardinal in the Church which had persecuted him and wrote flattering poems to the King of France and Richelieu.

The first version of *The City of the Sun* was written during his youth, when his body was bound but his mind was still free, and it is therefore more truly utopian than the others. Later, Campanella's vision was clouded by the fear of perpetual imprisonment and the necessity of compromise. It was, however, through the Latin versions that *The City of the Sun* became mostly known. It must have reached Germany before 1619, for it clearly influenced Andreae's *Christianopolis,* published in that year. It may have been taken there by Scioppio, a German scholar who had been converted to Catholicism and was leader of the counter-reformation in Germany. He tried hard to obtain Campanella's release, travelling from Italy to Germany in order to see the Emperor and win him to Campanella's cause, taking with him some of his manuscripts. *The City of the Sun* was published for the first time in 1623 in Frankfurt, by Tobias Adani, a German jurist who published most of Campanella's works from 1617 to 1629. An English translation (by T. W. Halliday) did not appear until 1886, when it was included in Henry Morley's *Ideal Commonwealths*. There is no indication from which Latin edition the translation was made, but it contains several obvious mistranslations which, in some cases, render the text meaningless. Some passages which have been left out are described by Morley as "one or two omissions of detail which can well be spared." These cuts seem to have been dictated by a Victorian sense of propriety rather than by considerations of space.

Ernst Bloch (essay date 1959)

SOURCE: "Counterpart to More: Campanella's *City of the Sun* or the Utopia of Social Order," in *The Principle of Hope,* 1959, translated by Neville Plaice,

Stephen Plaice, and Paul Knight, Basil Blackwell, 1986, pp. 523-34.

[*In the following excerpt from* The Principle of Hope, *originally published in German as* Das Prinzip Hoffnung, *Bloch contrasts the utopian vision of Campanella with that of More, arguing that these two writers influenced two opposing traditions of utopian writing: social order and freedom.*]

The Baroque is the age of centralized royal power, and it was progressive at that time. A totally authoritarian and also bureaucratic utopia: Campanella's *Civitas solis,* published in 1623, now corresponded to the harmony of bourgeois interests with the monarchy. Instead of freedom, as in More, the tune that now rings out is that of order, with rulers and supervisors. Instead of a president of the Utopians, in a simple Franciscan cloak, with a harvest crown, a ruler appears, a world pope. And what Campanella found most seductive about America was no longer, as in More, the paradisial innocence of the islanders, but the highly constructed Inca empire of the past. Lewis Mumford, in *The Story of Utopias,* 1922, calls Campanella's utopia nothing short of a 'marriage between Plato's *Republic* and the court of Montezuma'. After all, as noted above, Plato's *Republic* was the first utopianizing order, long before there was a novel of an ideal state based on freedom. In its title as in its geographical situation, Campanella's *City of the Sun* touches on that of Iamboulos; though the Sun in Campanella's City does not shine with effortless Hellenistic-oriental abundance, but simply with centralized rigour, of the sort which was also practised in truly Campanellan fashion by the artificial Jesuit state in Paraguay. Campanella's dreams as a whole were connected with contemporary power units; he projected these on to a utopian screen. Not in order to ideologize them, but he believed in the coming of his dream kingdom and emphasized the existing great powers solely as instruments for hastening its arrival. Although he spent twenty-seven years in the dungeons of Spanish reaction, which did not trust him, Campanella, who is first supposed to have had relations with the Turks, wildly acclaimed Spanish world-domination, and ultimately that of France, but in both cases exclusively as places of preparation for the messianic kingdom of the sun. He still characteristically ended the dedication to Richelieu of his work 'De sensu rerum et magia', newly published in 1637, with a messianic claim, not with courtly flattery: 'The city of the sun, devised by me, to be established by you'; in this arrogant hope Campanella also welcomed the birth of the future Louis XIV, who was later actually called the Sun King. Looking at it in more detail, the work about the 'City of the Sun' is a meticulous account given by a widely travelledGenoan to his host. The Gubernator Genuensis relates how on a voyage round the world he landed on the island of Taprobane (Ceylon) and fell into the hands of a band of armed men who had conducted him to the City of the Sun and explained its institutions to him. For all its boldness and the usual novelistic trappings, the account has a feel of technical engineering about it: the civitas is constructed like a contemporary plan of fortifications by Vauban. On the whole, Campanella's utopia must be understood in conformity with the world system of its creator; apart from Bacon and the Fichte of the 'Closed Commercial State', Campanella is the only philosopher among the more modern utopians. It was no accident that the *Civitas solis* was published as the appendix to a *Philosophia realis,* that is, as a paralipomenon, but also as a means of putting to the test a natural and moral philosophy. Just as man is a likeness of God, so is his extension, the state; accordingly, this social utopia descends from the supreme being to the state and seeks to show that the latter, conceived as perfect, resembles the radiations of a divine solar system. The communist features of such a utopia of domination may cause surprise; only in fact it is not a utopia of freedom at work here, but one of impersonal order, conceived in terms of an international state. Its thorough administrative organization was reflected in a model island, and the contradiction between a universal kingdom and an island city is suppressed. Life runs like clockwork in a military monarchic fashion, the strictest punctuality and pre-orderedness demonstrate their technical efficiency in terms of time, administration and economy. The incipient manufacturing system, which brought together workers and technological means of production in large workshops, is utopianized along the lines of state socialism. On the other hand, Campanella transfigures the Hispanicization of the continent at the time, the deliberate intolerance (though with contents of his own, not with those of the Inquisition). A state socialism appears, or rather: a popish one, with a lot of Byzantine and astrological pathos behind it. With the pathos of *the right time, the right situation, the right order of all people and things;* a commanding centre establishes order in a classless but extremely hierarchical way.

If things are run in this way, then there are neither rich nor poor, private property is abolished. All citizens have to work, a four-hour day is enough, exploitation and profit are unknown. Each trade is a communal enterprise, under supervision and without individual gain, the highest task is the common good.Current states are riddled with selfishness: 'But if there is no private property any more, then it becomes pointless and disappears.' The vices of poverty and the greater ones of wealth have vanished, the only quarrels are those on points of honour: 'The Solarians claim that poverty makes people low-minded, cunning, thieving, homeless and mendacious. But wealth makes them impudent, arrogant, ignorant, treacherous, boastful and heartless. In a true community, however, everybody is rich and poor at the same time—rich because they do not wish for anything that they do not have in common,—

poor because nobody possesses anything, and consequently the Solarians are not enslaved to things, but things serve them.' But while private property has thus died out, the state is not diminished as well, as it is in More, but it becomes instead the highest purpose of society; ascending from the provincia to the regnum, to the imperium, to the monarchia universalis and finally to the papal kingdom. The state guarantees precisely the pleasant part of order, the distribution of goods: 'The Solarians receive everything they need from the community, and the authorities strictly see to it that nobody gets an excessive amount, and nobody is denied anything they need.' Above all, Campanella's state also seeks its power in the present metaphysics it portrays, in the image of God, in accordance with Campanella's philosophy. The authorities reflect the primary forces of cosmic order, those three 'primalities' of being which govern human experiences and spheres of activity. These are Sapientia, Potentia, and Amor, their unity is God, they reach and emanate from God, through four worlds growing ever more corporeal, into their respective historical existence, the 'mundus situalis'. Within it the 'primalities' themselves need an embodiment to create the order which can always only be one of the right coordination: God becomes the papal world-ruler, also called Sol or Metaphysicus in Campanella's utopia. Subordinate to him are three princes whose sphere of activity exactly corresponds to the regions of Sapientia, Potentia, and Amor, as in a cabbalistic space. History becomes the production of this state space, which is the only veritable, i.e. vertical one; just as space in general is celebrated throughout Campanella, 'as an immortal and almost divine, all-pervading receptacle of things', which itself strives for fulfilment and fills the horror vacui, the horror of chaos and nothingness. Necessity as the expression of divine Potentia conquers the case of chance (contingentia), certainty (fatum) as the expression of divine Sapientia conquers the individual case (casus), but order (harmonia), above all, as the expression of divine Amor conquers the case of luck, of vicissitude (fortuna).Thus in Campanella (as earlier in Cusanus) the rising bourgeoisie stands firmly in the struggle against nothingness; unlike the declining, panchaotic bourgeoisie, wallowing in nothingness. But Campanella's order of wisdom, power and love, i.e. that of the three 'primalities', is opposed to the chaotic: to the case of chance, the individual case, and the case of vicissitude. And this order is precisely *active* in its opposition, since contingentia, casus, and fortuna are supposed to be merely 'a nihilo contracta', simply the remnants of the dead nothingness from which God called the world into existence. Though in a truly *emanatistic* fashion, Campanella ultimately sought to conquer the nothingness or non-ens in the world by an irradiation of the ens, the Sol, the solar essence. It therefore comes as no surprise that the further directive of such a thoroughly ruled world could become the myth of *astrology;* for it above all guarantees dependence on above. Astrolo-

gy corresponded to the fanaticism of this order, it casts man along with all things among planets and the ruling houses of the zodiac. Both the domestic and the public life of the Solarians, the traffic and the layout of the city, even baths, meals and the right moment for sexual intercourse are governed by the stars: 'Men and women sleep in two separate chambers, and await the moment of their fruitful union: at a specified time a matron opens both doors from outside. This time is specified by the doctor and the astrologer, who try to hit the moment in which Venus and Mercury stand east of the sun in a favourable house, in the auspicious aspect of Jupiter.' Freedom of choice and freedom in general are thus taken away from man, not in a mechanizing way but rather in the manner of a dictatorship of the stars, from above, on all sides. Nowadays astrology is just a ruin of superstitious architecture, but in those days it was still alive and accepted, a kind of class meeting-house, extending with its patriarchalisms through the whole world. And only incidentally do a few exemptions—not freedoms—lodge in the total hierarchy, they are solely missing prohibitions. There are several such missing prohibitions: 'The Solarian can spend his free time with pleasant studies, walks, mental and physical exercises and with pleasures.' Likewise the mount of Venus does not attain the height of the other pedantry, the astrological rules for sexual intercourse are only obligatory for prospective parents: 'The rest, who associate with those who are infertile or prostitutes either for pleasure or on doctor's orders or as a stimulant, disregard these customs.' In fact there is even an illusion of liberalism at the point where the state is most seriously in evidence, on the occasion of a death sentence: 'The man found guilty must in this case make his peace with hisaccuser and witness by kissing and embracing them, as the doctors of his illness so to speak. Moreover, the death sentence in Solaria is not carried out on any condemned man until he himself has become convinced by superior reasoning that it is necessary for him to die, and until he has been brought to the point of wishing for the death sentence to be carried out himself.' Rousseau's 'Contrat social' admittedly makes a similar demand, but the difference between the attitude of the latter and that of Campanella could not be greater. Rousseau wants to preserve self-determination even in the act which destroys it, whereas Campanella uses liberality as an aid to the strongest triumph of authority. For the rightly condemned individual here wants to see himself destroyed as a deviation, or in the language of the Church: laudabiliter se subjecit. Subjectivity precisely exists only in so far as it agrees to its own extermination. That is, it is even deprived of the refuge of being able to be a rebel or a persistent heretic. Thus total conformism triumphs exactly where it seems to suffer an exception; even in its humaneness, Campanella's *City of the Sun* represents the most extreme antithesis to the utopia of freedom. Order is virtue itself and its assembly: 'The Solarians have as many authorities as we have names of virtues: magnanimity, bravery, chastity, generosity, cheerfulness, sobriety and so on. And they are chosen for posts according to whether they betrayed the greatest tendency to this or that virtue even as children at school.' Even in this harsh utopia, happiness remains the summum bonum, but it is precisely the happiness of servitude, harnessed to a divine service which—with the total unity of spiritual and temporal power—is the same as service to the state. So much for Campanella's future state, it contains an intoxication of constraint which is unparalleled, it surpasses Plato's ideal of Sparta by using the whole Byzantine and Catholic hierarchy which had arisen since then. Apart from the distribution of property, life is only so bad because people are not in their place, because mundus situalis, the mere situational state of life, totters into the situational accidents of its semi-nothingness. Because no concord prevails and no agreement with the ruling celestial forces, no harmony with them; because the state is not on an even keel. This is time and again the basic contrast to the utopias of freedom, in such various forms, from the Cynics to Thomas More, and ultimately to anarchism; in Campanella the contrast breaks out consciously. The abolition of private property does not dissolve the contrast: for while in More this abolition overcomes subordination and superiority in general and posits total equality, in Campanella this equality becomes the very foundationsoil on which a new hierarchy arises, that of talents, virtues and 'primalities'. If we clarify this contrast between More and Campanella in terms of the two more competing than connected natural myths of their time, then we can say that More or the utopia of *freedom* corresponds almost as much to *alchemy* as Campanella or the utopia of *order* corresponds in fact to *astrology*. More never mentions alchemy, if only because gold is despised on his island and because the refining of metals in the symbolic sense, as a refining of the world, no longer seems to be necessary there. But when More relates right at the beginning that the founder of his island first blasted it away from the mainland, and when, as More says, it is isolated precisely from the world of the 'plumbei' or leaden ones, then these passages were soon interpreted alchemically and could be interpreted like this, in the sense of the later Rosicrucians or initiated 'general reformers' (Andreae, Comenius). 'Utopia' is distilled from the evil world like gold from lead,—alchemy was regarded as the mythology of this liberation. Campanella on the other hand certainly does mention alchemy, even the golden lustre in Sol and Civitas solis suggested this reminiscence, but the continuous pathos of astrology in his work prevented the liberation of social gold from breaking out of its pre-ordered space and exploding it. In Campanella, the harmony of the world below was also still to be founded, but the 'Civitas solis' remains strictly chained to the regency of the stars. Utopia does not have to be processed out here, but it is cosmic harmony, and there has been not too much but too

little government in society up to now, and consequently too little astrology. Thus the contrast between More's model and that of Campanella is also a mythological one; and it extends—without a mythological cloak—into all following utopias. Liberal-federative socialism (from Robert Owen onwards) has More as its ancestor, while centralist socialism (from Saint-Simon onwards) has points of contact with Campanella, with a broad-based, high-built system of rule, with social utopia as strictness and arranged happiness.

Bernardino M. Bonansea (essay date 1969)

SOURCE: "Political Theory: The Ideal State," in *Tommaso Campanella: Renaissance Pioneer of Modern Thought,* The Catholic University of America Press, 1969, pp. 264-98.

[*Reacting against interpretations of* The City of the Sun *as a communist or rationalist utopia, Bonansea views Campanella's utopian text as depicting an ideal society "in the pure order of nature," "modeled after the system of early Christian communities."*]

The City of the Sun, which in its Latin edition appears as an appendix to the treatise ***Politica in aphorismos digesta,*** is a fictional dialogue. In it a Genoese Sea Captain tells a Grandmaster of the Knights Hospitalers about his journey to the island of Taprobane under the equator. While there, he met a large group of armed men and women, many of whom understood his language, and they took him to the City of the Sun. The city, in the Captain's report, is largely built on a hill which rises out of an extensive plain, but its rings extend far beyond the base of the hill. The diameter of the city is over two miles and the circumference seven miles. Yet, because of the humped shape of the mountain, the area contains more buildings than it would if the city were built on a plain.

The city is divided into seven huge rings or circles named for the seven planets, and each ring is connected by four streets and gates facing the four points of the compass. The city is so built that if the first circle were stormed, it would take much more effort to storm the second, and still more to storm the others. Thus anyone wishing to capture the city must storm it seven times.

On top of the hill there arises a splendid temple built in the form of a circle and standing on thick columns beautifully grouped. It has a large dome containing in its center a small dome with an opening right over the altar. There is only one altar, and on it there is nothing but a large globe with the painting of the sky and a small globe with a representation of the earth.

The small dome at the top of the temple is surrounded

by several small cells, while larger cells are built behind the level space above the enclosures or arches of the inner and outer columns. These larger cells are occupied by priests and other religious officers.

An excerpt from Campanella's *The City of the Sun*:

Hospitaler: Tell me, what is that city like, and how is it ruled?

Genoese: Rising from a broad plain, there is a hill upon which the greater part of the city is situated, but its circling walls extend far beyond its base, so that the entire city is two miles and more in diameter and has a circumference of seven miles; but because it is on a rise, it contains more habitations than it would if it were on a plain.

The city is divided into seven large circuits, named after the seven planets. Passage from one to the other is provided by four avenues and four gates facing the four points of the compass. It is constructed in such a way that if the first circuit were taken by assault, more effort would be required to take the second, likewise again the third, and so forth, so that seven assaults would be needed to conquer it all. But in my opinion not even the first assault would be successful, so thick is the wall, which, moreover, is guarded by ramparts, towers, artillery, and surrounding moats.

Tommaso Campanella, in The City of the Sun: A Poetical Dialogue, *translated by Daniel J. Donno, University of California Press, 1981.*

The temporal and spiritual ruler of the city is a priest called Hoh or Sun, although in our language, the Captain remarks, he would be called Metaphysic. He is assisted by three princes, Pon, Sin, and Mor, names standing for *Potentia, Sapientia,* and *Amor,* that is, Power, Wisdom, and Love. Power takes care of all mattersrelating to war and peace and the military arts. He directs the military magistrates and the soldiers, and has the management of munitions, fortifications, and the storming of places. Wisdom has charge of the liberal and mechanical arts and all the sciences. He has as many magistrates and teachers under him as there are disciplines to be taught. To foster education, he has had the outer and inner walls of the city adorned with fine paintings and with illustrations of all the sciences. Love attends to the improvement of the race by providing that men and women unite to bring forth the best kind of offspring. Indeed they laugh at us for devoting so much care to the breeding of dogs and horses while neglecting the breeding of the human race. The education of children, along with stock raising, medicine, and agriculture, falls also under the care of Love.

Metaphysic treats all these matters with the three rulers, and nothing is done without him. Thus all the business of the state is discharged by the four together, but whatever Metaphysic says is always favorably accepted.

The inhabitants of the City of the Sun came originally from India, as they fled from the sword of the Moguls. Many among them were philosophers, and they decided to lead a philosophic life in common. There is among them a community of wives as well as of property. They hold, in fact, that private property is acquired because each man wants to have his own home and wife and children. This gives rise to self-love. Once self-love is abolished, there remains only love for the state.

They receive whatever they need from the community, and the magistrates take care that no one has more than he deserves. Yet no one is deprived of what is necessary. All young men call themselves brothers; those who are fifteen years older are called fathers, and those who are fifteen years younger are called sons.

They have magistrates corresponding to the name of each of our virtues, such as Magnanimity, Fortitude, Chastity, Liberality, Justice, and the like. Their selection is based on the excellence shown in the practice of the particular virtue they represent. Among them there is no robbery, murder, rape, incest, adultery, or other crimes that exist among us. They accuse themselves only of ingratitude, indolence, scurrility, lying, etc., for which they are duly punished.

Men and women wear almost the same kind of garment, which is suitable for war. The only difference is that the women's toga extends below the knee, while men's ends above the knee. Both sexes are educated together in all the arts. They learn the language when they are very young, and they are drilled in various kinds of gymnastics, so that their body is fully developed. They always go barefooted and bareheaded until they are seven years old. They are introduced to different trades, so that each one's talent may be discovered. After the seventh year they begin more serious and more specialized studies by attending lectures, engaging in disputations, and visiting the countryside with their teachers and judges. He who has learned several trades and knows how to practice them well is considered noble and superior to others.

Management of the race is for the good of the commonwealth and not for the benefit of private citizens. They maintain, in effect, that children are bred for the preservation of the species rather than for individual pleasure. Hence infants, by order of the physicians, are nursed by their mothers until they reach the age of two or more. Then girls are handed over to mistresses and boys to masters appointed by the state. As they grow older, their education is committed to the care of the magistrates, who also have charge of mating the best endowed male and female breeders according to the rules of philosophy. Women are forbidden under the death penalty to use cosmetics, high heeled shoes, or gowns with train.

Labor and other duties are so distributed among the inhabitants that each one works only for about four hours a day. The rest of the time is spent in study, reading, writing, walking, and lawful recreation. All citizens are rich because they desire no more than they have; at the same time all are poor because they own nothing in private. They have no fear of death, since they believe in the immortality of the soul and a future reward.

The inhabitants of the City of the Sun place great emphasis on agriculture, and no piece of ground is left uncultivated. They observe closely the winds and propitious stars, and attach great importance to the science of navigation. They travel abroad in order to become acquainted with other countries and peoples.

In diet, they make a distinction between useful and harmful foods, using them in accordance with medical science. They eat the most healthful foods which vary according to the different seasons of the year. They are very temperate in their use of wine, which is never given to the young until they reach nineteen, unless the state of their health demands it. After their nineteenth year they take it diluted with water, as do the women. When fifty or older the men take wine without water, except when they have to attend meetings. There are very few diseased among them, and for these they have special remedies, many of which are known only to them.

The rulers of the city hold regular meetings to decide on matters pertaining to the public welfare. Judges are constituted by the first masters in each trade. They observe the *lex talionis* or law of recompense and punish serious crimes with the death penalty. Secret confession is practiced in such a way that the citizens tell their sins to the magistrates, the magistrates to the three supreme chiefs, and these to Hoh himself, who offers sacrifices and prayers to God, but only after he has confessed publicly in the temple all the sins of his people. Human sacrifice is practiced on a voluntary basis. A man who volunteers to die for his country is treated with great benevolence and much honor; however, God does not require the death of the victim.

Priests, all of whom are over twenty-four years of age, offer prayers and sing hymns to God four times a day. They also observe the stars and note their motions and influences upon human affairs. In most cases, it is from among the priests that Hoh is elected.

The inhabitants of the City of the Sun regard the sun and the stars as living representations of God, which they honor but do not worship. They believe that the world is a huge animal in which men live just as worms live within men. They claim that it is not easy to know whether the world was made from nothing, from the ruins of other worlds, or from chaos; but they hold that it was made and did not exist from eternity. Hence they dislike Aristotle. They admit the existence of two physical principles: the sun as the father and the earth as the mother. Likewise, they admit two metaphysical principles: being, which is God; and nonbeing, which is the lack of being and the necessary condition for all created things. It is their conviction that evil and sin stem from a tendency toward nothingness. Sin has no efficient cause but only a deficient one; it shows a defect of the will, for it is in the will that sin resides.

They believe in the Trinity and say that God is Power, Wisdom, and Love. However, they do not distinguish the three divine persons by name, as Christians do, for they are not acquainted with revelation. They also say that all things are made of power, wisdom, and love inasmuch as they have being; of impotence, ignorance, and hatred inasmuch as they have nonbeing. They know that there is great corruption in the world, and from this fact they argue to the existence of some serious disorder in the past, but they do not believe it is due to Adam's sin. They acknowledge the freedom of the will and say that heresy is the work of the flesh. Finally, they teach that the true and holy law is the law of the First Reason.

As might be expected, many questions have been raised about *The City of the Sun*. Some of these questions concern the general theme of the work in the light of Campanella's entire literary production, and some concern particular issues, such as the practice of common use of goods and community of wives. There have been interpreters who claim to see in Campanella's ideal republic the model of state socialism and communism and hold that he is a forerunner of those doctrines. Others prefer to see in *The City of the Sun* a bold conception of a rationalistic state, in which man knows all faiths and religions, including the Christian religion, but accepts none of them. In this view, Campanella's ideal republic would show once more the heretical and rebellious spirit of its author, whom the Church never ceased to persecute. The fact that in many of his writings Campanella refers to *The City of the Sun* as a "dialogue on his own state" (*dialogo di propria repubblica*), is believed to lend support to the view that he stood for his own personal rationalistic theory even when he was contemplating a universal monarchy under the Pope, as described in the *Monarchia Messiae*.

Neither of these interpretations is acceptable. We believe that a great injustice is done to the author of **The City of the Sun** by those who like to present him as a harbinger of modern socialism and communism or as a champion of a purely rationalistic state theory. There is sufficient textual evidence in Campanella's works to support the contention that **The City of the Sun** is only a "poetical dialogue," as the subtitle of the work indicates, which depicts an imaginary community of men and women *in the pure order of nature*. Following the light of reason but unaided by Christian revelation, they organize themselves into an ideal society where all abuses—with due reservation for some questionable practices to be examined later—are eliminated and all citizens contribute effectively to the common welfare. To prove our point, we shall let Campanella speak for himself and present his case in his own terms. We shall add only those comments and observations that may help the reader better to understand Campanella's thought.

Anticipating the objections that the highly provocative character of **The City of the Sun** would raise among its readers, Campanella wrote a defense of the work to which he refers possible inquirers. This defense makes up the entire fourth question of the **Quaestiones politicae,** and is divided into three articles. In the first article he discusses the truth and usefulness of his political dialogue, while in the second and third articles he deals respectively with the controversial issues of community of goods and community of women. Answering the question whether the work would serve any purpose, since it is hardly conceivable that an ideal state like his could ever be brought into existence, he appeals to the authority of Thomas More, whose *Utopia* served as a blueprint for his own dialogue. Plato is also brought on the scene as the creator of an ideal republic that could not be fully realized in the state of corrupt nature but could have been in the state of innocence. Legislators are likewise known to issue laws that will never be fully observed; yet such laws serve their purpose, inasmuch as they set a pattern of action to be followed by the citizens in pursuing the common good of the state.

The ideal republic described in **The City of the Sun,** continues Campanella, is not like the Mosaic and Christian laws, which have been revealed to man by God. Rather, it represents the best form of government that philosophers can achieve by the light of reason alone. If in certain matters, such as the community of women, the inhabitants of the City of the Sun differ from the teaching of the Gospels, this is not due to ill will but to the weakness of the human mind, which considers as permissible certain practices that revelation proves to be faulty. The republic reflects the conditions of a people that is still *in gentilismo,* that is, in paganism, and looks forward to the revelation of a better way of life. They are, as it were, in a state of

preparation for Christianity (*in Catechismo ad vitam Christianam*), since, in the opinion of St. Cyril, it is the function of philosophy to prepare the gentiles for the evangelical truth.

These statements are so clear that they leave no doubt about the real nature of Campanella's dialogue. To see in **The City of the Sun** the realization of a naturalistic society that knew but rejected Christian revelation, is to distort Campanella's doctrine completely. One might object that he presents his ideal republic as a model also for Christians who have been enlightened by supernatural revelation and restored by Christ to the state of original innocence. He even expresses the hopes that such a republic may some day, after the downfall of the Antichrist, be established throughout the entire world. These statements, however, which follow almost immediately upon those we have just mentioned, should be interpreted in the light of the entire context and made to harmonize with the preceding doctrine rather than contradict it.

The point Campanella wants to make is that although his ideal republic can best be achieved by philosophers who have never come in contact with Christian revelation, it represents also the idealization of human nature in its striving for a perfect natural society. By restoring man to the state of original innocence and raising him to the supernatural order, Christ did not destroy human nature, which remains essentially the same even after Christ's redemption. Rather, He made it easier for men to organize themselves into an ideal society that, with the aid of grace and the sacraments, would help them better to attain their final end, both in the natural and supernatural orders. It is in this sense that Campanella can speak in the same article, and without contradicting himself, of an ideal state *in gentilismo,* modeled after Plato's *Republic* and Thomas More's *Utopia,* and an ideal state for all Christendom, inspired by the community system of early Christians and the monastic life of contemporary religious orders. It becomes likewise understandable how he can say that the Anabaptists, a contemporary religious sect of people living in common, cannot expect to make any real progress unless they decide to accept the teaching of the Catholic Church and rid themselves of their heretical beliefs.

Campanella has no doubt that the system of community of goods is in conformity with the natural law and that it contributes to the welfare of the state and its citizens. He defends this thesis in the second article of the fourth question of the **Quaestiones politicae,** where he argues against Aristotle and all philosophers who stand for the natural right of private property. To establish his position, he makes use of arguments from authority and from reason. Among the arguments from authority he cites statements by Pope St. Clement the Roman, St. Augustine, St. John Chrysostom, St. Ambrose, St. Thomas Aquinas, and others. However he takes some of these statements out of context and twists them to suit his own purpose. He also brings forward the teaching of the Apostles, the example of early Christians and churchmen, and the actual system of community life of the religious orders to show that the community of goods is a much better system than that which allows private property. In his opinion, the Church relaxed this law of nature at a later date, especially for the clergy, to avoid greater evils. It amounts in effect to a permission rather than to a real law.

The main reason for the abolition of private property is to prevent abuses that inevitably creep into society once the goods are divided among the citizens. Avarice, which is the root of all evils, fraud, theft, robbery, pride, egoism, jealousy, enmity and the like are only the most common abuses. To avoid them, goods must be distributed among the citizens on the basis of their natural talents and abilities. This will also help to uproot the social evils that result from a system based on heredity or an elective system in which ambition plays an important role. In conclusion, the doctrine of the community of goods, affirms Campanella, is definitely according to the law of nature. To hold the contrary is nothing short of heresy. Nor can it be said with Duns Scotus that the community of goods was of natural right in the state of innocence but not after Adam's fall. Original sin deprived man of the goods of the supernatural order, not of those which belong to the order of nature.

Thus, according to Campanella, community of goods is an ideal system for man both in the order of grace and the order of nature. Shall we say that his theory is an anticipation of modern socialistic and communistic collectivism? There are no doubt points of contact between the two doctrines, inasmuch as both defend some sort of state absolutism in regard to material goods. However, the doctrinal background and inspirational motive of the two systems, as well as the methods suggested for their establishment, make them very different. The state absolutism advocated by scientific socialism, and especially by Marxist communism, is a completely materialistic and atheistic conception of society that makes the state the supreme and absolute ruler over the goods and destinies of the citizens. It admits no spiritual or moral values and controls the citizens, who are reduced to almost insignificant units in the state machinery, by flashing before their imagination the mirage of an ideal temporal happiness that will never materialize.

Campanella's community system, on the other hand, is based on a completely different ideology. It is modeled after the system ofearly Christian communities and fashioned along the general lines of monastic life in the religious orders, where the abolition of private property is only a means to help the monks detach themselves from earthly goods and attend more completely to the things of the spirit. Furthermore, in *The City of the Sun* there is no indication whatsoever of violence or compulsion in enforcing the laws of the state. On the contrary, everything is done smoothly and in a most reasonable manner, since every citizen is asked to do what suits him best. Briefly, while Marxist communism attempts to achieve its purely materialistic ends by brute force, class warfare, and hatred, Campanella's collectivism aims at helping man to attain better the end for which he was created by fostering love and mutual understanding.

A second thorny question that Campanella discusses in his *Quaestiones politicae* is "Whether the community of women is more in agreement with nature and more helpful to generation, and hence to the state, than the possession of one wife and children." Here he faces the obvious objection, raised throughout the entire history of philosophy from Aristotle to his own time, that the community of women is against the natural law and destructive of marriage, the essential properties of which are unity and indissolubility.

Campanella is aware of the seriousness of the objection and proceeds carefully to justify the conduct of the dwellers in the City of the Sun. To avoid any misunderstanding, he cautions the reader at the beginning that not all kinds of community of women are legitimate, but only the particular type he describes in his political dialogue. There are, in effect, several ways of understanding the community of women. First of all, there is the so-called *concubitus vagus,* whereby a man is allowed to have sexual intercourse with any woman, at any time, with no restrictions whatsoever, as do certain animals. Promiscuity of this kind must be condemned, as it is against man's rational nature and leads to various abuses. There is another kind of promiscuity, continues Campanella, which consists in allowing a legally wed man to have sexual relations at certain definite times with a woman allotted to him, as has been the case in certain regions of France and Germany. This system, too, is to be condemned as against the natural law, or at least the divine positive law, for it promotes selfish gratification rather than the good of the offspring.

There is, however, a third kind of community of women, which isthe system followed by the inhabitants of the City of the Sun. It consists in matching only the best breeders, who will have sexual intercourse only at the time that is most suitable for generation and within certain age limits. This system, remarks Campanella, does not involve a breach of the natural law and is consistent with people who live *in puris naturalibus,* like the citizens in question, who have no knowledge of the divine positive law. Even if such a system were against the natural law, that fact could not be known by reason alone, since it cannot be inferred by way of conclusion from the natural law itself. It can only be known by a specific determination of the positive law, which of its nature is subject to change. Thus the doctrine of the community of women, as propounded in *The City of the Sun,* would become heretical only after the Church's condemnation; and those citizens, whose only rule and guide is the natural law known by reason, cannot be blamed for their conduct in regard to women.

Is this teaching inconsistent with the position that Campanella takes in his other works, such as the *Quaestiones occonomicae, Oeconomica,* and *Theologia,* where he proclaims that polygamy is against the natural law? Certain statements of the *Quaestiones politicae,* if taken separately, may seem to point toward a real conflict in his teaching. Yet, if we take a closer look at the context, we will see that the conflict is only apparent. In the works that have just been mentioned, where Campanella treats the doctrine of marriage specifically, he maintains that polygamy is only secondarily against the natural law, so that it is possible for God to dispense men from it. In the *Quaestiones politicae* he does not reject explicitly this doctrine; he simply emphasizes the difficulty for the inhabitants of the City of the Sun to discover it by the light of natural reason alone, prior to the positive decree of the Church. That this is Campanella's mind can be inferred from his insistence upon *the state of pure nature* in which those inhabitants are supposed to live, and from his explicit affirmation that the community of women may perhaps be against the natural law, but that this cannot be known by a philosopher. . . .

Although *The City of the Sun* is in the mind of its author a poetical dialogue describing an imaginary and hypothetic state, many of the ideas contained in it have a practical value. This was the intention of Campanella, who often refers to the dialogue in later and more serious works. . . . But even a cursory look at *The City of the Sun* will convince the reader that its author is to be credited with modern views on problems in the social, political, and educational fields. Thus Campanella appears once more as an original thinker and a forerunner of modern times.

Timothy J. Reiss (essay date 1973)

SOURCE: "Structure and Mind in Two Seventeenth-Century Utopias: Campanella and Bacon," in *Yale French Studies,* Vol. 49, 1973, pp. 82-95.

[*Reiss compares Campanella's and Bacon's utopian texts as illustrating two types of utopian vision—"the dynamic and the static."*]

The Utopian thinker, according to Marx, writes as a bourgeois who, in the silence of his study, gives free play at once to his reason and his imagination, and it may be supposed that this acknowledged duality of cause has its reflexion in the result. For the utopian ideal is at once a meditation upon history or an historical situation and a proposing of an "ideal" solution to that history. Indeed, to the extent that the utopia represents at once myth *and* the reasoned attempt to permit the insertion of that myth into the stream of History, it clearly partakes—as a literary text—of that epistemological division of thought which appears to characterize the sixteenth and seventeenth centuries in Europe. Insofar as the utopia is dynamic, it may offer an idealized *continuation* of that history, and it may thus be said to be adapted rather to the serial process of rational (logico-mathematical) thinking. Insofar as the utopia is static, it suggests a halt to History; and this halt can be found only in the creation of a myth, a retreat from social praxis into a mental figure of social stasis, the freezing of that praxis. In a way one may doubtless argue that an utopia is always static—as has recently Alexandre Cioranescu [in *L'Avenir du passé: Utopie et Littérature,* 1972]—since it always suggests to some degree the sublimation of a pre-existing social order, or of a model abstracted from that order. Nonetheless, that a profitable distinction can be made between the dynamic and the static utopia is what I hope to demonstrate in this essay.

The two best-known utopias of the early seventeenth century represent an almost exemplary demonstration of the two seemingly opposing thought systems which collide at this time. Campanella's *Civitas Solis* stands virtually as a paradigm of the process that seeks knowledge by analogies, Bacon's *New Atlantis* is as much aparadigmatic suggestion of the new experimentalism, of the reach for knowledge by the inductive process.

Certainly, Campanella was anything but ignorant of the expansion of knowledge and technical "know-how" occurring in his lifetime: he is aware (obviously) of the voyages—the form of his dialogue between the steersman and a "Grandmaster of the Knights Hospitallers" is reminiscent of Pigafetta's relation of Magellan's voyage to the Grandmaster of the Knights of Rhodes, his seaman served with Columbus—his Solarians have discovered flight, various forms of sea and land travel, and other mechanical devices; he hesitates between the systems of Ptolemy and Copernicus, recognizes Gilbert's work with magnets, avoids pronouncing on the question of the infinity of worlds, and refuses authority in learning, claiming preference for a direct experience of things. All this one may gather from the most superficial reading of no more than *The City of the Sun* itself. Campanella was also, of course, so ardent a supporter of Galileo as to offer himself in 1632 as the scientist's defender before the papal commission, and he had previously risked his life and successfully put a stop to the process leading to his own freedom by his *Apologia pro Galileo* (1622, commenced 1616), in which, as Santillana puts it, he "had called Aristotle and the Scholastics all sorts of names, had come out boldly for the Copernican system, and had propounded new and arbitrary interpretations of scripture."

However, as Santillana elsewhere observes, these particular "perilous fantasies" serve rather to affirm than deny that science is, if anything, the handmaiden of an humanism based in theological speculation and that its discoveries are more or less satisfactory explications, in the form of geometrical structures, of the miriad workings of divine providence. The Copernican system struck Campanella as a particularly happy model; but in this he varies scarcely at all from Osiander's position in his preface to the *De Revolutionibus*. He accepts the new cosmology as a suitable mathematical model for purposes of human knowledge, but denies that it is reality. This position, rather Renaissance humanist than medieval, is the very echo of the mode of thinking of the pre-Galilean philosopher. Speaking of Urban VIII, Santillana again makes the following remark:

> This is where his thinking was backed by the great schemes of the Renaissance and its hope in unknown harmonies. "There is nothing that is incredible," Marcilio Ficino had said. "For to God all things are possible, and nothing is impossible. There are numberless possibilities that we deny because we do not happen to know them." This was also what Pico della Mirandola had maintained, hinting at reaches of "natural magic" beyond our dreams; and Campanella, too, was supporting Galileo in the hope of results such as no scientist could ever produce. It was "Platonic theology" itself, urging man to extend his imagination beyond what he could see and test; it was Leonardo's belief in the creative power of artistic "fantasy."

Campanella's criticism of scholastic learning, when the Solarians argue that the bookman "has contemplated nothing but the world of books and has given his mind with useless result to the consideration of the dead signs of things", is in essence no different from his acquiescence in the Copernican system:

> They praise Ptolemy and admire Copernicus, but put Aristarchus and Philolaus ahead of him; but they say that the one counts with stones, the other with beans, while neither with the things themselves that are counted [*le stesse cose contate*], and they pay for the world with money of account, not with gold. But they research this transaction [*questo negozio*] with extreme subtlety, because it is important to know the workings [*le fabbrica*] of the world . . .

The signs of things serve only, he argues here, to conceal them. Between the bookmen's world of play-

ing with the signs for themselves, and that of the future technocrat, who will take the signs for their referent, the choice is that of two sides of the same coin. The phrase, *"stesse cose contate,"* is a revealing one, and it is to this goal that the Solarian will bend his energies: to the knowledge of things in themselves without the mediation of signs, whether monetary or linguistic. This, of course, brings us almost to Descartes' "idées claires et distinctes," the static knowledge at the center of all human knowing. Impossible goal, no doubt, but this is the reason for Campanella's dual rejection of signs.

This is why the form looks back to the concept of the great chain of being, and also why Campanella refers back to the *Critias,* and to the Renaissance utopias of Doni and Stiblin for the outward shape of his circular city. The structure of **Civitas Solis** is entirely directed inwards, and ultimately through the microcosm of the individual mind to God. In the light of the above brief commentary, there is little remarkable in that its theme is*ostensibly* directed more to the future and a knowledge of the natural sciences: "It represents an unlimited will to know [*Wissen-Wollen*], which is directed at all natural objects." For, in fact, the knowledge of nature is not simply a "will to know," but a will to know God, and it is to this end that the Solarians direct all their science.

The city "is divided into seven rings or huge circles named from the seven planets, and the way from one to the other of these is by four streets and through four gates, that look toward the four points of the compass". After the visitor has entered through the outer walls, of which, the traveller remarks: "so thick are the earthworks and so well fortified is it with breastworks, towers, guns, and ditches", that they would be impossible to storm, one arrives, by passing through the subsequent rings, at the foot of an ascent: "On the top of the hill is a rather spacious plain, and in the midst of this there rises a temple built with wondrous art". This temple is not divided from the city, but, like the intellect—or perhaps soul—that it appears to represent, it is opened to it, so that a constant intercommunication can, and does, take place: " . . . it is not girt with walls, but stands upon thick columns, beautifully wrought," and in its center is to be found the dome with, beneath it, the altar. The occupants of the temple are the 49 "priests and religious officers" of whom the principal is Sol: this is a godlike figure of all-knowing, not unlike the Cartesian image of human possibilities:

> The principal of the sciences, except Metaphysic, who is Hoh himself, and is, as it were, the architect of all science, having rule over all, are attached to Wisdom. Hoh is ashamed to be ignorant of any possible thing.

Indeed, the manner in which the priests, *who are named*

after various human virtues, moral, intellectual, and physical are described, is not unrevealing: for they are essentially the mediators between the ordinary citizens and the government of Sol or Hoh:

> The priests, moreover, determine the hours for breeding and the days for sowing, reaping, and gathering the vintage, and are, as it were, the ambassadors and intercessors and connection between God and man.

The situation of the city is such that we pass through the material walls to the pure intellect at the center, and thissystem informs life within the city in all its forms. The learning process, which we would expect to follow this pattern, is indeed impressed upon the citizens by it. The rejection, but the necessity for purposes of communication, of mere signs is also indicated in this process. The relegation of the purely human symbolic languages of alphabet and mathematics to the outer wall (though the latter are given pride of place on the inner surface) of the city would seem to suggest that though the way to knowledge must initially lie through them, we must, and can, so to speak, come out on the other side. Things are learned less by talking about them, than by direct observation; that is to say, "by walking around them" and through them. These symbols are replaced, as the visitor approaches the inner temple, by the depiction (perforce) of natural objects: successively, minerals, rivers and streams, vegetables, fish, birds and animals, until he comes to "the mechanical arts" and "the inventors in science, in warfare, in law", the prophets of natural religion, before arriving at the final resolution of the microcosm/ macrocosm tension with the world on the altar where is also to be found the central intellect, the ruler of the *City of the Sun*.

This plan is quite clearly the old one of the scholastics. And it is by a logic which accords with this that the city is communistic. Here the dynamism of the individual, the impulse behind possession, has no role. The static grandeur of nature which, properly, neither is controlled by man nor does it control him, informs the city. Within each step of the hierarchy there is equality of possession (save of honors), if not of talent: but each talent has its place in the *organized* hierarchy of the city. Given the static form of things, all works in harmony, and it is to be expected that things are done by the inhabitants only "when it is a pleasure to them", and because it is natural to do so: "each one [works] according to his natural propensity doing his duty well and pleasantly, because naturally".

Campanella's depiction of his city as a world in harmony (the outer surface of the first wall contains, not only alphabets, but also "an immense drawing of the whole earth", which is at the same time the individual mind and its way to knowledge, is summed up by one of the Solarian's pieces of wisdom: "The world is a great animal, and we live within it as worms live within us".

Campanella's city is indeed a static refuge (not, I would remark, a *retreat*) from the problems posed by a century about to confirm the adaptability of directed thought, with the concomitant problems of a metaphysical, ethical and social nature suddenly bursting in from a now strange outside. It is "an enchanted island, miraculously preserved at the Ocean's end, a perfect ark rediscovered at the end of a dream" [Jean Servier, *Histoire de l'utopie*]. Well aware of the new developments, the Solarians are bent on seeking knowledge:

> And when I asked with astonishment whence they had obtained our history, they told me that among them there was a knowledge of all languages, and that by perseverance they continually sent explorers and ambassadors over the whole earth, who learn thoroughly the customs, forces, rule and histories of the nations, bad and good alike.

This dynamism is absorbed into the monolithic structure of the city. Absorbed as a force of change into a form that can accept no change. Where the harmony is perfect, the only hope for survival is, very precisely, no change. The circles that are the image at once of the mind and of the world cannot but predicate their essential identity and continuity. This is why the movement to knowledge, the visitor's advancement, is inwards, toward the divine intellect, towards the spirit of the world, into the static knowledge at the center of being.

Speaking of the necessary structure of Utopian fiction, Cioranescu has noted that its articulation is most similar to that of a lawyer's brief: "The hypothesis is its basic fact: the deduction is its logical scaffolding." This, of course, forms the whole fiction—a static mass presented as a finished city. This may not be a wholly inapt characterization of the *Civitas Solis,* nor, come to that, of *Utopia* itself. But what if the fiction makes of deduction (or induction) not merely the means of its scaffolding, but also the subject of it? A most recent utopia, Skinner's *Walden Two* (1948), for instance, sets the idea of logical (experimental) progress at the very basis of its functioning; and what is most frightening *for us* about *Brave New World* or *1984* is just exactly their static nature and the quashing of the hope of experimentalism by extending it to one of its logical ends. Sir Francis Bacon lies at the other end of Huxley's and Orwell's dreary ladder, and in the *New Atlantis* it is to be expected that a serial progress should become its own subject. The essential structure controlling this utopia is based on a movement towards the outside, whether it be as voyage (and, in this connection, those of Columbus or Magellan are as symbolic as they were real), or as gaze. If the *Civitas Solis* can becompared to a contracted prey trapped in a corner—situated, may it be said, near the Taprobana of an already-outdated cosmogony—then the *New Atlantis* is the octopus, situated in a New World, sending out its tentacles to the Old.

Where Campanella dismisses the voyage itself in a word (as he does those of the Solarians), Bacon, on the contrary, insists upon it. In his fiction, this movement and its accompanying troubles take on what would at first appear to be an inordinate emphasis:

> We sailed from Peru (where we had continued by the space of one whole year) for China and Japan by the South Sea, taking with us victuals for twelve months, and had good winds from the east, though soft and weak, for five months' space and more. But then the wind came about and settled in the west for many days, so as we could make little or no way, and were sometimes in purpose to turn back. But then again there arose strong and great winds from the south with a point east, which carried us up (for all that we could do) towards the north, by which time our victuals failed us, though we had made good spare of them. So that finding ourselves in the midst of the greatest wilderness of waters in the world without victuals, we gave ourselves for lost men, and prepared for death.

In passing we may compare the tone of this passage to Pascal's anguished cry before the fearful silence of immense space which will come shortly after. It is an awe which fails to daunt Campanella, but certainly affects Bacon's travellers. For them, however, as initially for Pascal, the voyage comes to a halt at a land in an utterly unknown area of an unexplored sea. There they enter a welcome harbor before a beautiful city.

It is now, just when one would expect the journey to be at an end, that in fact there begins a whole series of journeys. The main voyage from the shelter of the old, safe world to this unknown region is to be repeated in several forms; and it is this dynamism of the voyage that becomes the central figure of *New Atlantis*. Anchored in port, they are not yet allowed to disembark, nor even approach the town, and it is only after several trips to-and-fro, after much discussion and ceremony, that the islanders permit them to land, and then only after a night's wait. From the prison their boat has become, they then make the short trip (in distance, but immense spiritually) which brings them to the "Strangers' House", where they will once againfind themselves sequestered; this time for five days.

After these five days, they do not yet leave. Instead there recommences the islanders' trips to-and-fro that characterized their wait in port: the governor of the House of Strangers comes for discussions. However, these are no less centered on sea-travel than the account itself to date: on the first day, he relates how a

mysterious "ark or chest of cedar" brought them by sea the word of an apostle of Christ, to which they owe their faith. The following day, he describes to them the state of navigation in the past, the Flood, and how his country was alone in maintaining a knowledge of foreign lands and the means to go there. He goes on to tell how one of the principal activities of New Atlantis is the dispatching every twelve years of two ships to go out into the world:

> appointed to several voyages; that in either of these ships there should be a mission of three of the Fellows or Brethren of Salomon's House, whose errand was only to give us knowledge of the affairs and state of those countries to which they were designed, and especially of the sciences, arts, manufactures, and inventions of all the world, and withal to bring unto us books, instruments, and patterns in every kind. . . .

It is only after the revelation of this archetypal voyage of research, that the visitors, strangers, begin to go out of their "refuge" to see the country. Ultimately, one of the voyagers from the House of Salomon comes back and they watch the ceremonial passage that he makes from the harbor, through the town, to some solitary retreat. There, after three days, the narrator is given permission to join him in discussions. This is followed by a kind of meditation upon the reason and justification for the House of Salomon, its activities, its journeys:

> The End of our Foundation is the knowledge of Causes and sacred motions of things, and the enlarging of the bounds of Human Empire, to the effecting of all things possible.

What follows is a description of a veritable experimental institution with its means and its experiments. "It is," as Cioranescu remarks, "a veritable programme, to the extent that all programmes remain open and leave the door open behind them. It was thus that it was understood immediately: and as early as1645 a philosophical College was founded at London, in the imitation of Salomon's House, and which was the ancestor of the illustrious Royal Society."

After this description, and after the traveller has left the narrator, the story comes to a close, or rather does not, with these words, "The Rest was not Perfected". But this end serves as an explication of the series of voyages within voyages, and suggests the goal obtained by the inductive movement. It is a journey which takes the traveller out towards the exterior to bring him back, ultimately, upon himself (here in the form of a second traveller) with the new knowledge he has acquired, and which will serve for the meditation I mentioned. The story, in a way, could not end otherwise. The experimental system must be an open-ended, repetitive one. The continual voyages, their halts for consideration, the arrival at empirical knowledge which leads the narrator back into another journey, and so on, are quite precisely the image of the experimental sequence. This dynamism is reinforced by the use throughout the fiction of the first person, both singular and plural; a use which may be contrasted with the almost exclusive use in the *Civitas Solis* of the third person, and that despite its superficial use of the dialogue.

Bacon's seeker is an individual "I" in search of knowledge which will allow him to enlarge "the bounds of Human Empire." It is a way to personal possession, with all the difficulties, hesitations, and fears that this may involve. The fellows of the House of Salomon are as much seekers of *personal* honor and riches as they are enrichers of the general store of knowledge: "For upon every invention of value we erect a statue to the inventor, and give him a liberal and honourable reward". It is not without significance that the narrator's own temerity is rewarded by a sum of money. To be sure, so were Campanella's Solarians rewarded: but these *all* could gain honors, and such as were no more than symbolic. Here they are represented by material possession, the image of that permitted by the invention itself. Here, moreover, the wise men do not consider the State an harmonious organism: it is an almost foreign body of which they are scarcely a part: "[they] take all an oath of secrecy for the concealing of those [inventions] which [they] think fit to keep secret, though some of those [they] do reveal sometimes to the state, and some not".

There is little doubt that [George] Uscatescu is right when he comments [in *Utopia y plenitud histórica,* 1963]: ". . .Machiavelli's conception of politics was in agreement with the fundamentals of the Baconian experimental philosophy. In addition, the idea Bacon has of politics is essentially utilitarian and activist." There is nothing new in a statement of identity between the politics of possessive individualism and the scientific stance of experimentalism: that the structure of Bacon's sea voyage should illustrate this is scarcely a cause for surprise. What is less generally remarked upon is that it is not only at the level of content that this attitude is revealed. The very form is built up from the impulse to control the other, to impose the self.

There is a fundamental difference of impulse between these two fictions. The access to both is by a long sea voyage, to be sure; but how speedily does Campanella jump the southern ocean to go to earth in his island, bound tight by its circular foundations, closed off as far as possible from the outside expansion of the sea. *The City of the Sun* is an attempt to create an unchanging world where all necessary knowledge has been not only acquired, but fixed for all time on its walls.

There is a more essential way, then, in which Campanella's structure recalls the Platonic, and that is not merely in its outward shape but in the very impulse of its functioning. In the *Republic* knowledge is equated with being itself: "And knowledge is relative to being and knows being". And absolute knowledge, knowledge of Unity, of Idea, is by definition accession to total being. Translated into Campanella's terms, the perfect knowledge aimed at by the City will be quite precisely coincident with that identity of the self with God found at the altar of Hoh. Just as Plato's State is ideal *because* it is at once the homologue *and* analogue of the ultimate guardian, the perfect philosopher, *because* its perfect harmony is that of the just soul (in the absolute sense given to *Justice* by Plato), so also with Campanella's City. Moreover, though it aims at this unity with the Divine, it can only do so in response to the aura of the Divine. Its light does not proceed from within. Although it must, of course, be completely receptive, it receives its light from without and beyond: "Then the sun is not sight, but the author of sight who is recognized by sight" (*Republic*).

Bacon has taken each of these terms and inverted them. For him, as he remarks in *The Advancement of Learning,* "the truth of being and the truth of knowing are one, differing no more than the direct beam and the beam reflected." This may well be, but however close he keeps them still, they are nonetheless divided: knowledge and being are split into two separate fields, and, for Bacon, their generalization into concepts is the responsibility of, and will result in, at least two different systems. His island has its base in two different motives. Furthermore, the sun of the New Atlantis is an entirely human one, and the mind, no longer recipient of light, is rather imposer of it. The twelve seekers who go out from Salomon's House are known as "Merchants of Light," while the three members of the House who are responsible for the formulation of "new experiments of a higher light" are known as "Lamps". If Salomon's House "is the very eye of the kingdom", it is a very self-contained eye, and quite unlike the reactive soul of Plato's State or Campanella's City.

Bacon's Atlantis is a city trying to have the best of both worlds: it, too, has its well-placed and long-lasting foundations. But its impulse is to the water. It is the travelling sages who are most honored and for whom there is most rejoicing. It is a city whose spirit is towards flux, danger, the transitory—in a word, progression: "The being destined to water is an ever-changing being [*un être en vertige*]. At each moment he is dying, some part of his substance is endlessly crumbling away." What is represented by these islands, lying in the midst of uncharted seas, is perhaps the attempt to seize the processes of intellection, a certain form of the unconscious. Each narrator sails through "an oneiric experience" towards "the revelation of his reality and of his ideality."

The utopian structure would appear to be understood best as the objectivization of a mode of thought, perhaps common to an era but certainly characterizing an individual view, and not as its opposite, a thinking about an object. Whatever may have been Campanella's attempts to externalize his ideal had the Calabrian revolt of 1599 been successful, alters this not in the least: our text would then have been in the field instead of in the library, but its form and meaning would have been the same. It would simply dramatize Cioranescu's point that "man's future remains still and always a mere literary image." That *New Atlantis* is without a conclusion emphasizes the apparent conflict between a static literary (and philosophical) mode, and the desire for the dynamism of possession; which perhaps suggests why Campanella's revolt had no conceivable hope of success. In that, it was the image of the mental structure which fostered it.

Kelly-Gadol on the persecution of Campanella:

Campanella's independent, restless, combative personality was undoubtedly as responsible for initiating his life of persecution as was the unorthodox character of his philosophical thought. A year after publishing his first book defending Telesio, he was imprisoned and tried by a Tribunal of the Dominican Order in Naples. His sentence reveals that it was not his Telesian ideas alone that led to this brush with the authorities, but the fact that he had left his rural monastery of Altomonte for the more congenial intellectual atmosphere of a secular house in Naples. From this point on, his life was never to be free of political danger, but he was to learn only slowly the political virtue of prudence. Released in 1592 after several months of confinement, he disobeyed the order to return to his Province, travelling instead to Rome, Florence, and Padua. He met Galileo in Padua and wrote a great deal (including another *Apologia pro Telesio*), but his efforts to secure a position which would afford him relative safety and independence came to nought. He failed to obtain from the Grand Duke Ferdinand II of Tuscany a Chair at Pisa or Siena, and renewed harassment was soon followed by a second incarceration. . . .

Joan Kelly-Gadol, "Tommaso Campanella: The Agony of Political Theory in the Counter-Reformation," in Philosophy and Humanism: Renaissance Essays in Honor of Paul Oskar Kristeller, *edited by Edward Mahoney, Columbia University Press, 1976.*

Jon Snyder (essay date 1985)

SOURCE: "*The City of the Sun* and the Poetics of the Utopian Dialogue," in *Stanford Italian Review,* Vol. 2, Fall, 1985, pp. 175-87.

[*In the following excerpt, Snyder examines the poetics of Campanella's utopian text, arguing that Campanella deliberately chose the dialogic form since dialogism is intrinsic to the liminal nature of all utopian fiction.*]

Tommaso Campanella (1568-1639) is known today chiefly for his famous work of utopian fiction, *La Città del Sole (The City of the Sun),* still widely considered among the most important texts in the Renaissance utopian tradition. Despite its status as a specifically literary work, though, *The City of the Sun* has yet to attract much critical attention to the problem of its poetics. This is not in itself surprising, given that the genre of utopian fiction has traditionally been studied solely in terms of its political and historical significance. Most utopian criticism concerns itself with thematics, not poetics; just as most of us can summarize what utopias are "about" (even if we have never read one) without ever touching upon the question of the forms of these fictions. Yet, as their paradoxical name indicates, utopias are first and foremost fictional texts, and therefore utopian fiction constitutes a linguistic code and a set of textual strategies. There is an urgent need to see utopian texts as being constructed according to conventions and text-rules which over time have forfeited their theoretical status and are no longer considered explicitly conventional by today's readers. One of the interesting things about *The City of the Sun* in this regard is that it explicitly proposes a reading of itself based upon rhetorical categories as well as upon political ones. For although its title includes the phrase "Idea Reipublicae Philosophicae" ("The Idea of a Philosophic Republic"), its unusual subtitle is "Un Dialogo Poetico" ("A Poetical Dialogue"), referring the reader to the long and extremely rich tradition of the *dialogue* in literature and philosophy. The following pages will examine the "forgotten" theoretical status of the discourse of *The City of the Sun* as a *utopian dialogue*—as a place of intersection between utopian fiction and the formal features of the dialogue—in order to open up the possibility of reading such a text for the first time in terms of its poetics.

The City of the Sun consists of a "poetical dialogue" between a Cavaliere dell'Ordine degli Ospitalieri di San Giovanni in Gerusalemme, called the "Ospitalario" in the text, and a Genoese sailor, identified as the "nochiero del Colombo"—that is, as Columbus' helmsman. The sailor's report about his visit to island of Taprobana, punctuated by questions from the Ospitalario, constitutes the body of the text. In it we learn of the fabulous City of the Sun, built on a hill in seven concentric circles, whose inhabitants—the Solarians—are knowledgeable in all the arts and sciences and live a totally communal existence without families or private property. Rather than paraphrase "what" the text tells us (which has been done elsewhere), it would seem more appropriate to ask "why" and "how" Campanella employed this particular form of discourse: in other words, to inquire into its textual motivations and formal mechanisms, in order to arrive at a provisional description of its utopian poetics. The traditional response to these questions conceives of *The City of the Sun* as an expression of thwarted idealism, either as a kind of compensation for a failed utopian revolution (the Calabrian uprising of 1599-1600), or as a blueprint for a future one. Luigi Firpo, for instance, the most important Campanellian critic of our time, remarks that "*The City of the Sun* becomes a document of clarification of intentions, a text designed to define and redeem his [Campanella's] own religious, philosophical, and social ideas, his own plans for a reform of the Church and political institutions. Only by starting here can we explain the genesis of the work as a literary document . . ." [*Lo stato ideale della Controriforma*]. It can be reasonably assumed (as Firpo does) that when Campanella decided upon a work of utopian fiction, writing under the most difficult conditions imaginable and with his life in doubt, the choice was not an innocent one. However, it still does not answer the question: why not another straightforward political or philosophical work such as *Articuli Prophetales, Monarchia di Spagna,* or *Monarchia Messiae,* all written during the early years of Campanella's long imprisonment? To claim that *The City of the Sun* "was first of all a rethinking of the beautiful but failed dream . . . that others had deformed and defiled without understanding its purity and dignity" [Firpo] is an act of critical mystification, linking "utopia" and "dream" together in a metadiscourse that says little or nothing about the discourse of the text itself. Campanella himself, on the other hand, pointed out that "if you seek a republic without abuses, you will have to go to Heaven, or simulate it ["o fingerla"] like Plato and Thomas More or like *The City of the Sun* . . .". *The City of the Sun,* then, in the words of its own author, appears as a part of a textual tradition, a term in the equation of utopian fiction, and it is to that equation that we now turn our attention.

The Dialogue as Textual Strategem

Any thematic reading or paraphrase of *The City of the Sun* leaves out the drama of the text's attempt to constitute itself as a work of utopian fiction. It is here that we must instead look to find the key to a less reductive reading: in the narrative situation, or locutionary framework, of the "dialogo poetico." Since the phrase appears at the head of the text, under the title and the author's name, it is apparent at once that one of its functions is to notify the reader of the sort of narrative activity involved here. It stands, in other words, as a signal of how the text is to be read, marking out—in elliptical fashion—the parameters of a performative program, and, implicitly, the conditions of its fulfillment. Let us look more closely at the textual function of the phrase "dialogo poetico." It is, first of all, an opening move. Although the analogy between chess

and literature is by now a banal one, the fact remains that, for both, the opening move determines much of what is to follow, limiting the players (the readers) to certain sets of options, while excluding others. Here the text designates itself as neither a strictly philosophical dialogue nor as a poetical imitation of "no place," but rather as something in between these two, i.e., as a *poetical dialogue.* Surely this is a problematic textual procedure, since it presents the reader at once with "the difficult task of seeing utopia as both similar and different," as both a part of the dialogical tradition and a transformation of it. The key to seeing the sameness and difference of Campanella's utopian fiction, then, is to be found in the dialogue itself as a textual stratagem.

A common rhetorical form both in Antiquity and in the Renaissance, the dialogue has its ancient roots in the concept of dialectic. The definition of dialectic, of course, has to do with discussion and reasoning by dialogue (*dialektikos* 'of conversation') as a method of philosophical investigation, based upon the supposed primacy of the spoken over the written. In Antiquity, the philosophical dialogue was generally considered the opposite of rhetoric, by dint of its association with dialectic: one need only think of Zeno's controversial definition of the difference between dialectic and rhetoric as the difference between a closed fist and an open hand. Despite its link with dialectic, though, the philosophical dialogue was and still is highly rhetorical in nature (as the Renaissance recognized): it can do no more than affirm the primacy of *inventio* over *elocutio*. In the case of *The City of the Sun,* the first thing to note from this perspective is that the text calls itself a "dialogo poetico" in order to point away from itself as a work of utopian fiction. Unlike More's *Utopia* or many of its epigones, the term "utopia" never appears in the text. In not identifying itself as a 'utopian' work at any point (except in its intertext, its implicit "dialogue" with More and Plato), *The City of the Sun* seems to use its tag "dialogo poetico" to indicate that it is not in fact a work of utopian fiction, but rather a dialogue of the traditional philosophical sort perfected by Plato. Yet at the same time the modifier "poetico" serves as asignal to the reader that this is not a dialogue of the sort normally associated with moral logic and dialectic: rather, it is to be read at least to some degree as a rhetorical (literary) work. Although it is true to some extent that "in subtitling his work *A Poetical Dialogue* Campanella meant only to call attention to its fictional character without intending to claim specifically literary merits for it," it is equally true that the subtitle calls attention to its dialogical discourse and the specific philosophical merits that are traditionally attributed to it. The tactical work of the term "dialogo poetico" is thus double-edged.

The fact that Campanella retains a problematical dialogical structure of discourse for his utopian fiction cannot be assigned solely to the intertextual "influence" of Plato's *Republic* and More's *Utopia* (or Doni's derivative *I Mondi*). It would not have been inconceivable for Campanella's versatile pen to have produced a work of utopian fiction in some other form familiar to the Italian Cinquecento and early Seicento, so rich in *prosatori*. He had already written other works in the form of collections of political aphorisms, methodological treatises, polemical essays, philosophical studies—including one written in Latin hexameters (the lost *Philosophia Pythagorica*), a *Dialogo politico contro Luterani, Calvinisti ed altri eretici,* a tragedy (also lost) entitled *Maria regina di Scozia,* poems, and vast quantities of letters, all before 1602, the presumed date of composition of *The City of the Sun*. Judging from the preceding list, it seems safe to conclude that *The City of the Sun* was not written as a "dialogo poetico" because its author lacked the technical means to write it otherwise, or because the literary production of the period had exhausted all other viable forms of discourse. If we instead look at the problem from a less crudely empirical perspective, the figure "dialogo poetico" can be seen to stand strategically at the head of the text *in place* of the term 'utopia' itself. To understand the text in such a light allows us to see that the ambivalent nature of the utopian figure itself—the fact that it both rhetorically calls attention to itself, in the form of a pun (*outopia/eutopia*), and points away from itself as a narrative fiction—is connected with the double nature of Campanella's poetical dialogue. In a general sense, what Campanella's hybrid form seems to be "about" is the boundary, or the lack of one, between fiction and nonfiction: it is a sort of *Schwellendialog,* a dialogue "on the threshold" that is also very much a dialogue about the threshold on which it stands.

The twofold strategy behind Campanella's hybrid term "dialogo poetico" depends in part upon the notion that as a *poetical* work it cannot be criticized or censored as pure political theory; as a *dialogical* work it can claim for itself the philosophically privileged status of nonfiction, investing the text with an aura of legitimacy. The rhetorical move of the "dialogo poetico" asserts that *The City of the Sun* is neither "pure" political theory nor, for that matter, "pure" fiction. The third term (missing in the text) which figures this is 'utopia' itself. The rhetoric of the "dialogo poetico" compels the reader to break down the encoded distinction between dialectic and rhetoric and to reinscribe it in the figure of 'utopia,' in which a code is in effect neutralized (this activity itself being far from neutral). As [Gary Saul] Morson [in *The Boundaries of Genre*, 1981] rightly remarks, ". . . utopias lie on the boundary between fiction and non-fiction because they are about that boundary or, to be precise, about the analogous boundary between social 'fact' and social 'fictions' . . . utopia describes the place that is no place in fiction that is not fiction."

Of course, not all Renaissance dialogues resemble each other for any reason other than the sharing of a common dialogical structure: the dialogue is not nearly as prescriptive a form as (let us say) the epithalamium or the eulogy. Even among works of utopian fiction the differences are as numerous as the similarities, More's *Utopia,* for instance, being radically different from Campanella's *The City of the Sun* both in its formal and thematic organization. Moreover, the term "dialogue" needs to be carefully defined when used to refer to Renaissance literature. For at least three distinct Renaissance modes of dialogue can be distinguished, all of which are based upon classical models or which borrow extensively from classical authors: these are the philosophical dialogue (Plato), the satirical dialogue (Lucian), and the didactic dialogue (Cicero). The point of this is not to describe exhaustively the history of the dialogue as a genre. Rather, in the case of the present discussion, it is to see that the first of these three—the philosophical dialogue—clearly concerns the reader of *The City of the Sun* most (given the Neoplatonic tradition behind Campanella) in considering the dialogue as a form of utopian discourse. *The City of the Sun* intersects with other Renaissance works of utopian fiction in the mutual use of the dialogue form, and the persistence with which these two forms accompany each other in the Renaissance is a sign that utopian discourse and dialogical discourse stand in a privileged relationship: the dialogical condition is the pre-text of utopian fiction.

The Reader in the Dialogue

Rudolf Hirzel, in his two-volume study of the literary history of the dialogue [*Der Dialog: Ein literarhistorischer Versuch*, 1895], defines the philosophical dialogue as a "mirror" of human existence, since it uses the speech of everyday life rather than the language of the rhetorician. However, he is forced to admit that the dialogue inevitably tends toward "literarization" as a result of its status as a text. For the dialogue shows us the process of thinking aloud, not thought itself: it is thought exteriorized and represented in language, and therefore alien to itself. The double-bind of Hirzel's analysis—that the dialogue both is and is not a part of the conventions of everyday speech (as opposed to literary or figurative language)—is symptomatic of a special difficulty found in theorizing about dialogical texts. For, although a fiction, the dialogue "presents itself as a formalization of real exchanges." A common dialogical convention, based upon the powerful figure of mimesis, is that it is the transcript of a conversation that actually occurred. In the case of utopian fiction, one of the chief advantages of the dialogue form is found precisely in the convention of its special referential status. The eyewitness account ("I saw") of the traveller who has returned from a visit to the utopian City acquires—as testimony, as reportage—a degree of ontological force which would otherwise be denied to the utopian fiction if it were instead, for instance, an epic poem or even a dramatic work. In epistemological terms, the rhetorically privileged, authentic mode of cognition is that of *seeing* the utopian City: all other understanding is by implication of a degraded sort. Consequently it is difficult, if not impossible, for the characters in the dialogue (or its readers) to question effectively the veracity of the traveller's report and, by the same token, the "reality" behind the utopian text. Thus the Renaissance convention that the dialogue actually took place, when accepted as part of a literal reading, "sanctions the reality of the 'other'" (i.e., the reality of the utopian City). The reader who does not "see" the utopian City is to be in effect shaken, perceptually and rhetorically, by the persuasiveness of the traveller's report and by the force of its referential claims.

Of course this is no more and no less than a convention: the dialogue is as highly mediated as any other complex form of fictional discourse. The self-reflexive nature of the dialogue is an essential part of its dialectic. In the process of bringing something else into presence (in this case, the utopian figure), things assert themselves as whatever particular thing they are. Thus, in raising utopian discourse into place, the dialogue foregrounds its own status as a literary text at the same time as it rhetorically denies itself that status. Utopian fiction operates in terms of the same dialectic: the reader comes up against the fact that utopian fiction, in its process of textualizing the present (the State), describes the very process by which it becomes itself a text to be read and interrogated.

Let us now consider the question of the audience in the dialogue and in utopian fiction: that is to say, the fictional "contract" between writer and reader (or between code and reader). Here we turn from rhetorical to pragmatic properties. First of all, the function of the utopian traveller or narrator, who engages in the dialogue with the interlocutor, is fairly clear:

> Utopias characteristically contain a fictional character—henceforth called a "delineator"—who explains the ideal society to an audience unfamiliar with it . . . Whether the utopia takes the form of a narrative, like *News from Nowhere,* or a dialogue, like Campanella's *City of the Sun;* whether it is set in the past, present, or future; and whether the delineator, like Socrates in the *Republic,* speculates on what the ideal society would be like or, like Campanella's sea captain, claims to have seen it . . . the delineator's social observations are designed not to portray the complex psychological ambiguities of a personal opinion, but rather to exploit the dramatic power of a truth revealed.
>
> [Morson, *The Boundaries of Genre,* 1981]

Yet is is equally legitimate to ask who or what the interlocutor himself represents. The same recent study

of utopian fiction asserts that the tactic of the utopian text is to place ". . . readers in the traveller's position, so that they can then be urged to repeat the traveller's conversion." But in **The City of the Sun** the reader does not journey (metaphorically speaking) with the traveller to the utopian City to encounter its inhabitants firsthand; the reader is instead the recipient of the traveller's report. So instead of identifying with the traveller, the reader identifies with the interlocutor: through the rhetorical figure of prosopopoiea, the questions are posed *by the reader* to the traveller. The reader is drawn, through this figural strategy, into the textual production of signification: only when the interlocutor has had the utopian world fully revealed to him will his point of view merge with the traveller's, and then and only then will the dialectic (as well as the dialogical text) of question and response cease. The figure of the interlocutor, then, represents the reader in the text, and, at the same time, the text represents (through the same figure of prosopopoeia) the anacretic process of its own reading. To read the utopian dialogue is to transform the language of knowledge (dialectic) into knowledge about language.

The question of the role of the reader in the dialogue has an added significance for the discourse of utopian fiction. For, through the rhetorical "code" of the philosophical dialogue, the utopian text not only claims for itself the privileged status of a dialectical argument (with its special access to "truth"), but assumes as its audience, through the symbolic and synechdochal figure of the interlocutor, an entire reading public. Each reader must, as a condition of performance of the text, take the place of the interlocutor, an act of substitution which constantly expands the dialogical exchange. The utopian text, as a dialogue, thus reaffirms its thematically explicit "social" function, since such a mode of representation possesses the contractual authority of consensus. In fact, as Francis Jacques points out [in *Dialogiques: recherches logiques sur le dialogue,* 1979], "Gadamer is right to correct that platitude that all dialogue prosupposes a common language. In reality all dialogue *constitutes itself* as a common language."

However, the "literariness" of the dialogue at the same time places a distance between the reader and the utopian text. In representing in the text the process of its own reading . . . through the figure of the interlocutor, the utopian dialogue foregrounds the fact that the reader's utopian "vision" or configuration, i.e., the new interpretive code that is the product of the dialogue, is at the same time pragmatically limited by the discourse of the text. The utopian dialogue removes from the reader the fictional possibility of complete participation in the text's process of interrogation and understanding. The role of the reader is restricted to the repetition of the original gesture of the interlocutor: there cannot be new exchanges of information each time the text is read. Utopian fiction does not invent a new code for both traveller and interlocutor as much as it reveals, in a dialogical framework, the code that the traveller has mastered and which the interlocutor/reader desires in turn to learn. What dialogue does in utopian fiction is to raise up the code of the utopian City into the light of "disconcealment," so that the reader can then learn how to see the authority of its new distinctions, and *only* those distinctions. The dialogue is thus a determining instance in the constitution of utopian discourse; to try to remove it as the scaffolding of the work would simply be to collapse it, like a body deprived of its bones, into something no longer identifiable as a utopian fiction (as happens, for example, in paraphrase).

The Politics of Opposition

The dialogical text implicates a logic of both distance and relation. The significance of dialogism for utopian fiction centers around this logic and its oppositional nature. The *heuristic* nature of the dialogue requires it to present two or more distinct frames of reference (or points of view) in the text. In supplying a (limited) set of alternatives, the structure of the text challenges the authority of any single speaker or perspective to make a definitive claim to the truth: even the Genoese sailor—under questioning—confesses that there are things about the life of the city that he does not know or completely understand. Stripped of its specifically Platonic endpoint, then, the dialectical process of the utopian dialogue is potentially infinite (saturation of the question-and-response system is practically impossible: there is always something else to ask, something more to learn, so that closure must be imposed upon it from the outside, as it is in *The City of the Sun,* where the sailor is forced to leave in order not to miss his ship): there is no final or ultimate truth to stop the dialogue in its tracks. Like any heuristic discourse, the dialogue is by its very nature incapable of proof: given the essential alterity of its structure of argumentation, it is unable to guarantee any specific transcendence of difference. Kushner [in "The Dialogue of the French Renaissance: Work of Art of Instrument of Inquiry?" 1977] calls this the dialogue's "epistemology of confrontation," so that if the reader finally sides with one particular voice in the dialogue, it is due primarily to persuasion and not to demonstration. In its presentation of the incompatible, of the fissures and the rifts between the speakers, the utopian dialogue takes the reader through a syncretic series of clashes and disruptions between frames of discourse, a plurivocal process which makes it, for the Renaissance utopographer, a "privileged mode of the quest for truth."

Finally, the intersubjective basis of the dialogue—the fiction that it is a rhetorical interchange or exchange—can be recuperated as a significant element of the thematics of utopian fiction, whose "subject" in the broadest sense is the theory of the social order of man (as he is not *now*). The utopian text claims as its referent a collective or collaborative human product (the utopian City), not the work of any given individual or deity: even Utopus could have done little without the Utopians. It is, therefore, a *political* fiction in the form of a dialogue; but it is also the political fiction *of* a dialogue. As we know from the dialectic, in the process of bringing something else into presence, the parts of the discourse reveal their real nature to us. Implicit in the work of textualizing the present (the "social text" of the State) is the utopia's own figural nature as an oppositional mode of writing, i.e., as a dialogical text. The operation by which the utopian text interrogates the social text is analogous to the structure of dialogue itself, based as the former is upon the interrogation of the present power-configuration of the State (it will be recalled that *The City of the Sun* is an exchange between a member of the State apparatus, the Cavaliere, and a "convert" to Solarian ways, the Genoese sailor). The dialogue thus becomes an extended figure for the political space of utopian fiction, which performs its interrogation of the State by introducing analogies and oppositions to it, a gesture that aims to subvert the authority of the social text's *récit,* which is another name for "history" itself. *The City of the Sun* is truly, as its complex of titles claims, not only a "Dialogo Poetico," but an "Appendix Politicae" ("An Appendix to the *Politics*"), precisely because its utopian poetics permit it, in the last analysis, to do what Campanella's political theory can never do in a climate of Inquisition and censorship. To uncover the "forgotten" textual principles and presuppositions of *The City of the Sun,* then, as we have tried to show, is to come to understand utopian fiction as the fusion of politics and poetics.

Jackson Spielvogel (essay date 1987)

SOURCE: "Reflections on Renaissance Hermeticism and Seventeenth-Century Utopias," in *Utopian Studies,* Vol. I, 1987, pp. 188-97.

[*In the following excerpt, Spielvogel traces the influence of Hermeticism on Campanella's philosophy in relation to the combination of science and magic that characterizes his ideal society.*]

Although modern historians rarely agree on any significant issue, there is a fair degree of unanimity on viewing the seventeenth century as the turning point in the emergence of modern Western history. It was a century full of plagues, constitutional crises, famines, population declines, economic depression, almost constant warfare, and widespread persecution of witches. But it also marked the emergence of the modern nation-state, a secular society and most important of all, a new view of reality, the universe and humankind that was embodied in the Scientific Revolution. The belief that material reality constitutes the only reality, resulting from the shift to a mechanistic universe, has become, after all, the modern Western way of viewing the world.

It is my feeling that seventeenth-century utopians have much to tell us about the significance of their century. They might also be able to enlighten us about what has gone wrong with out own twentieth century. Seventeenth-century utopians, as the Manuels [Frank E. and Fritzie P.] have pointed out in their masterful study on utopian thought in the Western world [*Utopian Thought in the Western World*, 1979], owed much to the legacy of Plato and Thomas More. But, as these authors have indicated, ". . . in the early seventeenth century the word 'utopia' came more and more to connote visions of an ideal state of man in this world, without restriction to the tale of a returned traveler reporting on a distant society to astonished Europeans." Indeed, Tommaso Campanella's *City of the Sun* and Johann Andreae's *Christianopolis* presented visions of reconstituted Christian commonwealths that would begin a universal millennium on earth, a millennium based on science as a way to God. It is clear from their early lives that both Campanella and Andreae believed in the possibility of actually creating their utopian Christian societies. Why were they so optimistic initially? And why did they so strongly emphasize the importance of science and mathematics? I believe that the revival of Hermeticism in the Renaissance and all the intellectual currents it spawned and became entangled with in the sixteenth and seventeenth centuries will help to answer these questions.

Renaissance Hermeticism had its beginning in Florence during the heyday of its cultural influence in fifteenth-century Italy. Upon the request of his financial patron Cosimo de' Medici, the Florentine Greek scholar Marsilio Ficino translated into Latin a Greek manuscript entitled the *Corpus Hermeticum*. Ficino and his contemporaries believed that the core of these writings was the work of Hermes Trismegistus, an ancient Egyptian priest. Ficino himself dated Hermes as living only two generations later than Moses and asserted that this author of Egyptian theology and philosophy had transmitted his wisdom in a line extending to Pythagoras and eventually to Plato. Actually, it was not recognized until the early part of the seventeenth century that the Hermetic treatises were written around 100-300 A.D. and were a product of the Neoplatonic mystery schools that flourished in the eastern part of the Roman Empire. However, as Frances Yates, the brilliant historian of Renaissance Hermeticism, has pointed out, we do not know precisely how old the sources of those mystery schools were, so that the *Corpus Hermeticum* could contain the essence of an older body of knowledge. In any case, our concern is what the Renaissance did with the ideas of the *Corpus Hermeticum*.

The Hermetic manuscripts basically contain two kinds of writings. One type stresses the occult sciences with emphasis on astrology, alchemy and magic. The other focuses on theological and philosophical beliefs and speculations. Some parts of the Hermetic writings are distinctly pantheistic, seeing divinity embodied in all aspects of nature, in the heavenly bodies as well as in earthly objects. As Giordano Bruno, one of the most prominent of the Hermeticists stated, "God as a whole is in all things." Other sections of the *Corpus Hermeticum* portray the universe in organic and animistic terms. Here the world is a living entity, full of life and constant movement. For Renaissance intellectuals, the Hermetic revival offered a new view of mankind. They saw man created as a divine being endowed with divine creative power. Although his basic essence was spiritual, man freely chose to enter the material world (Nature) and thus was of a double nature—mortal through his body, but immortal through his essential being. Man could recover his divinity through a regenerative experience, by purification of the soul. Thus regenerated, he became again a Son of God. This true sage or *magus,* as the Renaissance called him, then had knowledge of God and of truth. In regaining his original divinity he reacquired an intimate knowledge of nature and an ability to employ the powers of nature for beneficial purposes. The serious Renaissance *magus* believed in his ability to control nature and became involved in the practice of magic as a means of organizing and controlling his experience. Hermetic magic was basically a natural magic that sought to work with the normal powers of the cosmos. Hermeticists also revived a cabalistic magic, based on the Hebrew mystical tradition, that emphasized direct communication with and use of higher spiritual powers, such as angels. Nevertheless, Hermetic magic remained the most commonly practiced form of magic in the Renaissance.

Renaissance magic was the preserve of an intellectual elite from all of Europe. The most prominent *magi* were Marsilio Ficino, Pico della Mirandola and Giordano Bruno in Italy, Cornelius Agrippa and Paracelsus in Germany, and John Dee in England. By the end of the sixteenth century, Hermetic, cabalist and alchemical thought had become fused into an intellectual framework that Frances Yates has labelled Rosicrucian. In this Rosicrucian form Hermetic ideas had a major impact on the utopias of Campanella and Andreae.

Tommaso Campanella (1568-1639) was an Italian magician-philosopher, last in the line of Renaissance *magi* descending from Marsilio Ficino. At an early point in his life, he joined an occult group of researchers in the circle around Giambattista della Porta in Naples. Campanella is known to have practiced Ficino's brand of natural magic, including a famous magical operation to ward off the potential death of Pope Urban VIII at a time of the eclipse of the sun in 1628.

Based on astrological portents in 1598 and 1599 he came to believe in himself as one destined to lead the world into a new age. Taking his messianic inspirations seriously, Campanella helped to lead a revolt in his native Calabria in southern Italy against the ruling Spaniards. The revolt had universal aims. Spanish rule was to be replaced with a utopian republic, a magic Republic of the Sun with Campanella as head priest and prophet. This republic would then usher in universal reform and a new era with a new religion based on natural magic. But Campanella had little practical sense and few supporters and instead of heading a Republic of the Sun, he found himself in Spanish prisons for almost the next thirty years of his life.

In 1602 he wrote the first version of *City of the Sun*. This utopia is a model of the state that he had actually planned to create in Calabria. It is also a state ruled by essentially Hermetic priests who use scientific magic to keep the city prosperous and happy.

Campanella's republic is saturated with astrology. The City of the Sun is ruled by Sun or Metaphysic, a sun priest who knows how"God controls things" and the ways and customs of nature and nations. To help Sun, the temple in the center of the city houses a college of priests whose work it is to "gaze at the stars and . . . note all their movements and the effects these produce. In this manner, they learn what changes have taken place or are to take place in every country." Their knowledge of the stars and the influences emanating from the stars enables the priests to run the community to everyone's benefit. They determine by the stars the hours for breeding, not only of animals, but also for humans. Good human stock is produced for the community by selective breeding, not by genetics, but by the proper astrological timing for conception and by mating males and females on the basis of astrological temperaments, for the "constellation that was visible at their birth" determines their natural propensity. The priests also specify the days for planting and harvesting. The role of the priests as state astrologers makes them "mediators between God and man," a clear indication of the function of natural religion in Campanella's utopia. But it is also evident, in accordance with Hermetic doctrine, that astrology and the sciences went hand in hand. The priests were required to learn all the sciences and especially mathematics. Because of its magical and astrological elements, the Hermetic tradition had fostered a tradition of turning towards the world and investigating its secrets. Mathematics and mechanics were viewed as powerful instruments for magically operating on the world. The mathematics and mechanics of the *magus* may have been used with magical intentions, but their very use encouraged the development of those sciences.

There are also other examples of Hermetic influence in Campanella's *City of the Sun*. Animism, one of the basic building blocks of Hermetic magic, is seen in reference to the world as a living animal and to plants which have a sensitive feeling. The use of plants whose "powers and natures" resemble celestial objects and parts of the human body as medicines demonstrates an adoption of Paracelsian medicine. Inhabitants of the City of the Sun are referred to as followers of Pythagoras, the Greek philosopher considered by Hermeticists as one of the chief figures in the transmission of the Hermetic tradition of secret knowledge.

Campanella's *City of the Sun* can be seen then as a solid example of a magical type of religious Hermeticism. But due to the Christianizing of the Hermetic writings done by earlier *magi,* Campanella had no difficulty believing that the natural religion based on Hermeticism found in his republic could be harmonized with Christianity to create a new universal religion. Thus, "They believe what Christ said about the signs from the stars, the sun and the moon is true." Campanella's utopia held out the hope for a new synthesis of science and religion, made possible by Hermeticism, that would create the spiritual renovation of all mankind.

Anthony Stephens (essay date 1984)

SOURCE: "The Sun State and its Shadow: On the Condition of Utopian Writing," in *Utopias,* edited by Eugene Kamenka, Oxford University Press, Melbourne, 1987, pp. 1-19.

[*In the following essay, originally presented at the Fifteenth Annual Symposium of the Australian Academy of the Humanities in 1984, Stephens discusses the dystopian "shadow" in Campanella's* City of the Sun, *and contrasts the fictional techniques used by utopian writers of the Renaissance with those of later centuries.*]

Any beginning for an essay such as this has to be arbitrary. Rather than begin with Thomas More, I shall instead take one of his successors, who wrote about a century later, namely Fra Tommaso Campanella and his work, written first in Italian in 1602, entitled *La Città del Sole*. It was first published in Germany, in the author's own Latin version, in 1623 as *Civitas Solis*. I have chosen Campanella because he lends himself well to bringing out clearly the duality and contradiction inherent in positive Utopias as a genre. Campanella was a Dominican monk and a revolutionary who spent almost half of his seventy-one years in prison. Indeed, he composed his Utopia there after being condemned to life imprisonment in 1602 for his part in an abortive attempt to overthrow Spanish rule in Calabria. Initially a rebel against both church and state, he none the less began, from about 1606 onwards, to write on the necessity of the Pope's assuming world political supremacy. He later modified this to a two-stage design in which it was God's will that Spain should first acquire world sovereignty, in order then to relinquish it in favour of the Pope. Despite this, Campanella's name is inscribed among the fathers of the Russian Revolution on an obelisk in Red Square.

La Città del Sole is a city formed on the pattern of geometricUtopias with seven circular walls to represent the seven planets. But, as well, it is a state whose armies may engage in conquest and which may have its dependent satellites. It has a hierarchy chosen on the basis of individual merit alone, and male and female roles are merged in all vocations as far as possible. The state rests on the twin principles of the abolition of private property and the abolition of the family. The whole city is laid out as a giant educational machine. In the tradition of the Pansophists, 'all of the sciences [are] pictured on all of the walls'. Education for all children is equal and comprehensive. Youth is exposed to the whole gamut of possible vocations as part of its schooling; it is observed to find out which vocation each individual shows most inclination for. Moreover, work for all is limited to four hours a day and the dignity of labour is firmly enshrined in the system. 'The more laborious and utilitarian tasks, like those of the blacksmith and mason, are the more praiseworthy, and no one shuns them.' So the Sun State has, even to modern eyes, a great deal in its favour, if one contrasts it with, say, the two-tier Utopia designed by Leonardo da Vinci, of which the Manuels write in their comprehensive study:

> There would literally be two layers of existence: the nobles on the elevated platform in the sun, and the common people down below with the canals, sewers and carts . . . if the city were so constructed that carriers and workmen were relegated to the world underneath and the upper level was one vast area for free movement on foot by patricians, then the beauty of the superior parts would not be spoiled.

But society in the Sun State was nothing if not homogeneous. If we look at the distribution of power, then we find that the ruler was both prince and priest and called the Metafisico. Under him were three chief ministries, called Pon, Sin and Mor: 'that is to say Power, Wisdom and Love. Power has charge of war and peace and of military affairs . . . Wisdom has charge of all the sciences . . . has but one book in which all the sciences are treated . . . Love has charge of breeding and sees to the coupling of males and females who will produce healthy offspring.' If one cannot help thinking of Orwell's Minipax, Minitru and Miniluv, this is not altogether inapposite, for under Campanella's three ministries conformity in daily life is rigidly enforced. But his book is not without an awareness of the dangers of this. In his passage on the dignity of manual labour, Campanella is at pains to point out that 'in the division of labor no one is assigned to things that are destructive to hisindividuality but rather to things that preserve it'. There is, therefore, a clear concept of individuality and an awareness of what may threaten it. One of the obvious threats is the Sun State's eugenic programme, some salient features of which appear in the following description:

> On the appointed evening, the boys and girls prepare their beds and go to bed where the matron and senior direct them. Nor may they have intercourse until they have completely digested their food and have said their prayers. There are fine statues of illustrious men that the women gaze upon. Then both male and female go to a window to pray to the God of Heaven for good issue. They sleep in separate neighbouring cells until they are to have intercourse. At the proper time, the matron goes around and opens the cell doors. The exact hour when this must be done is determined by the Astrologer and the Physician who always endeavor to choose a time when Mercury and Venus are oriental to the Sun in a benefic house and are seen by Jupiter, Saturn and Mars with benefic aspect.

Astrology and physical characteristics dominate the eugenic programme to the exclusion of personality: 'fat girls are matched with thin men'—and vice versa—as Campanella says, 'so as to avoid extremes in their offspring'. The priests and those who are 'much given to speculation tend to be deficient in animal spirits and fail to bestow their intellectual powers upon their progeny because they are always thinking of other matters . . . As a consequence, they take care to mate with energetic, spirited, handsome women'.

Once more Campanella's text shows an awareness of the depersonalizing effects of all of this for, as a compensation, a kind of Platonic courtship is permitted in the Sun State between eugenically mismatched individuals, as long as it stops short of procreation: 'If a man becomes enamoured of a woman, he may speak and jest with her, send her verses, and make emblems out of flowers and branches for her. But if his having intercourse with her is deemed undesirable by reason of the offspring that might result, it will by no means be permitted unless she is already pregnant or is sterile.' If our sensitivity is conditioned by the twentieth-century dystopias of Zamyatin, Huxley and Orwell, or indeed by a passing acquaintance with eugenic programmes in Nazi Germany, then the dualism of the Sun State and its shadow is all too apparent.

The Utopian mind is essentially an ordering one, bent, as Zygmunt Bauman says, on 'the substitution of a human-made and human-desired order for the natural one'. It is almost a cliché of scholarly writing on Utopias that the same urge to symmetry that produces seven circular walls within each other, as a symbolic reflection of the order of the heavens, also produces an ideal of citizens as of all precisely the same size, as the result of carefully planned and guided copulations. It enforces on the people of the Sun State a relentlessly communal existence in dormitories and on a strict six-monthly rotation. While Campanella sees these principles of order and symmetry as sanctioned in moral and religious terms, he cannot but be uneasy about his Sun State even as he creates it. This uneasiness is betrayed by the text itself, for the shadow is darkest at those places where the text lapses into simple inconsistency.

As if wishing to be one up on Thomas More, whose *Utopia* notoriously did include slavery, Campanella says quite unambiguously of his Solarians: 'They keep no slaves, since they are sufficient unto themselves and more.' But further on in the text we find that this is not quite the whole truth: 'Slaves and aliens are not permitted to corrupt the manners of the city; thus those captured in war are sold, or they are put to digging ditches or performing other fatiguing tasks outside the city, where four squadrons of soldiers are regularly dispatched to supervise them and watch over the territory.' Since the Sun State is not averse to a bit of good healthy imperialism *vis-à-vis* its neighbours, the size of the slave-labour force on the city fringe might well be considerable. Now, any number of contemporary novels of science fiction use precisely the scenario of a revolt by such a slave population, commonly depicted as attractively feral humans, against a technologically superior élite of rulers who are often both more and less than human. At the least, the fact that Campanella's slave workers have to be kept under guard as they perform their labour in the fields marks a weak point in the whole system.

But where things get really sinister is when we start to look at the legal system of Campanella's Utopia, in particular at its punishments. Indeed, if one had to find a small corner for original endeavour in the already vastly overcrowded playground of Utopian scholarship, then the ways in which Utopias punish their wayward members would be a fascinating and revealing topic. By this I do not primarily mean instances such as Winston Smith and his ordeal in Room 101, but rather the mechanisms of punishment in the classical, positive Utopias. As with the issue of slavery, Campanella initially approaches the question of crime and punishment with great assurance:

> Now since theft, murder, rape, incest, adultery . . . do not exist among them, their offenses may only derive from ingratitude or malice, as when some person among them refuses to help another, or from lying, which they abhor more than the plague. Those who are guilty of these charges are punished by banishment from the common table or from intercourse with the opposite sex and are deprived of certain honors until the judge thinks they have been sufficiently punished.

Punishments that consist of temporary exclusion from the community are entirely appropriate to the benign role of the enlightened Metafisico, of whom it is said: 'But our Sun . . . would never be cruel or wicked or tyrannical, because he knows so much.' A little farther on, however, we find that there are male and female elders who have a supervisory role in the communal dwellings and 'who have authority to administer beatings (or have them administered by others) to anyone who is negligent or disobedient'. Flogging is also practised in the armed forces. Nor does it stop at that: 'Anyone who has disobeyed orders is given a club and placed in an enclosure containing wild beasts. If he succeeds in overcoming the lions and bears—almost an impossibility—he is restored to favor. In civil life, we find, the *lex talionis* applies in cases of serious bodily injury: "an eye for an eye, a nose for a nose—if the injuring involved premeditation."' Just as the Solarians' first principle of international law is compressed by Campanella into the pithy sentence, 'If the enemy will not bow to reason, war follows', so the *ultima ratio* of their judicial system is the death penalty. As the text blandly reveals, homicide is punished by death, as is persistent sodomy after other deterrents have proven ineffective. Still more bizarre is the dictum: 'It is a capital offense for women to use cosmetics . . . or to wear high heels and gowns with trains to cover the heels.'

While this may be dismissed as the personal quirk of an author who passed most of his life in monasteries and prisons, the way in which the death penalty is carried out must be taken seriously, since it is dictated by precisely the same logic of Utopian symmetry as pervades the whole structure of the state: 'Since there are no executioners, there can be no execution unless all the people take part in it, either by stoning or by-burning the condemned man, allowing him in the latter case to have gunpowder so as to hasten his dying.' So the perfectly integrated community becomes, at need, a community of executioners, and if we have a feeling of *déjà vu* here, then it may well be because we have read newspaper reports of the rationale of the execution of two students recently on the campus of the University of Tripoli, which was represented by official spokesmen as the enactment of the will of the whole student body, so that the outside world was in fact meant to understand the hangings as a kind of community execution.

Now, an allusion of this kind may provoke immediate accusations of ahistoricism and pleas to consider punishments in the world of 1602, which Campanella cannot help reflecting, whereas Colonel Gaddafi's Student Revolutionary Committee is all too plainly a twentieth-century phenomenon, and so on. But it is a fact of Utopias that almost the same scenarios recur repeatedly with scant respect for historical shifts, and Gaddafi's profession that he has placed all power directly in the hands of the masses has many antecedents in the mainstream Utopian tradition. Beyond this, Campanella's text shows again and again that its author has a very clear concept of *humane* behaviour, and this concept is perfectly applicable and intelligible today. We do not have to go so far as to treat Campanella as if he were a writer of this century. We need only apply the criterion of internal consistency to his text, to have the issues of slavery, warfare and punishment single themselves out in any attentive reading.

Thus the Sun State could be said to be accompanied, throughout the text which establishes it, by its shadow in the form of its own complete dystopia, and it requires only a shift of perspective, a reversal of emphasis, to see the negative side as dominant, the shadow as the substance. There is no lack of twentieth-century dystopias that do this, using many of the same elements as Campanella includes in his model. One might see this stemming from the fact that the tradition of Utopian writing is, perhaps to an even greater extent than other literary traditions, a parasite on itself, on its own past: reducing the most varied historical realities to much the same set of fictional simplifications, while their values may swing between the extremes of hope and admiration on the one hand, and fear and revulsion on the other.

It is a commonplace of definitions of Utopias that they negate a given social reality by offering a preferable alternative as fiction. But I think there is a too ready assumption that they do this in the name of an aggregate of humanistic ideals which is somehow inherent in the form—unless one turns the form on its head to make a dystopia, an act of violence which in turn only makes the cry of protest louder. But such an aggregate may itself be a fiction. Norbert Elias's recent analysis of Thomas More's *Utopia* administers a salutary corrective in this regard by pointing out how specific is the basis of More's protest in contemporary English social conditions and how narrowly defined is the target of More's main attack. Zygmunt Bauman [in *Socialism: The Active Utopia,* 1976] generalizes the point in an equally pertinent manner: 'Utopias, therefore, help to lay bare and make conspicuous the major divisions of interest within a society; . . . but by exposing their link to the predicament of various groups, utopias reveal also their class-committed nature . . . '. Bauman is in the main concerned with non-literary Utopias, that is, those in which the fictional element is mainly a convenience for offering a platform of social improvement. Hence he deals in the coherent interests of large groups and not with personal eccentricities. But there are no such restraints on Utopias in literature, which may be entirely dominated by the personal preoccupations of the author, irrespective of any representative value.

A German critic, Michael Winter, has analysed de Sade's *The 120 Days of Sodom* 1in terms of eighteenth-century Utopian writing and demonstrated its almost complete conformity of patterning and structure. De Sade has reproduced the pattern of the totally organized gratification of human wants. It is just that he has reversed the values of the structure in a way quite different from the dystopias of today. For while the common pattern of dystopias is to open a perspective onto a more humane world beyond the evil system, be this only through nostalgia or a conventional love story, in de Sade's world the system is that of human nature itself as he sees it, and there is no perspective that can be opened onto an alternative world, since the only world is human. De Sade thus achieves a dislocation of the Utopian model from the set of humane values to which it is conventionally attached, and couples it to his own vision of human nature as totally predatory, expressing itself completely in the endlessly repeated orgasm over the subjugated victim. De Sade's work shows that the linking of the Utopian structure to a core of humane values is conventional rather than necessary. There is no safeguard in the Utopian patterns that humane values will be preserved. Hitler's accession to power produced a sprinkling of Nazi Utopias, showing the blissful state of the *Reich* in various future projections.

The most common criticisms of Utopian writing are that Utopias are in the main both static and unrealistic. But I think a further significant criticism could well be that they are deceptive in terms of the values they communicate. The orthodox, positive Utopias set out to sell their worlds to the reader as wholly desirable, but in doing so they all too often block off any dimension of self-criticism in the text, particularly where they are fully self-consistent. One must be, in a sense, grateful for Campanella's inconsistencies as they do open the way to an appreciation of the dystopian subtext in his **Città del Sole**. It has been pointed out that this quality is also present in H. G. Wells's *A Modern Utopia* and the writings of Marge Piercy. Examples as extreme as de Sade's *The 120 Days of Sodom* are unlikely to convert any reader who does not already share the author's enthusiasms, but it is rather the works of the middle ground, the mainstream of positive Utopias that may well be pushing a highly specific and partisan line under the guise of an aggregate humanism. If we now look briefly at the two main criticisms, made over and over again of Utopias in general, then we shall take first the reproach that they are in the main static.

Utopian societies in fiction are not utterly devoid of history. The perfect state is frequently represented as having come about as a result of violent change, or as having been founded to offer a living contradiction to barbarous neighbours. But by and large they do not convince the reader that they have any real potential to evolve or mutate. Rather they have their own total conservatism. This is well brought out in a delightful passage from Zamyatin's *We,* first published in 1929. The hero, D-503, finds that his mild uneasiness with the system and his strong attraction to the lovely I-330 have brought him into contact with a group called the 'Mephis' who are bent on subversion. This shocks him profoundly and he shouts:

> It is inconceivable! It is absurd! Is it not clear to you that what you are planning is a revolution? Absurd, because a revolution is impossible! Because *our*—I speak for myself and for you—our revolution was the last one. No other revolutions may occur. Everybody knows that.

I-330 answers him:

> 'My dear, you are a mathematician, are you not? More than that a philosopher mathematician? Well then, name the last number.' 'What is . . . I . . . I cannot understand, which *last*.' 'The last one, the highest, the largest.' 'But I-330, that's absurd! Since the number of numbers is infinite, how can there be a last one?' 'And why then do you think there is a *last* revolution . . . their number is infinite . . . We may forget that someday. Of course, we shall certainly forget it when we grow old . . . Then we shall inevitably fall like autumn leaves from the trees, like you the day after tomorrow . . .'

In a very real sense, the Utopian imagination is caught out again and again defending its implicit status as author of the last conceivable revolution, a position which history makes untenable as a matter of course. The earliest Utopias already show an awareness of the problem. Both More and Campanella are careful to open their states to some extent to the outside world, if only by a system of spies reporting on innovations abroad so that Utopian states may import any new practices or technologies that seem to have positive advantages, and Bacon's *New Atlantis* is well nigh obsessed with scientific innovation. But what is universally lacking is any element of what might be called creative anarchy in the sphere of human relations. The total openness to technical innovations on the one hand and the inflexibility in human relations on the other is a weakness of the classical Utopias just as it is of middle-range science fiction today, which rarely gets into trouble with the gadgetry, but can only substitute for the organized inhumanity of the slave state or the prison planet the return to a homely, Norman-Rockwell-style banality. This is not to say that the best science fiction does the same, and one could point to positive exceptions such as Ursula K. Le Guin's *The Left Hand of Darkness,* which imaginatively breaks with sexual stereotypes, creating a race of 'aliens' from whom human readers might well have something to learn.

The criticism that Utopias are unrealistic seems rather

more used in slanging matches among Utopians than for attacks from outside the tribe. The most famous and influential of such attacks is that of Engels in the chapters from *Anti-Dühring* published separately as *The Development of Socialism from Utopia to Science.* There he says of the likes of Fourier and Saint-Simon: 'These new social systems were from the outset condemned to remain utopias; the more they were worked out in detail, the more they became dissipated in pure fantasy.' This view was not shared by the Utopian socialists themselves. Writing of his own system in 1820, Saint-Simon said that, apart from all its other advantages, it was the 'necessary result of all the advances of civilization up until the present day', and that if it was in no sense Utopian. That 'Utopia' should become virtually a term of abuse among the Utopian thinkers themselves in the early nineteenth century bears on the vexed question of the status of Utopias as fictions, which I should now like to pursue.

If we go back to Thomas More, then three things are clear about the conception of his work: first, that the positive model of the state is in part a Renaissance *jeu d'esprit,* an intellectual game in a well-established tradition of such pastimes; second, that the preface More wrote after the sketch of the ideal state attacks concrete social abuses of More's own time; third, that More does not expect any real mediation to occur between vision and reality. The work concludes with the sentence: 'But I readily admit that there are very many features in the Utopian commonwealth which it is easier for me to wish for in our countries than to have any hope of seeing realized.' Whilst the rather sketchy fictional element of More's *Utopia* is firmly in the service of ideas, the fictional status of Utopia does not of itself produce tensions, its value for the author and his contemporaries does not depend on the likelihood or otherwise of its becoming reality. If More's *Utopia* permits a more esoteric reading as a parable on the folly of counselling princes, then this seems, neither for contemporary readers nor in the centuries of the work's most vital reception, to have troubled its status as fiction. Campanella makes even less pretence of creating a believable fiction than More, and indeed wrote his Utopia in the wake of the failure of his revolutionary activity and at a time when, condemned to life imprisonment, he could scarcely look to any implementation of his ideas. Accordingly, ***La Città del Sole*** contains not the slightest indication as to how the social structure of the Sun State might relate to that of the author's own society, except in terms of static opposition—let alone begin to evolve within it.

The early Utopias see their fictional quality as absolute and unproblematical, and this is symbolized by their spatial isolation from Western Europe. Situated in some exotic and remote corner of the world, they are unlikely ever to initiate political interaction with the countries of Europe, and thus their fictional quality is under no pressure to shift in the direction of a programme for practical social change. In the latter part of the eighteenth century, this state of affairs changes significantly. The more the remoter parts of the world are explored and become known, the less they lend themselves to harbouring mythical, ideal commonwealths. The spatial isolation of Utopia on some distant island no longer seems an adequate representation of the disjunction between the ideal society and the author's real social context, and with the publication in 1770 of Mercier's novel *L'An 2440* there begins a trend to cast both Utopias and dystopias as temporal projections—a trend which has since become and remained dominant. The German historian Reinhart Koselleck sees in this shift a significant change in the criteria applied to Utopias, since the depiction of a future state of the author's own society commits the work to a set of linear projections from the shared experience of author and reader, which in turn depend on judgements as to probability and practicability. Whilst Campanella could with one stroke of the pen replace the whole system of hereditary nobility with a society in which families of any kind simply do not exist, Mercier's novel and its myriad successors must tailor their fictions according to a criterion of feasibility. They must be able to make *processes* of change credible, where the early Utopias simply posited oppositions. Obviously, this shift would not have come about without radical alteration in the ways in which European society viewed its own potential for change, initially in terms of the Enlightenment's doctrine of slow perfectibility and then, after 1789, in the perspective of the French Revolution. Thus by the early nineteenth century the questions: can this model be realized? *how* can it be realized? are in the forefront of all Utopian thinking and make the condition of Utopian fiction very much one of rational consensus between reader and author. The result is a division within Utopian writing itself, according to whether the criteria of feasibility and rational consensus are accepted or not. If they are, then we get programmes for social reform which appeal to historical necessity and are more or less devoid of fictional interest. If they are not, then Utopian writing may take leave of the tradition of devising model states altogether and transpose the Utopian impulse into purely aesthetic values, as happens in the German novel from the beginning of the nineteenth century onwards.

But this is only half the problem of fictionality in Utopian literature. For if the Utopias of the sixteenth and seventeenth centuries took precious little trouble to make their fictions believable, Utopian fiction of the eighteenth century tendedinstead to make Utopian ideas subservient to literary interest. German novelists of the eighteenth century, in particular, saw as a problem the apparent incompatibility between the preaching stance of the Utopian philosopher and the production of literary interest within the novel. So the question arose:

what can happen in Utopia to keep the readers on the edge of their seats? What changes can one ring in a Utopian society to create a gripping plot in terms of reader expectations? Solving this problem seems to have forced the Utopian novel into various kinds of sophistication which it might have preferred to avoid. In the case of the German novelist of the Enlightenment, Christoph Martin Wieland, the solution comes in the form of an ironic play of multiple perspectives. In France, the novel by the Abbé Prévost entitled *Le Philosophe anglois ou Histoire de Monsieur Cleveland* of 1739 is the first in the Utopian tradition to be explicitly written to show the failure of Utopian communities. The main characters, who are sophisticated Europeans, end up rejecting the emotional poverty of life in a society free of all conflict and passion.

Increasingly in the eighteenth century fictional texts explore the problem that, as we saw, is already implicit in Campanella's Utopia, even if it receives no analysis there, namely the degree to which the institutions of any Utopia pose a threat to the self-realization of the individual. As the concept of self-realization achieves more and more prominence in the eighteenth century, fictional Utopias take on more and more problematic forms. There is a growing reluctance to think in terms of whole states. Rather the Utopian models are explored in more modest and restricted settings, as, for example, the household of M. de Wolmar in the fourth part of Rousseau's novel *La Nouvelle Héloïse*. While Rousseau sketches with loving detail the vignette of a domestic Utopia, his main characters cannot help but find the Utopian atmosphere somewhat oppressive, and the author himself allows the awareness to come through that any Utopia contained within the framework of actual contemporary society and extrapolating from its premises can only represent a choice of evils.

Perhaps I can best sum up the problem of the fictionality of Utopias as it emerges towards the end of the eighteenth century as follows: the challenge of making a Utopian fiction into successful literature is not the same as ensuring that a programme for social reform in the Utopian mode is going to outpace its competitors in the race whose prize is the seal ofhistorical necessity. Both challenges can only be met by the exercise of the creative imagination, but it becomes apparent that in each case this takes place with different premises and goals. When arguing the pre-eminence of their 'scientific' extrapolations, Marx and Engels pointed up the tension in Utopianism between fantasy and fiction. Let us take as an example the following quotation from *The German Ideology:*

> As long as man remains in natural society, that is, as long as a cleavage exists between the particular and the common interest, as long, therefore, as activity is not voluntarily, but naturally, divided, man's own deed becomes an alien power opposed

to him, which enslaves him instead of being controlled by him. For as soon as the distribution of labour comes into being, each man has a particular, exclusive sphere of activity, which is forced upon him and which he cannot escape. He is a hunter, a fisherman, a shepherd, or a critical critic, and must remain so if he does not want to lose his means of livelihood; while in communist society, where nobody has one exclusive sphere of activity but each can become accomplished in any branch he wishes, society regulates the general production and thus makes it possible for me to do one thing today and another tomorrow, to hunt in the morning, to fish in the afternoon, rear cattle in the evening, criticise after dinner, just as I have a mind, without ever becoming hunter, fisherman, shepherd or critic.

This is clearly fantasy, and as such has its place within the author's scheme of things, its own force within his whole argument. But is it good fiction? Is it in any sense the possible basis for good fiction? I think not. For the point of literary fiction is not to be defensible as an intellectual hypothesis, but to be believable within the literary convention as a slice of simulated human experience. Now this, as I have said, is something that scarcely worried More or Campanella, as they simply adopted the model of the philosophical dialogue as a minimal and highly schematic fictional form. But it did worry novelists of the eighteenth century and after, as they took on the challenge of fleshing out schematic models of Utopia with more or less believable characters, evocative descriptions, enthralling plots and so on. In the nineteenth century this fictional dimension faded into irrelevance for those Utopian writers intent on pushing plans for action, recipes for concrete social change. But it remained a problem for novelists and is still very much one today. If we are given to reading science fiction for pleasure and in quantity, then we know that to the question already posed by Utopian fiction in the eighteenth century, namely, what plots are viable in a Utopian framework, the answer still seems to be, very few indeed. Moreover the dreariness of much science fiction shows that the further problem of embedding one's Utopia or anti-Utopia in a simulated reality that will hold a reader who is not prepared to put up with a theoretical disquisition remains quite intractable.

Now, the success of Orwell's *Nineteen Eighty-Four* shows that he must have solved this brilliantly. And yet, re-reading the novel again for the first time after twenty-odd years, I could not help being struck by what a crude piece of literary craftsmanship it is, if we compare it, say, with Kurt Vonnegut's *Player Piano.* Anthony Burgess published in 1978 a work entitled *1985,* the first part of which can best be described as a demolition job on Orwell's novel and the second part of which us Burgess's own pastiche of an English dystopia. While most of Burgess's criticism of Orwell seemed to me to hit the mark and very much con-

firmed my own reaction to Orwell revisited, it is equally my impression that Burgess's own dystopia of a Britain ruled haphazardly, if oppressively, by the omnipotent Trades Union Council is feeble in every respect in comparison with Orwell's. But among all his strictures, Burgess is very helpful in identifying the mainspring of Orwell's success:

> Orwell was good at things like working-class kitchens, nice cups of tea so strong as to be mahogany coloured, the latest murder in the *News of the World,* fish and chips, stopped up drains. He got the feel of 1948 all right. Physical grittiness. Weariness and privation . . . The meat ration was down to a couple of slices of fatty corned beef. One egg a month and the egg was usually bad. I seem to remember you could get cabbages easily enough. Boiled cabbage was a redolent staple of the British diet. You couldn't get cigarettes. Razor blades had disappeared from the market. I remember a short story that began, 'It was the fifty-fourth day of the new razor blade' . . . You saw the effects of German bombing everywhere, with London pride and loosestrife growing brilliantly in the craters. It's all in Orwell.

In a sense the smell of boiled cabbage is to *Nineteen Eighty-Four* what Proust's *madeleine* is to *A la recherche du temps perdu.* It is emblematic of the fiction which gives life in a literary sense to a model of totalitarianism whose intellectual shakiness and improbabilities a critic like Burgess can all tooeasily demonstrate. Its absence is what makes so many dystopias of contemporary science fiction synthetic and one-dimensional. Thus, this fictional dimension is in a way the necessary shadow of Utopia if it is to be effective as literature in the modern context. In literary terms at least, no matter how impeccable the sociology of a Utopia or dystopia may be, without the accompanying shadow of a credible fiction, which may draw its strength from the unrelieved banality of common experience, the schematic model is likely to be rejected by today's literary consumers as plain boring.

I hope that by cruelly, perhaps sadistically, exploiting the metaphor of the shadow I have shown something of the predicament of contemporary Utopian writing. Any Sun State, taken as literature rather than edifying theory, is today faced with the problems of a shadow that it does not want and a shadow it needs. The shadow it does not want is, as I tried to show with Campanella, the presence of a dystopia ready-made within any Utopian model, once the readers become sensitive to the incompatibility between what any positive Utopia exacts in the way of conformity and consistency and the concept of individual self-realization from which our own society shows no signs of moving away. Since Rousseau, the problem has forced itself into the foreground of literary Utopian writing. That it cannot be solved produces the state of affairs in which dystopias have become the most ready and dominant literary form.

The shadow that Utopian fiction needs to attach it to the ground of common experience seems to be something quite independent of the coherence or probability of the Utopian or anti-Utopian construct, but something which this cannot do without if it is to remain interesting, let alone entertaining. Perhaps we need a moratorium on dull dystopias, to give the genre a chance to revitalize itself. Ploughing through the deserts of not-quite-successful Utopian fiction, it is very hard to believe that Thomas More began his *Utopia* in one sensc at least as an exercise in wit. The tragedy of Utopian writing of the last two centuries is that the price one must pay for being witty on the subject is to write nonsense. I therefore close with an excerpt from my favourite piece of Utopian nonsense, namely Oscar Wilde's *The Soul of Man under Socialism.* Perceiving that the rift between rampant individualism on the one hand and the regimentation of any Utopian system on the other is total, Wilde cheerfully pretends that it does not exist. Aware of the increasing difficulty Utopias have in establishing their credibility asfiction, Wilde gives up and revels in the incredible:

> The chief advantage that would result from the establishment of Socialism is, undoubtedly, the fact that Socialism would relieve us from that sordid necessity of living for others which, in the present condition of things, presses so hardly upon almost everybody . . . Socialism itself will be of value simply because it will lead to individualism . . . The possession of private property is very often extremely demoralising, and that is, of course, one of the reasons why Socialism wants to get rid of the institution . . . If property had simply pleasures, we could stand it; but its duties make it unbearable. In the interest of the rich we must get rid of it . . . But I confess that many of the socialistic views I have come across seem to me tainted with ideas of authority, if not of actual compulsion. Of course, authority and compulsion are out of the question. It is only in voluntary associations that man is fine.

John M. Headley (essay date 1988)

SOURCE: "On the Rearming of the Heaven: The Machiavellism of Tommaso Campanella," in *Journal of the History of Ideas,* Vol. 49, No. 3, July-September, 1988, pp. 387-404.

[*Despite his avowed aversion of Machivellian philosophy, Campanella is often viewed as a Machiavellian writer. In the excerpt below, Headley concludes that despite seeming similarities between the two political philosophers, their differing historical contexts lead to fundamental ideological conflicts, especially with respect to the role of religion in civic society.*]

After Aristotle the greatest single intellectual antagonist of Campanella was Niccolò Machiavelli. Although Campanella was born forty years after the author of *The Prince* had died, he experienced a dramatic encounter with some of the immortal remains of his future archenemy. Campanella reports of his going to Florence in October 1592 in the hope of some university appointment: the Grand Duke Ferdinand I had given him permission to be escorted by the librarian Baccio Valori through the Laurentian, one of the first libraries of Europe, and, to the young Dominican, a treasury of learning that surpassed the much vaunted library of the Ptolemies at Alexandria. In the course ofthe tour Valori at one point took the intent visitor back to a secluded treasure chamber where the most precious codices and manuscripts were kept. There Campanella tells of being shown the books of Machiavelli written in his own hand, and as the librarian proceeded to regale him with an inaccurate biography of their writer, the already hunted friar stared down upon the manuscript books of the *Florentine History.* During his long life our aspiring world reformer would have cause to reflect upon this encounter.

Whatever the profound differences and opposition distinguishing the relationship between Tommaso Campanella and Niccolò Machiavelli, their strong affinities and even identity of interests most impressed contemporaries. Despite all his own disclaimers Campanella only managed further to convince his readers regarding this identity. In his immediately subsequent surviving letter, again to the Grand Duke Ferdinand, written two months later, Campanella recommended himself to the prince as a political expert and one whose special knowledge could enhance the Tuscan potentate's esteem and power. And in his most expressly anti-Machiavellian work, the notorious ***Atheism Conquered,*** which announced his antipathy in its original title, Campanella only confirmed the belief of many in his own and subsequent generations that he was himself both Machiavellian and atheist—in fact a "Second Machiavel" to his second English editor. Yet this very curious relationship to the cunning Florentine seemed to be a disease of the age. Two decades earlier Christopher Marlowe in the *Jew of Malta* had allowed his Machiavel to say: "Admir'd I am of those that hate me most." And Gabriel Naudé, Campanella's own friend and advocate, remarked that Machiavelli's doctrines were practiced by those who forbade them to be spread; to distrust all and dissimulate with each as he advises, would become the prescription for effective conduct in this Tacitean age. In short the relationship between the two apostles of guile was nothing if not ambiguous and complex.

It seems almost superfluous to rehearse here a subject that has been so beautifully treated by Friedrich Meinecke in one of the more memorable chapters of his classic *Machiavellism.* And yet for all its virtues Meinecke's effort to resolve the apparent enigma of Campanella's lifelong struggle with the idea of *ragione di stato* fails to get to the nub of the matter. Only at one point does his inquiry engage the question of religion as understood by the two combatants, but without pursuing it to a possible resolution. And it is upon the issue of religion that we need tofocus our attention. In fairness to Meinecke it should be noted that our inquiry is concerned less with the rival uses of *ragione di stato* by the two political thinkers than with the relationship of religion and politics for each.

Italian scholarship on the subject of our present controversy seems nearer the mark when it observes that for Campanella, Machiavelli represented not simply a political doctrine but a general conception of the world which has its distant roots in pagan philosophy, currently designated as gentilism, and its more recent associations with Renaissance Averroism and libertinism. For when Campanella claims that Machiavelli derives from Aristotlelianism, he means far more than what had become a virtual commonplace by 1600; namely, that Machiavelli had modelled his prince upon the tyrant of Aristotle appearing in the *Politics,* Book V. Rather, to Campanella Machiavellism meant an all too broad intellectual current, a cultural phenomenon which indeed was taking its toll upon Campanella himself. Machiavelli's beckoning of his generation to the *verità effettuale della cosa* had by the end of the sixteenth century broadened in its implications to involve a sharpened appreciation of the concrete, a tireless scrutiny of political and social phenomena, *a sapientia humana,* all contributing to the new autonomy of politics. Indeed the terrible, haunting vision of "an orphaned world" continued to obtrude itself, never completely to be suppressed or thrust aside. The *Atheism Conquered* can be seen as directed against its own author and as assuming the nature of an interior colloquy, thus implicitly making something of Machiavelli integral to Campanella. While incongruities abound, similarities, even correspondences, glare.

Any effort to achieve a more precise understanding of Campanella's relationship to Machiavelli as well as his very indebtedness to the Florentine must penetrate beyond both the obvious, pronounced points of opposition and also the express points of correspondence and appropriation to the basic assumptions and different frames of reference which motivate the thought of each. Standing in contrast to the crisp, refreshing clarity of Machiavelli's analysis, the ambiguities, obscurities, and tensions characteristic of any Baroque thinker suffer an abnormal accentuation in the tortuous existence of the Calabrian prophetic reformer, magus, and prisoner. If his social and political thought seems "to pull apart in opposite directions," if it undergoes an undeniable torquing there remains nevertheless throughout his work more than sufficient consistency, impelled byhis consuming world vision, to warrant an examination of the present problem and its peculiar relevance to the period of the early seventeenth century—this *machiavellisticum saeculum.*

Campanella's acquaintance with Machiavelli's works may well have extended beyond the *Prince* and the *Discourses,* but these alone are discernible in his own writings. Of course a dispassionate, impartial reading of *The Prince* was no more possible of Campanella's period than that of a comparably explosive work would be for our own. Campanella's controversy was as much with a Counter-Reformation image of Machiavelli as it was with the political thinker himself. According to this image successful politics required freedom from traditional moral and religious principles. To the sixteenth century Machiavelli was the teacher of evil, a vital commodity, for being evil was more useful than being good. The positive aspect of Machiavelli, his desire to promote civic virtue and public spirit, was quite lost on Campanella. The latter's formal effort to contend with the threat presented by *ragione di stato* to religion came in his **Atheism Conquered,** wherein Machiavelli emerges as the symbol of skepticism and cunning, and the Machiavellians as libertines undermining the profoundly natural and supernatural reality of all religion. Composed in the dreadful dungeon of San Elmo between April and July 1605 and written in Italian under the more revealing title of *The Philosophical Recognition of the True, Universal Religion against Antichristianism and Machiavellism,* this work first appeared in Rome in 1631 and then only to be suppressed by the censors. By his melding of Machiavelli with an Averroistic Aristotelianism, which he represented as being diametrically opposed to his own rationalized, naturalistic Christianity, Campanella saw the Florentine to be more than a political menace: indeed he assumed the proportions of a total and most hostile view of reality. In his desperate efforts to get the book approved and republished by meeting the individual censures, Campanella comes forth with some of his most extreme and exaggerated statements against Machiavelli.

These responses to censured passages conduct us beyond Machiavellism and allow us to approach Campanella's Machiavelli. All the evils of the present age in political and religious matters, he argues, derive from Machiavelli's *ragione di stato,* which perceives all faith to be just so many conspiracies and arts of *statisti.* Against the seventh censure Campanella has to explain his statement concerning the Duke of Valentinois; he says that he is writing against the Machiavelli who makes religion acraft of state and urges the prince to disregard veracity, oaths, and justice. On the contrary Campanella wishes to prove that this is not the true art of State because all who have followed such a doctrine have lost *lo stato* and their lives as well. He then proceeds to prove this point with all the historical examples that Machiavelli used, including Valentinois, Caesar Borgia himself, as an example of a prince who lost both the State and his life. Campanella would appear to be arguing, in the same vein as the current anti-Machiavellian moralists, that crime does not pay and that for the statesman honesty is the best policy and advantageous to the state. He now becomes still more vituperative: it is well known how much evil Machiavelli has done to *Cristianità*, legitimating and even prescribing to all princes injustice, treachery, perjury, the killing of parents and of any who are suspected by the *stato politico,* all for purposes of personal self-aggrandizement and not in the interest of the community. Machiavelli makes a trifle of religion and claims that Christ, the prophets, and Campanella's fellow Dominican Savonarola preached only to acquire *lo stato* for themselves, as do all tyrants, but that through their ignorance of politics, not knowing how to arm themselves, these unarmed prophets were killed. To which Campanella retorts that the unarmed prophets obtain an empire over the minds of men through their deaths, while the armed prophets, like John of Leyden at Münster, only manage to get themselves and their states destroyed. To the censors the recently freed prisoner explains that he seeks to remove the esteem in which Machiavelli is held by the *politici* and *heretici*—as well as by the unknown author of the *Three Impostors,* earlier ascribed to Campanella himself. Campanella desires to explode the claim that Machiavelli was learned in the sciences and to reveal him as knowledgeable only in human histories and in the practice of perverted politics. On the very same grounds which Machiavelli would be most appreciated by the modern age, namely his sense of the concrete, the historical, the experiential, and his basing of politics upon human history and experience, Campanella now takes violent issue, for here human cunning becomes *jus politiae.*

In conveying a further, somewhat more specifically political measurement of his enemy, Campanella addresses the issue of the Machiavellian ethos of power as it relates to political performance in his own day and what we have come to associate with the practices of the emerging absolute State. Struck by the increasing omnipresence of the political dimension, Campanella avers: "All the actions of men are directed to the state [*regnum*], as there is nothing that man does not do for its sake, since every prince transgresses religion and virtue, as they say for *ragion di stato,* because domination compensates one for all evils." To Machiavelli's praise of the wickedness of Caesar Borgia and Agathocles, Campanella objects that virtues are in conformity with nature and vices counter to it, and princes who violate religion and nature are ultimately the most unfortunate and condemned before God. Drawing closer to the political events of his own day, Campanella observes that religion, which should direct men to God, is abused for purposes of ruling and that princes change religion in accordance with the greater political utility, as is frequently evinced these days in

Germany. Campanella entertains the ideas that the Spaniards occupy the kingdoms of the new hemisphere for political gain, although under the pretext of religion, while a king of France for similar reasons will abjure his sectarian beliefs. To the statesmen and Machiavellists of his day Campanella says that unless at the outset they believe God to exist, to exercise his providence and to recompense us, by no means are we able to dispute with them. For who will dispute with the insane? Thus religion, however much embattled, is inescapably fundamental to the politics and the political consciousness of Campanella's thought.

At this time the term "religion" was undergoing a number of significant transformations in its meaning. Traditionally associated with the life of the monastic orders, the term less prominently referred to a worshipful attitude, a genuine fear or a love of God, a personal engagement with God first defined by Augustine and most recently expressed by some of the Protestant reformers. With the Reformation, however, had come a confessionalism, a bitter hostility between two religions which by the middle of the sixteenth century had made explicit what had long been threatening: religion becomes pluralized and reified; "a religion" begins to signify an assemblage of practices and beliefs, expressing a complex external reality distinct from its previous definitions. By the early seventeenth century a polemical work has for its title *Calvinismus bestiarum religio*: from a polemical context the age of the *-isms* had emerged. Yet within Italy itself such an important transformation in the understanding of the notion did not have to wait for the Reformation. Since the thirteenth century a primitive sociology of religions had been nursed at the University of Padua. There a heterodox form of Aristotelianism understood religion as *lex,* ushered in by an astral cycle, established by a *legifer,* and supported by a suitable allotment of miracles. Indeed PaduanAverroism had come to look upon religions as social and even naturalistic phenomena subject to growth, efflorescence, and decay. Crudely expressed, religion at its best served as necessary social-political cement. From the early fourteenth century with Pietro d'Abano to Pietro Pomponazzi in the early sixteenth century, Padua harbored a distinct tradition that makes more understandable Machiavelli's own ability to consider religion as an object of thought and a human phenomenon. Indeed in his political conception of religion Machiavelli represented only an aspect of a much larger development that had been in preparation for over two centuries and would continue to flow from its north Italian headwaters long after he had departed.

Campanella stands among a growing number in the early seventeenth century seeking to redefine religion as something rooted in the rational capacity of all men and therefore natural. Religion is the natural *virtus* with which we are all endowed by God: it is the natural return to God and thus can never be an *arte di stato*. Drawing on Stoic, Platonic, and Hermetic sources, he recognizes a universal rationality in mankind that serves as a preparation and basis for the overgrafting of Christ, who is seen in turn as the primal reason. Campanella readily admits the multiplicity of religions, all of which are established by the decree of nature; but in his view only Christianity is established by supernature, thereby making that religion uniquely true. In the current reshaping of science Campanella perceived a force which, by reinforcing and informing the Catholic religion, might decisively increase its possibilities for becoming not the religion of a special people but the religion of all. The world has one natural law in all peoples which no diversity can obliterate. Yet Thomist that he is, Campanella can claim that this natural law is fulfilled and elevated by the supernatural law evident in Christ. In Christianity alone, he concludes, can the perfect rationality be found.

The problem turns upon a controversy over the nature and purpose of religion. According to Campanella, Machiavelli transforms religion into a political art for retaining the people in hope of paradise and fear of hell. It becomes a means of political manipulation, the cunning of friars and clergy being applied to the rulers' domination of the people. Referring to Melchior Cano's *Loci* X, Campanella claims that the Florentine learned from Aristotle and more specifically from the Paduan Averroists that religion is instrumental in the art of ruling. Apparently horrified by Machiavelli's total subjection of religion to the principle of utility, the Calabrian prophet, gazing northwards, sees that in those kingdoms the *politici* have made religion a suit or hat that can be changed at will. Yet while rejecting this Machiavellian view of politicized religion, Campanella himself affirms religion's political utility, although on a different basis. He insists that no community can last a day without religion; in fact the social necessity of religion is axiomatic for Campanella. As the very soul of the political, religion exercises a natural magic in uniting members of a community. In the **Monarchia di Spagna** we learn that religion, whether true or false (*ò vera ò falsa*), possesses sovereign virtue commanding bodies, swords, and tongues, which are the instruments of empire. No ruler, he observes, is able to establish and retain *imperium* unless he is truly sent and authorized by God or at least is *believed* to be. Religion thus provides the necessary glue binding men to God and subjects to their rulers *in causa imperandi*. With Campanella the political uses of religion seem at times to strain perilously beyond whatever claims religion has to ultimate truth.

On points of detail and tactics he can also agree with Machiavelli: never at a loss for effective resort to cunning acts of political advantage to the state, he can advocate the prompt annihilation of opposition—a measure that would have received the approval of

Caesar Borgia. Other Machiavellian moments recur, expressive of political cunning: the lettered, the intelligentsia, should be kept occupied in the studying of nature, thereby diverted from such politically troubling matters as the study of theology and of philology—a point that would be echoed two generations later by the founders of the Royal Society; or again, so important is it for the Papacy to have a well stocked treasury that the church would be well-advised to raise money *sotto pretesto* of war against the Turk.

Does Campanella expressly tap those rich springs of political deception deriving from Plato, Averroes, and Padua, wherein the idea of the Noble Lie and deception as a necessary ingredient of political stability and order had received such important consideration and loving care? In the course of a lengthy treatment of religion that appears in Book XVI of the *Metaphysics* Campanella takes up the problem of deceivers as it pertains to a religion. After detailing ten criteria (*notae*) whereby the validity of one claiming to bear a *religio* and *lex* from God might be determined—all reasonable enough tests and for the most part applicable today—he addressed the problem of the deceived as well as the deceiving legislator, sent by demons or devils with God'spermission for the sake of a greater good. Among such are Muhammad, the Talmudists, and the gods of the pagans, contrary to nature and to the express prescriptions of God. As one sent by nature while being motivated by reason and love, Lycurgus bore holy laws regarding morals; nevertheless, deceived by the authority of the old religion, he established perverse laws on religious rites and doctrines.

> Among the deceivers are also some who are not themselves deceived, for while a pernicious deception is something to be fled, it is rather something to be esteemed when promotive of service and utility (*non autem officiosam et utilem*). Thus Pythagoras imagined himself for two years to have conversed with the gods and Numa meditated laws in a forest and then gave them to the Romans as if received from God. Varro praises this deception and reckons Romulus to have been killed and concealed by the fathers so that it might be believed that he had been taken up by God with the consequence that his laws would be observed as divine; thus Minos is believed to have done, imagining himself in a grotto speaking with Jove, unless deceived by the devil as was Muhammad from the very beginning. . . . But those who possess all the said marks are immune from suspicion of deception, passive or active. Indeed if God deceives them in having them bear a false religion and false dogmas, hellish and heavenly, so that men may be held to their duties thereby, nothing further must be disputed. For where God wants us to be deceived, we ought to obey. But because this dogma is perverse, that God might be a liar, I judge that religion ought to be embraced which is conferred by God with the ten marks until that religion should come forth having the same signs of God, which

have departed from the earlier one. For from this we know the Mosaic law to cease at the disposition of God because the prophets, miracles, martyrdom and the spiritualization of the believers ceased therein and they passed to Christianity, and the Jews have been given over to a reprobate understanding; they honor Talmudic impieties contrary to Moses, to God and to nature. But because with Muhammad these gifts of God have not passed from Christianity to Islam, therefore man has known by natural reason that Muhammad has not been sent by God against Christianity but rather by an impure demon which has not been able to give to him those charisms nor to deprive the Christians of theirs. Among the latter I daily see the saints accomplishing the same miracles, which in their time the apostles accomplished, and are refulgent with the same sanctity of life. If Porphyry might have considered this fact, he would not have preferred paganism to Christianity.

Campanella here appears to go well beyond Machiavelli in the *Discourses,* I, 11-12, in accepting the details of Paduan Averroism regarding the political utility and historical course of religions. While recognizing the social need for religious belief and savoring the utility of possible deception in this respect, he dissociates himself from affirming that God might inflict upon man an enduring deception merely for purposes of political order.

Nevertheless, on one significant issue the two clearly agree. In the vast heap of Campanella's writings and particularly in the work entitled **Philosophia realis,** it is easy to ignore the **Quaestiones . . . de politicis,** confusedly paginated, which had undergone several redactions since 1609 before appearing for the first time in Paris, 1637. The four questions constitute a criticism of Aristotle's *Politics* and most specifically his concept of the citizen as narrowed to the warriors and governors. In Campenella's repeated efforts to extend the concept to include artisans, peasants, and in fact all the people, we begin to expect from him an idealization of *il popolo* reminiscent of the heresiarch himself, Machiavelli. In fact that is precisely what we encounter:

> Truly workers constitute a great part of the State. We are not able to do without them. For that reason they must not be excluded from the body of citizens. . . . For if the peasants and workers are not so learned in Aristotle's logic, they nevertheless share a common nature and religion. Each artisan is king in his own craft as far as partaking in wisdom, as Solomon said. Justice and temperance however are more to be found in the common people (*plebe*) than in the nobility, for they believe in the law that is preached daily in the temple and what they hear from their mothers and fathers as well as in daily intercourse, and reverently they obey. The educated, in contrast, reliant on doctrine and agitated by conflicting syllogisms, are not as stalwart in justice,

temperance and fortitude. Even Machiavelli acknowledged this when he noted the people to be more just and trustworthy than princes.

Elsewhere in the same **Quaestio** Campanella can specifically attack Aristotle's portrait of the tyrant that culminates in *Politics* v, 11; he can also linger over a Thomistic understanding of deception that is neither hypocritical nor malign for the good of this same people "because we are still in the world and not yet in paradise." However, here he consciously and admittedly stands on common ground with Machiavelli in idealizing the populace.

If the two political thinkers are so apparently similar, how then does one account for the revulsion that Campanella experiences in confronting the Florentine? If to be Machiavellian means to be capable of resorting occasionally to the amoral, cunning act for purposes of maintaining political community, then Campanella is a Machiavellian. It was in this broad, shallow sense that his age understood Machiavelli and in this same sense that William Prynne, that provocative Puritan bigot, would refer to its author as a "Second Machiavel" in the second English edition of Campanella's **Monarchia di Spagna** (London, 1660). Yet this is hardly a very satisfactory understanding of Machiavelli, and in particular it fails to explain what Meinecke dramatically referred to as a sword, thrust into the flank of the body politic of Western humanity, from which it has been reeling ever since. The nature of that sword thrust has been perceptively defined by Isaiah Berlin [in "The Originality of Machiavelli," in *Against the Current*, 1982] in his observation that nothing is so offensive to one brought up in a monistic, religious system than a breach in it. To be confronted by a valid, even necessary, alternative to a hitherto total universal order can only prove devastating to an adherent of that order. For anyone "to attack and inflict lasting damage on a central assumption of an entire civilization is an achievement of the first order." By endowing politics with its own autonomous existence, its own moral and social order, Machiavelli opened the door to another world, another dimension of reality: he shattered the circle, the encyclopedia, the idealized unity of traditional medieval culture, and beckoned to the other provinces of life to follow.

Campanella saw this, although not with the precision that later hindsight may afford us. Rather he sensed himself struggling with something darkly monstrous, and what he lacked in clarity of perception he made up for in passion of conviction. For him the issues are what we would call pluralism and atheism. At the end of his **Atheism Conquered** he charges Machiavelli with not knowing that encyclopedia wherein all science is for the common use and edification; ethics, politics, the economy of the household are here one cake. When Machiavelli says that probity is good for saving souls but not states, he speaks not only against piety but also, according to the Calabrian, against nature, which through virtue, not through vice, saves all. Having continually referred to Machiavelli as an atheist; for he grants nothing to God butAristotle's formal initial motion, Campanella will add to the *Atheism Conquered,* composed around 1605, a preface in 1630 asserting that it is necessary to begin not with "I believe in the Holy Church" but "I believe in God," compelling him, Campanella, to demonstrate that God is, that He is one, that man is endowed with an immortal soul and that God is to be worshipped not fictitiously but by the true religion. For all its confusions the *Atheism Conquered* is a powerful document—confessional, apologetic, an inner dialogue. Here the great strands of heterodox Aristotelianism and Neoplatonic syncretism that constitute in large part the complex cultural formation of Campanella's youth compete for ascendancy, only to be resolved by the triumph of the latter. But Paduan Averroism as a somewhat heterodox form of Aristotelianism is never so displaced as not to be able to reassert itself at critical moments.

At this stage in our investigation a closer contrast can prove revealing. Campanella and Machiavelli, each driven by his political demon, differ both with respect to the right interpretation and use of a political Christianity as well as with respect to the context and frame of reference in which each finds himself. It would be wrong to assume that the autonomy won by Machiavelli for the expression of his political demon is devoid of all religion. On the contrary, religious bonds and habits of mind inhere to the new political enterprise as envisaged by the Florentine; they are for the rulers, however, divorced from any transcendental or metaphysical reference and to be exploited at will. Religion becomes entirely human, a civil matter, and like everything else is mortal. The notorious passage in which Machiavelli clearly prefers pagan religion to Christianity because of the former's greater capacity to generate public spirit will also include the haunting notion that there is no necessary reason for heaven now to be disarmed; and at present, political Christianity suffers to a significant extent from not having the proper leadership and from a false interpretation prompted by indolence. Indeed Machiavelli would appear to have room for the warrior saints and armed prophets as well as for St. Francis and St. Dominic— those popular leaders of a former age whose austerity, poverty, and sacrifice could move the first beginnings of urban masses in the Western world. Meanwhile, he scorns the canon lawyers, the curial administrators, and ecclesiastical lords of his own day. Yet whatever scattered evidence may lurk in the interstices of Machiavelli's writings for his espousal of a militant, crusading Christianity, the weight of his argument falls upon a church and clergy that need to attend to their properly pastoral function and upon a papacy which he vilifies for its excessive involvement in worldly pow-

er. Idealist and more specifically in this respect Marsilian, Machiavelli would reduce the church to its pastoral role and denounce what his friend Guicciardini referred to as those "wicked priests."

With his far-ranging imagination and aspirations, Campanella on the other hand understands the potentialities of the church for world rule and thus not only can make his peace with the fact of the Ecclesiastical State astride the peninsula but can also see it as the nucleus for a larger state, including the better part of Italy and thereby serving as an effective base for the exercise of a universal theocracy. More profoundly and astonishingly, early in his career he made the striking observation that Machiavelli, for all his cunning, while admiring papal stability, had failed to see it as a common ground for unity or unified action. Ten years later and almost a full century after the composition of the *Prince,* Campanella, living in the transformed Italy of the high Counter Reformation and the apparently imposing restored papacy, could turn with new eyes to Chapter XI, "On Ecclesiastical Principalities": there Machiavelli showed himself to be impressed by Alexander VI's demonstration of how a pope might prevail by recourse to money and to force. In the *Antiveneti* Campanella expressly takes issue with the claim made by the master of *ragione di stato* in the next chapter that the pope was the ruin of Italy; Machiavelli's observation pertaining to the Renaissance Papacy prior to the *Sacco* seemed to a shrewd observer of the early seventeenth century to be ignorant and unfounded.

Frankly espousing the vigorous exercise of a political Christianity, Campanella counters Machiavelli by preferring the political-administrative responsibilities of prelates to their pastoral function; in contradistinction to a papal pronouncement of 18 March 1624, Campanella recommends that if compelled to make the choice, cardinals who are bishops should remain in Rome to serve in the curia rather than pursue in their dioceses those pastoral functions prescribed by the Council of Trent. Linking *potestas* to *charitas* in the cleansing of the church itself, Campanella, despite his motley, magical heterodoxy, speaks with an authority and force which neither Guicciardini nor Machiavelli could muster: from the depths of his cell and from his inhuman physical suffering he can invoke not some assortment of armed prophets for purposes of clerical reform but rather God Himself,calling upon Christ to come, but to come armed!

> My life, my sufferings bear Thy stamp and
>   sign,
> If Thou return to earth, come armed; for lo,
> Thy foes prepare fresh crosses for thee, Lord!
> Not Turks, not Jews, but they who call them
>   Thine.

In what might be taken as an express reply to the

implicit challenge presented by Machiavelli in the *Discourses* II.2, Campanella avers that Christian laws, if not providing marvelous heroes like Caesar and Alexander, will produce a Moses, Peter, and Paul whose surpassing heroism is adored and resounds throughout the world. Yet Campanella's efforts go beyond trying to give more bite and greater snap to the athletes of the faith. Ever desirous of uniting faith with power, love with force, he occasionally alludes to the Moslem example of an armed high priest. Furthermore he will remain consistent throughout his life in advocating that the supreme pontiff should be armed: indeed the very wealth, magnificence, and power of the Papacy secure its position over all other princes.

Nevertheless it is in distinguishing the respective contexts of the two that we discover the decisive difference. Machiavelli's vision of politics is a product of long exposure to the rampant individuality and political illegitimacy of the Italian Renaissance brought to a pitch by the unhinging event of the French invasion of 1494. Fragmentation and permanent improvisation characterize this world:

> And as the observance of divine institutions is the cause of the greatness of republics, so the disregard of them produces their ruin; for where the fear of God is wanting, there the country will come to ruin, unless it be sustained by the fear of the prince, *which may temporarily supply the want of religion.*

And from this observation Machiavelli will go on to argue the greater value of good laws to a mortal prince, while admitting the improbability of ever attaining to the relatively solid ground provided by such good laws. If the Florentine knows neither the State nor *Raison d'Etat* as we today know, or think we know it, he grasps the essential temporality, the harsh necessities, the continuing improvisations that mark the life of that entity which we call the State, both product and attestation of a persisting emergency. On the other hand Campanella, venturing globally amongst vast imperial conglomerates that dwarf the restricted, intense view of his predecessor, never loses his holistic perspective, uniting religion with power, and remains thoroughly within a single universal order which he aspires to drive to an even greater, more effective realization.

There is yet another perspective in which we can better appreciate the controversy between these two political giants over the issue of religion and its relation to *ragione di stato*. Running through the *Discourses* and the *Prince* is a kind of nostalgia for an earlier age when a basic religious fervor infused civil society with greater fear, reverence, and natural discipline, so badly lacking in the Italy that Machiavelli experienced. In the cataclysm marked by the French invasion of Italy, partly explicable by the disappearance of religious customs, the astute Florentine reacted with a sense of

loss to an age wherein religious fervor was generally at a low ebb. A century later, however, Campanella stands at the height of the Catholic Church's revival in the Counter Reformation; thus he belongs to a time that could address more moralistically the problem of the wound in Europe's side. Machiavelli stood at the threshold of a new dimension divorced from religion as an ontological reality but eager to exploit its political utility. Campanella lived in the revival, no matter how inadequate, of Catholicism; and in his own political theory he would incorporate not only religion as a reinforced and expanded catholicity but the state itself into his church.

Yet whatever Campanella's moralistic ministrations to the wound in Christendom's side, his opposition to Machiavelli differed drastically from that of the contemporary anti-Machiavellians. The gulf separating the Calabrian prophet both from his own age and specifically from all the other self-proclaimed opponents of Machiavelli can best be appreciated under the category of time. With respect to time conceived as the potentiality for expectation or hope, for liberation or redemption, Campanella, despite all his magical, astrological, and naturalistic vagrancies, stood closer to the intrinsically Christian perspective on the future than did his contemporaries. For "an age without apocalypse" had from the beginning of the century come to settle upon Italy and gradually extend itself to the rest of Europe: by 1660 England seemed the last to succumb, following the death of the more florid Puritan dreams. It can well be urged that Europe certainly needed to cool off after the excess of apocalypses experienced during the long sixteenth century. The new age, however, placed worse than a low premium on such a destabilizing factor as eschatology or any tension toward the future. Implicitly the absolutist conception of time sought an obliteration of any challenging comparison or basis for criticism and amounted to a recrudescence of the harsh, mythic cycles of pagan naturalism, creating its own *aevum*: "in philosophy supporters and negators of Aristotelianism remain substantially enclosed in the iron circle of natural reality without opportunity for escape or final redemption; in politics Machiavellism, Tacitism, and *ragione di stato* likewise constitute expressions of a radical distrust in the possibility of subverting the empirical data of historic actuality; the religion, ecclesiology, and piety of the late Counter Reformation lack any suggestion of eschatological tension or criticism of the existent. *Il Seicento italiano* is in large part prisoner of man of the present." On the other hand both Machiavellians and anti-Machiavellians played the game within the constituted, recognized order. Little wonder that *il secolo senza apocalisse* would find it necessary to keep the exceptional, the radically prophetic, securely confined in the bottom of successive Neapolitan prisons for over a quarter of a century.

In concluding let us once more confront the question: in what sense can Campanella be understood to be a Machiavellian? For good reason did Campanella's English readers refer to him as a "second Machiavel" or as "that most politick friar." The actual indebtedness of Campanella to Machiavelli was more than peripheral, exceeding simply the incidental resort to cunning tactics. By profoundly appropriating the idea of religion's social and political utility, originally a product of Paduan Averroism, Campanella joined many political theorists of the Counter Reformation in judging religion by its effects, its utility, while nevertheless maintaining for himself its claims to truth. Similarly preoccupied with power and its effective exercise in this world, Machiavelli formulated and imparted to Campanella what became the central problem of his life: the empowerment of Christianity. The friar attempted to resolve for his own age the question which the secretary had hesitated to address in his own time; in his quest to achieve the predominance of a viable ecclesiastical state in Italy as well as papal theocracy throughout the world, Campanella in effect took up Machiavelli's challenge to realize a politically militant Christianity. That other interpretation of Christianity, to which Machiavelli occasionally alluded, Campanella would spend a lifetime pursuing in order that heaven might truly be rearmed.

Yet in the end Machiavelli and Campanella are worlds apart: the Florentine is willing to divorce himself from the traditional system in order to construct a new dimension of reality and to use religion for whatever it can provide: in contrast the Calabrian remains within the old system, using some of the new materials of the age not only to shore up but also to universalize the traditional, monistic order.

John M. Headley (essay date 1990)

SOURCE: "Tommaso Campanella and the End of the Renaissance," in *Journal of Medieval and Renaissance Studies,* Vol. 20, No. 2, Fall, 1990, pp. 157-74.

[*In the following excerpt, Headley argues that the contradictory elements in Campanella's philosophy are representative of a changing historical movement as the Renaissance gave way to the modern age at the beginning of the seventeenth century.*]

Do historical periods, or better yet historical movements, have an end, a definitive termination? It is hardly necessary to observe that historical periods exist in historians' heads as means of defining the past; such periods can only begin to have substantive meaning insofar as they are informed by a movement sufficiently self-conscious and coherent as to achieve contemporary identity over a succession of years, thereby demarcating a fairly distinct period, a historical period

to the later historian. Rather than as a period, the Renaissance can better be understood preeminently as a cultural movement, affecting and redefining the aristocracy during the years 1300 to 1600. Although the ambiguity of the term Renaissance as both historical movement and historical period remains, and in doing so serves a useful function, this paper treats the Renaissance primarily as a movement.

Thus to return to the question: Is there an end to that cultural movement that we call the Renaissance, and if so how and when? Obviously, historical movements do not end as do railroad tracks or a football game. For as a historical agent the movement itself has throughout been undergoing transmutation or transformation. In fact, transformation is certainly a more accurate term, for it preserves the historical texture of continuity, while employing chemical rather than mechanical imagery, whereby the fluidity and polyvalent character of a historical movement can be betterunderstood. The notion of terminus or end as used throughout this article only serves as an exhortation to define more clearly the various elements constituting this cultural movement and at what point they become dissociated and transformed, undermining the essential characteristics and integral features of that movement, while realigning themselves with different, even alien contemporary developments. Furthermore, it appears that historians have spent more time reflecting on the origins than defining the ends of movements. Therefore the task of trying to conceptualize the termination of anything so complex as the Renaissance, if dangerous, may prove useful.

A further venture into intellectual alchemy encourages the merging of the Renaissance with the medieval context in such a way that their confluence and contemporaneity can be entertained without dismissing the recognizable features of each. For the Renaissance as a lay, urban, patrician movement, evincing a more practical Christianity, assumes form and develops within the comprehensive medieval context of a preeminently clerical, ecclesiastical civilization from which had developed a chivalric, military culture. In Braudel's long sixteenth century that extends well into the seventeenth, we are reminded on the one hand by Marcel Bataillon [in "La herejía de Fray Francisco de la Cruz y la reacíon antilascasiana," *Études sur Bartolomé de las Casas*, 1965] that "the sixteenth century [is the] culmination of the Middle Ages in so many matters" and on the other hand by Marjorie Reeves [in *The Influence of Prophecy in the Later Middle Ages: A Study in Joachimism*, 1969] who suggests that only when the educated ceased to take prophecy seriously and the sense of involvement in the divine purposes of history disappeared did the Middle Ages truly end. Similar characteristics of what normally appear to be different ages and cultures coexist and can be readily recognized in such cases as the Dominican prophet and popular preacher Savonarola in his humanist, Florentine context; or the conservative nature of the Renaissance in Spain that under Cisneros clipped the wings of whatever might endanger church or monarchy; or, thirdly, the vigorous late medieval piety and religious consciousness of *Utopia*'s author, Thomas More. Likewise, apparently conflicting features and motifs can coexist in a single person, in a single age and culture.

What are the integral elements, the essential characteristics that constitute the cultural movement we call the Renaissance? Three suggest themselves, all of which are sufficiently evident in Petrarch: first, the conscious adoption of a perspective onthe past, as passed, and the quest to appeal initially to the aesthetic and eventually to the moral and philosophic norms in that past, identified as that of ancient Rome, all in order to evoke these norms as models or forms, to effect potential reform in the present; secondly, an affirmation of the primacy of the humanist, rhetorical tradition in contrast to the contemporary devotion to dialectic and to the emerging protoscientific interests evident in the arts and medical faculty at Padua; thirdly, the assertion of the authority of direct experience, evident in Leonardo da Vinci, the verification pursued by the Paracelsians and perhaps most pungently evinced by Sagredo's countering of Aristotle's authority with sensible experience, as presented at the beginning of the "Second Day" of Galileo's *Dialogue Concerning the Two Chief World Systems*. In all three elements the priority of will is present along with the enhanced integrity, autonomy, and authority of individual experience. As Petrarch claims in *On his own Ignorance,* he prefers "to will the good than to know the truth." Likewise rhetoric, ever conscious of its audience, seeks to capture and convince the total self, emotional as well as purely intellectual; the will and the affections become the proper object of eloquence. Similarly, with both Pico and Ficino, man relies primarily on himself and the right orientation of his will for salvation. Regarding the autonomy of man and its implications for the validity of individual experience, nominalism as well as some forms of mysticism of the late Middle Ages gives new depth, force, and definition to human individuality. A final point at this stage can be made: if principally evident during the first half of the Renaissance, these three characteristics persist throughout the movement with varying modifications, attaining in the case of experience, as evinced in Galileo, a decisive and momentous formulation conjoined with his mathematics.

In advancing the Dominican friar Tommaso Campanella as a terminal figure to the Renaissance, I am not suggesting any causal relationship of the former upon the movement. Nor am I arguing that there is something typical about him. Rather the encyclopedic, far-ranging mind of this Italian philosopher, prophet, and reformer affords a useful sort of lens whereby one can better apprise some of the complexities in the late, attenuated Renaissance as it encounters new currents at the beginning of the seventeenth century. For Campanella stands athwart that decisive transformation of learning occurring in the first third of the seventeenth century. His own intellectual formation derives essentially from the last third of the preceding century, yet is by no means impervious to the changes registered by the emerging new science. Despite his peculiar appropriations of Galileo and Machiavelli, however, the constant, the centerpiece of his entire thought, is a universal, hieratic order, a single monistic system. In fact, Campanella compels us to contend with the reassertion of medieval features, a sort of revenge of the medieval evident in the prophetic, the universal, the imperial, the monastic, and the encyclopedic working to snuff out the discrete, the critical, the republican (long since departed), the rhetorically exuberant, and the classically normative. He asserts a medieval monastic-apostolic Christianity permeating and penetrating the late Renaissance, curiously associable and associated with some of the latest currents of thought and intellectual endeavor.

In a quick assessment of Campanella against the present laundry list of Renaissance characteristics—turning to the first, the resort to the classical past for revival in the present, the very principle of renascence or renewal itself—one finds the Calabrian reformer standing in striking contrast: his prophetic, apocalyptic expectancy and his almost child-like delight and trust in the new, the innovative, orient him toward the future. Indeed, his truly emotional commitment to innovation and experimentation derives as much from this hunger for intellectual freedom as from his sensory epistemology. Witness his massive effort to mint a new philosophy to replace the Aristotelianism of his day, or his reaction to the appearance of Galileo's great *Dialogue* in 1632: "These innovations (*novità*) according to ancient truth, of new worlds, new stars, new systems, new peoples etc. are the beginning of a new age." Encouraged by Stoic and Origenistic themes, Campanella looks forward to a renovation of all things. He is a real modern in preferring recent deeds to those of Alexander the Great, Pyrrhus, and Jason.

If his departure from any sort of conscious Renaissance appeal to the past is abrupt, no less decisive is his abandonment of the humanist, rhetorical tradition. In the *City of the Sun* the Solarians pursue an education in the mathematical, physical, and astrological sciences, whose mastery is necessary for anyone to be considered for public office. It is true that a basic familiarity with the mechanical arts and the history of all peoples, their ceremonies, rites, and governments, together with the inventors of all the arts and laws is required. But history and the mechanical arts can each be learned in two days because both are clearly set forth graphically on the walls and arepracticed. The

Solarians deliberately eschew an Aristotelian sort of learning or, for that matter, the study of traditional literary authors as a "knowledge which requires only servile memory and which deprives the mind of vitality because it meditates upon books instead of things." Indeed he seems to express here an Americanism worthy of Henry Ford.

Likewise, in clearly preferring the study of the natural sciences to all other intellectual pursuits, Campanella appears to be driven not only by their utility but also because they divert minds from dangerous philosophical speculation and literary pursuits that beget social and political unrest. Such studies present so real a threat to political stability that he recommends importing a juggernaut of philosophers and philologists to destabilize the Ottoman empire. So evident is this theme in Campanella, especially in his ***Monarchia di Spagna,*** which saw English editions in 1654 and 1660, that in 1670 Henry Stubbs finds a case of "Campanella Revived" in the new Royal Society's conscious pursuit of a politically safe concentration upon the investigation of nature. Indeed the retreat from a high-flown rhetoric became general to Europe after 1660, but Campanella's own controversy with rhetoric at the beginning of the century proved instructive. As early as 1596, and again at the end of his life in 1634, Campanella lashed out at Ariosto and Tasso, who pursued the fabulous taste of the crowd. Preferring moral weight and religious depth to fashionable aesthetics, he celebrates Dante and his transcendence of the conventional. In seeking to define the proper subject for the poet, Campanella radically opposes classical mythology and expresses a contempt for the fables of Greece. Instead, the poet should honor true, public heroes, especially contemporaries: if someone might describe the seamanship of Columbus, with that of Magellan, Cortes' conquest of Mexico, or Drake's circumnavigation of the globe interposed as subordinate episodes, thereby imparting the marvelous novelty of the lands, customs, and new peoples, the great ardor and generous thoughts of the leader, then there would be no need to imagine new fables as the Greeks did in describing Jason. Campanella's own rough-hewn sonnets, massive in their moral and religious import, their political and social indignation, attest to this refreshing anomaly in an age of fashionable, prettified poetry. While it is true that Campanella appears to be taking issue not with Renaissance aesthetics but with what they had become in mannerism and the baroque, nevertheless, in his rupture with contemporary practices and the humanistic tradition, he asserts a political view of poetry: it is an instrument of doctrinal and moral management in the hands of the wise legislator. Clearly he is far removed from Renaissance aesthetics. Campanella exhibits a deliberate turning away from the humanist, rhetorical tradition because it is either frivolous or politically disruptive.

Though Campanella divorces himself from the first two characteristics of the Renaissance, he is an ardent champion of the third, the authority of direct experience. His own empiricism dictates such a position. He affirms that he learns more by examining the anatomy of an ant or a plant than by reading all the books in the world. One wonders what exactly his raw vision reveals. But more than anything else, he is most impressed by the epistemological implications of a single event. Recurring repeatedly throughout virtually all his work is the reference to Christopher Columbus. That the Genoan proved by his own achievement that the antipodes do exist, despite the claims of St. Augustine and Lactantius to the contrary, establishes definitively for the Calabrian the superiority of direct experience to the books and asseverations of the most august *auctoritates.* The fundamental reality of the individual's experience seems to have survived the vicissitudes of the Renaissance and awaits the disciplining and refinement of the new age. With respect to the naive enthusiasm of their empiricism, Campanella and Bacon share a common universe.

The immensity of the implications stemming from the authority of direct experience, if it possibly provides a clue to the central import of the Renaissance, is beyond the scope of this article. Nevertheless, to indulge momentarily in the fateful practice of the late sixteenth-century Paduans, the intermediate *negotiatio,* a reflection is in order before passing on. The new identity, singularity, and autonomy afforded to man by nominalism and the resulting implicit authority of the individual's experience promote an overarching reality that inheres to the Renaissance, making it, despite Troeltsch, the true threshold of modernity: namely, the integrity of an inner experience forged from the displacement occasioned by a new perspective and the emerging capacity to appropriate the intellectual attributes from that changed relationship. This perspective consciousness manifests itself most pungently and dramatically in Copernicus, who, through displacing the world from its central location in the universe, nevertheless affirms an anthropocentric consciousness whereby man can now achieve his ideal goal enunciated earlier by Anaxagoras, to become *contemplator caeli,* the contemplator of a universe that God has constructed, according to Copernicus, on man's account, *for us (propter nos).* Thus anthropocentrism becomes detached from physical location, from geocentrism, and finds its proper home in the newly excavated depths of man's thought with its idealization of the world's center. "The senses, not reason, have lost their Paradise." Perhaps this deepened consciousness is what Burckhardt intended when he spoke of man's subjectivity asserting itself so that he becomes an intellectual, spiritual individual (*geistiges Individuum*) and recognizes himself as such.

The argument here is historical and not just apparently logical, not resting merely upon the scattered witnesses of Pico and Ficino or even Giordano Bruno. The following texts from Campanella's great contemporary, Johann Kepler [in his *Astronomiae Pars Optica*], affirm the centrality of man's perception:

> Thus it is apparent that it was not proper for man, the inhabitant of this universe and its destined observer, to live in its inwards as though he were in a sealed room. Under those conditions he would never have succeeded in contemplating the heavenly bodies, which are so remote. On the contrary, by the annual revolution of the earth, his homestead, he is whirled about and transported in this most ample edifice, so that he can examine and with utmost accuracy measure the individual members of the house. . . . Moreover, as I said in the "Optics," in the interests of that contemplation for which man was created, and adorned and equipped with eyes, he could not remain at rest in the center. On the contrary, he must make an annual journey on this boat, which is our earth, to perform his observations. So surveyors, in measuring inaccessible objects, move from place to place for the purpose of obtaining from the distance between their positions an accurate base line for the triangulation.

Thus man is the observer, the measurer, the surveyor of God's creation. And similarly there comes from the depths of a Neapolitan dungeon the ringing affirmation of Campanella himself:

> Man's knowledge concerns this earth which, admittedly, is a point, if compared to the universe; nevertheless our knowledge pertains to this point, which *for us* is not a point.

Through the subjective experience of displacement and enforced perspective, the perceiving self is challenged to comprehend and reconstruct the universe imaginatively within its own consciousness. The emerging perspectival consciousness comprises that sense of distance and separation from the classical past which Panofsky defined as being comparable to the fixed distance between the eye and the object in focused perspective; at the same time this new depth to the self posits the need to master and control that other space.

By the beginning of the seventeenth century the Renaissance was an attenuated and fragmented movement, its front broken up by a number of emerging forces: the territorial state, the advance of confessionalism, the increasing preoccupation with natural philosophy. In southern Europe at least the contextual framework remained—the medieval hierarchical, clerical order of power—to be sure, more certain in Campanella's head than on the chessboard of European affairs.

Three prevailing characteristic features for the late Renaissance, though less distinct and internally coherent than those of the early Renaissance, suggest a tran-

sition from the late Renaissance toward a new ordering of reality. If the term did not itself connote a certain linear definition, one might recognize these most arguable features of the late Renaissance as being marginal to its original dynamic, extrinsic rather than intrinsic, more the result of external forces upon the movement than forces inherent in the movement itself. The three together constitute a filter through which European culture passed at the extreme attenuation of the Renaissance.

The first is a return to speculation and to metaphysics, a signal departure from the practical orientation of early humanism despite the very real affiliations of this new development with the original humanism. The conjunction of Medici rule and the abrupt importation of Platonic, or more precisely Neoplatonic, interests had coalesced in the capital of the Renaissance by the mid-quattrocento to make the concerns of a citizen in an urban republic less relevant in the changed context than the aspirations of a courtier. As evinced in the oration of Pico, there had turned out to be more than one past, in fact a bewildering number together with their sources. Once having turned to the past for its own sake, the Renaissance would press on to come up with not only Cicero and Plato, but also Epicurus, Archimedes, cabala, and even Christ—and the dark wealth of Hellenistic demonic cosmology that Alexandria inflicts ever anew upon Athens. The ontological extravagancies of FlorentinePlatonism produced such intoxicating and exuberant derivatives as Hermeticism, Paracelsism, and cabalism. Speculation and metaphysics, mystery, and the occult, together with a reinforced astrology, predominated.

Subsequently the second chief characteristic of the late Renaissance emerges: a delight in the singular, the arcane, the emblematic, the curious. This delight of the virtuoso in collecting rarities manifests a direct experience which has allowed perception and curiosity itself to run riot and to seed in a chance assemblage of curiosities. The oncoming mastery of nature certainly did not lie in this direction. Thus notable, even fateful, is an observation of Francis Bacon in the *New Organon*. Here he abjures those who forsake the ordinary and the common to investigate the less frequent and familiar. In contrast, Bacon's natural history incorporates an examination of the common:

> But I, who am well aware that no judgment can be passed on uncommon or remarkable things, much less anything new brought to light, unless the causes of common things, and the causes of those causes, be first duly examined and found out, am of necessity compelled to admit the commonest things into my history.

The statement is all the more striking in that Bacon shortly afterwards called for the compilation of all monsters and prodigies of nature, whatever rare and unusual. Although still a long way from Hume's belief that the passion for the marvelous is the hallmark of the ignorant, distinguishing the vulgar from the learned, nevertheless the Lord Chancellor's exhortation can be taken as the opening wedge of a movement that ultimately reduced the preternatural and the supernatural to the one natural order.

Finally, the third feature that emerged by the end of the sixteenth century is the discovery and impact of America. Does the dimension of space figure into an understanding of the Renaissance? Certainly the temporal dimension with its distinctive perspective upon the past is essential to any understanding of the Renaissance. But what of the spatial dimension? Whatever the actual parochialism of Christianity and of European culture at this stage of their development, there is nothing about the Renaissance, once extended beyond its northern Italian foundations, that must limit it to the European "stockade." Indeed, if any credence is to be given to Michelet'sRenaissance as the discovery of the world and of man, then America is the veritable fulfillment of that destiny. Had not Burckhardt begun his "Fourth Part" with Columbus? Yet it would seem that just as the Renaissance creation of a perspective upon the past led to a profusion of pasts that obscured and confused the ostensible clarity in perceiving the original norms and models of the movement, threatening to subvert its definition, so, in the very global outreach of the West, were the models of classical greatness surpassed, producing a liberation from ancient example and thus a further dissolution of this great cultural movement.

The discovery and impact of America promoted the growing recognition of a global unity and the community of mankind. The revival of Stoicism, especially in the hands of the Spanish moral theologians, made intellectual sense out of this immense and unique experience. But more profoundly, at the end of the sixteenth century, the self-experience and perception of Michel de Montaigne articulated the universal reality of the common human stamp. This late product of the Renaissance, if such it may be considered, the aspiration to world community, goes beyond that more benign and certainly nobler aspect of Western society, the passion to communicate and specifically to evangelize. For in its time an appalling amount of intellectual as well as material energy was mobilized to express that darker aspect inhering therein, the Western passion to exploit, to conquer, to master.

A challenging statement made forty years ago by the great historian of science, Alexandre Koyré [in "L'apport scientifique de la Renaissance," in *Études d'histoire de la pensée scientifique*,1966], here demands consideration:

> The epoch of the Renaissance was one of the periods least endowed with critical spirit that the world has known. It is the epoch of the grossest and most profound superstition, an epoch where the belief in magic and in witchcraft enjoyed a prodigious expansion and was infinitely more widespread than in the Middle Ages. . . . [A]strology plays in this epoch a far greater role than astronomy. . . . And if we consider the literary production of this epoch, it is evident that the beautiful volumes of translations from the classics coming from the Venetian presses do not constitute the great success of the book trade, but rather the works on demonology and magic; it is Cardano and later Della Porta who are the great authors universally read.

In the context of the present issues, Koyré's statement proves most illuminating both with respect to its insights and to its oversight. The preeminent source of such credulity is Florentine Platonism, which produced the great watershed in the development of this cultural movement. Revived Neoplatonism is the culprit. Admittedly, the witch craze cannot be directly attributed to this revival but, if to anything, the bull *Summis desiderantes affectibus* of Innocent VIII (1484) and the publication of the *Malleus maleficarum* (1486). Nevertheless, the recovery of Alexandrine thought provided the mental climate and supporting view of nature that helped to launch Europe on two centuries of fervid witch hunting. Renaissance Platonism's syncretistic, universalizing tendencies and the neglect of distinction and differentiation reflect a single comprehensive system in which all things are resemblances of one indwelling reality. Nevertheless, Koyré has taken a part of the Renaissance, perhaps the most influential part, for the whole. Despite its merits his statement overlooks the fact that before Renaissance Platonism there had been earlier developments within humanism that had possessed a sense of the discrete and had, in Lorenzo Valla and shortly thereafter in Poliziano and a wealth of great textual scholars, developed the critical, textual techniques associated with the emerging discipline of philology. Not only was the Renaissance, at least in one of its major aspects, not lacking in critical force, but this very critical talent of philology, in the person of Isaac Casaubon, ultimately punctured the inflated figure of Hermes Trismegistus and its accompanying myths.

For charting and assessing the course of the late Renaissance, Koyré's statement has considerable value. It suggests a break or serious deflection in this cultural movement occurring at the middle of the quattrocento. Beyond the immense impact of the Platonic reception occurring at the capital of the Renaissance, beyond the purely intellectual elements in this complex of forces, other developments contributed to the creation of this watershed: the advent of printing at the midpoint of this cultural movement and the beginning of that shift from the Renaissance urban, republican environment to the court, a harbinger of the later princely Baroque culture. Two further points emerge from Koyré's understanding of the Renaissance: first, while noting a boundless curiosity as a sort of obverse of the medal of Renaissance credulity, he posits as the prevailing formula for the Renaissance, *tout est possible,* which, to the extent that it was true at this stage in the movement, can onlyhasten the attenuation and incoherence of the Renaissance as a cultural reality; secondly, there occurred at another level a maturing of a disciplined, controlled experience culminating in the specifically designed and mathematically expressed *experimentum* of Galileo.

Briefly then, how does Tommaso Campanella relate to these later trends? To the first, the speculative, quite substantially. Though neither a Paracelsian nor a cabalist, Campanella does manifest some interest in Hermetic themes strengthened by his own affinity for Origen and for what appear to be neognostic influences. His long years in prison permitted him ample opportunity to give vent to his speculative instincts especially evident in his **Metaphysics** and **Theology.** And his pronounced involvement in astrology remains patent. The concept of man as microcosm, trumpeted by Pico and adhering to so much of the Hermetic as well as Paracelsian literature, does not, however, significantly penetrate Campanella's thought.

Campanella does not, however, share the age's developing interest in the obscure, the rare. Only in one instance, with respect to the subjects appropriate to true poetry, does he border on a baroque enthusiasm for the marvelous. In his **Poetica** of 1634/1638 Campanella urges that the poem as a magic instrument must be marvelous. The admirable or wondrous—as evinced in natural objects such as the sun, the stars, and monsters; or in human ingenuity such as bombards, the discovery of the new world and the new heavens and planets by Galileo, and Copernicus' construction of the world—all lend themselves immediately to the poet. Whatever is rare—Joshua's entry into Palestine, the beginning of the Roman empire, the Spanish entry into America, or above all the achievement of Columbus—offers itself. For whenever the marvelous is lacking, fables take over. Nor does Campanella limit his consideration to the West but is prepared to advance the religious rites and deeds of the Japanese and Chinese as suitable subjects, for the good poet ought to speak of all the world. Yet the total import and direction of Campanella's thought with its emphasis upon communication and the creation of a single coherent world order militate against any private lingering over the obscure for its own sake. The man who reduces all human learning to graphics and depicts them on the walls of his city has neither the patience nor the place for any private enjoyment of rarities.

With respect to the third characteristic of the late Re-

naissance, it is more accurate to speak of Campanella's identification rather than relationship; for his commitment to the unity of mankind, at least in the perspective of world evangelization, is total and fundamental. As a Dominican he belonged to a tradition of aggressive preaching and proselytizing. As part of the generation associated with and promotive of the *Congregatio de propaganda fide,* and perhaps personally influential in its founding in 1622, he shared in that vast momentum experienced by the Counter Reformation to win over the recently discovered populations of the earth. Both his apocalyptic vision and his naturalistic form of Christianity called for the salvation of all men and their incorporation into a single world order. His preoccupation with the realities of global unity is evident in many ways and in most of his works, although in none so specifically as in his **Quod reminiscentur** of 1615-18, one of his more important works and one that he prized above almost all others. Here in the second part he fastens upon the issue of the right to communicate with all peoples. His exhortation to the Emperor of China is profoundly and distinctively Western, rooted in Aristotle and impelled by Christian universalism; yet at the same time it is intimately Dominican and evangelical. For the great Dominican, Francisco de Vitoria, in his *De Indis,* had affirmed that whatever meager claims Spain had for being in the New World derived only from the natural right to society and to communication. Acting upon the commonly held European attitude, recently reasserted by Botero, that China had arrogantly turned away from all external associations and looked inward upon herself, Campanella abjures her emperor in a letter that was never delivered. Resorting to the image of the cheese and the worms, familiar enough in Campanella's own age and made familiar to a modern audience by Carlo Ginzburg, but used neither here nor elsewhere in Campanella's writings in the cosmogonic sense of Menocchio, Campanella admonishes the emperor:

> Those men [your subjects] are lacking in aspiration (*parvis contenti*); they seem not men but like worms born inside a cheese, who reckon nothing more nor better there to be in the world beyond their own cheese from which they are nourished, sustained, hidden, or as worms born in man's stomach who know nothing of man, nor his mind, cocooned away, not wanting to be disturbed. So, oh king, you seem to be to us. . . . Stick your head out beyond your cheese, beyond the stomach of your land.

And yet Campanella's total experience of the impending world unity is not limited to the spiritual and intellectualdimension; it embraces the material and the very instruments of power. In **The City of the Sun** he speaks of compass, printing press, and arquebus as *segni* of the imminent union of the world. He clearly celebrates a technological as well as a spiritual unification of the world.

How, then, do these characteristics of the end of the Renaissance stand with respect to Campanella? Professor Trevor-Roper has suggested and Professor Lewis Spitz has concurred that the Renaissance had spent itself by 1620. To have two historians concur on anything is a notable event worth celebrating and in this instance encourages one to seize a narrow ledge of time on which to construct an answer. One can draw some hazardous conclusions regarding that generation that came to maturity in the first decades of the seventeenth century. Campanella's own creative activity peaked during the first decade itself. I have tried to use his mind as a sort of lens to perceive the kaleidoscopic issues fanning out from one movement, while penetrating and dissolving or being reconstituted into another. If Campanella's mind does not always offer the most accurate and representative of lenses, it is intense and profound in its eccentricity, yet comprehensive in its sweep, revealing some often neglected, deep-seated forces.

Although in its undercurrents and indirect influences no historical movement is entirely obliterated but rather leaves a sediment of human experience for later inspiration, nevertheless as a conscious, coherent movement the Renaissance by the early seventeenth century was being overwhelmed both fore and aft, first by the quest for the new, by innovation with or without America, and secondly by the earlier forces of prophecy, apocalyptic, and confessionalism. The first casualty of these developments was the deliberate appeal to past norms for evocation in the present. While affirming a classical order, the age of growing absolutism presented a hostile face to any potential challenge offered by past models; the American experience and the forward orientation of the moderns further reduced the impact of such norms. Moreover, the development of philology, beyond the present survey, served to indicate both the inaccessibility as well as the inapplicability of the past and to freeze the classical authors in achievements of breathless scholarship. With respect to the humanistic, rhetorical tradition, it persisted, fragmented and attenuated, its individual members bowdlerized, slowly, ever so slowly giving ground to a new preoccupation and confidence working in itsmidst. This new sort of learning later defined itself as the scientific and technological tradition, broadly perceived and hailed, if misunderstood, by Campanella. The validity of direct experience did survive, even flourished and was developed and refined to become associated with a mathematics of which Campanella was quite innocent. At the same time that more profound, introspective experience of the anthropocentric, perspectival consciousness, already evinced in the high and late Renaissance, shortly received its baroque expression in the dreadful grandeur and terrible exaltation manifest in the awareness of that Cartesian *manqué,* Blaise Pascal, as he pondered the eternal silence of those infinite spaces. As for the unity of mankind, its spir-

itual realization, unachieved by Campanella and his age, continued to elude Western efforts, although technological unity was becoming a reality during Campanella's lifetime. We are reminded of the three primalities, amounting to the modes of God, a veritable Trinity that inspired Campanella's philosophy: Power, Wisdom, and Love, these three. But for Campanella—and here at least he was so expressive of the Western experience—the greatest of these is Power.

The undercurrents of the prophetic, astrological, and apocalyptic working through the medieval-Renaissance matrix had their ultimate resurgence at mid-century in the course of the English Civil War. But two decades earlier, in Paris, to which Campanella had removed as a final asylum, a new order was beginning to emerge. One can catch a fleeting glimpse of its nature in the correspondence of the newly appointed nuncio extraordinary to the court of Louis XIII, Giulio Mazzarini, soon to be known as Cardinal Mazarin. Having been sent to Paris with the express purpose, among others, of casting a cold eye upon the warm reception given to Campanella and of reporting on the doings of the Calabrian celebrity, Mazzarini worked to contain and reduce the influence of the prophet at court. At one point in the correspondence with his chief at Rome, the Secretary of State, and Cardinal-nephew, Francesco Barberini, the rising Roman ecclesiastic calculatingly observed 3 December 1634 in a statement portentous of the future: "I am persuaded, however, that the king will not be counseled to tie himself to any resolution based on good constellations and that he will consult what may be most advantageous for him with his prudence and effective powers rather than with those of celestial influence." At least for some in circles at Paris and also at Rome it may be said that the Middle Ages as well as the Renaissance had passed.

John M. Headley (essay date 1990)

SOURCE: "Tommaso Campanella and Jean de Launoy: The Controversy over Aristotle and his Reception in the West," in *Renaissance Quarterly,* Vol. XLIII, No. 3, Autumn, 1990, pp. 529-50.

[*Focusing on Campanella's polemic,* On the Gentilism that must not be adhered to, *Headley argues that Campanella's anti-Aristotelianism derives from his commitment to Christianity and the new spirit of empiricism.*]

In his first published work, the **Philosophy Demonstrated by the Senses** (Naples, 1591), Tommaso Campanella evinced at the outset of his long intellectual career that abiding and most pronounced feature of his entire philosophical position, namely, an opposition to Aristotle. The product of a twenty-one year old man, this book conveys a fresh empiricism and is significantly untainted by the impact of astrology or the occultism of G. B. Della Porta or the later political religious interests impelled by a personal messianism that would shape his thought. In combatting the detractors of Telesio against Aristotle, the ardent young Dominican charges the followers of the all highest Stagirite with embracing the sentences of others without bothering to scrutinize the nature of things. Our current affliction, he announces, is to excuse willingly the errors handed down by the ancients, as if bound to them, and to deny our own sensible experience. Chiefly to blame are certain books of dialectic with abstract names and obscure terms that beget great confusion. Their readers have not eyes for reality but only for what they find written in the pages of Aristotle. Without recourse to the country, to the sea, to the mountains, they bathe in the books of Aristotle muttering such words as accidents, potency, act. Science should consider things, not words. Like his English contemporary, Francis Bacon, Campanella will then go on to struggle manfully, if ineffectively, for a method based on sense and experience and at the same time express the need to find a different philosophical tradition upon which to support his Telesian propensities. Again, like Bacon, considering the West's long engagement with Aristotle as an aberrant deviation, he will turn to the pre-Socratics but also to the revival of Plato which had occurred at Florence in the previous century and most recently at Ferrara with Francesco Patrizi.

At this preliminary stage in our inquiry we may well ask whetherour youthful friar's quarrel is actually with Aristotle himself or simply with his contemporary practitioners or even with a particular brand of Aristotelianism. For it would be a mistake to treat Aristotelianism simplistically en bloc, particularly at a time of its great efflorescence during the course of the sixteenth century. We may affirm that Campanella's quarrel is from the start against all three: Aristotle himself, his current followers, and that school of heterodoxy or heresy known as Paduan Averroism. Enough has already been said to indicate that Campanella is profoundly disturbed by the way an Aristotelian terminology has penetrated the medieval universities, becoming the very furniture of men's minds, pervading the thought patterns of all university-trained scholars and corroding the entire intellectual establishment. Furthermore in this, his first published work, our young Dominican obviously feels it incumbent to defend his very real loyalty to Saint Thomas Aquinas. In doing so, he reveals the extent of the front upon which he will seek to engage the enemy. According to Campanella, Saint Thomas did not believe in the infallibility of Aristotle. Nevertheless, seeing the world dedicated to the Stagirite from whom it was possible to disentangle oneself, Aquinas, in order to avoid further occasion for error as exemplified by Averroes, sought an accommodation. As on later occasions during his life in dealing with this personally disturbing question, Campanella will

aver that Aquinas was not a follower of Aristotle but of Christ and sacred theology. And already at this time Campanella adumbrates a view that would shortly be expressed more explicitly in his *Atheism Conquered,* composed in 1605: namely, that Christian theology must not be allied with any of the traditional philosophies provided by the ancients and most certainly not by Aristotle; Saint Thomas reputes the Stoics, Pythagoras, and Socrates the best, while Augustine in looking to Plato recommends that Aristotle, Epicurus, and Democritus must be kept away from Christian philosophy.

Though Campanella's polemic against Aristotle and Aristotelianism pervades all his writings, only at one point and in a single work did his attack achieve anything like formal coherence. ***On the Gentilism that must not be adhered to*** (***De gentilismo non retinendo***) seems never to have received the attention that it deserves. Written in the less straitened conditions afforded by the Neapolitan prison of Castel dell'Uovo sometime between the end of 1609 and the beginning of 1610, it was originally intended as a preamble to the vast ***Quaestiones physiologicae, ethicae et politicae*** completed by 1613. The vicissitudes of imprisonment and shifting publishers prevented its appearance until its author was safely in Paris in 1636. The full title of the manifesto reads: "That especially the Peripatetic Philosophy of the Gentiles must not be adhered to: Whether it is expedient to formulate another Philosophy from the Gentiles and if so, what." Some of Campanella's Parisian friends apparently deemed it too explosive for publication. For as late as October 1635, Jean Bourdelot, the learned humanist and Master of Requests of Marie de Medici, writing to Peirese, observed that he, Bourdelot, had had the manuscript of what he called the ***Philosophia Ethica rejicienda*** in his possession for a very long time and that he believed that père Campanella would have ample trouble in getting it published. Nevertheless, published it was, with the license and approval of the Sorbonne. The issue was joined. Campanella's tract seemed a part of a growing tidal wave of opposition to the "Master of those that know"; rather, it crackled with implications.

According to the most authoritative appraisal of Renaissance Aristotelian currents, ***Gentilism*** was probably the closest intellectual heir to the *Examen vanitatis* of Gianfrancesco Pico, written a century earlier in 1520. Charles Schmitt [in *Gianfrancesco Pico della Mirandola (1469-1533),* 1967] finds in both works the same effort to show the vanity of profane learning and in Campanella's an even more pronounced return to emphasizing the early Church Fathers. Yet the intentions of the two authors are actually quite different. Forever the optimist, Campanella, transcending his own terrible sufferings, partakes of a rising mood of intellectual experimentation and innovation just on that momentous threshold when that "orb the optick glass the Tuscan artist views at evening from the top of Fiesole." He does not, however, share Pico's profound sense of the uniqueness of Christianity nor more significantly his scepticism, but has long had ready, made according to a Telesian patterning, a brand new philosophical suit to replace the old garb worn by Christianity. The new science presented theology with a crisis but also an opportunity.

A manifesto? And a long unpublished one at that? Only the singular circumstances of Campanella's existence might allow us to entertain such a possibility. Would that we knew the precise time of the first redaction. It would appear to be a relatively brief, compressed work, heavy in its import, fraught with ideas that had long been maturing in the prisoner's mind and now suddenly released by a singular event—the advent of the *Starry Messenger*. Having enjoyed since 1609 the less straitenedconfinement of the cell at Castel dell'Uovo, Campanella had been able to write, to study, and even to receive some visitors. Published in early March of 1610, Galileo's *Siderius Nuncius* achieved prompt notoriety. During the subsequent months Campanella could well have gathered something of its substance and surmised some implications before actually coming in contact with the book itself. Sometime in the last weeks of that year he received a visit from his old friend, the Telesian philosopher Antonio Persio, who placed between his hands a copy of the *Siderius Nuncius,* delivered at the request of Galileo himself. In two hours of reading the prisoner had consumed it. Soon afterwards he would write his exuberant letter of 13 January 1611 to Galileo. And the emerging philosophical epitome now bubbled with Galilean references. "Galileo's new stars," "the recent mathematicians," then scattered references to the telescope the name for which was soon to be minted in Prince Cesi's circle of Linceans and would have only at a later date been inserted into the text along with much else during the intervening quarter century. If the major import of **Gentilism** is the product of an incandescent moment of creativity, the composing of the work had enjoyed the maturing experience both of a release from the worst feature of his imprisonment and of a period of enforced fruitful expectation during the better part of 1610. Among the several innovations that Campanella now celebrated, the minting of a new Christian philosophy supportive of the new science was not the least important.

For such an immense undertaking as the dismantling of European Aristotelianism one might expect an authoritative instrument of biblical or Augustinian forging. Yet it is rather to a church council that Campanella resorts, thereby serving both to remind his readers as to the ecclesiastical authority present and at the same time managing to associate himself with an apparent rejection of humanism and an Aristotelianism that had both emerged contemporaneously with the scepticism of Gianfrancesco Pico. For Campanella appeals not only throughout this work but in other works to the eighth session of the Fifth Lateran Council, which affirmed for him that the philosophy and poetry of the pagans had produced for current learning "infected roots" (*radices infectas*): to the prisoner the provenance of the virulent infection was unquestionably Aristotelian. The question as to the precise intention of the framers of this decree, however, prompted conflicting interpretations at the time and has continued to puzzle scholars. The legislation of a philosophical explanation to buttress dogmatically the belief in the soul'simmortality seemed to be directed against Paduan Averroistic tendencies; while the rulings that those in holy orders could not linger more than five years over the sweets of philosophy or poetry without attending to the study of theology and canon law would suggest a reaction to current paganizing influences. Taken collectively, they appeared as a counterattack by theology and the theologians into the domain of philosophy. Yet the argument has been persuasively made that the inspirers of the decree, Vincenzo Quirini and Tommaso Giustiniani, were reacting more to the Aldine edition of Lucretius, published in 1500, than to Paudan controversies; together they sought to curtail humanism and the immoral overtones of classical poetry.

But Campanella does not share our doubts and hesitations regarding its import: the decree seeks to diminish the authority of the gentiles and to increase that of the Christians. It commands readers to condemn Aristotelian dogmas. It identifies an infection that is linked with Aristotle and the entire Aristotelian tradition, including the early Greek commentators, particularly Averroism, and the Renaissance commentators and expositors: Nifo, Pomponazzi, and Jandun, who believe more in the word of Averroes than in Scripture; likewise Zabarella, Cremonini, and other *Averroistae*. Despite the obvious rejection of Paduan Averroism, Campanella's quarrel is not just with Aristotelians and Averroists, past and present, but by the explicit listing of un-Christian Aristotelian dogmas he directs his attack against the Stagirite himself: the eternity of the world, the mortality of souls and consequently the denial of hell, paradise, purgatory, and the existence of demons and devils; the rejection of providence; and that God has no knowledge beyond himself. The denial of devils and angels except as motors or spheres and similarly the denial of the divine inspiration of sybils and prophets except by a melancholic spirit would pertain rather to Aristotle's scholastic followers. But Campanella will list the fathers who impugn Aristotle for the idea that the heavens do not have an elementary matter but are constituted of a quintessence, which Basil and Ambrose consider to conflict with sacred letters. On this last point in the first flush of Galileo's telescopic survey of the heavens, Campanella will thrust that early proponent of nature's uniformity, Empedocles, into the breach for good measure.

To the task of overhauling Christian philosophy Campanella brings two predispositions of quite unequal value: an emotional commitment to innovations and experimentation as an expressionnot simply of his sensory epistemology but also of his hunger for intellectual freedom; and secondly, in the possible relations of science and religion he subscribes to the widely held intellectual metaphor of the two Books, the one of Nature and the other of Scripture. Allowing even for later interpolations before the 1636 publication, we can understand the Calabrian prisoner's rhapsodizing over innovation and novelty in his *On Gentilism* as a product of that moment when he first hears of and discusses intensely the telescopic discoveries of Galileo, which he soon reports to the Florentine in a letter of January, 1611. The discovery of a new world by Columbus, new stars and a new astronomy from Copernicus, Tycho Brahe, and now Galileo, a new calendar from the pope as well as new artillery, the compass, and the windmill all seemed to reinforce the prophecy of Daniel 12:4—as the publisher of Bacon's own *Magna Instauratio* would soon note: namely, that in the final time there will be great concourse and agitation with a commensurate increase of knowledge.

In the second instance, given such a context a new philosophy is needed. To resist or do otherwise would be to abbreviate the hand of God in Christianity (*christianismo*) and remain stuck in the gentile philosophy. For the truth of philosophical sciences may be had more purely and certainly by Christian genius than by pagan. Deriving from the fathers the idea of the two quite different but supplementary sources of God's revelation—the Book of Nature and the Book of Holy Scripture, between which, according to Campanella's reading of Lateran V's decree, there is no quarrel—Campanella argued that just as Saint Jerome in translating the Bible surpassed the Septuagint, so must we now drop the other shoe and attend to the codex of nature and with an *instaurationem scientiarum* eradicate this former dependence on the pagans.

In a letter of mid-May, 1609, to Caspar Schopp, contemporaneous with the period of gestation for the composition of *On Gentilism,* Campanella had denounced Aristotelianism as the Antichristic font, the source of Machiavellists, heretics, and atheists because of its heretical dogmas. Proceeding further, he asserted that theology is not founded on the philosophy of Aristotle nor Plato nor Pythagoras but on natural philosophy wherever it is recognized. Now in his tract, impelled by the imperative that he believes he found in the decree of Lateran V to cleanse the infected roots of philosophy and banish Aristotelianism forever, he says that the new philosophy should adhere to the interests oftheology and canon law, while being guided by reason and utility. After listing the fathers who condemn Aristotle, Campanella cites Clement of Alexandria in his advice to select whatever has been rightly said by Stoics, Platonists, Epicureans as well as Aristotle.

Advocating, therefore, a broad eclecticism but with notable appeal to patristic theology, he turns in the second part of the tract to the question whether it is permissible to avert, contradict, or diminish Aristotle's authority. After appealing to Lateran V's apparent condemnation of Aristotle's dogmas, Campanella cites Ambrose and Origen's opinion that Aristotle is worse than Epicurus. Patristic authority also supports the belief of contemporary mathematicians regarding the falsity of a quintessence constituting the heavens. Aristotle sits as judge among us, a serpent in our midst and an embarrassment to all the efforts of our missionaries. Must we have Athenians as our teachers? In sum, no philosophy should be set up as teacher of indubitable trustworthiness in Christian schools. Here Campanella stretches again the authority of Lateran V to apply to any total commitment to a gentile philosophy—to Plato, Parmenides, or Aristotle. Columbus' discovery is used both to invalidate Aristotle totally and all philosophical authorities in general and to revive confidence in a new empiricism. Apparently aware of Quintilian's powerful image of language being a currency like money whose purity can be impaired or possibly alert to Lorenzo Valla's stringent application of this image to the pollution of Christian doctrine, Campanella announces the circulation of a counterfeit coinage of Aristotelian minting whose currency in the west he now proceeds to sketch.

In the very middle of his diatribe against Aristotelian philosophy, Campanella offers a brief sketch of the history of Aristotle's presence in the west. He had earlier noted that Aristotle had been in the schools seven hundred years. He presents the parallel of Aristotle's introduction into Christian schools with that of Antiochus Epiphanes' opening of the Greek philosophical gymnasia at Jerusalem in order to eliminate the law of God from Jewish minds, an event that would hasten the Maccabean revolt. Campanella depicts "our Roman Jerusalem" to have been the victim of barbarian invasions that laid waste the libraries of the philosophers in Italy, Gaul, Spain, and Africa, Saint Ambrose's commentary on the *Timaeus* becoming a notable casualty, together with Greek and Plato in general. But then with the victories of Charlemagne, schools were reopened; yet by thistime the clergy and even the cardinals themselves could hardly read. Here Giovanni Villani testifies that ignorance so prevailed that the later discovery of a mathematics book in the cell of Pope Sylvester and its being mistaken for necromantic activities on the part of the pope, served to queer the pontifical interment. It is in the context of this cultural barbarism that Aristotle, recovered by the Arabs, intrudes himself, the codices of the other philosophers having been lost. Entertaining the current belief that Saint Thomas is the author of the entirety of *De regimine principum,* Campanella can have the good scholastic doctor complaining about the absence of Plato in his own time. Only with the Council of Florence does Plato arrive by way of the Greeks. Yet despite the splendid efforts of the Medici princes to whom much is owed for the vindication of Christian spirits, the dominance of Aristotle is not broken, only his authority diminished. The opinion thus thrives that theology might be fallacious and contrary to natural philosophy concerning the eternity of the world, the mortality of the soul, religion, hell, heaven, angels, and demons. It is against such issues that Clement V at Vienne and Leo X at Lateran V have ruled. Campanella at this time in the development of his own thinking prior to 1637 will also include five Parisian synods as well as that at Rheims largely directed against Peter Abelard and Gilbert de la Porrée.

As with many other of his writings, Campanella was unable to publish the manuscript of the *On Gentilism* until he had fled to Paris in October 1634. No sooner had it appeared in print than its author recognized the need for an expanded version that would do justice to his own rapidly increasing appreciation of the issues which he had been treating. For in the learned circles of Paris, probably at the Dupuy and through the Bourdelots, he had encountered a young doctor of theology, Jean de Launoy, who had actually just received his doctorate from the Faculty of Theology at Paris in 1634 and had only recently returned from a visit to Rome; there he had befriended the distinguished scholars of the Vatican Library, Lucas Holstenius and Leone Alliacci, and entered into several learned conversations with them. In fact, Launoy stood at the threshold of a brilliant career wherein he would acquire a reputation for courage and responsibility, ever ready to sacrifice piety, especially of an extravagant sort, to truth, and would gain for himself the title of *dénicheur de saints.* Gallican, fearless in the pursuit of historical accuracy, and participating in that great surge of French learned scholarship that would culminate toward the end of the century in Mabillon, Du Cange, and Bayle, Launoy would now impart that second piece of evidence, that second authority that would assume its place beside that of Lateran V in Campanella's controversy with Aristotle.

Launoy managed at this time in 1636 to bring Campanella's attention to the fact that in 1231 Pope Gregory IX had ruled explicitly that the arts faculty should desist from reading the *Physics* of Aristotle and implicitly his *Metaphysics* until these books had been corrected. This action had been taken as confirmation of the archbishop of Sen's earlier condemnation of 1210, whereby in synod with his suffragan bishops he had called upon the schools for the elimination of Aristotle's works as fonts of error and impiety. Campanella seized upon this information, magnifying and treating as permanent its condemnation of Aristotle. Considering this material sufficiently important to re-

quire a new version of the *On Gentilism,* he incorporated it into the *Disputatio in prologum instauratarum scientiarum ad scholas christianas*. This work appeared as prefatory to his *Philosophia realis,* which he now published at another Paris printing house in 1637. Comparison of the second with the earlier version of the *De gentilismo* reveals that beside making four substantive additions to the 1636 version along with a number of minor clarifications, Campanella now introduced into his text in nine distinct places the new authority, linking Gregory IX with Lateran V. Thereby he made the Gregorian bull equal in authority with session eight of the Fifth Lateran Council as supporting evidence for the removal of Aristotle from the intellectual life of Christendom.

Given the fact that the relations between the Paris Dominicans and the university's doctors of theology had been less than cordial since the beginning of the sixteenth century, it was Campanella's good fortune to be able to converse with Launoy. Partly in reaction to Campanella's work and to the second version of *On Gentilism,* the Parisian doctor would be encouraged, if only for setting the record straight, to write seventeen years later his *On the Varying Fortunes of Aristotle at the University of Paris* that would see four editions. It is not, therefore, from this later work that Campanella derived the new material that will require a second edition of the *On Gentilism* and restore that tract to its commanding position as the propylacum to his philosophical works. Rather, as Campanella tells us in the additional material inserted toward the beginning of Article II, that most learned and intelligent theologian, Launoy, had recently given a report to Campanella and then shortly afterwards committed it to print in a work that proves by Launoy's later statement in the *fortuna* to have been his first publication (1636), the *Syllabus rationum quibus causa Durandi,* etc. From this last work, following upon their conversation, therefore, Campanella obtained the material for incorporation into his second edition of the *On Gentilism*.

In the Dominican's eager and indiscriminate appropriation of Launoy's research regarding Pope Gregory IX's ruling of 1231, we see the collision and contrast of two quite different worlds of learning: that magical, prophetic, syncretic one of what the late Renaissance had become, and the historical, critical, philological one of earlier humanism, now infused with contemporary currents of scepticism and scientific inquiry. For Robert Lenoble has found in Launoy's relentless pursuit of the historical fact and his examination of the credibility of witnesses a sense of the historically contingent that allows him to claim this theologian to be among the founders of modern history. Amidst the Jansenist turmoil Launoy asked the upsetting question as to whether Saint Augustine was an Augustinian and the church always Augustinian in its theology. In discovering that the Augustinian doctrine of grace appeared in the fourth century as a novelty and not as the traditional doctrine of the church, Launoy showed how a seeming _sensus communis_ could be a historical contingency. Like his two great friends Mersenne and Gassendi, Launoy followed the immanent logic of his discipline. Consequently, it is worthwhile at this juncture to examine briefly Launoy's later work _On the Varying Fortunes of Aristotle at the University of Paris_ both for his own account of the reception of Aristotle in the west and for his disagreements in retrospect with Campanella.

In 1653, Edmund Martin published together François Bernier's _Favilla ridiculi muris_ and Launoy's _De varia_ to defend Gassendi against J. B. Morin and his scholastic adversaries. Again in Launoy's pursuit of establishing a historical fact, the ostensibly established orthodoxy of Aristotle's persisting acceptance dissolves before the restitution of historicity. This sense of the historically contingent emerges from the very plurality of fortunes which do not describe a linear development. Launoy sees eight such shifts or fortunes of Aristotle at Paris. We need attend only to the first four: the beginning of the reception in 1200 that leads to the Parisian synod of 1209 to call for the burning of his books; the general prohibition but the admission of Aristotle's dialectic; Gregory IX's bull, seen as moderating on balance the prohibitions of the provincial council but explicitly forbidding any lecturing on the natural philosophy of Aristotle until the _Physics_ is corrected, while remaining silent on the dialectic and the _Metaphysics;_ and fourth, the renewal of the prohibition in 1265 by the Cardinal Legate Simon, until correction occurs, and now specifically including the _Metaphysics_. While Launoy's account is hardly a continuous narration or history, it is important to note that though he does indulge in providing a long list of patristic and early medieval opinions about Aristotle, beginning with Justin Martyr and Clement of Alexandria and extending down to Saint Bernard, the conscious presence of Aristotle in the West begins sharply and unaccountably in 1200. By forsaking the prevalent belief in the Carolingian origins of the university and Latin Aristotelianism, Launoy distanced himself from a myth that proved to be slower in dying than its dynastic counterpart, Pharamond, in medieval historiography. In contrast, Campanella's wildly inaccurate notion of the seven hundred years of Aristotle in the west at least has the merit, impelled by polemic, of attempting to provide some context and origins.

When, seventeen years after his encounter with Campanella, Launoy came to compose his account of Aristotle's reception at Paris, Campanella had long since been interred at the Jacobins. It is of some significance, however, that in his work the contemporary with whom the Paris theologian chose to enter into specific controversy and on two distinct matters was Campanella. In the first instance he accuses the Dominican "and

others ignorant of these events" of having abusively called Abelard heresiarch when the latter made his peace with the church and lived piously out his remaining days with Cluniac monks. The second accusation is more complicated, stemming from a problem that Launoy manages to create for himself. For he poses the question how Albert and Thomas were allowed to make commentaries on the prohibited books of Aristotle. Faced with this apparent lacuna in his evidence and unwilling to admit that truth might be shy and not announce herself, Launoy speculates: perhaps they were somewhere else than at Paris when they wrote and thus considered themselves immune; or that somehow they were simply ignorant of the Gregorian law. Aware that the theologians often sought special permission from Rome, Launoy remained distressed at not finding such a request. And thus he considered that the two princes of theology might in fact have been in violation of Gregory's specific admonition _fieri Theodidacti_. Complaining that Campanella would have it that Aquinas was not a peripatetic and that he mangled Launoy's own observation, the Parisian fastens upon the following passage in the revised version of _On Gentilism,_ only available as preface to the **_Philosophia realis_** of 1637:

> Less than a century earlier, Gregory IX had confirmed the condemnation of Aristotle effected by the University and the Synod of Paris and had ruled the burning of Aristotle's books and forbade his being lectured upon. But doctor Thomas was most observant of the authority of the pope and doctor[s] of the university. Thus in no way must he be considered to have Aristotelized but only to have exposed Aristotle, so that it might be made evident what evils had been introduced through Aristotle— and I would believe with the license of the pontiff. Wherefore skillfully yet not sufficiently prudently doctor Thomas was condemned by certain Parisians as being disobedient to council and to pope, and as being an Aristotelian most willingly.

Obviously indignant at these liberties and embroideries, Launoy confesses that he also would gladly believe, if only such a license might appear. But then he opines that "if the blessed doctor were alive now and should be condemned, without doubt he would prefer to be refuted with truth than to be excused with falsehood." Clearly unconvinced yet troubled, the Paris theologian remained open to more plausible explanations.

In assessing the exchange that took place between Campanella and Launoy in Paris in 1636, we can say that the credulous, eager friar with generous words for his learned benefactor persisted in his polemical position that Saint Thomas was not an Aristotelian. He shows himself prepared to seize upon any historical contingency in order to effect a distancing of his revered Aquinas from the poisonous Aristotle. For his part, the more critical Paris theologian appears some-what nettled by an encounter that led to the mauling of his evidence. Nevertheless, is it possible that Campanella, ever conscious of his friend Galileo and his recent condemnation at Rome, managed in this instance to deepen Launoy's appreciation of this case and the issues involved? For at the very end of his forthcoming *Syllabus rationum* (1636), Launoy introduced a problem or case of conscience in which, having reported the condemnation of the books of Aristotle by a synod of Paris and Gregory IX and the censure given at Rome on Copernicus and Galileo on the earth's movement, he proposes the following question for resolution: Whether the judgment rendered at Rome against the views of Galileo, *which has still not been sent, nor has the University of Paris been notified,* binds more the professors at this university than those that have been born by the synod of Paris and the bull of Gregory addressed to the doctors of the University of Paris against the books of Aristotle? Perhaps something like an exchange of ideas had occurred in the encounter of 1636 between the two clerics.

Fortified with his new evidence and authority, Campanella now reinforced some of his earlier arguments. Of capital importance is the relation between the two books:

> Gregory IX commands that they concentrate on becoming God-taught (*Theodidacti*), not philosophers, that is teachable by God and only then to explicate the divine books. Twofold however is the divine codex—one, the nature of things, and the other Scripture. These are to us the light and whoever bears witness from them is our master in the school of God; whoever supposes himself to be likewise a schoolfellow by sticking to his own individual fancies, although most honored by many, he must not be accepted but merely heard, as Augustine and other high ecclesiastics, when they deny the existence of the antipodes. Thus because philosophers claim to have accepted sciences from the first codex, namely that of nature (*natura rerum*), this first codex of God may not however conflict with the second for as the eighth session of the Fifth Lateran Council says: "Truths do not contradict each other;" likewise the apostle: "Has Christ been divided? No, for God is not the God of dissension, but of peace" [I Cor. 14:33]. They must be examined how they may have erred in conflict with the second or whether they might have erred in the first and they must be corrected by those who have accepted the charity of truth from Christ, the wisdom of God, unless we want to condemn all the holy doctors and Columbus and other discoverers of truths.

In both versions of his attack on Aristotle, Campanella's repeated recourse to the text of Daniel 12:4 that there will be great concourse and manifold increase of knowledge at the end and now the new emphasis upon *instauratio scientiarum* reminds us that the belief in

the millennial revival of knowledge together with the emancipation from the stranglehold of traditional Greek metaphysics had by the mid-thirties, especially in Paris, become a pan-European movement no longer limited to the Baconians. Certainly we cannot disallow, and indeed evidence supports, that Campanella, despite religious barriers, approached during the last years of his life the threshold of English intellectual and religious developments. The burgeoning movement that included such talents as Comenius and Gassendi, Mersenne and shortly Hobbes made clear enough the object to be attacked, namely traditionally received Greek metaphysics; the more positive demands of their program, such as the precise contours of the *instauratio* of learning, did not enjoy the same clarity. Yet in varying degrees most critics of the established system shared a buoyant optimism in a new intellectual order distinguished by three characteristics: a diverse, eclectic, preeminently empirical philosophy; a confidence in innovation; and a commitment to expand the new knowledge.

In concluding his second version of the **On Gentilism,** Campanella provides us with his clearest statement regarding the much desired revival of knowledge:

> Thus it is not useful to the commonweal [*Reipublicae*] to confine gifted temperaments to one Book, for thereby a person is dulled and deprived of the discovery of new things and new sciences. For the princes it is even expedient to occupy excellent minds in philosophizing so that their burning of the midnight oil may not prove inconvenient to the government. Multifold study is especially advantageous to the Papacy for the confirmation, increase and enlightenment of its people. Nor should we follow one doctor. . . . Daniel 12:4 says there will be much concourse together with manifold increase of knowledge. . . . As daily experience prompts, may the experience of new things indeed daily magnify and revive the sciences. Multifold study must not be denied; otherwise neither the new hemisphere, nor the new stars, nor the telescope, nor the compass, nor printing, nor the invention of cannon would have been discovered by us, if the inclinations for the entertainment of multiple philosophies had been precluded. Confusion and contention of sophists as well as those dogmas of faith, which are not unanimously adhered to, must be removed, saving however the study of philosophers. A single Codex appears for the young and for those of mediocre talent, not however for the advanced. In order to win the apt to the higher and better, one must therefore not be committed irrevocably to the words of one doctor, but it must be provided that the same books are not repeatedly published which the earliest teachers have taught *ad nauseam* in theology and by deviating from the Christian faith with respect to the laws of the internal and external forum. Let the way for discovery be precluded to none. The superfluous especially do not survive the inquiry of the ages, for they die

with their author. The new will inevitably always last and thus must not be feared. At the time of Vergil more than one hundred poets wrote, of whom hardly eight survive. After the Master of the Sentences more than sixty have written on his books; now hardly ten survive.

Certain points emerge as to the nature of the new Christian philosophy, the first of the two books or codices. It is consciously eclectic and diverse in its drawing upon any of the ancients. It is distinguished by a new empiricism, presumably Campanella's but also leaving room for what was believed to be Galileo's. Regarding the relation between the books, Lateran V asserts that there can be no quarrel; in fact, since Christ as the primal reason and wisdom is the author of both, there can be no conflict. Furthermore, philosophy is the catechism to the faith, not the impediment that the insipid Peripatetics have effected. Because theology calls all sciences as handmaidens to its cultivation, should there be a conflict, the opposition to faith must be rejected. Yet Campanella is confident that such innovators as Galileo with the telescope will produce no strain. The innovator does not form or reform the sciences contrary to the doctrine of the saints but from the two books he erects them from this collapsed condition under the gentiles.

When first composed in the course of 1610, Campanella's *De gentilismo* registered the initial impact of Galileo and his *Starry Messenger* upon an astounded and receptive European audience. During its own tortuous odyssey to print over a quarter of a century later the *De gentilismo* would anticipate the better known *Apologia* for Galileo of 1616, published at Frankfurt in 1622, wherein culminated the prisoner's intellectual support and tentative commitment to the program of the new science, howsoever misconstrued for his own astrological and apocalyptical purposes. Here he would carry further his efforts to set Saint Thomas at odds with Aristotle and to express his own impatience with the excessive over-commitment of current theology to Aristotelian natural philosophy. While Galileo prudently distanced himself from his irrepressibly generous admirer, Campanella, unwearied and never lacking for courage, continued to be frustrated in his efforts to draw closer to him. With that meeting of minds still unrealized and unrealizable at the end of his life, Campanella nevertheless could confidently take that first herald both of his own deepest philosophical disposition and of his commitment to the Galilean science and situate it as a portal to his entire thought. At Paris he had obtained not only its approval from the Faculty of Theology but also further important ammunition from amember of that august body. And whatever the differences between himself and Launoy the manifesto of his earlier life had now become sufficiently strengthened to reassume its former intended position as the propylaeum to his entire intellectual system and the trumpet call to the necessity for minting a new Christian philosophy.

Stephanie Laggini-Fiore (essay date 1992)

SOURCE: "Messianic Vision in the Poetry of Fra Tommaso Campanella," in *Romance Languages Annual*, Vol. 4, 1992, pp. 270-77.

[*Focusing on Campanella's poetry, Laggini-Fiore discusses the autobiographical aspects of Campanella's utopian vision.*]

Little has been written on what Franc Ducros [in *Tommaso Campanella Poète*, 1969] calls Fra Tommaso Campanella's *rôle messianique,* yet the messianic vision of the poet is central to both his poetry and his life. It was the direct result of his relationship with the world and with society: his poetry was written while he languished in the jails of the Inquisition for many years; his defense of Galileo was a response to the rulings of the Inquisition on matters of scientific research; his *Cittá del Sole* was simply the expression of his desire for a more perfect and a more just society. Campanella's poetry reflects the age, not on an external and superficial level, but with an internal and intimate one that will not be satisifed simply with commenting on the problems of the times but will go much further in seeking revolutionary solutions. He is no longer satisfied with the Renaissance solution of immobility and static perfection, and instead searches for a "new" solution to fit the new role of man. Through his poetry we shall find the evolution of a revolutionary vision that will begin by the anointment of himself as leader in a political fight against the Spanish. We must keep in mind that Campanella, though a friar, was no stranger to political intrigue: his religious habit did not confine his intellectual vigor. One should not ignore the fact that he was accused and condemned to life imprisonment for allegedly leading a popular revolt in Calabria. Campanella felt strongly his messianic role and, indomitably, he would pursue his goal of a *renovazion del secolo.* Motivated by the oppression of the times, by the exploitation of the people, and by the general injustice practiced everywhere around him, Campanella planned untiringly and preached continually in an almost propagandist manner for the execution of this revolutionary project. Together with a close group of collaborators, he worked for the instauration of a Calabrian republic founded on his principles of a natural Christian religion. The poet led no monastic, retiring life; he was religiously, politically, intellectually aware and active in a society that frowned on independent activity and thought.

During the entire period of his incarceration, 1599-1629, the astounding thing is that, amid horrendous torture, isolation, often terrible living conditions and lack of privacy, this man's writings would flourish. His philosophical, scientific, political, rhetorical and poetic writing would take root, grow, and proliferate in the nightmarish existence that he lived. He seemed to live outside his own body's deprivation, always keeping his sights leveled on his messianic vision, his destiny, the future world that would be created with his leadership. This messianic vision would eventually evolve from a political to a more philosophical approach to reform in which he would seek societal reform for all peoples. Perhaps more than any other writer of this age, Campanella reflects most clearly the feelings, the fears, and the ambitions of the intellectual in that society. Perhaps more than any other historian could, he outlines with clarity the nature of man in the turmoil of the epoch that was his.

Campanella's *Cantica* follows an autobiographical course. His life experiences are translated into poetic verse thereby giving us as readers a window not only into his personal life but into the life of the seventeenth century man. Franc Ducros calls *La Cantica* a "journal de l'existence du poète." In fact, he explains, not only does the poetry reflect the events of the poet's life, but the events of the poet's life are often inspired by the thought process which creates the poetry. Those bases on which the evolution of the poetry rests are: the exterior or objective ones, that is the life of the poet, the dramatic situations or events that shape his existence; and, the interior or subjective ones, that is "le monde d'idées" that lives and matures as Campanella's spiritual and philosophical life develops. His poetry, therefore, is constantly changing, constantly developing and maturing, according to what both his external and internal realities are at each period in his life. It is this dynamic quality that gives Campanella's poetry life and which gives it the ability to reach over the centuries and clarify for us the workings of the poet's mind and the formulation of his revolutionary ideas.

If, therefore, we are to follow coherently the progress of Campanella's poetry and of his "mission," then we must acknowledge that the external realities that play so great a role in the creation of his writings are essential to an understanding of the internal realities, that is the spiritual and philosophical realities reflected in his poetry and of the evolution of the poetry itself. Indeed, his earliest works dealt with his basic criticism of life, both political and social, as he knew it. Then, during the period of his politically active life, the "congiura," his poetry would espouse the tenets of his mission and his *Città del Sole* would propose a revolutionary model, a solution to the crisis at hand. After his arrest and his incarceration, one may easily follow through his poetry the course of that missionary ideal; its development and its evolution through time. Finally, and most importantly, we may use his poetry to determine the actual state of mind of the poet. In it, we may discover

his sufferings and doubts as well as his lucidity and strength of conviction.

Tommaso Campanella's poetic work commented directly on what he deemed were the abominations of the epoch: the corruption of the Church, the domination of the Spaniards in Italy, the apathy or inefficacy of the people to change the situation in which they lived, the ignorance even of the "learned" of society, the abundance of sins that were practiced daily from hypocrisy to self-love. Nothing was spared his scathing criticisms, for he felt that he must unmask the evils of society and government in order to clear the way for entrance into the *renovazion del secolo*. In the *Scelta* one poem in particular, **"Delle radici de' gran mali del mondo,"** sums up most effectively what Campanella felt were the obstacles to and the necessary elements of his goal:

> Io nacqui a debellar tre mali estremi:
> tirannide, sofismi, ipocrisia;
> ond'or m'accorgo con quanta armonia
> Possanza, Senno, Amor m'insegnò Temi.
>   Questi principii son veri e supremi
> della scoverta gran filosofia,
> rimedio contra la trina bugia,
> sotto cui tu piangendo, o mondo, fremi.
>   Carestie, guerre, pesti, invidia, inganno,
> ingiustizia, lussuria, accidia, sdegno,
> tutti a que' tre gran mali sottostanno,
>   che nel cieco amor proprio, figlio degno
> d'ignoranza, radice e fomento hanno:
> Dunque a diveller l'ignoranza io vegno.
>   (#8)

This poem clearly lays out Campanella's master plan; one might say it is the manifesto of his mission. It is a perfectly structured poem of syllogistic reasoning that works to reveal the logic of his plan for the *renovazion del secolo*. The three great evils of "tirannide, sofismi, ipocrisia" are placed in the first quatrain so as to parallel exactly what are the three metafisical *primalità* or *proprincipi* "Possanza, Senno, Amor." The first three are in effect the distortion of the three *primalità,* that is, "tirannide" is false "Possanza," "Sofismi" is false "Senno," and "ipocrisia" is false "Amor." Throughout the work, the parallelism of comparison continues as in verses 5 and 7, the "principi . . . veri e supremi" are contrasted to and suggested as a remedy to the "trina bugia" of "gran mali."

In the first terzina Campanella uses the Baroque technique of accumulation to create effect as he reveals the many problems that plagued his century, "carestie, guerre" and so forth, yet he again traces these back to the three great evils: "tutti a que' tre gran mali sottostanno." Not satisfied, Campanella digs further to find the "radice" of these three evils which he finds to be rooted in the greatest evil of all: "amor proprio" "figlio d'ignoranza." Most impressive is the sense of closure that pervades the poem and that illustrates the oppressiveness of a world anchored to the ground while it wallows in its own evil, and of a mind closed by its own ignorance to the wider mysteries of life. Structurally, this sense of closure is created by the poem itself, by the perfectly closed and balanced syllogism of which it is made. Stylistically, this crushing weight of oppressiveness is felt as the author places the world "sotto" the three evils, and again as he uses "sottostanno" to convey a feeling of closure. The adjective "cieco" conveys the image of the darkness of a world dominated by evil. In addition, the use of the word "radice" in reference to the greatest evil of all—"amor proprio"—and the apparent need of the prophet not just to eliminate but to "divellar" this evil translates to the reader not only the idea that it is a root that is anchored firmly in the darkest depths of man's being but it conveys also the difficulty of the prophet's task and the violence that may beneeded to accomplish it.

The poet's role in the poem is vital. As the prophet and bearer of "Possanza, Senno, Amor," he will fight to establish the three *proprincipi* in place of the three "gran mali" and thereby deliver the world to which this poem is addressed from its trembling state:

> sotto cui tu, piangendo, o mondo, fremi. (v.8)

and into a state of "armonia." The Baroque use of combat imagery appears here as Campanella begins and ends the poem with images of victory and of violence:

> Io nacqui a debellar tre mali estremi . . . (v.1)
> Dunque a diveller l'ignoranza io vegno. (v.14)

Through these same verses we see the strength of the presence of the author himself, as the poem begins and ends with "io." The poet as prophet presents himself as the "rimedio" for the world. With Christlike imagery, he reveals his destiny, for he was born—"io nacqui"—and he came—"io vegno"—to fulfill his mission: to triumph over evil and to eliminate the root of evil, that is ignorance. Against the trembling of the world, against the "fomento" of evil, against "bugia" that flourishes, he will be the source of "armonia."

These same themes of the "gran mali" and of the *proprincipi* will surface again and again throughout Tommaso Campanella's poetry. In these works, he will reaffirm his mission to eliminate the former and establish the latter in an effort to achieve his *renovazion del secolo*. In **"Accorgimento a tutte nazioni"**, the author speaks to all nations in an effort to urge them to follow the truth, the "Senno Primo," and repudiate the three evils. Here again the evils of "tirannia," "ipocrisia," and "sofismi" are presented as "l'empio, il falsario e l'ingiusto." More importantly, an element of trickery

or of false appearance is inserted here as tyranny masks itself in a "bel manto di nobiltà e valor" and as "sofismi" is imbued with an illusionary power of "incanto." Thus, Campanella makes these evils even more dangerous as they practice a transvestism that gives them an appearance of goodness.

Each of the three "gran mali" will have their place separately in the poet's collection of poetry. In his **"Sonetto sopra ilpresente stato d'Italia,"** Campanella laments the tyranny that dominates his homeland:

> Ahi cieca Italia nella tua rapina!
> sin quando il senno tuo sopito langue?
> (v.12-13)

Again, the reference to the darkness and blindness of the times appears and again the lack of "senno" is blamed. In fact, the two "gran mali" of "sofismo" or "poco senno" and "tirannia" are often linked together as cause and effect in Campanella's poetry. In "Che gli uomini seguono più il caso che la ragione nel governo politico, e poco imitan la natura," this concept of "poco senno" as responsible for the fact that tyrants govern the people while the bearers of truth are repressed is presented:

> Fa regi, sacerdoti, schiavi, eroi,
> di volgar opinioni ammascherati,
> con poco senno, come veggiam poi.
> Che gli empi spesso fûr canonizzati,
> gli santi uccisi, e gli peggior tra noi
> prìncipi finti contra i veri armati.
> (#15, v.9-14)

The adjective "ammascherati" underscores the concept of false appearance as these tyrants are no better than "schiavi" masquerading as "eroi." Interesting is the juxtaposition of "empi . . . canonizzati" and "santi uccisi" in a type of oxymoron that suggests clearly an image of a world in disorder, upside-down, inside-out, as saints are killed and false rulers are canonized. To round out the poem, Campanella gives his condemnation of these false rulers as "peggior tra noi" while he draws the battle lines between the tyrants and those who bring the truth: "i veri armati."

Perhaps the most bitterly scathing evaluation of the damaging effects of ignorance is "Della plebe," in which Campanella shows that the people are repressed because of their own ignorance:

> Il popolo è una bestia varia e grossa,
> ch'ignora le sue forze; e però stassi
> a pesi e botte di legni e di sassi,
> guidato da un fanciul che non ha possa,
> ch'egli potria disfar con una scossa:
> ma lo teme e lo serve a tutti spassi.
> Né sa quanto è temuto, ché i bombassi

fanno un incanto, che i sensi gli ingrossa.
  Cosa stupenda! e' s'appicca e imprigiona
con le man proprie, e si dà morte e guerra
per un carlin di quanti egli al re dona.
  Tutto è suo quanto sta fra cielo e terra,
ma nol conosce; e, se qualche persona
di ciò l'avvisa, e l'uccide al atterra.
                                                 (#33)

If, as Campanella says elsewhere, "il poco senno degli
assai ignoranti / fa noi meschini e tutto il mondo tris-
to" then this poem is the greatest proof of that. Campanella's Baroque tendencies come out in the striking
sensism that makes up this work. The imagery gives it
a tangibly passionate quality that helps the reader feel
distinctly such intangible qualities as fear, pain, ignorance and violence. We seem to witness the possibility
of that small "fanciul" being torn apart, "disfatto," by
the beast as we feel its beatings at his hands and then
immediately that violence changes to abject fear as the
beast cringes out of ignorance in front of its weaker
master. We feel the growing heaviness of the senses as
they swell—"ingrossa"—under the weight of the bom-
bastic rhetoric of the "fanciul." We feel also the cor-
poreality of the beast itself "varia e grossa" which seems
to lumber along heavily under the crushing weight of
his own ignorance. Finally, we feel the author's intervention: his disdain at the peoples' bestiality, that is,
inability to reason as human beings; his bitterness in
his obvious reference to himself as the persecuted bearer
of the truth: "se qualche persona di ciò l'avvisa, e'
l'uccide ed attera."

Most important in this poem is the imagery. Campanella
seems to be saying that he who does not use reason is
animalistic and deserves a fate equal to that of a non-
reasoning beast. The masses are such a beast and they
are constantly misguided. While mocking their lack of
"senno," he points to their potential: "ch'egli potria
disfar con una scossa," and makes an appeal to these
people to realize the power that lies in their own hands,
especially in the first terzina where he blames not the
tyrant but the people for their own misfortunes: "e'
s'appicca e imprigiona con le man proprie, e si dà
morte e guerra." Ignorant as this beast is, he does not
realize, "nol conosce," that the world is his for the
taking. The imagery referring to the tyrant, that of the
"fanciul," is interesting for Campanella strips awayall
pretentions. "Fanciul" suggests weakness, smallness and
immaturity while his actions in beating the beast suggest childish cruelty and bullying tactics. It is, in fact,
only the tyrant's armed strength, i "bombassi," and
never the moral and intellectual strength of a true leader that serves as an "incanto" to subjugate the people.
Here as in perhaps few other poems we capture a sense
of Campanella's frustration at what might have been
possible with the peoples' support.

In dealing with the evils of hypocrisy, the poet is no
less relentless. In "Contra gli ipocriti," Tommaso Campanella anoints himself as the one who will reveal to
the world the hypocrites that plague it. The poet-prophet
pleads to God, the source of "Senno" to help him in
this task. Here, his own search for "verità sincera e
pura" is juxtaposed against the "malizie" of the hypocrites. He stands for "sacrosanto ardore," and "benig-
nità" while the other stands for the complete opposite.
Again, one notices the concept of the difficulty of his
task as he asks God "dammi le forze" in his fight
against evil.

The obvious religious reference in the verse "il nome
di Giesù segnano in fronte" would seem to point to a
criticism of the clergy itself. In fact, in a note to this
poem, Giovanni Gentile points out that it is sometimes
entitled "Contro i Gesuiti." Their "malizie" are proven
in the last terzina for their apparently "sacrosanto e
divino" intentions are sharply contrasted to their sacre-
ligious actions: "chi spoglia pur gli morti in sepoltu-
ra." Once more, foremost in Campanella's treatment of
this evil is its falsified and therefore more dangerous
appearance. These hypocrites are the devil's messen-
gers disguised as servants of God. While "dalla scorze
in fuore" they make the sign of the cross and dress as
clergymen, in their "cuore" they carry "gli affetti di
Pluton." The damage disguise brings is underscored as
the poet asks: "Chi può più comportar tanta sciagura?"

Finally, in "Contra il proprio amore scoprimento stu-
pendo," is revealed the source of all evils, self-love.
From this egotism comes a lack of understanding of
nature, of other peoples different from oneself, God,
and true knowledge. In this poem, Campanella concludes that self-love creates in man such an egocentric
and distorted view that he does not see reality. He has,
in effect, fooled himself into thinking that his own
"astuzie" are really wisdom. In this manner, he de-
ludes himself that he is the center of the universe, that
he owns it.

The poet seems to make a checklist of the misconceptions engendered by self-love. He points out that although the stars and the other elements of nature are
"più forti e belle" than flawed man, the egotist sees
them only as servants of man. He erroneously believes
they are put into the universe to please and entertain
him; to create beauty for his enjoyment. Whereas this
man places nature in an inferior position to himself,
Campanella sees nature as far superior. Self-love is
also an exclusive quality that creates division and discord among peoples. The egotist sees himself again as
superior: he alone is loved by God, he alone is not
"barbare ed ignare." There is a sense of closure here
that conveys the idea of the elitist circle of the egotist
into which the "genti barbare ed ignare" are not invited. Interesting is Campanella's condemnation of the
insiders and of their ignorance in believing in their
own superiority. In the first terzina, the list continues:

E, per non travagliarsi, il saper schiva;
poi, visto il mondo a' suo' voti diverso,
nega la provvidenza o che Dio viva.
   Qui stima senno l'astuzie; e perverso,
per dominar, fa nuovi dèi. Poi arriva
a predicarsi autor dell'universo.
                              (Sonnet #9, v.9-14)

Here are the gravest of misconceptions for the egotist denies the importance of study and the existence of God. So as not to tax himself, "per non travagliarsi," since he is so busy loving himself, the egotist rejects study which leads to true knowledge. He bases his conclusions on "astuzie" instead of on true "senno." In this way, he falls into error, and into perversity. He believes there is no God since, in his opinion, life is made of chance. In his egotism, in his lack of true knowledge, he again places himself at the apex of power: he creates a new god—himself. As such, he believes himself "autor dell'universo." In this work, Tommaso Campanella details the problems that arise from the greatest evil, self-love. From it arise tyranny, sophism, hypocrisy and ignorance. If he is to create a new world, he must first act to obliterate these evils; he must replace these evils with virtue.

As has already been pointed out in the discussion on "Delle radici de' gran mali del mondo," the *proprincipi* "Possanza, Senno, Amor" represent the virtues that will save the world from evil. These same all-important *proprincipi* will be extolledthroughout the *Cantica*. In Madrigal 2 of **"Della medesima salmodia,"** Campanella names these three as the victors over disharmony and even over death:

   Per l'Unità ti priego viva e vera,
per cui disfarsi stimo
la discordia, la morte e l'empio inganno;
per la Possanza universal primera,
e per lo Senno primo
e per lo primo Amor, ch'un ente fanno:
togliene omai quel danno,
che da valor, da senno e d'amor finti,
tirannide, sofismi, ipocrisia,
spande pur tuttavia;
                              (#75, v. 1-10)

Once again the *proprincipi* are pitted against the great evils, yet here virtue seems to emerge triumphant. In Madrigal 2 of **"Canzon d'amor secondo la vera filosofia,"** Campanella specifies what is the true philosophy. He points out that "Possanza, Senno, Amor" are the virtues that created from a disordered world some sembalnce of harmony and of order. They were, in short, God's instruments to shape his universe. Every being, therefore, is imbued in his original state with these virtues. Campanella's job thus would be to return man to his natural state. The metaphor of the world as an animal—"Il perfetto animal, ch'or mondo è" (v.1)—is

common in this poet's work for he sees the world as a living organism, constantly changing and evolving. This is again a link with the baroque concept of metamorphism. In fact, Campanella is perhaps one of the strongest believers in true metamorphosis, for his very philosophy is filled with references to man's changing state. Death itself is seen as simply a shift to another form of life. Although he sees clearly the problems of his time, his is a positive and forward-looking vision. The living organism that is his world is filled with hope for betterment as a possibility for change is ever present. Never in Campanella's vision is evil set in stone; never can it not be vanquished. Thus, in this poem, we find a world in which "ogn'ente è perch'esser può, sa ed ama." The poet is affirming his belief that the potential for good is in all of us; that is our life-blood. In this way, his task is simply to draw out our "better half."

In **"Fede naturale del vero sapiente,"** Campanella reaffirms his strong faith in virtue and in the fact that all participate inthis virtue:

   Io credo in Dio, Possanza, Senno, Amore,
un, vita, verità, bontate, immenso,
primo ente, re degli enti e creatore.
   Non è parte, né tutto, inciso o estenso,
ma più somiglia al tutto, ond'ogni cosa
partecipò virtute, amore e senso.
                              (#3, v.1-6)

Here the poet ties his belief in a natural religion based on the *proprincipi* to God and from this bond issues forth truth, goodness without bounds, even life itself. Here again all of nature, the whole universe, participates in the virtue of his religion.

Tommaso Campanella's poetic and missionary task is to turn man from the state of blindness and darkness of the evil state in which he lives towards the light that leads to virtue. Already we have seen diverse references to this blindness. But Campanella goes further to describe what he sees as the transition from the darkness to the light under his leadership. In madrigal 5 of **"Orazioni tre in salmodia metafisicale congiunte insieme,"** Campanella describes himself thus in the first verse—"Deh! gran Pastor, il tuo can, la tua lampa"—and he equates "mia luce" with his "voce." it is clear that the poet sees himself as God's light on earth, as his mouthpiece. In Madrigal 4 of the same work, the reference is particularly striking as Campanella describes himself as the light in the midst of darkness:

   Stavamo tutti al buio. Altri sopiti
d'ignoranza nel sonno; e i sonatori
pagati raddolcîro il sonno infame.
Altri vegghianti rapivan gli onori,
la robba, il sangue, o si facean mariti
d'ogni sesso, e schernian le genti grame.

Io accesi un lume:

> (#73, Madrigal 4)

Campanella places himself in the shadows in verse 1 with the collective verb "stavamo" showing perhaps the strength of the evil that succeeded in covering even him. This same verb suggests a state of being, one of suspended animation in which ignorance is a state of sleep that hides beneath it horrors and that can only be described as "infame." The active nature of the verse "ioaccesi un lume," therefore, is rendered even more effective as it is in direct contrast to verse 1. Here Campanella stands on his own, alone—"io"—and not in with a group as before. The position of the personal pronoun "io" adds to its efficacy as it is placed in a position of prominence at the center of the work. The verb itself, "accesi," is strong: it no longer suggests a suspended state of being, a passive position. Instead, it is an active verb that suggests swift and sure vitality. The prophet has taken his stand—he has broken the darkness with his light.

This is Campanella's vision: to bring a light, knowledge, which will dispel the darkness of ignorance. The poet's continual usage of a chiaroscuro motif of the darkness of evil and the goodness of light focuses in particular on this very specific concept of knowledge. In fact, the emphasis on "il sapere" or "il Senno" is remarkable in Campanella's works. We discover that the "lampa" and the "luce" are a representation of knowledge itself. It is around this concept of knowledge that his entire vision revolves; that the solution to the evils of the world will be found. He, as the prophet, is the torchbearer and he will introduce to man the healing powers of knowledge. As such, he takes on a new and relevant role as Sage. In the Proemio of his *Cantica,* Campanella affirms immediately his role as the bringer of knowledge as he states:

> Io, che nacqui dal Senno e di Sofia (v.1)

and he reaffirms the power of that "senno" in the final verses:

> doglia, superbia e l'ignoranza vostra
> stemprate al fuoco ch'io rubbai dal sole.
>> (v.13-14)

Already in this first poem, Campanella states his case. He speaks of his fate as the prophet of "Senno." He was born to this destiny. From the "sole" of knowledge (and often he will use the sun as a metaphor for "Senno"), he emerged to bring to the world a fire that would melt away evil and pain. In **"Sonetto secondo del medesimo soggetto,"** the Sage pleads to his people to turn towards knowledge as their salvation:

> Ahi! s'ignoranza indusse tanti falli,
> tornate al Senno per la figliolanza.
>> (#48, v.13-14)

Here, he sets up a familial relationship among those who follow the truth and he puts "Senno" as the father of this family. Notice also the use of the verb "tornate" that would suggest that all men originated "al Senno" and therefore need only return to their original state to find salvation. This reiterates the beliefs espoused in #28 as seen previously that, indeed, man's natural state is to be found in the light. Again, in **"Al Primo Senno,"** Campanella states clearly that all men are born in the light: "così al Senno Primo unito nacque." At his birth, each entity receives from Mother Knowledge, knowledge in the amount that he needs to survive.

Senno is exalted in this poem to its highest status: not only does Campanella place it at the head of his religion of knowledge as "Senno Primo" but he calls it "sole," that is the lifeblood of man, and "Senno santo." Again, in **"A Tobia Adami filosofo"** the god knowledge is summoned as Campanella urges his friend Adami to use him as liberator from evil:

> Contra sofisti, ipocriti e tiranni
> d'armi del Primo Senno ornato vai
> la patria a liberar di tanti inganni.
>> (#70, v.9-11)

More important are perhaps the religious implications as Campanella describes Adami's sword as tempered in the "luce eterna" of knowledge and as he speaks of the "aurora degli eterni rai." The repetition of the adjective "eterno" as well as the presence of the godlike title "Primo Senno" can be understood as the indications of a declaration of a religion based on the God Knowledge. This becomes even clearer in #24 madrigal 1 in which the light of knowledge is defined in terms normally restricted to religious definitions of God. Not only is this a monotheistic religion ("La luce è una") but the god of this religion is omnipotent ("tutto vede e veder face in sua sfera"). In addition, he is able to spread its influence among others, that is, it is all-powerful.

Just as in #24 there is the reference to "il sole" as the source of knowledge, "Al Sole" is entirely dedicated to this idea. In **"Al Sole,"** Campanella, the Sage, places "Febo," the Sun, in the position of God as he prays to him for sustenance.

> . . . La giusta preghiera
> drizzola a te, Febo, ch'orni la scola mia.
> Veggoti nell'Ariete, levato a gloria, ed
>> ogni
> vital sostanza or emola farsi tua.
> Tu subblimi, avvivi e chiami a festa
>> novella
> ogni segreta cosa, languida, morta e pigra.
> Deh! avviva coll'altre me anche, o nume
>> potente,
> cui piu ch'agli altri caro ed amato sei.
>> (#89, v.1-9)

Campanella's use of religious terminology demonstrates how he viewed knowledge as the God of his mission: "preghiera" in verse 1 is an immediate indication as is the poet's vision of Febo "levato a gloria." The powers of this entity are outlined as Febo is seen as capable of making "ogni vital sostanza" his. More striking is the concept that he will transform evil, "ogni segreta cosa, languida, morta e pigra," into goodness. The use of "vital sostanza," "subblimi," and "avvivi" suggests the restorative powers of this "nume potente" and his ability to create from death life. Most revealing is the "festa novella" of which the poet speaks. This most certainly is a reference to the *renovazion del secolo,* to his vision of the new world that will be created by the influence of "il Senno." In verse 9, Campanella makes a direct reference to his love for this god who will be the salvation of the world and of which Campanella will be the chief messenger.

Only the followers of "il Senno," the "giudice ed autor di veritate" will achieve the happiness that comes from virtue—"Gran fortuna è 'l saper." "Gloria a colui che 'l tutto sape e puote!" says the poet, for man will be content:

> Viver dunque secondo il senno insegna
> felicità si tegna;
> per cui saper convegna
> tutte le cose che 'l mondo contiene.
> (#30, mad.8, v.9-12)

and will become, in fact, as a "dio secondo."

The triumphant, light-inspired poetry of Campanella cannot, however, erase the darker, more desperate poetry that co-exists with it in the *Cantica.* Although it is true that Campanella saw himself as the torch that would light the way to a *renovazion delsecolo,* and although it is also true that his poetry often reaches the heights of triumph and of inspired zeal; it is also true that his poetry descends into the depths of despair, loneliness, and doubt. While he was held aloft by his grand ideals, by his zeal to fulfill his mission as the prophet of knowledge; while he was encouraged to take action in the congiura by his strong belief that an alternative society was possible; he was also discouraged and at times almost crushed by the weight of reality: the tortures, his long imprisonment, the fact that he was not free to act on his role as Sage and that change was long in coming. If his poetry is a journal of his life experiences, then this darker side must also come into play, and indeed it does. We can trace effectively his various imprisonments, tortures, his period of false insanity through his poetry. One feels him fall into the depths of despair: physically, emotionally and spiritually.

The phase of imprisonment in Castel Sant'Elmo (1604) finds the poet at the peak of despair. Having been thrown into a subterranean "fossa," by far the worst of the prisons that he had been forced to endure, he suffered a life of discomfort, isolation, and pain. Madrigal 6 of "Della medesima salmodia," is a description of the horror that he experienced:

> . . . sei e sei anni, che 'n pena dispenso
> l'afflizion d'ogni senso,
> le membra sette volte tormentate,
> le bestemmie e le favole de' sciocchi,
> il sol negato agli occhi,
> i nervi stratti, l'ossa scontinoate,
> le polpe lacerate,
> i guai dove mi corco,
> li ferri, il sangue sparso, e 'l timor crudo,
> e 'l cibo poco e sporco . . .
> (#75, v.6-15)

Perhaps the most difficult of all of these afflictions was the "sol negato agli occhi" for that signified he was denied the light so dear to his state of mind, that he was forced to live in utter darkness and isolation. The **"Sonetto nel Caucaso"** written in July of 1604 is often seen as the turning point for Campanella, as the "sonetto della crisi." In this completely negative view of human life, there is no longer than familiar spark of hope and there is no longer that strong self-affirmation that existed in his previous poems:

> Temo che per morir non si migliora
> lo stato uman; per questo io non m'uccido:
> ché tanto è ampio di miserie il nido,
> che, per lungo mutar, non si va fuora.
> (v.1-4)

Up until this point, Campanella had almost denied the real presence of prison, refering to it as a place of the privileged in which he resided volontarily and to his glory. In this poem, instead, its presence in his life is all too real; it is, in fact, oppressively unavoidable. For the first time, Campanella names his tormentor, "Filippo," and names the place for what it is, "carcere." The sense of closeness in this place is suffocating as Campanella gives us an image of it as a "nido" that is crowded with misery—"ampio di miserie." It is a prison buried deep in the earth and the poem conveys to us the depths into which the poet has been placed and his sense of being in a place away from humanity and away from life. In the verses "ed io il presente grido / potrei obbliar, com'ho mill'altri ancora," the poet and his cries of despair seem buried deep within the earth where no man can hear. The previously strong poetic "io" is buried in the middle of a phrase and in the middle of the sonnet itself, just as the poet himself is buried. Indeed, the first word of the work, "temo," relays the message that his self-affermation has disappeared. The Lord himself is the only one who knows of the poet's existence: "Ma chi sa quel che di me fia, se tace Omnipotente?" as he is hidden deep within the bowels of the prison.

More frightening than the reality of the misery of the prison is the poet's belief that there is no escape for him. Previously, his mind and his soul always succeeded in escaping his imprisoned body through his poetry and through faith in the inevitability of his mission. Death itself was seen as simply another life form. Here, instead, there is no escape for body or mind and there is no better life after death. With deadened emotion, Tommaso Campanella pronounces his own and his mission's death sentence: "ogni spiaggia è come il nostro lido." His mission seems obliterated for he rejects change as risky and denies all hope of betterment. His final verses reveal his resigned heartbreak at God's silence in the face of Philip's cruelty.

The madrigals of "Lamentevole orazione profetale dal profondo della fossa dove stava incarcerato" emphasize these ideas. Campanella's state is described always as being in darkness, buried in the depths of the earth, hidden from view, as in madrigal 6 in which the poet describes himself as being "ne' ciechi chiostri . . . tra obblio e perdizion . . . ," or madrigal 2 in which he is "sepelita." The most striking madrigal is the following, in which he sees himself not simply as hidden but as dead, and more emphatically as murdered:

> Gli uccisi in sepoltura,
> dati da te in oblio,
> de' guai non hai piu cura,
> de' sotteranei laghi
> nell'infimo rinchiuso
> di morte fra le tenebre sembro io.
> 　　　(#78, madrigal 3, v.1-6)

He is the forgotten one, ignored by God, lost in the shadows of prison, buried deeply where nobody will see him. As he says in madrigal 2, he is one of the "perdute genti" as he lives a death-like life "peggior di mille morti."

Interesting in this work is the poet's attitude towards God. Since the power to escape prison is beyond Campanella's reach, he questions God's motives in causing him to be hidden there where he can do no good, where he cannot possibly carry out his mission.

> A te tocca, o Signore,
> se invan non m'hai creato,
> d'esser mio salvatore.
> Per questo notte e giorno
> a te lagrimo e grido.
> Quando ti parrà ben ch'io sia ascoltato?
> Piú parlar non mi fido,
> ché i ferri, c'ho d'intorno,
> ridonsi e fanmi scorno
> del mio invano pregare,
> degli occhi secchi e del rauco esclamare.
> 　　　(#78, madrigal 1)

The imagery in this poem of the "occhi secchi e del rauco esclamare" drives home the idea that prayer is useless, that all of his crying and praying aloud to God will have no effect. As the "ferri" of the prison represent the whole Inquisitorial system, Campanella is stating that not even the Inquisitorial clergy, those that are supposed to be his servants, believe that God will help the poet: "ridonsi e fanmi scorno / del mio invano pregare." His is a state of gradual loss of life, and it stands in marked contrast to his tormentors and to the prison itself, "i ferri," that are alive still and that laugh at the prophet. The presence of what Tommaso Campanella views as evil is as strong in this poetry as is the darkness in Sant'Elmo. And as we follow his life's course as it leads him from freedom to the "fossa" and back again we notice again the imagery of the "chiaroscuro." Here, however, often the light is obliterated by the darkness, the hope is dimmed by the despair, the cry of joy is drowned by the cry for mercy.

Despite the darkness, however, and despite the confusion that Campanella experiences concerning the reasons for his imprisonment when his leadership is needed outside in the world, despite his moments of doubt and of bitterness against God, not once does he deny the validity of the mission itself. Although he searches through his poetic and philosophical works for an answer to the problems that beset him, he never finds an alternative to his original vision. Franc Ducros points out:

> la "crise" . . . est comme l'épreuve
> du feu à laquelle on soumet l'or: elle le
> purifie mais n'en change pas la nature.

Indeed, the poet seems to come out of his worst ordeal stronger, purer, imbued with a sense of optimism that is borne of having faced reality and with having dealt with it well. Campanella seems to want to prove the theory of 1601:

> Se 'l quaglio si disfà, gran massa
> 　　apprende;
> e 'l fuoco, più soffiato, più s'accende,
> poi vola in alto e di stelle s'infiora.
> 　　　(#64, v.10-12)

In **"Al Sole,"** written between 1605 and 1607, Campanella again basks in the light of the sun of knowledge and finds that through it he may be reborn. In the icy hole in which the poet lived, only Senno succeeds in giving him warmth; only Febo can revive his withered roots.

> Esca io dal chiuso, mentre al tuo lume
> 　　sereno
> d'ime radici sorge la verde cima.
> 　Le virtù ascose ne'tronchi d'alberi, in alto
> in fior conversi, a prole soave tiri.

Le gelide vene ascose si risolvono in acqua
  pura,
che, sgorgando lieta, la terra riga.
  I tassi e ghiri dal sonno destansi lungo;
a' minimi vermi spirito e moto dài.
  Le smorte serpi al tuo raggio tornano vive:
    invidio, misero, tutta la schera loro.
  Muoiono in Irlanda per mesi cinque,
    gelando,
gli augelli, e mo pur s'alzano ad alto volo.
  Tutte queste opere son del tuo santo vigore,
a me conteso, fervido amante tuo.
  Credesi ch'ogge anche Giesú da morte
    resurse;
quando me vivo il rigido avello preme.
  L'olive secche han de te pur tanto favore:
rampolli verdi mandano spesso sopra.
  Vivo io, non morto, verde e non secco
    trovo,
benché cadavero per te seppelito sia.

(v.11-30)

In contrast to the poetry during his period of deepest crisis, this poem is quite a drastic change. Although he is still seen as "al buio," Campanella again finds his faith in "il sole." He again envisions the changes that take place under it's guidance and finds in it a hope for a change in his favor.

The vision of nature is quite different here than in the preceding period. Whereas before, the poet spoke of "laghi sotteranei," stagnant pools in which nothing lived, the nature of this poem is a living, vital one. It is a spring-time nature: as the sun of knowledge warms the earth, everything is reawakened and a new world is born out of the wintery freeze. Everything is movement and activity. Phrases such as "sgorgando lieta," "spirito e moto dài," "tornano vive," "s'alzano ad alto volo" tell us of the life-filled creatures and things of nature. The poet identifies himself with the natural surroundings in his vision as he sees himself being reawakened by the warmth of the same sun: "Esca io dal chiuso, mentre al tuo lume sereno / d'ime radici sorge la verde cima." Notice the constant references to "lume," the light that gives life. There is a tremendous aperture as Campanella leaves the close quarters of the prison and follows the path of the "augelli" that "s'alzano ad alto volo" into the vast natural world. Whereas before, he spoke of nothing but suffocating closeness, darkness, death, and the depths of the subteranean prison; now he sees vast spaces, light, life and an "alto volo" that will take him beyond that prison.

Laura Sanguineti White comments on the poet's vision of himself as he is metamorphised into a plant-like being. In the prison in which he lives, he has taken root and given fruit that is his poetry. There is a distinct imagery of the sprouting of a plant as it soaks up the light of the sun. Campanella speaks of himself in terms used for plantlife: "verde e non secco mi trovo." This imagery is revealing for in describing himself as "verde" the poet is saying that he is alive, that he is as vital a being as the other parts of nature. Almost surprised, he affirms "vivo io, e non morto." Although frozen, put into a state of suspended animation for a while by the darkness of the "fossa," he has not been killed. Indeed, he has emerged from the winter alive, and has been reborn. Most encouraging is the identification of the poet's rebirth with the resurrection of Christ. He, the prophet, the Sage, has risen from the dead to save the world from ignorance and evil, just as Christ did so many years before. In this identification lies the best indication to us that Tommaso Campanella's missionary dream had not withered away, but had simply been hibernating in search of a sunnier day.

In **"A Ridolfo Di Bina"** and **"A Tobia Adami filosofo,"** Tommaso Campanella urges these men to continue to fight towards realizing the vision:

Tu, con amino ardente, altiero e pio,
bandisci guerra alle falsarie scuole,
ch'io vincitor ti veggo, e veggo in Dio.
(#69, v.10-12)

Mal, se torci; gran ben, s'indrizzerai
virtue, diligenza, ingegno ed anni
verso l'aurora degli eterni rai.
(#68, v.10-12)

Noticeable is the strength of conviction and the optimism towards the outcome of the mission in these two passages. We see none of the desperation of the poetry in Sant'Elmo. Instead, there is again the militant tone towards evil, the sense that the Sages will fight to the end—"bandisci guerra"—to bring a *renovazion del secolo*. The vista of the birth of a new world is eloquently expressed as Campanella urges Ridolfo di Bina to apply all of his resources towards "l'aurora degli eterni rai."

Years after Campanella's imprisonment in Sant'Elmo, years after his first youthful dreams had been tested, years after his first convictions had been fought for, the vision had not changed. His hope for a better world, a *renovazion del secolo* remained with him and never diminished throughout the changes in his life. His was a revolutionary solution to the problems of his time. He constantly toiled to create what he deemed to be a fresh new world, one in which the "squilibri" of the Baroque Age would be reconciled and man would live in harmony. What is most impressive about him is that he was a man of thought but also of action. He was not content to simply write about a utopian society; he felt it was his duty to make it be realized. But what is perhaps most valuable to us is that his works reflected so closely the realities of his life; they give to us an unparalleled view of that epoch.

FURTHER READING

Criticism

Abramowitz, Isidore. *The Great Prisoners: The First Anthology of Literature Written in Prison.* New York: E. P. Dutton & Co., 1946, 879 p.

　Views Campanella's *City of the Sun* as the yoking together of the medieval world of astrology and the new spirit of enquiry and experimentation.

Blodgett, Eleanor Dickenson. "Bacon's *New Atlantis* and Campanella's *Civitas Solis:* A Study in Relationships." *PMLA* XLVI, No. 3 (September 1931): 763-80.

　Highlights the similarities between the two utopian texts and sees the differences as a product of the authors' differing life experiences.

Costa, Dennis. "Poetry and Gnosticism: The *Poetica* of Tommaso Campanella." *Viator* 15 (1984): 405-18.

　Argues that Campanella's philosophy was heavily influenced by Gnosticism.

Cro, Stelio. "Tommaso Campanella and the Poetry of the Baroque." *Romance Notes* XXII, No. 1 (Fall 1981): 88-93.

　Views Campanella's as one of the first modern Baroque poets who was convinced that the modern age was superior to the Classical ancient times.

Ernst, Germana. "From the watery Trigon to the fiery Trigon: Celestial Signs, Prophecies and History." In *'Astrologi hallucinati': Stars and the End of the World in Luther's Time,* edited by Paola Zambelli, pp. 265-80. New York and Berlin: Walter de Gruyter, 1986.

　Examines the role of astrology in Campanella's utopian thought.

Garin, Eugenio. "From Giordano Bruno to Tommaso Campanella." In *Italian Humanism: Philosophy and Civic Life in the Renaissance,* pp. 199-220. Translated by Peter Munz. Oxford: Basic Blackwell, 1965.

　Discusses Campanella's philosophy concerning sen-sory perception, feeling, and knowledge.

Grillo, Francesco. *Tommaso Campanella in America.* New York: S. F. Vanni, 1954, 109p.

　Attempts to reconcile the seeming contradictions between Campanella's rationalism and his alliegance to Catholicism.

Hertzler, Joyce Oramel. "Campanella's 'City of the Sun,'" In *The History of Utopian Thought,* pp. 153-65. New York: Macmillan, 1923.

　Provides an overview of Campanella's utopian vision of society in *City of the Sun.*

Mandel, Siegfried. "From the Mummelsee to the Moon: Refractions of Science in Seventeenth-Century Literature." *Comparative Literature Studies* IX, No. 4 (December 1972): 407-15.

　Argues that Campanella's utopia is based predominantly on his moralistic philosophy rather than his very limited knowledge of scientific truth.

Negley, Glenn Robert. "*The City of the Sun,* 1623." In *The Quest for Utopia,* pp. 314-17. New York: Henry Schuman, Inc., 1952.

　Argues that the many contradictory interpretations of *City of the Sun* arise from the complexity of the text and the tendency of critics to force utopian texts into their own ideological molds.

Ross, Harry. "The Birth of Modern Utopianism: Bacon, Campanella and Andreae." In *Utopias Old and New.* London: Nicholson and Watson, Ltd., 1938.

　Presents a close reading of *City of the Sun,* examining the curious mixture of aristocracy and democracy in Campanella's utopia.

Scalzo, Joseph. "Campanella, Foucault, and Madness in Late-Sixteenth-Century Italy." *Sixteenth Century Journal* XXI, No. 3 (Fall 1990): 359-71.

　Examines Campanella's alleged insanity in the light of Foucault's work on madness.

Walker, D. P. *Spiritual and Demonic Magic from Ficino to Campanella.* London: The Warburg Institute, 1958, 244p.

　Discusses Campanella's theories of astrological magic.

Utopia

Sir Thomas More

Latin prose dialogue and treatise on political philosophy.

INTRODUCTION

When Thomas More published *The Best State of a Commonwealth and the New Island of Utopia* (1516), he coined the word *utopia*, which has since become a common term in English. More's *Utopia* finds its origins in the "best commonwealth" dialogue, a rhetorical exercise practiced by ancient Greek philosophers in which the writer attempts to define an ideal society. The best-known examples of such dialogues are Plato's *Republic* and *Laws* and sections of Artistotle's *Poetics*. In *Utopia*, More explores a broad array of the elements that constitute any society—economic, legal, judicial, military, familial, and religious structures—all of which More envisions as closely regulated by the government. Over the years, political scientists have embraced *Utopia* as a work of creative political thought, ranking it with Plato's *Republic* and Machiavelli's *The Prince*. While most readers since the first publication have assumed that More advocated the social practices he ascribed to the fictional Utopia, many critics have pointed out that the author's intentions are not at all clear: the book could be either a best commonwealth exercise or a satire. In 1961, David Bevington noted that the "revered name of Thomas More has been invoked in support of the radical socialist states of the Soviet world empire, as well as in support of the anti-Communist position of the Papacy. Both interpretations purport to be founded on a critical reading of *Utopia*."

More was, in a time of religious upheaval, a devout Catholic; he was also an advisor to King Henry VIII, who ultimately broke England's tie to Catholicism. While More's work demonstrates an equal commitment to faith in divinity and faith in rationalism, his political allegiance to the king came into conflict with his religion when Henry VIII split from the Catholic Church and the Pope. Consequently, some critics have read the *Utopia* as a testament to More's efforts to negotiate between personal faith and duty to the government, although the conflict with Henry VIII occurred after More completed the book. More was executed in 1535 when he refused to comply with the king's wishes that he denounce Catholicism; the Catholic church canonized him in 1935.

Plot and Major Characters

More blended fact and fiction in the *Utopia*, creating characters based on real people (including himself) who encounter the purely fictional character Raphael Hythlodaeus, a traveler recently returned from the previously unknown island of Utopia. More bridged the gap from fact to fiction by prefacing the work with actual letters from friends and colleagues, all of whom endorse the book. These prefatory letters, also known as the *perarga*, constitute the first of three sections of the work. Book I, the second section, depicts the dialogue among Hythloday, More, and Peter Giles, which focuses on social conditions in sixteenth-century Europe, including agricultural economics and the penal system.

The discussion also features a debate about the philosopher's responsibility to government: Giles encourages Hythloday to become a political advisor in order to make his unique knowledge available to rulers; Hythloday suspects that a position as a counselor would force him to compromise his principles. Book II presents Hythloday's in-depth description of Utopia, taking the reader through all aspects of its social, political, and economic structure.

Textual History

More began his writing with the section ultimately published as Book II of the *Utopia* while serving as an ambassador in Antwerp in 1515; he composed Book I in 1516, back in England. The first edition of the complete work appeared late in 1516 and was followed by yearly editions printed in various European cities. Scholars requiring authoritative Latin manuscripts for their work usually rely on the first edition and one produced in November of 1518. Publication continued throughout the sixteenth and seventeenth centuries (notable editions appeared in 1548, 1555, 1563, 1565-66, 1601, 1613, 1629, 1663, and 1672). While most of these editions were in Latin, translations became more common during the nineteenth century. The Yale University Press *Complete Works of St. Thomas More* (1965) is an authoritative English-language edition, presenting the Latin and an English translation on facing pages; Cambridge University Press issued a new edition, with Latin and English versions, in 1995.

Critical Reception

In 1935 R. W. Chambers asserted that "few books have been more misunderstood than *Utopia*." The central question concerning the *Utopia* is the issue of authorial intent: any critic studying the *Utopia* must first try to determine whether the text is a sincere endorsement of the commonwealth described—truly More's "ideal" commonwealth—or a satirical commentary. The *Utopia*'s initial critical reception is that contained within the *perarga* of the volume: the letters from More's own friends and contemporaries endorsing the text. By and large, these thinkers received the *Utopia* as a wholly sincere best commonwealth exercise, and even occasionally treat Utopia as a real place. Much of the criticism leading into the twentieth century also treats the ideal as sincerely proposed; Frederick Seebohm (1867), for example, contends that the "point of the *Utopia* consisted in the contrast presented by its ideal commonwealth to the condition and habits of the European commonwealths of the period." Critics' attempts to determine if More endorsed the social policies he attributed to Utopia have produced lengthy discussions and debates, the most heated of which concern the subject of Utopia's economic communism. More describes the Utopians as living harmoniously without private property, which led Karl Marx and Frederich

Engels to name a specific variant of socialism for More in *The Communist Manifesto*, calling it "utopian socialism." Nonetheless, scholars disagree widely over More's intentions, the extremes in the debate exemplified by Karl Kautsky's painstaking demonstration of More's communism and H. W. Donner's assertion that More's portrayal of communism rejected the practice.

As the work of a religious martyr, the *Utopia* has also invited study by Catholic scholars concerned with the saint's principles. The book has often resisted such theologically oriented interpretation, however, because it presents the student with a society whose citizens are not Christians. Also problematic is the fact that throughout the work, the character Hythloday describes and idealizes many practices condemned by Catholic doctrine, such as divorce and suicide. Consequently, Catholic scholars were some of the first to approach the text as a "dialogic"—one in which the presentation of the debate carries more significance than the depiction of Utopia. These scholars point out that in the debates in Book I, the character with More's name often disagrees with Hythloday, suggesting that as appealing as Hythloday's rationalism may be, it is never quite enough without Christian faith. Other scholars have interpreted the same details, however, as an indictment of contemporary European Christianity, which was outstripped in virtue by a pagan society. Chambers exemplifies this view in his argument that the "underlying thought of *Utopia* always is, *With nothing save Reason to guide them, the Utopians do this; and yet we Christian Englishmen, we Christian Europeans . . . !*" Recently, this dialogic approach has also figured in the interpretations of scholars with more secular concerns, as later-twentieth-century scholars have tended to emphasize More's endorsement of specific problem-solving or intellectual mind-sets, rather than a particular social practice. David Bevington and Lee Khanna Cullen, for example, have focused on More's apparently positive portrayal of the intersection of different and often opposing viewpoints in open-minded discussion. Twentieth-century critics in general, however, have tended to perceive *Utopia* as a negative commentary—possibly a satiric figuration of contemporary Europe. This trend appears to be inspired by a critical focus on passages that seem contradictory: depictions of the Utopian practices of slavery and imperialism and political practices that amount to totalitarianism. Ironically, these same portions, as Schlomo Avineri has demonstrated, allowed some German critics sympathetic to Nazism in 1920s and 1930s to embrace the *Utopia*.

PRINCIPLE TRANSLATIONS

Utopia (translated by Gilbert Burnet) 1685
Utopia (translated by V. S. Ogden) 1949

Utopia (translated by Robert M. Adams) 1975
The Complete Works of St. Thomas More, Vol. IV
(translated by G. C. Richards) 1965

CRITICISM

Frederic Seebohm (essay date 1867)

SOURCE: "More's *Utopia*," in *The Oxford Reformers,*
1867. Reprint by ΛMS Press Inc., 1971, pp. 346-65.

*[In the following excerpt from his critical study, The
Oxford Reformers, Seebohm places* Utopia *in its political and historical context, contrasting what he believes to be More's ideal commonwealth with "the
condition and habits of the European commonwealths
of the period."]*

The point of the **Utopia** consisted in the contrast presented by its ideal commonwealth to the condition and
habits of the European commonwealths of the period.
This contrast is most often left to be drawn by the
reader from his own knowledge of contemporary politics, and hence the peculiar advantage of the choice
by More of such a vehicle for the bold satire it contained. Upon any other hypothesis than that the evils
against which its satire was directed were admitted to
be *real,* the romance of **Utopia** must also be admitted
to be harmless. To pronounce it to be dangerous was
to admit its truth.

Take, *e.g.,* the following passage relating to the international policy of the Utopians:—

> While other nations are always entering into leagues,
> and breaking and renewing them, the Utopians never
> enter into a league with any nation. For what is the
> use of a league? they say. As though there were no
> natural tie between man and man! and as though
> any one who despised this natural tie would,
> forsooth, regard mere words! They hold this opinion
> all the more strongly, because in that quarter of the
> world the leagues and treaties of princes are not
> observed as faithfully as they should be. For in
> *Europe,* and especially in those parts of it where
> the Christian faith and religion are professed, the
> sanctity of leagues is held sacred and inviolate;
> partly owing to the justice and goodness of princes,
> and partly from their fear and reverence of the
> authority of the Popes, who, as they themselves
> never enter into obligations which they do not most
> religiously perform [!], command other princes under
> all circumstances to abide by *their* promises, and
> punish delinquents by pastoral censure and
> discipline. For indeed, with good reason, it would
> be thought a most scandalous thing for those
> whose peculiar designation is "the faithful," to be

wanting in the faithful observances of treaties. But
in those distant regions . . . no faith is to be placed
in leagues, even though confirmed by the most
solemn ceremonies. Some flaw is easily found in
their wording whichis intentionally made ambiguous
so as to leave a loophole through which the parties
may break both their league and their faith. Which
craft—yes, *fraud* and *deceit*—if it were perpetrated
with respect to a contract between private parties,
they would indignantly denounce as sacrilege and
deserving the gallows, whilst those who suggest
these very things to princes, glory in being the
authors of them. Whence it comes to pass that justice
seems altogether a plebeian and vulgar virtue, quite
below the dignity of royalty; or at least there must
be two kinds of it, the one for common people and
the poor, very narrow and contracted, the other, the
virtue of princes, much more dignified and free, so
that *that* only is unlawful to *them* which they don't
like. The morals of princes being such in that region,
it is not, I think, without reason that the Utopians
enter into no leagues at all. Perhaps they would
alter their opinion if they lived amongst us.

Read without reference to the international history of
the period, these passages appear perfectly harmless.
But read in the light of that political history which,
during the past few years, had become so mixed up
with the personal history of the Oxford Reformers,
recollecting '*how* religiously' treaties had been made
and broken by almost every sovereign in Europe—
Henry VIII and the Pope included—the words in which
the justice and goodness of European princes is so
mildly and modestly extolled, become almost as bitter
in their tone as the cutting censure of Erasmus in the
Praise of Folly, or his more recent and open satire
upon kings.

Again, bearing in mind the wars of Henry VIII, and
how evidently the love of military glory was the motive which induced him to engage in them, the following passage contains almost as direct and pointed a
censure of the King's passion for war as the sermon
preached by Colet in his presence:—

> The Utopians hate war as plainly brutal, although
> practised more eagerly by man than by any other
> animal. And contrary to the sentiment of nearly
> every other nation, they regard nothing more
> inglorious than glory derived from war.

Turning from international politics to questions of internal policy, and bearing in mind the hint of Erasmus,
that More had in view chiefly the politics of his own
country, it is impossible not to recognise in the **Utopia**
the expression, again and again, of the *sense of wrong*
stirred up in More's heart, as he had witnessed how
every interest of the commonwealth had been sacrificed to Henry VIII's passion for war; and how, in
sharing the burdens it entailed, and dealing with the
social evils it brought to thesurface, the interests of the

poor had been sacrificed to spare the pockets of the rich; how, whilst the very wages of the labourer had been taxed to support the long-continued war expenditure, a selfish Parliament, under colour of the old 'statutes of labourers,' had attempted to cut down the amount of his wages, and to rob him of that fair rise in the price of his labour which the drain upon the labour market had produced.

It is impossible not to recognise that the recent statutes of labourers was the target against which More's satire was specially directed. . . .

The whole framework of the Utopian commonwealth bears witness to More's conviction, that what should be aimed at in his own country and elsewhere, was a true *community*—not a rich and educated aristocracy on the one hand, existing side by side with a poor and ignorant peasantry on the other—but *one people, well-to-do and educated throughout.*

Thus More's opinion was, that in England in his time, 'far more than four parts of the whole [people], divided into ten, could never read English,' and probably the education of the other six-tenths was anything but satisfactory. He shared Colet's faithin education, and represented that in Utopia *every child was properly educated.*

Again the great object of the social economy of Utopia was not to increase the abundance of luxuries, or to amass a vast accumulation in few hands, or even in national or royal hands, but to *lessen the hours of labour to the working man.* By spreading the burden of labour more evenly over the whole community—by taking care that there shall be no idle classes, be they beggars or begging friars—More expressed the opinion that the hours of labour to the working man might probably be reduced to *six.*

Again: living himself in Bucklersbury, in the midst of all the dirt and filth of London's narrow streets; surrounded by the unclean, ill-ventilated houses of the poor, whose floors of clay and rushes, never cleansed, were pointed out by Erasmus as breeding pestilence, and inviting the ravages of the sweating sickness; himself a commissioner of sewers, and having thus some practical knowledge of London's sanitary arrangements; More described the towns of Utopia as well and regularly built, with wide streets, waterworks, hospitals, and numerous common halls; all the houses well protected from the weather, as nearly as might be fireproof, three stories high, with plenty of windows, and doors both back and front, theback door always opening into a well-kept garden. All this was Utopian doubtless, and the result in Utopia of the still more Utopian abolition of private property; but the gist and point of it consisted in the contrast it presented with what he saw around him in Europe, and especially in England,

and men could hardly fail to draw the lesson he intended to teach.

It will not be necessary here to dwell further upon the details of the social arrangements of More's ideal commonwealth, or to enter at length upon the philosophical opinions of the Utopians; but a word or two will be needful to point out the connection of the latter with the views of that little band of friends whose joint history I am here trying to trace.

One of the points most important and characteristic is the *fearless faith in the laws of nature combined with a profound faith in religion,* which runs through the whole work, and which may, I think, be traced also in every chapter of the history of the Oxford Reformers. Their scientific knowledge was imperfect, as it needs must have been, before the days of Copernicus and Newton; but they had their eyes fearlessly open in every direction, with no foolish misgivings lest science and Christianity might be found to clash. They remembered (what is not always remembered in this nineteenthcentury), that if there be any truth in Christianity, Nature and her laws on the one hand and Christianity and her laws on the other, being framed and fixed by the same Founder, must be in harmony, and that therefore for Christians to act contrary to the laws of Nature, or to shut their eyes to facts, on the ground that they are opposed to Christianity, is—to speak plainly—to fight against one portion of the Almighty's laws under the supposed sanction of another; to fight, therefore, without the least chance of success, and with every prospect of doing harm instead of good.

Hence the moral philosophy of the Utopians was both Utilitarian and Christian. Its distinctive features, according to More, were—1st, that they placed *pleasure* (in the sense of 'utility') as the chief object of life; and 2ndly, that they drew their arguments in support of this as well from the principles of religion as from natural reason.

They defined 'pleasure' as 'every emotion or state of body or mind in which nature leads us to take delight.' And from reason they deduced, as modern utilitarians do, that not merely the pleasure of the moment must be regarded as the object of life, but what will produce the greatest amount and highest kind of pleasure in the long run; that, *e.g.* a greater pleasure must not be sacrificed toa lesser one, or a pleasure pursued which will be followed by pain. And from reason they also deduced that, nature having bound men together by the ties of Society, and no one in particular being a special favourite of nature, men are bound, in the pursuit of pleasure, to regard the pleasures of others as well as their own—to act, in fact, in the spirit of the golden rule; which course of action, though it may involve some immediate sacrifice, they saw clearly never costs so much as it brings back, both in the interchange of

mutual benefits, and in the mental pleasure of confer-
ring kindness on others. And thus they arrived at the
same result as modern utilitarians, that, while 'nature
enjoins *pleasure* as the end of all men's efforts,' she
enjoins such a reasonable and far-sighted pursuit of it
that 'to live by this rule is *"virtue."'*

In other words, in Utopian philosophy, *'utility'* was
recognised as *a* criterion of right and wrong; and from
experience of what, under the laws of Nature, is man's
real far-sighted interest, was derived *a* sanction to the
golden rule. And thus, instead of setting themselves
against the doctrine of utility, as some would do on the
ground of a supposed opposition to Christianity, they
recognised the identity between the two standards. They
recognised, as Mr. [John Stuart] Mill urges [in *Essay
on Utilitarianism,* 1863] that Christians ought to do
now, 'in the golden rule of Jesus of Nazareth, the complete spirit of the ethics of utility.'

The Utopians had no hesitation in defining 'virtue' as
'living according to nature'; for, they said, 'to this end
we have been created by God.' Their religion itself
taught them that 'God in his goodness created men for
happiness;' and therefore there was nothing unnatural
in his rewarding, with the promise of endless happiness hereafter, that 'virtue' which is living according
to those very laws of nature which He Himself established to promote the happiness of men on earth.

Nor was this, in More's hands, a merely philosophical
theory. He made the right practical use of it, in correcting those false notions of religion and piety which
had poisoned the morality of the middle ages, and
soured the devotion even of those mediaeval mystics
whose mission it was to uphold the true religion of the
heart. Who does not see that the deep devotion even of
a Tauler, or of a Thomas à Kempis, would have been
deepened had it recognised the truth that the religion
of Christ was intended to add heartiness and happiness
to daily life, and not to draw men out of it; that the
highest ideal of virtue is, not to stamp out those feelings and instincts which, under the rule of selfishness,
make a hell of earth, but so, as it were, to tune them
into harmony,that, under the guidance of a heart of
love, they may add to the charm and the perfectness of
life? The ascetic himself who, seeing the vileness and
the misery which spring out of selfish riot in pleasure,
condemns natural pleasure as almost in itself a sin,
fills the heaven of his dreams with white robes, golden
crowns, harps, music and angelic songs. Even *his* highest ideal of perfect existence is the unalloyed enjoyment of pleasure. He is a Utilitarian in his dreams of
heaven.

More, in his 'Utopia,' dreamed of this celestial morality as practised under earthly conditions. He had banished selfishness from his commonwealth. He was bitter
as any ascetic against vanity, and empty show, and

shams of all kinds, as well as all sensuality and excess;
but his definition of 'virtue' as 'living according to
nature' made him reject the ascetic notion of virtue as
consisting in crossing all natural desires, in abstinence
from natural pleasure, and stamping out the natural
instincts. The Utopians, More said, 'gratefully acknowledged the tenderness of the great Father of nature, who
hath given us appetites which make the things necessary for our preservation also agreeable to us. How
miserable would life be if hunger and thirst could only
be relieved by bitter drugs.' Hence, too, the Utopians
esteemed it not only 'madness,' but also *'ingratitude
to God,'* to waste the body by fasting, or toreject the
delights of life, unless by so doing a man can serve the
public or promote the happiness of others.

Hence also they regarded the pursuit of natural science, the 'searching out the secrets of nature,' not only
as an agreeable pursuit, but as 'peculiarly acceptable
to God.' Seeing that they believed that 'the first dictate
of reason is love and reverence for Him to whom we
owe all we have and all we can hope for,' it was natural that they should regard the pursuit of science rather as a part of their religion than as in any way antag-
onistic to it. But their science was not likely to be
speculative and dogmatic like that of the Schoolmen;
accordingly, whilst they were said to be very expert in
the mathematical sciences (*numerandi et metiendi sci-
entia*), they knew nothing, More said, 'of what even
boys learn here in the *"Parva logicalia"'*; and whilst,
by long use and observation, they had acquired very
exact knowledge of the motions of the planets and
stars, and even of winds and weather, and had invented very exact instruments, they had never dreamed,
More said, of those astrological arts of divination
'which are now-a-days in vogue among Christians.'

From the expression of so fearless a faith in the consistency of Christianity with science, it might be inferred that More would represent the religion of the
Utopians as at once broad and tolerant. It could not
logically be otherwise. The Utopians, we are told, differed very widely; but notwithstanding all their different objects of worship, they agreed in thinking that
there is one Supreme Being who made and governs the
world. By the exigencies of the romance, the Christian
religion had only been recently introduced into the
island. It existed there side by side with other and
older religions, and hence the difficulties of complete
toleration in Utopia were much greater hypothetically
than they would be in any European country. Still,
sharing Colet's hatred of persecution, More represented that it was one of the oldest laws of Utopia 'that no
man is to be punished for his religion.' . . .

T. E. Bridgett (essay date 1891)

SOURCE: "Treatment of Heretics," in *Life and Writ-*

The three main characters talking in the garden.

ings of Sir Thomas More, Lord Chancellor of England and Martyr Under Henry VIII, Burns & Oates, Ltd., 1891, pp. 253-72.

[*In the following essay, Bridgett discusses More's views on the subject of heresy and addresses accusations that More hypocritcally abandoned the principles of religious tolerance advocated in his* Utopia.]

In his epitaph More had designed and emphatically stated that he had been "troublesome to thieves, murderers, and heretics . . . ."

We have seen Erasmus's commentary on these words. It is necessary, however, to study their force, not as apologists, but as historians. Whom does More designate as heretics? In what way did he trouble or "molest" them? In molesting them, did he contradict the principles he had laid down in his *Utopia* about toleration? Did he remain within, or did he go beyond the law as it existed in his time?

There is a long-standing tradition that he was not merely severe, which may seem to be justified by his own words, but even arbitrary and unjust. And as his amiable and upright character is admitted on all hands, the blame of this warp in his character and blot on his fame is cast on the religion which he professed. We have seen Horace Walpole writing of "that cruel judge whom one knows not how to hate, who persecuted others in defence of superstitions he had himself exposed." it is probable that Walpole derived this view of Sir Thomas More from Burnet's *History of the Reformation.*

Burnet writes: "More was not governed by interest, nor did he aspire so to preferment as to stick at nothing that might contribute to raise him; nor was he subject to the vanities of popularity. The integrity of his whole life and the severity of his morals cover him from all these suspicions. If he had been formerly corrupted by a superstitious education, it had been no extraordinary thing to see so good a man grow to be misled by the force of prejudice. But how a man who had emancipated himself, and had got into a scheme of free thoughts, could be so entirely changed cannot be easily apprehended, nor how he came to muffle up his understanding and deliver himself up as a property to the blind and enraged fury of the priests. It cannot, indeed, be accounted for but by charging it on the intoxicating charms of that religion, that can darken the clearest understandings and corrupt the best natures; and since they wrought this effect on Sir Thomas More, I cannot but conclude the 'if these things were done in the green tree, what shall be done in the dry?'"

In our own day the same accusation of cruelty, and the same explanation, have been renewed by a popular historian. Mr. Froude writes [in *History of England*]: "Wolsey had chastised them [the innovators] with whips; Sir Thomas More would chastise them with scorpions, and the philosopher of the *Utopia,* the friend of Erasmus, whose life was of blameless beauty, whose genius was cultivated to the highest attainable perfection, was to prove to the world that the spirit of persecution is no peculiar attribute of the pedant, the bigot, or the fanatic, but may co-exist with the fairest graces of the human character. The lives of remarkable men usually illustrate some emphatic truth. Sir Thomas More may be said to have lived to illustrate the necessary tendencies of Romanism, in an honest mind convinced of the truth; to show that the test of sincerity in a man who professes to regard orthodoxy as an essential of salvation is not the readiness to endure persecution, but the courage that will venture to inflict it."

Such is the accusation. Let us now hear Sir Thomas''s own statement of the case, made in the spring of 1533 [in his *Apology*]: "As touching teretics, I hate that vice of theirs and not their persons, and very fain would I that the one were destroyed and the other saved. And that I have toward no man any other mind than this—how loudly soever these blessed new brethren and professors and preachers of heresy belie me—if all the favour and pity that I have used among them to their amendment were known, it would, I warrant you, well and plain appear; whereof, if it were requisite, I could bring forth witnesses more than men would ween.

"Howbeit, because it were neither right nor honesty that any man should look for more thank than he deserveth, I will that all the world wit it on the other side, that who so be so deeply grounded in malice, to the harm of his own soul and other men's too, and so set upon the sowing of seditious heresies, that no good means that men may use unto him can pull that malicious folly out of his poisoned, proud, obstinate heart, I would rather be content that he were gone in time, than overlong to tarry to the destruction of other."

If, then, sir Thomas More requires a defence, no such apology can be set up for him as may be valid for the judges, who administered our cruel penal code with regard to theft, in the early years of the present century—viz., that not being legislators they were not responsible for the barbarity of the laws, and that being judges they were bound to pass sentence according to the laws as they found them. Such a defence is not applicable to the case of Sir Thomas More. It would exonerate him from any charge of *injustice,* if it can be shown (as it certainly can) that he did not go beyond the law. But as regards the imputation of a cruel dis-

position, Sir Thomas would reject a defence based on the supposition that he was the reluctant administrator of laws, the existence of which he regretted. In his *Apology,* written after he had ceased to act as judge, he fully and heartily approves of the laws, both ecclesiastical and civil, that then existed in England against heresy, and he maintains that these laws had been administered with the utmost leniency and indeed with a dangerous laxity.

The first question then that occurs is with regard to More's consistency. Did his later theories and practice contradict the more generous philosophy of his youth? That the reader may judge for himself, I will give without abridgment a passage from *Utopia* in Burnet's translation.

After stating that in Utopia there were several sorts of religion—some idolatrous, some monotheistical—and that the higher views were gradually setting aside the others, Raphael (the supposed traveller) says that Christianity also had been lately introduced by himself and his companions. He then continues as follows:—

> "Those among them that have not received our religion do not fright any from it, and use none ill that goes over to it, so that all the while I was there one man only was punished on this occasion. He being newly baptised did, notwithstanding all that we could say to the contrary, dispute publicly concerning the Christian religion, with more zeal than discretion, and with so much heat, that he not only preferred our worship to theirs, but condemned all their rites as profane, and cried out against all that adhered to them as impious and sacreligious persons, that were to be damned to everlasting burnings. Upon his having frequently preached in this manner he was seized, and after trial he was condemned to banishment, not for having disparaged their religion, but for his inflaming the people to sedition; for this is one of their most ancient laws, that no man ought to be punished for his religion.

> "At the first constitution of their government, Utopus understood that, before his coming among them, the old inhabitants had been engaged in great quarrels concerning religion, by which they were so divided among themselves, that he found it an easy thing to conquer them, since, instead of uniting their forces against him, every different party in religion fought by themselves. After he had subdued them he made a law that every man might be of what religion he pleased, and might endeavour to draw others to it by the force of argument and by amicable and modest ways, but without bitterness against those of other opinions; but that he ought to use no other force but that of persuasion, and was neither to mix with it reproaches nor violence; and such as did otherwise were to be condemned to banishment or slavery.

"This law was made by Utopus, not only for preserving the public peace, which he saw suffered much by daily contentions and irreconcilable heats, but because he thought the interest of religion itself required it. He judged it not fit to determine anything rashly; and seemed to doubt whether those different forms of religion might not all come from God, who might inspire man in a different manner, and be pleased with this variety; he therefore thought it indecent and foolish for any man to threaten and terrify another to make him believe what did not appear to him to be true. And supposing that only one religion was really true, and the rest false, he imagined that the native force of truth would at last break forth and shine bright, if supported only by the strength of argument, and attended to with a gentle and unprejudiced mind; while, on the other hand, if such debates were carried on with violence and tumults, as the most wicked are always the most obstinate, so the best and most holy religion might be choked with supersition, as corn is with briars and thorns; he therefore left men wholly to their liberty, that they might be free to believe as they should see cause.

"Only he made a solemn and severe law against such as should so far degenerate from the dignity of human nature, as to think that our souls died with our bodies, or that the world was governed by chance, without a wise overruling Providence: for they all formerly believed that there was a state of rewards and punishments to the good and bad after this life; and they now look on those that think otherwise as scarce fit to be counted men, since they degrade so noble a being as the soul, and reckon it no better than a beast's: thus they are far from looking on such men as fit for human society, or to be citizens of a well-ordered commonwealth; since a man of such principles must needs, as oft as he dares do it, despise all their laws and customs: for there is no doubt to be made, that a man who is afraid of nothing but the law, and apprehends nothing after death, will not scruple to break through all the laws of his country, either by fraud or force, when by this means he may satisfy his appetites. They never raise any that hold these maxims either to honours or offices, nor employ them in any public trust, but despise them, as men of base and sordid minds. Yet they do not punish them, because they lay this down as a maxim, that a man cannot make himself believe whatever he likes."

This passage of the *Utopia* was no doubt in Burnet's mind when he referred to More's having once "got into a scheme of free thoughts." Sir James Mackintosh, a real lover of liberty, very different from Burnet, has written on this subject as follows:

"It is evident that the two philosophers (More and Erasmus), who found all their fair visions dispelled by noise and violence, deeply felt the injustice of citing against them, as a proof of inconsistency, that they departed from the pleasantries, the gay

dreams, at most the fond speculations, of their early days, when they saw these harmless visions turned into weapons of destruction in the blood-stained hands of the boors of Saxony, and of the ferocious fanatics of Munster. The virtuous love of peace might be more prevalent in More: the Epicurean desire of personal ease predominated more in Erasmus. But both were, doubtless from commendable or excusable causes, incensed against those odious disciples, who now, with no friendly voice, invoked their authority against themselves."

Though I have cited with pleasure this passage from an eminent writer, because it has a bearing on several things written by More in his *Utopia,* I can scarcely adopt it as regards the special matter of toleration we are now considering; for I do not find that More's early theories on this subject were ever brought as a reproach against him during his own lifetime, much less that the innovators whom he resisted and prosecuted ever appealed, in favour of their own liberty, to general principles of toleration. More himself has put the following wish into the mouth of his interlocutor in his *Dialogue*: "I would," says his friend, "all the world were agreed to take all violence and compulsion away, upon all sides, Christian and heathen, and that no man were constrained to believe but as he could be, by grace, wisdom and good works, induced; and then he that would go to God, go on in God's name, and he that will go to the devil, the devil go with him." This is perhaps the modern theory put in a homely way; but before giving More's answer, let me say that this was not the theory of the Lutherans with whom More had to do. They pleaded for liberty as having exclusively the truth, but they never thought of giving liberty to Catholics. The Mass was to be forcibly abolished as a horrible idolatry, the monks to be dragged from their cloisters, and if necessary whipped at a cart's tail till they would marry and work, and the gospel of Luther forced by the civil power upon the world. The state of things that More supposes in his Utopia had nothing parallel in that age either among Catholics or Protestants. Some may think that he approximately describes the present state of England; in which case, could he rise again, himself unchanged, in our changed state of society, he would doubtless plead for quiet and mutual forbearance, as did his Portuguese friend, Raphael, in the conversation at Antwerp.

For my own part, I can find no evidence of change of views, or of inconsistency in the author of the *Utopia.* In that work More is discoursing of people who had no revelation from God, and he condemns their acrimonious disputes and intolerance in matters of pure reason or natural tradition. Before he can be accused of inconsistency, it should be shown that the social and religious problems, discussed by him in his later English writings, were analogous to those contemplated by King Utopus, and if so, that he solved them differently. Did he, in later years, teach that men left by God to the pure exercise of their reason, should not also be left free by their rulers, "to seek God, if happily they may feel after Him and find Him"? Did he ever teach that the unbaptised heathen should be compelled by force to accept the true faith? Did he ever teach that men brought up from childhood in heresy, and in atheism and materialism, and dazed and bewildered by the multitude of opinions around them, should be punished because they could not see their way to certainty or unity? On the contrary, it was because he foresaw this very state of things as the result of Luther's revolt, and grieved over it; because he foresaw that if once unity were broken up, and the Catholic faith called in question, the people would be "tossed about with every wind of doctrine, by the wickedness of men, by cunning craftiness, by which they lie in wait to deceive," he therefore met these innovations with an energy inspired no less by his love of freedom of thought, than by his love of his country. He thought, and he worte over and over again, that there was no slavery like the slavery of sectarianism, and no freedom like that enjoyed where all have on unchangeable faith. Did More understand the word heretic as it is generally understood in England at the present day? I am not proposing a theological, but a historical question. I am not asking whether More was right or wrong in his judgment regarding heresy, but what did he mean by it? To most Protestants, orthodoxy can only mean for each man his private opinion or conviction in matters of religion, while heresy can only be a nickname for his neighbour's views. It does not require a mind of More's acuteness, or a character of his fairness, to see at a glance that, in such circumstances, mutual forbearance is the strictest of duties, and that no one should be violently repressed but he who violently disturbs his neighbour.

To More the word heresy conveyed a very different meaning. It was the private choice, by an individual, of a doctrine contradictory to that held to be clearly revealed by the divinely guided society to which that individual had belonged. More himself points out (and it is his views we are discussing), that according to St. Paul, not only is heresy or faction in religion classed with grievous sins like murder, theft, and adultery, but it is supposed by him to be as easily recognised and proved; so that the ruler of the spiritual society can admonish and reprove and ultimately reject the criminal, and cast him forth from the society, either delivering him over to Satan, like Hymeneus and Alexander, that he may learn not to blaspheme, or at least warning and commanding the society to avoid him as a pestilence.

To More a heretic was neither a simple man erring by ignorance, nor a learned man using his freedom in doubtful points: he was a man whose heart was "proud, poisoned, and obstinate," because he denied the Divine guidance of the Church into which he had been baptised, while he claimed special Divine inspiration for himself.

But this is not an adequate explanation of More's aversion to Lutheranism and of his conduct towards it. What has been said would apply to all heresy, though it were limited to the most abstruse points of revelation, and though its holder took no pains to propagate it. The zeal, the indignation and the horror of Sir Thomas More were aroused, because to him the Lutheran doctrines, as they first came before the world, appeared as the denial of everything that the Christian people had hitherto held in veneration, and as uprooting the foundation of all morals. We have seen what he wrote about it in his Latin work, under the name of Ross. As time went on he painted it in still darker colours, as fuller accounts came of the excesses in Germany and Switzerland. "Is it not a wonderful thing," he asks, in his *Dialogue,* written in 1528—"Is it not a wonderful thing, that we should now see a lewd friar so bold and shameless to marry a nun and bide thereby, and be taken still for a Christian man, and over that, for a man meet to be the beginner of a sect, whom any honest man would vouchsafe to follow? If our Lord God, whose wisdom is infinite, should have set and studied to devise a way whereby He might cast in our face the confusion of our folly, how might He have founden a more effectual than to suffer us that call ourselves Christian folk, to see such a rabble springing up among us, as let not to set at nought all the doctors of Christ's Church, and lean to the only authority of Friar Tuck and Maid Marion?"

We have not, however, yet reached the full motive of More's conduct. It was because the buffooneries and infamies of Friar Tuck were united with the outrages and violence of Robin Hood that More justified their suppression by force. This is the answer he gives to his friend who wished that everyone might be left free to go to the devil if he chose. Yes, replies More, but he shall not drag society with him. It is here I find a perfect consistency with the opinions he had expressed in *Utopia.* King Utopus, he says, having no means of attaining unity, enforced moderation and mutual toleration, where he had found nothing but confusion and bitterness, because that contention had weakened the country and laid it open to foreign conquest. More, on the contrary, was the highest magistrate in a country hitherto in perfect peace and unity in religious matters. The Catholic Church had held exclusive possession of England for nearly a thousand years, and its doctrines, discipline, and institutions had leavened every part of English life. The policy of Utopus would certainly have allowed no heated dissensions to be introduced to break up this unity. He who would not allow the materialists to propagate their opinions, would have given no licence to false spiritualists "to bring in sects blaspheming."

This is the contention of Sir Thomas More throughout his many voluminous works of controversy. He says [in *English Works*] that "it was the violent cruelty first used by the heretics themselves against good Catholic folk that drove good princes thereto, for preservation not of the faith only, but also of peace among the people." He enters fully into the history of the treatment of heretics. The Church, he maintains, had in no age punished them by death. The State had done it in self-defence, and had called on the Church to define heresy, to judge the fact and deliver the relapsed heretic into the hands of the civil power. The State (he maintains) only did this when it had attained peace and unity by means of the Church, and when it was found by experience that heretics ever stirred up sedition and rebellion, and if allowed to spread, brought about division and ruin. He points to the history of Lollardy in England in the time of Henry IV and Henry V; and to the fearful results of Lutheranism in Germany, in the violent destruction of the Catholic Church in some lands, the wars of the peasants in others; to the division of the empire making it unable to resist the threatened invasion of the Turks; and to that general breakup of what was called Christendom, which would be the inevitable consequence of the spread of these principles.

Let us now turn from the theories of More to his personal practice. Was he ever cruel or unjust? It is surely a bold thing to accuse him of this after his own challenge. In 1532 an anonymous writer under the character of a peace-maker had thrown great blame on the proceedings of the clergy, but always in general terms, as, "Some say," "Many say," etc. Sir Thomas writes: "Let this pacifier come forth and appear before the king's Grace and his Council, or in what place he list, and there prove, calling me thereto, that any one of all these had wrong—but if it were for that they were burned no sooner. And because he shall not say that I bid him trot about for naught, this shall I proffer him, that I will bind myself for surety, and find him other twain besides of better substance than myself, that for every one of these whom he proveth wronged, his ordinary or his other officer by whom the wrong was done, shall give this pacifier all his costs about the proof and a reasonable reward besides. And yet now, though no man would give him nothing, it were his part, perdie! to prove it for his own honesty, since he hath said so far."

This public challenge met with no response in More's lifetime. Thirty years after his death the Protestant martyrologist Foxe brought forward some stories of More's cruelty, which are the sole foundation on which Burnet and other writers have grounded their accusations of his having "delivered himself up as a property to the blind and enraged fury of the priests."

In his account of John Tewkesbury, a pouchmaker or leather-seller of London, Foxe writes as follows:

> He was sent from the Lollard's Tower to my Lord Chancellor's, called Sir Thomas More, to Chelsea, with all his articles [*i.e.,* the articles of accusation], to see whether he could turn him, and that he might accuse others; and there he lay in the porter's lodge, hand, foot and head in the stocks, six days without release. Then was he carried to Jesu's Tree in his privy garden, where he was whipped and also twisted in his brows with a small rope, that the blood started out of his eyes, and yet would not accuse no man. Then was he let loose in the house for a day, and his friends thought to have him at liberty the next day. After this he was sent to be racked in the Tower, till he was almost lame and there promised to recant.

Again, of James Bainham, a lawyer, Foxe writes that he also was whipped in Sir Thomas's garden at the Tree of Truth, and then sent to the Tower to be racked, "and so he was, Sir Thomas More being present himself, till in a manner he had lamed him."

Burnet says that Sir Thomas "looked on, and saw him put to the rack."

Foxe wrote in the time of Elizabeth, and he has been proved to have picked up every bit of traditional gossip, and to have added so many inventions and embellishments of his own, that unless where he gives documents his testimony is of no value.

As regards Tewkesbury, his first examination, after which he retracted, was on 8th May, 1529, and this was several months before Sir Thomas was chancellor. The story, therefore, of his torture in More's garden is clearly mythical. Foxe has strangely mixed up the stories of Tewkesbury and Bainham; both are whipped at a tree in Sir Thomas More's garden, though whether the Tree of Jesus was the same as the Tree of Truth we are not told; both are sent to the Tower and racked; both retract; both are afterwards overcome by remorse, and publicly bewail their retraction to their friends in a conventicle in Bowe Lane, and then afterwards make a public protest in a church, and so both are condemned to be burnt. These are strange coincidences; but it is still more strange that a part of what Foxe had written of Tewkesbury in one edition, in another edition he omitted, and tacked on to his account of Bainham. The accuracy of Foxe may be judged from the fact that he imputes the death of Frith to More, yet Frith died in 1533, and More had resigned his office a year before.

Foxe does not seem to have been the inventor of the sotry of the whippings and racking, for in the 36th chapter of his *Apology* Sir Thomas refers to some such lies as then in circulation. The passage is very important, and shall be given with little abridgment:

"They that are of this brotherhood be so bold and so shameless in lying, that whoso shall hear them speak, and knoweth not what sect they be of, shall be very sore abused [misled] by them. Myself have good experience, for the lies are neither few nor small that many of the blessed brethren have made, and daily yet make by me.

"Divers of them have said that of such as were in my house while I was chancellor I used to examine them with torments, causing them to be bound to a tree in my garden, and there piteously beaten. And this tale had some of those good brethren so caused to be blown about, that a right worshipful friend of mine did of late, within less than this fortnight, tell unto another near friend of mine that he had of late heard much speaking thereof.

"What cannot these brethren say that can be so shameless to say thus? For of very truth, albeit that for a great robbery or a heinous murder, or sacrilege in a church, with carrying away the pix with the Blessed Sacrament, or villainously casting it out, I caused sometimes such things to be done by some officers of the Marshalsea, or of some other prisons, with which ordering of them, and without any great hurt that afterwards should stick by them, I found out and repressed many such desperate wretches as else had not failed to have gone farther; yet, saving the sure keeping of heretics, I never did cause any such thing to be done to any of them in all my life, except only twain. Of which the one was a child and a servant of mine in mine own house, whom his father had, ere ever he came with me, nursled up in such matters, and had set him to attend upon George Jay or Gee, otherwise called Clerk, which is a priest, and is now for all that wedded in Antwep, into whose house there the two nuns were brought which John Birt, otherwise called Adrian, stole out of their cloister to make them harlots. This George Jay did teach this child his ungracious heresy against the Blessed Sacrament of the altar, which heresy this child afterwards, being in service with me, began to teach another child in my house, which uttered his counsel. And upon that point perceived, I caused a servant of mine to stripe him like a child before mine household, for amendment of himself and ensample of such other.

"Another was one, which after that he had fallen into that frantic heresy, fell soon after into plain open frenzy besides." More then tells how he was confined in bedlam, and when set free disturbed public service in churches, and committed acts of great indecency: "Whereupon I, being advertised of these pageants, and being sent unto and required by very devout religious folk to take some other order with him, caused him, as he came wandering by my door, to be taken by the constables and bound to a tree in the street before the whole town, and there they striped him with rods till he waxed weary, and somewhat longer. And it appeared well that his remembrance was good enough, save that it went about grazing till it was beaten home. For he could then very well rehearse his faults himself, and speak and treat very well, and promise to do afterwards as well. And verily God be thanked, I hear none harm of him now.

"And of all that ever came in my hand for heresy, as help me God, saving (as I said) the sure keeping of them, had never any of them any stripe or stroke given them, so much as a fillip on the forehead.

"But now tell the brethren many marvellous lies, of much cruel tormenting that heretics had in my house, so far forth that one Segar, a bookseller of Cambridge, which was in mine house about four or five days, and never had either bodily harm done him, or foul word spoken him, hath reported since, as I hear say, to divers, that he was bound to a tree in my garden, and thereto too piteously beaten, and yet besides that bound about the head with a cord and wrung till he fell down dead in a swoon. And this tale of his beating did Tyndale tell to an old acquaintance of his own, and to a good lover of mine, with one piece farther yet, that while the man was in beating, I spied a little purse of his hanging at his doublet, wherin the poor man had, as he said, five marks, and that caught I quickly to me, and pulled it from his doublet and put it in my bosom, and that Segar never saw it after, and therein I trow he said true, for no more did I neither, nor before neither, nor I trow no more did Segar himself."

From this it would seem that Tindale's report of Segar's false tale of the whipping and the twisted cord had, by the time of Foxe, got into the legend of Tewkesbury. On this declaration of Sir Thomas More, Sir James Mackintosh writes as follows:

This statement, so minute, so easily contradicted, if in any part false, was made public after his fall from power, when he was surrounded by enemies and could have no friends but the generous. He relates circumstances of public notoriety, or at least, so known to all his household, which it would have been rather a proof of insanity than of imprudence to have alleged in his defence, if they had not been indisputably and confessedly true. Wherever he touches this subject, there is a quietness and a circumstantiality, which are among the least equivocal marks of a man who adheres to the temper most favourable to the truth, because he is conscious that the truth is favourable to him. . . . Defenceless and obnoxious as More then was, no man was hardy enough to dispute his truth. Foxe was the first who, thirty years afterwards, ventured to oppose it in a vague statement, which we know to be in some respects inaccurate; and on this slender authority alone has rested such an imputation on the veracity of the most sincere of men.

Since the days of Sir James Mackintosh another charge has been made against More. Mr. Anthony Froude writes: "I do not intend in this place to relate the stories of his cruelties in his house at Chelsea, which he himself partially denied, and which at least we may hope were exaggerated"; but Mr. Froude goes on to relate what he asserts to have been acts of illegal imprisonment committed by More. The first is that of Thomas Philips; the second, that of John Field. The evidence against Sir Thomas is merely that Mr. Froude found petitions to the king drawn up by the men themselves. Of the result of Field's petition Mr. Froude call tell nothing; of that of Philips he has to tell that his complaint was against the Bishop of London rather than against More, and that it was cast aside by the House of Lords as frivolous.

Mr. Froude does not seem to be aware that More himself has spoken of these very petitions. In the 38th chapter of his *Apology* he relates how Thomas Philips, a leatherseller, was brought before him when he was chancellor; he was examined with great leniency ("in as hearty loving manner as I could") and at last "I by indenture delivered him to his ordinary," but afterwards, for reasons enumerated,

> I advised, and by my means helped that he was received prisoner into the Tower. And yet after that he complained thereupon, not against me but against the ordinary. Whereupon the king's highness commanded certain of the greatest lords of his Council to know how the matter stood; which known and reported, his highness gave unto Philips such answer as, if he had been half so good as I would he were, of half so wise as himself weeneth he were, he would forthwith have followed, and not stand still in his obstinacy so long, as he hath now put himself thereby in another deeper peril.

Sir Thomas continues:

> Others have besides this complained that they have been unjustly handled, and they have nothing gotten but rebuke and shame. And some hath been heard upon importunate clamour, and the cause and handling examined by the greatest lords temporal of the king's most honourable council, and that since I left the office, and the complainour found in his complaining so very shameless false, that he hath been answered that he was too easily dealth with, and had wrong that he was no worse served.

Sir Thomas does not mention the names in these latter cases, nor does he say that the petitions of redress were made against himself; yet it seems likely that Field's complaint is the one last enumerated. In any case history contains no record that when Cromwell and the Earl of Wiltshire, and More's other enemies, were seeking charges against him, Field's complaints were considered worthy of attention. Yet Mr. Froude takes the fact that complaints were made as equivalent to a proof that they were well founded. Surely the great chancellor's integrity can survive a ruder shock than this. In the Debellacion of Salem and Bizance, Sir Thomas More again referred to the accusations of harshness as follows:

> The untruth of such false fame hath been before the king's honourable council of late well and plainly proved, upon sundry such false complaints by the king's gracious commandment examined. And albeit that this is a thing notoriously known, and that I have myself in mine Apology spoken thereof, and that, since that book gone abroad, it hath been in likewise before the lords well and plainly proved in more matters afresh, and albeit that this water washeth away all his matter, yet goeth ever this water over this goose's back, and for anything that any man can do, no man can make it sink unto the skin, that she may once feel it, but ever she shaketh such plain proofs off with her feathers of 'Some say,' and 'They say' the contrary.

The goose is still shaking her feathers in Mr. Froude's pages.

From all that has been gathered together in this chapter, I venture to conclude that there is no evidence of change in More's views as regards religious liberty, nor did his genial character become deteriorated or soured. He held strongly that the dogmatising heretics of those days, in the then circumstances of England and Christendom, should be forcibly repressed, and if necessary punished even by death, according to the existing laws. Yet in the administration of those laws he was not only rigidly upright, but as tender and merciful as is compatible with the character and office of a judge. "What other controversialist can be named," asks Sir James Mackintosh [in *Life of More*], "who, having the power to crush antagonists whom he viewed as the disturbers of the quiet of his own declining years, the destroyers of all the hopes which he had cherished for mankind, contented himself with severity of language?"

Karl Kautsky (essay date 1927)

SOURCE: "The Mode of Production of the Utopians: Criticism," in *Thomas More and His Utopia,* translated by H. J. Stenning, A. & C. Black, Ltd., 1927, pp. 204-14.

[*Kautsky, as the following chapter from his book demonstrates, is known among More scholars for present-*

ing the first significant argument that More's Utopia described and advocated a socialist state. Below, he contrasts More's "communist" Utopia with the aims of modern Socialism.]

Nobody with any knowledge of the subject would assert that More's aims are in complete agreement with the tendencies of modern scientific Socialism, which is based on two factors: the development of the proletariat as a class and the development of large-scale machine production, which enlists science in its service and to-day imposes a scheme of systematically organised social labour within each undertaking. Large-scale industry constitutes the technical foundation upon which, as modern Socialism holds, the proletariat will shape production in accordance with its interests, when it becomes a politically decisive factor.

The capitalist mode of production, however, developed its evils at an earlier time than it created the elements which are destined to remove them. The proletariat must become a permanent institution and an important section of the people before it is conscious of itself as a class and can reveal itself to the investigator as the power which will bear the burden of social reorganisation. On the other hand, under the system of commodity production, large-scale industry can only develop in the capitalistic form; it only becamepossible when large masses of capital had accumulated in a few hands, which were confronted with an army of propertyless, work-seeking proletarians.

Capital and proletariat, mass poverty and great wealth must exist for a long time before they develop the seeds of a new society. So long as such seeds are not disclosed, all attempts to remove the evils of the capitalist mode of production by the introduction of an alternative system are futile, and Socialism is doomed to remain of a Utopian character.

This was still the position at the beginning of the nineteenth century. How much more unfavourable was it in More's time! At the beginning of the nineteenth century there was already a Labour Movement with definite aims; the only Labour Movement that More was acquainted with consisted of a few secret leagues and despairing revolts of artisan and peasant elements. At the beginning of the nineteenth century the transition from capitalist manufacture to large-scale industry could be clearly perceived. In More's time capitalism was just beginning to gain the upper hand over the industry and agriculture of England. Its domination had not lasted long enough to effect a technical revolution; the difference between capitalist and simple commodity production was of degree rather than of kind. The worker who wove wool for the merchant did so in the same way as the members of the Weavers' Guild. The difference consisted merely in the fact that the merchant employed more workers than the master weaver,

and that the master weaver's journeymen had every prospect of becoming masters themselves, while the wage worker of the capitalist merchant had no chance of ever becoming a capitalist. The distinction between the capitalist and the guild mode of production was then only of a social, not of a technical character: handicraft was the basis of one as of the other.

Agriculture was in a like case. The undertakings of capitalist farmers were at first distinguished from those of feudal settlers by their magnitude. There was little to be seen of improvements in methods of cultivation or the use of perfected tools. Men were made superfluous, not by an increase in the productivity of agricultural labour, but by the transition to a ruder form of agricultural production, from cornfields to pasturage.

However obvious, therefore, certain of the evils of capitalism were in More's time, the technical foundations upon which it was based, and upon which More was obliged to build up his anti-capitalist commonwealth, were still handicraft and peasant agriculture.

It is clear that More could not avoid deviating in many points from modern Socialism. Reactionary as he seems to us in many respects, if one is so foolish as to measure him by the standards of the twentieth and not by the sixteenth century—being, in consequence of the backwardness of the proletariat, an opponent of every popular movement and a champion of constitutional monarchy—More's Socialism often appears retrogressive in an economic respect. The surprising thing is, however, that in spite of the unfavourable conditions, More's Socialism does exhibit so many of the most essential features of modern Socialism that he may rightly be counted among modern Socialists.

The unmodern aspects of More's Communism are the necessary consequences of the mode of production he was obliged to take as his starting-point. The chief of these reactionary features is the attachment of every man to a specific handicraft.

The most important work in modern large-scale industry is assigned to science, which methodically investigates the mechanical and chemical forces employed in production, and also investigates the mechanical and chemical properties of the various materials whose transformation is the object of production, and finally directs the application of the technical principles it has investigated. Onlya few easily learned movements in connection with supervising the machinery or the chemical processes are left to the hand worker.

This vacuity and simplicity of manual labour is to-day one of the most important causes of its degrading tendency. It no longer employs or attracts the mind, and is repellent and blunting in its effect. It permits skilled labour to be replaced by unskilled, and strong workers by weak workers. It also frees the capitalists to an increasing extent from the necessity of keeping a staff of skilled workers. And simultaneously the conditions of production are constantly being transformed by the application of science to production, for science does not rest, nor does the pressure of competition to effect new improvements. The machine of yesterday is obsolete to-day, and out of the running to-morrow.

When the proletariat directs production, it will transform these causes of the degradation of the working class into so many instruments for its elevation. The simplification of machine movements renders it possible for the worker to change his work from time to time, bringing into play a number of muscles and nerves whose harmonious activity will impart vitality just as unproductive gymnastics do to-day. Successively engaged in the most diverse occupations, he will then become conscious of his latent capabilities, and from a machine will become a free man. And the simultaneous preoccupation with the sciences, which will come with a shorter working day, will restore intellectual meaning to his work, by disclosing its connection with the totality of technical and economic processes and their roots.

Instead of changes of work, which is only possible with large-scale production, and will also be necessary if the working class is not to degenerate, More prescribes the attachment of every worker to a specific handicraft. In handicraft the handling of the tool and the knowledge of its effect upon the raw material is not the result of methodical and scientific investigation, but is the accumulation of personal, often haphazard, experiences. This is also the case with manufacture, where, however, each division of production is split up into various detail processes, to each of which a worker is permanently assigned, and to learn which does not, of course, require as much time as is necessary to learn all the movements and methods of a specific process of production. While it is necessary in manufacture to keep a worker for a long time at his detail process, in order to acquire the needful skill to make his labour as productive as possible, in handicraft it is a technical necessity to put a worker to a certain trade in youth, so that from constant intercourse with a skilled master, he may become acquainted with all the traditions of the trade. This apprenticeship did not appear an evil, as handicraft still possessed a certain charm.

But how shall we deal with the work of day labourers, who were already very numerous in More's time, with the dirty work—slaughtering, sanitary services, etc.? These unpleasant labours, a favourite objection of the Philistine to Socialism, have been a thorn in the flesh for all Utopists. Fourier tried to solve the problem by introducing psychological motives, often very ingeniously contrived, into work. More attempted to achieve

something similar, as we have seen, by the lever of religion, which was so strong in his time. But as he did not consider this sufficient, he was obliged to have recourse to the compulsory labour of slaves, and to introduce into his commonwealth a class without property and rights working for others. He resorts to all kinds of devices to soften this institution by pointing to persons in that class who might otherwise have been overtaken by a worse fate. To remove the degraded class entirely was impossible for him, given the technical foundation of his speculations. Only modern large-scale industry provides the full opportunity for adjusting the various kinds of work, and so simplifying the residue of unpleasant work as to permit of its alternate performance by all capable of labour, thus abolishing any special compulsion upon an unfortunate class of workers. The distinction between pleasant and unpleasant work has largely disappeared, inasmuch as work which was formerly pleasant has been divested of every attraction. But modern technology has also succeeded in lightening or abolishing many unpleasant tasks. On the whole, however, technology has not hitherto accomplished very much in this direction. To make work more pleasant is not the task which capitalism assigns to it. Capitalism desires a saving of labour-power, even though the unpleasantness of work be increased. Only when the working class exercises a decisive influence upon the mode of production, will science be utilised to throw its whole weight into solving the problem of abolishing unpleasant labours. And there is no problem of this kind which modern technology could not solve as soon as it seriously applied itself thereto. Moreover, a great part of the unpleasant work of to-day will be abolished by the transfer of industry to the countryside, of which we shall have to speak.

A third feature which contradicts modern Socialism may be referred to in this connection: the frugality of the Utopians.

More's intention is—and this is quite a modern feature—to free the citizens of his commonwealth as much as possible from physical labour, in order to procure them leisure for intellectual and social activity. His chief means to this end are the organisation of labour, to avoid all the useless work which the existing anarchy introduces into the economic life, and which was comparatively slight in More's time, and finally the restriction of wants.

The first two points More has in common with modern Socialism, but not the last. To speak to-day of the necessity of restricting wants, in order to shorten working hours, would imply a strange misconception of the conditions of our age of over-production, where one technical improvement follows another, where the mode of production has reached such a level of productivity that it theatens to burst the framework of capitalism, in order to develop without hindrance.

It was different in More's time. The productivity of handicraft developed very slowly, and sometimes completely ossified. And so it was with peasant agriculture. No considerable increase of production in relation to the number of workers could be expected from a communism established on this foundation. Consequently, wants had to be limited if it was desired to reduce hours of labour.

The effect of capitalism, as More saw it, was not over-production, but scarcity. Pasturage was extended at the expense of agriculture, resulting in a rise in the prices of food, which was partly caused by the flow of silver and gold from America to Europe. What, however, was of greater weight with More in making his Utopians of frugal manners was the senseless luxury of his age. A luxury in clothing as in the furnishing of houses, an excessive pomp, developed, which served not for the satisfaction of an artistic need, but the display of wealth. It is easy to understand why More combated this with great vigour, and why he went to the opposite extreme in clothing his Utopians with skins and uniform woollen garments.

Do not, however, believe that More preached a monkish asceticism. On the contrary, we shall see him revealed as a true Epicurean in respect of harmless enjoyments which did not impose superfluous work upon the community.

Here, as elsewhere, his unmodern ideas appear as limitations imposed upon him by the backwardness of his age, without influencing him to the extent of obscuring the essentially modern character of his ideals.

This becomes obvious when we consider what features More's Socialism has in common with present-day Socialism, in contrast both to primitive communism, with whose vestiges More became acquainted, and to Plato's communism, with which, as we know, he was familiar.

We have already noted how world commerce broke down the exclusiveness and restrictions of the primitive community, beyond which even Plato did not advance, as he put the nation as an economic unity in place of the village community.

But world trade also broke down the caste system of the primitive communities.

Like the medieval towns, the Platonic Republic was divided into rigidly defined castes, and Plato's communism was a privilege of the supreme caste.

On the other hand, the vital principle of capitalism is free competition: equality of competitive conditions for everybody, and therefore abolition of caste distinctions. If capitalism united the small communities into a na-tion, it also tended to absorb all castes into one nation.

This tendency of capitalism also coincides with More's communism. It is national in contrast to the local and caste communism of the past, with which More was acquainted by experience and study. In this, he was more modern than present-day Anarchism, which aims at splitting up the nation into independent groups and communes.

We have seen that the Senate of the Utopians consists of delegates from the various communities; it is this representative body of the nation which organises production, estimates the needs which it is to supply, and divides the labour produce according to the results of these statistics. The local communities are not commodity producers, exchanging their products for those of other communities. Each one produces for the whole nation. The nation, and not the local community, is also the owner of the means of production; above all, of the land. And not the local community, but the Commonwealth as a whole sells to foreign countries the superfluity of products and receives the proceeds of such sale. Gold and silver constitute the war chest of the nation.

The equality of all members of the community, however, which under capitalism only implies an equality of competitive conditions, becomes, under More's communism, an equal obligation of all to labour. This great principle connects it most closely with modern Socialism, and distinguishes it most sharply from Plato's communism, which is a communism of non-workers, of exploiters. The privileged class of the Platonic Republic, the "guardians," who alone practise communism, regarded work as something degrading; they lived on the tribute from the working citizens.

There is only one unimportant exception from the equal obligation to labour in *Utopia:* among the able-bodied a few scholars are exempted. This exception was necessary under the system of handicraft, where manual work was too onerous to leave time for mental activity.

The existence of compulsory labour, of course, contravenes the equality of the Utopians. We have seen what the explanation of this contradiction is. Moreover, More himself, in making this concession to the backwardness of the contemporary mode of production, preserved the modern character as much as possible, inas much as he made the bondsmen, not a hereditary caste, but a class. The bondsmen are either foreign wage workers, who may change their position if they desire, or declassed persons condemned to forced labour, owing to their misconduct, with the chance of retrieving their characters.

Specially noteworthy and completely in line with present-day Socialism is the equal obligation to work imposed on man and woman, the assigning to woman an industrial vocation. Women as well as men must learn a handicraft. . . .

An important and characteristic feature of the mode of production of the Utopians has yet to be mentioned: the removal of the antagonism between town and country.

This problem is a wholly modern one, due to the concentration of industry in the towns. In More's time the solution of the problem was not so pressing as it is today. Yet the antagonism between town and country had already developed pretty considerably in many countries. This may be inferred from the rise of pastoral poetry (first in Italy in the fifteenth century) which expressed the longing of the townsman for the country.

More had a particularly good opportunity to observe the tendency of the modern mode of production to increase the size of the great towns, for London was one of the most rapidly growing towns of that time.

More himself left London as often as he could to stay in the village of Chelsea.

The conditions of London and More's own inclinations combined to convince him of the necessity for abolishing the antagonism between town and country.

This can only be done by transferring industry to the countryside, by combining industrial with agricultural labour. If, however, this adjustment is not to lead to general rustication, the technical means must exist to remove that isolation which is necessarily bound up with small peasant farming, means for the communication of ideas by other methods than personal intercourse—newspapers, post, telegraph, telephone, must be highly developed, as well as means for the transport of products, machines, raw materials, and persons: railways, steamers, motor traffic. Finally, every agricultural undertaking must be so extensive as to permit of the concentration of a larger number of workers in one spot.

All these preliminary conditions were entirely absent in More's time. His aim, however, was a higher level of mental culture, not the rustication of the whole people. This combination of agricultural with industrial labour was, therefore, impossible for him, and he was obliged to content himself with prescribing a certain period of agricultural labour for every citizen, making children familiar with it from an early age, and setting a limit to the size of the towns. We shall learn that no town might number more or less than 6,000 families, comprising ten to sixteen adults. These devices do not, of course, harmonise with modern Socialism, but they were a necessity imposed upon More by the small-scale production of his time.

We observe again that More's aims are modern, but their realisation was prevented by the backwardness of the mode of production of his time. This was sufficiently developed to enable an observer like More, methodically trained and specially cognisant of the economic conditions, and under the particularly favourable circumstances which England then offered, to perceive its tendencies, but not far enough developed to disclose the means of overcoming these tendencies.

Thus More's communism is modern in most of its tendencies, and unmodern in most of its expedients.

H. W. Donner (essay date 1945)

SOURCE: "Communism?" and "Solution," in *Introduction to Utopia*, Sidgwick & Jackson, Ltd., 1945, pp. 66-83.

[*In the following chapters from his critical study* Introduction to Utopia, *Donner addresses the debate concerning More's portrayal of communism; he concludes that the* Utopia *indirectly rejects communism as a solution to social ills, arguing that human behavior, rather than social institutions, must change.*]

So far the apparent tendency of the *Utopia* seems to agree tolerably well with what we know of that "righteous and holy judge" who was its author. But we are not going to escape so easily. Of all the features of the Utopian commonwealth the most notable is the community of ownership. Yet we possess a most emphatic contradiction of the very principle of communism from the pen of More himself. In the **Dialogue of Comfort against Tribulation,** written during his imprisonment in the Tower, in expectancy of martyrdom, at a moment when he was opening his heart wholly to God, More wrote:

> But, cousin, men of substance must there be, for else shall you have more beggars, pardie, than there be, and no man left able to relieve another. For this I think in my mind a very sure conclusion, that if all the money that is in this country, were to-morrow next brought together out of every man's hand, and laid all upon one heap, and then divided out unto every man alike, it would be on the morrow after worse than it was the day before. For I suppose when it were all equally thus divided among all, the best should be left little better then, than almost a beggar is now. And yet he that was a beggar before, all that he shall be the richer for that he should thereby receive, shall not make him much above a beggar still, but many one of the rich men, if their riches stood but in moveable substance, shall be safe enough from riches for all their life after.

> Men cannot, you wot well, live here in this world, but if that some one man provide a mean of living for some other many. Every man cannot have a ship of his own, nor every man be a merchant withouta stock; and these things, you wot well, must needs be had; nor every man cannot have a plough by himself. And who might live by the tailor's craft, if no man were able to put a gown to make? Who by the masonry or who could live a carpenter, if no man were able to build neither church, nor house? Who should be makers of any manner cloth, if there lacked men of substance to set sundry sorts a work? Some man that hath but two ducats in his house, were better forbear them both and leave himself not a farthing, but utterly lose all his own, than that some rich man, by whom he is weekly set a work should of his money lose the one half; for then were himself like to lack work. For surely the rich man's substance is the wellspring of the poor man's living. And therefore here would it fare by the poor man, as it fared by the woman in one of Æsop's fables, which had an hen that laid her every day a golden egg; till on a day she thought she would have a great many eggs at once, and therefore she killed her hen, and found but one or twain in her belly, so that for covetise of those few, she lost many.

In the course of nearly twenty years that had passed between the writing of **Utopia** and the **Dialogue of Comfort** More might have changed his mind, as [Karl] Kautsky believed. For a long time that was the accepted view. And in fact, even in his life-time he was charged with inconsistency by [William] Tyndale. The accusation didnot concern communism, it is true, but it presents the same problem. Twitting him with the *Encomium Moriae,* written in his house and dedicated to him by his "darling" Erasmus, Tyndale wants to show that More did not always look with any great reverence upon the images and relics of the saints. More answered the charge. After quoting Tyndale's words he writes:

> If this be true, then the more cause have I to thank God for amendment. But surely this is untrue. For, God be thanked! I never had that mind in my life to have holy saints' images or their holy relics out of reverence. Nor, if there were any such thing in *Moria,* that thing could not yet make any man see that I were myself of that mind, the book being made by another man, though he were my darling never so dear. Howbeit, that book of *Moria* doth indeed but jest upon the abuses of such things, after the manner of the disour's part in a play.

The **Utopia** was not written by another man, but the praises of communism were certainly laid in another man's mouth. Was Raphael Hythloday playing the Jester's part in the comedy of **Utopia**?

How important is the question of interpretation we may gather from the continuation. "In these days", More goes on to say,

> in which men by their own default, misconstrue, and take harm of the very scripture of God, until men better amend, if any man would now translate *Moria* into English, or some works either that I have myself written ere this, albeit there be none harm therein, folk yet being (as they are) given to take harm of that that is good, I would not only my darling's books but mine own also, help to burn them both with mine own hands, rather than folk should (though through their own fault) take any harm of them, seeing that I see them likely in these days so to do.

More does not repudiate **Utopia,** but times have changed, and he seems to fear lest it should be misinterpreted.

In his **Apology,** published in 1533, when after his resignation he stood alone and in need of making his position clear beyond doubt, there is an interesting passage concerning private ownership, which takes us back at any rate two years nearer the publication of *Utopia*. Refuting the "Pacifyer" who had suggested the confiscation of the superfluous property of the Church, More answers with passion: "But by what right men may take away from any man, spiritual or temporal, against his will, the land that is already lawfully his own, that thing this pacifyer telleth us not yet." Then More goes on to relate the amusing experiences he has had inmaking people imagine instances where a change of ownership might seem suitable. At first they had always been enthusiastic, but on second thoughts they had usually had to give up the attempt of introducing a better order of things.

> Not for that we might not always find other enough content to enter into their possessions, though we could not always find other men enough content to enter into their religions, but for that in devising what way they should be better bestowed, such ways as at the first face seemed very good, and for the comfort and help of poor folk very charitable, appeared after upon reasoning, more likely within a while to make many beggars more than to relieve them that are already.

The argument is the same as in the *Dialogue of Comfort,* and for a more detailed statement of his views on the question of the confiscation of property More refers us to the lengthier argumentation of his own *Supplication of Souls,* which had been published as early as 1530.

More's arguments are chiefly two. One is that no improvement would result if one man's goods were taken away from him and given to other people. The second is that it would be against the law. Remembering with what determination, not to say ferocity even, the Utopians upheld the law, it may be worth while going back to the argumentation which introduces the description of communist Utopia in the first book.

Raphael takes up the question of a redistribution of property, limiting the share of each private citizen and each officer of the crown—even of the king himself, as Fortescue had indeed suggested—to a certain statutory amount. But, he says, this would not solve the problem, for people would start enriching themselves anew and "while you go about to do your cure of one part, you shall make bigger the sore of another part: so the help of one causeth another's harm, forasmuch as nothing can be given to any man, unless it be taken from another". As to the utility of such an attempt there seems to be complete agreement between the opinion voiced by Hythloday and More's own. And in point of law also, surprising as this may seem, there seems to be a considerable amount of unison. For Hythloday says that "here among us, every man hath

his possessions several to himself", a statement of fact, comparable to More's phrase concerning "the land that is already lawfully his own", just quoted from the *Apology*. About the legality of this arrangement there is as little doubt in the mind of Hythloday as in More's own. Nor does Raphael even question the justice of it, unless we attribute to his words a meaning which they do not seem to contain. All that he denies is: "that justice is there executed where all things come into the hands of evil men"; and where all except very few are compelled to "live miserably, wretchedly, and beggarly". This is the real problem.

Reasoning in favor of communism, Raphael argues that "where every man under certain titles and pretences draweth and plucketh to himself as much as he can, and so a few divide among themselves all the riches that there is" (the problem in England at that time), "be there never so much abundance and store, there to the residue is left lack and poverty". And, as if he had said that private property is the cause of greed and covetousness, he concludes that "wheresoever possessions be private, where money beareth all the stroke, it is hard and almost impossible that there the weal public may justly be governed and prosperously flourish". He seems to blame the institution of private property for making men evil. More has met that argument in his *Apology,* and he could have contradicted it most emphatically in the *Utopia,* had he wanted to do so. For the sake of argument, however, he lets Hythloday score the point and confines his objections in the dialogue to the utility of communism.

> But I am of a contrary opinion (quod I) for methinks that all men shall never there live wealthily where all things be common. For how can there be abundance of goods, or of anything, where every man withdraweth his hand from labour? whom the regard of his own gains driveth not to work, and the hope that he hath in other men's travails maketh him slothful. Then when they be pricked with poverty, and yet no man can by any law or right defend that for his own, which he hath gotten with the labour of his own hands, shall not there of necessity be continual sedition and bloodshed? specially the authority and reverence of magistrates being taken away; which what place it may have with such men, among whom is no difference, I cannot devise.

The objection that there would be no respect for authority if all were made equal, is particularly interesting, for More's battle in life was always in defence of authority against the anarchy that was threatening, a defence to which he stuck even on the scaffold. In the dialogue he argues also that the institution of private property may encourage people to virtue, whereas community of goods might lead them to indulge in the sin of slothfulness, thus meeting Hythloday on his own ground, and making the reader forget how he got there.

Raphael, however, shows no surprise at these objections. His answer is ready: nobody who has not seen the Utopian commonwealth can know anything about communism, his views are prejudiced and of no validity. And so Raphael tells his story. Yet even at the end the More of the dialogue remains sceptical. "Many things", he says,

> came to my mind which in the manners and laws of that people seemed to be instituted and founded of no good reason, . . . and chiefly, in that which is the principal foundation of all their ordinaces, that is to say, in the community of their life and living.

It must be admitted, I think, that More could not have argued more strongly against communism without destroying his own fiction. We accept it as a potential reality because More tricks us to accept it. Evincing a consummate skill in the manipulation of the dialogue he makes us first accept reason, and not human ability, as the standard by which to judge whether something may be realised or no. Secondly he deliberately deceives us into blaming institutions, instead of human nature, as the cause of abuses and injustice. In this way he persuades us that society can be cured of all the evils besetting it, if only the institutions were reasonable. Raphael Hythloday's argument in favour of "cure" is allowed to get the better of More's own, which is that we should so contrive that"what you cannot turn to good, so to order it that it be not very bad", and which is dismissed by Raphael as effecting at the best no more than a "mitigation" of evil. This is the manner in which More brings about his brilliant *jeu d'esprit*. Without this deception there would have been no Utopia, or if there had, it must have been taken to be More's own ideal.

It is possible to marshal even more arguments against the identification of Hythloday's Utopian fiction with More's practical suggestions for reform. When at the end he says that he must "needs confess and grant, that many things be in the Utopian weal public, which in our cities I may rather wish for than hope after", More uses a phrase (*optarim verius quam sperarim*) which in Humanist terminology means that it would be too good to be true. He expresses it very similarly earlier on when he says that "it is not possible for all things to be well, unless all men were good: which I think will not be yet this good many years". More's "twin spirit" Erasmus had used a similar locution in his *Institutio principis Christiani,* where he said that "it is too much even to hope that all men will be good". And the phrase returns in More's *Apology:* "Would God the world were such as every man were good . . . But sith that this is more easy to wish, than likely to look for" . . . the cure is not as simple as that, and does not lie in a change-over from one political system to another.

As for communism it is instructive to glance for a moment at the opinions of other members of that group of humanists whose unison of thought is such that one can often use the words of one to express the ideas of another. In his criticism of the doctrines of the Anabaptists Vives, Erasmus' pupil and More's friend who so warmly recommended the *Utopia,* puts the argument against communism more strongly than either of them, when he protests against "the recent iniquitous wars" and the demand of the rebels for property to be held in common,

> whereas you cannot by any promulgation transfer the virtue of man's mind, or his wisdom, judgment, memory, into common property. Or even if you limit the demand to material things, the taking of the student's books away from him for the use of the soldier will not be recompensed by the student's joint use of the implements of war.

Erasmus also, speaking on the same subject, says that the communism attempted in practice "was only possible when the Church was small, and then not among all Christians: as soon as the Gospel spread widely, it became quite impossible. The best way towardsagreement is that property should be in the hands of lawful owners, but that out of charity we should share one with another".

During the last years of More's life communism was no joking matter, as indicated in the *Confutation,* and when he tackles the problem of how to reconcile private property with Christianity in his *Dialogue of Comfort,* More reaches much the same conclusion as Erasmus though as always he evinces an appreciation of the practical difficulties which escaped his learned friend. And in reading this extract we must not forget that More was "the best friend the poor e'er had."

> But now, cousin, to come to your doubt, how it may be that a man may with conscience keep riches with him, when he seeth so many poor men upon whom he may bestow it; verily that might he not with conscience do, if he must bestow it upon as many as he may. And so must of truth every rich man do, if all the poor folk that he seeth be so specially by God's commandment committed unto his charge alone, that because our Saviour saith, *Omni petenti te, da,* Give every man that asketh thee, therefore he be bounden to give out still to every beggar that will ask him, as long as any penny lasteth in his purse. But verily, cousin, that saying hath (as St. Austin saith other places in Scripture hath) need of interpretation. For as holy St. Austin saith: Though Christ say, Give every man that asketh thee, he saith not yet, give them all that they will ask thee. But surely all were one, if he meant to bind me by commandment, to give every man without exception somewhat; for so should I leave myself nothing.

Our Saviour in that place of the 6th chapter of St. Luke, speaketh both of the contempt that we should in heart have of these worldly things, and also of the manner that men should use toward their enemies. For there he biddeth us love our enemies, give good words for evil, and not only suffer injuries patiently, both by taking away of our good and harm done unto our body, but also to be ready to suffer the double, and over that to do them good again that do us the harm. And among these things, he biddeth us give every man that asketh, meaning, that in the thing that we may conveniently do a man good, we should not refuse it, what manner of man soever he be, though he were our mortal enemy, namely where we see, that but if we help him ourself, the person of the man should stand in peril of perishing. And therefore saith St. Paul, *Si esurierit inimicus tuus, da illi cibum,*—If thine enemy be in hunger give him meat. But now, though I be bounden to give every manner man in some manner of his necessity, were he my friend or my foe, Christian man or heathen; yet am I not unto all men bounden alike, nor unto any man in every case alike. But, as I began to tell you, the differences of the circumstances make great change in the matter.

St. Paul saith, *Qui non providet suis, est infideli deterior,*—He that provideth not for those that are his, is worse than an infidel. Those are ours that are belonging to our charge, either by nature, or law, or any commandment of God.

In this passage we come extraordinarily near to the meaning of *Utopia* and may be able to judge better of that unique consistency which marks More's life and writings. *Utopia* was not a programme either for imperialist expansion, as Oncken would have it, nor for a communist revolution, as Kautsky thought. If it had been understood as a plea for a communist state, would not this have been held against him by his enemies when More stood friendless at his trial? What he actually says in his own person in the dialogue of the first book is that if you want to improve things and influence ministers of state "you must not labour to drive into their heads new and strange informations". You must accept what order you find established and go slow about improving on it, lest you should end by marring rather than mending. This Hythloday admits, inasmuch as he says: "If so be that I should speak those things that Plato feigneth in his weal public, or that the Utopians do in theirs; these things though they were (as they be in deed) better, yet they might seem spoken out of place." Even Hythloday does not conceive of communism as a practical programme of reform, but what he has so far pleaded for, is that the greed and luxury of the rich should be restrained, that work should be provided for the poor, that kings should obstain from wars and conquest and seek peace and the welfare of their subjects. These recommendations he wants to push home, and so illustrates them with examples from the history and practice of fictitious peoples like the Polylerites and the Achorians. To More and Peter Giles, however, he tells his story of the happy state of the Utopians, and, the reader's mind being sufficiently prepared to accept the fiction, More publishes Hythloday's story as something "whereby these our cities, nations, countries, and Kingdoms may take example". It was More's manner to teach by means of examples, and like a modern Aesop he tells his fables about men instead of animals, but we must not forget that examples may be of various kinds and different application. They may encourage imitation, but they may warn us against it also. Even in the second book of *Utopia* More does not always point the way of the ascent to heaven, but that of the descent also into that hell whose glare flickers over its pages. And so he chose that double manner of praise and parody, making some things good in his ideal commonwealth and some things "very absurd", leaving it to the good sense of his readers to decide where he was in earnest and where he was speaking "in sport".

Returning now to the parallels that it is possible to draw between Utopia and Europe, we find that in the self-abnegating and austere communism of Utopia there lies concealed more than a vague likeness to the Christian monasteries, already threatened by the onslaught of a new age with "new and strange informations". Even more than in the common land agriculture, communism existed in the monasteries of Europe, and so the Utopian example becomes in this light a defence of the monasteries. Where it existed More did not want to see communism abolished, but he did not believe it was possible everywhere in this wretched state of the world. More did not believe in "cure", as did his own Raphael Hythloday, but he regarded it as the duty of all to try and "mitigate" the ills of this world. Nor has he left us in ignorance of the manner in which it should be undertaken. . . .

The Utopian commonwealth is ingeniously built up from suggestions in the narratives of Vespucci and Peter Martyr, combined with hints from Plato's *Republic* and *Laws,* the *Germania* of Tacitus, and other sources which describe the workings of a primitive society, if by primitive is meant a society living according to the law of nature. All Utopian institutions are founded on reason, and on reason alone. More has been careful never to exceed this self-imposed limitation. The Utopians have learned everything that the ancient philosophers can teach us, and even in their religion there is nothing for which there was no precedent in classical antiquity. Like their institutions, their philosophy and religion also are founded on reason. Their virtue consists in living according to nature, and the law of nature regulates their private and public life, their actions in peace as well as in war. As a synthesis of the best pagan customs and philosophical systems, of the political and religious thought of the pagan world, Utopia is an achievement of no small significance, a *tour de force* which delighted the humanists of the Renaissance and gained for its author a position among the foremost men of learning in Europe, excelling in wit, erudition, and style. To the learned it was not least for its scholarship that *Utopia* became an object of admiration. With a consistency that must impress minds trained in the school of the Platonic Academy of Florence and stimulated by the constructions of Pico and Reuchlin, More assigned to the Utopians a definite place in the order of the universe and in the history of mankind. To the common reader no such complexities need detract from his enjoyment of the book as a production of humanist wit, a *jeu d'esprit* of an uncommonly accessible nature.

Against the background of Europe ruled by Folly, as described by Erasmus in the *Moriae Encomium* or by More himself in the first book, Utopia is described as ruled by Reason. It is a picture that must stimulate even the most unthinking to some searching of heart. As the late R. W. Chambers put it, "the virtues of heathen Utopia show up by contrast the vices of Christian Europe". It is as a plea for Reason that the *Utopia* must strike the reader most forcibly. Against the background of insane tyranny and senseless war, Utopia enjoys both peace and freedom. Instead of lawlessness and anarchy in Europe, law and order in Utopia. It is an order based on respect for the dignity of man and the freedom of conscience, trampled under foot in contemporary Europe. Instead of the selfishness and greed of a few rich men depriving the European masses of their means of livelihood, collaboration for the common good providing plenty for all Utopian citizens. Instead of concentrating on material gains, the Utopians prefer the pleasures of the mind. Learning is there the property of all, whereas in Europe ignorance in the cloak of priesthood was persistently trying to stop the expansion of the mind. In Utopia there is no such contradiction, and, in words strongly reminiscent of Pico, More sets out the Utopian conviction of the agreement between the conclusions of an enquiring reason and the truths of a divinely inspired religion.

> For whilst they by the help of this Philosophy search out the secret mysteries of nature, they think that they not only receive thereby wonderful great pleasure, but also obtain great thanks and favour of the author and maker thereof. Whom they think, according to the fashion of other artificers, to have set forth the marvellous and gorgeous frame of the world for man to behold; whom only he hath made of wit and capacity to consider and understand the excellency of so great a work. And therefore, say they, doth he bear more good will and love to the curious and diligent beholder and viewer of his work, and marveller at the same, than he doth to him, which like a very beast without wit and reason, or as one without sense or moving, hath no regard to so great and so wonderful a spectacle.

Lest, however, we should be misled by the parallel to disapprove of the religious orders as such, More has given Utopia her monks also, who prefer hard manual labour to the contemplation of nature. For even the Utopians recognize that reason is not sufficient for the understanding of all mysteries in nature, and so in their philosophy they call on religion for the confirmation of the fundamental truths of the existence of God and man's immortality, postulated by reason. While from the nature of his sources he had to make his Utopians embrace an Epicurean doctrine of pleasure which might seem to conflict with the mediæval ideal of asceticism, More with his supreme intellectual facility dissolves the difficulty by making them recognize the insufficiency of reason to decide in what the felicity of man consists and so they come naturally to found morality on religion.

> They reason of virtue and pleasure. But the chief and principal question is in what thing, be it one or more, the felicity of man consisteth. But in this point they seem almost too much given and inclined to the opinion of them which defend pleasure; wherein they determine either all or the chiefest part of man's felicity to rest. And (which is more to be marvelled at) the defence of this so dainty and delicate an opinion they fetch even from their grave, sharp, bitter, and rigorous religion. For they never dispute of felicity or blessedness, but they join to the reasons of Philosophy certain principles taken out of religion; without the which, to the investigation of true felicity, they think reason of itself weak and unperfect.

It is in the spirit that inspires the Utopian commonwealth that we must seek the key to the interpretation of its meaning. This is to be found neither in its laws nor in its institutions. Utopia is not a country where everybody acts reasonably from choice only, but under a compulsion intolerable to modern minds. Utopian law is indeed a law as "ungentle and sharp" as it is inexorable. To Europe, however, God has given "the new law of clemency and mercy, under the which he ruleth us with fatherly gentleness, as his dear children". In our appreciation of Utopia we must consequently understand that her citizens labour under the handicap of that "ungentle and sharp law" which reflects their "grave, sharp, bitter, and rigorous religion," whereas to us Christians God has given not only reason to guide us, but he has also revealed to us his own law, which is love, and peace, and justice.

"Reason is servant to Faith and not enemy", said More, and so faith rises on the foundations of reason, like the pinnacles and spires from the roof of a cathedral. But reason alone can never arrive at the "fruition of the sight of God's glorious majesty face to face". To a disciple of St. Thomas Aquinas, Pico, and Colet, the most elevated pagan philosophy and religion could only be a preparation for the revelation of Christianity, and the first rungs on Jacob's ladder. The law of reason, which governs Utopia, is subservient to the Divine law, which ought to rule the behaviour of all Christians. Raphael Hythloday consequently tells us that we must not "wink at the most part of all those things which Christ taught us and so straitly forbade them to be winked at, that those things also which he whispered in the ears of his disciples, he commanded to be proclaimed openly on the house-tops". However ideal it might appear by contrast with the contemporary Europe, Utopia does not represent More's ultimate ideal. It is a state founded only upon reason and ruled by the "ungentle and sharp" law of nature. It does not embody the religion of Christ with its "new law of clemency and mercy". It is a state where slavery is permitted, although in a milder form than in classical antiquity, but it is not a state where all are brethren, as Christ would have it. It is a community where grievous offences against the law are punished with death, but "God commandeth us that we shall not kill".

Reason by itself is "weak and unperfect". Only God's guidance can bring man to the perfection for which He created him. Hence pagan behaviour cannot be a model for Christians to imitate, or as Erasmus put it in his *Institutio principis Christiani:* "Whenever you think of yourself as a prince, remember that you are a Christian prince! You should be as different from even the noble pagan princes as a Christian is from a pagan." Providence had not granted to the Utopians the privilege of Revelation, and so their manners cannot serve as models for those who have received revealed religion, even if the Utopian welcome extended to the Christians in Hythloday's party seems to indicate that they have not much farther to travel on the road of preparation for the reception of the mystery. So far they remain on the level of pagan philosophy, and the ultimate ideal is very much higher. Speaking of the great princes of antiquity, Erasmus says: "As it would be most disgraceful to be surpassed by them in any honorable deed of theirs, so it would be the last degree of madness for a Christian prince to wish to imitate them without change. The disgrace of being surpassed by the heathen was keenly felt by Vives in comparing the *Legenda Aurea* with the classical masterpieces of literature, relating not the lives of saints but of cruel soldiers and generals. Yet how much greater shame must not we feel, seeing that whereas we live at constant enmity one against the other, the Utopians have achieved a state of law and order. In spite of their hard laws they have surpassed us, not only in the perfection of their institutions, but in their mutual help and generosity and unreserved collaboration. Even in the instance of punishments they seem to have surpassed us, for whereas the Utopians inflict capital punishment only on hardened sinners, Europeans punish the loss of a little money with "the loss of man's life." In this manner of interpretation Raphael's arguments in the first book of *Utopia* derive the strongest possible support from the institutions of the Utopians, not in the likeness but in the differences between a Christian and a pagan state. Whereas the pagan Utopians may employ serfs to meet the needs of labour, the disgrace to Europe is almost inconceivable inasmuch as servitude in Utopia should be found preferable to so called "freedom" elsewhere. In attempting to understand More's meaning we must always remember this, that reason alone supports the Utopian laws and institutions, but reason has a claim on Europe also. It is not enemy to Faith, but servant. In the likeness of Utopia More shows how certain institutions in Europe, threatened by destruction, are founded on reason and so worth preserving, because where there is reason there is hope of religion. But for Christians to try and imitate Utopian institutions without change "would be the last degree of madness".

When therefore sociologists are concerned to show to what extent the Utopian ideal has been realised in modern society and to what degree it still remains unfulfilled, they are merely breaking up the Coloseum in order to build the Farnese Palace. They have seen only the stones and forgotten the vision. It was not the constitution of commonwealths that More desired to reform, but the spirit. The Utopian institutions can be nothing except "very absurd" without the spirit that informs them. They must not be copied, but surpassed by Christian institutions. The community of goods that reason recommends to the Utopians, must be excelled in the spiritual community of all Christians. It was the Christian monasteries that provided the pattern for the Utopian republic, and in More's mind it was they that represented the mundane revelation of the ultimate ideal.

It might be exemplified in concrete instances how far short of the Christian standard the Utopians actually fall. When the priests in Utopia are allowed to marry, this must not be understood as More's scheme for the reformation of the Church; it is merely that God has not granted them that personal intimacy which has only been made possible through the Incarnation. Utopian religious customs are no more models for the Christian Church than are the political institutions of that commonwealth, and so must not be taken literally. The fact that in Utopia God is worshipped under different names, is certainly not served up by More for imitation by the Catholic Church, to which in More's view God had alone revealed himself. The Utopians with reason as their sole guide can only convince themselves of the existence of God; about his nature they can know nothing. Hence toleration is natural to them. Yet I cannot agree with those who would have it not apply where Christianity is concerned, being a revealed religion and so admitting of no doubt as to the truth of its doctrine. The Divine law is a law "of clemency and mercy", and the Utopian toleration requires its counterpart in Christian charity. Whatever ideas he may have entertained concerning the reformation of the Church, and it would carry us too far to go into the question of its details, More left it to the Church itself. Even in the first part of *Utopia* where he so sharply criticizes European conditions, not sparing ecclesiastics any more than laymen, it is the abuses he condemns, not the institutions. What he is asking for, is that in the same way as reason was allowed to regulate life in Utopia, so reason illuminated by Divine revelation should be given a hearing in European affairs. Just as the Utopians live in strict obedience to the law of nature, so must we be ruled by the law of Christ. Temporal justice is "the strongest and surest bond of a commonwealth", says More, and he does not want us to set it aside, but man-made law must be tempered by the law of Christ which is itself the highest justice.

Such has long been the Roman Catholic interpretation of *Utopia,* and it has been convincingly restated during recent years. It has been maintained with characteristic vigour and eloquence by the late R. W. Chambers in his great biography of More. This was also the way in which his contemporaries understood More's intention, as plainly appears from Budé's remark that if only the three principles of Utopia, which he accurately defined as equality, love of peace, and contempt of gold, could be "fixed in the minds of all men, . . . We should soon see pride, covetousness, insane competition, and almost all other deadly weapons of our adversary the devil, fall powerless." By showing how far short of the Utopians contemporary Europe fell in the practice of the four cardinal virtues of wisdom, fortitude, temperance, and justice, More wanted to stimulate us not only in the exercise of mundane virtue but of the Christian virtues also of faith, hope, and charity. In St. Augustine's terminology we may say that in Utopia More gives us such a description of a *vita socialis,* based only on the four pagan virtues, as must most forcibly remind us of our duty by means of an ardent exercise of the three Christian virtues to prepare for the *Civitas Dei.* Self-love, according to St. Augustine, is the opposite to the love of God, and so it is the love of self in all its utterances from mere vanity to cruel tyranny that More attacks most violently in the first book of Utopia, showing us in the second how the noble Utopians have eschewed self from all their dealings and find their greatest pleasure in working for the good of all and in actively helping their fellows. We cling to our worldly treasure, but the Utopians gladly give up their houses every ten years. More does not want us to imitate this custom, which no doubt he would have described as "very absurd", but he did want us to feel that one house is "as nigh heaven" as another. More did not want us to give everything away, but he did want us to use our wealth in such a way that it should not be said that in our states "money beareth all the stroke"; not for the increase of our own luxury, but for the relief of poverty, so that the prosperity of our society might rival that of Utopia itself. The love of power, which in the guise of the new Machiavellian statecraft was ruining Europe, was in More's view but another outcome of the love of self. In Utopia, however, aggressors are so cruelly punished that they are not likely to disturb the peace a second time.

Religion must reinforce the arguments of reason and Christian society surpass the pagan. It is not our institutions that we must destroy, but those evil passions which are at the root of the abuses. More's programme of reform was one of personal amelioration. "There is nothing better", John Colet, his teacher and confessor, had written to Erasmus, "than that we should lead a pure and holy life, which in my judgment will never be attained but by the ardent love and imitation of Jesus". Had not St. Matthew told us also, that "the disciple is not above his master, nor the servant above his lord". More had not forgotten the lesson, and his own passion bears witness to his pious striving to imitate his Master.

In his *Apology* More did not omit pointing to the personal responsibility of each individual for the good of all. Speaking of the "faults, enormities, and errors" that beset both state and church, he says these he would wish to have amended, "and every man specially labour to mend himself". This is the advice also that Raphael Hythloday would have wished to give his king—to "let him rather amend his own life, renounce unhonest pleasures, and forsake pride". And in the next instance More asks all to work together to eliminate the faults of society, "observed in the doing evermore such order and fashion as may stand and agree with reason and justice, the king's laws of the realm, the Scripture of God, and the laws of Christ's Church, ever keeping love and concord. . . . This has been hitherto the whole sum of my writing." Neither did More neglect to rub in the lesson, "for I think every man's duty toward God is so great, that very few folk serve him as they should do".

If, then, one should want to sum up the *Utopia* in a few inadequate words—for the subject is interminable—one may say that:

In the first book More analyses the evils that beset early sixteenth century English society—and to some extent these are the evils of all human society—and makes suggestions how they might be mitigated. The second book is a moral fable, intended to delight with its wit and ingenuity while it teaches a lesson in private and public morals by means of an example. It does not describe the ultimate ideal, but one that is practicable enough, which we are asked not slavishly to copy, but to surpass and excel. The *Utopia* does not attempt a final solution of the problems of human society—for More was too wise to attempt the impossible—but it contains an appeal addressed to all of us, which allows of no refusal, that we should try and do each one his share to mend our own selves and ease the burden of our fellow-men, to improve mankind and prepare for the life to come. In this lies its enduring power, that however high we may fix the ideal, to whatever perfection we may attain, More points higher still, from matter to the spirit, and from man to God.

Kaufmann asserts *Utopia's* historical singularity:

[Three] hundred and sixty years ago, shortly before the outburst of popular discontent, social, political, and religious, culminating in the Reformation, there appeared a small book, creating no little stir in the learned world of the day, the "Utopia" of Sir Thomas More, who became presently Lord Chancellor of England under King Henry VIII. In that book were reflected, in a wonderful manner, the social discontents and aspirations of the age. It has been called the only work of genius of that age in England, and its merit consisted in producing, in thoughtful and cultured language, the undefined ideas and longings of the people all over Europe.

M. Kaufmann, in Utopias; or, Schemes of Social Improvement, *C. Kegan, Paul & Co., 1879.*

David Bevington (essay date 1961)

SOURCE: "The Dialogue in *Utopia:* Two Sides of the Question," in *Studies in Philology,* Vol. 58, No. 1, January, 1961 pp. 496-509.

[*In the following essay, Bevington suggests that the dialogue form of the* Utopia *provides a clue to the author's opinions: More identified with neither Hythloday nor the character named More, but used the discussion to present "a dialogue of the mind with itself."*]

Students of *Utopia* are divided in their interpretation of Thomas More's political and economic opinions. Is More himself for oragainst common ownership of property? Writers on the question have tended to fall into two clearly defined camps, according to mankind's innate tendency to be born into this world as "either a little Liberal, Or else a little Conservative," and the polemical conflict between the factions has assumed in the context of our uneasy modern world the proportions of ideological warfare. The revered name of Thomas More has been invoked in support of the radical socialist states of the Soviet world empire, as well as in support of the anti-Communist position of the Papacy. Both interpretations purport to be founded on a critical reading of *Utopia.*

One literary reason why *Utopia* has lent itself to such divergence of opinion is its basic genre: the dialogue. More's island community is essentially the focal point for an extended discussion on government and society between various speakers or *personae,* each a character created by the author and having his individual point of view: Peter Giles, Hythloday, and the *persona* More who may or may not represent the views of Thomas More the writer. Giles's part in the discussion is minor, but Hythloday and *persona* More present two fundamental sides to the question. Hythloday's platform is the common ownership of property, and he refuses to concede the feasibility of gradual reform in a monarchical society. The *persona* More is often forthrightly opposed to the doctrine of common ownership, and argues instead for a policy of compromise and slow change within the limitations of practical politics. Their dialogue concludes in apparent lack of reconciliation of these opposing points of view. Accordingly, the critic can choose his hero. If Thomas More speaks directly for himself through the name of More, as he does in his later dialogues against Tyndale, then Hythloday is a dangerous public enemy like Tyndale whose dogmas are explicated only to be exploded. If on the other hand Thomas More uses his own name merely as a protective device in order to propound through Hythloday an essentially subversive political philosophy, then the *persona* More may be viewed as a dupe or stooge, setting up straw men to be demolished in orderly succession by the invincible progressive.

Between the cry of voices from both sides, the middle position of regarding *Utopia* as the impartial presentation of two points of view, as a dialogue of the mind with itself, has received less attention than it deserves. The moderate stand is an unglamorous one. It does not have the ineluctable force of an idea carried to its logical absolute. Nevertheless the moderate position has much to commend itself in the writings of the eminently fairminded and humorously wise Thomas More. Our present purpose is to suggest thecritical basis for supposing that Hythloday and *persona* More represent the two polarities of More's own mind, by an analysis of *Utopia* in terms of its genre and its historical perspective.

As a literary technique, the dialogue is often used for purposes of refutation, for demonstrating the patent superiority of one idea over another. In this method the creator of the dialogue possesses the enviable advantage of being able to speak on behalf of his opponent, and to order his arguments in a fashion best suited to his own case. To such a type More's diatribes against Tyndale unquestionably belong. Abstractly considered, however, literary dialogue would seem to lend itself equally well to a rendering of two balanced sides of a question. Such dialogue partakes of the nature of the drama: its author can create characters who speak as representatives of the many divisions of humanity. In analyzing a dramatic work we guard ourselves against identifying its author with any one of the characters, however much we may want to believe that some character summarizes our view of the author's mind. In this connection it is worth noting the kinds of early sixteenth-century drama with which More was most likely to be familiar: e.g., *Fulgens and Lucrece* (printed by John Rastell, More's brother-in-law), and a little later the interludes of John Heywood (More's nephew by marriage). Nearly all of these interludes are characterized primarily by the element of rhetorical debate rather than dramatic action, and often present several sides of a question without preference for one side over the others. For example, Heywood's *Play of the Weather* reconciles all of Jove's petitioners with complete impartiality.

A balanced, two-sided dialogue is also analogous to the proceedings of a court trial, suggesting a parallel with the renowned impartiality of More's own judicial career. He served both as lawyer and judge on many occasions, and is known to have refused as a lawyer cases that he considered not worth a day in court. His overpowering sense of fairness inevitably found its way into his writings. Except for the occasions when he was refuting what he viewed as a palpable and gross public danger to society—such as a Tyndale or a Luther—More as a person was temperamentally inclined to grant any worthy cause a hearing and to arrive at the truth of the matter by the legal process of approaching every issue from two opposing viewpoints. As lawyer, More learned to argue for a case; as magistrate, he learned to receive conflicting arguments and to weigh them with justice.

More was capable, then, both of polemical dialogue and of a dialogue of genuine debate wherein real issues are to be decided. Which sort did he choose to employ in *Utopia?* An analysis of the literary method of this dialogue suggests that he viewed with detachment and fairness the presentation of both sides. The dialogue in Book I of *Utopia* contains a good deal more agreement than is generally supposed or recognized. Furthermore, the discussion moves in the direction of agreement. Amicable debate always is, or should be, a process of coming together, of discarding irrelevancies, of untangling those misunderstandings which are the artificial product of imperfect communication, of determining a basis of agreement in order to narrow the dispute to its elemental refinement of difference. The proponents concede points when convinced, until they have arrived at the distillation of their respective stands. Hythloday and *persona* More follow this generalized pattern, with the result that by the time they have discovered their ultimate positions they have left behind them a vast area of consent. They agree particularly with respect to their analysis of the historical facts: the condition of European society and government in the years of the early sixteenth century.

It is actually Peter Giles who begins the central discussion of Book I by posing the first major question, and accordingly it is important to account for More's literary purpose in introducing this third person to the conversation:

> Then Peter, much marvelling at the man: Surely, Master Raphael, quoth he, I wonder greatly why you get you not into some king's court.

Giles is indeed something of an innocent, for he supplements his query with two reasons for joining a king's court which are immediately demolished: (1) an official position in the government will enable a man to assist all his friends and kinsmen, and (2) public power will give a man an opportunity to bring himself "in a very good case," that is, to line his own pocket. These considerations are raised only to be answered, and Hythloday wastes little time or effort in doing so. Concerning favoritism and personal aggrandizement there could be no dispute, nor would it have been appropriate for either of the two main contenders to have proposed such possibilities. We may see here the usefulness of having a third person present at a dialogue essentially between two persons. Giles's function is to pose the question and to state the superficial arguments that would be unsuited to either of his companions. Thereafter his part in the discussion dwindles to nothing. Throughout the rest of Book I Hythloday continually addresses "Master More" with only one mention of Giles, and Peter's only speech in all this time is another touch of simpleheaded complacency: "Surely, quoth Master Peter, it shall be hard for you to make me believe that there is better order in that new land than is here in these countries that we know."

It is doubtful that More wished deliberately to portray his good friend Giles as an intellectual lightweight. Clearly, More is consciously distinguishing between the *persona* and the actual man. Giles speaks in such conventional terms for dramatic reasons only. His function is an important one, for it is in the discrediting of Giles's suggestions of personal advantage and favoritism that Hythloday and *persona* More come to their first agreement. In fact, the very earliest utterance of *persona* More in the discussion is in support of Hythloday's deft answers to Giles:

> Well, I perceive plainly, friend Raphael, quoth I, that you be desirous neither of riches nor of power; and truly I have in no less reverence and estimation a man of your mind than any of them all that be so high in power and authority.

Whenever we find an agreement between the two principals, we are surely safe in assuming the author's concurrence. In the analogy of the courtroom, it is as though plaintiff and defendant have stipulated concerning some fact that is plainly incontrovertible. Thus, at the beginning of his trial on the meritsand limitations of counselling a king, More rejects out of hand the consideration of private gain. In fact, the case is put far more strongly: Hythloday and *persona* More agree that court service, if it is to be undertaken, must prove a real personal sacrifice on the part of the philosopher. The greatest loss will be liberty, insists Hythloday: "Now I live at liberty after mine own mind and pleasure, which I think very few of these great states and peers of realms can say." And *persona* More readily concedes that public office will be "somewhat to your own pain and hindrance." The only point of contention between them is whether or not the result would be worth the self-sacrifice; that is, whether court service would prove to be a public benefit. Both speakers agree that personal comfort must never stand in the way of "the profit of the weal-public," but they differ as to whether the philosopher can be of use at all, no matter what the individual cost.

The chief question is: if the philosopher offers counsel, will the king take heed and will he translate good advice into wise policy? Which way does monarchy tend, to tyranny or to benevolence? Hythloday and *persona* More take sides from the start. For Hythloday, the record is almost entirely on the side of tyranny. To *persona* More, monarchy is at least a potential source of good, although he freely recognizes even at the beginning of thediscussion the equal power for evil: "For from the prince, as from a perpetual well-spring, cometh among the people the flood of all that is good *or evil*" (italics mine). *Persona* More's position is not naive, like that of Giles. His statement is cautious but hopeful. Hythloday also speaks with qualifications about "the most part of all princes." In neither case is monarchy absolutely good or absolutely bad. Once again we find the spokesmen not so far apart as it first seemed. They agree that monarchy exists in various degrees of quality. The question hereupon becomes, for the philosopher who is to make the personal decision whether or not to offer counsel, what are the specific historical conditions at the time and place of his choice? In Thomas More's case, this meant England under the reign of Henry VIII.

Unquestionably an ambiguity existed in More's mind concerning the nature of the reigning monarch. Henry VIII was a young king of many virtues and liabilities. To More's sorrow Henry vain-gloriously insisted on emulating his great ancestor Henry V in "delight in warlike matters and feats of chivalry" to the neglect of home administration and to the depletion of the treasury. Yet at his succession in 1509 Henry was immensely popular. He was amiable and generous, skillful in archery and tennis. He was competent in Latin, French, and Italian, was a musician and encourager of thearts, and a friend to new sciences and Humanism. Hence there was a contemporary validity in each of the respective stands of Hythloday and *persona* More.

More, the lawyer and judge, argues each case as one who understands the issues involved. His presentation takes the form of a comprehensive and orderly historical survey of recent issues and events, embracing three chief areas of governmental activity: (1) domestic policy: unemployment, the farm problem, the penal code and question of capital punishment, and vagabondage (2) foreign policy, principally concerning foreign conquest and colonization and (3) fiscal policy: the valuation of money, benevolences and forced loans, monopoly grants, extortion, and bribery.

In the technique of literary dialogue, the factor which distinguishes the discussion of domestic policy from the other two major headings is that it does not take place between Hythloday and *persona* More. Hythloday relates it to his companions as an argument that took place many years before, in 1497, among himself, Cardinal Morton, and "also a certain layman cunning in the laws of your realm." The possible reasons for this removal in time are several. One obvious suggestion is that it is a form of self-protection for the author, an attack on Henry VIII under the guise of criticizing a former reign. Another possibility is that the author is payingcareful heed to his fictitious chronology, and accordingly dates Hythloday's visit to England at a time consonant with his voyages under the flag of Amerigo Vespucci. In the context of our discussion, however, a third reason may be offered: that the writer More's chief motivation is a removal of these specific issues from the immediacy of the Hythloday-*persona* More debate. Hythloday and *persona* More are enumerating the counts for and against English monarchy in 1515-16; we shall see, however, that domestic policy was not an issue wherein either of them found Henry VIII seriously at fault. Hence it was no longer a live issue in terms of the debate between More's two *personae*. We never actually learn *persona* More's opinion on the question of enclosure. At the conclusion of Hythloday's account he acknowledges that the narrator has spoken "wittily and so pleasantly," but implies that the entire matter of the speech has been slightly irrelevant to their debating point:

> But yet, all this notwithstanding, I can by no means change my mind, but that I must needs believe that you, if you be disposed and can find in your heart to follow some prince's court, shall with your good counsels greatly help and further the commonwealth.

In other words, *persona* More gently reproves his friend for beating a dead horse, and proposes that they proceed to mattersthat will really test the nature of Henry VIII's intentions. Why does he consider the discussion of enclosure to be irrelevant?

When we read Hythloday's stirring pleas on behalf of the husbandman, and his defiance of the rich, we instinctively conjecture a denunciation of complacent governmental policy, and suppose that Hythloday has scored a telling point against Henry VIII. In point of fact, however, by 1515-16 the government was attempting to handle the crisis on a large scale, under the direction of Wolsey. Royal commissioners were appointed to study the problem, and they reported a need for positive action. Hythloday urges the government to "make a law"; important legislation was passed in 1514, 1515, and 1516. These acts were directed particularly against the evils which Hythloday mentions: engrossing and forestalling (i.e., buying up in advance to force up the market price), and the plucking down of farms and villages by rich men who were exploiting the demand for wool at the expense of other types of agriculture. The government actually ordered rebuilding, as Hythloday demands, and restrained numberless attempts at further enclosure. The problem continued, because it was too large an agricultural revolution to be stayed by any governmental policy; but there was at least no ambiguity in the government's position on the farm problem. Hythloday's strictures would have been relevant in 1497, but not in 1516. Hence More removes this topic from the present conversation not only in time but in persons involved in the discussion.

The debate on domestic policy is a discussion within a discussion, and in many ways it mirrors in microcosm the larger plan. The most striking resemblance is that we again find three persons present at a dialogue (the scoffer and the friar appear from nowhere much later in the conversation). Once again the function of the third party—the irascible lawyer—is to serve as spokesman for the wrong point of view, and thus provide a basis of agreement between the principal characters. *Persona* Morton, like *persona* More, tends somewhat to the cautious side, but he receives Hythloday's declamation on enclosure reform without an objection. He is also willing to give the Polylerites' penal code a practical trial by deferring death sentences in England for a period of time, and adds his own suggestion that "vagabonds may very well be ordered after the same fashion." This amicable talk ends in a quarrel between the scoffer and the friar which has all the appearances of a digression. Hythloday afterwards apologizes to his hearers for a "long and tedious . . . tale." A digression it may be, but it is not without purpose. The sharp tongues and short tempers of lawyer, scoffer, and friar provide a meaningful contrast to the sane and considerate conduct of Hythloday, Morton, and *persona* More. The primary object of the satire in this digression is not the court or the clergy, but the folly of unreasonable argument.

The proposals concerning social legislation and penal reform are included in the Morton-Hythloday conversation for a very different reason from that suggested for the inclusion of the enclosure problem in this same section. In this latter instance the reason was that governmental policy seemed to be entirely in accord with More's wishes. The same could hardly be said to hold true for relaxation of the death penalty or improvement of regulations concerning vagabondage. Paradoxically, the precise opposite was true. In exploring these possibilities More was centuries ahead of his time, and his suggestions clearly extended beyond what he was ready to ask realistically of Henry VIII. No sixteenth-century government considered such social benevolence as its proper sphere of activity, much less as its duty. Hence it was an unfair test in distinguishing between a tyrant and a true prince at that point in history. More evidently had no doubt as to the essential rightness of this stand—both Hythloday and Morton agree to this—but More was not ready to propound such an advanced degree of enlightenment as a necessary condition of the philosopher's endorsement of any particular administration. In order to distinguish between the attainable and the unattainable, he relegated the latter to an abstracted conversation in a past reign. In summary, then, the material for the debate on domestic policy consists of a settled issue—enclosure—and an essentially impractical issue—social humanitarianism, both lying outside the realm of the central controversy concerning the nature of Tudor monarchy. It is for these disparate reasons that *persona* More can conclude the entire section with the easy dismissal, "But yet, all this notwithstanding, I can by no means change my mind." The crucial issues in the debate of the mind with itself lay yet ahead.

Plainly, it was to be in foreign and fiscal policy that monarchy would reveal its true inclination towards benevolence or despotism. The weight of evidence here would be decisive in persuading the philosopher to aid a government or to avoid its hopeless contamination. Policies of war and reckless expenditure were unavoidably interrelated, and were anathema to the Humanist scholar and supporter of London commercial interests. If, however, one could reason that a young king's sabre-rattling had stemmed from the effusion of adolescent vanity, one might pray for a change of temperament and for an era of peace at home. *Persona* More and Hythloday characteristically take sides. In the former's view any possibility for improvement, no matter how slight, would oblige the philosopher to assist and encourage the humane instinct. Hythloday is more inclined to expect the worst, and hints darkly at the incorrigible example of King Dionysius—with its obvious moral for the philosopher whose fate it is to be involved in duplicity beyond his control. Here is an issue that would influence one's choice, unlike the uncontroversial issue of domestic policy.

Consequently, in his consideration of foreign and fiscal policy the author shifts his scene from 1497 to the present (1516) and from the abstraction of a discussion within a discussion to the immediacy of the Hythloday-*persona* More debate. The foreign policy debate centers upon the example of the King of France, while fiscal policy is discussed abstractly with relation to "some king and his council." In neither case, obviously, is Henry VIII actually mentioned, and the extent to which his own actions partook of these evil examples is left unstated. The historical factors lie outside the scope of this study; we are interested in the literary method of debate and the extent of agreement between the two speakers.

In these terms, the fact of prime significance is that *persona* More and Hythloday agree entirely on the dangers involved. Although they implicitly differ as to whether Henry VIII in 1516 fell irretrievably into these categories of aggressive foreign policy and reckless spending, the two speakers do not question the essential perniciousness of these categories. In foreign policy the French king is plainly charged with meddling in affairs that are none of his business: laying claim to foreign dominions under pretext of an ancient hereditary line of succession, buying soldiers and alliances, encouraging pretenders to the enemy's throne, and the like. *Persona* More makes no pretence of finding a glimmer of hope in such a situation. When asked how well he thinks the French king would receive the philosopher's advice to "tarry still at home" and govern his own kingdom wisely, *persona* More readily concedes the point: "So God help me, not very thankfully, quoth I." In a case like this, any philosopher would show his greatest wisdom in sparing his breath and saving his own skin.

Similarly in fiscal policy *persona* More has no answer for Hythloday's example of "some king and his council" who indulge in extortion, bribery, "benevolences" and forced loans, creating exorbitant taxes (largely at the expense of the middle class) for the purpose of levying unneeded troops. After stating his proposals and objections, Hythloday concludes:

> These, and such other information, if I should use among men wholly inclined and given to the contrary part, how deaf hearers think you should I have?

> Deaf hearers doubtless, quoth I, and in good faith no marvel.

When confronted with completely "deaf hearers," *persona* More is ready to abandon the cause of counselling a monarch, and to live in philosophic retirement with Hythloday, pondering an impractical but ideal world across the oceans. But who is to say that an administration at any particular moment in history is entirely hopeless? Hythloday's examples of evil are as theoretical in their way as his picture of the ideal life of Utopia in Book II.

Somewhere between the ideally good and the perfectly evil stood Henry VIII, and his intentions were as yet uncertain. Thomas More had to make a decisive choice in answer to Henry's request for his wise counsel. The actual decision is beyond our present scope, but it is central to an understanding of the dialogue to realize that in 1515-16 More perceived a dilemma. He gave expression to it in a pattern of two alternatives: Hythloday's wariness of all Machiavellianism as an earnest of future ill intent, and *persona* More's cautiously idealistic tendency to seize upon any ray of hope as a basis for gradual improvement.

Now that the historical evidence is in, More's spokesmen proceed to their summations, to the concluding arguments of counsel for both sides. If one spokesman is merely serving as devil's advocate for the other, it is difficult to understand why both addresses to the jury are so coherent, rational, convincing, and essentially moderate in tone. *Persona* More labels the distinction between their points of view with the terms "school philosophy" (Hythloday's) and "another philosophy, more civil" (his own). He does not use the term "school philosophy" pejoratively; it is "not unpleasant among friends in familiar communication." Its only fault is that it is too forthright, too uncompromising; it lacks the quality of tact and diplomacy, of knowing when to speak and when to remain silent. "Civil" philosophy is the ability to "make the best of it," to "handle the matter wittily and handsomely for the purpose; and that which you cannot turn to good, so to order it that it be not very bad." This is no idle and naive humor, to be overturned and made ridiculous by Hythloday. More as a responsible public servant had long known the meaning of "compromise" in its best sense. He was eminently a practical man of policies.

Yet a man of principle knows where compromise leaves off and appeasement begins. At least, he knows in theory. More's beloved classical master Seneca found the dividing line to be exasperatingly thin and hard to locate. A policy of compromise involves a frightening element of chance. In a very real sense, compromise is a braver course for the true man of principle than stoical indifference. The counsellor of state is forever in need of reappraising the situation, while the man of principle stands fast on his logic. The worst that can befall the latter is martyrdom. The counsellor is in danger of personal dishonor and ridicule. Nero's reign might well have been the worse without Seneca's attempts at compromise, but the stigma of "appeaser" will live forever with Seneca's name. More evidently had Seneca's example in mind as he wrote **Utopia**, for he refers to the passage "out of *Octavia* the place wherein Seneca disputeth with Nero."

It is possible to be at the same time a counsellor of state and a man of principle—possible but dangerous. At every moment in history such a man must decide whether to acquiesce or to stand fast. He holds as incontrovertible the axiom that "You must not forsake the ship in a tempest because you cannot rule and keep down the winds." On the other hand, no sane man would undertake to contravene Plato's similitude of the philosophers who, being unable to persuade others to come in out of the rain, "do keep themselves within their houses, being content that they be safe themselves, seeing they cannot remedy the folly of the people." More, in hisown life, applied both courses of action to differing problems. The problem relevant to the dialogue in *Utopia* was a complex one, and depended on a great many variables. The choice was not easy, and by all indications it came months or even years after the composition of the work. What we hear in *Utopia* is the dispassionate voice of the author, laying before the world his view of the facts and of the philosophical basis for a decision.

Avineri comments on the depiction of imperialism and military engagements in More's *Utopia*:

The quest for empire and colonisation is thus elevated into a law of nature, and fighting against the Utopians becomes tantamount to fighting against nature itself. If one adds to this, that on the rare occasions when the Utopians fight their wars with their owncitizens, women fight along with men—we get here, *prima facie* at least, a picture of a modern, total and rationalized war. It is being waged in utmost cynicism with all possible means, without any regard for ordinary ethics and morality, justifying ruthless expansion, genocide, subversion and political assassination, along with the unscrupulous use of allies which are really utterly dependent. If Utopia is a paradise for its own inhabitants, it is causing life to be very much like hell to all other nations.

It has to be admitted that the surprise at finding such descriptions in More's *Utopia* is possible only if the book is conceived as a description of an *ideal* commonwealth, depicting More's *summun bonum*. To be sure, this is the most current and prevailing opinion, and the *Utopia* is presented in most general textbooks on political theory not just as *Nowhere*, but also as a *desideratum*, and this is difficult to square with the chapter on war, which seems to run the dream into a nightmare.

Shlomo Avineri, "War and Slavery in More's Utopia," in International Review of Social History, *Vol. VII, No. 2, 1962.*

The description of the island of Utopia in Book II deals similarly with the problem of the philosopher in deciding whether or not to participate in a government. The respective stands of *persona* More and of Hythloday are merely the obverse of their previous positions concerning tyranny. The former, who always tries to "make the best of it," is skeptical of a system that would overthrow entirely the established order of things. He is skeptical but not hostile; he is anxious to hear his friend's account of Utopia in all its details: "you shall think us desirous to know whatsoever we know not yet." Hythloday, who considers most princes to be beyond hope, is ready to try a more severe remedy. Yet even he does not reject the moderate solution out of hand. He readily grants that wise statutes may help somewhat to ease inequality of wealth, so that "these evils also might be lightened and mitigated. But that they may be perfectly cured, and brought to a good and upright state, it is notto be hoped for, whiles every man is master of his own to himself." The description of Utopia is a body of theoretical material towards which More's inquiring mind develops a polarity of rational attitudes. The philosophical mind must contain within itself always a Platonic ideal as a frame of reference. Notwithstanding, the Platonist in his worldly life is a practical man, recognizing the need for temporizing with human imperfection. *Persona* More is this practical man. It is he who accentuates mortal frailty: "For it is not possible for all things to be well unless all men were good, which I think will not be yet this good many years." Still, Utopia belongs to the future; and *persona* More's practicality remained a living force for its author in his life's application of Utopian ideals to English society. The two sides of the question continued for More to be valid and essentially unanswerable.

J. H. Hexter (essay date 1965)

SOURCE: "*Utopia* and Its Historical Milieu," in *The Complete Works of St. Thomas More, Vol. 4*, edited by Edward Surtz and J. H. Hexter, Yale University Press, 1965, pp. xxiii-cxxiv.

[*Hexter's essay, "*Utopia *and Its Historical Milieu" has been recognized since its publication as a groundbreaking contribution to More scholarship. The excerpt that follows presents Hexter's observations on Christian Humanism as the context for the* Utopia; *in the concluding section, "The Radicalism of* Utopia," *Hexter argues that More's vision transcended its time in its image of social equality.*]

CHRISTIAN HUMANISM

The years of the most intense and fertile development of Christian humanism coincide with the years of most intensive communication between Erasmus, its most active propagator, and More. And near the end of those fruitful years, in 1515-16, More wrote *Utopia*. These facts suggest a possible, indeed a probable, connection between the book and its author on the one hand and Christian humanism as it was being propounded in those years by Erasmus on the other. Yet two very persuasive expositions of *Utopia,* each deserving serious and careful consideration, tend to separate it from the Christian humanism of Erasmus and to assimilate it to modes of understanding either opposite or unrelated to his. The first exposition [P. Albert Duhamel, "Medievalism of More's *Utopia,*" *Studies in Philology,* 1955] proceeds by counterposing two opposite methods of attaining knowledge—the analytical method of the medieval schools and the rhetorical method of the humanists. The former moves by means of logical argumentation from presumably irrefragable premises to putatively ineluctable conclusions. It is substantially metaphysical and formally dialectical. By its very nature the scholastic method fragments whatever literary texts it uses—whether Cicero or St. Paul—employing bits and pieces of them as premises or supporting statements or conclusions for its sequence of syllogistically connected trains of reasoning. The rhetorical (or historical) method of the humanists on the other hand takes a literary text and by studying it at once internally as a coherent expression of its author's intention and externally in connection with its setting in time and space, with its historical milieu, aims to achieve a sympathetic understanding of the work as a whole and of the whole intention of its author. For this purpose a most careful study of the language of the text is indispensable, so that philology and history replace dialectic and classification as the instruments of investigation. For the literature of pagan antiquity this kind of study began in the age of Petrarch. It was the great achievement of the northern Christian humanists, beginning with John Colet, to apply the methods hitherto focused on classical literature to Scripture itself. Now there is none of this sort of thing in *Utopia,* no philological investigation, no *explication de texte,* no historical orientation. There is, however, especially in the Discourse, a considerable amount of what can be construed as systematic logical exposition. Therefore, it is argued, far from being a humanist work *Utopia* is More's most medieval effort.

This argument, presented with far more erudition and persuasiveness than the above inadequate summary conveys, nevertheless is not entirely convincing. In the first place the very mode of demonstration by which the argument for the scholastic character of *Utopia* is put forward is itself a trifle scholastic; it would better satisfy a medieval logician than a Renaissance humanist. It tends to break the text of the Discourse on Utopia to bits and reshuffle those bits into a structure dialectically adequate, rather than to examine the work as the expression of a living man at a moment in his life, and to discern the meaning and intention of the work in terms of the interplay between a personality and its historical milieu. Moreover the argument rests on a conception of Christian humanism which would exclude not only *Utopia* but also Erasmus' *Colloquies, The Education of a Christian Prince,* even *The Complaint of Peace* and *The Praise of Folly,* since they are

not *explications de texte* while, perhaps a trifle oddly, it would find room for Luther's *Lectures on the Epistle to the Romans.* Under the circumstances the dissociation of *Utopia* from Christian humanism seems less likely to be the consequence of More's intention than of an arbitrarily meager image of Christian humanism on the part of the scholar who makes the dissociation.

But as soon as one places *Utopia* in its chronological setting, in its relation to More's own activities and those of his friends, the likelihood that at that point More's habits of thought assumed a scholastic cast begins to evaporate. In England, with the patronage and encouragement of the circle who were More's warm friends, Erasmus was engaged on the task that above all others defined the Christian humanist's method and goal, the emendation of the Greek text of the New Testament and the provision of a new Latin paraphrase. More's mission to the Netherlands in 1515 did not take him out of the Christian humanist circle, for Cuthbert Tunstal was one of his colleagues, and he spent time during his stay with Jerome Busleyden and Peter Giles.

To get an idea of the degree to which common outlook, common purpose, and common sentiment bound More and Erasmus together in 1515, we need to turn first to More's long letter to Martin Dorp, a professor at Louvain. Apparently urged on by fellow theologians there, Dorp in an exchange of letters with Erasmus had taken exception to some of the satire, especially that against theologians and the theology of the schools, in *The Praise of Folly.* He had also expressed alarm at the implication, latent in Erasmus' editorial work on the New Testament, that, on occasion, a towering medieval theological structure might rest on a foundation no more firm than a copyist's error. To combat both these views More took up his pen, rushing to the defense of his friend in what he wryly called a laconic note—a letter-apologia of more than 15,000 words.

The letter is a vigorous defense of two positions, one embodied in *The Praise of Folly,* the other in the edition of the New Testament. Those positions were the key points in the propaganda of Christian humanism as Erasmus conceived it. The first position was that one of the best and most effective ways to combat stupidity, fatuousness, and even in some instances evil itself was through satire. The second position, as we have already seen, was that to bring about a revival of religion and a reform of society men needed to know the teaching of Christ, and that to achieve this knowledge the study of His words and those of the Apostles as they were first spoken and written was indispensable. Exhaustively and exhaustingly in his letter to Dorp, More offers a detailed defense of satire and of the philological study of scripture. The length of his apologia measures the depth of his conviction: he had had his introduction to the Christian humanist method of studying the New Testament from John Colet more than a decade before, and he made evident his high valuation of satire as early as 1506, when jointly with Erasmus he translated several of Lucian's dialogues. He may have been able to dash off the long letter to Dorp in jig time because, besides being saturated with the subject, he had seen Dorp's first letter and Erasmus' answer well before he composed his apologia. The letter to Drop is a hasty, rambling composition, but it expresses a long-ripening, coherent and firmly held judgment.

More's concern with the Erasmus-Dorp controversy and his composition of *Utopia* were continuous if not indeed stimultaneous. But this increases the difficulty of thinking of *Utopia* as a work predominantly scholastic rather than humanist in character. It requires us to suppose that while one part of More's mind was most intensely focused on the sort of thing that most concerned Christian humanists in his letter to Dorp, the other part of his mind dealing with *Utopia* fell or had just fallen into a pattern of thinking which at that very time he was holding up to ridicule andcontempt. For in his letter to Dorp one of the stratagems by which More defended Christian humanism was a devastating and unqualified attack on school philosophy from Peter Lombard on. The suppositions above stated subject our credulity to excessive and unnecessary stress.

The same observation applies to a second way of thinking about *Utopia* and its author which emphasizes their medieval orientation and dissociates them from Erasmus. The Utopian commonwealth, the argument goes, was patently a heathen, not a Christian, state. To anyone reared as More had been in Catholic orthodoxy there was an obvious distinction between the four pagan virtues, which were accessible to heathen reason, and the three Christian virtues, which were not. By basing his *Utopia* on the distinction between Temperance, Courage, Wisdom, and Justice on the one hand and Faith, Hope, and Charity on the other, More both follows the medieval tradition and gives point to his satire on contemporary abuses in Christian Europe. "The underlying thought of *Utopia* always is, *With nothing save reason to guide them, the Utopians do this; and yet we Christian Englishmen, we Christian Europeans* . . . ! The virtues of heathen Utopia show up by contrast the vices of Christian Europe. But the Four Cardinal Virtues are subsidiary to, not a substitute for, the Christian virtues. More has done his best to make thisclear. It is not his fault if he has been misunderstood" [Chambers, *Thomas More,* 1935].

Yet in *Utopia* itself one vainly seeks any such distinction. If More indeed did his best to make this point, he did it so badly that for four hundred years no one recognized it as being his point. Fortunately, there is another alternative: that what stood to the fore of its author's mind as he wrote the *Utopia* may not have

been the contrast of the virtuous heathen and the wicked professed Christian. This turns . . . to the question of historical milieu. And . . . the region of More's historical milieu which is pertinent to our present inquiry is the one we have designated Christian humanism.

What preoccupation of Christian humanists, especially of Erasmus and of More himself, at the time the latter was writing *Utopia,* most satisfactorily explains the unmistakable and invidious comparison which More insistently makes between the Christian realms of Europe and his imaginary commonwealth? In raising this question we again follow the method of the humanists themselves rather than that of their opponents, the philosophers of the schools. It would not be much use, after the scholastic fashion, to try to contrive the particular set of logically interrelated doctrinal propositions to which, if they were put to the question, most Christian humanists might assent. For such assent would tell us little about the matter of paramount interest to us (and to them): what *at a given moment* did they feel a serious Christian should especially concern himself about? what did Christendom *at that moment* most need to worry about? The moment or time span to which our inquiry is directed is 1515-16.

The question that Erasmus believed was paramount in those years was at once great and simple: "What is it to be a Christian?" Concerning that question he had two powerful convictions. The first was that the answers to it represented in much of the teaching and most of the common practice of his day were worse than wrong, that they were an outrageous parody of the truth, perpetuated by men narrow of mind and blinded by self-interest. The second was that the true answer was already in a large measure accessible and that it could be made more readily accessible. Erasmus believed that it was his vocation, with the help of his evergrowing circle of friends through all Christendom, unremittingly to strive to discredit the wrong answers to the question "What is a Christian?" and to give men the best chance possible to know the right one.

These two convictions Erasmus most strikingly juxtaposes in theadage *Dulce Bellum Inexpertis.* In early editions of the *Adages* from 1508 on, the *Dulce Bellum* had received less than forty words of comment. In the edition of 1515 it becomes the subject of a vigorous invective essay of about 11,000 words. Although particular major facets of Erasmus' way of thinking receive fuller and more coherent expression elsewhere, in no work does the relation of those facets appear more clearly. The ills of his world, Erasmus believed, resulted from a deadly interplay of wrong thinking and bad acting. The wrong thinking was in part the result of the principal ends that the universities of Erasmus' day, and for centuries before his day, had set for the education they provided. Those ends were the assimilation of knowledge to the patterns provided by the corpus of Aristotle's philosophy and the Roman *Corpus Juris*. The propagators of this kind of education were the professors of theology and law at the universities of Christendom. In effect the philosophy of the schools accommodated the teaching of Christ to the doctrines of Aristotle, to theories of Roman lawyers, and by extension to the notions of all sorts of pagan writers. To achieve this accommodation the faculties of the universities had literally torn the word of God to tatters. When it did not engage professional logicians in noisy but sterile arguments, this process led them to something worse. It set them to seeking ways to bring the teaching of the Son of God, who setHimself over against the ways of the world, into accord with Aristotle's philosophy and Roman law, which accepted the world, never looking or thinking beyond it.

For those who lived by their rules, Aristotle and the Roman jurists aimed only to make life within a worldly framework as satisfactory and orderly as could be. Following Aristotle, the school philosophers taught that no society where all things were common could flourish; to attain perfect happiness men must have the goods of the body and of fortune. And masking Roman law under the cloak and name of equity, the civilians supported the schoolmen, allowing force to be met with force, approving the pursuit of gain and even moderate usury, and declaring war, if just, to be a splendid thing. To seek to bring such teaching into agreement with that of Christs was to mix fire and water. The pursuit of honor, the pursuit of riches, the pursuit of power became acceptable, and with them greed, pride, and tyranny. And so the teaching of Christ, dismantled bit by bit, was scattered with scarcely a trace in a world that called itself Christian.

But ideas have consequences. What is Christianity in a world that disregards Christ's teaching? In such a world, what does a man mean when he professes to be a Christian? When one takes the heart outof Christianity, all that is left, all that can be left, is a dead body. To simulate life in such a body it must be put through ever more exacting and ever more numerous formal and mechanical motions. What are the motions? Pilgrimages, worship of relics, hagiolatry, fasts, rites of all sorts, degenerating at the worst into sheer superstition and magic-mongering. And who beat the drums for this vain parade? The beneficiaries of course: the monks with their collections of relics, the ignorant friars, the lordly bishops. It cannot be otherwise. Once the teaching of Christ is rationalized away, there is nothing left but external acts of sacerdotally certified and clerically sponsored busy-work.

The price of the reduction of Christianity to a mockery of what Christ came for is high; it is also inevitable: it is the war of Christian against Christian. The mystical body of Christ becomes a battleground; Christians burn and loot; they rape and murder other Christians. For war is the culminating act of corrupted man, the colligation of all his evil propensities. The teachers of Christendom had given over their true vocation in order to become apologists at retail for each particular kind of worldliness, provisioners of counterfeited Christian licenses to allow base men to do what they would, and therefore the final wickedness of war was sure to follow. Those teachers were not merely silent in theface of war among Christians, the ultimate treason to the Prince of Peace; they even sanctioned that treason. If they did not quite dare to make war as such into a positive good, they so managed matters as to relieve every warrior, from the hated mercenaries to the insatiable soldier-princes, of any qualms of conscience for a course of conduct as congenial to their vile appetites as it was disastrous to the Christian commonwealth and contrary to the Savior's teaching and example.

Though the learned of Europe had long engaged in what Erasmus took to be a conspiracy to misguide men as to what it meant to be a Christian, he had no doubt about what being a Christian meant. To be a Christian was not first and foremost to assent to a creed, or to participate in a particular routine of pious observances; it was to *do* as a Christian; to be a Christian was a way of life. To help them to discover this way of life men had of all guides the best—the very Son of God, Jesus Christ Himself. He still taught men how to be Christians, as He had taught His disciples hundreds and hundreds of years before, by His words, preserved in the Gospels and expressed in the letters of the Apostles. He also taught by His own life, for Christ was the first and perfect Christian. What men needed then was not new teaching; it was to find again the best teaching of all; and having found it to make it their way ofliving. The most important work a man of letters could do was to rescue the Gospel from the theologians and canon lawyers who had torn it to shreds and thus prevented men from knowing it. Erasmus believed he had notably advanced this work by editing and translating the New Testament. The philosophy of Christ which he speaks of often in the Paraclesis has nothing to do with the philosophy of the schools. It rests more on feeling than on syllogism; it is life rather than discourse, inspiration rather than erudition. And the simple man inspired by the Gospel is a far better teacher of that philosophy than the learned worldly-wiseman. For the philosophy of Christ belongs to the heart not to the head; it is a matter of spirit and action rather than of ceremonies and maxims. What men do, not what they say, what they practice, not what they profess, makes them Christian; and the best Christian is he whose doings, whose whole life, comes nearest the teaching and example of the Master.

We need not inquire whether on the critical or on the constructive side Erasmus' judgment was sound and his history accurate, whether school philosophy, Roman law, and formalism in religious observance were related to one another and to the early sixteenth-century world as Erasmus believed them to be. For present purposes it is enough to recognize that at the time of their publication withouta single explicit qualification Thomas More accepted the main positions which Erasmus took in the two crucial works just examined—the *Dulce Bellum Inexpertis* and the Paraclesis. Indeed to say that More accepted Erasmus' positions is to understate and perhaps to misstate the matter in at least two ways. In the first place he did far more than passively accept the positions; in the second place to describe those positions merely as those of Erasmus implies a view of their origin which might be hard to sustain.

From 1515 to 1520 More not only "accepted" Erasmus' views; he was their most pertinacious and combative defender, in one instance indeed more combative than Erasmus himself. Aside from *Utopia* and an unfortunate and tiresome squabble with the French humanist Germain de Brie, More directed his literary efforts for five years into a defense of his friend, or rather into an all-out assault on his friend's detractors. During these years he wrote four important letters. In the one to Oxford University, using what over the distance of four hundred years looks like a mallet to crush a gnat, he threatened the "Trojans," the opponents of Erasmus' New Learning there, with the displeasure of the Archbishop of Canterbury, of the Cardinal-Archbishop of York and Lord Chancellor, and of the King himself. In the three other letters—to Dorp, to Edward Lee, and to a Monk—More gave himself over to energetic attacks on those whodoubted the wisdom or the worth of Erasmus' work on the New Testament. The letter to Dorp gives More a chance to flay the school theologians, the letter to a Monk gives him a chance to do the like to the regular clergy—for a long time two choice targets of Erasmian satire. More with great zest seizes both chances. The sophistic pedantry of the dialecticians, their wanderings in a confused labyrinth of *questiunculae,* their absorption in "the petty casuistry of the moderns," which is to Scripture as a kitchen maid to the queen, are the objects of his unmeasured and unqualified contempt. And the life of the professed religious of his day fares no better. Lately much has been said about More's admiration of the monastic life, and what has been said is part of the truth, but in his letter to a Monk he shows small respect for the notion that "to reside forever in the same spot and, like a clam or sponge, to cling eternally to the same rock is the last word in sanctity." The occasion of this tirade was monkish criticism of Erasmus for his perpetual wanderings over the face of Europe, and More seizes on the opportunity to appraise the character and work of the chief of Christian humanists. It is an appraisal which should give pause to recent scholars who have tried to impute major differences in outlook to the two friends as early as 1515.

The lazy, More says, would no doubt rather squat with the monksthan roam with Erasmus, who "does more work in one day than you people do in several months. . . . He sometimes has done more for the whole Church in one month than you have in several years, unless you suppose that anybody's fastings or pious prayers have as deep and wide an influence as his brilliant works, which are educating the entire world to the meaning of true holiness." Erasmus "defies stormy seas and savage skies and the scourges of land travel, provided it furthers the common cause." He bears "seasickness, the tortures of tossing waves, the threat of deadly storms, and faces the ever present danger of shipwreck." He plods "through dense forest and wild woodland, over rugged hilltops and steep mountains, along roads beset with bandits." He is ever "tattered by the winds, spattered with mud, travel-weary, worn out by hardships." And the body that Erasmus subjects to these torments "is growing old and has lost its strength from hard study and toil." Clearly Erasmus must have long since succumbed to these hardships "had not God preserved him for the benefit of an ungrateful people. No matter where his journeys take him, he always comes back bearing wonderful gifts for everyone else, while he gets nothing but shattered health and the insults of wicked men, occasioned by his beneficence." Erasmus is forced to travel in the interest of his studies, "that is, for the common good. . . . As the sun spreads its rays, so wherever Erasmus is, he spreads hiswonderful riches." Dedicated wholly to the service of others, he expects no personal reward here below. Surely there is a more than accidental parallel between this account of the tribulations of Erasmus in his valiant propagation of the philosophy of Christ, and Paul's tale of his hardships in behalf of the gospel of Christ [in II Corinthians], "in journeyings often, in perils of waters, in perils of robbers . . . in perils in the city, in perils in the wilderness, in perils in the sea . . . in weariness and painfulness . . . in hunger and thirst . . . in cold."

Returning again to the relative value of the monk's service to God and the service Erasmus was rendering, More continues, "God will prefer his speech to your silence, his silence to your prayers, his eating to your fasting, and in short everything you proudly despise about Erasmus' way of life God will value more highly than all that you find most sweet in your own way of life." The tree may be known by its fruit and the fruit of Erasmus' ceaseless toil and travel has been the publication of more works "abounding not merely in learning but in solid piety than any other man has written for many centuries." And the advances made in sacred as in secular learning are due as much to the unflagging efforts of Erasmus as to "anyone else in the past several centuries." This is why in every land in Christendom men of true intellectual and moral worth seek to outdo one another in their thanks to Erasmus for what his work has done for them.

The scholarly proficiency and the unremitting, almost ruthless, dedication of Erasmus' enormous output were unique. But the ideas and beliefs that inspired that output were probably less the achievement of Erasmus' individual genius than the product of the mutually fructifying interplay of a number of like minds. A very important phase of that interplay had begun with Erasmus' first journey to England in 1499. More had a part in it from the beginning; and one of its consequences over two decades seems to have been an ever closer congruence in the outlooks of the two men. Even before 1506 a friend of theirs had remarked on a likeness of "mind, tastes, feelings, and interest such that twin brothers could not more closely resemble one another." At the center of this common ground shared by the two men was the conviction that to be a Christian was first of all to live like a Christian, to take as the model of day-to-day conduct the words and acts of Christ.

During the very year when Erasmus quoted the above comment on the similarity of their outlook, More in his dedication letter to his translation of Lucian observed that in *The Cynic* that satirist was praising Christian living, those Christian virtues of "simplicity, temperance and frugality that make up the straight and narrow path which leads to life." There is no distinction here between pagan virtues and Christian. All virtues that men must practice in order to live righteously are Christian virtues. The distinction that concerns More is not one between types of virtue but between kinds of men—the men who live the rigorous disciplined life commanded and exemplified by Christ and the men who—whatever their assiduity in lip service to orthodoxy—live like pigs and hyenas.

Nine years before he wrote *Utopia*, then, More, like his friend Erasmus, saw Christianity as a way of life. Whatever moves men toward that way of life is Christian. And if it comes from Lucian, who was not a Christian, it is no less Christian for that. This indeed follows from the Christian humanist propensity to see Christ primarily as a teacher, as the most effective of all teachers of virtue, who perfectly embodied in action what others, whether pagan or Jew, had offered as precept. In the sphere of conduct particularly, the boundary between the region of nature and the region of grace is not very sharp. This is especially so if Christ's mission was, as Erasmus and perhaps More believed, the renewal of a nature once wholly good but corrupted by evil custom beyond the power of mere men to restore it.

In 1515 More and Erasmus and many of their friends were full of the excitement of new discovery—the discovery, they believed, of a method of understanding the message of Christianity and the life and teaching of their Lord Jesus far superior to the method current in their own day. Into a world gone stale and sour they hoped they could bring a sense of the good and the true, which would freshen and sweeten it. The method of understanding espoused by the humanists was new, but not the understanding itself. The method—philological investigation and "rhetorical" apprehension of Christ's teaching—had to be new because the old method, so the adherents of the New Learning contended, had buried both understanding and the thing to be understood under a pile of sophistical scholastic debris and futile formalism. The thing to be understood was of course as old as, in some matters older than, the Apostles, and as new as tomorrow. It was the eternal word of God's revelation of His Truth, His Will, and His Love to men.

Our inquiry about the relation between More and Erasmus and about the substance of Christian humanism has revealed that in 1515-16 the two men stood in complete agreement on precisely those matters which at the time both regarded as of primary importance—especially on the need to deploy the talents and the erudition of humanists in order to remold the world in conformity to Christ's rule. Was this Christian humanist outlook which More so fully shared with Erasmus reflected in *Utopia,* and particularly in that contrast, sometimes implicit, sometimes explicit, between Europeans and Utopians which pervades the book? Not if the question that the contrast raises is merely: how can Christians behave so badly when heathen Utopians behave so well? That question smacks a little too strongly of the medieval schools. But the contrast may raise another question, at once shocking and more in line with Christian humanist habits of thought: as between the Europeans and the Utopians, *which are truly Christian*? Such a question would bring *Utopia* into positive and central relation to the defense and propagation of Christian humanism which was More's primary commitment when he wrote the book. For in wrestling with the question about Europeans and Utopians in the context More provides, one also by inference wrestles with the question: what, truly, is it to be a Christian?

There is a reasonable amount of evidence that these questions were among those with which More intended to confront the reader in *Utopia*. Comments by both Budé and Erasmus indicate that they sense such an intent. Budé calls Utopia *Hagnopolis,* a holy community. He describes Utopia as a place where, as by a miracle, men have achieved Christianity without revelation. In a marginal note Erasmus calls it a holy commonwealth. In those notes, too, he observes how the Utopians surpass European Christians in several matters characteristically Christian—Utopian rejection of astrological superstition, Utopian belief in immortality, and the sanctity of the Utopian priesthood.

In its content and occasionally even in its language the Discourse on Utopia keeps before the reader the problem of balancing the nominal Christianity of Europeans against the way of thinking and acting of the Utopians. The Utopians not only possess in the highest measure the virtues More had described as Christian a decade earlier—simplicity, temperance, frugality; they also have faith in a God in whose goodness and mercy they trust. Along with that faith goes *spes,* hope for life eternal. And along with faith and hope goes *charitas,* or love. The Utopians repay their benefactors with *charitas* and share a *mutuus amor charitasque* while magistrates and citizens deal with one another lovingly like fathers and children. The institutions of Utopia are not only *prudentissima,* the most prudent; they are also *sanctissima,* the most holy. And their social order established the rules of life which Christ had taught as the right way for men, but which, according to Erasmus' *Dulce Bellum,* had been reasoned away in Christian Europe by Aristotelian theologians and Romanist lawyers in order to permit the pursuit of profit, usury, private property. Nowhere does More make the community of spirit between true Christians and Utopians more explicit than at the point of the story where one would expect the contrast to be sharpest—the point where Hythlodaeus and his band convert many Utopians to Christianity. For beside Christ's miracles and the martyrs, what draws the Utopians to Christianity is His teachings and character. The *contrast* of Christian teaching with what they know by reason is not what moves so many Utopians to accept baptism in the faith nor does More say anything about such a contrast. Quite to the contrary, they become converts because the teaching of Christ accords with their most cherished beliefs. It is of special weight with them that "His disciples' common *way of life* had been pleasing to Christ and that it is still in use among the truest societies of Christians". The italics are mine, the emphasis is More's. It is the emphasis of the Christian humanists. The teaching and the way of life are what count above all else. In their teaching, the Utopians are very like Christians; and in their way of life they are far closer than any European Christian people to the way of the first and best Christians of all. Their whole society indeed exemplifies the chief Christian virtue—*charitas.* More than any other Christian institution the family embodies giving without demanding an equivalent in return. And this is the very essence of *charitas,* of that Christian love of which Christ's giving of Hislife for sinners is the supreme symbol and perfect example. Fulfilling the Gospel command of Christian brotherhood—"*mutuum date nihil inde sperantes,* Give, seeking nothing in return"—in Utopia "they make up the scarcity of one place with the surplus of another. This service they perform without payment, receiving nothing in return from those to whom they give." And so, More concludes, driving his point home, "the whole island is like a single family". If in the light of all this one wonders today whether the Utopians were not better Christians than the formal Christians of More's time and place, it seems likely that More's contemporaries wondered the same thing, and

that this is what More intended should happen.

From the description of the conversion of the Utopians More might have meant to suggest that even before Hythlodaeus instructed them in Christian teaching and baptized them with water, the Utopians already enjoyed what Catholic theologians call the baptism of desire. This, however, might impute to More in 1516 a stronger preoccupation with the niceties of school theology than the evidence seems to warrant. It is more likely that he was reaching for a less technical distinction—that between those who know God in the bottom of their heart and those who merely acknowledge Him with the top of their head. The latter avowed their faith and performedthe required ritual motions of a Christian but denied Christ in every other act of their lives. The former, not having heard Christ preached or seen the sacraments administered, did not know how to produce any of the outward and visible signs of an inward and spiritual grace, but that grace was nevertheless in them and showed itself in their relations to their fellowmen. The great commandment was not two separate injunctions but one. Truly to "love the Lord thy God" and not to "love thy neighbor as thyself" was impossible; thus their own deeds gave the lie to all the Christian professions of the princes and great ones of Europe. But the reverse was also true. Men could not truly love their neighbors without having God in Christ at the bottom of their hearts, no matter what the errors with which the top of their heads might be furnished. And such a people loving God and their neighbors were the Utopians. Surely for men not heavily committed to any formal school of philosophy—and none of the Christian humanists seems to have been so committed—the most pertinent fact about the Utopians was not merely that they discoursed like reasonable pagans but that they lived like very good Christians. When they heard about Christ for the first time, they experienced not so much revelation as recognition. For the first time they recognized the truth that had inspired their actions and their institutions and that made Utopia the best of commonwealths. If this is so, then in 1515 More like Erasmus was preoccupied with the central problem of the Christian humanists, "What, truly, is it to be a Christian?" And *Utopia* reflects his preoccupation. The conclusion which *Utopia* suggests without flatly stating it is that Christianity was not a mere occasional flurry of formal deeds demanded by authority but a way of life that emanated from every heart where Christ had found a home.

The peculiar twist More gives to that problem—the Utopians living in the New World had been out of the range of the spoken and written Word—testifies to his early perception of what was to become a difficult psychological problem for the Christian world. The untold millions of men who had never heard the gospel preached were only slowly emerging into the consciousness of Christians in the wake of the great discoveries and explorations. Increasing contact with and awareness of these millions were to impose on Christians a crisis of creed and conscience altogether different from that raised by contact with overtly anti-Christian Moslems in the Middle Ages. For these new millions were not anti-Christian, at least not in the beginning; they were non-Christian. In *Utopia* More had started to nudge Western men into a posture that might have spared non-Europeans much suffering and spared Christian Churches from assuming, toward the unconverted, attitudes that were to impede and in places wholly frustrate the Christian mission ofconversion and that were one day to help drive Western men of sensitive conscience from the Christian fold. But it was not to be. . . .

Did More believe that there was in Europe a group of men suitable to serve as its rulers? If so, what was this group? How could these men be found?

One way to find them is to start with a dream—a dream of the author of *Utopia*. To try to solve a problem in social history by the analysis of a dream is not a procedure likely to commend itself very often to a sober historian; it is the sort of thing he is likely to expect from the more desperate varieties of social scientist. But in this case we confront special circumstances. *Utopia*, after all, is fantasy; and—many of the difficulties in interpreting the book result from this—fantasy itself dwells where the boundary between dreaming and waking, imagery and actuality, is not a sharp line but a broad, indistinct twilight region. Indeed we cannot be sure whether the dream of Thomas More which we are about to look into was a true dream or a daydream, another bit of sheer fantasy. He tells of his dream in a letter to Erasmus of December 1516. When More wrote Erasmus, he was still waiting "for our *Utopia*, with the feelings with which a mother awaits the return ofher boy from foreign parts." His letter goes this way:

> You have no idea how thrilled I am; I feel so expanded, and I hold my head high. For in my daydreams I have been marked out by my Utopians to be their king forever; I can see myself now marching along, crowned with a diadem of wheat, very striking in my Franciscan frock, carrying a handful of wheat as my sacred scepter, thronged by a distinguished retinue of Amaurotians, and, with this huge entourage, giving audience to foreign ambassadors and sovereigns; wretched creatures they are, in comparison with us, as they stupidly pride themselves on appearing in childish garb and feminine finery, laced with that despicable gold, and ludicrous in their purple and jewels and other baubles. Yet, I would not want either you or our friend, Tunstal, to judge me by other men, whose character shifts with fortune. Even if heaven has decreed to waft me from my lowly estate to this soaring pinnacle which, I think, defies comparison with that of kings, still you will never find me

> forgetful of that old friendship I had with you when I was but a private citizen. And if you do not mind making the short trip to visit me in Utopia, I shall definitely see to it that all mortals governed by my kindly rule will show you the honor due to those who, they know, are very dear to the heart of their king.

> I was going to continue with this fascinating vision, but the rising Dawn has shattered my dream—poor me!—and shaken me off my throne and summons me back to the drudgery of the courts. But at least this thought gives me consolation: real kingdoms do not last much longer.

With every due allowance for the fanciful element in the letter, something about More's yearnings emerges from this unusually distinct dream or vision. For to the heart's desire of a man what better guide can there be than his dreams? When More let his imagination range freely it did not reveal ascetic flight from the world or a purely contemplative immersion in scholarship to be the ultimate desire of his heart; More saw himself most completely fulfilled as a ruler, or prince. But he saw himself as a prince in Utopia; it was with the rulers of his own imaginary commonwealth that he identified himself. And this meant that, save for the fact of ruling, he would in every way differ from the rulers of Europe, the leaders of the cosmopolitan military élite, the primary target of his most savage satire.

What manner of men were these rulers of Utopia of whom he would be one? The letter itself tells us something about them. They are contemptuous of finery and wealth; and they themselves wear onlythe simple habit in which all Utopians dress. The emblem of office borne before them is not the sword, the symbol of power, destruction, war; it is the sheaf of wheat, symbol of peace, prosperity—and work. Simplicity, sobriety, industry, love of peace—the virtues of the rulers of Utopia begin to seem a bit bourgeois after all! Until, of course, we recall that the medieval bourgeoisie had not undergone purgation by Calvinism, that in the centers of urban life in More's day—the Netherlands and Italy—the town rulers were distinguished neither for their austerity nor for their addiction to the ways of peace. The list omits two indispensable bourgeois traits—craftiness and love of gain. The Utopian magistrates with their sobriety and appetite for hard work are modeled not on the moneygrubber but on the scholar; the end of their way of life is not to maximize gain or profit or wealth, but to maximize leisure—*otium* in the good sense of time free for study and contemplation. *Industria* and *studium* have as their ends not the accumulation of riches but *cultus* and *humanitas,* culture and humanity, *libertas* and *cultus animi,* spiritual freedom and culture. The very pastimes of Utopians are steeped in the pursuit of learning, and possession of it is the prime qualification for office.

The rulers of Utopia did not buy office or inherit it or receive it as a favor from a king as was the common European practice. Indeed anyone caught soliciting office was forever banned from it. Their fellow citizens elected them to office for life because they were the best men in the land—the best not because they were the strongest, the richest, or the craftiest, or because they had had great and renowned forbears, but because they were chosen from a select group of men. For their excellence, and by the recommendation of the priests and the secret vote of the lesser magistrates, the members of this group, which was about one-thousandth of the population, were exempted from the common Utopian requirement of six hours of labor a day. During good conduct and when not required for government service, this very small band of men devoted itself wholly to study. It was therefore for extraordinary merit attained in the life of learning that the highest office was awarded in Utopia, the place which beyond all others would have satisfied Thomas More's freest fantasy of the best life a man could have on earth.

In the Europe of his own day, were there any men who for More represented living analogues to the rulers of the Utopian commonwealth? There were indeed, and our previous investigation of the relationship between More and Erasmus allows us to infer who they were. We need not, however, rely altogether on inference, for in a letter More comes close to identifying them for us explicitly. While still nervously awaiting the publication of his book, More wrote Erasmus:

> I am anxious to find out if it meets with the approval of Tunstal, and Busleyden, and your Chancellor; but their approval is more than I could wish for, since they are so fortunate as to be top-ranking officials in their own governments, although they might be won over by the fact that in this commonwealth of mine the ruling class would be completely made up of such men as are distinguished for learning and virtue. No matter how powerful those men are in their present governments—and, true, they are very powerful—still they have some high and mighty clowns as their equals, if not their superiors, in authority and influence. I do not think that men of this caliber are swayed by the fact that they would not have many under them as subjects, as the term is now used by kings to refer to their people, who are really worse off than slaves; for it is a much higher honor to rule over free people; and good men, such as they, are far removed from that spiteful feeling which desires others to suffer while they are well off themselves.

When More thought of ruling and rulers in connection with *Utopia,* among the names which came to his mind were those of Busleyden, Tunstal, Jean Le Sauvage, Chancellor of Prince Charles—and himself. The first three men were already serving their rulers in impor-

tant offices; he was under pressure from his King to do the like. In Utopia such men would not be servants of rulers, but rulers themselves "in authority and power." Here indeed are the true analogues in Christendom to the rulers of Utopia. Or rather, to align the fantasy with the facts, the rulers of Utopia are the analogues of such men as Busleyden, Tunstal, Le Sauvage, and More—analogues, that is to say, of the Christian humanists. It is hardly surprising that More felt that the one group of men suited for rule in Europe was the group which shared his convictions on those matters that at the moment he deemed of paramount importance. . . .

Utopia and the Christian revival

. . . In the powerful currents of religious reform of his day, More was deeply involved, and never more deeply than in 1515 when he was composing the Discourse on Utopia. In one of its aspects the Discourse is thus the fruit of More's meditations, begun long before he conceived and wrote **Utopia,** on the necessary conditions of a society in which Christ's will was man's rule, the conditions of the *regnum Christi.* So in 1515 in the matter of the *regnum Christi,* as in so many other matters, More shared the concern of his friend Erasmus. Yet in this matter at this time the differences between the two friends were considerable. It is possible to discern these differences very clearly, for within a few months of the writing of the Utopian Discourse Erasmus wrote *The Education of a Christian Prince.* It afforded him an opportunity, if he chose to take it, to set forth his conception of the right ordering of a good society.

Contemporary and recent works with which to compare Erasmus' tract abound. Indeed, leaving aside its plea for Christian peace, that tract, distinguished from the rest, if at all, only by the amenity of its style, tends to vanish into the endlessly tepid puddle of hortatory treatises addressed to Christian princes. When Erasmus turns from his two central preoccupations, the restoration of Christian letters and the maintenance of Christian peace, his social observations are invertebrate; they are unconnected, particular responses to social malaises, because he has only a very slight awareness of the interpenetration of social institutions and social structures.

On the other hand, to find an earlier literary work with which to compare **Utopia** one must go back almost two thousand years to Plato's *Republic.* We have already been at considerable pains to point out the divergences of **Utopia** and the *Republic,* but we had to be at such pains because of the unmistakable likenesses between the two books. The significant fact in this context is that there is no similar felt need to point out the difference between **Utopia** and any book written between the fourth century B.C. and 1515. The differences are obvious to the hastiest reader.

To his meditations on the problems of the *regnum Christi,* More's Netherlands mission brought a new dimension, almost literally. It enabled More to see in depth, in perspective, and in mutual relation problems which his contemporaries saw in the flat and as a disjointed series. In 1515 More sees European society as a whole, and this enables him to achieve his vision of the best commonwealth, Utopia. For Utopia is a sort of anti-Europe, a reverse-Europe, whose institutional organization at all levels above the family is the opposite of that of Europe. Whether he made sense of Utopia because he had already made sense of Europe or whether, as the sequence of the composition of *Utopia* suggests, it was the other way about, More does achieve a clarity of vision about the world he lives in unsurpassed by any contemporary but Machiavelli and perhaps Guicciardini, and a range of insight into that world of which neither of his Italian contemporaries wascapable.

And yet in *Utopia* he does not ultimately ascribe the troubles of the world to impersonal forces, to the underlying patterns of history, to chance, or to human error and the natural insufficiency of human understanding—not once, not ever. His way of explaining and understanding contemporary social pathology bears the imprint of the evangelical and prophetic outlook which he shared with other men affected by the Christian revival: for him social ills resulted from sin. And, among the sins, sloth, greed, and pride above all infect More's world, as it is set forth in *Utopia*—the sloth of the idle retainer and his more idle master; the monstrous greed of the usurer, the fat abbot, and the enclosing landlord; the insatiable pride of the rich and the powerful, displayed in rich clothing, in gems and baubles, but above all in a passionate and ruthless pursuit of social place. For man's pride glories in the subjection and servility of others, it knows no limit and no satisfaction because it is the result of no natural need. It grows hungrier from what it feeds on because it is rooted in the ultimate and infinite emptiness of the sinful soul turned away from God. It is the shame of Christians that despite the clear teaching of Christ, which they profess to follow, they have erected their so-called commonwealths on foundations made of the very stuff that human sinfulness andespecially pride feeds on—the glorification of force and violence, rewards for successful chicanery, tolerance of individual and private aggrandizement at the expense of the common good and the public welfare. Actual Christian societies are therefore faulty in their foundations, in the very structure of their laws; to try to raise the *regnum Christi* on such a footing is to build on sand. Such is the explicit judgment passed in *Utopia* on the world More lived in; and it is a judgment not explicitly made by any of More's intellectual comrades-in-arms.

Under such circumstances pious exhortation and instruction are ineffectual, since they run completely counter to men's deeds and the laws which sanction them. Nowhere in *Utopia* does More suggest that propagands for reform directed at individual consciences is of itself enough to raise Europe from its slough. When law, by sanctioning iniquity, renders it easy for bad men to satisfy appetites offensive to God at the expense of their fellow men, mere words are not enough to counter its force. The only sure foundation of a righteous society is the bond of law. Thus it is in Utopia. There the human propensity to sin, instead of being fattened by the very rules of the commonwealth, is starved and weakened by those rules. No man can seek a false prestige for himself by personal adornment, because all clothing is the same and unadorned. No mancan waste the substance of society on what a later writer was to call conspicuous leisure and what More with greater directness calls idleness, because by the laws of that holy commonwealth he who does not work does not eat. No man can lord it over others by making them his servants because in Utopia no adult freeman, indeed no slave, has a man for a master or a lord, not even for a landlord. Service, bond or free, military or civil, is rendered to or for the commonwealth only.

Finally, consider that institution of Utopia which not only is most striking to the casual reader but which was most striking to some of the shrewdest of More's contemporaries, the institution which he himself singled out as the chief difference between Utopia and all European societies—Utopian communism. Of all the measures to crush the monster Pride it is the most important and most effective, because it goes to the root of the evil, which is man's chronic sense of insecurity, insufficiency and anxiety. In Europe, men's endless pursuit of money and ruthless victimization of their fellows resulted largely from the sin of pride; but the institutions of Europe often enough encouraged men to act in such ways and did nothing serious to discourage them. To acquire more than one's fellows had acquired was legally possible and socially advantageous; from this fact followed the worst of the social-malaises that afflicted Christian Europe. Utopian communism made such acquisition socially absurd and legally impossible; from this followed the potentiality for a decent society. Thus attacked at its roots, pride is a sin that "can have no place at all in the Utopian scheme of things."

As we have already seen in another connection, the overall effect of the structure of Utopian law is the elimination of all social organisms intermediate between the commonwealth on the one hand and the patriarchal family on the other. What is left are two institutions, one by definition public, the other by nature providing minimal scope to individual idiosyncrasy. Men live, eat, travel, work, study, and play (if the no doubt elevating but rather stuffy recreations permitted in Utopia can be called play) according to public regulation, in public places, under public authority. They drink, brawl, gamble, and fornicate nowhere, at least not without danger from Utopia's harsh laws. In Utopia there is no "pretext to evade work", and men live all the time under everyone's eyes. Truly there is no place to hide in the land Budé called Hagnopolis, the City of Saints.

Utopia then is a society at once religious and austere. Its austerities, however, are not those of a withdrawn community of spiritual athletes performing special feats of self-mortification to win thereby from the divine spectator some transmundane guerdon for themselves or for their spiritual beneficiaries. The austerities of Utopia are imposed on all Utopians, the laws of a commonwealth, not the rules of a cloister. They are also the laws *for* a commonwealth, neither arbitrary nor useless. The laws for a holy commonwealth, of course; their vigor is the indispensable prop of social righteousness; the asceticism of Utopia is an asceticism of this world, an *innerweltliche askese,* directed toward securing that, on earth by mortal men as in heaven by saints and angels, God's will be done and His Name thereby glorified.

In such a holy commonwealth the problem of the Dialogue of Counsel vanishes. The Christian humanists of the early sixteenth century were caught, as we have seen, on the horns of a dilemma, the dilemma of the prophet to whom the greatest danger turns out to be honor in his own country. Most of them acknowledged the duty and responsibility of an active life; but their range of choice in carrying out their duty was narrow and, to the more conscientious among them, painful. They could serve the commonwealth with only the pen as unattached intellectuals or they could enter the council of a prince, where the power of decision lay. Once there, they would have to "approve the worst counsels and subscribe to the mostruinous decrees," since to give "only faint praise to evil counsels" is to be counted "a spy, and almost a traitor." But in Utopia the Christian humanist would have the duty, which then would be the privilege, too, of serving by ruling the kind of society that it was his prophetic mission to set before Christians as a goal and an example. In that society Christ's law of love of God and neighbor prevailed, and public service meant something better than active participation in "a kind of conspiracy of the rich, who are aiming at their own interests under the name and title of the commonwealth." Earlier we saw that in a vision More imagined himself a prince in Utopia, and found the vision good, because Utopia was ruled by cosmopolitan intellectuals, in effect by humanists like himself. But More found the vision good not only because of who ruled but also because of what the rulers ruled—an austere laic commonwealth whose ordinances struck at the roots of sin, a commonwealth where Christ's teaching of equality, righteous-

ness, and love toward God through love toward one's neighbor was the custom of the land and its law. Thus *Utopia* expressed the highest aspirations not only of early sixteenth-century men of letters but especially of Christian humanists. It also figured forth some of the hopes of that Christian Revival which was an important element in its historical matrix.

More ingeniously conceived a mode of organizing human affairs which would resolve many of the spiritual dilemmas of his day, of his friends, of his own, which would incorporate within itself a broad band of the spectrum of religious renewal as the most ardent reformers of the age envisaged that renewal. Having performed this rather remarkable imaginative feat, More put it in a book. There was nothing much else to do with it. So slight was the likelihood that the only people—the princes and the popes—who could do anything forceful to bring the *regnum Christi* closer to actuality would do anything, that some have doubted the seriousness of **Utopia,** especially since a little after the book was published its author took a course quite contrary to the one Hythlodaeus prescribed. In hopes, no doubt, of ameliorating the evils of his day along the lines that he suggested in his stories about the Achorians, the Polylerites and the Macarians in the Dialogue of Counsel, More entered the service of his prince. In a fashion almost too pat, his experience vindicated Hythlodaeus' wisdom; his hopes were quite baseless. Under a rather heavy veneer of humane learning and geniality Henry VIII was the very model of the predatory leader of a predatory semi-military ruling class; he was magnificent, splendid, spendthrift, idle, envious, treacherous, rapacious, and stupidly and stupefyingly vainglorious. His chief minister and alter ego, Wolsey, made up for Henry's idleness by hisown tireless activity; in all other respects he shared in full measure his master's traits of character.

As a councilor of his prince during the decade before Wolsey's fall, More was an intimate witness of much that he most detested in the doings of Europe's rulers—notably the judicial murder of the Duke of Buckingham and the fruitless and inordinately costly war against France. As speaker of the House of Commons in 1523, he helped Wolsey bully and cajole a large grant from Parliament for a military venture which he must have detested; and he received, for his "faithful diligence" in helping his master extort money from his subjects, a reward of £200. The English got only humiliation and heavy financial loss from Henry's misbegotten enterprise against France. After Francis' disaster at Pavia, however, the French paid Henry's councilors off for their good offices in truce negotiations with the Emperor. Sir Thomas was in the book for a pension of 150 crowns. Whether in these douceurs, the common rewards of the servants of kings, the delicate spiritual sensorium of More caught a whiff of blood-money, one cannot say. There is no evidence that he refused to accept payment. In any case he may have felt more poignantly than when he wrote it the force of Hythlodaeus' remark that although in a prince's council it might barely be possible to keep "your own integrity and innocence, you will be made a screen for the wickedness and folly of others." He learned soon enough in person what his own literary creation could have told him: what happens to a would-be prophet who puts his faith in princes. The route to the *regnum Christi* did not pass through the courts of Renaissance rulers.

A window to the future: the radicalism of Utopia

As we have just seen, More's perception of the requirements of a holy commonwealth, more astute than that of his contemporaries, projected his vision beyond theirs. *Utopia* transcended its milieu in another way, however, a way that justifies speaking with appropriate reservations of its modernity. . . .

The modernity of *Utopia* lies in the institutions of the Utopian commonwealth; it is there that More clearly transcends his historical milieu, there that he stands on the margins of modernity. The conditions for righteous living in Utopia were achieved by means of its institutions, and its central institution is Utopian communism. What fascinated and still fascinates so many people about *Utopia*, what has kept the book selling, what is new about it, is precisely this Utopian communism. This assertion, however, opens the door wide to an onrush of objections anddenials. Surely in the sixteenth century there is nothing new about communism. We find it in Plato's *Republic*, and in *Utopia* More acknowledges his debt to that book. We find it in that "common way of life . . . pleasing to Christ and . . . still in use among the truest societies of Christians", that is, the better monasteries which, says Hythlodaeus, made it easier to convert the Utopians to Christianity. We find it in the later Stoic conception of man's natural condition, which included the community of all possessions. This conception was taken up by the early Church Fathers and by canon lawyers and theologians in the Middle Ages; and More was far too well-read not to have come across it in one or several of the forms thus given it.

But although the idea of communism was very old in More's day, it is not with communism as such that we are concerned. We are concerned not with the genus communism or with other species of the genus: Platonic, Stoic, early Christian, monastic, canonist, or theological communism; we are concerned with Utopian communism—that is, simply communism as it appears in the imaginary commonwealth of Utopia, as More conceived it. Perhaps one way to sharpen our sense of the modernity of Utopian communism is to contrast it with the principal earlier types of communistic theory.

The contrast in substance between Utopian communism and the communism of the *Republic* is especially notable because of the very odd formal relationship between *Utopia* and the *Republic*, More and Plato. The enthusiasm for Plato as against Aristotle was well-rooted among many Renaissance philosophers of the generation or two before More's own. More himself surely knew about the Platonic Academy in Florence with which Colet had had direct contact. He even translated the biography of one of the most famous members of that group, Pico della Mirandola. But although well-acquainted with the *Republic* the Renaissance Platonists showed little interest in the political theme of that work or in the ordering of Plato's imaginary commonwealth. What drew them were those parts of the *Republic* which could be made to fit their Neoplatonic preoccupations and their desire to set Christianity on a Platonic rather than an Aristotelian philosophical foundation. And this preoccupation is very remote from a concern with the best condition of a commonwealth. This view of Plato is quite evident in John Colet. Colet, deeply moved by the sinfulness of humanity in contrast to the righteousness of God, spoke out sharply against some of the social iniquities of his day. But for all the connection he made between his social views and the *Republic*, or for that matter any of the dialogues preoccupied with man as a political animal, he need not have known Plato at all. On the otherhand, it would take a very fine mesh indeed to sift out of *Utopia* any discernible residue of Renaissance Neoplatonism. Yet in the book More explicitly refers to Plato five times, more often than to any other man of letters. Four of his five references are to Plato's political views, and all those four are to the *Republic*. But—and this is an extreme oddity—while three of the four political references report the substance of their source with reasonable accuracy, a fourth does not. In that fourth reference Hythlodaeus says that if he told the advisers of princes about "the kind of things which Plato creates in his republic or which the Utopians actually put in practice in theirs . . . such institutions . . . might appear odd because here individuals have the right of private property, there all things are common." As we have seen, this is simply not so: in Utopia private property is indeed altogether abolished; in the *Republic* it is not.

In Plato's *Republic* communism is—to speak anachronistically—a communism of Janissaries. Its function is to separate from the ruled mass, among whom private ownership prevails, the governing warrior élite. Moreover, it is too readily forgotten that in the *Republic* what gave the initial impetus to Plato's excursus into the construction of an imaginary commonwealth was his quest for a canon for the proper ordering of the individual human psyche; and it isto this problem that the *Republic* ultimately returns. In More's *Utopia* communism is not a means of separating out a warrior élite from the lumpish mass. Utopian communism applies to all Utopians. And in the economy of the book it is not peripheral but central. As specified in its title, the concern of *Utopia* is directly with the *optimo reipublicae statu,* the best ordering of a civil society or commonwealth; and it is again and again made clear that Utopian communism provides the institutional array indispensable to that best ordering.

To derive Utopian communism from the Jerusalem community of the apostolic age or from its medieval successors-in-spirit, the monastic communities, is as misleading as to derive it from Plato's *Republic:* in the *Republic* we have to do with an élite of physical and intellectual athletes, in the apostolic and monastic communities with an élite of spiritual and religious athletes. The apostolic community was literally an élite: personally chosen by Christ himself. And the monastic communities were supposed to be made up of volunteers selected only after a novitiate which would test their religious aptitude for monastic rigors. But Utopians were not selected for citizenship in Utopia, they were born there.

Nor can More's emphasis on Utopian communism as the very root of the matter be ascribed merely to his involvement in Christian humanism and the Christian Revival. It is true of course that a spiritual impulse which moves men to listen open-eared to the Gospels has latent in it radical possibilities. But to find in the Gospel one of the sources of inspiration for the radicalism of *Utopia* is by no means to exhaust that radicalism. The effect of the Gospels taken seriously is to deracinate old habits of thought about the way life should be lived; but to one concerned with the civil life of men it does not provide unambiguous guidance or any clear mandate. Men who in the name of the Gospel have rejected the way of living of their daily world have arrived at the most diverse conclusions as to what the Gospel requires them to put in its place. More was surely moved to his criticism of his own world by his share in the concern of his day with biblical Christianity. But the bare fact of the matter is that no one else involved in Christian humanism or the Christian Revival achieved the sort of modern conception of society which manifests itself in Utopian communism.

Finally, the conception of the *natural* community of all possessions which originated with the Stoics was firmly fixed in tradition by More's time, although it was not accepted by all the theologian-philosophers of the Middle Ages. It moved its communism back to the safe distance of the age of innocence, but it did not serve to contrast the existing order of society with a possible alternative order, because, for the Christian, the age of innocence was not a possible alternative once man had sinned. The actual function of patristic-civilian-canonist-scholastic communism was set forth by St. Gregory almost a millennium before More wrote *Utopia*. "The soil is common to all men; when we give the necessities of life to the poor, we restore to them what is already theirs. We should think of it more as an act of justice than compassion" [Gregory the Great, "Regulae Pastoralis Liber," *Patrologia Latina,* ed. J.-P. Migne, 1896].

Because community, not severalty, of property is the law of nature no man can assert an absolutely unalterable right to private possessions. Indeed, every man is by nature and reason and therefore by conscience obligated to regard himself as a custodian. He is a trustee for the common good, however feeble may be the safeguards which the positive or public law of property provides against his misuse of that share of the common fund wisely or unwisely entrusted to his keeping. In contrast to this Stoic-patristic view, *Utopia* implies that the nature of man is such that to rely on individual conscience to supply the deficiencies of public law is to embark in a sieve on the bottomless sea of humansinfulness. The Utopians brace conscience with legal sanctions. In a properly ordered society the massive force of public law performs the function which in natural law is ineptly left altogether to a small voice so often still.

In all the ways shown above, Utopian communism differs from previous conceptions in which community of possessions and living plays a role. Neither from one of these conceptions nor from a combination of them can it be deduced; it remains an integral whole, original—a new thing. And Utopian communism is one of the few new things in *Utopia*; much of the rest is medieval or Christian humanist or part of an old tradition of social criticism. But to say that at a moment in history something is *new* is not necessarily to say that it is modern; and for this statement the best evidence comes within the five years following the publication of *Utopia,* when Martin Luther elaborated a new vision of the nature of God's encounter with man. New, indeed, was Luther's vision, but not modern, as anyone knows who has ever tried to make intelligible to modern students what Luther was getting at.

Although Utopian communism is both new in 1516 and also modern, it is not modern communism or even modern socialism, as they exist or have ever existed in theory or in practice. Consider the featuresof Utopian communism: generous public provisions for the infirm; democratic and secret elections of all officers including priests; meals taken publicly in common refectories; a common habit or uniform prescribed for all citizens; even houses changed once a decade; six hours of manual labor a day for all but a handful of magistrates and scholars and careful measures to prevent anyone from shirking; no private property, no money; no sort of pricing at all for any goods or services, and therefore no market in the economic sense of the term. Indeed by the standards of economists—capitalist or socialist—the Utopian commonwealth is quite hopeless. It is not properly geared to maximizing utilities, to satisfying men's wants. On the contrary, so many things that a good many people want are banned in Utopia that Calvin's Geneva looks a bit frivolous and frisky by comparison. We have already had a clue to the reason for the deficiencies of Utopia as an economy. More's interest was not in the most effective organization of economic resources for the satisfaction of human wants because he was not concerned with the best economy or with the satisfaction of wants, and probably he had no clear conception of an economy distinct from the other relations of men in a community. He was primarily concerned, as he said on the title page of his book, with the best condition of a commonwealth, with the common well-being. And this well-being could be attained not by seeing that men, oftencorrupted and certainly corruptible, had what they wanted, but by seeing that those same men, often good, and certainly improvable, had what they needed for their welfare.

So, although Utopian communism diverges substantially from any communist tradition of thought or action with which More was acquainted, it also differs in detail and outlook from present-day socialist and communist economic theory and economic practice. It is not the details, however, that make *Utopia* modern; it is the bent of the spirit, the attitude of mind which informs and gives structure to those details. What that bent and that attitude were we will understand better if we examine more carefully the character of their contrast with the bent and attitude of the communist theory, familiar to More, with the longest continuous tradition. That was the theory which reached Christianity by way of Stoicism through the Church Fathers of late antiquity.

As one examines closely what the Fathers had to say about communism one is struck by something beside the substance of their views. The two obvious gross facts about those views—so obvious that they have tended to be overlooked—is that, first, they are scattered and, second, they are meager. When the Fathers deal with the communism which they suppose existed in a state of nature, it is rarely inconjunction with other arrangements that they assume existed in that state—equality of all men, universal liberty, and so on. They tend to come at the question casually and obliquely, if at all, in conjunction with some other matters of larger and more present concern—the sin of avarice, for example. Most of them probably believed that, like slavery, private property was at once the result and the corrective for sin after humanity had fallen through the disobedience of the first man. Yet this fact usually has to be inferred from the general tenor of their remarks: rarely do the Fathers make wholly explicit and unambiguous the relationship between communism and the state of innocence on the one hand, and private property and sin on the other.

Moreover, the Fathers' observations on communism before the Fall are so sketchy and vague that one can never gather from them the faintest conception of how it worked. Perhaps they felt that in a region so scantily populated and so abundantly endowed by Nature as the Earthly Paradise, detailed arrangements were otiose. But the more certain and significant reason for the meagerness of the Fathers' observations on the organization of a society in which possessions were held in common was, as we previously indicated, that not even as an act of imagination did they conceive of such a society as an alternative to the one in which they lived.

In the Church Fathers' view of the matter, then, as a consequence of human sinfulness, men are at once punished and safeguarded by, among other things, the severalty of property; and communism and a number of other desirable human arrangements have slipped from beyond the grasp of men because of that sinfulness. *Utopia* does to this view what Karl Marx did to Hegel; it turns it upside down. Private property is not a partial prophylaxis to human sinfulness—quite the contrary. Though not perhaps the unique cause, private property and the dense mass of inequalities which are ancillary to it are the most blatant occasions of human iniquity; they provide the rich black rottenness in which man's sins most abundantly flourish. And the way to deal with the evils which flourish under a regime of money and markets, private property, and inequality is simply to destroy that regime; without destroying it there will be no cure for the ills it engenders. Although a certain amount of patchwork may keep a sick society from falling into utter decay, patching one part often weakens another, and really "there is no hope . . . of a cure . . . as long as each individual is master of his own property." Here we get to the heart of what is modern about *Utopia*. It has as one of its central preoccupations not the amelioration of a sick society but the conditions indispensable to a sane one. Moreover, a nature essentially different from the ordinary nature of ordinary men emphatically wasnot one of the conditions of a sane society. The occidentals "are inferior" to the Utopians, says Hythlodaeus, "neither in brains nor in resources." The Utopians themselves had once been a "rude and rustic people," who lived in "mere cabins and huts, haphazardly made with any wood at hand, with mudplastered walls." The basis for the transformation of this barbarous folk to "such a perfection of culture and humanity as makes them now superior to almost all other mortals" was a drastic, a radical transformation of their institutions. That transformation drew out of the private sphere and into the domain of public law matters that in More's time were left to the desires and decisions of unregulated or lightly regulated individuals and groups—costume, meals, care of the aged and infirm, education, work and the hours of labor, the distribution of goods, the allocation of what a later generation was to call the factors of production, even the consumption of leisure.

The contrast between this way of looking at human affairs and the way most widely current in the Middle Ages and still widespread in More's own day could hardly be sharper. In that earlier perspective men through their misdoings had lost the capacity for a rational ordering of their affairs, so that for their present scarcely civil condition there was no real remedy on earth; and they had betteraccept the bad that was, in fear of the worse that might be. This older perspective Martin Luther shared with St. Augustine. In the perspective of *Utopia,* however, the irrational ordering of their affairs provided the incentive for men's misdoing; but they could escape from their present scarcely civil condition if they would undertake a resolute, rational, and radical reordering of their affairs. This is the point of view precisely set forth by Hythlodaeus. In More's sixteenth-century world, he says, self-seeking is as rational as concern for the common good is in Utopia. In a corrupt society, corrupt action is reasonable; in a decent society, decent action is reasonable. In its intense perception and presentation of community of goods as a conceivably viable alternative to private property and in its insistence that communism, not private property, is prophylactic against human wickedness, *Utopia* stands on the margins of modernity.

Another indication of the peculiarity of *Utopia,* of its deviation from the traditional norm, is provided by its diametrical contrast to the common medieval Christian attitude toward the broad spectrum of doings and ways of living which continuously or sporadically have strongly attracted large numbers of men. Professor [R. H.] Tawney summarizes the medieval view [in *Religion and the Rise of Capitalism,* 1947] as follows: "Society is an organism of differentgrades, and human activities form a hierarchy of functions which differ in kind and in significance, but each of which is of value on its own plane, provided that it is governed, however remotely, by the end which is common to all." This is a most spacious and accommodating attitude toward human affairs; it enabled the custodians of medieval values to accept a very wide range of activities as proper to man, if only some way could be found to construct for those activities sets of rules which did not manifestly run counter to divine law.

In effect, during the medieval centuries the social function assumed by the Christian Church, acting primarily through the clergy, was to Christianize society as it found it. By and large with only occasional and unsystematic eruptions of queasiness it simply accepted the hierarchical order, the domination of society by a warrior élite, chivalry, serfdom, romantic love, a market economy. By subjecting all Christians to auricular confession and to the sacrament of penance, the ecclesiastical hierarchy sought to infuse all existing legitimatized relations with a Christian spirit; and by setting forth penitential rules based on experience and on a detailed casuistry it brought each new sort of human activity as it emerged under the surveillance and, hopefully, the restraint of Christian morality. In a sense this stance affectswith a presumption of rightness, or at least of non-wrongness, the things that at any time men are currently doing and customarily have done. Concerning any human activity the medieval question becomes, "Is there any compelling reason why this should not be permitted in moderation?" On the other hand, the Utopian question is, "Why should a society consistently aiming at the best pursue or permit the pursuit of this activity?" In answering the medieval question it is easy to find room for the chase, the game of chance, the tavern, the gorgeous costume, the jewels, and the gold. In answering More's question it is hard to find room for any of these. In Utopia there are practically no *adiaphora,* practically no things indifferent.

The shift from the medieval stance of initial acceptance of the variety of human desires to the Utopian position which tests the admissibility of every desire by its congruity with the needs of a society rationally conceived generates radicalism of the modern kind. But Utopian communism does not tie in with any of the varieties of scientific socialism originating in Marx or with the anarchists' apocalyptic. It rather anticipates the radical egalitarianism which flared up fitfully in the Enlightenment. This egalitarianism gained force during the French Revolution among the Jacobins and later in England among the utilitarians. During thenineteenth century, radical egalitarians came to recognize that other kinds of equality became meaningless when traversed by the fierce inequality of the rich and the poor. They concluded that the effects of such inequality could be destroyed only by eradicating the inequality itself, by applying curbs of law in the interest of justice to the force of power and wealth. Thus modern egalitarian radicalism arrived at the point where Hythlodaeus began his Discourse on Utopia.

Once we have linked Utopian communism with its proper modern analogue, the way in which *Utopia* projects its vision into a later age becomes clearer. Nevertheless it is a quite curious way. Erasmus has often been identified as a precursor of the *philosophes* of the Enlightenment. Indeed, in some measure, the inhabitants of Utopia in their outlook *are* Enlightenment *philosophes*. The fund of moral conceptions common to most of the *philosophes* was after all the residue of centuries of Christianity; it was largely Christian ethics minus Christian mystery. The *philosophes* held as evil almost everything (except unbelief) which Christian ethics deemed sinful, as good almost everything Christian ethics deemed righteous (except faith in Christian dogma). In the main they dredged up a more or less plausible non-Christian rationale to provide shoring for a Christian morality for which they sought no substitute. What the *philosophes* did because they rejected Christian revelation, More had done over two centuries earlier because technically his Utopians could not know Christian revelation. The equation *reason equals nature equals virtue,* the deism precariously perched on rational foundations of doubtful solidity, the feeble and slightly apologetic hedonism wavering between the logical need for a this-worldly base and the psychological need for other-worldly sanctions—all these positions, common to so many eighteenth-century *philosophes,* recapitulate the "philosophy" of the Utopians.

More important, the author of *Utopia* combines certain traits and habits of thought in a pattern that was to become part of the ordinary stock in trade of the modern radical. More's contemporaries, especially the humanists, were inhibited from making a like combination by the very form in which they usually cast their writing on politics. That form is the *Fürstenspiegel,* the Mirror of Princes. . . . The form was venerable, and in innumerable treatises "over a period of ten centuries" from A.D. 500 to 1500, "the most striking and prominent thought that we find is the personal attitude toward rulership and rulers. Every one of the writers lays great stress upon the personal moral virtues of the prince. It is from him alone that good or evil, as he wills it, is visited on the land" [Erasmus, *Institutio*]. The question to which this sort of work addresses itself is, "What should the best prince do?" Given the habitual patterns of thought of almost ten centuries, this question had concealed within it a peculiar limitation. What a good prince did not do, so said the unvarying voice of traditional wisdom for a millennium, was to take the law into his own hands. He administered the law, he amended the law, occasionally he even dictated the law; but he did not abolish the law and replace it with a totally different law. Under such circumstances it is no wonder that most of the Mirrors of Princes of the Middle Ages and Renaissance go on at great length about the moral qualities of a good ruler and his proper style of conduct but are stonily silent about the substance of his actions. Consequently, in the context of the Middle Ages and the Renaissance, the question, "What ought the prince to do?" does not lead to the question, "What ought a good society to be?" On the contrary it prevents the latter question from being raised by focusing its entire attention on the personality and wisdom of the prince and giving no heed to the structure of society.

Giles offers Hythlodaeus the standard humanist princebook gambit early in *Utopia*: a "truly philosophic spirit" ought to be a royal councilor because "from the monarch, as from a never-failing spring flows a stream of all that is good or evil over the whole nation."The result might be described as prince-book gambit declined. The protagonist of the Dialogue, Hythlodaeus, refuses to turn it into a disquisition on the character of the virtuous prince. Of course, given the order of com-

position of *Utopia,* he was bound to refuse the gambit. The discourse on Utopia had already made pivotal a question that earlier humanists scarcely asked, "What is the best way to order a commonwealth—a polity-economy-society?" And by a significant inversion the princely *deus ex machina* of Utopia, King Utopus, does precisely what the ideal princes of the *Fürstenspiegel* literature never do and what even Machiavelli's prince never does: instead of maintaining the law that he finds among his subjects, he utterly abolishes it. Thus More breaks out of the circle which limited so much humanist writing about politics to platitudinous trivia and futile moralistic incantation.

Having escaped the confines of the humanist prince-books, More's thinking about the commonwealth was free to assume a new pattern. The components of that thinking in fact took a form which strikingly anticipates that of modern radicalism; not only are there a number of identifiable elements common to both, but the colligation of those elements seems similar. Separately these elements are 1) humanitarianism, 2) in connection with problems of human conduct a preference for arguments based on reason againstarguments based on tradition or custom, 3) belief in the efficacy of good law and good education as a remedy for the ills of the commonwealth, 4) environmentalism, 5) the sense that drastic change is necessary to deal with current ills. Readers of the literature of the Enlightenment and of English radicalism will surely recognize that a considerable part of the story that that literature has to tell can be organized under these five rubrics. It remains to identify them in Utopia. The humanitarian element is of course unmistakable—touching sympathy for men dogged by the insecurities and anxieties of life in More's own society, pity for the overburdened working people, concern for decent provision for the aged and infirm. Most clearly symptomatic, however, of More's transcendence of his own milieu is his preoccupation with crime and punishment. Both in the Discourse and the Dialogue there is evidence of his concern with a rational penology—in his description of how the Utopians treat their bondmen, in his contempt for England's harsh penal law, in his conception of punishment as a means of both deterrence and correction rather than of vengeance. Indeed Hythlodaeus' description of the organization of penal servitude among the Polylerites is perhaps the first of those attempts to conceive a wholly rational penology of which the Panopticon of that radical of radicals, Jeremy Bentham, was to be the most notorious, though not the last.

In *Utopia* the humanitarian quest for a rational penology is of a piece with a preference there made explicit for the rational over the merely customary and traditional. Writing in a world that, in matters of property and power, habitually identified right with custom and tradition, More gives short shrift to both. It is well enough to let the "wisest provisions" of the forefathers be; it is another matter in the face of a rational propos-al for improvement to say, "Our forefathers were hap-py with that sort of thing, and would to heaven we had their wisdom." This kind of nonsense, rampant among the councilors of Europe's rulers, is unknown in Uto-pia. There, any new thing that may make life better, whether proposed by a traveler or learned from books, is eagerly seized on and tried. While nature and reason are the sure guides to the good life, perverse habit hardened into custom leads to vice. But more signifi-cant than any detail, the whole project of the Discourse on Utopia is by its nature an unlimited exercise in rationality; its underlying presupposition is that the best ordering of human affairs can be discerned by subject-ing all merely human institutions to rational criticism, rational consideration, and rational reconstruction.

The extreme rationality of *Utopia* in respect to the ordering of society is as distinctively marked on the negative as on thepositive side. Even more curious than what *Utopia* says is its silence. Wholly lacking through-out the book is any hankering, explicit or implicit, for the good old days, a hankering that seems to have been pandemic in More's time and that is so deeply rooted in the stuff men are made of that it survived into an age dominated by the idea of progress. Indeed it sur-vived among such passionate exponents of progress as William Morris and Friedrich Engels. Even though the best days were coming, good days there had been; it was now that was truly awful. In More's own time the good old days might mean the dream world of chival-ry, and obviously he had no time for that. It might also mean, and in More's intellectual milieu usually did mean, Greco-Roman antiquity; but oddly enough there is not a trace in *Utopia* of that worship of ancient civilization (as distinct from admiration for an ancient literature) which was common coin among humanists. For the apostolic community of the first century after Christ, More indeed obliquely indicated his admira-tion, but in antiquity, as he well knew, that community was not a civilization; it was a group separated off, living in the world but not of it.

The means by which the best society is kept best are good institutions and good education—again a recipe after the heart of Bentham and of the generations of radicals who walked along andwidened the path he opened. Thus the indifference of Utopians to gold, their aversion to a money economy, and their abomination of the "madness of men who pay almost divine honors to the rich" have two sources. One is *doctrina* and *literae,* teaching and letters, for some schooling is giv-en to all; the other is their *educatio,* their upbringing in a commonwealth whose institutions are far removed from such folly. Their very fighting spirit in war de-rives its force from the institutions of Utopia, from its radical communism. In other lands concern about their livelihood at home and about the future of their fam-ilies saps the courage of the bravest. The Utopian in arms has no such worry, and consequently is more ready to fight to the finish. Finally it is the institutions of Utopia that make it at once most happy and most stable; and (so goes the last sentence of the Peroration) as long as its institutions remain sound no external enemy can destroy it.

Clearly More, like all good modern radicals, is a social environmentalist. This does not imply in either case a belief that men can so manipulate their social environ-ment as to eliminate the need for external controls and coercion. The anarchists have dreamed such a dream; but very few garden-variety radicals have done so. And More certainly did not; he was both too good a Chris-tian and too widely experienced a man to suffer delu-sionsabout human perfectibility. Nevertheless the ob-vious implication of his sketch of a society made ex-cellent by its laws, institutions, and education is that human happiness can be increased in a very large way by rules and teaching that repress men's evil impulses and foster their good ones, that do not subject them to temptations which are beyond the capacity of ordinary mortals to resist. More is very careful to note that the vast difference between the good way affairs are or-dered in Utopia and the ill way they are ordered in Europe has nothing to do with any difference in nat-ural endowment between Europeans and Utopians. It is in the use to which they put their natural gifts that the Utopians surpass the people of Europe.

In effect Utopia provides an environment in which men's natural gifts flourish, Europe an environment which causes them to grow twisted and rot. For exam-ple, in England the law which calls for thieves to be hanged simply gives them an incentive to murder, since if they are caught the penalty will be no greater. The condition which makes thieves is poverty and unem-ployment; and yet the English "ordain grievous and terrible punishments for a thief when it would have been much better to provide some means of getting a living, that no one should be under this terrible neces-sity first of stealing and then of dying for it." Again "you allow your youths to be badly brought up and their characters, even from early years, to become more and more corrupt. . . ." To punish men for crimes "which from boyhood they had shown every prospect of committing" is first to "create thieves and then become the very agents of their punishment." The rem-edies proposed to reform the penal law are like the ones built into the institutions of Utopia. They aim to achieve the security of life and means of livelihood which will take away the temptation to theft. The emphasis is all away from mere sermonizing before the criminal event and mere retribution after, all in the direction of prophylaxis by wise social controls. Since those controls are sound in Utopia, all Utopians "hav-ing had an excellent rearing to a virtuous life," they subject their fellow-countrymen convicted of heinous crimes to the harshest bondage. It is because men respond rationally to their environment that Europe is racked with social ills. For 'there men talk freely of the common interest—but look after their private interest only. In Utopia, where nothing is private, they seriously concern themselves with public affairs. *Assuredly in both cases they act reasonably* (italics mine).' The social arrangements of Europe drive sensible men, of necessity, to take care of themselves, and the public be damned. It is the social environment of Europe, its laws and customs, that leads Christian men to prey on Christian men in a society based not on community but on the thinly masked oppression of the poor by the rich.

The analysis in *Utopia* is radical. It stands at the opposite pole to the best-known piece of social analysis in Tudor literature—Ulysses' apostrophe to the principle of hierarchy in *Troilus and Cressida*. Shakespeare's splendid lines are only the most superb exemplar of the current orthodoxy. That human nature was red in tooth and claw, that by inclination men were wolves to other men, that they continually tended to fall into the savage war of each against each and that the sole safeguard against such horrors was the maintenance of the serried array of the existing order of society under its current rulers, was the firm conviction set forth to and for those who ruled in Renaissance Europe, to whom it doubtless made good listening. Concerning the conviction of those who were ruled in Renaissance Europe our evidence is scanty. The fundamental social conviction expressed in *Utopia* is that, far from being worth preserving, the social order based on hierarchy is only worth eradicating; that outside the family the true principle of the good commonwealth is the very opposite of hierarchy; it is equality.

The idea of eradicating, deracinating, pulling up by the roots—the starting point of radicalism—is not only implicit in *Utopia,* it is sporadically explicit. To attain justice, property must be utterly cast down. In Europe pride is too solidly fixed in men to be ripped out easily, but the Utopians have extirpated the roots of ambition. When the Utopians abolish the use of money they cut away a mass of troubles and pull a crop of crimes up by the roots. *Subferre, evellere, radicibus extirpare, subferre* again, *rescindere, radicatus evellere*—the vernacular equivalents of such terms are the standard coins of intellectual commerce with the modern radical.

The radicalism of *Utopia* is not a bit of *trompe-l'oeil,* a trick of perspective, the results of staring too long at a sixteenth-century book from some place in the twentieth century. The relation of the order of composition of the parts of *Utopia* to the completed book confirms the radical character of the work. Our analysis of the structure of the book indicated that the Dialogue of Counsel, including the Exordium in Book I, and the Conclusion, including the Peroration in Book II, were written after More's return to London, and most likely in about that order, since the effectiveness of both the Exordium and the Peroration indicates that More had the whole work—Dialogue as well as Discourse—clearly in mind and probably on paper when he set them down. In other words these sections of *Utopia,* though certainly not written at leisure, were composed after More had a chance to ruminate a bit on what he had already written in the Netherlands. He was free to proceed in a wide variety of possible ways, or, if he chose, not to proceed any further at all, but simply to pack up the job with the Introduction and Discourse. So in a way, what More writes in London is his own judgment on what he wrote earlier in the Netherlands. The Discourse was a work of many facets, both of mood and of substance. In the parts of *Utopia* he wrote subsequently in London, More could continue the variety of mood or assume a particular one, could select some substantial elements of the Discourse to the neglect of others for emphasis by reiteration or development.

With respect to mood, the range is narrower while the intensity is greater in the later-written parts of *Utopia* than in the Discourse. In the Discourse there is wit, considerable whimsy, a good bit of detailed but somewhat fanciful elaboration, many touches of humor, and some disengaged intellectual play, as well as harsh satire and angry social comment. In the parts of *Utopia* written in London there is only a trace of whimsy, no intellectual play, no elaboration of detail for the sheer pleasure of elaborating, and only a few bits of humor. There is wit, but the wit is sardonic, at times even savage. The Dialogue is also a diatribe; and whatever shreds of doubt may remain about More's own attitude toward his imaginary commonwealth of Utopia, the Dialogue leaves none at all about his detestation of the way of life of sixteenth-century Europe. The *festivus,* the gay, aspect of the *libellus* about Utopia is almost wholly confined to the Discourse; the Dialogue, the Exordium, and the Peroration are very sober. The satire, of which there is a great deal, is rarely playful; it is often grim, even bitter. It is the almost unbroken sobriety and earnestness of the exchanges between Hythlodaeus, More, and Giles and of Hythlodaeus' peroration that gives them their extraordinary intensity.

All this suggests that More may well have taken the Discourse more seriously after he thought it over in London than he did while he was writing it in the Netherlands. Or rather that he took more seriously those substantial elements of the Discourse which in the Dialogue, the Exordium, and the Peroration he chose to emphasize by reiteration and development. And what elements were these? Not the philosophy of the Utopians. In what he wrote in London More simply stopped fitting the social commentary of *Utopia* to the peculiar exigencies of a specious Epicureanism. Even in the

Exordium and the Peroration, where Hythlodaeus is specifically contrasting Europe and Utopia, decrying the former, lauding the latter, he has nothing to say about the Utopian philosophy of pleasure. Indeed the word *voluptas,* which in the Discourse More skillfully wove into Hythlodaeus' praise of Utopian institutions, occurs scarcely at all in the rest of the book. Nor in the Dialogue, Exordium, and Peroration is there any reference to the religious creeds and practices of the Utopians. More did not take the religions of the Utopians, their diverse beliefs and formal practices, seriously any more than he took their philosophy seriously. In the Dialogue he castigates the appetite for ruinous war among Christian princes; he denounces rulers who were wolves devouring their subjects through outrageous exactions rather than shepherds watching over them; he attacks the English penal system for its inhumanity. In effect he inveighs against the sins of the whole ruling class of the West—especially against its sloth, its greed, and its pride.

Campbell describes More's timelessness:

Sir Thomas More is one of those great figures that stand at the parting ways of history. He was as genuinely linked with the classical and patristic and mediaeval past as he was with the scientific future in which so many now put their hopes. But while he was as intellectually committed as the best minds in each of these periods were to the special interests of each, he had, what some of them had not, a never-failing and an ever-deepening supernatural faith. None can rightly understand More who do not understand this, and likewise understand, at the same time, that because he had this supernatural faith he also had faith in natural reason. Thus he differed, on the one hand, from the reformers who, in the name of faith, despised natural reason, and, on the other, from the later rationalists of the French Revolution, who in the name of reason despised supernatural faith. But with him faith came first, "the comen knowen faith" as he called it, "of all Christian men for this fifteen hundred year." "Reason," he also wrote, "so far from being an enemy to faith, is servant to faith."

More, therefore, was neither wholly of the past, as some have said, nor of the future, as others have believed, but really of the eternal present. . . .

W. E. Campbell, in More's Utopia and His Social Teaching, *Eyre & Spottiswoods, 1930.*

It is the Exordium and the Conclusion (including the Peroration) rather than the Discourse or even the Dialogue that bring the radical character of *Utopia* into the sharpest focus, all the more significantly because these appear to be the sections of the book that More wrote last. In both, the emphasis is the same; in both

the colligation of elements that makes the pattern of modern radicalism holds the center of attention. Mild measures, ameliorations are rejected; they may prevent utter disaster, but they are inadequate. If human nature is to grow straight and clean instead of twisted and foul it must be transplanted into a society which will foster such growth. Such a society is Utopia, where there is no money, no private property, no mine and thine. Without Utopian equality in all things, all the evils that plague a commonwealth by destroying the characters of its citizens will again take possession of the body politic, rendering transitory and ultimately futile all reforms and making the commonwealth once more a mere conspiracy of the rich against the poor. Community of property and abolition of money are *the only means* for achieving true equality. They are also *only the means*; the end is equality. For the final equations are simple and radical: the equitable is the good; equality is justice.

Equality is justice. That is the cutting edge of More's thought in *Utopia*. It frees him of the unexamined assumption, nearly universal in his day, about men's relations to men, the assumption not merely of difference, but of inequality, of status, of hierarchy. It envisages equality not as the lost prize of a golden age forever gone, but as the indispensable condition for a righteous social order. Its orientation is not toward the past but toward the future; and it impels the thinking of More into the future, and toward a particular point in that future—toward modern radicalism. Not toward Marx and scientific socialism. More would have found little congenial to him in the combination of economic analysis, German speculative thought, and the worship of science so conspicuous in the Marxian canon. One quotation from an eminent modern historian is enough to indicate where *Utopia* fits in the crazy quilt of modernity, and to summarize the whole structure of More's radicalism, with each element so distinct and sharp that it needs no further clarification here:

> The reality of a class struggle in modern society . . . is . . . insistent and the indignation aroused by the phrase is itself evidence of the fact. But to suppose that such phenomena are preordained and unavoidable—to find their sources in inexorable historical tendencies . . . instead of in the obvious, commonplace operations of folly and greed, which can either be indulged till they bring their nemesis, or chastened and repressed—is not science but superstition. . . . Democracy . . . can be used to correct inequalities. . . . Contrasts of environment, and inherited wealth, and educational opportunity and economic security, with the whole sad business of snobbery and servility which such contrasts produce, are the creation, not of nature, but of social convention. . . . Men have given one stamp to their institutions; they can give another. They have ideal-ized money and power; they can "choose" equality [R. H. Tawney, *Equality*, 1931].

Lee Cullen Khanna (essay date 1971)

SOURCE: "*Utopia:* The Case for Open-Mindedness in the Commonwealth," in *Moreana,* No. 31-32, November, 1971, pp. 91-105.

[In the following essay, Khanna contends that More recommends open-mindedness in his text, exemplifying it both in the Utopians and in the dialogue between the characters of Hythloday, More, and Peter Giles.]

The *Utopia* has been read as an economic, social or political treatise, hailed as a precursor of communism, and praised for its illustration of medieval and monastic virtues. Some critics have analyzed its philosophic precepts, while others have seen it as a light-hearted *jeu d'esprit*. More's major work has fascinated and puzzled readers for generations.

The continuous popular appeal of the work may itself indicate, however, a more fundamental and universal meaning than that attributed to it by most critics. I believe that the dramatic emphasis of *Utopia* does not depend upon any philosophical or political system. Rather the two books form a self-contained literary unit whose consistent theme is the importance of open-mindedness for the improvement of the social order. The ability to experiment, learn, and change is more important to *Utopia* than any particular new institution or custom presented.

The importance of the experimental attitude is often overlooked, because critical debate frequently centers upon a reader's preference for Hythloday's or More's opinions. But a close reading indicates that both are created characters serving More's larger purpose. Hythloday's fictional nature is usually accepted, but, as early as the prefatory letter to Giles, the author begins to establish a fictional "Thomas More" as well. In that letter More portrays himself as a scrupulously honest, literal reporter when in fact, as his humanist readers realized, he was a sophisticated feigner. Throughout *Utopia* More exists as a persona distinct from the author. He is literal-minded and pragmatic, occasionally almost fatalistic. This character confronts Raphael Hythloday, idealist, extremist, and revolutionary. The two personalities are deliberately played against one another, but finally neither has the upper hand. The reader is faced, directly and dramatically, with two different perspectives. He need accept neither "More" nor Hythloday as the author's spokesman nor, indeed, *Utopia* itself as a blueprint for the perfect order.

Although this uncertainty about how seriously to take the characters and the society they discuss has troubled many critics, it seemed to pose little problem to More's humanist readers. Their commendatory letters and verses, published with the first four editions of *Utopia,* share in its spirit and enhance its meaning.

The prefatory letters are not dogmatic, but, as Peter Allen notes [*Studies in the Renaissance,* 1963], they praise *Utopia* as "both a delightful literary game and an important philosophic work." Many ideas, practical and impractical, are espoused in a highly imaginative fashion, and readers are invited to participate in this wise and witty discussion about society.

The tone of the prefatory material indicates that More's humanist readers did respond as he had intended. Guillaume Budé, for example, does not provide any absolute interpretation but adopts various points of view. First, in the manner of Hythloday, he attacks the vices of Europe; then, philosophically, he speculates on the nature of Utopia. Finally, although he seems to suggest that the island is ideal, Budé's closing advice to Europeans is not athoughtless imitation of Utopia but a receptive attitude. He says that the present age and those succeeding will "hold his [More's] account as a nursery of correct and useful institutions from which every man may introduce and *adapt* transplanted customs to his own society" (italics mine).

Further evidence of reactions that point toward More's basic meaning is given by Erasmus and Giles, the humanists most closely associated with *Utopia.* In a letter to William Cop Erasmus indicates his reaction to the work. Interestingly enough he does not commend it as the depiction of an ideal republic. By reading More's book, he says, you will be amused and simultaneously discover "the very sources from which almost all the evils of society rise." A modern reader cannot be sure precisely what Erasmus meant by the "sources" of social evils. But the similarity of this remark to that of Peter Giles is striking. In his prefatory letter to Jerome Busleyden Giles does not know whether to admire most More's "happy memory" or the conversation with Hythloday "or the sagacity with which he has noted the sources from which all evils actually arise in the commonwealth or from which all blessings possibly could arise . . ."

Giles provided a clue to his meaning by the quatrain in the "Utopian vernacular" he contributed to the first edition. In that little poem "Utopia" speaks, saying she represents the philosophical city for mortals but does so without the aid of any "abstract philosophy." No particular system or systems are mentioned to account for her greatness. The last lines of the verse reveal the actual source of Utopia's strength. "Ungrudgingly do I share my benefits with others; undemurringly do I adopt whatever is better from others." The willingness to learn and change is the origin of Utopian blessings, just as the narrow-mindedness shown in the council scenes of Book One is the source of the evils that afflict Europe.

The two men closest to the *Utopia,* Erasmus and Giles, do not hold it up as a model, nor do they isolate any of its institutions for special praise or imitation. Rather they admire the expanded awareness afforded by More's book. The *Utopia* illustrates a certain plasticity of attitude, a fundamental insight which illuminates the causes of evil in the social order. Agreeing on a generalized tribute to More's insight rather than to the particular constitution of the island, Erasmus and Giles perhaps also agreed on the crucial importance of tolerance and receptivity expressed in the lines of Giles' quatrain.

Although later commentators tended to dismiss Utopia as unreal or dogmatically assert, with Hythloday, that it was totally ideal, More probably desired more flexibility from his reader. His use of two fictional characters served this end.

In traditional voyage tales the reader responds solely to the point of view of the adventurer himself. He may dismiss the traveler's stories as far-fetched, the strange customs as simply wrong, the lands as unreal. Even if he fully approves the new institutions, he may not see any hope of applying them to his nation. By using two narrators, however, More incorporated some of these very "realistic" reactions into the work itself. As a practical man of affairs the character "More" points out the extremism of many of Hythloday's views and often voices persuasive reasons for compromise. Thus he often emphasizes the potential relevance of Utopian institutions. But his final resignation to the status quo expresses the very reaction that readers of *Utopia* might have had without him. By incorporating this passive reaction into the work More revealed its inadequacy. Such apparent apathy, following as it does Hythloday's persuasive peroration contrasting Utopian industry and European complacency, pushes the reader toward a positive "Utopian" response. Let us see, he might say, if we cannot profit from these new ways and appropriate to ourselves "whatever seemsbetter." The contrasting personalities of More's two characters thus might make the reader affirm the necessity for change. Confronted by opposites and given no definite solution, the reader is freed to react with his own suggestions for reform—to participate in the process of devising a better society.

If opening the reader's mind to social change was More's purpose, the form of *Utopia* suits his aim. The unresolved opposition between "More" and Hythloday leaves both books open-ended. In addition, contrasts are established on multiple levels between Europe and Utopia. These numerous differences do not, however, lead to an absolute choice between the two societies. Just as the exchange between Hythloday and "More" is inconclusive, the merits of the two governments remain relative. This relativity is emphasized through the dialogue form of Book One, and the conflicts there prepare the reader to see contrasts between Utopia and Europe implied in Book Two. Thus a tension between opposites tends to shape both sections to More's purpose.

The open-ended form created by More's controlled use of contrast advances the theme of *Utopia* as well as its purpose. A textual analysis of both books should show that the importance of experimental attitudes is the real subject of the work.

This theme finds dramatic focus at the end of each book. At the conclusion of his debate with Giles and "More", Hythloday reveals what is actually most important about Utopia. Denying the usefulness of counsel in a corrupt state, he summarizes his position by contrasting the "holy institutions of the Utopians" with the injustices of European society. When "More" objects to communism, Hythloday's response is significant. He tells "More" that he should have seen Utopia, not because of its communism, but because of the people's "industry". It is not their intelligence but their willingness to apply new ideas that causes the citizens of Utopia to surpass Europeans. "I hold for certain," Hythloday says, "that even though we surpass them in brains, we are far inferior to them in application and industry."

Although Utopians have had little contact with distant countries, their chronicles do report the landing of shipwrecked Romans and Egyptians some twelve hundred years earlier. "Now mark what good advantage their industry took of this one opportunity," says Hythloday. "The Roman empire possessed no art capable of any use which they did not either learn from the shipwrecked strangers or discover for themselves after receiving the hints for investigation—so great a gain was it to them that on a single occasion some persons were carried to their shores from ours."Hythloday draws the important parallel with European response to his landing and the new information he brings. "But if any like fortune has ever driven anyone from their shores to ours, the event is as completely forgotten as future generations will perhaps forget that I had once been there. And just as they immediately at one meeting appropriated to themselves every good discovery of ours, so I suppose it will be long before we adopt anything that is better arranged with them than with us. *This trait, I judge, is the chief reason why, though we are inferior to them neither in brains nor in resources, their commonwealth is more wisely governed and more happily flourishing than ours*" (italics mine). It is Utopian ability to change, to heed and apply new ideas that Hythloday lauds as their chief quality—not their communism, Epicureanism, nor any of their customs.

Utopian open-mindedness comes dramatically to the fore again at the end of Book Two. At this point it is not Hythloday's opinions but a vision of the Utopians themselves that emphasizes their chief virtue. The account of their religious belief has become increasingly more impressive and is finally crowned by the description of the Utopians at prayer. These people, who have achieved so much in the way of material well-being and philosophic sanity, humbly beg further instruction. The Utopian thanks God for "benefits received, particularly that by divine favor he has chanced on that commonwealth which is the happiest and has received that religion which he hopes to be the truest." Then the Utopian adds, "If he errs in these matters or if there is anything better and more approved by God than that commonwealth or that religion, he prays that He will, of His goodness, bring him to the knowledge of it, for he is ready to follow in whatever path He may lead him." Despite all his justifiable reasons for pride and a strong sense of self-assurance, the Utopian readily admits the limits of his knowledge. He prefaces his belief with a conditional and is able to qualify even his religious views. Addressing God he says, "*if* this form of a commonwealth be the best and his religion the truest, he prays that then He may give him steadfastness and bring other mortals to the same way of living and the same opinion of God—*unless* there be something in this variety of religions which delights His inscrutable will" (italics mine). The humility that allows such qualification also fosters progress. This is the point brought out in a variety of ways and climactically espoused at the end of each book.

Even as these dramatic high-points reveal the importance of a receptive attitude, so too does the chief line of argument in the body of each book. This consistency of theme welds the somewhat disparate forms of the two sections into an effective whole. An analysis first of the dialogue and then of Hythloday's monologue—the description of Utopia—should reveal this underlying thematic unity.

The conversation between Giles, "More" and Hythloday in Book One centers ostensibly on the value of service at a royal court. After the introduction to "More" is completed and the three are comfortably seated, Giles says, "Why, my dear Raphael, I wonder that you do not attach yourself to some king." The debate is on. It is concluded, although not resolved, at the end of the book when Hythloday says that service in any state other than Utopia is futile.

Perhaps, then, a critic of *Utopia* should concentrate on external information about More's own decision to enter the court circle. Presumably he decided to enter Henry's service soon after the composition of *Utopia*. The danger is, however, that the analysis may lead away from the work itself toward More's "probable" thinking and "possible" conversations with friends around 1515. When J.H. Hexter, for example, tries to ascertain the "furniture of More's mind" in 1515, he fails to see the relevance of the actual dialogue in Book One to the whole of *Utopia*.

Why, in fact, is there such a conflict about the merit of royal service? The debate arises from the underlying recognition of the difficulty of provoking change. European kings, courtiers, and even ordinary citizens are not ready to receive new ideas. The dialogue in Book One brings out the importance of this issue in several ways.

After Giles has urged Raphael to join some court in order to benefit himself and his friends, "More" then tries to persuade him on the basis of public service. Hythloday modestly denies the ability More ascribes to him, but adds the real reason why he disdains councilorship. He says, "Among royal councilors everyone is actually so wise as to have no need of profiting by another's counsel, or everyone seems so wise in his own eyes as not to condescend to profit by it . . . If anyone, when in the company of people who are jealous of others' discoveries or prefer their own, should propose something which he either has read of as done in other times or has seen done in other places, the listeners behave as if their whole reputation for wisdom were jeopardized and as if afterwards they would deserve to be thought plain blockheads unless they could lay hold of something to find fault with in the discoveries of others. When all other attempts fail, their last resource is a remark such as this: 'Our forefathers were happy withthat sort of thing, and would to heaven we had their wisdom.'" In this fashion Hythloday points out the destructiveness of provincialism and insists that while it exists, no counsel can be useful.

After the disadvantage of excessive respect for tradition has been pointed out, Book One falls roughly into three council scenes: the one at Cardinal Morton's remembered by Hythloday, and the imaginary councils of the French king and those of another, unidentified ruler. In each case Hythloday explores some particular English or European evil and offers remedies for it. He supports his arguments by examples from history and from travel. But his final point in each case is that his proposals make no difference, since they will not be heeded. When he opposes capital punishment for theft at Cardinal Morton's and indicates the evils of enclosure and of idle retainers, he is immediately dismissed by a supposedly learned lawyer—a representative of English justice. After he suggests bondage as a punishment for theft, Hythloday adds that he sees "no reason why this method might not be adopted even in England . . ." The lawyer replies: "Never could that system be established in England without involving the commonwealth in a very serious crisis . . ." Hythloday recalls, not without bitterness, that "all who were present gave him their assent." Although the Cardinal sways his courtiers to a more favorable reception, Hythloday realizes that the primary reaction to his new ideas is based on traditionalism, national pride, and preference for one's own opinions.

Apologizing to "More" for the length of his tale, Hythloday points out, "This conversation I had to relate, though somewhat concisely, to exhibit the attitude of those who had rejected what I had said at first yet who, immediately afterward, when the Cardinal did not disapprove of it, also gave their approval, flattering him . . . From this reaction you may judge what little regard courtiers would pay to me and my advice." When "More" still demurs, Hythloday offers a hypothetical case. The French king decides to meet with his council to determine the most successful method of waging war on Italy. His councilors argue about which plan will best further the king's goal. Suppose I, asks Hythloday, suggested that Italy be left alone. Suppose I opposed war in general. "What reception from my listeners, my dear More, do you think this speech of mine would find?" "More" must concede Hythloday's reiterated point. "'To be sure, not a very favorable one,' I granted." Hythloday proceeds to make his case about the narrow-mindedness of European rulers still stronger. "Picture the councilors of some king or other," he continues, "debating with him and devising by what schemes they may heap up treasure for him." "At this point suppose I were again to rise and maintain that these counsels are both dishonorable and dangerous for the king, whose very safety, not merely his honor, rests on the people's resources rather than his own." Hythloday returns to the purpose of his hypothesis: "To sum it all up, if I tried to obtrude these and like ideas on men strongly inclined to the opposite way of thinking, to what deaf ears should I tell the tale!" Again "More" concedes the point, "Deaf indeed, without doubt, I agreed."

As the book closes, Hythloday reiterates his position about the futility of advising kings who will not listen. Then he contrasts Utopia. His climactic testimony to Utopian open-mindedness bears directly on the issue at the heart of the entire book. Hythloday's fundamental frustration with Europeans is not their private property, but their "deaf ears". By the time the reader reaches the end of Book One and learns of the readiness with which Utopians heed new ideas, he might well agree that "this trait" could be "the chief reason" why a commonwealth might be "more wisely governed and more happily flourishing."

In spite of Hythloday's consistent disparagement of European courts, however, the question of counsel remains open. "More" argues for the necessity of setting forth new ideas even in a hostile atmosphere. And some hope of response is offered. In the first council scene, cited by Hythloday to prove the futility of advice, one major source for optimism exists—Morton himself. The lawyer and the rest of the company dismiss Hythloday's suggestions, to be sure, but the Cardinal quells the disapproval with these words: "It is not easy to guess whether it would turn out well or ill inasmuch as absolutely no experiment has been made."

In his willingness to experiment, the Cardinal foreshadows the Utopian attitude lauded in Book Two. He also offers a positive counter to Hythloday's pessimistic view on the fruits of counsel in Europe. The uncompromising Hythloday is too much angered by the general lack of response to appreciate the importance of the Cardinal's interest. But the Cardinal gives weight to More's argument—the possibility of effecting some change. After recalling his conversation at Morton's, Hythloday points out the futility of his service, but "More", without openly disagreeing, dwells on the Cardinal and his happiness at his court as a boy. Later "More" does voice his opinion. He admits that Hythloday's radical advice would encounter deaf ears. But he adds, "and by heaven I am not surprised. Neither, to tell the truth, do I think that such ideas should be thrust on people, or such advice given, as you are positive will never be listened to." "More" then argues that some good can be achieved by working through the convictions of the hearers—and not in direct opposition. He actually states the basic assumption about human nature presupposed by his view. He tells Hythloday that by "the indirect approach you must seek and strive to the best of your power to handle matters tactfully. What you cannot turn to good you must make as little bad as you can. For it is impossible that all should be well unless all men were good, a situation which I do not expect for a great many years to come!"

"More", accepting the severe limits of human nature, is willing to adapt to a given situation. Rather than pessimism, he urges gratitude for whatever small change might be effected. Hythloday, on the other hand, insists that a favorable climate of opinion is a necessary base for any improvement. Both, however, recognize the fundamental importance of receptive attitudes to the welfare of the state, and both make the primacy of this issue apparent to the reader. They differ only in the degree which each deems acceptable for progress. The confrontation of Hythloday, the radical idealist, and "More", the practical man of affairs, provides the reader a complete spectrum of possibilities on the issue of change in an established state. The question of whether or not to advise kings is necessarily based on the possible effect of such advice. And it is this issue that relates the dialogue intrinsically to Hythloday's discourse.

In the course of Hythloday's description of the island, constituting Book Two, Utopian willingness to take advice is seen as a vital factor in their achievement. For instance, Hythloday points out the eagerness with which Utopians adopted the ideas introduced by his company. They learned Greek, discovered the art of printing and manufacture of paper, and received the religious doctrine of Christianity from Hythloday and his companions. Appropriately enough, Hythloday stresses the teachableness of the Utopians in his discussion of Utopian travel. The citizens travel little, but can take full advantage of new experiences, whether their own journeys or, as in the case of Hythloday and his friends, the travels of others. "When they had heard from us about the literature and learning of the Greeks," Hythloday says, "it was wonderful to see their extreme desire for permission to master them through our instruction." At first the Portuguese adventurers only humored their hosts, doubting their ability to grasp so difficult a tongue. Yet, Hythloday confesses his astonishment, "in less than three years they were perfect in the language and able to peruse good authors without any difficulty unless the text had faulty readings."

In the case of printing on paper, the Utopians did not even wait for explicit instruction. So ready were they to respond to new methods that they seized the initiative. In Europe it might be necessary to explain painstakingly the advantages of something different, and then justify the cost and labor involved in conversion to such new methods. In Utopia the citizens were so intrigued by the very sight of Aldine printing that they promptly set to work on the problem of reproducing it. Hythloday tells the reader that neither he nor any of his companions were "expert in either art". With "the greatest acuteness" the Utopians guessed how it was done. The most important factor in their success, however, was not their intelligence, but, as Hythloday had suggested earlier, their open-mindedness and industry. Hythloday says, "Their first attempts were not very successful, but by frequent experiment they soon mastered both." His closing remarks seem to emphasize the most important aspect of his comments on travel. "Whoever, coming to their land on a sightseeing tour, is recommended by any special intellectual endowment or is acquainted with many countries through long travel, is sure of a hearty welcome, for they delight in hearing what is happening in the whole world."

The observations about travel are not the only points in Book Two that indicate the over-riding virtues of Utopians. In his account of their religion Hythloday gives another example of the educability of the island's citizens. He says, "After they had heard from us the name of Christ, His teaching, His character . . . you would not believe how readily disposed they, too, were to join it [the Christian religion]." Many Utopians were baptized, persuaded to love the sacraments and "desire them with the greatest eagerness." In religion, as in more earth-bound affairs, the Utopians were eager to appropriate whatever seemed better.

In the case of the Utopian interest in Christianity, however, Hythloday rounds out his account with a particularly interesting story. First he pays tribute even to those Utopians who did not adopt Christianity. Even those, he says, "who do not agree with the religion of Christ do not try to deter others from it. They do not attack any who have made their profession." More remarkable, still, than this tribute to pagan tolerance

and maturity coming from a Christian, is its juxtaposition with the account which follows. "Only one of our company, while I was there, was interfered with. As soon as he was baptized, in spite of our advice to the contrary, he spoke publicly of Christ's religion with more zeal than discretion. He began to grow so warm in his preaching that not only did he prefer our worship to any other but he condemned all the rest. He proclaimed them to be profane in themselves and their followers to be impious and sacrilegious and worthy of everlasting fire." The fiery neophyte oversteps the forms of decorum observed by his fellow Utopians. He abandons reason and the sense of his own finite limitation to impose his views on others. In the end he is sentenced to exile, not for his Christianity, but for his bigotry.

The over-zealous Utopian described in Book Two corresponds to the friar at Cardinal Morton's mentioned in Book One. Like the friar, the Utopian becomes destructive through his excessive partisanship. He damns all who do not agree with him just as the friar threatens all who scorn friars with excommunication. Because he forsakes the tolerance that made his nation great, the baptized Utopian is made to look as foolish as the friar.

In both books, then, More discloses the folly of narrow-mindedness and also reveals the value of tolerance for social improvement. In addition, he gives evidence that Utopians themselves recognize the importance of maintaining receptive attitudes and make notable efforts to preserve them.

The founder of the island avoided rigid precepts and showed a profound personal tolerance. Utopus readily admitted the limits of human knowledge and was, says Hythloday, "uncertain whether God did not desire a varied and manifold worship and therefore did not inspire people with different views." He was open to all possibilities but felt the best approach was ideological freedom. "Even if it should be the case that one single religion is true and all the rest are false, he foresaw that, provided the matter was handled reasonably and moderately, truth by its own natural force would finally emerge sooner or later and stand forth conspicuously." He felt it his duty to promote free exchange and control any violent suppression of views, for, he observed, "the worst men are always the most unyielding." Here, as in the rest of *Utopia*, flexibility seems to be a necessary condition for the emergence of the best. With such premises Utopus, says Hythloday, "made the whole matter of religion an open question. . . ."

The citizens' common life, often held up as the most important aspect of Utopia, also contributes to flexibility. In so far as communism encourages detachment, it encourages change. Possessions tend to generate protective or acquisitive attitudes that limit the actions and even the thinking of the owner. Hythloday notes one social result of common life when he says, "No city has any desire to extend its territory, for they consider themselves the tenants rather than the masters of what they hold."

Since the Utopians have no need—either personal or national—to acquire more land or goods, they do not rush into war. They decide to do battle only if they judge it to be in the best interest of the commonwealth or of their allies. Once the decision is made, they endeavor to accomplish their goals with as little bloodshed as possible. They devise new military strategies, because they are no more bound by concepts of honor than they are by desire for land. Encouraging treachery within the enemy ranks, the Utopians capture their leaders and so demoralize their opponents. They do not disdain such betrayal, because it saves lives on both sides. Hythloday says, "They boast themselves as having acted with valor and heroism whenever their victory is such as no animal except man could have won, that is by strength of intellect. . . ." They do not consider it heroic or honorable to die unnecessarily. Life is not cheap in a state where each citizen has equal access to pleasure—material and intellectual.

If the society as a whole adopts new approaches to age-old human problems, the ordinary citizen is likely to be receptive to new methods too. Hythloday often comments on those aspects of Utopian common life that encourage individual pliancy. For example, he points out that men alternate between rural and urban life on a regular basis. Each man thus has the experience of two quite different ways of life on which to base his judgments. He does not have to defend his profession, since he has at least two. Nor is he limited to the virtues of town or country life and so likely to scorn one or the other.

His personal flexibility is encouraged by other, apparently diverse, Utopian customs. For example, Hythloday notes that the Utopians change their homes by lot every ten years. He does not explain the purpose of this rotation, yet it surely discourages attachment. In this communistic society no one becomes so concerned about his home that he is not willing to risk losing it if the occasion demands. In only one aspect of Utopian life is the competitive drive mentioned. The Utopians do take pride in the beauty of the gardens behind their homes. Yet even this rivalry is skillfully contrived to hinder individual vanity. For the "keen competition" which Hythloday observes in the case of gardens is "between blocks."

The family structure is also designed to discourage protective self-interest. Members may be transferred from one family unit to another on the basis of the size of each group. A major result of this regulation, too,

must be to free the individual to think about the good of the community. He need not fearfully resist change lestit endanger his family or his goods.

Just as many features of Utopian communism encourage receptive attitudes, so too does Utopian natural philosophy. Much has been written about Epicurean and Stoic elements in the *Utopia* and the sources of More's version of them. Yet what is important in Hythloday's lengthy description of Utopian philosophy is not just its relationship to classical schools of thought, but its relevance to More's basic purpose. When the Utopians define virtue as living according to nature's precept, they are espousing a system that tends to discourage an accretion of irrational traditions. Nature, reason, and use afford a yardstick against which to measure customs, institutions, and ideas.

Hythloday illustrates the function of their philosophy in his discussion of false pleasure. He notes that when fashion is artificially determined, men tend to measure their own value by the quality of their clothes. Yet, as Hythloday observes, "If you consider the use of the garment, why is wool of finer thread superior to that of thicker?" He goes on to question the worth of "empty and unprofitable honors", asking "what natural and true pleasure can another's bared head or bent knees afford you? Will this behavior cure the pain in your own knees or relieve the lunacyin your own head?" In Utopia citizens are honored in proportion to their contributions to society, their strength of intellect, or their virtue. Freed from the bonds of artificial social conventions, Utopians are able to respond to new customs or ideas on the basis of their natural utility.

Utopian conclusions about dress, ways of showing honor, and other issues are not meant to be wholeheartedly embraced by the reader, but the fresh perspective their system offers is of great significance. Hythloday summarizes his presentation of Utopian philosophy by saying, "This is their view of virtue and pleasure. They believe that human reason can attain to no truer view, unless a heaven-sent religion inspire man with something more holy. Whether in this stand they are right or wrong, time does not permit us to examine—*nor is it necessary*. We have taken upon ourselves only to describe their principles, and not also to defend them" (italics mine).

It is not necessary or important to establish the absolute validity of the Utopian system. In fact the whole method of *Utopia* tends to confute absolutism. Hythloday himself had expressed hesitation about the high estimation of pleasure in Utopia, and the qualification about "heaven-sent religion" in the passage quoted-probably indicates a Christian reservation about a pagan state. But Hythloday's main emphasis is on the triumphant result of Utopian attitudes. He commends their "nimbleness" of body and their nimbleness of mind after discussing their philosophy. It is at this point in fact that he praises their quick comprehension of Greek, printing, and papermaking. Because they are no more bound by provincial pride in their own techniques than they are by an artificially established nobility, Utopians can experiment freely with new methods, even as they can value men for their minds.

Utopian religion, communism, and moral philosophy all contribute to the inquisitiveness and intellectual agility of the citizens. Humility before God's superior wisdom forbids an absolutist acceptance of manmade dogma, and an eagerness to know the divine will encourages an exploration of nature. Hythloday observes that when the Utopians investigate "the secrets of nature, they appear to themselves not only to get great pleasure in doing so but also to win the highest approbation of the Author and Maker of nature." The Utopian system of communism frees citizens from the worries of private property, and the business of accumulating goods for oneself and one's family, and it frees the state from deleterious wars. Consequently, individual and national efforts may be turned to intellectual and cultural improvements. And, finally, Utopiannatural philosophy offers the perspective of nature and reason by which to judge individual and social endeavors.

These three major aspects of Utopian society foster the willingness to change that both "More" and Hythloday agree is crucial for the good state. In addition, the Utopians preserve their social pliancy in many incidental ways. For example, they do not establish a rigid schedule for labor. Normally they work six hours a day, but if production needs do not require the fruits of any particular trade, the men are freed for more useful work. If the roads need repair, the unoccupied workers may do that. If no work remains to be done, then "they announce publicly that there will be fewer hours of work. For the authorities do not keep the citizens against their will at superfluous labor. . . ." Regulations like these indicate a kind of built-in flexibility in the Utopian system. Another example is a rather remarkable rule for debate in the Utopian senate. Utopians refuse to discuss any proposition on the same day it is laid before the body. In this case, the officials reveal their awareness of the dangers of dogmatic stands and try to avoid them. As Hythloday explains, "This is their rule lest anyone, after hastily blurting out the first thought that popped into his head, should afterwards give more thought to defending his opinions than to supporting what is good for the commonwealth. . . ."

Not only does Hythloday describe regulations in Utopian society which indicate the citizenry's own appreciation of pliancy and respect for learning, he also relates humorous tales about the state which, even as they amuse, suggest the value of such attitudes. In the first chapter of Book Two, for example, the Utopian method of hatching eggs is introduced. In the midst of the serious discussion of agriculture and the duties of farmers, the reader is suddenly confronted with the startling image of chickens pursuing human beings as their parents. Some readers might have heard of the ancient Egyptian method of artificial incubation via Pliny, Diodorus Siculus, or Mandeville, although the practice did not yet exist in Europe. But the suggestion that the newly hatched chickens followed "humans as their mothers" probably seemed strange and funny. In many of their institutions Utopians were wholly admirable, a reader might well observe, but in cases like this they were just peculiar. Yet even this amusing Utopian phenomenon contributes subtly to More's larger purpose. On a level more of entertainment than of Platonic discussion, the artificial incubation of chickens gives a striking alternative to something as apparently standardized as the way of raising fowl. The crowning touch is of course the claim that chicks follow humans as mothers. In other words, chickens adapt to the situation in which they find themselves; their custom is modified by experience—not maintainedin spite of it. With a laugh then, More says, look here, even chickens can change.

There are many other whimsical tales in the *Utopia,* such as the story of the Anemolian ambassadors, the legend about the creation of the island from a peninsula, the strange methods of Utopian courtship, the description of the outlandish garb worn by Utopian priests, and Herculean methods of placing raw materials near urban centers. These accounts of strange Utopian customs all give fresh perspective to traditional European values. The legend about Utopus' conquest and his subsequent excavation of fifteen miles of land connecting the island to the peninsula shows the fruit of cooperative effort. As the marginal note points out, "What Is Common to All Is Borne Lightly". The "light work" of course is of heroic proportions and so serves to remove Utopians from the realm of a purely practical discussion of the best state—even as it testifies to the advantages of communism.

The laughter evoked by such strange tales serves its own purpose. A sober discussion of the best state of the commonwealth might well seem to forbid purely experimental ideas. Such a ponderous subject seems to call for only the most prudent suggestions. But the humorous stories and occasional excesses of Utopian customs lend alighter tone. In this atmosphere, one feels, there is the freedom to make mistakes. Engaged by the wit as well as the subject of the discussion, a reader might well respond with his own ideas for an improved commonwealth. To awaken this response was surely More's primary intent in the *Utopia.*

The amusing aspects of Utopia also serve to limit the land as an ideal, and, in fact, Hythloday's final remarks do not simply hold up the vision of a perfect state. Instead his closing statement contrasts Europe and Utopia and then points to the source of European failure—pride. Europe might long ago have admitted the superiority of such just methods as those practiced in Utopia, Hythloday says, "had not one single monster, the chief and progenitor of all plagues, striven against it—I mean Pride." The angry diatribe against pride which follows is intrinsically related to the entire movement of More's work. Since More's fundamental message is the vital importance of receptive attitudes, it is logical that his protagonist should finally lash out against the enemy of change. It is the vanity of nationalism and delight in one's own opinions that prevent Europeans from heeding a fresh suggestion. Pride is a "serpent from hell" because she closes men's minds to improvement for the community at large. Under her influence people foolishly exalt the status quo, like the lawyer at Cardinal Morton's. Because she drains men's objectivity and capacity to "see life whole," pride, says Hythloday, "acts like the suckfish in preventing and hindering them from entering on a better way of life." Hythloday's final anger is consistent with his frustration at the inflexibility of European thinking seen throughout Book One. In his early conversation with "More", Hythloday suggests the relationship between pride and the refusal to accept new ideas. He will not offer his counsel to European governments because "everyone seems so wise in his own eyes as not to condescend to profit by it [another's counsel]. . . ." Excessive self-esteem prevents most men from listening to others. Or if the proud do deign to hear anyone else, they only criticize. As Hythloday says, "The listeners behave as if their whole reputation for wisdom were jeopardized . . . unless they could lay hold of something to find fault with in the discoveries of others." Pride is therefore the vice most to be feared in the royal councils of Europe, the reason for Hythloday's own unwillingness to enter public service, and the appropriate subject of his final denunciation.

The pertinence of Hythloday's final attack on pride is only one indication of the unity between the two books of *Utopia*. Positing the basic need for experimentation in all efforts for the "beststate of a commonwealth", More skillfully interlocks both sections. The dialogue, concentrating as it does on Hythloday's account of European ills, tends to stress the negative—the disadvantages of pride and provincialism. The reversed image, Utopia, affords a view of positive achievement. Here is a society where a flexible outlook is fostered and preserved—by the religion, the economy, and a variety of regulations and customs.

The contrast is not that simple, however. As if to illustrate formally the substance of his work, More never shuts the door to debate. Therefore Book One is not wholly taken up with the limited vision of Europeans. Cardinal Morton testifies to the possibility of change. And More argues that improvement might be effected, even in England. Similarly, Book Two does not present a perfect state. Not only is Utopia pagan, but some of its rules are excessive, some of its customs absurd. Finally, neither the positive vision of the imaginary Utopian at prayer nor the negative attack on European pride predominates. Rather, the contrast itself, like more subtle juxtapositions throughout the text, creates the lasting impression and serves to encourage a realistic approach to social problems.

More includes a discussion of actual contemporary evils in the larger context of urging experimental attitudes. By way of indicating English pride Hythloday points out specific injustices, like capital punishment for theft. And although he denies that partial remedies to such problems have any real utility, he does suggest ways to alleviate this evil. In Book Two Utopian humility, teachableness, and the conscious effort to preserve flexibility are revealed again and again. In the process, however, the particular achievements possible in such a society are noted. Practices like bondage as a punishment for crime, electoral representation of the people, and the provision of adequate hospital facilities relate pertinently to European ills. Throughout his work, then, More is trying both to point out the general social advantages of flexibility and to bring about a willingness to change in the case of specific practical problems.

The very existence of *Utopia* reveals Thomas More's hope that new ideas could have some effect in the European state. The depiction of the conflict between "More" and Hythloday, like Hythloday's surprising admission that he left Utopia only "to make known that new world," indicates a basic optimism about the possibility of creating—not a perfect commonwealth—but a better one.

Alice Morgan (essay date 1973)

SOURCE: "Philosophical Reality and Human Construction in the *Utopia*," in *Moreana*, Vol. 9/10, No. 39, September, 1973, pp. 15-23.

[*In the following essay, Morgan examines More's treatment of the theme of "the natural" versus "the artificial" in* Utopia, *emphasizing his concern with "the distinguishing of true from false values."*]

In More's imaginary commonwealth the structure of Catholic feudal Europe is overwhelmingly challenged. There is no inherited social hierarchy, no single approved religion. Economic and political equality are maintained by the institutions of communism and the election of public officials; material parity is assured by uniform dress, lodging, and meals. Utopia is a radical change from the society mercilessly anatomized in the first book.

The chief question about *Utopia* is the extent to which we, and More, find sympathetic this radical reorganization. That Utopia is a perfect ideal for a Christian is clearly untenable: suicide, for example, is even hypothetically acceptable only in the absence of Revelation. More cannot have meant his model as a full and particular moral guide. But when Utopia is seen as a state organized without the aid of Revelation, by man for himself, it appears superior to contemporary Europe in most respects. In Utopia, man creates a structure which answers his natural and civil needs adequately. This positive view of More's Utopia has recently been challenged in particular by Harry Berger, Jr. and by Robbin Johnson, and, of utopias in general, by Lewis Mumford. The rigidity of Utopia, its inhospitality to change, and its inorganic relation to history, are seen as negative, even destructive, forces. Yet this view seems a modern imposition on an age which sought stability, and which considered the universe to be rigidly structured, on the cosmic model rather than on the organic. The problem was to find a proper structure, one conforming to the organization of nature, and equally immutable in all but particulars. This is the great achievement of the Utopian commonwealth: its fundamental structure follows Nature, and More makes the relation between nature and artifice a central issue.

The way in which the natural and the artificial are related is of course a major Renaissance theme, and it is no surprise to find it in *Utopia*. More uses it as an index of the profound difference between his constructed, or model world, and the 'real' world of both his created and actual audiences. One of the first details we learn about Utopia is that it is an island. A. L. Morton offers a typical response to this information [in *The English Utopia,* 1952]: "It is as an island that we always think of Utopia. The fact that an island is self-centered, finite, and may be remote, gives it just the qualities we require to set our imagination to work." Islands, of course, have a vast literature of their own, as "other worlds", and, more obviously, England too is an island. But Utopia is not a natural island: it has been transformed into one, like Plato's Atlantis. King Utopus is responsible for this feat, as he is for two related acts of reconstruction. One is, of course, the establishment of the government itself, the other is the renaming of the nation, "Utopia" replacing "Abraxa". The three are parallel acts, or the same act on different planes, the simply physical, the political, and the verbal. Whether one sees this as a necessary fresh start, or, with Johnson, as "discontinuity with [the] past . . . isolation" [*More's Utopia: Ideal and Illusion,* 1969], it shows a characteristic coherence among the realms of human action. Utopia is defined by construction: its physical qualities, its institutions, and its name are the work of man. This suggests its relationship to the work *Utopia* itself, a relationship hinted at in the introductory quatrain as it is translated from the made-up language of this imaginary world: Vtopus me dux ex non

insula fecit insulam. Literally, 'Ruler Utopus made me an island out of a non-island', and "me" can be the island, or the work in which the island is postulated.

Despite this assertive naming and creation, More's position is not that of a nominalist. The name or the term is not arbitrary, but is a verbal reflection of an essential reality—hence 'Utopia' or 'nowhere', and all the other names whose covert statements about reality More emphasizes in the concluding letter to Giles. It is characteristic of Utopia that the right terms are in common use: language is not a form of deception. The ironic constrast is the European peace treaty or alliance, where the word and the reality are so distant that one must make a formal treaty with one who is, nominally, a brother! The treaties themselves, of course, are always deceptive. But in Utopia, where no treaties are necessary, and where their paradoxical quality is apparent, definitions are always accurate. 'Pleasure', for example, is correctly understood; it does not lead to what a European would consider a 'life of pleasure'. True pleasure follows "the guidance of nature" and is contrasted with "spurious" or false pleasures. In these, the word 'pleasure' is being used inaccurately: these pleasures, in short, are not pleasures at all, and hence in Utopia are not *called* pleasures, for here word and reality conform. The reality of 'pleasure' is an absolute: the Utopians explicitly reject a subjective theory of pleasure, noting that apparent pleasures which "inspire in the sense a feeling of enjoyment—which seems to be the function of pleasure—" "have nothing to do with true pleasuresince there is nothing sweet in them by nature". Context is unimportant: pleasure is immutable and inherent in the natural qualities of the 'thing itself'—if a man values something not really pleasurable, it is because he is perverse: " . . . it is impossible for any man's judgment, depraved either by disease or by habit, to change the nature of pleasure any more than that of anything else".

It is highly significant that the treatment of false pleasures focuses on economic issues, for Utopia's economic philosophy is closely related to the principles which underlie the definition of pleasure. The first spurious pleasure Hythlodaeus mentions is that derived from the possession of fine clothing. This pleasure is based on a double misapprehension of reality. First of all, a man's own worth is not altered by his clothes, or any other thing external to himself. His value is absolute and inherent in himself alone. Secondly, "fine" clothes are of themselves no more valuable than coarse clothes: the value of clothing is determined by its natural function, to cover warmly. "If you consider the use of the garment, why is wool of finer thread superior to that of thicker?" This is one of Hythlodaeus' many invocations of an extreme theory of use value: we see it most clearly in the Utopian's treatment of gold and jewels. The man with rich clothes is worth no more thanthe poor man because, first, the clothes are not part of his nature, and second, both sets of clothes fulfill the same function and should be equally valued. We may recall Lear's disquisition on this theme, taking the opposing view:

> Oh reason not the need; . . .
> Allow not nature more than nature needs,
> Man's life is cheap as beast's. Thou art a
>   lady:
> If only to go warm were gorgeous,
> Why, nature needs not what thou gorgeous
>   wear'st,
> Which scarcely keeps thee warm . . .
>
>   (II. iv. 266-272)

The Utopians hold with nature's needs, and reject the pleasures of the gorgeous as they reject this concept of "lady". An item of clothing, then, is given value not by accidents of context—rare gems, difficult and time-consuming embroidery, a cut especially new or flattering—but by its capacity to keep the wearer warm or suitably modest, which is its natural use or function. Use value (as opposed to exchange value) is thus an absolute: "Exchange value comes to a thing from outside; it is a value bestowed upon it by other things . . . Use value . . . is inherent in the thing" [Everett Hall, *Modern Science and Human Values,* 1966].

To accord an item a value other than use value, as in the case of elegant clothes, is to substitute an imaginary value for a true one. To desire these elegant clothes is to seek a false pleasure rather than a true pleasure. Characteristically, Utopians see the fallacy of fine clothes, and also ensure that no one will desire them by virtually eliminating all distinctions among garments.

If the theory of use value is pushed to its limit, it suggests that all considerations of supply and demand be obliterated. This was not a part of the Aristotelian or medieval formulation, but it is just what occurs in Utopia, where, as Hythlodaeus takes pains to emphasize, there is always abundant supply, and hence never excessive demand. The contemporary attack on money was based on its value as investment capital:

> The natural purpose of exchange, the more abundant satisfaction of wants, is lost sight of; the accumulation of money becomes an end in itself. The worst form of money-making is that which uses money itself as the source of accumulation: usury. Money is intended to be used in exchange, but not to increase at interest; it is by nature barren; through usury it breeds, and this must be the most unnatural of all ways of making money [Erich Roll, *A History of Economic Thought,* 1940].

Hythlodaeus goes beyond this standard formulation by treating *all* of money's functions as unnatural, thus putting money in the role of a construction neither required by, nor consonant with nature:

> So easily might men get the necessities of life if that blessed money, supposedly a grand invention to ease access to those necessities, was not in fact the only barrier to our getting what we need.

The concept 'invention' is vital: money, as we tell ourselves, doesn't grow on trees. It is a construct, and an unhealthy one; it has no place in Utopia.

Utopia, then, is fortunate in the operation of human ordainments. Typically, artifice works to reinforce nature, not to oppose it. The elaborate legal system of England, for example, is without Utopian parallel. Laws in Utopia are simple, few, and just, and there are no lawyers. The legal system depends upon the natural intelligence of man for its interpretation: in this way it contrasts with the obscurity and complexity of English law. In this discussion the emphasis is on the untrained, or natural, intelligence, which is all that is necessary for comprehension of Utopian law. A later attack on the European legal system is more radical, as it suggests that the laws are not only difficult to understand, but positively unjust: the rich "invent and devise all ways and means by which . . . they may keep . . . all that they have amassed . . . These devices become law . . .". The law in Utopia is not a conglomeration of "ways and means" to benefit the rich at the expense of the poor; in accordance with Utopia's institutional integrity, law serves to advance justice and not to eliminate or obscure it.

The legal system is thus another example of the beneficent use of the artificial. Utopians welcome the capacity of artifice to bring nature into useful civil order. Although the citizens despise the use of cosmetics as a deception they accept the disguising of nature when, for instance, they add to their naturally risky harbor a series of guides. These make navigation safe for Utopians, but can be shifted about to deceive and destroy hostile visitors. Similarly, cities are consciously ordained and constructed; their location, size and layout are not matters of chance. The farmhouses too are planned, and, within limits, the size of the family is also a construct. Poultry is bred by incubation; the river at Amaurotum is elaborated by engineering so that drinking water will be accessible even if an enemy dams it up. The farthest reach of Utopian ingenuity (and More's delight in hyperbolic action) is the transplanting of a forest so that it will be nearer to the destination of its lumber. These are all benign, indeed exemplary, uses of the human capacity to ordain, alter, construct—like the Utopian commonweal itself. This is perhaps the defining characteristic of Utopia, and one that makes it particularly unrealistic, for while there are evil acts in Utopia, and evil people, there are no evil institutions.

Northrup Frye, in discussing utopias [in "Varieties of Literary Utopias," *Daedalus,* 1965] links More's work with *The Prince* and *The Courtier.* As might be expected, both these books show concern for the issues dealt with above. Machiavelli stresses a political version of the supply-and-demand economy: value is determined by context, not by inherent worth. A man's success is largely dependent on his times: they may be unpropitious for one of his temperament, and nothing can alter that fact. Correspondingly, Machiavelli is free to advise his readers to construct a public image, although it does not conform to the private reality. And, not surprisingly, he displays particular interest in the man whose ultimate station is not one he is born to: the prince who begins as a private man has displayed more force in achieving his role of leader than one whose position was inherited. The man, in short, who is least dominated by nature or fortune (i.e. by his personal outlook, his capacities, his birth) and who most dominates his surroundings, is the man Machiavelli finds most exciting. With this we may compare an early discussion in *The Courtier,* where the issue is whether a courtier's skills are most praiseworthy in one of good birth or in one of no particular standing. The argument for the latter is that such a man is to be judged on his personal qualities, not on his ancestry; the argument for the former depends on a sense of harmony between the outer and inner man. We may sense that Machiavelli would have preferred the man who must take his position entirely by himself, while the consensus in *The Courtier* is "that good should spring of good" and that nobility of birth is most consonant with nobility of action. Both works deal constantly with the idea of artifice, treating it now as an ornament, now as a deception. But Machiavelli accepts it in both its forms, while Castiglione must at least appear to condemn it when it is meant to deceive. And yet he is far more flexible than is Hythlodaeus, allowing his courtier to follow orators who, "dissembling their cunning, made semblant their Orations to be made verie simply, and rather as nature and truth ledde them, than studie and arte . . .". The ramifications of this issue are too great to consider in detail here, but they are based on the same alternatives as those of *Utopia:* art or skill can be seen as cohering with nature or as opposing nature. Castiglione in general is more tolerant of art as mask than is Hythlodaeus; Machiavelli goes so far as to recommend it. For Renaissance writers the archetype of cooperation between the natural and the artificial is the garden: it will not do to dwell on Shakespeare's many garden scenes, or to more than drop the names of Spenser, Bacon and Marvell. We may note, rather, that in Utopia where all men wear the same clothing, and where houses are exchanged every ten years to prevent their being too much personalized, gardening is a favorite pastime, and competition in creating gardens is not only permitted but is encouraged. This seems to be a symbolic statement of the ideal relation between nature and art

in that favored nation.

Outside Utopia, constructions are likely to be falsifications. Fine clothing is followed in the list of false pleasures by "empty and unprofitable honors":

> What natural and true pleasure can another's bared head or bent knees afford you? Will this behavior cure the pain in your own knees or relieve the lunacy in your own head?

Again the valuable is the useful, and not the hard-to-get. Nobility, jewels, superfluous wealth are all subject to the same derision: their value lies not in their use but in the (disordered) imagination of men: such value is a construct, and a vicious one. Gambling and hunting too are worthless in themselves, for "there is nothing sweet in them by nature". In Utopia true pleasure is recognized and rationally pursued. Outside Utopia the organization of society ordains untrue pleasures as goals and these also are rationally pursued:

> . . . outside Utopia, how many are there who do not realize that, unless they make some separate provision for themselves, however flourishing the commonwealth, they will themselves starve? For this reason, necessity compels them to hold that they must take account of themselves rather than of the people, that is, of others.

Reason, in Utopia, is the pursuit of true pleasure, and the establishment of ordinances and institutions in accord with nature. In the light of this definition, we can see the general coherence of the Utopians' religious preferences. With few exceptions, reason tells them that nature includes a God. As is generally the case in Utopia, those who disagree with this proposition, while they are tolerated, are not permitted to create institutions of any sort. Their unreasonable behavior is punished by isolation, but not so harshly as to lead to their adopting a religious stance simply to avoid punishment: this would be a deceit, and is hence to be avoided. The only formal structure for religion is the non-denominational church with its few and holy priests. Zealous proselytizing or derogation are alike forbidden, so that religious quarreling will not occur. The reason for this is given in a telling simile: "But if the struggle [between religions] were decided by arms and riots, since the worst men are always the most unyielding, the best and holiest religion would be overwhelmed because of the conflicting false religions, like grain choked by thorns and underbrush". In this borrowing from husbandry we are once again reminded that while nature is the ethical absolute, and reason a guide to nature, there is still the need for human disposition and imposed structure. It is the Utopians' great good fortune to have only such structures as match the true reality of nature.

The necessity for some 'artificial' impositions derives from More's basic view of man as fallen. The villain of the piece is that cardinal sin, Pride: Hythlodaeus makes this clear at the very end of his discourse. "Pride is too deeply fixed in men to be easily plucked out". Only in Utopia has it been, at least, kept under control: "They have adopted such institutions of life as have laidthe foundations of the commonwealth not only most happily, but also to last forever . . .". And More the listener at once begins to muse on "the customs and laws of the people described" in a critical fashion. His unspoken objection recalls to us the way in which the philosophical, the economic, and the institutional are related in Utopia:

> Many things came to my mind which seemed very absurdly established . . . most of all in that feature which is the principal foundation of their whole structure, I mean their common life and subsistance—without any exchange of money.

(More emphatically underlines this construct as the fundamental one in Utopia).

> This latter alone utterly overthrows all the nobility, magnificence, splendor, and majesty which are, in the estimation of the common people, the true glories and ornaments of the commonwealth.

In this, which Hexter rightly considers an intentionally weak response, the focus is not on communism per se (in contrast the Aristotelian objection offered earlier, is basically economic). Atissue, instead, is the distinguishing of true from false values. The Latin words make this clearer: "vera . . . decora atque ornamenta"—in Utopia the goals *are* the true ornaments of a commonwealth; in England and Europe the opinion of the public is vitiated, and the goals are false pleasures, mere imaginary constructions, ornaments that deceive philosophically and divert economically from the Natural and hence the Good.

Wayne A. Rebhorn (essay date 1976)

SOURCE: "Thomas More's Enclosed Garden: *Utopia* and Renaissance Humanism," in *English Literary Renaissance,* Vol. 6, 1976, pp. 140-55.

[*In the essay that follows, Rebhorn investigates the parallels between More's* Utopia *and Renaissance humanist ideals, exploring how the* Utopia *draws upon and extends humanist agricultural metaphors associated with education and social improvement.*]

Thomas More has generally been paired with Erasmus as one of the leading representatives of Renaissance humanism, and his *Utopia* has been widely read as a provocative expression of humanist ideals.With the works of fifteenth-century humanist educators like Vittorino da Feltre and Aeneas Silvius and of contemporaries like Erasmus, the book shares certain fundamental doctrines: a faith in man's educability; a conviction of his potential goodness, rationality, and willingness to cooperate with his fellows; and a belief in social planning and the transformation of social institutions as the best means both to improve society as a whole and to raise the individual to the heights of human possibility. However, while More's *Utopia* reveals a clear relationship to Renaissance humanism through its sharing of such basic doctrines and assumptions, it also possesses a deeper relationship to the tradition than the existence of doctrinal similarities alone might suggest.

Going beneath the level of doctrine, More is linked to the humanist tradition at the fundamental level of language. His *Utopia* is organized about a few key images which not only generate his conception of human nature but also inform his vision of the natural order, dictate the construction of Utopia's social institutions, and even determine the distinctive features of the island's topography. One critic [Michael Holquist, "How To Play Utopia," in *Game, Play, Literature,* 1968] has argued that for the utopian writer generally, "anthropology leads necessarily toecology," and this cryptic maxim, I would claim, is especially applicable to More precisely because in his work he perceives both human nature (anthropology) and the natural world (ecology) through the same set of images—both are *terrain* to be *cultivated* or *farmed,* transformed by the human art of *agriculture* into a perfect, almost paradisical, *garden.* More shares with his humanist predecessors and contemporaries these images and the sets of terms they generate in the course of being elaborated, and if he differs from them in any way, it is in the degree to which the images dominate his thought and receive concrete embodiment in his vision of Utopia. Where the humanists thought of education as a kind of agriculture and longed for a world transformed at least metaphorically into a garden of innocence, More's artistic imagination treats those metaphors literally, making the Utopians into a race of farmers and the Utopian state into an immense walled garden.

More's *Utopia* is based on a particularly unsentimental, Christian view of nature as fallen and in need of human management and labor if it is to be fertile and bear fruit. To be sure, the Utopians speak of it as a good parent because it supplies in abundance all those things truly needful for human existence and buries away underground useless commodities such as gold and silver; nevertheless, Hythloday stresses that Utopia does not possessparticularly fertile soil or especially good weather, and he alludes obliquely to the existence of swamps and mountains which certainly could not provide comfortable sites for human habitation. Contrary to the opinion of several modern critics, Utopia is clearly not a nostalgically envisioned Golden Age where a benevolent Mother Nature makes life soft and easy. Rather, its success is due to its inhabitants' persistent labor, planning, and care, which alone have turned a potential desert into a garden paradise.

From the very first pages of Book II More emphasizes the absolute importance of human art to the success of his Utopian state. He describes how his ideal citizens have complemented the natural defenses of their central bay and exterior shores with fortresses and garrisons, have thoughtfully designed their houses and cities to keep out chill winds, and to protect themselves from the attacks of their neighbors have excavated the huge ditch which severed their state completely from the mainland. Within all these protective walls and barriers, the Utopians engage in one art more than any other which epitomizes what all the arts mean for them—the art of agriculture. Defining themselves primarily as "agricolae", rather than lords over the land, they all practice this art which assumes that the imperfections of the natural world can be remedied to a large degree by human planning and industry, an art which thus easily serves as a resonant symbolic center for the basic images and values of More's work. Essentially, agriculture involves nothing less than the incorporation of nature into culture; literally, the word means the cultivation of the fields, the human act of dwelling upon, possessing, and thus transforming a piece of brute and virgin wilderness into a settled suburb of the city of man. Agriculture stands symbolically at the center of More's work because it is the primal act by which civilization defines itself.

Appropriately, More describes his Utopian isle in such a way that agriculture seems to determine totally the features of its topography. Since all its cities are situated twenty-four miles from one another and surrounded by twelve miles of cultivated fields, almost the entire space between them must logically be occupied by cultivated fields and pastures. Looking at Utopia from above, one would see an endless succession of fields, interrupted only occasionally at regular intervals by cities, and descending lower, one would see within those cities rows and rows of houses all enclosing their own sets of interior gardens. Gardens within gardens, all surrounded by protective walls and barriers, all symmetrically laid out within those almost mathematically regular boundaries—Utopia is an immense Renaissance garden where man's art has civilized and domesticated practically every aspect of the natural world.

Instructively, in the one passage where the existence of a Utopian forest receives passing attention, Hythloday is actually praising the Utopians for having transplanted it from one location to another on the isle. Traditionally, from Dante to Shakespeare, the forest was presented as antithetical to the city and its gardens; it was outside the boundaries of human culture. Evaluated positively, it could be seen as a place of refuge, an oasis into which one might retreat or flee, if only temporarily, from an oppressive or perverted civilization. But it was also depicted as a savage wilderness dangerous to man's body, a dark wood of error perilous for his soul. In every case, the forest, whether Arden or Dante's "selva oscura," was never considered man's home. In the passage from *Utopia* alluded to above, More effectively obliterates the dichotomy between forest and civilization by incorporating the former into the latter. The forest becomes something man plants and transplants at will. It is put under the control of human agriculture which neutralizes its dangers, transforming it into just one more fertile precinct within the Utopian walled garden which is man's best home on earth.

In depicting Utopia as a walled garden, More deliberately invokes comparisons with the earthly paradise. He even suggestively locates his island, to follow one interpreter of his text, at the Antipodes, where some medieval and Renaissance cartographers thought the earthly paradise to be. More's garden differs, to be sure, from Eden in one absolutely crucial respect: it is not the result of God's benevolent creation and maintenance on behalf of man, but is due to human effort, intelligence, and perseverance. Utopia is fallen man's attempt to re-create something of Eden in the midst of a fallen world.

As testimony to the fundamental, imagistic unity of More's *Utopia,* human nature is presented in the same agricultural terms used for the natural world. Man is conceived metaphorically as soil which must be cultivated if he is to prosper and bear fruit, and the cultivation of Utopia's citizens, for which Hythloday commends them, is every bit as thorough as that which their island receives at their hands. The repressive social institutions and constant monitoring of behavior which mark Utopia testify to a fear that nature—human or otherwise—will never be fruitful if left to its own devices and will be drawn to evil more easily than to good. Thus travel is restricted and idleness discouraged; only slaves are allowed to hunt or butcher meat, lest good citizens come to enjoy the act of slaughter; and marriage is protected by rigorous laws, since men would naturally prefer the pleasures of casual fruition. Finally, just as the Utopians have eliminated wild and dangerous natural terrain by subjecting it to cultivation, so they have subjected human society to a process of total cultivation, eliminating all those wild and hidden places—taverns, alehouses, brothels—into which men might slip away from the ever-watchful eyes of their fellows in order to dally joyfully with vice.

Agriculture and the terms describing its operations thus effectively determine the moral categories of *Utopia*. From the very start of the book, when More recounts

Hythloday's travels in the New World, he establishes the basic moral opposition between the cultivated and the rude and rustic as he contrasts the savage lands and peoples of the torrid zone with the more civilized lands and peoples of the temperate. Later, he will criticize the Zapoletans (Swiss mercenaries) who live in wild and rugged mountains and have become so "agrestis" that the Utopians rejoice whenever one of them is killed. Most strikingly, More's basic moral dichotomy appears in his praise of Utopian colonization which has aroused the ire of more than one modern critic of the book. Colonization, it should be remembered, derives from "colo," which means "to cultivate," and by extension, "to settle land," and those individuals who carry it out are called "coloni," a word which means both farmers and colonists and which More uses interchangeably with "agricolae." Thus, since colonization and cultivation are really the same process, it should hardly be surprising that More would praise it through Hythloday's mouth. Colonization is not presented as the suppressing of an inferior by a more powerful people, but essentially as the extension of Utopian agriculture, civilizing an otherwise barren land by transforming it into yet another garden.

More's basic moral opposition between the cultivated and the uncultivated underlies Hythloday's vitriolic attack on sheep-raising in England. He paints a depressing picture of a land where no soil is tilled and the farmers, the "coloni", have been forced into work condemned as sterile and unfruitful. They have been replaced by sheep whose wool they cannot afford to buy and whose meat does not serve to nourish them. Those sheep are depicted as monsters which devour not only men, but *cities* and *fields* as well. England, once a green and pleasant land, has become a parodic inversion of civilization, a dreary "solitudo" unfertile because uncultivated. No wonder More places Utopia at the Antipodes from his native land!

If agriculture generates an opposition between the cultivated and the uncultivated, it also generates one between domestication and wildness, between the taming of nature, whether animal or human, which allows it to be brought safely within the walls of the city or garden, and an untamed, wild, bestial nature which presents a constant threat to man and his culture. Thus the torrid zone near the equator is described not only as uncultivated, but also as full of wild beasts ("effera" and "belua"), whereas in the temperate zone all things grow mild and tame ("omnia mansuefacere"). Similarly, the Zapoletans are condemned as ferocious ("ferox") creatures who love war, an activity twice deplored as fit only for beasts. Even worse, the English have become a race of beast-men: the landlord class serves the serpent of hell ("Averni serpens"), the wild beast of pride; their idle retainers and mercenaries are labeled, respectively, drones ("fuci") and wild animals ("beluas"); and the poor peasants, whom all the others

have chased from the land and the civilizing pursuit of agriculture, have become mere beasts of burden ("iumenta") whose lives are pitied as even worse than those of beasts. England offers a monstrous inversion of the whole process of domestication where sheep, normally tamed and raised to provide men with clothing and food, have become wild again ("indomitae") and metaphorically devour those who should literally devour them. In this context, it is entirely appropriate to recall how More praised Hythloday for not coming to Europe with strange tales of monsters which eat men—the monsters were already there!

By contrast, the Utopians receive great praise as domesticators. They breed poultry and utilize the ox for both farming and food. But what is more important, they constantly strive to domesticate themselves and set up institutions for monitoring behavior lest the beast lurking in every man take possession of him. Appropriately, the Utopians condemn as beasts ("pecuini") those citizens who commit crimes like theft and violence as well as those who simply reject fundamental religious tenets. Criminals who rebel against the just punishment of servitude are "untamed beasts" ("indomitae beluae"), and the Utopians feel no qualms about slaughtering ("trucidantur") creatures who have fallen so far beneath the dignity of human behavior. On the other hand, they willingly release those slaves whom servitude has rendered tame ("domiti") and thus restored to the proper condition of man.

Agriculture also involves a third set of opposed terms in *Utopia,* since it means not only cultivation and domestication, but also effective segregating of the clean and healthy from the dirty and diseased. Living in a fallen world ever ready to invade and corrupt their island paradise, the Utopians have to maintain a constant vigilance against the evils that could easily contaminate them. They must build walls around their communal gardens and set rock barriers and fortresses around their island. They must constantly weed and chase away pests that would impair the fertility and productivity of their land, and they must similarly protect and guard their physical and moral life from contamination by disease and evil. Many Utopian institutions reflect an intense concern with the segregation of good and ill. Amaurotum, the model for all Utopian cities, is located on a river which insures an abundant supply of pure, fresh water, and all animals are slaughtered *outside* the city so that their filthy remains ("tabum acsordes") can be washed away at once in another river, thus preserving the purity of the city and the entire island. Similarly, the sick are quarantined in hospitals located *outside* the walls of each city, and unclean things are not allowed inside lest they infect the air the Utopians breathe. Nor should it seem surprising that a people so obsessed with excluding dirt and disease from their world would require prospective marriage partners to inspect one another naked, a practice justified by the argument that one would not buy a horse unless one checked it first for disease.

If the Utopians seem anxious to avoid contact with filth and disease which corrupt the body, they are equally anxious to protectthe mind from moral infection. Thus slaves perform all kinds of dirty work, lest free citizens develop bad habits. To extinguish the monster of pride, which elsewhere takes pleasure in piling up gold at others' expense, the Utopians teach an utter disdain for gold by using it not only for children's toys, thus identifying pride as infantile, but also to make chamber pots, thus identifying it with excrement. Similarly, they condemn all those who fall below their standards of humanity as filth or disease or excrement. The Zapoletans are scornfully dismissed as "that dregs of a people" ("illa colluvie populi"). Suicides who commit their desperate act when not terminally ill are thrown into swamps, a symbolic consigning of the foul to the foul. Most strikingly, the Utopians develop their own philosophy in which health is considered something positive and good in itself, not merely the absence of disease and pain or a precondition for other, real pleasures. The word for health, "sanitas," moreover, applies not only to man's physical, but also to his moral and spiritual, condition. Finally, the Utopians think of their entire state as a collective entity which can enjoy health or be afflicted with disease ("pernicies"), and they recognize their own responsibility in choosing magistrates and instructing the people so that health and salvation are maintained.

This imagery of sickness and health, filth and cleanliness, dominates Hythloday's description of Utopia and fits perfectly his conception of Europe's problem and his personal role as a healer of souls (Raphael means the "healing of God"). Hythloday explicitly criticizes European monarchs as *infected* from childhood with perverse opinions ("perversis opinionibus . . . infecti"), and sees himself proposing "decreta sana" in order to cure the disease. He characterizes the sheep which trouble England as a plague ("pestis"), and attacks the idlers who abound in Europe as just so much filth. Most effectively, he argues that one cannot cure the basic disease of Europe, its pride and greed and inhumanity, merely by treating symptoms or local infections. To achieve public "salus," the entire system must be changed and vice eradicated from Europe as completely as possible.

While images of filth and cleanliness, disease and health, may seem intrinsically unrelated to agriculture, in More's thought at least the connection is established frequently and with compelling force. For instance, in condemning the Zapoletans, More attacks them for their lack of cultivation and their wildness and dismisses them as filth, thus utilizing all three of his basic categories almost as through they were completely interchangeable in his mind. Similarly, the English sheep

are fearful monsters who have reversedthe processes of cultivation and domestication and are excoriated as a "pestis." This last term actually admits of two translations which demonstrate the interpenetration of these categories in More's thought, for "pestis" means both "plague" and "pest," both disease and destructive, wild animal. In another passage concerned with the fear of contagion felt by the Utopians, disease is described as creeping like a snake from person to person ("ab alio ad alium serpere"). Disease thus becomes a sly and dangerous serpent, a "pestis" of particular malignancy, and this image is echoed later when pride is labeled the prince and parent of all "pestes" and is identified as the serpent of hell. By contrast, when More praises the Utopians for transforming their not particularly fertile soil into fruitful fields, he speaks of their *curing* the land ("terrae sic *medentur* industria"), as though lack of fertility were some sort of disease. Finally, when Hythloday speaks of curing the ills of Europe, he repeatedly uses agricultural metaphors: cure vices, he insists, by tearing up the roots which the weeds of depraved opinion have sent down from evil seeds; pluck out pride; and by ending the use of money, uproot an entire crop of evils. Thus More's language reveals the basic connections he accepted between sound agriculture, health, and cleanliness, connections which demonstrate the profound, imaginative unity of his work.

All these basic categories—cultivation and domestication, health and cleanliness—relate More's work directly to the humanist tradition. Although there is no firm evidence that he knew of Italian educators like Vittorino da Feltre and Guarino da Verona or that he had read the writings of Leonardo Bruni and Aeneas Silvius, it is unlikely that he was entirely ignorant of the doctrines and concepts they had propounded. On the other hand, it is almost a certainty that he knew Quintilian and Plutarch, on whom those Renaissance humanists depended for many of their educational conceptions. Moreover, it is quite unlikely that an admirer of Pico della Mirandola and of Florentine Neoplatonism generally would have missed the optimistic note in their assessment of man which they shared with the humanist thinkers and educators mentioned above. Most effective in establishing More's connection with the thought of Renaissance humanism, however, are his deep and abiding friendship, frequent conversations and letters, and all the labors shared with the greatest of the humanists, Desiderius Erasmus. Consequently, it should appear no more than reasonable to place More within the humanist camp, to seek parallels and analogues for his major concepts and images in the works of men like Vergerius, Aeneas Silvius, and Erasmus, and ultimately to argue that the *Utopia* can be read as a brilliant articulation of humanist ideals.

From Vergerius to Erasmus, the humanists argued that nature generally, and human nature in particular, although impaired by the Fall and thus never completely perfectible by human efforts alone, nevertheless were granted a freedom and a potential to develop in almost any conceivable direction. Like their ancient mentors, Cicero, Plutarch, and Quintilian, the humanists never tired of praising the liberal arts as those worthy a free man ("liber"), but where the ancient writers thought of freedom primarily in a political sense, the Renaissance saw it as metaphysical, moral, and existential. Vergerius, for instance, declared that while a man's place of birth and family were inevitably determined beyond his control, he could nevertheless distinguish and define himself by means of his virtue acquired through education and training. Erasmus envisaged the newly created infant's mind as a "tabula complanata," thus anticipating Locke's "tabula rasa" by two hundred years. This blank tablet was morally neutral, dangerously open to the possibility of degenerating to bestial levels, but equally capable of rising up almost to divinity. This double potentiality received its most eloquent expression in the myth which Pico used to open his famous *Oratio,* but Erasmus himself summarized it succinctly in one of his treatises on education: "Nature, when it gives you a child, hands over nothing other than a crude mass. . . . If you disregard it, you will have a wild beast; if you watchover it, you will have, if I may speak thus, a god." Essentially, the humanists felt that before being transformed by man's art, nature was rough and imperfect, filled with unrealized potentialities, and man as man did not yet exist. Erasmus declared simply, "men are not born, but made"; with a defective—or a missing—education, they could never move beyond the level of the brutes, could never hope to repair the defects of their fallen condition, but with proper care they could indeed realize the potential they possessed, in spite of the Fall, for goodness and rationality and could thus, in a limited measure, cooperate in their own salvation, which God's grace alone could ultimately insure.

As the humanists elaborated their conception of the art of education, they repeatedly had recourse to the same basic metaphors which lie at the center of More's thought in *Utopia.* Vergerius, for example, sees education as the implanting of the seeds of virtue in the child's mind, and, developing this idea of agriculture even further, Aeneas Silvius tells the young prince to whom he addresses his treatise: "just as farmers ('colini') surround their hedges with little trees, so admonishments and arrangements ('instituta') consonant with a praiseworthy life ought to surround you, so that the most upright seeds of mores may germinate, for the fountainheadand root of honesty is legitimate discipline." Erasmus likewise considers the child's mind a fertile field which has the potential to become a magnificent garden, although he cannot decide whether the seeds of virtue already lie dormant in the soil or are planted by the preceptor, who, in either case, must, like a good farmer, care for them and remove noxious weeds.

Just as the humanists thought of education as a process of cultivating the soil of the mind, they also conceived it as domestication, a taming of the mind. This conception was doubtless suggested by the notion of education as "disciplina," a restraining, limiting, or even punishing, and it must have been influenced by the striking comparisons ancient writers like Plutarch made between animals' educability and man's. The identification of education with the domestication and taming of man's potentially wild and bestial nature received its most powerful presentation in a short colloquy entitled *Ars notoria* which Erasmus wrote to attack the popular "art of memory" ("ars notoria") because it promised an easy, painless method for acquiring knowledge of all the liberal arts. On the contrary, Erasmus has his spokesman declare that wisdom and learning can be had only through labor, which can indeed come to seem reasonably agreeable, but only after the mind has been *tamed* so that it cancarry out the exercises involved without resistance. Thus, he declares, "Let your first care be that you understand the thing deeply and then that you rehearse and repeat it to yourself. And in this, as they say, the mind is to be tamed, as often as is necessary, so that it can fix itself in cogitation. For if there's any mind so rustic that it cannot be tamed to do such a thing, then it is scarcely fit for learning."

Finally, all the humanists conceive of evil as filth or disease from which the individual must be segregated. Leonardo Bruni, for instance, speaks of evil as filth ("tabes") which befouls or pollutes the mind ("mentem . . . coinquinat"), and Francesco Barbaro, in his treatise on woman, which includes a long chapter on child-rearing, sees the helpless infant as sucking wickedness and impure diseases ("impuras aegritudines") along with the milk of a corrupt nurse, thus suffering both body and spirit to be simultaneously infected by the contagious disease of evil ("pernicioso contagio"). And, of course, More's close friend Erasmus has recourse to the same characteristic metaphors when he warns of the ease with which the young child's tender mind may be infected by passions and desires ("amoribus aliisque cupiditatibus inficiatur").

The humanists do more, however, than merely anticipate the essential metaphors which underlie More's *Utopia* and receive concrete expression in its topography, institutions and, philosophies. They also anticipate in a limited fashion both the idea of creating an ideal environment to produce and suitably house ideal men, and they characteristically tend to visualize that environment as a garden, especially a garden contained within an ideal palace or city.

Although the humanists praised man's potential for self-improvement, they, like More, distrusted the natural in man: men were considered weak, frail beings whose fallen natures exposed them openly and continually to vice and passion, disease and sloth. In the fifteenth century, Aeneas Silvius asserted the characteristic position: man was always prone to sin, but youth especially possessed a particular propensity to imitate evil.

Erasmus later claimed that young children clung to evil more readily and easily than to good and were more given to passion than reason, and he explained these defects as the result of man's fallen condition:

> . . . that early age, led more by its natural sense than by judgment, will imbibe evil as easily as good, or more easily. . . . The pagan philosophers understood this matter and marveled at it. They could not find the cause which Christian philosophy has offered us, for it teaches that this propensity toward evil was planted in us by Adam, the founder of the human race.

Man's fallen nature expressed itself not only in terms of a predilection for vice and an indulgence of the passions, but also in an ultimate uneducability afflicting some members of the species. Finally, the humanists worried that all men were physically weak, exposed to disease and danger, and thus terribly in need of developing strong, healthy bodies to complement their strong, healthy minds.

Although confronted with man's physical, intellectual, and moral weaknesses, the humanists remained confident that education could overcome almost all obstacles to human improvement. However defective nature might be, they felt that man's art could remedy it within very large and generous limits. "Nature is an efficacious thing," admits Erasmus, "but a more efficacious education will conquer it." Considering the importance agricultural metaphors had in their thought, it is striking that the humanists turned their particular attention to the *environment* in which the child would be raised. They saw the creation of an ideally moral and intellectually stimulating environment as essential if education were really to triumph over a less than cooperative human nature. Moreover, they felt that this ideal environment had to be segregated from the fallen world about it if any traces of the child's Adamic innocence were to be preserved and his potential for rationality and goodness realized. According to Erasmus, "it is most true that the largest portion of . . . evil in us derives from impure associations and a depraved education, especially in that period of life when we are weak and easily moved in all directions." The segregation of the child from evil, a proposition all the humanists endorsed in more or less radical forms, meant essentially a careful selection of schoolbooks, nurses, tutors, playments, and companions, as well as a specially purified and moral home and school. Fearfully aware of man's tendencies toward evil, the humanists

kept pushing back the point at which the child was to be placed in this environment, until someone like Erasmus could even write prescriptions for the proper method of sexual intercourse. Moreover, the humanists wanted the child's behavior within his ideal world to be carefully and continuously monitored by parents and educators. They particularly distrusted unsupervised leisure, believing with Alberti—and clearly with More—that "l'ozio si è balia de' vizii," and urging the playing of instructional games, healthy exercises, and reading during time spent away from studies. In effect, what the humanists wanted for the child's education was nothing less than the transformation of the world—or at least a piece of it—into an ideal kinder-garten, an edenic schoolroom, thoroughly moral, separated by firm boundaries from the fallen world about it, and rigorously monitored for any appearance of vice.

Just as important for More's conception of his ideal state, the humanists came increasingly to feel that an immense and unbridgeable gap lay open between their schoolroom-garden and the rest of the world. Where Italian humanists in the fifteenth century could still envisage an education that led directly to public service and social activity, the education imagined by Erasmus and his contemporaries was designed less to prepare the child for the active life in society than to make him an upright Christian. Moreover, as humanism developed between the fifteenth and sixteenth centuries, thinkers also came increasingly to feel the need to extend the time of education—and hence its ideal environment—further and further into adult life, until Erasmus could imagine the whole of life as being a continual process of education. It is hardly surprising, therefore, that in his *Convivium religiosum* he should imagine an ideal adult existence spent in an enclosed garden that maintained the essential features of the child's educational environment intact.

In the light of all these humanist ideals, More's Nowhere does indeed appear to be Somewhere. Although clearly influenced by Plato's *Republic,* ideas of ancient Sparta, and accounts of kingdoms in the New World, Utopia can also be seen as an imaginative extension of the ideal enclosed garden which several generations of humanists had desired and even, in limited ways, had attempted to create. *Utopia* simply expands the humanist schoolhouse until its walls reach the borders of the entire state. In its institutions it enshrines the basic features of that ideal environment. Where the humanists wanted a purified, clean, healthy school away from the smoky cities of the fallen world, Utopia totally separates itself from that world and sets up barriers of rocks and fortresses to prevent any intrusion of vice of disease or filth from its neighbors. Where the humanists wanted the child exposed to only the best books and people in order to insure his moral perfection, the Utopians constantly offer models of virtue to their children, erecting statues commemorating good men and ridiculing slaves by means of gold chains and ornaments. Filled with a cautious faith in man's potential for goodness and rationality, but fearing his ever-present inclination to vice, More follows in the footsteps of the humanists and designs a rigidly controlled environment where freedom of movement, religious dissension, and sexual association are carefully restricted. Not trusting men to amuse themselves honestly, he has their leisure-time activities supervised so that only constructive games, work like gardening, and self-improvement through continuing education are really tolerated. Finally, More takes the constant monitoring the humanists desired to the point where no one in Utopia can ever escape public scrutiny. No wonder Erasmus and Giles, Busleiden and Budé wrote admiringly of More's work—the enclosed garden of Utopia is a colossal version of the educational environment they all desired for their children and dreamed of as a model for a brave new world.

George M. Logan (essay date 1983)

SOURCE: *"Utopia,"* in *The Meaning of More's "Utopia,"* Princeton University Press, 1983, pp. 131-253.

[*In the following excerpt, Logan describes* Utopia *as a "best commonwealth exercise" in the classical tradition, pointing to the echoes of Plato and Aristotle in the work.*]

To examine the theoretical questions advanced at the end of Book I of *Utopia,* More employed the original and central exercise of Greek political philosophy, the determination of the best form of the commonwealth. [In a footnote, the author adds: "To preclude misunderstanding, let me say at once that this statement does not imply that Utopia must be More's ideal commonwealth. The exercise can . . . be undertaken for reasons other than elaborating one's own ideal."] This exercise, which has its ancestry in the inveterate Greek practice of comparing polities, and its literary antecedents in such passages as the debate among spokesmen for monarchy, aristocracy, and democracy in Herodotus' *Histories,* entered political philosophy in Plato's *Republic.* In their attempt to specify the nature of the perfectly just man, Socrates and his companions are led into discussion of the perfectly just polis. The resulting exchanges delineate in effect the Idea of the polis. "Perhaps," Socrates suggests, the Republic "is laid up as a pattern in heaven, where those who wish can see it and found it in their own hearts." Although there is small chance that this polis will ever actually exist, the determination of its form has practical value. Like the image of the just man, the Republic provides a model to guide action: "By looking at these perfect patterns and the measure of happiness . . . they would enjoy, we force ourselves to admit that the nearer we approximate to them the more nearly we share their

lot."

In the *Republic,* Plato's earliest political work, speculative development is untrammeled by practical considerations. In particular, Plato does not acknowledge that the recalcitrance of human nature imposes constraints on the realization of political ideals. The most important reflection of this fact is found in the circumstance that the Republic is a government of men—the philosopher-rulers—rather than of law. Indeed, Plato always regarded government by wise men as preferable to even the best government by law. In the *Laws,* however, a late work, he takes account of the fact that it is in practice extremely difficult to assure a supply of wise men and elaborates the optimal pattern for a polis governed by law—his "second-best state." It is this work rather than the *Republic* that provided, as [George H.] Sabine says [in *A History of Political Theory,* 1961], the "point of departure" for the third and last of the great best-commonwealth exercises of Greek theory, the discussion of the ideal polis in the seventh and unfinished eighth books of Aristotle's *Politics.* For Aristotle is acutely aware of the constraints that empirical fact places upon theory. According to Aristotle, Plato erred in the *Republic* by not considering "the teaching of actual experience." Even in discussing a nonexistent, ideal polis "it cannot be right to make any assumption which is plainly impossible," since in order for a pattern of an ideal polis to be useful, the ideal conditions "must be capable of fulfilment as well as being ideal."

It is crucial to understand that the best-commonwealth exercise is not, for Plato and Aristotle, simply a matter of piling together seemingly ideal features of a polis. As the quintessential manifestation of the rationalistic and holistic character of Greek political theory, the exercise has at its core the conception of the polis as a system of reciprocally-affecting parts. Since the polis aims at self-sufficiency, its ideal form is a structure of just those elements that will constitute a self-sufficient unit. Plato's pronouncement that "society originates . . . because the individual is not self-sufficient" leads immediately to the specification of the human needs—food, shelter, clothing—that must be supplied within the polis, and this list, in turn, leads to the development of a list of essential occupations. Superfluity in any component of the polis is as harmful as deficiency. One manifestation of social pathology is "a multitude of occupations none of which is concerned with necessaries." The provision of the luxuries produced by these professions means that "the territory which was formerly enough to support us will now be too small," a circumstance that fosters aggression: "If we are to have enough for pasture and plough, we shall have to cut a slice off our neighbours' territory. And if they too are no longer confining themselves to necessities and have embarked on the pursuit of unlimited material possessions, they will want a slice of ours too." By contrast, in the ideal polis "the land must be extensive enough to support a given number of people in modest comfort, and not a foot more is needed."

The method of Aristotle's best-commonwealth exercise is essentially the same as that of the *Republic* and *Laws,* but Aristotle characteristically articulates the principles of this method in a much more explicit and systematic fashion. Book VII of the *Politics* opens, as I pointed out earlier, with a statement of the relation between ethics and politics: "Before we can undertake properly the investigation of our next theme—the nature of an ideal constitution—it is necessary for us first to determine the nature of the most desirable way of life [for the individual]. As long as that is obscure, the nature of the ideal constitution must also remain obscure." There follows a recapitulation of Aristotle's views on the best life. Axiomatically, the end of life is happiness. The constituent elements of the best life, then, are "external goods; goods of the body; and goods of the soul," for "no one would call a man happy" who was seriously deficient in respect of any of these classes of goods. But "differences begin to arise when we ask, 'How much of each good should men have? And what is the relative superiority of one good over another?'" The truth is that external goods and goods of the body are merely instrumental. Thus, "like all other instruments, [they] have a necessary limit of size": "any excessive amount of such things must either cause its possessor some injury or, at any rate, bring him no benefit." On the contrary, "the greater the amount of each of the goods of the soul, the greater is its utility."

It is evident that the goal of the polis is to facilitate the achievement of happiness by its citizens: "There is one thing clear about the best constitution: it must be a political organization which will enable all sorts of men to be at their best and live happily." There follows an argument against the idea that the happiness of the polis lies in war and conquest, which concludes with a restatement of the view that the goal of the polis is to secure the good life for its citizens:

> if military pursuits are . . . to be counted good, they are good in a qualified sense. They are not the chief end of man, transcending all other ends: they are means to his chief end. The true end which good law-givers should keep in view, for any state or stock or society with which they may be concerned, is the enjoyment of partnership in a good life and the felicity thereby attainable.

The formulation of the goal of the polis leads in turn to discussion of the physical and institutional components necessary to secure the attainment of this goal. It is made clear early in the discussion that the governing principle is, as in Plato, self-sufficiency, which implies certain demographic and geographic requirements and

the fulfillment of a specific list of occupational functions. The polis requires "such an initial amount of population as will be self-sufficient for the purpose of achieving a good way of life in the shape and form of a political association." Population may exceed this number, but not by so much that the citizens are unable to "know one another's characters," something that is necessary "both in order to give decisions in matters of disputed rights, and to distribute the offices of government according to the merit of candidates." Thus the "optimum standard of population . . . is, in a word, 'the greatest surveyable number required for achieving a life of self-sufficiency.'" Similarly, the territory of the polis must be such as to ensure "the maximum of self-sufficiency":

> and as that consists in having everything, and needing nothing, such a territory must be one which produces all kinds of crops. In point of *extent* and *size,* the territory should be large enough to enable its inhabitants to live a life of leisure which combines liberality with temperance. . . . What was said above of the population—that it should be such as to be surveyable—is equally true of the territory.

In addition to having an appropriate population and territory, the polis must provide six "services": food, the required arts and crafts, arms, "a certain supply of property, alike for domestic use and for military purposes," "an establishment for the service of the gods," and "a method of deciding what is demanded by the public interest and what is just in men's private dealing." Thus the polis must include specific occupational groups: "a body of farmers to produce the necessary food; craftsmen; a military force; a propertied class; priests; and a body for deciding necessary issues and determining what is the public interest." Discussion of the best arrangements for fulfilling and maintaining these requirements (including a long discussion of the proper education of citizens) occupies the remainder of Aristotle's treatment of the ideal polis.

The best-commonwealth exercise, then, is made up of four sequential steps, which underlie the design of the *Republic* and *Laws* and are clearly articulated in the *Politics.* On the basis of a conception of man's nature (both Plato and Aristotle devote some space to this topic, which properly belongs to psychology and physiology), one first determines the best life of the individual (the principal subject of ethics and the starting point of politics). The second step involves the determination, given these conclusions about the individual, of the overall goal of the commonwealth and of the contributory goals the joint attainment of which will result in the attainment of the overall goal. The third step constitutes the elaboration of the required components of a self-sufficient polis. Finally, the theorist must determine the particular form that each of these components should be given in order to assure that, collectively, they will constitute the best polis, that truly self-sufficient entity that achieves all the contributory goals, and thus the overall goal, of the polis.

It has always been recognized that *Utopia* is related to Plato's and Aristotle's accounts of the ideal polis. But treatments of the relation, when they have gone beyond general statements that More was inspired by these works, have usually been restricted to the enumeration of particular geographic, demographic, and-institutional parallels between Utopia and the ideal poleis of Greek theory (especially that of the *Republic*). More is thought, that is, simply to have appropriated a selection of desirable-sounding features from the Greek works, a view of the relation that fits comfortably with the common notion that the Utopian construct is a collection of randomly-chosen and whimsically-ordered features that seemed (for the most part) ideal to More. [Edward L.] Surtz, for example, writes that More goes to the *Republic* "for the broad bases of the *Utopia,* e.g. the search for justice . . . [and] the introduction of communism into the best state," while "for many of his details he turns to the more realistic and practical *Laws*." The *Politics* "may be the ultimate, though remote, source for such items as the following: condemnation of wars of conquest and dedication to peacetime pursuits, . . . the end of government as the good of the citizens, . . . the objections to communism, the traditional case for democracy, and education as the foundation of the state because of the importance of early impressions." In his Commentary, Surtz annotates numerous specific parallels (and differences) between More and Plato, as well as a good many between More and Aristotle.

Among his annotations of Aristotelian parallels, however, is a scattered series of notes that suggests that the choice of topics in the account of Utopia reflects, and follows roughly the order of, Aristotle's list of the six necessary services of the polis—a fact that should have made Surtz wonder whether Utopia might owe an underlying constructional schema, as well as some materials that flesh it out, to Greek theory. And indeed [Thomas I.] White has recently shown [in "Aristotle and Utopia," *Rensaissance Quarterly,* 1976] not only that More's debts to the *Politics* are direct and extensive but also that many of them reflect the fact that the design of the Utopian construct is fundamentally informed by the concept of self-sufficiency:

> Self-sufficiency is not an explicitly avowed goal of Utopia, but it should be clear that simply because of Utopia's avowedly ideal, or at least superior, nature, self-sufficiency is a necessary aim of the society. That is, it seeks both the end (full human development) and the means (self-reliance and a static culture) implied by [*autarkeia*]. More has at least implicitly and quite possibly consciously adopted Aristotle's idea as the basis of Utopia. And

there are a number of similarities between specific institutions or practices described by these two thinkers which demonstrate their general agreement on self-sufficiency as the fundamental goal of the state.

One can in fact go a good deal further and say simply that More's Utopian construct embodies the results of a best-commonwealth exercise performed in strict accordance with the Greek rules. The construct includes all the parts of the exercise, and it includes nothing of substance that is not either a part of it or of More's comments on his results. This fact, which provides the quietus for the view of the account of Utopia as whimsical mélange, would be obvious were it not that More decided to present his best-commonwealth exercise in a form that doubly disguised it. First, unlike Plato and Aristotle, he offers not dialectics but a model that embodies the end-product of dialectics. Second, the model is presented as a fictional travelogue. The choice of this mode of presentation entailed suppressing or disguising the various components of the dialectical substructure of the model—its generative postulates and the arguments involved in the four steps of the best-commonwealth exercise—and a partial abandonment of the logical order of topics in the exercise for the rather different order (or disorder) of the traveler's tale—geography, and then any number of topics in any associative order. The crucial arguments deducing the best life of the individual from human nature are presented out of their logical place and attributed not to the author (nor to Hythloday, who is only recording what he saw and heard) but to the Utopian moral philosophers, and they are offered not as a step in the generation of the Utopian construct but simply as supposedly interesting incidental information about Utopian philosophy. The conclusion about the goal of the commonwealth that follows from this view of the best life of the individual is presented in one sentence at the end of the account of Utopian occupations: "the constitution of their commonwealth looks in the first place to this sole object: that for all the citizens, as far as the public needs permit, as much time as possible should be withdrawn from the service of the body and devoted to the freedom and culture of the mind." The contributory goals of the commonwealth, and the arguments about the array of features calculated to facilitate the attainment and maintenance of these goals, can for the most part be inferred only by examining the individual features of Utopia and their interrelations.

It is clear that the best-commonwealth exercise offered a perfect way of exploring the questions raised in Book I. The question whether social justice necessitates communism had been the most conspicuous concern of the original best-commonwealth exercises. Moreover, the degree of compatibility between the politically expedient and the imperatives of morality and religion can be precisely determined by examining the institutions and policies of an ideal commonwealth constructed according to Greek principles, since by definition such a commonwealth is characterized by perfect expediency: the best-commonwealth exercise is designed to generate the constitution of a polis that acts with perfect rationality to assure that its citizens individually and collectively pursue their real interests.

These considerations suggest the solution to the much-discussed problem of why More made Utopia non-Christian. More and all his contemporaries—including Machiavelli and Guicciardini—knew that moral, and Christian, behavior is advisable on suprarational, religious grounds. The liveliest question in early (pre-Reformation) sixteenth-century political thought, however, is that raised in Book I of *Utopia:* how far, in political life, is this kind of behavior advisable, or unadvisable, on purely prudential grounds? More realized that this question could be answered by seeing what a society pursuing perfect expediency through perfectly rational calculations would be like. This realization was doubtless prompted by the fact that, as I noted above, the political works of Plato and Aristotle in which the best-commonwealth exercise originates also provide the most authoritative bases for the claim that the expedient sometimes differs from the moral. If one wants to refute or modify these conclusions, then, a most effective way is to show that the best-commonwealth exercise, if performed more correctly, does not in fact lead to them.

It is also clear why More chose to present his results as a fictionalized model. He presents them as a model because he feels, as he indicates in Book I, that this form of presentation represents an important methodological advance in the systemic approach to social analysis. He disguises the model as a fiction for the same reason that *Utopia* as a whole is presented as a fiction. Fictional dialogue is conventional in humanist philosophical writing; underlying this convention is the valid observation that the appeal, hence the utility, of a learned work is enhanced if its lessons are dressed in the sugar-coat of fiction. Sidney's later description of the poet's calculations applies to the humanist tradition as a whole:

> he doth not only show the way, but giveth so sweet a prospect into the way, as will entice any man to enter into it. . . . He beginneth not with obscure definitions, which must blur the margent with interpretations and load the memory with doubtfulness; but . . . with a tale forsooth he cometh unto you. . . . And, pretending no more, doth intend the winning of the mind from wickedness to virtue. . . . for even those hard-hearted evil men who think virtue a school name, and know no other good but *indulgere genio,* and therefore despise the austere admonitions of the philosopher, . . . yet will be content to be delighted—which is all the good-fellow poet seemeth to promise—and so steal to see the

form of goodness (which seen they cannot but love) ere themselves be aware, as if they took a medicine of cherries. (*An Apology for Poetry*)

In his second letter to Giles More acknowledges that such considerations underlie the mode of presentation of the Utopian construct: "I do not pretend that if I had determined to write about the commonwealth and had thought of such a story as I have recounted, I should have perhaps shrunk from a fiction [*fictio*] whereby the truth, as if smeared with honey, might a little more pleasantly slide into men's minds."

Ann W. Astell (essay date 1985)

SOURCE: "Rhetorical Strategy and the Fiction of Audience in More's *Utopia*," in *The Centennial Review,* Vol. XXIX, No. 3, Summer, 1985, pp. 302-19.

[*In the essay that follows, Astell focuses on the letters, or* parerga, *that introduce More's text, using them to study how the fiction constructs its audience and, specifically, how the dialogues achieve their purpose through "indirection."*]

St. Thomas More's *Utopia,* whether considered as dialogue or discourse, is a self-consciously rhetorical work, and critics tend to approach it accordingly. Scholars primarily interested in *logos* as a means of persuasion typically characterize *Utopia* either as an argument upholding the superiority of the "philosophical city" so vividly described in Book II, or as a carefully balanced (and unresolved) debate about "The Best State of a Commonwealth." Critics especially sensitive to the pathetic appeal describe More's book as a satire against England. Still others, concerned with the personal appeal, have argued that More qualifies the *ethos* of Raphael Hythloday in a way that discredits him, disassociates him from More, and renders Utopia itself suspect as an ideal state.

Despite this kind of critical interest in the rhetoric of *Utopia,* practically no attempt has been made to relate the moving power of the text to its effect upon its intended, historical audience: the circle of More's Latinist friends whose response to the work is recorded in the so-called *parerga*—the letters, poems, and marginalnotes that accompanied the editions of 1516, 1517, and 1518. Indeed, there has been relatively little scholarly interest in the humanist writings on *Utopia*. In J. H. Hexter's brilliant 1952 study [*More's Utopia: The Biography of an Idea*] he relied upon the opinions expressed in the *parerga* to set forth an "unimpeachably orthodox" interpretation of More's social doctrine. In 1963 Peter R. Allen called attention to the prefatory letters and verses as a way of identifying *Utopia* to the reader as a specifically "humanist document within the growing forces of the movement" ["*Utopia* and European Humanism: The Function of the Prefatory Letters and Verses," *Studies in the Renaissance* X (1963)]. In the 1965 Yale edition all the supplementary material that accompanied the first three editions of More's *Utopia* was reprinted for the first time. Four years later R. S. Sylvester complained [in *Si Hythlodaeo Credimus*: Vision and Revision in Thomas More's *Utopia*," Soundings, 1969] that the comments of More's humanist friends had been "rather unjustly neglected" and urged that their attitude toward the work be reconsidered as a model for reader response.

Like Sylvester I believe that the *parerga* provides a means for us to recover the rhetorical context within which the book's symbols are to be understood. *Quid* and *guibus* belong together. More addresses his *Utopia* to a particular, historical, humanist audiencewhom he fictionalizes within the work itself as the auditors of Raphael Hythloday. Through the fiction of audience More delights his readers, engages their imaginative cooperation with the narrative, and directs their response, step by step, from within the text. He does so in order to achieve a particular rhetorical objective: the moral education of his audience towards humility, the single most important virtue for a servant of the commonwealth. The writings of the *parerga,* which according to More's wish should accompany *Utopia* into print, provide a guide for reader response and remind us that artifact and audience, structure and rhetorical strategy, must be considered together.

More himself attached great importance to the *parerga* as a way of placing *Utopia* within its proper rhetorical context. His 1516 correspondence with Erasmus reveals that the desired the soon-to-be-published *Utopia* to be "handsomely set off" by the "highest of recommendations", and that he actively solicited written responses to the book from "both intellectuals and distinguished statesmen." He himself supplied two of the letters within the *parerga*. More's second letter to Peter Giles, published in the 1517 Paris edition, alerts the reader to clues in the text which disclose the nature of *Utopia* to be "truth under the guise of fiction," and urges him to read it accordingly. Two other items in the *parerga,* the poems of Gerhard Geldenhauer and Cornelis de Schrijver, are specifically addressed to the general reader, telling him what he may expect to find in the book and what benefits he will surely derive from the reading experience. All of the supplementary material, including the marginalia, was certainly approved by More for publication in the 1518 Basel edition, and there is every reason to believe that More expected the humanist commentary to lead, not mislead, the reader.

As *causa exemplaris* for the larger reading audience, the humanist circle makes a typical and therefore supra-temporal response to More's *Utopia* in the writings of the *parerga* which preface the text proper,

Map of Utopia from the 1516 edition.

interpenetrate it in the form of marginalia, and follow it as an appendix. The *parerga* continually invite the reader to respond as others have responded before him; to take up membership in an audience that already exists, and generally agrees, about the meaning of *Utopia;* to sit down, as it were, in company with Erasmus, Froben, Budé, Lupset, Giles, Busleyden, Desmarais, Geldenhauer, de Schrijver, Rhenanus, and More himself. Indeed, the *parerga* present the humanist circle as an audience capable of assimilating the individual reader who makes their response his own.

This outer audience, moreover, functions as an extension of the fictive humanist audience More creates within *Utopia* itself. More effects that rhetorical extension of audience into audience by fictionalizing himself and Peter Giles as the auditors of Raphael Hythloday. As a rhetorical device, the frame audience provides More with a self-conscious way of doing what Father Walter Ong insists the writer always does—i.e., he casts his readers in a particular role, directs them toward the discovery of their part, and invites them to play it. As model and teacher, More himself assumes

Map of Utopia from the 1518 edition.

University of Louvain, proposes in playful earnestness that "a number of distinguished and invincible theologians . . . betake themselves to the island". More himself continues the fiction in his correspondence, asking Giles to contact Raphael and find out from him the exact length of the bridge spanning the River Anydrus at Amaurotum.

The enthusiastic willingness of representative humanists to play the part of Raphael's audience reflects their understanding that the benefit to be gained from the reading experience depends on their imaginative cooperation with the fiction, their tasting the honey where More has hid the moral truths he wishes to convey. Indeed, the reader only learns the lesson More teaches if he plays the part of Raphael's auditor in company with More and Giles.

The response of that fictive audience to Hythloday's discourse is guided, in turn, by the responses of other groups who have supposedly given Hythloday a hearing in the past: Cardinal Morton and his associates, and the Utopians themselves. A series of hypothetical audiences, introduced by Hythloday during the Dialogue of Counsel, also influences the response of More and Giles. As the various responses of all these audiences to Hythloday's speeches are recorded and evaluated, the range of possible reader responses is simultaneously explored, with certain responses being systematically excluded as inappropriate. The textual directives constrain the reader to respond with increasing openness and humility to Hythloday's speech.

At the same time Hythloday's success or failure with each group of auditors becomes eventful. The hero Hythloday is in search of an audience that will pay heed to his message. Indeed, there is no other plot and, as Elizabeth McCutcheon notes [in "Thomas More, Raphael Hythlodaeus, and the Angel Raphael," *Studies in English Literature,* 1969], "the most dramatic moment in all of **Utopia** occurs in the last few paragraphs" when the reader finds out whether or not Raphael Hythlodaeus succeeds with that most promising of audiences, More and Giles. To the extent that the reader's sympathy for Hythloday is aroused, he wishes him success—even to the point of becoming himself the audience Hythloday seeks. The reader who does so eventually confronts his own pride and, in that confrontation, achieves the self-knowledge that makes it possible for him to be both a rhetor and a reformer.

In the moral education of his audience toward humility, More points to a solution of the problem posed in the Dialogue of Counsel when Hythloday denies, and More affirms, that a reformer can reach his goals in a court culture opposed to his views by way of rhetorical indirection and accommodation. Hythloday insists that one cannot proceed *obliquo ductu* without coming "to share the madness" of those he sought to cure, and

the part he expects his readers to play. Ambrosius Holbein's delightful woodcut, which headed the text proper in the 1518 edition, suggests that the reader's place is on the garden bench, next to More and Giles, facing the bearded Hythloday, and listening to him as he speaks. The title, directly below the garden scene, invites the reader to read a transcription of the very discourse More has heard, to join company with the trustworthy reporter.

The *parerga* reveals that More's original audience, the circle of European humanists, delighted in the role More had assigned to them, and responded by fictionalizing themselves even further. The scholar William Budé, for instance, in his letter to Thomas Lupset, contends that he has conducted a personal investigation as to the whereabouts of Utopia. Peter Giles contributes two poems, aquatrain and a hexastichon, that he claims to have translated into Latin from the Utopian vernacular. Giles also reports to Jerome Busleyden that the island's exact location is unknown to him because someone coughed very loudly just at the moment when Raphael described it. John Desmarais, the orator of the

More does not deny that that danger exists. Striving "to handle things tactfully" can easily lead to a compromise of principles and the loss of one's prophetic mission. In many ways this problem—the necessity of using rhetoric to attain one's goal and the near impossibility of doing so—is a specifically humanist version of a universal Christian problem: how is it possible to be in the world without being of it?

The Dialogue throws into relief the difficult rhetorical situation actually confronting the humanist reformer at court in a moral climate fraught with "many and great dangers". More observes in his October 31, 1516 letter to Erasmus that Cuthbert Tunstal, Jerome Busleyden, and Jean le Sauvage have to endure "some high and mighty clowns as their equals, if not superiors, in authority and influence." The *parerga* includes Budé's complaint that most of thepeople in positions of authority "to give definitive replies on what is good and fair" achieved that status by accumulating dishonest wealth. Busleyden, too, writes with a certain poignancy that More is one of a very few men "who not only sincerely want to serve the commonwealth, but also have the learning to know how, the trust of others to be able, and the prestige with the corresponding power, and who consequently can serve" with loyalty, honesty, and wisdom.

John Cardinal Morton has the qualities Busleyden names, and his presence in the Dialogue symbolizes the solution to the dilemma it poses. Hythloday's high esteem for Morton endears him to More, who has admired the Cardinal from the days of his youth. As he tells Hythloday, "Since you are strongly devoted to his memory, you cannot believe how much more attached I feel to you on that account". Remembering Morton, then, produces a certain harmony between the disputants. Indeed, in his person the issues that divide More and Hythloday are transcended. What is impossible for Hythloday (and, indeed, for most men) is possible for Morton. Hythloday describes the Cardinal as a man "who deserved respect as much for his prudence and virtue as for his authority", and observes that "the King placed the greatest confidence in his advice, and the commonwealth seemed to depend on him when I was there". Morton, then, represents the possibility of combining service to the King with genuine service to the commonwealth, a position of public influence with nobility of character, experience with youthfulness, eloquence ("his speech was polished and pointed") with honor, rhetoric with moral philosophy, tact with the ability to effect reform.

Hythloday notes that Morton had come directly from school to the court where, during the course of a long political career filled with "many and great dangers", he has acquired "a statesman's sagacity." In the wolfish court circle he has learned to be cunning as a serpent, gentle as a dove. Through hard and humiliating experience with the ways of the world, he has come to know his own worst tendencies, and to guard against them.

The lesson Morton learned by passing through "many and great dangers" is the same lesson More wishes to teach his readers. Knowing "the original causes of the world's evils" and "the very sources of right and wrong", the reader will be in a position to serve the commonwealth and lighten the burden that "cannot be removed entirely" even in Utopia because it belongs to the condition of fallen man.

More's second letter to Giles, included in the *parerga* of 1517, suggests that human nature is such that the hard truths of failure and sin, the experiential knowledge of one's own, and England's, wickedness, can only "slide into men's minds" if it is "smeared with honey". The poet as moral teacher, then, must use the "indirect approach" More recommends to Hythloday. More's *obliquo ductu*, like Cicero's *de insinuatione*, names the rhetorical strategy one must employ in the face of an audience that is opposed to one's view, or offended and alienated by the subject of one's speech. In such a case the rhetor must proceed by way of indirection—*"dissimulatione et circumitione obscure,"* as Cicero puts it in his *De Inventione*—gradually approaching his true subject, stealing into the minds of his auditors (*"subiens auditoris animum"*) who are surprised, or even tricked, into assent.

Utopia as a whole is a masterpiece of rhetorical indirection. It is More's book, but it is entitled "The Discourse of the Extraordinary Character, Raphael Hythlodaeus." It pretends to make known the "manners and customs" of a distant people when it actually lays bare our own pride as the fountainhead of all injustice. It purports to be about Utopia when its true subject is Europe, and England in particular. Erasmus testifies to this in his famous July 23, 1519 letter to Ulrich Hutten when he states that More's "*Utopia* was published with the aim of showing the causes of the bad conditions of states; but was chiefly a portrait of the British state." Similarly, Gerhard Geldenhauer's verse address to the reader maintains, "In this book the very sources of right and wrong are revealed by the eloquent More". And Cornelis de Schrijver's poem preface advises the reader to "read these pages which the celebrated More has given us" if he wants to "uncover the original causes of the world's evils and to experience the great emptiness lying concealed at the heart of things".

In order to disclose the emptiness of vainglory, More first conceals that truth in the honey of his fiction. In order to teach true humility, he identifies himself with his audience and plays with them the part of Hythloday's pupil. When the reader first encounters More he finds him in the company of Cuthbert Tunstal, a humanist statesman well-known for his "integrity and learning". They are negotiating with Georges de Themsecke, the shrewd and eloquent representative of Charles, Prince of Castile, on behalf of a "model monarch," Henry VIII. When the Provost of Cassel temporarily breaks off the negotiations, More goes to Antwerp where he meets Giles, "an honorable man of high position in his home town" who is "distinguished equally by learning and character." These brief sketches serve to establish the *ethos* of Hythloday'simmediate audience for the reader. Certainly the humanist scholars and statesmen who read More's *Utopia* found it easy to identify with these men whom they knew by reputation, if not personally, as leading exponents of their own high ideals.

When Giles introduces the sunburnt and bearded Hythloday to More, he describes him as a wayfaring philosopher, more conversant in Greek than Latin, who has just returned from a voyage like "that of Ulysses or . . . of Plato". Giles informs More that Hythloday, an associate of Amerigo Vespucci, can tell him much about "unknown peoples and lands," adding that this is a subject about which More is "always most greedy to hear." Thus the reader's curiosity is piqued along with More's, and directed by his interest in the "excellent institutions" of foreign commonwealths away from a trivial concern with "stale travelers' wonders". Indeed, More rather pointedly remarks that "those wise and prudent provisions" which Hythloday noticed in his travels through various civilized nations are the sort of facts which "would be useful to readers". Not only are the "well and wisely trained citizens" of other nations useful to our own people as *exempla* leading to the "correction of . . . errors"; they are also, More observes, more rare, wonderful, and interesting than the "scyllas and greedy Celaenos and folk-devouring Laestrygones" that are the subjects ofpopular travelogues. Remarks of this sort prepare the reader for what is to come by defining the genre of Hythloday's discourse, appeal to the reader's sense of civic responsibility, and incorporate the reader's motives for reading into More's own reasons for listening to Hythloday.

According to Hexter's reconstruction, Hythloday launches into his account "of the manners and customs of the Utopians" immediately after this brief introduction in More's original draft of the *Utopia*. More, however, apparently felt the need to provide a more fully developed rhetorical context for the speech Hythloday delivers in Book II. Therefore, in his revised draft, More added the so-called Dialogue of Counsel—"the talk which drew and led [Hythloday] on to mention that commonwealth".

The discussion begins with Giles' naive suggestion that the knowledgeable and wise Hythloday attach himself to some king in order to profit the commonwealth while securing personal gain and "the advancement of all [his] relatives and friends." In words echoing Luke 9: 25, Hythloday replies that he does not want to become

"prosperous by a way which [his] soul abhors", and More commends him for his personal integrity: "It is plain that you, my dear Raphael, are desirous neither of riches nor of power. Assuredly, I reverence and look up to a man of your mind." Thus, at the very beginning of the Dialogue, Hythloday's high moral character is affirmed, and the reader is invited to respond to him as More does, the *ethos* of the speaker appealing to the *ethos* of the audience.

More proceeds to make an ethical appeal to Hythloday, telling him that his own "generous and truly philosophic spirit" should motivate him to apply his "talent and industry to the public interest," even at the cost of "personal disadvantages." More stresses that he who influences the king affects the people as a whole, the monarch being, like a "never-failing spring," the source of "good and evil" for the nation. Hythloday modestly replies that he lacks the great abilities More ascribes to him, and that he would not be able to accomplish any good anyway in the king's service because neither the king nor his courtiers would listen to his counsel.

Hythloday proceeds to call up a number of possible audiences for himself as test-cases. He imagines himself making an innovative proposal "in the company of people who are jealous of others' discoveries or prefer their own". He pictures himself arguing for measures of reform in the presence of a long-winded lawyer, ahanger-on, an unholy friar, and a flock of other flatterers surrounding John Cardinal Morton. He imagines himself advocating peace to the King of France before "a circle of his most astute councilors" at a meeting called for the express purpose of planning military aggression against Italy, Flanders, Brabant, and Burgundy. He pictures himself admonishing a king against arrogance and greed at a session when the other councilors are busy "devising by what schemes they may heap up treasure for him". He concludes that his opinions would surely meet with an unfavorable reception from each of these audiences, exclaiming, "if I tried to obtrude these and like ideas on men strongly inclined to the opposite way of thinking, to what deaf ears should I tell my tale!" More can only shake his head and agree with Hythloday that he surely would not succeed if he tried to "force upon people new and strange ideas which . . . carry no weight with persons of opposite conviction".

This series of strange and difficult audiences has proved troublesome to critics of *Utopia* who usually conclude, as David Bevington does, that Hythloday is proposing extreme cases that are irrelevant to the topic actually under discussion: the Tudor monarchy. In his introduction to the Yale edition, Father Surtz suggests, moreover, that Hythloday's hypothetical audiences have no relationship to *Utopia's* real audience, outside of defining theintended readership by negation.

The ending of the Dialogue and the conclusion of Book II, however, suggest that these fictive audiences do have an inner relationship to *Utopia's* intended audience, and that the discovery of that relationship belongs to the *gnosis* imparted by the poet as moral teacher. Certainly More expects his high-minded readers to suppose that the corrupt court circles, who would reward Hythloday with banishment or ridicule for his attempt to "uproot . . . the seeds of evil and corruption", are far-removed from themselves. Indeed, he cultivates that response by awakening in his (and Hythloday's) audience moral outrage against kings and councilors who have inflicted so much suffering on the peoples of Europe through their schemes, deceptions and warmongering.

Suddenly, however, the audience is asked to direct that same moral outrage toward themselves when, at the end of the Dialogue, Hythloday candidly reveals his "heart's sentiments" and tells More that such abuses are inevitable in a society based on private property— i.e., the unequal distribution of goods: "wherever you have private property and all men measure things by cash values, there it is scarcely possible for a common-wealth to have justice or prosperity". Hythloday's conclusion challenges the value system of More's readers, all of whom are property owners, and suggests that they are not untainted by the selfishness and pride which manifests itself so blatantly in the wealthy and powerful. *Persona* More adds weight to Hythloday's charge when, at the end of the Utopian discourse, he remarks that the "estimation of the common people" places a high value on worldly goods—"nobility, magnificence, splendor and majesty"—as "the true glories and ornaments of the commonwealth".

When Hythloday connects the moral ills of the court in a causal relationship with an economic system based on private ownership that encourages fallen man's propensity toward covetousness, his auditors in the garden suddenly find themselves among the "persons of opposite conviction" whom Hythloday had addressed hypothetically before. More declares that he is "of the contrary opinion" and proceeds to enumerate the usual arguments against communism. When Hythloday refutes More's objections by citing his happy experience among the Utopians, Giles, equally on the defensive, says that he finds it hard to believe "that a better-ordered people is to be found in that new world than the one known to us". The notion of common ownership is thrust upon them as one of Hythloday's "novel ideas".

As threatened as More and Giles may feel by Hythloday's position, they can hardly respond in any of the ways that have previously been rejected as reflecting "proud, ridiculous and obstinate prejudices". They cannot reject Hythloday's view out-of-hand as the punctilious lawyer had. They cannot respond with

contempt, as the Cardinal's courtiers did. They can hardly treat the matter as a jest, as did the foolish hanger-on. Nor can they turn a deaf ear like the wicked kings and courtiers. More himself makes a direct connection between his possible response as an auditor and the responses of Hythloday's other audiences at the conclusion of the afternoon discourse when he recalls Hythloday's "censure of others on account of their fear that they might not appear wise enough, unless they found some fault to criticize in other men's discoveries", and decides (at least for the time being) not to voice any opposition to Hythloday's views. If at the end of the long Utopian discourse More still recalls Hythloday's other audiences and measures his response by theirs, we may be sure that they are much closer to his thoughts at the end of the Dialogue. The reader, like More and Giles, finds himself constrained to respond with greater humility and open-mindedness to Hythloday's "novel ideas" than others have.

In Book I More provides his readers with two models for that kind of magnanimous response to Hythloday's message in the Utopians themselves and in the person of John Cardinal Morton. The Cardinal, as Lord Chancellor of England, listens attentively to Hythloday's impassioned harangue on the injustice of the death penalty for thieves, the disastrous consequences of maintaining a standing militia, and the multiple problems stemming from the policy of enclosing arable farmland for grazing sheep. After silencing the lawyer who is about to reply to Hythloday "in the usual manner of disputants", Morton offers the opportunity for further discussion at a later meeting. When, in response to the Cardinal's sincere question about what penalty, other than the death penalty, Hythloday would propose for theft, he suggests an adaptation of the penal system used by the Romans and the Polylerites, the Cardinal agrees with Hythloday that there is no reason "why this method might not be adopted . . . in England". Indeed, Morton immediately conceives a plan for experimenting with Hythloday's proposal, even extending its application to vagrants as well as thieves. Morton's wisdom keeps him from clinging to old practices that have proven ineffectual, and from rejecting new ways that have not been tested. He serves as a model for the reader who is asked, not to ape him as the blind courtiers do, but to assume his fundamental attitude toward Hythloday's "novel ideas".

At the end of the Dialogue, however, Hythloday is not merely opposing the abuses of the rich and powerful; he is challenging private ownership itself, an institution cherished even by the common man, and suggesting that justice will never be achieved by a society that fails to counteract fallen man's root tendency toward greed, sloth, and pride by taking Utopian measures. Despite the example of openness set by Cardinal Morton, More and Giles are in obvious disagreement with Hythloday even before he begins to describe "the manners and customs of the Utopians".

Ultimately he secures their attentiveness by appealing to their civic pride and supplying them with the example of yet another model audience, the Utopians themselves. Hythloday reports that the islanders "immediately at one meeting appropriated to themselves every good discovery of ours". This openness to change and willingness to "adopt whatever is better from others" is, Hythloday asserts, the chief reason why "their commonwealth is more wisely governed and more happily flourishing than ours".

More responds by begging and beseeching Raphael to describe the island:

> Do not be brief, but set forth in order the terrain, therivers, the cities, the inhabitants, the traditions, the customs, the laws, and, in fact, everything which you think we should like to know. And you must think we wish to know everything of which we are still ignorant.

The sincerity of More's request gains symbolic expression when he reserves the whole afternoon for listening to Hythloday's account, commands the servants to leave them in peace, and takes up his seat anew in the same place, on the same bench. Both Giles and More urge Raphael to "fulfill his promise," and he sees them "intent and eager to listen".

At the end of Book I, then, Hythloday has gained an audience for himself through the use of other audiences: the censured audiences whose response arises out of "proud, ridiculous and obstinate prejudices" and the commended audiences, outstanding for their good will, attentiveness and docility. More has also gained an audience for Book II of his *Utopia* by fictionalizing himself and his fellow humanists (represented by Giles) as Hythloday's attentive listeners. The part More expects his audience to play is clear enough: they are to set aside their prejudgments about how a society is to be ordered, and seriously entertain the possibility of a better way of doing things as a way of reorienting themselvestoward the ideal, and directing their energies in everyday life toward the achievement of "the best state of a commonwealth."

The writings of the *parerga* indicate that More's original audience read Book II in just that way. The reader hears no more of More and Giles until the very last paragraphs, and their less-than-wholehearted response to Hythloday's discourse is concealed from the reader until the very end. Throughout almost all of Book II the only audience directing the reader's response is the enthusiastic outer circle of humanists whose side-comments in the margins either capsule Hythloday's description, express admiration for the Utopian ways, or pass judgment against European practices that fall short

of the ideal. When, for instance, Hythloday reports that no city on the blessed island "has any desire to extend its territory", the comment in the opposite margin reads, "Yet Today the Desire for Expansion Is the Curse of All Commonwealths." When Raphael notes that the Utopians are unacquainted with dice "and that kind of foolish and ruinous game", the unseen audience whose voice is recorded in the marginal comment exclaims, "Yet Now Dicing Is the Amusement of Kings." At other points the humanist response is a burst of exclamatory praise: "O Holy Commonwealth—and Worthy of Imitation Even by Christians!", "How Much Wiser the Utopians Are than the Common Run of Christians!", "O Priests Far More Holy thanOurs!". Page by page, paragraph by paragraph, the marginal comments render the outer audience present and invite the reader to enter into its ranks by appropriating the canonical response.

At times, too, the reader is directly addressed. When Hythloday notes that the Utopian religion is the best to which human reason, unaided by revelation, can attain, the side comment reads: "Careful Attention Must be Paid Also to This Point". And when Hythloday in his *peroratio* surveys the European status quo and denounces it as a "conspiracy of the rich" who only pretend to serve the commonwealth, the speaker in the margin urges, "Reader, Take Notice of These Words!"

More's ultimate goal—the bringing of his humanist audience to a new self-knowledge and humility that will safeguard and increase their fruitfulness as advocates of reform—can only be accomplished if the reader cooperates with the text, fictionalizes himself as Hythloday's audience and (at least for a while) believes that there is a Utopia somewhere. Only if the reader takes the blessed island seriously, and imaginatively perceives it as an ideal state that other men have actually achieved, will the on-going comparison with England bring about the desired effect. More wants the reader to experience the failure of England and Christian Europe keenly. Therefore he uses Utopia, "the best state of a commonwealth," as a standard of comparison; he holds up the fictive island as a Golden World before the eyes of his readers so that they can realize anew that they have fallen short of the communal ideal to which they are called. Indeed, Hythloday, Budé, and Erasmus all describe Utopia as the embodiment of Christ's social teaching, which remains the ultimate standard by which all human conduct is judged and found wanting.

At the end of the Dialogue of Counsel Hythloday draws a causal relationship between the abuses of the nobility and the self-seeking generally encouraged by the economics of private ownership. At the end of the Utopian Discourse he goes a step further and declares that men have institutionalized the unequal distribution of goods and rejected communism (even though the latter has obvious benefits and has been recommended to us by Christ Himself) because of the urgings of "one single Monster, the chief and progenitor of all plagues", Pride. The progression is rhetorically potent, beginning with an evil that is distant from the reader and localized in the king and his court, proceeding to a systemic evil in which the individual participates, and ending at the the threshold of each heart with the personal sin of pride, the chief sin which is the root cause of all the others, includingcovetousness. The broad outline of this progression reveals to what an extent the rhetor More has taken the philosopher Hythloday into his service and used him to accomplish the education and formation of *Utopia's* audience. More, the "arranger of the materials" supposedly presented by Hythloday, proceeds by way of indirection, first arousing the reader's indignation at unjust laws and the corrupt practices of others, and then gradually redirecting that same indignation toward his own moral shortcomings.

Having brought the reader into a confrontation with his own pride and achieved his educational aim, More calls attention to the rhetorical strategy he has used by discarding its devices, distancing his reading audience from the fictive audience, and himself from Hythloday. In the very last paragraphs of Book II *persona* More confides to the reader that he finds many of the Utopian customs and laws to be "very absurdly established"; he admits that he "cannot agree with all" that Hythloday said; and he says that he has little if any "hope of being realized" in Europe those features which he admires in the Utopian commonwealth. While he may be provoked to thought and desirous of further discussion, he is certainly not persuaded, not moved to action, by what he has heard.

In Hythloday's failure with More and Giles, the poet More dramatizes the failure of unadorned philosophy to move men, and addresses the very problem Sir Philip Sidney accuses him of having overlooked when he patterned a "most absolute commonwealth." With a certain shock the reader recalls that the book he has been reading is not, after all, a transcription of the talk given by Raphael Hythlodaeus, but a fiction of Thomas More. Like Sidney, More believed that "the fayned image of Poesie" has a greater power than "the regular instruction of Philosophy" to move men. Accordingly he retells Hythloday's facts as fictions, translates his Greek into Latin, turns his "philosophical city" into a "phantom", changes his Somewhere into a No-Where, and thus transforms even the philosopher Hythloday (much against his will, no doubt) into a rhetor and poet.

Thus it is that while *persona* More responds in a reserved and almost patronizing way to Hythloday's afternoon discourse, the humanist writers of the *parerga* respond with an unqualified enthusiasm to the

book which purports to be nothing more than a reporting of that same talk. All of them praise More for his eloquence, and attribute to his artistry the moving power of the book. At the same time they attribute the philosophical function of revelation to Hythloday, calling him "the discoverer" of Utopia.They distinguish, however, only in order to unite, and thus pay tribute to the perfect poetry of the *Utopia* that delights even as it moves and teaches. They know, after all, that "Utopia lies outside the limits of the known world, . . . perhaps close to the Elysian Fields" and that Hythloday himself belongs to the realm of More's imagination. On the other hand, they know that *Utopia* has a serious message for the reader who is willing to enter into the game and play along with More himself the part of Hythloday's audience.

Peter Iver Kaufman (essay date 1987)

SOURCE: "Humanist Spirituality and Ecclesial Reaction: Thomas More's *Monstra*," in *Church History,* Vol. 56, No. 1, March, 1987, pp. 25-38.

[*In the following essay, Kaufman takes issue with the traditional reading of* Utopia *as a direct embodiment of humanist ideals, calling it instead "a gentle ecclesial remonstrance" to the principles of More's humanist colleagues.*]

"Do you want to see new marvels (*monstra*)? Do you want to seestrange ways of life, to find the sources of virtue or the causes of all evil; to sense the vast emptiness that commonly goes unnoticed?"

Cornelius Grapheus was responsible for this sales promotion. Along with other prefatory material, it introduced Thomas More's *Utopia* to readers in 1516. More's friend, Erasmus of Rotterdam, had collected endorsement, and either he or Peter Giles had approached Grapheus, then secretary to the municipal government at Antwerp. It is reasonable to assume that Grapheus jumped at the chance to associate his name with the new work. He had published nothing before this time, save for some devotional verse in 1514, yet careers were launched, patrons found, and reputations ennobled by promotional material as well as by the material promoted.

But Grapheus appears oddly equivocal when he cheers More's *monstra*. The inducement hardly seems compatible with what we know, or with what we think we know of humanists' sunny and optimistic dispositions. What are we to make of that "vast emptiness?" Did Grapheus smuggle some skepticism into his assignment? Could *"nova monstra"* mean both "marvelous new things" and "monstrous new things?"

Small questions such as these often summon us to

reassess larger issues. In this instance, the apparent equivocation of humanist correspondents tempted me to review the character of renaissance humanism in northern Europe and to offer a reappraisal of the *Utopia*'s place in the history of renaissance spirituality. I shall argue that Thomas More carefully traced the trajectory of humanist idealism and discovered that it led humanists back to the religious formalism that they ostensibly deplored but that he was increasingly willing to defend. Hence, we may think of the *Utopia* as an ecclesial reaction.

Equivocation in the prefatory material does not settle the question of humanist discontent. In fact, traces of the correspondents' bafflement are difficult to detect. Friends were eager to flatter one another. Bounders were happy to hurl hyperbole at distinguished colleagues. Peter Giles was delighted with the *Utopia* and wrote to that effect to Jerome Busleyden, whose greetings to More were also incorporated in the first edition. William Budé composed a favorable review for the second edition, and Erasmus's own imprimatur surfaced with the third edition in 1518. Still, one wonders why Erasmus waited so long.

Jean Desmarais, who wrote for the earliest printing, offered arather curious suggestion that hints at some humanist dissatisfaction with Thomas More's dream commonwealth. Utopian government, Desmarais conceded, had much to teach Europeans. Since the unleavened people on the remote island were fascinated with Christianity, Desmarais proposed that the church's "invincible" theologians be sent to expedite conversions, to sift the natives' laws and customs, and to return with strategies for the improvement of public administration. But the mission is packed with irony, for Erasmus, More, and their friends considered those "invincible" theologians arrogant, unteachable, and insufferable. Had humanists been able to lease their antagonists to the Utopians, they would have cared little for their recovery. If only to keep the fiction working, Desmarais might have volunteered himself or some more itinerant humanist—Erasmus, perhaps. But the prospect of travelling to More's island was unwelcome. Utopian order was too perfect, uncomfortably perfect. William Budé averred that the community of saints or hagnopolis was not simply a utopia or "no place" but a "never-to-be land" (*"Udepotia"*) as well.

Would Desmarais have volunteered to export the invincible scholastics, and would Budé, in this intance, have seemed so despairing, if the *Utopia* were the culmination of the humanist "program" for social and religious reform? Would Grapheus haveinvited fellow humanists to "see strange ways," if Utopian society had been conjured as the hypostasis of humanist spirituality? Before answering, of course, one must consider the character of the humanist "program" as well as the character of humanist spirituality, and these

considerations require a review of the nature of northern renaissance humanism.

The prefatory endorsements provide a fine place to start. Nearly every correspondent applauds Thomas More for his scholarly attention to antiquity. Desmarais thought England exceedingly fortunate to have such a citizen who was equally at home in ancient Greece and Rome. Desmarais also announced that the study of classical literature flowered elsewhere, but he guessed that the *Utopia* would be a goad to greater achievement on the continent. More's fabulous commonwealth was certainly an occasion for several parts of the community united by a devotion to classical literature to join in celebration and mutual encouragement. The prefatory letters borrow ideas and superlatives from one another, much as neighbors might trade recipes. The point to be remembered, however, is that the correspondents were not neighbors. Their friendships were choreographed and often, I suspect, contained by the letters that crisscrossed Europe.

The epistolary evidence is difficult to read. If northern renaissance humanism was a "movement," the direction in which it was moving at any given time is not always clear. What is clear and incontestable is that the prolific, refined, and usually charming Erasmus of Rotterdam occupied the center of the friendship network. Yvonne Charlier remarked that Erasmus attracted friends as light attracts insects. The simile is rather patronizing, yet scholars who have lavished years and pages on other northern European scholars of the period generally concede Erasmus's preeminence. For his part, Erasmus tirelessly stressed the importance of friendship for the success of Europe's belletristic revival and for religious renewal. His famous and frequently anthologized adage, *Dulce bellum inexpertis* ("War is Sweet to those who have not tried it"), insists that nature made humans companionable and that "she added also the love of learning and the pursuit of knowledge. And this, just as it is instrumental in drawing the mind of man away from all savagery, has the greatest power of knitting up friendships. Indeed, neither family connections nor blood relationship bind souls together in closer or firmer bond of friendship than does a shared enthusiasm for noble studies."

Erasmus's very first letters reveal his own craving for friendship and collegiality. "If you love me," he wrote to Cornelius Gerard, "pray let me have some share in your own studies." Yet it was soon obvious to Gerard and to other correspondents that Erasmus would not be content to fall in as one oarsman among many. He wanted to determine his friends' tastes, to prescribe their reading, as well as to encourage their writing. He harassed Gerard, for example, to alter his unfavorable estimate of Laurentius Valla, whom Erasmus himself admired tremendously. But Erasmus could afford only to be mildly censorious when he pestered corespondents, for friendships were fragile and, above all, precious. Terms of endearment and assurances of unflinching admiration punctuate his petitions: only disreputable barbarians libel Valla, and surely Gerard, "most faithful devotee of literary culture," dazzling poet, and perfect friend, will not long be misled. Erasmus's overtures were compelling. His perseverance and compassion seem commendable, even now. He circulated among his friends in Paris a manuscript by Gerard's nephew, Williams Hermans, "the first and chief hope of our Holland," in order to find a patron and launch a friend's career.

To those same ends, Erasmus composed a dedication to his own patron, the bishop of Cambrai, to accompany Hermans's odes. The dedication tells us a great deal about Erasmus's belletristic prejudices, so it is a shame to leave so much of it unglossed. But one particular fiction takes us directly to our principal concernwith the character of northern renaissance humanism. When a smaller perjury would have sufficed to stress his friend's modesty, Erasmus retailed at considerable length the fable that he had taken and circulated the manuscript without Hermans's permission. He pleaded guilty to the theft. He confessed that he had manufactured summerweight stories to cover the text's disappearance, tales that would not hold together once the *Silva odarum* had reappeared in print. Erasmus also incriminated colleagues in Paris who had agreed to review the manuscript. Finally, he invoked antiquity's experts to exculpate his accomplices and himself, for Cicero, among others, had suggested that friendships made meaningless such distinctions as mine and thine: friends have all things in common.

Erasmus took some liberties with his Cicero. Ownership and copyright had no place in Cicero's *De amicitia,* which contends that lasting and satisfying friendships depends on common interests, common tastes, common opinions—on consensus. Informed readers would have known that Erasmus's fable referred to that *consensio studiorum,* and they would have understood that Erasmus was industriously trying to mortar a humanist consensus with his own letters and dedications. Manuscripts were exchanged, patrons shared, books promoted, egos inflated, and the network of friends grew because Erasmus was shrewd and entrepreneurial. He cultivated the impression that his correspondents were engaged in a momentous battle against "barbarians" who discredited learning that exceeded their own narrow range. His friends joined the chant, villified barbarous educators, and scolded indifferent ecclesiastical officials. Erasmus had generated something of a siege mentality that gave humanists a sense of solidarity and that braced their consensus. The idea that they were surrounded by hostile forces and left to their mercy by listless authorities fashioned a scholarly association of humanists who seldom assembled in one place long enough to be surrounded.

Erasmus's interwoven exhiliration and alarm filled the early letters. Not only was he alarmed by barbarous critics. He was distressed as well at the prospect of losing a single colleague. The consensus, he figured, must be sufficiently broad and ambiguous to accommodate friends who most certainly would have squabbled with one another over refinements. Erasmus's letters reflect his latitudinarian approach. His epistolography enshrines his impatience with rules and restrictions that inhibit expression. The earliest drafts of his *Opus de conscribendis epistolis,* composed for his students in Paris shortly before 1500, caution stylists against following too slavishly the formulae prescribed by medieval epistolographers, who seemed to have a tried and true phrase forevery occasion. Erasmus kept to his theme in his revisions of the *De conscribendis,* yet the nature of his complaint had changed. True, he had lobbied relentlessly for a belletristic revival, but that was no reason to lie low while classical literature was made an idol, while personal expression was sacrificed to imitation. Correspondence was too important for the *consensio studiorum* to be encumbered by prescriptions or to be stuffed with salutations and exordia imported from antiquity.

Erasmus could not very well have purged all commonplaces. Even humanist correspondents hardly knew how to console without echoing well-worn assurances and without pronouncing on life's uncertainty and God's inscrutability. Erasmus's remarks and examples *de consolatione* merely suggest that condolences crammed with clichés were less effective than letters conditioned by circumstance. Neither Cicero nor custom ranked higher in humanist epistolography than utility and inventiveness. Erasmus replaced formulae and detailed prescriptions with a set of general standards.

To the extent that letters became the instruments for social and religious reform, as humanists gained some influence at court and among leading prelates, the very contribution of the northern renaissance hinged on this epistolographic reform. But that is notthe main reason for having paused here over Erasmus's *Opus de conscribendis.* Imagine that the formulae that guaranteed epistolographic decorum are analogous to religious formalism that steadied the ecclesiastical order. Erasmus thought it necessary to debase the former, patterned expression and imitation, in order to assure authentic, meaningful communication. He believed it necessary to minimize the latter, patterned action, in order to revive and dignify lay spirituality.

On that count, the church's ceremonies and sanctions seemed ineffective to Erasmus. As far as he could tell, penances, pilgrimages, indulgences, and oblations had not improved lay behavior at all. Such complaints were not new, yet learned critics like Erasmus had a knack for entertaining while complaining, so humanist grievances had a greater chance to reach influential ears than the related charges that unsociable heretics gripped to their graves.

This was certainly the case in England. While a guest of Thomas More in London, Erasmus composed his justly famous *Praise of Folly,* which targets the clergy for criticism and lists Europe's leading prelates among Europe's principle purveyors of (and slaves to) foolishness. Erasmus accused the clergy of peddling superstition, of harnessing guileless Christians to an assortment of worthless customs. Even the mendicants, once the church's resident crusaders against greed and indolence, had learned to empty merchants' purses and to seduce their wives with pretentious nonsense. *Folly* probably was not as subversive as it initially appears. Eramus poked fun at pride and power and was not content to confine his criticisms to one institution or one class. Nonetheless, his irreverence for the church in *Folly* may be paired with several of his less playful comments—especially with his indifference to ritual and ecclesiastical structure—in the *Enchiridion militis christiani.* The *Enchiridion* sets aside all the machinery that enabled the church to define and to maintain discipline, from confessionals to consistory courts. It stands as a rough equivalent of a self-help manual. An armload of imperatives and a vague sense of lay perfectability eclipse the little that remains of the Christian cult.

"Free yourself from the errors of this world," the *Enchiridion* urges; "find your way into the light of spiritual living." Erasmus seems to have implied that the church's arbiters of morality, both theorists and officials, were meddlesome yet ineffective. Even when driven by the best intentions, clerical Christianity had failed to inspire (or appropriately reward) piety. Erasmus and his humanist friends were persuaded fully that Christianity without vows, rules,and rituals would not leave Christendom rudderless, any more than human intelligence without formulae would be left speechless. Laurentius Valla, for instance, noted that *religiosi* sealed their promises to be chaste and obedient with elaborate consecrations, yet he pronounced that the piety behind the promises meant far more than the profession that confirmed them. John Colet implied that those same promises transformed virtuous laypeople into a spiritual priesthood that might do more for the spread of righteousness than the ordained clergy. No need, then, to stand on ceremony or to be awed by clerical status. Christ and the apostles abundantly supplied laypeople with the sturdiest standards for Christian conduct. Lay spirituality could flourish without constant ecclesiastical review and restraints.

But not without grace! Spiritual living required divine empowerment, for human determination, at its best, faltered. Erasmus was not one to sour on the vast capacities of humankind, but his *Enchiridion* does not undervalue the formidable temptations that Christians

confront. Powers that belong exclusively to the phenomenal world cannot long hold them off or quiet them. Spiritual living, therefore, must be a divine gift and a divine force rather than a human achievement. Erasmus's conclusion, on this matter, might have come from observation, to the extent that consistentlyexceptional conduct seemed then, as it always does, inconsistent with lives crafted month by month from crisis and routine. In this case, however, he and other humanists extrapolated from their sacred texts—on the question of spiritual empowerment, principally from the pauline epistles. Paul enabled them to tailor the meaning of moral autonomy to fit their understandings of lay spirituality. They readily incorporated his proclamation that Christ was the consummation of the law (*finis legis*) into their protests against religious formalism. Paul also saved them from extreme Pelagianism. In the context of moral theology, both Colet and Erasmus revived what they took to have been the apostle's stipulation that genuine piety originated with spiritual assistance and was reducible to constant spiritual empowerment. Before Martin Luther stirred violent reactions against the rhetoric of reform, Erasmus implied that some release from ecclesiastical regimentation was perfectly appropriate for some mature Christians (and that some forms of regimentation were inappropriate for all Christians), but neither Erasmus nor his humanist friends suggested that Christians were (or should be) ultimately independent.

Humanists were disinclined to fight for their adaptations of the Pauline materials with irascible colleagues who often brought time-honored philosophical categories to bear upon their biblicaltexts. By responding "so as to seem not to respond," Erasmus hoped to disarm Jacob Latomus, one of his more stubborn scholastic critics. To humanists who eschewed theology as it was then practiced, there seemed no surer sign that God had abandoned theologians to their own devices than their willingness to engage in interminable and disagreeable disputes about the darker corners of doctrine. Controversies over categories too long had obscured the straightforward ethical application of Paul's distinctions to moral regeneration, from which humanists expected the free and joyous fulfillment of the law in personal love for God and for neighbor. Erasmus believed that Paul had called for precisely this "fulfillment" when he had called Christ the consummation of the law.

Scholasticism, then, occasionally came under heavy fire. Sometimes humanists were polite when they replied directly to their scholastic critics, but cruel comments and jokes about those "invincible theologians" circulated in their letters to one another and, of course, in Erasmus's satires. Scholastic exegesis was ridiculed, yet scriptural study *per se* was above reproach. Georges Chantraine goes to great lengths to make explicit and more or less systematic humanism's sanctification of informed exegesis, which began with training in languages and exposure to the literature of classical antiquity and proceeded as "a progressive initiation into God's mysteries." One can argue that Chantraine has overdrawn his account, but there is enough evidence to suggest that the scholar's study had acquired the standing of a church. There, God's mysteries and God's spirit were accessible without clerical mediation. With this understanding in mind, whether one continues to explore Erasmus's "exegetical mysticism" or reassesses his remarks on spiritual empowerment, considerable ground should be yielded to those who have underscored the importance of humanist anticlericalism or, let us say, the importance of extra-ecclesial dimensions of humanist spirituality.

"Free yourself from the errors of this world." Stow that directive and others like it, and a very different picture of humanist spirituality materializes. Stress Erasmus's imperative, as I have done, and two choices present themselves. One might travel south to locate the origins of the humanists' "lay sermons," satires, and spirituality in order to test Charles Trinkaus's impression [in *The Scope of Renaissance Humanism*, 1983] that Erasmus and his friends "most perfectly fulfill the promises and programs of the religious thought and studies of the Italian humanists." Yet the other avenue quite conveniently brings us back to the remarks that introduced this essay, and it leads to some strangely reactionary sentiments that were formulated in Thomas More's *Utopia* and therefore leads close to the center of the humanists' campaigns for consensus without conformity.

The *Utopia* is usually thought to have been the capstone of the humanist position and protest. But I shall argue that More's fantasy was a gentle ecclesial remonstrance. Thomas More appears to me to have invited his humanist friends to reconsider the cultural and institutional consequences of their imperatives and, perhaps, to temper their optimism. Even as More gave fresh vitality to humanist convictions, he recommended that his colleagues contemplate outcomes as well as "oughts."

At the outset, one has to concede that More's *Utopia* is a mystifying text. The author created Raphael Hythloday, an opinionated tourist, to tell readers of a fabulous island, a medieval Lake Wobegone, where citizens were "easy-going," "good-tempered," and truly "ingenious": a place where minds invariably were alert, bodies were healthy and nimble (*agili vegetoque*). Greed had been suppressed. In fact, Utopians permitted no private ownership. Citizens were diligent and disciplined workers, whose leisure was arranged and spent most cleverly and whose love for literature was intense. Priests' conduct was unexceptionable; their piety, unpretentious. Hythloday admired Utopian culture uncritically, perhaps too much so for his maker,

who allows a second character, "Morus," to insert something of a disclaimer. The *Utopia*'s second book closes with Morus's suggestion that many things on the island were "very absurdly established." But the disclaimer confuses rather than enlightens, for Morus's reservations are immediately followed by a brief yet bewildering defense of opulence and ostentation, as if Thomas More meant to discredit his Morus. More himself was troubled by the swagger of the Tudor aristocracy and somewhat embarrassed by the affluence of the Tudor church. If he intended Morus to introduce his own criticisms of Utopia ("Very absurdly established"), why burden Morus with a preposterous vindication of wealth and pomp? If he admired the Utopians as assiduously as Hythloday, why tax them with Morus's opinions? The conclusion only muddles an already complicated problem. After pages of Hythloday's rapturous recollections and after centuries of interpretation, we cannot say with confidence how much of Thomas More was transported to his *Utopia*.

If, as was once claimed, the *Utopia* is only a humanist conceit, the answer has been permanently shelved beyond reach. If the *Utopia* had been composed as serious social criticism, perhaps one or more of the Thomas Mores already lured from this teeming document someday will tower over the others. For now, however, each reader finds a favorite facsimile, and none appears to have distinct and decisive advantages. More the humanist and humorist competes with More the puritan. More the communist jostles More the apologist for bourgeois capitalism. To this collection, add More the imperialist, the monk, the phrase-cradling exhibitionist, the master of "self-cancellation," the unflinching secularist, the "deeply divided soul." The proliferation has been staggering, and who can tell what contraband character the next reading will drag into the assembly?

Several of the interpretations, especially those that speak of "self-cancellation," pathological disorders, and divided souls, have touched upon the contradiction in the *Utopia*. Many of the Utopians' peppery opinions endorsed by Hythloday recast humanism's faith in education and reflect humanism's preoccupation with virtue. Yet virtue and learning in Utopia are purchased at a price that would have outraged most humanists. The Utopians, it seems, had discreet doubts about human nature. They prized education and literature, yet they suspected that character was tractable to a point beyond which learning was unlikely to have had any wholesome effect. What, then, should be done? The author was reluctant to lace Utopian social order with laws and lawyers (few humanist satires concluded without a slap at solicitors, summoners, and self-important justices); still, the *Utopia* asks rules and regulations to do what literary culture and self-discipline could not. They kept Utopians at work, determined their vocations, shaped their leisure, bridled their lusts, framed their courtships, preserved their marriages, set out their wardrobes, and designed their homes. The *Utopia*'s totalist approach to social control swerved from humanism's fascination with freedoms.

More's approach in the *Utopia* was also demonstrably ecclesial. There was nothing remarkable in his pragmatic regard for religion. Much as humanists, Utopia's moral theorists insisted that citizens be ever mindful of the afterlife and moderate their pursuits of pleasure accordingly. Hythloday reported that no serious discussion of moral philosophy in Utopia floated free from religion. But the *Utopia* does more than wrap religion in its program for moral improvement and civic virtue. It stands as the preamble of More's impassioned defense of ecclesiastical structure and ritual in his *Responsio ad Lutherum,* which was composed six years later, after he had been persuaded that Martin Luther's *ecclesia diffusa* or "invisible church" was a dangerous abstraction. The *Response,* particularly More's revision of the original draft in 1523, barkedremorselessly at Luther's irreverence and purported inconsistencies. It seemed to More that, once Rome, her officials, her traditions, and her pronouncements were discredited, any cadre of eccentrics could call itself a church.

It could be argued that late medieval anxieties and aversions to anarchy commissioned and fueled More's *Response.* "Give us a rule" to control exegesis, he badgered Luther. *"Det nobis regulam"* or your rhetoric will seem insubstantial as well as subversive. Reckless assertions about the sole authority of scripture, when hitched to a destabilizing ecclesiology, seemed to Thomas More to invite trouble. One compelling rogue could challenge with impunity understandings that had developed over the centuries. And Luther had opened scriptures to everyone (*viam aperit omnibus*), the rogues and the righteous.

Thomas More was unimpressed by Luther's talk of universal faith. To him, it was a paper consensus. The first gust of common sense would make short work of it. Genuine consensus was fastened by a pervasive rationality (in the *Utopia*) or by some spiritual bond and *sensus fidelium* (in the *Response*). And genuine consensus, for More, rested on rules and rituals devised to prevent the decline of public morality.

The *Utopia* and the *Response* are variations on a theme, which reduces to the triumph of ritual and routine over rhetoric. In the *Response,* the triumph is explicitly ecclesiological. Ecclesial elements and a fund of ecclesial characters in the *Utopia* suggest that the distance between the two works is less than one might think. J. H. Hexter, for instance, inventoried the patently monastic features of Utopian life [in *More's Utopia: The Biography of an Idea,* 1952], from the distribution of resources to the regimentation of livery. Ordinarily, the similarities are referred exclusively to Thomas More's nostalgia for the Charterhouse, which he left more than twelve years before he manufactured Hythloday. Without splitting the *Utopia*'s seams, however, one also might relate the fictional commonwealth's monastic habits to the subsequent development of More's sense of ecclesial order. The same should be said of Utopia's clergy, for Thomas More, it turned out, was incapable of conjuring a priestless republic. In the *Utopia*'s first book, Hythloday complained that a gang of good-for-nothing priests had been allowed to prey upon European society. Utopian prelates were different in some respects, but not in all, yet Hythloday quickly warmed to them. They educated the young, scolded delinquents, and consulted with politicians on moral policy. They were able and admirable. Usually men, they took the realm's finest women as wives (*uxores selectissimae*). Utopians revered their priests, and they exempted them from normal duties and routines.

Utopian priests also escaped criminal prosecution simply because they were clerics. This was a telling concession for More to have made in 1515, for the issue of clerical immunity was caked with controversy in late medieval England. After acrimonious debate, parliament had just reinstated the practice of extending protection to clerics *in minoribus*. This is not to imply that the *Utopia* was written as an editorial on the parliamentary debates. Still, it is worth noting the conserving and conservative character of the text as well as its radical displacements. In essence, the partnership between politicians and priests, as it had been contracted in northern Europe, was not substantially altered in Utopia, though the commonwealth was churchless. Collaboration sustained discipline. Priests drafted projects for citizens' consciences. Magistrates intervened when excommunicated malcontents resisted their clergy's plans for their penance.

At one point, the *Utopia* seems to endorse direct prelatical involvement in politics. More's closest friends cautioned against it. John Colet wrote squeamishly and sometimes angrily about the clerical worldliness that inspired priests' political careers. Erasmus celebrated Archbishop Warham's retirement as chancellor in1515 as a release from prison. Hythloday's sense of the corruption of court life and his fear of contamination, should he stoop to public service, compress the opinions of several influential humanists, though More may not have scripted them for that purpose. But Hythloday also eulogized John Morton, Archbishop of Canterbury and, from 1487 to 1500, Lord Chancellor. That tribute, the monastic cast of Utopia social order, and the civic responsibilities of Utopia's priests are the text's most overtly ecclesial elements. Along with the rituals of citizenship, the rules, restraints, and routines, they constitute a reaction to humanism's obsessions with learned conversation, correspondence, self-discipline, and consensus without conformity.

Two biographical observations appear to capsize this conclusion. In the first place, epistolary evidence proves that More did not decamp and leave his friends to campaign without him. Scholastic critics, notably Martin Dorp, learned that to contend with Erasmus was to contend with More. And More continued to file briefs, *amicus curiae,* favoring Erasmus's biblical and patristic scholarship and furthering the humanists' belletristic revival. The *Utopia*'s *nova monstra,* then, started no feuds. But brawls are not required to make the point that equivocation and apparent discontent, submerged in the prefatory materials, mark More's text as a departure fromother humanists' extra-ecclesial orientations. The *Utopia* was not a shrill manifesto that immediately made friends and enemies. It was a muted recognition of the ecclesial frontiers of humanist spirituality.

A second bit of biography takes us from evidence to assessment. Brian Gogan most succinctly puts the problem in his recent study of ecclesiological themes in More's work [*The Common Corps of Christendom,* 1982]. Gogan declares at the start that "Martin Luther killed off the More of *Utopia,*" and that More is entombed in his own introduction, never to return and haunt the remaining pages. John Headley's account [in "Thomas Murner, Thomas More, and the First Expression of More's Ecclesiology," *Studies in the Renaissance,* 1967] is more provident. He maintains that Henry VIII started More thinking seriously about ecclesiological issues when the king asked for assistance with his *Assertio* against Luther (1521). Thomas Murner, then in England, alerted More to the magnitude of the crisis on the continent. The *Responsio ad Lutherum* soon followed, according to Headley, as "the first expression of More's ecclesiology." We must grant that no amount of prowling through Utopia's churchless commonwealth will produce an ecclesiology. Still, we find that the ecclesial dimensions of the *Utopia* make the *Response*'s "first expression" rather predictable.

Biographies continue to provide us with many Thomas Mores. The variety itself signals that *the* meaning of the *Utopia* may not be recoverable as long as that meaning is construed in terms of generative intentions. The course followed in this paper has been a different one. It started with several readers' responses to the *Utopia* and pressed ahead to define the discourse in which humanist spirituality and the *Utopia*'s ecclesial reaction might best be understood. Here, the method contributes principally to the *unwriting* of biography. Erasmus's rehearsal of More's life, as Heinz Holeczek has shown [in "Die humanistische Bildung des Thomas More und ihre Beurteilung durch Erasmus von Rotterdam," *Zeitschrift für historische Forschung,* 1976], suppressed (*verwischt*) anything that threatened the author's image of the immaculate humanist. Many of Erasmus's heirs similarly launder More's "lives" as humanist and as saint in order to

cinch complete compatibility. Others insist that the incompatibility was so conspicuous that it can be accommodated biographically only by two contrary phases. The *Utopia,* as we may read it now, should inhibit progress along either of these two lines, though it does not suggest an infallible alternative. Perhaps our reading accords only with Stephen Greenblatt's sense that Thomas More stubbornly yearned "to be absorbed" in "the total institution" all his life [*Renaissance Self-fashioning: More to Shakespeare,* 1980].

But our business has been with texts rather than with psychologies. The conclusion is simply that the *Utopia*'s ecclesial reaction is most fully disclosed and appreciated as part of the discourse constituted by our particular evaluations of Erasmus's *Enchiridion,* humanists' epistles and epistolography, and Thomas More's own *Response* to Luther. But it seems fair to say as well that our knowledge of humanist spirituality would be wanting, were we incurious about More's marvelous *and* monstrous new things.

Quentin Skinner (essay date 1987)

SOURCE: "Sir Thomas More's *Utopia* and the Language of Renaissance Humanism," in *The Languages of Political Theory in Early-Modern Europe,* edited by Anthony Pagden, Cambridge University Press, 1987, pp. 123-57.

[*In the essay below, Skinner examines the values and conventions that characterized Renaissance discussions of political theory in order to determine the* Utopia*'s place in that discussion and to argue that the work is More's vision of a "best commonwealth".*]

Almost everything about More's *Utopia* is debatable, but at least the general subject-matter of the book is not in doubt. More announces his theme on the title page, which reads: *De optimo reipublicae statu deque nova insula Utopia.* His concern, that is, is not merely or even primarily with the new island of Utopia; it is with 'the best state of a commonwealth'.

To say that this is More's concern is at once to raise what has always been seen as the main interpretative puzzle about his book. Does he intend us to take the description of Utopia in Book II as an account of a commonwealth in its best state? Are we intended to share and ratify the almost undounded enthusiasm that Raphael Hythloday, the traveller to Utopia, displays for that island and its way of life?

Until recently More's interpreters tended to answer in the affirmative. One theory has been that More aimed to picture the best state that reason can hope to establish in the absence of revelation. Another suggestion has been that he not only sought to portray a perfectly virtuous commonwealth, but wished at the same time to convey that, in spite of their heathenism, the Utopians are more truly and genuinely Christian than the nominally Christian states of western Europe. While disagreeing on the extent to which More holds up Utopia as an ideal, both schools of thought acceptthat Utopia must in some sense be regarded as an ideal commonwealth.

Of late, however, the best scholarship on *Utopia* has instead laid all its emphasis on the doubts and equivocations in More's text. Some commentators have stressed the inherently ambiguous character of the dialogue form that More chooses to employ; others have underlined the points at which he seems to criticise his own analysis of the 'best state', and even to treat it as a futile theory which is doomed to 'get nowhere'. From several different perspectives, scholars have thus converged on the suggestion that (as [Brendan] Bradshaw [in "More on Utopia," *The Historical Journal,* 1981] puts it) More must be taken to be expressing 'serious reservations about the ideal system' which Hythloday describes. More's final aim (in [W.S.] Allen's words [in 'The tone of More's farewell to Utopia: a reply to J. H. Hexter', *Moreana,* 1976]) must have been to leave us 'with an ambivalent and puzzled view' about Utopian life as a whole.

There can be no doubt that this new approach has added significantly to our understanding of More's text, especially by insisting on the implications of the fact that the figure of More in the dialogue disagrees with Hythloday at several importantpoints. Nevertheless, the new orthodoxy seems to me to embody an unacceptable view of More's basic purposes. I shall accordingly try in what follows to restate the case for saying that, for all the ironies and ambiguities in More's text, his main aim was to challenge his readers at least to consider seriously whether Utopia may not represent the best state of a commonwealth.

Otium and *Negotium*

More's handling of the theme of the *optimus status reipublicae* undoubtedly contains many unusual and puzzling elements. But it is important to note at the outset that there was nothing unusual about More's decision to consider that particular theme. More's text is sometimes approached as if he introduced a completely new topic into Renaissance political thought. But in fact the question of what constitutes the best state of a commonwealth was a standard subject of debate throughout the era of the Renaissance. We find the question being raised by a number of scholastic political philosophers in the wake of Aristotle's discussion in the *Politics.* And we find the same question being raised, and the same phraseology used, by an even wider range of so-called 'humanist' political writers—that is, by writers whose primary intellectual

allegiances were owed to the *studia humanitatis,* and hence to themoral and political philosophy of Rome rather than Greece.

This in turn suggests a way of approaching the complexities of More's text. If *Utopia* is an instance of a familiar genre of Renaissance political theory, it may be best to begin not with More's text itself but rather with some attempt to indicate the assumptions and conventions characteristic of the genre as a whole. Beginning in this way, we may eventually be able to gain some sense of More's own basic purposes. For we may be able to see how far he is accepting and reiterating common assumptions, or perhaps rephrasing and reworking them, or perhaps criticising and repudiating them altogether in order to attain a new perspective on a familiar theme. It is this approach which I shall now attempt to put to work.

Among political theorists of the Renaissance, whether scholastic or humanist in allegiance, there was little debate about what constitutes the *optimus status reipublicae.* A state will be in its best state, it was widely agreed, if and only if two claims can appropriately be made about it. One is that its laws are just, and thereby serve to promote the common good of its citizens. The other is that its citizens are in consequence able to pursue their own happiness, 'living and living well' in the manner most befitting the nature and dignity of man.

As soon as writers of this period turn, however, to ask how these conditions can be brought about, large differences of opinion begin to emerge. Among these, the most basic concerned the form of government that needs to be set up if a commonwealth is to have any chance of attaining and remaining in its best state. One widely held belief was that the only sure method is to assign all the affairs of the *res publica* to a wise guardian, a *Pater patriae.* His duty is to take upon himself all the burdens of the *vita activa,* leaving everyone else free to pursue their own higher purposes and so attain their happiness. This was the view of the earliest generation of self-styled humanists, including Petrarch himself in his last political testament, and of such younger contemporaries as Pier Paolo Vergerio and Giovanni da Ravenna, both of whom lived and wrote—as did Petrarch in the closing years of his life—under the patronage of the Carrara lords of Padua in the final decades of the fourteenth century.

It was the belief of all these writers that, as Giovanni expresses it, 'the government of a single individual is always to be preferred, even when the person in question is only a moderately good man'. One of his grounds for this belief is that 'where oneperson is in complete control, everyone else is able to pursue his own affairs in an untroubled way, and remains entirely free from public business'. One reason for supposing this to be a highly desirable state of affairs is that a life of *otium,* of freedom from public duty, is indispensable for the achievement of our highest ends and hence our greatest happiness. But a further reason derives from the fact that the alternative, the life of *negotium* as lived by courtiers, public servants and advisers to princes, is said to be inherently corrupt. 'No life is more miserable, more uncertain, more self-deceiving.' Flattery takes the place of truth, while approval is constantly sought for the most disgraceful policies, including violations of peace and betrayals of trust. The moral is said to be obvious: 'if you wish to remain pious, just, a respecter of truthfulness and innocence, remove yourself from the life of the court'.

These commitments remained an enduring element in humanist political theory, and became increasingly popular after Ficino's translations in the 1480s made Plato's political doctrines widely available for the first time. We find the ideal of the philosopher-king being espoused even by a number of Florentine humanists in this period. The connected suggestion that, under any less perfect system, the philosopher must remain aloof frompolitics recurs even more prominently among northern humanists in the opening decades of the sixteenth century.

Within More's own intellectual circle, for example, we find the claim that a princely regime is always to be preferred, together with the claim that a life of *otium* is best for everyone else, both being eloquently defended. Erasmus's *Institutio principis christiani,* published in the same year as More's **Utopia,** is founded on the assumption that the only means to attain the *optimus status reipublicae* is to ensure 'that there is a prince whom everyone obeys, that the prince obeys the laws and that the laws answer to our ideals of *honestas* and equity'. Similarly, More's younger contemporary, Thomas Starkey, writing his *Dialogue* between Pole and Lupset in the early 1530s, begins by presenting the related ideal of *otium* as the outlook to be expected from a fashionable humanist intellectual trained in Italy. Pole opens the discussion by announcing that he desires no part in public life. Instead he wishes to imitate 'the old and antique philosophers', who 'forsook the meddling with matters of common weals, and applied themselves to the secret studies and searching of nature'. He offers two main reasons for his preference, both very familiar by this stage in the development of humanist culture. One is that the life of *negotium* inhibits us from attaining our highest ends and thereby cheats usof our fullest happiness. This is because 'the perfection of man resteth in the mind and in the chief and purest part thereof', and in consequence requires a life dedicated to *otium* and the pursuit of truth. The other reason 'which hath caused many great, wise and politic men to abhor from common weals' is that the life of *negotium* forces the philosopher, whose concern is with truth, into a world of compromise,

hypocrisy and lies. It leaves the wise man 'nothing obtaining but only to be corrupt with like opinions as they be which meddle therewith' and is therefore to be shunned in the same way that a good man shuns the company of thieves.

This strand of humanism was always opposed, however, by a school of thought which argued that it can never be safe or even just to entrust our happiness to others. The exponents of this position generally concluded, by contrast, that the only possible means of bringing about the *optimus status reipublicae* must be to train an active citizenry and cleave to a fully participative system of republican government.

This so-called 'civic' humanism has been associated in particular with the great city-republics of Renaissance Italy, and above all with *Quattrocento* Florence. But the movement was of course of much broader significance than this, and even penetrated the princelycourts of northern Europe in the early years of the sixteenth century. For example, while Starkey's *Dialogue* opens with Pole's Platonist defence of *otium,* the figure of Lupset quickly replies that if anyone allows himself to be 'drawn by the sweetness of his studies' away from 'the cure of the common weal', then 'he doth manifest wrong to his country and friends, and is plain unjust and full of iniquity, as he that regardeth not his office and duty, to the which above all he is most bounden by nature'.

Nor of course was this 'civic' scale of values simply a product of the Renaissance. The ideals in question, as well as the vocabulary used for expressing them, were taken more or less wholesale from the last great defenders of the Roman republic—from Livy, Sallust and above all from Cicero, whose *De officiis* furnished virtually the whole framework for civic humanist discussions of the active life.

The *De officiis* had taught in the first place that the highest aim of a good man must be to embrace the four cardinal virtues, since these are the qualities needed for the effective performance of our duties. To possess these qualities is to be *honestus,* Cicero's general and most honorific term for someone who succeeds in cultivating the virtues and performing the *officia* they prescribe. For Cicero, however, it was also a crucial principle that 'all the praise of *virtus* derives from action'. From this he inferred that our highest earthly duty must always be to place our talents in the service of our community. We must learn to recognise that 'every duty which tends to preserve society and uphold the unity of men must be given preference over any duty to forward knowledge and science'. Acting on this insight, we must train ourselves to discharge with *industria* all the *officia* of war and peace. We must labour for our *res publica* in everything that conduces to *honestas* and a well-ordered life. We must, in short, make it our principal task 'to respect, defend and preserve concord and unity within the whole community of men'.

But what of the Platonist objection that this will cheat us of happiness, since it will carry us away from the life of *otium,* the way of life best suited to the nature and dignity of man? Cicero directly addresses himself to this central contention of Greek ethics in Book I of the *De officiis,* and offers an answer that was later to be endlessly cited by civic humanists of the Renaissance.

He admits that 'the noblest and greatest philosophers' have always 'withdrawn themselves from public affairs'. They have held that, if you are a sage, it is essential 'that you should be able to live asyou wish' (*sic vivere, ut velis*). But he firmly repudiates this scale of priorities. Near the start of his discussion he roundly declares that 'it is contrary to one's duty to permit oneself to be drawn away by one's studies from taking an active part in public life'. And later he reiterates the same point in far more positive terms. The life of *negotium* is not merely of more importance than that of *otium,* but also calls for greater abilities. As a result it is not only 'more fruitful' as a way of life; it is also capable of bringing us greater fulfilment and happiness. 'So it appears that what Plato says about philosophers is not really adequate. Although they secure one kind of justice, in that they do no positive harm, in another way they fail; for their studies prevent them from living an active life, so causing them to abandon those whom they ought to defend.'

What of the further objection that the life of *negotium* will degrade the philosopher, since he will be obliged, in an imperfect world, to abandon the cause of truth in the name of playing a part and accommodating to the times? Again Cicero has a direct answer, and again it was endlessly echoed by civic humanists of the Renaissance.

The truly wise man, Cicero retorts, is someone who recognises thatall the world's a stage. 'Actors select for themselves not the best plays, but those in which they are best able to accommodate their talents.' The relevance of the image is that 'if a player looks to this consideration in selecting his roles, should not a wise man look to the same consideration in his entire way of life?' Surely we must recognise that 'necessity will sometimes thrust roles upon us which we do not in the least feel to be suitable'. But we must recognise at the same time that our duty in such a situation is to do the best we can, 'serving with as little indecorousness as can be mustered' in the adverse circumstances.

These debates about the form of *regimen* best suited to bringing about the *optimus status reipublicae* provide us, I suggest, with a context for understanding some at least of the complexities of More's text. In particular, they help us to make sense of what he is doing in Book I, the dialogue between Hythloday and the figure of More himself. We can now hope to recognise some of what is at stake in their argument: what orthodoxy More is questioning, what response he is offering, what exact position on the spectrum of political debate he is seeking to defend.

Like his younger contemporary Thomas Starkey, More begins by allowing a fashionably Platonist commitment to be fully stated. This is done through the figure of Hythloday. When we first encounter him, we are told that he is no ordinary traveller; rather he is a voyager in the manner of Plato, a man in search of the truth about political life. After this introduction, the next fact we learn about him is that he adopts an unequivocal stance on what we have seen to be one of the major topics of debate in Renaissance moral and political philosophy: whether the truth about political life is more readily to be gleaned from Greek or from Roman sources. Hythloday 'is by no means ignorant of the Latin language', we are told, 'but he is exceptionally learned in Greek, which he has studied with far greater attention than Latin. This is because he has devoted himself completely to philosophy, and in Latin has found nothing of the least significance in that subject except for some bits of Seneca and Cicero.'

Hythloday then begins to recount what he has learnt on his travels, at which point his interlocutors urge him to place his wisdom at the disposal of the public by entering the service of a king. Hythloday responds in precisely the tones which, as we have seen, Cicero had particularly associated with the admirers of Platonic philosophy. According to Cicero, the view adopted by that greatest of all philosophers had been that, if you are a sage, you must seek your happiness by living as you please—*vivere, ut velis.* Hythlodaycompletely agrees. 'I live as I please' (*vivo ut volo*), he replies, and in consequence live more happily (*felicior*) than a life of public service would ever permit.

When the figure of More presses him, he later offers a further—and again a purely Platonist—reason for refusing to enter public life. Being a philosopher, he says, 'I wish to speak the truth.' If I were to become a courtier, 'I should instead have to approve openly of the worst possible decisions and endorse the most disgraceful decrees'. The invariable outcome of such a way of life, he insists, is that 'rather than being able to do any good, you find yourself among colleagues who are easily able to corrupt even the best of men before reforming themselves'. Plato was right, he concludes: he showed us 'why wise men are right to take no part in public affairs'.

Having allowed these standard arguments in favour of *otium* to be fully laid out, however, the figure of More in the dialogue then attacks them point by point. He does so, moreover, not merely from the general perspective of a Ciceronian civic humanist, but in precisely the vocabulary which, as we have seen, Cicero had originally put into currency in his defence of the active life.

More first assures Hythloday that 'if only you could induce yourself not to shun the courts of princes, you would be able to do the greatest good for the commonwealth by means of your advice'. To this he adds in sterner tones—echoing the *De officiis* almost word for word—that 'there is in fact no greater duty than this one incumbent upon you as a good man'. The Platonist objection that such a life cheats us of happiness is met with the lie direct. A life of public service 'not only constitutes the means by which you can help people both as private individuals and as members of the community, but is also the means to secure your own greater happiness'. Finally, the Platonist fear that this will betray the cause of truth by forcing the philosopher to accommodate to the times is met with a strong rebuke, one that again echoes the sentiments and even the imagery of the *De officiis* almost word for word. All that this betrays, More retorts, is a kind of scholasticism, whereas a wise man knows 'that there is another and more practical kind of philosophy, one that understands its place on the stage, accommodates itself to whatever play is already in hand, and seeks to discharge whatever roles are assigned to it as decorously as possible'. The same considerations, he goes on, 'apply equally in the case of the commonwealth and in the matter of giving advice to princes. Even if you cannot pull out evil opinions by the roots, even if you cannot manage to reform well-entrenched vices according to your own beliefs, you must never on that account desert the cause of the commonwealth.'

There are, I think, two morals to be drawn from this first part of the story. The first is that the labels 'humanist' and even 'Christian humanist' have come to be applied too loosely to More's text even in some of the best recent scholarship. More's stance in the opening Book of *Utopia* is undoubtedly that of a humanist, and includes some explicit criticism of scholastic philosophy. But we cannot simply speak of Hythloday as 'the ideal type of Christian humanist'; nor can we say that, in defending the importance of counselling princes, More's position is 'in all respects the orthodox humanist one'. The question whether philosophers ought to counsel princes was a subject of intense debate among Christian humanists; no specific answer to the question can properly be called orthodox. If we are to speak more precisely, we must recognise that what More is doing in Book I is reviving one particular set of humanist beliefs—those of a 'civic' or Ciceronian humanism—and sharply opposing them to a more fashionable and broadly Platonist outlook which was threatening to undermine the element of political commitment in the humanism of More's own time. More is restating the case for a humanist ideal to which the courts of northern Europe were proving increasingly inhospitable: theideal of civic self-government, based on an active and politically educated citizenship.

The other moral suggested by this first part of the story concerns the relationship which has often been noted between Book I of *Utopia* and More's own personal circumstances at the time of writing it. In 1515, the year when *Utopia* was conceived, More was employed on an embassy to Flanders; in 1516, the year of its publication, he was first offered a pension by Henry VIII; in the course of 1518, after much apparent hesitation, he accepted a place on the privy council and embarked on his career at court. The arguments about *otium* and *negotium* in Book I have often been seen as a dramatisation of the 'moral tension' induced by the 'temptation' to give up the ideals of humanism embodied in the figure of Hythloday in favour of just such a worldly life.

It is arguable, however, that this is to misunderstand the nature of More's humanist allegiances. So far from viewing the choice of a public career as a temptation, the figure of More in the dialogue clearly regards it, in good Ciceronian style, as the one means of fulfilling the highest *officium* of a true humanist philosopher. If we are to relate this first half of *Utopia* to More's own life, my suggestion is that More should not be seen as expressing doubts about the decision he was himself in the process of making; he should rather be seen as offering a justification for that decision as the outcome of a true understanding of the proper relationship between philosophy and public life.

Vera nobilitas

I now turn to a second debate among Renaissance political theorists about the *optimus status reipublicae*. This arose within the ranks of those who agreed that the best state can only be attained if we live as active citizens within a self-governing commonwealth. The further question they raised concerns the range of attributes that citizens need to possess if they are to discharge their civic *officia* to the best effect. To phrase it in the form in which it was habitually discussed, the question is about the qualities that make a citizen best fitted to serve the common good, and in consequence most deserving of honour, esteem and praise. Or, to put it in the precise vocabulary the Renaissance writers liked to use, the question is about the qualities that go to make a truly noble citizen, a citizen of *vera nobilitas* whose conduct is worthy of honour, esteem and praise.

The humanists inherited an unambiguous answer to these questions from scholastic and ultimately Aristotelian sources. It became a favourite literary tactic of theirs to dramatise their doubts about this intellectual inheritance by way of writing dialogues about the concept of *vera nobilitas,* dialogues in which they counterpoised their own ideal against the more commonly accepted point of view. This genre first attained widespread popularity among the civic humanists of *Quattrocento* Florence. Buonaccorso de Montemagna's *Controversia de nobilitate* (*c.* 1420) provides one of the earliest examples, while Poggio Bracciolini's *De nobilitate* (*c.* 1440) is perhaps the most celebrated. Thereafter the topic became a standard one, with many leading humanists of the second half of the *Quattrocento* contributing to the debate. For example, such well-known figures as Cristoforo Landino, Bartolomeo Sacchi and Antonio de Ferrariis all wrote dialogues on the meaning of true nobility.

If we turn to the first exponents of the *studia humanitatis* in England, and thus to More's immediate intellectual background, we find the same topic being widely taken up. John Tiptoft made a translation of Buonaccorso's *Controversia* as early as the 1460s, and by the start of the new century the question of *vera nobilitas* was much discussed in Erasmian humanist circles. Erasmus himself raises the issue in his *Institutio principis christiani,* and withina few years we find it recurring in such works as *Fulgens and Lucrece,* Heywood's *Gentleness and nobility,* Elyot's *Book of the Governor* and many other writings of a similar humanist character.

The problem all these writers address—as Tiptoft's translation of Buonaccorso puts it—is to identify who should hold 'of right' the various 'offices of estate and worship' in the commonwealth. According to the commonly accepted view, the answer is that those citizens who are noblest and worthiest to occupy such honourable positions will be those who are possessed of high lineage and ancient wealth. As Tiptoft more succinctly expresses it, the suggestion is that 'noblesse resteth in blood and riches'.

Although lineage is held to be important, the defence of this position principally centred on the claim that wealth is one of the conditions of true nobility. One point on which everyone agreed was that, if wealth is indeed a criterion, it must be inherited wealth. If it is instead the product of one's own acquisitive talents, this robs one of any title to be regarded as a citizen of the highest worthiness. As Niccolo explains in Poggio's *De nobilitate,* 'I certainly cannot see what kind of nobility can be acquired by trade, for trade is judged by wise men to be vile and base, and nothing that can be regarded as contemptible can be related tonobility in any way.'

The positive argument purporting to connect nobility with wealth was essentially Aristotelian in character. To possess extensive riches, but without exercising the contemptible abilities required to amass them, is to be in a position to serve and benefit one's friends and community in a truly noble style of splendour and magnificence altogether denied to those who live in more modest circumstances. As Lorenzo de' Medici— the protagonist of the Aristotelian case—emphasises in Poggio's dialogue, a rich man is in a unique position, 'both in time of war and peace, whenever the spending of money is of the utmost importance, to acquire glory for himself by that means, thereby winning the nobility that arises from that source'.

The underlying assumption is that wealth, far from being a hindrance to civic virtue, is one of the means to ensure its effective exercise. This had been Aristotle's contention in the *Politics,* and Aquinas had very influentially restated and developed the argument under the title *De honestate* in the *Summa theologiae.* Beginning with the claim that 'honour is due to many other things besides virtue', Aquinas had declared in his *responsio* that this position is essentially correct. Some objects other than virtue arerightly honoured because, like God, they are of even greater significance than virtue itself. 'But others are rightly honoured, even though they are of lesser significance, on the grounds that they are helpful to the exercise of virtue, and these include nobility, power and wealth.'

As will by now be evident, this scholastic view of true nobility rests not merely on strong beliefs about the importance of inheritance, but also on aristocratic assumptions about the proper uses of extensive wealth. As in Aristotle, an ethic of display and splendour, of liberality and magnificence, lies at the heart of the argument. Again, Aquinas was to prove a highly influential intermediary in the transmission of these values. As his title *De magnificentia* in the *Summa* insists, 'the achievement of anything great—from which the term 'magnificent' arises—appropriately relates to the idea of virtue, from which it follows that the term 'magnificent' denotes a virtue'.

The same assumptions generally reappear in humanist dialogues about *vera nobilitas,* where they usually figure not merely as scholastic arguments but as commonly accepted beliefs. In Buonaccorso's *Controversia,* for example, the first speaker ends by explaining that his reason for treating wealth as a criterion for true nobility is that 'the chief and highest part of noblesse must rest in liberality', and that 'he paineth himself vainly to exercise liberality to other folks which hath not whereof to use it to himself'. 'If you deny this view', as Lorenzo adds in Poggio's dialogue, 'you will be rejecting what is agreed about this matter by everyone.'

Among humanist intellectuals, however, this view was in fact denied. It was challenged with a claim that soon became almost a slogan of humanist political thought:

the claim that *virtus vera nobilitas est,* that the possession of virtue constitutes the only possible grounds for regarding someone as a person of true nobility.

This is not to say that the humanists in general had any quarrel with the basic assumptions about private property and its hereditability that underpinned the Aristotelian and scholastic case. On the contrary, they strongly endorsed Aquinas's classic account of the indispensability of private property in any well-ordered commonwealth. Drawing once more on Aristotle, Aquinas had argued in his title *De furto et rapina* in the *Summa* that private property is not merely legitimate but essential to the satisfactory conduct of political life. One reason he gave wasthat, if all things are instead held in common, everyone will avoid working and in consequence help to bring about a state of gratuitous poverty. But his main contention was that, in the absence of private property, endless confusion and quarrelling will be sure to arise, a state of disorder that can never be regulated and stabilised except by recognising that some goods must be held privately and not treated as part of the common stock.

The humanists found little to say about the first of these claims, although Cicero in the *De officiis* had argued that one of the prime duties of our rulers must be to ensure that there is an abundance of goods, a point he had made in the course of his own defence of private property. But they firmly underlined Aquinas's second point, making it a commonplace of humanist political theory to insist that no political order can ever be maintained unless the values of 'degree, priority and place' are firmly upheld. As always, Cicero's arguments in the *De officiis* furnished them with their highest authority, and on this issue Cicero had spoken with exceptional vehemence. 'What plague could ever be worse', he had written, than to favour an equal distribution of goods? Those who do so 'are undermining the foundations of the commonwealth, for in the first place they are destroying harmony, which cannot possibly be sustained where money is taken from one person and given tosomeone else; and in the second place they are subverting equity, which will altogether collapse if it ceases to be lawful for people to hold their own goods'.

Despite their endorsement of these widely accepted beliefs about the social basis of nobility, the humanists completely repudiated the related claim that the quality of nobility itself is in any way connected with lineage or inherited wealth. They permitted themselves a tone of pure amazement at the idea that ancient lineage might be supposed relevant. As Niccolo puts it in Poggio's dialogue, 'what can conceivably be thought noble about a man who merely has numerous ancestors and a long account of his family history?' Erasmus in his *Institutio* was later to allow himself a similar note of surprise. He concedes that he has no wish 'to take away honour from those of high lineage, provided they are formed in the image of their ancestors and excel in those qualities that originally made them members of the nobility' But he adds that this gives us no reason at all 'for allowing the title of nobility' to those who merely happen to be members of a leisured class and live a life of *iners otium,* 'sluggish idleness'.

The main point the humanists make, however, is that it is even more ridiculous to suppose that the possession of inherited wealth canin any way entitle someone to be regarded as truly noble. Niccolo flatly declares in Poggio's dialogue that 'riches cannot in the least ennoble us', while Erasmus in the *Institutio* offers an anatomy of true nobility which serves to underline the same point. 'There are three forms of nobility,' he maintains, 'one of which arises from virtue and good deeds, while the next derives from an understanding of those studies which are *honestissimae* and the third from ancestral portraits and long lineage, or else from the possession of wealth. But this third and lowest degree is so low that it really amounts to nothing at all unless it has arisen out of virtue itself.

If lineage and inherited wealth are both irrelevant, what gives rise to the quality of true nobility? Erasmus's analysis already gives the answer, and in offering it he was able to draw on a century of civic humanist argument. As Niccolo had declared in triumph at the end of Poggio's dialogue, 'it is virtue that constitutes the one and only nobility', a conclusion he takes both Seneca and 'our Cicero' to have demonstrated beyond doubt. 'It is thus the judgment of wise men', he adds, 'that nobility arises neither from a life of *otium* nor from contemplative solitude, nor even from the possession of great wealth; it arises exclusively from the study of virtue, a quality we are much better able toexercise when living in cities and amid the fellowship of mankind.'

As before, my suggestion is that this aspect of the debate about the *optimus status reipublicae* supplies us with a context that helps to make sense of some of the further complexities of More's **Utopia.** In particular, it helps us to explain the connections between the two Books into which **Utopia** is divided, and at the same time enables us to reconsider what has always been the chief interpretative question about the book, the question of how far More intends us to admire the portrait of Utopian society sketched by Hythloday in Book II. What emerges, I suggest, if we turn to these aspects of the work—and especially to the exact vocabulary More employs—is that one of his main concerns in **Utopia** is to intervene in the precise debate we have so far been considering, the debate about the meaning of true nobility. To grasp the nature of that intervention, I shall argue, is at the same time to uncover the serious message that underlies the seemingly detached and ironic surface of his text.

Hythloday engages with the issue of *vera nobilitas* at two connected but distinguishable points. First of all, he provides us simply with a picture of what he describes as the true and the counterfeit images of nobility, together with a description of the contrasting social consequences that naturally flow from espousing one or other of them.

The moment at which he draws this contrast most forcefully is in the closing pages of the book. After outlining the Utopian way of life, Hythloday ends by discussing with the figure of More the significance of the story he has told. The first claim Hythloday makes at this juncture is that, in his judgement, the Utopians have in fact attained the *optimus status reipublicae*. Their laws and institutions seriously aim at the common good, as a result of which they are able to live *felicissime*, as happily as possible.

How have they managed it? Hythloday answers in essentially negative terms. They have managed by not organising their society 'according to the unjust ideas of justice that prevail everywhere else'. These unjust ideas take the form of 'lavishing great gifts' upon nobles, rich merchants and other 'so-called gentlemen' who either live a life of *otium* and 'do no work at all', or else occupy themselves with 'wholly superfluous *negotium*' that contributes nothing of value to the commonwealth. 'For this they are rewarded with a luxurious and a splendid life.' By contrast, no thanks, no benefits, no feelings of kindness are shown to those who work 'with unceasing labour' at tasks 'so essential to the commonwealth that it would not last a single year without them'. 'The lives they lead are so full of misery that the condition of beasts of burden might seem altogether preferable.'

We may say, then, that what Hythloday appears to be claiming, at this summarising point in his argument, is that the Utopians owe their happiness to their avoidance of mistaken beliefs about the qualities that truly deserve to be regarded as noble and praiseworthy, as opposed to the qualities that merely happen to be displayed by the so-called gentry and nobility. Nor is this to put words into Hythloday's mouth. If we turn back to the account he gives in Book II of the Utopians' social attitudes, we find him phrasing his description in exactly these terms. The Utopians are distinguished by their belief that to connect nobility with *splendor,* with richness of apparel or other conspicuous displays of wealth, 'such that someone will think himself nobler if the texture of his garments is finer', is nothing but insane. The Utopians 'not only think it extraordinary, they actually detest the insanity of those who pay almost divine honours to the rich, especially when those who do so owe the rich nothing, are under no obligation to them, but behave towards them in that fashion simply because they happen to be rich'.

Rejecting this counterfeit view of nobility, the view the Utopians espouse is exactly the one we have already encountered in Cicero and his humanist disciples, and is couched in exactly the same terms. The Utopians believe that what is alone noble and deserving of honour is a willingness to labour for the common good. The qualities they think of as truly noble are accordingly the qualities of virtue that are indispensable for performing such civic tasks. As a result, the laws and customs of Utopia not only forbid *otium* and require *negotium* from everyone; they are also designed to ensure that the elements of civic virtue are encouraged, praised and admired above all. Thus we learn that the Utopians are all trained in virtue. They are all encouraged to follow a virtuous way of life by the fact that virtue is so highly honoured in their society. They are especially incited to virtue by the fact that statues of great men who have performed outstanding services to the community are erected in their marketplaces. Magistrates who serve with the highest virtue are rewarded with honour and praise. And the priests, who are chosen for their outstanding virtue, are regarded for that reason as persons of true *maiestas*. The whole society is portrayed as one in which the quality of virtue has been made the ruling principle. It is a society in which the women, the magistrates and the heads of families are all described as possessing *honestas,* the highest term of praise among Ciceronian humanists for those who attain the full range of the virtues and deploy them upon the betterment of our common life.

As a result of substituting this view of what is truly noble for the commonly accepted one, the Utopians have managed at the same time to avoid a number of baleful social consequences that stem, according to Hythloday, from accepting the counterfeit belief. Hythloday lists them when first mentioning the existence of Utopia at the end of Book I, and reiterates them when summarising his argument in the closely parallel passage at the end of Book II. One is poverty, which is unknown in Utopia, a society in which 'it has dwindled away completely', leaving 'no poor men, no beggars', but 'abundance of everything for everyone'. The other is social disorder, the inevitable concomitant of poverty. This too has 'perished completely' in Utopia, leaving 'a people so well-ordered', according to Hythloday, 'that if you had seen them, you would say that there is no good order anywhere else'.

We can summarise the entire scale of values Hythloday is describing—as he does himself when first mentioning Utopia—by saying that Utopia is a society in which *virtuti precium sit,* in which 'virtue has its reward'. For it is a society in which virtue is regarded, as it ought to be, as the one quality truly deserving of honour, esteem and praise.

I am suggesting, then, that Hythloday's description of

Utopia in Book II should be read as an account of the social benefits that flow from espousing the true instead of the counterfeit view of nobility. By contrast, his famous analysis of the injustices of English society in Book I forms a perfectly balanced account of the dire effects that stem from accepting the counterfeit view in its place.

That the English endorse the counterfeit view is emphatically asserted in the course of Book II, especially at the point where Hythloday compares 'what is now believed' about this question with the Utopian attitudes we have just examined. 'What is now believed is that nothing else counts as nobility' except 'being descended from a long line of ancestors who have been rich over a long period of time, especially if they have been rich in landed estates'. The result is that men of high lineage and inherited wealth 'believe themselves to be noble' in the sense of being entitled to honour and respect, entitled to be met with bared heads and bent knees,

Hythloday not only characterises this belief as 'sweetly insane'; he also treats it as the cause of all the woes afflicting English society that are analysed in Book I. Not only does he start by directing his accusations specifically against 'the great number of nobles' and their 'immense crowds of idle retainers'; he subsequently confines himself almost entirely to illustrating how these particular social groups have been the ruin of English society.

The most obvious consequence of their ascendancy is widespread poverty. Recognising that their title to respect depends on their capacity to live a life of *splendor* and magnificence, the nobles are driven into 'evil greed' as the only means of satisfying their pride. 'They are not content, living in *otium* and luxury, to do no good for their community; they actually do it positive harm.' To ensure the highest profits from their lands, 'they leave no arable at all, but enclose everything for pasture, demolishing houses, destroying towns' and evicting tenants who are then left to starve. Desperate and gratuitous hardship is the price that others pay for their aristocratic way of life.

The other and consequential outcome is endemic social unrest. The armies of retainers kept by the aristocracy form a serious part of the problem, for they live in idleness, never learn any kind of trade, devote themselves to the arts of war and 'continually make trouble and disturb the peace'. Finally, even worse disorders are caused by those evicted from their lands and livelihoods. 'For what remains for them, in the last resort, but to steal and then be hanged—justly, no doubt—or else to wander and beg?'

Hythloday completes this aspect of his argument when he points, at the end of Book II, to the principles that must inevitably govern any society founded on this view of nobility. As we have seen, to base a society on the true view, as the Utopians do, is to make virtue its ruling principle. By contrast, to base a society on the counterfeit view is to ensure that its citizens cultivate the worst of the vices. Of these the deadliest is pride, 'that serpent from hell which coils itself round the hearts of mortal men'. To connect nobility with wealth is to place 'this chief and progenitor of all plagues' at the centre of our social life. For pride 'measures prosperity not by her own advantages, but by the disadvantages suffered by others', and therefore loves to live 'in circumstances where her happiness can shine more brightly by comparison with their miseries'. Finally, once the life of magnificence demanded by pride becomes our highest aspiration, the other ruling passion of our society can only be avarice. For everyone will then be forced to act 'with insatiable cupidity' if the demands of pride are to be adequately satisfied.

So far, then, Hythloday has simply reiterated and defended a conventional humanist equation between virtue and true nobility. As I began by observing, however, his contrast between the rival views of nobility only represents one of two ways in which he engages with the debate about *vera nobilitas*. When we turn to the further claim he wishes to make, we find ourselves moving beyond the confines of humanist orthodoxy, confronting an argument at once more radical and explicitly Platonist in character.

Hythloday signals this further commitment in the form of two metaphors introduced at the end of Book I. He remarks that hitherto he has been talking about the diseases of bodies politic; he now wishes to consider 'how to return them to a healthy state'. But there is no hope of such a cure, he adds, unless we can first identify the seeds of evil in social life and pluck them out by the roots.

What then is the evil that needs to be rooted out? After surveying the Utopian system, Hythloday answers his own question in a single word. At the root of social injustice lies a mistaken belief about what should count as *privatus,* the realm of private as opposed to public interests. Describing Utopia as a community in which the *optimus status reipublicae* has in fact been reached, Hythloday at once adds that it is a society of which it can also be said that *nihil privati est,* there is nothing of the private about it at all.

This explains why there is such a strong suspicion of privacy in Utopia. The Utopians never eat in private, but always in public halls; they seem to prefer public to private worship; they live in private houses, but these are kept public by virtue of a design that 'gives admission to anyone who wishes to enter'; and they even insist that, before marriage, the private parts of the body must be made public to the partner involved.

What they have recognised above all, however, is that no community can ever hope to attain its best state unless the institution of private property, and the money economy sustaining it, are both abolished. We can now see the force of Hythloday's metaphor: money, he is saying, is the root of all evil, and must be eradicated if there is to be any prospect of serving public as opposed to private interests. As Hythloday declares at the end of Book I, this is what Plato recognised. 'As that wisest of all men easily foresaw, the one and only road to public welfare is by way of an equality of goods.' Hythloday emphatically agrees, and goes on to spell out the implications of the argument. 'I am fully persuaded that no just and equal distribution of goods will ever be possible, nor will happiness ever be found in mortal affairs, until the institution of private property is totally overthrown.' To put his point at its simplest and most resonant, what he is saying is that we have no hope of establishing a genuine commonwealth unless we base it on a system of common wealth.

As Book II goes on to show, this is the insight the Utopians have put into practice. As a result, Hythloday affirms at the close of his account, they not only live *felicissime,* as happily as possible; it also seems likely that their happiness will last *aeternum duratura.* And the right way to translate that last phrase is surely by observing that Hythloday ends in just the way that such stories are supposed to end, by assuring us that the heroes lived happily ever after.

The optimus status reipublicae

Hythloday's conclusion is a sufficiently resounding one, but it still leaves us with the problem of assessing where the author of ***Utopia*** stands in relation to it. Are we to take it that More endorses the claim that the Utopians have succeeded in establishing a perfectly rational society? Are we even to suppose, as some commentators have lately argued, that the description of Utopia is intended as the portrait of a perfectly Christian commonwealth? Or must we conclude, as the best recent scholarship has claimed, that More's irony and indirection reflect his own deep feelings of ambiguity about the Utopian way of life?

If we are to reconsider these questions, we need to start by reminding ourselves of the precise topic More addresses in the book. As I began by observing, it is surely uncontentious to say that More's basic concern is with the character of the best state of a commonwealth. But to say that this is his theme is at the same time to insist that he is not primarily concerned with a number of other distinct though closely related questions that also preoccupied Erasmian humanists at the time. He does not begin—as Erasmus does in the *Enchiridion*—by telling us that his topic will be 'the right way of life, such that, if you are instructed in it, you can attain that state of mind which is worthy of a true Christian'. Nor does he announce—as, for example, Starkey does in his *Dialogue*—that his aim will be to examine the relationship between the best state of a commonwealth and the attainment of that way of life 'wherein lieth the perfection of man'. More's concern, as his title page tells us, is purely and simply with the best state of a commonwealth in itself.

Once we recognise the precise focus of More's inquiry, and the need to distinguish it from other topics of debate within the Christian humanist movement, we can hope to re-examine some of the interpretations of More's text suggested by recent scholarship. In particular, we can hope to reconsider Hexter's thesis that, for all the heathenism of Utopia, it was More's intention to portray the Utopians as living a perfectly virtuous and hence a truly Christian way of life.

This interpretation cannot survive an examination of what Hythloday tells us about the place of religion in Utopian life. The chief point he makes is that, insofar as the Utopians have any shared religion, their religious beliefs are at the same time dictates of rationality. They all think it obvious that the world is governed by divine providence. Likewise, they all agree 'that the soul is immortal; that it is destined by God's mercy for a life of happiness; and that there will be punishments after this present life for our crimes as well as rewards for our virtues and good deeds'. But they think that 'although these principles belong to religion, reason also leads us to the judgement that they are worthy to be believed and accepted'. This makes the Utopians willing to enforce these particular principles, for they feel that to deny them 'would be to sink below the dignity of human nature.' But it also leads them to acknowledge that, apart from these obvious exceptions, nothing about religion is certain and everything ought therefore to be tolerated.

The first comment Hythloday offers on this outlook is that even the Utopians admit that it may not be altogether satisfactory. They recognise that moral arguments depend in part on religious premises. 'They also concede without hesitation that, if religious sanctions were to be withdrawn, no one would be so foolish as not to pursue his own pleasure by fair means or foul.' They think the religious principles they introduce into their own discussions about human happiness are such that 'no truer viewpoint can be attained by the processes of human reasoning alone'. But they emphasise that their conclusions have been arrived at 'in the absence of a heaven-sent religion'. Finally, they acknowledge that such a religion might well be able 'to inspire men with something more holy' than the beliefs they currently accept.

Moreover, Hythloday himself—a fervent Christian no less than a Platonist—makes it clear that in his view the religious and in consequence the moral attitudes of the Utopians are in factseriously flawed. He thereby introduces into his analysis a distinction familiar to classical humanists: a distinction between the optimal conduct of public affairs on the one hand and the optimal conduct of one's own individual life on the other. The former he believes the Utopians have already attained; on the latter point, however, he feels that they still need to be further instructed.

Hythloday is quite explicit in the first place about the incompleteness of religious understanding in Utopia. Before his arrival the Utopians knew nothing of the Incarnation, being wholly ignorant of 'the name and the doctrine and the nature and the miracles of Christ'. Even after his voyages they still lacked any access to the Sacraments or the Scriptures, thus remaining cut off from the Church's mediating powers and from any understanding of the divine positive law and the soteriological scheme outlined in the Bible.

Hythloday is equally emphatic about the resulting limitations of the Utopian moral code. These derive from the one feature of Utopian life he directly criticises, namely their view of human happiness. Basing themselves on reason alone, and knowing nothing of God's purposes as disclosed in the Bible, 'they show themselvesmore inclined than is right' to conclude that individual happiness must simply consist 'in leading as carefree and joyful a life as possible while helping others do the same'. One implication of their outlook is that in certain circumstances they are ready to permit and even encourage both suicide and euthanasia. 'If someone has a disease which is not only incurable but a source of continual agony and distress', then 'the priests and magistrates exhort the man' either to commit suicide and 'free himself from this bitter life' or else 'voluntarily to allow others to free him from it'. Such decisions are regarded not merely as wise but as 'pious and holy', and those who take them are honoured for doing so.

Given their view of human happiness, this attitude strikes the Utopians as perfectly reasonable. But it is a case in which their reliance on reason alone, without the benefit of Christian revelation, leads them seriously astray. Although they have no means of knowing it, the actions they regard as pious and honourable are at once mortal sins and a negation of an important aspect of Christian soteriology. The Utopians lack any understanding of the intrinsic value of suffering, a value which—under the symbol of the Cross—is central to the soteriological scheme presented in the New Testament. At the same time they fail to recognise, as Hythloday remarks in his tiradeagainst the English practice of hanging thieves, that 'God has not only forbidden us to kill', but 'has withdrawn from us the right to bring about our own death as well as the death of others'. Although reason might incline us to allow certain exceptions—as the Utopians do in their igno-

rance—the divine positive law made known by God in the Mosaic Code, and renewed by Christ in the New Testament, is completely unambiguous. It simply tells us 'Thou shalt not kill.'

It cannot, then, have been More's intention, in emphasising the heathenism of Utopia, to point ironically to the fact that the heathen Utopians, 'far more than the nominal Christians of Europe, have succeeded in establishing a truly Christian commonwealth'. The irony of the situation seems rather to be registered by the figure of More himself when he first tells us at the start of Book I about his conversations with Hythloday. He reports that Hythloday 'told me of many mistaken customs to be found among the newly-discovered peoples'. But he adds at once that Hythloday 'also informed me of not a few customs that could well serve as examples to our own cities, nations, peoples and kingdoms, thereby enabling us to correct our own mistakes'. Possessing as we do the benefits of revelation as well as reason, we ought to be able to surpass such heathern communities in all respects. The irony—and the scandal—lies in the fact that we have so much to learn from them.

The Utopians have not attained for themselves the ideal of a perfectly Christian life. But it does not follow that they have not attained the best state of the commonwealth. Reason and revelation are both indispensable for the first, but reason alone suffices for the second, and reason is a universal possession of mankind, one common to heathens and Christians alike. It is certainly possible, therefore, that More intends us to accept that the Utopians have in fact achieved a correct view of what constitutes true nobility, have avoided the baleful consequences of espousing the counterfeit view instead, and have arrived as a result at the *optimus status reipublicae*.

As we have seen, it is certainly Hythloday's belief that this is the case. But the question, as before, is whether More intends us to endorse that belief. The answer appears to be contained in a single highly charged passage at the end of the book, a passage in which the figure of More comments directly on the lessons Hythloday has drawn from his own narrative. 'When Raphael finished his story, many things occurred to me which seemed absurdly established in the customs and laws of the people he had described.' Of these, More goes on, 'the one that struck me most was the feature that constitutes the foundation of their entire social structure: their common life and mode of subsistence, based on having no moneytransactions at all. If this were to be established, it would overthrow all the nobility, magnificence, splendour and majesty that represent, according to the commonly accepted opinion, the true decorations and ornaments of a commonwealth.'

This is a highly ambiguous as well as a highly charged

passage. But it certainly contains one objection to Hythloday's analysis to be expected from a good Ciceronian humanist—the persona that, as we have seen, the figure of More sustains throughout the dialogue. The objection More implicitly raises is in fact no different from the one we have already seen him making at the end of Book I. Philosophy, he had told Hythloday, must seek to be useful in civic life. But in order to be useful it must be willing to accommodate to the times. It must work with commonly accepted opinions and try to make them 'as little bad as possible'. But, as we have seen, the most commonly accepted opinion in More's time about nobility, magnificence, splendour and majesty was that they are all connected together. It is precisely Hythloday's contention, however, that the ideal of nobility will have to be separated from these other values if the *optimus status reipublicae* is ever to be attained. More's objection is, therefore, in part a purely practical one: what is absurd about Hythloday's advocacy is the fact that it takes no account whatever of what is generally believed.

It seems clear, however, that More is also offering a deeper comment on the story Hythloday has told, and the question of what further comment he wishes to make has become a subject of intense debate. Recent commentators have suggested that More's remarks must simply be taken at face value: he is criticising the absurdity of the Utopian system for failing to recognise the importance of nobility, magnificence, splendour and majesty in social life. But this thesis has I think nothing to recommend it. In the first place it is not what More says in the crucial passage. All he says is that the Utopian system would overthrow 'the commonly accepted opinion' of these values—the opinion that they are all indissolubly linked with each other. As I have laboured to demonstrate, however, it was one of the characteristic ambitions of humanist political theory to dissolve those very links in the name of upholding the rival opinion that true nobility derives from virtue alone. To suppose that More, at this crucial summarising point in his argument, was aligning himself with the very orthodoxy his fellow humanists were overwhelmingly concerned to attack is not merely to go beyond anything he actually says in the text; it is also to make nonsense of the fundamentally humanist allegiances he displays throughout the book.

The clue to More's meaning lies instead, I suggest, in examiningthe implications of his argument from the point of view of his fellow humanists. His argument itself (to repeat) is that if the Utopian system were to be instituted—forbidding the use of money and abolishing private property—the effect would be to overthrow the values conventionally attached to the concepts of nobility, magnificence, splendor and majesty. As I have been emphasising, however, it was precisely the ambition of More's fellow humanists to overthrow just those conventional values. The implication seems

inescapable: More is pointing out that, although the Utopian system may look absurd at first sight, it provides a means of overturning those very values which, according to the humanists themselves, were standing in the way of their own equation between virtue and true nobility, and in consequence standing in the way of enabling the best state of the commonwealth to be realised.

It appears, then, that what More is doing in this crucial passage is putting a challenge to his fellow humanists, and in particular raising a doubt about the coherence of their political thought. On the one hand they liked to claim that they wanted above all to prevent inherited wealth from being treated as a criterion of true nobility. But on the other hand they continued to insist on the indispensability of private property, of hereditability and in general of 'degree, priority and place' as preconditions of any well-ordered society. The question we are left with at the end of *Utopia* is whether we can really have it both ways. If we are serious about the claim that virtue constitutes the only true nobility, it may be incoherent simply to endorse the usual justifications for private property. It may instead be necessary to consider the Utopian case for abolishing it in the name of ensuring that virtue alone is honoured, and that the best state of the commonwealth is thereby attained.

There is one very obvious objection, however, to supposing that this is the fundamental message More intends to leave with us at the end of *Utopia*. This is the fact that the figure of More appears throughout the book in the guise of a good Ciceronian humanist. As I have shown, that school of thought consistently and vehemently opposed the Platonist claim that the attainment of the *optimus status reipublicae* might require the abolition of private property. Moreover, when Hythloday first presents the Platonist point of view at the end of Book I, the figure of More responds in precisely the terms I have shown to be characteristic of humanist (and scholastic) theories about the indispensability of private property in any well-ordered commonwealth. 'It is quite impossible to live a satisfactory way of life', More retorts, 'where everything is held in common.' One reason is that gratuitous poverty will result.'For how can there ever be an adequate supply of goods where individuals are no longer spurred onwards by the motive of personal gain, and become sluggish through trusting to the industry of others?' A further reason is that 'endless quarrelling and sedition' will be sure to arise, 'especially since the authority of magistrates and any reverence for their office will have been completely undermined'.

But the point which has not been sufficiently noticed about the structure of More's *Utopia* is that Hythloday's entire contribution can—and I think should—be read as an ironic inversion of precisely these two central assumptions of scholastic as well as humanist political thought. What Hythloday shows us in Book I is that, even if you uphold the rights of private property, you do not necessarily avoid the twin dangers of poverty and disorder. For in England, where the rights of property-holders are defended with extreme violence, the country nevertheless suffers, as we have seen, from exactly these two social diseases. By contrast, what Hythloday shows us in Book II is that, even if you abolish private property, you do not necessarily contract these social diseases at all. For in Utopia, where everything is held in common, the community is nevertheless described as one in which—as Hythloday very revealingly puts it in his summary—there is no disorder, andwhere there is abundance of everything for everyone.

There is, moreover, a carefully contrived asymmetry between More's response to these claims at the end of Book I and his later response to exactly the same claims at the end of Book II. At the end of Book I he confidently replies by putting the standard case in favour of private property. By the end of Book II, however, his confidence has completely evaporated in the face of Hythloday's arguments. He makes no attempt to restate his earlier case, but instead brings the discussion to a close by making fully explicit the two points we have seen to be implicit in his earlier comments on Hythloday's narrative. On the one hand he reiterates his purely practical doubts. 'I cannot have any hope', he says, of seeing many features of the Utopian commonwealth adopted. But on the other hand he leaves us to wonder whether this may not be entirely to our loss. For the book ends with More saying that 'I readily confess that there are very many features of the Utopians' commonwealth which, although I cannot have any hope of seeing, I should nevertheless like to see, realised in our own communities.'

Like his fellow-humanists, More acknowledges the impracticability of seeking to abolish the institution of private property. Unlike them, however, he implies that such realism is purchased at a highprice. To concede the point, he shows us, is to close off one of the means—perhaps even, Hythloday insists, 'the one and only means'—of bringing about the *optimus status reipublicae*. As a result, *Utopia* ends on a wistful and elegiac note. Doubtless we have no hope of ever living in the manner of the Utopians; but the thought we are left with is that, for all that, theirs may nevertheless be the best state of a commonwealth.

James Romm (essay date 1991)

SOURCE: "More's Strategy of Naming in the *Utopia*," in *Sixteenth Century Journal,* Vol. XXII, No. 2, Summer, 1991, pp. 173-83.

[In the following essay, Romm examines the significance of naming in the Utopia, *arguing that More used irony and ambiguity in an effort to demonstrate the unreliability of language.]*

Like his fellow humanists, Thomas More was deeply interested in both philology and semiology, and in particular in the ways these two disciplines overlapped. For him Greek and Latin, or language in general, could at times become a kind of code, the meanings ofwhich could be extracted only imperfectly or not at all. Concerns over the relationship between language and meaning are particularly prominent in the *Utopia,* a work which opens with a "decoding" of a nonsensical quatrain, and which contains numerous proper names said on the one hand to derive from ancient Greek and on the other to be mere "barbarisms" signifying nothing at all. Such paradoxes, and the various obstacles met by critics attempting to resolve them, offer occasion for a new consideration of More's strategy of naming in the *Utopia,* and thereby of his relationship to Lucian's *Vera Historia*—the source and model for this kind of linguistic play. I hope to show that the frustration of critics who have attempted a systematic analysis of *Utopia's* names—in particular the seventeenth-century Dutch philologist Gerhard J. Vossius—is in fact exactly the response More meant to evoke, in imitation of the strategies of contradiction and incongruity he, like other humanist authors, had found in Lucian.

Vossius, in a letter entitled "De Utopia Mori ac paradoxis in illa vocabulis agit," conducts an extensive inquiry into the proper names of the *Utopia,* but ends by complaining to his addressee that More himself has rendered the task impossible:

> I hope I have made an adequate response to your requestregarding these matters. Except perhaps you will deem that some of these names seem to be less successfully composed, if we analyze them in the above manner. I won't deny it; but we must not be made to take the blame off of More's shoulders.

Other, more recent commentators have attempted to pick up the analysis where Vossius left off, but their efforts at schematization, especially in regard to the names of *Utopia's* famous peoples, have been similarly unsuccessful. Thus, most scholars have found that More's ethnologic names break down into two broad categories: those which, like "Utopians," ironically negate the peoples they describe, and those like "Macarians" which identify some prominent moral or ethical quality. Complicating this scheme, however, are a handful of invented names which do not fit comfortably into either category, and others which have been variously assigned, by different commentors, to both. Should these anomalies, as Vossius suggests above, be attributed to a *culpam Mori?* And if so, what was

More's purpose in creating such linguistic obfuscation?

Let us begin, as Vossius does, by distinguishing a group of invented names for which More supplies his own translations, thereby himself raising the problem of how names convey meanings. For example, the two titles for Utopian state officers, "syphogrant" and "tranibor" in the "ancient tongue" of the island, have since been modernized by the Utopians themselves to "phylarch" and "protophylarch." Vossius believes that, by supplying Greek equivalents for these words, More effectively precludes the possibility that their meanings could be independently derived from the verbal elements they contain, and indeed this seems to be the case; commentary on "tranibor," for instance, has produced no more convincing translation than "bench eater," and that only by stretching the word's morphology rather badly out of shape. Later in his letter, however, Vossius violates his own not unreasonable principle by supplying an etymological analysis of a name which More has already translated: "Buthrescas," as he notes, is composed of *threskos,* an obscure adjective meaning "religious," and the intensifying prefix *bou-,* to give the very sense which Hythlodaeus supplies, "religiosos." In at least this one instance, More's translation paradoxically confirms that his coinage indeed derives from standard Greek roots.

In setting up these two models of noun construction, More seems to be elaborating an inconsistency common to Greek ethnographic writing, where foreign names are occasionally recorded in their original language but at other times are given in translation. *Utopia's* nominal play becomes more complex than this, however, when the two kinds of signification are blended together, as in the case of the Utopian festival names, "cynemernos" and "trapemernos." These have been translated by More, via Hythlodaeus, as "primifesti" ("first feasts") and "finifesti" ("last feasts"), but their verbal elements also seem, at least to Vossius, vaguely Hellenic:

> One might have suspected that the name should be written "Cynemerinos," as if it came from the word *kunos* ["dog"] and *hémerinos* ["days"], so that it would refer to the dog days. Similarly the other name can be thought to derive from the same *hémerinos* and the word *tropés* ["winter solstice"], so that "winter days" would be understood. But these analyses must cease, since the words would in that case be from Greek, which More did not intend; otherwise he would not have included his own translation, *primifesti* and *finifesti*. This explanation does not fit well with the idea of a Greek origin. The same is true of the names "syphogrant" and "tranibor". . . . It would be an empty labor, to derive the roots of these names from the Greek.

This halting, on-again-off-again attempt at etymological explication reveals the incongruity built into More's nomenclatural scheme: the festival names seem to Vossuis to hint at a deeper meaning than that which Hythlodaeus supplies, but the counterexample of "tranibor" and "syphogrant" puts an abrupt end to this type of speculation. Variations in nominal construction therefore create larger discontinuities in the meanings of names, derailing the commentator's quest for coherence.

Similar discontinuities, moreover, can be observed within larger groups of More's coined names, especially in the largest group, those which designate the countries and peoples described by his narrator Hythlodaeus. Here we must reject the view of Dorsch that all of *Utopia's* coined names serve, like the title itself, to disclaim or ironize the entities for which they stand. "Macarians" in Book I, for instance, has no such function, unless we presume that a "blessed" race is a self-evident impossibility in More's scheme of things. A more prominent case is that of "Zapoletans" or "Profiteers" in Book II, the name of the mercenary people who hire themselves out to any paying customer. Here, in fact, More has fashioned the name not as an ironic jest but as an attack on a practice which, to judge by the vehemence of Hythlodaeus' several remarks on the subject, he clearly detested. Granted, the construction of this name is more obscure than that of "Macarians," since its first element, *za-,* represents a rare dialectical variantof the intensifying prefix *dia-,* and *poletae,* a nonce-word from the verb *poleó* ("to sell"), looks rather confusingly like the suffix *politai* ("citizens") more common in ethnographic contexts. Nevertheless "Zapoletans" finally admits of only one interpretation, so that we must presume its obscurity to be another strategy in More's etymological game. Like the "cynemernos" which so tempted Vossius, puzzle-words of this type invite us to come after them in search of larger significance, suggesting a kind of encryption which must be decoded to be understood.

Indeed, the arcane construction of "Zapoletans" seems to imply that Hythlodaeus' critique of mercenary soldiery is aimed at some particular race within More's own purview; such, a least, was the inference drawn by the author of *Utopia's* marginal notes (perhaps Erasmus), who here remarks, in his only attempt to reveal specific referents below the surface of the text, "gens haud ita dissimilis Eluetis." Whether or not the Swiss are indeed More's target, it is significant that *Utopia's* earliest reader saw in this invented name a veiled polemic against a very real and proximate political abuse. The more specific and prescriptive More's verbal coinages, the more closely they border on code, just as—to extend the same principle to topographical inventions—his detailed descriptions of the Utopian landscape have seemed to some interpreters to demand correlation with that of England. Such particulars engage a heuristic impulse in the reader which struggles to systematize and assign significance; we find it difficult to believe that they may have been composed at random, or without any larger pattern in mind.

Some interpreters have indeed attempted to apply the model established by "Zapoletans" more widely; James Simmonds, for example, suggests [in "More's Use of Names in Book II of *Utopia*," *Neueren Sprachen,* 1961] that the names of all the non-Utopian peoples in Book II of *Utopia* have a similarly opaque ethical meaning, while those that describe the Utopians themselves are entirely of the self-negating variety. The scheme holds true only in its very loosest outlines. Simmonds' etymologies, derived in part from an English translation attributed to Goitein, often require us to impart strained or unnatural meanings to More's Greek; and he neglects to explain why no comparable scheme governs *Utopia's* first book, where, for example, we find the names "Macarians" as well as "Achorians" ("Nowherites") both assigned to non-Utopians. Worse, Simmonds ignores the fact that the poet-laureate of Utopia, Anemolius, shares his name with a foreign race, the Anemolians of the Book II embassy scene. The coincidence invalidates the idea that More linguistically distinguishes Utopian and non-Utopian names, even though the contrast between "Utopians" and "Zapoletans"—the former a name which proclaims its referent to be nonexistent, the latter seemingly a pointed reference to a very real European nation—might have led us to that conclusion. In Simmonds' case, then, as in that of Vossius, an initially promising analysis of More's naming breaks down if we attempt to apply it more widely.

The flaws in Simmonds' scheme become especially apparent in the case of names like "Nephelogetae," which although clearly Greek in origin do not easily fit either the pattern of Utopian self-negation or of non-Utopian ethical satire. Vossius again reveals the nature of the problem when he attempts to recast this name, using even more force here than he had done earlier with "cynemernos":

> I would prefer "Nephelogenetae"; [*vefeloyevetai*] would be "those born from cloud," that is, as unreal as the centaurs of poetry, of whom you would say [*vefeloyeveiv*] and [*vefeloyevetai*] because they are said to have been begotten by Ixion from a cloud.

Vossius correctly points out that the second element here, *getés,* has no evident meaning, although it comes maddeningly close to *genetae,* a form that would have made the resulting name perfectly intelligible. Instead we are left with an indeterminate sense of "cloud" that does not apply to its referent in any readily apparent way, yet which, in its very obscurity, seems to require some sort of explanation. That is, the half-formed name leaves us dangling between intelligibility and nonsense, a median position from which any heuristically-minded reader, like Vossius, strives immediately to extricate himself.

Vossius' frustration can moreover be replicated by modern readers, who attempt to analyze "Nephelogetae" with the help of the Yale commentary. The editors of this work cite a variety of possible meanings for the name, including the one Vossius attempted to create, "born from a cloud" (derived from what is termed a "syncopated" form of *genetae*), and that proposed by Simmonds and Goitein, "'people under a cloud,' i.e. a cloud of oppression" (because they are set upon by their foes the Alaopolitans). That is to say, we are faced with the same unresolved dichotomy we encountered earlier, between a self-negating meaning and a reference to a particular social abuse, contained this time within the various explanations of a single name. Nor do the literary parallels cited by Surtz and Hexter help to alleviate our distress: for we are given the examples of Lucian's Nephelokentauroi or "Cloud-centaurs," and Aristophanes' Nephelokokkygia or "Cloud-cuckooland," alongside Homer's august and grandiloquent epithet for the god Zeus, *nephelégereta* or "cloud-gatherer." Here our editors yoke together the ironically self-negating sense of the *nephelos* verbal element in Greek comedy and satire, with the far more stately and substantive Homeric usage, replicating at the level of literary reminiscence the split between sense and nonsense.

The Yale editors, while offering no clear preference of their own from among these alternatives, imply that it is incumbent upon us to make such a choice; but in this, I believe, they have missed the importance of More's carefully constructed verbal ambiguity. Surely it is no accident that "Nephelogetae" here can be analyzed as either a self-negation or as a meaningful ethical critique, since the *Utopia* as a whole consistently and deliberately treads a median line between these two poles. Meaning and nonsense are carefully held in equipoise throughout the work, a form of irony cultivated by More, and other humanist authors, from out of the pages of Lucian. It is the same ambiguity, moreover, which presents itself in *Utopia's* very title, another paradox which has caused Vossius, as well as Scaliger before him, to throw up his hands in despair. With its first element balanced perfectly between *ou* and *eu,* as Anemolius' opening hexastich reveals, the name can mean either "Noplace" or "Fine place"—or rather, as was undoubtedly More's intent, both at once. The fact that "Nephelogetae" also invites interpretation at both the ethical and ironic level, therefore, seems to be part of *Utopia's* larger strategy of assigning double-edged significance to its inventions; the text always seeks to place us in this median zone where meanings suggest themselves but fail to emerge fully.

In fact, once this duplicitous strategy has been recognized, we can discern it in several of *Utopia's* more puzzling names. Thus "Anemolians," like "Nephelogetae," mixes a substantive, ethically oriented meaning taken from Homer with a self-negating one found in

Lucian: In their vain desire to impress the Utopians, the Anemolians are certainly "windy" in the Homeric sense of "boastful," but at the same time they share in the meaning Lucian suggests when referring to astrology as *logon pseudea kai anemólion,* a "false and windy discipline." Both connotations of the adjective were certainly known to More, and he seems to have preserved the ambiguity between them quite intentionally. Similarly "Alaopolitans" can be analyzed, as Vossius points out, either as *a-lao-politai* or *alao-politai,* so as to refer either to "'dwellers in the city of the blind,' given to a people who oppress anotherwith 'an unjust accusation under the colour of justice'" [Simmonds, "More's Use of Names," quoting Goitein], or more simply, as "cives ex nullo regionis populo" (Vossius). Here, in other words, an ambiguity of formation, rather than connotation, creates another 'toss-up' situation in which an ethically pointed meaning is held in suspension with a self-negating one; and again, More's duplicity is perfectly mirrored in the ambivalence of subsequent interpretive efforts.

More's model for this catch-me-if-you-can etymological game was undoubtedly Lucian, and in particular the one Lucianic work which peers out from behind *Utopia's* ironic veils at every turn, the *Vera Historia.* This fantastical travelogue delights in coining compound names for foreign places and peoples, but, if we look for a consistent scheme of thought governing these names, we shall come away as frustrated as Vossius; Lucian simply does not make things that easy. To take one prominent example, the description of the world inside a whale's belly at the end of *Vera Historia* I, creates names for a wide array of peoples, most of which blend human physiology with that of marine creatures: "Crab-hands," "Tuna-heads," "Flounder-feet," and the like. But amid this list occurs the more troublesome "Tritonomendetes," seemingly a compound of *Tritón,* the monstrous Greek sea god, and *Mendes,* an obscure Egyptian word meaning "goat." Whatever meaning (if any) this word is meant to convey, the anomaly it creates throws an otherwise coherent series of names into disarray. And again, as in More's case, the effect of this disruption can be gauged by the division it has caused among interpreters:

> Quelques commentateurs demandent ici quelle analogie il peut y avoir entre des pieds de bouc et la forme d'une belette; mais nous pensons que le mot *Tritono-mendetes* est ici une dénomination vague et qu'on ne doit point toujours chercher une exacte analogie entre la définition d'une chose et sa dénomination. [Jean Baudoin in the 1613 translation of the Oeuvres de Lucien de Samosate]

The debate recorded here closely parallels that over *Utopia's* toponymy, in that here as well the arcanity of an invented name poses itself, at least to some commentators, as a puzzle that demands an arcane solution; while others, like the editor quoted above, sense that the text's entire scheme of signification has simply fallen apart.

Perhaps the most telling of the paradoxical names employed by More in the *Utopia,* "morosophi" or "wise fools," was taken straight outof Lucian, although in this case from the *Alexander* rather than the *Vera Historia.* Although the word is not used by Lucian as a proper noun, More practically converts it into one by capitalizing it in the one passage where it appears, a discussion of the French practice of employing a standing army even during times of peace:

> Evidently it seems to the Morosophi that their public safety lies in this: Whether they have a strong and stable garrison at the ready, made up in particular of veterans.

The absence of any demonstrative pronoun here makes "Morosophi" a virtual stand-in for "French," who have been identified only as a country rather than as a polity in the passage just prior to this. Here, then, is yet another twist in More's nomenclatural game: by renaming a very real people with a Lucianic coinage, in this very first instance of ironical naming, he further undermines our sense that names will allow us to distinguish between real and fantastic entities, or to properly locate nodes of signification.

For the reader, of course, the temptation to meddle in these nomenclatural mysteries is quite strong, especially since several of them seem to be verging on a solution. More lures us into hisgame by arousing our instinctive desire for verbal signification, but then frustrates that desire by keeping fulfillment just out of reach. Like the commentator whose marginal note attempts to identify the referent of "Zapoletans," we sense incipient meanings taking shape out of recognizable verbal elements, but if we grasp at these meanings in an effort to articulate them fully we find nothing in our hands but formless putty. In this way the names of *Utopia* are only a single, especially illustrative instance of the larger strategies which govern the work as a whole, and which are, moreover, an integral aspect of all fabulous voyage literature: our need to create a one-to-one mapping of words onto things, or of real places onto invented ones, is first invoked, then defeated when those mappings fail to cohere. If we play the game in the same spirit of "merry jest" in which the author offers it to us, the tension of the unresolved meanings can be a source of pleasure; if we take it too seriously, however, we will end, like Vossius, by stamping out feet in frustration and walking away.

Baker on the translation of More's Utopia:

Sixteenth-century translators in particular could exercise a good deal of latitude in their interpretations of texts. The second English translator of *Utopia,* Gilbert Burnet, wrote in 1684 that he initially suspected More himself of having been the first translator of Utopia because that first "[t]ranslator has taken a liberty that seems too great for any but the author himself, who is Master of his own Book." Indeed, in the *Confutation of Tyndale's Answer* (1532), More at least anticipated one form that such "liberty" might take. For there he appeared willing to see both *Utopia* and Erasmus's *Moriae Encomium* consigned to the flames rather than translated into English and, like Tyndale's at that time heretical text, so More imagined the possibility of another master of *Utopia* transforming his book in an equally dire way. The Reformation and, in particular, the terrifying spectacle of the German Peasants Revolt (1525)—for which More blamed Luther—provide the political context in which More's remark must be understood. It is one thing to discuss the possibility of a communistic society in a language that few can read, but any expansion of this readership raised the specter of widespread disorder and revolt for More. Indeed, both More and Luther, who vehemently disassociated himself fom the peasants, viewed popular rebellion as the ultimate horizon of radicalism, and neither wanted challenges to authority to reach this horizon.

David Weil Baker, "Topial Utopias: Radicalizing Humanism in Sixteenth-Century England," in Studies in English Literature, 1500-1900, *Winter, 1996.*

To conclude, then, we can see that Vossius, and other commentators like him, have become lost in the verbal labyrinth More constructs out of *Utopia's* names, vainly following avenues of interpretation that eventually turn into blind alleys. Furthermore More has ingeniously baited them with their own most cherished pursuit, philology; for what linguistic scholar can resist the challenge of a code, especially one based on familiar Greek roots? In fact, More's own last word on the subject of nomenclature, contained in a letter to Peter Giles appended to the 1517 edition, reveals that the more learned members of the audience had been the particular butt of his joke:

> Thus if I had done nothing else than simply insert the names of prince, river, city, island so as to warn the more expert readers that the island was nowhere, the city invisible, and the river waterless, the prince lacking a people—which would not have been hard to do, and would have been much cleverer than what I actually did—I am not so obtuse as to have wished to use those barbarous and meaningless names, Utopia, Anydrus, Amaurotum, and Ademus,

unless the need to observe historical accuracy had compelled me.

By casting himself as the bumbling "stupidus," in contrast to the learned "peritiores" who have become caught in his etymological trap, More dons the familar mask of Socrates, the sage whose wisdom comes out of not knowing: ultimately, he seems to say, the only interpretation of his names which carries any weight is that which reveals no meaning in them at all. However, the contorted grammar of the sentence in which this is expressed defies our efforts topin down his precise meaning, and moreover seems to give more weight to the naming strategy the author claims to reject than that which he actually uses. Evidently More intended his one retrospective statement on the nomenclatural problem to increase, rather than resolve, its complexity, and thereby to poke fun at those already attempting a solution.

One name I have not discussed herein is that of the narrator, Raphael Hythlodaeus, but it should be clear by this point how this coinage establishes a pattern which governs the others we have examined. In a work largely dedicated to showing that "'Nonsense' is well worth hearing out, well worth arguing with" [John Traugott, "A Voyage to Nowhere with Thomas More and Jonathan Swift," *Sewanee Review,* 1971], it should not surprise us to find the very signifying power of language called into question by the irregular and irrelevant operations performed on its constitutive elements. The struggles of subsequent philologists, like Vossius, to decipher these riddles serve to prove More's larger point, that a naïve faith in inflexible linguistic—or political—systems only leads to befuddled perplexity when those systems prove less regular and more open-ended than had been apparent. The victory in this game of etymological hide-and-go-seek finally belongs to More himself, who has hidden his nominal meanings in a way which seems to require that we uncover them, but who gives us shifting and contradictory clues as to where we should look; and who, moreover, only watches in detached amusement as we blunder about in the wrong direction.

John Freeman (essay date 1992)

SOURCE: "More's Place in 'No Place': The Self-Fashioning Transaction in *Utopia,*" in *Texas Studies in Literature and Language,* Vol. XXXIV, No. 2, Summer, 1992, pp. 197-217.

[*Freeman interprets the* Utopia *as an autobiographical text in the essay that follows, finding in it an expression of More's "desire to strike a proper balance between what is private and what is public."*]

Long the reverenced object of hagiographers, from the

humanist saint of William Roper to the socialist martyr of Karl Kautsky, Thomas More is undergoing a second martyrdom at the hands of modern biographers. They have argued for a lack of integration between More's life and its literary productions. The image of the utopian idealist and dreamer is refuted, for instance, by claims that the fury of the polemical works reveals More's "true personality." A point to irremediable contradictions between Thomas More, the humanist idealist, and what Stephen Greenblatt [in *Renaissance Self-Fashioning: From More to Shakespeare,* 1980] labels "Morus," the public servant on an embassy for Henry VIII. In his *The Public Career of Thomas More* [1980], J. A. Guy portrays More as a sycophantic courtier. Guy argues that More dissembled his intentions to enter court employment even from his dear friend Erasmus. For Guy, More's entry into court service was the culmination of savvy political stagecrafting, "the climax of a progression by which he gained the attention of Henry and Wolsey." Focusing on More's activities in the Netherlands during the time of the writing of *Utopia,* Richard Marius points out [in *Thomas More,* 1984] that the embassy upon which More had embarked was intended

> to increase commerce, especially in wool, and . . . while he penned these immortal lines, he was working hard to add to the wealth of those classes in English society whom Raphael castigates for their heartless greed. . . . Whether More recognized these ironies himself is an unanswerable question, but at least they reveal what we learn from a study of his other works, that when he wrote he built a world he could control and that, like most writers, he did not always take care to make that created world correspond entirely with the world where he had to make his way.

In his *Utopia* [1984], Louis Marin concurs that *Utopia* in its detachment relates "in a different way to the historical and geographic world whose contradictory consciousness produced it." Marin even argues that More "erased" himself as the author of the text by pointing at himself as both "a character in his book and, even better, as a *historically* existing figure, as a real representation." In these critics' estimation, More's place in No Place is by no means assured.

Differing with Marius and Marin, I wish to argue that the "created world" of *Utopia* corresponds very closely to the world in which More had to find his place; in fact, Book I represents both England and More's historical and biographical situations, and Book II offers an allegorization of those terms. Moreover, a central problem for *Utopia* involves the question of how one authors oneself, how one authorizes oneself to speak. More's perceived lack of an *integer vita,* marking *Utopia* itself as a disintegrative text, is belied by the offering of the text itself as a discursive space (*topos*) for transacting the terms of More's self-fashioning. A

literary *topos* in Book II, this *topos* becomes historically determined with the addition of Book I. Far from being situated nowhere, *Utopia* represents a transaction of values that link the formation of social identity to the agrarian crisis of More's day. Restoring a sense of place to the literary topos by filling in these agrarian values will demonstrate a greater integration of the "created world" of *Utopia* with the historical circumstances surrounding its composition. This restored topography will also lead to a fuller understanding of the conflicting elements of More's social identity being played out in *Utopia* (the various *bioi* constituting life in the private, communal, and state domains). While the utopian text may not have succeeded in integrating these conflicting *bioi* in a satisfactory fashion, its two books can be read as a convertibility formula for working them out.

One reason biographers have difficulty placing More in No Place is that the text itself is situated on the very fault line of shifting topographical values. In More's period, the individual is being redefined, particularly in terms of that individual's relationship to the land. As J. H. Hexter has shown [in "*Utopia* and Its Historical Milieu," in *The Complete Works of Thomas More,* 1965], More writes a text that plays a sense of personal crisis against the historical backdrop of an England plagued by problems of class divisions and social injustice. Stephen Greenblatt, citing Marin, notes the existence of ruptures in the Utopian text, "ruptures betrayed by subtle inconsistencies and contradictions in topography, economic exchange, the exercise of power," and other factors. Far from "tearing the canvas" of the work (Marin's estimation), such ruptures in Greenblatt's view represent the artist's self-consciousness about fashioning himself in "the presence of those sociohistorical forces to which Utopia owes its existence." More's individualism, the place he will occupy in his society, is forged from the conflict of those forces.

In tracing the emergence of the individual in the early Renaissance [in "The Land Speaks: Cartography, Chorography, and Subversion in Renaissance England," *Representations,* 1986], Richard Helgerson examines the role of the Renaissance cartographer and asserts that cartography not only served to free the land from royal ownership in diminishing the signs of that royal ownership but also allowed cartographers in their power of representation to gain a growing measure of authorial autonomy. Helgerson maintains that the emergence of the land from royal dominance and the emergence of the individual authorial self are parallel phenomena "deeply implicated in one another." This parallel development begins with "a common term of difference," the royal absolutism from which each is beginning to detach itself. Helgerson maintains that, although neither the land nor the authorial self explicitly rejects this royal absolutism, "they nevertheless edge toward a different sense—a sense of words and images caught in a complex and mutually self-constituting exchange between individual authors and the land they represent." Helgerson proclaims the mapmaker as *"novus homo chorographicus,"* a prophetic being who in his self-asserting, nascent autonomy signals growing challenges to that royal absolutism.

Although *Utopia* precedes by some one hundred years the period on which Helgerson concentrates, it serves as an interesting early text in evaluating Helgerson's assertions. The ideological differences that arise from the splitting of the island of Utopia from the once historically contingent England are an initial indication of the power of the author to remake the map, to work at the margins of history in reformulating England in an image far different from that envisioned or sanctioned by any historical monarch. A disciple of Vespucci, bringing word of a New World with a new ordering of society, Hythloday offers in his account of Utopia the possibilities of a new vision not only of society but of the individual as well.

A strategy of displacement governs the operations of Book II, the neologism "utopia" expressing a detaching of the land from royal absolutism. Pure escapism, the book inscribes the character of the land in the mythic figure of King Utopus. Utopus—or Eutopos, "the Good King of the Land"—has conferred positive value upon the land and its people by breaking the land link and effectively enclosing that land. Textually, he exists in the fullness of the letter, enclosed entirely from history in his total self-referencing in the figure of the mythically displaced land of Utopia.

As long as Utopia remains No Place, a merely literary *topos* in a long tradition of Golden Age lands, Eutopos can operate as a mythic Lycurgus. Autonomous in the purest etymological sense of the word, he is a law unto himself. His identity is not contingent upon history, nor is it contingent upon the vagaries and royal prerogatives of a Henry VIII. Indeed, Eutopos serves in many ways as an absolute contrast to the historically contingent figure of Henry VIII. As a point of departure from history, the absolutism of Utopus is benign, in sharp contrast to that exercised by Henry VIII. A ruler who would phase out monarchy in his own land represents a bit of wistful thinking on More's part when we consider the fanatical preoccupation Henry VIII had in providing himself an heir. In establishing the terms of these two forms of royal absolutism, Morus and Raphael define the terms between the restrictive royal absolutism of Henry VIII and the possibilities of self-creation represented by the royal absolutism of Utopus (an absolutism that elevates the individual to his own kingly status). In his more fanciful moments, More actually imagined himself as king of Utopia. At the height of his enthusiasm for Utopia, he confides to Erasmus:

"You have no idea how thrilled I am; I feel so expanded, and I hold my head high. For in my daydreams I have been marked out by my Utopians to be their king forever; I can see myself now marching along, crowned with a diadem of wheat, very striking in my Franciscan frock, carrying a handful of wheat as my sacred scepter, thronged by a distinguished retinue of Amaurotians, and, with this huge entourage, giving audience to foreign ambassadors and sovereigns; wretched creatures they are, in comparison with us, as they stupidly pride themselves on appearing in childish garb and feminine finery, laced with that despicable gold, and ludicrous in their purple and jewels and other baubles."

This "fascinating vision" or "dream" is broken up by the light of day, "deposing poor me from my sovereignty." More's only consolation is that "real kingdoms are not much more lasting."

Not only do we witness in this remarkable exaltation a personal dissatisfaction with the royal imperative, but we can also witness the fundamental nature of *Utopia,* specifically Book II, as the place in which an overreaching individuality is mounted against that royal imperative. In this light, Marie-Claude Rousseau writes [in *"Utopies, 1516-1977," Moreana,* 1979] of the utopist as "the demiurge of his world and his work, a psychodrama where his dreams are projected." The modest symbols of this Utopian kingship, emblems of which Raphael certainly would approve, mark More, at least in this momentary fancy, as sympathetic to the peasant. Expressing a subversive, momentary desire for absolute autonomy, More is the farthest possible from Morus, the court servant; at the same moment, he is closest to Raphael in Hythloday's championing of the oppressed and his hatred for gold and the trappings of courtly spectacle and excess. In this dream, More does not see himself in the image of the aspiring courtier, trained in the Inns of Court for a career as a royal servant and adviser. The desire projected here, given free play in the utopian field wherein all things are possible, is one in which More can momentarily find a place for himself and his longing for the monastic life (symbolized by the Franciscan frock). This dream marks the autonomizing appeal Utopia had for More in its glorifying of the private individual. More's assurance to Erasmus that his fanciful rise from his "lowly estate to this soaring pinnacle" will not threaten their friendship indicates that his concerns about entering Henry's court and compromising his humanist principles are also scripted into this psychodrama. This vision suggests that elements of the historical More are incorporated in the text, that Raphael embodies impulses in More contradictory to the Morus persona.

What might make one a king in fiction would not necessarily serve to advance one in the more practical world of court politics. The limits to self-fashioning in fiction and imagination were indeed boundless, not so the limitations placed upon self-fashioning in the very real and dangerous world presided over by Henry VIII. Even on its own terms, however, the created world of Utopia reflects the historically contingent circumstances surrounding its composition.

Those critics who see rifts between the created world of *Utopia* and the life More led fail to recognize that More's text is a more faithful mirror of his life and England's historical circumstances than a superficial investigation reveals. In seeking to situate *Utopia* in the discursive space between the concept and history, Marin asks a series of provocative questions: "To what reality or to what absent term does it ["utopia"] finally refer? What figure—fraught with incoherencies of its own—traverses it? What discursive conclusion opens up as soon as the thesis of historical truth, from whose posture it speaks, is lacking?" In posing Morus against Raphael, the historical figure against the mythic figuration, More has hedged his bet. I use the term "hedged" advisedly, for it is the figure of enclosure—"fraught with incoherencies of its own"—that traverses the text as a constant equation in the self-fashioning transaction. It mediates the conversion of values between the private and the public, between opposing class identities.

The bet that More is hedging is that involving his own self-fashioning, and its broadest values are those represented by the opposing figures of Morus and Raphael. The self-fashioning that must be worked out between the opposing terms of Morus and Raphael points toward class conflict, a conflict between an expropriating class and an expropriated class in which More represents the very middle class that was being defined in this conflict. Morus, the representative of the expropriators of land, and Raphael, representative of the dispossessed, cause this topographical discourse to be extended into the narrative structure of the text as their two voices bring the historical notions of improvement and impoverishment into that text.

If we reexamine the myth of Utopia's founding, for example, we find that in his conquering of the Abraxians, King Utopus acts out of a myth whose plot is very much grounded in a history vexed with the problems as well as the opportunities of enclosure. The "incoherencies" of enclosure expose Eutopos as Outopos in demonstrating just how closely the created world of Utopia is linked to historical contingencies. The "problem" that the text of *Utopia* seeks to solve is that of enclosure, particularly the large-scale pastoral enclosure occurring in More's day. Lying along a fault line that represents a break in historical continuity occasioned by the irreconcilable programs of large-scale enclosers, small-scale improvers, and subsistence-level farmers, *Utopia* must mediate the class conflicts that arise from shifts in agrarian values. The myth of Utopia's founding is not at all divorced from the prob-

lems of English history; in fact, the king's conquering of the Abraxians is simply the telling and enactment of that history over again, its characters disguised in myth.

The improver, Utopus, is not merely conducting a raid upon a fictional people; he is, in essence, raiding history, for his conquering of the Abraxians allows him to redefine and reshape English history for his own ends. This reworking of history begins with a forcible expropriation of people from their land. While we are not told specifically whether that part of the conquered Utopians who resist are killed or expelled, this initial expropriation of Abraxa sets an obvious precedent and model for the Utopians' spillover colonization of lands outside their territory. In these seizures of territory, those who refuse to be ordered by the Utopians' laws are driven "out of those bounds which they [the Utopians] have limited and defined for themselves" (*Reneuntes ipsorum legibus uiuere, propellunt his finibus quos sibi ipsi describunt*"; note the initial surveying that has occurred before eviction, a surveying not unlike that preparatory to the evictions of historical enclosure). Like their historical counterparts, the enclosers, the Utopians justify their expropriation of others' lands by arguing their ability to improve them by a fuller utilization than that practiced by the natives. These vanquished people, their rights of landholding extinguished, are the fictional counterparts of England's squatter population evicted by enclosure. Those who do comply join with their conquerors in enclosing the peninsula of Utopia as an island. They, along with the conquering Utopians, become the class of improvers, their historical counterparts.

The plot of Book II thus offers a careful reenactment of English history in this conquering and evicting of one part of the Abraxians. This is the overt content of Book I, the historical injustice perpetrated against a displaced class. As the problem of Book I, it gets little play here, for the myth of Book II must work toward finding an intermediate term between the displaced yeomanry and the large-scale encloser. To insist too strongly upon the historical identity of any of the players in this mythic reenactment would undermine the myth of improvement so dear to Raphael. Obliquely, the text addresses the problems of vagrancy and idleness by enclosing the wastes of the "New World." As a means of implementing and expanding social control in More's England, enclosures of the unenclosed wastes were advocated, for these wastes were commonly characterized as "nurseries of beggars." Enclosed lands were reputed to breed a more prosperous, better quality citizenry; they also yielded a higher parliamentary subsidy. Those who block Utopus's "improvement" are evicted, the counterparts of the historically dispossessed (and their voicelessness in Raphael's account of Utopia's founding corresponds to the voicelessness of their counterparts in history). If we consider the problem of history beyond the confines of Book I, we shall find that this glossing over the evicted Abraxians allows Book II to redefine history not as a conflict between the expropriated and the large-scale encloser but as a collusion between the small-scale improver and the large-scale encloser.

This collusion, constituting the myth of Book II, is essential if the text is to recapture the historical value of improvement for itself. As Rodney Hilton indicates [in *Class Conflict and the Crisis of Feudalism,* 1985], within the peasantry a split was developing as this peasantry began to separate into "elements with differing economic interests." Unlike the "poor and middling peasants" involved in subsistence farming, a wealthier class of entrepreneurial peasants had accumulated both movable and landed property and were increasingly the beneficiaries of any new economic ordering (the improvements which could be had through enclosure, for example). These were what Hilton labels the "upper stratum of the peasantry, benefiting from the crisis in the seigneurial economy." With the impetus of the textile industry, these peasants would play an important role in constituting the class of capitalist farmers that emerged in the sixteenth and seventeenth centuries. Hilton closely links the growth of this class, which struck against all forms of seigneurial control, with the emergence of capitalism.

Historically within the English "tribe," a widening separation was occurring between the upper- and lower-strata peasantry, a division very much rooted in the political and economic shifts that occurred in sixteenth-century England. The "wolves"—large-scale enclosers—not only expropriated the land of the poorer peasantry—the sheep—but they have also disrupted the orderly historical shift being brought on by the small-scale enclosers. The plans of the large-scale encloser and the small-scale improver are merged in Book II, as the remaining Abraxians are subsumed into one common identity with their conquerors, both henceforward known as Utopians. This merger runs counter to history, for Hilton has shown that the programs of these two groups ran directly counter to one another. In this respect, Utopus raids history twice over, for he both expropriates one element of the peasant class while co-opting the program of another. Most important, this conquering and transformation of the "compliant" element of the Abraxians allow Utopus to wrest the historical value of improvement from the program of the small-scale enclosers and to reinvest it in the large-scale enclosing of Utopia.

Utopus and, by association, Raphael rework historical situations and identities in a fashion that does not bear close scrutiny; indeed, the myth of Utopia is undermined when one converts the values expressed in Book II into those more historically oriented ones of Book I. The myth of Utopia's founding by enclosure risks being exposed if it is not disguised. The expropriation of the Abraxians is thus muted, displaced, and "alienated" in the example of Utopus's conquering of foreign lands. The historical expulsion of peasants from private land by members of the yeomanry and nobility might not seem to equate to the conquest of an alien territory and the expulsion of some part of its people by a king; however, the digging out of the land link, transforming the mythic Abraxian peninsula into a figuration of the English island, reminds us that there is a strong sense of the familiar in the alien. It also marks Book II as a prophetic text in a sense quite contrary to Kautsky's celebration of *Utopia* as a precursor to socialism. The text's transfer of the enclosing function from the levels of yeomanry and nobility to that of the state predicts the link between large-scale Acts of Enclosure and the growth of the modern state.

The charge of duplicity that Marius brings against More is offset and answered by the double text of *Utopia,* for Book I provides many keys for reading and deciphering the myth offered in Book II. Indeed, unwound from the historical materials of More's own embassy is another embassy, uniting history and myth, that brings Raphael forth. Raphael argues on behalf of the dispossessed yeoman who appeared many times before More in Chancery court; Hythloday sets forth—this time quite pointedly and eloquently—the rights of the expropriated. As Richard Sylvester points out in *"Si Hythlodaeo Credimus"* [in *Essential Articles: Thomas More,* 1977], Hythloday is "both uprooted himself and an uprooter of others. His most urgent pleas for reform bristle with metaphors of deracination and eradication." In service to the interests of royalty and the wool merchants, More is suddenly confronted in the Netherlands with the very spokesperson for those less powerful, competing interests: the dispossessed yeomanry. Contrary to Marius's and Marin's assertions, Thomas More provides a text entirely contingent to history and to his personal circumstances at the time of its composition. *Utopia* exemplifies Jean Howard's dictum [in "The New Historicism in Renaissance Studies," *English Literary Renaissance,* 1986] that literary texts do not constitute "monologic, organically unified wholes" but "sites where many voices of culture and many systems of intelligibility interact." Raphael's curious—and untenable—position as a spokesperson for the expropriated and a representative of Utopus, a large-scale encloser, bears witness to the text's rootedness in the history it allegorizes. Morus himself, representing a collusion between monarchy and merchants in an embassy that sought to improve trade equally advantageous to both, offers yet another voice in the text's encoding of dissonant cultural interactions.

The historical contingency of *Utopia,* a text that uses enclosure both as a theme and as a principle of its own organization, provides a better sense of place for More in his text. It should cause some revision of critical stances that argue that More led a duplicitous and inauthentic life. Stephen Greenblatt, for instance, sees More's life as "nothing less than this: the invention of a disturbingly unfamiliar form of consciousness . . . poised between engagement and detachment." He notes further a distinction between text and "lived reality . . . precisely abrogated by More's mode of existence." Raphael, summoned forth by this *rupture* between lived reality and self-fashioning, stands between More and the "achieved" identity of Morus, marking within that identity "the signs of its own subversion or loss." As an abrogation of More's mode of existence, Raphael stands in the place of that marginalized existence. Nonetheless, the enclosing of Book II in Book I brings that which is marginal into the enclosure of the text. Critics who emphasize the gaps between the text and lived reality fail to recognize that the two books, taken together, offer a full presentation, if not an integration, of Thomas More. In fact, in hedging the text as a bet between Morus and Raphael, More reveals an authorial intention bent upon confrontation.

If history has not been erased from the text, then it is reasonable to assume that traces of the historical Thomas More yet linger. For Marin, the initial erasure of the author from his book and the attendant gap that opens up thereby are repaired only at the end of the Book II. Here, Marin indicates, the historical figure of Thomas More reappears "to initiate an ambiguous transition toward the author of the book, *to exit the book.*" Between the two identical signatures, the last of which will reunify narrator and author, Marin sees More's historical identity as having been suspended. Marginalized for the space of the text is the public identity of "Thomas More, Citizen and Sheriff of the Famous City of Great Britain, London," a representative of the London merchants. This public identity, inscribed at both margins of the text, provides the topical circumstance in which *Utopia* was composed, for it was as the popular under-sheriff of London that More was called upon by the merchants of the city to travel to the Netherlands to negotiate matters of trade in English wool and Flemish cloth.

The opening lines of Book I, however, point toward the potentially divisive nature of More's embassy as both a representative of the London mercers and as an ambassador from Henry VIII ("The most invincible King of England, Henry the eighth of that name, who is distinguished by all the accomplishments of a model monarch, had certain weighty matters recently in dispute with His Serene Highness, Charles, Prince of Castile"). At this time, the interests of king and merchants coincided, but there is a disturbance lying just beneath this officious, laudatory opening to Book I. Indeed, More has struck an uneasy balance here between Ambassador Thomas More and what Russell Ames labels Citizen Thomas More. As Ames indicates in his *Citizen Thomas More,* the middle class "campaigned" against feudalism as a decaying system,

employing the merchants "as its chief economic power and the humanists as its ideological shock troops—with More active in both groups." A member of the Company of London Mercers, their "chosen mouthpiece" sent, as [William] Roper tells us [in *The Lyfe of Sir Thomas More, Knighte*], "at the suite and instaunce of the Englishe marchauntes," More was embarked upon a mission that represented "the interests of all English exporters of wool." At this point, at least, More was not a king's man but, as Ames asserts, someone far more "attached to town republican political principles than [to] monarchist principles." That More himself felt an opposition here is a matter of historical record, for he turned down a pension offered him by Henry, feeling that acceptance would cause him to come into a conflict of interest in fulfilling his role of sheriff. As he writes to Erasmus in 1515, "Should any question arise between them and the King about their privileges (as sometimes happens) they might have less confidence in me as a pensioner of the King."

At each margin of the text, the reiterated signature of "Citizen and Sheriff" encloses the two identities of Morus and Raphael, hedging in the dialectic they represent. Far from representing an exclusion of biographical detail or an incomplete self-presentation, the text reclaims one part of More's split and marginalized identity in the figure of Raphael, making it part of the self-fashioning transaction that is usually discussed in terms of Morus alone. The narrative splitting of Thomas More between Morus's narration of Book I and Raphael's narration of Book II makes the two appear to be marginal to one another. Upon closer examination, however, a certain convertibility formula exists between the two books as well as between *Utopia* and the marginalized identity that constitutes its circumambient context.

When we consider the relationship between Morus and Raphael, we find a contradictory pairing in which there is both a sense of identification and denial. Dialectically opposed, there seems to be very little the two can agree upon. More defends service to the state; Raphael shows that "servitude" and "service" are divided from each other by an easily removed prefix (*"servias"* versus *"inservias"*). Morus is in the Netherlands representing the wool industry and the interests of enclosers; Raphael appears as the advocate of the threatened yeomanry, offering a stinging attack against those very interests.

Commenting upon the relationship between the two as presented in Book I, critics have spoken of Raphael as More's alter ego, someone radically different from More coming at a critical moment to challenge him. That More fashioned part of Raphael from himself becomes clear when Raphael tells us that he was brought up in the household of John Morton, Thomas More's mentor at the Inns of Court. As the author of *Social England*

[Henry Duff Traill, 1902] indicates, Morton was an unrelenting reformer of the decaying Church, and his influence upon More would be a lasting one:

> From him it may well be that More learnt first to view with sympathetic eyes the sorrows of the people, and to speak what was in his mind so boldly and clearly. He belongs half to the past, half to the future: in him the interests of the Middle Ages and those of Tudor times, if not of modern life, seem to find a connecting link.

This shared biography denotes some of the affinities Raphael bears to More; of course, the More we encounter in Book I—Morus—serves as the antithesis to Raphael in reflecting the practical and politically ambitious side of Thomas More. If Morus represents More's tendency toward royal service, then the portrayal of Raphael is a hedge against that bet. The product of four separate voyages to the New World, Raphael cuts a figure in striking contrast to what we can imagine of Morus's own person as the courtly representative that negotiates for English wool merchants. The ambassador, locked in technical and interminable negotiations of international commerce, finds himself in an unexpected, face-to-face encounter with Hythloday, "a man of advanced years, with sunburnt countenance and long beard and cloak hanging carelessly from his shoulder." Indeed, there is no more striking a contrast imaginable than this between Raphael, with his future course already set on the New World, and Thomas More, who, in his embassy to Flanders, represents the new "economic" man being created from the dissolution of feudalism and the rise of capitalism. And yet, the more Raphael's mythic mask is stripped away, the clearer it becomes that the negotiations undertaken in *Utopia* represent a crisis that involves all elements of More's self-fashioning.

The sense of crisis to which *Utopia* is a response represents for More an uncertainty about his place, the role he should play in his society. This sense of dislocation can be expressed in terms of the social identity that modern society has inherited from the Greek city-state. As Hannah Arendt asserts in *The Human Condition* [1959], the rise of this city-state meant, according to Aristotle, "that man received besides his private life a sort of second life, his *bios politikos.* Now every citizen belongs to two orders of existence; and there is a sharp distinction in his life between what is his own (*idiom*) and what is communal (*koinon*)." Arendt catalogs the three ways of life (*bioi*) that Aristotle thought were the choices allotted to the free man:

> the life of enjoying bodily pleasures in which the beautiful, as it is given, is consumed; the life devoted to the matters of the *polis,* in which excellence produces beautiful deeds, and the life of the philosopher devoted to inquiry into, and contemplation of,

things eternal, whose everlasting beauty can neither be brought about through the producing interference of man nor be changed through his consumption of them.

The influence of the first *bios* occurs in the discussion of pleasure in Book II, in which we are told that the Utopians maintain "that a person would be stupid not to seek pleasure by fair means or foul," the only restriction being that this pleasure should not "interfere with a greater nor . . . follow after a pleasure which would bring pain in retaliation." The influence of the life devoted to matters of the polis, the second *bios,* is a central concern for Citizen Thomas More as representative of the mercers. The third *bios,* the life of philosophic contemplation and detachment, is the path advocated by Raphael in his rejection of royal service as a form of servitude. In particular, this second and third *bioi* define the conflict between Morus and Raphael. As Greenblatt indicates, the *vita activa* or *vita negotiosa* is an essential concern in *Utopia,* where More argues with Raphael about the choice of a detached and philosophic existence versus the choice of a more engaged life devoted to public-political affairs. What is central to this question is how much of one's own life should one preserve in the face of public demands upon one's time and even upon one's very self. To what extent is one a private individual and to what extent a public one? Thomas More tries to fashion himself amid the counterweights of three different possible fashionings: private, communal, and state.

The presence of these three identities in *Utopia* suggests a far more complete self-presentation than what is often characterized. Representing a mixture of the private and philosophic *bioi,* Raphael, as the narrator of Book II, offers More a tempting escape from the world of historical circumstance and political compromise. As Robbin S. Johnson argues [in *More's Utopia: Ideal and Illusion,* 1969], Raphael's disengagement from the political realm is isolative, for "the individual utopian dreamer . . . tends to withdraw from any socially common cause. He merges his own being into the ideal [thereby turning] all expression inward." She finds Raphael's idealism "self-serving." Arendt also notes the limitations of an excessive privatizing and isolating of oneself from the community. The ancients, she argues, stressed "the private trait of privacy. . . . A man who lived only a private life, who like the slave was not permitted to enter the public realm, or like the barbarian had chosen not to establish such a realm, was not fully human."

It is little wonder that, faced with these two identities of Morus and Raphael, More seems to have insisted on the middle term, of Citizen Thomas More, for he resisted both the extreme detachment of Raphael's elevation of the individual as well as the emptying out of one's private life involved in committing oneself to royal service. The essential problem in *Utopia,* however, remains one of demarcating the boundary between the private and the public that, for Arendt, signifies "the world itself, in so far as it is common to all of us and distinguished from our privately owned place in it." What is one's own and what part of oneself is public? What boundary should one set around oneself in terms of maximizing what one could achieve in both realms?

In each of these three elements of a self-fashioning, one can find limitations and risks. As Arendt notes, "The rise of the city-state and the public realm occurred at the expense of the private realm of family and household." More felt this opposition, noting at one point that he could remain an ambassador only by starving his family. The problem for More in this period was that of establishing the boundary of his own private sphere while maximizing the benefits to be derived from participating in the larger spheres of communal and state life. This is, of course, an essential concern in Raphael's and Morus's argument about the desirability of public service. Morus argues in behalf of such service, even though it often intrudes upon the private preserve. He invokes Raphael's "generous and truly philosophic spirit" in arguing that he "apply your talent and industry to the public interest, even if it involves some personal disadvantages to yourself."

In Utopia there is an overriding concern with balancing what is private and one's own with what is the public interest (*"publicum rem"*). The communality stressed in Utopia ("Nature calls all men to help one another to a merrier life") is tempered by an allowance for individuality so long as that individuality does not move the person to further his own advantage to the disadvantage of his neighbors. Especially in terms of contracts and laws, Utopia offers a fine resolution of tensions between the private and public spheres, a resolution seemingly unobtainable in the litigious times of More's England:

> Therefore they hold that not only ought contracts between private persons to be observed but also public laws for the distribution of vital commodities, that is to say, the matter of pleasure. . . . As long as such laws are not broken, it is prudence to look after your own interests, and to look after those of the public in addition is a mark of devotion. But to deprive others of their pleasure to secure your own, this is surely an injustice. On the contrary, to take away something from yourself and to give it to others is a duty of humanity and kindness which never takes away as much advantage as it brings back.

Here, pleasure itself is viewed as a "commodity" for distribution as the Utopians seek to balance equality of "ownership" with each individual's exercising of a private right. There is a sense of fluidity between private and public; indeed, the boundaries that compose what is private display an open face to the public interest, in the fashion of the Utopian houses that are "permeable" structures in allowing for both private as well as public accessibility. What is private can be easily merged with the public domain in Utopia, a merger and lack of conflict that surely must have appealed to a Thomas More striving to strike a proper balance between the private and the public in his own life.

In working out the proper equation between the public and the private, Arendt does not believe it is accidental "that the whole discussion has eventually turned into an argument about the desirability of or undesirability of privately owned property." The conflict between private property and communal right is, of course, a crucial one for *Utopia*. Raphael is a strident critic of private property: "When every man aims at absolute ownership of all the property he can get, be there never so great abundance of goods, it is all shared by a handful who leave the rest in poverty." This privatizing of land takes the land out of communal ownership; it separates individuals from the community in freeing them from many of the communal obligations previously situated in the very character of that land. Morus's counterargument to Raphael—"Life cannot be satisfactory where all things are common"—emphasizes "the motive of personal gain" as a necessary inducement for making individuals productive and not slothfully dependent upon the industry of others. At the root of this conflict is the fact that More's complete self-fashioning into Morus, the public *bios,* cannot be achieved without retrieving private property from Raphael's condemnation; equally true is that the self-fashioning represented by Raphael cannot be achieved without the total rejection of the public *bios* that Morus advances.

Greenblatt indicates the topographical basis of this conflict when he states that "private ownership of property is causally linked in *Utopia* to private ownership of self" (what C. B. Macpherson calls 'possessive individualism'). The conflict in *Utopia* is that the abolition of private property advocated by Raphael is for Morus, a representative of the propertied interests, a threat to that very self he seeks to fashion ("to abolish private property is to render such self-conscious individuality obsolete," Greenblatt). Enclosure, with its asserting of individual rights over communal rights, is at the very heart of More's embassy to the Netherlands. The privatizing of land resulted in the privatizing of individuals, the creation of a middle class whose very identity had been formed through its claim to private ownership of property. This is the class from which Citizen Thomas More had emerged. The class conflict entailed by enclosures becomes personalized in the choices More had to make among these possible *bioi*. Citizen Thomas More, forming the hedge between a private and enclosed life and a more public and expansive life, must decide upon the costs involved in converting the private into the public (Morus's position) or the public into the private (Raphael's position).

The absolutist positions taken by Raphael and Morus produce the dialectic from which More must work out his place in society. Raphael's freedom from private property—he very early gave away wealth and possessions in disengaging himself from all familial obligation and expectation—guarantees him an absolute privacy. The willingness of Morus to surrender personal misgivings in entering court service, to sacrifice what is private for the public good, compromises that very privacy. Here, the surrender of the private ownership of oneself is repaid by improvement, either the improvement gained for oneself or, more idealistically, for the collective state. As Peter Giles argues, the two forms of improvement can be compatible, just as the private gain to be won from his embassy could be compatible with the public good. The advantage of operating between the two domains is argued by Morus himself, for an insider and adviser retains the option of subverting the aims of the ruling order ("What you cannot turn to good you must make as little bad as you can"). The problem with working as a private individual within the margins of the dominant ideology is that More runs the risk of being subverted himself, deprived (de-privatus) of that private ownership of himself by the co-optive force of that ideology. This is the direction in which Morus heads him. Indeed, in his final justification of royal absolutism, Morus points toward a total refunding of the common (and private) good in the deifying adulation that commoners paid to that royalty, a transaction that is negated by the Utopians' moneyless economy and communal life.

For Thomas More, maintaining a right to his private opinion came into conflict with Henry VIII's idea of what was "owned" by the state. We can find even in as early a text as *Utopia* a desire to strike a proper balance between what is private and what is public. Enclosure, of course, is the very embodying principle of this conflict. In "The Property Rights Paradigm," [*Journal of Economic History,* 1973], Armen A. Alchian and Harold Demsetz point toward this commingling of property rights and privacy in arguing that "what is *owned* are *rights* to use resources, including one's body and mind, and these rights are always circumscribed, often by the prohibition of certain activities." The state, for instance, can regulate and limit a person's right to own certain ideas and opinions even to the point of violating the most private preserves, the home and the individual's very person.

While Citizen Thomas More might retain some independence in the conflicts between the propertied interests and the expropriated, Morus the royal appointee would undoubtedly find himself at times personally compromised by this public identity. Still, the publication of *Utopia*, particularly the Dialogue of Counsel, suggests an optimism about freely expressing one's ideas at Henry's court. That More also includes a healthy dose of Raphael's skepticism about court service demonstrates a desire on More's part to weigh carefully the risks and rewards of courtly service against the security and detachment offered by Raphael. Even though Morus argues in such a way as to emphasize what the individual could accomplish in the court, the truth was that Henry VIII had already begun to shape humanists like More to his own ends, as ideologists for the court in terms of influencing public opinion. As Kautsky notes, no bureaucracy had yet been formed for carrying on such vital functions. Thus, as Morus, More faced the very real prospect of being an instrument of public policy shaped to the strong-willed Henry's ends. As a spokesperson for that very class that was being expropriated, Raphael threatens More's self-fashioning as Morus. As a representative of Utopus, however, Raphael also serves as a reminder that More cannot seek his place in No Place, for there is ultimately no escape from historical contingency and the conflicting choices to be found there. To be expropriated, to be removed from one's own proper sense of oneself, is a conflict of both a personal and a historically agrarian nature in *Utopia*.

The working out of a place for oneself, the making of a place for oneself, is the underlying theme of the Dialogue of Counsel in Book I. More's negotiation of his place in society is ultimately traceable to the landed values reflected in the agrarian crisis from which *Utopia* has risen. Raphael and Utopus reflect the ironies of finding a place, ironies that Marius felt were excluded from the text. On the contrary, More's place in No Place can never be fixed beyond the land surveyor's measure. "The genius of a place," Raymond Williams informs us [in *The Country and the City,* 1979], "was the making of a place." This "socially resonant word" was as important in More's day as it was in the eighteenth century. The improvement of land became tied to the improvement of one's own social position; however, the large-scale enclosure behind More's ambassadorship often improved one class at the expense of impoverishing another. The capital accumulation it engendered was part of what Williams labels "an ambiguous process: increasing real wealth but distributing it unevenly"—quite contrary to the impulse of small-scale enclosure. Williams, who remarks upon "a continuing contrast between the extraordinary improvement of the land and the social consequences of just this process," speaks in the same voice for the dispossessed and vagrant of the eighteenth century that is Raphael's for the expropriated of the sixteenth century. Raphael, of course, speaks in Book I for the marginal and the displaced, subverting that dominant ideology represented by Morus. Morus argues not only for the improvement of society—along with More—but also for the improvement of one's own position, the bettering of one's place in society. Representing wool-trading interests in negotiations whose success would only serve to spur the progress of enclosures, More already faced an ethical and moral dilemma in choosing between the two positions.

In hedging the text within the doubly inscribed identity of Citizen Thomas More and allowing the engaged and public self of Morus to dispute with the detached and private self of Raphael, More has recreated the sense of personal crisis from which the text has risen. "Citizen Thomas More," the proper middle term in this self-fashioning, provides the middle ground for these marginalized identities to be defined and valued through the enclosure transaction (for enclosure involved the claiming of the marginal). In this respect, autobiography is expressed in the conflict among these various *bioi*: the private, communal, and state ownership that, derived from the larger discourse of the sixteenth-century agrarian crisis, is particularized in More's own personalsituation. The negotiating of wool contracts becomes for More, often idled by long breaks in these negotiations, a negotiating of his own particular place in society. In this sense, the total work represents More's efforts to take possession of himself, to define what was private against that which was the special province of the communal or state. Books I and II, representing respectively the external and internal components of the enclosure formula, thus serve in their dialectical opposition to establish the boundary lines of what More hoped to call his own.

The biographical gaps that critics perceive between the life More led and the "created world" of his text are surveyors' errors in failing to measure a seemingly mythic and alien landscape in real world terms. The error is not entirely their own, for the text faithfully represents a world in transition whose shifting values are difficult to represent. Until those values are fully restored to *Utopia*, autobiography can only present itself as auto-{ }-graphy; historically, a gap has opened up between self-reference or self-presentation (*eautos*) and the authorizing power of the letter to inscribe (*graphein*) that identity. One of the primary bases of social identity (*topos:* land) is shifting along with class boundaries, a fact signified by the uncertain, indeterminate prefix of "utopia." Expressed as auto-{ }-graphy, this term underscoresboth the importance of land in forming social identity and self-referencing as well as the effect of that land (absent, an undecided value) in preventing the possibility of self-reference, of individualization, and of self-fashioning. If scholars are to accomplish more than mere second-guessing about the fashioning of More's life, then they are going to have to do their reconstructions from the ground up, employing the complex set of terms that More himself had to negotiate. More's place in No Place can be determined by a formula through which the apparent

terms of difference between the mythic island of Book II and the historical England of Book I are demonstrated to be convertible values.

Neologism institutes a new term: autopography. Awkward, certainly, but no other term better expresses the complex oppositions of exclusion and inclusion, privatization and communalism, that constitute the utopian dialectic. Conjoining the two discourses of autobiography and topography, this neologism fills in the suspended, bracketed term of the former (*bios*) with an important determiner of social place in More's day (*topos*). It constantly keeps before us the supplementary nature of the utopian text. If the figure of the land is mythically displaced, the possibility of self-referencing exists once more in the text, but only through the mediation of the land as it has been restored in the creation of Utopia by King Utopus. If the figure of the land remains historically situated, under the absolutism of Henry VIII and the state, then there is the risk of expropriation. Raphael's vision of improvement as expropriative and self-corrupting wars against that of Morus, who represents the privileges and prerogatives of courtly service. Each figure seeks to shape More to his own ends, to bring that which is marginal within the special enclosure of each one's vision of improvement.

As More's autobiography, *Utopia* represents the serious work of determining identity amid the special set of circumstances for making this determination in early sixteenth-century England. If Raphael's vision is less preferable to what Morus offers, it is because the utopian myth ultimately points to the incontrovertible evidence of history. Rather than disguise that incontrovertible evidence in myth and wish-fulfillment, More staked out a claim to a life whose course he could not always control like a work of art. While More's most recent antihagiographical critic, Jonathan V. Crewe, speaks [in "The 'Encomium Moriae' of William Roper," *English Literary History*, 1988] of the "theatricality" of his martyrdom, exposing William Roper's "figure of saintly constancy," he at least recognizes the encircling ring of threats and pressures that drove More increasingly inward at the end of his life. For Crewe, "Roper's More is one who finally inhabits its [the text's] structure of simultaneous total masculine empowerment and implied dependence, of familial enclosure beyond both power and law." In his final days, within this familial enclosure, More sought to preserve his private conscience from the intrusions of the state. But this time the wolf would not go from his door.

As More's autobiography, *Utopia* is a text through which much of what Greenblatt calls "social energy" is circulated in terms of historical identities and situations newly coined into myth and refunded once again into history. The dynamics of this circulation had to have been an abiding concern for Thomas More as he sought to find his place in his tumultuous times. Those critics who look for inconsistencies and faults in More might do well to make sure their own moral bookkeeping is in order. At least they might recognize that there is only one place where these conflicts between public and private can be fully resolved and transcended. This is the martyr's *topos,* the saint's burial place, where More now lies. Our scholarly exhumings of the historical Thomas More have invoked an unquiet spirit, restlessly wandering between our heaven and earth of sanctification and vilification. "The unburied dead are covered by the sky" is the consolation the well-traveled Raphael would offer More today. The small consolation that I have to offer is neither a monument nor an urn. It is simply a restoring of the narrower historical confines in which this controversy can be worked out, a modest plot of land, indeed.

FURTHER READING

Bibliography

Gibson, R. W. *St. Thomas More: A Preliminary Bibliography of His Works and of Moreana to the Year 1750.* New Haven: Yale University Press, 1961, 499 p.

> A descriptive bibliography of early editions of More's works and Moreana, with a bibliography of Utopiana by Gibson and J. Max Patrick.

Criticism

Allen, Peter R. "*Utopia* and European Humanism: The Function of the Prefatory Letters and Verses." *Studies in the Renaissance* X (1963): 91-107.

> Discusses the letters and poems written for early editions of *Utopia* by More and his fellow humanists. Allen concludes: "The appended letters and verses . . . share in both the fictional aspect of *Utopia* and its serious intent, and commend it as both a delightful literary game and an important philosophic work."

Berger, Harry, Jr. "Utopian Folly: Erasmus and More on the Perils of Misanthropy." *English Literary Renaissance* 12, No. 3 (Autumn 1982): 271-90.

> Maintains that "in their very different ways both *The Praise of Folly* and *Utopia* dramatize the same vitiated attitude toward life, and explore its consequences."

Boewe, Charles. "Human Nature in More's *Utopia*." *The Personalist* XLI, No. 3 (Summer 1960): 303-09.

> Investigates More's beliefs concerning the social influence of heredity and environment as they are implied in *Utopia.*

Bradshaw, Brendan. "More on Utopia." In *Historical Journal* 24, No. 1 (1981): 1-27.

Determines More's proper place in the context of Renaissance and Christian humanism, concluding that *Utopia* is a story of "a process of conversion: evangelization, producing intellectual assent and followed by sacramental initiation."

Davis, J. C. "The Re-emergence of Utopia: Sir Thomas More." In *Utopia and the Ideal Society: A Study of English Utopian Writing, 1516-1700*, pp. 41-61. Cambridge: Cambridge University Press, 1981.

> Presents *Utopia* as a radical text, emphasizing in particular More's attack on the status quo of Renaissance aristocracy.

Elliott, Robert C. "The Shape of *Utopia*." In *The Shape of Utopia: Studies in a Literary Genre*, pp. 25-49. Chicago and London: University of Chicago Press, 1970.

> While addressing the "Catholic interpretation" of *Utopia*, argues the need for more analysis of *Utopia* as a literary work and less effort to reach More's mind through that work.

Frye, Northop. "Natural and Revealed Communities." In *Myth and Metaphor: Selected Essays, 1974-1988*, 289-306. Charlottesville: University Press of Virginia, 1990.

> Presents a range of reflections on *Utopia* and humanism.

Heiserman, A. R. "Satire in the *Utopia*." *PMLA* LXXVIII, No. 3 (June 1963): 163-74.

> Argues that "only an application of the satiric principle . . . explains the apparent discrepancies between More's career and his 'ideal' state, and accounts for the fact that *Utopia* has seemed a *jeu d'esprit*, a philosophical argument, a program for political reform, and an enigmatic document in the history of ideas."

Johnson, Robbin S. *More's Utopia: Ideal and Illusion.* New Haven: Yale University Press, 1969, 166 p.

> Approaches the text as More's personal attempt to negotiate "the role of social myth or utopian idealism in the real world."

Kinney, Arther F. *Rhetoric and Poetic in Thomas More's "Utopia."* Humana Civilitas: Sources and Studies relating to the Middle Ages and the Renaissance, Vol. 5. Malibu, CA: Udena Publications, 1979, 36 p.

> Studies the rhetorical complexity of *Utopia.*

Ludwig, Hans-Werner. "Thomas More's *Utopia*: Historical Setting and Literary Effectiveness." In *Intellectuals and Writers in Fourteenth-Century Europe*, edited by Piero Boitani and Ann Torti, pp. 244-63. Tübingen, Germany: Gunter Narr Verlag Tübingen, 1986.

> Praises the literary form of *Utopia*, claiming that this enables the work to transcend its historical context and its status as historical document or social commentary.

McCutcheon, Elizabeth. "Time in More's *Utopia*." In *Acta Conventus Neo-Latini Turonensis: Troisième Congrès International d'Études Néo-Latins, Tours*, edited by Jean-Claude Margolin, pp. 697-707. Paris: Librairie Philosophique J. Vrin, 1980.

>An in-depth analysis of the role of time in *Utopia* and its moral and spiritual implications.

Mason, H. A. "More's 'Utopia': The Vindication of Christian Humanism." *Humanism and Poetry in the Early Tudor Period*. London: Routledge and Kegan Paul, 1959, 296 p.

>Presents More as straddling two epochs, the medieval and the modern, in his Utopian construct of Christian humanism.

Metscher, Thomas. "The Irony of Thomas More: Reflections on the Literary and Ideological Status of *Utopia*." *Shakespeare Jahrbuch* 118 (1982): 120-30.

>Discusses the concept of ideal social order in *Utopia*, commenting as well on More and the traditions of radical literature.

Pineas, Rainer. "Thomas More's Use of the Dialogue Form as a Weapon of Religious Controversy." *Studies in the Renaissance* VII (1960): 193-206.

>A close survey of More's use of the dialogue form in his controversial works, concluding: "By using the dialogue to discuss the issues rather than just to ridicule his opponents' beliefs, More widened the scope of the Renaissance dialogue of religious controversy."

——. "Thomas More's Use of Humor as a Weapon of Religious Controversy." *Studies in Philology* LVIII, No. 2 (April 1961): 97-114.

>Explains More's controversial works, arguing that "in his bitter struggle to preserve the Catholic faith, More made humor one of his main weapons."

Raitiere, Martin N. "More's *Utopia* and *The City of God*." *Studies in the Renaissance* XX (1973): 144-68.

>Probes the dichotomy of "natural right and patriarchal authority" in *Utopia*, suggesting that More was influenced by St. Augustine's *The City of God*.

Rexroth, Kenneth. "Thomas More's *Utopia*." In *Classics Revisited*, pp. 154-59. Chicago: Quadrangle Books, 1968.

>A brief review of *Utopia*, describing the work as "a kind of perfected and purified Old Testament."

Additional coverage of More's life and career is contained in the following sources published by Gale Research: Literature Criticism 1400-1800, Vol. 10.

Literature Criticism from 1400 to 1800

Cumulative Indexes

How to Use This Index

The main references

Calvino, Italo
1923-1985.....CLC 5, 8, 11, 22, 33, 39,
73; SSC 3

list all author entries in the following Gale Literary Criticism series:

BLC = *Black Literature Criticism*
CLC = *Contemporary Literary Criticism*
CLR = *Children's Literature Review*
CMLC = *Classical and Medieval Literature Criticism*
DA = *DISCovering Authors*
DC = *Drama Criticism*
HLC = *Hispanic Literature Criticism*
LC = *Literature Criticism from 1400 to 1800*
NCLC = *Nineteenth-Century Literature Criticism*
PC = *Poetry Criticism*
SSC = *Short Story Criticism*
TCLC = *Twentieth-Century Literary Criticism*
WLC = *World Literature Criticism, 1500 to the Present*

The cross-references

See also CANR 23; CA 85-88;
obituary CA 116

list all author entries in the following Gale biographical and literary sources:

AAYA = *Authors & Artists for Young Adults*
AITN = *Authors in the News*
BEST = *Bestsellers*
BW = *Black Writers*
CA = *Contemporary Authors*
CAAS = *Contemporary Authors Autobiography Series*
CABS = *Contemporary Authors Bibliographical Series*
CANR = *Contemporary Authors New Revision Series*
CAP = *Contemporary Authors Permanent Series*
CDALB = *Concise Dictionary of American Literary Biography*
CDBLB = *Concise Dictionary of British Literary Biography*
DLB = *Dictionary of Literary Biography*
DLBD = *Dictionary of Literary Biography Documentary Series*
DLBY = *Dictionary of Literary Biography Yearbook*
HW = *Hispanic Writers*
JRDA = *Junior DISCovering Authors*
MAICYA = *Major Authors and Illustrators for Children and Young Adults*
MTCW = *Major 20th-Century Writers*
NNAL = *Native North American Literature*
SAAS = *Something about the Author Autobiography Series*
SATA = *Something about the Author*
YABC = *Yesterday's Authors of Books for Children*

Literary Criticism Series
Cumulative Author Index

Author Index

Asturias, Miguel Angel
1899-1974 .... **CLC 3, 8, 13; HLC**
See also CA 25-28; 49-52; CANR 32;
CAP 2; DAM MULT, NOV; DLB 113;
HW; MTCW

Atares, Carlos Saura
See Saura (Atares), Carlos

Atheling, William
See Pound, Ezra (Weston Loomis)

Atheling, William, Jr.
See Blish, James (Benjamin)

Atherton, Gertrude (Franklin Horn)
1857-1948 .... **TCLC 2**
See also CA 104; DLB 9, 78

Atherton, Lucius
See Masters, Edgar Lee

Atkins, Jack
See Harris, Mark

Atticus
See Fleming, Ian (Lancaster)

Atwood, Margaret (Eleanor)
1939- ..... **CLC 2, 3, 4, 8, 13, 15, 25, 44, 84; DA; DAB; DAC; PC 8; SSC 2; WLC**
See also AAYA 12; BEST 89:2; CA 49-52;
CANR 3, 24, 33; DAM MST, NOV,
POET; DLB 53; INT CANR-24; MTCW;
SATA 50

Aubigny, Pierre d'
See Mencken, H(enry) L(ouis)

Aubin, Penelope 1685-1731(?) .... **LC 9**
See also DLB 39

Auchincloss, Louis (Stanton)
1917- .... **CLC 4, 6, 9, 18, 45**
See also CA 1-4R; CANR 6, 29;
DAM NOV; DLB 2; DLBY 80;
INT CANR-29; MTCW

Auden, W(ystan) H(ugh)
1907-1973 ...... **CLC 1, 2, 3, 4, 6, 9, 11, 14, 43; DA; DAB; DAC; PC 1; WLC**
See also CA 9-12R; 45-48; CANR 5;
CDBLB 1914-1945; DAM DRAM, MST,
POET; DLB 10, 20; MTCW

Audiberti, Jacques 1900-1965 ...... **CLC 38**
See also CA 25-28R; DAM DRAM

Audubon, John James
1785-1851 .... **NCLC 47**

Auel, Jean M(arie) 1936-........... **CLC 31**
See also AAYA 7; BEST 90:4; CA 103;
CANR 21; DAM POP; INT CANR-21

Auerbach, Erich 1892-1957 .... **TCLC 43**
See also CA 118

Augier, Emile 1820-1889 .... **NCLC 31**

August, John
See De Voto, Bernard (Augustine)

Augustine, St. 354-430 ...... **CMLC 6; DAB**

Aurelius
See Bourne, Randolph S(illiman)

Austen, Jane
1775-1817 ..... **NCLC 1, 13, 19, 33, 51; DA; DAB; DAC; WLC**
See also CDBLB 1789-1832; DAM MST,
NOV; DLB 116

Auster, Paul 1947-............... **CLC 47**
See also CA 69-72; CANR 23

Austin, Frank
See Faust, Frederick (Schiller)

Austin, Mary (Hunter)
1868-1934 .... **TCLC 25**
See also CA 109; DLB 9, 78

Autran Dourado, Waldomiro
See Dourado, (Waldomiro Freitas) Autran

Averroes 1126-1198 .... **CMLC 7**
See also DLB 115

Avicenna 980-1037 .... **CMLC 16**
See also DLB 115

Avison, Margaret 1918-.... **CLC 2, 4; DAC**
See also CA 17-20R; DAM POET; DLB 53;
MTCW

Axton, David
See Koontz, Dean R(ay)

Ayckbourn, Alan
1939- .... **CLC 5, 8, 18, 33, 74; DAB**
See also CA 21-24R; CANR 31;
DAM DRAM; DLB 13; MTCW

Aydy, Catherine
See Tennant, Emma (Christina)

Ayme, Marcel (Andre) 1902-1967... **CLC 11**
See also CA 89-92; CLR 25; DLB 72

Ayrton, Michael 1921-1975 .... **CLC 7**
See also CA 5-8R; 61-64; CANR 9, 21

Azorin........................ **CLC 11**
See also Martinez Ruiz, Jose

Azuela, Mariano
1873-1952 .... **TCLC 3; HLC**
See also CA 104; 131; DAM MULT; HW;
MTCW

Baastad, Babbis Friis
See Friis-Baastad, Babbis Ellinor

Bab
See Gilbert, W(illiam) S(chwenck)

Babbis, Eleanor
See Friis-Baastad, Babbis Ellinor

Babel, Isaak (Emmanuilovich)
1894-1941(?) ...... **TCLC 2, 13; SSC 16**
See also CA 104

Babits, Mihaly 1883-1941 .... **TCLC 14**
See also CA 114

Babur 1483-1530.................. **LC 18**

Bacchelli, Riccardo 1891-1985 ..... **CLC 19**
See also CA 29-32R; 117

Bach, Richard (David) 1936-....... **CLC 14**
See also AITN 1; BEST 89:2; CA 9-12R;
CANR 18; DAM NOV, POP; MTCW;
SATA 13

Bachman, Richard
See King, Stephen (Edwin)

Bachmann, Ingeborg 1926-1973..... **CLC 69**
See also CA 93-96; 45-48; DLB 85

Bacon, Francis 1561-1626 .... **LC 18, 32**
See also CDBLB Before 1660; DLB 151

Bacon, Roger 1214(?)-1292 ...... **CMLC 14**
See also DLB 115

Bacovia, George................. **TCLC 24**
See also Vasiliu, Gheorghe

Badanes, Jerome 1937-........... **CLC 59**

Bagehot, Walter 1826-1877 ...... **NCLC 10**
See also DLB 55

Bagnold, Enid 1889-1981 .... **CLC 25**
See also CA 5-8R; 103; CANR 5, 40;
DAM DRAM; DLB 13, 160; MAICYA;
SATA 1, 25

Bagritsky, Eduard 1895-1934 ..... **TCLC 60**

Bagrjana, Elisaveta
See Belcheva, Elisaveta

Bagryana, Elisaveta............... **CLC 10**
See also Belcheva, Elisaveta
See also DLB 147

Bailey, Paul 1937- .... **CLC 45**
See also CA 21-24R; CANR 16; DLB 14

Baillie, Joanna 1762-1851 .... **NCLC 2**
See also DLB 93

Bainbridge, Beryl (Margaret)
1933- .... **CLC 4, 5, 8, 10, 14, 18, 22, 62**
See also CA 21-24R; CANR 24;
DAM NOV; DLB 14; MTCW

Baker, Elliott 1922-............... **CLC 8**
See also CA 45-48; CANR 2

Baker, Nicholson 1957-.......... **CLC 61**
See also CA 135; DAM POP

Baker, Ray Stannard 1870-1946... **TCLC 47**
See also CA 118

Baker, Russell (Wayne) 1925-...... **CLC 31**
See also BEST 89:4; CA 57-60; CANR 11,
41; MTCW

Bakhtin, M.
See Bakhtin, Mikhail Mikhailovich

Bakhtin, M. M.
See Bakhtin, Mikhail Mikhailovich

Bakhtin, Mikhail
See Bakhtin, Mikhail Mikhailovich

Bakhtin, Mikhail Mikhailovich
1895-1975 .... **CLC 83**
See also CA 128; 113

Bakshi, Ralph 1938(?)-............ **CLC 26**
See also CA 112; 138

Bakunin, Mikhail (Alexandrovich)
1814-1876 .... **NCLC 25**

Baldwin, James (Arthur)
1924-1987 ...... **CLC 1, 2, 3, 4, 5, 8, 13, 15, 17, 42, 50, 67, 90; BLC; DA; DAB; DAC; DC 1; SSC 10; WLC**
See also AAYA 4; BW 1; CA 1-4R; 124;
CABS 1; CANR 3, 24;
CDALB 1941-1968; DAM MST, MULT,
NOV, POP; DLB 2, 7, 33; DLBY 87;
MTCW; SATA 9; SATA-Obit 54

Ballard, J(ames) G(raham)
1930- .... **CLC 3, 6, 14, 36; SSC 1**
See also AAYA 3; CA 5-8R; CANR 15, 39;
DAM NOV, POP; DLB 14; MTCW

Balmont, Konstantin (Dmitriyevich)
1867-1943 .... **TCLC 11**
See also CA 109

Balzac, Honore de
1799-1850 .... **NCLC 5, 35, 53; DA; DAB; DAC; SSC 5; WLC**
See also DAM MST, NOV; DLB 119

Bambara, Toni Cade
1939- ..... **CLC 19, 88; BLC; DA; DAC**
See also AAYA 5; BW 2; CA 29-32R;
CANR 24, 49; DAM MST, MULT;
DLB 38; MTCW

Beagle, Peter S(oyer) 1939-........ CLC 7
See also CA 9-12R; CANR 4; DLBY 80;
INT CANR-4; SATA 60

Bean, Normal
See Burroughs, Edgar Rice

Beard, Charles A(ustin)
1874-1948 .... TCLC 15
See also CA 115; DLB 17; SATA 18

Beardsley, Aubrey 1872-1898 ..... NCLC 6

Beattie, Ann
1947- .... CLC 8, 13, 18, 40, 63; SSC 11
See also BEST 90:2; CA 81-84; DAM NOV,
POP; DLBY 82; MTCW

Beattie, James 1735-1803 .... NCLC 25
See also DLB 109

Beauchamp, Kathleen Mansfield 1888-1923
See Mansfield, Katherine
See also CA 104; 134; DA; DAC;
DAM MST

Beaumarchais, Pierre-Augustin Caron de
1732-1799 .... DC 4
See also DAM DRAM

Beaumont, Francis 1584(?)-1616...... DC 6
See also CDBLB Before 1660; DLB 58, 121

Beauvoir, Simone (Lucie Ernestine Marie
Bertrand) de
1908-1986 .... CLC 1, 2, 4, 8, 14, 31, 44,
50, 71; DA; DAB; DAC; WLC
See also CA 9-12R; 118; CANR 28;
DAM MST, NOV; DLB 72; DLBY 86;
MTCW

Becker, Jurek 1937-............ CLC 7, 19
See also CA 85-88; DLB 75

Becker, Walter 1950-............. CLC 26

Beckett, Samuel (Barclay)
1906-1989 ...... CLC 1, 2, 3, 4, 6, 9, 10,
11, 14, 18, 29, 57, 59, 83; DA; DAB;
DAC; SSC 16; WLC
See also CA 5-8R; 130; CANR 33;
CDBLB 1945-1960; DAM DRAM, MST,
NOV; DLB 13, 15; DLBY 90; MTCW

Beckford, William 1760-1844 .... NCLC 16
See also DLB 39

Beckman, Gunnel 1910-........... CLC 26
See also CA 33-36R; CANR 15; CLR 25;
MAICYA; SAAS 9; SATA 6

Becque, Henri 1837-1899........ NCLC 3

Beddoes, Thomas Lovell
1803-1849 .... NCLC 3
See also DLB 96

Bedford, Donald F.
See Fearing, Kenneth (Flexner)

Beecher, Catharine Esther
1800-1878 .... NCLC 30
See also DLB 1

Beecher, John 1904-1980.......... CLC 6
See also AITN 1; CA 5-8R; 105; CANR 8

Beer, Johann 1655-1700............ LC 5

Beer, Patricia 1924-.............. CLC 58
See also CA 61-64; CANR 13, 46; DLB 40

Beerbohm, Henry Maximilian
1872-1956 .... TCLC 1, 24
See also CA 104; DLB 34, 100

Beerbohm, Max
See Beerbohm, Henry Maximilian

Beer-Hofmann, Richard
1866-1945 .... TCLC 60
See also DLB 81

Begiebing, Robert J(ohn) 1946-..... CLC 70
See also CA 122; CANR 40

Behan, Brendan
1923-1964 .... CLC 1, 8, 11, 15, 79
See also CA 73-76; CANR 33;
CDBLB 1945-1960; DAM DRAM;
DLB 13; MTCW

Behn, Aphra
1640(?)-1689 ...... LC 1, 30; DA; DAB;
DAC; DC 4; PC 13; WLC
See also DAM DRAM, MST, NOV, POET;
DLB 39, 80, 131

Behrman, S(amuel) N(athaniel)
1893-1973 .... CLC 40
See also CA 13-16; 45-48; CAP 1; DLB 7,
44

Belasco, David 1853-1931 .... TCLC 3
See also CA 104; DLB 7

Belcheva, Elisaveta 1893- .... CLC 10
See also Bagryana, Elisaveta

Beldone, Phil "Cheech"
See Ellison, Harlan (Jay)

Beleno
See Azuela, Mariano

Belinski, Vissarion Grigoryevich
1811-1848 .... NCLC 5

Belitt, Ben 1911-................. CLC 22
See also CA 13-16R; CAAS 4; CANR 7;
DLB 5

Bell, James Madison
1826-1902 .... TCLC 43; BLC
See also BW 1; CA 122; 124; DAM MULT;
DLB 50

Bell, Madison (Smartt) 1957- ...... CLC 41
See also CA 111; CANR 28

Bell, Marvin (Hartley) 1937-..... CLC 8, 31
See also CA 21-24R; CAAS 14;
DAM POET; DLB 5; MTCW

Bell, W. L. D.
See Mencken, H(enry) L(ouis)

Bellamy, Atwood C.
See Mencken, H(enry) L(ouis)

Bellamy, Edward 1850-1898 ...... NCLC 4
See also DLB 12

Bellin, Edward J.
See Kuttner, Henry

Belloc, (Joseph) Hilaire (Pierre)
1870-1953 .... TCLC 7, 18
See also CA 106; DAM POET; DLB 19,
100, 141; YABC 1

Belloc, Joseph Peter Rene Hilaire
See Belloc, (Joseph) Hilaire (Pierre)

Belloc, Joseph Pierre Hilaire
See Belloc, (Joseph) Hilaire (Pierre)

Belloc, M. A.
See Lowndes, Marie Adelaide (Belloc)

Bellow, Saul
1915- ...... CLC 1, 2, 3, 6, 8, 10, 13, 15,
25, 33, 34, 63, 79; DA; DAB; DAC;
SSC 14; WLC
See also AITN 2; BEST 89:3; CA 5-8R;
CABS 1; CANR 29; CDALB 1941-1968;
DAM MST, NOV, POP; DLB 2, 28;
DLBD 3; DLBY 82; MTCW

Belser, Reimond Karel Maria de
See Ruyslinck, Ward

Bely, Andrey .... TCLC 7; PC 11
See also Bugayev, Boris Nikolayevich

Benary, Margot
See Benary-Isbert, Margot

Benary-Isbert, Margot 1889-1979... CLC 12
See also CA 5-8R; 89-92; CANR 4;
CLR 12; MAICYA; SATA 2;
SATA-Obit 21

Benavente (y Martinez), Jacinto
1866-1954 .... TCLC 3
See also CA 106; 131; DAM DRAM,
MULT; HW; MTCW

Benchley, Peter (Bradford)
1940-...................... CLC 4, 8
See also AAYA 14; AITN 2; CA 17-20R;
CANR 12, 35; DAM NOV, POP;
MTCW; SATA 3

Benchley, Robert (Charles)
1889-1945 .... TCLC 1, 55
See also CA 105; DLB 11

Benda, Julien 1867-1956 .... TCLC 60
See also CA 120

Benedict, Ruth 1887-1948 .... TCLC 60

Benedikt, Michael 1935- .... CLC 4, 14
See also CA 13-16R; CANR 7; DLB 5

Benet, Juan 1927-................ CLC 28
See also CA 143

Benet, Stephen Vincent
1898-1943 .... TCLC 7; SSC 10
See also CA 104; DAM POET; DLB 4, 48,
102; YABC 1

Benet, William Rose 1886-1950 ... TCLC 28
See also CA 118; DAM POET; DLB 45

Benford, Gregory (Albert) 1941-.... CLC 52
See also CA 69-72; CANR 12, 24, 49;
DLBY 82

Bengtsson, Frans (Gunnar)
1894-1954 .... TCLC 48

Benjamin, David
See Slavitt, David R(ytman)

Benjamin, Lois
See Gould, Lois

Benjamin, Walter 1892-1940..... TCLC 39

Benn, Gottfried 1886-1956........ TCLC 3
See also CA 106; DLB 56

Bennett, Alan 1934- ..... CLC 45, 77; DAB
See also CA 103; CANR 35; DAM MST;
MTCW

Bennett, (Enoch) Arnold
1867-1931 .... TCLC 5, 20
See also CA 106; CDBLB 1890-1914;
DLB 10, 34, 98, 135

Bennett, Elizabeth
See Mitchell, Margaret (Munnerlyn)

Bennett, George Harold 1930-
See Bennett, Hal
See also BW 1; CA 97-100

Bennett, Hal . . . . **CLC 5**
See also Bennett, George Harold
See also DLB 33

Bennett, Jay 1912- . . . . **CLC 35**
See also AAYA 10; CA 69-72; CANR 11,
42; JRDA; SAAS 4; SATA 41;
SATA-Brief 27

Bennett, Louise (Simone)
1919- . . . . **CLC 28; BLC**
See also BW 2; DAM MULT; DLB 117

Benson, E(dward) F(rederic)
1867-1940 . . . . **TCLC 27**
See also CA 114; DLB 135, 153

Benson, Jackson J. 1930- . . . . **CLC 34**
See also CA 25-28R; DLB 111

Benson, Sally 1900-1972 . . . . **CLC 17**
See also CA 19-20; 37-40R; CAP 1;
SATA 1, 35; SATA-Obit 27

Benson, Stella 1892-1933 . . . . **TCLC 17**
See also CA 117; DLB 36

Bentham, Jeremy 1748-1832 . . . . . **NCLC 38**
See also DLB 107, 158

Bentley, E(dmund) C(lerihew)
1875-1956 . . . . **TCLC 12**
See also CA 108; DLB 70

Bentley, Eric (Russell) 1916- . . . . **CLC 24**
See also CA 5-8R; CANR 6; INT CANR-6

Beranger, Pierre Jean de
1780-1857 . . . . **NCLC 34**

Berendt, John (Lawrence) 1939- . . . . **CLC 86**
See also CA 146

Berger, Colonel
See Malraux, (Georges-)Andre

Berger, John (Peter) 1926- . . . . . . **CLC 2, 19**
See also CA 81-84; DLB 14

Berger, Melvin H. 1927- . . . . **CLC 12**
See also CA 5-8R; CANR 4; CLR 32;
SAAS 2; SATA 5

Berger, Thomas (Louis)
1924- . . . . **CLC 3, 5, 8, 11, 18, 38**
See also CA 1-4R; CANR 5, 28;
DAM NOV; DLB 2; DLBY 80;
INT CANR-28; MTCW

Bergman, (Ernst) Ingmar
1918- . . . . **CLC 16, 72**
See also CA 81-84; CANR 33

Bergson, Henri 1859-1941 . . . . **TCLC 32**

Bergstein, Eleanor 1938- . . . . **CLC 4**
See also CA 53-56; CANR 5

Berkoff, Steven 1937- . . . . **CLC 56**
See also CA 104

Bermant, Chaim (Icyk) 1929- . . . . . . **CLC 40**
See also CA 57-60; CANR 6, 31

Bern, Victoria
See Fisher, M(ary) F(rances) K(ennedy)

Bernanos, (Paul Louis) Georges
1888-1948 . . . . **TCLC 3**
See also CA 104; 130; DLB 72

Bernard, April 1956- . . . . **CLC 59**
See also CA 131

Berne, Victoria
See Fisher, M(ary) F(rances) K(ennedy)

Bernhard, Thomas
1931-1989 . . . . **CLC 3, 32, 61**
See also CA 85-88; 127; CANR 32;
DLB 85, 124; MTCW

Berriault, Gina 1926- . . . . **CLC 54**
See also CA 116; 129; DLB 130

Berrigan, Daniel 1921- . . . . **CLC 4**
See also CA 33-36R; CAAS 1; CANR 11,
43; DLB 5

Berrigan, Edmund Joseph Michael, Jr.
1934-1983
See Berrigan, Ted
See also CA 61-64; 110; CANR 14

Berrigan, Ted . . . . **CLC 37**
See also Berrigan, Edmund Joseph Michael,
Jr.
See also DLB 5

Berry, Charles Edward Anderson 1931-
See Berry, Chuck
See also CA 115

Berry, Chuck . . . . **CLC 17**
See also Berry, Charles Edward Anderson

Berry, Jonas
See Ashbery, John (Lawrence)

Berry, Wendell (Erdman)
1934- . . . . **CLC 4, 6, 8, 27, 46**
See also AITN 1; CA 73-76; CANR 50;
DAM POET; DLB 5, 6

Berryman, John
1914-1972 . . . . . . **CLC 1, 2, 3, 4, 6, 8, 10,
13, 25, 62**
See also CA 13-16; 33-36R; CABS 2;
CANR 35; CAP 1; CDALB 1941-1968;
DAM POET; DLB 48; MTCW

Bertolucci, Bernardo 1940- . . . . **CLC 16**
See also CA 106

Bertrand, Aloysius 1807-1841 . . . . **NCLC 31**

Bertran de Born c. 1140-1215 . . . . . **CMLC 5**

Besant, Annie (Wood) 1847-1933 . . . **TCLC 9**
See also CA 105

Bessie, Alvah 1904-1985 . . . . **CLC 23**
See also CA 5-8R; 116; CANR 2; DLB 26

Bethlen, T. D.
See Silverberg, Robert

Beti, Mongo . . . . **CLC 27; BLC**
See also Biyidi, Alexandre
See also DAM MULT

Betjeman, John
1906-1984 . . . **CLC 2, 6, 10, 34, 43; DAB**
See also CA 9-12R; 112; CANR 33;
CDBLB 1945-1960; DAM MST, POET;
DLB 20; DLBY 84; MTCW

Bettelheim, Bruno 1903-1990 . . . . . . **CLC 79**
See also CA 81-84; 131; CANR 23; MTCW

Betti, Ugo 1892-1953 . . . . **TCLC 5**
See also CA 104

Betts, Doris (Waugh) 1932- . . . . **CLC 3, 6, 28**
See also CA 13-16R; CANR 9; DLBY 82;
INT CANR-9

Bevan, Alistair
See Roberts, Keith (John Kingston)

Bialik, Chaim Nachman
1873-1934 . . . . **TCLC 25**

Bickerstaff, Isaac
See Swift, Jonathan

Bidart, Frank 1939- . . . . **CLC 33**
See also CA 140

Bienek, Horst 1930- . . . . **CLC 7, 11**
See also CA 73-76; DLB 75

Bierce, Ambrose (Gwinett)
1842-1914(?) . . . . **TCLC 1, 7, 44; DA;
DAC; SSC 9; WLC**
See also CA 104; 139; CDALB 1865-1917;
DAM MST; DLB 11, 12, 23, 71, 74

Billings, Josh
See Shaw, Henry Wheeler

Billington, (Lady) Rachel (Mary)
1942- . . . . **CLC 43**
See also AITN 2; CA 33-36R; CANR 44

Binyon, T(imothy) J(ohn) 1936- . . . . **CLC 34**
See also CA 111; CANR 28

Bioy Casares, Adolfo
1914- . . . **CLC 4, 8, 13, 88; HLC; SSC 17**
See also CA 29-32R; CANR 19, 43;
DAM MULT; DLB 113; HW; MTCW

Bird, Cordwainer
See Ellison, Harlan (Jay)

Bird, Robert Montgomery
1806-1854 . . . . **NCLC 1**

Birney, (Alfred) Earle
1904- . . . . **CLC 1, 4, 6, 11; DAC**
See also CA 1-4R; CANR 5, 20;
DAM MST, POET; DLB 88; MTCW

Bishop, Elizabeth
1911-1979 . . . . . . **CLC 1, 4, 9, 13, 15, 32;
DA; DAC; PC 3**
See also CA 5-8R; 89-92; CABS 2;
CANR 26; CDALB 1968-1988;
DAM MST, POET; DLB 5; MTCW;
SATA-Obit 24

Bishop, John 1935- . . . . **CLC 10**
See also CA 105

Bissett, Bill 1939- . . . . **CLC 18; PC 14**
See also CA 69-72; CAAS 19; CANR 15;
DLB 53; MTCW

Bitov, Andrei (Georgievich) 1937- . . . **CLC 57**
See also CA 142

Biyidi, Alexandre 1932-
See Beti, Mongo
See also BW 1; CA 114; 124; MTCW

Bjarme, Brynjolf
See Ibsen, Henrik (Johan)

Bjornson, Bjornstjerne (Martinius)
1832-1910 . . . . **TCLC 7, 37**
See also CA 104

Black, Robert
See Holdstock, Robert P.

Blackburn, Paul 1926-1971 . . . . . . **CLC 9, 43**
See also CA 81-84; 33-36R; CANR 34;
DLB 16; DLBY 81

Black Elk 1863-1950 . . . . **TCLC 33**
See also CA 144; DAM MULT; NNAL

Black Hobart
See Sanders, (James) Ed(ward)

Blacklin, Malcolm
See Chambers, Aidan

Blackmore, R(ichard) D(oddridge)
  1825-1900 .... **TCLC 27**
  See also CA 120; DLB 18

Blackmur, R(ichard) P(almer)
  1904-1965 .... **CLC 2, 24**
  See also CA 11-12; 25-28R; CAP 1; DLB 63

Black Tarantula, The
  See Acker, Kathy

Blackwood, Algernon (Henry)
  1869-1951 .... **TCLC 5**
  See also CA 105; DLB 153, 156

Blackwood, Caroline 1931- .... **CLC 6, 9**
  See also CA 85-88; CANR 32; DLB 14;
  MTCW

Blade, Alexander
  See Hamilton, Edmond; Silverberg, Robert

Blaga, Lucian 1895-1961 .... **CLC 75**

Blair, Eric (Arthur) 1903-1950
  See Orwell, George
  See also CA 104; 132; DA; DAB; DAC;
  DAM MST, NOV; MTCW; SATA 29

Blais, Marie-Claire
  1939- .... **CLC 2, 4, 6, 13, 22; DAC**
  See also CA 21-24R; CAAS 4; CANR 38;
  DAM MST; DLB 53; MTCW

Blaise, Clark 1940- .... **CLC 29**
  See also AITN 2; CA 53-56; CAAS 3;
  CANR 5; DLB 53

Blake, Nicholas
  See Day Lewis, C(ecil)
  See also DLB 77

Blake, William
  1757-1827 .... **NCLC 13, 37; DA; DAB;
  DAC; PC 12; WLC**
  See also CDBLB 1789-1832; DAM MST,
  POET; DLB 93; MAICYA; SATA 30

Blake, William J(ames) 1894-1969 ... **PC 12**
  See also CA 5-8R; 25-28R

Blasco Ibanez, Vicente
  1867-1928 .... **TCLC 12**
  See also CA 110; 131; DAM NOV; HW;
  MTCW

Blatty, William Peter 1928- .... **CLC 2**
  See also CA 5-8R; CANR 9; DAM POP

Bleeck, Oliver
  See Thomas, Ross (Elmore)

Blessing, Lee 1949- .... **CLC 54**

Blish, James (Benjamin)
  1921-1975 .... **CLC 14**
  See also CA 1-4R; 57-60; CANR 3; DLB 8;
  MTCW; SATA 66

Bliss, Reginald
  See Wells, H(erbert) G(eorge)

Blixen, Karen (Christentze Dinesen)
  1885-1962
  See Dinesen, Isak
  See also CA 25-28; CANR 22, 50; CAP 2;
  MTCW; SATA 44

Bloch, Robert (Albert) 1917-1994 ... **CLC 33**
  See also CA 5-8R; 146; CAAS 20; CANR 5;
  DLB 44; INT CANR-5; SATA 12;
  SATA-Obit 82

Blok, Alexander (Alexandrovich)
  1880-1921 .... **TCLC 5**
  See also CA 104

Blom, Jan
  See Breytenbach, Breyten

Bloom, Harold 1930- .... **CLC 24**
  See also CA 13-16R; CANR 39; DLB 67

Bloomfield, Aurelius
  See Bourne, Randolph S(illiman)

Blount, Roy (Alton), Jr. 1941- ..... **CLC 38**
  See also CA 53-56; CANR 10, 28;
  INT CANR-28; MTCW

Bloy, Leon 1846-1917............ **TCLC 22**
  See also CA 121; DLB 123

Blume, Judy (Sussman) 1938-... **CLC 12, 30**
  See also AAYA 3; CA 29-32R; CANR 13,
  37; CLR 2, 15; DAM NOV, POP;
  DLB 52; JRDA; MAICYA; MTCW;
  SATA 2, 31, 79

Blunden, Edmund (Charles)
  1896-1974 .... **CLC 2, 56**
  See also CA 17-18; 45-48; CAP 2; DLB 20,
  100, 155; MTCW

Bly, Robert (Elwood)
  1926- .... **CLC 1, 2, 5, 10, 15, 38**
  See also CA 5-8R; CANR 41; DAM POET;
  DLB 5; MTCW

Boas, Franz 1858-1942........... **TCLC 56**
  See also CA 115

Bobette
  See Simenon, Georges (Jacques Christian)

Boccaccio, Giovanni
  1313-1375 .... **CMLC 13; SSC 10**

Bochco, Steven 1943- .... **CLC 35**
  See also AAYA 11; CA 124; 138

Bodenheim, Maxwell 1892-1954 ... **TCLC 44**
  See also CA 110; DLB 9, 45

Bodker, Cecil 1927- .... **CLC 21**
  See also CA 73-76; CANR 13, 44; CLR 23;
  MAICYA; SATA 14

Boell, Heinrich (Theodor)
  1917-1985 .... **CLC 2, 3, 6, 9, 11, 15, 27,
  32, 72; DA; DAB; DAC; WLC**
  See also CA 21-24R; 116; CANR 24;
  DAM MST, NOV; DLB 69; DLBY 85;
  MTCW

Boerne, Alfred
  See Doeblin, Alfred

Boethius 480(?)-524(?) .... **CMLC 15**
  See also DLB 115

Bogan, Louise
  1897-1970 ...... **CLC 4, 39, 46; PC 12**
  See also CA 73-76; 25-28R; CANR 33;
  DAM POET; DLB 45; MTCW

Bogarde, Dirk .... **CLC 19**
  See also Van Den Bogarde, Derek Jules
  Gaspard Ulric Niven
  See also DLB 14

Bogosian, Eric 1953- .... **CLC 45**
  See also CA 138

Bograd, Larry 1953-............... **CLC 35**
  See also CA 93-96; SAAS 21; SATA 33

Boiardo, Matteo Maria 1441-1494 .... **LC 6**

Boileau-Despreaux, Nicolas
  1636-1711 .... **LC 3**

Boland, Eavan (Aisling) 1944-... **CLC 40, 67**
  See also CA 143; DAM POET; DLB 40

Bolt, Lee
  See Faust, Frederick (Schiller)

Bolt, Robert (Oxton) 1924-1995 .... **CLC 14**
  See also CA 17-20R; 147; CANR 35;
  DAM DRAM; DLB 13; MTCW

Bombet, Louis-Alexandre-Cesar
  See Stendhal

Bomkauf
  See Kaufman, Bob (Garnell)

Bonaventura.................... **NCLC 35**
  See also DLB 90

Bond, Edward 1934-........ **CLC 4, 6, 13, 23**
  See also CA 25-28R; CANR 38;
  DAM DRAM; DLB 13; MTCW

Bonham, Frank 1914-1989......... **CLC 12**
  See also AAYA 1; CA 9-12R; CANR 4, 36;
  JRDA; MAICYA; SAAS 3; SATA 1, 49;
  SATA-Obit 62

Bonnefoy, Yves 1923-........ **CLC 9, 15, 58**
  See also CA 85-88; CANR 33; DAM MST,
  POET; MTCW

Bontemps, Arna(ud Wendell)
  1902-1973 .... **CLC 1, 18; BLC**
  See also BW 1; CA 1-4R; 41-44R; CANR 4,
  35; CLR 6; DAM MULT, NOV, POET;
  DLB 48, 51; JRDA; MAICYA; MTCW;
  SATA 2, 44; SATA-Obit 24

Booth, Martin 1944-.............. **CLC 13**
  See also CA 93-96; CAAS 2

Booth, Philip 1925-................ **CLC 23**
  See also CA 5-8R; CANR 5; DLBY 82

Booth, Wayne C(layson) 1921- ..... **CLC 24**
  See also CA 1-4R; CAAS 5; CANR 3, 43;
  DLB 67

Borchert, Wolfgang 1921-1947 ..... **TCLC 5**
  See also CA 104; DLB 69, 124

Borel, Petrus 1809-1859........ **NCLC 41**

Borges, Jorge Luis
  1899-1986 ... **CLC 1, 2, 3, 4, 6, 8, 9, 10,
  13, 19, 44, 48, 83; DA; DAB; DAC;
  HLC; SSC 4; WLC**
  See also CA 21-24R; CANR 19, 33;
  DAM MST, MULT; DLB 113; DLBY 86;
  HW; MTCW

Borowski, Tadeusz 1922-1951...... **TCLC 9**
  See also CA 106

Borrow, George (Henry)
  1803-1881 .... **NCLC 9**
  See also DLB 21, 55

Bosman, Herman Charles
  1905-1951 .... **TCLC 49**

Bosschere, Jean de 1878(?)-1953... **TCLC 19**
  See also CA 115

Boswell, James
  1740-1795 ...... **LC 4; DA; DAB; DAC;
  WLC**
  See also CDBLB 1660-1789; DAM MST;
  DLB 104, 142

Bottoms, David 1949-............. **CLC 53**
  See also CA 105; CANR 22; DLB 120;
  DLBY 83

Boucicault, Dion 1820-1890...... **NCLC 41**

Boucolon, Maryse 1937-
  See Conde, Maryse
  See also CA 110; CANR 30

Bourget, Paul (Charles Joseph)
1852-1935 .... **TCLC 12**
See also CA 107; DLB 123

Bourjaily, Vance (Nye) 1922- .... **CLC 8, 62**
See also CA 1-4R; CAAS 1; CANR 2;
DLB 2, 143

Bourne, Randolph S(illiman)
1886-1918 .... **TCLC 16**
See also CA 117; DLB 63

Bova, Ben(jamin William) 1932- .... **CLC 45**
See also AAYA 16; CA 5-8R; CAAS 18;
CANR 11; CLR 3; DLBY 81;
INT CANR-11; MAICYA; MTCW;
SATA 6, 68

Bowen, Elizabeth (Dorothea Cole)
1899-1973 ...... **CLC 1, 3, 6, 11, 15, 22;**
SSC 3
See also CA 17-18; 41-44R; CANR 35;
CAP 2; CDBLB 1945-1960; DAM NOV;
DLB 15; MTCW

Bowering, George 1935- .... **CLC 15, 47**
See also CA 21-24R; CAAS 16; CANR 10;
DLB 53

Bowering, Marilyn R(uthe) 1949- ... **CLC 32**
See also CA 101; CANR 49

Bowers, Edgar 1924- .... **CLC 9**
See also CA 5-8R; CANR 24; DLB 5

Bowie, David .... **CLC 17**
See also Jones, David Robert

Bowles, Jane (Sydney)
1917-1973 .... **CLC 3, 68**
See also CA 19-20; 41-44R; CAP 2

Bowles, Paul (Frederick)
1910- .... **CLC 1, 2, 19, 53; SSC 3**
See also CA 1-4R; CAAS 1; CANR 1, 19,
50; DLB 5, 6; MTCW

Box, Edgar
See Vidal, Gore

Boyd, Nancy
See Millay, Edna St. Vincent

Boyd, William 1952- .... **CLC 28, 53, 70**
See also CA 114; 120

Boyle, Kay
1902-1992 ..... **CLC 1, 5, 19, 58; SSC 5**
See also CA 13-16R; 140; CAAS 1;
CANR 29; DLB 4, 9, 48, 86; DLBY 93;
MTCW

Boyle, Mark
See Kienzle, William X(avier)

Boyle, Patrick 1905-1982 .... **CLC 19**
See also CA 127

Boyle, T. C. 1948-
See Boyle, T(homas) Coraghessan

Boyle, T(homas) Coraghessan
1948- .... **CLC 36, 55, 90; SSC 16**
See also BEST 90:4; CA 120; CANR 44;
DAM POP; DLBY 86

Boz
See Dickens, Charles (John Huffam)

Brackenridge, Hugh Henry
1748-1816 .... **NCLC 7**
See also DLB 11, 37

Bradbury, Edward P.
See Moorcock, Michael (John)

Bradbury, Malcolm (Stanley)
1932- .... **CLC 32, 61**
See also CA 1-4R; CANR 1, 33;
DAM NOV; DLB 14; MTCW

Bradbury, Ray (Douglas)
1920- .... **CLC 1, 3, 10, 15, 42; DA;**
DAB; DAC; WLC
See also AAYA 15; AITN 1, 2; CA 1-4R;
CANR 2, 30; CDALB 1968-1988;
DAM MST, NOV, POP; DLB 2, 8;
INT CANR-30; MTCW; SATA 11, 64

Bradford, Gamaliel 1863-1932..... **TCLC 36**
See also DLB 17

Bradley, David (Henry, Jr.)
1950- .... **CLC 23; BLC**
See also BW 1; CA 104; CANR 26;
DAM MULT; DLB 33

Bradley, John Ed(mund, Jr.)
1958- .... **CLC 55**
See also CA 139

Bradley, Marion Zimmer 1930-..... **CLC 30**
See also AAYA 9; CA 57-60; CAAS 10;
CANR 7, 31; DAM POP; DLB 8;
MTCW

Bradstreet, Anne
1612(?)-1672 ...... **LC 4, 30; DA; DAC;**
PC 10
See also CDALB 1640-1865; DAM MST,
POET; DLB 24

Brady, Joan 1939- .... **CLC 86**
See also CA 141

Bragg, Melvyn 1939- .... **CLC 10**
See also BEST 89:3; CA 57-60; CANR 10,
48; DLB 14

Braine, John (Gerard)
1922-1986 .... **CLC 1, 3, 41**
See also CA 1-4R; 120; CANR 1, 33;
CDBLB 1945-1960; DLB 15; DLBY 86;
MTCW

Brammer, William 1930(?)-1978 .... **CLC 31**
See also CA 77-80

Brancati, Vitaliano 1907-1954..... **TCLC 12**
See also CA 109

Brancato, Robin F(idler) 1936- ..... **CLC 35**
See also AAYA 9; CA 69-72; CANR 11,
45; CLR 32; JRDA; SAAS 9; SATA 23

Brand, Max
See Faust, Frederick (Schiller)

Brand, Millen 1906-1980.......... **CLC 7**
See also CA 21-24R; 97-100

Branden, Barbara .... **CLC 44**
See also CA 148

Brandes, Georg (Morris Cohen)
1842-1927 .... **TCLC 10**
See also CA 105

Brandys, Kazimierz 1916- .... **CLC 62**

Branley, Franklyn M(ansfield)
1915- .... **CLC 21**
See also CA 33-36R; CANR 14, 39;
CLR 13; MAICYA; SAAS 16; SATA 4,
68

Brathwaite, Edward Kamau 1930-... **CLC 11**
See also BW 2; CA 25-28R; CANR 11, 26,
47; DLB 125

Brautigan, Richard (Gary)
1935-1984 .... **CLC 1, 3, 5, 9, 12, 34, 42**
See also CA 53-56; 113; CANR 34;
DAM NOV; DLB 2, 5; DLBY 80, 84;
MTCW; SATA 56

Braverman, Kate 1950- .... **CLC 67**
See also CA 89-92

Brecht, Bertolt
1898-1956 ...... **TCLC 1, 6, 13, 35; DA;**
DAB; DAC; DC 3; WLC
See also CA 104; 133; DAM DRAM, MST;
DLB 56, 124; MTCW

Brecht, Eugen Berthold Friedrich
See Brecht, Bertolt

Bremer, Fredrika 1801-1865 ..... **NCLC 11**

Brennan, Christopher John
1870-1932 .... **TCLC 17**
See also CA 117

Brennan, Maeve 1917- .... **CLC 5**
See also CA 81-84

Brentano, Clemens (Maria)
1778-1842 .... **NCLC 1**
See also DLB 90

Brent of Bin Bin
See Franklin, (Stella Maraia Sarah) Miles

Brenton, Howard 1942- .... **CLC 31**
See also CA 69-72; CANR 33; DLB 13;
MTCW

Breslin, James 1930-
See Breslin, Jimmy
See also CA 73-76; CANR 31; DAM NOV;
MTCW

Breslin, Jimmy .... **CLC 4, 43**
See also Breslin, James
See also AITN 1

Bresson, Robert 1901- .... **CLC 16**
See also CA 110; CANR 49

Breton, Andre 1896-1966... **CLC 2, 9, 15, 54**
See also CA 19-20; 25-28R; CANR 40;
CAP 2; DLB 65; MTCW

Breytenbach, Breyten 1939(?)- .. **CLC 23, 37**
See also CA 113; 129; DAM POET

Bridgers, Sue Ellen 1942- .... **CLC 26**
See also AAYA 8; CA 65-68; CANR 11,
36; CLR 18; DLB 52; JRDA; MAICYA;
SAAS 1; SATA 22

Bridges, Robert (Seymour)
1844-1930 .... **TCLC 1**
See also CA 104; CDBLB 1890-1914;
DAM POET; DLB 19, 98

Bridie, James.................... **TCLC 3**
See also Mavor, Osborne Henry
See also DLB 10

Brin, David 1950-................ **CLC 34**
See also CA 102; CANR 24;
INT CANR-24; SATA 65

Brink, Andre (Philippus)
1935- .... **CLC 18, 36**
See also CA 104; CANR 39; INT 103;
MTCW

Brinsmead, H(esba) F(ay) 1922- .... **CLC 21**
See also CA 21-24R; CANR 10; MAICYA;
SAAS 5; SATA 18, 78

Chatterji, Saratchandra .... TCLC 13
  See also Chatterje, Sarat Chandra

Chatterton, Thomas 1752-1770 ...... LC 3
  See also DAM POET; DLB 109

Chatwin, (Charles) Bruce
    1940-1989 .... CLC 28, 57, 59
  See also AAYA 4; BEST 90:1; CA 85-88;
  127; DAM POP

Chaucer, Daniel
  See Ford, Ford Madox

Chaucer, Geoffrey
    1340(?)-1400 ... LC 17; DA; DAB; DAC
  See also CDBLB Before 1660; DAM MST,
  POET; DLB 146

Chaviaras, Strates 1935-
  See Haviaras, Stratis
  See also CA 105

Chayefsky, Paddy .... CLC 23
  See also Chayefsky, Sidney
  See also DLB 7, 44; DLBY 81

Chayefsky, Sidney 1923-1981
  See Chayefsky, Paddy
  See also CA 9-12R; 104; CANR 18;
  DAM DRAM

Chedid, Andree 1920-............. CLC 47
  See also CA 145

Cheever, John
    1912-1982 ...... CLC 3, 7, 8, 11, 15, 25,
              64; DA; DAB; DAC; SSC 1; WLC
  See also CA 5-8R; 106; CABS 1; CANR 5,
  27; CDALB 1941-1968; DAM MST,
  NOV, POP; DLB 2, 102; DLBY 80, 82;
  INT CANR-5; MTCW

Cheever, Susan 1943-.......... CLC 18, 48
  See also CA 103; CANR 27; DLBY 82;
  INT CANR-27

Chekhonte, Antosha
  See Chekhov, Anton (Pavlovich)

Chekhov, Anton (Pavlovich)
    1860-1904 ..... TCLC 3, 10, 31, 55; DA;
              DAB; DAC; SSC 2; WLC
  See also CA 104; 124; DAM DRAM, MST

Chernyshevsky, Nikolay Gavrilovich
    1828-1889 .... NCLC 1

Cherry, Carolyn Janice 1942-
  See Cherryh, C. J.
  See also CA 65-68; CANR 10

Cherryh, C. J. .... CLC 35
  See also Cherry, Carolyn Janice
  See also DLBY 80

Chesnutt, Charles W(addell)
    1858-1932 .... TCLC 5, 39; BLC; SSC 7
  See also BW 1; CA 106; 125; DAM MULT;
  DLB 12, 50, 78; MTCW

Chester, Alfred 1929(?)-1971...... CLC 49
  See also CA 33-36R; DLB 130

Chesterton, G(ilbert) K(eith)
    1874-1936 .... TCLC 1, 6; SSC 1
  See also CA 104; 132; CDBLB 1914-1945;
  DAM NOV, POET; DLB 10, 19, 34, 70,
  98, 149; MTCW; SATA 27

Chiang Pin-chin 1904-1986
  See Ding Ling
  See also CA 118

Ch'ien Chung-shu 1910-.......... CLC 22
  See also CA 130; MTCW

Child, L. Maria
  See Child, Lydia Maria

Child, Lydia Maria 1802-1880 .... NCLC 6
  See also DLB 1, 74; SATA 67

Child, Mrs.
  See Child, Lydia Maria

Child, Philip 1898-1978 .... CLC 19, 68
  See also CA 13-14; CAP 1; SATA 47

Childress, Alice
    1920-1994 .. CLC 12, 15, 86; BLC; DC 4
  See also AAYA 8; BW 2; CA 45-48; 146;
  CANR 3, 27, 50; CLR 14; DAM DRAM,
  MULT, NOV; DLB 7, 38; JRDA;
  MAICYA; MTCW; SATA 7, 48, 81

Chislett, (Margaret) Anne 1943-.... CLC 34

Chitty, Thomas Willes 1926-....... CLC 11
  See also Hinde, Thomas
  See also CA 5-8R

Chivers, Thomas Holley
    1809-1858 .... NCLC 49
  See also DLB 3

Chomette, Rene Lucien 1898-1981
  See Clair, Rene
  See also CA 103

Chopin, Kate
    .... TCLC 5, 14; DA; DAB; SSC 8
  See also Chopin, Katherine
  See also CDALB 1865-1917; DLB 12, 78

Chopin, Katherine 1851-1904
  See Chopin, Kate
  See also CA 104; 122; DAC; DAM MST,
  NOV

Chretien de Troyes
    c. 12th cent. - .... CMLC 10

Christie
  See Ichikawa, Kon

Christie, Agatha (Mary Clarissa)
    1890-1976 ...... CLC 1, 6, 8, 12, 39, 48;
                            DAB; DAC
  See also AAYA 9; AITN 1, 2; CA 17-20R;
  61-64; CANR 10, 37; CDBLB 1914-1945;
  DAM NOV; DLB 13, 77; MTCW;
  SATA 36

Christie, (Ann) Philippa
  See Pearce, Philippa
  See also CA 5-8R; CANR 4

Christine de Pizan 1365(?)-1431(?) .... LC 9

Chubb, Elmer
  See Masters, Edgar Lee

Chulkov, Mikhail Dmitrievich
    1743-1792 .... LC 2
  See also DLB 150

Churchill, Caryl 1938-... CLC 31, 55; DC 5
  See also CA 102; CANR 22, 46; DLB 13;
  MTCW

Churchill, Charles 1731-1764........ LC 3
  See also DLB 109

Chute, Carolyn 1947-............. CLC 39
  See also CA 123

Ciardi, John (Anthony)
    1916-1986 .... CLC 10, 40, 44
  See also CA 5-8R; 118; CAAS 2; CANR 5,
  33; CLR 19; DAM POET; DLB 5;
  DLBY 86; INT CANR-5; MAICYA;
  MTCW; SATA 1, 65; SATA-Obit 46

Cicero, Marcus Tullius
    106B.C.-43B.C. .... CMLC 3

Cimino, Michael 1943-............ CLC 16
  See also CA 105

Cioran, E(mil) M. 1911-........... CLC 64
  See also CA 25-28R

Cisneros, Sandra 1954-...... CLC 69; HLC
  See also AAYA 9; CA 131; DAM MULT;
  DLB 122, 152; HW

Clair, Rene....................... CLC 20
  See also Chomette, Rene Lucien

Clampitt, Amy 1920-1994 .... CLC 32
  See also CA 110; 146; CANR 29; DLB 105

Clancy, Thomas L., Jr. 1947-
  See Clancy, Tom
  See also CA 125; 131; INT 131; MTCW

Clancy, Tom....................... CLC 45
  See also Clancy, Thomas L., Jr.
  See also AAYA 9; BEST 89:1, 90:1;
  DAM NOV, POP

Clare, John 1793-1864 ...... NCLC 9; DAB
  See also DAM POET; DLB 55, 96

Clarin
  See Alas (y Urena), Leopoldo (Enrique
  Garcia)

Clark, Al C.
  See Goines, Donald

Clark, (Robert) Brian 1932-........ CLC 29
  See also CA 41-44R

Clark, Curt
  See Westlake, Donald E(dwin)

Clark, Eleanor 1913- .... CLC 5, 19
  See also CA 9-12R; CANR 41; DLB 6

Clark, J. P.
  See Clark, John Pepper
  See also DLB 117

Clark, John Pepper
    1935- .... CLC 38; BLC; DC 5
  See also Clark, J. P.
  See also BW 1; CA 65-68; CANR 16;
  DAM DRAM, MULT

Clark, M. R.
  See Clark, Mavis Thorpe

Clark, Mavis Thorpe 1909-........ CLC 12
  See also CA 57-60; CANR 8, 37; CLR 30;
  MAICYA; SAAS 5; SATA 8, 74

Clark, Walter Van Tilburg
    1909-1971 .... CLC 28
  See also CA 9-12R; 33-36R; DLB 9;
  SATA 8

Clarke, Arthur C(harles)
    1917- ...... CLC 1, 4, 13, 18, 35; SSC 3
  See also AAYA 4; CA 1-4R; CANR 2, 28;
  DAM POP; JRDA; MAICYA; MTCW;
  SATA 13, 70

Clarke, Austin 1896-1974........ CLC 6, 9
  See also CA 29-32; 49-52; CAP 2;
  DAM POET; DLB 10, 20

Clarke, Austin C(hesterfield)
    1934- .... CLC 8, 53; BLC; DAC
  See also BW 1; CA 25-28R; CAAS 16;
  CANR 14, 32; DAM MULT; DLB 53,
  125

Clarke, Gillian 1937-............. CLC 61
  See also CA 106; DLB 40

Clarke, Marcus (Andrew Hislop)
　　1846-1881 .... **NCLC 19**

Clarke, Shirley　1925- .... **CLC 16**

Clash, The
　　See Headon, (Nicky) Topper; Jones, Mick;
　　Simonon, Paul; Strummer, Joe

Claudel, Paul (Louis Charles Marie)
　　1868-1955 .... **TCLC 2, 10**
　　See also CA 104

Clavell, James (duMaresq)
　　1925-1994 .... **CLC 6, 25, 87**
　　See also CA 25-28R; 146; CANR 26, 48;
　　DAM NOV, POP; MTCW

Cleaver, (Leroy) Eldridge
　　1935- .... **CLC 30; BLC**
　　See also BW 1; CA 21-24R; CANR 16;
　　DAM MULT

Cleese, John (Marwood)　1939- ..... **CLC 21**
　　See also Monty Python
　　See also CA 112; 116; CANR 35; MTCW

Cleishbotham, Jebediah
　　See Scott, Walter

Cleland, John　1710-1789 .... **LC 2**
　　See also DLB 39

Clemens, Samuel Langhorne　1835-1910
　　See Twain, Mark
　　See also CA 104; 135; CDALB 1865-1917;
　　DA; DAB; DAC; DAM MST, NOV;
　　DLB 11, 12, 23, 64, 74; JRDA;
　　MAICYA; YABC 2

Cleophil
　　See Congreve, William

Clerihew, E.
　　See Bentley, E(dmund) C(lerihew)

Clerk, N. W.
　　See Lewis, C(live) S(taples)

Cliff, Jimmy..................... **CLC 21**
　　See also Chambers, James

Clifton, (Thelma) Lucille
　　1936- .... **CLC 19, 66; BLC**
　　See also BW 2; CA 49-52; CANR 2, 24, 42;
　　CLR 5; DAM MULT, POET; DLB 5, 41;
　　MAICYA; MTCW; SATA 20, 69

Clinton, Dirk
　　See Silverberg, Robert

Clough, Arthur Hugh　1819-1861.. **NCLC 27**
　　See also DLB 32

Clutha, Janet Paterson Frame　1924-
　　See Frame, Janet
　　See also CA 1-4R; CANR 2, 36; MTCW

Clyne, Terence
　　See Blatty, William Peter

Cobalt, Martin
　　See Mayne, William (James Carter)

Cobbett, William　1763-1835 ..... **NCLC 49**
　　See also DLB 43, 107, 158

Coburn, D(onald) L(ee)　1938- ...... **CLC 10**
　　See also CA 89-92

Cocteau, Jean (Maurice Eugene Clement)
　　1889-1963 .... **CLC 1, 8, 15, 16, 43; DA;**
　　　　　　　　　　　　DAB; DAC; WLC
　　See also CA 25-28; CANR 40; CAP 2;
　　DAM DRAM, MST, NOV; DLB 65;
　　MTCW

Codrescu, Andrei　1946- .... **CLC 46**
　　See also CA 33-36R; CAAS 19; CANR 13,
　　34; DAM POET

Coe, Max
　　See Bourne, Randolph S(illiman)

Coe, Tucker
　　See Westlake, Donald E(dwin)

Coetzee, J(ohn) M(ichael)
　　1940- .... **CLC 23, 33, 66**
　　See also CA 77-80; CANR 41; DAM NOV;
　　MTCW

Coffey, Brian
　　See Koontz, Dean R(ay)

Cohan, George M.　1878-1942 ..... **TCLC 60**

Cohen, Arthur A(llen)
　　1928-1986 .... **CLC 7, 31**
　　See also CA 1-4R; 120; CANR 1, 17, 42;
　　DLB 28

Cohen, Leonard (Norman)
　　1934- .... **CLC 3, 38; DAC**
　　See also CA 21-24R; CANR 14;
　　DAM MST; DLB 53; MTCW

Cohen, Matt　1942- .... **CLC 19; DAC**
　　See also CA 61-64; CAAS 18; CANR 40;
　　DLB 53

Cohen-Solal, Annie　19(?)- .... **CLC 50**

Colegate, Isabel　1931- .... **CLC 36**
　　See also CA 17-20R; CANR 8, 22; DLB 14;
　　INT CANR-22; MTCW

Coleman, Emmett
　　See Reed, Ishmael

Coleridge, Samuel Taylor
　　1772-1834 .... **NCLC 9; DA; DAB;**
　　　　　　　　　　　DAC; PC 11; WLC
　　See also CDBLB 1789-1832; DAM MST,
　　POET; DLB 93, 107

Coleridge, Sara　1802-1852....... **NCLC 31**

Coles, Don　1928- .... **CLC 46**
　　See also CA 115; CANR 38

Colette, (Sidonie-Gabrielle)
　　1873-1954 ...... **TCLC 1, 5, 16; SSC 10**
　　See also CA 104; 131; DAM NOV; DLB 65;
　　MTCW

Collett, (Jacobine) Camilla (Wergeland)
　　1813-1895 .... **NCLC 22**

Collier, Christopher　1930- .... **CLC 30**
　　See also AAYA 13; CA 33-36R; CANR 13,
　　33; JRDA; MAICYA; SATA 16, 70

Collier, James L(incoln)　1928- ..... **CLC 30**
　　See also AAYA 13; CA 9-12R; CANR 4,
　　33; CLR 3; DAM POP; JRDA;
　　MAICYA; SAAS 21; SATA 8, 70

Collier, Jeremy　1650-1726.......... **LC 6**

Collier, John　1901-1980........... **SSC 19**
　　See also CA 65-68; 97-100; CANR 10;
　　DLB 77

Collins, Hunt
　　See Hunter, Evan

Collins, Linda　1931- .... **CLC 44**
　　See also CA 125

Collins, (William) Wilkie
　　1824-1889 .... **NCLC 1, 18**
　　See also CDBLB 1832-1890; DLB 18, 70,
　　159

Collins, William　1721-1759 .... **LC 4**
　　See also DAM POET; DLB 109

Colman, George
　　See Glassco, John

Colt, Winchester Remington
　　See Hubbard, L(afayette) Ron(ald)

Colter, Cyrus　1910- .... **CLC 58**
　　See also BW 1; CA 65-68; CANR 10;
　　DLB 33

Colton, James
　　See Hansen, Joseph

Colum, Padraic　1881-1972........ **CLC 28**
　　See also CA 73-76; 33-36R; CANR 35;
　　CLR 36; MAICYA; MTCW; SATA 15

Colvin, James
　　See Moorcock, Michael (John)

Colwin, Laurie (E.)
　　1944-1992........ **CLC 5, 13, 23, 84**
　　See also CA 89-92; 139; CANR 20, 46;
　　DLBY 80; MTCW

Comfort, Alex(ander)　1920-........ **CLC 7**
　　See also CA 1-4R; CANR 1, 45; DAM POP

Comfort, Montgomery
　　See Campbell, (John) Ramsey

Compton-Burnett, I(vy)
　　1884(?)-1969 ...... **CLC 1, 3, 10, 15, 34**
　　See also CA 1-4R; 25-28R; CANR 4;
　　DAM NOV; DLB 36; MTCW

Comstock, Anthony　1844-1915 .... **TCLC 13**
　　See also CA 110

Conan Doyle, Arthur
　　See Doyle, Arthur Conan

Conde, Maryse　1937-............. **CLC 52**
　　See also Boucolon, Maryse
　　See also BW 2; DAM MULT

Condillac, Etienne Bonnot de
　　1714-1780 .... **LC 26**

Condon, Richard (Thomas)
　　1915- .... **CLC 4, 6, 8, 10, 45**
　　See also BEST 90:3; CA 1-4R; CAAS 1;
　　CANR 2, 23; DAM NOV;
　　INT CANR-23; MTCW

Congreve, William
　　1670-1729 .... **LC 5, 21; DA; DAB;**
　　　　　　　　　　　DAC; DC 2; WLC
　　See also CDBLB 1660-1789; DAM DRAM,
　　MST, POET; DLB 39, 84

Connell, Evan S(helby), Jr.
　　1924- .... **CLC 4, 6, 45**
　　See also AAYA 7; CA 1-4R; CAAS 2;
　　CANR 2, 39; DAM NOV; DLB 2;
　　DLBY 81; MTCW

Connelly, Marc(us Cook)
　　1890-1980 .... **CLC 7**
　　See also CA 85-88; 102; CANR 30; DLB 7;
　　DLBY 80; SATA-Obit 25

Connor, Ralph .... **TCLC 31**
　　See also Gordon, Charles William
　　See also DLB 92

Conrad, Joseph
　　1857-1924 .... **TCLC 1, 6, 13, 25, 43, 57;**
　　　　　　　　　　DA; DAB; DAC; SSC 9; WLC
　　See also CA 104; 131; CDBLB 1890-1914;
　　DAM MST, NOV; DLB 10, 34, 98, 156;
　　MTCW; SATA 27

Conrad, Robert Arnold
See Hart, Moss

Conroy, Pat 1945-............. CLC 30, 74
See also AAYA 8; AITN 1; CA 85-88;
CANR 24; DAM NOV, POP; DLB 6;
MTCW

Constant (de Rebecque), (Henri) Benjamin
1767-1830 .... NCLC 6
See also DLB 119

Conybeare, Charles Augustus
See Eliot, T(homas) S(tearns)

Cook, Michael 1933- .... CLC 58
See also CA 93-96; DLB 53

Cook, Robin 1940- .... CLC 14
See also BEST 90:2; CA 108; 111;
CANR 41; DAM POP; INT 111

Cook, Roy
See Silverberg, Robert

Cooke, Elizabeth 1948- .... CLC 55
See also CA 129

Cooke, John Esten 1830-1886 ..... NCLC 5
See also DLB 3

Cooke, John Estes
See Baum, L(yman) Frank

Cooke, M. E.
See Creasey, John

Cooke, Margaret
See Creasey, John

Cooney, Ray .... CLC 62

Cooper, Douglas 1960- .... CLC 86

Cooper, Henry St. John
Scc Creasey, John

Cooper, J. California .... CLC 56
See also AAYA 12; BW 1; CA 125;
DAM MULT

Cooper, James Fenimore
1789-1851 .... NCLC 1, 27
See also CDALB 1640-1865; DLB 3;
SATA 19

Coover, Robert (Lowell)
1932- .. CLC 3, 7, 15, 32, 46, 87; SSC 15
See also CA 45-48; CANR 3, 37;
DAM NOV; DLB 2; DLBY 81; MTCW

Copeland, Stewart (Armstrong)
1952- .... CLC 26

Coppard, A(lfred) E(dgar)
1878-1957 .... TCLC 5; SSC 21
See also CA 114; YABC 1

Coppee, Francois 1842-1908 ...... TCLC 25

Coppola, Francis Ford 1939-....... CLC 16
See also CA 77-80; CANR 40; DLB 44

Corbiere, Tristan 1845-1875 ..... NCLC 43

Corcoran, Barbara 1911-.......... CLC 17
See also AAYA 14; CA 21-24R; CAAS 2;
CANR 11, 28, 48; DLB 52; JRDA;
SAAS 20; SATA 3, 77

Cordelier, Maurice
See Giraudoux, (Hippolyte) Jean

Corelli, Marie 1855-1924......... TCLC 51
See also Mackay, Mary
See also DLB 34, 156

Corman, Cid .... CLC 9
See also Corman, Sidney
See also CAAS 2; DLB 5

Corman, Sidney 1924-
See Corman, Cid
See also CA 85-88; CANR 44; DAM POET

Cormier, Robert (Edmund)
1925- ..... CLC 12, 30; DA; DAB; DAC
See also AAYA 3; CA 1-4R; CANR 5, 23;
CDALB 1968-1988; CLR 12; DAM MST,
NOV; DLB 52; INT CANR-23; JRDA;
MAICYA; MTCW; SATA 10, 45, 83

Corn, Alfred (DeWitt III) 1943-.... CLC 33
See also CA 104; CANR 44; DLB 120;
DLBY 80

Corneille, Pierre 1606-1684.... LC 28; DAB
See also DAM MST

Cornwell, David (John Moore)
1931- .... CLC 9, 15
See also le Carre, John
See also CA 5-8R; CANR 13, 33;
DAM POP; MTCW

Corso, (Nunzio) Gregory 1930-... CLC 1, 11
See also CA 5-8R; CANR 41; DLB 5, 16;
MTCW

Cortazar, Julio
1914-1984 ...... CLC 2, 3, 5, 10, 13, 15,
33, 34; HLC; SSC 7
See also CA 21-24R; CANR 12, 32;
DAM MULT, NOV; DLB 113; HW;
MTCW

CORTES, HERNAN 1484-1547..... LC 31

Corwin, Cecil
See Kornbluth, C(yril) M.

Cosic, Dobrica 1921- .... CLC 14
See also CA 122; 138

Costain, Thomas B(ertram)
1885-1965 .... CLC 30
See also CA 5-8R; 25-28R; DLB 9

Costantini, Humberto
1924(?)-1987 .... CLC 49
See also CA 131; 122; HW

Costello, Elvis 1955-.............. CLC 21

Cotter, Joseph Seamon Sr.
1861-1949 .... TCLC 28; BLC
See also BW 1; CA 124; DAM MULT;
DLB 50

Couch, Arthur Thomas Quiller
See Quiller-Couch, Arthur Thomas

Coulton, James
See Hansen, Joseph

Couperus, Louis (Marie Anne)
1863-1923 .... TCLC 15
See also CA 115

Coupland, Douglas 1961-..... CLC 85; DAC
See also CA 142; DAM POP

Court, Wesli
See Turco, Lewis (Putnam)

Courtenay, Bryce 1933-........... CLC 59
See also CA 138

Courtney, Robert
See Ellison, Harlan (Jay)

Cousteau, Jacques-Yves 1910-...... CLC 30
See also CA 65-68; CANR 15; MTCW;
SATA 38

Coward, Noel (Peirce)
1899-1973 .... CLC 1, 9, 29, 51
See also AITN 1; CA 17-18; 41-44R;
CANR 35; CAP 2; CDBLB 1914-1945;
DAM DRAM; DLB 10; MTCW

Cowley, Malcolm 1898-1989 ...... CLC 39
See also CA 5-8R; 128; CANR 3; DLB 4,
48; DLBY 81, 89; MTCW

Cowper, William 1731-1800....... NCLC 8
See also DAM POET; DLB 104, 109

Cox, William Trevor 1928- ... CLC 9, 14, 71
See also Trevor, William
See also CA 9-12R; CANR 4, 37;
DAM NOV; DLB 14; INT CANR-37;
MTCW

Coyne, P. J.
See Masters, Hilary

Cozzens, James Gould
1903-1978 .... CLC 1, 4, 11
See also CA 9-12R; 81-84; CANR 19;
CDALB 1941-1968; DLB 9; DLBD 2;
DLBY 84; MTCW

Crabbe, George 1754-1832....... NCLC 26
See also DLB 93

Craig, A. A.
See Anderson, Poul (William)

Craik, Dinah Maria (Mulock)
1826-1887 .... NCLC 38
See also DLB 35; MAICYA; SATA 34

Cram, Ralph Adams 1863-1942.... TCLC 45

Crane, (Harold) Hart
1899-1932 .... TCLC 2, 5; DA; DAB;
DAC; PC 3; WLC
See also CA 104; 127; CDALB 1917-1929;
DAM MST, POET; DLB 4, 48; MTCW

Crane, R(onald) S(almon)
1886-1967 .... CLC 27
See also CA 85-88; DLB 63

Crane, Stephen (Townley)
1871-1900 .... TCLC 11, 17, 32; DA;
DAB; DAC; SSC 7; WLC
See also CA 109; 140; CDALB 1865-1917;
DAM MST, NOV, POET; DLB 12, 54,
78; YABC 2

Crase, Douglas 1944-............. CLC 58
See also CA 106

Crashaw, Richard 1612(?)-1649...... LC 24
See also DLB 126

Craven, Margaret
1901-1980 .... CLC 17; DAC
See also CA 103

Crawford, F(rancis) Marion
1854-1909 .... TCLC 10
See also CA 107; DLB 71

Crawford, Isabella Valancy
1850-1887 .... NCLC 12
See also DLB 92

Crayon, Geoffrey
See Irving, Washington

Creasey, John 1908-1973.......... CLC 11
See also CA 5-8R; 41-44R; CANR 8;
DLB 77; MTCW

Crebillon, Claude Prosper Jolyot de (fils)
1707-1777 .... LC 28

Credo
See Creasey, John

Creeley, Robert (White)
1926- ..... **CLC 1, 2, 4, 8, 11, 15, 36, 78**
See also CA 1-4R; CAAS 10; CANR 23, 43;
DAM POET; DLB 5, 16; MTCW

Crews, Harry (Eugene)
1935- .... **CLC 6, 23, 49**
See also AITN 1; CA 25-28R; CANR 20;
DLB 6, 143; MTCW

Crichton, (John) Michael
1942- .... **CLC 2, 6, 54, 90**
See also AAYA 10; AITN 2; CA 25-28R;
CANR 13, 40; DAM NOV, POP;
DLBY 81; INT CANR-13; JRDA;
MTCW; SATA 9

Crispin, Edmund .... **CLC 22**
See also Montgomery, (Robert) Bruce
See also DLB 87

Cristofer, Michael 1945(?)- .... **CLC 28**
See also CA 110; DAM DRAM; DLB 7

Croce, Benedetto 1866-1952 ...... **TCLC 37**
See also CA 120

Crockett, David 1786-1836 .... **NCLC 8**
See also DLB 3, 11

Crockett, Davy
See Crockett, David

Crofts, Freeman Wills
1879-1957 .... **TCLC 55**
See also CA 115; DLB 77

Croker, John Wilson 1780-1857 .. **NCLC 10**
See also DLB 110

Crommelynck, Fernand 1885-1970 .. **CLC 75**
See also CA 89-92

Cronin, A(rchibald) J(oseph)
1896-1981 .... **CLC 32**
See also CA 1-4R; 102; CANR 5; SATA 47;
SATA-Obit 25

Cross, Amanda
See Heilbrun, Carolyn G(old)

Crothers, Rachel 1878(?)-1958..... **TCLC 19**
See also CA 113; DLB 7

Croves, Hal
See Traven, B.

Crowfield, Christopher
See Stowe, Harriet (Elizabeth) Beecher

Crowley, Aleister................. **TCLC 7**
See also Crowley, Edward Alexander

Crowley, Edward Alexander 1875-1947
See Crowley, Aleister
See also CA 104

Crowley, John 1942-.............. **CLC 57**
See also CA 61-64; CANR 43; DLBY 82;
SATA 65

Crud
See Crumb, R(obert)

Crumarums
See Crumb, R(obert)

Crumb, R(obert) 1943-............. **CLC 17**
See also CA 106

Crumbum
See Crumb, R(obert)

Crumski
See Crumb, R(obert)

Crum the Bum
See Crumb, R(obert)

Crunk
See Crumb, R(obert)

Crustt
See Crumb, R(obert)

Cryer, Gretchen (Kiger) 1935-...... **CLC 21**
See also CA 114; 123

Csath, Geza 1887-1919.......... **TCLC 13**
See also CA 111

Cudlip, David 1933- .... **CLC 34**

Cullen, Countee
1903-1946 ...... **TCLC 4, 37; BLC; DA;**
DAC
See also BW 1; CA 108; 124;
CDALB 1917-1929; DAM MST, MULT,
POET; DLB 4, 48, 51; MTCW; SATA 18

Cum, R.
See Crumb, R(obert)

Cummings, Bruce F(rederick) 1889-1919
See Barbellion, W. N. P.
See also CA 123

Cummings, E(dward) E(stlin)
1894-1962 ...... **CLC 1, 3, 8, 12, 15, 68;**
DA; DAB; DAC; PC 5; WLC 2
See also CA 73-76; CANR 31;
CDALB 1929-1941; DAM MST, POET;
DLB 4, 48; MTCW

Cunha, Euclides (Rodrigues Pimenta) da
1866-1909 .... **TCLC 24**
See also CA 123

Cunningham, E. V.
See Fast, Howard (Melvin)

Cunningham, J(ames) V(incent)
1911-1985 .... **CLC 3, 31**
See also CA 1-4R; 115; CANR 1; DLB 5

Cunningham, Julia (Woolfolk)
1916- .... **CLC 12**
See also CA 9-12R; CANR 4, 19, 36;
JRDA; MAICYA; SAAS 2; SATA 1, 26

Cunningham, Michael 1952- .... **CLC 34**
See also CA 136

Cunninghame Graham, R(obert) B(ontine)
1852-1936 .... **TCLC 19**
See also Graham, R(obert) B(ontine)
Cunninghame
See also CA 119; DLB 98

Currie, Ellen 19(?)-............... **CLC 44**

Curtin, Philip
See Lowndes, Marie Adelaide (Belloc)

Curtis, Price
See Ellison, Harlan (Jay)

Cutrate, Joe
See Spiegelman, Art

Czaczkes, Shmuel Yosef
See Agnon, S(hmuel) Y(osef Halevi)

Dabrowska, Maria (Szumska)
1889-1965 .... **CLC 15**
See also CA 106

Dabydeen, David 1955- .... **CLC 34**
See also BW 1; CA 125

Dacey, Philip 1939- .... **CLC 51**
See also CA 37-40R; CAAS 17; CANR 14,
32; DLB 105

Dagerman, Stig (Halvard)
1923-1954 .... **TCLC 17**
See also CA 117

Dahl, Roald
1916-1990 ...... **CLC 1, 6, 18, 79; DAB;**
DAC
See also AAYA 15; CA 1-4R; 133;
CANR 6, 32, 37; CLR 1, 7; DAM MST,
NOV, POP; DLB 139; JRDA; MAICYA;
MTCW; SATA 1, 26, 73; SATA-Obit 65

Dahlberg, Edward 1900-1977... **CLC 1, 7, 14**
See also CA 9-12R; 69-72; CANR 31;
DLB 48; MTCW

Dale, Colin...................... **TCLC 18**
See also Lawrence, T(homas) E(dward)

Dale, George E.
See Asimov, Isaac

Daly, Elizabeth 1878-1967........ **CLC 52**
See also CA 23-24; 25-28R; CAP 2

Daly, Maureen 1921-.............. **CLC 17**
See also AAYA 5; CANR 37; JRDA;
MAICYA; SAAS 1; SATA 2

Damas, Leon-Gontran 1912-1978 ... **CLC 84**
See also BW 1; CA 125; 73-76

Dana, Richard Henry Sr.
1787-1879 .... **NCLC 53**

Daniel, Samuel 1562(?)-1619........ **LC 24**
See also DLB 62

Daniels, Brett
See Adler, Renata

Dannay, Frederic 1905-1982 .... **CLC 11**
See also Queen, Ellery
See also CA 1-4R; 107; CANR 1, 39;
DAM POP; DLB 137; MTCW

D'Annunzio, Gabriele
1863-1938 .... **TCLC 6, 40**
See also CA 104

d'Antibes, Germain
See Simenon, Georges (Jacques Christian)

Danvers, Dennis 1947-............ **CLC 70**

Danziger, Paula 1944- .... **CLC 21**
See also AAYA 4; CA 112; 115; CANR 37;
CLR 20; JRDA; MAICYA; SATA 36,
63; SATA-Brief 30

Da Ponte, Lorenzo 1749-1838.... **NCLC 50**

Dario, Ruben 1867-1916 .... **TCLC 4; HLC**
See also CA 131; DAM MULT; HW;
MTCW

Darley, George 1795-1846........ **NCLC 2**
See also DLB 96

Daryush, Elizabeth 1887-1977.... **CLC 6, 19**
See also CA 49-52; CANR 3; DLB 20

Dashwood, Edmee Elizabeth Monica de la
Pasture 1890-1943
See Delafield, E. M.
See also CA 119

Daudet, (Louis Marie) Alphonse
1840-1897 .... **NCLC 1**
See also DLB 123

Daumal, Rene 1908-1944........ **TCLC 14**
See also CA 114

Davenport, Guy (Mattison, Jr.)
1927- .... **CLC 6, 14, 38; SSC 16**
See also CA 33-36R; CANR 23; DLB 130

Denby, Edwin (Orr) 1903-1983 ..... **CLC 48**
See also CA 138; 110

Denis, Julio
See Cortazar, Julio

Denmark, Harrison
See Zelazny, Roger (Joseph)

Dennis, John 1658-1734 .... **LC 11**
See also DLB 101

Dennis, Nigel (Forbes) 1912-1989 .... **CLC 8**
See also CA 25-28R; 129; DLB 13, 15;
MTCW

De Palma, Brian (Russell) 1940- .... **CLC 20**
See also CA 109

De Quincey, Thomas 1785-1859 ... **NCLC 4**
See also CDBLB 1789-1832; DLB 110; 144

Deren, Eleanora 1908(?)-1961
See Deren, Maya
See also CA 111

Deren, Maya .... **CLC 16**
See also Deren, Eleanora

Derleth, August (William)
1909-1971 .... **CLC 31**
See also CA 1-4R; 29-32R; CANR 4;
DLB 9; SATA 5

Der Nister 1884-1950 .... **TCLC 56**

de Routisie, Albert
See Aragon, Louis

Derrida, Jacques 1930- .... **CLC 24, 87**
See also CA 124; 127

Derry Down Derry
See Lear, Edward

Dersonnes, Jacques
See Simenon, Georges (Jacques Christian)

Desai, Anita 1937- ...... **CLC 19, 37; DAB**
See also CA 81-84; CANR 33; DAM NOV;
MTCW; SATA 63

de Saint-Luc, Jean
See Glassco, John

de Saint Roman, Arnaud
See Aragon, Louis

Descartes, Rene 1596-1650 .... **LC 20**

De Sica, Vittorio 1901(?)-1974 ..... **CLC 20**
See also CA 117

Desnos, Robert 1900-1945 .... **TCLC 22**
See also CA 121

Destouches, Louis-Ferdinand
1894-1961 .... **CLC 9, 15**
See also Celine, Louis-Ferdinand
See also CA 85-88; CANR 28; MTCW

Deutsch, Babette 1895-1982 .... **CLC 18**
See also CA 1-4R; 108; CANR 4; DLB 45;
SATA 1; SATA-Obit 33

Devenant, William 1606-1649 .... **LC 13**

Devkota, Laxmiprasad
1909-1959 .... **TCLC 23**
See also CA 123

De Voto, Bernard (Augustine)
1897-1955 .... **TCLC 29**
See also CA 113; DLB 9

De Vries, Peter
1910-1993 .... **CLC 1, 2, 3, 7, 10, 28, 46**
See also CA 17-20R; 142; CANR 41;
DAM NOV; DLB 6; DLBY 82; MTCW

Dexter, Martin
See Faust, Frederick (Schiller)

Dexter, Pete 1943- .... **CLC 34, 55**
See also BEST 89:2; CA 127; 131;
DAM POP; INT 131; MTCW

Diamano, Silmang
See Senghor, Leopold Sedar

Diamond, Neil 1941- .... **CLC 30**
See also CA 108

Diaz del Castillo, Bernal 1496-1584 .. **LC 31**

di Bassetto, Corno
See Shaw, George Bernard

Dick, Philip K(indred)
1928-1982 .... **CLC 10, 30, 72**
See also CA 49-52; 106; CANR 2, 16;
DAM NOV, POP; DLB 8; MTCW

Dickens, Charles (John Huffam)
1812-1870 ...... **NCLC 3, 8, 18, 26, 37,
50; DA; DAB; DAC; SSC 17; WLC**
See also CDBLB 1832-1890; DAM MST,
NOV; DLB 21, 55, 70, 159; JRDA;
MAICYA; SATA 15

Dickey, James (Lafayette)
1923- .... **CLC 1, 2, 4, 7, 10, 15, 47**
See also AITN 1, 2; CA 9-12R; CABS 2;
CANR 10, 48; CDALB 1968-1988;
DAM NOV, POET, POP; DLB 5;
DLBD 7; DLBY 82, 93; INT CANR-10;
MTCW

Dickey, William 1928-1994 ...... **CLC 3, 28**
See also CA 9-12R; 145; CANR 24; DLB 5

Dickinson, Charles 1951- .... **CLC 49**
See also CA 128

Dickinson, Emily (Elizabeth)
1830-1886 .... **NCLC 21; DA; DAB;
DAC; PC 1; WLC**
See also CDALB 1865-1917; DAM MST,
POET; DLB 1; SATA 29

Dickinson, Peter (Malcolm)
1927- .... **CLC 12, 35**
See also AAYA 9; CA 41-44R; CANR 31;
CLR 29; DLB 87, 161; JRDA; MAICYA;
SATA 5, 62

Dickson, Carr
See Carr, John Dickson

Dickson, Carter
See Carr, John Dickson

Diderot, Denis 1713-1784 .... **LC 26**

Didion, Joan 1934- ..... **CLC 1, 3, 8, 14, 32**
See also AITN 1; CA 5-8R; CANR 14;
CDALB 1968-1988; DAM NOV; DLB 2;
DLBY 81, 86; MTCW

Dietrich, Robert
See Hunt, E(verette) Howard, (Jr.)

Dillard, Annie 1945- .... **CLC 9, 60**
See also AAYA 6; CA 49-52; CANR 3, 43;
DAM NOV; DLBY 80; MTCW;
SATA 10

Dillard, R(ichard) H(enry) W(ilde)
1937- .... **CLC 5**
See also CA 21-24R; CAAS 7; CANR 10;
DLB 5

Dillon, Eilis 1920-1994 .... **CLC 17**
See also CA 9-12R; 147; CAAS 3; CANR 4,
38; CLR 26; MAICYA; SATA 2, 74;
SATA-Obit 83

Dimont, Penelope
See Mortimer, Penelope (Ruth)

Dinesen, Isak .... **CLC 10, 29; SSC 7**
See also Blixen, Karen (Christentze
Dinesen)

Ding Ling .... **CLC 68**
See also Chiang Pin-chin

Disch, Thomas M(ichael) 1940- ... **CLC 7, 36**
See also AAYA 17; CA 21-24R; CAAS 4;
CANR 17, 36; CLR 18; DLB 8;
MAICYA; MTCW; SAAS 15; SATA 54

Disch, Tom
See Disch, Thomas M(ichael)

d'Isly, Georges
See Simenon, Georges (Jacques Christian)

Disraeli, Benjamin 1804-1881 .. **NCLC 2, 39**
See also DLB 21, 55

Ditcum, Steve
See Crumb, R(obert)

Dixon, Paige
See Corcoran, Barbara

Dixon, Stephen 1936- ..... **CLC 52; SSC 16**
See also CA 89-92; CANR 17, 40; DLB 130

Dobell, Sydney Thompson
1824-1874 .... **NCLC 43**
See also DLB 32

Doblin, Alfred .... **TCLC 13**
See also Doeblin, Alfred

Dobrolyubov, Nikolai Alexandrovich
1836-1861 .... **NCLC 5**

Dobyns, Stephen 1941- .... **CLC 37**
See also CA 45-48; CANR 2, 18

Doctorow, E(dgar) L(aurence)
1931- .... **CLC 6, 11, 15, 18, 37, 44, 65**
See also AITN 2; BEST 89:3; CA 45-48;
CANR 2, 33; CDALB 1968-1988;
DAM NOV, POP; DLB 2, 28; DLBY 80;
MTCW

Dodgson, Charles Lutwidge 1832-1898
See Carroll, Lewis
See also CLR 2; DA; DAB; DAC;
DAM MST, NOV, POET; MAICYA;
YABC 2

Dodson, Owen (Vincent)
1914-1983 .... **CLC 79; BLC**
See also BW 1; CA 65-68; 110; CANR 24;
DAM MULT; DLB 76

Doeblin, Alfred 1878-1957 .... **TCLC 13**
See also Doblin, Alfred
See also CA 110; 141; DLB 66

Doerr, Harriet 1910- .... **CLC 34**
See also CA 117; 122; CANR 47; INT 122

Domecq, H(onorio) Bustos
See Bioy Casares, Adolfo; Borges, Jorge
Luis

Domini, Rey
See Lorde, Audre (Geraldine)

Dominique
See Proust, (Valentin-Louis-George-Eugene-)
Marcel

Don, A
See Stephen, Leslie

Donaldson, Stephen R. 1947- .... **CLC 46**
See also CA 89-92; CANR 13; DAM POP;
INT CANR-13

Donleavy, J(ames) P(atrick)
1926- . . . . **CLC 1, 4, 6, 10, 45**
See also AITN 2; CA 9-12R; CANR 24, 49;
DLB 6; INT CANR-24; MTCW

Donne, John
1572-1631 . . . . **LC 10, 24; DA; DAB;**
DAC; PC 1
See also CDBLB Before 1660; DAM MST,
POET; DLB 121, 151

Donnell, David 1939(?)- . . . . **CLC 34**

Donoghue, P. S.
See Hunt, E(verette) Howard, (Jr.)

Donoso (Yanez), Jose
1924- . . . . **CLC 4, 8, 11, 32; HLC**
See also CA 81-84; CANR 32;
DAM MULT; DLB 113; HW; MTCW

Donovan, John 1928-1992 . . . . **CLC 35**
See also CA 97-100; 137; CLR 3;
MAICYA; SATA 72; SATA-Brief 29

Don Roberto
See Cunninghame Graham, R(obert)
B(ontine)

Doolittle, Hilda
1886-1961 . . . . . **CLC 3, 8, 14, 31, 34, 73;**
DA; DAC; PC 5; WLC
See also H. D.
See also CA 97-100; CANR 35; DAM MST,
POET; DLB 4, 45; MTCW

Dorfman, Ariel 1942- . . . . **CLC 48, 77; HLC**
See also CA 124; 130; DAM MULT; HW;
INT 130

Dorn, Edward (Merton) 1929- . . . **CLC 10, 18**
See also CA 93-96; CANR 42; DLB 5;
INT 93-96

Dorsan, Luc
See Simenon, Georges (Jacques Christian)

Dorsange, Jean
See Simenon, Georges (Jacques Christian)

Dos Passos, John (Roderigo)
1896-1970 . . . . . . **CLC 1, 4, 8, 11, 15, 25,**
34, 82; DA; DAB; DAC; WLC
See also CA 1-4R; 29-32R; CANR 3;
CDALB 1929-1941; DAM MST, NOV;
DLB 4, 9; DLBD 1; MTCW

Dossage, Jean
See Simenon, Georges (Jacques Christian)

Dostoevsky, Fedor Mikhailovich
1821-1881 . . . . . . **NCLC 2, 7, 21, 33, 43;**
DA; DAB; DAC; SSC 2; WLC
See also DAM MST, NOV

Doughty, Charles M(ontagu)
1843-1926 . . . . **TCLC 27**
See also CA 115; DLB 19, 57

Douglas, Ellen . . . . **CLC 73**
See also Haxton, Josephine Ayres;
Williamson, Ellen Douglas

Douglas, Gavin 1475(?)-1522 . . . . **LC 20**

Douglas, Keith 1920-1944 . . . . **TCLC 40**
See also DLB 27

Douglas, Leonard
See Bradbury, Ray (Douglas)

Douglas, Michael
See Crichton, (John) Michael

Douglass, Frederick
1817(?)-1895 . . . . . . **NCLC 7; BLC; DA;**
DAC; WLC
See also CDALB 1640-1865; DAM MST,
MULT; DLB 1, 43, 50, 79; SATA 29

Dourado, (Waldomiro Freitas) Autran
1926- . . . . **CLC 23, 60**
See also CA 25-28R; CANR 34

Dourado, Waldomiro Autran
See Dourado, (Waldomiro Freitas) Autran

Dove, Rita (Frances)
1952- . . . . **CLC 50, 81; PC 6**
See also BW 2; CA 109; CAAS 19;
CANR 27, 42; DAM MULT, POET;
DLB 120

Dowell, Coleman 1925-1985 . . . . **CLC 60**
See also CA 25-28R; 117; CANR 10;
DLB 130

Dowson, Ernest Christopher
1867-1900 . . . . **TCLC 4**
See also CA 105; DLB 19, 135

Doyle, A. Conan
See Doyle, Arthur Conan

Doyle, Arthur Conan
1859-1930 . . . . **TCLC 7; DA; DAB;**
DAC; SSC 12; WLC
See also AAYA 14; CA 104; 122;
CDBLB 1890-1914; DAM MST, NOV;
DLB 18, 70, 156; MTCW; SATA 24

Doyle, Conan
See Doyle, Arthur Conan

Doyle, John
See Graves, Robert (von Ranke)

Doyle, Roddy 1958(?)- . . . . **CLC 81**
See also AAYA 14; CA 143

Doyle, Sir A. Conan
See Doyle, Arthur Conan

Doyle, Sir Arthur Conan
See Doyle, Arthur Conan

Dr. A
See Asimov, Isaac; Silverstein, Alvin

Drabble, Margaret
1939- . . . . **CLC 2, 3, 5, 8, 10, 22, 53;**
DAB; DAC
See also CA 13-16R; CANR 18, 35;
CDBLB 1960 to Present; DAM MST,
NOV, POP; DLB 14, 155; MTCW;
SATA 48

Drapier, M. B.
See Swift, Jonathan

Drayham, James
See Mencken, H(enry) L(ouis)

Drayton, Michael 1563-1631 . . . . **LC 8**

Dreadstone, Carl
See Campbell, (John) Ramsey

Dreiser, Theodore (Herman Albert)
1871-1945 . . . . **TCLC 10, 18, 35; DA;**
DAC; WLC
See also CA 106; 132; CDALB 1865-1917;
DAM MST, NOV; DLB 9, 12, 102, 137;
DLBD 1; MTCW

Drexler, Rosalyn 1926- . . . . **CLC 2, 6**
See also CA 81-84

Dreyer, Carl Theodor 1889-1968 . . . . **CLC 16**
See also CA 116

Drieu la Rochelle, Pierre(-Eugene)
1893-1945 . . . . **TCLC 21**
See also CA 117; DLB 72

Drinkwater, John 1882-1937 . . . . . **TCLC 57**
See also CA 109; 149; DLB 10, 19, 149

Drop Shot
See Cable, George Washington

Droste-Hulshoff, Annette Freiin von
1797-1848 . . . . **NCLC 3**
See also DLB 133

Drummond, Walter
See Silverberg, Robert

Drummond, William Henry
1854-1907 . . . . **TCLC 25**
See also DLB 92

Drummond de Andrade, Carlos
1902-1987 . . . . **CLC 18**
See also Andrade, Carlos Drummond de
See also CA 132; 123

Drury, Allen (Stuart) 1918- . . . . **CLC 37**
See also CA 57-60; CANR 18;
INT CANR-18

Dryden, John
1631-1700 . . . . **LC 3, 21; DA; DAB;**
DAC; DC 3; WLC
See also CDBLB 1660-1789; DAM DRAM,
MST, POET; DLB 80, 101, 131

Duberman, Martin 1930- . . . . **CLC 8**
See also CA 1-4R; CANR 2

Dubie, Norman (Evans) 1945- . . . . . . **CLC 36**
See also CA 69-72; CANR 12; DLB 120

Du Bois, W(illiam) E(dward) B(urghardt)
1868-1963 . . . . . . **CLC 1, 2, 13, 64; BLC;**
DA; DAC; WLC
See also BW 1; CA 85-88; CANR 34;
CDALB 1865-1917; DAM MST, MULT,
NOV; DLB 47, 50, 91; MTCW; SATA 42

Dubus, Andre 1936- . . . **CLC 13, 36; SSC 15**
See also CA 21-24R; CANR 17; DLB 130;
INT CANR-17

Duca Minimo
See D'Annunzio, Gabriele

Ducharme, Rejean 1941- . . . . **CLC 74**
See also DLB 60

Duclos, Charles Pinot 1704-1772 . . . . . **LC 1**

Dudek, Louis 1918- . . . . **CLC 11, 19**
See also CA 45-48; CAAS 14; CANR 1;
DLB 88

Duerrenmatt, Friedrich
1921-1990 . . . . . . **CLC 1, 4, 8, 11, 15, 43**
See also CA 17-20R; CANR 33;
DAM DRAM; DLB 69, 124; MTCW

Duffy, Bruce (?)- . . . . **CLC 50**

Duffy, Maureen 1933- . . . . **CLC 37**
See also CA 25-28R; CANR 33; DLB 14;
MTCW

Dugan, Alan 1923- . . . . **CLC 2, 6**
See also CA 81-84; DLB 5

du Gard, Roger Martin
See Martin du Gard, Roger

Duhamel, Georges 1884-1966 . . . . **CLC 8**
See also CA 81-84; 25-28R; CANR 35;
DLB 65; MTCW

Author Index

Author Index

Forster, E(dward) M(organ)
1879-1970 ..... **CLC 1, 2, 3, 4, 9, 10, 13, 15, 22, 45, 77; DA; DAB; DAC; WLC**
See also AAYA 2; CA 13-14; 25-28R; CANR 45; CAP 1; CDBLB 1914-1945; DAM MST, NOV; DLB 34, 98; DLBD 10; MTCW; SATA 57

Forster, John 1812-1876 .... **NCLC 11**
See also DLB 144

Forsyth, Frederick 1938-...... **CLC 2, 5, 36**
See also BEST 89:4; CA 85-88; CANR 38; DAM NOV, POP; DLB 87; MTCW

Forten, Charlotte L. .... **TCLC 16; BLC**
See also Grimke, Charlotte L(ottie) Forten
See also DLB 50

Foscolo, Ugo 1778-1827.......... **NCLC 8**

Fosse, Bob .... **CLC 20**
See also Fosse, Robert Louis

Fosse, Robert Louis 1927-1987
See Fosse, Bob
See also CA 110; 123

Foster, Stephen Collins
1826-1864 .... **NCLC 26**

Foucault, Michel
1926-1984 .... **CLC 31, 34, 69**
See also CA 105; 113; CANR 34; MTCW

Fouque, Friedrich (Heinrich Karl) de la Motte
1777-1843 .... **NCLC 2**
See also DLB 90

Fourier, Charles 1772-1837 ...... **NCLC 51**

Fournier, Henri Alban 1886-1914
See Alain-Fournier
See also CA 104

Fournier, Pierre 1916-............ **CLC 11**
See also Gascar, Pierre
See also CA 89-92; CANR 16, 40

Fowles, John
1926- ...... **CLC 1, 2, 3, 4, 6, 9, 10, 15, 33, 87; DAB; DAC**
See also CA 5-8R; CANR 25; CDBLB 1960 to Present; DAM MST; DLB 14, 139; MTCW; SATA 22

Fox, Paula 1923-................ **CLC 2, 8**
See also AAYA 3; CA 73-76; CANR 20, 36; CLR 1; DLB 52; JRDA; MAICYA; MTCW; SATA 17, 60

Fox, William Price (Jr.) 1926- ..... **CLC 22**
See also CA 17-20R; CAAS 19; CANR 11; DLB 2; DLBY 81

Foxe, John 1516(?)-1587 .... **LC 14**

Frame, Janet .... **CLC 2, 3, 6, 22, 66**
See also Clutha, Janet Paterson Frame

France, Anatole................... **TCLC 9**
See also Thibault, Jacques Anatole Francois
See also DLB 123

Francis, Claude 19(?)- .... **CLC 50**

Francis, Dick 1920- .... **CLC 2, 22, 42**
See also AAYA 5; BEST 89:3; CA 5-8R; CANR 9, 42; CDBLB 1960 to Present; DAM POP; DLB 87; INT CANR-9; MTCW

Francis, Robert (Churchill)
1901-1987 .... **CLC 15**
See also CA 1-4R; 123; CANR 1

Frank, Anne(lies Marie)
1929-1945 .... **TCLC 17; DA; DAB; DAC; WLC**
See also AAYA 12; CA 113; 133; DAM MST; MTCW; SATA-Brief 42

Frank, Elizabeth 1945-........... **CLC 39**
See also CA 121; 126; INT 126

Franklin, Benjamin
See Hasek, Jaroslav (Matej Frantisek)

Franklin, Benjamin
1706-1790 ..... **LC 25; DA; DAB; DAC**
See also CDALB 1640-1865; DAM MST; DLB 24, 43, 73

Franklin, (Stella Maraia Sarah) Miles
1879-1954 .... **TCLC 7**
See also CA 104

Fraser, (Lady) Antonia (Pakenham)
1932-....................... **CLC 32**
See also CA 85-88; CANR 44; MTCW; SATA-Brief 32

Fraser, George MacDonald 1925-.... **CLC 7**
See also CA 45-48; CANR 2, 48

Fraser, Sylvia 1935-.............. **CLC 64**
See also CA 45-48; CANR 1, 16

Frayn, Michael 1933-...... **CLC 3, 7, 31, 47**
See also CA 5-8R; CANR 30; DAM DRAM, NOV; DLB 13, 14; MTCW

Fraze, Candida (Merrill) 1945-..... **CLC 50**
See also CA 126

Frazer, J(ames) G(eorge)
1854-1941 .... **TCLC 32**
See also CA 118

Frazer, Robert Caine
See Creasey, John

Frazer, Sir James George
See Frazer, J(ames) G(eorge)

Frazier, Ian 1951-................ **CLC 46**
See also CA 130

Frederic, Harold 1856-1898...... **NCLC 10**
See also DLB 12, 23; DLBD 13

Frederick, John
See Faust, Frederick (Schiller)

Frederick the Great 1712-1786 ...... **LC 14**

Fredro, Aleksander 1793-1876..... **NCLC 8**

Freeling, Nicolas 1927- .... **CLC 38**
See also CA 49-52; CAAS 12; CANR 1, 17, 50; DLB 87

Freeman, Douglas Southall
1886-1953 .... **TCLC 11**
See also CA 109; DLB 17

Freeman, Judith 1946-............ **CLC 55**
See also CA 148

Freeman, Mary Eleanor Wilkins
1852-1930 .... **TCLC 9; SSC 1**
See also CA 106; DLB 12, 78

Freeman, R(ichard) Austin
1862-1943 .... **TCLC 21**
See also CA 113; DLB 70

French, Albert 1943- .... **CLC 86**

French, Marilyn 1929-...... **CLC 10, 18, 60**
See also CA 69-72; CANR 3, 31; DAM DRAM, NOV, POP; INT CANR-31; MTCW

French, Paul
See Asimov, Isaac

Freneau, Philip Morin 1752-1832.. **NCLC 1**
See also DLB 37, 43

Freud, Sigmund 1856-1939 .... **TCLC 52**
See also CA 115; 133; MTCW

Friedan, Betty (Naomi) 1921-...... **CLC 74**
See also CA 65-68; CANR 18, 45; MTCW

Friedlaender, Saul 1932- .... **CLC 90**
See also CA 117; 130

Friedman, B(ernard) H(arper)
1926-.................... **CLC 7**
See also CA 1-4R; CANR 3, 48

Friedman, Bruce Jay 1930-.... **CLC 3, 5, 56**
See also CA 9-12R; CANR 25; DLB 2, 28; INT CANR-25

Friel, Brian 1929-........... **CLC 5, 42, 59**
See also CA 21-24R; CANR 33; DLB 13; MTCW

Friis-Baastad, Babbis Ellinor
1921-1970 .... **CLC 12**
See also CA 17-20R; 134; SATA 7

Frisch, Max (Rudolf)
1911-1991 ..... **CLC 3, 9, 14, 18, 32, 44**
See also CA 85-88; 134; CANR 32; DAM DRAM, NOV; DLB 69, 124; MTCW

Fromentin, Eugene (Samuel Auguste)
1820-1876 .... **NCLC 10**
See also DLB 123

Frost, Frederick
See Faust, Frederick (Schiller)

Frost, Robert (Lee)
1874-1963 .... **CLC 1, 3, 4, 9, 10, 13, 15, 26, 34, 44; DA; DAB; DAC; PC 1; WLC**
See also CA 89-92; CANR 33; CDALB 1917-1929; DAM MST, POET; DLB 54; DLBD 7; MTCW; SATA 14

Froude, James Anthony
1818-1894 .... **NCLC 43**
See also DLB 18, 57, 144

Froy, Herald
See Waterhouse, Keith (Spencer)

Fry, Christopher 1907-....... **CLC 2, 10, 14**
See also CA 17-20R; CANR 9, 30; DAM DRAM; DLB 13; MTCW; SATA 66

Frye, (Herman) Northrop
1912-1991 .... **CLC 24, 70**
See also CA 5-8R; 133; CANR 8, 37; DLB 67, 68; MTCW

Fuchs, Daniel 1909-1993 .... **CLC 8, 22**
See also CA 81-84; 142; CAAS 5; CANR 40; DLB 9, 26, 28; DLBY 93

Fuchs, Daniel 1934-.............. **CLC 34**
See also CA 37-40R; CANR 14, 48

Fuentes, Carlos
1928- ...... **CLC 3, 8, 10, 13, 22, 41, 60; DA; DAB; DAC; HLC; WLC**
See also AAYA 4; AITN 2; CA 69-72; CANR 10, 32; DAM MST, MULT, NOV; DLB 113; HW; MTCW

Fuentes, Gregorio Lopez y
See Lopez y Fuentes, Gregorio

Fugard, (Harold) Athol
1932- .... **CLC 5, 9, 14, 25, 40, 80; DC 3**
See also AAYA 17; CA 85-88; CANR 32;
DAM DRAM; MTCW

Fugard, Sheila 1932- .... **CLC 48**
See also CA 125

Fuller, Charles (H., Jr.)
1939- .... **CLC 25; BLC; DC 1**
See also BW 2; CA 108; 112;
DAM DRAM, MULT; DLB 38;
INT 112; MTCW

Fuller, John (Leopold) 1937- .... **CLC 62**
See also CA 21-24R; CANR 9, 44; DLB 40

Fuller, Margaret .... **NCLC 5, 50**
See also Ossoli, Sarah Margaret (Fuller
marchesa d')

Fuller, Roy (Broadbent)
1912-1991 .... **CLC 4, 28**
See also CA 5-8R; 135; CAAS 10; DLB 15,
20

Fulton, Alice 1952- .... **CLC 52**
See also CA 116

Furphy, Joseph 1843-1912 .... **TCLC 25**

Fussell, Paul 1924- .... **CLC 74**
See also BEST 90:1; CA 17-20R; CANR 8,
21, 35; INT CANR-21; MTCW

Futabatei, Shimei 1864-1909 ...... **TCLC 44**

Futrelle, Jacques 1875-1912 ...... **TCLC 19**
See also CA 113

Gaboriau, Emile 1835-1873 ...... **NCLC 14**

Gadda, Carlo Emilio 1893-1973 .... **CLC 11**
See also CA 89-92

Gaddis, William
1922- ..... **CLC 1, 3, 6, 8, 10, 19, 43, 86**
See also CA 17-20R; CANR 21, 48; DLB 2;
MTCW

Gaines, Ernest J(ames)
1933- .... **CLC 3, 11, 18, 86; BLC**
See also AITN 1; BW 2; CA 9-12R;
CANR 6, 24, 42; CDALB 1968-1988;
DAM MULT; DLB 2, 33, 152; DLBY 80;
MTCW

Gaitskill, Mary 1954- .... **CLC 69**
See also CA 128

Galdos, Benito Perez
See Perez Galdos, Benito

Gale, Zona 1874-1938 .... **TCLC 7**
See also CA 105; DAM DRAM; DLB 9, 78

Galeano, Eduardo (Hughes) 1940-... **CLC 72**
See also CA 29-32R; CANR 13, 32; HW

Galiano, Juan Valera y Alcala
See Valera y Alcala-Galiano, Juan

Gallagher, Tess 1943-.... **CLC 18, 63; PC 9**
See also CA 106; DAM POET; DLB 120

Gallant, Mavis
1922- ...... **CLC 7, 18, 38; DAC; SSC 5**
See also CA 69-72; CANR 29; DAM MST;
DLB 53; MTCW

Gallant, Roy A(rthur) 1924- .... **CLC 17**
See also CA 5-8R; CANR 4, 29; CLR 30;
MAICYA; SATA 4, 68

Gallico, Paul (William) 1897-1976 ... **CLC 2**
See also AITN 1; CA 5-8R; 69-72;
CANR 23; DLB 9; MAICYA; SATA 13

Gallup, Ralph
See Whitemore, Hugh (John)

Galsworthy, John
1867-1933 ...... **TCLC 1, 45; DA; DAB;**
DAC; WLC 2
See also CA 104; 141; CDBLB 1890-1914;
DAM DRAM, MST, NOV; DLB 10, 34,
98

Galt, John 1779-1839 .... **NCLC 1**
See also DLB 99, 116, 159

Galvin, James 1951-.............. **CLC 38**
See also CA 108; CANR 26

Gamboa, Federico 1864-1939 ..... **TCLC 36**

Gandhi, M. K.
See Gandhi, Mohandas Karamchand

Gandhi, Mahatma
See Gandhi, Mohandas Karamchand

Gandhi, Mohandas Karamchand
1869-1948 .... **TCLC 59**
See also CA 121; 132; DAM MULT;
MTCW

Gann, Ernest Kellogg 1910-1991.... **CLC 23**
See also AITN 1; CA 1-4R; 136; CANR 1

Garcia, Cristina 1958- .... **CLC 76**
See also CA 141

Garcia Lorca, Federico
1898-1936 ... **TCLC 1, 7, 49; DA; DAB;**
DAC; DC 2; HLC; PC 3; WLC
See also CA 104; 131; DAM DRAM, MST,
MULT, POET; DLB 108; HW; MTCW

Garcia Marquez, Gabriel (Jose)
1928- .... **CLC 2, 3, 8, 10, 15, 27, 47, 55,**
68; DA; DAB; DAC; HLC; SSC 8; WLC
See also AAYA 3; BEST 89:1, 90:4;
CA 33-36R; CANR 10, 28, 50;
DAM MST, MULT, NOV, POP;
DLB 113; HW; MTCW

Gard, Janice
See Latham, Jean Lee

Gard, Roger Martin du
See Martin du Gard, Roger

Gardam, Jane 1928-.............. **CLC 43**
See also CA 49-52; CANR 2, 18, 33;
CLR 12; DLB 14, 161; MAICYA;
MTCW; SAAS 9; SATA 39, 76;
SATA-Brief 28

Gardner, Herb.................... CLC 44

Gardner, John (Champlin), Jr.
1933-1982 ..... **CLC 2, 3, 5, 7, 8, 10, 18,**
28, 34; SSC 7
See also AITN 1; CA 65-68; 107;
CANR 33; DAM NOV, POP; DLB 2;
DLBY 82; MTCW; SATA 40;
SATA-Obit 31

Gardner, John (Edmund) 1926-..... **CLC 30**
See also CA 103; CANR 15; DAM POP;
MTCW

Gardner, Noel
See Kuttner, Henry

Gardons, S. S.
See Snodgrass, W(illiam) D(e Witt)

Garfield, Leon 1921-.............. **CLC 12**
See also AAYA 8; CA 17-20R; CANR 38,
41; CLR 21; DLB 161; JRDA; MAICYA;
SATA 1, 32, 76

Garland, (Hannibal) Hamlin
1860-1940 .... **TCLC 3; SSC 18**
See also CA 104; DLB 12, 71, 78

Garneau, (Hector de) Saint-Denys
1912-1943 .... **TCLC 13**
See also CA 111; DLB 88

Garner, Alan 1934-.......... **CLC 17; DAB**
See also CA 73-76; CANR 15; CLR 20;
DAM POP; DLB 161; MAICYA;
MTCW; SATA 18, 69

Garner, Hugh 1913-1979 .... **CLC 13**
See also CA 69-72; CANR 31; DLB 68

Garnett, David 1892-1981 .... **CLC 3**
See also CA 5-8R; 103; CANR 17; DLB 34

Garos, Stephanie
See Katz, Steve

Garrett, George (Palmer)
1929- .... **CLC 3, 11, 51**
See also CA 1-4R; CAAS 5; CANR 1, 42;
DLB 2, 5, 130, 152; DLBY 83

Garrick, David 1717-1779 .... **LC 15**
See also DAM DRAM; DLB 84

Garrigue, Jean 1914-1972 .... **CLC 2, 8**
See also CA 5-8R; 37-40R; CANR 20

Garrison, Frederick
See Sinclair, Upton (Beall)

Garth, Will
See Hamilton, Edmond; Kuttner, Henry

Garvey, Marcus (Moziah, Jr.)
1887-1940 .... **TCLC 41; BLC**
See also BW 1; CA 120; 124; DAM MULT

Gary, Romain .... CLC 25
See also Kacew, Romain
See also DLB 83

Gascar, Pierre .... CLC 11
See also Fournier, Pierre

Gascoyne, David (Emery) 1916- .... **CLC 45**
See also CA 65-68; CANR 10, 28; DLB 20;
MTCW

Gaskell, Elizabeth Cleghorn
1810-1865 .... **NCLC 5; DAB**
See also CDBLB 1832-1890; DAM MST;
DLB 21, 144, 159

Gass, William H(oward)
1924- ... **CLC 1, 2, 8, 11, 15, 39; SSC 12**
See also CA 17-20R; CANR 30; DLB 2;
MTCW

Gasset, Jose Ortega y
See Ortega y Gasset, Jose

Gates, Henry Louis, Jr. 1950-...... **CLC 65**
See also BW 2; CA 109; CANR 25;
DAM MULT; DLB 67

Gautier, Theophile
1811-1872 .... **NCLC 1; SSC 20**
See also DAM POET; DLB 119

Gawsworth, John
See Bates, H(erbert) E(rnest)

Gaye, Marvin (Penze) 1939-1984 ... **CLC 26**
See also CA 112

Gebler, Carlo (Ernest) 1954-....... **CLC 39**
See also CA 119; 133

Gee, Maggie (Mary) 1948-........ **CLC 57**
See also CA 130

Gee, Maurice (Gough) 1931- .... **CLC 29**
See also CA 97-100; SATA 46

Gelbart, Larry (Simon) 1923- ... **CLC 21, 61**
See also CA 73-76; CANR 45

Gelber, Jack 1932- .... **CLC 1, 6, 14, 79**
See also CA 1-4R; CANR 2; DLB 7

Gellhorn, Martha (Ellis) 1908- ... **CLC 14, 60**
See also CA 77-80; CANR 44; DLBY 82

Genet, Jean
1910-1986 ... **CLC 1, 2, 5, 10, 14, 44, 46**
See also CA 13-16R; CANR 18;
DAM DRAM; DLB 72; DLBY 86;
MTCW

Gent, Peter 1942- .... **CLC 29**
See also AITN 1; CA 89-92; DLBY 82

Gentlewoman in New England, A
See Bradstreet, Anne

Gentlewoman in Those Parts, A
See Bradstreet, Anne

George, Jean Craighead 1919- ...... **CLC 35**
See also AAYA 8; CA 5-8R; CANR 25;
CLR 1; DLB 52; JRDA; MAICYA;
SATA 2, 68

George, Stefan (Anton)
1868-1933 .... **TCLC 2, 14**
See also CA 104

Georges, Georges Martin
See Simenon, Georges (Jacques Christian)

Gerhardi, William Alexander
See Gerhardie, William Alexander

Gerhardie, William Alexander
1895-1977 .... **CLC 5**
See also CA 25-28R; 73-76; CANR 18;
DLB 36

Gerstler, Amy 1956- .... **CLC 70**
See also CA 146

Gertler, T. .... **CLC 34**
See also CA 116; 121; INT 121

Ghalib 1797-1869 .... **NCLC 39**

Ghelderode, Michel de
1898-1962 .... **CLC 6, 11**
See also CA 85-88; CANR 40;
DAM DRAM

Ghiselin, Brewster 1903- .... **CLC 23**
See also CA 13-16R; CAAS 10; CANR 13

Ghose, Zulfikar 1935- .... **CLC 42**
See also CA 65-68

Ghosh, Amitav 1956- .... **CLC 44**
See also CA 147

Giacosa, Giuseppe 1847-1906 ...... **TCLC 7**
See also CA 104

Gibb, Lee
See Waterhouse, Keith (Spencer)

Gibbon, Lewis Grassic .... **TCLC 4**
See also Mitchell, James Leslie

Gibbons, Kaye 1960- .... **CLC 50, 88**
See also DAM POP

Gibran, Kahlil
1883-1931 .... **TCLC 1, 9; PC 9**
See also CA 104; DAM POET, POP

Gibson, William
1914- .... **CLC 23; DA; DAB; DAC**
See also CA 9-12R; CANR 9, 42;
DAM DRAM, MST; DLB 7; SATA 66

Gibson, William (Ford) 1948- ... **CLC 39, 63**
See also AAYA 12; CA 126; 133;
DAM POP

Gide, Andre (Paul Guillaume)
1869-1951 .... **TCLC 5, 12, 36; DA;
DAB; DAC; SSC 13; WLC**
See also CA 104; 124; DAM MST, NOV;
DLB 65; MTCW

Gifford, Barry (Colby) 1946- .... **CLC 34**
See also CA 65-68; CANR 9, 30, 40

Gilbert, W(illiam) S(chwenck)
1836-1911 .... **TCLC 3**
See also CA 104; DAM DRAM, POET;
SATA 36

Gilbreth, Frank B., Jr. 1911- .... **CLC 17**
See also CA 9-12R; SATA 2

Gilchrist, Ellen 1935- .. **CLC 34, 48; SSC 14**
See also CA 113; 116; CANR 41;
DAM POP; DLB 130; MTCW

Giles, Molly 1942- .... **CLC 39**
See also CA 126

Gill, Patrick
See Creasey, John

Gilliam, Terry (Vance) 1940- .... **CLC 21**
See also Monty Python
See also CA 108; 113; CANR 35; INT 113

Gillian, Jerry
See Gilliam, Terry (Vance)

Gilliatt, Penelope (Ann Douglass)
1932-1993 .... **CLC 2, 10, 13, 53**
See also AITN 2; CA 13-16R; 141;
CANR 49; DLB 14

Gilman, Charlotte (Anna) Perkins (Stetson)
1860-1935 .... **TCLC 9, 37; SSC 13**
See also CA 106

Gilmour, David 1949- .... **CLC 35**
See also CA 138, 147

Gilpin, William 1724-1804 ...... **NCLC 30**

Gilray, J. D.
See Mencken, H(enry) L(ouis)

Gilroy, Frank D(aniel) 1925- .... **CLC 2**
See also CA 81-84; CANR 32; DLB 7

Ginsberg, Allen
1926- ...... **CLC 1, 2, 3, 4, 6, 13, 36, 69;
DA; DAB; DAC; PC 4; WLC 3**
See also AITN 1; CA 1-4R; CANR 2, 41;
CDALB 1941-1968; DAM MST, POET;
DLB 5, 16; MTCW

Ginzburg, Natalia
1916-1991 .... **CLC 5, 11, 54, 70**
See also CA 85-88; 135; CANR 33; MTCW

Giono, Jean 1895-1970 .... **CLC 4, 11**
See also CA 45-48; 29-32R; CANR 2, 35;
DLB 72; MTCW

Giovanni, Nikki
1943- ...... **CLC 2, 4, 19, 64; BLC; DA;
DAB; DAC**
See also AITN 1; BW 2; CA 29-32R;
CAAS 6; CANR 18, 41; CLR 6;
DAM MST, MULT, POET; DLB 5, 41;
INT CANR-18; MAICYA; MTCW;
SATA 24

Giovene, Andrea 1904- .... **CLC 7**
See also CA 85-88

Gippius, Zinaida (Nikolayevna) 1869-1945
See Hippius, Zinaida
See also CA 106

Giraudoux, (Hippolyte) Jean
1882-1944 .... **TCLC 2, 7**
See also CA 104; DAM DRAM; DLB 65

Gironella, Jose Maria 1917- .... **CLC 11**
See also CA 101

Gissing, George (Robert)
1857-1903 .... **TCLC 3, 24, 47**
See also CA 105; DLB 18, 135

Giurlani, Aldo
See Palazzeschi, Aldo

Gladkov, Fyodor (Vasilyevich)
1883-1958 .... **TCLC 27**

Glanville, Brian (Lester) 1931- ...... **CLC 6**
See also CA 5-8R; CAAS 9; CANR 3;
DLB 15, 139; SATA 42

Glasgow, Ellen (Anderson Gholson)
1873(?)-1945 .... **TCLC 2, 7**
See also CA 104; DLB 9, 12

Glaspell, Susan (Keating)
1882(?)-1948 .... **TCLC 55**
See also CA 110; DLB 7, 9, 78; YABC 2

Glassco, John 1909-1981 .... **CLC 9**
See also CA 13-16R; 102; CANR 15;
DLB 68

Glasscock, Amnesia
See Steinbeck, John (Ernst)

Glasser, Ronald J. 1940(?)- .... **CLC 37**

Glassman, Joyce
See Johnson, Joyce

Glendinning, Victoria 1937- .... **CLC 50**
See also CA 120; 127; DLB 155

Glissant, Edouard 1928- .... **CLC 10, 68**
See also DAM MULT

Gloag, Julian 1930- .... **CLC 40**
See also AITN 1; CA 65-68; CANR 10

Glowacki, Aleksander
See Prus, Boleslaw

Glueck, Louise (Elisabeth)
1943- .... **CLC 7, 22, 44, 81**
See also CA 33-36R; CANR 40;
DAM POET; DLB 5

Gobineau, Joseph Arthur (Comte) de
1816-1882 .... **NCLC 17**
See also DLB 123

Godard, Jean-Luc 1930- .... **CLC 20**
See also CA 93-96

Godden, (Margaret) Rumer 1907- ... **CLC 53**
See also AAYA 6; CA 5-8R; CANR 4, 27,
36; CLR 20; DLB 161; MAICYA;
SAAS 12; SATA 3, 36

Godoy Alcayaga, Lucila 1889-1957
See Mistral, Gabriela
See also BW 2; CA 104; 131; DAM MULT;
HW; MTCW

Godwin, Gail (Kathleen)
1937- .... **CLC 5, 8, 22, 31, 69**
See also CA 29-32R; CANR 15, 43;
DAM POP; DLB 6; INT CANR-15;
MTCW

Godwin, William 1756-1836 ..... **NCLC 14**
See also CDBLB 1789-1832; DLB 39, 104,
142, 158

Author Index

Gray, Amlin 1946- . . . . **CLC 29**
See also CA 138

Gray, Francine du Plessix 1930- . . . . **CLC 22**
See also BEST 90:3; CA 61-64; CAAS 2;
CANR 11, 33; DAM NOV;
INT CANR-11; MTCW

Gray, John (Henry) 1866-1934 . . . . **TCLC 19**
See also CA 119

Gray, Simon (James Holliday)
1936- . . . . **CLC 9, 14, 36**
See also AITN 1; CA 21-24R; CAAS 3;
CANR 32; DLB 13; MTCW

Gray, Spalding 1941- . . . . **CLC 49**
See also CA 128; DAM POP

Gray, Thomas
1716-1771 . . . . . . **LC 4; DA; DAB; DAC;**
PC 2; WLC
See also CDBLB 1660-1789; DAM MST;
DLB 109

Grayson, David
See Baker, Ray Stannard

Grayson, Richard (A.) 1951- . . . . **CLC 38**
See also CA 85-88; CANR 14, 31

Greeley, Andrew M(oran) 1928- . . . . **CLC 28**
See also CA 5-8R; CAAS 7; CANR 7, 43;
DAM POP; MTCW

Green, Brian
See Card, Orson Scott

Green, Hannah
See Greenberg, Joanne (Goldenberg)

Green, Hannah . . . . **CLC 3**
See also CA 73-76

Green, Henry . . . . **CLC 2, 13**
See also Yorke, Henry Vincent
See also DLB 15

Green, Julian (Hartridge) 1900-
See Green, Julien
See also CA 21-24R; CANR 33; DLB 4, 72;
MTCW

Green, Julien . . . . **CLC 3, 11, 77**
See also Green, Julian (Hartridge)

Green, Paul (Eliot) 1894-1981 . . . . . . **CLC 25**
See also AITN 1; CA 5-8R; 103; CANR 3;
DAM DRAM; DLB 7, 9; DLBY 81

Greenberg, Ivan 1908-1973
See Rahv, Philip
See also CA 85-88

Greenberg, Joanne (Goldenberg)
1932- . . . . **CLC 7, 30**
See also AAYA 12; CA 5-8R; CANR 14,
32; SATA 25

Greenberg, Richard 1959(?)- . . . . **CLC 57**
See also CA 138

Greene, Bette 1934- . . . . **CLC 30**
See also AAYA 7; CA 53-56; CANR 4;
CLR 2; JRDA; MAICYA; SAAS 16;
SATA 8

Greene, Gael . . . . **CLC 8**
See also CA 13-16R; CANR 10

Greene, Graham
1904-1991 . . . . **CLC 1, 3, 6, 9, 14, 18, 27,**
37, 70, 72; DA; DAB; DAC; WLC
See also AITN 2; CA 13-16R; 133;
CANR 35; CDBLB 1945-1960;
DAM MST, NOV; DLB 13, 15, 77, 100;
DLBY 91; MTCW; SATA 20

Greer, Richard
See Silverberg, Robert

Gregor, Arthur 1923- . . . . **CLC 9**
See also CA 25-28R; CAAS 10; CANR 11;
SATA 36

Gregor, Lee
See Pohl, Frederik

Gregory, Isabella Augusta (Persse)
1852-1932 . . . . **TCLC 1**
See also CA 104; DLB 10

Gregory, J. Dennis
See Williams, John A(lfred)

Grendon, Stephen
See Derleth, August (William)

Grenville, Kate 1950- . . . . **CLC 61**
See also CA 118

Grenville, Pelham
See Wodehouse, P(elham) G(renville)

Greve, Felix Paul (Berthold Friedrich)
1879-1948
See Grove, Frederick Philip
See also CA 104; 141; DAC; DAM MST

Grey, Zane 1872-1939 . . . . **TCLC 6**
See also CA 104; 132; DAM POP; DLB 9;
MTCW

Grieg, (Johan) Nordahl (Brun)
1902-1943 . . . . **TCLC 10**
See also CA 107

Grieve, C(hristopher) M(urray)
1892-1978 . . . . **CLC 11, 19**
See also MacDiarmid, Hugh; Pteleon
See also CA 5-8R; 85-88; CANR 33;
DAM POET; MTCW

Griffin, Gerald 1803-1840 . . . . **NCLC 7**
See also DLB 159

Griffin, John Howard 1920-1980 . . . . **CLC 68**
See also AITN 1; CA 1-4R; 101; CANR 2

Griffin, Peter 1942- . . . . **CLC 39**
See also CA 136

Griffiths, Trevor 1935- . . . . **CLC 13, 52**
See also CA 97-100; CANR 45; DLB 13

Grigson, Geoffrey (Edward Harvey)
1905-1985 . . . . **CLC 7, 39**
See also CA 25-28R; 118; CANR 20, 33;
DLB 27; MTCW

Grillparzer, Franz 1791-1872 . . . . . . **NCLC 1**
See also DLB 133

Grimble, Reverend Charles James
See Eliot, T(homas) S(tearns)

Grimke, Charlotte L(ottie) Forten
1837(?)-1914
See Forten, Charlotte L.
See also BW 1; CA 117; 124; DAM MULT,
POET

Grimm, Jacob Ludwig Karl
1785-1863 . . . . **NCLC 3**
See also DLB 90; MAICYA; SATA 22

Grimm, Wilhelm Karl 1786-1859 . . **NCLC 3**
See also DLB 90; MAICYA; SATA 22

Grimmelshausen, Johann Jakob Christoffel
von 1621-1676 . . . . **LC 6**

Grindel, Eugene 1895-1952
See Eluard, Paul
See also CA 104

Grisham, John 1955- . . . . **CLC 84**
See also AAYA 14; CA 138; CANR 47;
DAM POP

Grossman, David 1954- . . . . **CLC 67**
See also CA 138

Grossman, Vasily (Semenovich)
1905-1964 . . . . **CLC 41**
See also CA 124; 130; MTCW

Grove, Frederick Philip . . . . **TCLC 4**
See also Greve, Felix Paul (Berthold
Friedrich)
See also DLB 92

Grubb
See Crumb, R(obert)

Grumbach, Doris (Isaac)
1918- . . . . **CLC 13, 22, 64**
See also CA 5-8R; CAAS 2; CANR 9, 42;
INT CANR-9

Grundtvig, Nicolai Frederik Severin
1783-1872 . . . . **NCLC 1**

Grunge
See Crumb, R(obert)

Grunwald, Lisa 1959- . . . . **CLC 44**
See also CA 120

Guare, John 1938- . . . . **CLC 8, 14, 29, 67**
See also CA 73-76; CANR 21;
DAM DRAM; DLB 7; MTCW

Gudjonsson, Halldor Kiljan 1902-
See Laxness, Halldor
See also CA 103

Guenter, Erich
See Eich, Guenter

Guest, Barbara 1920- . . . . **CLC 34**
See also CA 25-28R; CANR 11, 44; DLB 5

Guest, Judith (Ann) 1936- . . . . **CLC 8, 30**
See also AAYA 7; CA 77-80; CANR 15;
DAM NOV, POP; INT CANR-15;
MTCW

Guevara, Che . . . . **CLC 87; HLC**
See also Guevara (Serna), Ernesto

Guevara (Serna), Ernesto 1928-1967
See Guevara, Che
See also CA 127; 111; DAM MULT; HW

Guild, Nicholas M. 1944- . . . . **CLC 33**
See also CA 93-96

Guillemin, Jacques
See Sartre, Jean-Paul

Guillen, Jorge 1893-1984 . . . . **CLC 11**
See also CA 89-92; 112; DAM MULT,
POET; DLB 108; HW

Guillen (y Batista), Nicolas (Cristobal)
1902-1989 . . . . . **CLC 48, 79; BLC; HLC**
See also BW 2; CA 116; 125; 129;
DAM MST, MULT, POET; HW

Guillevic, (Eugene) 1907- . . . . **CLC 33**
See also CA 93-96

Guillois
See Desnos, Robert

Guiney, Louise Imogen
1861-1920 .... TCLC 41
See also DLB 54

Guiraldes, Ricardo (Guillermo)
1886-1927 .... TCLC 39
See also CA 131; HW; MTCW

Gumilev, Nikolai Stephanovich
1886-1921 .... TCLC 60

Gunn, Bill .... CLC 5
See also Gunn, William Harrison
See also DLB 38

Gunn, Thom(son William)
1929- .... CLC 3, 6, 18, 32, 81
See also CA 17-20R; CANR 9, 33;
CDBLB 1960 to Present; DAM POET;
DLB 27; INT CANR-33; MTCW

Gunn, William Harrison 1934(?)-1989
See Gunn, Bill
See also AITN 1; BW 1; CA 13-16R; 128;
CANR 12, 25

Gunnars, Kristjana 1948-.......... CLC 69
See also CA 113; DLB 60

Gurganus, Allan 1947-............ CLC 70
See also BEST 90:1; CA 135; DAM POP

Gurney, A(lbert) R(amsdell), Jr.
1930- .... CLC 32, 50, 54
See also CA 77-80; CANR 32;
DAM DRAM

Gurney, Ivor (Bertie) 1890-1937 ... TCLC 33

Gurney, Peter
See Gurney, A(lbert) R(amsdell), Jr.

Guro, Elena 1877-1913........... TCLC 56

Gustafson, Ralph (Barker) 1909-.... CLC 36
See also CA 21-24R; CANR 8, 45; DLB 88

Gut, Gom
See Simenon, Georges (Jacques Christian)

Guthrie, A(lfred) B(ertram), Jr.
1901-1991 .... CLC 23
See also CA 57-60; 134; CANR 24; DLB 6;
SATA 62; SATA-Obit 67

Guthrie, Isobel
See Grieve, C(hristopher) M(urray)

Guthrie, Woodrow Wilson 1912-1967
See Guthrie, Woody
See also CA 113; 93-96

Guthrie, Woody................... CLC 35
See also Guthrie, Woodrow Wilson

Guy, Rosa (Cuthbert) 1928-........ CLC 26
See also AAYA 4; BW 2; CA 17-20R;
CANR 14, 34; CLR 13; DLB 33; JRDA;
MAICYA; SATA 14, 62

Gwendolyn
See Bennett, (Enoch) Arnold

H. D. .... CLC 3, 8, 14, 31, 34, 73; PC 5
See also Doolittle, Hilda

H. de V.
See Buchan, John

Haavikko, Paavo Juhani
1931- .... CLC 18, 34
See also CA 106

Habbema, Koos
See Heijermans, Herman

Hacker, Marilyn 1942- .... CLC 5, 9, 23, 72
See also CA 77-80; DAM POET; DLB 120

Haggard, H(enry) Rider
1856-1925 .... TCLC 11
See also CA 108; 148; DLB 70, 156;
SATA 16

Hagiwara Sakutaro 1886-1942 .... TCLC 60

Haig, Fenil
See Ford, Ford Madox

Haig-Brown, Roderick (Langmere)
1908-1976 .... CLC 21
See also CA 5-8R; 69-72; CANR 4, 38;
CLR 31; DLB 88; MAICYA; SATA 12

Hailey, Arthur 1920- .... CLC 5
See also AITN 2; BEST 90:3; CA 1-4R;
CANR 2, 36; DAM NOV, POP; DLB 88;
DLBY 82; MTCW

Hailey, Elizabeth Forsythe 1938-... CLC 40
See also CA 93-96; CAAS 1; CANR 15, 48;
INT CANR-15

Haines, John (Meade) 1924-....... CLC 58
See also CA 17-20R; CANR 13, 34; DLB 5

Hakluyt, Richard 1552-1616........ LC 31

Haldeman, Joe (William) 1943-..... CLC 61
See also CA 53-56; CANR 6; DLB 8;
INT CANR-6

Haley, Alex(ander Murray Palmer)
1921-1992 .... CLC 8, 12, 76; BLC; DA;
DAB; DAC
See also BW 2; CA 77-80; 136; DAM MST,
MULT, POP; DLB 38; MTCW

Haliburton, Thomas Chandler
1796-1865 .... NCLC 15
See also DLB 11, 99

Hall, Donald (Andrew, Jr.)
1928- .... CLC 1, 13, 37, 59
See also CA 5-8R; CAAS 7; CANR 2, 44;
DAM POET; DLB 5; SATA 23

Hall, Frederic Sauser
See Sauser-Hall, Frederic

Hall, James
See Kuttner, Henry

Hall, James Norman 1887-1951 ... TCLC 23
See also CA 123; SATA 21

Hall, (Marguerite) Radclyffe
1886(?)-1943 .... TCLC 12
See also CA 110

Hall, Rodney 1935- .... CLC 51
See also CA 109

Halleck, Fitz-Greene 1790-1867 .. NCLC 47
See also DLB 3

Halliday, Michael
See Creasey, John

Halpern, Daniel 1945- .... CLC 14
See also CA 33-36R

Hamburger, Michael (Peter Leopold)
1924- .... CLC 5, 14
See also CA 5-8R; CAAS 4; CANR 2, 47;
DLB 27

Hamill, Pete 1935- .... CLC 10
See also CA 25-28R; CANR 18

Hamilton, Alexander
1755(?)-1804 .... NCLC 49
See also DLB 37

Hamilton, Clive
See Lewis, C(live) S(taples)

Hamilton, Edmond 1904-1977....... CLC 1
See also CA 1-4R; CANR 3; DLB 8

Hamilton, Eugene (Jacob) Lee
See Lee-Hamilton, Eugene (Jacob)

Hamilton, Franklin
See Silverberg, Robert

Hamilton, Gail
See Corcoran, Barbara

Hamilton, Mollie
See Kaye, M(ary) M(argaret)

Hamilton, (Anthony Walter) Patrick
1904-1962 .... CLC 51
See also CA 113; DLB 10

Hamilton, Virginia 1936-.......... CLC 26
See also AAYA 2; BW 2; CA 25-28R;
CANR 20, 37; CLR 1, 11; DAM MULT;
DLB 33, 52; INT CANR-20; JRDA;
MAICYA; MTCW; SATA 4, 56, 79

Hammett, (Samuel) Dashiell
1894-1961 .... CLC 3, 5, 10, 19, 47;
SSC 17
See also AITN 1; CA 81-84; CANR 42;
CDALB 1929-1941; DLBD 6; MTCW

Hammon, Jupiter
1711(?)-1800(?) .... NCLC 5; BLC
See also DAM MULT, POET; DLB 31, 50

Hammond, Keith
See Kuttner, Henry

Hamner, Earl (Henry), Jr. 1923- ... CLC 12
See also AITN 2; CA 73-76; DLB 6

Hampton, Christopher (James)
1946- .... CLC 4
See also CA 25-28R; DLB 13; MTCW

Hamsun, Knut .... TCLC 2, 14, 49
See also Pedersen, Knut

Handke, Peter 1942- .. CLC 5, 8, 10, 15, 38
See also CA 77-80; CANR 33;
DAM DRAM, NOV; DLB 85, 124;
MTCW

Hanley, James 1901-1985 ... CLC 3, 5, 8, 13
See also CA 73-76; 117; CANR 36; MTCW

Hannah, Barry 1942-....... CLC 23, 38, 90
See also CA 108; 110; CANR 43; DLB 6;
INT 110; MTCW

Hannon, Ezra
See Hunter, Evan

Hansberry, Lorraine (Vivian)
1930-1965 ...... CLC 17, 62; BLC; DA;
DAB; DAC; DC 2
See also BW 1; CA 109; 25-28R; CABS 3;
CDALB 1941-1968; DAM DRAM, MST,
MULT; DLB 7, 38; MTCW

Hansen, Joseph 1923-............. CLC 38
See also CA 29-32R; CAAS 17; CANR 16,
44; INT CANR-16

Hansen, Martin A. 1909-1955..... TCLC 32

Hanson, Kenneth O(stlin) 1922-.... CLC 13
See also CA 53-56; CANR 7

Hardwick, Elizabeth 1916- .... CLC 13
See also CA 5-8R; CANR 3, 32;
DAM NOV; DLB 6; MTCW

Hardy, Thomas
1840-1928 ...... **TCLC 4, 10, 18, 32, 48,**
53; DA; DAB; DAC; PC 8; SSC 2; WLC
See also CA 104; 123; CDBLB 1890-1914;
DAM MST, NOV, POET; DLB 18, 19,
135; MTCW

Hare, David 1947- .... **CLC 29, 58**
See also CA 97-100; CANR 39; DLB 13;
MTCW

Harford, Henry
See Hudson, W(illiam) H(enry)

Hargrave, Leonie
See Disch, Thomas M(ichael)

Harjo, Joy 1951- .... **CLC 83**
See also CA 114; CANR 35; DAM MULT;
DLB 120; NNAL

Harlan, Louis R(udolph) 1922- ..... **CLC 34**
See also CA 21-24R; CANR 25

Harling, Robert 1951(?)- .... **CLC 53**
See also CA 147

Harmon, William (Ruth) 1938- ..... **CLC 38**
See also CA 33-36R; CANR 14, 32, 35;
SATA 65

Harper, F. E. W.
See Harper, Frances Ellen Watkins

Harper, Frances E. W.
See Harper, Frances Ellen Watkins

Harper, Frances E. Watkins
See Harper, Frances Ellen Watkins

Harper, Frances Ellen
See Harper, Frances Ellen Watkins

Harper, Frances Ellen Watkins
1825-1911 .... **TCLC 14; BLC**
See also BW 1; CA 111; 125; DAM MULT,
POET; DLB 50

Harper, Michael S(teven) 1938- .. **CLC 7, 22**
See also BW 1; CA 33-36R; CANR 24;
DLB 41

Harper, Mrs. F. E. W.
See Harper, Frances Ellen Watkins

Harris, Christie (Lucy) Irwin
1907- .... **CLC 12**
See also CA 5-8R; CANR 6; DLB 88;
JRDA; MAICYA; SAAS 10; SATA 6, 74

Harris, Frank 1856(?)-1931 .... **TCLC 24**
See also CA 109; DLB 156

Harris, George Washington
1814-1869 .... **NCLC 23**
See also DLB 3, 11

Harris, Joel Chandler
1848-1908 .... **TCLC 2; SSC 19**
See also CA 104; 137; DLB 11, 23, 42, 78,
91; MAICYA; YABC 1

Harris, John (Wyndham Parkes Lucas)
Beynon 1903-1969
See Wyndham, John
See also CA 102; 89-92

Harris, MacDonald .... **CLC 9**
See also Heiney, Donald (William)

Harris, Mark 1922- .... **CLC 19**
See also CA 5-8R; CAAS 3; CANR 2;
DLB 2; DLBY 80

Harris, (Theodore) Wilson 1921- .... **CLC 25**
See also BW 2; CA 65-68; CAAS 16;
CANR 11, 27; DLB 117; MTCW

Harrison, Elizabeth Cavanna 1909-
See Cavanna, Betty
See also CA 9-12R; CANR 6, 27

Harrison, Harry (Max) 1925- ...... **CLC 42**
See also CA 1-4R; CANR 5, 21; DLB 8;
SATA 4

Harrison, James (Thomas)
1937- .... **CLC 6, 14, 33, 66; SSC 19**
See also CA 13-16R; CANR 8; DLBY 82;
INT CANR-8

Harrison, Jim
See Harrison, James (Thomas)

Harrison, Kathryn 1961- .... **CLC 70**
See also CA 144

Harrison, Tony 1937- .... **CLC 43**
See also CA 65-68; CANR 44; DLB 40;
MTCW

Harriss, Will(ard Irvin) 1922- ...... **CLC 34**
See also CA 111

Harson, Sley
See Ellison, Harlan (Jay)

Hart, Ellis
See Ellison, Harlan (Jay)

Hart, Josephine 1942(?)- .... **CLC 70**
See also CA 138; DAM POP

Hart, Moss 1904-1961 .... **CLC 66**
See also CA 109; 89-92; DAM DRAM;
DLB 7

Harte, (Francis) Bret(t)
1836(?)-1902 .... **TCLC 1, 25; DA; DAC;**
SSC 8; WLC
See also CA 104; 140; CDALB 1865-1917;
DAM MST; DLB 12, 64, 74, 79;
SATA 26

Hartley, L(eslie) P(oles)
1895-1972 .... **CLC 2, 22**
See also CA 45-48; 37-40R; CANR 33;
DLB 15, 139; MTCW

Hartman, Geoffrey H. 1929- .... **CLC 27**
See also CA 117; 125; DLB 67

Hartmann von Aue
c. 1160-c. 1205 .... **CMLC 15**
See also DLB 138

Hartmann von Aue 1170-1210 .... **CMLC 15**

Haruf, Kent 1943- .... **CLC 34**
See also CA 149

Harwood, Ronald 1934- .... **CLC 32**
See also CA 1-4R; CANR 4; DAM DRAM,
MST; DLB 13

Hasek, Jaroslav (Matej Frantisek)
1883-1923 .... **TCLC 4**
See also CA 104; 129; MTCW

Hass, Robert 1941- .... **CLC 18, 39**
See also CA 111; CANR 30, 50; DLB 105

Hastings, Hudson
See Kuttner, Henry

Hastings, Selina .... **CLC 44**

Hatteras, Amelia
See Mencken, H(enry) L(ouis)

Hatteras, Owen .... **TCLC 18**
See also Mencken, H(enry) L(ouis); Nathan,
George Jean

Hauptmann, Gerhart (Johann Robert)
1862-1946 .... **TCLC 4**
See also CA 104; DAM DRAM; DLB 66,
118

Havel, Vaclav
1936- .... **CLC 25, 58, 65; DC 6**
See also CA 104; CANR 36; DAM DRAM;
MTCW

Haviaras, Stratis .... **CLC 33**
See also Chaviaras, Strates

Hawes, Stephen 1475(?)-1523(?) ..... **LC 17**

Hawkes, John (Clendennin Burne, Jr.)
1925- ...... **CLC 1, 2, 3, 4, 7, 9, 14, 15,**
27, 49
See also CA 1-4R; CANR 2, 47; DLB 2, 7;
DLBY 80; MTCW

Hawking, S. W.
See Hawking, Stephen W(illiam)

Hawking, Stephen W(illiam)
1942- .... **CLC 63**
See also AAYA 13; BEST 89:1; CA 126;
129; CANR 48

Hawthorne, Julian 1846-1934 ..... **TCLC 25**

Hawthorne, Nathaniel
1804-1864 .... **NCLC 39; DA; DAB;**
DAC; SSC 3; WLC
See also CDALB 1640-1865; DAM MST,
NOV; DLB 1, 74; YABC 2

Haxton, Josephine Ayres 1921-
See Douglas, Ellen
See also CA 115; CANR 41

Hayaseca y Eizaguirre, Jorge
See Echegaray (y Eizaguirre), Jose (Maria
Waldo)

Hayashi Fumiko 1904-1951 .... **TCLC 27**

Haycraft, Anna
See Ellis, Alice Thomas
See also CA 122

Hayden, Robert E(arl)
1913-1980 ...... **CLC 5, 9, 14, 37; BLC;**
DA; DAC; PC 6
See also BW 1; CA 69-72; 97-100; CABS 2;
CANR 24; CDALB 1941-1968;
DAM MST, MULT, POET; DLB 5, 76;
MTCW; SATA 19; SATA-Obit 26

Hayford, J(oseph) E(phraim) Casely
See Casely-Hayford, J(oseph) E(phraim)

Hayman, Ronald 1932- .... **CLC 44**
See also CA 25-28R; CANR 18, 50;
DLB 155

Haywood, Eliza (Fowler)
1693(?)-1756 .... **LC 1**

Hazlitt, William 1778-1830 ...... **NCLC 29**
See also DLB 110, 158

Hazzard, Shirley 1931- .... **CLC 18**
See also CA 9-12R; CANR 4; DLBY 82;
MTCW

Head, Bessie 1937-1986 ... **CLC 25, 67; BLC**
See also BW 2; CA 29-32R; 119; CANR 25;
DAM MULT; DLB 117; MTCW

Headon, (Nicky) Topper 1956(?)- ... **CLC 30**

Heaney, Seamus (Justin)
1939- .... **CLC 5, 7, 14, 25, 37, 74; DAB**
See also CA 85-88; CANR 25, 48;
CDBLB 1960 to Present; DAM POET;
DLB 40; MTCW

Hearn, (Patricio) Lafcadio (Tessima Carlos)
1850-1904 .... **TCLC 9**
See also CA 105; DLB 12, 78

Hearne, Vicki 1946- .... **CLC 56**
See also CA 139

Hearon, Shelby 1931- .... **CLC 63**
See also AITN 2; CA 25-28R; CANR 18,
48

Heat-Moon, William Least .... **CLC 29**
See also Trogdon, William (Lewis)
See also AAYA 9

Hebbel, Friedrich 1813-1863 ..... **NCLC 43**
See also DAM DRAM; DLB 129

Hebert, Anne 1916- ... **CLC 4, 13, 29; DAC**
See also CA 85-88; DAM MST, POET;
DLB 68; MTCW

Hecht, Anthony (Evan)
1923- .... **CLC 8, 13, 19**
See also CA 9-12R; CANR 6; DAM POET;
DLB 5

Hecht, Ben 1894-1964 .... **CLC 8**
See also CA 85-88; DLB 7, 9, 25, 26, 28, 86

Hedayat, Sadeq 1903-1951 .... **TCLC 21**
See also CA 120

Hegel, Georg Wilhelm Friedrich
1770-1831 .... **NCLC 46**
See also DLB 90

Heidegger, Martin 1889-1976 ...... **CLC 24**
See also CA 81-84; 65-68; CANR 34;
MTCW

Heidenstam, (Carl Gustaf) Verner von
1859-1940 .... **TCLC 5**
See also CA 104

Heifner, Jack 1946- .... **CLC 11**
See also CA 105; CANR 47

Heijermans, Herman 1864-1924 ... **TCLC 24**
See also CA 123

Heilbrun, Carolyn G(old) 1926- ..... **CLC 25**
See also CA 45-48; CANR 1, 28

Heine, Heinrich 1797-1856 .... **NCLC 4**
See also DLB 90

Heinemann, Larry (Curtiss) 1944- .. **CLC 50**
See also CA 110; CAAS 21; CANR 31;
DLBD 9; INT CANR-31

Heiney, Donald (William) 1921-1993
See Harris, MacDonald
See also CA 1-4R; 142; CANR 3

Heinlein, Robert A(nson)
1907-1988 ...... **CLC 1, 3, 8, 14, 26, 55**
See also AAYA 17; CA 1-4R; 125;
CANR 1, 20; DAM POP; DLB 8; JRDA;
MAICYA; MTCW; SATA 9, 69;
SATA-Obit 56

Helforth, John
See Doolittle, Hilda

Hellenhofferu, Vojtech Kapristian z
See Hasek, Jaroslav (Matej Frantisek)

Heller, Joseph
1923- .... **CLC 1, 3, 5, 8, 11, 36, 63; DA;**
DAB; DAC; WLC
See also AITN 1; CA 5-8R; CABS 1;
CANR 8, 42; DAM MST, NOV, POP;
DLB 2, 28; DLBY 80; INT CANR-8;
MTCW

Hellman, Lillian (Florence)
1906-1984 ...... **CLC 2, 4, 8, 14, 18, 34,**
44, 52; DC 1
See also AITN 1, 2; CA 13-16R; 112;
CANR 33; DAM DRAM; DLB 7;
DLBY 84; MTCW

Helprin, Mark 1947- ..... **CLC 7, 10, 22, 32**
See also CA 81-84; CANR 47; DAM NOV,
POP; DLBY 85; MTCW

Helvetius, Claude-Adrien
1715-1771 .... **LC 26**

Helyar, Jane Penelope Josephine 1933-
See Poole, Josephine
See also CA 21-24R; CANR 10, 26;
SATA 82

Hemans, Felicia 1793-1835 ...... **NCLC 29**
See also DLB 96

Hemingway, Ernest (Miller)
1899-1961 .... **CLC 1, 3, 6, 8, 10, 13, 19,**
30, 34, 39, 41, 44, 50, 61, 80; DA; DAB;
DAC; SSC 1; WLC
See also CA 77-80; CANR 34;
CDALB 1917-1929; DAM MST, NOV;
DLB 4, 9, 102; DLBD 1; DLBY 81, 87;
MTCW

Hempel, Amy 1951- .... **CLC 39**
See also CA 118; 137

Henderson, F. C.
See Mencken, H(enry) L(ouis)

Henderson, Sylvia
See Ashton-Warner, Sylvia (Constance)

Henley, Beth .... **CLC 23; DC 6**
See also Henley, Elizabeth Becker
See also CABS 3; DLBY 86

Henley, Elizabeth Becker 1952-
See Henley, Beth
See also CA 107; CANR 32; DAM DRAM,
MST; MTCW

Henley, William Ernest
1849-1903 .... **TCLC 8**
See also CA 105; DLB 19

Hennissart, Martha
See Lathen, Emma
See also CA 85-88

Henry, O. .... **TCLC 1, 19; SSC 5; WLC**
See also Porter, William Sydney

Henry, Patrick 1736-1799 .... **LC 25**

Henryson, Robert 1430(?)-1506(?).... **LC 20**
See also DLB 146

Henry VIII 1491-1547 .... **LC 10**

Henschke, Alfred
See Klabund

Hentoff, Nat(han Irving) 1925- ..... **CLC 26**
See also AAYA 4; CA 1-4R; CAAS 6;
CANR 5, 25; CLR 1; INT CANR-25;
JRDA; MAICYA; SATA 42, 69;
SATA-Brief 27

Heppenstall, (John) Rayner
1911-1981 .... **CLC 10**
See also CA 1-4R; 103; CANR 29

Herbert, Frank (Patrick)
1920-1986 ...... **CLC 12, 23, 35, 44, 85**
See also CA 53-56; 118; CANR 5, 43;
DAM POP; DLB 8; INT CANR-5;
MTCW; SATA 9, 37; SATA-Obit 47

Herbert, George
1593-1633 .... **LC 24; DAB; PC 4**
See also CDBLB Before 1660; DAM POET;
DLB 126

Herbert, Zbigniew 1924- .... **CLC 9, 43**
See also CA 89-92; CANR 36;
DAM POET; MTCW

Herbst, Josephine (Frey)
1897-1969 .... **CLC 34**
See also CA 5-8R; 25-28R; DLB 9

Hergesheimer, Joseph
1880-1954 .... **TCLC 11**
See also CA 109; DLB 102, 9

Herlihy, James Leo 1927-1993 ...... **CLC 6**
See also CA 1-4R; 143; CANR 2

Hermogenes fl. c. 175- .... **CMLC 6**

Hernandez, Jose 1834-1886...... **NCLC 17**

Herodotus c. 484B.C.-429B.C..... **CMLC 17**

Herrick, Robert
1591-1674 ..... **LC 13; DA; DAB; DAC;**
PC 9
See also DAM MST, POP; DLB 126

Herring, Guilles
See Somerville, Edith

Herriot, James 1916-1995 .... **CLC 12**
See also Wight, James Alfred
See also AAYA 1; CA 148; CANR 40;
DAM POP

Herrmann, Dorothy 1941- .... **CLC 44**
See also CA 107

Herrmann, Taffy
See Herrmann, Dorothy

Hersey, John (Richard)
1914-1993 .... **CLC 1, 2, 7, 9, 40, 81**
See also CA 17-20R; 140; CANR 33;
DAM POP; DLB 6; MTCW; SATA 25;
SATA-Obit 76

Herzen, Aleksandr Ivanovich
1812-1870 .... **NCLC 10**

Herzl, Theodor 1860-1904........ **TCLC 36**

Herzog, Werner 1942- .... **CLC 16**
See also CA 89-92

Hesiod c. 8th cent. B.C.- .... **CMLC 5**

Hesse, Hermann
1877-1962 .... **CLC 1, 2, 3, 6, 11, 17, 25,**
69; DA; DAB; DAC; SSC 9; WLC
See also CA 17-18; CAP 2; DAM MST,
NOV; DLB 66; MTCW; SATA 50

Hewes, Cady
See De Voto, Bernard (Augustine)

Heyen, William 1940- .... **CLC 13, 18**
See also CA 33-36R; CAAS 9; DLB 5

Heyerdahl, Thor 1914- .... **CLC 26**
See also CA 5-8R; CANR 5, 22; MTCW;
SATA 2, 52

Heym, Georg (Theodor Franz Arthur)
1887-1912 . . . . **TCLC 9**
See also CA 106

Heym, Stefan 1913- . . . . **CLC 41**
See also CA 9-12R; CANR 4; DLB 69

Heyse, Paul (Johann Ludwig von)
1830-1914 . . . . **TCLC 8**
See also CA 104; DLB 129

Heyward, (Edwin) DuBose
1885-1940 . . . . **TCLC 59**
See also CA 108; DLB 7, 9, 45; SATA 21

Hibbert, Eleanor Alice Burford
1906-1993 . . . . **CLC 7**
See also BEST 90:4; CA 17-20R; 140;
CANR 9, 28; DAM POP; SATA 2;
SATA-Obit 74

Higgins, George V(incent)
1939- . . . . **CLC 4, 7, 10, 18**
See also CA 77-80; CAAS 5; CANR 17;
DLB 2; DLBY 81; INT CANR-17;
MTCW

Higginson, Thomas Wentworth
1823-1911 . . . . **TCLC 36**
See also DLB 1, 64

Highet, Helen
See MacInnes, Helen (Clark)

Highsmith, (Mary) Patricia
1921-1995 . . . . **CLC 2, 4, 14, 42**
See also CA 1-4R; 147; CANR 1, 20, 48;
DAM NOV, POP; MTCW

Highwater, Jamake (Mamake)
1942(?)- . . . . **CLC 12**
See also AAYA 7; CA 65-68; CAAS 7;
CANR 10, 34; CLR 17; DLB 52;
DLBY 85; JRDA; MAICYA; SATA 32,
69; SATA-Brief 30

Higuchi, Ichiyo 1872-1896 . . . . . . **NCLC 49**

Hijuelos, Oscar 1951- . . . . . . **CLC 65; HLC**
See also BEST 90:1; CA 123; CANR 50;
DAM MULT, POP; DLB 145; HW

Hikmet, Nazim 1902(?)-1963 . . . . . . **CLC 40**
See also CA 141; 93-96

Hildesheimer, Wolfgang
1916-1991 . . . . **CLC 49**
See also CA 101; 135; DLB 69, 124

Hill, Geoffrey (William)
1932- . . . . **CLC 5, 8, 18, 45**
See also CA 81-84; CANR 21;
CDBLB 1960 to Present; DAM POET;
DLB 40; MTCW

Hill, George Roy 1921- . . . . **CLC 26**
See also CA 110; 122

Hill, John
See Koontz, Dean R(ay)

Hill, Susan (Elizabeth)
1942- . . . . **CLC 4; DAB**
See also CA 33-36R; CANR 29;
DAM MST, NOV; DLB 14, 139; MTCW

Hillerman, Tony 1925- . . . . **CLC 62**
See also AAYA 6; BEST 89:1; CA 29-32R;
CANR 21, 42; DAM POP; SATA 6

Hillesum, Etty 1914-1943 . . . . **TCLC 49**
See also CA 137

Hilliard, Noel (Harvey) 1929- . . . . . . **CLC 15**
See also CA 9-12R; CANR 7

Hillis, Rick 1956- . . . . **CLC 66**
See also CA 134

Hilton, James 1900-1954 . . . . **TCLC 21**
See also CA 108; DLB 34, 77; SATA 34

Himes, Chester (Bomar)
1909-1984 . . . . **CLC 2, 4, 7, 18, 58; BLC**
See also BW 2; CA 25-28R; 114; CANR 22;
DAM MULT; DLB 2, 76, 143; MTCW

Hinde, Thomas . . . . **CLC 6, 11**
See also Chitty, Thomas Willes

Hindin, Nathan
See Bloch, Robert (Albert)

Hine, (William) Daryl 1936- . . . . **CLC 15**
See also CA 1-4R; CAAS 15; CANR 1, 20;
DLB 60

Hinkson, Katharine Tynan
See Tynan, Katharine

Hinton, S(usan) E(loise)
1950- . . . . . . **CLC 30; DA; DAB; DAC**
See also AAYA 2; CA 81-84; CANR 32;
CLR 3, 23; DAM MST, NOV; JRDA;
MAICYA; MTCW; SATA 19, 58

Hippius, Zinaida . . . . **TCLC 9**
See also Gippius, Zinaida (Nikolayevna)

Hiraoka, Kimitake 1925-1970
See Mishima, Yukio
See also CA 97-100; 29-32R; DAM DRAM;
MTCW

Hirsch, E(ric) D(onald), Jr. 1928- . . . **CLC 79**
See also CA 25-28R; CANR 27; DLB 67;
INT CANR-27; MTCW

Hirsch, Edward 1950- . . . . **CLC 31, 50**
See also CA 104; CANR 20, 42; DLB 120

Hitchcock, Alfred (Joseph)
1899-1980 . . . . **CLC 16**
See also CA 97-100; SATA 27;
SATA-Obit 24

Hitler, Adolf 1889-1945 . . . . **TCLC 53**
See also CA 117; 147

Hoagland, Edward 1932- . . . . **CLC 28**
See also CA 1-4R; CANR 2, 31; DLB 6;
SATA 51

Hoban, Russell (Conwell) 1925- . . **CLC 7, 25**
See also CA 5-8R; CANR 23, 37; CLR 3;
DAM NOV; DLB 52; MAICYA;
MTCW; SATA 1, 40, 78

Hobbs, Perry
See Blackmur, R(ichard) P(almer)

Hobson, Laura Z(ametkin)
1900-1986 . . . . **CLC 7, 25**
See also CA 17-20R; 118; DLB 28;
SATA 52

Hochhuth, Rolf 1931- . . . . **CLC 4, 11, 18**
See also CA 5-8R; CANR 33;
DAM DRAM; DLB 124; MTCW

Hochman, Sandra 1936- . . . . **CLC 3, 8**
See also CA 5-8R; DLB 5

Hochwaelder, Fritz 1911-1986 . . . . . . **CLC 36**
See also CA 29-32R; 120; CANR 42;
DAM DRAM; MTCW

Hochwalder, Fritz
See Hochwaelder, Fritz

Hocking, Mary (Eunice) 1921- . . . . . **CLC 13**
See also CA 101; CANR 18, 40

Hodgins, Jack 1938- . . . . **CLC 23**
See also CA 93-96; DLB 60

Hodgson, William Hope
1877(?)-1918 . . . . **TCLC 13**
See also CA 111; DLB 70, 153, 156

Hoffman, Alice 1952- . . . . **CLC 51**
See also CA 77-80; CANR 34; DAM NOV;
MTCW

Hoffman, Daniel (Gerard)
1923- . . . . **CLC 6, 13, 23**
See also CA 1-4R; CANR 4; DLB 5

Hoffman, Stanley 1944- . . . . **CLC 5**
See also CA 77-80

Hoffman, William M(oses) 1939- . . . **CLC 40**
See also CA 57-60; CANR 11

Hoffmann, E(rnst) T(heodor) A(madeus)
1776-1822 . . . . **NCLC 2; SSC 13**
See also DLB 90; SATA 27

Hofmann, Gert 1931- . . . . **CLC 54**
See also CA 128

Hofmannsthal, Hugo von
1874-1929 . . . . **TCLC 11; DC 4**
See also CA 106; DAM DRAM; DLB 81,
118

Hogan, Linda 1947- . . . . **CLC 73**
See also CA 120; CANR 45; DAM MULT;
NNAL

Hogarth, Charles
See Creasey, John

Hogg, James 1770-1835 . . . . **NCLC 4**
See also DLB 93, 116, 159

Holbach, Paul Henri Thiry Baron
1723-1789 . . . . **LC 14**

Holberg, Ludvig 1684-1754 . . . . **LC 6**

Holden, Ursula 1921- . . . . **CLC 18**
See also CA 101; CAAS 8; CANR 22

Holderlin, (Johann Christian) Friedrich
1770-1843 . . . . **NCLC 16; PC 4**

Holdstock, Robert
See Holdstock, Robert P.

Holdstock, Robert P. 1948- . . . . **CLC 39**
See also CA 131

Holland, Isabelle 1920- . . . . **CLC 21**
See also AAYA 11; CA 21-24R; CANR 10,
25, 47; JRDA; MAICYA; SATA 8, 70

Holland, Marcus
See Caldwell, (Janet Miriam) Taylor
(Holland)

Hollander, John 1929- . . . . . . **CLC 2, 5, 8, 14**
See also CA 1-4R; CANR 1; DLB 5;
SATA 13

Hollander, Paul
See Silverberg, Robert

Holleran, Andrew 1943(?)- . . . . **CLC 38**
See also CA 144

Hollinghurst, Alan 1954- . . . . **CLC 55**
See also CA 114

Hollis, Jim
See Summers, Hollis (Spurgeon, Jr.)

Holmes, John
See Souster, (Holmes) Raymond

Holmes, John Clellon 1926-1988 . . . . **CLC 56**
See also CA 9-12R; 125; CANR 4; DLB 16

Holmes, Oliver Wendell
1809-1894 . . . . NCLC 14
See also CDALB 1640-1865; DLB 1;
SATA 34

Holmes, Raymond
See Souster, (Holmes) Raymond

Holt, Victoria
See Hibbert, Eleanor Alice Burford

Holub, Miroslav 1923- . . . . CLC 4
See also CA 21-24R; CANR 10

Homer
c. 8th cent. B.C.- . . . . . CMLC 1, 16; DA;
DAB; DAC
See also DAM MST, POET

Honig, Edwin 1919- . . . . CLC 33
See also CA 5-8R; CAAS 8; CANR 4, 45;
DLB 5

Hood, Hugh (John Blagdon)
1928- . . . . CLC 15, 28
See also CA 49-52; CAAS 17; CANR 1, 33;
DLB 53

Hood, Thomas 1799-1845. . . . . . . NCLC 16
See also DLB 96

Hooker, (Peter) Jeremy 1941- . . . . . . CLC 43
See also CA 77-80; CANR 22; DLB 40

Hope, A(lec) D(erwent) 1907- . . . . CLC 3, 51
See also CA 21-24R; CANR 33; MTCW

Hope, Brian
See Creasey, John

Hope, Christopher (David Tully)
1944- . . . . CLC 52
See also CA 106; CANR 47; SATA 62

Hopkins, Gerard Manley
1844-1889 . . . . NCLC 17; DA; DAB;
DAC; WLC
See also CDBLB 1890-1914; DAM MST,
POET; DLB 35, 57

Hopkins, John (Richard) 1931- . . . . . . CLC 4
See also CA 85-88

Hopkins, Pauline Elizabeth
1859-1930 . . . . TCLC 28; BLC
See also BW 2; CA 141; DAM MULT;
DLB 50

Hopkinson, Francis 1737-1791 . . . . . . LC 25
See also DLB 31

Hopley-Woolrich, Cornell George 1903-1968
See Woolrich, Cornell
See also CA 13-14; CAP 1

Horatio
See Proust, (Valentin-Louis-George-Eugene-)
Marcel

Horgan, Paul (George Vincent O'Shaughnessy)
1903-1995 . . . . CLC 9, 53
See also CA 13-16R; 147; CANR 9, 35;
DAM NOV; DLB 102; DLBY 85;
INT CANR-9; MTCW; SATA 13;
SATA-Obit 84

Horn, Peter
See Kuttner, Henry

Hornem, Horace Esq.
See Byron, George Gordon (Noel)

Hornung, E(rnest) W(illiam)
1866-1921 . . . . TCLC 59
See also CA 108; DLB 70

Horovitz, Israel (Arthur) 1939- . . . . . CLC 56
See also CA 33-36R; CANR 46;
DAM DRAM; DLB 7

Horvath, Odon von
See Horvath, Oedoen von
See also DLB 85, 124

Horvath, Oedoen von 1901-1938. . . TCLC 45
See also Horvath, Odon von
See also CA 118

Horwitz, Julius 1920-1986. . . . . CLC 14
See also CA 9-12R; 119; CANR 12

Hospital, Janette Turner 1942- . . . . . CLC 42
See also CA 108; CANR 48

Hostos, E. M. de
See Hostos (y Bonilla), Eugenio Maria de

Hostos, Eugenio M. de
See Hostos (y Bonilla), Eugenio Maria de

Hostos, Eugenio Maria
See Hostos (y Bonilla), Eugenio Maria de

Hostos (y Bonilla), Eugenio Maria de
1839-1903 . . . . TCLC 24
See also CA 123; 131; HW

Houdini
See Lovecraft, H(oward) P(hillips)

Hougan, Carolyn 1943- . . . . CLC 34
See also CA 139

Household, Geoffrey (Edward West)
1900-1988 . . . . CLC 11
See also CA 77-80; 126; DLB 87; SATA 14;
SATA-Obit 59

Housman, A(lfred) E(dward)
1859-1936 . . . . . . TCLC 1, 10; DA; DAB;
DAC; PC 2
See also CA 104; 125; DAM MST, POET;
DLB 19; MTCW

Housman, Laurence 1865-1959 . . . . . TCLC 7
See also CA 106; DLB 10; SATA 25

Howard, Elizabeth Jane 1923- . . . CLC 7, 29
See also CA 5-8R; CANR 8

Howard, Maureen 1930- . . . . . CLC 5, 14, 46
See also CA 53-56; CANR 31; DLBY 83;
INT CANR-31; MTCW

Howard, Richard 1929- . . . . . . CLC 7, 10, 47
See also AITN 1; CA 85-88; CANR 25;
DLB 5; INT CANR-25

Howard, Robert Ervin 1906-1936. . . TCLC 8
See also CA 105

Howard, Warren F.
See Pohl, Frederik

Howe, Fanny 1940- . . . . CLC 47
See also CA 117; SATA-Brief 52

Howe, Irving 1920-1993. . . . . CLC 85
See also CA 9-12R; 141; CANR 21, 50;
DLB 67; MTCW

Howe, Julia Ward 1819-1910 . . . . . TCLC 21
See also CA 117; DLB 1

Howe, Susan 1937- . . . . CLC 72
See also DLB 120

Howe, Tina 1937- . . . . CLC 48
See also CA 109

Howell, James 1594(?)-1666 . . . . LC 13
See also DLB 151

Howells, W. D.
See Howells, William Dean

Howells, William D.
See Howells, William Dean

Howells, William Dean
1837-1920 . . . . TCLC 7, 17, 41
See also CA 104; 134; CDALB 1865-1917;
DLB 12, 64, 74, 79

Howes, Barbara 1914- . . . . CLC 15
See also CA 9-12R; CAAS 3; SATA 5

Hrabal, Bohumil 1914-. . . . . CLC 13, 67
See also CA 106; CAAS 12

Hsun, Lu
See Lu Hsun

Hubbard, L(afayette) Ron(ald)
1911-1986 . . . . CLC 43
See also CA 77-80; 118; CANR 22;
DAM POP

Huch, Ricarda (Octavia)
1864-1947 . . . . TCLC 13
See also CA 111; DLB 66

Huddle, David 1942- . . . . CLC 49
See also CA 57-60; CAAS 20; DLB 130

Hudson, Jeffrey
See Crichton, (John) Michael

Hudson, W(illiam) H(enry)
1841-1922 . . . . TCLC 29
See also CA 115; DLB 98, 153; SATA 35

Hueffer, Ford Madox
See Ford, Ford Madox

Hughart, Barry 1934-. . . . . CLC 39
See also CA 137

Hughes, Colin
See Creasey, John

Hughes, David (John) 1930- . . . . CLC 48
See also CA 116; 129; DLB 14

Hughes, (James) Langston
1902-1967 . . . . . CLC 1, 5, 10, 15, 35, 44;
BLC; DA; DAB; DAC; DC 3; PC 1;
SSC 6; WLC
See also AAYA 12; BW 1; CA 1-4R;
25-28R; CANR 1, 34; CDALB 1929-1941;
CLR 17; DAM DRAM, MST, MULT,
POET; DLB 4, 7, 48, 51, 86; JRDA;
MAICYA; MTCW; SATA 4, 33

Hughes, Richard (Arthur Warren)
1900-1976 . . . . CLC 1, 11
See also CA 5-8R; 65-68; CANR 4;
DAM NOV; DLB 15, 161; MTCW;
SATA 8; SATA-Obit 25

Hughes, Ted
1930- . . . . CLC 2, 4, 9, 14, 37; DAB;
DAC; PC 7
See also CA 1-4R; CANR 1, 33; CLR 3;
DLB 40, 161; MAICYA; MTCW;
SATA 49; SATA-Brief 27

Hugo, Richard F(ranklin)
1923-1982 . . . . CLC 6, 18, 32
See also CA 49-52; 108; CANR 3;
DAM POET; DLB 5

Hugo, Victor (Marie)
1802-1885 . . . . NCLC 3, 10, 21; DA;
DAB; DAC; WLC
See also DAM DRAM, MST, NOV, POET;
DLB 119; SATA 47

Huidobro, Vicente
See Huidobro Fernandez, Vicente Garcia

Huidobro Fernandez, Vicente Garcia
　1893-1948 .... **TCLC 31**
　See also CA 131; HW

Hulme, Keri　1947- .... **CLC 39**
　See also CA 125; INT 125

Hulme, T(homas) E(rnest)
　1883-1917 .... **TCLC 21**
　See also CA 117; DLB 19

Hume, David　1711-1776. .... **LC 7**
　See also DLB 104

Humphrey, William　1924- .... **CLC 45**
　See also CA 77-80; DLB 6

Humphreys, Emyr Owen　1919-..... **CLC 47**
　See also CA 5-8R; CANR 3, 24; DLB 15

Humphreys, Josephine　1945-.... **CLC 34, 57**
　See also CA 121; 127; INT 127

Hungerford, Pixie
　See Brinsmead, H(esba) F(ay)

Hunt, E(verette) Howard, (Jr.)
　1918- .... **CLC 3**
　See also AITN 1; CA 45-48; CANR 2, 47

Hunt, Kyle
　See Creasey, John

Hunt, (James Henry) Leigh
　1784-1859 .... **NCLC 1**
　See also DAM POET

Hunt, Marsha　1946-............ **CLC 70**
　See also BW 2; CA 143

Hunt, Violet　1866-1942 .... **TCLC 53**

Hunter, E. Waldo
　See Sturgeon, Theodore (Hamilton)

Hunter, Evan　1926- .... **CLC 11, 31**
　See also CA 5-8R; CANR 5, 38;
　DAM POP; DLBY 82; INT CANR-5;
　MTCW; SATA 25

Hunter, Kristin (Eggleston)　1931-... **CLC 35**
　See also AITN 1; BW 1; CA 13-16R;
　CANR 13; CLR 3; DLB 33;
　INT CANR-13; MAICYA; SAAS 10;
　SATA 12

Hunter, Mollie　1922-........... **CLC 21**
　See also McIlwraith, Maureen Mollie
　Hunter
　See also AAYA 13; CANR 37; CLR 25;
　DLB 161; JRDA; MAICYA; SAAS 7;
　SATA 54

Hunter, Robert　(?)-1734........... **LC 7**

Hurston, Zora Neale
　1903-1960 .... **CLC 7, 30, 61; BLC; DA;
　DAC; SSC 4**
　See also AAYA 15; BW 1; CA 85-88;
　DAM MST, MULT, NOV; DLB 51, 86;
　MTCW

Huston, John (Marcellus)
　1906-1987 .... **CLC 20**
　See also CA 73-76; 123; CANR 34; DLB 26

Hustvedt, Siri　1955-.............. **CLC 76**
　See also CA 137

Hutten, Ulrich von　1488-1523....... **LC 16**

Huxley, Aldous (Leonard)
　1894-1963 ..... **CLC 1, 3, 4, 5, 8, 11, 18,
　35, 79; DA; DAB; DAC; WLC**
　See also AAYA 11; CA 85-88; CANR 44;
　CDBLB 1914-1945; DAM MST, NOV;
　DLB 36, 100; MTCW; SATA 63

Huysmans, Charles Marie Georges
　1848-1907
　See Huysmans, Joris-Karl
　See also CA 104

Huysmans, Joris-Karl.............. **TCLC 7**
　See also Huysmans, Charles Marie Georges
　See also DLB 123

Hwang, David Henry
　1957- .... **CLC 55; DC 4**
　See also CA 127; 132; DAM DRAM;
　INT 132

Hyde, Anthony　1946-............. **CLC 42**
　See also CA 136

Hyde, Margaret O(ldroyd)　1917-... **CLC 21**
　See also CA 1-4R; CANR 1, 36; CLR 23;
　JRDA; MAICYA; SAAS 8; SATA 1, 42,
　76

Hynes, James　1956(?)-............ **CLC 65**

Ian, Janis　1951- .... **CLC 21**
　See also CA 105

Ibanez, Vicente Blasco
　See Blasco Ibanez, Vicente

Ibarguengoitia, Jorge　1928-1983.... **CLC 37**
　See also CA 124; 113; HW

Ibsen, Henrik (Johan)
　1828-1906 ...... **TCLC 2, 8, 16, 37, 52;
　DA; DAB; DAC; DC 2; WLC**
　See also CA 104; 141; DAM DRAM, MST

Ibuse Masuji　1898-1993........... **CLC 22**
　See also CA 127; 141

Ichikawa, Kon　1915-.............. **CLC 20**
　See also CA 121

Idle, Eric　1943-.................. **CLC 21**
　See also Monty Python
　See also CA 116; CANR 35

Ignatow, David　1914-...... **CLC 4, 7, 14, 40**
　See also CA 9-12R; CAAS 3; CANR 31;
　DLB 5

Ihimaera, Witi　1944- .... **CLC 46**
　See also CA 77-80

Ilf, Ilya........................ **TCLC 21**
　See also Fainzilberg, Ilya Arnoldovich

Immermann, Karl (Lebrecht)
　1796-1840 .... **NCLC 4, 49**
　See also DLB 133

Inclan, Ramon (Maria) del Valle
　See Valle-Inclan, Ramon (Maria) del

Infante, G(uillermo) Cabrera
　See Cabrera Infante, G(uillermo)

Ingalls, Rachel (Holmes)　1940-..... **CLC 42**
　See also CA 123; 127

Ingamells, Rex　1913-1955 .... **TCLC 35**

Inge, William Motter
　1913-1973 .... **CLC 1, 8, 19**
　See also CA 9-12R; CDALB 1941-1968;
　DAM DRAM; DLB 7; MTCW

Ingelow, Jean　1820-1897 .... **NCLC 39**
　See also DLB 35; SATA 33

Ingram, Willis J.
　See Harris, Mark

Innaurato, Albert (F.)　1948(?)- .. **CLC 21, 60**
　See also CA 115; 122; INT 122

Innes, Michael
　See Stewart, J(ohn) I(nnes) M(ackintosh)

Ionesco, Eugene
　1909-1994 .... **CLC 1, 4, 6, 9, 11, 15, 41,
　86; DA; DAB; DAC; WLC**
　See also CA 9-12R; 144; DAM DRAM,
　MST; MTCW; SATA 7; SATA-Obit 79

Iqbal, Muhammad　1873-1938 ..... **TCLC 28**

Ireland, Patrick
　See O'Doherty, Brian

Iron, Ralph
　See Schreiner, Olive (Emilie Albertina)

Irving, John (Winslow)
　1942- .... **CLC 13, 23, 38**
　See also AAYA 8; BEST 89:3; CA 25-28R;
　CANR 28; DAM NOV, POP; DLB 6;
　DLBY 82; MTCW

Irving, Washington
　1783-1859 ..... **NCLC 2, 19; DA; DAB;
　SSC 2; WLC**
　See also CDALB 1640-1865; DAM MST;
　DLB 3, 11, 30, 59, 73, 74; YABC 2

Irwin, P. K.
　See Page, P(atricia) K(athleen)

Isaacs, Susan　1943- .... **CLC 32**
　See also BEST 89:1; CA 89-92; CANR 20,
　41; DAM POP; INT CANR-20; MTCW

Isherwood, Christopher (William Bradshaw)
　1904-1986 .... **CLC 1, 9, 11, 14, 44**
　See also CA 13-16R; 117; CANR 35;
　DAM DRAM, NOV; DLB 15; DLBY 86;
　MTCW

Ishiguro, Kazuo　1954- ...... **CLC 27, 56, 59**
　See also BEST 90:2; CA 120; CANR 49;
　DAM NOV; MTCW

Ishikawa Takuboku
　1886(?)-1912 .... **TCLC 15; PC 10**
　See also CA 113; DAM POET

Iskander, Fazil　1929- .... **CLC 47**
　See also CA 102

Ivan IV　1530-1584 .... **LC 17**

Ivanov, Vyacheslav Ivanovich
　1866-1949 .... **TCLC 33**
　See also CA 122

Ivask, Ivar Vidrik　1927-1992....... **CLC 14**
　See also CA 37-40R; 139; CANR 24

Jackson, Daniel
　See Wingrove, David (John)

Jackson, Jesse　1908-1983 .... **CLC 12**
　See also BW 1; CA 25-28R; 109; CANR 27;
　CLR 28; MAICYA; SATA 2, 29;
　SATA-Obit 48

Jackson, Laura (Riding)　1901-1991
　See Riding, Laura
　See also CA 65-68; 135; CANR 28; DLB 48

Jackson, Sam
　See Trumbo, Dalton

Jackson, Sara
　See Wingrove, David (John)

Jackson, Shirley
　1919-1965 .... **CLC 11, 60, 87; DA;
　DAC; SSC 9; WLC**
　See also AAYA 9; CA 1-4R; 25-28R;
　CANR 4; CDALB 1941-1968;
　DAM MST; DLB 6; SATA 2

Jacob, (Cyprien-)Max　1876-1944 ... **TCLC 6**
　See also CA 104

Kaufman, George S. 1889-1961..... CLC 38
See also CA 108; 93-96; DAM DRAM;
DLB 7; INT 108

Kaufman, Sue .... CLC 3, 8
See also Barondess, Sue K(aufman)

Kavafis, Konstantinos Petrou 1863-1933
See Cavafy, C(onstantine) P(eter)
See also CA 104

Kavan, Anna 1901-1968...... CLC 5, 13, 82
See also CA 5-8R; CANR 6; MTCW

Kavanagh, Dan
See Barnes, Julian

Kavanagh, Patrick (Joseph)
1904-1967 .... CLC 22
See also CA 123; 25-28R; DLB 15, 20;
MTCW

Kawabata, Yasunari
1899-1972 ..... CLC 2, 5, 9, 18; SSC 17
See also CA 93-96; 33-36R; DAM MULT

Kaye, M(ary) M(argaret) 1909-..... CLC 28
See also CA 89-92; CANR 24; MTCW;
SATA 62

Kaye, Mollie
See Kaye, M(ary) M(argaret)

Kaye-Smith, Sheila 1887-1956..... TCLC 20
See also CA 118; DLB 36

Kaymor, Patrice Maguilene
See Senghor, Leopold Sedar

Kazan, Elia 1909-........... CLC 6, 16, 63
See also CA 21-24R; CANR 32

Kazantzakis, Nikos
1883(?)-1957 .... TCLC 2, 5, 33
See also CA 105; 132; MTCW

Kazin, Alfred 1915- .... CLC 34, 38
See also CA 1-4R; CAAS 7; CANR 1, 45;
DLB 67

Keane, Mary Nesta (Skrine) 1904-
See Keane, Molly
See also CA 108; 114

Keane, Molly..................... CLC 31
See also Keane, Mary Nesta (Skrine)
See also INT 114

Keates, Jonathan 19(?)- .... CLC 34

Keaton, Buster 1895-1966 .... CLC 20

Keats, John
1795-1821 .... NCLC 8; DA; DAB;
DAC; PC 1; WLC
See also CDBLB 1789-1832; DAM MST,
POET; DLB 96, 110

Keene, Donald 1922- .... CLC 34
See also CA 1-4R; CANR 5

Keillor, Garrison .... CLC 40
See also Keillor, Gary (Edward)
See also AAYA 2; BEST 89:3; DLBY 87;
SATA 58

Keillor, Gary (Edward) 1942-
See Keillor, Garrison
See also CA 111; 117; CANR 36;
DAM POP; MTCW

Keith, Michael
See Hubbard, L(afayette) Ron(ald)

Keller, Gottfried 1819-1890 .... NCLC 2
See also DLB 129

Kellerman, Jonathan 1949- .... CLC 44
See also BEST 90:1; CA 106; CANR 29;
DAM POP; INT CANR-29

Kelley, William Melvin 1937-...... CLC 22
See also BW 1; CA 77-80; CANR 27;
DLB 33

Kellogg, Marjorie 1922-........... CLC 2
See also CA 81-84

Kellow, Kathleen
See Hibbert, Eleanor Alice Burford

Kelly, M(ilton) T(erry) 1947-...... CLC 55
See also CA 97-100; CAAS 22; CANR 19,
43

Kelman, James 1946-.......... CLC 58, 86
See also CA 148

Kemal, Yashar 1923- .... CLC 14, 29
See also CA 89-92; CANR 44

Kemble, Fanny 1809-1893 .... NCLC 18
See also DLB 32

Kemelman, Harry 1908-............ CLC 2
See also AITN 1; CA 9-12R; CANR 6;
DLB 28

Kempe, Margery 1373(?)-1440(?) ..... LC 6
See also DLB 146

Kempis, Thomas a 1380-1471 .... LC 11

Kendall, Henry 1839-1882....... NCLC 12

Keneally, Thomas (Michael)
1935- ...... CLC 5, 8, 10, 14, 19, 27, 43
See also CA 85-88; CANR 10, 50;
DAM NOV; MTCW

Kennedy, Adrienne (Lita)
1931- .... CLC 66; BLC; DC 5
See also BW 2; CA 103; CAAS 20; CABS 3;
CANR 26; DAM MULT; DLB 38

Kennedy, John Pendleton
1795-1870 .... NCLC 2
See also DLB 3

Kennedy, Joseph Charles 1929-
See Kennedy, X. J.
See also CA 1-4R; CANR 4, 30, 40;
SATA 14

Kennedy, William 1928-... CLC 6, 28, 34, 53
See also AAYA 1; CA 85-88; CANR 14,
31; DAM NOV; DLB 143; DLBY 85;
INT CANR-31; MTCW; SATA 57

Kennedy, X. J.................... CLC 8, 42
See also Kennedy, Joseph Charles
See also CAAS 9; CLR 27; DLB 5

Kenny, Maurice (Francis) 1929- .... CLC 87
See also CA 144; CAAS 22; DAM MULT;
NNAL

Kent, Kelvin
See Kuttner, Henry

Kenton, Maxwell
See Southern, Terry

Kenyon, Robert O.
See Kuttner, Henry

Kerouac, Jack ..... CLC 1, 2, 3, 5, 14, 29, 61
See also Kerouac, Jean-Louis Lebris de
See also CDALB 1941-1968; DLB 2, 16;
DLBD 3

Kerouac, Jean-Louis Lebris de 1922-1969
See Kerouac, Jack
See also AITN 1; CA 5-8R; 25-28R;
CANR 26; DA; DAB; DAC; DAM MST,
NOV, POET, POP; MTCW; WLC

Kerr, Jean 1923-................ CLC 22
See also CA 5-8R; CANR 7; INT CANR-7

Kerr, M. E.................... CLC 12, 35
See also Meaker, Marijane (Agnes)
See also AAYA 2; CLR 29; SAAS 1

Kerr, Robert .... CLC 55

Kerrigan, (Thomas) Anthony
1918- .... CLC 4, 6
See also CA 49-52; CAAS 11; CANR 4

Kerry, Lois
See Duncan, Lois

Kesey, Ken (Elton)
1935- ...... CLC 1, 3, 6, 11, 46, 64; DA;
DAB; DAC; WLC
See also CA 1-4R; CANR 22, 38;
CDALB 1968-1988; DAM MST, NOV,
POP; DLB 2, 16; MTCW; SATA 66

Kesselring, Joseph (Otto)
1902-1967 .... CLC 45
See also DAM DRAM, MST

Kessler, Jascha (Frederick) 1929-.... CLC 4
See also CA 17-20R; CANR 8, 48

Kettelkamp, Larry (Dale) 1933- .... CLC 12
See also CA 29-32R; CANR 16; SAAS 3;
SATA 2

Keyber, Conny
See Fielding, Henry

Keyes, Daniel 1927-.... CLC 80; DA; DAC
See also CA 17-20R; CANR 10, 26;
DAM MST, NOV; SATA 37

Khanshendel, Chiron
See Rose, Wendy

Khayyam, Omar
1048-1131 .... CMLC 11; PC 8
See also DAM POET

Kherdian, David 1931-........... CLC 6, 9
See also CA 21-24R; CAAS 2; CANR 39;
CLR 24; JRDA; MAICYA; SATA 16, 74

Khlebnikov, Velimir .... TCLC 20
See also Khlebnikov, Viktor Vladimirovich

Khlebnikov, Viktor Vladimirovich 1885-1922
See Khlebnikov, Velimir
See also CA 117

Khodasevich, Vladislav (Felitsianovich)
1886-1939 .... TCLC 15
See also CA 115

Kielland, Alexander Lange
1849-1906 .... TCLC 5
See also CA 104

Kiely, Benedict 1919-.......... CLC 23, 43
See also CA 1-4R; CANR 2; DLB 15

Kienzle, William X(avier) 1928- .... CLC 25
See also CA 93-96; CAAS 1; CANR 9, 31;
DAM POP; INT CANR-31; MTCW

Kierkegaard, Soren 1813-1855.... NCLC 34

Killens, John Oliver 1916-1987..... CLC 10
See also BW 2; CA 77-80; 123; CAAS 2;
CANR 26; DLB 33

Killigrew, Anne 1660-1685........... LC 4
See also DLB 131

Kim
See Simenon, Georges (Jacques Christian)

Kincaid, Jamaica 1949- ... **CLC 43, 68; BLC**
See also AAYA 13; BW 2; CA 125;
CANR 47; DAM MULT, NOV;
DLB 157

King, Francis (Henry) 1923- ..... **CLC 8, 53**
See also CA 1-4R; CANR 1, 33;
DAM NOV; DLB 15, 139; MTCW

King, Martin Luther, Jr.
1929-1968 .... **CLC 83; BLC; DA; DAB;
DAC**
See also BW 2; CA 25-28; CANR 27, 44;
CAP 2; DAM MST, MULT; MTCW;
SATA 14

King, Stephen (Edwin)
1947- ...... **CLC 12, 26, 37, 61; SSC 17**
See also AAYA 1, 17; BEST 90:1;
CA 61-64; CANR 1, 30; DAM NOV,
POP; DLB 143; DLBY 80; JRDA;
MTCW; SATA 9, 55

King, Steve
See King, Stephen (Edwin)

King, Thomas 1943- .... **CLC 89; DAC**
See also CA 144; DAM MULT; NNAL

Kingman, Lee...................... **CLC 17**
See Natti, (Mary) Lee
See also SAAS 3; SATA 1, 67

Kingsley, Charles 1819-1875 ..... **NCLC 35**
See also DLB 21, 32; YABC 2

Kingsley, Sidney 1906-1995........ **CLC 44**
See also CA 85-88; 147; DLB 7

Kingsolver, Barbara 1955- ...... **CLC 55, 81**
See also AAYA 15; CA 129; 134;
DAM POP; INT 134

Kingston, Maxine (Ting Ting) Hong
1940- .... **CLC 12, 19, 58**
See also AAYA 8; CA 69-72; CANR 13,
38; DAM MULT, NOV; DLBY 80;
INT CANR-13; MTCW; SATA 53

Kinnell, Galway
1927- .... **CLC 1, 2, 3, 5, 13, 29**
See also CA 9-12R; CANR 10, 34; DLB 5;
DLBY 87; INT CANR-34; MTCW

Kinsella, Thomas 1928- .... **CLC 4, 19**
See also CA 17-20R; CANR 15; DLB 27;
MTCW

Kinsella, W(illiam) P(atrick)
1935- .... **CLC 27, 43; DAC**
See also AAYA 7; CA 97-100; CAAS 7;
CANR 21, 35; DAM NOV, POP;
INT CANR-21; MTCW

Kipling, (Joseph) Rudyard
1865-1936 ...... **TCLC 8, 17; DA; DAB;
DAC; PC 3; SSC 5; WLC**
See also CA 105; 120; CANR 33;
CDBLB 1890-1914; CLR 39; DAM MST,
POET; DLB 19, 34, 141, 156; MAICYA;
MTCW; YABC 2

Kirkup, James 1918- .... **CLC 1**
See also CA 1-4R; CAAS 4; CANR 2;
DLB 27; SATA 12

Kirkwood, James 1930(?)-1989 ...... **CLC 9**
See also AITN 2; CA 1-4R; 128; CANR 6,
40

Kirshner, Sidney
See Kingsley, Sidney

Kis, Danilo 1935-1989 .... **CLC 57**
See also CA 109; 118; 129; MTCW

Kivi, Aleksis 1834-1872 .... **NCLC 30**

Kizer, Carolyn (Ashley)
1925- .... **CLC 15, 39, 80**
See also CA 65-68; CAAS 5; CANR 24;
DAM POET; DLB 5

Klabund 1890-1928............... **TCLC 44**
See also DLB 66

Klappert, Peter 1942-............. **CLC 57**
See also CA 33-36R; DLB 5

Klein, A(braham) M(oses)
1909-1972 .... **CLC 19; DAB; DAC**
See also CA 101; 37-40R; DAM MST;
DLB 68

Klein, Norma 1938-1989 .... **CLC 30**
See also AAYA 2; CA 41-44R; 128;
CANR 15, 37; CLR 2, 19;
INT CANR-15; JRDA; MAICYA;
SAAS 1; SATA 7, 57

Klein, T(heodore) E(ibon) D(onald)
1947- .... **CLC 34**
See also CA 119; CANR 44

Kleist, Heinrich von
1777-1811 .... **NCLC 2, 37**
See also DAM DRAM; DLB 90

Klima, Ivan 1931-................ **CLC 56**
See also CA 25-28R; CANR 17, 50;
DAM NOV

Klimentov, Andrei Platonovich 1899-1951
See Platonov, Andrei
See also CA 108

Klinger, Friedrich Maximilian von
1752-1831 .... **NCLC 1**
See also DLB 94

Klopstock, Friedrich Gottlieb
1724-1803 .... **NCLC 11**
See also DLB 97

Knebel, Fletcher 1911-1993........ **CLC 14**
See also AITN 1; CA 1-4R; 140; CAAS 3;
CANR 1, 36; SATA 36; SATA-Obit 75

Knickerbocker, Diedrich
See Irving, Washington

Knight, Etheridge
1931-1991 ...... **CLC 40; BLC; PC 14**
See also BW 1; CA 21-24R; 133; CANR 23;
DAM POET; DLB 41

Knight, Sarah Kemble 1666-1727 ..... **LC 7**
See also DLB 24

Knister, Raymond 1899-1932...... **TCLC 56**
See also DLB 68

Knowles, John
1926- ...... **CLC 1, 4, 10, 26; DA; DAC**
See also AAYA 10; CA 17-20R; CANR 40;
CDALB 1968-1988; DAM MST, NOV;
DLB 6; MTCW; SATA 8

Knox, Calvin M.
See Silverberg, Robert

Knye, Cassandra
See Disch, Thomas M(ichael)

Koch, C(hristopher) J(ohn) 1932- ... **CLC 42**
See also CA 127

Koch, Christopher
See Koch, C(hristopher) J(ohn)

Koch, Kenneth 1925- .... **CLC 5, 8, 44**
See also CA 1-4R; CANR 6, 36;
DAM POET; DLB 5; INT CANR-36;
SATA 65

Kochanowski, Jan 1530-1584....... **LC 10**

Kock, Charles Paul de
1794-1871 .... **NCLC 16**

Koda Shigeyuki 1867-1947
See Rohan, Koda
See also CA 121

Koestler, Arthur
1905-1983 .... **CLC 1, 3, 6, 8, 15, 33**
See also CA 1-4R; 109; CANR 1, 33;
CDBLB 1945-1960; DLBY 83; MTCW

Kogawa, Joy Nozomi 1935-... **CLC 78; DAC**
See also CA 101; CANR 19; DAM MST,
MULT

Kohout, Pavel 1928-.............. **CLC 13**
See also CA 45-48; CANR 3

Koizumi, Yakumo
See Hearn, (Patricio) Lafcadio (Tessima
Carlos)

Kolmar, Gertrud 1894-1943....... **TCLC 40**

Komunyakaa, Yusef 1947-......... **CLC 86**
See also CA 147; DLB 120

Konrad, George
See Konrad, Gyoergy

Konrad, Gyoergy 1933- ...... **CLC 4, 10, 73**
See also CA 85-88

Konwicki, Tadeusz 1926-..... **CLC 8, 28, 54**
See also CA 101; CAAS 9; CANR 39;
MTCW

Koontz, Dean R(ay) 1945-......... **CLC 78**
See also AAYA 9; BEST 89:3, 90:2;
CA 108; CANR 19, 36; DAM NOV,
POP; MTCW

Kopit, Arthur (Lee) 1937- .... **CLC 1, 18, 33**
See also AITN 1; CA 81-84; CABS 3;
DAM DRAM; DLB 7; MTCW

Kops, Bernard 1926-.............. **CLC 4**
See also CA 5-8R; DLB 13

Kornbluth, C(yril) M. 1923-1958.... **TCLC 8**
See also CA 105; DLB 8

Korolenko, V. G.
See Korolenko, Vladimir Galaktionovich

Korolenko, Vladimir
See Korolenko, Vladimir Galaktionovich

Korolenko, Vladimir G.
See Korolenko, Vladimir Galaktionovich

Korolenko, Vladimir Galaktionovich
1853-1921 .... **TCLC 22**
See also CA 121

Korzybski, Alfred (Habdank Skarbek)
1879-1950 .... **TCLC 61**
See also CA 123

Kosinski, Jerzy (Nikodem)
1933-1991 .... **CLC 1, 2, 3, 6, 10, 15, 53,
70**
See also CA 17-20R; 134; CANR 9, 46;
DAM NOV; DLB 2; DLBY 82; MTCW

Kostelanetz, Richard (Cory) 1940- .. **CLC 28**
See also CA 13-16R; CAAS 8; CANR 38

Lane, Patrick 1939- .... **CLC 25**
  See also CA 97-100; DAM POET; DLB 53;
  INT 97-100

Lang, Andrew 1844-1912 .... **TCLC 16**
  See also CA 114; 137; DLB 98, 141;
  MAICYA; SATA 16

Lang, Fritz 1890-1976 .... **CLC 20**
  See also CA 77-80; 69-72; CANR 30

Lange, John
  See Crichton, (John) Michael

Langer, Elinor 1939- .... **CLC 34**
  See also CA 121

Langland, William
  1330(?)-1400(?) ...... **LC 19; DA; DAB;**
                                              DAC
  See also DAM MST, POET; DLB 146

Langstaff, Launcelot
  See Irving, Washington

Lanier, Sidney 1842-1881 .... **NCLC 6**
  See also DAM POET; DLB 64; DLBD 13;
  MAICYA; SATA 18

Lanyer, Aemilia 1569-1645 ...... **LC 10, 30**
  See also DLB 121

Lao Tzu .... **CMLC 7**

Lapine, James (Elliot) 1949- .... **CLC 39**
  See also CA 123; 130; INT 130

Larbaud, Valery (Nicolas)
  1881-1957 .... **TCLC 9**
  See also CA 106

Lardner, Ring
  See Lardner, Ring(gold) W(ilmer)

Lardner, Ring W., Jr.
  See Lardner, Ring(gold) W(ilmer)

Lardner, Ring(gold) W(ilmer)
  1885-1933 .... **TCLC 2, 14**
  See also CA 104; 131; CDALB 1917-1929;
  DLB 11, 25, 86; MTCW

Laredo, Betty
  See Codrescu, Andrei

Larkin, Maia
  See Wojciechowska, Maia (Teresa)

Larkin, Philip (Arthur)
  1922-1985 .... **CLC 3, 5, 8, 9, 13, 18, 33,**
                                    39, 64; DAB
  See also CA 5-8R; 117; CANR 24;
  CDBLB 1960 to Present; DAM MST,
  POET; DLB 27; MTCW

Larra (y Sanchez de Castro), Mariano Jose de
  1809-1837 .... **NCLC 17**

Larsen, Eric 1941- .... **CLC 55**
  See also CA 132

Larsen, Nella 1891-1964 ..... **CLC 37; BLC**
  See also BW 1; CA 125; DAM MULT;
  DLB 51

Larson, Charles R(aymond) 1938-... **CLC 31**
  See also CA 53-56; CANR 4

Las Casas, Bartolome de 1474-1566.. **LC 31**

Lasker-Schueler, Else 1869-1945 .. **TCLC 57**
  See also DLB 66, 124

Latham, Jean Lee 1902-.......... **CLC 12**
  See also AITN 1; CA 5-8R; CANR 7;
  MAICYA; SATA 2, 68

Latham, Mavis
  See Clark, Mavis Thorpe

Lathen, Emma .... **CLC 2**
  See also Hennissart, Martha; Latsis, Mary
  J(ane)

Lathrop, Francis
  See Leiber, Fritz (Reuter, Jr.)

Latsis, Mary J(ane)
  See Lathen, Emma
  See also CA 85-88

Lattimore, Richmond (Alexander)
  1906-1984 .... **CLC 3**
  See also CA 1-4R; 112; CANR 1

Laughlin, James 1914-........... **CLC 49**
  See also CA 21-24R; CAAS 22; CANR 9,
  47; DLB 48

Laurence, (Jean) Margaret (Wemyss)
  1926-1987 .... **CLC 3, 6, 13, 50, 62;**
                                      DAC; SSC 7
  See also CA 5-8R; 121; CANR 33;
  DAM MST; DLB 53; MTCW;
  SATA-Obit 50

Laurent, Antoine 1952- .... **CLC 50**

Lauscher, Hermann
  See Hesse, Hermann

Lautreamont, Comte de
  1846-1870 .... **NCLC 12; SSC 14**

Laverty, Donald
  See Blish, James (Benjamin)

Lavin, Mary 1912- ...... **CLC 4, 18; SSC 4**
  See also CA 9-12R; CANR 33; DLB 15;
  MTCW

Lavond, Paul Dennis
  See Kornbluth, C(yril) M.; Pohl, Frederik

Lawler, Raymond Evenor 1922- .... **CLC 58**
  See also CA 103

Lawrence, D(avid) H(erbert Richards)
  1885-1930 .... **TCLC 2, 9, 16, 33, 48, 61;**
                    DA; DAB; DAC; SSC 4, 19; WLC
  See also CA 104; 121; CDBLB 1914-1945;
  DAM MST, NOV, POET; DLB 10, 19,
  36, 98; MTCW

Lawrence, T(homas) E(dward)
  1888-1935 .... **TCLC 18**
  See also Dale, Colin
  See also CA 115

Lawrence of Arabia
  See Lawrence, T(homas) E(dward)

Lawson, Henry (Archibald Hertzberg)
  1867-1922 .... **TCLC 27; SSC 18**
  See also CA 120

Lawton, Dennis
  See Faust, Frederick (Schiller)

Laxness, Halldor .... **CLC 25**
  See also Gudjonsson, Halldor Kiljan

Layamon fl. c. 1200-............ **CMLC 10**
  See also DLB 146

Laye, Camara 1928-1980 ... **CLC 4, 38; BLC**
  See also BW 1; CA 85-88; 97-100;
  CANR 25; DAM MULT; MTCW

Layton, Irving (Peter)
  1912- .... **CLC 2, 15; DAC**
  See also CA 1-4R; CANR 2, 33, 43;
  DAM MST, POET; DLB 88; MTCW

Lazarus, Emma 1849-1887........ **NCLC 8**

Lazarus, Felix
  See Cable, George Washington

Lazarus, Henry
  See Slavitt, David R(ytman)

Lea, Joan
  See Neufeld, John (Arthur)

Leacock, Stephen (Butler)
  1869-1944 .... **TCLC 2; DAC**
  See also CA 104; 141; DAM MST; DLB 92

Lear, Edward 1812-1888 .... **NCLC 3**
  See also CLR 1; DLB 32; MAICYA;
  SATA 18

Lear, Norman (Milton) 1922- ...... **CLC 12**
  See also CA 73-76

Leavis, F(rank) R(aymond)
  1895-1978 .... **CLC 24**
  See also CA 21-24R; 77-80; CANR 44;
  MTCW

Leavitt, David 1961-............... **CLC 34**
  See also CA 116; 122; CANR 50;
  DAM POP; DLB 130; INT 122

Leblanc, Maurice (Marie Emile)
  1864-1941 .... **TCLC 49**
  See also CA 110

Lebowitz, Fran(ces Ann)
  1951(?)-................... **CLC 11, 36**
  See also CA 81-84; CANR 14;
  INT CANR-14; MTCW

Lebrecht, Peter
  See Tieck, (Johann) Ludwig

le Carre, John .... **CLC 3, 5, 9, 15, 28**
  See also Cornwell, David (John Moore)
  See also BEST 89:4; CDBLB 1960 to
  Present; DLB 87

Le Clezio, J(ean) M(arie) G(ustave)
  1940- .... **CLC 31**
  See also CA 116; 128; DLB 83

Leconte de Lisle, Charles-Marie-Rene
  1818-1894 .... **NCLC 29**

Le Coq, Monsieur
  See Simenon, Georges (Jacques Christian)

Leduc, Violette 1907-1972......... **CLC 22**
  See also CA 13-14; 33-36R; CAP 1

Ledwidge, Francis 1887(?)-1917 ... **TCLC 23**
  See also CA 123; DLB 20

Lee, Andrea 1953- .... **CLC 36; BLC**
  See also BW 1; CA 125; DAM MULT

Lee, Andrew
  See Auchincloss, Louis (Stanton)

Lee, Don L. .... **CLC 2**
  See also Madhubuti, Haki R.

Lee, George W(ashington)
  1894-1976 .... **CLC 52; BLC**
  See also BW 1; CA 125; DAM MULT;
  DLB 51

Lee, (Nelle) Harper
  1926- .... **CLC 12, 60; DA; DAB; DAC;**
                                                WLC
  See also AAYA 13; CA 13-16R;
  CDALB 1941-1968; DAM MST, NOV;
  DLB 6; MTCW; SATA 11

Lee, Helen Elaine 1959(?)- .... **CLC 86**
  See also CA 148

Lee, Julian
  See Latham, Jean Lee

Lee, Larry
  See Lee, Lawrence

Lee, Laurie 1914-. . . . . **CLC 90; DAB**
See also CA 77-80; CANR 33; DAM POP;
DLB 27; MTCW

Lee, Lawrence 1941-1990. . . . . **CLC 34**
See also CA 131; CANR 43

Lee, Manfred B(ennington)
1905-1971 . . . . **CLC 11**
See also Queen, Ellery
See also CA 1-4R; 29-32R; CANR 2;
DLB 137

Lee, Stan 1922-. . . . . **CLC 17**
See also AAYA 5; CA 108; 111; INT 111

Lee, Tanith 1947-. . . . . **CLC 46**
See also AAYA 15; CA 37-40R; SATA 8

Lee, Vernon. **TCLC 5**
See also Paget, Violet
See also DLB 57, 153, 156

Lee, William
See Burroughs, William S(eward)

Lee, Willy
See Burroughs, William S(eward)

Lee-Hamilton, Eugene (Jacob)
1845-1907 . . . . **TCLC 22**
See also CA 117

Leet, Judith 1935- . . . . **CLC 11**

Le Fanu, Joseph Sheridan
1814-1873 . . . . **NCLC 9; SSC 14**
See also DAM POP; DLB 21, 70, 159

Leffland, Ella 1931- . . . . **CLC 19**
See also CA 29-32R; CANR 35; DLBY 84;
INT CANR-35; SATA 65

Leger, Alexis
See Leger, (Marie-Rene Auguste) Alexis
Saint-Leger

Leger, (Marie-Rene Auguste) Alexis
Saint-Leger 1887-1975. . . . . . . **CLC 11**
See also Perse, St.-John
See also CA 13-16R; 61-64; CANR 43;
DAM POET; MTCW

Leger, Saintleger
See Leger, (Marie-Rene Auguste) Alexis
Saint-Leger

Le Guin, Ursula K(roeber)
1929- . . . . . . **CLC 8, 13, 22, 45, 71; DAB;
DAC; SSC 12**
See also AAYA 9; AITN 1; CA 21-24R;
CANR 9, 32; CDALB 1968-1988; CLR 3,
28; DAM MST, POP; DLB 8, 52;
INT CANR-32; JRDA; MAICYA;
MTCW; SATA 4, 52

Lehmann, Rosamond (Nina)
1901-1990 . . . . **CLC 5**
See also CA 77-80; 131; CANR 8; DLB 15

Leiber, Fritz (Reuter, Jr.)
1910-1992 . . . . **CLC 25**
See also CA 45-48; 139; CANR 2, 40;
DLB 8; MTCW; SATA 45;
SATA-Obit 73

Leimbach, Martha 1963-
See Leimbach, Marti
See also CA 130

Leimbach, Marti . . . . **CLC 65**
See also Leimbach, Martha

Leino, Eino . . . . **TCLC 24**
See also Loennbohm, Armas Eino Leopold

Leiris, Michel (Julien) 1901-1990. . . **CLC 61**
See also CA 119; 128; 132

Leithauser, Brad 1953-. . . . . **CLC 27**
See also CA 107; CANR 27; DLB 120

Lelchuk, Alan 1938-. . . . . **CLC 5**
See also CA 45-48; CAAS 20; CANR 1

Lem, Stanislaw 1921-. . . . . . . **CLC 8, 15, 40**
See also CA 105; CAAS 1; CANR 32;
MTCW

Lemann, Nancy 1956-. . . . . **CLC 39**
See also CA 118; 136

Lemonnier, (Antoine Louis) Camille
1844-1913 . . . . **TCLC 22**
See also CA 121

Lenau, Nikolaus 1802-1850 . . . . . **NCLC 16**

L'Engle, Madeleine (Camp Franklin)
1918- . . . . **CLC 12**
See also AAYA 1; AITN 2; CA 1-4R;
CANR 3, 21, 39; CLR 1, 14; DLB 52;
JRDA; MAICYA; MTCW; SAAS 15;
SATA 1, 27, 75

Lengyel, Jozsef 1896-1975. . . . . **CLC 7**
See also CA 85-88; 57-60

Lennon, John (Ono)
1940-1980 . . . . **CLC 12, 35**
See also CA 102

Lennox, Charlotte Ramsay
1729(?)-1804 . . . . **NCLC 23**
See also DLB 39

Lentricchia, Frank (Jr.) 1940-. . . . . . **CLC 34**
See also CA 25-28R; CANR 19

Lenz, Siegfried 1926-. . . . . **CLC 27**
See also CA 89-92; DLB 75

Leonard, Elmore (John, Jr.)
1925- . . . . **CLC 28, 34, 71**
See also AITN 1; BEST 89:1, 90:4;
CA 81-84; CANR 12, 28; DAM POP;
INT CANR-28; MTCW

Leonard, Hugh. . . . . **CLC 19**
See also Byrne, John Keyes
See also DLB 13

Leopardi, (Conte) Giacomo
1798-1837 . . . . **NCLC 22**

Le Reveler
See Artaud, Antonin (Marie Joseph)

Lerman, Eleanor 1952-. . . . . **CLC 9**
See also CA 85-88

Lerman, Rhoda 1936-. . . . . **CLC 56**
See also CA 49-52

Lermontov, Mikhail Yuryevich
1814-1841 . . . . **NCLC 47**

Leroux, Gaston 1868-1927. . . . . **TCLC 25**
See also CA 108; 136; SATA 65

Lesage, Alain-Rene 1668-1747. . . . . . **LC 28**

Leskov, Nikolai (Semyonovich)
1831-1895 . . . . **NCLC 25**

Lessing, Doris (May)
1919- . . . . . **CLC 1, 2, 3, 6, 10, 15, 22, 40;
DA; DAB; DAC; SSC 6**
See also CA 9-12R; CAAS 14; CANR 33;
CDBLB 1960 to Present; DAM MST,
NOV; DLB 15, 139; DLBY 85; MTCW

Lessing, Gotthold Ephraim
1729-1781 . . . . **LC 8**
See also DLB 97

Lester, Richard 1932-. . . . . **CLC 20**

Lever, Charles (James)
1806-1872 . . . . **NCLC 23**
See also DLB 21

Leverson, Ada 1865(?)-1936(?) . . . . **TCLC 18**
See also Elaine
See also CA 117; DLB 153

Levertov, Denise
1923- . . . . . . **CLC 1, 2, 3, 5, 8, 15, 28, 66;
PC 11**
See also CA 1-4R; CAAS 19; CANR 3, 29,
50; DAM POET; DLB 5; INT CANR-29;
MTCW

Levi, Jonathan. . . . . **CLC 76**

Levi, Peter (Chad Tigar) 1931-. . . . . **CLC 41**
See also CA 5-8R; CANR 34; DLB 40

Levi, Primo
1919-1987 . . . . **CLC 37, 50; SSC 12**
See also CA 13-16R; 122; CANR 12, 33;
MTCW

Levin, Ira 1929-. . . . . **CLC 3, 6**
See also CA 21-24R; CANR 17, 44;
DAM POP; MTCW; SATA 66

Levin, Meyer 1905-1981 . . . . **CLC 7**
See also AITN 1; CA 9-12R; 104;
CANR 15; DAM POP; DLB 9, 28;
DLBY 81; SATA 21; SATA-Obit 27

Levine, Norman 1924-. . . . . **CLC 54**
See also CA 73-76; CANR 14; DLB 88

Levine, Philip 1928-. . **CLC 2, 4, 5, 9, 14, 33**
See also CA 9-12R; CANR 9, 37;
DAM POET; DLB 5

Levinson, Deirdre 1931-. . . . . **CLC 49**
See also CA 73-76

Levi-Strauss, Claude 1908- . . . . **CLC 38**
See also CA 1-4R; CANR 6, 32; MTCW

Levitin, Sonia (Wolff) 1934- . . . . **CLC 17**
See also AAYA 13; CA 29-32R; CANR 14,
32; JRDA; MAICYA; SAAS 2; SATA 4,
68

Levon, O. U.
See Kesey, Ken (Elton)

Lewes, George Henry
1817-1878 . . . . **NCLC 25**
See also DLB 55, 144

Lewis, Alun 1915-1944. . . . . **TCLC 3**
See also CA 104; DLB 20

Lewis, C. Day
See Day Lewis, C(ecil)

Lewis, C(live) S(taples)
1898-1963 . . . . . **CLC 1, 3, 6, 14, 27; DA;
DAB; DAC; WLC**
See also AAYA 3; CA 81-84; CANR 33;
CDBLB 1945-1960; CLR 3, 27;
DAM MST, NOV, POP; DLB 15, 100,
160; JRDA; MAICYA; MTCW;
SATA 13

Lewis, Janet 1899-. . . . . **CLC 41**
See also Winters, Janet Lewis
See also CA 9-12R; CANR 29; CAP 1;
DLBY 87

Mann, (Luiz) Heinrich   1871-1950... **TCLC 9**
See also CA 106; DLB 66

Mann, (Paul) Thomas
1875-1955 .... **TCLC 2, 8, 14, 21, 35, 44,**
60; DA; DAB; DAC; SSC 5; WLC
See also CA 104; 128; DAM MST, NOV;
DLB 66; MTCW

Manning, David
See Faust, Frederick (Schiller)

Manning, Frederic   1887(?)-1935 ... **TCLC 25**
See also CA 124

Manning, Olivia   1915-1980 ..... **CLC 5, 19**
See also CA 5-8R; 101; CANR 29; MTCW

Mano, D. Keith   1942- .... **CLC 2, 10**
See also CA 25-28R; CAAS 6; CANR 26;
DLB 6

Mansfield, Katherine
..... **TCLC 2, 8, 39; DAB; SSC 9; WLC**
See also Beauchamp, Kathleen Mansfield

Manso, Peter   1940- .... **CLC 39**
See also CA 29-32R; CANR 44

Mantecon, Juan Jimenez
See Jimenez (Mantecon), Juan Ramon

Manton, Peter
See Creasey, John

Man Without a Spleen, A
See Chekhov, Anton (Pavlovich)

Manzoni, Alessandro   1785-1873 .. **NCLC 29**

Mapu, Abraham (ben Jekutiel)
1808-1867 .... **NCLC 18**

Mara, Sally
See Queneau, Raymond

Marat, Jean Paul   1743-1793 .... **LC 10**

Marcel, Gabriel Honore
1889-1973 .... **CLC 15**
See also CA 102; 45-48; MTCW

Marchbanks, Samuel
See Davies, (William) Robertson

Marchi, Giacomo
See Bassani, Giorgio

Margulies, Donald .... **CLC 76**

Marie de France   c. 12th cent. -.... **CMLC 8**

Marie de l'Incarnation   1599-1672.... **LC 10**

Mariner, Scott
See Pohl, Frederik

Marinetti, Filippo Tommaso
1876-1944 .... **TCLC 10**
See also CA 107; DLB 114

Marivaux, Pierre Carlet de Chamblain de
1688-1763 .... **LC 4**

Markandaya, Kamala .... **CLC 8, 38**
See also Taylor, Kamala (Purnaiya)

Markfield, Wallace   1926- .... **CLC 8**
See also CA 69-72; CAAS 3; DLB 2, 28

Markham, Edwin   1852-1940 ...... **TCLC 47**
See also DLB 54

Markham, Robert
See Amis, Kingsley (William)

Marks, J
See Highwater, Jamake (Mamake)

Marks-Highwater, J
See Highwater, Jamake (Mamake)

Markson, David M(errill)   1927- .... **CLC 67**
See also CA 49-52; CANR 1

Marley, Bob .... **CLC 17**
See also Marley, Robert Nesta

Marley, Robert Nesta   1945-1981
See Marley, Bob
See also CA 107; 103

Marlowe, Christopher
1564-1593 ..... **LC 22; DA; DAB; DAC;**
DC 1; WLC
See also CDBLB Before 1660;
DAM DRAM, MST; DLB 62

Marmontel, Jean-Francois
1723-1799 .... **LC 2**

Marquand, John P(hillips)
1893-1960 .... **CLC 2, 10**
See also CA 85-88; DLB 9, 102

Marquez, Gabriel (Jose) Garcia
See Garcia Marquez, Gabriel (Jose)

Marquis, Don(ald Robert Perry)
1878-1937 .... **TCLC 7**
See also CA 104; DLB 11, 25

Marric, J. J.
See Creasey, John

Marrow, Bernard
See Moore, Brian

Marryat, Frederick   1792-1848 .... **NCLC 3**
See also DLB 21

Marsden, James
See Creasey, John

Marsh, (Edith) Ngaio
1899-1982 .... **CLC 7, 53**
See also CA 9-12R; CANR 6; DAM POP;
DLB 77; MTCW

Marshall, Garry   1934- .... **CLC 17**
See also AAYA 3; CA 111; SATA 60

Marshall, Paule
1929- .... **CLC 27, 72; BLC; SSC 3**
See also BW 2; CA 77-80; CANR 25;
DAM MULT; DLB 157; MTCW

Marsten, Richard
See Hunter, Evan

Martha, Henry
See Harris, Mark

Martial   c. 40-c. 104 .... **PC 10**

Martin, Ken
See Hubbard, L(afayette) Ron(ald)

Martin, Richard
See Creasey, John

Martin, Steve   1945- .... **CLC 30**
See also CA 97-100; CANR 30; MTCW

Martin, Valerie   1948- .... **CLC 89**
See also BEST 90:2; CA 85-88; CANR 49

Martin, Violet Florence
1862-1915 .... **TCLC 51**

Martin, Webber
See Silverberg, Robert

Martindale, Patrick Victor
See White, Patrick (Victor Martindale)

Martin du Gard, Roger
1881-1958 .... **TCLC 24**
See also CA 118; DLB 65

Martineau, Harriet   1802-1876.... **NCLC 26**
See also DLB 21, 55, 159; YABC 2

Martines, Julia
See O'Faolain, Julia

Martinez, Jacinto Benavente y
See Benavente (y Martinez), Jacinto

Martinez Ruiz, Jose   1873-1967
See Azorin; Ruiz, Jose Martinez
See also CA 93-96; HW

Martinez Sierra, Gregorio
1881-1947 .... **TCLC 6**
See also CA 115

Martinez Sierra, Maria (de la O'LeJarraga)
1874-1974 .... **TCLC 6**
See also CA 115

Martinsen, Martin
See Follett, Ken(neth Martin)

Martinson, Harry (Edmund)
1904-1978 .... **CLC 14**
See also CA 77-80; CANR 34

Marut, Ret
See Traven, B.

Marut, Robert
See Traven, B.

Marvell, Andrew
1621-1678 ...... **LC 4; DA; DAB; DAC;**
PC 10; WLC
See also CDBLB 1660-1789; DAM MST,
POET; DLB 131

Marx, Karl (Heinrich)
1818-1883 .... **NCLC 17**
See also DLB 129

Masaoka Shiki .... **TCLC 18**
See also Masaoka Tsunenori

Masaoka Tsunenori   1867-1902
See Masaoka Shiki
See also CA 117

Masefield, John (Edward)
1878-1967 .... **CLC 11, 47**
See also CA 19-20; 25-28R; CANR 33;
CAP 2; CDBLB 1890-1914; DAM POET;
DLB 10, 19, 153, 160; MTCW; SATA 19

Maso, Carole   19(?)- .... **CLC 44**

Mason, Bobbie Ann
1940- .... **CLC 28, 43, 82; SSC 4**
See also AAYA 5; CA 53-56; CANR 11,
31; DLBY 87; INT CANR-31; MTCW

Mason, Ernst
See Pohl, Frederik

Mason, Lee W.
See Malzberg, Barry N(athaniel)

Mason, Nick   1945- .... **CLC 35**

Mason, Tally
See Derleth, August (William)

Mass, William
See Gibson, William

Masters, Edgar Lee
1868-1950 ...... **TCLC 2, 25; DA; DAC;**
PC 1
See also CA 104; 133; CDALB 1865-1917;
DAM MST, POET; DLB 54; MTCW

Masters, Hilary   1928- .... **CLC 48**
See also CA 25-28R; CANR 13, 47

Mastrosimone, William   19(?)- ...... **CLC 36**

Mathe, Albert
See Camus, Albert

Matheson, Richard Burton 1926- ... **CLC 37**
See also CA 97-100; DLB 8, 44; INT 97-100

Mathews, Harry 1930-......... **CLC 6, 52**
See also CA 21-24R; CAAS 6; CANR 18, 40

Mathews, John Joseph 1894-1979... **CLC 84**
See also CA 19-20; 142; CANR 45; CAP 2; DAM MULT; NNAL

Mathias, Roland (Glyn) 1915-..... **CLC 45**
See also CA 97-100; CANR 19, 41; DLB 27

Matsuo Basho 1644-1694........... **PC 3**
See also DAM POET

Mattheson, Rodney
See Creasey, John

Matthews, Greg 1949-............ **CLC 45**
See also CA 135

Matthews, William 1942-......... **CLC 40**
See also CA 29-32R; CAAS 18; CANR 12; DLB 5

Matthias, John (Edward) 1941-...... **CLC 9**
See also CA 33-36R

Matthiessen, Peter
1927-............ **CLC 5, 7, 11, 32, 64**
See also AAYA 6; BEST 90:4; CA 9-12R; CANR 21, 50; DAM NOV; DLB 6; MTCW; SATA 27

Maturin, Charles Robert
1780(?)-1824 .... **NCLC 6**

Matute (Ausejo), Ana Maria
1925-....................... **CLC 11**
See also CA 89-92; MTCW

Maugham, W. S.
See Maugham, W(illiam) Somerset

Maugham, W(illiam) Somerset
1874-1965 ...... **CLC 1, 11, 15, 67; DA;**
DAB; DAC; SSC 8; WLC
See also CA 5-8R; 25-28R; CANR 40; CDBLB 1914-1945; DAM DRAM, MST, NOV; DLB 10, 36, 77, 100; MTCW; SATA 54

Maugham, William Somerset
See Maugham, W(illiam) Somerset

Maupassant, (Henri Rene Albert) Guy de
1850-1893 ..... **NCLC 1, 42; DA; DAB;**
DAC; SSC 1; WLC
See also DAM MST; DLB 123

Maurhut, Richard
See Traven, B.

Mauriac, Claude 1914-............. **CLC 9**
See also CA 89-92; DLB 83

Mauriac, Francois (Charles)
1885-1970 .... **CLC 4, 9, 56**
See also CA 25-28; CAP 2; DLB 65; MTCW

Mavor, Osborne Henry 1888-1951
See Bridie, James
See also CA 104

Maxwell, William (Keepers, Jr.)
1908-....................... **CLC 19**
See also CA 93-96; DLBY 80; INT 93-96

May, Elaine 1932- .... **CLC 16**
See also CA 124; 142; DLB 44

Mayakovski, Vladimir (Vladimirovich)
1893-1930 .... **TCLC 4, 18**
See also CA 104

Mayhew, Henry 1812-1887 ...... **NCLC 31**
See also DLB 18, 55

Mayle, Peter 1939(?)-............. **CLC 89**
See also CA 139

Maynard, Joyce 1953-............ **CLC 23**
See also CA 111; 129

Mayne, William (James Carter)
1928-....................... **CLC 12**
See also CA 9-12R; CANR 37; CLR 25; JRDA; MAICYA; SAAS 11; SATA 6, 68

Mayo, Jim
See L'Amour, Louis (Dearborn)

Maysles, Albert 1926- .... **CLC 16**
See also CA 29-32R

Maysles, David 1932-............. **CLC 16**

Mazer, Norma Fox 1931- .... **CLC 26**
See also AAYA 5; CA 69-72; CANR 12, 32; CLR 23; JRDA; MAICYA; SAAS 1; SATA 24, 67

Mazzini, Guiseppe 1805-1872 .... **NCLC 34**

McAuley, James Phillip
1917-1976 .... **CLC 45**
See also CA 97-100

McBain, Ed
See Hunter, Evan

McBrien, William Augustine
1930-....................... **CLC 44**
See also CA 107

McCaffrey, Anne (Inez) 1926-...... **CLC 17**
See also AAYA 6; AITN 2; BEST 89:2; CA 25-28R; CANR 15, 35; DAM NOV, POP; DLB 8; JRDA; MAICYA; MTCW; SAAS 11; SATA 8, 70

McCall, Nathan 1955(?)-.......... **CLC 86**
See also CA 146

McCann, Arthur
See Campbell, John W(ood, Jr.)

McCann, Edson
See Pohl, Frederik

McCarthy, Charles, Jr. 1933-
See McCarthy, Cormac
See also CANR 42; DAM POP

McCarthy, Cormac 1933-..... **CLC 4, 57, 59**
See also McCarthy, Charles, Jr.
See also DLB 6, 143

McCarthy, Mary (Therese)
1912-1989 ... **CLC 1, 3, 5, 14, 24, 39, 59**
See also CA 5-8R; 129; CANR 16, 50; DLB 2; DLBY 81; INT CANR-16; MTCW

McCartney, (James) Paul
1942-....................... **CLC 12, 35**
See also CA 146

McCauley, Stephen (D.) 1955- ..... **CLC 50**
See also CA 141

McClure, Michael (Thomas)
1932-....................... **CLC 6, 10**
See also CA 21-24R; CANR 17, 46; DLB 16

McCorkle, Jill (Collins) 1958-...... **CLC 51**
See also CA 121; DLBY 87

McCourt, James 1941-............. **CLC 5**
See also CA 57-60

McCoy, Horace (Stanley)
1897-1955 .... **TCLC 28**
See also CA 108; DLB 9

McCrae, John 1872-1918............ **TCLC 12**
See also CA 109; DLB 92

McCreigh, James
See Pohl, Frederik

McCullers, (Lula) Carson (Smith)
1917-1967 .... **CLC 1, 4, 10, 12, 48; DA;**
DAB; DAC; SSC 9; WLC
See also CA 5-8R; 25-28R; CABS 1, 3; CANR 18; CDALB 1941-1968; DAM MST, NOV; DLB 2, 7; MTCW; SATA 27

McCulloch, John Tyler
See Burroughs, Edgar Rice

McCullough, Colleen 1938(?)-...... **CLC 27**
See also CA 81-84; CANR 17, 46; DAM NOV, POP; MTCW

McDermott, Alice 1953- .... **CLC 90**
See also CA 109; CANR 40

McElroy, Joseph 1930- .... **CLC 5, 47**
See also CA 17-20R

McEwan, Ian (Russell) 1948- ... **CLC 13, 66**
See also BEST 90:4; CA 61-64; CANR 14, 41; DAM NOV; DLB 14; MTCW

McFadden, David 1940-........... **CLC 48**
See also CA 104; DLB 60; INT 104

McFarland, Dennis 1950- .... **CLC 65**

McGahern, John
1934-........... **CLC 5, 9, 48; SSC 17**
See also CA 17-20R; CANR 29; DLB 14; MTCW

McGinley, Patrick (Anthony)
1937-....................... **CLC 41**
See also CA 120; 127; INT 127

McGinley, Phyllis 1905-1978 .... **CLC 14**
See also CA 9-12R; 77-80; CANR 19; DLB 11, 48; SATA 2, 44; SATA-Obit 24

McGinniss, Joe 1942-............. **CLC 32**
See also AITN 2; BEST 89:2; CA 25-28R; CANR 26; INT CANR-26

McGivern, Maureen Daly
See Daly, Maureen

McGrath, Patrick 1950-........... **CLC 55**
See also CA 136

McGrath, Thomas (Matthew)
1916-1990 .... **CLC 28, 59**
See also CA 9-12R; 132; CANR 6, 33; DAM POET; MTCW; SATA 41; SATA-Obit 66

McGuane, Thomas (Francis III)
1939-................ **CLC 3, 7, 18, 45**
See also AITN 2; CA 49-52; CANR 5, 24, 49; DLB 2; DLBY 80; INT CANR-24; MTCW

McGuckian, Medbh 1950-......... **CLC 48**
See also CA 143; DAM POET; DLB 40

McHale, Tom 1942(?)-1982....... **CLC 3, 5**
See also AITN 1; CA 77-80; 106

McIlvanney, William 1936-......... **CLC 42**
See also CA 25-28R; DLB 14

McIlwraith, Maureen Mollie Hunter
See Hunter, Mollie
See also SATA 2

Author Index

Millar, Kenneth 1915-1983 . . . . **CLC 14**
See also Macdonald, Ross
See also CA 9-12R; 110; CANR 16;
DAM POP; DLB 2; DLBD 6; DLBY 83;
MTCW

Millay, E. Vincent
See Millay, Edna St. Vincent

Millay, Edna St. Vincent
1892-1950 . . . . . . **TCLC 4, 49; DA; DAB;
DAC; PC 6**
See also CA 104; 130; CDALB 1917-1929;
DAM MST, POET; DLB 45; MTCW

Miller, Arthur
1915- . . . . **CLC 1, 2, 6, 10, 15, 26, 47, 78;
DA; DAB; DAC; DC 1; WLC**
See also AAYA 15; AITN 1; CA 1-4R;
CABS 3; CANR 2, 30;
CDALB 1941-1968; DAM DRAM, MST;
DLB 7; MTCW

Miller, Henry (Valentine)
1891-1980 . . . . **CLC 1, 2, 4, 9, 14, 43, 84;
DA; DAB; DAC; WLC**
See also CA 9-12R; 97-100; CANR 33;
CDALB 1929-1941; DAM MST, NOV;
DLB 4, 9; DLBY 80; MTCW

Miller, Jason 1939(?)- . . . . **CLC 2**
See also AITN 1; CA 73-76; DLB 7

Miller, Sue 1943- . . . . **CLC 44**
See also BEST 90:3; CA 139; DAM POP;
DLB 143

Miller, Walter M(ichael, Jr.)
1923- . . . . **CLC 4, 30**
See also CA 85-88; DLB 8

Millett, Kate 1934- . . . . **CLC 67**
See also AITN 1; CA 73-76; CANR 32;
MTCW

Millhauser, Steven 1943- . . . . **CLC 21, 54**
See also CA 110; 111; DLB 2; INT 111

Millin, Sarah Gertrude 1889-1968 . . **CLC 49**
See also CA 102; 93-96

Milne, A(lan) A(lexander)
1882-1956 . . . . **TCLC 6; DAB; DAC**
See also CA 104; 133; CLR 1, 26;
DAM MST; DLB 10, 77, 100, 160;
MAICYA; MTCW; YABC 1

Milner, Ron(ald) 1938- . . . . **CLC 56; BLC**
See also AITN 1; BW 1; CA 73-76;
CANR 24; DAM MULT; DLB 38;
MTCW

Milosz, Czeslaw
1911- . . . **CLC 5, 11, 22, 31, 56, 82; PC 8**
See also CA 81-84; CANR 23; DAM MST,
POET; MTCW

Milton, John
1608-1674 . . . . . . **LC 9; DA; DAB; DAC;
WLC**
See also CDBLB 1660-1789; DAM MST,
POET; DLB 131, 151

Min, Anchee 1957- . . . . **CLC 86**
See also CA 146

Minehaha, Cornelius
See Wedekind, (Benjamin) Frank(lin)

Miner, Valerie 1947- . . . . **CLC 40**
See also CA 97-100

Minimo, Duca
See D'Annunzio, Gabriele

Minot, Susan 1956- . . . . **CLC 44**
See also CA 134

Minus, Ed 1938- . . . . **CLC 39**

Miranda, Javier
See Bioy Casares, Adolfo

Mirbeau, Octave 1848-1917 . . . . . . **TCLC 55**
See also DLB 123

Miro (Ferrer), Gabriel (Francisco Victor)
1879-1930 . . . . **TCLC 5**
See also CA 104

Mishima, Yukio
. . . . . . **CLC 2, 4, 6, 9, 27; DC 1; SSC 4**
See also Hiraoka, Kimitake

Mistral, Frederic 1830-1914 . . . . . . **TCLC 51**
See also CA 122

Mistral, Gabriela . . . . **TCLC 2; HLC**
See also Godoy Alcayaga, Lucila

Mistry, Rohinton 1952- . . . . . . **CLC 71; DAC**
See also CA 141

Mitchell, Clyde
See Ellison, Harlan (Jay); Silverberg, Robert

Mitchell, James Leslie 1901-1935
See Gibbon, Lewis Grassic
See also CA 104; DLB 15

Mitchell, Joni 1943- . . . . **CLC 12**
See also CA 112

Mitchell, Margaret (Munnerlyn)
1900-1949 . . . . **TCLC 11**
See also CA 109; 125; DAM NOV, POP;
DLB 9; MTCW

Mitchell, Peggy
See Mitchell, Margaret (Munnerlyn)

Mitchell, S(ilas) Weir 1829-1914 . . **TCLC 36**

Mitchell, W(illiam) O(rmond)
1914- . . . . **CLC 25; DAC**
See also CA 77-80; CANR 15, 43;
DAM MST; DLB 88

Mitford, Mary Russell 1787-1855 . . **NCLC 4**
See also DLB 110, 116

Mitford, Nancy 1904-1973 . . . . **CLC 44**
See also CA 9-12R

Miyamoto, Yuriko 1899-1951 . . . . . **TCLC 37**

Mo, Timothy (Peter) 1950(?)- . . . . . . **CLC 46**
See also CA 117; MTCW

Modarressi, Taghi (M.) 1931- . . . . . . **CLC 44**
See also CA 121; 134; INT 134

Modiano, Patrick (Jean) 1945- . . . . . **CLC 18**
See also CA 85-88; CANR 17, 40; DLB 83

Moerck, Paal
See Roelvaag, O(le) E(dvart)

Mofolo, Thomas (Mokopu)
1875(?)-1948 . . . . **TCLC 22; BLC**
See also CA 121; DAM MULT

Mohr, Nicholasa 1935- . . . . . . **CLC 12; HLC**
See also AAYA 8; CA 49-52; CANR 1, 32;
CLR 22; DAM MULT; DLB 145; HW;
JRDA; SAAS 8; SATA 8

Mojtabai, A(nn) G(race)
1938- . . . . **CLC 5, 9, 15, 29**
See also CA 85-88

Moliere
1622-1673 . . . . . **LC 28; DA; DAB; DAC;
WLC**
See also DAM DRAM, MST

Molin, Charles
See Mayne, William (James Carter)

Molnar, Ferenc 1878-1952 . . . . **TCLC 20**
See also CA 109; DAM DRAM

Momaday, N(avarre) Scott
1934- . . . **CLC 2, 19, 85; DA; DAB; DAC**
See also AAYA 11; CA 25-28R; CANR 14,
34; DAM MST, MULT, NOV, POP;
DLB 143; INT CANR-14; MTCW;
NNAL; SATA 48; SATA-Brief 30

Monette, Paul 1945-1995 . . . . **CLC 82**
See also CA 139; 147

Monroe, Harriet 1860-1936 . . . . **TCLC 12**
See also CA 109; DLB 54, 91

Monroe, Lyle
See Heinlein, Robert A(nson)

Montagu, Elizabeth 1917- . . . . **NCLC 7**
See also CA 9-12R

Montagu, Mary (Pierrepont) Wortley
1689-1762 . . . . **LC 9**
See also DLB 95, 101

Montagu, W. H.
See Coleridge, Samuel Taylor

Montague, John (Patrick)
1929- . . . . **CLC 13, 46**
See also CA 9-12R; CANR 9; DLB 40;
MTCW

Montaigne, Michel (Eyquem) de
1533-1592 . . . . . . **LC 8; DA; DAB; DAC;
WLC**
See also DAM MST

Montale, Eugenio
1896-1981 . . . . **CLC 7, 9, 18; PC 13**
See also CA 17-20R; 104; CANR 30;
DLB 114; MTCW

Montesquieu, Charles-Louis de Secondat
1689-1755 . . . . **LC 7**

Montgomery, (Robert) Bruce 1921-1978
See Crispin, Edmund
See also CA 104

Montgomery, L(ucy) M(aud)
1874-1942 . . . . **TCLC 51; DAC**
See also AAYA 12; CA 108; 137; CLR 8;
DAM MST; DLB 92; JRDA; MAICYA;
YABC 1

Montgomery, Marion H., Jr. 1925- . . **CLC 7**
See also AITN 1; CA 1-4R; CANR 3, 48;
DLB 6

Montgomery, Max
See Davenport, Guy (Mattison, Jr.)

Montherlant, Henry (Milon) de
1896-1972 . . . . **CLC 8, 19**
See also CA 85-88; 37-40R; DAM DRAM;
DLB 72; MTCW

Monty Python
See Chapman, Graham; Cleese, John
(Marwood); Gilliam, Terry (Vance); Idle,
Eric; Jones, Terence Graham Parry; Palin,
Michael (Edward)
See also AAYA 7

Moodie, Susanna (Strickland)
1803-1885 . . . . **NCLC 14**
See also DLB 99

Mooney, Edward 1951-
See Mooney, Ted
See also CA 130

Mooney, Ted . . . . CLC 25
  See also Mooney, Edward

Moorcock, Michael (John)
  1939- . . . . CLC 5, 27, 58
  See also CA 45-48; CAAS 5; CANR 2, 17,
  38; DLB 14; MTCW

Moore, Brian
  1921- . . . . . . CLC 1, 3, 5, 7, 8, 19, 32, 90;
                          DAB; DAC
  See also CA 1-4R; CANR 1, 25, 42;
  DAM MST; MTCW

Moore, Edward
  See Muir, Edwin

Moore, George Augustus
  1852-1933 . . . . TCLC 7; SSC 19
  See also CA 104; DLB 10, 18, 57, 135

Moore, Lorrie . . . . CLC 39, 45, 68
  See also Moore, Marie Lorena

Moore, Marianne (Craig)
  1887-1972 . . . . CLC 1, 2, 4, 8, 10, 13, 19,
                  47; DA; DAB; DAC; PC 4
  See also CA 1-4R; 33-36R; CANR 3;
  CDALB 1929-1941; DAM MST, POET;
  DLB 45; DLBD 7; MTCW; SATA 20

Moore, Marie Lorena   1957-
  See Moore, Lorrie
  See also CA 116; CANR 39

Moore, Thomas   1779-1852 . . . . NCLC 6
  See also DLB 96, 144

Morand, Paul   1888-1976 . . . . CLC 41
  See also CA 69-72; DLB 65

Morante, Elsa   1918-1985 . . . . CLC 8, 47
  See also CA 85-88; 117; CANR 35; MTCW

Moravia, Alberto . . . . . . CLC 2, 7, 11, 27, 46
  See also Pincherle, Alberto

More, Hannah   1745-1833 . . . . NCLC 27
  See also DLB 107, 109, 116, 158

More, Henry   1614-1687 . . . . LC 9
  See also DLB 126

More, Sir Thomas   1478-1535 . . . . LC 10, 32

Moreas, Jean . . . . TCLC 18
  See also Papadiamantopoulos, Johannes

Morgan, Berry   1919- . . . . CLC 6
  See also CA 49-52; DLB 6

Morgan, Claire
  See Highsmith, (Mary) Patricia

Morgan, Edwin (George)   1920- . . . . . CLC 31
  See also CA 5-8R; CANR 3, 43; DLB 27

Morgan, (George) Frederick
  1922- . . . . CLC 23
  See also CA 17-20R; CANR 21

Morgan, Harriet
  See Mencken, H(enry) L(ouis)

Morgan, Jane
  See Cooper, James Fenimore

Morgan, Janet   1945- . . . . CLC 39
  See also CA 65-68

Morgan, Lady   1776(?)-1859 . . . . . . NCLC 29
  See also DLB 116, 158

Morgan, Robin   1941- . . . . CLC 2
  See also CA 69-72; CANR 29; MTCW;
  SATA 80

Morgan, Scott
  See Kuttner, Henry

Morgan, Seth   1949(?)-1990 . . . . CLC 65
  See also CA 132

Morgenstern, Christian
  1871-1914 . . . . TCLC 8
  See also CA 105

Morgenstern, S.
  See Goldman, William (W.)

Moricz, Zsigmond   1879-1942 . . . . . TCLC 33

Morike, Eduard (Friedrich)
  1804-1875 . . . . NCLC 10
  See also DLB 133

Mori Ogai . . . . TCLC 14
  See also Mori Rintaro

Mori Rintaro   1862-1922
  See Mori Ogai
  See also CA 110

Moritz, Karl Philipp   1756-1793 . . . . . . LC 2
  See also DLB 94

Morland, Peter Henry
  See Faust, Frederick (Schiller)

Morren, Theophil
  See Hofmannsthal, Hugo von

Morris, Bill   1952- . . . . CLC 76

Morris, Julian
  See West, Morris L(anglo)

Morris, Steveland Judkins   1950(?)-
  See Wonder, Stevie
  See also CA 111

Morris, William   1834-1896 . . . . NCLC 4
  See also CDBLB 1832-1890; DLB 18, 35,
  57, 156

Morris, Wright   1910- . . . CLC 1, 3, 7, 18, 37
  See also CA 9-12R; CANR 21; DLB 2;
  DLBY 81; MTCW

Morrison, Chloe Anthony Wofford
  See Morrison, Toni

Morrison, James Douglas   1943-1971
  See Morrison, Jim
  See also CA 73-76; CANR 40

Morrison, Jim . . . . CLC 17
  See also Morrison, James Douglas

Morrison, Toni
  1931- . . . . CLC 4, 10, 22, 55, 81, 87;
                 BLC; DA; DAB; DAC
  See also AAYA 1; BW 2; CA 29-32R;
  CANR 27, 42; CDALB 1968-1988;
  DAM MST, MULT, NOV, POP; DLB 6,
  33, 143; DLBY 81; MTCW; SATA 57

Morrison, Van   1945- . . . . CLC 21
  See also CA 116

Mortimer, John (Clifford)
  1923- . . . . CLC 28, 43
  See also CA 13-16R; CANR 21;
  CDBLB 1960 to Present; DAM DRAM,
  POP; DLB 13; INT CANR-21; MTCW

Mortimer, Penelope (Ruth)   1918- . . . . CLC 5
  See also CA 57-60; CANR 45

Morton, Anthony
  See Creasey, John

Mosher, Howard Frank   1943- . . . . . . CLC 62
  See also CA 139

Mosley, Nicholas   1923- . . . . CLC 43, 70
  See also CA 69-72; CANR 41; DLB 14

Moss, Howard
  1922-1987 . . . . CLC 7, 14, 45, 50
  See also CA 1-4R; 123; CANR 1, 44;
  DAM POET; DLB 5

Mossgiel, Rab
  See Burns, Robert

Motion, Andrew (Peter)   1952- . . . . . . CLC 47
  See also CA 146; DLB 40

Motley, Willard (Francis)
  1909-1965 . . . . CLC 18
  See also BW 1; CA 117; 106; DLB 76, 143

Motoori, Norinaga   1730-1801 . . . . NCLC 45

Mott, Michael (Charles Alston)
  1930- . . . . CLC 15, 34
  See also CA 5-8R; CAAS 7; CANR 7, 29

Moure, Erin   1955- . . . . CLC 88
  See also CA 113; DLB 60

Mowat, Farley (McGill)
  1921- . . . . CLC 26; DAC
  See also AAYA 1; CA 1-4R; CANR 4, 24,
  42; CLR 20; DAM MST; DLB 68;
  INT CANR-24; JRDA; MAICYA;
  MTCW; SATA 3, 55

Moyers, Bill   1934- . . . . CLC 74
  See also AITN 2; CA 61-64; CANR 31

Mphahlele, Es'kia
  See Mphahlele, Ezekiel
  See also DLB 125

Mphahlele, Ezekiel   1919- . . . . . CLC 25; BLC
  See also Mphahlele, Es'kia
  See also BW 2; CA 81-84; CANR 26;
  DAM MULT

Mqhayi, S(amuel) E(dward) K(rune Loliwe)
  1875-1945 . . . . TCLC 25; BLC
  See also DAM MULT

Mr. Martin
  See Burroughs, William S(eward)

Mrozek, Slawomir   1930- . . . . CLC 3, 13
  See also CA 13-16R; CAAS 10; CANR 29;
  MTCW

Mrs. Belloc-Lowndes
  See Lowndes, Marie Adelaide (Belloc)

Mtwa, Percy   (?)- . . . . CLC 47

Mueller, Lisel   1924- . . . . CLC 13, 51
  See also CA 93-96; DLB 105

Muir, Edwin   1887-1959 . . . . TCLC 2
  See also CA 104; DLB 20, 100

Muir, John   1838-1914 . . . . TCLC 28

Mujica Lainez, Manuel
  1910-1984 . . . . CLC 31
  See also Lainez, Manuel Mujica
  See also CA 81-84; 112; CANR 32; HW

Mukherjee, Bharati   1940- . . . . CLC 53
  See also BEST 89:2; CA 107; CANR 45;
  DAM NOV; DLB 60; MTCW

Muldoon, Paul   1951- . . . . CLC 32, 72
  See also CA 113; 129; DAM POET;
  DLB 40; INT 129

Mulisch, Harry   1927- . . . . CLC 42
  See also CA 9-12R; CANR 6, 26

Mull, Martin   1943- . . . . CLC 17
  See also CA 105

Mulock, Dinah Maria
  See Craik, Dinah Maria (Mulock)

Munford, Robert 1737(?)-1783 .... **LC 5**
See also DLB 31

Mungo, Raymond 1946-........... **CLC 72**
See also CA 49-52; CANR 2

Munro, Alice
1931- ... **CLC 6, 10, 19, 50; DAC; SSC 3**
See also AITN 2; CA 33-36R; CANR 33;
DAM MST, NOV; DLB 53; MTCW;
SATA 29

Munro, H(ector) H(ugh) 1870-1916
See Saki
See also CA 104; 130; CDBLB 1890-1914;
DA; DAB; DAC; DAM MST, NOV;
DLB 34; MTCW; WLC

Murasaki, Lady.................. **CMLC 1**

Murdoch, (Jean) Iris
1919- ...... **CLC 1, 2, 3, 4, 6, 8, 11, 15,
22, 31, 51; DAB; DAC**
See also CA 13-16R; CANR 8, 43;
CDBLB 1960 to Present; DAM MST,
NOV; DLB 14; INT CANR-8; MTCW

Murnau, Friedrich Wilhelm
See Plumpe, Friedrich Wilhelm

Murphy, Richard 1927-........... **CLC 41**
See also CA 29-32R; DLB 40

Murphy, Sylvia 1937-............. **CLC 34**
See also CA 121

Murphy, Thomas (Bernard) 1935-... **CLC 51**
See also CA 101

Murray, Albert L. 1916- .... **CLC 73**
See also BW 2; CA 49-52; CANR 26;
DLB 38

Murray, Les(lie) A(llan) 1938- ..... **CLC 40**
See also CA 21-24R; CANR 11, 27;
DAM POET

Murry, J. Middleton
See Murry, John Middleton

Murry, John Middleton
1889-1957 .... **TCLC 16**
See also CA 118; DLB 149

Musgrave, Susan 1951- .... **CLC 13, 54**
See also CA 69-72; CANR 45

Musil, Robert (Edler von)
1880-1942 .... **TCLC 12; SSC 18**
See also CA 109; DLB 81, 124

Muske, Carol 1945- .... **CLC 90**
See also Muske-Dukes, Carol (Anne)

Muske-Dukes, Carol (Anne) 1945-
See Muske, Carol
See also CA 65-68; CANR 32

Musset, (Louis Charles) Alfred de
1810-1857 .... **NCLC 7**

My Brother's Brother
See Chekhov, Anton (Pavlovich)

Myers, L. H. 1881-1944.......... **TCLC 59**
See also DLB 15

Myers, Walter Dean 1937- ... **CLC 35; BLC**
See also AAYA 4; BW 2; CA 33-36R;
CANR 20, 42; CLR 4, 16, 35;
DAM MULT, NOV; DLB 33;
INT CANR-20; JRDA; MAICYA;
SAAS 2; SATA 41, 71; SATA-Brief 27

Myers, Walter M.
See Myers, Walter Dean

Myles, Symon
See Follett, Ken(neth Martin)

Nabokov, Vladimir (Vladimirovich)
1899-1977 ..... **CLC 1, 2, 3, 6, 8, 11, 15,
23, 44, 46, 64; DA; DAB; DAC; SSC 11;
WLC**
See also CA 5-8R; 69-72; CANR 20;
CDALB 1941-1968; DAM MST, NOV;
DLB 2; DLBD 3; DLBY 80, 91; MTCW

Nagai Kafu..................... **TCLC 51**
See also Nagai Sokichi

Nagai Sokichi 1879-1959
See Nagai Kafu
See also CA 117

Nagy, Laszlo 1925-1978............ **CLC 7**
See also CA 129; 112

Naipaul, Shiva(dhar Srinivasa)
1945-1985 .... **CLC 32, 39**
See also CA 110; 112; 116; CANR 33;
DAM NOV; DLB 157; DLBY 85;
MTCW

Naipaul, V(idiadhar) S(urajprasad)
1932- .... **CLC 4, 7, 9, 13, 18, 37; DAB;
DAC**
See also CA 1-4R; CANR 1, 33;
CDBLB 1960 to Present; DAM MST,
NOV; DLB 125; DLBY 85; MTCW

Nakos, Lilika 1899(?)-............. **CLC 29**

Narayan, R(asipuram) K(rishnaswami)
1906-............... **CLC 7, 28, 47**
See also CA 81-84; CANR 33; DAM NOV;
MTCW; SATA 62

Nash, (Frediric) Ogden 1902-1971 .. **CLC 23**
See also CA 13-14; 29-32R; CANR 34;
CAP 1; DAM POET; DLB 11;
MAICYA; MTCW; SATA 2, 46

Nathan, Daniel
See Dannay, Frederic

Nathan, George Jean 1882-1958... **TCLC 18**
See also Hatteras, Owen
See also CA 114; DLB 137

Natsume, Kinnosuke 1867-1916
See Natsume, Soseki
See also CA 104

Natsume, Soseki .... **TCLC 2, 10**
See also Natsume, Kinnosuke

Natti, (Mary) Lee 1919-
See Kingman, Lee
See also CA 5-8R; CANR 2

Naylor, Gloria
1950- ..... **CLC 28, 52; BLC; DA; DAC**
See also AAYA 6; BW 2; CA 107;
CANR 27; DAM MST, MULT, NOV,
POP; MTCW

Neihardt, John Gneisenau
1881-1973 .... **CLC 32**
See also CA 13-14; CAP 1; DLB 9, 54

Nekrasov, Nikolai Alekseevich
1821-1878 .... **NCLC 11**

Nelligan, Emile 1879-1941....... **TCLC 14**
See also CA 114; DLB 92

Nelson, Willie 1933-............. **CLC 17**
See also CA 107

Nemerov, Howard (Stanley)
1920-1991 .... **CLC 2, 6, 9, 36**
See also CA 1-4R; 134; CABS 2; CANR 1,
27; DAM POET; DLB 5, 6; DLBY 83;
INT CANR-27; MTCW

Neruda, Pablo
1904-1973 ..... **CLC 1, 2, 5, 7, 9, 28, 62;
DA; DAB; DAC; HLC; PC 4; WLC**
See also CA 19-20; 45-48; CAP 2;
DAM MST, MULT, POET; HW; MTCW

Nerval, Gerard de
1808-1855 ..... **NCLC 1; PC 13; SSC 18**

Nervo, (Jose) Amado (Ruiz de)
1870-1919 .... **TCLC 11**
See also CA 109; 131; HW

Nessi, Pio Baroja y
See Baroja (y Nessi), Pio

Nestroy, Johann 1801-1862...... **NCLC 42**
See also DLB 133

Neufeld, John (Arthur) 1938- ...... **CLC 17**
See also AAYA 11; CA 25-28R; CANR 11,
37; MAICYA; SAAS 3; SATA 6, 81

Neville, Emily Cheney 1919-........ **CLC 12**
See also CA 5-8R; CANR 3, 37; JRDA;
MAICYA; SAAS 2; SATA 1

Newbound, Bernard Slade 1930-
See Slade, Bernard
See also CA 81-84; CANR 49;
DAM DRAM

Newby, P(ercy) H(oward)
1918-..................... **CLC 2, 13**
See also CA 5-8R; CANR 32; DAM NOV;
DLB 15; MTCW

Newlove, Donald 1928- .... **CLC 6**
See also CA 29-32R; CANR 25

Newlove, John (Herbert) 1938-..... **CLC 14**
See also CA 21-24R; CANR 9, 25

Newman, Charles 1938-.......... **CLC 2, 8**
See also CA 21-24R

Newman, Edwin (Harold) 1919- .... **CLC 14**
See also AITN 1; CA 69-72; CANR 5

Newman, John Henry
1801-1890 .... **NCLC 38**
See also DLB 18, 32, 55

Newton, Suzanne 1936-........... **CLC 35**
See also CA 41-44R; CANR 14; JRDA;
SATA 5, 77

Nexo, Martin Andersen
1869-1954 .... **TCLC 43**

Nezval, Vitezslav 1900-1958 ...... **TCLC 44**
See also CA 123

Ng, Fae Myenne 1957(?)-.......... **CLC 81**
See also CA 146

Ngema, Mbongeni 1955- .... **CLC 57**
See also BW 2; CA 143

Ngugi, James T(hiong'o)........ **CLC 3, 7, 13**
See also Ngugi wa Thiong'o

Ngugi wa Thiong'o 1938-..... **CLC 36; BLC**
See also Ngugi, James T(hiong'o)
See also BW 2; CA 81-84; CANR 27;
DAM MULT, NOV; DLB 125; MTCW

Nichol, B(arrie) P(hillip)
1944 1988 .... **CLC 18**
See also CA 53-56; DLB 53; SATA 66

O'Donovan, Michael John
1903-1966 . . . . **CLC 14**
See also O'Connor, Frank
See also CA 93-96

Oe, Kenzaburo
1935- . . . . **CLC 10, 36, 86; SSC 20**
See also CA 97-100; CANR 36, 50;
DAM NOV; DLBY 94; MTCW

O'Faolain, Julia 1932- . . . . **CLC 6, 19, 47**
See also CA 81-84; CAAS 2; CANR 12;
DLB 14; MTCW

O'Faolain, Sean
1900-1991 . . . . **CLC 1, 7, 14, 32, 70;**
SSC 13
See also CA 61-64; 134; CANR 12;
DLB 15; MTCW

O'Flaherty, Liam
1896-1984 . . . . **CLC 5, 34; SSC 6**
See also CA 101; 113; CANR 35; DLB 36;
DLBY 84; MTCW

Ogilvy, Gavin
See Barrie, J(ames) M(atthew)

O'Grady, Standish James
1846-1928 . . . . **TCLC 5**
See also CA 104

O'Grady, Timothy 1951- . . . . **CLC 59**
See also CA 138

O'Hara, Frank
1926-1966 . . . . **CLC 2, 5, 13, 78**
See also CA 9-12R; 25-28R; CANR 33;
DAM POET; DLB 5, 16; MTCW

O'Hara, John (Henry)
1905-1970 . . . . **CLC 1, 2, 3, 6, 11, 42;**
SSC 15
See also CA 5-8R; 25-28R; CANR 31;
CDALB 1929-1941; DAM NOV; DLB 9,
86; DLBD 2; MTCW

O Hehir, Diana 1922- . . . . **CLC 41**
See also CA 93-96

Okigbo, Christopher (Ifenayichukwu)
1932-1967 . . . . . **CLC 25, 84; BLC; PC 7**
See also BW 1; CA 77-80; DAM MULT,
POET; DLB 125; MTCW

Okri, Ben 1959- . . . . **CLC 87**
See also BW 2; CA 130; 138; DLB 157;
INT 138

Olds, Sharon 1942- . . . . **CLC 32, 39, 85**
See also CA 101; CANR 18, 41;
DAM POET; DLB 120

Oldstyle, Jonathan
See Irving, Washington

Olesha, Yuri (Karlovich)
1899-1960 . . . . **CLC 8**
See also CA 85-88

Oliphant, Laurence
1829(?)-1888 . . . . **NCLC 47**
See also DLB 18

Oliphant, Margaret (Oliphant Wilson)
1828-1897 . . . . **NCLC 11**
See also DLB 18, 159

Oliver, Mary 1935- . . . . **CLC 19, 34**
See also CA 21-24R; CANR 9, 43; DLB 5

Olivier, Laurence (Kerr)
1907-1989 . . . . **CLC 20**
Scc also CA 111; 129

Olsen, Tillie
1913- . . . . . **CLC 4, 13; DA; DAB; DAC;**
SSC 11
See also CA 1-4R; CANR 1, 43;
DAM MST; DLB 28; DLBY 80; MTCW

Olson, Charles (John)
1910-1970 . . . . . **CLC 1, 2, 5, 6, 9, 11, 29**
See also CA 13-16; 25-28R; CABS 2;
CANR 35; CAP 1; DAM POET; DLB 5,
16; MTCW

Olson, Toby 1937- . . . . **CLC 28**
See also CA 65-68; CANR 9, 31

Olyesha, Yuri
See Olesha, Yuri (Karlovich)

Ondaatje, (Philip) Michael
1943- . . . **CLC 14, 29, 51, 76; DAB; DAC**
See also CA 77-80; CANR 42; DAM MST;
DLB 60

Oneal, Elizabeth 1934-
See Oneal, Zibby
See also CA 106; CANR 28; MAICYA;
SATA 30, 82

Oneal, Zibby . . . . **CLC 30**
See also Oneal, Elizabeth
See also AAYA 5; CLR 13; JRDA

O'Neill, Eugene (Gladstone)
1888-1953 . . . . . . **TCLC 1, 6, 27, 49; DA;**
DAB; DAC; WLC
See also AITN 1; CA 110; 132;
CDALB 1929-1941; DAM DRAM, MST;
DLB 7; MTCW

Onetti, Juan Carlos 1909-1994 . . . **CLC 7, 10**
See also CA 85-88; 145; CANR 32;
DAM MULT, NOV; DLB 113; HW;
MTCW

O Nuallain, Brian 1911-1966
See O'Brien, Flann
See also CA 21-22; 25-28R; CAP 2

Oppen, George 1908-1984 . . . . **CLC 7, 13, 34**
See also CA 13-16R; 113; CANR 8; DLB 5

Oppenheim, E(dward) Phillips
1866-1946 . . . . **TCLC 45**
See also CA 111; DLB 70

Orlovitz, Gil 1918-1973 . . . . **CLC 22**
See also CA 77-80; 45-48; DLB 2, 5

Orris
See Ingelow, Jean

Ortega y Gasset, Jose
1883-1955 . . . . **TCLC 9; HLC**
See also CA 106; 130; DAM MULT; HW;
MTCW

Ortese, Anna Maria 1914- . . . . **CLC 89**

Ortiz, Simon J(oseph) 1941- . . . . **CLC 45**
See also CA 134; DAM MULT, POET;
DLB 120; NNAL

Orton, Joe . . . . **CLC 4, 13, 43; DC 3**
See also Orton, John Kingsley
See also CDBLB 1960 to Present; DLB 13

Orton, John Kingsley 1933-1967
See Orton, Joe
See also CA 85-88; CANR 35;
DAM DRAM; MTCW

Orwell, George
. . . . . **TCLC 2, 6, 15, 31, 51; DAB; WLC**
See also Blair, Eric (Arthur)
See also CDBLB 1945-1960; DLB 15, 98

Osborne, David
See Silverberg, Robert

Osborne, George
See Silverberg, Robert

Osborne, John (James)
1929-1994 . . . . . **CLC 1, 2, 5, 11, 45; DA;**
DAB; DAC; WLC
See also CA 13-16R; 147;
CDBLB 1945-1960; DAM DRAM, MST;
DLB 13; MTCW

Osborne, Lawrence 1958- . . . . **CLC 50**

Oshima, Nagisa 1932- . . . . **CLC 20**
See also CA 116; 121

Oskison, John Milton
1874-1947 . . . . **TCLC 35**
See also CA 144; DAM MULT; NNAL

Ossoli, Sarah Margaret (Fuller marchesa d')
1810-1850
See Fuller, Margaret
See also SATA 25

Ostrovsky, Alexander
1823-1886 . . . . **NCLC 30**

Otero, Blas de 1916-1979 . . . . **CLC 11**
See also CA 89-92; DLB 134

Otto, Whitney 1955- . . . . **CLC 70**
See also CA 140

Ouida . . . . **TCLC 43**
See also De La Ramee, (Marie) Louise
See also DLB 18, 156

Ousmane, Sembene 1923- . . . . **CLC 66; BLC**
See also BW 1; CA 117; 125; MTCW

Ovid 43B.C.-18(?) . . . . **CMLC 7; PC 2**
See also DAM POET

Owen, Hugh
See Faust, Frederick (Schiller)

Owen, Wilfred (Edward Salter)
1893-1918 . . . . . . **TCLC 5, 27; DA; DAB;**
DAC; WLC
See also CA 104; 141; CDBLB 1914-1945;
DAM MST, POET; DLB 20

Owens, Rochelle 1936- . . . . **CLC 8**
See also CA 17-20R; CAAS 2; CANR 39

Oz, Amos 1939- . . . **CLC 5, 8, 11, 27, 33, 54**
See also CA 53-56; CANR 27, 47;
DAM NOV; MTCW

Ozick, Cynthia
1928- . . . . **CLC 3, 7, 28, 62; SSC 15**
See also BEST 90:1; CA 17-20R; CANR 23;
DAM NOV, POP; DLB 28, 152;
DLBY 82; INT CANR-23; MTCW

Ozu, Yasujiro 1903-1963 . . . . **CLC 16**
See also CA 112

Pacheco, C.
See Pessoa, Fernando (Antonio Nogueira)

Pa Chin . . . . **CLC 18**
See also Li Fei-kan

Pack, Robert 1929- . . . . **CLC 13**
See also CA 1-4R; CANR 3, 44; DLB 5

Padgett, Lewis
See Kuttner, Henry

Padilla (Lorenzo), Heberto 1932- . . . **CLC 38**
See also AITN 1; CA 123; 131; HW

Page, Jimmy 1944- . . . . **CLC 12**

Page, Louise 1955- . . . . CLC 40
See also CA 140

Page, P(atricia) K(athleen)
1916- . . . . CLC 7, 18; DAC; PC 12
See also CA 53-56; CANR 4, 22;
DAM MST; DLB 68; MTCW

Paget, Violet 1856-1935
See Lee, Vernon
See also CA 104

Paget-Lowe, Henry
See Lovecraft, H(oward) P(hillips)

Paglia, Camille (Anna) 1947- . . . . CLC 68
See also CA 140

Paige, Richard
See Koontz, Dean R(ay)

Pakenham, Antonia
See Fraser, (Lady) Antonia (Pakenham)

Palamas, Kostes 1859-1943 . . . . TCLC 5
See also CA 105

Palazzeschi, Aldo 1885-1974 . . . . CLC 11
See also CA 89-92; 53-56; DLB 114

Paley, Grace 1922- . . . . CLC 4, 6, 37; SSC 8
See also CA 25-28R; CANR 13, 46;
DAM POP; DLB 28; INT CANR-13;
MTCW

Palin, Michael (Edward) 1943- . . . . . CLC 21
See also Monty Python
See also CA 107; CANR 35; SATA 67

Palliser, Charles 1947- . . . . CLC 65
See also CA 136

Palma, Ricardo 1833-1919 . . . . TCLC 29

Pancake, Breece Dexter 1952-1979
See Pancake, Breece D'J
See also CA 123; 109

Pancake, Breece D'J . . . . CLC 29
See also Pancake, Breece Dexter
See also DLB 130

Panko, Rudy
See Gogol, Nikolai (Vasilyevich)

Papadiamantis, Alexandros
1851-1911 . . . . TCLC 29

Papadiamantopoulos, Johannes 1856-1910
See Moreas, Jean
See also CA 117

Papini, Giovanni 1881-1956 . . . . TCLC 22
See also CA 121

Paracelsus 1493-1541 . . . . LC 14

Parasol, Peter
See Stevens, Wallace

Parfenie, Maria
See Codrescu, Andrei

Parini, Jay (Lee) 1948- . . . . CLC 54
See also CA 97-100; CAAS 16; CANR 32

Park, Jordan
See Kornbluth, C(yril) M.; Pohl, Frederik

Parker, Bert
See Ellison, Harlan (Jay)

Parker, Dorothy (Rothschild)
1893-1967 . . . . CLC 15, 68; SSC 2
See also CA 19-20; 25-28R; CAP 2;
DAM POET; DLB 11, 45, 86; MTCW

Parker, Robert B(rown) 1932- . . . . . . CLC 27
See also BEST 89:4; CA 49-52; CANR 1,
26; DAM NOV, POP; INT CANR-26;
MTCW

Parkin, Frank 1940- . . . . CLC 43
See also CA 147

Parkman, Francis, Jr.
1823-1893 . . . . NCLC 12
See also DLB 1, 30

Parks, Gordon (Alexander Buchanan)
1912- . . . . CLC 1, 16; BLC
See also AITN 2; BW 2; CA 41-44R;
CANR 26; DAM MULT; DLB 33;
SATA 8

Parnell, Thomas 1679-1718 . . . . LC 3
See also DLB 94

Parra, Nicanor 1914- . . . . CLC 2; HLC
See also CA 85-88; CANR 32;
DAM MULT; HW; MTCW

Parrish, Mary Frances
See Fisher, M(ary) F(rances) K(ennedy)

Parson
See Coleridge, Samuel Taylor

Parson Lot
See Kingsley, Charles

Partridge, Anthony
See Oppenheim, E(dward) Phillips

Pascoli, Giovanni 1855-1912 . . . . . . TCLC 45

Pasolini, Pier Paolo
1922-1975 . . . . CLC 20, 37
See also CA 93-96; 61-64; DLB 128;
MTCW

Pasquini
See Silone, Ignazio

Pastan, Linda (Olenik) 1932- . . . . . . CLC 27
See also CA 61-64; CANR 18, 40;
DAM POET; DLB 5

Pasternak, Boris (Leonidovich)
1890-1960 . . . . . . CLC 7, 10, 18, 63; DA;
DAB; DAC; PC 6; WLC
See also CA 127; 116; DAM MST, NOV,
POET; MTCW

Patchen, Kenneth 1911-1972 . . . CLC 1, 2, 18
See also CA 1-4R; 33-36R; CANR 3, 35;
DAM POET; DLB 16, 48; MTCW

Pater, Walter (Horatio)
1839-1894 . . . . NCLC 7
See also CDBLB 1832-1890; DLB 57, 156

Paterson, A(ndrew) B(arton)
1864-1941 . . . . TCLC 32

Paterson, Katherine (Womeldorf)
1932- . . . . CLC 12, 30
See also AAYA 1; CA 21-24R; CANR 28;
CLR 7; DLB 52; JRDA; MAICYA;
MTCW; SATA 13, 53

Patmore, Coventry Kersey Dighton
1823-1896 . . . . NCLC 9
See also DLB 35, 98

Paton, Alan (Stewart)
1903-1988 . . . . . . CLC 4, 10, 25, 55; DA;
DAB; DAC; WLC
See also CA 13-16; 125; CANR 22; CAP 1;
DAM MST, NOV; MTCW; SATA 11;
SATA-Obit 56

Paton Walsh, Gillian 1937-
See Walsh, Jill Paton
See also CANR 38; JRDA; MAICYA;
SAAS 3; SATA 4, 72

Paulding, James Kirke 1778-1860 . . NCLC 2
See also DLB 3, 59, 74

Paulin, Thomas Neilson 1949-
See Paulin, Tom
See also CA 123; 128

Paulin, Tom . . . . CLC 37
See also Paulin, Thomas Neilson
See also DLB 40

Paustovsky, Konstantin (Georgievich)
1892-1968 . . . . CLC 40
See also CA 93-96; 25-28R

Pavese, Cesare
1908-1950 . . . . . TCLC 3; PC 13; SSC 19
See also CA 104; DLB 128

Pavic, Milorad 1929- . . . . CLC 60
See also CA 136

Payne, Alan
See Jakes, John (William)

Paz, Gil
See Lugones, Leopoldo

Paz, Octavio
1914- . . . . CLC 3, 4, 6, 10, 19, 51, 65;
DA; DAB; DAC; HLC; PC 1; WLC
See also CA 73-76; CANR 32; DAM MST,
MULT, POET; DLBY 90; HW; MTCW

Peacock, Molly 1947- . . . . CLC 60
See also CA 103; CAAS 21; DLB 120

Peacock, Thomas Love
1785-1866 . . . . NCLC 22
See also DLB 96, 116

Peake, Mervyn 1911-1968 . . . . CLC 7, 54
See also CA 5-8R; 25-28R; CANR 3;
DLB 15, 160; MTCW; SATA 23

Pearce, Philippa . . . . CLC 21
See also Christie, (Ann) Philippa
See also CLR 9; DLB 161; MAICYA;
SATA 1, 67

Pearl, Eric
See Elman, Richard

Pearson, T(homas) R(eid) 1956- . . . . CLC 39
See also CA 120; 130; INT 130

Peck, Dale 1967- . . . . CLC 81
See also CA 146

Peck, John 1941- . . . . CLC 3
See also CA 49-52; CANR 3

Peck, Richard (Wayne) 1934- . . . . . . CLC 21
See also AAYA 1; CA 85-88; CANR 19,
38; CLR 15; INT CANR-19; JRDA;
MAICYA; SAAS 2; SATA 18, 55

Peck, Robert Newton
1928- . . . . CLC 17; DA; DAC
See also AAYA 3; CA 81-84; CANR 31;
DAM MST; JRDA; MAICYA; SAAS 1;
SATA 21, 62

Peckinpah, (David) Sam(uel)
1925-1984 . . . . CLC 20
See also CA 109; 114

Pedersen, Knut 1859-1952
See Hamsun, Knut
See also CA 104; 119; MTCW

Plato
428(?)B.C.-348(?)B.C..... **CMLC 8; DA; DAB; DAC**
See also DAM MST

Platonov, Andrei .... **TCLC 14**
See also Klimentov, Andrei Platonovich

Platt, Kin 1911- .... **CLC 26**
See also AAYA 11; CA 17-20R; CANR 11;
JRDA; SAAS 17; SATA 21

Plautus c. 251B.C.-184B.C. .... **DC 6**

Plick et Plock
See Simenon, Georges (Jacques Christian)

Plimpton, George (Ames) 1927-..... **CLC 36**
See also AITN 1; CA 21-24R; CANR 32;
MTCW; SATA 10

Plomer, William Charles Franklin
1903-1973 .... **CLC 4, 8**
See also CA 21-22; CANR 34; CAP 2;
DLB 20; MTCW; SATA 24

Plowman, Piers
See Kavanagh, Patrick (Joseph)

Plum, J.
See Wodehouse, P(elham) G(renville)

Plumly, Stanley (Ross) 1939- ...... **CLC 33**
See also CA 108; 110; DLB 5; INT 110

Plumpe, Friedrich Wilhelm
1888-1931 .... **TCLC 53**
See also CA 112

Poe, Edgar Allan
1809-1849 ..... **NCLC 1, 16; DA; DAB; DAC; PC 1; SSC 1; WLC**
See also AAYA 14; CDALB 1640-1865;
DAM MST, POET; DLB 3, 59, 73, 74;
SATA 23

Poet of Titchfield Street, The
See Pound, Ezra (Weston Loomis)

Pohl, Frederik 1919- .... **CLC 18**
See also CA 61-64; CAAS 1; CANR 11, 37;
DLB 8; INT CANR-11; MTCW;
SATA 24

Poirier, Louis 1910-
See Gracq, Julien
See also CA 122; 126

Poitier, Sidney 1927-............. **CLC 26**
See also BW 1; CA 117

Polanski, Roman 1933- .... **CLC 16**
See also CA 77-80

Poliakoff, Stephen 1952- .... **CLC 38**
See also CA 106; DLB 13

Police, The
See Copeland, Stewart (Armstrong);
Summers, Andrew James; Sumner,
Gordon Matthew

Polidori, John William
1795-1821 .... **NCLC 51**
See also DLB 116

Pollitt, Katha 1949- .... **CLC 28**
See also CA 120; 122; MTCW

Pollock, (Mary) Sharon
1936- .... **CLC 50; DAC**
See also CA 141; DAM DRAM, MST;
DLB 60

Polo, Marco 1254-1324 .... **CMLC 15**

Polybius c. 200B.C.-c. 118B.C. .... **CMLC 17**

Pomerance, Bernard 1940-........ **CLC 13**
See also CA 101; CANR 49; DAM DRAM

Ponge, Francis (Jean Gaston Alfred)
1899-1988 .... **CLC 6, 18**
See also CA 85-88; 126; CANR 40;
DAM POET

Pontoppidan, Henrik 1857-1943 ... **TCLC 29**

Poole, Josephine .... **CLC 17**
See also Helyar, Jane Penelope Josephine
See also SAAS 2; SATA 5

Popa, Vasko 1922-1991 .... **CLC 19**
See also CA 112; 148

Pope, Alexander
1688-1744 ...... **LC 3; DA; DAB; DAC; WLC**
See also CDBLB 1660-1789; DAM MST,
POET; DLB 95, 101

Porter, Connie (Rose) 1959(?)- ..... **CLC 70**
See also BW 2; CA 142; SATA 81

Porter, Gene(va Grace) Stratton
1863(?)-1924 .... **TCLC 21**
See also CA 112

Porter, Katherine Anne
1890-1980 ...... **CLC 1, 3, 7, 10, 13, 15, 27; DA; DAB; DAC; SSC 4**
See also AITN 2; CA 1-4R; 101; CANR 1;
DAM MST, NOV; DLB 4, 9, 102;
DLBD 12; DLBY 80; MTCW; SATA 39;
SATA-Obit 23

Porter, Peter (Neville Frederick)
1929- .... **CLC 5, 13, 33**
See also CA 85-88; DLB 40

Porter, William Sydney 1862-1910
See Henry, O.
See also CA 104; 131; CDALB 1865-1917;
DA; DAB; DAC; DAM MST; DLB 12,
78, 79; MTCW; YABC 2

Portillo (y Pacheco), Jose Lopez
See Lopez Portillo (y Pacheco), Jose

Post, Melville Davisson
1869-1930 .... **TCLC 39**
See also CA 110

Potok, Chaim 1929-....... **CLC 2, 7, 14, 26**
See also AAYA 15; AITN 1, 2; CA 17-20R;
CANR 19, 35; DAM NOV; DLB 28, 152;
INT CANR-19; MTCW; SATA 33

Potter, Beatrice
See Webb, (Martha) Beatrice (Potter)
See also MAICYA

Potter, Dennis (Christopher George)
1935-1994 .... **CLC 58, 86**
See also CA 107; 145; CANR 33; MTCW

Pound, Ezra (Weston Loomis)
1885-1972 ...... **CLC 1, 2, 3, 4, 5, 7, 10, 13, 18, 34, 48, 50; DA; DAB; DAC; PC 4; WLC**
See also CA 5-8R; 37-40R; CANR 40;
CDALB 1917-1929; DAM MST, POET;
DLB 4, 45, 63; MTCW

Povod, Reinaldo 1959-1994 .... **CLC 44**
See also CA 136; 146

Powell, Adam Clayton, Jr.
1908-1972 .... **CLC 89; BLC**
See also BW 1; CA 102; 33-36R;
DAM MULT

Powell, Anthony (Dymoke)
1905- .... **CLC 1, 3, 7, 9, 10, 31**
See also CA 1-4R; CANR 1, 32;
CDBLB 1945-1960; DLB 15; MTCW

Powell, Dawn 1897-1965 .... **CLC 66**
See also CA 5-8R

Powell, Padgett 1952-............. **CLC 34**
See also CA 126

Powers, J(ames) F(arl)
1917- .... **CLC 1, 4, 8, 57; SSC 4**
See also CA 1-4R; CANR 2; DLB 130;
MTCW

Powers, John J(ames) 1945-
See Powers, John R.
See also CA 69-72

Powers, John R. .... **CLC 66**
See also Powers, John J(ames)

Pownall, David 1938-............. **CLC 10**
See also CA 89-92; CAAS 18; CANR 49;
DLB 14

Powys, John Cowper
1872-1963 .... **CLC 7, 9, 15, 46**
See also CA 85-88; DLB 15; MTCW

Powys, T(heodore) F(rancis)
1875-1953 .... **TCLC 9**
See also CA 106; DLB 36

Prager, Emily 1952-............. **CLC 56**

Pratt, E(dwin) J(ohn)
1883(?)-1964 .... **CLC 19; DAC**
See also CA 141; 93-96; DAM POET;
DLB 92

Premchand .... **TCLC 21**
See also Srivastava, Dhanpat Rai

Preussler, Otfried 1923-........... **CLC 17**
See also CA 77-80; SATA 24

Prevert, Jacques (Henri Marie)
1900-1977 .... **CLC 15**
See also CA 77-80; 69-72; CANR 29;
MTCW; SATA-Obit 30

Prevost, Abbe (Antoine Francois)
1697-1763 .... **LC 1**

Price, (Edward) Reynolds
1933- .... **CLC 3, 6, 13, 43, 50, 63**
See also CA 1-4R; CANR 1, 37;
DAM NOV; DLB 2; INT CANR-37

Price, Richard 1949- .... **CLC 6, 12**
See also CA 49-52; CANR 3; DLBY 81

Prichard, Katharine Susannah
1883-1969 .... **CLC 46**
See also CA 11-12; CANR 33; CAP 1;
MTCW; SATA 66

Priestley, J(ohn) B(oynton)
1894-1984 .... **CLC 2, 5, 9, 34**
See also CA 9-12R; 113; CANR 33;
CDBLB 1914-1945; DAM DRAM, NOV;
DLB 10, 34, 77, 100, 139; DLBY 84;
MTCW

Prince 1958(?)- .... **CLC 35**

Prince, F(rank) T(empleton) 1912- .. **CLC 22**
See also CA 101; CANR 43; DLB 20

Prince Kropotkin
See Kropotkin, Peter (Aleksieevich)

Prior, Matthew 1664-1721.......... **LC 4**
See also DLB 95

Pritchard, William H(arrison)
1932- . . . . **CLC 34**
See also CA 65-68; CANR 23; DLB 111

Pritchett, V(ictor) S(awdon)
1900- . . . . **CLC 5, 13, 15, 41; SSC 14**
See also CA 61-64; CANR 31; DAM NOV;
DLB 15, 139; MTCW

Private 19022
See Manning, Frederic

Probst, Mark 1925- . . . . **CLC 59**
See also CA 130

Prokosch, Frederic 1908-1989 . . . . **CLC 4, 48**
See also CA 73-76; 128; DLB 48

Prophet, The
See Dreiser, Theodore (Herman Albert)

Prose, Francine 1947- . . . . **CLC 45**
See also CA 109; 112; CANR 46

Proudhon
See Cunha, Euclides (Rodrigues Pimenta) da

Proulx, E. Annie 1935- . . . . **CLC 81**

**Proust, (Valentin-Louis-George-Eugene-)
Marcel**
1871-1922 . . . . **TCLC 7, 13, 33; DA;
DAB; DAC; WLC**
See also CA 104; 120; DAM MST, NOV;
DLB 65; MTCW

Prowler, Harley
See Masters, Edgar Lee

Prus, Boleslaw 1845-1912 . . . . **TCLC 48**

Pryor, Richard (Franklin Lenox Thomas)
1940- . . . . **CLC 26**
See also CA 122

Przybyszewski, Stanislaw
1868-1927 . . . . **TCLC 36**
See also DLB 66

Pteleon
See Grieve, C(hristopher) M(urray)
See also DAM POET

Puckett, Lute
See Masters, Edgar Lee

Puig, Manuel
1932-1990 . . . **CLC 3, 5, 10, 28, 65; HLC**
See also CA 45-48; CANR 2, 32;
DAM MULT; DLB 113; HW; MTCW

Purdy, Al(fred Wellington)
1918- . . . . **CLC 3, 6, 14, 50; DAC**
See also CA 81-84; CAAS 17; CANR 42;
DAM MST, POET; DLB 88

Purdy, James (Amos)
1923- . . . . **CLC 2, 4, 10, 28, 52**
See also CA 33-36R; CAAS 1; CANR 19;
DLB 2; INT CANR-19; MTCW

Pure, Simon
See Swinnerton, Frank Arthur

Pushkin, Alexander (Sergeyevich)
1799-1837 . . . . . **NCLC 3, 27; DA; DAB;
DAC; PC 10; WLC**
See also DAM DRAM, MST, POET;
SATA 61

P'u Sung-ling 1640-1715 . . . . **LC 3**

Putnam, Arthur Lee
See Alger, Horatio, Jr.

Puzo, Mario 1920- . . . . **CLC 1, 2, 6, 36**
See also CA 65-68; CANR 4, 42;
DAM NOV, POP; DLB 6; MTCW

Pym, Barbara (Mary Crampton)
1913-1980 . . . . **CLC 13, 19, 37**
See also CA 13-14; 97-100; CANR 13, 34;
CAP 1; DLB 14; DLBY 87; MTCW

Pynchon, Thomas (Ruggles, Jr.)
1937- . . . . . **CLC 2, 3, 6, 9, 11, 18, 33, 62,
72; DA; DAB; DAC; SSC 14; WLC**
See also BEST 90:2; CA 17-20R; CANR 22,
46; DAM MST, NOV, POP; DLB 2;
MTCW

Qian Zhongshu
See Ch'ien Chung-shu

Qroll
See Dagerman, Stig (Halvard)

Quarrington, Paul (Lewis) 1953- . . . . **CLC 65**
See also CA 129

Quasimodo, Salvatore 1901-1968 . . . **CLC 10**
See also CA 13-16; 25-28R; CAP 1;
DLB 114; MTCW

Queen, Ellery . . . . **CLC 3, 11**
See also Dannay, Frederic; Davidson,
Avram; Lee, Manfred B(ennington);
Sturgeon, Theodore (Hamilton); Vance,
John Holbrook

Queen, Ellery, Jr.
See Dannay, Frederic; Lee, Manfred
B(ennington)

Queneau, Raymond
1903-1976 . . . . **CLC 2, 5, 10, 42**
See also CA 77-80; 69-72; CANR 32;
DLB 72; MTCW

Quevedo, Francisco de 1580-1645 . . . . **LC 23**

Quiller-Couch, Arthur Thomas
1863-1944 . . . . **TCLC 53**
See also CA 118; DLB 135, 153

Quin, Ann (Marie) 1936-1973 . . . . **CLC 6**
See also CA 9-12R; 45-48; DLB 14

Quinn, Martin
See Smith, Martin Cruz

Quinn, Simon
See Smith, Martin Cruz

Quiroga, Horacio (Sylvestre)
1878-1937 . . . . **TCLC 20; HLC**
See also CA 117; 131; DAM MULT; HW;
MTCW

Quoirez, Francoise 1935- . . . . **CLC 9**
See also Sagan, Francoise
See also CA 49-52; CANR 6, 39; MTCW

Raabe, Wilhelm 1831-1910 . . . . **TCLC 45**
See also DLB 129

Rabe, David (William) 1940- . . . **CLC 4, 8, 33**
See also CA 85-88; CABS 3; DAM DRAM;
DLB 7

Rabelais, Francois
1483-1553 . . . . . . **LC 5; DA; DAB; DAC;
WLC**
See also DAM MST

Rabinovitch, Sholem 1859-1916
See Aleichem, Sholom
See also CA 104

Racine, Jean 1639-1699 . . . . **LC 28; DAB**
See also DAM MST

Radcliffe, Ann (Ward) 1764-1823 . . **NCLC 6**
See also DLB 39

Radiguet, Raymond 1903-1923 . . . . **TCLC 29**
See also DLB 65

Radnoti, Miklos 1909-1944 . . . . **TCLC 16**
See also CA 118

Rado, James 1939- . . . . **CLC 17**
See also CA 105

Radvanyi, Netty 1900-1983
See Seghers, Anna
See also CA 85-88; 110

Rae, Ben
See Griffiths, Trevor

Raeburn, John (Hay) 1941- . . . . **CLC 34**
See also CA 57-60

Ragni, Gerome 1942-1991 . . . . **CLC 17**
See also CA 105; 134

Rahv, Philip 1908-1973 . . . . **CLC 24**
See also Greenberg, Ivan
See also DLB 137

Raine, Craig 1944- . . . . **CLC 32**
See also CA 108; CANR 29; DLB 40

Raine, Kathleen (Jessie) 1908- . . . **CLC 7, 45**
See also CA 85-88; CANR 46; DLB 20;
MTCW

Rainis, Janis 1865-1929 . . . . **TCLC 29**

Rakosi, Carl . . . . **CLC 47**
See also Rawley, Callman
See also CAAS 5

Raleigh, Richard
See Lovecraft, H(oward) P(hillips)

Raleigh, Sir Walter 1554(?)-1618 . . . . **LC 31**
See also CDBLB Before 1660

Rallentando, H. P.
See Sayers, Dorothy L(eigh)

Ramal, Walter
See de la Mare, Walter (John)

Ramon, Juan
See Jimenez (Mantecon), Juan Ramon

Ramos, Graciliano 1892-1953 . . . . . **TCLC 32**

Rampersad, Arnold 1941- . . . . **CLC 44**
See also BW 2; CA 127; 133; DLB 111;
INT 133

Rampling, Anne
See Rice, Anne

Ramsay, Allan 1684(?)-1758 . . . . **LC 29**
See also DLB 95

Ramuz, Charles-Ferdinand
1878-1947 . . . . **TCLC 33**

Rand, Ayn
1905-1982 . . . . . . **CLC 3, 30, 44, 79; DA;
DAC; WLC**
See also AAYA 10; CA 13-16R; 105;
CANR 27; DAM MST, NOV, POP;
MTCW

Randall, Dudley (Felker)
1914- . . . . **CLC 1; BLC**
See also BW 1; CA 25-28R; CANR 23;
DAM MULT; DLB 41

Randall, Robert
See Silverberg, Robert

Ranger, Ken
See Creasey, John

Richards, Keith 1943-
See Richard, Keith
See also CA 107

Richardson, Anne
See Roiphe, Anne (Richardson)

Richardson, Dorothy Miller
1873-1957 . . . . **TCLC 3**
See also CA 104; DLB 36

Richardson, Ethel Florence (Lindesay)
1870-1946
See Richardson, Henry Handel
See also CA 105

Richardson, Henry Handel. . . . . **TCLC 4**
See also Richardson, Ethel Florence
(Lindesay)

Richardson, Samuel
1689-1761 . . . . . . **LC 1; DA; DAB; DAC;
WLC**
See also CDBLB 1660-1789; DAM MST,
NOV; DLB 39

Richler, Mordecai
1931- . . . . **CLC 3, 5, 9, 13, 18, 46, 70;
DAC**
See also AITN 1; CA 65-68; CANR 31;
CLR 17; DAM MST, NOV; DLB 53;
MAICYA; MTCW; SATA 44;
SATA-Brief 27

Richter, Conrad (Michael)
1890-1968 . . . . **CLC 30**
See also CA 5-8R; 25-28R; CANR 23;
DLB 9; MTCW; SATA 3

Ricostranza, Tom
See Ellis, Trey

Riddell, J. H. 1832-1906 . . . . **TCLC 40**

Riding, Laura. . . . . **CLC 3, 7**
See also Jackson, Laura (Riding)

Riefenstahl, Berta Helene Amalia 1902-
See Riefenstahl, Leni
See also CA 108

Riefenstahl, Leni. . . . . **CLC 16**
See also Riefenstahl, Berta Helene Amalia

Riffe, Ernest
See Bergman, (Ernst) Ingmar

Riggs, (Rolla) Lynn 1899-1954 . . . . **TCLC 56**
See also CA 144; DAM MULT; NNAL

Riley, James Whitcomb
1849-1916 . . . . **TCLC 51**
See also CA 118; 137; DAM POET;
MAICYA; SATA 17

Riley, Tex
See Creasey, John

Rilke, Rainer Maria
1875-1926 . . . . **TCLC 1, 6, 19; PC 2**
See also CA 104; 132; DAM POET;
DLB 81; MTCW

Rimbaud, (Jean Nicolas) Arthur
1854-1891 . . . . . **NCLC 4, 35; DA; DAB;
DAC; PC 3; WLC**
See also DAM MST, POET

Rinehart, Mary Roberts
1876-1958 . . . . **TCLC 52**
See also CA 108

Ringmaster, The
See Mencken, H(enry) L(ouis)

Ringwood, Gwen(dolyn Margaret) Pharis
1910-1984 . . . . **CLC 48**
See also CA 148; 112; DLB 88

Rio, Michel 19(?)- . . . . **CLC 43**

Ritsos, Giannes
See Ritsos, Yannis

Ritsos, Yannis 1909-1990 . . . . . **CLC 6, 13, 31**
See also CA 77-80; 133; CANR 39; MTCW

Ritter, Erika 1948(?)- . . . . **CLC 52**

Rivera, Jose Eustasio 1889-1928 . . . **TCLC 35**
See also HW

Rivers, Conrad Kent 1933-1968 . . . . . . **CLC 1**
See also BW 1; CA 85-88; DLB 41

Rivers, Elfrida
See Bradley, Marion Zimmer

Riverside, John
See Heinlein, Robert A(nson)

Rizal, Jose 1861-1896 . . . . **NCLC 27**

Roa Bastos, Augusto (Antonio)
1917- . . . . **CLC 45; HLC**
See also CA 131; DAM MULT; DLB 113;
HW

Robbe-Grillet, Alain
1922- . . . . . . **CLC 1, 2, 4, 6, 8, 10, 14, 43**
See also CA 9-12R; CANR 33; DLB 83;
MTCW

Robbins, Harold 1916- . . . . **CLC 5**
See also CA 73-76; CANR 26; DAM NOV;
MTCW

Robbins, Thomas Eugene 1936-
See Robbins, Tom
See also CA 81-84; CANR 29; DAM NOV,
POP; MTCW

Robbins, Tom. . . . . **CLC 9, 32, 64**
See also Robbins, Thomas Eugene
See also BEST 90:3; DLBY 80

Robbins, Trina 1938- . . . . **CLC 21**
See also CA 128

Roberts, Charles G(eorge) D(ouglas)
1860-1943 . . . . **TCLC 8**
See also CA 105; CLR 33; DLB 92;
SATA-Brief 29

Roberts, Kate 1891-1985 . . . . **CLC 15**
See also CA 107; 116

Roberts, Keith (John Kingston)
1935- . . . . **CLC 14**
See also CA 25-28R; CANR 46

Roberts, Kenneth (Lewis)
1885-1957 . . . . **TCLC 23**
See also CA 109; DLB 9

Roberts, Michele (B.) 1949- . . . . **CLC 48**
See also CA 115

Robertson, Ellis
See Ellison, Harlan (Jay); Silverberg, Robert

Robertson, Thomas William
1829-1871 . . . . **NCLC 35**
See also DAM DRAM

Robinson, Edwin Arlington
1869-1935 . . . . **TCLC 5; DA; DAC; PC 1**
See also CA 104; 133; CDALB 1865-1917;
DAM MST, POET; DLB 54; MTCW

Robinson, Henry Crabb
1775-1867 . . . . **NCLC 15**
See also DLB 107

Robinson, Jill 1936- . . . . **CLC 10**
See also CA 102; INT 102

Robinson, Kim Stanley 1952- . . . . . . **CLC 34**
See also CA 126

Robinson, Lloyd
See Silverberg, Robert

Robinson, Marilynne 1944- . . . . **CLC 25**
See also CA 116

Robinson, Smokey. . . . . **CLC 21**
See also Robinson, William, Jr.

Robinson, William, Jr. 1940-
See Robinson, Smokey
See also CA 116

Robison, Mary 1949- . . . . **CLC 42**
See also CA 113; 116; DLB 130; INT 116

Rod, Edouard 1857-1910 . . . . **TCLC 52**

Roddenberry, Eugene Wesley 1921-1991
See Roddenberry, Gene
See also CA 110; 135; CANR 37; SATA 45;
SATA-Obit 69

Roddenberry, Gene. . . . . **CLC 17**
See also Roddenberry, Eugene Wesley
See also AAYA 5; SATA-Obit 69

Rodgers, Mary 1931- . . . . **CLC 12**
See also CA 49-52; CANR 8; CLR 20;
INT CANR-8; JRDA; MAICYA;
SATA 8

Rodgers, W(illiam) R(obert)
1909-1969 . . . . **CLC 7**
See also CA 85-88; DLB 20

Rodman, Eric
See Silverberg, Robert

Rodman, Howard 1920(?)-1985 . . . . . **CLC 65**
See also CA 118

Rodman, Maia
See Wojciechowska, Maia (Teresa)

Rodriguez, Claudio 1934- . . . . **CLC 10**
See also DLB 134

Roelvaag, O(le) E(dvart)
1876-1931 . . . . **TCLC 17**
See also CA 117; DLB 9

Roethke, Theodore (Huebner)
1908-1963 . . . . . . **CLC 1, 3, 8, 11, 19, 46**
See also CA 81-84; CABS 2;
CDALB 1941-1968; DAM POET; DLB 5;
MTCW

Rogers, Thomas Hunton 1927- . . . . . **CLC 57**
See also CA 89-92; INT 89-92

Rogers, Will(iam Penn Adair)
1879-1935 . . . . **TCLC 8**
See also CA 105; 144; DAM MULT;
DLB 11; NNAL

Rogin, Gilbert 1929- . . . . **CLC 18**
See also CA 65-68; CANR 15

Rohan, Koda. . . . . **TCLC 22**
See also Koda Shigeyuki

Rohmer, Eric. . . . . **CLC 16**
See also Scherer, Jean-Marie Maurice

Rohmer, Sax. . . . . **TCLC 28**
See also Ward, Arthur Henry Sarsfield
See also DLB 70

Saba, Umberto 1883-1957 .... **TCLC 33**
See also CA 144; DLB 114

Sabatini, Rafael 1875-1950 ...... **TCLC 47**

Sabato, Ernesto (R.)
1911- .... **CLC 10, 23; HLC**
See also CA 97-100; CANR 32;
DAM MULT; DLB 145; HW; MTCW

Sacastru, Martin
See Bioy Casares, Adolfo

Sacher-Masoch, Leopold von
1836(?)-1895 .... **NCLC 31**

Sachs, Marilyn (Stickle) 1927- ..... **CLC 35**
See also AAYA 2; CA 17-20R; CANR 13,
47; CLR 2; JRDA; MAICYA; SAAS 2;
SATA 3, 68

Sachs, Nelly 1891-1970 .... **CLC 14**
See also CA 17-18; 25-28R; CAP 2

Sackler, Howard (Oliver)
1929-1982 .... **CLC 14**
See also CA 61-64; 108; CANR 30; DLB 7

Sacks, Oliver (Wolf) 1933- .... **CLC 67**
See also CA 53-56; CANR 28, 50;
INT CANR-28; MTCW

Sade, Donatien Alphonse Francois Comte
1740-1814 .... **NCLC 47**

Sadoff, Ira 1945- .... **CLC 9**
See also CA 53-56; CANR 5, 21; DLB 120

Saetone
See Camus, Albert

Safire, William 1929- .... **CLC 10**
See also CA 17-20R; CANR 31

Sagan, Carl (Edward) 1934- .... **CLC 30**
See also AAYA 2; CA 25-28R; CANR 11,
36; MTCW; SATA 58

Sagan, Francoise .... **CLC 3, 6, 9, 17, 36**
See also Quoirez, Francoise
See also DLB 83

Sahgal, Nayantara (Pandit) 1927- ... **CLC 41**
See also CA 9-12R; CANR 11

Saint, H(arry) F. 1941- .... **CLC 50**
See also CA 127

St. Aubin de Teran, Lisa 1953-
See Teran, Lisa St. Aubin de
See also CA 118; 126; INT 126

Sainte-Beuve, Charles Augustin
1804-1869 .... **NCLC 5**

Saint-Exupery, Antoine (Jean Baptiste Marie
Roger) de
1900-1944 .... **TCLC 2, 56; WLC**
See also CA 108; 132; CLR 10; DAM NOV;
DLB 72; MAICYA; MTCW; SATA 20

St. John, David
See Hunt, E(verette) Howard, (Jr.)

Saint-John Perse
See Leger, (Marie-Rene Auguste) Alexis
Saint-Leger

Saintsbury, George (Edward Bateman)
1845-1933 .... **TCLC 31**
See also DLB 57, 149

Sait Faik .... **TCLC 23**
See also Abasiyanik, Sait Faik

Saki .... **TCLC 3; SSC 12**
See also Munro, H(ector) H(ugh)

Sala, George Augustus .... **NCLC 46**

Salama, Hannu 1936- .... **CLC 18**

Salamanca, J(ack) R(ichard)
1922- .... **CLC 4, 15**
See also CA 25-28R

Sale, J. Kirkpatrick
See Sale, Kirkpatrick

Sale, Kirkpatrick 1937- .... **CLC 68**
See also CA 13-16R; CANR 10

Salinas, Luis Omar 1937- ... **CLC 90; HLC**
See also CA 131; DAM MULT; DLB 82;
HW

Salinas (y Serrano), Pedro
1891(?)-1951 .... **TCLC 17**
See also CA 117; DLB 134

Salinger, J(erome) D(avid)
1919- ...... **CLC 1, 3, 8, 12, 55, 56; DA;
DAB; DAC; SSC 2; WLC**
See also AAYA 2; CA 5-8R; CANR 39;
CDALB 1941-1968; CLR 18; DAM MST,
NOV, POP; DLB 2, 102; MAICYA;
MTCW; SATA 67

Salisbury, John
See Caute, David

Salter, James 1925- .... **CLC 7, 52, 59**
See also CA 73-76; DLB 130

Saltus, Edgar (Everton)
1855-1921 .... **TCLC 8**
See also CA 105

Saltykov, Mikhail Evgrafovich
1826-1889 .... **NCLC 16**

Samarakis, Antonis 1919- .... **CLC 5**
See also CA 25-28R; CAAS 16; CANR 36

Sanchez, Florencio 1875-1910 ..... **TCLC 37**
See also HW

Sanchez, Luis Rafael 1936- .... **CLC 23**
See also CA 128; DLB 145; HW

Sanchez, Sonia 1934- ... **CLC 5; BLC; PC 9**
See also BW 2; CA 33-36R; CANR 24, 49;
CLR 18; DAM MULT; DLB 41;
DLBD 8; MAICYA; MTCW; SATA 22

Sand, George
1804-1876 ..... **NCLC 2, 42; DA; DAB;
DAC; WLC**
See also DAM MST, NOV; DLB 119

Sandburg, Carl (August)
1878-1967 .... **CLC 1, 4, 10, 15, 35; DA;
DAB; DAC; PC 2; WLC**
See also CA 5-8R; 25-28R; CANR 35;
CDALB 1865-1917; DAM MST, POET;
DLB 17, 54; MAICYA; MTCW; SATA 8

Sandburg, Charles
See Sandburg, Carl (August)

Sandburg, Charles A.
See Sandburg, Carl (August)

Sanders, (James) Ed(ward) 1939- ... **CLC 53**
See also CA 13-16R; CAAS 21; CANR 13,
44; DLB 16

Sanders, Lawrence 1920- .... **CLC 41**
See also BEST 89:4; CA 81-84; CANR 33;
DAM POP; MTCW

Sanders, Noah
See Blount, Roy (Alton), Jr.

Sanders, Winston P.
See Anderson, Poul (William)

Sandoz, Mari(e Susette)
1896-1966 .... **CLC 28**
See also CA 1-4R; 25-28R; CANR 17;
DLB 9; MTCW; SATA 5

Saner, Reg(inald Anthony) 1931- .... **CLC 9**
See also CA 65-68

Sannazaro, Jacopo 1456(?)-1530 ...... **LC 8**

Sansom, William
1912-1976 .... **CLC 2, 6; SSC 21**
See also CA 5-8R; 65-68; CANR 42;
DAM NOV; DLB 139; MTCW

Santayana, George 1863-1952 ..... **TCLC 40**
See also CA 115; DLB 54, 71; DLBD 13

Santiago, Danny .... **CLC 33**
See also James, Daniel (Lewis)
See also DLB 122

Santmyer, Helen Hoover
1895-1986 .... **CLC 33**
See also CA 1-4R; 118; CANR 15, 33;
DLBY 84; MTCW

Santos, Bienvenido N(uqui) 1911- ... **CLC 22**
See also CA 101; CANR 19, 46;
DAM MULT

Sapper .... **TCLC 44**
See also McNeile, Herman Cyril

Sappho fl. 6th cent. B.C.- .... **CMLC 3; PC 5**
See also DAM POET

Sarduy, Severo 1937-1993 .... **CLC 6**
See also CA 89-92; 142; DLB 113; HW

Sargeson, Frank 1903-1982 .... **CLC 31**
See also CA 25-28R; 106; CANR 38

Sarmiento, Felix Ruben Garcia
See Dario, Ruben

Saroyan, William
1908-1981 ..... **CLC 1, 8, 10, 29, 34, 56;
DA; DAB; DAC; SSC 21; WLC**
See also CA 5-8R; 103; CANR 30;
DAM DRAM, MST, NOV; DLB 7, 9, 86;
DLBY 81; MTCW; SATA 23;
SATA-Obit 24

Sarraute, Nathalie
1900- .... **CLC 1, 2, 4, 8, 10, 31, 80**
See also CA 9-12R; CANR 23; DLB 83;
MTCW

Sarton, (Eleanor) May
1912- .... **CLC 4, 14, 49**
See also CA 1-4R; CANR 1, 34;
DAM POET; DLB 48; DLBY 81;
INT CANR-34; MTCW; SATA 36

Sartre, Jean-Paul
1905-1980 .... **CLC 1, 4, 7, 9, 13, 18, 24,
44, 50, 52; DA; DAB; DAC; DC 3; WLC**
See also CA 9-12R; 97-100; CANR 21;
DAM DRAM, MST, NOV; DLB 72;
MTCW

Sassoon, Siegfried (Lorraine)
1886-1967 .... **CLC 36; DAB; PC 12**
See also CA 104; 25-28R; CANR 36;
DAM MST, NOV, POET; DLB 20;
MTCW

Satterfield, Charles
See Pohl, Frederik

Saul, John (W. III) 1942- .... **CLC 46**
See also AAYA 10; BEST 90:4; CA 81-84;
CANR 16, 40; DAM NOV, POP

Saunders, Caleb
See Heinlein, Robert A(nson)

Saura (Atares), Carlos 1932- .... CLC 20
See also CA 114; 131; HW

Sauser-Hall, Frederic 1887-1961.... CLC 18
See also Cendrars, Blaise
See also CA 102; 93-96; CANR 36; MTCW

Saussure, Ferdinand de
1857-1913 .... TCLC 49

Savage, Catharine
See Brosman, Catharine Savage

Savage, Thomas 1915- .... CLC 40
See also CA 126; 132; CAAS 15; INT 132

Savan, Glenn 19(?)- .... CLC 50

Sayers, Dorothy L(eigh)
1893-1957 .... TCLC 2, 15
See also CA 104; 119; CDBLB 1914-1945;
DAM POP; DLB 10, 36, 77, 100; MTCW

Sayers, Valerie 1952- .... CLC 50
See also CA 134

Sayles, John (Thomas)
1950- .... CLC 7, 10, 14
See also CA 57-60; CANR 41; DLB 44

Scammell, Michael .... CLC 34

Scannell, Vernon 1922- .... CLC 49
See also CA 5-8R; CANR 8, 24; DLB 27;
SATA 59

Scarlett, Susan
See Streatfeild, (Mary) Noel

Schaeffer, Susan Fromberg
1941- .... CLC 6, 11, 22
See also CA 49-52; CANR 18; DLB 28;
MTCW; SATA 22

Schary, Jill
See Robinson, Jill

Schell, Jonathan 1943- .... CLC 35
See also CA 73-76; CANR 12

Schelling, Friedrich Wilhelm Joseph von
1775-1854 .... NCLC 30
See also DLB 90

Schendel, Arthur van 1874-1946 ... TCLC 56

Scherer, Jean-Marie Maurice 1920-
See Rohmer, Eric
See also CA 110

Schevill, James (Erwin) 1920- .... CLC 7
See also CA 5-8R; CAAS 12

Schiller, Friedrich 1759-1805 .... NCLC 39
See also DAM DRAM; DLB 94

Schisgal, Murray (Joseph) 1926- ..... CLC 6
See also CA 21-24R; CANR 48

Schlee, Ann 1934- .... CLC 35
See also CA 101; CANR 29; SATA 44;
SATA-Brief 36

Schlegel, August Wilhelm von
1767-1845 .... NCLC 15
See also DLB 94

Schlegel, Friedrich 1772-1829 .... NCLC 45
See also DLB 90

Schlegel, Johann Elias (von)
1719(?)-1749 .... LC 5

Schlesinger, Arthur M(eier), Jr.
1917- .... CLC 84
See also AITN 1; CA 1-4R; CANR 1, 28;
DLB 17; INT CANR-28; MTCW;
SATA 61

Schmidt, Arno (Otto) 1914-1979.... CLC 56
See also CA 128; 109; DLB 69

Schmitz, Aron Hector 1861-1928
See Svevo, Italo
See also CA 104; 122; MTCW

Schnackenberg, Gjertrud 1953- ..... CLC 40
See also CA 116; DLB 120

Schneider, Leonard Alfred 1925-1966
See Bruce, Lenny
See also CA 89-92

Schnitzler, Arthur
1862-1931 .... TCLC 4; SSC 15
See also CA 104; DLB 81, 118

Schopenhauer, Arthur
1788-1860 .... NCLC 51
See also DLB 90

Schor, Sandra (M.) 1932(?)-1990 ... CLC 65
See also CA 132

Schorer, Mark 1908-1977 .... CLC 9
See also CA 5-8R; 73-76; CANR 7;
DLB 103

Schrader, Paul (Joseph) 1946- ...... CLC 26
See also CA 37-40R; CANR 41; DLB 44

Schreiner, Olive (Emilie Albertina)
1855-1920 .... TCLC 9
See also CA 105; DLB 18, 156

Schulberg, Budd (Wilson)
1914- .... CLC 7, 48
See also CA 25-28R; CANR 19; DLB 6, 26,
28; DLBY 81

Schulz, Bruno
1892-1942 .... TCLC 5, 51; SSC 13
See also CA 115; 123

Schulz, Charles M(onroe) 1922- .... CLC 12
See also CA 9-12R; CANR 6;
INT CANR-6; SATA 10

Schumacher, E(rnst) F(riedrich)
1911-1977 .... CLC 80
See also CA 81-84; 73-76; CANR 34

Schuyler, James Marcus
1923-1991 .... CLC 5, 23
See also CA 101; 134; DAM POET; DLB 5;
INT 101

Schwartz, Delmore (David)
1913-1966 ... CLC 2, 4, 10, 45, 87; PC 8
See also CA 17-18; 25-28R; CANR 35;
CAP 2; DLB 28, 48; MTCW

Schwartz, Ernst
See Ozu, Yasujiro

Schwartz, John Burnham 1965- .... CLC 59
See also CA 132

Schwartz, Lynne Sharon 1939- ..... CLC 31
See also CA 103; CANR 44

Schwartz, Muriel A.
See Eliot, T(homas) S(tearns)

Schwarz-Bart, Andre 1928- .... CLC 2, 4
See also CA 89-92

Schwarz-Bart, Simone 1938- .... CLC 7
See also BW 2; CA 97-100

Schwob, (Mayer Andre) Marcel
1867-1905 .... TCLC 20
See also CA 117; DLB 123

Sciascia, Leonardo
1921-1989 .... CLC 8, 9, 41
See also CA 85-88; 130; CANR 35; MTCW

Scoppettone, Sandra 1936- .... CLC 26
See also AAYA 11; CA 5-8R; CANR 41;
SATA 9

Scorsese, Martin 1942- .... CLC 20, 89
See also CA 110; 114; CANR 46

Scotland, Jay
See Jakes, John (William)

Scott, Duncan Campbell
1862-1947 .... TCLC 6; DAC
See also CA 104; DLB 92

Scott, Evelyn 1893-1963............ CLC 43
See also CA 104; 112; DLB 9, 48

Scott, F(rancis) R(eginald)
1899-1985 .... CLC 22
See also CA 101; 114; DLB 88; INT 101

Scott, Frank
See Scott, F(rancis) R(eginald)

Scott, Joanna 1960- .... CLC 50
See also CA 126

Scott, Paul (Mark) 1920-1978.... CLC 9, 60
See also CA 81-84; 77-80; CANR 33;
DLB 14; MTCW

Scott, Walter
1771-1832 .... NCLC 15; DA; DAB;
DAC; PC 13; WLC
See also CDBLB 1789-1832; DAM MST,
NOV, POET; DLB 93, 107, 116, 144, 159;
YABC 2

Scribe, (Augustin) Eugene
1791-1861 .... NCLC 16; DC 5
See also DAM DRAM

Scrum, R.
See Crumb, R(obert)

Scudery, Madeleine de 1607-1701..... LC 2

Scum
See Crumb, R(obert)

Scumbag, Little Bobby
See Crumb, R(obert)

Seabrook, John
See Hubbard, L(afayette) Ron(ald)

Sealy, I. Allan 1951- .... CLC 55

Search, Alexander
See Pessoa, Fernando (Antonio Nogueira)

Sebastian, Lee
See Silverberg, Robert

Sebastian Owl
See Thompson, Hunter S(tockton)

Sebestyen, Ouida 1924- .... CLC 30
See also AAYA 8; CA 107; CANR 40;
CLR 17; JRDA; MAICYA; SAAS 10;
SATA 39

Secundus, H. Scriblerus
See Fielding, Henry

Sedges, John
See Buck, Pearl S(ydenstricker)

Sedgwick, Catharine Maria
1789-1867 .... NCLC 19
See also DLB 1, 74

Sherburne, Zoa (Morin) 1912-...... CLC 30
See also AAYA 13; CA 1-4R; CANR 3, 37;
MAICYA; SAAS 18; SATA 3

Sheridan, Frances 1724-1766........ LC 7
See also DLB 39, 84

Sheridan, Richard Brinsley
1751-1816 .... NCLC 5; DA; DAB;
DAC; DC 1; WLC
See also CDBLB 1660-1789; DAM DRAM,
MST; DLB 89

Sherman, Jonathan Marc........... CLC 55

Sherman, Martin 1941(?)-......... CLC 19
See also CA 116; 123

Sherwin, Judith Johnson 1936-... CLC 7, 15
See also CA 25-28R; CANR 34

Sherwood, Frances 1940-......... CLC 81
See also CA 146

Sherwood, Robert E(mmet)
1896-1955 .... TCLC 3
See also CA 104; DAM DRAM; DLB 7, 26

Shestov, Lev 1866-1938 .... TCLC 56

Shiel, M(atthew) P(hipps)
1865-1947 .... TCLC 8
See also CA 106; DLB 153

Shiga, Naoya 1883-1971.......... CLC 33
See also CA 101; 33-36R

Shilts, Randy 1951-1994 .... CLC 85
See also CA 115; 127; 144; CANR 45;
INT 127

Shimazaki Haruki 1872-1943
See Shimazaki Toson
See also CA 105; 134

Shimazaki Toson................. TCLC 5
See also Shimazaki Haruki

Sholokhov, Mikhail (Aleksandrovich)
1905-1984 .... CLC 7, 15
See also CA 101; 112; MTCW;
SATA-Obit 36

Shone, Patric
See Hanley, James

Shreve, Susan Richards 1939-...... CLC 23
See also CA 49-52; CAAS 5; CANR 5, 38;
MAICYA; SATA 46; SATA-Brief 41

Shue, Larry 1946-1985........... CLC 52
See also CA 145; 117; DAM DRAM

Shu-Jen, Chou 1881-1936
See Lu Hsun
See also CA 104

Shulman, Alix Kates 1932-...... CLC 2, 10
See also CA 29-32R; CANR 43; SATA 7

Shuster, Joe 1914-.............. CLC 21

Shute, Nevil.................... CLC 30
See also Norway, Nevil Shute

Shuttle, Penelope (Diane) 1947- ..... CLC 7
See also CA 93-96; CANR 39; DLB 14, 40

Sidney, Mary 1561-1621 .... LC 19

Sidney, Sir Philip
1554-1586 ..... LC 19; DA; DAB; DAC
See also CDBLB Before 1660; DAM MST,
POET

Siegel, Jerome 1914- .... CLC 21
See also CA 116

Siegel, Jerry
See Siegel, Jerome

Sienkiewicz, Henryk (Adam Alexander Pius)
1846-1916 .... TCLC 3
See also CA 104; 134

Sierra, Gregorio Martinez
See Martinez Sierra, Gregorio

Sierra, Maria (de la O'LeJarraga) Martinez
See Martinez Sierra, Maria (de la
O'LeJarraga)

Sigal, Clancy 1926-............... CLC 7
See also CA 1-4R

Sigourney, Lydia Howard (Huntley)
1791-1865 .... NCLC 21
See also DLB 1, 42, 73

Siguenza y Gongora, Carlos de
1645-1700 .... LC 8

Sigurjonsson, Johann 1880-1919... TCLC 27

Sikelianos, Angelos 1884-1951 .... TCLC 39

Silkin, Jon 1930- .... CLC 2, 6, 43
See also CA 5-8R; CAAS 5; DLB 27

Silko, Leslie (Marmon)
1948- .... CLC 23, 74; DA; DAC
See also AAYA 14; CA 115; 122;
CANR 45; DAM MST, MULT, POP;
DLB 143; NNAL

Sillanpaa, Frans Eemil 1888-1964... CLC 19
See also CA 129; 93-96; MTCW

Sillitoe, Alan
1928- .... CLC 1, 3, 6, 10, 19, 57
See also AITN 1; CA 9-12R; CAAS 2;
CANR 8, 26; CDBLB 1960 to Present;
DLB 14, 139; MTCW; SATA 61

Silone, Ignazio 1900-1978 .... CLC 4
See also CA 25-28; 81-84; CANR 34;
CAP 2; MTCW

Silver, Joan Micklin 1935- .... CLC 20
See also CA 114; 121; INT 121

Silver, Nicholas
See Faust, Frederick (Schiller)

Silverberg, Robert 1935- .... CLC 7
See also CA 1-4R; CAAS 3; CANR 1, 20,
36; DAM POP; DLB 8; INT CANR-20;
MAICYA; MTCW; SATA 13

Silverstein, Alvin 1933- .... CLC 17
See also CA 49-52; CANR 2; CLR 25;
JRDA; MAICYA; SATA 8, 69

Silverstein, Virginia B(arbara Opshelor)
1937- .... CLC 17
See also CA 49-52; CANR 2; CLR 25;
JRDA; MAICYA; SATA 8, 69

Sim, Georges
See Simenon, Georges (Jacques Christian)

Simak, Clifford D(onald)
1904-1988 .... CLC 1, 55
See also CA 1-4R; 125; CANR 1, 35;
DLB 8; MTCW; SATA-Obit 56

Simenon, Georges (Jacques Christian)
1903-1989 .... CLC 1, 2, 3, 8, 18, 47
See also CA 85-88; 129; CANR 35;
DAM POP; DLB 72; DLBY 89; MTCW

Simic, Charles 1938-... CLC 6, 9, 22, 49, 68
See also CA 29-32R; CAAS 4; CANR 12,
33; DAM POET; DLB 105

Simmons, Charles (Paul) 1924-..... CLC 57
See also CA 89-92; INT 89-92

Simmons, Dan 1948-............. CLC 44
See also AAYA 16; CA 138; DAM POP

Simmons, James (Stewart Alexander)
1933- .... CLC 43
See also CA 105; CAAS 21; DLB 40

Simms, William Gilmore
1806-1870 .... NCLC 3
See also DLB 3, 30, 59, 73

Simon, Carly 1945-.............. CLC 26
See also CA 105

Simon, Claude 1913-...... CLC 4, 9, 15, 39
See also CA 89-92; CANR 33; DAM NOV;
DLB 83; MTCW

Simon, (Marvin) Neil
1927- .... CLC 6, 11, 31, 39, 70
See also AITN 1; CA 21-24R; CANR 26;
DAM DRAM; DLB 7; MTCW

Simon, Paul 1942(?)- .... CLC 17
See also CA 116

Simonon, Paul 1956(?)- .... CLC 30

Simpson, Harriette
See Arnow, Harriette (Louisa) Simpson

Simpson, Louis (Aston Marantz)
1923- .... CLC 4, 7, 9, 32
See also CA 1-4R; CAAS 4; CANR 1;
DAM POET; DLB 5; MTCW

Simpson, Mona (Elizabeth) 1957-... CLC 44
See also CA 122; 135

Simpson, N(orman) F(rederick)
1919- .... CLC 29
See also CA 13-16R; DLB 13

Sinclair, Andrew (Annandale)
1935- .... CLC 2, 14
See also CA 9-12R; CAAS 5; CANR 14, 38;
DLB 14; MTCW

Sinclair, Emil
See Hesse, Hermann

Sinclair, Iain 1943-.............. CLC 76
See also CA 132

Sinclair, Iain MacGregor
See Sinclair, Iain

Sinclair, Mary Amelia St. Clair 1865(?)-1946
See Sinclair, May
See also CA 104

Sinclair, May.................. TCLC 3, 11
See also Sinclair, Mary Amelia St. Clair
See also DLB 36, 135

Sinclair, Upton (Beall)
1878-1968 ...... CLC 1, 11, 15, 63; DA;
DAB; DAC; WLC
See also CA 5-8R; 25-28R; CANR 7;
CDALB 1929-1941; DAM MST, NOV;
DLB 9; INT CANR-7; MTCW; SATA 9

Singer, Isaac
See Singer, Isaac Bashevis

Singer, Isaac Bashevis
1904-1991 .... CLC 1, 3, 6, 9, 11, 15, 23,
38, 69; DA; DAB; DAC; SSC 3; WLC
See also AITN 1, 2; CA 1-4R; 134;
CANR 1, 39; CDALB 1941-1968; CLR 1;
DAM MST, NOV; DLB 6, 28, 52;
DLBY 91; JRDA; MAICYA; MTCW;
SATA 3, 27; SATA-Obit 68

Singer, Israel Joshua 1893-1944 ... TCLC 33

Singh, Khushwant 1915-.......... **CLC 11**
  See also CA 9-12R; CAAS 9; CANR 6

Sinjohn, John
  See Galsworthy, John

Sinyavsky, Andrei (Donatevich)
  1925- .... **CLC 8**
  See also CA 85-88

Sirin, V.
  See Nabokov, Vladimir (Vladimirovich)

Sissman, L(ouis) E(dward)
  1928-1976 .... **CLC 9, 18**
  See also CA 21-24R; 65-68; CANR 13;
  DLB 5

Sisson, C(harles) H(ubert) 1914-..... **CLC 8**
  See also CA 1-4R; CAAS 3; CANR 3, 48;
  DLB 27

Sitwell, Dame Edith
  1887-1964 .... **CLC 2, 9, 67; PC 3**
  See also CA 9-12R; CANR 35;
  CDBLB 1945-1960; DAM POET;
  DLB 20; MTCW

Sjoewall, Maj 1935-.............. **CLC 7**
  See also CA 65-68

Sjowall, Maj
  See Sjoewall, Maj

Skelton, Robin 1925-............. **CLC 13**
  See also AITN 2; CA 5-8R; CAAS 5;
  CANR 28; DLB 27, 53

Skolimowski, Jerzy 1938-........ **CLC 20**
  See also CA 128

Skram, Amalie (Bertha)
  1847-1905 .... **TCLC 25**

Skvorecky, Josef (Vaclav)
  1924- .... **CLC 15, 39, 69; DAC**
  See also CA 61-64; CAAS 1; CANR 10, 34;
  DAM NOV; MTCW

Slade, Bernard................ **CLC 11, 46**
  See also Newbound, Bernard Slade
  See also CAAS 9; DLB 53

Slaughter, Carolyn 1946-.......... **CLC 56**
  See also CA 85-88

Slaughter, Frank G(ill) 1908- ...... **CLC 29**
  See also AITN 2; CA 5-8R; CANR 5;
  INT CANR-5

Slavitt, David R(ytman) 1935-.... **CLC 5, 14**
  See also CA 21-24R; CAAS 3; CANR 41;
  DLB 5, 6

Slesinger, Tess 1905-1945 .... **TCLC 10**
  See also CA 107; DLB 102

Slessor, Kenneth 1901-1971........ **CLC 14**
  See also CA 102; 89-92

Slowacki, Juliusz 1809-1849 ..... **NCLC 15**

Smart, Christopher
  1722-1771 .... **LC 3; PC 13**
  See also DAM POET; DLB 109

Smart, Elizabeth 1913-1986........ **CLC 54**
  See also CA 81-84; 118; DLB 88

Smiley, Jane (Graves) 1949- .... **CLC 53, 76**
  See also CA 104; CANR 30, 50;
  DAM POP; INT CANR-30

Smith, A(rthur) J(ames) M(arshall)
  1902-1980 ....**CLC 15; DAC**
  See also CA 1-4R; 102; CANR 4; DLB 88

Smith, Anna Deavere 1950-........ **CLC 86**
  See also CA 133

Smith, Betty (Wehner) 1896-1972... **CLC 19**
  See also CA 5-8R; 33-36R; DLBY 82;
  SATA 6

Smith, Charlotte (Turner)
  1749-1806 .... **NCLC 23**
  See also DLB 39, 109

Smith, Clark Ashton 1893-1961 .... **CLC 43**
  See also CA 143

Smith, Dave.................... **CLC 22, 42**
  See also Smith, David (Jeddie)
  See also CAAS 7; DLB 5

Smith, David (Jeddie) 1942-
  See Smith, Dave
  See also CA 49-52; CANR 1; DAM POET

Smith, Florence Margaret 1902-1971
  See Smith, Stevie
  See also CA 17-18; 29-32R; CANR 35;
  CAP 2; DAM POET; MTCW

Smith, Iain Crichton 1928- .... **CLC 64**
  See also CA 21-24R; DLB 40, 139

Smith, John 1580(?)-1631 .... **LC 9**

Smith, Johnston
  See Crane, Stephen (Townley)

Smith, Joseph, Jr. 1805-1844 .... **NCLC 53**

Smith, Lee 1944-.............. **CLC 25, 73**
  See also CA 114; 119; CANR 46; DLB 143;
  DLBY 83; INT 119

Smith, Martin
  See Smith, Martin Cruz

Smith, Martin Cruz 1942-......... **CLC 25**
  See also BEST 89:4; CA 85-88; CANR 6,
  23, 43; DAM MULT, POP;
  INT CANR-23; NNAL

Smith, Mary-Ann Tirone 1944-..... **CLC 39**
  See also CA 118; 136

Smith, Patti 1946- .... **CLC 12**
  See also CA 93-96

Smith, Pauline (Urmson)
  1882-1959 .... **TCLC 25**

Smith, Rosamond
  See Oates, Joyce Carol

Smith, Sheila Kaye
  See Kaye-Smith, Sheila

Smith, Stevie .... **CLC 3, 8, 25, 44; PC 12**
  See also Smith, Florence Margaret
  See also DLB 20

Smith, Wilbur (Addison) 1933-..... **CLC 33**
  See also CA 13-16R; CANR 7, 46; MTCW

Smith, William Jay 1918- .... **CLC 6**
  See also CA 5-8R; CANR 44; DLB 5;
  MAICYA; SATA 2, 68

Smith, Woodrow Wilson
  See Kuttner, Henry

Smolenskin, Peretz 1842-1885.... **NCLC 30**

Smollett, Tobias (George) 1721-1771 .. **LC 2**
  See also CDBLB 1660-1789; DLB 39, 104

Snodgrass, W(illiam) D(e Witt)
  1926- .... **CLC 2, 6, 10, 18, 68**
  See also CA 1-4R; CANR 6, 36;
  DAM POET; DLB 5; MTCW

Snow, C(harles) P(ercy)
  1905-1980 .... **CLC 1, 4, 6, 9, 13, 19**
  See also CA 5-8R; 101; CANR 28;
  CDBLB 1945-1960; DAM NOV; DLB 15,
  77; MTCW

Snow, Frances Compton
  See Adams, Henry (Brooks)

Snyder, Gary (Sherman)
  1930- .... **CLC 1, 2, 5, 9, 32**
  See also CA 17-20R; CANR 30;
  DAM POET; DLB 5, 16

Snyder, Zilpha Keatley 1927-...... **CLC 17**
  See also AAYA 15; CA 9-12R; CANR 38;
  CLR 31; JRDA; MAICYA; SAAS 2;
  SATA 1, 28, 75

Soares, Bernardo
  See Pessoa, Fernando (Antonio Nogueira)

Sobh, A.
  See Shamlu, Ahmad

Sobol, Joshua.................... **CLC 60**

Soderberg, Hjalmar 1869-1941 .... **TCLC 39**

Sodergran, Edith (Irene)
  See Soedergran, Edith (Irene)

Soedergran, Edith (Irene)
  1892-1923 .... **TCLC 31**

Softly, Edgar
  See Lovecraft, H(oward) P(hillips)

Softly, Edward
  See Lovecraft, H(oward) P(hillips)

Sokolov, Raymond 1941-.......... **CLC 7**
  See also CA 85-88

Solo, Jay
  See Ellison, Harlan (Jay)

Sologub, Fyodor .... **TCLC 9**
  See also Teternikov, Fyodor Kuzmich

Solomons, Ikey Esquir
  See Thackeray, William Makepeace

Solomos, Dionysios 1798-1857 ... **NCLC 15**

Solwoska, Mara
  See French, Marilyn

Solzhenitsyn, Aleksandr I(sayevich)
  1918- ...... **CLC 1, 2, 4, 7, 9, 10, 18, 26,
  34, 78; DA; DAB; DAC; WLC**
  See also AITN 1; CA 69-72; CANR 40;
  DAM MST, NOV; MTCW

Somers, Jane
  See Lessing, Doris (May)

Somerville, Edith 1858-1949 ...... **TCLC 51**
  See also DLB 135

Somerville & Ross
  See Martin, Violet Florence; Somerville,
  Edith

Sommer, Scott 1951- .... **CLC 25**
  See also CA 106

Sondheim, Stephen (Joshua)
  1930- .... **CLC 30, 39**
  See also AAYA 11; CA 103; CANR 47;
  DAM DRAM

Sontag, Susan 1933-... **CLC 1, 2, 10, 13, 31**
  See also CA 17-20R; CANR 25;
  DAM POP; DLB 2, 67; MTCW

Stephen, Sir Leslie
See Stephen, Leslie

Stephen, Virginia
See Woolf, (Adeline) Virginia

Stephens, James 1882(?)-1950 ...... **TCLC 4**
See also CA 104; DLB 19, 153

Stephens, Reed
See Donaldson, Stephen R.

Steptoe, Lydia
See Barnes, Djuna

Sterchi, Beat 1949- .... **CLC 65**

Sterling, Brett
See Bradbury, Ray (Douglas); Hamilton, Edmond

Sterling, Bruce 1954- .... **CLC 72**
See also CA 119; CANR 44

Sterling, George 1869-1926 .... **TCLC 20**
See also CA 117; DLB 54

Stern, Gerald 1925- .... **CLC 40**
See also CA 81-84; CANR 28; DLB 105

Stern, Richard (Gustave) 1928-... **CLC 4, 39**
See also CA 1-4R; CANR 1, 25; DLBY 87; INT CANR-25

Sternberg, Josef von 1894-1969..... **CLC 20**
See also CA 81-84

Sterne, Laurence
1713-1768 ...... **LC 2; DA; DAB; DAC; WLC**
See also CDBLB 1660-1789; DAM MST, NOV; DLB 39

Sternheim, (William Adolf) Carl
1878-1942 .... **TCLC 8**
See also CA 105; DLB 56, 118

Stevens, Mark 1951- .... **CLC 34**
See also CA 122

Stevens, Wallace
1879-1955 .... **TCLC 3, 12, 45; DA; DAB; DAC; PC 6; WLC**
See also CA 104; 124; CDALB 1929-1941; DAM MST, POET; DLB 54; MTCW

Stevenson, Anne (Katharine)
1933- .... **CLC 7, 33**
See also CA 17-20R; CAAS 9; CANR 9, 33; DLB 40; MTCW

Stevenson, Robert Louis (Balfour)
1850-1894 ..... **NCLC 5, 14; DA; DAB; DAC; SSC 11; WLC**
See also CDBLB 1890-1914; CLR 10, 11; DAM MST, NOV; DLB 18, 57, 141, 156; DLBD 13; JRDA; MAICYA; YABC 2

Stewart, J(ohn) I(nnes) M(ackintosh)
1906-1994 .... **CLC 7, 14, 32**
See also CA 85-88; 147; CAAS 3; CANR 47; MTCW

Stewart, Mary (Florence Elinor)
1916- .... **CLC 7, 35; DAB**
See also CA 1-4R; CANR 1; SATA 12

Stewart, Mary Rainbow
See Stewart, Mary (Florence Elinor)

Stifle, June
See Campbell, Maria

Stifter, Adalbert 1805-1868 ...... **NCLC 41**
See also DLB 133

Still, James 1906- .... **CLC 49**
See also CA 65-68; CAAS 17; CANR 10, 26; DLB 9; SATA 29

Sting
See Sumner, Gordon Matthew

Stirling, Arthur
See Sinclair, Upton (Beall)

Stitt, Milan 1941- .... **CLC 29**
See also CA 69-72

Stockton, Francis Richard 1834-1902
See Stockton, Frank R.
See also CA 108; 137; MAICYA; SATA 44

Stockton, Frank R. .... **TCLC 47**
See also Stockton, Francis Richard
See also DLB 42, 74; DLBD 13; SATA-Brief 32

Stoddard, Charles
See Kuttner, Henry

Stoker, Abraham 1847-1912
See Stoker, Bram
See also CA 105; DA; DAC; DAM MST, NOV; SATA 29

Stoker, Bram .... **TCLC 8; DAB; WLC**
See also Stoker, Abraham
See also CDBLB 1890-1914; DLB 36, 70

Stolz, Mary (Slattery) 1920- .... **CLC 12**
See also AAYA 8; AITN 1; CA 5-8R; CANR 13, 41; JRDA; MAICYA; SAAS 3; SATA 10, 71

Stone, Irving 1903-1989 .... **CLC 7**
See also AITN 1; CA 1-4R; 129; CAAS 3; CANR 1, 23; DAM POP; INT CANR-23; MTCW; SATA 3; SATA-Obit 64

Stone, Oliver 1946- .... **CLC 73**
See also AAYA 15; CA 110

Stone, Robert (Anthony)
1937- .... **CLC 5, 23, 42**
See also CA 85-88; CANR 23; DLB 152; INT CANR-23; MTCW

Stone, Zachary
See Follett, Ken(neth Martin)

Stoppard, Tom
1937- ...... **CLC 1, 3, 4, 5, 8, 15, 29, 34, 63; DA; DAB; DAC; DC 6; WLC**
See also CA 81-84; CANR 39; CDBLB 1960 to Present; DAM DRAM, MST; DLB 13; DLBY 85; MTCW

Storey, David (Malcolm)
1933- .... **CLC 2, 4, 5, 8**
See also CA 81-84; CANR 36; DAM DRAM; DLB 13, 14; MTCW

Storm, Hyemeyohsts 1935- .... **CLC 3**
See also CA 81-84; CANR 45; DAM MULT; NNAL

Storm, (Hans) Theodor (Woldsen)
1817-1888 .... **NCLC 1**

Storni, Alfonsina
1892-1938 .... **TCLC 5; HLC**
See also CA 104; 131; DAM MULT; HW

Stout, Rex (Todhunter) 1886-1975 ... **CLC 3**
See also AITN 2; CA 61-64

Stow, (Julian) Randolph 1935- .. **CLC 23, 48**
See also CA 13-16R; CANR 33; MTCW

Stowe, Harriet (Elizabeth) Beecher
1811-1896 ..... **NCLC 3, 50; DA; DAB; DAC; WLC**
See also CDALB 1865-1917; DAM MST, NOV; DLB 1, 12, 42, 74; JRDA; MAICYA; YABC 1

Strachey, (Giles) Lytton
1880-1932 .... **TCLC 12**
See also CA 110; DLB 149; DLBD 10

Strand, Mark 1934- ...... **CLC 6, 18, 41, 71**
See also CA 21-24R; CANR 40; DAM POET; DLB 5; SATA 41

Straub, Peter (Francis) 1943- ...... **CLC 28**
See also BEST 89:1; CA 85-88; CANR 28; DAM POP; DLBY 84; MTCW

Strauss, Botho 1944- .... **CLC 22**
See also DLB 124

Streatfeild, (Mary) Noel
1895(?)-1986 .... **CLC 21**
See also CA 81-84; 120; CANR 31; CLR 17; DLB 160; MAICYA; SATA 20; SATA-Obit 48

Stribling, T(homas) S(igismund)
1881-1965 .... **CLC 23**
See also CA 107; DLB 9

Strindberg, (Johan) August
1849-1912 ...... **TCLC 1, 8, 21, 47; DA; DAB; DAC; WLC**
See also CA 104; 135; DAM DRAM, MST

Stringer, Arthur 1874-1950 .... **TCLC 37**
See also DLB 92

Stringer, David
See Roberts, Keith (John Kingston)

Strugatskii, Arkadii (Natanovich)
1925-1991 .... **CLC 27**
See also CA 106; 135

Strugatskii, Boris (Natanovich)
1933- .... **CLC 27**
See also CA 106

Strummer, Joe 1953(?)- .... **CLC 30**

Stuart, Don A.
See Campbell, John W(ood, Jr.)

Stuart, Ian
See MacLean, Alistair (Stuart)

Stuart, Jesse (Hilton)
1906-1984 .... **CLC 1, 8, 11, 14, 34**
See also CA 5-8R; 112; CANR 31; DLB 9, 48, 102; DLBY 84; SATA 2; SATA-Obit 36

Sturgeon, Theodore (Hamilton)
1918-1985 .... **CLC 22, 39**
See also Queen, Ellery
See also CA 81-84; 116; CANR 32; DLB 8; DLBY 85; MTCW

Sturges, Preston 1898-1959 .... **TCLC 48**
See also CA 114; 149; DLB 26

Styron, William
1925- .... **CLC 1, 3, 5, 11, 15, 60**
See also BEST 90:4; CA 5-8R; CANR 6, 33; CDALB 1968-1988; DAM NOV, POP; DLB 2, 143; DLBY 80; INT CANR-6; MTCW

Suarez Lynch, B.
See Bioy Casares, Adolfo; Borges, Jorge Luis

Su Chien 1884-1918
  See Su Man-shu
  See also CA 123

Suckow, Ruth 1892-1960 . . . . **SSC 18**
  See also CA 113; DLB 9, 102

Sudermann, Hermann 1857-1928 . . **TCLC 15**
  See also CA 107; DLB 118

Sue, Eugene 1804-1857 . . . . **NCLC 1**
  See also DLB 119

Sueskind, Patrick 1949- . . . . **CLC 44**
  See also Suskind, Patrick

Sukenick, Ronald 1932- . . . . . **CLC 3, 4, 6, 48**
  See also CA 25-28R; CAAS 8; CANR 32;
  DLBY 81

Suknaski, Andrew 1942- . . . . **CLC 19**
  See also CA 101; DLB 53

Sullivan, Vernon
  See Vian, Boris

Sully Prudhomme 1839-1907 . . . . . **TCLC 31**

Su Man-shu . . . . **TCLC 24**
  See also Su Chien

Summerforest, Ivy B.
  See Kirkup, James

Summers, Andrew James 1942- . . . . . **CLC 26**

Summers, Andy
  See Summers, Andrew James

Summers, Hollis (Spurgeon, Jr.)
  1916- . . . . **CLC 10**
  See also CA 5-8R; CANR 3; DLB 6

Summers, (Alphonsus Joseph-Mary Augustus)
  Montague 1880-1948 . . . . **TCLC 16**
  See also CA 118

Sumner, Gordon Matthew 1951- . . . . **CLC 26**

Surtees, Robert Smith
  1803-1864 . . . . **NCLC 14**
  See also DLB 21

Susann, Jacqueline 1921-1974 . . . . **CLC 3**
  See also AITN 1; CA 65-68; 53-56; MTCW

Su Shih 1036-1101 . . . . **CMLC 15**

Suskind, Patrick
  See Sueskind, Patrick
  See also CA 145

Sutcliff, Rosemary
  1920-1992 . . . . **CLC 26; DAB; DAC**
  See also AAYA 10; CA 5-8R; 139;
  CANR 37; CLR 1, 37; DAM MST, POP;
  JRDA; MAICYA; SATA 6, 44, 78;
  SATA-Obit 73

Sutro, Alfred 1863-1933 . . . . **TCLC 6**
  See also CA 105; DLB 10

Sutton, Henry
  See Slavitt, David R(ytman)

Svevo, Italo . . . . **TCLC 2, 35**
  See also Schmitz, Aron Hector

Swados, Elizabeth (A.) 1951- . . . . **CLC 12**
  See also CA 97-100; CANR 49; INT 97-100

Swados, Harvey 1920-1972 . . . . **CLC 5**
  See also CA 5-8R; 37-40R; CANR 6;
  DLB 2

Swan, Gladys 1934- . . . . **CLC 69**
  See also CA 101; CANR 17, 39

Swarthout, Glendon (Fred)
  1918-1992 . . . . **CLC 35**
  See also CA 1-4R; 139; CANR 1, 47;
  SATA 26

Sweet, Sarah C.
  See Jewett, (Theodora) Sarah Orne

Swenson, May
  1919-1989 . . . . **CLC 4, 14, 61; DA; DAB;**
                              DAC; PC 14
  See also CA 5-8R; 130; CANR 36;
  DAM MST, POET; DLB 5; MTCW;
  SATA 15

Swift, Augustus
  See Lovecraft, H(oward) P(hillips)

Swift, Graham (Colin) 1949- . . . . **CLC 41, 88**
  See also CA 117; 122; CANR 46

Swift, Jonathan
  1667-1745 . . . . . . **LC 1; DA; DAB; DAC;**
                              PC 9; WLC
  See also CDBLB 1660-1789; DAM MST,
  NOV, POET; DLB 39, 95, 101; SATA 19

Swinburne, Algernon Charles
  1837-1909 . . . . . . **TCLC 8, 36; DA; DAB;**
                              DAC; WLC
  See also CA 105; 140; CDBLB 1832-1890;
  DAM MST, POET; DLB 35, 57

Swinfen, Ann . . . . **CLC 34**

Swinnerton, Frank Arthur
  1884-1982 . . . . **CLC 31**
  See also CA 108; DLB 34

Swithen, John
  See King, Stephen (Edwin)

Sylvia
  See Ashton-Warner, Sylvia (Constance)

Symmes, Robert Edward
  See Duncan, Robert (Edward)

Symonds, John Addington
  1840-1893 . . . . **NCLC 34**
  See also DLB 57, 144

Symons, Arthur 1865-1945 . . . . **TCLC 11**
  See also CA 107; DLB 19, 57, 149

Symons, Julian (Gustave)
  1912-1994 . . . . **CLC 2, 14, 32**
  See also CA 49-52; 147; CAAS 3; CANR 3,
  33; DLB 87, 155; DLBY 92; MTCW

Synge, (Edmund) J(ohn) M(illington)
  1871-1909 . . . . **TCLC 6, 37; DC 2**
  See also CA 104; 141; CDBLB 1890-1914;
  DAM DRAM; DLB 10, 19

Syruc, J.
  See Milosz, Czeslaw

Szirtes, George 1948- . . . . **CLC 46**
  See also CA 109; CANR 27

Tabori, George 1914- . . . . **CLC 19**
  See also CA 49-52; CANR 4

Tagore, Rabindranath
  1861-1941 . . . . **TCLC 3, 53; PC 8**
  See also CA 104; 120; DAM DRAM,
  POET; MTCW

Taine, Hippolyte Adolphe
  1828-1893 . . . . **NCLC 15**

Talese, Gay 1932- . . . . **CLC 37**
  See also AITN 1; CA 1-4R; CANR 9;
  INT CANR-9; MTCW

Tallent, Elizabeth (Ann) 1954- . . . . . **CLC 45**
  See also CA 117; DLB 130

Tally, Ted 1952- . . . . **CLC 42**
  See also CA 120; 124; INT 124

Tamayo y Baus, Manuel
  1829-1898 . . . . **NCLC 1**

Tammsaare, A(nton) H(ansen)
  1878-1940 . . . . **TCLC 27**

Tan, Amy 1952- . . . . **CLC 59**
  See also AAYA 9; BEST 89:3; CA 136;
  DAM MULT, NOV, POP; SATA 75

Tandem, Felix
  See Spitteler, Carl (Friedrich Georg)

Tanizaki, Jun'ichiro
  1886-1965 . . . . . . **CLC 8, 14, 28; SSC 21**
  See also CA 93-96; 25-28R

Tanner, William
  See Amis, Kingsley (William)

Tao Lao
  See Storni, Alfonsina

Tarassoff, Lev
  See Troyat, Henri

Tarbell, Ida M(inerva)
  1857-1944 . . . . **TCLC 40**
  See also CA 122; DLB 47

Tarkington, (Newton) Booth
  1869-1946 . . . . **TCLC 9**
  See also CA 110; 143; DLB 9, 102;
  SATA 17

Tarkovsky, Andrei (Arsenyevich)
  1932-1986 . . . . **CLC 75**
  See also CA 127

Tartt, Donna 1964(?)- . . . . **CLC 76**
  See also CA 142

Tasso, Torquato 1544-1595 . . . . **LC 5**

Tate, (John Orley) Allen
  1899-1979 . . . . **CLC 2, 4, 6, 9, 11, 14, 24**
  See also CA 5-8R; 85-88; CANR 32;
  DLB 4, 45, 63; MTCW

Tate, Ellalice
  See Hibbert, Eleanor Alice Burford

Tate, James (Vincent) 1943- . . . **CLC 2, 6, 25**
  See also CA 21-24R; CANR 29; DLB 5

Tavel, Ronald 1940- . . . . **CLC 6**
  See also CA 21-24R; CANR 33

Taylor, C(ecil) P(hilip) 1929-1981 . . . **CLC 27**
  See also CA 25-28R; 105; CANR 47

Taylor, Edward
  1642(?)-1729 . . . **LC 11; DA; DAB; DAC**
  See also DAM MST, POET; DLB 24

Taylor, Eleanor Ross 1920- . . . . **CLC 5**
  See also CA 81-84

Taylor, Elizabeth 1912-1975 . . . **CLC 2, 4, 29**
  See also CA 13-16R; CANR 9; DLB 139;
  MTCW; SATA 13

Taylor, Henry (Splawn) 1942- . . . . . . **CLC 44**
  See also CA 33-36R; CAAS 7; CANR 31;
  DLB 5

Taylor, Kamala (Purnaiya) 1924-
  See Markandaya, Kamala
  See also CA 77-80

Taylor, Mildred D. . . . . CLC 21
See also AAYA 10; BW 1; CA 85-88;
CANR 25; CLR 9; DLB 52; JRDA;
MAICYA; SAAS 5; SATA 15, 70

Taylor, Peter (Hillsman)
1917-1994 . . . . . CLC 1, 4, 18, 37, 44, 50,
71; SSC 10
See also CA 13-16R; 147; CANR 9, 50;
DLBY 81, 94; INT CANR-9; MTCW

Taylor, Robert Lewis 1912- . . . . CLC 14
See also CA 1-4R; CANR 3; SATA 10

Tchekhov, Anton
See Chekhov, Anton (Pavlovich)

Teasdale, Sara 1884-1933 . . . . TCLC 4
See also CA 104; DLB 45; SATA 32

Tegner, Esaias 1782-1846 . . . . NCLC 2

Teilhard de Chardin, (Marie Joseph) Pierre
1881-1955 . . . . TCLC 9
See also CA 105

Temple, Ann
See Mortimer, Penelope (Ruth)

Tennant, Emma (Christina)
1937- . . . . CLC 13, 52
See also CA 65-68; CAAS 9; CANR 10, 38;
DLB 14

Tenneshaw, S. M.
See Silverberg, Robert

Tennyson, Alfred
1809-1892 . . . . NCLC 30; DA; DAB;
DAC; PC 6; WLC
See also CDBLB 1832-1890; DAM MST,
POET; DLB 32

Teran, Lisa St. Aubin de . . . . CLC 36
See also St. Aubin de Teran, Lisa

Terence 195(?)B.C.-159B.C. . . . . . . CMLC 14

Teresa de Jesus, St. 1515-1582 . . . . . . LC 18

Terkel, Louis 1912-
See Terkel, Studs
See also CA 57-60; CANR 18, 45; MTCW

Terkel, Studs . . . . CLC 38
See also Terkel, Louis
See also AITN 1

Terry, C. V.
See Slaughter, Frank G(ill)

Terry, Megan 1932- . . . . CLC 19
See also CA 77-80; CABS 3; CANR 43;
DLB 7

Tertz, Abram
See Sinyavsky, Andrei (Donatevich)

Tesich, Steve 1943(?)- . . . . CLC 40, 69
See also CA 105; DLBY 83

Teternikov, Fyodor Kuzmich 1863-1927
See Sologub, Fyodor
See also CA 104

Tevis, Walter 1928-1984 . . . . CLC 42
See also CA 113

Tey, Josephine . . . . TCLC 14
See also Mackintosh, Elizabeth
See also DLB 77

Thackeray, William Makepeace
1811-1863 . . . . NCLC 5, 14, 22, 43; DA;
DAB; DAC; WLC
See also CDBLB 1832-1890; DAM MST,
NOV; DLB 21, 55, 159; SATA 23

Thakura, Ravindranatha
See Tagore, Rabindranath

Tharoor, Shashi 1956- . . . . CLC 70
See also CA 141

Thelwell, Michael Miles 1939- . . . . . CLC 22
See also BW 2; CA 101

Theobald, Lewis, Jr.
See Lovecraft, H(oward) P(hillips)

Theodorescu, Ion N. 1880-1967
See Arghezi, Tudor
See also CA 116

Theriault, Yves 1915-1983 . . . . CLC 79; DAC
See also CA 102; DAM MST; DLB 88

Theroux, Alexander (Louis)
1939- . . . . CLC 2, 25
See also CA 85-88; CANR 20

Theroux, Paul (Edward)
1941- . . . . CLC 5, 8, 11, 15, 28, 46
See also BEST 89:4; CA 33-36R; CANR 20,
45; DAM POP; DLB 2; MTCW;
SATA 44

Thesen, Sharon 1946- . . . . CLC 56

Thevenin, Denis
See Duhamel, Georges

Thibault, Jacques Anatole Francois
1844-1924
See France, Anatole
See also CA 106; 127; DAM NOV; MTCW

Thiele, Colin (Milton) 1920- . . . . CLC 17
See also CA 29-32R; CANR 12, 28;
CLR 27; MAICYA; SAAS 2; SATA 14,
72

Thomas, Audrey (Callahan)
1935- . . . . CLC 7, 13, 37; SSC 20
See also AITN 2; CA 21-24R; CAAS 19;
CANR 36; DLB 60; MTCW

Thomas, D(onald) M(ichael)
1935- . . . . CLC 13, 22, 31
See also CA 61-64; CAAS 11; CANR 17,
45; CDBLB 1960 to Present; DLB 40;
INT CANR-17; MTCW

Thomas, Dylan (Marlais)
1914-1953 . . . TCLC 1, 8, 45; DA; DAB;
DAC; PC 2; SSC 3; WLC
See also CA 104; 120; CDBLB 1945-1960;
DAM DRAM, MST, POET; DLB 13, 20,
139; MTCW; SATA 60

Thomas, (Philip) Edward
1878-1917 . . . . TCLC 10
See also CA 106; DAM POET; DLB 19

Thomas, Joyce Carol 1938- . . . . CLC 35
See also AAYA 12; BW 2; CA 113; 116;
CANR 48; CLR 19; DLB 33; INT 116;
JRDA; MAICYA; MTCW; SAAS 7;
SATA 40, 78

Thomas, Lewis 1913-1993 . . . . CLC 35
See also CA 85-88; 143; CANR 38; MTCW

Thomas, Paul
See Mann, (Paul) Thomas

Thomas, Piri 1928- . . . . CLC 17
See also CA 73-76; HW

Thomas, R(onald) S(tuart)
1913- . . . . CLC 6, 13, 48; DAB
See also CA 89-92; CAAS 4; CANR 30;
CDBLB 1960 to Present; DAM POET;
DLB 27; MTCW

Thomas, Ross (Elmore) 1926- . . . . . . CLC 39
See also CA 33-36R; CANR 22

Thompson, Francis Clegg
See Mencken, H(enry) L(ouis)

Thompson, Francis Joseph
1859-1907 . . . . TCLC 4
See also CA 104; CDBLB 1890-1914;
DLB 19

Thompson, Hunter S(tockton)
1939- . . . . CLC 9, 17, 40
See also BEST 89:1; CA 17-20R; CANR 23,
46; DAM POP; MTCW

Thompson, James Myers
See Thompson, Jim (Myers)

Thompson, Jim (Myers)
1906-1977(?) . . . . CLC 69
See also CA 140

Thompson, Judith . . . . CLC 39

Thomson, James 1700-1748 . . . . . . LC 16, 29
See also DAM POET; DLB 95

Thomson, James 1834-1882 . . . . . . NCLC 18
See also DAM POET; DLB 35

Thoreau, Henry David
1817-1862 . . . . . NCLC 7, 21; DA; DAB;
DAC; WLC
See also CDALB 1640-1865; DAM MST;
DLB 1

Thornton, Hall
See Silverberg, Robert

Thucydides c. 455B.C.-399B.C. . . . . CMLC 17

Thurber, James (Grover)
1894-1961 . . . . CLC 5, 11, 25; DA; DAB;
DAC; SSC 1
See also CA 73-76; CANR 17, 39;
CDALB 1929-1941; DAM DRAM, MST,
NOV; DLB 4, 11, 22, 102; MAICYA;
MTCW; SATA 13

Thurman, Wallace (Henry)
1902-1934 . . . . TCLC 6; BLC
See also BW 1; CA 104; 124; DAM MULT;
DLB 51

Ticheburn, Cheviot
See Ainsworth, William Harrison

Tieck, (Johann) Ludwig
1773-1853 . . . . NCLC 5, 46
See also DLB 90

Tiger, Derry
See Ellison, Harlan (Jay)

Tilghman, Christopher 1948(?)- . . . . . CLC 65

Tillinghast, Richard (Williford)
1940- . . . . CLC 29
See also CA 29-32R; CANR 26

Timrod, Henry 1828-1867 . . . . NCLC 25
See also DLB 3

Tindall, Gillian 1938- . . . . CLC 7
See also CA 21-24R; CANR 11

Tiptree, James, Jr. . . . . CLC 48, 50
See also Sheldon, Alice Hastings Bradley
See also DLB 8

Titmarsh, Michael Angelo
See Thackeray, William Makepeace

Tocqueville, Alexis (Charles Henri Maurice
Clerel Comte) 1805-1859 . . . . . NCLC 7

Tolkien, J(ohn) R(onald) R(euel)
1892-1973 . . . . . . **CLC 1, 2, 3, 8, 12, 38;**
DA; DAB; DAC; WLC
See also AAYA 10; AITN 1; CA 17-18;
45-48; CANR 36; CAP 2;
CDBLB 1914-1945; DAM MST, NOV,
POP; DLB 15, 160; JRDA; MAICYA;
MTCW; SATA 2, 32; SATA-Obit 24

Toller, Ernst 1893-1939 . . . . **TCLC 10**
See also CA 107; DLB 124

Tolson, M. B.
See Tolson, Melvin B(eaunorus)

Tolson, Melvin B(eaunorus)
1898(?)-1966 . . . . **CLC 36; BLC**
See also BW 1; CA 124; 89-92;
DAM MULT, POET; DLB 48, 76

Tolstoi, Aleksei Nikolaevich
See Tolstoy, Alexey Nikolaevich

Tolstoy, Alexey Nikolaevich
1882-1945 . . . . **TCLC 18**
See also CA 107

Tolstoy, Count Leo
See Tolstoy, Leo (Nikolaevich)

Tolstoy, Leo (Nikolaevich)
1828-1910 . . . . . . **TCLC 4, 11, 17, 28, 44;**
DA; DAB; DAC; SSC 9; WLC
See also CA 104; 123; DAM MST, NOV;
SATA 26

Tomasi di Lampedusa, Giuseppe 1896-1957
See Lampedusa, Giuseppe (Tomasi) di
See also CA 111

Tomlin, Lily . . . . **CLC 17**
See also Tomlin, Mary Jean

Tomlin, Mary Jean 1939(?)-
See Tomlin, Lily
See also CA 117

Tomlinson, (Alfred) Charles
1927- . . . . **CLC 2, 4, 6, 13, 45**
See also CA 5-8R; CANR 33; DAM POET;
DLB 40

Tonson, Jacob
See Bennett, (Enoch) Arnold

Toole, John Kennedy
1937-1969 . . . . **CLC 19, 64**
See also CA 104; DLBY 81

Toomer, Jean
1894-1967 . . . . . . **CLC 1, 4, 13, 22; BLC;**
PC 7; SSC 1
See also BW 1; CA 85-88;
CDALB 1917-1929; DAM MULT;
DLB 45, 51; MTCW

Torley, Luke
See Blish, James (Benjamin)

Tornimparte, Alessandra
See Ginzburg, Natalia

Torre, Raoul della
See Mencken, H(enry) L(ouis)

Torrey, E(dwin) Fuller 1937- . . . . **CLC 34**
See also CA 119

Torsvan, Ben Traven
See Traven, B.

Torsvan, Benno Traven
See Traven, B.

Torsvan, Berick Traven
See Traven, B.

Torsvan, Berwick Traven
See Traven, B.

Torsvan, Bruno Traven
See Traven, B.

Torsvan, Traven
See Traven, B.

Tournier, Michel (Edouard)
1924- . . . . **CLC 6, 23, 36**
See also CA 49-52; CANR 3, 36; DLB 83;
MTCW; SATA 23

Tournimparte, Alessandra
See Ginzburg, Natalia

Towers, Ivar
See Kornbluth, C(yril) M.

Towne, Robert (Burton) 1936(?)- . . . . **CLC 87**
See also CA 108; DLB 44

Townsend, Sue 1946- . . **CLC 61; DAB; DAC**
See also CA 119; 127; INT 127; MTCW;
SATA 55; SATA-Brief 48

Townshend, Peter (Dennis Blandford)
1945- . . . . **CLC 17, 42**
See also CA 107

Tozzi, Federigo 1883-1920 . . . . **TCLC 31**

Traill, Catharine Parr
1802-1899 . . . . **NCLC 31**
See also DLB 99

Trakl, Georg 1887-1914 . . . . **TCLC 5**
See also CA 104

Transtroemer, Tomas (Goesta)
1931- . . . . **CLC 52, 65**
See also CA 117; 129; CAAS 17;
DAM POET

Transtromer, Tomas Gosta
See Transtroemer, Tomas (Goesta)

Traven, B. (?)-1969 . . . . **CLC 8, 11**
See also CA 19-20; 25-28R; CAP 2; DLB 9,
56; MTCW

Treitel, Jonathan 1959- . . . . **CLC 70**

Tremain, Rose 1943- . . . . **CLC 42**
See also CA 97-100; CANR 44; DLB 14

Tremblay, Michel 1942- . . . . . . **CLC 29; DAC**
See also CA 116; 128; DAM MST; DLB 60;
MTCW

Trevanian . . . . **CLC 29**
See also Whitaker, Rod(ney)

Trevor, Glen
See Hilton, James

Trevor, William
1928- . . . . . **CLC 7, 9, 14, 25, 71; SSC 21**
See also Cox, William Trevor
See also DLB 14, 139

Trifonov, Yuri (Valentinovich)
1925-1981 . . . . **CLC 45**
See also CA 126; 103; MTCW

Trilling, Lionel 1905-1975 . . . . **CLC 9, 11, 24**
See also CA 9-12R; 61-64; CANR 10;
DLB 28, 63; INT CANR-10; MTCW

Trimball, W. H.
See Mencken, H(enry) L(ouis)

Tristan
See Gomez de la Serna, Ramon

Tristram
See Housman, A(lfred) E(dward)

Trogdon, William (Lewis) 1939-
See Heat-Moon, William Least
See also CA 115; 119; CANR 47; INT 119

Trollope, Anthony
1815-1882 . . . . . **NCLC 6, 33; DA; DAB;**
DAC; WLC
See also CDBLB 1832-1890; DAM MST,
NOV; DLB 21, 57, 159; SATA 22

Trollope, Frances 1779-1863 . . . . . **NCLC 30**
See also DLB 21

Trotsky, Leon 1879-1940 . . . . **TCLC 22**
See also CA 118

Trotter (Cockburn), Catharine
1679-1749 . . . . **LC 8**
See also DLB 84

Trout, Kilgore
See Farmer, Philip Jose

Trow, George W. S. 1943- . . . . **CLC 52**
See also CA 126

Troyat, Henri 1911- . . . . **CLC 23**
See also CA 45-48; CANR 2, 33; MTCW

Trudeau, G(arretson) B(eekman) 1948-
See Trudeau, Garry B.
See also CA 81-84; CANR 31; SATA 35

Trudeau, Garry B. . . . . **CLC 12**
See also Trudeau, G(arretson) B(eekman)
See also AAYA 10; AITN 2

Truffaut, Francois 1932-1984 . . . . . . **CLC 20**
See also CA 81-84; 113; CANR 34

Trumbo, Dalton 1905-1976 . . . . **CLC 19**
See also CA 21-24R; 69-72; CANR 10;
DLB 26

Trumbull, John 1750-1831 . . . . **NCLC 30**
See also DLB 31

Trundlett, Helen B.
See Eliot, T(homas) S(tearns)

Tryon, Thomas 1926-1991 . . . . **CLC 3, 11**
See also AITN 1; CA 29-32R; 135;
CANR 32; DAM POP; MTCW

Tryon, Tom
See Tryon, Thomas

Ts'ao Hsueh-ch'in 1715(?)-1763 . . . . **LC 1**

Tsushima, Shuji 1909-1948
See Dazai, Osamu
See also CA 107

Tsvetaeva (Efron), Marina (Ivanovna)
1892-1941 . . . . **TCLC 7, 35; PC 14**
See also CA 104; 128; MTCW

Tuck, Lily 1938- . . . . **CLC 70**
See also CA 139

Tu Fu 712-770 . . . . **PC 9**
See also DAM MULT

Tunis, John R(oberts) 1889-1975 . . . **CLC 12**
See also CA 61-64; DLB 22; JRDA;
MAICYA; SATA 37; SATA-Brief 30

Tuohy, Frank . . . . **CLC 37**
See also Tuohy, John Francis
See also DLB 14, 139

Tuohy, John Francis 1925-
See Tuohy, Frank
See also CA 5-8R; CANR 3, 47

Turco, Lewis (Putnam) 1934- . . . **CLC 11, 63**
See also CA 13-16R; CAAS 22; CANR 24;
DLBY 84

Turgenev, Ivan
1818-1883 . . . . **NCLC 21; DA; DAB;
DAC; SSC 7; WLC**
See also DAM MST, NOV

Turgot, Anne-Robert-Jacques
1727-1781 . . . . **LC 26**

Turner, Frederick 1943- . . . . **CLC 48**
See also CA 73-76; CAAS 10; CANR 12,
30; DLB 40

Tutu, Desmond M(pilo)
1931- . . . . **CLC 80; BLC**
See also BW 1; CA 125; DAM MULT

Tutuola, Amos 1920- . . . **CLC 5, 14, 29; BLC**
See also BW 2; CA 9-12R; CANR 27;
DAM MULT; DLB 125; MTCW

Twain, Mark
. . . . . **TCLC 6, 12, 19, 36, 48, 59; SSC 6;
WLC**
See also Clemens, Samuel Langhorne
See also DLB 11, 12, 23, 64, 74

Tyler, Anne
1941- . . . . **CLC 7, 11, 18, 28, 44, 59**
See also BEST 89:1; CA 9-12R; CANR 11,
33; DAM NOV, POP; DLB 6, 143;
DLBY 82; MTCW; SATA 7

Tyler, Royall 1757-1826 . . . . **NCLC 3**
See also DLB 37

Tynan, Katharine 1861-1931 . . . . **TCLC 3**
See also CA 104; DLB 153

Tyutchev, Fyodor 1803-1873 . . . . . **NCLC 34**

Tzara, Tristan . . . . **CLC 47**
See also Rosenfeld, Samuel
See also DAM POET

Uhry, Alfred 1936- . . . . **CLC 55**
See also CA 127; 133; DAM DRAM, POP;
INT 133

Ulf, Haerved
See Strindberg, (Johan) August

Ulf, Harved
See Strindberg, (Johan) August

Ulibarri, Sabine R(eyes) 1919- . . . . . **CLC 83**
See also CA 131; DAM MULT; DLB 82;
HW

Unamuno (y Jugo), Miguel de
1864-1936 . . . . **TCLC 2, 9; HLC; SSC 11**
See also CA 104; 131; DAM MULT, NOV;
DLB 108; HW; MTCW

Undercliffe, Errol
See Campbell, (John) Ramsey

Underwood, Miles
See Glassco, John

Undset, Sigrid
1882-1949 . . . . **TCLC 3; DA; DAB;
DAC; WLC**
See also CA 104; 129; DAM MST, NOV;
MTCW

Ungaretti, Giuseppe
1888-1970 . . . . **CLC 7, 11, 15**
See also CA 19-20; 25-28R; CAP 2;
DLB 114

Unger, Douglas 1952- . . . . **CLC 34**
See also CA 130

Unsworth, Barry (Forster) 1930- . . . . **CLC 76**
See also CA 25-28R; CANR 30

Updike, John (Hoyer)
1932- . . . . . . **CLC 1, 2, 3, 5, 7, 9, 13, 15,
23, 34, 43, 70; DA; DAB; DAC; SSC 13;
WLC**
See also CA 1-4R; CABS 1; CANR 4, 33;
CDALB 1968-1988; DAM MST, NOV,
POET, POP; DLB 2, 5, 143; DLBD 3;
DLBY 80, 82; MTCW

Upshaw, Margaret Mitchell
See Mitchell, Margaret (Munnerlyn)

Upton, Mark
See Sanders, Lawrence

Urdang, Constance (Henriette)
1922- . . . . **CLC 47**
See also CA 21-24R; CANR 9, 24

Uriel, Henry
See Faust, Frederick (Schiller)

Uris, Leon (Marcus) 1924- . . . . . . **CLC 7, 32**
See also AITN 1, 2; BEST 89:2; CA 1-4R;
CANR 1, 40; DAM NOV, POP; MTCW;
SATA 49

Urmuz
See Codrescu, Andrei

Urquhart, Jane 1949- . . . . **CLC 90; DAC**
See also CA 113; CANR 32

Ustinov, Peter (Alexander) 1921- . . . . **CLC 1**
See also AITN 1; CA 13-16R; CANR 25;
DLB 13

Vaculik, Ludvik 1926- . . . . **CLC 7**
See also CA 53-56

Valdez, Luis (Miguel)
1940- . . . . **CLC 84; HLC**
See also CA 101; CANR 32; DAM MULT;
DLB 122; HW

Valenzuela, Luisa 1938- . . . **CLC 31; SSC 14**
See also CA 101; CANR 32; DAM MULT;
DLB 113; HW

Valera y Alcala-Galiano, Juan
1824-1905 . . . . **TCLC 10**
See also CA 106

Valery, (Ambroise) Paul (Toussaint Jules)
1871-1945 . . . . **TCLC 4, 15; PC 9**
See also CA 104; 122; DAM POET; MTCW

Valle-Inclan, Ramon (Maria) del
1866-1936 . . . . **TCLC 5; HLC**
See also CA 106; DAM MULT; DLB 134

Vallejo, Antonio Buero
See Buero Vallejo, Antonio

Vallejo, Cesar (Abraham)
1892-1938 . . . . **TCLC 3, 56; HLC**
See also CA 105; DAM MULT; HW

Valle Y Pena, Ramon del
See Valle-Inclan, Ramon (Maria) del

Van Ash, Cay 1918- . . . . **CLC 34**

Vanbrugh, Sir John 1664-1726 . . . . . . **LC 21**
See also DAM DRAM; DLB 80

Van Campen, Karl
See Campbell, John W(ood, Jr.)

Vance, Gerald
See Silverberg, Robert

Vance, Jack . . . . **CLC 35**
See also Vance, John Holbrook
See also DLD 8

Vance, John Holbrook 1916-
See Queen, Ellery; Vance, Jack
See also CA 29-32R; CANR 17; MTCW

Van Den Bogarde, Derek Jules Gaspard Ulric
Niven 1921-
See Bogarde, Dirk
See also CA 77-80

Vandenburgh, Jane . . . . **CLC 59**

Vanderhaeghe, Guy 1951- . . . . **CLC 41**
See also CA 113

van der Post, Laurens (Jan) 1906- . . . **CLC 5**
See also CA 5-8R; CANR 35

van de Wetering, Janwillem 1931- . . **CLC 47**
See also CA 49-52; CANR 4

Van Dine, S. S. . . . . **TCLC 23**
See also Wright, Willard Huntington

Van Doren, Carl (Clinton)
1885-1950 . . . . **TCLC 18**
See also CA 111

Van Doren, Mark 1894-1972 . . . . . **CLC 6, 10**
See also CA 1-4R; 37-40R; CANR 3;
DLB 45; MTCW

Van Druten, John (William)
1901-1957 . . . . **TCLC 2**
See also CA 104; DLB 10

Van Duyn, Mona (Jane)
1921- . . . . **CLC 3, 7, 63**
See also CA 9-12R; CANR 7, 38;
DAM POET; DLB 5

Van Dyne, Edith
See Baum, L(yman) Frank

van Itallie, Jean-Claude 1936- . . . . . . **CLC 3**
See also CA 45-48; CAAS 2; CANR 1, 48;
DLB 7

van Ostaijen, Paul 1896-1928 . . . . . **TCLC 33**

Van Peebles, Melvin 1932- . . . . . . **CLC 2, 20**
See also BW 2; CA 85-88; CANR 27;
DAM MULT

Vansittart, Peter 1920- . . . . **CLC 42**
See also CA 1-4R; CANR 3, 49

Van Vechten, Carl 1880-1964 . . . . . . **CLC 33**
See also CA 89-92; DLB 4, 9, 51

Van Vogt, A(lfred) E(lton) 1912- . . . . **CLC 1**
See also CA 21-24R; CANR 28; DLB 8;
SATA 14

Varda, Agnes 1928- . . . . **CLC 16**
See also CA 116; 122

Vargas Llosa, (Jorge) Mario (Pedro)
1936- . . . . **CLC 3, 6, 9, 10, 15, 31, 42, 85;
DA; DAB; DAC; HLC**
See also CA 73-76; CANR 18, 32, 42;
DAM MST, MULT, NOV; DLB 145;
HW; MTCW

Vasiliu, Gheorghe 1881-1957
See Bacovia, George
See also CA 123

Vassa, Gustavus
See Equiano, Olaudah

Vassilikos, Vassilis 1933- . . . . **CLC 4, 8**
See also CA 81-84

Vaughan, Henry 1621-1695 . . . . **LC 27**
See also DLB 131

Vaughn, Stephanie . . . . **CLC 62**

Walker, Alice (Malsenior)
1944- ...... **CLC 5, 6, 9, 19, 27, 46, 58;**
BLC; DA; DAB; DAC; SSC 5
See also AAYA 3; BEST 89:4; BW 2;
CA 37-40R; CANR 9, 27, 49;
CDALB 1968-1988; DAM MST, MULT,
NOV, POET, POP; DLB 6, 33, 143;
INT CANR-27; MTCW; SATA 31

Walker, David Harry 1911-1992.... **CLC 14**
See also CA 1-4R; 137; CANR 1; SATA 8;
SATA-Obit 71

Walker, Edward Joseph 1934-
See Walker, Ted
See also CA 21-24R; CANR 12, 28

Walker, George F.
1947- .... **CLC 44, 61; DAB; DAC**
See also CA 103; CANR 21, 43;
DAM MST; DLB 60

Walker, Joseph A. 1935- .... **CLC 19**
See also BW 1; CA 89-92; CANR 26;
DAM DRAM, MST; DLB 38

Walker, Margaret (Abigail)
1915- .... **CLC 1, 6; BLC**
See also BW 2; CA 73-76; CANR 26;
DAM MULT; DLB 76, 152; MTCW

Walker, Ted .... **CLC 13**
See also Walker, Edward Joseph
See also DLB 40

Wallace, David Foster 1962-....... **CLC 50**
See also CA 132

Wallace, Dexter
See Masters, Edgar Lee

Wallace, (Richard Horatio) Edgar
1875-1932 .... **TCLC 57**
See also CA 115; DLB 70

Wallace, Irving 1916-1990 ...... **CLC 7, 13**
See also AITN 1; CA 1-4R; 132; CAAS 1;
CANR 1, 27; DAM NOV, POP;
INT CANR-27; MTCW

Wallant, Edward Lewis
1926-1962 .... **CLC 5, 10**
See also CA 1-4R; CANR 22; DLB 2, 28,
143; MTCW

Walley, Byron
See Card, Orson Scott

Walpole, Horace 1717-1797......... **LC 2**
See also DLB 39, 104

Walpole, Hugh (Seymour)
1884-1941 .... **TCLC 5**
See also CA 104; DLB 34

Walser, Martin 1927-............. **CLC 27**
See also CA 57-60; CANR 8, 46; DLB 75,
124

Walser, Robert
1878-1956 .... **TCLC 18; SSC 20**
See also CA 118; DLB 66

Walsh, Jill Paton................. **CLC 35**
See also Paton Walsh, Gillian
See also AAYA 11; CLR 2; DLB 161;
SAAS 3

Walter, Villiam Christian
See Andersen, Hans Christian

Wambaugh, Joseph (Aloysius, Jr.)
1937- .... **CLC 3, 18**
See also AITN 1; BEST 89:3; CA 33-36R;
CANR 42; DAM NOV, POP; DLB 6;
DLBY 83; MTCW

Ward, Arthur Henry Sarsfield 1883-1959
See Rohmer, Sax
See also CA 108

Ward, Douglas Turner 1930-....... **CLC 19**
See also BW 1; CA 81-84; CANR 27;
DLB 7, 38

Ward, Mary Augusta
See Ward, Mrs. Humphry

Ward, Mrs. Humphry
1851-1920 .... **TCLC 55**
See also DLB 18

Ward, Peter
See Faust, Frederick (Schiller)

Warhol, Andy 1928(?)-1987........ **CLC 20**
See also AAYA 12; BEST 89:4; CA 89-92;
121; CANR 34

Warner, Francis (Robert le Plastrier)
1937- .... **CLC 14**
See also CA 53-56; CANR 11

Warner, Marina 1946-............ **CLC 59**
See also CA 65-68; CANR 21

Warner, Rex (Ernest) 1905-1986.... **CLC 45**
See also CA 89-92; 119; DLB 15

Warner, Susan (Bogert)
1819-1885 .... **NCLC 31**
See also DLB 3, 42

Warner, Sylvia (Constance) Ashton
See Ashton-Warner, Sylvia (Constance)

Warner, Sylvia Townsend
1893-1978 .... **CLC 7, 19**
See also CA 61-64; 77-80; CANR 16;
DLB 34, 139; MTCW

Warren, Mercy Otis 1728-1814... **NCLC 13**
See also DLB 31

Warren, Robert Penn
1905-1989 .... **CLC 1, 4, 6, 8, 10, 13, 18,**
39, 53, 59; DA; DAB; DAC; SSC 4; WLC
See also AITN 1; CA 13-16R; 129;
CANR 10, 47; CDALB 1968-1988;
DAM MST, NOV, POET; DLB 2, 48,
152; DLBY 80, 89; INT CANR-10;
MTCW; SATA 46; SATA-Obit 63

Warshofsky, Isaac
See Singer, Isaac Bashevis

Warton, Thomas 1728-1790........ **LC 15**
See also DAM POET; DLB 104, 109

Waruk, Kona
See Harris, (Theodore) Wilson

Warung, Price 1855-1911........ **TCLC 45**

Warwick, Jarvis
See Garner, Hugh

Washington, Alex
See Harris, Mark

Washington, Booker T(aliaferro)
1856-1915 .... **TCLC 10; BLC**
See also BW 1; CA 114; 125; DAM MULT;
SATA 28

Washington, George 1732-1799...... **LC 25**
See also DLB 31

Wassermann, (Karl) Jakob
1873-1934 .... **TCLC 6**
See also CA 104; DLB 66

Wasserstein, Wendy
1950- .... **CLC 32, 59, 90; DC 4**
See also CA 121; 129; CABS 3;
DAM DRAM; INT 129

Waterhouse, Keith (Spencer)
1929- .... **CLC 47**
See also CA 5-8R; CANR 38; DLB 13, 15;
MTCW

Waters, Frank (Joseph) 1902-...... **CLC 88**
See also CA 5-8R; CAAS 13; CANR 3, 18;
DLBY 86

Waters, Roger 1944-.............. **CLC 35**

Watkins, Frances Ellen
See Harper, Frances Ellen Watkins

Watkins, Gerrold
See Malzberg, Barry N(athaniel)

Watkins, Paul 1964-.............. **CLC 55**
See also CA 132

Watkins, Vernon Phillips
1906-1967 .... **CLC 43**
See also CA 9-10; 25-28R; CAP 1; DLB 20

Watson, Irving S.
See Mencken, H(enry) L(ouis)

Watson, John H.
See Farmer, Philip Jose

Watson, Richard F.
See Silverberg, Robert

Waugh, Auberon (Alexander) 1939-.. **CLC 7**
See also CA 45-48; CANR 6, 22; DLB 14

Waugh, Evelyn (Arthur St. John)
1903-1966 ...... **CLC 1, 3, 8, 13, 19, 27,**
44; DA; DAB; DAC; WLC
See also CA 85-88; 25-28R; CANR 22;
CDBLB 1914-1945; DAM MST, NOV,
POP; DLB 15; MTCW

Waugh, Harriet 1944- .... **CLC 6**
See also CA 85-88; CANR 22

Ways, C. R.
See Blount, Roy (Alton), Jr.

Waystaff, Simon
See Swift, Jonathan

Webb, (Martha) Beatrice (Potter)
1858-1943 .... **TCLC 22**
See also Potter, Beatrice
See also CA 117

Webb, Charles (Richard) 1939-...... **CLC 7**
See also CA 25-28R

Webb, James H(enry), Jr. 1946-.... **CLC 22**
See also CA 81-84

Webb, Mary (Gladys Meredith)
1881-1927 .... **TCLC 24**
See also CA 123; DLB 34

Webb, Mrs. Sidney
See Webb, (Martha) Beatrice (Potter)

Webb, Phyllis 1927-.............. **CLC 18**
See also CA 104; CANR 23; DLB 53

Webb, Sidney (James)
1859-1947 .... **TCLC 22**
See also CA 117

Webber, Andrew Lloyd............. **CLC 21**
See also Lloyd Webber, Andrew

White, Walter F(rancis)
1893-1955 . . . . **TCLC 15**
See also White, Walter
See also BW 1; CA 115; 124; DLB 51

White, William Hale 1831-1913
See Rutherford, Mark
See also CA 121

Whitehead, E(dward) A(nthony)
1933- . . . . **CLC 5**
See also CA 65-68

Whitemore, Hugh (John) 1936- . . . . . **CLC 37**
See also CA 132; INT 132

Whitman, Sarah Helen (Power)
1803-1878 . . . . **NCLC 19**
See also DLB 1

Whitman, Walt(er)
1819-1892 . . . . . **NCLC 4, 31; DA; DAB;**
DAC; PC 3; WLC
See also CDALB 1640-1865; DAM MST,
POET; DLB 3, 64; SATA 20

Whitney, Phyllis A(yame) 1903- . . . . **CLC 42**
See also AITN 2; BEST 90:3; CA 1-4R;
CANR 3, 25, 38; DAM POP; JRDA;
MAICYA; SATA 1, 30

Whittemore, (Edward) Reed (Jr.)
1919- . . . . **CLC 4**
See also CA 9-12R; CAAS 8; CANR 4;
DLB 5

Whittier, John Greenleaf
1807-1892 . . . . **NCLC 8**
See also CDALB 1640-1865; DAM POET;
DLB 1

Whittlebot, Hernia
See Coward, Noel (Peirce)

Wicker, Thomas Grey 1926-
See Wicker, Tom
See also CA 65-68; CANR 21, 46

Wicker, Tom . . . . **CLC 7**
See also Wicker, Thomas Grey

Wideman, John Edgar
1941- . . . . **CLC 5, 34, 36, 67; BLC**
See also BW 2; CA 85-88; CANR 14, 42;
DAM MULT; DLB 33, 143

Wiebe, Rudy (Henry)
1934- . . . . **CLC 6, 11, 14; DAC**
See also CA 37-40R; CANR 42;
DAM MST; DLB 60

Wieland, Christoph Martin
1733-1813 . . . . **NCLC 17**
See also DLB 97

Wiene, Robert 1881-1938. . . . . **TCLC 56**

Wieners, John 1934- . . . . **CLC 7**
See also CA 13-16R; DLB 16

Wiesel, Elie(zer)
1928- . . . . . . **CLC 3, 5, 11, 37; DA; DAB;**
DAC
See also AAYA 7; AITN 1; CA 5-8R;
CAAS 4; CANR 8, 40; DAM MST,
NOV; DLB 83; DLBY 87; INT CANR-8;
MTCW; SATA 56

Wiggins, Marianne 1947- . . . . **CLC 57**
See also BEST 89:3; CA 130

Wight, James Alfred 1916-
See Herriot, James
See also CA 77-80; SATA 55;
SATA-Brief 44

Wilbur, Richard (Purdy)
1921- . . . **CLC 3, 6, 9, 14, 53; DA; DAB;**
DAC
See also CA 1-4R; CABS 2; CANR 2, 29;
DAM MST, POET; DLB 5;
INT CANR-29; MTCW; SATA 9

Wild, Peter 1940- . . . . **CLC 14**
See also CA 37-40R; DLB 5

Wilde, Oscar (Fingal O'Flahertie Wills)
1854(?)-1900 . . . . **TCLC 1, 8, 23, 41; DA;**
DAB; DAC; SSC 11; WLC
See also CA 104; 119; CDBLB 1890-1914;
DAM DRAM, MST, NOV; DLB 10, 19,
34, 57, 141, 156; SATA 24

Wilder, Billy . . . . **CLC 20**
See also Wilder, Samuel
See also DLB 26

Wilder, Samuel 1906-
See Wilder, Billy
See also CA 89-92

Wilder, Thornton (Niven)
1897-1975 . . . . . . **CLC 1, 5, 6, 10, 15, 35,**
82; DA; DAB; DAC; DC 1; WLC
See also AITN 2; CA 13-16R; 61-64;
CANR 40; DAM DRAM, MST, NOV;
DLB 4, 7, 9; MTCW

Wilding, Michael 1942- . . . . **CLC 73**
See also CA 104; CANR 24, 49

Wiley, Richard 1944- . . . . **CLC 44**
See also CA 121; 129

Wilhelm, Kate . . . . **CLC 7**
See also Wilhelm, Katie Gertrude
See also CAAS 5; DLB 8; INT CANR-17

Wilhelm, Katie Gertrude 1928-
See Wilhelm, Kate
See also CA 37-40R; CANR 17, 36; MTCW

Wilkins, Mary
See Freeman, Mary Eleanor Wilkins

Willard, Nancy 1936- . . . . **CLC 7, 37**
See also CA 89-92; CANR 10, 39; CLR 5;
DLB 5, 52; MAICYA; MTCW;
SATA 37, 71; SATA-Brief 30

Williams, C(harles) K(enneth)
1936- . . . . **CLC 33, 56**
See also CA 37-40R; DAM POET; DLB 5

Williams, Charles
See Collier, James L(incoln)

Williams, Charles (Walter Stansby)
1886-1945 . . . . **TCLC 1, 11**
See also CA 104; DLB 100, 153

Williams, (George) Emlyn
1905-1987 . . . . **CLC 15**
See also CA 104; 123; CANR 36;
DAM DRAM; DLB 10, 77; MTCW

Williams, Hugo 1942- . . . . **CLC 42**
See also CA 17-20R; CANR 45; DLB 40

Williams, J. Walker
See Wodehouse, P(elham) G(renville)

Williams, John A(lfred)
1925- . . . . **CLC 5, 13; BLC**
See also BW 2; CA 53-56; CAAS 3;
CANR 6, 26; DAM MULT; DLB 2, 33;
INT CANR-6

Williams, Jonathan (Chamberlain)
1929- . . . . **CLC 13**
See also CA 9-12R; CAAS 12; CANR 8;
DLB 5

Williams, Joy 1944- . . . . **CLC 31**
See also CA 41-44R; CANR 22, 48

Williams, Norman 1952- . . . . **CLC 39**
See also CA 118

Williams, Sherley Anne
1944- . . . . **CLC 89; BLC**
See also BW 2; CA 73-76; CANR 25;
DAM MULT, POET; DLB 41;
INT CANR-25; SATA 78

Williams, Shirley
See Williams, Sherley Anne

Williams, Tennessee
1911-1983 . . . . . **CLC 1, 2, 5, 7, 8, 11, 15,**
19, 30, 39, 45, 71; DA; DAB; DAC;
DC 4; WLC
See also AITN 1, 2; CA 5-8R; 108;
CABS 3; CANR 31; CDALB 1941-1968;
DAM DRAM, MST; DLB 7; DLBD 4;
DLBY 83; MTCW

Williams, Thomas (Alonzo)
1926-1990 . . . . **CLC 14**
See also CA 1-4R; 132; CANR 2

Williams, William C.
See Williams, William Carlos

Williams, William Carlos
1883-1963 . . . . **CLC 1, 2, 5, 9, 13, 22, 42,**
67; DA; DAB; DAC; PC 7
See also CA 89-92; CANR 34;
CDALB 1917-1929; DAM MST, POET;
DLB 4, 16, 54, 86; MTCW

Williamson, David (Keith) 1942- . . . . **CLC 56**
See also CA 103; CANR 41

Williamson, Ellen Douglas 1905-1984
See Douglas, Ellen
See also CA 17-20R; 114; CANR 39

Williamson, Jack . . . . **CLC 29**
See also Williamson, John Stewart
See also CAAS 8; DLB 8

Williamson, John Stewart 1908-
See Williamson, Jack
See also CA 17-20R; CANR 23

Willie, Frederick
See Lovecraft, H(oward) P(hillips)

Willingham, Calder (Baynard, Jr.)
1922-1995 . . . . **CLC 5, 51**
See also CA 5-8R; 147; CANR 3; DLB 2,
44; MTCW

Willis, Charles
See Clarke, Arthur C(harles)

Willy
See Colette, (Sidonie-Gabrielle)

Willy, Colette
See Colette, (Sidonie-Gabrielle)

Wilson, A(ndrew) N(orman) 1950- . . **CLC 33**
See also CA 112; 122; DLB 14, 155

Wilson, Angus (Frank Johnstone)
1913-1991 . . **CLC 2, 3, 5, 25, 34; SSC 21**
See also CA 5-8R; 134; CANR 21; DLB 15,
139, 155; MTCW

Literary Criticism Series
Cumulative Topic Index

This index lists all topic entries in Gale's *Classical and Medieval Literature Criticism, Contemporary Literary Criticism, Literature Criticism from 1400 to 1800, Nineteenth-Century Literature Criticism,* and *Twentieth-Century Literary Criticism.*

Topic Index

LC Cumulative Nationality Index

AFGHAN
Babur **18**

AMERICAN
Bradstreet, Anne **4, 30**
Edwards, Jonathan **7**
Eliot, John **5**
Franklin, Benjamin **25**
Hopkinson, Francis **25**
Knight, Sarah Kemble **7**
Munford, Robert **5**
Penn, William **25**
Taylor, Edward **11**
Washington, George **25**
Wheatley (Peters), Phillis **3**
Winthrop, John **31**

BENINESE
Equiano, Olaudah **16**

CANADIAN
Marie de l'Incarnation **10**

CHINESE
Lo Kuan-chung **12**
P'u Sung-ling **3**
Ts'ao Hsueh-ch'in **1**
Wu Ch'eng-en **7**
Wu Ching-tzu **2**

DANISH
Holberg, Ludvig **6**
Wessel, Johan Herman **7**

DUTCH
Erasmus, Desiderius **16**
Lipsius, Justus **16**
Spinoza, Benedictus de **9**

ENGLISH
Addison, Joseph **18**
Andrewes, Lancelot **5**
Arbuthnot, John **1**
Aubin, Penelope **9**
Bacon, Francis **18, 32**
Behn, Aphra **1, 30**
Boswell, James **4**
Bradstreet, Anne **4, 30**
Brooke, Frances **6**
Bunyan, John **4**
Burke, Edmund **7**
Butler, Samuel **16**
Carew, Thomas **13**
Cary, Elizabeth, Lady Falkland **30**
Cavendish, Margaret Lucas **30**
Caxton, William **17**
Chapman, George **22**
Charles I **13**
Chatterton, Thomas **3**
Chaucer, Geoffrey **17**
Churchill, Charles **3**
Cleland, John **2**
Collier, Jeremy **6**
Collins, William **4**
Congreve, William **5, 21**
Crashaw, Richard **24**
Daniel, Samuel **24**
Davys, Mary **1**
Day, Thomas **1**
Dee, John **20**
Defoe, Daniel **1**
Dekker, Thomas **22**
Delany, Mary (Granville Pendarves) **12**
Dennis, John **11**
Devenant, William **13**
Donne, John **10, 24**
Drayton, Michael **8**
Dryden, John **3, 21**

Elyot, Sir Thomas **11**
Equiano, Olaudah **16**
Fanshawe, Ann **11**
Farquhar, George **21**
Fielding, Henry **1**
Fielding, Sarah **1**
Foxe, John **14**
Garrick, David **15**
Gray, Thomas **4**
Hakluyt, Richard **31**
Hawes, Stephen **17**
Haywood, Eliza (Fowler) **1**
Henry VIII **10**
Herbert, George **24**
Herrick, Robert **13**
Howell, James **13**
Hunter, Robert **7**
Johnson, Samuel **15**
Jonson, Ben(jamin) **6**
Julian of Norwich **6**
Kempe, Margery **6**
Killigrew, Anne **4**
Kyd, Thomas **22**
Langland, William **19**
Lanyer, Aemilia **10, 30**
Lilly, William **27**
Locke, John **7**
Lovelace, Richard **24**
Lyttelton, George **10**
Malory, (Sir) Thomas **11**
Manley, (Mary) Delariviere **1**
Marlowe, Christopher **22**
Marvell, Andrew **4**
Milton, John **9**
Montagu, Mary (Pierrepont) Wortley **9**
More, Henry **9**
More, Sir Thomas **10, 32**
Parnell, Thomas **3**
Pepys, Samuel **11**

LC Cumulative Title Index

Title Index

Title Index

See *El Conde Alarcos*
Count d'Irlos (Castro) **19**:4
The Counterfeit Bridegroom; or, The Defeated Widow (Behn) **1**:33; **30**:71, 80
The Counterfeit Christian Detected and the Real Quaker Justified (Penn) **25**:287, 291
The Countess of Dellwyn (Fielding) **1**:273, 278
"Countess of Denbigh" (Crashaw)
See "Address to the Noblest and Best of Ladies, the Countess Denbigh Against Irresolution and Delay in Matters of Religion"
The Countess of Pembroke's Arcadia (*Arcadia*) (Sidney) **19**:318-27, 329-30, 334-36, 338-45, 347-49, 351-58, 360-62, 364-74, 376-80, 389-91, 396-97, 399-415, 420-30, 432-33
The Countess of Mountgomeries Urania (Wroth) **30**:334-38, 340, 342-44, 346-59, 363-65, 367, 369, 371, 383, 393
The Country Girl (Garrick) **15**:122-23
The Country House (Vanbrugh) **21**:293, 319
"The Country Lass" (Burns) **3**:85; **29**:49
"Country Life" (Philips) **30**:326
"A Country Life: To His Brother, Master Thomas Herrick" (Herrick) **13**:377-82
"The Country Life, to the Honoured Master Endimion Porter, Groome of the Bed-Chamber to His Majesty" (Herrick) **13**:327, 364, 368, 377, 395
The Country Parson (Herbert) **24**:225-26, 255, 266-67
The Country-Wife (Wycherley) **8**:379-81, 383, 385-92, 394, 396-97, 400-02, 406, 409-16, 419-23, 425-26, 428-29; **21**:347, 355-57, 359-70, 372-76, 379-80, 383, 387-88, 390-91, 393-98
Courage (Grimmelshausen)
See *Die Erzbetrugerin und Landstortzerin Courasche*
"Courante Monsieur" (Lovelace) **24**:327
Cours d'étude (Condillac) **26**:7, 10, 29, 31, 47, 54
"The Court Life. To a Friend, Disswading Him from Attending for Places" (Wycherley) **8**:416
"The Court of Death: a Pindarique Poem, dedicated to the memory of her Most Sacred Majesty, Queen Mary" (Dennis) **11**:14, 49-50
"The Court of Equity" (Burns)
See "Libel Summons"
"Court of Honor" (Addison) **18**:27
The Court of the King of Bantam (Behn) **1**:34, 38, 45-6, 48; **30**:88
Court Poems (*Town Eclogues*) (Montagu) **9**:276
The Courtesan (Aretino)
See *Cortigiana errante*
The Courtier (Castiglione)
See *Il libro del cortegiano*
The Courtier's Library (Donne) **10**:82
"Courtship" (Erasmus) **16**:193
The Cousins (Davys) **1**:97
The Covent-Garden Tragedy (Fielding) **1**:239
"A Covetous Man" (Butler) **16**:50
"The Coy Mistress" (Marvell)
See "To His Coy Mistress"
The Crafty Whore (Aretino) **12**:21, 25
"The Craven Street Gazette" (Franklin) **25**:141
"The Cricket" (P'u Sung-ling)
See "Tsu-chih"

Criminal Legislation (Marat)
See *Plan de législation criminelle, ouvrage dans lequel on traite des délits et des peines, de la force des preuves et des présomptions . . .*
"Cripples" ("On Cripples") (Montaigne) **8**:221
The Crisis (Steele) **18**:352, 354
Crispin, rival de son maître (Lesage) **2**:182, 201; **28**:199-202, 209, 211-12, 215
The Critic (Gracian y Morales)
See *El Criticón*
"The Critic and the Writer of Fables" (Winchilsea) **3**:443, 457
Critical Examination of the Apologists of the Christian Religion (Holbach) **14**:167
The Critical History of Jesus Christ; or, Reasoned Analysis of the Gospels (Holbach)
See *Ecce Homo! or, A Critical Inquiry into the History of Jesus of Nazareth; Being a Rational Analysis of the Gospels*
Critical Observations (Dennis)
See *Remarks on a Book, entituled Prince Arthur, an Heroick Poem*
El Criticón (*The Critic*; *The Master Critic*) (Gracian y Morales) **15**:136-52, 154-55, 157-72, 174-75
La critique de L'école des femmes (*The School for Wives Criticized*) (Moliere) **10**:278, 281, 283, 287, 297, 311, 321; **28**:255-56, 258, 274
Critique de l'Opera (Perrault) **2**:259
Critique de Turcaret (Lesage) **28**:204
The Critique upon Milton (Addison) **18**:7
Le crocheteur borgne (Voltaire) **14**:359
"Cromwell" (Drayton)
See "Thomas Cromwell, Earle of Essex"
"The Crosse" (Donne) **10**:16, 40, 84; **24**:165, 167, 198-99
"The Crosse" (Herbert) **24**:268. 272-74
"Crowne of Sonnets" (Wroth) **30**:342, 390, 399
De cruce (Lipsius)
See *De cruce libi tres*
De cruce libi tres (*De cruce*) (Lipsius) **16**:269
"Crucifying" (Donne) **24**:167
The Cruel Brother (Davenant) **13**:175, 216
"The Cruel Mistress" (Carew) **13**:11
"The Cruell Maid" (Herrick) **13**:364
The Cruelty of the Spaniards in Peru (Davenant) **13**:190
"The Crusade" (Warton) **15**:432-33, 442, 445, 454
The Cry: A New Dramatic Fable (Fielding) **1**:270, 273
"The Cryer" (Drayton) **8**:27
The Cub at Newmarket. A Letter to the People of Scotland (Boswell) **4**:50, 52-3
El Cubo de la Almundena (Calderon de la Barca) **23**:14
Cuento de cuentos (Quevedo) **23**:154
El cuerdo loco (Vega) **23**:393
La cuerva de Salamanca (*The Cave of Salamanca*) (Cervantes) **6**:189-92; **23**:139, 142
"Culex" (Spenser) **5**:312
"A Cully" (Butler) **16**:50
La cuna y la sepultura (Quevedo) **23**:190
"Cupid and Ganymede" (Prior) **4**:461
"Cupid Fargone" (Lovelace) **24**:340
"Cupid, I Hate Thee, Which I'de Have Thee Know" (Drayton)
See "Sonnet 48"

"Cupid's Conflict" (More) **9**:298, 302
The Cure and the Sickness (Calderon de la Barca) **23**:9
De Curiositatis pernicic (Andreae) **32**:100
"El curioso" (Cervantes) **23**:95
El curioso impertinente (*The Tale of the Foolish Curiosity*) (Cervantes) **23**:99, 130, 141, 144-45
"A Curious Man" (Butler) **16**:52
"The Curse" (Donne) **10**:52, 82
"The Curse" (Herrick) **13**:341
"A Custom of the Island of Cea" (Montaigne) **8**:238
"Cyclops" (Erasmus) **16**:154
Cymon (Garrick) **15**:124
"Cymon and Iphigenia" (Dryden) **3**:184, 205, 213, 243
"Cynthia" (Jonson) **6**:322
Cynthia's Revels (Jonson) **6**:300, 302, 306, 308, 311, 335-36, 342
The Czar of Muscovy (Pix) **8**:260-61, 263, 269, 271-72, 276
"Czego chcesz od nas, panie?" (Kochanowski)
See "Pieśń"
"The Daft Days" (Fergusson) **29**:170-71, 175, 178, 181, 189, 194, 198, 205, 214, 234-37
"Les daimons" ("Demonology") (Ronsard) **6**:407, 411, 422, 424
"Daintie Davie" (Burns) **3**:56
D'Alembert's Dream (Diderot)
See *Le Rêve de d'Alembert*
La dama boba (*The Silly Lady*) (Vega) **23**:372, 393
La dama duende (*The Phantom Lady*) (Calderon de la Barca) **23**:38, 41-2, 44, 46, 57, 59, 64, 66
"A Damask Rose Sticking upon a Lady's Breast" ("On a Damaske Rose") (Carew) **13**:18, 30
D'Ambois (Chapman)
See *The Tragedy of Bussy D'Ambois*
"Damon the Mower" (Wheatley) **3**:410-11, 441-42
"Damon to his Friends" (Fergusson) **29**:201
"The Dampe" (Donne) **10**:36-7, 82; **24**:154
The Dancing-Master (Wycherley)
See *The Gentleman Dancing-Master*
The Danger of Priestcraft to Religion and Government (*Priestcraft Dangerous to Religion and Government*) (Dennis) **11**:26
"The dangers of speaking and of not speaking and the function of language in silence" (Quevedo)
See "Peligros de habler y de caller y lenguaje en el silencio"
"Dangers wait on Kings" (Herrick) **13**:394
Dannemarks og Norges beskrivelse (*Description of Denmark and Norway*) (Holberg) **6**:266, 281
Dannemarks riges historie (*History of the Kingdom of Denmark*) (Holberg) **6**:266, 278, 281-82
Den danske comoedies ligbegænglese (Holberg) **6**:278
"Daphnaida" (Spenser) **5**:312-13
"Daphnis and Chloe" (Marvell) **4**:408-10
"Dark Night of the Soul" (John of the Cross)
See "Noche Oscura del alma"
The Dark Night of the Soul (John of the Cross)
See *Noche Escura del Alma*
"Date Obolum Belesario" (Hopkinson) **25**:251, 255

Title Index

Title Index

Title Index

Title Index

Title Index

Title Index

Title Index

Title Index

Title Index

Title Index

Title Index

Title Index

Title Index

Title Index

ISBN 0-8103-9277-1

9 780810 392779